POLICE MISCONDUCT, COMPLAINTS, AND PUBLIC REGULATION

POLICE MISCONDUCT, COMPLAINTS, AND PUBLIC REGULATION

John Beggs QC
Hugh Davies

OXFORD
UNIVERSITY PRESS

OXFORD

UNIVERSITY PRESS

Great Clarendon Street, Oxford OX2 6DP

Oxford University Press is a department of the University of Oxford.
It furthers the University's objective of excellence in research, scholarship,
and education by publishing worldwide in

Oxford New York

Auckland   Cape Town Dar es Salaam   Hong Kong   Karachi
Kuala Lumpur Madrid Melbourne Mexico City   Nairobi
New Delhi Shanghai Taipei Toronto
With offices in
Argentina Austria Brazil Chile Czech Republic France Greece
Guatemala Hungary Italy Japan South Korea Poland Portugal
Singapore Switzerland Thailand Turkey Ukraine Vietnam

Oxford is a registered trade mark of Oxford University Press
in the UK and in certain other countries

Published in the United States
by Oxford University Press Inc., New York

© John Beggs QC and Hugh Davies 2009

The moral rights of the author have been asserted

Database right Oxford University Press (maker)

Reprinted 2010

Crown copyright material is reproduced under Class Licence
Number C01P0000148 with the permission of OPSI
and the Queen's Printer for Scotland.

ISBN 978-0-19-954618-3

Printed and bound by CPI Group (UK) Ltd,
Croydon, CR0 4YY

For

Sarah, Maria, Liz, George, Lorna, Millie, Jack, and Harry

Claire, Millie, Tom, and Martha

FOREWORD

'Policing is too important to leave to the police alone' is a common mantra in the annals of British policing—most often expressed by members of the police service. Inherent in the phrase is not only recognition of the importance of help from, and the support of, the community at large, but also the need for oversight and accountability. This book addresses a number of aspects of both these latter concepts, setting them out for the informed reader and those coming to the issues with a lesser awareness of an historical and current context to aid understanding.

Confidence in the police has always been key to successful community support, and that reality has been thrust further into the 'limelight' by the Government adopting 'raising public confidence' as the single national target for policing. All other targets—and there was an extensive number—have been dropped.

To a great extent that confidence is also secured by the public knowing that the police operate to a very high standard of integrity and ethics that goes beyond simply working within the law. As a great deal of discretion and independence is afforded to the police then so should the conduct and disciplinary procedures under which they operate command support and confidence.

The two authors of this book have an enormous range of knowledge and experience of 'conduct and discipline' in the police arena—viewed from a wide range of perspectives. They are well placed to set the scene and then go on to advise and inform on what recent changes have taken place, how they will operate, and comment on their strengths and weaknesses. Thus the end product is more than a textbook.

Having led the recent review of police conduct and discipline for Government (ably assisted by representatives from a wide range of interested parties), I agree with a comment by the authors that the changes represent a 'seismic shift' in the processes and procedures. That shift also occurred in relation to the prevailing philosophy and culture of police behaviour and conduct, and was the consequence of a careful look at the impact and effectiveness of the existing law and mechanisms. While perhaps not inevitable, for me, it was a timely, worthy, and therefore a welcome outcome.

Two factors set the police apart from the citizen as an 'employee'. The first is that police officers can exercise lethal force on behalf of the State, and the second is that they can be required to control dangerous and life threatening situations (eg riots) with the risk of prosecution or disciplinary measures if they do not. This singular position also strongly suggests that Parliament should retain the controlling hand in setting the rules and regulations governing the behaviour of police. While the 'normal employment framework' as represented in the ACAS model is apposite, it needs adjustment for the policing context. In other words, the concept of the 'office of constable' should be left untouched. It is seen by many as sacrosanct in that it offers confirmation of the constitutional independence of the constable who is answerable 'to the law alone'. This position is singular to policing in England and Wales, and is still regarded by most observers as being worthy of protection.

The previous approach to conduct and discipline, at worst, reflected all the elements of a criminal investigation and prosecution or, at best, was similar to the approach in a military Courts Martial. Both features were a product of a history and culture which were no longer applicable, if ever they had been.

The essential elements of the proposed new approach signal a significant shift of emphasis towards development and improvement over blame and sanction. It is anticipated that the issue of officer capability will be more to the fore, with the range of outcomes that such a process offers for securing public satisfaction and improving individual and organizational service delivery.

Equally, if not more important, is the intention to make the process clearer and more acceptable to the public by seeking workable solutions to matters of complaint (and differences of opinion) in a timely and proportionate way, with the minimum of bureaucracy. At the heart of this is local action where supervisors are allowed to do just that: manage and supervise.

If the benefits that the seismic change is intended to deliver are to be achieved then all those with a role in the conduct and disciplinary process must exercise an individual and collective responsibility. They must ensure that the change in philosophy remains on course; maintain a firm level of resolve and courage to make the reforms work as intended; and be ready to defend the 'new world' against inappropriate challenge.

By raising understanding and 'nailing' responsibilities this book goes a long way in offering a guiding touchstone.

William Taylor
Author of *Taylor Review of Police Discipline in England and Wales*
Former Commissioner of Police for the City of London and
Chief Inspector of Constabulary for Scotland

PREFACE

The public is interested in the police behaving badly. So are we. The Sweeney is more compelling than Dixon of Dock Green. Alleged misconduct by serving police officers—particularly of the most serious kind—invariably adds an extra human interest ingredient to the conduct of any case. Proceedings are routinely controversial, played out in public, and adopted (occasionally perhaps hijacked) as vehicles for wider agendas on all sides. Equally, regulation of police misconduct, and accountability in public for the exercise of powers by the police, are manifestly in the public interest. One can expect a progression to more public hearings—to date there has been only one—of the most serious allegations of police misconduct.

The world in this context is also changing in other respects. Regulation of police forces through police authorities and the relevant Secretary of State is not new but has become progressively more political. American-style elected police authorities are not inconceivable. The IPCC not only enjoys greater powers than the predecessor PCA, but has proved more pro-active in the use of such powers and transparent as to the product of investigations. Inquests—particularly those where Article 2 is engaged—have become de-facto public inquiries frequently lasting months. The draft Coroners and Justice Bill 2009 does not itself remedy the serious intrinsic flaws in the existing procedures. Time will tell whether new draft Rules will do better.

In terms of internal misconduct proceedings the 2008 regime is intended to replace the old culture of blame and punishment with one of learning and improvement of performance. In the continued absence of fixed-term contracts officers hold office until retirement. The procedures should achieve the objective of promoting competence. Unless all sides embrace the philosophy underpinning change the new regime—which is as, if not more, complicated than the old—will simply not work or be trusted in practice.

We met when appearing against each other in August 2005 on a police misconduct case. Not unusually, misconduct proceedings were used in preference to serious criminal charges to litigate evidence of systemic corruption. We have appeared regularly against each other ever since. As the volume of police misconduct cases grows, together with the greater number of Article 2 inquests involving the police, it became obvious to us that the police service and other (in Government-speak) 'stakeholders' in the complaints and misconduct system required a convenient and compendious source of the regulatory framework covering police complaints, misconduct and public regulation. Some understanding of the complex national framework of police regulation is the necessary context, as is treatment of core principles of law relating to professional regulation and concepts of general application such as disclosure, abuse of process, judicial review, and the definitions of crime. We have tried to create just such a book, and are grateful to our publishers for allowing us to include extensive extracts from the relevant statutes, regulations, and guidance.

Our perspective has been that of barristers who each both prosecute and defend in police misconduct cases and who, between us, appear regularly in high-profile police related cases in both the criminal and civil jurisdictions. We hope that our ambition to produce a balanced, neutral, and objective guide to law and practice in this field has been met. We welcome constructive criticism if not.

The 2008 regime, primarily the product of the Taylor Review, provides the police service with a golden opportunity to manage its complaints and internal conduct matters in a more intelligent and purposive manner. Disproportionate investigations of one force by another should be history: perspective has too often been lost in an attempt to demonstrate the necessary independence. We must hope that the police service will start better to calibrate its resources and responses to complaints. Truly bad officers, namely those unfit to hold office (of whom there are inevitably some in all forces) should be removed effectively and efficiently by fair processes. Officers who make honest or isolated mistakes in good faith should be supported and encouraged to learn and improve. Few officers will serve for 30 years without committing some such honest operational error. The expectation of loss of office in such circumstances proves not only unfair but counter-productive.

It is in the public interest that most on duty matters should be managed as performance-related rather than necessitating a misconduct investigation or charge. To make the performance regulations work the senior echelons of the police service need to offer strong leadership and to invest heavily in the training and development of its supervisors. In our experience supervisory failure, whether of individuals or the local culture, is usually documented as part of the narrative leading to more serious subsequent misconduct. Equally individual officers, and their representatives, must acknowledge that regulation of performance is intended to operate in a constructive spirit. This demands co-operation rather than confrontation.

We gratefully acknowledge the contribution of others to this book. Research was conducted by various individual pupils at 3 Raymond Buildings, including but not limited to Stephen Foster, Rachel Kapila (now tenants), and Robert Morris, and, at 3 Serjeants' Inn, James Berry. Other expert practitioners from whom we received valuable input include Katriona Swan at the IPCC, Colin Reynolds at Reynolds Dawson, Scott Ingram at Russell Jones and Walker, and PC David Bennett of the Police Federation. Detective Superintendent Vic Marshall is a central architect in the process and philosophy of reform, and constant source of assistance in our attempts to articulate what was intended in these respects. Inspector Mustaqa Patala of Lancashire Constabulary prepared the process maps in chapter 4, which are in turn reproduced by kind permission of the Chief Constable of Lancashire Constabulary. Our publishers—primarily Jane Kavanagh and Faye Judges—have demonstrated expertise and patience in equal measure, and the painful process of converting the flattery of commission to the reality of publication would simply not have been concluded without their support and encouragement.

John Beggs QC
3 Serjeants' Inn
London

Hugh Davies
Gray's Inn
London
16 March 2009

CONTENTS—SUMMARY

Table of Cases   xxix
Table of Statutes   xxxvii
Table of Statutory Instruments   xlvii
Table of European Treaties and Conventions   lvii
List of Abbreviations   lix

1. The Organization of Policing in England and Wales,
    and the Regulation of Police Forces   1

2. The Suspension and Removal of Chief Officers by
    Police Authorities and the Secretary of State   37

3. Complaints and Misconduct I: The Independent Police
    Complaints Commission (IPCC)   49

4. Complaints and Misconduct II: Overview
    of the 2004 and 2008 Conduct and Performance
    Regulations, and Associated Appeals   89

5. The Police (Performance) Regulations 2008   111

6. Standards of Professional Behaviour and the
    Initial Handling of a Report   155

7. Investigations under Schedule 3 of the 2002 Act
    and the 2008 Conduct Regulations   197

8. Misconduct Proceedings under the Police (Conduct)
    Regulations 2008   257

9. The Police (Conduct) Regulations 2004   295

10. Special ('Fast-track') Cases under the Police (Conduct)
    Regulations 2004 and 2008   329

11. Chief Officer Reviews, Internal Appeals, and
    Police Appeals Tribunals   351

12. Abuse of Process   379

13. Probationers   395
14. Inquests   403
15. Police-related Criminal Offences   453

Appendices   499

Index   753

CONTENTS

Table of Cases   xxix
Table of Statutes   xxxvii
Table of Statutory Instruments   xlvii
Table of European Treaties and Conventions   lvii
List of Abbreviations   lix

1. **The Organization of Policing in England and Wales,
    and the Regulation of Police Forces**

    A. Overview   1.01
        Direction and control   1.04
        Direction and control: local procedures under Home Office
            Circular 19/2005   1.07

    B. The Organization of the Police   1.11
        Police areas and forces   1.11
        Rank structure   1.17
        Basic conditions of service   1.18
        Inter-force activity   1.19
        Police authorities and collaborative arrangements   1.23

    C. The Role of the Secretary of State   1.26
        The Secretary of State: general duties   1.28
        Setting 'strategic priorities'   1.32
        The setting of objectives and performance targets
            by the Home Secretary   1.36
        The Police Standards Unit (PSU) and the Police and Crime
            Standards Directorate (PCSD)   1.40
        The power to give directions to police authorities   1.45
        The revised powers of direction under s 40 of the Police Act 1996   1.50
        Police Act 1996, ss 41A and 41B   1.60
        Reports to the Secretary of State from police authorities and
            chief constables   1.61
        Regulations for police forces   1.62
        Codes of practice and statutory guidance issued by the Secretary
            of State   1.66
        Home Office Guidance on Police Unsatisfactory Performance,
            Complaints and Misconduct Procedures   1.68

The removal of chief officers   1.76
The Police Negotiating Board (PNB) and the Police Advisory Boards   1.78
Other miscellaneous powers of regulation   1.82

D. Police Authorities   1.86
History and membership   1.86
General functions   1.94
Obligations to consult the local community and status as a
    'best value authority'   1.98
Questions to a police authority nominee at council meetings   1.99
Crime and disorder partnerships, and councils'
    duties to obtain 'best value'   1.100
Association of Police Authorities (APA) published guidance   1.102
Equality and diversity   1.103
The funding of legal representation for members of the force
    and others   1.105
Police authorities: a summary of specific statutory duties
    in relation to complaints and misconduct   1.110

E. The National Policing Improvement Agency (NPIA)   1.119

F. Conclusion   1.129

2. **The Suspension and Removal of Chief Officers**
by Police Authorities and the Secretary of State

A. Overview   2.01

B. Statutory Framework   2.07
The powers and duties of police authorities   2.07
The powers of the Secretary of State   2.11

C. Home Office Protocol (March 2004)   2.14

D. Analysis of the Combined Procedure   2.16
The initial decision to use the procedure and the rights
    of the officer   2.16
The obligation to consult HMIC/HMCIC   2.19
Suspension   2.20
The procedures preceding the requirement to retire or resign   2.27

E. Conclusion   2.38

3. **Complaints and Misconduct I: The Independent**
Police Complaints Commission (IPCC)

A. Overview   3.01

B. Complaints and Misconduct: The Police Reform Act 2002—
The Overall Statutory Structure   3.13

The structure of the Police Reform Act 2002   3.13

C. The Legal Character of the IPCC   3.22
    Legal status   3.22

D. The Commission: The Chairman, the Members,
    and the Staff   3.41
    The Commission as a public authority   3.41
    The Constitution   3.44

E. The General Functions and Duties of the Commission   3.51
    Its role contrasted with that of the PCA   3.51
    The 'Learning the Lessons Committee'   3.54
    The IPCC's statutory functions and duties   3.57
    Other statutory duties   3.70
    The statutory guidance   3.71

F. The IPCC Complaints and Discipline Process   3.91
    Overview   3.91
    Statutory provision: members of the Commission,
       including the chair and deputy chair   3.97
    Non-statutory procedures   3.102
    The chairman   3.109
    The deputy chairs   3.112
    The ordinary members of the Commission   3.114
    Suspension   3.129
    The IPCC stages   3.132
    The Commission staff   3.167

G. Conclusion   3.195

**4. Complaints and Misconduct II: Overview of the 2004
    and 2008 Conduct and Performance Regulations,
    and Associated Appeals**

A. Overview   4.01
    Introduction and the history of reform   4.01
    The Taylor Review and parliamentary intent   4.10
    Summary of central changes under the 2008 regime   4.14
    The structure of subsequent associated chapters   4.15

B. Process Charts   4.18

5. The Police (Performance) Regulations 2008

A. Overview   5.01
    Background   5.01
    The structure of the Regulations   5.23

B. Preliminaries   5.34
    Definitions   5.34
    'Police friend'   5.46
    Procedure at meetings under the Regulations   5.49
    'Nominated persons' (reg 9)   5.54

C. The First Stage   5.57
    Pre-regulatory action   5.59
    Unsatisfactory performance   5.63
    Unsatisfactory attendance   5.71
    Chapter 4 of the Home Office Guidance   5.80
    Invoking the Regulations   5.92
    The circumstances in which a first-stage meeting may
        be required (reg 12)   5.93
    Arrangement of the first-stage meeting (reg 13)   5.96
    Procedure at the first-stage meeting (reg 14)   5.104
    Procedure following the first-stage meeting (reg 15)   5.112
    Appeals against the finding and outcome of a first-stage
        meeting (regs 16–18)   5.123
    The first-stage appeal meeting (reg 18)   5.131

D. The Second Stage   5.136
    The circumstances in which a second-stage meeting may be
        required (reg 19)   5.136
    Arrangement of the second-stage meeting (reg 20)   5.145
    Procedure at and after the second-stage meeting (regs 21 and 22)   5.148
    Appeals against the finding and outcome of the second-stage
        meeting (regs 23–25)   5.151

E. The Third Stage   5.155
    Arrangement of the third-stage meeting (reg 27)   5.160
    Gross incompetence (regs 28 and 29)   5.161
    Procedure on receipt of notice of the third-stage meeting (reg 32)   5.167
    The management of witnesses (reg 33)   5.174
    The timing and notice of the third-stage meeting (reg 34)   5.177
    Panel members (regs 30 and 31)   5.178
    Procedure at the third-stage meeting (regs 35 and 36)   5.188
    The finding (reg 37)   5.190
    Outcomes (reg 38)   5.194
    Assessment of performance or attendance following third-stage
        meetings (regs 39–41)   5.201

F. Police Appeals Tribunals   5.208

G. Conclusion   5.209

6. **Standards of Professional Behaviour and the Initial**
   Handling of a Report

A. Overview   6.01

B. The New Standards of Professional Behaviour   6.26
   Context: the commencement of the Police (Conduct) Regulations 2008   6.26
   Further guidance as to the Standards of Professional Behaviour
       in the Home Office Guidance   6.44

C. Initial Handling: The Police Reform Act 2002, Sch 3,
   or the Police (Conduct) Regulations 2008   6.61
   The application of Sch 3 to the 2002 Act   6.64

D. The Police Reform Act 2002, Pt 2: Complaints,
   Conduct Matters, and DSI Matters   6.71
   Complaints   6.72
   Conduct matters   6.76
   DSI matters   6.77
   A person serving with the police   6.80
   The application of Pt 2 to officers who have ceased to serve   6.81
   The exclusion from Sch 3 of direction and control matters   6.82
   Schedule 3 to the Police Reform Act 2002   6.83

E. Police Reform Act 2002, Sch 3, Pt 1: The Handling
   of Complaints   6.85
   Local resolution (Sch 3, para 6)   6.100
   Appeals relating to local resolution (Sch 3, para 9)   6.116
   Dispensation by the IPCC   6.119

F. Police Reform Act 2002, Sch 3, Pt 2: The Handling
   of Conduct Matters   6.125
   Civil proceedings involving a conduct matter   6.126
   The recording of conduct matters in other cases   6.128
   A conduct matter disclosed during DSI investigation   6.131
   Other mandatory referrals to the IPCC by the appropriate
       authority   6.132
   Discretionary referrals by the appropriate authority to the IPCC   6.133

G. Police Reform Act 2002, Sch 3, Pt 2A: The Handling
   of DSI Matters   6.140

H. Police Reform Act 2002, Sch 3: Miscellaneous Aspects   6.146
   Restrictions on proceedings   6.146
   Special cases (Sch 3, paras 20A–20I)   6.149
   The power of the IPCC to discontinue an investigation
       (Sch 3, para 21)   6.151

I. Conclusion   6.157

7. **Investigations under Schedule 3 of the 2002 Act and the 2008 Conduct Regulations**

A. Overview of the Investigatory Regimes and the Police
(Conduct) Regulations 2008   7.01
The Police (Conduct) Regulations 2008 and the associated
Home Office Guidance: a summary   7.05
Part 1: 'Preliminary'   7.07
The harm test and the implied duty of disclosure (reg 4)   7.14
Interpretation of the prescribed reg 4 'harm test'   7.31
Part 2: 'General'   7.35
The status and role of a police friend (reg 6)   7.36
Legal and other representation (reg 7)   7.46
The effect of outstanding or possible
criminal proceedings (reg 9)   7.50
Suspension (reg 10)   7.55

B. Determination of the Investigatory Regime   7.63
Introduction   7.63
Forms of investigation   7.67
Independent investigations under para 19: additional points   7.71

C. Assessment of Conduct   7.74
Schedule 3 matters: 'severity assessment'   7.76
Assessment of conduct under Part 3 of the 2008 Conduct
Regulations   7.83

D. The Appointment of the Investigator   7.91
The definition and the enhanced role of the investigator
in the 2008 regime   7.91
The appointment of the investigator in Sch 3 investigations   7.96
Investigators under the 2008 Conduct Regulations   7.103
Investigators under paras 16–18 of Sch 3 to the 2002 Act   7.105

E. The Purpose of the Investigation   7.110

F. Written Notices of Investigation   7.113
The history and purpose of 'notices of investigation'   7.113
The content of notices of investigation   7.120
Matters specific to reg 15 notices   7.122

G. Representations to the Investigator   7.126
Schedule 3 matters   7.127
2008 Conduct Regulations   7.129

H. Interviews   7.134
Pre-interview procedures   7.137
Discretion as to interviews   7.144

Criminal and misconduct interviews as part of a single investigation 7.145
Application of the Regulation of Investigatory Powers Act 2000
(RIPA) 7.155

I. The Report of the Investigation 7.167
The 2008 Conduct Regulations 7.167
Investigation reports for Sch 3 investigations 7.169
Action by the IPCC in response to an investigation report from a
managed or IPCC investigation (Sch 3, para 23) 7.173
Notification requirements on the IPCC 7.178
Procedures following the service of a para 23(6) notification 7.179
Action by the IPCC in response to an investigation report from a
local or supervised investigation (Sch 3, para 24) 7.182
Final reports on other DSI matters (Sch 3, paras 24A–24C) 7.186
Appeals to the IPCC in relation to an investigation (Sch 3, para 25) 7.189
Reviews and reinvestigations following an appeal (Sch 3, para 26) 7.196
The duties and IPCC powers of recommendation and direction
in relation to disciplinary proceedings (Sch 3, para 27) 7.198
Information for the complainant about disciplinary recommendations
(Sch 3, para 28) 7.203

J. Conclusion 7.206

8. Misconduct Proceedings under the Police (Conduct)
Regulations 2008

A. Referral of Case 8.01
The referral of the case to misconduct proceedings 8.07
Withdrawal of the case 8.18
Disclosure of the investigator's report to the officer concerned 8.21
Notice of referral to misconduct proceedings and panel membership:
reg 21 8.23
Form of written notice and particularity of 'charge' 8.25
The identity of, and objection to, panel members 8.31

B. Procedure on Receipt of Notice 8.35

C. Witnesses 8.40
The timing and notice of misconduct proceedings 8.45
Persons conducting misconduct proceedings for non-senior officers:
reg 25 8.51
Documents to be supplied: reg 28 8.61

D. Rights of Attendance and Participation in Misconduct
Proceedings 8.66
The nature of 'private' misconduct proceedings 8.66
The officer concerned 8.67

The IPCC   8.68
The investigator   8.69
Hearings in public   8.70
Complainants and interested persons   8.76

E. Procedure at Misconduct Proceedings   8.86
The power of the chair to determine the procedure at misconduct
    proceedings   8.86
Adverse inferences   8.89
The questioning of witnesses   8.96
The prescribed task of the person conducting or chairing
    the proceedings   8.104
The burden and standard of proof   8.105
The relevance of previous good character to fact finding   8.109
Majority findings   8.111

F. Outcomes   8.112
Mitigation   8.125
The approach to outcomes   8.129
Notification of outcomes   8.138

G. Appeals from Misconduct Proceedings   8.142
Appeals against the outcome of a misconduct meeting   8.143
Appeals from the outcomes of misconduct hearings   8.155

9. The Police (Conduct) Regulations 2004

A. Overview   9.01
The Police (Conduct) Regulations 2004 and the application
    of Home Office Guidance   9.01
The purpose of proceedings under the 2004 Conduct Regulations   9.07
The relationship between the 2004 and 2008 Home Office
    Guidance   9.12
The application of the 2004 Conduct Regulations   9.16

B. The Structure, Purpose, and Application of the Regulations
and the Home Office Guidance   9.22
The structure and purpose   9.22
Application   9.25
The Code of Conduct   9.32

C. General Points and Procedural Challenges   9.45

D. Non-senior Officers   9.54
Initial handling: informal resolution outside misconduct procedures   9.54
Local resolution and the role of a 'friend'   9.59
Words of advice and written warnings as part of local resolution   9.63

Formal investigation: notifications and the duties of disclosure	9.69
Notice of investigation under reg 9: service	9.74
The investigation and use of criminal interviews	9.79
The investigating officer's report and procedure on its receipt	9.80
Withdrawal of a case	9.82
Autrefois acquit	9.83
Joint hearings and legal representation at joint hearings	9.85
Disclosure and drafting charges (reg 14)	9.87
Drafting charges under reg 14	9.90
The role of the presenting officer	9.94
Other procedural steps before a hearing	9.97
Witness notification and attendance	9.98
Officers conducting the hearing	9.101
Procedure at the hearing	9.106
Sanctions	9.111
Reviews and appeals	9.114

E. Senior Officers Under the 2004 Conduct Regulations — 9.115

F. Conclusion — 9.117

10. Special ('Fast-track') Cases Under the Police (Conduct) Regulations 2004 and 2008

A. Overview — 10.01

B. The Role of the Independent Police Complaints Commission (IPCC) and Crown Prosecution Service (CPS) — 10.09
  Providing information to the affected officer and the complainant in Sch 3 cases — 10.24

C. Special Cases Under the 2004 Conduct Regulations — 10.43
  Criteria for special cases under the 2004 Conduct Regulations — 10.48
  The procedure for consideration in advance of the hearing — 10.54
  The procedure for the hearing (paras 17–27 of the Appendix to ch 3 of the Home Office Guidance) — 10.64
  Chief constable's review, special constables, and non-senior officers — 10.70
  Appeal to the police appeals tribunals from a fast-track review — 10.75

D. Special Cases Under the 2008 Conduct Regulations — 10.77
  Pre-hearing procedures — 10.83
  Procedure following the decision to certify and refer to a special-case hearing — 10.87
  Procedure at the special-case hearing — 10.98
  Outcomes and notification — 10.108

E. Conclusion — 10.110

11. **Chief Officer Reviews, Internal Appeals, and Police Appeals Tribunals**

A. Overview   11.01

B. Chief Officer's Review Under the 2004 Conduct Regulations   11.08
   Chief officer reviews: core provisions under the 2004
      Conduct Regulations and the Home Office Guidance   11.10
   The officer conducting the review   11.12
   Who may attend   11.21
   The scope of the review   11.26
   The interpretation of chief officer review provisions
      by the Administrative Court   11.33
   The right to participate in the hearing   11.38
   The outcome of the review   11.39

C. Senior Officer Appeals   11.44

D. The Police Appeals Tribunals   11.45
   Statutory basis   11.45
   Common features: Police Act 1996, s 85 and Sch 6   11.49
   Appeals under the 1999 PAT Rules   11.54
   Appeals under the 2008 PAT Rules   11.72

E. Conclusion   11.112

12. **Abuse of Process**

A. Overview   12.01

B. The Police as a Regulated Profession   12.08
   The primacy of regulations   12.08
   Examples of consequences of failing to follow the regulatory
      framework   12.17
   The timing and availability of judicial review   12.24

C. Jurisdiction   12.27
   Ex p Bennett and executive unlawfulness   12.27
   The practicability of a fair hearing and regulatory departure   12.36
   Exceptional remedy   12.45
   Burden   12.47

D. Regulatory Departure   12.49

E. Delay   12.55

F. 'Fair Hearing Impossible'   12.57

G. Article 6 of the European Convention on Human Rights
   (ECHR)   12.59

H. Conclusion   12.65

13. Probationers

A. Overview   13.01

B. Regulation 13 of the Police Regulations 2003   13.03
   Decided authorities   13.14
   Conclusions from the case law   13.23
   Procedure   13.24

C. Conclusion   13.26

14. Inquests

A. Overview   14.01
   Introduction   14.01
   Coronial law, policing, and the engagement of Art 2 of the ECHR   14.14

B. The Nature and Purpose of an Inquest   14.25
   Statutory purpose: statutory provisions   14.28
   Jamieson and *Middleton* inquests: general observations   14.33
   Inquests distinguished from other forms of proceeding   14.37

C. The Duty to Hold, and the Timing of, an Inquest   14.43
   The duty to hold an inquest (s 8(1))   14.47
   Summoning a jury (s 8(3) and (4))   14.52
   Inquests and criminal proceedings (s 16)   14.59
   Inquests following a public inquiry   14.68
   The scope of the inquest if resumed   14.71
   Challenging decisions regarding resumption or the conduct
      of an inquest   14.74

D. The Scope of the Inquest: *Jamieson*, *Middleton*, and Art 2   14.77
   Introduction and central conclusions in *Jamieson*   14.77
   Article 2 and *Middleton*   14.84
   Subsequent developments in the context of Art 2 inquests   14.87
   Participation, *Amin*, and disclosure   14.89
   Middleton, narrative verdicts, and restrictions on narrative verdicts 14.95
   Rule 43 and the Coroners (Amendment) Rules 2008   14.105

E. Fundamental Points of Procedure   14.110
   Qualification as an interested person   14.110
   The funding of interested persons   14.112

Anonymity 14.127
Presence in court for other witnesses and the privilege against
    self-incrimination 14.142
Witness summons and the admissibility of disputed evidence 14.147

F. Verdicts 14.153
Withdrawing a verdict from the jury: *Galbraith* and *Douglas-Williams* 14.156
Leaving verdicts at inquests 14.162
Unlawful killing and the lethal use of firearms 14.168
Challenging decisions as to verdicts 14.179

G. Conclusion 14.180

15. Police-related Criminal Offences

A. Overview 15.01
Common issues 15.01
The relationship with misconduct charges 15.08

B. Misconduct in Public Office 15.10
A summary of the elements 15.15
'1. A public officer acting as such (paragraph 54)' 15.20
'2. Wilfully neglects to perform his duty and/or wilfully
    misconducts himself (paragraphs 28, 30, 45 and 55)' 15.45
'3. To such a degree as to amount to an abuse of the public's trust
    in the office holder (paragraphs 46 and 56 to 59)' 15.66
'4. Without reasonable excuse or justification (paragraph 60)' 15.70
Conclusions in relation to misconduct in public office 15.73

C. Unlawful Killing 15.75
Introduction 15.75
An overview of the forms of homicide 15.78
The duty of care 15.81
Causation 15.84
Self-defence and reasonable use of force in the performance
    of a legal duty 15.88
Unlawful and dangerous act manslaughter 15.91
Gross negligence manslaughter 15.96
Corporate manslaughter 15.114

D. Driving-related Offences 15.128
The law 15.133
Section 87 exemption 15.138
The application of the exemption to police response drivers 15.141

Milton   15.146
   A summary of the liability of the police driver and the associated duty
     of other road users   15.159
  E. Conclusions   15.163

Appendix A: A Table of Force Statistics   501
Appendix B: The Police Appeals Tribunals Rules 1999, SI 1999/818   504
Appendix C: The Police (Conduct) Regulations 2004, SI 2004/645   510
**Appendix D: The Police (Complaints and Misconduct)
   Regulations 2004, SI 2004/643, as amended**   532
Appendix E: The Police Reform Act 2002, Schedule 3, Part 1   554
**Appendix F: The Police (Performance) Regulations 2008,
   SI 2008/2862**   587
**Appendix G: The Police (Conduct) Regulations 2008,
   SI 2008/2864**   613
**Appendix H: The Police Appeals Tribunals Rules 2008,
   SI 2008/2863**   646
Appendix I: Home Office Guidance (2008) *Police Officer Misconduct,*
   Unsatisfactory Performance and Attendance Management
   Procedures   656
**Appendix J: The Police (Amendment) Regulations 2008,
   SI 2008/2865**   749

Index   753

TABLE OF CASES

A v Secretary of State for the Home Department [2005] UKHL 71, [2006] 2 AC 221 . . . . . 12.34
Aitken v Yarwood [1965] 1 QB 327, QBD 15.156
Alexandrou v Oxford [1993] 4 All ER 328, CA 15.83
Andrews v DPP [1937] AC 576, (1938) 26 Cr App R 34, HL 15.92, 15.111
Ashley v Chief Constable of Sussex [2008] UKHL 25, [2008] 3 All ER 573 . . . . 15.83
Attorney General v Barker (Civil Proceedings Order) [2000] 1 FLR 759, DC 12.35
Attorney General of the British Virgin Islands v Hartwell [2004] UKPC 12,
    [2004] 1 WLR 1273 (BVI) 15.83
Attorney General's Reference (No 1 of 1990), [1992] QB 630, CA 7.117, 12.40,
                                   12.45, 12.47, 12.55
Attorney General's Reference (No 3 of 2003), [2004] EWCA Crim 868, [2005]
    QB 73, [2004] Cr App R 23, [2004] 3 WLR 451 . . . . 9.41, 15.12, 15.15, 15.18,
                    15.19, 15.28, 15.32, 15.46, 15.49, 15.52, 15.54, 15.62, 15.65
Attorney General's Reference (No 4 of 2000), [2001] EWCA Crim 780,
    [2001] 2 Cr App R 417 . . . . 15.149
AWG Group Ltd (formerly Anglian Water Plc) v Morrison [2006] EWCA Civ 6,
    [2006] 1 All ER 967 . . . . 5.38, 11.17
B (Children) (Sexual Abuse: Standard of Proof), [2008] UKHL 35,
    [2009] 1 AC 11 . . . . 8.106
Bennett v Officers A and B [2004] EWCA Civ 1439, [2005] UKHRR 44 . . . . 14.134
Bijl v General Medical Council [2001] UKPC 42, [2002] Lloyd's Rep Med 60 (UK) 8.133
Blackburn (No 3) [1973] QB 241, [1973] 1 All ER 324, CA 1.05
Bolt v Chief Constable of Merseyside. *See* R (Bolt) v Chief Constable of Merseyside
Bolton v Law Society [1994] 1 WLR 512, CA 8.131, 8.136
Brooks v Commissioner of Police of the Metropolis [2005] UKHL 24,
    [2005] 1 WLR 1495 . . . . 15.83
Bryant v Law Society [2007] EWHC 3043 (Admin), [2009] 1 WLR 163 . . . . 6.37, 9.36
Bubbins v United Kingdom (50196/99) (2005) 41 EHRR 458 . . . . 14.101
C v Police and Secretary of State for the Home Department, IPT/03/02H 7.163
Calveley v Chief Constable of Merseyside [1989] AC 1228, HL 12.52, 15.83
Caparo Industries Plc v Dickman [1990] 2 AC 605, HL 15.83
Carroll v West Midlands Police (CA, 10 May 1994) 13.17
Carter v Chief Constable of Cumbria Police [2008] EWHC 1072 (QB) 15.63
Chief Constable of North Wales v Evans. *See* R v Chief Constable of
    North Wales, ex p Evans
Clayton v HM Coroner for South Yorkshire (East District). *See* R (Clayton) v
    HM Coroner for South Yorkshire (East District)
Compagnie Financiere du Pacific v Peruvian Guano Co [1882] 11 QBD 55 . . . . 7.34
Condron v United Kingdom (35718/97) (2001) 31 EHRR 1, [2000] Crim LR 679 . . . . . . 8.95
Connelly v DPP [1964] AC 1254 . . . . 12.46
Council for the Regulation of Healthcare Professionals v General Medical
    Council and Saluja [2006] EWHC 2784 (Admin),
    [2007] 1 WLR 3094 . . . . 12.06, 12.41, 12.42
Crowther's Case (1600) Cro Eliz 654 . . . . 15.22

Doherty, Re [2008] UKHL 33 [2008] 1 WLR 1499 . . . . 8.106
Donkin v Law Society [2007] EWHC 414 (Admin), (2007) 157 NLJ 402, DC 6.37, 8.109
DPP v Milton (No 1) [2006] EWHC 242 (Admin), (2006) 170 JP 319, DC 15.145,
15.149–15.153, 15.155, 15.158
DPP v Newbury ([1977] AC 500, HL 15.91, 15.94
Ebrahim v Feltham Magistrates Court, sub nom Mouat v DPP [2001]
2 Cr App R 23 . . . . 12.58
Elguzouli-Daf v Commissioner of Police of the Metropolis [1995]
QB 335, CA 15.83
Farmer v British Transport Police (CA, 30 July 1999) 13.21, 13.22, 13.23
Fatnani v General Medical Council [2007] EWCA Civ 46, [2007]
1 WLR 1460 . . . . 8.131
Friedl v Austria (A/305-B) (1996) 21 EHRR 83 . . . . 7.162
Gee v General Medical Council [1987] 1 WLR 564, HL 8.26
Ghosh v General Medical Council [2001] UKPC 29, [2001] 1 WLR 1915 (UK) 11.59
Green, Re (Southwark Crown Court, 7 January 2008) 15.25
H (Minors) (Sexual Abuse: Standard of Proof), Re [1996] AC 563, HL 8.106
Heagren v Chief Constable of Norfolk [1997] EWCA Civ 2044 . . . . 15.83
Henly v Lyme Corp (1828) 5 Bing 91 . . . . 15.33
Hill v Chief Constable of West Yorkshire [1989] AC 53, HL 15.83
Hodgson v South Wales Police Authority. *See* R (Hodgson) v
South Wales Police Authority
Howell v Lees Millais [2007] EWCA Civ 720, (2007) 104(29) LSG 24 . . . . 5.38
Howlett v HM Coroner for Devon [2006] EWHC 2570 (Admin), [2006]
Inquest LR 176 . . . . 14.21, 14.94
Johnson and Maggs v Professional Conduct Committee of the Nursing and
Midwifery Council [2008] EWHC 885 (Admin) 12.41
Jones v Warwick University [2003] EWCA Civ 151, [2003] 1 WLR 954 . . . . 7.165
Jordan v United Kingdom (2001) EHRR 52 . . . . 14.89, 14.102, 14.103
Khan v United Kingdom (35394/97) (2001) 31 EHRR 45 . . . . 7.162
Kirkham v Chief Constable of Greater Manchester, sub nom
Kirkham v Anderton [1990] 2 QB 283, CA 15.107, 15.108
Knightley v Johns [1982] 1 WLR 349, CA 15.83
Laker Airways Ltd v Department of Trade [1977] QB 643, CA 11.22
Lancaster and Worrall (1890) 16 Cox CC 739 . . . . 15.34
Lee v United Kingdom (53429/99) [2000] Po LR 170 ECHR 12.61, 12.63
McCann v United Kingdom (A/324) (1996) 21 EHRR 97 . . . . 14.103
McCaughey, Re application for judicial review [2004] NIQB 2 . . . . 14.94
Mackalley's Case (1611) 9 Co Rep 656 . . . . 15.22
McKerr's Application for Judicial Review, Re [2004] UKHL 12,
[2004] 1 WLR 807, [2004] 2 All ER 409 (NI) 14.34
McNern v Commissioner of Police of the Metropolis [2000] Po LR 117 CA 15.83
Maddison (Deceased), Re [2002] EWHC 2567 (Admin), The Times,
28 November 2002, DC 14.94
Marshall v Osmond [1983] QB 1034, CA 15.143
Milton v Crown Prosecution Service [2007] EWHC 532 (Admin),
[2008] 1 WLR 2481 . . . . 6.39, 15.145, 15.149, 15.153
Murray v United Kingdom (Right to Silence) (18731/91)
(1996) 22 EHRR 29 . . . . 8.95
Musumeci v Attorney General of New South Wales [2002] NSWSC 425 . . . . 14.94
N v Secretary of State for the Home Department [2005] UKHL 31,
[2005] 2 AC 296 . . . . 14.103
Officer L, Re [2007] UKHL 36, [2007] 1 WLR 2135, [2007]
4 All ER 965 . . . . 14.134, 14.135

Osman v United Kingdom (23452/94) (2000) 29 EHRR 245 . . . . 14.15, 14.130,
14.135, 14.140
Palmer (Sigismund) v R [1971] AC 814 PC (Jam). 15.02
Paul v Deputy Coroner of the Queen's Household [2007]
EWHC 408 (Admin); [2008] QB 172 . . . . 14.54
Pellegrin v France (2001) 31 EHRR 651 . . . . 7.27, 9.08, 12.59
Porter v Magill [2001] UKHL 67, [2002] 2 AC 357. . . . . 5.38, 11.17
Powell v United Kingdom (Admissibility) (45305/99) (2000)
30 EHRR CD 362 . . . . 14.103
Practice Direction (Crown Ct: Defendant's Evidence) [1995] 2 Cr App R 192
Sup Ct 8.92
R v Adomako [1995] 1 AC 171, HL. 15.66, 15.96, 15.100,
15.105, 15.108, 15.112
R v Argent [1997] 2 Cr App R 27, CA. 8.95
R v Bateman (1925) 19 Cr App R 8 . . . . 15.111
R v Bembridge (1738) 3 Doug 327, CA 15.32
R v Borron (1820) 3 B&Ald 432, KB 15.47
R v Boston (1923) 33 CLR 386, HC (Aus) 15.31, 15.35
R v Bowden [1996] 1 WLR 98, [1996] 1 Cr App R 104, CA. 15.32, 15.38
R v Cato (1976) 62 Cr App R 41. . . . . 15.85
R v Chief Constable of Avon and Somerset, CO/2425/00, 10 July 2000 . . . . 8.33
R v Chief Constable of Devon and Cornwall, ex p Hay [1996] 2 All ER 711 . . . . 12.39
R v Chief Constable of Merseyside, ex p Calveley [1986] QB 424, CA. 7.114, 7.116,
7.119, 12.52
R v Chief Constable of Merseyside, ex p Merrill [1989] 1 WLR 1077, CA. 7.116–7.118,
12.03, 12.04, 12.24, 12.26, 12.37, 12.38, 12.40, 12.50
R v Chief Constable of North Wales, ex p Evans, sub nom
Chief Constable of North Wales v Evans [1982] 1 WLR 1155, HL 12.22, 13.15
R v Chief Constable of Sussex ex p International Trader's Ferry [1999]
2 AC 415, [1999] 1 All ER 129, [1998] 3 WLR 260, HL 1.05
R v Church [1966] 1 QB 59, CCA. 15.94
R v Clegg [1995] 1 AC 482. . . . . 15.02
R v Collins [1997] RTR 439, CA 15.149, 15.151, 15.154
R v Cowan [1996] Cr App R 1, CA. 8.95
R v Curley (1909) 2 Cr App R 109, CCA 15.85
R v Currie (Central Criminal Court, 1992). 15.31
R v Daniel (1754) 1 Leach 44, (1754) 1 East PC 333 . . . . 15.84
R v Davies [2008] UKHL 36 . . . . 14.40
R v Davis [2008] UKHL 36, [2008] 1 AC 1128 . . . . 14.129
R v DPP, ex p Duckenfield [1999] 2 All ER 873, [2000] 1 WLR 55, CA 1.03, 1.25, 1.105
R v Dytham [1979] QB 722, CA. 15.22, 15.32
R v Evans (Gemma) [2009] EWCA Crim 650; [2009] WLR (D) 118, CA 15.83
R v G [2003] UKHL 50, [2004] 1 AC 1034 . . . . 15.55, 15.58, 15.69
R v Galbraith [1981] 2 All ER 1060, (1981) 73 Cr App R
124, CA. 14.157, 14.162, 14.164, 14.166, 14.173
R v General Medical Council, ex p Toth [2000] 1 WLR 2209, QBD. 12.43
R v Grant (Edward) [2005] EWCA Crim 1089, [2006] QB 60, [2005]
3 WLR 437, [2005] 2 Cr App R 28, [2005] Crim. LR 955 . . . . 7.165
R v GS [2005] EWCA Crim 887 . . . . 7.155
R v H [2004] UKHL 3, [2004] 2 AC 134 . . . . 7.22, 7.155
R v Hedgcock [2007] EWCA Crim 3486 . . . . 14.161
R v Hennigan (1971) 55 Cr App R 262, CA (Crim Div) 15.85
R v Hickinbottom (Hull Crown Court, 19 April 2005). 15.102
R v HM Coroner for Cardiff, ex p Thomas [1970] 1 WLR 1475, DC 14.154

R v HM Coroner for East Kent, ex p Spooner (The Herald of Free Enterprise)
(1988) 152 JP 115 . . . . 14.179
R v HM Coroner for East Sussex Western District, ex p Homberg (1994)
158 JP 357 . . . . 14.82
R v HM Coroner for Exeter and East Devon, ex p Palmer [1997] EWCA 2951 . . . . 14.179
R v HM Coroner for Greater London Southern District ex p Driscoll R (1995)
159 JP 45, DC 14.111
R v HM Coroner for Hammersmith, ex p Peach [1980] QB 211, CA 3.147, 14.55
R v HM Coroner for Inner London North District, ex p Koto (Diesa) (1993)
157 JP 857, DC 14.179
R v HM Coroner for Inner London West District, ex p Dallaglio [1994]
4 All ER 139, CA 14.27, 14.63, 14.81, 14.82
R v HM Coroner for North Humberside and Scunthorpe, ex p Jamieson
[1995] QB 1, [1994] 3 WLR 82, [1994] 3 All ER 972. . . . . 14.31, 14.33, 14.41,
14.63. 14.77, 14.78, 14.80–14.82
R v HM Coroner for South London, ex p Thompson (1982)
126 SJ 625, DC 14.41
R v HM Coroner for Southwark, ex p Hicks [1987] 1 WLR 1624, QBD. 3.147
R v HM Coroner for Southwark, ex p Kendall [1988] 1 WLR 1186, QBD 14.76
R v HM Coroner for the City of London, ex p Barber [1975] 1 WLR 1310,
[1975] 3 All ER 538, [1975] Crim LR 515; (1975) 119 SJ 697 DC. 14.154
R v Horseferry Road Magistrates Court, ex p Bennett (No 1) [1994]
1 AC 42, HL 12.03, 12.27, 12.28. 12.33
R v Lang [2005] EWCA Crim 2864, [2006] 2 Cr App R (S) 3. . . . . 10.38
R v Larkin (1942) 29 Cr App R 18, CA. 15.91
R v Latif [1996] 1 WLR 104, HL 12.33, 12.46
R v Lesley [1996] 1 Cr App R 39, CA 14.160
R v Llewellyn-Jones [1968] 1 QB 429, CA 15.66
R v Looseley: Attorney General's Reference (No 3 of 2000) [2001] UKHL 53,
[2002] 1 Cr App R 29, [2001] 1 WLR 2060 . . . . 12.34
R v Lord Saville of Newdigate, ex p B (No 2), sub nom R v Lord Saville of
Newdigate, ex p A [2000] 1 WLR 1855; [1999] 4 All ER 860, CA 14.134
R v Lowe [1973] QB 702, (1973) 57 Cr App R 365, CA. .15.93, 15.111
R v Marison ([1997] RTR 457. . . . . 15.153
R v McInnes (1971) 55 Cr App R 551, CA 15.02
R v Mellor [1996] 2 Cr App R 245, The Times, 29 February 1996. . . . . 15.86
R v Commissioner of Police of the Metropolis, ex p Blackburn [1968]
2 QB 118, [1968] 1 All ER 763, CA 1.04, 1.05
R v Misra [2004] EWCA Crim 2375, [2005]
1 Cr App R 21 . . . . 15.96–15.98, 15.105, 15.112
R v Newton (1983) 77 Cr App R 13, CA. 8.30
R v North and East Devon HA, ex p Coughlan [2001] QB 213, [2000]
2 WLR 622, CA 6.42, 12.19
R v Pagett (1983) 76 Cr App R 279. . . . . 15.87
R v Pitts (1842) C&Mar 248 . . . . 15.85
R v Police Complaints Board, ex p Madden; R v Police Complaints Board,
ex p Rhone [1983] 2 All RE 353, [1983] Crim LR 263 . . . . 1.73
R v Russell-Jones (Kenneth) [1995] 3 All ER 239, [1995] 1 Cr App R 538, CA 9.94
R v Secretary of State for the Home Office, ex p Northumbria Police Authority [1989]
1 QB 26, CA 1.03
R v Sheppard [1981] AC 394, HL. 15.52, 15.53
R v Shippey [1988] Crim LR 767, QBD. 14.160
R v Stephens; R v Mujuru [2007] EWCA Crim 1249, [2007]
2 Cr App R 26 . . . . 10.39

R v Surrey Coroner, ex p Campbell [1982] QB 661, DC. 14.143
R v Whitaker [1914] 3 KB 1283, (1914) 10 Cr App R 245, CCA 15.34, 15.38
R v Woodward [1995] RTR 130, CA 15.153
R (A) v Lord Saville of Newdigate (Bloody Sunday Inquiry) [2001]
     EWCA Civ 2048, [2002] 1 WLR 1249. . . . . 14.134
R (Amin) v Secretary of State for the Home Department [2003]
     UKHL 51, [2004] 1 AC 653, [2003] WLR 1169 . . . . .14.42, 14.66, 14.71,
                                                                                         14.89, 14.95
R (Anderson) v HM Coroner for Inner North Greater London [2004]
     EWHC 2729 (Admin); [2004] Inquest LR 155 . . . . .14.169, 14.170
R (Bennett) v HM Coroner for Inner South London [2007] EWCA Civ 617,
     [2007] Inquest LR 163 . . . . .6.50, 7.58, 14.164, 14.170, 14.172, 14.175
R (Bennion) v Chief Constable of Merseyside [2001] EWCA Civ 638,
     [2001] IRLR 442, [2002] ICR 136. . . . . 11.38
R (Bentley) v HM Coroner for Avon [2001] EWHC Admin 170,
     (2002) 166 JP 297 . . . . .14.21, 14.94
R (Bolt) v Chief Constable of Merseyside [2007] EWHC 2607 (QB) 6.45, 10.70,
                                                                                    11.15, 11.34, 11.42
R (Campbell) v General Medical Council [2005] EWCA Civ 250,
     [2005] 1 WLR 3488. . . . . 8.110
R (Canning) v HM Coroner for Northampton [2006] EWCA Civ 1225,
     [2006] Inquest LR 155 . . . . .14.47, 14.48
R (Cash) v HM Coroner for Northamptonshire [2007] EWHC 1354 (Admin),
     [2007] 4 All ER 903 . . . . .14.36, 14.102
R (Challender) v Legal Services Commission [2004] EWHC 925 (Admin),
     [2004] Inquest LR 58 . . . . 14.124
R (Chief Constable of Avon and Somerset Police) v Police Appeals Tribunal
     [2004] EWHC 220 (Admin), (2004) Times, 11 February, [2004]
     All ER (D) 17 (Feb) 1.72, 3.160, 7.26, 8.99, 8,131, 9.05,
                                                                                   11.54, 11.69, 11.75
R (Clayton) v HM Coroner for South Yorkshire (East District) [2005]
     EWHC 1196 (Admin), [2005] Inquest LR 110, DC. 14.76, 14.96, 14.104
R (Coghlan) v Chief Constable of Greater Manchester [2004] EWHC 2801
     (Admin), [2005] 2 All ER 890 . . . . .1.72, 12.16
R (Coker) v HM Coroner for Inner South London [2006] EWHC 614
     (Admin), [2006] Inquest LR 98 . . . . 14.21, 14.37, 14.94, 14.146
R (Commissioner of Police of the Metropolis) v HM Coroner for Greater London
     Southern District [2003] EWHC 1829 (Admin); [2003] Inquest
     LR 132; [2003] ACD 87. . . . . 14.100
R (Craik) v Coroner for Wiltshire and Swindon [2004]
     EWHC 2653 (Admin) 14.179
R (D) v Secretary of State for the Home Department [2006] EWCA Civ
     143 [2006] 3 All ER 946. . . . . 14.88
R (Da Silva) v DPP [2006] EWHC 3204 (Admin); [2006] Inquest
     LR 224, DC. 15.100, 15.113
R (Douglas-Williams) v HM Coroner for Inner London South District
     [1999] 1 All ER 344, (1998) 162 JP 751, CA 14.163, 14.166
R (Gibson) v General Medical Council [2004] EWHC 2781 (Admin) 12.43
R (Green) v Police Complaints Authority [2004] UKHL 6, [2004]
     1 WLR 725 . . . . 3.30, 3.34, 7.93
R (Hodgson) v South Wales Police Authority [2008] EWHC 1183 (Admin),
     [2008] ACD 78 . . . . 12.22
R (Hurst) v HM Coroner for Northern District London [2007] UKHL 13,
     [2007] 2 AC 189 . . . . 14.34

R (Independent Police Complaints Commission) v Assistant Commissioner
  Hayman [2008] EWHC 2191 (Admin) 8.106, 9.12
R (Independent Police Complaints Commission) v Chief Constable of West Mercia
  [2007] EWHC 1035 (Admin), [2007] Inquest LR 95. . . . . 3.28
R (Independent Police Complaints Commission) v Chief Constable of
  West Midlands (Re Howarth) [2007] EWHC 2715 (Admin) 3.158, 10.73,
                                                                          11.22, 11.32, 11.34
R (Independent Police Complaints Commission) v Hayman [2007]
  EWHC 2136 (Admin) 11.34
R (Kasperowicz) v Plymouth Coroner [2005] EWCA Civ 44 . . . . 14.50
R (Khan) v HM Coroner for West Hertfordshire [2002] EWHC 302 . . . . 14.179
R (Khan) v Secretary of State for Health [2003] EWCA Civ 1129, [2004]
  1 WLR 971 . . . . .14.122, 14.123
R (Lewis) v HM Coroner for the Mid and North Division of the
  County of Shropshire, [2009] EWHC 661 (Admin). 14.103
R (Longfield Care Homes Ltd) v HM Coroner for Blackburn [2004]
  EWHC 2467 (Admin), [2004] Inquest LR 50 . . . . .14.83, 14.97
R (Main) v Minister for Legal Aid [2007] EWCA Civ 1147,
  [2008] HRLR 8 . . . . 14.125
R (Maria Otone de Menezes) v Assistant Deputy Coroner for Inner South London,
  [2008] EWHC 3356 (Admin), 3 December 2008. . . . . 14.104
R (Middleton) v HM Coroner for Western Somerset [2004] UKHL 10,
  [2004] 2 AC 182 . . . . 1.108, 14.30, 14.33, 14.34, 14.36,
                                    14.39, 14.41, 14.42, 14.66, 14.77, 14.83–14.85, 14.95,
                                    14.98, 14.99, 14.101, 14.104, 14.105, 14.179
R (Mullen) v Secretary of State for the Home Department [2000] QB 529, CA. 12.34
R (O'Leary) v Chief Constable of Merseyside [2001] EWHC Admin 57,
  [2001] Po LR 10. . . . . 12.17
R (Pamplin) v Law Society [2001] EWHC Admin 300 . . . . .7.150, 7.151
R (Paul) v Assistant Deputy Coroner of Inner West London [2007]
  EWCA Civ 1259, [2008] 1 WLR 1335. . . . . .3.147, 14.150
R (Pekkelo) v HM Coroner for Central and South East Kent [2006]
  EWHC 1265 (Admin); [2006] Inquest LR 119 . . . . 14.103
R (Reynolds) v Chief Constable of Sussex [2008] EWCA Civ 1160, (2008)
  105(42) LSG 22. . . . . 6.17, 14.20, 14.91
R (Rowley) v DPP [2003] EWHC 693 (Admin); [2003]
  Inquest LR 96 DC 15.101
R (Sacker) v HM Coroner for West Yorkshire [2004] UKHL 11, [2004]
  1 WLR 796 . . . . .14.13, 14.105
R (Saunders) v Independent Police Complaints Commission [2008]
  EWHC 2372 (Admin), [2009] 1 All ER 379. . . . . 3.33, 6.17, 10.26, 10.40,
                                                                          14.20, 14.92
R (Scholes) v Secretary of State for the Home Department [2006]
  EWCA Civ 1343, [2006] HRLR 44 . . . . 14.13, 14.99, 14.105
R (Secretary of State for the Home Department) v Humberside Police Authority
  [2004] EWHC 1642 (Admin), [2004] ACD 92 . . . . .1.77, 2.21
R (Sharman) v HM Coroner for Inner North London, sub nom
  Sharman v HM Coroner for Inner North London [2005] EWCA Civ 967,
  [2005] Inquest LR 168. . . . . 14.08, 14.104, 14.168, 14.170,
                                                                          14.173, 14.175, 14.176
R (Smith) v Oxfordshire Assistant Deputy Coroner [2008]
  EWHC 694 (Admin), [2008] 3 WLR 1284 . . . . .14.21, 14.94
R (Takoushis) v HM Coroner for Inner North London [2005]
  EWCA Civ 1440, [2006] 1 WLR 461. . . . . .14.27, 14.53

R (Touche) v HM Coroner for Inner North London District [2001]
  EWCA Civ 383, [2001] QB 1206. . . . . .14.47, 14.49
R (Wheeler) v Assistant Commissioner of Police of the Metropolis [2008]
  EWHC 439 (Admin) 5.99, 6.38, 8.27, 8.29, 9.90, 11.39
R (Whitehead) v Chief Constable of Avon and Somerset; R
  (on the application of Daglish) v Chief Constable of Avon and Somerset
  [2001] EWHC Admin 433, [2001] Po LR 174 . . . . 12.63
R (Wilkinson) v Chief Constable of West Yorkshire [2002] EWHC 2353
  (Admin); [2002] Po LR 328 . . . . 7.117, 12.03, 12.04, 12.24, 12.26, 12.37
R (Woodhams) v AC Ghaffur, CO/6155/2008 . . . . 11.35
Raissi v Commissioner of Police of the Metropolis [2008] EWCA Civ 1237,
  (2008) 105(45) LSG 19 . . . . 7.158
Rao v State of India [1999] 3 LRC 297, Sup Ct (India) 15.31, 15.36
Redgrave v Commissioner of Police of the Metropolis [2003] EWCA Civ 4,
  [2003] 1 WLR 1136. . . . . 8.131, 9.11, 9.83, 12.06, 12.39,
                                                                     12.43, 12.47, 15.09
Reynolds v CC Sussex [2008] EWHC 1240 (Admin). *See* R (Reynolds)
  v Chief Constable of Sussex
Reza v General Medical Council [1991] 12 AC 181, HL. 8.25
Rigby v Chief Constable of Northamptonshire [1985] 1 WLR 1242, QBD. 15.83
S (A Child) v Keyse [2001] EWCA Civ 715, [2001] Po LR 169. . . . . 15.144, 15.155, 15.160
Salsbury v Law Society [2008] EWCA Civ 1285, (2008) 105(47) LSG 18. . . . . 8.131
Scholes v Secretary of State for the Home Department. *See* R (Scholes) v Secretary
  of State for the Home Department
Shields, Re [2003] UKHL 3, [2003] NO 161, [2003] All ER (D) 81 (Feb) 1.65
Shum Kwok Sher v Hong Kong Special Administrative Region [2002]
  5 HKCSAR 381 . . . . 15.17
Sin Kam Wah v Hong Kong Special Administrative Region [2005]
  2 HKLRD 375 . . . . .15.18, 15.43
Southwark LBC v Dennett [2007] EWCA Civ 1091, [2008] HLR 23. . . . . 15.63
Stockwell v Society of Lloyd's [2007] EWCA Civ 390 . . . . 15.63
Surrey Police Authority v Beckett [2001] EWCA Civ 1253, [2002] ICR 257. . . . . 7.111
Taylor v Anderton [1995] 1 WLR 447, CA. 7.93
Three Rivers DC v Bank of England (No 3) [2003] 2 AC 1, HL 15.62
Tucker v National Crime Squad [2003] EWCA Civ 57 . . . . 12.26
Twinsectra Ltd v Yardley [2002] UKHL 12, [2002] 2 AC 164. . . . . .6.37, 9.36
Van Colle v Chief Constable of Hertfordshire [2008] UKHL 50, [2008]
  3 WLR 593, [2008] 3 All ER 977 . . . . .14.130, 15.83
Varma v General Medical Council [2008] EWHC 753 (Admin) [2008]
  LS Law Medical 313 . . . . 12.41
Walker v Royal College of Veterinary Surgeons [2007] UKPC 64 (UK). 8.136, 11.59
Wilkinson v Chief Constable of West Yorkshire. *See* R (Wilkinson)
  v Chief Constable of West Yorkshire
Woolgar v Chief Constable of Sussex [2000] 1 WLR 25, CA. 7.150, 7.151

TABLE OF STATUTES

Access to Justice Act 1999 . . . . 14.117
  s 6 . . . . 14.117
    (8) 14.117
  s 71(1) 14.68
  Sch 2 . . . . 14.117
Births and Deaths Registration
  Act 1953 . . . . 14.28
British Transport Commission
  Act 1949 . . . . 1.02
Children and Young Persons
  Act 1933 . . . . 15.52
  s 1 . . . . 15.52, 15.93
Commissioners for Revenue
  and Customs Act 2005
  s 28 . . . . 3.05
Constitutional Reform Act 2005
  s 12(2) 14.28
  Sch 1, Pt 2, para 19 . . . . 14.28
    para 20 . . . . 14.28
Coroners Act 1988 . . . . . 3.06, 14.94, 14.101
  s 8 . . . . 14.43
    (1) 14.44, 14.45, 14.47–14.49,
                                        14.52, 14.58
    (3) 14.46, 14.52, 14.57
      (b) 14.53
      (d) 14.53–14.56, 14.58, 14.81
    (4) 14.46, 14.52, 14.56, 14.57
  s 10(2) 14.147
    (4) 14.147
  s 11 . . . . 14.25, 14.28
    (3) 14.28
    (4) 14.28
    (5)(c) 14.28
    (6) 14.31, 14.32
  s 12(2) 14.108, 14.153
  s 13 . . . . 14.75, 14.76
  s 16 . . . . 14.43, 14.58, 14.59
    (1) 14.59
    (3) 14.61, 14.62
  s 17 . . . . 14.58
  s 17A 14.68
    (1) 14.68–14.70
    (4) 14.69
    (5) 14.70
  s 19 . . . . 14.45, 14.50

Sch 4 . . . . 14.26
Corporate Manslaughter and Corporate
  Homicide Act 2007 . . . . 15.77, 15.114
  s 1 . . . . 15.77, 15.118
  s 2 . . . . 15.82, 15.119
    (1)(a) 15.124
      (b) 15.124
      (d) 15.115, 15.121,
                                      15.124, 15.126
  s 3 . . . . 15.120
  s 4 . . . . 15.120
  s 5 . . . . 15.115, 15.120, 15.121
    (2) 15.123
      (c) 15.123
    (3) 15.124
    (4) 15.122
  s 6 . . . . 15.120
  s 7 . . . . 15.120
  s 8 . . . . 15.110, 15.125
  s 13 . . . . 15.117
    (1) 15.117
    (2) 15.119
  s 18 . . . . 15.116
  s 19 . . . . 15.116
  s 25 . . . . 15.116
  s 26 . . . . 14.32
  Sch 2, para 1(1) 14.32
    (2)(a) 14.32
Crime and Disorder Act 1998 . . . 1.27, 1.100
Criminal Damage Act 1971
  s 1 . . . . 15.58
Criminal Justice Act 1988
  ss 35–36 . . . . 15.102
Criminal Justice Act 2003
  s 170(9) 15.11
  s 172 . . . . 15.11
  ss 224–229 . . . . 10.38
Criminal Justice and Immigration Act
  2008 . . . . 10.17, 10.18
  s 76 . . . . 6.50, 14.168, 15.02,
                                        15.89, 15.90
  s 126 . . . . 1.13
  s 127 . . . . 1.13
  Sch 22 . . . . 1.13, 11.51
    para 2 . . . . 1.28

Criminal Justice and Immigration Act
  2008 (*cont.*)
  Sch 22 (*cont.*)
    para 3 . . . . .1.64
    para 6 . . . . .1.80
    para 8 . . . . .11.49, 11.72, 11.110
    (2)(2) 11.110
    para 9 . . . . .1.26, 1.69, 11.75
    (3) 1.69
    (4) 1.69
    para 11 . . . . .11.45
    (2) 11.51
    (3) 11.51
    (5) 11.51, 11.111
  Sch 23 . . . . .1.13, 3.15, 4.14, 6.66,
                                    6.83, 7.176
    para 5 . . . . .7.76
    paras 6–10 . . . . .10.11
    para 23 . . . . .6.106
Criminal Justice and Police Act 2001
  Pt 4 . . . . .1.34
  s 122 . . . . .2.08
  s 123 . . . . .2.07
Criminal Justice and Public Order Act 1994
  s 34 . . . . .1.81, 8.92, 8.95
  s 38(3) 8.95
Criminal Law Act 1967
  s 3 . . . . 6.50, 15.88
Criminal Law Act 1977
  s 3 . . . . .14.171
Criminal Procedure and Investigations
  Act 7.14, 7.18–7.21, 7.26,
              7.32, 8.24, 8.37, 9.08, 12.12
  s 3 . . . . 7.21, 7.22
    (1) 7.33
    (a) 7.22
  s 7A 7.21
Disability Discrimination
  Act 1995 . . . . .1.103, 5.79, 5.88
Domestic Violence, Crimes and
  Disorder Act 2004
  s 5 . . . . .10.39
Employment Rights Act 1996 . . . . . 5.08, 6.60
  s 42K 6.05
Equalities Act 2006 . . . . .1.103
Greater London Authority Act 1999
  s 310 . . . . .1.86
  s 318 . . . . .2.08
  s 319 . . . . .2.08
  s 320 . . . . .2.08
  Sch 27, para 28 . . . . .1.105
Health and Safety at Work etc
  Act 1974 . . . . .15.116

Human Rights Act 1998 . . . . .1.103, 3.31,
              3.32, 3.147, 7.162, 14.01,
              14.34, 14.65, 14.77, 14.83
  s 6 . . . . .3.42
    (2) 3.42
    (3)(b) 3.42
Immigration Act 2006 . . . . .1.26
Interpretation Act 1978
  s 5 . . . . .1.14
  Sch 1 . . . . .1.14
Local Government Act 1972 . . . . .1.105
  s 111(1) 1.105
  s 146A 1.105
  s 250(2) 11.67, 11.102
    (3) 11.67, 11.102
Local Government Act 1985
  Sch 14 . . . . .1.105
Local Government Act 1999
  s 1(1)(d) 1.101
  s 4 . . . . .1.34
London Government Act 1963
  s 76 . . . . .1.15
Local Government and Public
    Involvement in Health Act 2007
  s 241 . . . . .1.101
  s 245(5) 1.101
  Sch 18, Pt 8 . . . . .1.101
Medical Act 1983
  s 40 . . . . .8.133
Mental Health Act 1983
  s 136 . . . . .14.169
Ministry of Defence Police
  Act 1987 .1.02
Official Secrets Act 1989 . . . . .3.11
Police Act 1964 . . . . .1.03, 1.80, 1.86
Police Act 1996 . . . . 1.03, 1.26, 1.29,
          1.34, 1.51, 1.52, 1.72, 1.82, 1.104,
          1.110, 2.05, 2.29, 3.26, 3.30,
                              3.82, 11.19
  Preamble 1.03
  Pt 1 . . . . 1.12, 1.13
  Pts 1–3 . . . . .1.31
  Pt 2 . . . . .1.12, 1.13, 1.28
  Pt 3 . . . . 1.12, 1.31
  Pt 4 . . . . .1.12
    Ch 1 . . . . 3.28, 3.39
    Ch 2 . . . . .1.31
  Pt 5 . . . . 1.12, 1.31
  s 1 . . . . 1.14, 1.26
    (1) 1.14, 1.94
  s 2 . . . . 1.14, 1.76
    (2)(a) 1.14
    (b) 1.14

s 3 . . . . 1.30, 1.66, 1.86–1.88
s 4 . . . . .1.86
s 5B 1.86
s 5C 1.86
s 6 . . . . .1.94
 (1) 1.105, 1.110
 (2) 1.94
 (3) 1.94
 (5) 1.94
s 6A 1.96
s 6ZA 1.24, 1.96
 (2)(b) .1.24
s 6ZB 1.96
s 6ZC 1.96
s 7 . . . . .1.96
ss 7–9 . . . . .1.96
s 8 . . . . .1.96
s 8A 1.97
s 9 . . . . 1.104, 1.110
s 9E 1.76, 2.08, 2.09
ss 9E–9G 9.27
s 9F 2.08
s 9FA 2.08
s 9G 2.08
s 10 . . . . 11.17, 11.36, 11.42,
              11.84, 12.19, 13.08
 (1) 1.25, 1.104
s 11 . . . . . . 1.76, 1.104, 1.110, 2.07, 2.09,
       2.10, 2.14, 2.24, 2.28, 2.33, 9.27
 (2) 2.28
 (3) 2.28
 (3A) .2.20
s 11A 2.07
s 12 . . . . 1.104, 1.110, 2.07, 9.27
s 12A(1) 11.13
 (2) 11.13, 11.13
s 20 . . . . .1.99
s 20A 1.99
s 22 . . . . .1.61
 (3) 1.110
s 23 . . . . .1.19
 (1) 1.20
 (2) 1.20
 (3) 1.20
 (4) 1.20
 (7) 1.20
 (7A) .1.19
 (7B) .1.19
s 24 . . . . 1.19, 1.21
 (1) 1.21
 (2) 1.21
 (3) 1.21
 (4) 1.21

 (5) 1.21
s 25 . . . . .1.19
s 26 . . . . .1.19
s 32 . . . . 1.15, 2.09
s 33 . . . . .1.15
s 36(1) .1.28
 (2) 1.31
 (d) 1.28
ss 36–53 . . . . .1.28
s 36A 1.32
 (6)(a) .1.34
 (b) 1.34
 (7) 1.33, 1.34
s 37 . . . . .1.32, 1.34, 1.36
 (1) 1.36
 (2) 1.33
 (3) 1.36
s 37A 1.32, 1.33, 1.37, 1.94, 1.96
s 38 . . . . 1.32, 1.36, 1.37, 1.94
 (1) 1.37
 (2) 1.37
 (3) 1.37
 (4) 1.37
 (5) 1.38
s 39 . . . . 1.66, 1.94
s 39A 1.67
 (3) 1.74
 (4) 1.74
 (7) 1.73
s 40 . . . . .1.39, 1.45, 1.50–1.52,
             1.54, 1.58, 1.59, 2.16
 (1)(a) 1.52, 1.53
 (b) 1.52, 1.53
 (2) 1.53
 (4) 1.55, 1.56
 (a) 1.57
 (5) 1.56
 (6) 1.57
 (7) 1.57
s 40A 1.45, 1.58, 1.59, 2.16
 (4) 1.58
 (5) 1.58
s 40B 1.59, 2.16
 (1) 1.59
 (3) 1.59
 (6) 1.59
 (7) 1.59
s 41 . . . . .1.82
s 41A 1.60, 2.16
 (12) 1.60
s 41B 1.60
s 42 . . . . .2.11, 2.12, 2.14, 2.16,
             2.24, 2.29, 2.33, 9.27

Police Act 1996 (*cont.*)
(1) 1.76
(1A) 1.77, 2.20, 2.23
(3) 2.16, 2.29, 2.30
(3A) 2.29
s 43 ....1.61
s 44 ....1.61
(4) 1.61
s 45 .... 1.39, 1.82
s 46 ....1.82
s 48 ....1.82
s 49 ....1.82
s 50 ....1.68, 1.79, 1.80, 1.81,
5.01, 7.178, 7.184, 11.55
(1) 1.62
(2) 1.62
(3) 7.172
(7) 1.81
(3) 1.63, 1.64
s 51 ....1.70, 1.79, 1.80, 1.82,
5.01, 7.178, 7.184
(2A) 7.172
s 52 ....1.82
s 53 ....1.82
s 53A 1.82
s 54 ....1.45, 1.46, 1.54
(1) 1.46
(2) 1.46
(3) 1.46
(4) 1.46
s 54(2B) 1.47
(2B)–(3B) 1.47
(3) 1.47
s 55 ....1.48
(1) 1.48
(3) 1.48
(4) 1.49
(5) 1.49
(6) 1.49
s 57 ....1.82
s 60 ....1.82
s 61 .... 1.31, 1.79
(1) 1.31, 1.80
s 62 ....1.31
(1) 1.79
(1D) 1.79
(1E) 1.79
s 63 ....1.80
(1) 1.80
(1C) 1.80
(3) 1.31, 1.80
s 64 ....1.82
ss 66–76 ....1.110
s 68(1) 3.39

s 71 ....3.28
s 74 ....3.39
s 75 ....3.39
s 77 ....1.104
s 78 ....3.46
s 84 .... 1.28, 5.01
s 85 ....1.28, 1.31, 4.08, 5.01,
5.193, 5.208, 11.04, 11.06,
11.45, 11.49, 11.58, 11.72,
11.74, 11.110
(1) 1.31, 11.110
(2) 11.110, 11.111
(5) 1.31
(6) 1.31
s 87 ....1.26, 1.63, 1.68, 4.02,
9.01, 9.04, 11.55, 11.75
(1) 1.69, 5.09, 6.10, 12.50
(1A) 1.68, 1.70
(2) 1.68
(2)–(5) 1.68
(5) 1.70, 7.13
s 95 ....1.31
s 96(1) 1.98
(6)–(10) 1.98
s 97(1)(a) 6.07
(d) 6.07
(8) 7.72
s 98 .... 1.19, 1.83
s 101 ....1.16, 1.26, 1.76, 1.122
(1) 1.14, 1.76
s 102 .... 1.29, 1.36
s 103 ....1.14
s 105(1) 1.86
(4) 1.67
Sch 1 ....1.12, 1.14, 1.16, 1.17,
1.26, 2.01, 3.81
Sch 2 .... 1.12, 1.87
para 1(2) 1.88
(5) 1.88
para 2 .... 1.87, 1.88
para 3 ....1.88
para 4 .... 1.87, 1.88
para 6 ....1.87
Sch 2A 1.87
para 1 ....1.89
(2) 1.88
(3) 1.88
para 2 ....1.93
para 3 ....1.88
(a) 1.88
para 4(1)(a) 1.93
(2) 1.93
Sch 3 .... 1.12, 1.87
Sch 3A 1.87

Sch 4 . . . . .1.12
Sch 5 . . . . .1.12
Sch 6 . . . . . 1.12, 1.31, 11.45, 11.49, 11.51
  para 1 . . . . .11.51
  para 2 . . . . .11.51
  para 6 . . . . .11.51, 11.64, 11.65
    (1) 11.51
    (2) 11.51
  para 7 .11.111
    (1) 11.51, 11.52
  para 9(1) 11.51
  para 10(a) 1.76
Sch 7, para 32 . . . . .1.14
Sch 8 . . . . .1.12
Police Act 1997
  s 54(1) 11.13
Police and Criminal Evidence
    Act 1984 . . . . .12.12
  Pt IX 1.03
  s 78 . . . . .7.162
  s 96 . . . . .3.46
  s 103 . . . . .11.55
  s 117 . . . . 6.50, 15.88
Police and Justice Act 2006 . . . . . .1.03, 1.13,
                1.26, 1.30, 1.51, 1.82,
                1.83, 1.89, 1.98
  Pt 1 . . . . .1.119
  Pt 4 . . . . .1.121
  s 1 . . . . .1.121
    (1) 1.119
    (2) 1.119
    (3) 1.79, 3.05
  s 2 . . . . 1.24, 1.45, 1.51,
              1.58, 1.60, 1.88, 1.96,
              1.98, 2.16
  s 4 . . . . 1.01, 1.101
  s 6 . . . . 1.30, 1.102
    (1) 15.28
    (2) 1.30
    (3) 1.30
  s 32 . . . . .1.121
  s 52 . . . . .1.96
  s 53(1) 1.32
  Sch 1 . . . . .1.120
    Pt 1 . . . . 1.120, 1.126
    Pt 2 . . . . .1.120
    Pt 3 . . . . 1.120, 1.128
    Pt 4 . . . . .1.120
    Pt 5 . . . . .1.120
    Pt 6 . . . . .1.120
    Pt 7 . . . . .1.120, 1.127, 3.05
    para 1 . . . . 1.121, 1.124
      (e) 1.124
      (ea) 1.121

    paras 1–6 . . . . .1.120
    para 2 . . . . .1.123
      (1) 1.123
      (2)(a)(i)–(iii) 1.124
      (b) 1.124
      (3) 1.124
      (4) 1.123, 1.124
      (5) 1.123
    para 3 . . . . .1.122
    para 4 . . . . .1.126
    para 5 . . . . .1.126
    para 6 . . . . .1.126
      (4) 1.126
    para 7 . . . . .1.127
    paras 7–27 . . . . .1.120
    para 19 .1.127
    para 28 .1.128
    para 29 .1.128
    paras 29–32 . . . . .1.120
    para 30 .1.128
      (1) 1.121
      (2) 1.121
      (3) 1.121, 1.128
    para 32 .1.128
    paras 33–36 . . . . .1.120
    paras 37–46 . . . . .1.120
    paras 47–48 . . . . .1.120
    paras 49–92 . . . . .1.120
    para 61 .1.79
    para 67(1) 1.79
      (3) 1.79
    para 80 .3.05
    para 81 .1.127
    para 87 .3.05
  Sch 2 . . . . .1.51
    para 2 . . . . .1.88
    para 4 . . . . .1.88
    para 8 . . . . 1.24, 1.96
    para 9 . . . . .1.96
    para 10 .1.96
    para 27 . . . . 1.45, 1.51, 1.58, 2.16
    para 30 .1.83
      (1) 1.98
      (2) 1.98
      (4) 1.98
  Sch 4 . . . . 1.30, 1.102
    para 13 .15.28
  Sch 6, para 2 . . . . .1.16
    para 3 . . . . .1.16
  Sch 15, Pt 1(B), para 10 . . . . .1.96
Police and Magistrates' Courts
    Act 1994
  Pt 1 Ch 1 . . . . .1.03
  Sch 4 . . . . .1.105

Police Reform Act 2002 . . . . .1.03, 1.13,
　　　　1.26, 1.52, 1.82, 1.83, 1.85, 1.104,
　　　　1.111, 3.03, 3.04, 3.07, 3.13, 3.15,
　　　　3.24, 3.28, 3.32–3.34, 3.36,
　　　　3.41, 3.80, 3.84, 3.105, 4.03, 6.07,
　　　　7.73, 7.93, 9.45, 10.09,
　　　　11.14, 14.90
Preamble 3.02
Pt 1 . . . . 3.16,
Pt 2 . . . . . . 1.34, 1.67, 1.80, 1.111, 1.114,
　　　　1.116, 3.01, 3.17, 3.19, 3.20, 3.28,
　　　　3.31, 3.35, 3.37, 3.59, 3.68, 3.76,
　　　　3.78, 6.61, 6.71, 6.72, 6.80,
　　　　6.81, 7.13, 15.27
Pt 2A 6.79
Pt 3 . . . . 3.18, 3.76
Pt 4 Ch 1 . . . . 1.34, 3.21, 3.24
　Ch 2 . . . . .3.21
Pts 4–7 . . . . .3.21
Pt 5 . . . . .3.21
Pt 6 . . . . .3.21
Pt 7 . . . . .3.21
s 1 . . . . 1.32, 7.194
ss 1–9 . . . . .3.16
s 3 . . . . 1.45, 1.47
s 4 . . . . .1.45
s 5 . . . . .1.60
s 7 . . . . .1.82
s 9 . . . . 3.97, 3.160
　(1) 3.41
　(2) 3.44
　　(a) 3.98
　　(b) 3.98
　(3) 1.127, 3.45, 3.46
　(5) 3.41
　(7) 1.36, 3.22
ss 9–11 . . . . 3.17, 3.19
s 10 . . . . .3.30, 3.51, 3.59
　(1) 3.60
　　(a)–(e) 3.69
　　(b) 3.86
　　(c) 3.97
　　(d) 3.87
　　(e) 3.62, 3.69, 3.70, 3.89,
　　　　　　　　　　　　　　　3.90, 7.188
　　(e)–(h) 3.69
　　(f) 3.61, 3.69
　　(g) 3.62
　　(h) 3.62
　(2) 3.63
　(3) 3.64
　(4) 3.65, 3.66
　(5) 3.65, 3.67
　(6) 3.68

　(7) 3.69
　　(a) 3.69
　　(b) 3.69
　(8) 3.59
s 11 . . . . 3.70, 3.86
　(3) 3.89
　(4) 3.89
　(5)(b) 15.128
　(6) 3.88, 3.89
　　(b) 3.88
s 12 . . . . .1.112, 3.17, 9.45
　(1) 6.64, 6.72
　(2) 6.06, 6.64, 6.76, 6.126
　(2A) 6.64, 6.77
　(2A)–(2D) 6.78
　(2B) 6.77
　(2C) 6.77
　(3) 6.73
　(4) 6.73
　(5) 6.74
　(6) 6.75
　(7) 6.06, 6.67, 6.80
s 13 . . . . .6.82
ss 13–14 . . . . .3.17
s 14 . . . . 1.81, 1.85, 1.111, 3.80, 6.82
　(1) 6.82
　(2) 1.81
　(3) 1.81
s 15 . . . . 1.04, 1.114, 1.118, 3.35
　(6)–(10) .1.114
ss 15–27 . . . . .3.17
s 16 . . . . 1.114, 3.35
s 16A 1.114, 3.35
s 17 . . . . .1.118, 3.70, 3.86
　(1) 1.115
　(2) 1.115
　(4) 1.115
s 18 . . . . 1.116, 1.118, 3.70, 3.86
　(2) 1.116
　　(a) 1.117
　(3) 1.117
　(4)(b) 1.117
　(5) 1.118
s 20 . . . . 3.29, 10.24, 10.34,
　　　　　　　　　　　　　　　14.20, 14.91
　(1) 10.34, 10.36, 14.90
　(2) 10.34, 10.36, 14.20, 14.90
　(4) 10.34, 14.20, 14.90
　(5) 7.193, 10.35
　(5)–(7) 7.181, 10.34
　(6)–(9) .10.24
s 20F 10.34
s 20E(3) 10.34
s 20H 10.34

s 21 . . . . .6.155, 7.175, 7.181, 7.184,
7.185, 7.191, 10.25, 10.28,
10.34, 10.41, 14.20, 14.91
(5) 7.10
(6) 10.36, 14.90
(7) 10.36, 14.90
s 22 . . . . 1.85, 3.55, 3.57, 3.71,
3.74, 3.75, 3.80, 3.86, 6.4,
6.91, 7.67, 7.189, 9.17
(1) 3.72
(2) 3.72, 3.77, 3.78
(3) 3.58, 3.71
(4) 3.71
(5) 3.77, 3.79
(6) 3.71
(7) 3.58, 3.73
(8) 3.73
s 26 . . . . 1.11, 3.46, 3.64, 3.82
s 26A 1.11, 3.05, 3.64
s 26B 1.11, 3.05, 3.64
s 27 . . . . .3.167, 3.169, 3.170
(4) 3.169
s 28 . . . . 3.17, 3.23
(3) 3.24
s 29 . . . . . . .1.76, 1.111, 3.17, 8.76, 11.12
(1) 7.13
(3) 6.07, 6.67
(4) 6.07
(a) 6.07
s 30 . . . . 2.07, 2.08
ss 30–32 . . . . 2.10, 9.27
ss 30–33 . . . . 2.05, 2.14
ss 30–34 . . . . .3.18
s 31 . . . . .2.07
s 33 . . . . .2.11
ss 35–37 . . . . .3.18
s 36 . . . . .1.81
s 37 . . . . 6.05, 6.60
s 38 . . . . 15.23, 15.24, 15.29, 15.30
(1) 15.25
(2) 15.25
ss 38–47 . . . . .3.21
ss 38–108 . . . . .3.21
s 39 . . . . .3.46, 3.64, 15.26, 15.27,
15.29, 15.30
(1) 15.26
(1)–(8) 15.28
(2) 15.26, 15.27
(a) 15.26
(b) 15.26
(9) 15.28
(10) 15.28
(11)(a) 15.28
(b) 15.28

(c) 15.28
(d) 15.28
(12) 15.28
(13) 15.28
s 41 . . . . .3.46
s 41A 3.46
s 43 . . . . .7.06
ss 48–78 . . . . .3.21
s 77 . . . . .1.110
s 78 . . . . .1.02
ss 78–81 . . . . .3.21
s 79 . . . . .1.02
ss 82–104 . . . . .3.21
ss 82–91 . . . . .3.21
s 83 . . . . .1.12
s 87(1) 7.06, 8.10
ss 92–102 . . . . .3.21
s 103(7) 1.22
ss 103–104 . . . . .3.21
s 105 . . . . .1.36
(4) 1.36, 3.167
ss 105–108 . . . . .3.21
s 107(1) 1.68
s 108 . . . . .1.36
Sch 2 . . . . .3.17, 3.19, 3.45, 3.97, 3.160
Pt 3 . . . . .3.20
para 1 . . . . .3.50
(1) 3.98
(3) 3.47
(4) 3.99
(5) 3.99
(6) 3.100
para 2 . . . . .3.50
(1) 3.98
(5) 3.100
(6) 3.100
(f) 3.116, 3.165
(g) 3.116, 3.165
(7) 3.100
para 24 . . . . .1.32
para 25 . . . . 1.32, 1.33
para 26 . . . . .1.32
Sch 3 . . . . .1.81, 1.111, 3.17, 3.20,
3.91, 4.11, 4.14, 6.01, 6.09, 6.15,
6.17, 6.18, 6.22, 6.25, 6.61,
6.63–6.68, 6.70, 6.82, 6.83, 6.120,
6.136, 6.146, 7.01–7.03, 7.05, 7.76,
7.78, 7.89, 7.96, 7.113, 7.122, 7.127,
7.137, 7.147, 7.169, 7.187,
8.01, 8.16, 8.78, 9.03, 9.17, 9.25,
9.45, 9.102, 9.115, 10.24, 10.26,
12.13, 12.49, 12.54
Pt 1 . . . . .1.112, 3.20, 4.14, 6.25,
6.61, 6.83, 6.85, 6.140, App E

Police Reform Act 2002 (*cont.*)
Pt 2 . . . . 1.113, 3.20, 6.25, 6.61,
6.78, 6.83, 6.125, 6.139, 6.140
Pt 2A 1.113, 3.06, 3.20, 6.25,
6.61, 6.83, 6.140
Pt 3 . . . . 3.20, 4.14, 6.01, 6.04,
6.14, 6.16, 6.25, 6.61, 6.98,
7.01, 7.63, 7.64, 7.74,
10.10, 10.26, 10.28
para 1 . . . . 6.85, 6.143
paras 1–9 .3.20
para 2 . . . . 1.112, 6.86–6.88
paras 2–4 . . . . .1.112
para 3 . . . . 1.112, 6.87
(3) 3.40
(7) 6.89
para 4 . . . . 1.112, 6.25, 6.90,
6.98, 6.114
(1) 6.91, 6.94, 6.132
(c) 3.87, 6.93
(2) 6.92, 6.94, 6.133
(3) 6.94, 6.95, 6.134
(4) 6.96
(6) 6.97
para 5 . . . . 6.98, 6.138
(2) 6.100
para 6 . . . . 6.99, 6.100, 6.119, 8.07
(2) 6.102, 6.123
(3) 6.105
(4) 6.106
(a)(ii) 6.106
(b)(ii) 6.106
para 7 . . . . . . 6.102, 6.119, 6.121–6.123
(1) 6.121
para 8 . . . . .6.110
(3) 6.10
(4) 6.113, 6.114
(5) 6.114
(b) 6.114
(6) 6.115
para 9 . . . . .6.109, 6.116, 6.118
(1) 6.116
(2) 6.116
(7) 6.118
(8) 6.116
para 10 . . . . .1.113, 3.40,
6.126–6.128, 9.45
(2)(b) 6.126
(3) 6.126
(6) 6.126
paras 10–13 . . . . .1.113
paras 10–14 . . . . .3.20
para 11 . . . . 3.40, 6.128, 6.131,
7.187, 9.45

(3)(b) 8.07
(5) 6.129
para 12 . . . . 6.137, 6.143
para 13 . . . . .6.25
(1) 6.130–6.134
(c) .3.87
(2) 6.130, 6.133, 6.134
(3) 6.95, 6.134
(6) 6.136
para 14 . . . . .6.138
para 14A(1) 6.141
(2) 6.142
paras 14A–14D 3.20
para 14B .6.143
para 14C 6.144
para 14D 6.145
para 15 . . . . .6.98, 6.118, 9.25
(3) 7.82
(3)–(7) 7.197
(4) 6.14, 6.64, 7.05, 7.61,
7.63, 7.67, 7.68, 10.12
(5) 6.14
para 16 . . . . 6.14, 6.64, 7.68, 7.97,
7.169, 7.182, 8.68,
8.69, 8.154
(3) 7.97
paras 16–17 . . . . .7.06
paras 16–18 . . . . .7.105
paras 16–19 . . . . .6.25, 6.65,
7.04–7.06, 7.63, 8.01,
8.07, 8.22, 8.55, 8.76, 10.96
para 17 . . . . 6.14, 6.64, 7.68, 7.169,
7.182, 8.68, 8.154, 9.45
(2) 7.98
(3)–(5) 7.98
(6) 7.98
(6A) 7.98
paras 17–19 . . . . 7.61, 8.69, 9.75,
9.101, 11.107
para 18 . . . . 6.14, 6.64, 7.68, 7.169,
8.68, 8.154, 9.45, 10.20
(2) 7.171
paras 18–19 . . . . .7.06
para 19 . . . . 1.118, 6.14, 6.64, 6.153,
7.68, 7.71, 7.76, 7.169, 8.68, 8.70,
8.154, 9.45, 10.20
(4) 7.72
(7) 7.73
para 19A .7.77
paras 19A–19E . . . 4.14, 6.65, 6.69, 7.76
para 19B 7.77, 7.81, 7.83
(1) 7.78, 7.170, 8.149, 10.96
(a) 8.76
(4) 7.79

(5) 7.80
(7) 7.120, 7.127
(9) 7.75, 7.81
(10) 7.75, 7.81
paras 19B–19E. 7.77
para 19C 7.81, 7.127, 7.133, 8.89
  (1)(a) .7.170
    (b) .7.170
  (2) 7.81, 7.127
para 19D 7.81
para 20. . . . . 6.146, 10.10
para 20A. 6.149, 10.11
  (3) .10.29
  (7) 7.06, 10.17
  (8) .10.17
paras 20A–20H 4.16
paras 20A–20I 6.66, 6.149
paras 20A–20L. 10.10
para 20B. 10.11, 10.29
  (2) .10.17
  (3) 6.17, 6.150, 10.14,
                          10.15, 10.21
    (a) .10.17
  (5) 10.17, 10.18
  (6) 10.17, 10.28
  (7) 10.14, 10.19, 10.21
  (8) .10.19
para 20C 10.28
  (3) .10.34
  (4) .10.32
para 20D(2) 10.11
para 20E. 10.11, 10.30
  (2) .10.31
  (3) .10.30
para 20F(2) 10.30
  (4) .10.32
para 20G 10.11
  (1) .10.18
para 20H 10.10, 10.14, 10.15,
                          10.19, 10.22
  (1) 6.18, 6.150, 10.21
  (6) .10.21
  (7) 6.18, 6.150, 10.16, 10.22,
                          10.82, 10.86
para 20I(2). 10.15, 10.22
para 21 . . . . .6.151, 6.154–6.156
  (2) .6.153
para 21A. 6.25, 6.131
  (2) .7.186
  (4) .7.186
  (6) .6.131
para 22. . . . . 3.79, 4.14, 6.69,
              6.146, 8.07, 10.24, 14.20
  (2) .7.182

(3) 7.173, 7.182
(5) .7.173
(7) .7.170
paras 22–27 . . . . .6.70
para 23 . . . . . . .3.79, 6.25, 7.172, 7.182,
                          7.199, 7.201
  (2)(b) 7.176
    (c) .7.176
  (2A) .7.174
  (2B)(a) 7.174, 7.176
    (b) 7.174
  (3) .7.178
  (6) 7.178–7.180
    (b) 7.176
  (7) 7.180, 8.07
  (8) .7.181
    (b) 7.181
  (9) 7.181, 10.36
para 24. . . . . 6.25, 7.182
  (2)(a) 7.190
  (2A) .7.182
  (2B) .7.182
  (3) .7.184
  (5A) .7.183
  (5B) .7.183
  (5C). 7.183
  (6) 7.184, 7.185, 8.07
    (a)(ii) 7.184
    (b) 7.184
  (7) .10.36
para 24A. 6.146, 7.186
  (4) .7.188
paras 24A–24C. 7.186
para 24B(1) 7.187
para 25. . . . . 3.79, 7.185, 7.189,
                          7.194, 7.199, 7.201
  (2) .7.191
    (a) .7.193
  (3) .7.194
  (6) .7.193
  (8) .7.193
    (a) .7.196
  (9) .7.193
  (9A) .7.193
  (10) .7.194
  (12) .7.195
  (13) .7.189
para 26. . . . . 7.196, 7.197
  (1) .7.196
para 27. . . . . 7.180, 7.181, 7.193,
              7.198, 7.199, 7.203–7.205,
                                    10.10
  (3) 8.68, 8.69, 8.154
  (4) .11.43

Police Reform Act 2002 (*cont.*)
     (a) 8.68, 8.69, 8.154,
                  9.116, 10.12
     (5) 10.23
     (6) 10.23
     (7) 7.201
   para 28 . . . . .7.203
   Sch 7 para 18 . . . . .1.68
Police (Scotland) Act 1967 . . . . .1.16
Race Relations Act 1976 . . . . .1.103
Race Relations (Amendment)
   Act 2000 .1.103
Railways, Transport and Safety
   Act 2003 .1.02
   s 28 15.28
   s 77(3) 15.28
Regulation of Investigatory
   Powers Act 2000 . . . . .3.48, 7.155,
              7.161, 7.162, 7.164,
              7.165, 12.12
   Pt I 7.155–7.158
   Pt II 7.155, 7.156, 7.162
   s 1(5)(c) 7.158
   s 3 . . . . .7.158
   s 4 . . . . 7.158–7.160
     (2) 7.159
     (7) 7.160
   s 17 . . . . .7.158
   s 18 . . . . .7.158
     (4) 7.158
   s 26 . . . . 7.163, 7.164
     (2)(a) 7.163
   s 27(1) 7.162
   s 71 . . . . .7.155, 7.157, 7.162
   s 80 . . . . .7.162
Road Safety Act 2006 . . . . .15.131
   s 19 . . . . 15.138, 15.140

s 20 . . . . 15.131, 15.135
s 23 . . . . .15.131
s 30 . . . . 15.131, 15.136
s 33 . . . . .15.131
s 61 . . . . .15.136
   (1) 14.59
Road Traffic Act 1988 . . . . .15.134
   s 1 . . . . .15.134
   ss1–3 . . . . .15.134
   s 2 . . . . .15.34
   s 2A(1) 15.149
     (3) 15.145, 15.153
   s 2B 15.135
   s 3ZA 15.136
     (3) 15.137
Road Traffic Act 1991 . . . . .15.134
Road Traffic Regulations Act 1984
   s 87 . . . . .15.138, 15.139, 15.145
     (3) 15.138
Serious Crime Act 2007
   Pt 2 . . . . .15.116
   s 74(2)(g) 1.121
   s 94(1) 1.121
   Sch 8, Pt 7, para 177(1) 1.121
     (2)(a) 1.121
Serious Organised Crime and
   Police Act 2005 . . . . 1.13, 3.07
   s 55 . . . . .3.05
   s 157 . . . . .1.97
   s 160 . . . . .1.113, 3.06, 6.140
   Sch 2 . . . . .3.05
   Sch 12 . . . . .6.140
     para 1 . . . . 1.113, 3.06
     para 3 . . . . 6.77, 6.78
     para 11 . . . . 1.113, 3.06
     para 12 . . . . 1.113, 3.06
Sex Discrimination Act 19 . . . . .761.103

TABLE OF STATUTORY INSTRUMENTS

Civil Partnership Act 2004 (Amendments
    to Subordinate Legislation) Order
    2005 (SI 2005/2114)
    art 1 . . . . 14.110
    art 2(1) 14.110
    Sch 1, para 4 . . . . 14.110
Civil Procedure Rules 1998
    (SI 1998/3132)
    r 3.4 . . . . 6.120
    (2) 12.35
Community Legal Service (Funding)
    Regulations 2000
    (SI 2000/516) 14.123
Constitutional Reform Act 2005
    (Commencement No 5)
    Order 2006 (SI 2006/1014)
    art 2(a) 14.28
    Sch 1, para 7 . . . . 14.28
Coroners (Amendment) Rules 2005
    (SI 2005/420)
    r 1(1) 14.110
    r 5 . . . . 14.110
Coroners (Amendment) Rules 2008
    (SI 2008/1652) 14.13, 14.65,
                            14.105, 14.106
Coroners Rules 1984
    (SI 1984/552) 14.37, 14.104
    r 20(2) 14.110, 14.147
    (d) 14.112
    r 22 . . . . 14.144
    (2) 14.146
    r 36 . . . . 14.25, 14.29
    r 37 . . . . 3.147, 14.14, 14.150, 14.151
    (2) 14.148, 14.151
    (5) 14.149
    r 40 . . . . 14.39
    r 42 . . . . 14.10, 14.29, 14.30
    r 43 . . . . 14.13, 14.27, 14.65, 14.105,
                            14.107, 14.109
    r 43A 14.106
    r 43B 14.106
    r 60 . . . . 14.26
Corporate Manslaughter and
    Corporate Homicide Act 2007
    (Commencement No 1) Order 2008
    (SI 2008/401) 15.77, 15.114

art 2(1) 14.32
Criminal Justice and Immigration
    Act 2008 (Commencement No 3
    and Transition Provisions)
    Order 2008 (SI 2008/2712)
    art 2 . . . . 7.76
    Sch 1, para 17(b) 7.76
Criminal Justice and Immigration
    Act 2008 (Commencement No 4
    and Saving Provision) Order 2008
    (SI 2008/2993) 6.106
    art 2(1)(i) 7.76
    (ii) 7.76
Criminal Justice and Police Act 2001
    (Consequential Amendments)
    (Police Ranks) Regulations 2001
    (SI 2001/3888) 1.81, 11.44
Greater London Authority Act 1999
    (Consequential Amendments)
    (Police) Order 2000
    (SI 2000/1549) 11.44
Health and Safety at Work
    (Northern Ireland) Order 1978
    (SI 1978/1039) 15.116
Independent Police Complaints
    Commission (Investigatory Powers)
    Order 2004 (SI 2004/815) 3.48
Independent Police Complaints
    Commission (Staff Conduct)
    Regulations 2004
    (SI/2004/660) 3.167,
                            3.170, 3.192
    reg 2(2) 3.170, 3.171
    (3) 3.170–3.172, 3.176
    (a)(i) 3.173
    (4) 3.173
    reg 3 . . . . 3.170, 3.173, 3.176
    (3) 3.177
    regs 3–5 . . . . 3.175
    reg 4 . . . . 3.178
    (2) 3.178
    reg 5 . . . . 3.180
    (1) 3.178, 3.180, 3.183
    (2) 3.181
    (3) 3.183
    (4) 3.183

Independent Police Complaints
    Commission (Staff Conduct)
    Regulations 2004
    (SI 2004/2004/660) (*cont.*)
    (5) 3.184
    reg 6. . . . . .3.174
    reg 7. . . . . .3.174
    reg 8. . . . . .3.174
Independent Police Complaints
    Commission (Transitional Provisions)
    (Amendment) Order 2004
    (SI 2004/1092). 3.23
    art 2(5). 3.40
Independent Police Complaints
    Commission (Transitional Provisions)
    Order 2004 (SI 2004/671) 3.23
    art 2 . . . . 3.26, 3.28
    (1) 3.28
    (2) 3.28, 3.31
    (3) 3.28
    (4) 3.29
    art 3 . . . . 3.37, 15.27
    (a) 3.37, 3.38
    art 4 . . . . .3.39
    (1) 3.39, 3.40
    (2) 3.40
    (3) 3.40
Metropolitan Police Authority
    Regulations 2008
    (SI 2008/631). 1.89
    reg 1(2). 1.91
    reg 6. . . . . .1.90
    (3). 1.90, 1.93
    reg 10(1). 1.90
    reg 20(1). 1.90
National Crime Squad (Complaints)
    Regulations 1998 (SI 1998/638)
    reg 19. . . . . .3.39
National Crime Squad (Dispensation
    from Requirement to Investigate
    Complaints) Regulations 2003
    (SI 2003/2601)
    reg 4. . . . . .3.39
Official Secrets Act 1989 (Prescription)
    (Amendment) Order 2007
    (SI 2007/2148). 3.11
Police (Amendment) Regulations 2003
    (SI 2003/2594). 1.81
Police (Amendment) Regulations 2004
    (SI 2004/3216). 1.81
Police (Amendment) Regulations 2005
    (SI 2005/2834). 1.81, 4.14, 8.114
Police (Amendment) Regulations 2006
    (SI 2006/1467). 1.81

Police (Amendment) (No 2)
    Regulations 2006
    (SI 2006/3449). 1.81, 4.14, 8.114
Police (Amendment) Regulations 2007
    (SI 2007/1160). 1.81
Police (Amendment) Regulations 2008
    (SI 2008/2865). 4.14, 7.12,
        8.114, 9.65, 9.66, App J
Police and Justice Act 2006
    (Commencement No 1,
    Transitional and Saving Provisions)
    (Amendment) Order
    (SI 2008/617). 1.91
Police and Justice Act 2006
    (Commencement No 1,
    Transitional and Saving Provisions)
    Order 2006 (SI 2006/3364) 1.87
    art 2(a) 1.24
    (b) 1.24, 1.96
Police and Justice Act 2006
    (Commencement No 2, Transitional
    and Saving Provisions) Order 2007
    (SI 2007/709)
    art 3 . . . . .1.30, 1.51, 1.119
    (a) 1.79, 3.05, 3.35
    (b) 1.45, 1.58, 2.16
    (c) 1.58, 2.16
    (d) 15.28
Police and Justice Act 2006
    (Commencement No 3)
    Order 2007 (SI 2007/1614)
    art 2(g). 3.05
Police and Justice Act 2006
    (Commencement No 4)
    Order 2007 (SI 2007/2754)
    art 2 . . . . .3.05
Police and Justice Act 2006
    (Commencement No 7 and Savings
    Provision) Order 2008 (SI 2008/311)
    art 2(b). 1.96
    art 3 . . . . .1.96
Police and Justice Act 2006
    (Commencement No 9)
    Order 2007 (SI 2007/709)
    art 2 . . . . .1.101
    art 5 . . . . .1.101
Police and Justice Act 2006
    (Supplementary and Transitional
    Provisions) (Amendment) Order 2008
    (SI 2008/619). 1.91
Police and Justice Act 2006
    (Supplementary and
    Transitional Provisions) Order
    (SI 2006/3365). 1.87

Police (Anonymous, Repetitious Etc.
    Complaints) Regulations 1985
    (SI 2985/672)
reg 3 . . . . 3.39
Police Appeals Tribunals (Amendment)
    Rules 2003 (SI 2003/2597) 11.01
Police Appeals Tribunals Rules 1999
    (SI 1999/818) 11.01, 11.04,
                11.06, 11.44, 11.46, 11.48,
                11.49, 11.50, 11.54, 11.56,
                11.76, 11.101, App B
  r 4 . . . . 11.61
  r 5 . . . . 11.63
    (1) 11.62
    (2) 11.62
    (3) 11.63
  r 6 . . . . 11.63, 11.64
    (1) 11.64
    (2) 11.64
    (3) 11.64
    (5) 11.64
      (c) 11.65
    (6) 11.64
    (8) 11.65
  r 7 . . . . 11.63
  r 8 . . . . 11.65, 11.66
    (1) 11.66
    (3) 11.67
  r 9 . . . . 11.65, 11.66, 11.67
    (4) 11.66
  r 10 . . . . 11.66, 11.69
    (1) 11.69
    (2) 11.69
    (3) 11.69
    (5) 11.71
  r 11 . . . . 11.67
  r 12 . . . . 11.67
    (4) 11.67
  r 13 . . . . 11.70
    (1) 11.70
    (3) 11.70
    (4) 11.70
Police Appeals Tribunals Rules 2008
    (SI 2008/2863) 4.02, 4.03, 4.08,
              4.15, 5.31, 7.05, 8.155, 10.112,
              11.01, 11.04, 11.06, 11.44,
              11.46, 11.48–11.50, 11.58,
              11.69, 11.72, 11.74–11.76,
              11.101, 11.112, App H
  r 2(2) 11.74
  r 3 . . . . 11.107
  r 4 . . . . 11.76, 11.109
    (3) 11.77
    (4) 11.78

    (b) 11.93, 11.96
  r 5 . . . . 11.76,
                       11.81, 11.109
    (4) 11.82
    (5) 11.83
    (6) 11.85
    (b) 11.93, 11.96
  r 6 . . . . 11.87
    (1) 11.88
    (2) 11.88
    (3) 11.88
  r 7 . . . . 11.87, 11.88
    (4) 11.89
  r 8 . . . . 11.90
  r 9 . . . . 11.87, 11.90
    (2) 11.90
    (4) 11.91, 11.102
    (5)(a) 11.93
      (b) 11.93
    (6)(a) 11.91
      (b) 11.91
    (7) 11.95
    (8) 11.95, 11.102
      (a) 11.97
      (b) 11.97
      (c) 11.97
      (d) 11.97
    (9) 11.96
    (10) 11.97
  r 10 . . . . 11.87, 11.97
  r 11 . . . . 11.92, 11.98,
                       11.99, 11.101
    (2)(a) 11.99
      (b) 11.98, 11.99
  r 12 . . . . 11.101
  r 13 . . . . 11.98, 11.102
    (3) 11.98
  rr 13–21 . . . . 11.101
  r 14(1) 11.103
    (2) 11.103
  r 15 . . . . 11.104
  r 16 . . . . 11.105
    (1) 11.105, 11.107
    (2) 11.105
    (3) 11.105
  r 17 . . . . 11.106
  r 18(1) 11.106
  r 19 . . . . 11.106
    (6) 11.107
  r 20 . . . . 11.106
  r 21 . . . . 11.107
  r 22(1) 11.109
    (3) 11.109
    (4)–(6) 11.109

Police Authorities (Particular Functions
  and Transitional Provisions)
  Order 2007 (SI 2008/82) 1.24
Police (Complaints and Misconduct)
  (Amendment) Regulations 2006
  (SI 2006/1406). . . 3.07, 6.04, 6.25, 6.96
  reg 2(4). 6.25
Police (Complaints and Misconduct)
  (Amendment) Regulations 2008
  (SI 2008/2866). 3.07, 4.02,
                        6.04, 6.25
  reg 3 . . . . 3.91, 4.14, 6.25, 6.66
Police (Complaints and Misconduct)
  Regulations 2004
  (SI 2004/643). 3.07, 6.04,
        6.25, 7.99, 10.36, App D
  reg 1 . . . . .6.25
  reg 2 . . . . 3.06, 6.25
    (2) 6.91
    (3) 6.96
  reg 3 . . . . .6.25
    (2) 6.120
    (3) 6.120
    (6) 6.121
    (7) 6.121
  reg 4 . . . . 6.25, 6.111
    (1) 6.09, 6.111
  reg 5 . . . . .6.25
  reg 5A 6.25
  reg 6 . . . . 6.25, 7.99
  reg 7 . . . . .6.25, 6.151, 8.22
    (2) 6.152, 6.153
    (3) 6.153
    (4) 6.154
    (5) 6.154
    (7) 6.156
    (8) 6.156
    (9) 6.156
  reg 8 . . . . 6.25, 6.89
  reg 9 . . . . 6.25, 6.116
    (7) 6.118
  reg 10 . . . . 6.25, 7.189
  reg 11 . . . . .6.25
    (2)(a) 14.91
    (b) 14.91
  reg 12 . . . . 6.25, 10.24, 10.36,
                 10.41, 14.91
    (3) 10.37
  reg 13 . . . . .6.25
  reg 14 . . . . 6.25, 7.110
  reg 14A 3.91, 4.14, 6.04, 6.15,
    6.25, 6.66, 7.01, 7.06, 7.38, 7.81,
    7.92, 7.113, 7.120, 7.122,
    7.127, 8.14, 8.89, 8.116, 12.53

    (1) 7.120, 7.122
    (h) 7.128, 7.140
    (7) 7.141
    (8) 7.142
  regs 14A–14E 6.04, 6.65
  reg 14B 6.04, 6.25
  reg 14C 6.04, 6.25
  reg 14D 6.04, 6.25, 7.137, 7.138
    (5) 7.138
    (6) 7.139
  reg 14E 6.04, 6.25, 7.167,
                   7.171, 12.51
  reg 15 . . . . 6.25, 6.66
  reg 16 . . . . .6.25
  reg 17 . . . . .6.25
  reg 18 . . . . 6.25, 7.105
    (1)(a) 7.104
  reg 19 . . . . .6.25
  reg 20 . . . . .6.25
  reg 21 . . . . 6.25, 6.81
  reg 22 . . . . .6.25
  reg 23 . . . . .6.25
    (2) 7.194
  reg 24 . . . . .6.25
  reg 25 . . . . .6.25
    (2) 6.25
  reg 26 . . . . .6.25
  reg 27 . . . . .6.25
  reg 28 . . . . .6.25
  reg 29 . . . . .6.25
  reg 30 . . . . .6.25
Police (Complaints) (Informal
  Resolution) Regulations 1985
  (SI 1985/671). 3.39
Police (Conduct) Regulations 1985 . . . . . .1.71
Police (Conduct) Regulations 1999
  (SI 1999/730). 1.71, 4.01, 6.26,
                8.105, 9.01, 9.34
  reg 7 . . . . .5.96
  reg 9 . . . . .12.51
Police (Conduct) Regulations 2004
  (SI 2004/645). 1.71, 1.81, 3.07,
    3.149, 4.01, 4.03, 4.16, 5.38,
    6.02, 6.20, 6.21, 6.23, 6.27, 6.26,
    6.61–7.07, 7.06, 7.85, 7.87, 7.113,
    7.135, 8.02, 8.13, 8.14, 8.26, 8.53,
    8.55, 8.61, 8.63, 8.75, 8.86, 8.92,
    8.105, 8.112, 8.114, 8.142, 9.01–9.03,
    9.07, 9.12, 9.13, 9.15–9.17, 9.20,
    9.21, 9.22, 9.24, 9.26, 9.34, 9.61,
    9.92, 9.96, 9.105, 9.113, 9.115, 10.04,
    10.05, 10.08, 10.48, 10.77, 10.78,
    10.82, 11.06–11.08, 11.44,
    11.75, 11.108, 15.09, App C

reg 1 . . . . .9.01
reg 2 . . . . .9.01
reg 3 . . . . .8.76, 9.01, 9.25
 (1) 9.116
 (2) 9.27
 (3)(a) 9.28, 9.29
  (b) 9.28, 9.30
reg 4 . . . . 9.01, 9.54
 (3) 9.116
 (5)(d) 9.116
reg 5 . . . . 9.01, 9.54
 (1)(b) 9.116
 (3) 9.116
reg 6 . . . . .9.01
reg 7 . . . . 9.01, 9.56, 9.73, 9.79, 9.116
 (1) 9.75
 (3) 9.56
reg 8 . . . . .9.01, 9.68, 9.73, 9.76, 9.77, 9.79
 (1) 9.75
 (6) 9.116
 (8) 9.116
reg 9 . . . . . . 3.91, 5.96, 6.15, 7.113, 7.121,
     9.18, 9.01, 9.61, 9.62, 9.68, 9.70,
     9.74, 9.77, 9.78, 9.81, 12.51
reg 10 . . . . 9.01, 9.80
regs 10–12 .9.116
reg 11 . . . . 9.01, 9.66, 9.79, 9.81
 (7) 9.81
reg 12 . . . . 9.01, 10.56
 (1) 9.82
reg 13 . . . . .9.01
 (1) 9.116
 (4) 9.116
reg 14 . . . . 9.01, 9.87, 9.91, 9.92,
     9.98, 9.104, 10.47, 10.57, 10.58
 (1) 9.08, 9.71
  (b) 9.88
 (2) 9.88, 9.90, 9.104
 (4) 9.116
reg 15 . . . . .9.01, 9.66, 10.53
reg 16 . . . . .9.01, 9.97, 10.58
reg 17 . . . . .9.01, 9.86, 9.97, 9.98,
     9.110, 11.21
reg 18 . . . . 9.01, 9.91, 9.98, 10.58
 (2) 9.99
 (3) 9.100
reg 19 . . . . 9.01, 9.101
 (5) 9.102
reg 20 . . . . .9.01, 9.116, 10.64
 (2)(a)–(c) 9.116
reg 21 . . . . . . 9.01, 9.08, 9.72, 9.91–9.93,
     9.104, 9.105
 (3) 9.91
reg 22 . . . . 8.61, 9.01, 9.104, 9.105

 (b) 9.93
reg 23 . . . . 9.01, 9.98
reg 24 . . . . .9.01
 (1) 9.116
reg 25 . . . . 9.01, 9.116
 (1) 10.12
 (2)(a) 9.98
reg 26 . . . . 9.01, 10.59
reg 27 . . . . .9.01, 9.52, 9.106
 (1) 9.86, 9.108
 (2) 9.52, 9.106
 (7) 9.52, 9.107
 (8) 9.116
reg 28 . . . . 9.01, 9.109
reg 29 . . . . 9.01, 9.109
reg 30 . . . . 9.01, 9.109
reg 31 . . . . 9.01, 9.109
reg 32 . . . . 9.01, 9.109
reg 33 . . . . 9.01, 9.110, 9.116,
     11.14, 11.19
 (5) 9.110
reg 34 . . . . .9.01
reg 35 . . . . 4.14, 9.01, 9.116, 11.08
 (2) 9.111, 10.63, 11.21
 (3) 9.116, 10.63
 (4) 9.116
 (6) 9.112
reg 36 . . . . .9.01
reg 37 . . . . .9.01
 (1) 11.11
 (2) 9.116
 (3)(a) 9.116
reg 38 . . . . .9.01
reg 39 . . . . 9.01, 11.62
reg 40 . . . . 9.01, 9.114, 11.02,
     11.08, 11.10, 13.16
reg 41 . . . . .9.01, 11.10, 11.21
reg 42 . . . . 9.01, 11.10
 (1) 11.43
 (2) 11.21
 (4) 11.43
 (5) 11.43
reg 43 . . . . 9.01, 11.10
 (2) 11.13
reg 44 . . . . .9.01
reg 45 . . . . .9.105, 10.43, 10.48
Sch 1 . . . . 1.18, 6.32, 9.01,
     9.22, 9.32
 para 1 . . . . .6.32
 para 6 . . . . .9.46
Sch 2 . . . . 9.22, 9.54
 Pt 1 . . . . 10.43, 10.48
 Pt 2 . . . . 10.43, 10.44
 para 2 . . . . .10.56

Police (Conduct) Regulations 2008
   (SI 2008/2864). 1.18, 1.35, 1.64,
     1.71, 3.08, 3.149, 3.177, 3.96, 4.02,
     4.06, 4.09, 4.14, 4.16, 5.05, 5.23,
     5.36, 5.44, 5.52, 5.62, 6.02, 6.20,
     6.21, 6.24, 6.26, 6.28, 6.41, 6.61, 6.63,
     6.67, 6.69, 6.105, 6.106, 7.02, 7.05,
     7.07, 7.10, 7.13, 7.43, 7.50, 7.59, 7.103,
     7.104, 7.165, 7.167, 7.178, 7.184, 7.207,
     8.01, 8.10, 8.19, 8.26, 8.36, 8.40, 8.45,
     8.46, 8.53, 8.55, 8.74, 8.76, 8.92, 9.08,
     9.20, 9.42, 9.80, 9.98, 9.105, 9.108,
     10.02, 10.04, 10.05, 10.08, 10.77,
     10.89, 10.109, 11.02, 11.04, 11.06,
     11.07, 11.09, 11.51, 11.74, 11.77,
     12.08, 12.49, 12.54, 15.09, App G
   Pt 1 . . . . .7.05
   Pt 2 . . . . 7.05, 7.35
   Pt 3 . . . . 4.14, 6.61, 6.64, 7.01, 7.05,
     7.63, 7.64, 7.74, 7.76, 7.122
   Pt 4 . . . . 6.62, 6.70, 7.04, 7.05, 8.01,
     8.02, 8.06, 10.85, 10.86, 10.89,
     10.91, 10.98, 10.103, 10.107, 10.111
   Pt 5 . . . . .6.66, 6.150, 7.05, 10.77,
     10.98, 10.104
   reg 1. . . . . 7.07, 7.06
     (1) 6.26
   reg 2. . . . . 7.07, 7.06, 10.77, 10.98
   reg 3. . . . . 7.06, 7.08, 8.18, 8.33, 8.52,
     10.79, 10.83, 11.16
     (1) 4.14, 6.26, 6.28, 6.30, 6.31,
     6.67, 7.09, 7.39, 7.46, 10.79
     (f)(b) 7.89
     (2) 6.31
     (c) 10.79
     (3) 7.12
     (5) 7.08
     (4) 7.12
     (6) 7.08
     (7) 7.13
     (8) 7.13
   reg 4. . . . . 7.05, 7.06, 7.14, 7.20, 7.26,
     7.31, 8.23, 9.96, 10.57, 10.87, 10.94
   reg 5. . . . . 6.28, 6.67, 6.131,
     7.06, 7.61, 7.64
   reg 6. 7.35, 7.36
     (1) 7.38
     (2) 7.39, 7.41
     (3) 7.39
   reg 7. . . . . 7.06, 7.35, 7.46, 7.121, 8.25
     (1) 7.46
     (1)–(3) 8.87
     (3) 8.87
     (4) 8.87, 8.126

     (5) 7.47, 8.31
     (5)–(8) 8.87
   reg 8. . . . . 7.06, 7.35
   reg 9. . . . . 6.147, 7.06, 7.35, 7.50
     (1) 7.50
     (2) 7.51, 7.53
     (3) 7.51, 8.08, 8.15, 8.16, 10.84
     (4) 7.53
     (5) 7.53
   reg 10 . . . . 7.08, 7.06, 7.35, 7.55, 7.59
     (5) 7.61
     (6) 7.62
     (7) 7.62
     (8) 7.62
     (9) 7.62
   reg 11 . . . . .6.64, 7.06, 7.63
   reg 12 . . . . 4.14, 7.06, 7.77, 7.83,
     7.89, 7.103, 8.16
     (1) 4.14, 7.84, 8.14, 8.116
     (2) 7.85
     (2)–(4) 7.83
     (3) 7.86
     (a) 7.88
     (b) 7.90
     (4) 7.84
     (5) 4.14, 7.75, 7.89
     (6) 7.85
   reg 13 . . . . .7.06, 7.87, 7.103
     (a) 7.87
     (2) 7.103
     (4) 7.104
   reg 14 . . . . .7.06
   reg 15 . . . . 3.91, 4.14, 5.96, 6.15,
     7.01, 7.06, 7.81, 7.88, 7.92,
     7.113, 7.120–7.123, 7.132,
     9.18, 9.70, 9.74, 12.51, 12.53
     (1) 7.129, 8.89
     (h) 7.128, 7.130, 7.140
     (2) 7.125
     (4) 7.124
   reg 16 . . . . .7.06, 7.121, 7.133
     (1) 7.129, 8.89
     (2) 7.131, 7.132
     (3) 7.132
   reg 17 . . . . 7.06, 7.46, 7.137, 7.138
     (5) 7.138
     (6) 7.139
     (7) 7.141
     (8) 7.142
   reg 18 . . . . 4.14, 6.69, 7.06, 7.169, 8.07
     (2) 7.167
     (3) 7.168, 10.83
   reg 19 . . . . .6.70, 7.02, 7.04, 7.06,
     7.11, 8.06, 8.07

(1) 4.14, 6.70
(2) 8.08
(4) 8.15
(5) 8.11, 8.17
(8) 8.12
　(a) 8.14
(9)(a) 7.87
　(b) 7.87, 8.14
reg 19B(10) 8.16
reg 20 . . . . 7.06, 8.18, 8.18, 8.22
(2) 8.19
reg 21 . . . . 7.06, 8.26, 8.32, 8.47
(1) 8.36, 8.45, 8.61
　(c)(ii) 7.14
(2) 8.31
(3) 8.146
reg 22 . . . . 7.06, 8.35, 8.38, 8.42
(2) 7.121, 8.36, 8.41, 8.61,
　　　　　　　　　　8.89, 8.90, 12.66
(3) 7.121, 8.37, 8.61,
　　　　　　　　　　　　8.89, 8.90
(4) 8.41, 8.43
(5) 8.42, 8.43
reg 23 . . . . 7.06, 8.43
(3) 8.43
reg 24 . . . . .7.06
(2) 8.47
(4)–(8) 8.50
reg 25 . . . . 7.06, 8.34
(5) 8.56
reg 26 . . . . .7.06, 8.56, 11.07
reg 27 . . . . .7.06, 8.56, 8.60
(3) 8.16
(4) 8.16
reg 28 . . . . 7.06, 8.61, 9.105, 11.07
(1)(c) 8.62, 9.105
reg 29 . . . . 7.06, 8.67
regs 29–33 . . . . .8.66
reg 30 . . . . 7.06, 7.47
(1) 8.126
(2) 8.68
(4) 8.75
reg 31 . . . . 7.06, 7.47, 8.76, 8.82
(5) 8.80
(7) 8.79
regs 31–34 .7.04
reg 32 . . . . .7.06, 8.73, 8.82
(3) 8.83
(4) 8.84
(5) 8.70, 10.98
(6) 8.70
(8) 8.82
regs 32–34 .7.47
reg 33 . . . . 7.06, 8.85

reg 34 . . . . .7.06, 8.83, 8.87, 8.88,
　　　　　　　　　　　8.103, 12.55
(1) 7.29, 8.86
(5) 8.87
　(v) 8.96, 8.98
(8) 8.96–8.99
(10) 8.89
(10)–(12) 8.38
(12) 8.89
(13) 8.104
(14) 8.105
(15) 8.111
reg 35 . . . . .4.14, 7.06, 8.152
(2)(a) 8.113
　(b) 8.113
(5) 8.119
(6) 8.120
　(b) 7.12
(7) 7.13, 8.123
(8) 7.13, 8.121
(10) 8.125, 8.126
　(a) 8.125
　(b) 8.125
　(c) 8.125
　(ii) 8.126
regs 35–37 .8.112
reg 36 . . . . 7.06, 8.138
(1) 8.138
(2) 8.139
(3) 8.139
reg 37 . . . . 7.06, 8.140
reg 38 . . . . .7.06, 8.139, 8.142
(2) 8.143, 8.144
(3) 8.145
(4) 8.145
(6)–(12) 8.146
(8) 8.150
regs 38–40 . . . . 7.06, 8.143
reg 39 . . . . 7.06, 8.147
(2) 8.147
(3)–(6) 8.148
(7) 8.149
reg 40 . . . . .7.06
(2) 8.151
(3) 8.151
(4) 8.152
(5) 8.153
(6) 8.153
(7) 8.154
reg 41 . . . . .7.06, 7.08, 10.83
(1) 10.87
(2) 10.83, 10.84
(3) 10.83, 10.84
(5) 10.83

Police (Conduct) Regulations 2008
  (SI 2008/2864) (*cont.*)
  regs 41–57 . . . . .10.77
  reg 42 . . . . .7.06, 10.86, 10.91
    (1) 10.105
  reg 43 . . . . 7.06, 10.87
    (3) 10.88
  reg 44 . . . . .7.06
  reg 45 . . . . .7.06, 10.89. 10.95
  reg 46 . . . . .7.06
  reg 47 . . . . .7.06
  reg 48 . . . . .7.06
  reg 49 . . . . 7.06, 10.93
  reg 50 . . . . 7.06, 10.96
  reg 51 . . . . 7.06, 10.96
    (3) 10.96
  reg 52 . . . . .7.06, 10.96, 10.98
  reg 53 . . . . 7.06, 10.96
    (1) 10.98
  reg 54 . . . . 7.06, 10.99
    (1) 10.94, 10.99
    (3) 10.99
    (4) 10.99
    (5) 10.100
    (6) 10.102
    (8) 10.100
    (9) 10.99
    (10) 10.101
    (11) 10.101
    (13) 10.103
  reg 55 . . . . 7.06, 10.108
    (2)(b) 7.12
    (5) 10.103
    (8) 10.109
  regs 55–58 . . . . .10.108
  reg 56 . . . . 7.06, 10.108
  reg 57 . . . . 7.06, 10.108
  reg 58 . . . . .7.06, 10.78, 10.108
  Sch 6.31, 6.44, 7.06
  Annex N. 8.130
Police (Conduct) (Senior Officers)
  (Amendment) Regulations 2003
  (SI 2003/2596). 11.44
Police (Conduct) (Senior Officers)
  Regulations 1999
  (SI 1999/731). 9.01, 11.44
  reg 25 . . . . .11.62
Police (Discipline) Regulations 1977
  (SI 1977/580). 4.01, 6.26,
                       7.113, 9.74
  reg 7 . . . . 7.113, 9.74
Police (Discipline) Regulations 1985
  (SI 1985/518). 6.26, 12.38
  reg 7 . . . . .12.51

  reg 14(1). .11.19
    (2). 11.19
  reg 24 . . . . .12.17
Police (Efficiency) (Amendment)
  Regulations 2003
  (SI 2003/528). 4.01, 5.02
Police (Efficiency) (Amendment No 2)
  Regulations 2003
  (SI 2003/2600). 1.81, 5.02
Police (Efficiency) Regulations 1999 (SI
  1999/732) 1.81, 3.07, 4.01, 4.03,
             4.04, 5.02–5.04, 5.14, 5.31,
          5.33, 5.123, 6.02, 9.23, 11.06,
                      11.07, 11.74
  regs 19–22 . . . . .5.23
Police (Fingerprints) Regulations 2007
  (SI 2007/1162). 1.81
Police (Minimum Age for Appointment)
  Regulations 2006
  (SI 2006/2278). 1.81
Police Pension Regulations 1987
  (SI 1987/257). 7.163, 12.08
Police (Performance) Regulations
  2008 (SI 2008/2862) 3.08, 3.196,
      4.02, 4.04, 4.09, 4.14, 4.16, 5.01,
      5.04, 5.05, 5.07, 5.23, 5.30, 5.31,
      5.33, 5.34, 5.36, 5.38, 5.54, 5.59,
    5.62, 5.71, 5.82, 5.117, 5.123, 5.209,
    5.210, 6.02, 6.12, 7.01, 7.50, 7.85, 8.09,
    8.10, 8.19, 8.20, 11.03, 11.04, 11.06,
        11.07, 11.81, 12.08, App F
  Pt 1 . . . . .5.24
  Pt 2 . . . . .5.24
  Pt 3 . . . . 5.24, 5.57, 5.94, 5.144
  Pt 4 . . . . .5.24
  Pt 5 . . . . .5.24
  reg 1 . . . . 5.33, 5.58
  regs 1–4 . . . . .5.24
  reg 2 . . . . .5.33
  reg 3 . . . . .5.33
    (2) 5.01
  reg 4 . . . . .5.32–5.35, 5.165
    (3) 5.45
  reg 5 . . . . 5.33, 5.46
    (2) 5.47
    (3) 5.46
  regs 5–9 . . . . .5.24
  reg 6 . . . . .5.33
  reg 7 . . . . .5.33
  reg 8 . . . . 5.33, 5.148
    (2) 5.49
    (3) 5.50
      (b) 5.51
    (6) 5.51

(8)(a) 5.52
(9) 5.53
reg 9 . . . . 5.33, 5.54, 5.94
    (1) 5.55
reg 10 . . . . .5.33
reg 11 . . . . .5.33
reg 12 . . . . 5.33, 5.93, 5.100
regs 12–18 .5.24
reg 13 . . . . 5.04, 5.33, 5.96, 5.97
    (3)–(6) 5.96, 5.101
    (8) 5.102
reg 14 . . . . 5.33, 5.106
    (3) 5.104
    (4) 5.105
    (6)(c) 5.115
reg 15 . . . . 5.33, 5.112
    (3) 5.114
reg 16 . . . . 5.33, 5.113, 5.117, 5.124
    (3) 5.125
    (4) 5.127
        (d) 5.100
regs 16–18 . . . . .5.123
reg 17 . . . . .5.33
reg 18 . . . . 5.33, 5.108
    (7) 5.133
reg 19 . . . . .5.33, 5.136, 5.201
    (2) 5.140, 5.143
    (3) 5.141, 5.143
    (4) 5.141
    (6) 5.98, 5.143
regs 19–25 . . . . .5.24
reg 20 . . . . 5.33, 5.145
reg 21 . . . . 5.33, 5.148
reg 22 . . . . 5.33, 5.148
reg 23 . . . . .5.33
regs 23–25 . . . . .5.151
reg 24 . . . . .5.33
reg 25 . . . . .5.33
reg 26 . . . . .5.33
reg 27 . . . . .5.33
reg 28 . . . . 5.31, 5.32, 5.33,
                                            5.35, 11.83
reg 26 . . . . .11.82
    (2) 5.33
    (4) 5.33
    (6) 5.98
regs 26–41 . . . . .5.24
reg 27 . . . . 5.33, 5.159, 5.160,
                                            5.177, 5.204
reg 28 . . . . 5.33, 5.161, 5.162, 5.190
reg 29 . . . . 5.33, 5.161, 5.163,
                                            5.164, 5.177
reg 30 . . . . 5.33, 5.178, 5.186, 5.205
reg 31 . . . . .5.33, 5.178, 5.205

    (1) 5.184
    (3) 5.182
reg 32 . . . . .5.33, 5.167, 5.174
reg 33 . . . . 5.33, 5.174
    (4) 5.176
reg 34 . . . . 5.33, 5.177
reg 35 . . . . 5.33, 5.188
reg 36 . . . . .5.33, 5.188, 5.189
    (4) 5.208
reg 37 . . . . .5.33, 5.190, 5.191
reg 38 . . . . 5.33, 5.191, 5.194,
                                  5.200–5.202, 5.207
reg 39 . . . . .5.33, 5.201, 5.206
regs 39–41 . . . . .5.201
reg 40 . . . . 5.33, 5.202
reg 41 . . . . 5.33, 5.206
Police (Promotion) (Amendment)
    Regulations 2002 (SI 2002/767) 1.81
Police (Promotion) (Amendment)
    Regulations 2003
    (SI 2003/2595) 1.81
Police (Promotion) (Amendment)
    Regulations 2005 (SI 2005/178) 1.81
Police (Promotion) (Amendment)
    Regulations 2006
    (SI 2006/1442) 1.81
Police Reform Act 2002
    (Commencement No 1)
    Order (SI 2002/2306) 1.51
    art 2(d)(i) 15.28
        (f)(ii) 1.12
Police Reform Act 2002 (Commencement
    No 4) Order 2003 (SI 2003/808)
    art 2(b) 15.28
Police Reform Act 2002 (Commencement
    No 8) Order 2004 (SI 2004/913)
    art 2(e) 1.68
Police Reform Act 2002 (Commencement
    No 9) Order 2004
    (SI 2004/1319) 2.10
Police Regulations 2003
    (SI 2003/527) 1.81, 12.08
    reg 3(1) 1.18
    reg 6(1) 1.18
    reg 7 . . . . 1.18, 6.57
    reg 8 . . . . 1.18, 12.22
    reg 13 . . . . .13.03, 13.07–13.09, 13.11,
                                  13.13–13.17, 13.21–13.27
        (1) 13.03
    reg 15 . . . . 4.14, 7.12, 8.114,
                                            8.125, 9.65
    reg 28 . . . . .5.88
    reg 29 . . . . .1.18
    Sch 2, para 1 . . . . .7.59

Revenue and Customs (Complaints
  and Misconduct) Regulations 2005
  (SI 2005/3311). 3.05
Road Safety Act 2006 (Commencement
  No 2) Order 2007 (SI 2007/2472)
  art 2(h). 15.136
Road Safety Act 2006 (Commencement
  No 4) Order 2008
  (SI 2008/1918). 15.135
Serious and Organised Crime and
  Police Act 2005 (Commencement
  No 1, Transitional and Transitory
  Provisions) Order 2005
  (SI 2005/1521)
  art 3(1)(w) 1.113, 3.06, 6.140
  art 5(2). 1.97
Serious and Organised Crime and
  Police Act 2005 (Commencement
  No 5, Transitional and Transitory
  Provisions and Savings) Order 2006
  (SI 2006/378)

art 3(2)(e). 3.05
Serious and Organised Crime and
  Police Act 2005 (Consequential
  and Supplementary Amendments
  to Secondary Legislation) 2006
  (SI 2006/594). 9.01, 11.01
Sch 1, para 43(1) 6.25
Special Constables (Amendment)
  Regulations 2002
  (SI 2002/3180). 1.81
Telecommunications (Lawful Business
  Practice) (Interception of
  Communications) Regulations 2000
  (SI 2000/2699). 7.160
  reg 2(d) 7.161
Traffic Signs Regulations and General
  Directions 1994 (SI 1994/1519)
  reg 15(2). .15.138
  reg 33(2). .15.138

TABLE OF EUROPEAN TREATIES AND CONVENTIONS

Convention on Mutual Assistance
 in Criminal Matters between
 Member States of the
 European Union 1.22
Protocol 1.22
European Convention on
 Human Rights 6.48
Pt 1 . . . . 14.84
Art 1 . . . . 14.15, 14.84
Art 2 . . . . . 1.108, 3.33, 3.43, 14.01, 14.14,
     14.15, 14.22, 14.27, 14.34,
     14.36, 14.62, 14.65–14.67,
    14.77, 14.83, 14.84, 14.87, 14.94,
      14.97, 14.100, 14.101,
   14.120–14.122, 14.126, 14.134,
  14.135, 14.138, 14.140, 14.172, 15.07
 (1) 14.15
 (2) 6.50

Art 3 . . . . 6.46
Art 5 . . . . 14.15
Art 6 . . . . 7.27, 9.08, 12.42,
     12.59, 12.62, 12.63, 12.64
 (1) 12.62
Art 8 . . . . 7.162, 7.165, 12.42, 14.15
 (1) 7.162
 (2) 7.162, 7.165
Art 14 . . . . 6.48

Treaty on European Union
 Art 34 . . . . 1.22

LIST OF ABBREVIATIONS

ACAS	Advisory, Conciliation and Arbitration Service
ACPO	Association of Chief Police Officers
APA	Association of Police Authorities
BCU	Basic Command Unit
BTP	British Transport Police
Centrex	Central Police Training and Development Authority
CLSF	Community Legal Services Fund
CNC	Civil Nuclear Constabulary
CPIA	Criminal Procedures and Investigation Act 1996
CPOSA	Chief Police Officers' Staff Association
CPS	Crown Prosecution Service
CRE	Commission for Racial Equality
CSEW	Coroner's Society of England and Wales
DPP	Director of Public Prosecutions
DRC	Disability Rights Commission
DSI	death and serious injury
ECHR	European Convention on Human Rights
ECtHR	European Court of Human Rights
EHRC	Equality and Human Rights Commission
EOC	Equal Opportunities Commission
GLA	Greater London Authority
GMC	General Medical Council
HMCIC	Her Majesty's Chief Inspector of Constabulary
HMIC	Her Majesty's Inspectorate of Constabulary
HMRC	Her Majesty's Revenue and Customs
HOCR	Home Office Counting Rules
HRA	Human Rights Act 1998
HRP	human resources professional
IO	investigating officer
IPCC	Independent Police Complaints Commission
JSB	Judicial Studies Board
KPI	key performance indicator
LSC	Legal Services Commission
MDP	Ministry of Defence Police
MP	Member of Parliament
MPA	Metropolitan Police Authority
MPS	Metropolitan Police Service

NCIS	National Crime Intelligence Service
NCRS	National Crime Reporting Standards
NCS	National Crime Squad
NDGB	non-departmental government body
NPIA	National Policing Improvement Agency
NPP	National Policing Plan
PABEW	Police Advisory Board for England and Wales
PACE	Police and Criminal Evidence Act 1984
PAT	police appeals tribunal
PAT Rules	Police Appeals Tribunals Rules (1999 or 2008)
PCA	Police Complaints Authority
PCSD	Police and Crime Standards Directorate
PCSO	police community support officer
PDR	performance and development review
PFEW	Police Federation of England and Wales
PITO	Police Information Technology Organisation
PNB	Police Negotiating Board
PNC	Police National Computer
PPAF	Policing Performance Assessment Framework
PPSG	Home Office Police Performance Steering Group
PSAEW	Police Superintendents' Association of England and Wales
PSU	Home Office Police Standards Unit
RAFP	Royal Air Force Police
RIPA	Regulation of Investigatory Powers Act 2000
RMP	Royal Military Police
RPC	Royal Parks Constabulary
SCS	Senior Civil Service
SGC	Sentencing Guidelines Council
SMART	specific, measurable, achievable, relevant, and time-related
SOCA	Serious Organised Crime Agency
SPSA	Scottish Police Services Authority
SWPI	significant wider public interest
UPPs	unsatisfactory performance procedures
WIN	written improvement notice

1

THE ORGANIZATION OF POLICING IN ENGLAND AND WALES, AND THE REGULATION OF POLICE FORCES

A. Overview	1.01		Complaints and Misconduct	
Direction and control	1.04		Procedures	1.68
Direction and control: local			The removal of chief officers	1.76
procedures under Home			The Police Negotiating Board (PNB)	
Office Circular 19/2005	1.07		and the Police Advisory Boards	1.78
B. The Organization of the Police	1.11		Other miscellaneous powers	
Police areas and forces	1.11		of regulation	1.82
Rank structure	1.17	**D.**	**Police Authorities**	1.86
Basic conditions of service	1.18		History and membership	1.86
Inter-force activity	1.19		General functions	1.94
Police authorities and collaborative			Obligations to consult the local	
arrangements	1.23		community and status as a	
C. The Role of the Secretary of State	1.26		'best value authority'	1.98
The Secretary of State: general duties	1.28		Questions to a police authority	
Setting 'strategic priorities'	1.32		nominee at council meetings	1.99
The setting of objectives and			Crime and disorder partnerships,	
performance targets by the			and councils' duties to obtain	
Home Secretary	1.36		'best value'	1.100
The Police Standards Unit (PSU)			Association of Police Authorities	
and the Police and Crime Standards			(APA) published guidance	1.102
Directorate (PCSD)	1.40		Equality and diversity	1.103
The power to give directions to police			The funding of legal representation	
authorities	1.45		for members of the force	
The revised powers of direction			and others	1.105
under s 40 of the Police Act 1996	1.50		Police authorities: a summary	
Police Act 1996, ss 41A and 41B	1.60		of specific statutory duties	
Reports to the Secretary of State			in relation to complaints	
from police authorities and			and misconduct	1.110
chief constables	1.61		The Police Act 1996	1.110
Regulations for police forces	1.62		The Police Reform Act 2002	1.111
Codes of practice and statutory		**E.**	**The National Policing**	
guidance issued by the Secretary			**Improvement Agency**	
of State	1.66		**(NPIA)**	1.119
Home Office Guidance on Police		**F.**	**Conclusion**	1.129
Unsatisfactory Performance,				

A. Overview

1.01 Regulation of the police is most readily understood at the level of failures by individual police officers. There are different regulations to address misconduct and performance, respectively, which are considered in detail in subsequent chapters of this book. Necessarily, however, there are layers of regulation above these, which are directed at controlling the conduct and performance of police forces, and those that act as chief officers of individual police forces. This involves considerations of efficiency, effectiveness, and the setting and achievement of strategic priorities.

1.02 At this level, there is, for most police forces, a historically tripartite structure involving the Secretary of State, usually for the Home Department ('the Home Secretary'), police authorities, and chief officers of police.[1] These legal personalities function alongside other statutory bodies, including Her Majesty's Inspectorate of Constabulary (HMIC), the National Policing Improvement Agency (NPIA), and the Independent Police Complaints Commission (IPCC). Whilst there is some political momentum towards greater community involvement in policing (the so-called 'new localism') and the election of chiefs of police, individual office holders within these legal personalities continue to owe their respective offices to appointment rather than to popular election.

1.03 The tripartite structure was preserved by the Police Act 1996[2] (the 1996 Act), the Police Reform Act 2002 (the 2002 Act), and the Police and Justice Act 2006 (the 2006 Act). The Court of Appeal characterized the distribution of responsibilities between the three bodies in *R v DPP, ex p Duckenfield*[3] as:

> Looking at the whole picture displayed by these provisions it is clear that the Chief Constable is in charge of day to day policing. The police authority has a role in relation to policy or strategy; but this is subject to the overall direction of the Secretary of State.

---

[1] Certain forces are regulated according to different structures. For example, the British Transport Police Force has a police authority (under the Railways, Transport and Safety Act 2003), but is regulated by the Secretary of State for Transport: see the British Transport Commission Act 1949. The Ministry of Defence Police (MDP) has no police authority and is regulated by the Secretary of State for Defence: see the Ministry of Defence Police Act 1987. Disciplinary matters are reflected in ss 78 and 79 of the 2002 Act, and the Ministry of Defence (Conduct) Regulations 2004, SI 2004/653. The Serious Organised Crime Agency (SOCA) has a board and director general.

[2] Expressed in the Preamble as an Act to consolidate the Police Act 1964, Pt IX of the Police and Criminal Evidence Act 1984, Ch 1 of Pt 1 of the Police and Magistrates' Courts Act 1994, and certain other enactments relating to the police. In fact, in part, it introduced new provisions.

[3] [1999] 2 All ER 873, [2000] 1 WLR 55, *per* Laws LJ at 78G.

The degree of overlap was the subject of *R v Secretary of State for the Home Office, ex p Northumbria Police Authority*.[4] In the modern context, the division between strategy and day-to-day direction and control is becoming increasingly complex.

Direction and control

Direction and control by the chief officer is an important concept within the regulation of policing. It is the duty of the chief officer of police to secure the preservation of the Queen's Peace and the enforcement of law in his area. This may include specific other duties according to the statutory function of a particular force. The chief officer is responsible for the disposition and control of his force.[5] **1.04**

In relation to these operational matters, he acts on his own responsibility **1.05** ('he knows through his officers the local situation, the availability of officers and his financial resources, the other demands on the police in the area at different times'),[6] and may not be given instructions by either his police authority or a Minister of the Crown.[7] He is accountable for implementing strategy, and this may impact on his direction and control of the force. Many of his managerial decisions will lack the requisite public element to attract judicial review (see 12.26).

He is also subject to codes of practice and guidance in relation to the discharge **1.06** of these functions. Direction and control matters are outside the scope of the discipline and complaints system. As will be seen (see 1.76–1.77 below, and Chapter 2), the chief officer is accountable, and may be removed, under provisions directed at effectiveness and efficiency of the force, without personal misconduct being established.

Direction and control: local procedures under Home Office Circular 19/2005

Direction and control is defined in para 8 of Home Office Circular 19/2005 **1.07** ('Guidance on the handling of complaints relating to the direction and control of a police force by a chief officer') as 'the legitimate independent operational responsibility and discretion that is held by a chief officer'. The Circular defines as included within a complaint as to direction and control—whether by the chief officer or his delegate, such as a Basic Command Unit (BCU) commander— matters that relate to: (i) operational policing policies (where there is no issue of

---

[4] [1989] 1 QB 26.

[5] *R v Commissioner of Police of the Metropolis, ex p Blackburn* [1968] 2 QB 118, 135F–136G, [1968] 1 All ER 763, CA.

[6] *R v Chief Constable of Sussex, ex p International Trader's Ferry Ltd* [1999] 2 AC 418, 430D, [1999] 1 All ER 129, 136–7, 140–1, [1998] 3 WLR 1260, 1268, 1272, HL.

[7] *R v Commissioner of Police of the Metropolis, ex p Blackburn* [1968] 2 QB 118, 135–6, [1968] 1 All ER 763, CA; *Blackburn (No 3)* [1973] QB 241, [1973] 1 All ER 324, CA.

conduct); (ii) organizational decisions; (iii) general policing standards in the force; and (iv) operational management decisions (where there is no issue of conduct).

1.08 Paragraphs 6 and 7 of the Circular reflect a right 'to ask questions about the way in which policing is delivered locally and if dissatisfied to complain about that service'. A person serving with the force (whether as police officer, staff member, member of the Special Constabulary, volunteer or contractor, or those acting on their behalf) is not a member of the public for this purpose. Complaints cannot include matters to do with 'internal management and organisational support, practices and procedures' (see paras 7 and 17), or the 'general functions of a police authority'.

1.09 Circular 19/2005 requires the chief officer to issue a written local procedure and guidance within this defined 'scope'. The purpose of such a local procedure (essentially, promoting early local resolution at the lowest level possible) and procedural matters that must be addressed are rehearsed at para 11 of the Circular. In relation to the local procedure, the Circular also addresses duties as to categorizing and recording complaints generally, which must be read alongside (and subordinate to) statutory duties in relation to the same matters.

1.10 Clearly, much of the resultant regulation by, and division of functions between, these parties relates to policing considerations other than misconduct by individual officers, and is accordingly not addressed in detail in this book. Whilst discipline and misconduct are ordinarily within the immediate direction and control of chief officers, any consideration of the direct roles of the Secretary of State and police authorities in the regulation of complaints about police performance, whether in respect of the force or individual officers, demands that the essential statutory provisions defining the basic parameters of the relationship between these parties are rehearsed in outline.

B. The Organization of the Police

Police areas and forces

1.11 With some exceptions, including the Serious Organised Crime Agency (SOCA), the British Transport Police (BTP), and the Ministry of Defence Police (MDP), policing in England and Wales is organized on a geographical basis. These forces and the NPIA *must* enter into arrangements with the IPCC; other forces maintained other than by police authorities *may* do so.[8]

---

[8] Police Reform Act 2002, ss 26, 26A (SOCA), and 26B (NPIA).

The essential statutory provisions—particularly in respect of regulation of per- **1.12**
formance, misconduct, and discipline—are found in Pt I of the 1996 Act
('Organisation of police forces'), coupled with Schs 1 ('Police areas', with amended
descriptions in Sch 8), 2 ('Police authorities established under section 3'), and 3
('Police authorities: selection of independent members'). Part II of the 1996 Act
addresses 'Central supervision, direction and facilities'; Pt III, 'Police representative institutions'; Pt IV, 'Complaints, disciplinary proceedings, etc'; Pt V,
'Miscellaneous and general'. Schedule 4 provides the form of attestation made
when assuming the office of constable,[9] Sch 5, the Police Complaints Authority
(replaced from 1 April 2004 by the IPCC), and Sch 6, appeals to police appeals
tribunals.

Significant additions, substitutions, and repeals were made to these provisions—in **1.13**
particular, to Pts I ('Powers of the Secretary of State') and II ('Complaints and
misconduct', including the IPCC)—by the 2002 and 2006 Acts. Related changes
arose under the Serious Organised Crime and Policing Act 2005, which created
SOCA. Further amendments were made by the Criminal Justice and Immigration
Act 2008, ss 126 and 127, and, in particular, the provisions of Schs 22 and 23 of
that Act.

Section 1(1) of the 1996 Act provides that England and Wales shall be divided **1.14**
into police areas that shall be (s 2) the areas prescribed in Sch 1, and the Metropolitan
police district (s 2(2)(a)) and the City of London police area (s 2(2)(b)). The definition of 'police area' is applied to any other Act unless the contrary intention
appears.[10] Under s 101(1) of the 1996 Act, a 'police force' is defined for the purpose of that Act as one that is maintained by a police authority. A 'police area'
means an area provided for by s 1 of the 1996 Act. There are forty-three such
areas,[11] the parameters of which are also set out in Sch 1. Whether the force uses

---

[9] 'I . . . of . . . do solemnly and sincerely declare and affirm that I will well and truly serve the
Queen in the office of constable, with fairness, integrity, diligence and impartiality, upholding
fundamental human rights and according equal respect to all people; and that I will, to the best of
my power, cause the peace to be kept and preserved and prevent all offences against people and property; and that while I continue to hold the said office I will, to the best of my skill and knowledge,
discharge all the duties thereof faithfully according to law.' Substituted by the Police Reform Act
2002, s 83, in force 1 October 2002: see SI 2002/2306, art 2(f)(ii).

[10] Interpretation Act 1978, s 5, Sch 1 (amended by the Police Act 1996, s 103, Sch 7, para 32).

[11] The areas are: (1) Avon and Somerset; (2) Bedfordshire; (3) Cambridgeshire; (4) Cheshire; (5)
Cleveland; (6) Cumbria; (7) Derbyshire; (8) Devon and Cornwall; (9) Dorset; (10) Durham; (11) Essex;
(12) Gloucestershire; (13) Greater Manchester; (14) Hampshire; (15) Hertfordshire; (16)
Humberside; (17) Kent; (18) Lancashire; (19) Leicestershire; (20) Lincolnshire; (21) Merseyside; (22)
Norfolk; (23) Northamptonshire; (24) Northumbria; (25) North Yorkshire; (26) Nottinghamshire;
(27) South Yorkshire; (28) Staffordshire; (29) Suffolk; (30) Surrey; (31) Sussex; (32) Thames Valley;
(33) Warwickshire; (34) West Mercia; (35) West Midlands; (36) West Yorkshire; (37) Wiltshire;
(38) Dyfed Powys; (39) Gwent; (40) North Wales; (41) South Wales; (42) the Metropolitan Police
District; (43) the City of London police area.

'Constabulary', 'Police', or 'Service' as a suffix in its corporate name is not defined in Sch 1. The force areas, names, and numbers of officers and other staff are set out in App 1.

1.15 The Secretary of State (which, for these police forces, is the Home Secretary) has power to alter these police areas (other than the City of London police) and the number of police areas by Order under s 32, although there is no provision for alterations that result in the abolition of the Metropolitan police district.[12] Duties of consultation are rehearsed in the residue of s 32, and associated procedures to object by s 33. Government proposals to merge force areas in 2006 were abandoned in favour of promoting initiatives for greater cross-border cooperation in specific areas by police forces.

1.16 There are numerous policing entities outside those set out in Sch 1 to the 1996 Act, such as SOCA, the BTP, and MDP. These forces ('entities') have procedures adapted to function, but are, for example, within the role of the NPIA.[13]

Rank structure

1.17 Police forces covered by Sch 1, excepting the Metropolitan Police Service (MPS), and most other policing entities, are organized under a rank structure, as follows: chief constable; deputy chief constable;[14] assistant chief constable; chief superintendent; superintendent; chief inspector; inspector; sergeant; constable. The MPS hierarchy is the same between constable and chief superintendent, but above this is structured as follows: commissioner; deputy commissioner; assistant commissioner; deputy assistant commissioner; commander. Officers holding any rank above that of chief superintendent are 'senior officers' in all of the applicable

---

[12] As defined by the London Government Act 1963, s 76.

[13] Police and Justice Act 2006, Sch 6, paras 2 and 3. The other entities are the Royal Naval Regulating Branch, the Royal Military Police (RMP), the Royal Air Force Police (RAFP), the Royal Marines Police, the Civil Nuclear Constabulary (CNC), any person listed as a police force by order of the Secretary of State, any police force maintained under or by virtue of the Police (Scotland) Act 1967, the Scottish Police Services Authority (SPSA), the Police Service of Northern Ireland, the Police Service of Northern Ireland Reserve, the States of Jersey Police Force, the salaried police force of the Island of Guernsey, the Isle of Man Constabulary, and any person engaged outside the United Kingdom in the carrying on of activities similar to any carried on by a police force within the meaning of s 101. Forces listed as a police force by the Secretary of State include the Epping Forest Keepers, the Kensington and Chelsea Parks Police, numerous ports and harbours police forces (Mersey Tunnels, Port of Bristol, Port of Dover, Port of Falmouth, Port of Felixstowe, Port of Liverpool, Port of Tilbury, and Tees and Hartlepool Harbour), the RAFP Provost Branch, the Kew Constabulary (formerly the Royal Botanic Gardens Constabulary), Royal Marines Police, RMP, Royal Navy Regulating Branch, Royal Parks Constabulary (RPC), CNC, Universities of Oxford and Cambridge Constables, Wandsworth Parks Constabulary, and the York Minster Police.

[14] Under the Sheehy recommendations, this rank was to have been phased out, but has now been restored. Certain forces lacked a deputy chief constable for the period between.

legislation, and eligible for membership of the Association of Chief Police Officers (ACPO).

Basic conditions of service

Members of a police force (which includes a member suspended under the con- **1.18**
duct regulations) are subject to certain restrictions on taking office. These are rehearsed primarily in the Police Regulations 2003,[15] and considered in greater detail in the context of the Code of Conduct laid out in the Police (Conduct) Regulations 2004,[16] and (more comprehensive) 'Standards of Professional Behaviour' under the Schedule to the Police (Conduct) Regulations 2008,[17] but they include restrictions on private life,[18] public rights and duties, business interests incompatible with membership of a police force,[19] and an obligation to carry out lawful orders.[20]

Inter-force activity

The 1996 Act makes express provision for 'collaboration agreements' between **1.19**
police forces[21] to promote the more efficient and effective discharge of police functions (s 23), mutual aid of one police force by another (s 24), provision of special services at the request of any person (s 25), and the provision of advice and assistance to international organizations (s 26). Cross-border arrangements between police forces in England and Wales, Scotland, and the Police Service of Northern Ireland are reflected in s 98.

Collaboration agreements under s 23(1) are made between chief constables, with **1.20**
the approval of their police authorities, 'if it appears any police functions can more efficiently or effectively be discharged by members of the forces acting jointly'. Section 23 collaboration agreements are made between police authorities and may extend to the use of premises, equipment, or other material or facilities (subs (2)). Expenditure is as agreed between the parties, or, in the absence of agreement, as determined by the Secretary of State (subs (3)). The Secretary of State can direct that police forces enter into such agreements (subs (4)). Subsection (7) allows for discretion in police authorities to cooperate in any other way with any person where to do so is calculated to facilitate, or is conducive or incidental to, the discharge of any of the authority's functions.

---

[15] SI 2003/527, reg 3(1).
[16] SI 2004/645, Sch 1
[17] SI 2008/2864.
[18] SI 2003/527, reg 6(1).
[19] Ibid, regs 7 and 8.
[20] Ibid, reg 20.
[21] Including the BTP (s 23(7A)) and the CNC (s 23(7B)).

1.21 Section 24 is contingent (subs (1)) on an application by one chief officer to that of another force for the latter to provide constables or other assistance for the purpose of enabling the other force to meet any special demands on its resources. The Secretary of State can specify such aid by direction if to do so is 'expedient in the interests of public safety or order' (subs (2)). Constables provided under this section come under the direction and control of the receiving force (subss (3) and (4)). The difficult question of funding is addressed by subs (5): it is either by agreement, as provided for by any subsisting agreement between all police authorities generally, or, in the absence of general agreement, as may be determined by the Secretary of State. Applied to misconduct and discipline, the expenditure inherent in an IPCC investigation conducted by an outside force—for example, following a death in custody, fatal shooting, or alleged serious criminal conduct by officers—may be very substantial, and a difficult matter in terms of budgeting for a police authority.

1.22 Other provisions apply as to liability for the wrongful acts of those attached to international joint investigation teams 'formed under the leadership of a constable', meaning (s 103(7) of the 2002 Act) any investigation team formed in accordance with:

(i) any framework decision on joint investigation teams adopted under Art 34 of the Treaty on European Union;

(ii) the Convention on Mutual Assistance in Criminal Matters between the Member States of the European Union, and the Protocol to that Convention, established in accordance with that Article of that Treaty; or

(iii) any international agreement to which the United Kingdom is a party and which is specified for the purposes of this section in an Order made by the Secretary of State.

Police authorities and collaborative arrangements

1.23 The momentum is towards greater collaborative working, and police authorities and chief officers are expected to increase this both operationally and in respect of 'back office' matters, specifically, in respect of 'protective policing services'— namely, counter-terrorism, serious organized crime, public order, major crime, critical incidents, road policing, and civil contingencies. As the Home Office put it in a letter to all police authorities and chief officers dated 14 February 2007: '[T]he Government's vision for policing has developed and reflects the need to ensure public protection through national and gross force action as well as locally.'

1.24 By virtue of a power provided by s 6ZA of the 1996 Act, the Secretary of State may confer particular functions on police authorities by an Order, including a requirement to secure arrangements for its force to cooperate with other police forces where necessary or expedient (s 6ZA(2)(b)).[22] The draft statutory instrument—that is, the Police Authorities (Particular Functions and Transitional Provisions) Order 2007—provides, at para 4, that:

> A police authority shall secure that arrangements are made for that force to co-operate with other police forces where such co-operation be – (a) in the interests of the efficiency and effectiveness of that force; or (b) in the interests of the efficiency or effectiveness of one or more police forces maintained for the areas of other authorities.

Whilst it has been held that the duty to secure the maintenance of an efficient and effective police force for its area includes doing things that reasonably support that duty, whilst stopping short of invading the provinces of the chief officer,[23] marrying these recent statutory obligations with the discretion afforded to chief officers under s 10(1) of the 1996 Act as to direction and control is far from straightforward. The observation is well made that there are 'obvious ambiguities in these arrangements'[24] in relation to responsibility for policing policies as distinct from operational control.   **1.25**

C. The Role of the Secretary of State

The Secretary of State referred to is usually the Home Secretary, although this may not be the case for forces outside those established under ss 1 and 101 of, and Sch 1 to, the 1996 Act. The Secretary of State's role is reflected primarily in the Police Act 1996, and was extended (and amended) by the Police Reform Act 2002 and the Police and Justice Act 2006. Paragraph 9 of Sch 22 to the Criminal Justice and Immigration Act 2008 extends the power to issue guidance concerning disciplinary proceedings under s 87 of the 1996 Act.   **1.26**

Certain additional powers were created under the Crime and Disorder Act 1998. These relate to crime and disorder reduction partnerships, and give the Home Secretary power to merge partnership areas, and to require the reduction of particular crimes and forms of disorder. The relevant partnerships are those between councils, police authorities, fire authorities, and primary care trusts/health authorities.   **1.27**

---

[22] Inserted by the Police and Justice Act 2006, s 2, Sch 2, para 8, in force 15 January 2007: see SI 2006/3364, art 2(a) and (b).

[23] *R v DPP, ex p Duckenfield* [2000] 1 WLR 55, 79E-F, CA.

[24] Marshall, G. and Loveday, B. (1994) 'The Police: Independence and Accountability' in J. Jowell and D. Oliver (eds) *The Changing Constitution*, 3rd edn, Oxford: OUP, ch 11, pp 300–1.

The Secretary of State: general duties

1.28   The starting point for the Secretary of State's functions is Pt 2 of the Police Act 1996, entitled 'Central Supervision, Direction and Facilities'. The 'Functions of the Secretary of State' are set out in ss 36–53. Section 36(1) defines the 'general duty' in the terms that the Secretary of State 'shall exercise his powers under the provisions of this Act referred to in subsection (2) in such manner and to such extent as appears to him to be best calculated to promote the efficiency and effectiveness of the police'. Paragraph 2 of Sch 22 to the Criminal Justice and Immigration Act 2008 extends the s 36(2)(d) power under the general duty to include s 84, as well as s 85, of the 1996 Act.

1.29   By s 102, any power of the Secretary of State to make Orders, rules, or regulations under the 1996 Act shall be exercisable by statutory instrument.

1.30   A significant number of the provisions require consultation with 'persons whom he considers to represent the interests' of, respectively, police authorities under s 3, and the chief constables maintained by those authorities. Section 6 of, and Sch 4 to, the 2006 Act define these persons as the Association of Police Authorities (APA) and ACPO, respectively.[25] Whilst Sch 4 simply rehearses the provisions that will remain in force after the 2006 Act is implemented in full, s 6(2) and 6(3) provide that the Secretary of State may, by Order, make the appropriate consequential amendment to any statutory provision. This accommodates matters including a change of name by either organization.

1.31   The provisions under s 36(2) are Pts I–III of the Police Act 1996, excluding: ss 61 and 62 in Pt III ('Police representative institutions—that is, the Police Negotiating Board, or PNB, for the United Kingdom and its functions with respect to regulations');[26] s 85 ('Appeals against dismissal, etc') within Ch II ('Disciplinary and other proceedings') of Pt IV ('Complaints, disciplinary proceedings, etc), and Sch 6 (appeals to the police appeals tribunals); and s 95 (payments out of the Metropolitan and City of London police funds for special constables and cadets) in Pt V ('Miscellaneous and general'). Section 85(1) creates the statutory right of appeal to a police appeals tribunal to any officer that is dismissed, required to resign, or reduced in rank; by s 63(3), the Secretary of State may make rules as

---

[25] In force from 1 April 2007: The Police and Justice Act 2006 (Commencement No 2, Transitional and Saving Provisions) Order 2007, SI 2007/709, art 3.

[26] The PNB considers questions relating to hours of duty, leave, pay and allowances, pensions, or the issue, use, and return of police clothing, personal equipment, and accoutrements (s 61(1)). It considers those representing police authorities, members of forces, and cadets, the Commissioner of Police of the Metropolis, and the Secretary of State. The Secretary of State is required, other than of pensions, 'to take into consideration' the advice of the Board. Although provision is made anticipating arrangements to produce an agreed recommendation, if necessary by arbitration (s 62(2)), the Secretary of State ultimately has discretion.

to the procedure on such appeals, which must be laid before Parliament after being made (s 85(5)). By s 85(6), Sch 6 shall have effect: rules created under s 85(5) are subject to that limitation. Appeals to the police appeals tribunal are considered in greater detail in Chapter 11.

Setting 'strategic priorities'

Section 1 of the Police Reform Act 2002 inserted s 36A into the 1996 Act, impos- **1.32** ing a duty on the Secretary of State to produce annually (subject to exceptional circumstances) a National Policing Plan (NPP) before the beginning of each financial year. From 8 November 2006,[27] para 24 of Sch 2 to the 2006 Act, arising under s 2, repealed ss 36A and 37 (the setting of objectives for police authorities). Paragraph 25 of Sch 2 inserted a new section into the 1996 Act—namely, s 37A—directed at the 'setting of strategic priorities for police authorities', and para 26 amended s 38 of the 1996 Act (the setting of performance targets). The language of 'setting objectives' is replaced with that of 'giving effect' to 'strategic priorities'.

Familiar duties of consultation with the APA, ACPO, and 'such other persons as **1.33** he thinks fit' were provided for in s 36A(7), and for representatives of police authorities and chief constables under s 37(2). Under para 25 of Sch 2, the new s 37A provides that the Secretary of State shall consult the APA and ACPO. Although not stated as such other than in the explanatory notes, this does not exclude others at his discretion.

More generally, the new provisions, simply empowering the setting of undefined **1.34** strategic priorities, are less prescriptive than those they replace and impose fewer mandatory duties on the Secretary of State. Section 36A(6)(a) provided that the NPP 'must set out whatever the Secretary of State considers to be the strategic policing priorities generally' for the qualifying police forces for a period of three years. Subsection (6)(b) provided that it must have 'described' what, in relation to that period, the Secretary of State was 'intending or proposing' so far as specified matters were concerned.[28] Section 36A(7) provided a broad textured right for the Secretary of State to include 'such other information, plans and advice' as he considered relevant to the priorities set out in the Plan.

---

[27] Police and Justice Act 2006, s 53(1).
[28] These being: (i) the setting of objectives under s 37 of the 1996 Act, and the giving of general directions in relation to any objective so set; (ii) the specification of performance indicators for police authorities under the Local Government Act 1999, s 4; (iii) the making of regulations under the 1996 Act, Pt 4 of the Criminal Justice and Police Act 2001 (police training), and by Pt 2 of the 2002 Act (complaints, etc); (iv) the issuing of guidance under any provision of the 1996 Act or Pt 2 of the 2002 Act; and (v) the issuing and revision of codes of practice under the 1996 Act and Ch 1 of Pt 4 of the 2002 Act (powers exercisable by civilians).

1.35 Under the new provisions, the obligation to produce such plans has effectively shifted to police authorities and chief officers. To some extent, these generic strategic 'objectives' or 'priorities' are less significant than the detail of any specific regulation produced—particularly when applied to matters of misconduct and discipline, where the 'strategy' of maintaining a well and efficiently disciplined force is uncontroversial, and unlikely to be the subject of key performance indicators (KPIs). Any NPP should leave, and generally did leave, discretion to police authorities and chief officers in respect of local priorities, although tensions inevitably existed. That said, a discipline strategy driven by efficiency may promote procedures that reduce the delay between complaint and resolution of the complaint, as is apparent from the (arguably ambitious) timescales rehearsed in the Police (Conduct) Regulations 2008.

The setting of objectives and performance targets by the Home Secretary

1.36 Sections 37 (before it was repealed) and 38 of the 1996 Act respectively enabled and enable the Secretary of State to set objectives for qualifying police authorities, and to set performance targets for individual police authorities. By s 37(1), the Secretary of State 'may by order[29] have determined objectives for the policing of the areas of all police authorities established under section 3'. This may have implied that an objective created by such an Order could not isolate individual police areas. In practice, the point is probably academic. Section 102 of the 1996 Act simply provides that powers to make Orders, rules, or regulations under the Act shall be by statutory instrument. This is mirrored by s 105 of the 2002 Act, but by s 105(4), other than Orders under ss 9(7) or 108, this includes power to make different provisions for different areas, to make them subject to exemptions, and to make such incidental, supplemental, consequential, or transitional arrangement as the Secretary of State thinks fit.

1.37 Greater specificity arises with respect to setting performance targets under s 38. Under s 38(1), where an objective has been set under s 37A, the Secretary of State may direct police authorities to establish levels of performance (performance targets) to be 'aimed at' in order to achieve the objective. This may, under s 38(2), be directed either at all, or one or more, particular authorities; a direction may impose conditions with which the performance targets 'must conform', and these may differ as between authorities (subs (3)). The Secretary of State determines in what manner these directions are published (subs (4)).

1.38 Additionally, a wholly new subsection (s 38(5)) is inserted, stating that 'a police authority that is given a direction under this section shall comply with it'. Although this

---

[29] By s 37(3), a statutory instrument containing an Order under this section shall be laid before Parliament after being made.

is a strengthening of language relative to 'shall have regard to it', what practical difference this makes remains to be seen.

These provisions are associated with a recording and reporting structure that includes the Home Office Counting Rules (HOCR) and the National Crime Reporting Standards (NCRS) for measuring performance, and the duty on a chief officer under s 45 of the 1996 Act to maintain and transmit to the Secretary of State such criminal particulars (statistics) as to offences, offenders, criminal proceedings, and the state of crime in a police area as he may require. In practice, the HOCR and NCRS are complicated, and define the circumstances in which a crime is recorded and 'detected'. Some contend that these targets and methods tend to distort practical policing to the disadvantage of the public. There is no direct sanction for failing to meet a target as such, although powers exist to address inefficient or ineffective performance under s 40 of the 1996 Act. There are, additionally, other highly tuned measures of performance developed through Home Office units and ACPO initiatives.

1.39

The Police Standards Unit (PSU) and the Police and Crime Standards Directorate (PCSD)

In 2001, the Home Office, under the then Home Secretary David Blunkett, published a White Paper on police reform titled *Policing a New Century*. The proposals were not without controversy, and included the creation of the Home Office Police Standards Unit (PSU). The proposals heralded a more aggressive approach to intervention in actual policing by the Home Office. In September 2004, it published—in conjunction with management consultants Accenture, and 'in association with' the APA, ACPO, HMIC, and the Police Superintendents' Association of England and Wales (PSAEW)—a detailed guide entitled *Managing Police Performance: A Practical Guide to Performance Management*.[30]

1.40

The 'key drivers' to performance management are identified as: public sector reform; public service agreements; the Policing Performance Assessment Framework (PPAF); iQuanta,[31] HMIC baseline assessments; the Home Office Police Performance Steering Group (PPSG); and PSU engagement activity. Each of these heads is considered in detail in the guide.

1.41

---

[30] Available online at <http://police.homeoffice.gov.uk>.

[31] Defined as 'a web-based data analysis tool that provides users with easy access to unified policing performance information based on common data and agreed analyses'. The Guide contends that 'iQuanta has been crucial in providing clear analysis of performance to a variety of police performance stakeholders'.

1.42   As to the PPSG, the guide provides that:

> Informed by PPAF, iQuanta, and HMIC's baseline assessments, the Home Office is taking a more robust and analytical look at police performance than ever before. The Police Performance Steering Group (PPSG) – chaired by the Home Office's director of policing policy and attended by representatives from ACPO, APA, HMIC, PSU and the Prime Minister's Delivery Unit, takes a strategic view on the issues affecting policing performance. As well as scanning the police performance horizon, PPSG also considers comprehensive assessments of force and BCU performance. These assessments are the basis on which PSU becomes engaged with forces in order to help deliver specific performance improvements.

1.43   The last head, 'PSU engagement activity', represents the most direct form of intervention by the PSU in actual policing on the ground. The guide describes the nature of 'engagement activity' as follows:

> A key part of the new police performance landscape is the 'engagement' work of the Police Standards Unit. On the basis of the comprehensive performance assessments described above PSU has been tasked to work with a number of forces and BCUs to leverage specific performance improvements. This 'engagement activity' – which is complemented by the involvement of HMIC – has entailed PSU working with forces to address organisational, tactical or geographically specific problems to bring about specific performance improvements. The 'monitoring to intervention framework', drawn up in consultation with ACPO and APA, explains the four stages of 'engagement' (monitoring, engagement, collaboration and intervention). It has been a crucial development in making the process of engagement and disengagement as open and transparent as possible. The framework sets out the criteria for moving from one stage to another, and crucially details what PSU expect from forces at each stage of the process and similarly what forces can expect from PSU.

1.44   Individual forces have seen 'engagement' at one or more of these levels since the introduction of the PSU. The PSU now operates as part of the wider Home Office Police and Crime Standards Directorate (PCSD), created in July 2006. The 2005–06 Director's Report[32] identifies the structure of the Directorate, and its purpose as 'a single point of delivery for the information, scrutiny and support required to maintain excellence in police and partnership performance in relation to crime reduction and community safety'. It sets out that, in the relevant preceding year, the PSU was engaged with forces in Cleveland, Northamptonshire, Nottinghamshire, and Humberside. The purpose and extent of the engagement varied.

The power to give directions to police authorities

1.45   The relevant power to 'engage' is that of directing a police authority to take specific remedial action in relation to its force if the force is failing, or would fail,

---

[32]   Available online at <http://police.homeoffice.gov.uk>.

to carry out a particular function in an effective manner. Until amendments under the 2006 Act,[33] the exercise of this power was contingent on the Secretary of State receiving an adverse report by HMIC under s 54 of the 1996 Act, as amended by s 3 of the 2002 Act.[34] Section 40 of the 1996 Act (the power to give directions to police authorities after adverse reports) was as substituted by s 4 of the 2002 Act. Section 40A, introduced by the 2006 Act, introduces a separate, but related, power of the Secretary of State to direct the police authority to take specified measures if satisfied that the police authority is failing to discharge its functions in an effective manner.

Section 54 of the 1996 Act provides for the appointment of inspectors and a **1.46** chief inspector (subs (1)), and that such inspectors shall inspect and report as to the efficiency and effectiveness of every qualifying police force (subs (2)), and carry out such other duties to promote this as the Secretary of State may, from time to time, direct (subs (3)). There is a duty to report annually in such manner as the Secretary of State directs. This report is laid before Parliament (subs (4)).

These powers were extended by s 3 of the 2002 Act (inserting s 54(2B)–(3B) to **1.47** the 1996 Act) to include the power to require an inspection, and associated duty to report, in circumstances confined to a particular part of, particular matters relating to, or particular activities of a qualifying force (s 54(2B)). Section 54(3) requires the inspectors to carry out such other duties for the purpose of furthering police efficiency and effectiveness as the Secretary of State may, from time to time, direct.

The publication of such reports is addressed by s 55 of the 1996 Act. Publication **1.48** is within the discretion of the Secretary of State (subs (1)), although parts may be excluded on the grounds of national security or if it may jeopardize the safety of any person. By subs (3), the Secretary of State is required to send a copy of the published report to each of the police authority and the chief officer affected.

The police authority is required to invite the chief officer to submit comments **1.49** on the published report by such date as it may specify (s 55(4)), and shall publish, in 'such manner as appears to it to be appropriate', its comments, comments by the chief officer, and the authority's response to the chief officer's comments (subs (5)). The police authority is required to send the subs (5) document so published to the Secretary of State (subs (6)). In theory, this may mean that the police authority will not publish the whole of any document, and hence may not send the whole document to the Secretary of State. What is 'appropriate'

---

[33] Police and Justice Act 2006, s 2, Sch 2, para 27, in force 1 April 2007: SI 2007/709, art 3(b) and (c).
[34] See further 1.52 *et seq* below.

for publication is not defined, although there is undoubtedly a strong public interest in transparency, and discretion must be exercised reasonably according to established principles of public law.

The revised powers of direction under s 40 of the Police Act 1996

1.50   A decision to give mandatory directions—as distinct from strategic guidance—to a police authority is a serious measure of some political sensitivity. It encroaches upon the presumption that chief officers will enjoy operational independence in the management (or, as expressed in the Act, 'direction and control') of a police force, subject to the separate power to remove the chief officer for culpable failures of performance. The sensitivity of the position is reflected in a number of safeguards to the exercise of the power within s 40 of the 1996 Act, as amended.

1.51   Section 40 was amended, from 1 October 2002, by s 4 of the 2002 Act.[35] The 2006 Act introduces further amendments to the 1996 Act, which are set out in Sch 2 to the Act. Section 2 of the 2006 Act simply provides that Sch 2 shall have effect. The amendments rehearsed in Sch 2 are coming into force on different dates through a series of commencement Orders. In relation to amendments to s 40 of the 1996 Act, the substituted s 40, introduced by para 27 of Sch 2 to the 2006 Act, came into force on 1 April 2007.[36]

1.52   Some of the safeguards contained in the 1996 Act, as amended by the 2002 Act ('the original system'), have been removed. In particular, under the original system, the first (and, arguably, fundamental) such safeguard was that the Secretary of State must have received a s 54 HMIC report concluding that, in the opinion of the author of that report, either the whole or any part of the force inspected was, whether generally or in particular respects, not efficient or effective (the original s 40(1)(a)), or that the whole or part of a force would cease to be efficient or effective, whether generally or in particular respects, unless remedial action was taken (the original s 40(1)(b)). If so, the Secretary of State may have directed the relevant police authority to take such remedial action as may be specified in the direction. Without an HMIC report meeting either of these criteria, however, the Secretary of State under s 40 could have given no such direction.

1.53   The point was reinforced by the original s 40(2), which provided that the remedial measures in the direction must not have related to any matter other than a matter by reference to which the report contained a statement of opinion falling within subs (1)(a) or (b), or a matter that the Secretary of State 'consider[ed] relevant to

---

[35]   SI 2002/2306.
[36]   The Police and Justice Act 2006 (Commencement No 2, Transitional and Saving Provisions) Order 2007, SI 2007/709, art 3.

any matter falling within' that statement of opinion. This obviously permitted some latitude.

Under the new procedure, the exercise of the power to give directions in relation **1.54** to a police force is not contingent on the terms of any s 54 report by HMIC. The relevant new provisions in this respect are as follows.

POLICE ACT 1996

40 Power to give directions in relation to police force

(1) Where the Secretary of State is satisfied that the whole or any part of a police force is failing to discharge any of its functions in an effective manner, whether generally or in particular respects, he may direct the police authority responsible for maintaining the force to take specified measures for the purpose of remedying the failure.

(2) Where the Secretary of State is satisfied that the whole or any part of a police force will fail to discharge any of its functions in an effective manner, whether generally or in particular respects, unless remedial measures are taken, he may direct the police authority responsible for maintaining the force to take specified measures in order to prevent such a failure occurring.

(3) The measures that may be specified in a direction under subsection (1) or (2) include the submission to the Secretary of State of an action plan setting out the measures which the person or persons submitting the plan propose to take for the purpose of remedying the failure in question or (as the case may be) preventing such a failure occurring.

Certain procedural safeguards are preserved under the substituted section. To a **1.55** substantial extent, they follow the provisions under the original system. The central provision is s 40(4), which provides as follows.

(4) The Secretary of State shall not give a direction under this section in relation to any police force unless—

   (a) the police authority responsible for maintaining the force and the chief officer of police of that force have each been given such information about the Secretary of State's grounds for proposing to give that direction as he considers appropriate for enabling them to make representations or proposals under the following paragraphs of this subsection;

   (b) that police authority and chief officer have each been given an opportunity of making representations about those grounds;

   (c) that police authority and chief officer of police have each had an opportunity of making proposals for the taking of remedial measures that would make the giving of the direction unnecessary; and

   (d) the Secretary of State has considered any such representations and proposals.

By s 40(5), subs (4) does not apply where the police authority and the chief officer 'have already been made aware of the matters constituting' the grounds for **1.56** proposing to give a direction, where the information that they had about those matters was sufficient to enable them to identify remedial measures that would make the giving of a direction unnecessary, and where they have had a reasonable opportunity to take such measures.

1.57 By s 40(6), the Home Secretary shall not give a direction unless Her Majesty's Chief Inspector of Constabulary (HMCIC) has been given the same subs (4)(a) information and an opportunity to make written representations about those grounds. The effect of these provisions is that it should be relatively rare for a formal direction to be given. Specific concerns will be addressed through proposals, and counterproposals, between the respective parties. Assuming that a direction is given, subs (7) provides that a police authority shall comply with it.

1.58 The s 40 powers in relation to giving directions in relation to a police force are mirrored in s 40A[37] in respect of giving directions in relation to police authorities. The difference is that the chief officer is removed from the list of mandatory consultees under subss (4) and (5).

1.59 Section 40B provides for the regulation of the procedures applicable to directions under ss 40 and 40A. Subsections (6) and (7) provide that, where a direction is given, the Home Secretary will prepare a report on his exercise of that power in relation to the affected force, which shall be laid before Parliament. The timing of the report, which may relate to more than one exercise of the power, is at such time as the Home Secretary considers appropriate. The content of the report is not prescribed by statute, although it could be reflected in procedural regulations arising under s 40B(1) and (3).

Police Act 1996, ss 41A and 41B

1.60 These sections, giving the Secretary of State power to require a police authority to submit an action plan to address conduct judged by HMIC to be inefficient or ineffective (or that would be), enjoyed a short life. They were introduced by s 5 of the 2002 Act from 1 October 2002, and repealed by s 2 of the 2006 Act from 1 April 2007. Section 41A(12) specifically excluded the use of a direction in relation to particular individuals or cases.

Reports to the Secretary of State from police authorities and chief constables

1.61 Sections 43 and 44 of the 1996 Act provide that the Secretary of State may require police authorities and/or chief constables (including the Commissioner of the City of London police) to submit a report on such matters connected with the discharge of the authority's functions or the policing of the chief constable's police area as he may specify, in such form as he specifies, and published in a manner he considers appropriate. Additionally, mandatory annual reports by the chief constable to the police authority under s 22 of the 1996 Act must be submitted to the Secretary of State (s 44(4)).

---

[37] Police and Justice Act 2006, s 2, Sch 2, para 27, in force 1 April 2007: SI 2007/709, art 3(b) and (c).

Regulations for police forces

Section 50(1) of the 1996 Act empowers (but does not require) the Secretary of **1.62**
State to make regulations as to the government, administration, and conditions
of service of police forces. Under subs (2), this discretionary power includes,
without prejudice to the generality of subs (1):

(a) the ranks to be held by members of police forces;
(b) the qualifications for appointment and promotion of members of police forces;
(c) periods of service on probation;
(d) voluntary retirement of members of police forces;
(e) the conduct, efficiency and effectiveness of members of police forces and the maintenance
of discipline;
(f) the suspension of members of a police force from membership of that force and from their
office as constable;
(g) the maintenance of personal records of members of police forces;
(h) the duties that are or are not to be performed by members of police forces;
(i) the treatment as occasions of police duty of attendance at meetings of the Police Federations
and of any body recognized by the Secretary of State for the purposes of section 64;
(j) the hours of duty, leave, pay and allowances of members of police forces; and
(k) the issue, use, and return of police clothing, personal equipment and accoutrements.

Section 50(3) requires the Secretary of State to produce regulations to: **1.63**

(a) establish, or make provision for the establishment of, procedures for cases in which a member of a police force may be dealt with by dismissal, requirement to resign, reduction in
rank, reduction in rate of pay, fine, reprimand or caution;
(b) make provision for securing that any case in which a senior officer may be dismissed or dealt
with in any of the other ways mentioned in paragraph (a) is decided—
[. . .]
(ii) . . . by the police authority which maintains the force or by a committee of that
authority.

This is coupled with the power to issue guidance concerning disciplinary proceedings under s 87 (see 1.68 below).

Section 50(3) is substituted by para 3 of Sch 22 to the Criminal Justice and **1.64**
Immigration Act 2008. There is a more general power consistent with the loss
of certain sanctions under the 2008 Conduct Regulations. The language is now
to establish, or to make provision for the establishment of, procedures for the
taking of disciplinary proceedings in respect of the conduct, efficiency, and
effectiveness of members of police forces, including procedures for cases in which
such persons may be dealt with by dismissal.

Where regulations are made, chief officers of police may not issue orders that **1.65**
conflict with those regulations, but they may issue orders that supplement the
regulations.[38]

---

[38] See *Re Shields* [2003] UKHL 3, [2003] NI 161, [2003] All ER (D) 81 (Feb).

Codes of practice and statutory guidance issued by the Secretary of State

1.66 Section 39 of the 1996 Act gave the Secretary of State power to issue codes of practice to police authorities in relation to the discharge of any functions under s 3. This power, which extends to the power to revise the whole or part of any such code, was subject only to the duty to lay a copy before Parliament. There is no express obligation to consult.

1.67 Section 39A of the 1996 Act, inserted by s 2 of the 2002 Act, extended the power to cover codes of practice for chief officers. The power exists where the Secretary of State 'considers it necessary to do so for the purpose of promoting the efficiency and effectiveness generally' of the police forces maintained for police areas in England and Wales. In theory, it appears that such a code could apply to one or more of the police areas (see s 105(4)).

Home Office Guidance on Police Unsatisfactory Performance, Complaints and Misconduct Procedures

1.68 In relation to disciplinary proceedings, s 87 of the 1996 Act empowers the Secretary of State to issue guidance concerning disciplinary proceedings. The Home Office's Guidance on *Police Unsatisfactory Performance, Complaints and Misconduct Procedures* arises under the s 50 powers. Section 87 provides[39] as follows.

(1) The Secretary of State may issue guidance to police authorities, chief officers of police and other members of police forces concerning the discharge of their functions under regulations made under section 50 in relation to the matters mentioned in subsection (2)(e) of that section, and they shall have regard to any such guidance in the discharge of their functions.

(1A) The Secretary of State may also issue guidance to the Independent Police Complaints Commission concerning the discharge of its functions under any regulations under section 50 in relation to disciplinary proceedings.

(2) Nothing in this section shall authorise the issuing of any guidance about a particular case.

(3) It shall be the duty of every person to whom any guidance under this section is issued to have regard to that guidance in discharging the functions to which the guidance relates.

(4) A failure by a person to whom guidance under this section is issued to have regard to the guidance shall be admissible in evidence in any disciplinary proceedings or on any appeal from a decision taken in any such proceedings.

(5) In this section "disciplinary proceedings" means any proceedings under any regulations under section 50 that are identified as disciplinary proceedings by those regulations.

1.69 Paragraph 9 of Sch 22 to the Criminal Justice and Immigration Act 2008 substitutes the following for subs 1:

(1) The Secretary of State may issue relevant guidance to—
   (a) police authorities,
   (b) chief officers of police,

---

[39] Subsections (1A), (2)–(5), substituted, for subs (2) as originally enacted, by the Police Reform Act 2002, s 107(1), Sch 7, para 18, in force 1 April 2004: see SI 2004/913, art 2(e).

 (c) other members of police forces,

 (d) special constables, and

 (e) persons employed by a police authority who are under the direction and control of the chief officer of police of the police force maintained by that authority.

[. . .]

(1ZA) "Relevant guidance" is guidance as to the discharge of functions under regulations under section 50 or 51 or in relation to the matters mentioned in section 50(2)(e) or 51(2)(ba).

Paragraph 9(3) and (4) adds s 51 to s 87(1A) and (5) (guidance concerning disciplinary proceedings, etc). **1.70**

Home Office Guidance has been issued in relation to each of the 1985, 1999, 2004, and 2008 Conduct Regulations. The guidance in relation to the 2008 Regulations is reproduced at Appendix I. A reasoned departure from guidance, in the interests of justice given the purpose of disciplinary proceedings, is permissible. **1.71**

The statutory guidance must, of course, be consistent with the law—in this case, the terms of the Police Act 1996. If guidance is not within the terms of the statute, the legal effect has to be determined by reference to general principles of interpretation and administrative law.[40] Home Office Guidance purporting to limit the powers of the police appeals tribunals under the 1996 Act was accordingly invalid.[41] **1.72**

By s 39A(7) of the 1996 Act, in discharging any function to which such a code relates, a chief officer 'shall have regard to it'. A requirement to 'have regard to' a code, or guidance, means no more than that a person is required to take it into account when discharging his functions and does not mean that he is obliged to comply with it.[42] Obviously, an arbitrary refusal to follow guidance (by any decision maker, whether in this context or otherwise), rather than a reasoned departure from it, may generate a challenge that it has not been taken into account at all. **1.73**

These powers are subject to a duty to require the NPIA[43] to prepare a draft (s 39A(3)) of any code or revision, and that Agency is, in turn, required to consult with police authorities, chief officers, and such other persons as it thinks fit (s 39A(4)). **1.74**

---

[40] *R (Coghlan) v Chief Constable of Greater Manchester Police* [2004] EWHC 2801 (Admin), [2005] 2 All ER 890, [2004] All ER (D) 26 (Dec).

[41] *R (Chief Constable of Avon and Somerset Police) v Police Appeals Tribunal* [2004] EWHC 220 (Admin), (2004) Times, 11 February, [2004] All ER (D) 17 (Feb).

[42] *R v Police Complaints Board, ex p Madden; R v Police Complaints Board, ex p Rhone* [1983] 2 All ER 353, [1983] Crim LR 263.

[43] These functions were formerly exercised by the Central Police Training and Development Authority (Centrex).

1.75 Applied to discipline and misconduct, these codes of practice are of general application and cannot be issued only in relation to an individual case.

The removal of chief officers

1.76 The removal of chief officers (as defined in s 101 of the 1996 Act)[44] and 'senior officers' (that is, those holding the rank above chief superintendent)[45] in the interests of efficiency and effectiveness, rather than for personal misconduct, is addressed in detail in Chapter 2, because it is primarily the function of the police authority under s 11 of the 1996 Act (s 9E in relation to the Commissioner and Deputy Commissioners of the MPS). Under s 42(1) of the Act, however, the Secretary of State has the power to require a police authority to exercise its powers to call upon the chief officer to retire in the interests of efficiency or effectiveness.

1.77 Under s 42(1A), he can require the suspension of a chief officer pending resolution of these procedures in any case in which he considers it necessary for 'the maintenance of public confidence in the force in question'. In determining the public interest, the Secretary of State is entitled to take into account the confidence of the public at large in a force rather than confining his attention to the public within the area of the particular police force.[46]

The Police Negotiating Board (PNB) and the Police Advisory Boards

1.78 Subject to the character of the regulation, the Secretary of State is required to consult either the PNB for the United Kingdom, or the Police Advisory Board for England and Wales (PABEW), and the Police Advisory Board for Scotland.

1.79 Section 61 of the 1996 Act makes provision for the PNB for the United Kingdom for the purpose of consideration of 'questions relating to hours of duty, leave, pay and allowances, pensions or the issue, use and return of police clothing, personal equipment and accoutrements' (subs (1)). By s 62(1), ('Functions of the Board with respect to regulations'), other than in relation to pensions, the Secretary of State is required, before making any regulation under ss 50 or 51 in relation to these issues, to consult the Board, to 'take into consideration' any recommendation made by it, and to supply the Board with a draft of the regulations. Section 62(1D)

---

[44] Police Act 1996, s 101(1), meaning: (a) in relation to a police force maintained under s 2, the chief constable; (b) in relation to the MPS, the Commissioner of Police of the Metropolis; and (c) in relation to the City of London police force, the Commissioner of Police for the City of London.

[45] Schedule 6, para 10(a), to the 1996 Act; s 29 of the 2002 Act.

[46] See *R (Secretary of State for the Home Department) v Humberside Police Authority, David Westwood* [2004] ACD 92, [2004] EWHC 1642 (Admin).

and (1E) extends this to terms and conditions affecting the constables and civilians employed by the NPIA.[47]

Section 63 of the 1996 Act provides for the PABEW (and that for Scotland), origi- **1.80** nally reflected in statute under the Police Act 1964. Subsection (1) provides that it continues 'for the purpose of advising the Secretary of State on general questions affecting the police in those countries respectively'. Subsection (1C) extends the reach to the NPIA. The constitution and proceedings of the Police Advisory Boards are determined by the Secretary of State following consultation with organizations representing the interests of police authorities, and of members of police forces and police cadets (s 63(3)). Subsection (3) reproduces the obligations on the Secretary of State to consult before making any regulation[48] under ss 50 and 51 as apply to the PNB, other than regulations covered under s 61(1) by the PNB, and extends the duty to any regulations under Pt 2 of the 2002 Act (complaints and misconduct, including the IPCC) and the NPIA.

A series of regulations, some directly concerning efficiency and misconduct **1.81** regulations, have arisen under s 50.[49] Section 36 of the 2002 Act further extended the generality of the s 50 powers to include the power to regulate the participation of the IPCC and others in disciplinary proceedings, and the application of s 34 of the Criminal Justice and Public Order Act 1994 (inferences to be drawn from a failure to mention a fact when questioned or charged) to disciplinary proceedings. Additionally, s 14 of the 2002 Act takes so much of any complaint as relates to the direction and control by a chief officer (or someone performing that role) out of Sch 3 to that Act ('Handling of complaints'). Section 14(2), however, empowers the Secretary of State to issue guidance to chief officers and police authorities as to handling such a matter, and each is required to have regard to

---

[47] Inserted by the Police and Justice Act 2006, s 1(3), Sch 1, Pt 7, paras 61 and 67(1) and (3), in force 1 April 2007: SI 2007/709, art 3(a).

[48] Extended to include 'rules' by para 6 of Sch 22 to the Criminal Justice and Immigration Act 2008.

[49] As at January 2008: the Police (Efficiency) Regulations 1999, SI 1999/732; the Criminal Justice and Police Act 2001 (Consequential Amendments) (Police Ranks) Regulations 2001, SI 2001/3888; the Police (Promotion) (Amendment) Regulations 2002, SI 2002/767; the Special Constables (Amendment) Regulations 2002, SI 2002/3180 (made under subs (7)); the Police Regulations 2003, SI 2003/527; the Police (Amendment) Regulations 2003, SI 2003/2594; the Police (Promotion) (Amendment) Regulations 2003, SI 2003/2595; the Police (Efficiency) (Amendment No 2) Regulations 2003, SI 2003/2600; the Police (Conduct) Regulations 2004, SI 2004/645; the Police (Amendment) Regulations 2004, SI 2004/3216; the Police (Promotion) (Amendment) Regulations 2005, SI 2005/178; the Police (Amendment) Regulations 2005, SI 2005/2834; the Police (Promotion) (Amendment) Regulations 2006, SI 2006/1442; the Police (Amendment) Regulations 2006, SI 2006/1467; the Police (Minimum Age for Appointment) Regulations 2006, SI 2006/2278; the Police (Amendment) (No 2) Regulations 2006, SI 2006/3449; the Police (Amendment) Regulations 2007, SI 2007/1160; and the Police (Fingerprints) Regulations 2007, SI 2007/1162.

such guidance (subs (3)). HOC 19/2005 addresses local procedures in terms of direction and control (see 1.07–1.09 above).

Other miscellaneous powers of regulation

1.82 Each of the 1996, 2002, and 2006 Acts provide a number of other functions and powers for the Secretary of State, including the power to produce regulations. Under the 1996 Act, these include the power to produce regulations relating to: setting a minimum budget (s 41); providing criminal statistics (s 45); the police grant (s 46); grants for capital expenditure (s 46); expenditure on safeguarding national security (s 48); local inquiries into policing (s 49); special constables (s 51); police cadets (s 52); standard of equipment (s 53), extended by s 7 of the 2002 Act (inserting s 53A to the 1996 Act) to include regulation of procedures and practices; common services (s 57); and regulations for Police Federations[50] (s 60).

1.83 Powers under the 2002 and 2006 Acts directly relevant to misconduct and discipline are identified as and where they arise in other chapters in this book. Paragraph 30 of Sch 2 to the 2006 Act, when in force, will give the Secretary of State the power to regulate the arrangements for obtaining the views of the community on policing under s 98 of the 1996 Act.

1.84 The Secretary of State enjoys the power to regulate police forces in other respects under a wide range of statutory provisions. These are only reflected in this text in so far as they relate to misconduct and discipline matters.

1.85 Section 22 of the 2002 Act gives the IPCC the power to issue statutory guidance in respect of the discharge of its functions. The explanatory notes to the 2002 Act (which are of non-statutory status) rehearse that, apart from guidance issued by the Secretary of State under s 14 relating to complaints dealing with direction and control by a chief officer, the Secretary of State will no longer issue guidance in relation to complaints.

D. Police Authorities

History and membership

1.86 Police authorities date back to the Police Act 1964 and, by s 3[51] of the 1996 Act, are bodies corporate that shall be established for every police area listed in Sch 1.

---

[50] Express limitations on the rights on a member of a police force to be a member of any trade union are set out in s 64 of the 1996 Act. The Police Federation is not within s 64.

[51] Which does not extend to Scotland (see s 105(1)).

Authorities other than the Metropolitan Police Authority (MPA) shall consist of seventeen members, which may be extended to any odd number above that by the Secretary of State (s 4). The MPA, which was established in 2000 by the Greater London Authority Act 1999,[52] shall consist of twenty-three members, which number may be reduced by the Secretary of State to any odd number not less than seventeen (s 5C).

Further provision as to the membership of police authorities arose under Schs 2, 2A, 3, and 3A to the 1996 Act. According to the explanatory note to the regulations, the White Paper *Building Communities, Beating Crime*, published in November 2004, proposed to strengthen the skills and experience base of police authorities, partly by removing the separate category of lay justice members. Accordingly, Schs 2 and 2A were substituted, and Schs 3 and 3A repealed, by paras 2, 4, and 6 of Sch 2 to the 2006 Act. The central changes produced (from 1 April 2008 for police authorities established under s 3, and 3 July 2008 for the MPA)[53] are to remove the requirement of fixed relative numbers of members of the council/Greater London Authority (GLA) and independent members, and to reduce from three to one (four to one in the MPA) the minimum number of lay justice members. Regulations must still provide for the numbers, and process of selection, of 'other persons'. **1.87**

In headline terms, authorities established under s 3 shall consist of: (a) persons who are members of a relevant council; and (b) other persons, including at least one lay justice.[54] The MPA shall consist of: (a) persons appointed from among the Mayor of London and members of the London Assembly; and (b) other persons, including at least one lay justice.[55] The substituted Schedules make allowance for further detailed regulation of the membership.[56] Within this flexibility are some minimum requirements. For authorities under s 3, the council members are appointed by the relevant council(s) (Sch 2, para 2), and other members by existing members of an authority from a shortlist of persons prepared by selection panel (Sch 2, para 3). Members appoint the chairman from among their number at each annual general meeting (Sch 2, para 4). **1.88**

Applied to the MPA, para 1 of Sch 2A to the Police Act 1996 (as amended by the Police and Justice Act 2006) provides that the Secretary of State will make **1.89**

---

[52] Section 310 of the 1999 Act, inserting s 5B to the 1996 Act.

[53] See the Police and Justice Act 2006 (Commencement No 1, Transitional and Saving Provisions) Order 2006, SI 2006/3364, and the Police and Justice Act 2006 (Supplementary and Transitional Provisions) Order 2006, SI 2006/3365.

[54] Schedule 2, para 1(2), to the 1996 Act, as amended by s 2 of, and para 2 of Sch 2 to, the 2006 Act.

[55] Schedule 2A, para 1(2) and (3), to the 1996 Act, as amended by s 2 of, and para 4 of Sch 2 to, the 2006 Act.

[56] Schedule 2, para 1(5); Sch 2A, para 3.

regulations governing membership of the MPA. The Metropolitan Police Authority Regulations 2008[57] (MPA Regulations) have been made by the Secretary of State.

1.90 By reg 6(3) of the MPA Regulations, the Mayor of London may appoint himself as a member of MPA, and by reg 10(1), where the Mayor is a member of the MPA, he is to be chairman. By reg 20(1), where the Mayor is so appointed under reg 6, he shall cease to be a member of the MPA if he ceases to be Mayor and does not on the same day again become Mayor.

1.91 The MPA Regulations came into force on 1 April 2008—but by reg 1(2), they apply only in respect of appointments of members of the MPA that take effect on, or after, 1 October 2008. The Police and Justice Act 2006 (Commencement No 1, Transitional and Savings Provisions) (Amendment) Order 2008[58] and the Police And Justice Act 2006 (Supplementary And Transitional Provisions) (Amendment) Order 2008[59] provide that the existing system for police authority appointments will continue to apply to appointments that take effect up until 30 September 2008.

1.92 Under these provisions, the Mayor—on the basis that he appointed himself as a member of the MPA—became chairman of the MPA on 1 October 2008.

1.93 Members appointed from the London Assembly are to be appointed by the Mayor of London (Sch 2A, para 2). As regards other members of the MPA: one of the members shall be appointed by the Secretary of State (Sch 2A, para 3(a)); others, by existing members of the MPA from a shortlist prepared by a selection panel. As stated, if the Mayor of London is a member of the MPA,[60] he is to be chairman (Sch 2A, para 4(1)(a)); if not, he appoints from among the members of the MPA. He may also appoint vice-chairmen (Sch 2A, para 4(2)).

General functions

1.94 The general functions of all police authorities, including the MPA,[61] are set out in s 6 of the 1996 Act. Each shall: (a) secure the maintenance of an efficient and effective police force for its area; and (b) hold the chief officer of police of that force to account for the exercise of his functions, and those of persons under his direction and control (s 1(1)). In discharging these basic functions, the authority shall have regard to any strategic objectives determined by the Secretary of State under s 37A, any performance targets established by the authority, whether in

---

[57] SI 2008/631.
[58] SI 2008/617.
[59] SI 2008/619.
[60] See the Metropolitan Police Authority Regulations SI 2008/631, reg 6(3).
[61] Police Act 1996, s 6(5).

compliance with a direction from the Secretary of State under s 38 or otherwise (s 6(2)), and, where the discharge of a function is affected by a code issued under s 39, to that code (s 6(3)).

The application of these basic duties to arrangements between forces was considered at 1.19–1.22 above. **1.95**

There is, additionally, obligation to have regard to any objectives determined by the authority under s 7, and any local policing plan issued by the authority under s 8. The obligations on police authorities under ss 7 and 8, as well as the obligation under s 6A to produce a three-year strategy plan, and that under s 9 to produce an annual report, were repealed by the 2006 Act.[62] Section 6ZA of the 1996 Act (powers to confer particular functions on a police authority, including that requiring reports on specific matters from the chief officer) was introduced by para 8 of Sch 2 to the 2006 Act with effect from 15 January 2007. Once the repeal takes practical effect, these are replaced by s 6ZB (annual 'plans by police authorities', including policing objectives—framed so as to be consistent with strategic objectives under s 37A—and proposed three-year arrangements to achieve them), and s 6ZC ('reports by police authorities', by Order of the Secretary of State, concerning the policing of their areas).[63] **1.96**

From 1 April 2006, police authorities have been required to produce an annual 'local policing summary', the content of which may be regulated by the Secretary of State, consisting of a report for members of the public in the authority's area on matters relating to the policing of that area for the year.[64] **1.97**

Obligations to consult the local community and status as a 'best value authority'

There is an obligation on the police authority to make arrangements for obtaining the views of people in that area about matters concerning the policing of that area, and their cooperation with the police in preventing crime in that area (s 96(1) of the 1996 Act). When in force, the 2006 Act will extend this to antisocial behaviour.[65] As matters stand (s 96(6)–(10)), the Secretary of State may require **1.98**

---

[62] Police and Justice Act 2006, ss 2 and 52, Sch 2, para 10, Sch 15, Pt 1(B). Paragraph 10 repealed ss 6A and 7–9 of the 1996 Act from 14 March 2008: Police and Justice Act 2006 (Commencement No 7 and Savings Provision) Order 2008, SI 2008/311, arts 2(b) and 3.

[63] Ibid, s 2, Sch 2, para 8: Police and Justice Act (Commencement No 1, Transitional and Saving Provisions) Order 1006, SI 2006/3364, art 2(b), in force 14 December 2006; Sch 2, para 9 (introducing ss 6ZB and 6ZC): Police and Justice Act (Commencement No 7 and Savings Provision) Order 2008, SI 2008/311, art 2(b), in force 14 March 2008.

[64] Police Act 1996, s 8A, inserted by the Serious and Organised Crime Act 2005, s 157, and the Serious and Organised Crime Act 2005 (Commencement No 1, Transitional and Transitory Provisions) Order 2005, SI 2005/1521, art 5(2).

[65] Police and Justice Act 2006, s 2, Sch 2, para 30(1) and (2).

reports as to the adequacy of these arrangements. This limited power will be strengthened, to a degree, by substitute provisions under the 2006 Act,[66] when in force, giving the Secretary of State power to regulate the procedure.

Questions to a police authority nominee at council meetings

1.99 Under s 20 of the 1996 Act, each relevant council must make arrangements for enabling questions on the discharge of the functions of a police authority to be put by members of the council at a meeting of the council for answer by a person nominated by the authority for that purpose. Equivalent provisions apply to the MPA (s 20A).

Crime and disorder partnerships, and councils' duties to obtain 'best value'

1.100 The Crime and Disorder Act 1998 created crime and disorder reduction partnerships, under the auspices of which the police force, police authorities, local authorities, and a large number of other agencies are required to devise a strategy for tackling crime and disorder after widespread consultation with the public. Ordinarily, members of the partnership will include probation services, health agencies, voluntary groups, residents' associations, and other bodies of that nature.

1.101 Under s 1(1)(d) of the Local Government Act 1999, a police authority is a 'best value' authority with the obligation (s 3) 'to make arrangements to secure continuous improvement in the way in which its functions are exercised, having regard to a combination of economy, efficiency and effectiveness'. The practical implications of this are restricted by subsequent legislation.[67] The Home Office publishes[68] guidance to police authorities as to the 'best value' philosophy.

Association of Police Authorities (APA) published guidance

1.102 As has been set out, the APA is the body that the Secretary of State must consult before discharging particular functions, including issuing regulations, guidance, and codes of practice in relation to policing.[69] Police authorities are also required to cooperate with other statutory bodies, including HMIC and the IPCC. In May 2007, the APA published guidance entitled *Oversight and Scrutiny of*

---

[66] Ibid, s 2, Sch 2, para 30(1) and (4).

[67] Police and Justice Act 2006, s 4, in force 31 March 2007: see the Police and Criminal Justice Act 2006 (Commencement No 9) Order 2007, SI 2007/709, art 2. For transitional provisions and savings having effect for the financial years ending 31 March 2008 and 31 March 2009, see art 5. Section 4 will be repealed by the Local Government and Public Involvement in Health Act 2007, s 241, Sch 18, Pt 8, date in force to be appointed: see s 245(5).

[68] Online at <http://police.homeoffice.gov.uk>.

[69] Police and Justice Act 2006, s 6 and Sch 4.

Professional Standards Matters: The Role of Police Authorities.[70] Elements of this non-statutory, declaredly 'non-prescriptive', guidance include an analysis of 'strategic oversight of professional standards matters', and 'promoting efficiency and effectiveness—and learning the lessons'.

Equality and diversity

Police authorities have specific duties under different Acts in relation to equality **1.103** and diversity, including those under the Human Rights Act 1998, the Race Relations Act 1976 (as amended by the Race Relations (Amendment) Act 2000), the Disability Discrimination Act 1995 (as amended in 2005), and the Equalities Act 2006, which amends the Sex Discrimination Act 1976. The APA's published guidance adopts as approved practice many of the recommendations of the March 2005 report by the Commission for Racial Equality (CRE),[71] *The Police Service in England and Wales: Final Report of a Formal Investigation.*

More generally, 'key activities' are recommended in the Executive Summary to **1.104** promote the basic objective of ensuring a high-quality level of oversight of professional standards. Police authorities are required, by s 15 of the 2002 Act (and s 77 of the 1996 Act), to ensure that they are kept informed as to all matters about complaints and misconduct matters. Other than in somewhat exceptional circumstances in relation to the removal of chief and other qualifying senior officers to ensure the effective and efficient provision of policing in a police area,[72] considered in detail in the next chapter, police authorities do not have a direct role in the investigation or determination of individual misconduct cases. This reflects the fact that direction and control matters are for the chief officer,[73] including the appointment and removal of officers. There are, however, specific statutory duties under the 1996 and 2002 Acts that may be summarized.

The funding of legal representation for members of the force and others

It has been held[74] that a police authority is empowered by the Local Government **1.105** Act 1972, s 111(1)[75] (power to take action calculated to facilitate, or which is

---

[70] Available online at <http://www.apa.police.uk>.

[71] Merged in 2007 with the Disability Rights Commission (DRC) and the Equal Opportunities Commission (EOC) to create the Equality and Human Rights Commission (EHRC).

[72] Police Act 1996, ss 9, 11, and 12.

[73] Ibid, s 10(1).

[74] *R v DPP, ex p Duckenfield; R v South Yorkshire Police Authority, ex p Chief Constable of South Yorkshire Police* [1999] 2 All ER 873, [2000] 1 WLR 55.

[75] Local Government Act 1972, s 111(1), applies to all police authorities (except the City of London police) by virtue of s 146A of the 1972 Act (as inserted by Sch 14 to the Local Government Act 1985 and amended by Sch 4 to the Police and Magistrates' Courts Act 1994). It applies to the MPA by virtue of para 28 of Sch 27 to the Greater London Authority Act 1999. As regards the City of London police, the Common Council of the City is the police authority and s 111(1) of

conducive or incidental to, the discharge of any of its functions), to support its general function under s 6(1) of the Police Act 1996 so as to fund officers' legal costs in criminal and judicial review proceedings. In practice, this extends to inquests and public inquiries. The exercise of the power may be controversial, and in the judicial review proceedings following the inquest verdict relating to the death of Roger Sylvester, the MPA funded the costs of both the appellant police officers and the family of the deceased. The family had contended that it had no alternative source of funding.

1.106 Considerations relating to the exercise of the discretion as to funding are supplemented by HOC 43/2001. Paragraph 1 of this document provides as follows:

> It is important that police officers should be able to carry out their duties in the confidence that their police authority will support them by providing financial assistance in legal proceedings taken against them and progressed by them, if they act in good faith and exercise their judgement reasonably. The following guidance, which has been prepared in consultation with ACPO, CPOSA, the Superintendents' Association, the Police Federation and the Association of Police Authorities, should be read against this.

1.107 Although the Circular allows for discretion, it concludes (para 11) as follows:

> In summary, police officers must be confident that Police Authorities will provide financial support for officers in legal proceedings where they have acted in good faith and have exercised their judgement reasonably. Police Authorities will need to decide each case on its own merits, but subject to that there should be a strong presumption in favour of payment where these criteria are met.

1.108 Considerations of funding are becoming highly significant in the context of inquests post-dating *Middleton*,[76] which must discharge the investigative ('adjectival') obligation under Art 2 of the European Convention on Human Rights (ECHR), as enacted by the Human Rights Act 1998. These costs can be significant, and very often the force will itself be an interested person, alongside, and in addition to, police officers. The same proposition obviously applies to public inquiries.

1.109 Even if there is not a direct conflict between the officers and the force, in practice separate representation is very often necessary. The approach taken to particular evidence, and force policies, will often differ as a matter of strategy and interpretation. The affected police officer may, quite legitimately, hold a different opinion of training and system issues from that of the force. Such an officer, it is contended, has no less acted in good faith or exercised his or her judgement reasonably,

---

the 1972 Act applies to the Common Council directly, ie without application by any subsequent enactment.

[76] *R (Middleton) v West Somerset Coroner and anor* [2004] 2 AC 182, HL.

and should be funded. Additionally, the affected officer will often have received separate representation during the preceding investigation and continuity of representation is a legitimate consideration for the police authority.

Police authorities: a summary of specific statutory duties in relation to complaints and misconduct

The Police Act 1996

These matters have already been addressed, but include: the general duty for a **1.110** police authority to secure the maintenance of an efficient and effective police force in its area (s 6(1)); a specific duty to keep itself informed of the operation of ss 66 to 76 of the 1996 Act (relating to the handling of complaints, as amended by the 2002 Act, s 77); the obligation on a chief officer to report on matters relating to efficiency and effectiveness (s 22(3)); and the power to require an officer of ACPO rank to retire or resign on the grounds of efficiency or effectiveness, with the approval of the Secretary of State (ss 9A-H, 11 and 12).

The Police Reform Act 2002

Whilst a police authority never becomes the investigator, specific duties arise **1.111** with respect to the referral of particular complaints and conduct in the police authority's role as appropriate authority under Pt 2 ('Complaints and Misconduct') of the 2002 Act. The duty extends to taking steps to preserve evidence. By s 29 (the interpretation section), the police authority is the appropriate authority responsible for determining procedures under the 2002 Act in relation to senior officers—that is, those above the rank of chief superintendent; if below that rank, the appropriate authority is the chief officer. Section 14 provides that nothing in Sch 3 shall have effect to so much of any complaint as relates to the direction and control of a police force by the chief officer or someone acting in that capacity.

The duties of an authority in terms of handling other complaints, as defined **1.112** by s 12 of the 2002 Act, are set out in Pt 1 of Sch 3 to the 2002 Act, and, in particular, paras 2–4. In summary (the procedures are addressed in greater detail in Chapters 4–8), under para 2, where a complaint is referred to an authority, it should determine whether or not it is the appropriate authority, and, if it is not, notify the appropriate authority of the complaint. It must then so inform the complainant. The procedure, if it elects either not to notify or record a complaint, is addressed by para 3. Paragraph 4 provides for the circumstances in which the authority has a duty to refer a complaint to the IPCC.

In relation to 'conduct matters' (Pt 2 of Sch 3 to the 2002 Act), para 10 provides **1.113** for the duties, when a civil complaint is notified, on the police authority to consider whether it involves a conduct matter and to record/inform appropriately.

The duties and functions of the police authority in respect of other conduct matters are addressed in Chapters 4–8. They are rehearsed at paras 10–13 of Pt 2 of Sch 3 to the 2002 Act. Similar duties arise in respect of handling death and serious injury (DSI) matters, as rehearsed in Pt 2A of Sch 3 to the 2002 Act.[77]

1.114 Section 15 sets out general duties on an authority (shared with chief officers, inspectors of constabulary, SOCA, and the NPIA)[78] to ensure that it is kept informed of matters under any provision of Pt 2 of the 2002 Act—namely, complaints and misconduct. Where a police authority requires a chief officer of its own or any other force to provide a member of that force to investigate a matter in relation to which it is the appropriate authority, or if the IPCC is managing or supervising the investigation, that chief officer must do so. A police authority must provide anyone so appointed with all such assistance and cooperation that he or she may reasonably require.[79] Payment for such required assistance is addressed by s 16.

1.115 Police authorities and chief officers are required to provide information to the IPCC as may be specified by regulation (s 17(1)), and as appears to the IPCC to be required by it for the purposes of the carrying out of any of its functions (s 17(2)). The obligation does not require the provision of information 'before the earliest time at which it is practicable for that authority or chief officer to do so', or 'in which it never becomes practicable' to do so (s 17(4)). 'Practicability' is not further defined.

1.116 Section 18 establishes the duties of a police authority for, and chief officer of, a force to allow a person nominated for that purpose by the IPCC to have access to any premises occupied for the purposes of that force, and to documents and other things on those premises to allow access to the nominated person. The qualifying purposes are defined by s 18(2)—namely: (a) the purposes of any examination by the IPCC of the efficiency and effectiveness of the arrangements made by the force in question for handling complaints, or dealing with recordable conduct matters or DSI matters; and (b) the purposes of any investigation by the IPCC under Pt 2 of the 2002 Act, or of any investigation carried out under its supervision or management.

1.117 There are, however, some limitations. By s 18(3), a requirement imposed under this section for the purposes mentioned in subs (2)(a) must be notified to the

---

[77] Inserted by the Serious Organised Crime and Police Act 2005, s 160, Sch 12, paras 1, 11, and 12, in force 1 July 2005: see the Serious and Organised Crime Act 2005 (Commencement No 1, Transitional and Transitory Provisions) Order 2005, SI 2005/1521, art 3(1)(w).

[78] There are some limitations on this duty and the approval of the relevant 'directing officer' may be required: see s 15(6)–(10).

[79] In relation to the NPIA, see s 16A.

authority or chief officer at least forty-eight hours before the time at which access is required. By subs (4)(b), where there are reasonable grounds for not allowing that person to have the required access at the time at which he seeks it, the obligation to secure that the required access is allowed shall have effect as an obligation to secure that the access is allowed to that person at the earliest practicable time after there cease to be any such grounds as that person may specify. This appears to leave the decision, ultimately, with the IPCC and there are no additional provisions protecting the party required to provide access.

Section 18(5) provides that the s 18 provisions are in addition to, and without **1.118** prejudice to, the rights of entry, search, and seizure that are, or may be, conferred on a person designated for the purposes of para 19 of Sch 3, or any person who otherwise acts on behalf of the IPCC, in his capacity as a constable or as a person with the powers and privileges of a constable, or the obligations of police authorities and chief officers under ss 15 and 17.

E. The National Policing Improvement Agency (NPIA)

Part 1 of the 2006 Act ('Police reform') created (s 1(1)) a new statutory body **1.119** corporate—the NPIA—with effect from 1 April 2007.[80] The NPIA replaced the Central Police Training and Development Authority (Centrex), and the Police Information Technology Organisation (PITO), which were both abolished by s 1(2).

The detailed provisions as to the NPIA are in Sch 1 to the 2006 Act, which is in **1.120** seven Parts:

- Part 1—'Objects and powers' (paras 1–6);
- Part 2—'Membership, etc' (paras 7–27);
- Part 3—'Accountability and supervision' (paras 29–32);
- Part 4—'Financial provision' (paras 33–36);
- Part 5—'Transfer schemes' (paras 37–46);
- Part 6—'Interpretation and modification' (paras 47–48); and
- Part 7—'Consequential amendments' (paras 49–92).

Other than para 30(3),[81] the whole Schedule is effective, as with s 1, from 1 April **1.121** 2007. Part 1, para (1), provides as follows.

---

[80] The Police and Justice Act 2006 (Commencement No 2, Transitional and Saving Provisions) Order 2007, SI 2007/709, art 3; transitional arrangements are found in art 6.

[81] Under para 30(1) and (2), the Secretary of State may require HMCIC to inspect, and report on, the efficiency and effectiveness of the NPIA, either generally or on a particular matter. Paragraph 30(3) will apply s 32 of the Act (power of a person conducting an inspection) to these paragraphs in the same way as it applies to an inspection under Pt 4 of the Act ('Inspectorates').

PART I

OBJECTS AND POWERS

The Agency's objects

(1) The objects of the Agency are—

    (a) the identification, development and promulgation of good practice in policing;

    (b) the provision to listed police forces of expert advice about, and expert assistance in connection with, operational and other policing matters;

    (c) the identification and assessment of—

        (i) opportunities for, and

        (ii) threats to,

    police forces within the meaning given by section 101 of the Police Act 1996 (c 16) (police forces for police areas in England and Wales), and the making of recommendations to the Secretary of State in the light of its assessment of any opportunities and threats;

    (d) the international sharing of understanding of policing issues;

    (e) the provision of support to listed police forces in connection with—

        (i) information technology,

        (ii) the procurement of goods, other property and services, and

        (iii) training and other personnel matters;

    [(ea) the carrying out of its functions under section 3 of the Proceeds of Crime Act 2002 (c 29) (accreditation and training of financial investigators);][82]

    (f) the doing of all such other things as are incidental or conducive to the attainment of any of the objects mentioned in paragraphs (a) to (e) [(ea)].

1.122 The forces and entities in respect of which the NPIA exercises these powers are divided into 'listed' and 'restrictively listed' police forces by para 3. 'Restrictedly listed police forces' include any police force maintained under or by virtue of the Police (Scotland) Act 1967, the Scottish Police Services Authority (SPSA), the Police Service of Northern Ireland, the Police Service of Northern Ireland Reserve, the States of Jersey Police Force, the salaried police force of the Island of Guernsey, the Isle of Man Constabulary, and any person engaged outside the United Kingdom in the carrying on of activities similar to any carried on by a police force within the meaning of s 101. Others—including all forces under s 101 of the 1996 Act, SOCA, BTP, military police forces, and the Civil Nuclear Constabulary (CNC)—are simply 'listed'.

1.123 'The Agency's principal power' is set out in para 2. Under sub-para (1), it may (subject to sub-paras (4) and (5)) 'do anything it considers appropriate to achieve its objectives'. By sub-para (5), in the case of a restrictedly listed police force, the NPIA may provide advice, assistance, or support to the force only with the consent of the entity that is comprised in the force, the person whose control that entity is under, or the authority responsible for maintaining the force.

---

[82] Sub-paragraph (ea) inserted by the Serious Crime Act 2007, s 74(2)(g), Sch 8, Pt 7, para 177(1) and (2)(a), date in force to be appointed: see the Serious Crime Act 2007, s 94(1).

In the exercise of powers under para 1, the NPIA is able to accept gifts, and **1.124** loans, of money and other property (para 2(2)(b)), including provision for commercial sponsorship (para 2(3)), although it may only borrow money or other property with the consent of the Secretary of State (para 2(4)). For para 1(e) support (provision of support in information technology, procurement of goods, other property and services, and training and other personnel matters), it may carry on activities itself with a view to forces making use of what is provided through the carrying on of the activities, may support forces in their carrying on of activities themselves, and may support forces in any other way that it considers appropriate (para 2(a)(i)–(iii)).

Self-evidently, these are broad-textured objects and powers. The NPIA declares on **1.125** its website[83] that it is 'police owned and led and will work with police forces and authorities to ensure that [its] activities are fully aligned with the needs of policing'. It is effectively another policing entity for the purposes of the IPCC. Its headquarters are in London and there are some eleven other regional centres. The range and depth of activity is apparent from the website, and is clearly intended to represent a step change in the quality of delivery of national policing services, including workforce modernization and training. High-quality specialist officers from other forces are being seconded to the Agency to promote informed input.

Part 1 of Sch 1 provides some regulation of the Agency's objects and powers. **1.126** Paragraph 4 requires consultation with identified parties in the exercise of powers in relation to Scotland or Northern Ireland. Paragraph 5 requires the production of an annual plan setting out priorities, strategic priorities set by the Secretary of State under para 6, how it intends to give effect to such priorities, performance targets, and financial resources. The Agency is required to consult with the Secretary of State, the APA, and ACPO before finalizing the plan. The Secretary of State, after consulting the Agency, and (other than for Scottish forces under para 6(4), when Scottish Ministers must be consulted) the APA and ACPO, may 'determine' strategic priorities for the Agency under para 6.

Membership, in terms of the chairman and other members, is regulated under **1.127** para 7. The Agency is to consist of a chairman appointed by the Secretary of State, a chief executive, and other members. These parties are ineligible for membership of the IPCC.[84] The APA and ACPO must each nominate at least one of the other members, and one must be a member of the Home Civil Service.

---

[83] <http://www.npia.police.uk>.
[84] Police and Justice Act 2006, Sch 1, Pt 7, para 81, amending s 9(3) of the 2002 Act to this effect.

Paragraph 19 addresses regulations for constables employed by, or seconded to, the Agency.

1.128 Part 3 provides for accountability and supervision. The Agency is required to submit an annual report (para 28), and the Secretary of State may, at any time, require additional reports on specified matters connected with the carrying out of the Agency's functions (para 29). Paragraph 30 enables the Secretary of State to require HMCIC to inspect the Agency,[85] and he may give post-inspection directions to the Agency if it is failing to carry out any of its functions efficiently and effectively, or if it will cease to do so unless remedial action is taken (para 32).

F. Conclusion

1.129 This overview of national arrangements serves to demonstrate the complexity of the existing position. Policing has become a political matter, with elected politicians willing to stretch statutory powers over chief officers to the limit. Concurrently, there is some momentum towards elected, rather than appointed, chief officers and members of police authorities. The Policing and Crime Bill 2009 proposes reform of the process of appointment of senior officers and greater collaboration between forces.

1.130 The intrinsic merit of these developments and how the inevitable tensions will play out in practice is a matter of debate. In some forces, there is an open move away from meeting government performance targets in favour of delivering practical local policing. A chief officer on the ground may be justified in following his instinct, and providing genuine direction and control over his forces. As the dual role of an elected politician as Mayor of London and MPA chairman is tending to demonstrate, those in central government advocating change should be careful what they wish for.

---

[85] Paragraph 30(3) is not in force.

2

THE SUSPENSION AND REMOVAL
OF CHIEF OFFICERS BY POLICE
AUTHORITIES AND THE SECRETARY
OF STATE

A. **Overview**	2.01	The obligation to consult	
B. **Statutory Framework**	2.07	HMIC/HMCIC	2.19
The powers and duties of police		Suspension	2.20
authorities	2.07	The procedures preceding the	
Police Act 1996, s 11,		requirement to retire or resign	2.27
as amended: the appointment		'Explanations' to the affected	
and removal of chief constables	2.10	senior officer	2.31
The powers of the Secretary of State	2.11	'Representations' by the	
C. **Home Office Protocol**		affected senior officer	2.33
(March 2004)	2.14	The Secretary of State's approval	2.35
D. **Analysis of the Combined**		Inquiries	2.36
Procedure	2.16	Discretion as to which	
The initial decision to use the		requirement is imposed	2.37
procedure and the rights		E. **Conclusion**	2.38
of the officer	2.16		

A. Overview

The powers of removal and suspension reflected in this chapter relate to chief **2.01**
constables, deputy chief constables, and assistant chief constables of police areas
listed in Sch 1 of the Police Act 1996, and the Commissioner, Deputy
Commissioner, Assistant Commissioners, and Commanders of the Metropolitan
Police Service (MPS).

The powers and procedures rehearsed are somewhat more theoretical than real. **2.02**
Their use represents a police authority and/or the Secretary of State having to
take the proverbial 'nuclear option' when: (i) all other alternatives have been
exhausted; and (ii) they are presented with an obdurate senior officer. The vast

majority of problems associated with the efficiency and effectiveness of a force will be managed by earlier police authority intervention, or (more rarely) engagement by the Home Office Police Standards Unit (PSU). Powers and functions in these respects were addressed in Chapter 1.

2.03 These procedures are not directed at alleged misconduct by a senior or chief officer. Such alleged misconduct is addressed through normal misconduct regulations for senior officers. Additionally, the statutory procedures largely pre-date the declared intention of central government to play a more active role in the management of police performance, as also considered in Chapter 1.

2.04 That said, the procedures have been used historically, and their potential use against the Commissioner of the Metropolitan Police, following the conviction of his office under health and safety legislation in 2007 in connection with the operation surrounding the shooting of Jean Charles de Menezes, was a matter of political debate. The procedures provide the context in which other negotiated removals from office take place. The somewhat protracted theoretical process may be said to promote early settlement with a chief officer who is demonstrating a reluctance to accept that a removal from office on the basis of his force's failure to achieve efficiency or effectiveness is justified on merit.

2.05 The basic statutory provisions are set out in Part B of this chapter. These provisions were supplemented by a Protocol dated March 2004 for the implementation of ss 30–33 of the Police Reform Act 2002 (which amended the relevant powers under the 1996 Act) agreed between the Home Office, the Association of Police Officers (ACPO), the Chief Police Officers' Staff Association (CPOSA), and the Association of Police Authorities (APA). The effect of the non-statutory Protocol is addressed in Part C, and is reflected in a flow chart (based on Annex B of the Protocol) reproduced in Figure 2.1.

2.06 There exists a distinction between the 'maintenance of public confidence' criterion determining the power to suspend, and the 'interests of efficiency and effectiveness' criteria used in respect of the ultimate power to require resignation or retirement.

B. Statutory Framework

The powers and duties of police authorities

2.07 The legislative framework for action by police authorities to require the resignation/retirement of chief constables in the interests of efficiency or effectiveness is set out in s 11 of the Police Act 1996, as amended by ss 30 and 31 of the Police Reform Act 2002. Corresponding powers for authorities to remove deputy chief constables are provided for in s 11A of the 1996 Act, as inserted by s 123 of the Criminal Justice and Police Act 2001. Equivalent powers with respect to assistant chief constables are provided for in s 12 of the 1996 Act.

A corresponding power for the Metropolitan Police Authority (MPA) to remove **2.08** the Commissioner or Deputy Commissioner of the MPS is provided for in s 9E of the 1996 Act (also amended by ss 30 and 31 of the 2002 Act), as inserted by s 318 of the Greater London Authority Act 1999. With respect to Assistant Commissioners and Commanders of the MPS, the same power is provided for in ss 9F and 9G of the 1996 Act, as inserted by ss 319 and 320 of the Greater London Authority Act 1999. For Deputy Assistant Commissioners, the power is provided for in s 9FA of the 1996 Act, as inserted by s 122 of the Criminal Justice and Police Act 2001.

The power to allow for the suspension of individual senior officers in certain **2.09** circumstances is provided for in ss 9E and 11 of the 1996 Act, as amended and introduced by s 32 of the 2002 Act.

Police Act 1996, s 11, as amended: the appointment and removal of chief constables

From 1 June 2004, s 11 provides as follows.[1]   **2.10**

11 Appointment and removal of chief constables

(1) The chief constable of a police force maintained under section 2 shall be appointed by the police authority responsible for maintaining the force, but subject to the approval of the Secretary of State and to regulations under section 50.

(2) Without prejudice to any regulations under section 50 or under the Police Pensions Act 1976, the police authority, acting with the approval of the Secretary of State, may call upon the chief constable [in the interests of efficiency or effectiveness, to retire or to resign].

(3) Before seeking the approval of the Secretary of State under subsection (2), the police authority shall give the chief constable [—
   (a) an explanation in writing of the authority's grounds for calling upon him, in the interests of efficiency or effectiveness, to retire or to resign; and
   (b) an opportunity to make representations;
   and the authority shall consider any representations made by or on behalf of the chief officer.
   The opportunity given to the chief constable to make representations must include the opportunity to make them in person].

[(3A) A police authority maintaining a police force under section 2, acting with the approval of the Secretary of State, may suspend from duty the chief constable of that force if—
   (a) it is proposing to consider whether to exercise its power under subsection (2) to call upon the chief constable to retire or to resign and is satisfied that, in the light of the proposal, the maintenance of public confidence in that force requires the suspension; or
   (b) having been notified by the Secretary of State that he is proposing to consider whether to require the police authority to exercise that power, it is satisfied that, in the light of

---

[1] The words in square brackets were introduced by ss 30–32 of the 2002 Act (SI 2004/1319).

the Secretary of State's proposal, the maintenance of public confidence in that force requires the suspension; or

(c) it has exercised that power or been sent under section 42(2A) a copy of a notice of the Secretary of State's intention to require it to exercise that power, but the retirement or resignation has not yet taken effect;

and it shall be the duty of a police authority maintaining such a force (without reference to the preceding provisions of this subsection) to suspend the chief constable of that force from duty if it is required to do so by the Secretary of State under section 42(1A).]

(4) A chief constable who is called upon to retire under subsection (2) shall [retire or resign under subsection (2), shall retire or resign with effect from such date as the police authority may specify, or with effect from such earlier date] as may be agreed upon between him and the authority.

The powers of the Secretary of State

2.11 The Secretary of State has powers to instigate action by police authorities to remove chief constables, or the Commissioner or Deputy Commissioner of the MPS. These powers are provided for in s 42 of the 1996 Act, as amended by s 33 of the 2002 Act. Section 33 of the 2002 Act also provides for the Secretary of State to require the MPA to suspend the Commissioner or Deputy Commissioner of the MPS from duty, and other police authorities to suspend a chief constable from duty.

2.12 Section 42 of the 1996 Act, as amended, provides as follows.

42 Removal of chief constables, etc

[(1) The Secretary of State may—
  (a) require the Metropolitan Police Authority to exercise its power under section 9E to call upon the Commissioner or Deputy Commissioner, in the interests of efficiency or effectiveness, to retire or to resign; or
  (b) require a police authority maintaining a police force under section 2 to exercise its power under section 11 to call upon the chief constable of that force, in the interests of efficiency or effectiveness, to retire or to resign.

(1A) The Secretary of State may also, in any case falling within subsection (1B) in which he considers that it is necessary for the maintenance of public confidence in the force in question—
  (a) require the Metropolitan Police Authority to suspend the Commissioner or Deputy Commissioner from duty; or
  (b) require a police authority maintaining a police force under section 2 to suspend the chief constable of that force from duty.

(1B) The cases falling within this subsection are—
  (a) where the Secretary of State is proposing to exercise his power under subsection (1) in relation to the Metropolitan Police Authority or, as the case may be, the other police authority in question, or is proposing to consider so exercising that power;
  (b) where the Metropolitan Police Authority or the other police authority in question is itself proposing to exercise its power to call upon the Commissioner or Deputy Commissioner or, as the case may be, the chief constable of the force in question to retire or to resign, or is proposing to consider so exercising that power; and

   (c) where the power mentioned in paragraph (a) or (b) has been exercised but the retirement or resignation has not yet taken effect.

(2) Before requiring the exercise by the Metropolitan Police Authority or any other police authority of its power to call upon the Commissioner or Deputy Commissioner or the chief constable of the force in question to retire or to resign, the Secretary of State shall—

   (a) give the officer concerned a notice in writing—

      (i) informing him of the Secretary of State's intention to require the exercise of that power; and

      (ii) explaining the Secretary of State's grounds for requiring the exercise of that power; and

   (b) give that officer an opportunity to make representations to the Secretary of State.

(2A) Where the Secretary of State gives a notice under subsection (2)(a), he shall send a copy of the notice to the Metropolitan Police Authority or other police authority concerned.

(2B) The Secretary of State shall consider any representations made to him under subsection (2).]

(3) [Where the Secretary of State proposes to require the exercise of a power mentioned in subsection (1), he] shall, appoint one or more persons (one at least of whom shall be a person who is not an officer of police or of a Government department) to hold an inquiry and report to him and shall consider any report made under this subsection.

[(3A) At an inquiry held under subsection (3)—

   (a) the Commissioner, Deputy Commissioner or, as the case may be, the chief constable in question shall be entitled, in accordance with any regulations under section 42A, to make representations to the inquiry;

   (b) the Metropolitan Police Authority or, as the case may be, the police authority concerned shall be entitled, in accordance with any regulations made under section 42A, to make representations to the inquiry.

(3B) The entitlement of the Commissioner, Deputy Commissioner or, as the case may be, the chief constable in question to make representations shall include the entitlement to make them in person.]

(4) The costs incurred by [the Commissioner, the Deputy Commissioner or a chief constable] in respect of an inquiry under this section, taxed in such manner as the Secretary of State may direct, shall be defrayed out of the police fund.

[(4A) If the Secretary of State exercises the power conferred by subsection (1) in relation to the Commissioner or the Deputy Commissioner or a chief constable, the Metropolitan Police Authority or other police authority concerned—

   (a) shall not be required to seek the Secretary of State's approval before calling upon the Commissioner or Deputy Commissioner or chief constable in question, in the interests of efficiency or effectiveness, to retire or to resign; and

   (b) shall not be required to give the Commissioner, the Deputy Commissioner or the chief constable a written explanation of the authority's grounds for calling upon him to retire or to resign, to give him an opportunity to make representations to it or to consider any representations made by him.

(4B) In this section "the Commissioner" means the Commissioner of Police of the Metropolis and "the Deputy Commissioner" means the Deputy Commissioner of Police of the Metropolis.

(4C) In this section a reference to the police authority concerned, in relation to a chief constable, is to the police authority which maintains the police force of which he is chief constable.]

These statutory procedures are supplemented by the March 2004 Protocol.   **2.13**

C. Home Office Protocol (March 2004)

2.14 By way of background, Annex B of the Police Negotiating Board Agreement on Pay and Conditions of Chief Police Officers ('The operation and financial consequences of the expiry of FTAs,[2] early retirement and retirement and resignation in the interests of efficiency and effectiveness') details the uses and financial consequences of ss 11 and 42 of the 1996 Act, as amended by ss 30–33 of the 2002 Act. In March 2004, the Home Office, APA, ACPO, and the CPOSA agreed a Protocol.

2.15 The following central features of the procedure emerge if the statutory provisions are read alongside the March 2004 Protocol.

D. Analysis of the Combined Procedure

The initial decision to use the procedure and the rights of the officer

2.16 Paragraphs 11 and 12 of the Protocol provide that whilst the Secretary of State may initiate action under s 42 without having first issued direction under ss 40[3] and 41A, where he does so, the reasons for this will be considered by the s 42(3) independent inquiry.

2.17 Paragraph 13 of the Protocol provides that, apart from in exceptional cases, senior officers must have been alerted to any concerns about their impact on efficiency or effectiveness, and given a reasonable amount of time to address the matter prior to any action being taken against them under the suspension and removal powers. In cases involving assistant commissioners, and deputy commissioners, and commanders, the views of the Commissioner will be taken into account, and where the Secretary of State initiates the action the views of police authorities will be taken into account.

2.18 By para 14, affected officers must be given the 'earliest possible opportunity' to make representations to the relevant decision maker, and 'reasonable access to relevant materials in order to make their representations'.

The obligation to consult HMIC/HMCIC

2.19 Paragraph 15 introduces a requirement of 'consultation' with HM Inspectorate of Constabulary (HMIC) for the relevant force before taking or instigating

---

[2] Fixed-term appointments.
[3] The Protocol precedes the substitutions to ss 40, 40A, and 40B, made under the Police and Justice Act 2006, s 2, Sch 2, para 27, from 1 April 2007 (see SI 2007/709, art 3(b) and (c)).

action under the suspension and removal powers. This applies equally to the Secretary of State and to the police authority. Where consideration is being given to taking or instigating action with respect to the Commissioner or Deputy Commissioner of the MPS, or the chief constable of another force, HM Chief Inspector of Constabulary (HMCIC) will also be consulted. By para 16, the required consultation 'should be fully documented and copies retained for consideration by the Secretary of State where the authority is initiating action or by the independent inquiry where the Secretary of State is instigating it'.

Suspension

It will be seen that whilst a qualifying officer may be suspended by the police **2.20** authority (with the approval of the Secretary of State) when suspension is 'required' to maintain public confidence (s 11(3A)), in the context of other procedures, there is a duty to do so when directed by the Secretary of State in the exercise by the latter of powers under s 42(1A). Under s 42(1A), the test is that suspension is 'necessary' for the maintenance of public confidence in the force in question.

As set out in 1.77 above, in determining the public interest, the Secretary of **2.21** State is entitled to take into account the confidence of the public at large rather than confining his attention to the public within the area of the particular police force.[4] The 2004 Bichard Inquiry was a public inquiry on child protection procedures in Humberside Police and Cambridgeshire Constabulary—particularly, the effectiveness of relevant intelligence-based record keeping, vetting practices since 1995, and information sharing with other agencies. It made recommendations on matters of local and national relevance, and arose from perceived acute policing failures in the context of the investigation of the murders of Jessica Chapman and Holly Wells by Ian Huntley.

The Inquiry Report (published 22 June 2004) identified long-standing and **2.22** serious failures of policing. Amongst other criticisms of Humberside Police, characterized by the judge as 'extremely strong', it found:[5]

> The process of creating records on their main local intelligence system (called 'CIS Nominals') was fundamentally flawed throughout the relevant period. Police officers at various levels were alarmingly ignorant of how records were created and how the system worked. The guidance and training available were inadequate and this fed the confusion which surrounded the review and deletion of records once they had been created.

---

[4] See *R (Secretary of State for the Home Department) v Humberside Police Authority, David Westwood* [2004] ACD 92, [2004] EWHC 1642 (Admin).
[5] HMSO (2004) *The Bichard Inquiry Report*, 22 June, HC 653, para 10.

2.23 Certain improvements had been made—and were recognized as having been made—by the date of the publication of the Inquiry Report. Humberside Police Authority maintained confidence in its chief constable (David Westwood), whereas the Home Secretary did not. The Court held that the Home Secretary's powers under s 42(1A) were correctly exercised, given his assessment of the state of public confidence nationally (that is, outside the police authority area) in Humberside Police. It was not suggested at the hearing that the criticisms were insufficient to give reasonable grounds for the exercise of the power.[6]

2.24 The Protocol rehearses the statutory bases of the power to suspend, which arise in point of time when either the police authority or the Secretary of State is considering whether to exercise the relevant powers under either s 11 or 42. Paragraph 20 provides, consistently with the statute, that the Secretary of State may not instigate the suspension from duty of any senior officer below the rank of chief constable or, in the MPS, the Commissioner or Deputy Commissioner.

2.25 Paragraphs 21 and 22 provide as follows:

> 21. A senior officer should only ever be suspended from duty under section 9E(2A), section 11(3A) or section 42(1A) of the 1996 Act where this is required for the maintenance of public confidence in the force. Suspension is a grave matter and the authority or the Secretary of State will need to make a judgement about whether suspension would enhance or diminish public confidence.
> 22. Once a senior officer has been suspended, he or she will normally remain suspended until a final decision has been taken. However, the suspension will be reviewed on a monthly basis to ensure that its continuation is still appropriate. The fact that a senior officer has been suspended should not of course imply any pre-judgement of a case.

2.26 Under para 23, authorities should 'fully document' their reasons for suspending a senior officer from duty, and the Secretary of State should similarly fully document his reasons for requiring an authority to suspend a chief officer.

The procedures preceding the requirement to retire or resign

2.27 It will be seen that the exercise of these powers is subject to a number of statutory stages, which vary according to whether it is the police authority or Secretary of State that has initiated the process. The expression 'in the interests of efficiency or effectiveness' is not further defined. This makes it an uncertain threshold criterion.

2.28 If the s 11 power is initiated by the relevant police authority, it may only exercise the power with the approval of the Secretary of State (s 11(2)) in relation to requiring resignation or removal. In terms of the statute, without reference to the

---

[6] See [4] of the judgment.

associated Protocol, the rights of the affected officer are prescribed simply by reference to s 11(3), amounting fundamentally to little more than the right to: (a) an explanation in writing of the authority's grounds for calling upon him, in the interests of efficiency or effectiveness, to retire or to resign; and (b) an opportunity to make representations in person.

The statutory process under the 1996 Act is more protracted if the Secretary **2.29** of State initiates it under s 42. In substance, in addition to the rights of notification and participation in the process for the affected officer, the Secretary of State is required to hold an inquiry (s 42(3) and (3A)). If the exercise of the s 42(1) power is in relation to a chief constable, or either of the Commissioner or Deputy Commissioner of the MPS, the police authority is not required to obtain approval before exercising the relevant power to require retirement or resignation.

To date, no actual inquiry has arisen under s 42(3). Given the contractual terms **2.30** of appointment, and the increased use of powers of engagement by the PSU with failing forces, the exercise of the power is unlikely save for in another exceptional situation such as highlighted by the Bichard Inquiry. It is to be observed that the departure of the affected chief constable, even in that case, was successfully negotiated following his suspension and no statutory inquiry was necessary.

'Explanations' to the affected senior officer

The Protocol offers the affected officer some more 'concrete' rights than provided **2.31** for in the statute. Under 'explanations', addressed under paras 24–26 of the Protocol, the decision maker is required to provide a full written explanation of the grounds for taking the decision to require resignation or retirement, which will include the evidence on which it is based, and may include the material 'fully documenting' the decision required under paras 16 and 23. This may include the material from the relevant HMIC, HMCIC, or Home Office official.

By para 26, the affected officer will 'always' receive a full written explanation **2.32** before any public statement is made: 'a balance will need to be struck between legitimate public interest and the senior officer's "right to privacy"'. The latter assertion is not addressed further in practical terms.

'Representations' by the affected senior officer

Under 'representations' (Protocol paras 27–30), an affected officer has fourteen **2.33** days from notification that s 11 or s 42 is invoked in which to indicate that they wish to make representations, and a further fourteen days in which to prepare to make them. The officer must be ready to make the representations after that period. These representations can be made in person or in writing, and may, in either case, be made through a third party, which presumably includes a legal representative. The actual timing after that period is a matter for the determining police authority or Secretary of State.

2.34   The Protocol continues that it will, in all cases, be incumbent upon the police authority, or the Secretary of State, to consider and respond in writing to any representations made by or on behalf of the senior officer in question. As with the advice that the police authority or the Secretary of State receives from HMIC for the force concerned, HMCIC or Home Office officials, a senior officer's representations, and the authority or the Secretary of State's response to the representations, should be fully documented.

The Secretary of State's approval

2.35   In addition to the statutory obligations, paras 31 and 32 of the Protocol provide that police authorities will put their proposals to the Secretary of State in writing, enclosing copies of all of the documentation referred to in paras 16, 23, and 30 (see 2.36 below). Where the authority has taken action without the senior officer in question having previously been alerted to any concerns, the Secretary of State will consider the reasons for this.

Inquiries

2.36   The Protocol (paras 33–35) adds to the statutory provisions to the effect that the inquiry will have access to the material fully documenting decisions/reviews under paras 16 (HMIC/HMCIC consultation), 23 (reasons for suspension), and 30 (senior officer's representations and the authority/Secretary of State's response to it). Where the Secretary of State has instigated action without having made prior use of his powers of direction, or without the senior officer in question having previously been alerted to any concerns, the inquiry will consider the reasons for this.

Discretion as to which requirement is imposed

2.37   Paragraphs 36 and 37 of the Protocol provide that, in exercising their power to remove senior officers, it will, in all cases, be for police authorities to specify whether the requirement is for the senior officer to retire or to resign, and the date upon which the retirement or resignation is to have effect. Senior officers may agree with their authorities to leave the service at an earlier date than that originally specified by the authority.

E.   Conclusion

2.38   As has been observed, these powers have been little used in practice. This may simply reflect a reality that the circumstances justifying their use seldom arise in practice and the alternative means of resolving policing difficulties. In future, any increased politicization of the appointment and role of the chief officer may encourage use of the procedures.

The relevant procedures are summarized in Figure 2.1.   **2.39**

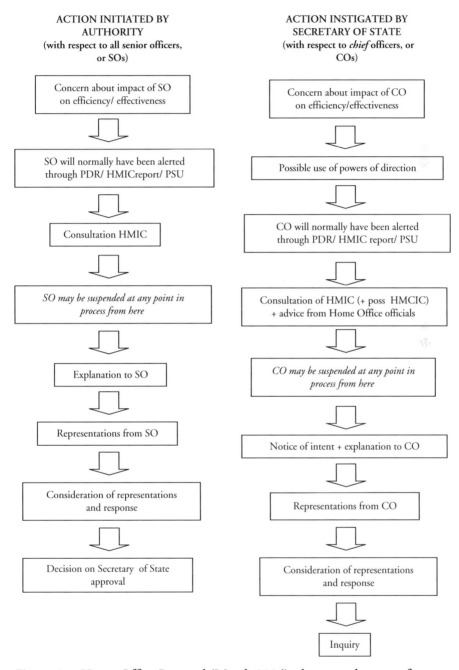

Figure 2.1 Home Office Protocol (March 2004): the normal process for action under suspension and removal powers.

3

COMPLAINTS AND MISCONDUCT I:
THE INDEPENDENT POLICE
COMPLAINTS COMMISSION (IPCC)

A. Overview	3.01	operation of the police complaints system'	3.86
B. Complaints and Misconduct: The Police Reform Act 2002— The Overall Statutory Structure	3.13	'2. Promoting confidence in the complaints system, among the public and the police'	3.87
The structure of the Police Reform Act 2002	3.13	'3. Ensuring the accessibility of the complaints system'	3.88
General	3.13	'4. Promoting policing excellence by drawing out and feeding back learning'	3.89
Parts 1–3: structure	3.16		
Schedules 2 and 3	3.19		
Parts 4–7	3.21	F. The IPCC Complaints and Discipline Process	3.91
C. The Legal Character of the IPCC	3.22	Overview	3.91
Legal status	3.22	Statutory provision: members of the Commission, including the chair and deputy chair	3.97
Creation and transitional arrangements	3.22	Non-statutory procedures	3.102
Referrals to the Police Complaints Authority (PCA) pre-dating 1 April 2004	3.26	The chairman	3.109
		The deputy chair	3.112
Referrals and complaints recorded after 1 April 2004	3.36	The ordinary members of the Commission	3.114
D. The Commission: The Chairman, the Members, and the Staff	3.41	Suspension	3.129
The Commission as a public authority	3.41	The IPCC stages	3.132
		'1. The preliminary examination'	3.132
The Constitution	3.44	'2A. Complaint investigation and findings'	3.141
E. The General Functions and Duties of the Commission	3.51	'2B. Investigation review'	3.153
Its role contrasted with that of the PCA	3.51	'3A. Sanctions consideration (for allegations of a serious nature)'	3.161
The 'Learning the Lessons Committee'	3.54		
The IPCC's statutory functions and duties	3.57	'3B. Sanctions decision'	3.165
Other statutory duties	3.70	The Commission staff	3.167
The statutory guidance	3.71	Statutory regulation	3.167
'1. Setting, monitoring, inspecting and reviewing standards for the		Internal procedures	3.185
		G. Conclusion	3.195

A. Overview

3.01 The Independent Police Complaints Commission (IPCC) was created by Pt 2 of the Police Reform Act 2002 (the 2002 Act) and assumed power on 1 April 2004. The IPCC's functions and duties are considerably wider and deeper than those of its predecessor—namely, the Police Complaints Authority (PCA).

3.02 The Preamble to the 2002 Act provides that it is an Act 'to make new provision about the supervision, administration, functions and conduct of police forces, police officers and other persons serving with, or carrying out functions in relation to, the police'. For its part, the IPCC claims[1] that it 'began work' with 'a wide range of new, stronger powers to radically change [sic] the way complaints against the police are handled in England and Wales'. It identifies the 'core beliefs' of justice and respect for human rights, independence, valuing diversity, integrity, and openness.

3.03 The creation of the IPCC certainly met widespread, and long-standing, demands for reform. There had been calls for a wholly independent body to oversee and investigate police complaints at least as early as Lord Scarman's Inquiry relating to the Brixton riots in the early 1980s.[2] His Inquiry Report recommended both an independent element to any investigation into alleged police misconduct, and greater provision for early conciliation in respect of such a complaint. The then Home Secretary, William Whitelaw, acknowledged in response the necessity of 'substantial reform' of the police complaints system. The recommendations are reflected, albeit twenty-one years later, both in the IPCC's investigative functions and in the prominence given to local resolution in the 2002 Act.

3.04 Lord Scarman's approach was echoed by Sir William MacPherson in the Stephen Lawrence Inquiry into matters arising from the death of Stephen Lawrence in 1993.[3] His Inquiry Report was published in February 1999. In 2000, the government issued a Consultation Paper on the issue of complaints against the police, the recording and investigation of complaints, police discipline, and the disclosure of reports and other information. In response to the consultation exercise, the government issued a framework document titled *Complaints Against the Police: Framework for a New System*. Following further consultation, the 2002 Act was enacted on 24 July 2002.

---

[1] IPCC Statutory Guidance, *Making the New Complaints System Work Better*, para 1.1.
[2] Lord Scarman's Report into the 'Brixton Disorders', published 25 November 1981, following widespread public disorder in April 1981.
[3] The Stephen Lawrence Inquiry, 24 February 1999.
[4] Reflecting, in turn, an existing Home Office study, *Feasibility of an Independent System for Investigating Complaints Against the Police*, and an extensive document produced by the campaigning organization Liberty, entitled *An Independent Police Complaints Commission*.

The resultant IPCC is a national body with powers extending significantly **3.05**
beyond the narrow investigation of complaints against police officers. Leaving
aside the subsequent extension of its powers over organizations including the
Serious Organised Crime Agency (SOCA) and HM Revenue and Customs
(HMRC),[5] the IPCC enjoys powers over a wide range of police officers and civilian staff, and in circumstances not limited to the traditional 'complaint' or 'conduct' situation. These terms, and the extended role of the IPCC, are respectively
defined and addressed in Chapters 4–8.

In qualifying circumstances (including complaints, conduct matters,[6] and all **3.06**
circumstances involving the police in which death or serious injury arises),[7] the
IPCC is involved in the investigation and resolution of the investigation. This
involvement extends from determining appeals against a local resolution of a
complaint to conducting an investigation wholly independently of any police
force. In appropriate circumstances, the IPCC determines whether discipline
charges are brought, and can be represented (and even present the relevant
evidence) before the misconduct tribunal. It is invariably an interested person for
the purposes of inquest proceedings following a qualifying (police-related) death
under the Coroners Act 1988.

The creation of the IPCC was coupled with important associated legislation— **3.07**
notably, the Police (Complaints and Misconduct) Regulations 2004[8] (in force

---

[5] The jurisdiction of the IPCC was extended, from 28 December 2005, to cover HMRC—see
s 28 of the Commissioners for Revenue and Customs Act 2005, and the Revenue and Customs
(Complaints and Misconduct) Regulations 2005, SI 2005/3311—and from 1 April 2006, to cover
SOCA—see s 26A of the 2002 Act, inserted by s 55 of, and Sch 2 to, the Serious Organised Crime
and Police Act 2005, and the Serious Organised Crime and Police Act 2005 (Commencement
No 5 and Transitional and Transitory Provisions and Savings) Order 2006, SI 2006/378, art 3(2)(e).
Jurisdiction was extended to the enforcement and removal functions of the Immigration and
Nationality Directorate (the 'Border and Immigration Agency') by s 41 of the Police and Justice
Act 2006, from 29 June 2007 in relation to England and Wales (see the Police and Justice Act 2006
(Commencement No 3) Order 2007, SI 2007/1614, art 2(g)), and from 10 October 2007 in
relation to Scotland and Northern Ireland (see the Police and Justice Act 2006 (Commencement
No 4) Order 2007, SI 2007/2754, art 2). It was extended to include the NPIA from 1 April 2007
(s 26B of the 2002 Act, inserted by the Police and Justice Act 2006, s 1(3), Sch 1, Pt 7, paras 80
and 87, and the Police and Justice Act 2006 (Commencement No 2, Transitional and Saving
Provisions) Order 2007, SI 2007/709, art 3(a); for transitional provisions and savings, see
art 6(1).
[6] Police (Complaints and Misconduct) Regulations 2004, SI 2004/643, reg 2, considered in
Chapter 6.
[7] From 1 July 2005, any qualifying death or serious injury (DSI) matter must be referred to the
IPCC even where there is no complaint or evidence of a conduct matter: see Sch 3, Pt 2A, of the
2002 Act, reflecting the Serious Organised Crime and Police Act 2005, s 160, Sch 12, paras 1, 11,
and 12, and the Serious Organised Crime and Police Act 2005 (Commencement No 1, Transitional
and Transitory Provisions) Order 2005, SI 2005/1521, art 3(1)(w).
[8] SI 2004/643.

from the same date as the 2002 Act, with material amendments in 2006[9] and 2008),[10] the Serious Organised Crime and Police Act 2005, and statutory guidance issued by the IPCC in respect of its purpose and functions.[11] A materially revised system regulating misconduct proceedings for police officers[12] was also brought into force on 1 April 2004. These measures promoted greater transparency, including the right of a complainant to question witnesses (including the accused officer) at misconduct hearings, and (where determined by the IPCC) the possibility of public access to the hearing.

3.08 These, and subsequent, measures—notably, the Police (Performance) Regulations 2008[13] and the Police (Conduct) Regulations 2008[14]—represent an attempted change of culture in terms of the regulation of police conduct and performance. The legislative material at times reflects this, introducing concepts such as the IPCC's 'guardianship' role, and defining the wider purpose of the IPCC in 'promoting confidence in the complaints system as a whole among the public and police'.

3.09 The IPCC is required to operate independently of complainants, affected police officers (or others within its jurisdiction), police forces, police authorities, the Secretary of State, and other interested parties. Necessarily, however, it must discharge its various functions in cooperation with them, on a directed basis or otherwise.

3.10 The wider inquisitorial purpose—that is, a role not limited to identifying and prosecuting misconduct, and instead making recommendations as appropriate for systematic reform—brings with it associated statutory duties in terms of disclosure and transparency. These duties produce corresponding rights for the complainant, the officer subject to investigation, and the wider public. The statutory framework makes provision as to duties and responsibilities, including disclosure, recording, and reporting.

3.11 The work of Commission staff is regularly controversial and demands confidentiality. The improper and deliberate leak of information by a member of Commission staff, in respect of the investigation into the circumstances of the shooting by police of Jean Charles de Menezes, precipitated a change such

---

[9] Police (Complaints and Misconduct) (Amendment) Regulations 2006, SI 2006/1406.
[10] Police (Complaints and Misconduct)(Amendment) Regulations 2008, SI 2008/2866, in force 1 December 2008.
[11] IPCC Statutory Guidance, *Making the Complaints System Work Better*, issued 1 December 2005.
[12] The Police (Conduct) Regulations 2004, SI 2004/645. See Chapters 4 and 5.
[13] SI 2008/2862.
[14] SI 2008/2864.

that, in future,[15] members of staff will be bound by the provisions of the Official Secrets Act 1989. Breach of this Act may incur criminal prosecution and imprisonment.

Any consideration of the resultant system requires an understanding of the constitutional framework underpinning the IPCC and its statutory purpose as defined in the legislation.   **3.12**

B. Complaints and Misconduct: The Police Reform Act 2002—The Overall Statutory Structure

The structure of the Police Reform Act 2002

General

The Act consists of 108 sections divided into seven Parts. There are eight associated Schedules. Reference must be made to the relevant Schedule in respect of any section of the Act. These provisions are supplemented by detailed subordinate legislation and IPCC-issued statutory guidance.   **3.13**

Where formal misconduct proceedings arise from any investigation, these are subject to discrete conduct regulations, addressed in Chapters 6–9 of this book. The relevant conduct regulations will necessarily be contingent on the status of the affected officer/staff member, the date of the conduct, and the nature of the conduct.   **3.14**

All of the provisions must now be read in the context of Sch 23 of the Criminal Justice and Immigration Act 2008, which makes material amendments to the procedures governing investigations under the 2002 Act.   **3.15**

Parts 1–3: structure

Part 1 (ss 1–9) addresses the powers of the Secretary of State and was covered in Chapter 1.   **3.16**

Part 2, entitled 'Complaints and misconduct', covers: 'The IPCC' (ss 9–11, coupled with Sch 2); 'Application of Part 2' (s 12); 'Handling of complaints, conduct matters and DSI[16] matters' (ss 13–14, coupled with Sch 3); 'Co-operation, assistance and information' (ss 15–27); 'Transitional provisions' (s 28); and 'Interpretation of Part 2' (s 29).   **3.17**

---

[15] The Official Secrets Act 1989 (Prescription)(Amendment) Order 2007, SI 2007/2148.
[16] Death and serious injury.

3.18 Part 3, entitled 'Removal, suspension and disciplining of senior officers', covers 'Removal and suspension of senior officers' (ss 30–34, 'senior officers' being those above the rank of chief superintendent),[17] and 'Disciplinary proceedings and protected disclosures' (ss 35–37).

Schedules 2 and 3

3.19 Sections 9–11 of Pt 2 ('The IPCC') must be read in conjunction with Sch 2 to the Act (similarly headed 'The IPCC').

3.20 The residue of Pt 2 must be read in conjunction with Sch 3, headed 'Handling of complaints and conduct matters, etc'. Schedule 3 is subdivided into parts. Part 1 (paras 1–9) is concerned with the handling of complaints. Part 2 (paras 10–14) is concerned with the handling of conduct matters. Part 2A (paras 14A–14D) is concerned with the handling of death and serious injury (DSI) matters. Part 3 of Sch 2 to the Act is of general application to complaint, conduct, and DSI matters, and is concerned with 'investigations and subsequent proceedings' dealt with in Chapter 6.

Parts 4–7

3.21 Parts 4–7 of the Act (ss 38–108) are of less direct relevance to complaints and misconduct.[18] Where relevant, reference is made in the narrative of this work.

C. The Legal Character of the IPCC

Legal status

Creation and transitional arrangements

3.22 The IPCC was created with effect from 1 April 2004, coincident with the Police Complaints Authority (PCA) ceasing to exist.[19]

3.23 Transitional provisions in relation to misconduct and discipline are addressed in this work in detail as and where relevant. The essential provisions in terms of assuming the powers of the PCA are s 28 of the 2002 Act ('Transitional arrangements connected with establishing the Commission, etc') and the IPCC (Transitional Provisions) Order 2004[20] ('the basic transitional Order'), coupled

---

[17] Section 29.
[18] Part 4 ('Police powers etc), Chs 1 (ss 38–47, 'Exercise of police powers by civilians') and 2 (ss 48–78, 'Provisions modifying and supplementing police powers'); Pt 5 (ss 78–81, 'The Ministry of Defence Police'); Pt 6 (ss 82–104, headed 'Miscellaneous', with subheadings at ss 82–91, 'Appointment and attestation of police officers, etc', ss 92–102, 'Bodies with functions in relation to the police', and ss 103–104, 'International joint investigation teams'); Pt 7 (ss 105–108, 'Supplemental').
[19] Police Reform 2002 Act, s 9(7).
[20] SI 2004/671, in force 1 April 2004.

with the IPCC (Transitional Provisions)(Amendment) Order 2004[21] ('the amendment Order').

Section 28(3) provides that any transitional provisions made by order of the **3.24** Secretary of State shall include—pending the coming into force of any repeal by the 2002 Act of an enactment contained in Ch 1 of Pt 4 of the 1996 Act (complaints), or for transitional purposes connected with the coming into force of any such repeal—that the functions of the PCA under an enactment so contained are to be carried out by the Commission.

These so-called 'legacy cases' were numerous. The IPCC took over some 5,217 **3.25** cases, either on an existing basis, or qualifying under the old system although recorded after 1 April 2004. As at August 2007, only eighty-seven remained to be completed, with an estimated thirty yet to be received from local forces;[22] now, only a small rump of legacy cases remain.

Referrals to the Police Complaints Authority (PCA) pre-dating 1 April 2004

The more significant provisions are found in the associated statutory instru- **3.26** ments. Article 2 of the basic transitional Order effectively provides that, where an investigation into a complaint was ongoing on 1 April 2004, the complaint would continue to be handled under the Police Act 1996, but that the Commission would perform the functions of the PCA under that Act.

The subsequent amendment Order corrected an omission from the basic transi- **3.27** tional Order by including not only complaints referred to the PCA before 1 April 2004, but also the supervision of other matters that had been voluntarily referred to the PCA by a police authority or chief officer of police. Where the PCA had already dealt with such a matter, it may not then be recorded as a complaint or a conduct matter under the new regime.

The language of art 2 of the basic transitional Order operates to exclude all **3.28** of the provisions of the 2002 Act for investigations assumed on this transitional basis. Under art 2(2), 'nothing in or made under Part 2 of the 2002 Act shall apply in relation to that complaint [or matter]' (that being, under art 2(1), a complaint received before 1 April 2004, or matter referred to the PCA under s 71 of the Police Act 1996 before that date), and, under art 2(3), 'notwithstanding the repeal of Chapter 1 of Part 4 of the Police Act 1996, and subject to paragraph (4), that Chapter shall continue to have effect in relation to that complaint [or matter] as if there had been no such repeal'.[23]

---

[21] SI 2004/1092, in force 15 April 2004.
[22] IPCC Annual Report 2006–07, p 40.
[23] See *R (IPCC) v Chief Constable of West Mercia and PC Walton* [2007] EWHC 1035 (Admin), [8].

3.29   In practical terms, and consistent with art 2(4) of the basic transitional Order, the IPCC simply assumed the functions of the PCA. This materially qualifies the powers and duties of the IPCC in respect of both the conduct of the investigation and associated statutory duties in relation to disclosure, including, under s 20, the duty to keep the complainant informed.

3.30   Considerations relating to disclosure by the PCA were considered in detail by the House of Lords in *R (Green) v Police Complaints Authority*.[24] In summary, it was not necessary to the discharge of the PCA's functions, as defined, to disclose witness statements to a complainant at the stage under the 1996 Act at which either criminal or disciplinary charges were under consideration. The purpose of the PCA was not defined in the statute and the House of Lords provided a more restrictive interpretation than the Court of Appeal. This contrasts with the statutory declaration of purpose in relation to the IPCC under s 10 of the 2002 Act.

3.31   As to disclosure, however, it may be that considerations of public law arising from the Human Rights Act 1998 qualify, and extend, the duties on the IPCC even when narrowly discharging functions of the PCA. Article 2(2) of the basic transitional Order simply provides that: 'Nothing in or made under Part 2 of the 2002 Act shall apply in relation to that complaint [or matter]'.

3.32   If a contended obligation is strictly outside this parameter, it may be arguable that the IPCC should adopt either: (i) the practice under the residue of the 2002 Act; or, if different, (ii) such procedure as discharges its obligation under the Human Rights Act 1998, which is engaged on 1 October 2000.[25] For example, the practice has arisen of reflecting the reasoning of the investigating officer in communications by the IPCC with complainants without (the IPCC contends) thereby disclosing the investigating officer's report.

3.33   The obvious competing consideration is that there is no control over the use made of disclosed material by the complainant, or third parties, and it is liable, if misused, to compromise either the investigation—including the investigative element inherent in an inquest under Art 2 of the European Convention on Human Rights (ECHR)—or any associated criminal or disciplinary proceedings. There is a 'harm' test under the statutory guidance under the 2002 Act and the test of what is 'necessary' may involve some flexibility. These matters

---

²⁴   [2004] 1 WLR 725.
²⁵   The difference in practice was demonstrated in the IPCC decision relating to the death in custody of Roger Sylvester. A 'legacy' case, the Metropolitan Police Service (MPS)—ie the affected officers' force—refused disclosure of the independent (Essex) investigating officer's report to the deceased's family. The IPCC had no power to compel it. Subject to certain exceptions, disclosure under the 2002 Act is mandatory.

were considered in *R (Saunders)(Tucker) v IPCC and ors*,[26] as discussed at
14.91–14.94.

The reasoning in *Green* relating to disclosure may be said to apply with equal **3.34**
force to the proper limits, and timing, of disclosure to complainants (and, to a
degree, affected police officers) by the IPCC under the 2002 Act. This is considered in detail in Chapters 6–8.

There is a duty of cooperation with the IPCC imposed on third parties, including **3.35**
police authorities, chief officers, and inspectors, under Pt 2 of the 2002 Act,[27]
and the associated arrangements prescribing payment for assistance with investigations (s 16) and the duties imposed on the National Policing Improvement
Agency (NPIA) (s 16A).[28] These are strictly determined under the relevant
applicable statutory scheme.

Referrals and complaints recorded after 1 April 2004

These transitional arrangements relate to complaints or referrals to the PCA pre- **3.36**
ceding 1 April 2004. In respect of police constables, if the appropriate authority received the complaint/reference after that date, even if the conduct or matter
complained of took place before 1 April 2004, the 2002 Act applies.

The situation in such a context is different in respect of a civilian employee of the **3.37**
police, a special constable, or a person designated as a detention officer or
escort officer.[29] In respect of a 'complaint received', or 'a conduct matter coming
to the attention of an appropriate authority' after 1 April 2004, but relating to
conduct before that date by such persons, by art 3 of the basic transitional Order,
nothing in or made under Pt 2 of the 2002 Act applies in relation to that complaint or conduct matter.

No allowance is made for situations, readily foreseeable, wherein the conduct **3.38**
complained of incorporates a common factual background and a combination
of police constables and other persons as defined by art 3(a).

Article 4 ('Repeated complaints') provides that complaints that have already been **3.39**
submitted and closed under the old system, or which were held not to qualify
for recording under that system (for example, because they related to the direction
or control of a police force by its chief officer), cannot be reopened under the

---

26 [2008] EWHC 2372 (Admin).
27 See, inter alia, ss 15 (general duties of police authorities, chief officers, and inspectors) and
17 (provision of information to the Commission).
28 From 1 April 2007: SI 2007/709, art 3(a).
29 IPCC (Transitional Provisions) Order 2004, SI 2004/671, art 3(a): '. . . a person falling within
section 12(7)(b) or (c) of the 2002 Act (employees of a police authority and special constables), or
designated under section 39(2) of that Act (police powers for contracted-out staff)'.

new system. Article 4(1) rehearses the five qualifying mechanisms for a matter to be deemed closed:

(i) that the requirements of ss 74 or 75 of the Police Act 1996 (steps to be taken after investigation) were complied with;

(ii) that the complaint was informally resolved in accordance with:

(a) the Police (Complaints) (Informal Resolution) Regulations 1985;[30] or

(b) reg 19 of the National Crime Squad (Complaints) Regulations 1998;[31]

(iii) the PCA dispensed with the requirements of Ch 1 of Pt 4 of the Police Act 1996 under either:

(a) reg 3 of the Police (Anonymous, Repetitious Etc. Complaints) Regulations 1985;[32] or

(b) reg 4 of the National Crime Squad (Dispensation from Requirement to Investigate Complaints) Regulations 2003;[33]

(iv) the complainant gave notification that he withdrew the complaint; or

(v) the appropriate authority concluded that the complaint did not fall to be recorded under s 68(1) of the Police Act 1996.

3.40 Further, under art 4(2), there is no right of appeal to the Commission under para 3(3) of Sch 3 to the 2002 Act (the right to appeal to the Commission against a failure by the police authority or chief officer to record anything, etc) against a decision of an appropriate authority not to record such a closed complaint. By art 4(3),[34] a conduct matter shall not be recorded under paras 10 or 11 of Sch 3 to the 2002 Act if previously submitted and resolved in any of the mechanisms set out in art 4(1).

D. The Commission: The Chairman, the Members, and the Staff

The Commission as a public authority

3.41 The IPCC is a body corporate referred to throughout the 2002 Act as 'the Commission'.[35] It is not to be regarded as the servant or agent of the Crown, and does not enjoy any status, privilege, or immunity of the Crown.[36] It is a

---

[30] SI 1985/671.

[31] SI 1998/638.

[32] SI 1985/672.

[33] SI 2003/2601.

[34] Inserted by the amendment Order, SI 2004/1092, art 2(5).

[35] Police Reform Act 2002, s 9(1).

[36] Ibid, s 9(5).

non-departmental government body (NDGB), funded by the Home Office, but operationally independent of it and any other interested party.

The IPCC is a 'public authority' within the Human Rights Act 1998.[37] Under **3.42** s 6 of the 1998 Act it is, subject to the subs 6(2) exceptions, unlawful for it to act in a way that is incompatible with a Convention right. It follows that its formal decisions will invariably have the requisite public quality for the purpose of challenge by way of judicial review.

These rights include the substantive, and (of greater application) investigative **3.43** (procedural or adjectival), duties and obligations under Art 2 of the ECHR (the right to life). The nature of these rights is considered in greater detail in Chapter 14.

The Constitution

The Commission must consist of a chairman and not fewer than ten other mem- **3.44** bers.[38] As at March 2009, the Commission comprised the chair, two deputy chairs, and ten 'operational' Commissioners, with two part-time non-executive Commissioners, divided between four regional centres, with individual Commissioners retaining responsibility for particular police forces and/or organizations under its jurisdiction.

The imperative to create a body independent of those under scrutiny is reflected **3.45** in the detailed provisions as to the appointment of the chairman and members of the Commission. The regulations are rehearsed in s 9(3) of, and Sch 2 to, the 2002 Act. The net effect of these provisions is that the perceived necessity of independence from those under investigation disqualifies any person who has had a qualifying role within the any force or organization under the jurisdiction of the Commission from acting as chairman or 'ordinary member' of the Commission (commonly referred to as a 'Commissioner').

Those disqualified from acting as chairman or as another member of the **3.46** Commission are prescribed by s 9(3). In summary, this disqualifies any person who:

- at any time, has held the office of constable;
- has been under the direction and control of a chief officer or equivalent in Scotland or Northern Ireland;

---

[37] Human Rights Act 1998, s 6(3)(b): a 'public authority' includes 'any person certain of whose functions are functions of a public nature'.
[38] Police Reform Act 2002, s 9(2). The chairman is appointed by Her Majesty; members are appointed by the Secretary of State.

- has been designated under ss 39 (contracted staff), or 41 and 41A (designated community safety, and weights and measures inspectors);
- has been chairman, chief executive, member, or member of staff of either SOCA, the NPIA, the National Criminal Intelligence Service (NCIS), or the National Crime Squad (NCS); or
- has been a member of a body of constables under s 26 of the 2002 Act (forces maintained otherwise than by police authorities) or equivalent predecessors.[39]

3.47 The terms of appointment of the chairman were contended to be significant in promoting independence. By para 1(3) of Sch 2, the appointment of the chairman shall be for a term not exceeding five years, but the chairman shall become eligible for reappointment at the end of his term of office. As a Royal appointment (ordinary members are appointed by the Secretary of State), there is, theoretically, a reduced risk of political interference in the exercise of the chairman's functions.

3.48 The chairman does not, however, enjoy any greater rights than ordinary members of the Commission in terms of operational decision-making. He appears to have no statutory right to override a decision of another ordinary member. He and the deputy chairs have specific roles in terms of authorizing surveillance under the applicable provisions of the Regulation of Investigatory Powers Act 2000 (RIPA). The specific powers in this respect are set out in the IPCC (Investigatory Powers) Order 2004.[40] The conduct of investigations (particularly independent investigations) by the IPCC is considered in detail in Chapter 6.

3.49 These disqualifications from appointment do not apply to other employees of the IPCC, including investigating officers and legal advisers: to extend disqualification beyond Commission members would have excluded many with qualifying expertise. The necessary independence is preserved through discretion ultimately residing with Commission members as to all material decisions, and the statutory obligation to keep complainants and interested persons informed as to the conduct and progress of investigations.

3.50 The grounds for removing the chairman and an ordinary member of the Commission, respectively, are set out in paras 1 (chairman) and 2 (ordinary members) of Sch 2 to the 2002 Act, and considered in detail from 3.97 below.

---

[39] Specifically, s 78 of the 1996 Act and s 96 of the 1984 Act.
[40] SI 2004/815, in force from 1 April 2004.

E. The General Functions and Duties of the Commission

Its role contrasted with that of the PCA

In simple terms, the general functions and duties of the IPCC are prescribed by **3.51** s 10 of the 2002 Act, coupled with the associated Schedules to the Act, and statutory guidance issued under the same by the Commission. To an unusual degree, this legislation provides for purposive and policy matters in respect of the Commission's role.

The prescribed statutory functions and duties provide an important context for **3.52** the investigative and reporting functions of the Commission. Central to any interpretation is recognition that the Commission's purpose extends beyond the simple investigation, and supervision of the prosecution (criminal or discipline), of reported misconduct by qualifying police personnel. The Commission is responsible for promoting improvements in procedures generally where these are identified, even in the absence of misconduct.

These matters have been interpreted to include identifying, and addressing, **3.53** chronic difficulties with policing. For example, the IPCC presently identifies policing and diversity, and policing and mental health, within this category. In principle, a coherent, evidence-based, analysis of recurrent policing difficulties— notably, the procedures and resources applied to those with acute mental health difficulties, and/or those acutely affected by alcohol or drug intoxication—may result in benefits to operational police officers nationally. Such reporting, and associated recommendations for national implementation, was, in practice, not characteristic of the PCA.

The 'Learning the Lessons Committee'

The IPCC set up a committee, known as the 'Learning the Lessons Committee', **3.54** which first met in June 2006.[41] It has representatives from the Association of Chief Police Officers (ACPO), the Association of Police Authorities (APA), Her Majesty's Inspectorate of Constabulary (HMIC), the Home Office, and the NPIA.

The IPCC says that the Committee will receive reports and information on **3.55** investigations for consideration. It will then distribute bulletins to stakeholders and via its website.[42] As distinct from s 22 statutory guidance (considered below), such bulletins clearly have no statutory status as such.

---

[41] IPCC Annual Report, 2006–07, ch 4.
[42] The first such bulletin was directed at the policing of complaints of domestic violence. Subsequent bulletins have covered a range of useful and relevant policing topics.

3.56 Certain new practices were tested in the Wales and south-west regions, including: standard terms of reference for investigations; a separate section in each investigation report directed at 'learning recommendations'; the opportunity for the local force to respond to learning recommendations in a draft report; a review of national recommendations by the dedicated specialist Commissioner; and a distinction between 'suggestions' and 'recommendations'. Changes are likely to be implemented nationally at some point during 2009.

The IPCC's statutory functions and duties

3.57 Whilst a central tenet of the statutory guidance issued by the IPCC ('Making the new police complaints system work better'), the 'guardianship function' of the Commission is not referred to as such in either the statute or the Schedules to the Act. The power to issue statutory guidance derives from s 22 of the 2002 Act, and the particular guidance came into force on 1 December 2005. It is under review and a new version is anticipated in 2009, which will presumably take effect immediately for all new investigations.

3.58 The statutory guidance, produced after mandatory statutory consultation,[43] must be understood in its statutory context. Functions and duties are defined in the statute in broad, although not unlimited, purposive language. By s 22(7) of the 2002 Act, it 'shall be the duty' of every person to whom any guidance under the section is issued 'to have regard to that guidance' in exercising or performing the powers and duties to which the guidance relates. This envisages the possibility of discretionary departure from statutory guidance having had regard to it.

3.59 The 'general functions of the Commission' (including defined duties) are prescribed by s 10. By subs (8), nothing in Pt 2 of the 2002 Act confers any function on the Commission 'in relation to so much of any complaint or conduct matter as relates to the direction and control of a police force by the chief officer of police of that force', or a person for the time being carrying out that function. The exclusion of direction and control matters preserves the operational independence of chief officers. What constitutes direction and control was addressed in Chapter 1.

3.60 Section 10(1) provides, in material part, as follows.

> (1) The functions of the Commission shall be—
>   (a) to secure the maintenance by the Commission itself, and by police authorities and chief
>   officers, of suitable arrangements with respect to the matters mentioned in subsection (2);
>   (b) to keep under review all arrangements maintained with respect to those matters;

---

[43] Police Reform Act 2002, s 22(3): the IPCC is required to consult the APA, ACPO, and 'such other persons as it thinks fit'.

(c) to secure that arrangements maintained with respect to those matters comply with the requirements of the following provisions of this Part, are efficient and effective and contain and manifest an appropriate degree of independence;

(d) to secure that public confidence is established and maintained in the existence of suitable arrangements with respect to those matters and with the operation of the arrangements that are in fact maintained with respect to those matters;

(e) to make recommendations, and to give such advice, for the modification of the arrangements maintained with respect to those matters, and also of police practice in relation to other matters, as appear, from the carrying out by the Commission of its other functions, to be necessary or desirable.

Subsection (1)(f) imposes these functions on the Commission in respect of bodies of constables other than those maintained by police authorities to such extent as may be required by regulations made by the Secretary of State. **3.61**

Subsections (1)(g) and (h) provide that the Commission shall carry out functions in relation to, respectively, SOCA and the NPIA, which correspond to those set out in subs (1)(e) in relation to police forces. **3.62**

The subsection (2) matters are as follows: **3.63**

(a) the handling of complaints made about the conduct of persons serving with the police;

(b) the recording of matters from which it appears that there may have been conduct by such persons which constitutes or involves the commission of a criminal offence or behaviour justifying disciplinary proceedings;

[(ba) the recording of matters from which it appears that a person has died or suffered serious injury during, or following, contact with a person serving with the police;]

(c) the manner in which any such complaints or any such matters as are mentioned in paragraph (b) [or (ba)] are investigated or otherwise handled and dealt with.

Subsection (3) imposes on the Commission any functions conferred by statutory agreement relating to other bodies of constables, SOCA, and the NPIA,[44] regulations in relation to contracted-out staff,[45] and disciplinary or similar proceedings against any body of constables maintained other than by a police authority.[46] **3.64**

Further, broad-textured, duties are imposed on the Commission by subss (4) and (5). **3.65**

Under subs (4), the obligation is imposed on the Commission 'to exercise the powers and perform the duties conferred on it by the following provisions of this Part in the manner it considers best calculated for the purpose of securing the **3.66**

---

[44] 2002 Act, ss 26, 26A, and 26B, respectively.

[45] Section 39.

[46] The jurisdiction of the IPCC was extended, from 28 December 2005, to cover HMRC, from 1 April 2006 to SOCA, and to the enforcement and removal functions of the Immigration and Nationality Directorate (the 'Border and Immigration Agency') from 29 June 2007 in relation to England and Wales, and 10 October 2007 in relation to Scotland and Northern Ireland, and to the NPIA from 1 April 2007. See n 5 above for the implementing legislation.

proper carrying out of its functions under subsections (1) and (3)', and 'to secure that arrangements exist which are conducive to, and facilitate, the reporting of misconduct by persons in relation to whose conduct the Commission has functions'.

3.67 Subsection (5) imposes a positive duty in terms of cooperation and arrangements with HM Chief Inspector of Constabulary (HMCIC) in the carrying out of their respective functions.

3.68 Subsection (6), subject only to the other provisions of Pt 2, extends these specific duties and powers, and enables the Commission to 'do anything which it appears to it to be calculated to facilitate, or is incidental or conducive to, the carrying out of its functions'.

3.69 Subsection (7) gives the Commission discretion to impose a charge 'as it thinks fit' on any person in connection with the making of any recommendation or the giving of any advice to that person, for the purposes of, or in connection with, carrying out its functions under subss (1)(e)–(h). In practice, this probably limits recovery in all cases to subs (1)(e) recommendations and advice.[47]

Other statutory duties

3.70 Apart from these functions and duties, and the flexibility of role and purpose inherent in s 10(1)(e) in particular, the relevant background to the s 22 statutory guidance includes powers of inspection (s 18), the obligation to produce an annual report and any specific report requested by the Secretary of State (s 11), and monitoring the system by calling for information from police authorities and forces (s 17). These powers and duties were addressed in Chapter 1.

The statutory guidance

3.71 The power of the Commission to issue guidance is contained within s 22 of the 2002 Act. The duty to consult is contained in subs (3), and by subs (4), the approval of the Secretary of State shall be required for the issue by the Commission of any guidance under the section. The guidance is of general application, and subs (6) expressly provides that nothing in the section shall authorize the issuing of any guidance about a particular case. Guidance is to be distinguished from a direction as part of a particular investigation in this sense.

---

[47] Police Reform Act 2002, s 10(1)(f), relating to bodies of constables other than those maintained by police authorities, imposes functions that 'broadly correspond to' the preceding paragraphs of the subsection, including, by implication, subss (1)(a)–(e). Subsection (7)(a) provides for recovery in relation to the Commission's function under subs (1)(e), and subs (7)(b) for 'any corresponding function conferred on it by virtue of subsection (1)(f)'. On one view, promoting consistency, this may be read as corresponding to subs (7)(a).

The guidance may be issued, pursuant to subs (1), to police authorities, to chief **3.72** officers, and to persons who are serving with the police other than as chief officers, concerning the exercise or performance by the persons to whom the guidance is issued, of any of the powers or duties specified in subs (2). To this extent, it would seem that the guidance is not issued to the Commission itself.

This may be relevant to complaints against the Commission or its staff in **3.73** relation to alleged failures to implement its own guidance. As has been stated, subs (7) imposes a duty on every person to whom the guidance is issued 'to have regard to that guidance in exercising or performing the powers and duties to which the guidance relates'. Subsection (8) provides that 'a failure by a person to whom guidance is issued to have regard to the guidance shall be admissible in evidence in any disciplinary proceedings or on any appeal from a decision taken in any such proceedings'.

Paragraph 4.1 of the statutory guidance, however, asserts that 'the IPCC is part **3.74** of the police complaints system and therefore the principles set out in this guidance apply to the IPCC as well as the police service'. Members of the Commission, and Commission employees, whilst discharging powers and duties under Pt 2, are not 'serving with the police' in any capacity. It follows that s 22 statutory guidance cannot, strictly, be issued to them. In that the Commission has adopted the relevant principles, however, there is a legitimate expectation that the Commission will apply its own guidance.

More generally, for persons to whom advice is issued within s 22, the duty is to **3.75** 'have regard to' the guidance, rather than necessarily follow it prescriptively; to that end, the guidance is admissible at disciplinary proceedings rather than determinative of them.

Liability to a discipline charge is therefore contingent on the purported justifi- **3.76** cation for departing, as a matter of discretion, from the statutory guidance in any particular case. The threshold for such departure to be reasonable is not clear and will be case-specific. Different principles may apply if a chief officer (or other relevant officer) refuses to act on directions properly within the power of the Commission as to any matter within Pts 2 or 3 of the 2002 Act.

The powers and duties that may be covered by guidance are narrowly defined by **3.77** s 22(2), and more broadly within subs (5). It is observed that, although of general application, the guidance may appear to extend to matters of operational policing (such as protecting a scene) even for investigations that are not strictly independent investigations. The contended justification may be to promote a common national approach to matters including the operative procedures following deaths in custody, fatal shootings, and road traffic accidents involving police vehicles.

3.78 Section 22(2) defines the powers and duties as:

(i) those that are conferred or imposed by or under Pt 2 of the 2002 Act; and

(ii) those that are otherwise conferred or imposed, but relate to:

(a) the handling of complaints;

(b) the means by which recordable matters, including DSI matters, are dealt with; or

(c) the detection or deterrence of misconduct by persons serving with the police.

3.79 Section 22(5) provides, without prejudice to the generality of the preceding provisions, that guidance may be issued as to:

- handling complaints (covering, in each case, complaints and recordable conduct matters, including DSI matters) that have not been recorded;
- the procedure to be followed when recording a complaint;
- determining whether a complaint is suitable for local resolution and the procedure to be followed;
- how to protect the scene of an incident or alleged incident that may become the subject of a complaint;
- the circumstances of disclosure of information/documentation about the investigation of any complaint; and
- matters to be included in a memorandum under paras 23 (action by the Commission in response to an investigation report under para 22) or 25 (appeals to the Commission with respect to an investigation) of Sch 3 to the 2002 Act.

3.80 As was observed in Chapter 1, the transfer of responsibility to the IPCC from the Secretary of State in terms of guidance in relation to complaints is reflected in the explanatory notes to the 2002 Act. This states that the latter will—following the creation of the IPCC and, specifically, its power to issue guidance under s 22—only give guidance in relation to the resolution of direction and control matters under s 14 of the Act, and not in relation to complaints.

3.81 Paragraph 4 of the resultant IPCC statutory guidance, headed 'Application of the guidance', states that it applies fully to each of the forty-three police forces in England and Wales under Sch 1 of the Police Act 1996. All police officers, police staff, and special constables working for these forces are covered, as are contracted staff who have been designated under the Act as custody or escort officers.

3.82 Forces within s 26 agreements are covered, but subject to agreed flexibility and possible exemptions. Consistent with the statute, PCA legacy cases being dealt with under the 1996 Act are not covered (para 4.2).

3.83 Under para 4.1, the guidance:

. . . is primarily addressed to a police service audience, particularly Chief Police Officers and Professional Standards Departments. However, under the Police

Reform Act, police authorities must investigate complaints against officers of ACPO rank and discharge specific statutory functions. Where the guidance is not explicitly addressed to a police authority, the IPCC expects all authorities to adopt the principles set out within it.

The purposive language of the statute finds its reflection in the Commission's **3.84** self-styled role within the guidance as 'Safeguarding the police complaints system—the IPCC's guardianship function'. The guidance contends that:

> the IPCC's general duty under the Police Reform Act 2002 to increase confidence in the police complaints system in England and Wales and in so doing, to contribute to increasing public confidence as a whole, is the basis of the IPCC's guardianship function.

The 'legislative framework of guardianship' sets out four 'elements' for these **3.85** purposes, which are not reflected directly in the original statute. These are rehearsed in the guidance, and below, with the associated (IPCC-contended) legislative derivation.

'1. Setting, monitoring, inspecting and reviewing standards for the operation of the police complaints system'

Under this element, the guidance lists: **3.86**

- the power to issue statutory guidance (s 22);
- inspection powers (s 18);
- the annual report and any specific reports requested by the Secretary of State (s 11);
- monitoring the system by calling for information from police authorities and forces (s 17);
- keeping the complaints system under review (s 10(1)(b)).

'2. Promoting confidence in the complaints system, among the public and the police'

Under this element, the guidance lists: **3.87**

- securing public confidence in the complaints system (s 10(1)(d));
- ensuring that arrangements are efficient and effective, and demonstrate an appropriate degree of independence (s 10(1)(c));
- the IPCC's power to call in for consideration complaints or allegations of misconduct (Sch 3, para 4(1)(c), and Sch 3, para 13(1)(c)).

'3. Ensuring the accessibility of the complaints system'

Under this element, the guidance lists: **3.88**

- designating gateways into the police complaints system (s 12(6));
- promoting third party reporting of complaints (s 12(6)(b)).

'4. Promoting policing excellence by drawing out and feeding back learning'

3.89 Under this element, the guidance lists:

- the ability to make recommendations and give advice on police complaints arrangements, and also on other matters of police practice that appear, from the IPCC's work, to be necessary or desirable (s 10(1)(e));
- reporting to the Secretary of State on matters that should be drawn to his or her attention, including reasons of gravity or exceptional circumstances (s 11(3) and (4));
- that, within its legal powers, the IPCC can do anything that helps to facilitate its functions (s 10(6)).

3.90 As can be seen, the statutory language (notably, s 10(1)(e)) has been exploited to provide a vehicle for an expansive role for the Commission. In that the existing statutory guidance is the product of statutory consultation, and approved by the Secretary of State, it is unlikely that material aspects of it will be susceptible to challenge as ultra vires.

F. The IPCC Complaints and Discipline Process

Overview

3.91 The intrinsic nature of the public functions and duties of the IPCC inevitably attracts repeated complaint. This probably arises in equal measure from complainants and the subjects of complaint. Unmeritorious complaints (or, more particularly, routine investigations of any recordable matter even without a complaint) are shown to take a considerable period of time, particularly when the Crown Prosecution Service (CPS) is asked to determine whether to bring criminal charges. The careers of affected police officers are directly prejudiced by such delay, particularly where precautionary reg 9 notices have been served under the Police (Conduct) Regulations 2004[48] and will be under the equivalent reg 15 of the 2008 Conduct Regulations,[49] or, for Sch 3 investigations, reg 14A of the Police (Complaints and Misconduct) Regulations 2004,[50] as amended by reg 3 of the Police (Complaints and Misconduct) (Amendment) Regulations 2008.[51]

3.92 The delay in decision taking can be measured in years and is routinely compounded by further delay listing substantive hearings, such as criminal trials,

---

[48] SI 2004/645.
[49] SI 2008/2864.
[50] SI 2004/643.
[51] SI 2008/2866.

inquests, and associated disciplinary hearings. Whilst not always avoidable, the consequences are manifestly unfair to all affected parties. The IPCC is often held responsible for the delays, albeit not always fairly. Tension with police authorities and chief officers is also inevitable. As with any substantial organization, there will be a proportion of internal workplace complaints.

Self-evidently, whilst there must be accountability for those in public office, a **3.93** proportionate response is required to complaints if the process of resolution is not to operate so as to frustrate the performance of the IPCC's various functions.

Given a qualifying complaint, different schemes apply to: (i) the chairman; **3.94** (ii) deputy chairmen; (iii) ordinary members of the Commission ('Commissioners'); and (iv) staff (including lawyers and investigators) of the Commission.

It may be observed that complainants in such a context enjoy fewer rights, and **3.95** that the procedures are less transparent, than complaints against police officers handled by the Commission. Much is left unanswered by the non-statutory existing material.

Further, the actual non-statutory procedures appear capable of change at the **3.96** discretion of, respectively, the Home Office, or a Commission meeting, without any obligation to consult.

Statutory provision: members of the Commission, including the chair and deputy chair

There appears to be no direct provision in the statute. The Home Secretary **3.97** enjoys powers generally under s 9 of, and Sch 2 to, the 2002 Act in relation to appointment and termination. Members of the Commission (including the chairman and deputy chairs) are subject to the Commissioners' Code of Conduct. This document is common to anyone assuming public office of this type, and adds little substantive to self-evident principles of integrity and purpose in the discharge of public office.[52]

As stated, in terms of appointment, the Queen appoints the chairman, and the **3.98** Secretary of State appoints other members of the Commission.[53] This affects rights to appeal if removed from office: it would appear that there is no right to

---

[52] The Commissioners' Code of Conduct was agreed by the Commission in January 2004 and revised in March 2005. It incorporates the 'Seven Principles of Public Life' set out by the Parliamentary Committee on Standards in Public Life—namely, selflessness, integrity, objectivity, accountability, openness, honesty, and leadership.

[53] Police Reform Act 2002, s 9(2)(a) (chairman) and (b) (other members).

issue a claim for wrongful or unlawful dismissal, because the post is an appointed office rather than employment as such.[54]

3.99 The statutory grounds for removing a chairman are set out in para 1(4) and (5) of Sch 2 to the 2002 Act. These provide as follows.

(4) The chairman of the Commission may be removed from office by Her Majesty either—
   (a) at his own request; or
   (b) on being advised by the Secretary of State that there are grounds falling with sub-paragraph (5) for the removal of the chairman.

(5) The following are grounds for removing the chairman from office—
   (a) that he has failed without reasonable excuse to carry out the functions of his office for a continuous period of three months;
   (b) that he has become a person falling within one or more paragraphs of section 9(3);
   (c) that he has, since his appointment, been sentenced to imprisonment for a term of three months or more;
   (d) that he is a person who—
     (i) has had a bankruptcy order made against him;
     (ii) has had his estate sequestrated; or
     (iii) has made a composition or arrangement with, or granted a trust deed for, his creditors;
   (e) that he is subject to—
     (i) a disqualification order under the Company Directors Disqualification Act 1986 (c 46) or under Part 2 of the Companies (Northern Ireland) Order 1989 (SI 1989/2404 (NI 18)); or
     (ii) an order made under section 429(2)(b) of the Insolvency Act 1986 (c 45) (failure to pay under county court administration order);
   (f) that he has acted improperly in relation to his duties; or
   (g) that he is otherwise unable or unfit to perform his duties.

(6) For the purposes of this paragraph a sentence of imprisonment for any term the whole or part of which is suspended shall be taken to be a sentence of imprisonment for the whole term.

3.100 The statutory grounds for the resignation of, or for removing, a Commissioner are set out in para 2(5) and (6) of Sch 2 to the 2002 Act. It will be seen that the criteria are, to a degree, different from those applying to the chairman:

(5) An ordinary member may at any time resign his office as a member of the Commission by notice in writing to the Secretary of State.

(6) The Secretary of State may at any time remove a person from office as an ordinary member if he is satisfied that that person—
   (a) has failed without reasonable excuse to carry out the functions of his office for a continuous period of three months beginning not earlier than six months before that time;
   (b) has become a person falling within one or more paragraphs of section 9(3);
   (c) has, since his appointment, been sentenced to imprisonment for a term of three months or more;

---

[54] See, for chairman, para 1(1) of Sch 2 to the 2002 Act ('. . . shall hold office as chairman of the Commission in accordance with the terms of his appointment') and, for other members, para 2(1), expressed in identical terms.

(d) is a person who—
  (i) has had a bankruptcy order made against him;
  (ii) has had his estate sequestrated; or
  (iii) has made a composition or arrangement with, or granted a trust deed for, his creditors;
(e) is subject to—
  (i) a disqualification order under the Company Directors Disqualification Act 1986 (c 46) or under Part 2 of the Companies (Northern Ireland) Order 1989 (SI 1989/2404 (NI 18)); or
  (ii) an order made under section 429(2)(b) of the Insolvency Act 1986 (c 45) (failure to pay under county court administration order);
(f) has acted improperly in relation to his duties; or
(g) is otherwise unable or unfit to perform his duties.[55]

There is no statutory procedure or regulation prescribing any aspect of the process **3.101** preceding such removal. Such procedure as does exist is provided by an unhappy combination of poorly drafted Commission documents, the limitations of which are likely to become obvious when they are first tested in contentious proceedings.

Non-statutory procedures

At a Commission meeting on 26 May 2004, a document setting out guidance for **3.102** use in the event of an allegation of misconduct or impropriety by IPCC Commissioners, including the chair and deputy chairs, was produced ('the May 2004 Commission document').[56]

This was supplemented by a document agreed by the Commission, although **3.103** not apparently formally by the Home Office, entitled *Procedure for Handling Complaints of Misconduct Against Commissioners*, dated, as agreed by the Commission, on 27 September 2006 ('the September 2006 Commission document'). Neither the genesis nor authorship of these Commission documents is clear. The September 2006 Commission document does not refer to the May 2004 Commission document. The statutory language of 'chairman' and 'deputy chairman' is replaced with 'chair' and 'deputy chair'.[57]

Paragraph 1 of the May 2004 Commission document contends that it does **3.104** not apply to any of the matters that would not be regarded as a complaint under the IPCC 'principal complaints scheme', nor is it 'designed' for complaints about 'corporate decisions of the Commission or its committees or in relation to individual cases'.[58] A formal complaint is not required, and an expression of dissatisfaction can amount to a complaint.

---

[55] Paragraph 2(7) reproduces para 1(6) in terms of suspended sentences.
[56] 'Complaints against, and disciplinary proceedings for, IPCC Commissioners'.
[57] The text of this work uses the statutory language unless rehearsing the original document.
[58] The documents are available online at <http://www.ipcc.gov.uk>.

3.105 The 'principal complaints scheme' is not defined. It is, presumably, complaints about police officers under the 2002 Act. It may be that the intention is to require the statutory procedure to be followed in respect of IPCC decisions under the Act. The language, however, is ambiguous.

3.106 What is excluded under 'individual cases' is neither defined, nor readily comprehended. Self-evidently, certain IPCC decisions in respect of individual cases may attract either appeal or judicial review: others, however, will not. The misconduct complained of may relate to an individual case, yet not affect directly a particular formal decision. The complainant's remedy in such a context is not obvious.

3.107 A complaint may be made by a member of the public, by a person serving with the police, by another Commissioner, or by a member of the Commission staff. There is no direct provision permitting the chairman to make a complaint, which may either be simple oversight or, more likely, reflect his role in the process of determining a complaint.

3.108 There is a duty on a Commissioner who suspects misconduct by himself or another Commissioner to report it to a deputy chair and the Commission Secretary.[59] This duty does not, by implication, extend either to staff or the suspected misconduct of staff.

The chairman

3.109 The guidance does not apply if the complaint relates to the alleged misconduct of the chairman. If it does, para 22 of the guidance simply provides that the Commission Secretary (after informing the chairman and deputy chairmen about the making and the nature of the complaint) shall pass the complaint to the Home Office 'for it to take such action as its considers appropriate'. This is not further defined.

3.110 Paragraph 27 of the September 2006 Commission document sets out that complaints against the chairman will be considered at the (so-called) 'IPCC stages' (see 3.132 *et seq* below):

> ... by a senior (SCS) Home Office employee or by a Home Office Appointee. If undertaken by a Home Office Appointee, it will need to be from a different panel from that used for sanctions consideration. This is partly a matter of matching skills, those for conducting an investigation being different from those required for consideration of sanctions; but also to ensure continued separation of functions.

3.111 No further detail is set out. There are no published Home Office criteria as to the selection of an appointee.

---

[59] May 2004 Commission document, para 3.

The deputy chairs

The procedures applicable to ordinary members of the Commission(see 3.114 **3.112** *et seq* below) effectively apply to a complaint against a deputy chair: see paras 16–21 of the May 2004 Commission document. The difference is that the chairman performs the role in relation to a non-serious complaint against a deputy that the deputy performs in respect of a complaint against a member of the Commission.

By para 26, all of the 'IPCC stages' under the September 2006 Commission **3.113** document will be considered by the chairman, 'supplemented as appropriate by independent reviewers'.

The ordinary members of the Commission

The May 2004 Commission document prescribes duties of recording and **3.114** reporting in relation to complaints received in relation to the conduct of all Commissioners. However received, the complaint must be recorded by the Commission Secretary and placed on a complaints file.[60]

There is an overlapping duty, under paras 1 and 3 of the September 2006 **3.115** Commission document, which places an obligation on the deputy chair to record the circumstances of every complaint and the resolution, and 'is intended to apply to allegations of misconduct from employees of the IPCC, fellow Commissioners or third parties alike'.

The complaint is then passed to the chairman for him to determine whether the **3.116** complaint is a 'serious complaint'.[61] A complaint is a serious complaint 'where made by or on behalf of the public or a person serving with the police who has been adversely affected by the conduct complained of', and would, if proved, be likely to result in the dismissal of the Commissioner concerned under para 2(6)(f) or (g) of Sch 2 to the 2002 Act.[62]

It is not clear if complaints made by Commissioners and staff members are delib- **3.117** erately excluded from the paragraph, or are said to be implicit in 'made by or on behalf of a member of the public'. This interpretation may be impossible if no member of the public was adversely affected.

Paragraph 3 of the September 2006 Commission document provides that 'these **3.118** actions and the processes described are intended to apply to allegations of misconduct from employees of [the] IPCC, fellow Commissioners or third parties alike'.

---

[60] Ibid, paras 4 and 5.
[61] Ibid, para 6.
[62] Ibid, para 7.

3.119   A person is 'adversely affected' if he suffers 'any form of loss or damage, distress or inconvenience, if he or she is put in danger or is otherwise unduly put at risk of being adversely affected. A person is not adversely affected by the conduct by reason only of having witnessed the conduct'.[63]

3.120   By para 8 of the May 2004 Commission document, if the chairman determines that the complaint is serious, then the Home Office will be notified, and 'thereafter the complaint shall be dealt with in accordance with procedures to be agreed with the Home Office'.

3.121   By para 9, if the chairman determines that the complaint is not a serious complaint, the complaint will be passed to one of the deputy chairmen. In either case, the subsequent September 2006 Commission document appears to apply. This produces a measure of duplication, although not necessarily consistency.

3.122   As will be seen, in resolving the competing considerations of securing an effective complaints system for complainants, on the one hand, with the necessity of reducing the practical demands of administering such a system on the IPCC and affected Commissioners, on the other, the alleged conduct must be sufficiently serious to warrant dismissal before the process of investigation imports any wholly independent element.

3.123   This decision is with the IPCC. As will be seen, the level of genuine independence inherent in the process is also restricted to a limited review. A system that has IPCC Commissioners of one rank determining complaints about other IPCC Commissioners of another is unlikely to enjoy significant confidence from complainants.

3.124   Subject to the necessary amendments applicable to the chairman and deputy chairmen, complaints are determined in respect of all Commissioners according to the stated three-stage process rehearsed in the September 2006 Commission document.

3.125   The three-stage process consists of:

- '1. The preliminary examination';
- '2A. Complaint investigation and findings';
- '2B. Investigation review';
- '3A. Sanctions consideration'; and
- '3B. Sanctions decision'.

3.126   The 'overview' that precedes the 'detail' baldly asserts that 'the first two stages are the responsibility of the IPCC' and that 'an appeal avenue is provided for in the second stage'. By implication, no such appeal exists from the important first stage.

---

[63] Ibid.

Matters of general application are addressed, including timeliness[64] ('. . . the strong **3.127** expectation of this procedure is that timeliness should be an important ingredient'), and confidentiality[65] (including the possibility of a written undertaking by the complainant, 'until the complaint is fully resolved or the parties otherwise agree').

The consequences of a complainant not agreeing to such confidentiality are **3.128** not clear. It is difficult to see that the IPCC could, in every case, require confidentiality as a condition precedent to determining a complaint.

Suspension

Suspension is addressed at para 32 of the September 2006 Commission docu- **3.129** ment. It appears to apply equally to the chairman, deputy chairmen, and ordinary members, although the only specific provision is that 'a Commissioner may be suspended by the Chair'. The power to suspend the chairman and deputy chairmen is not addressed.

Suspension is contended not to be a sanction 'in this context' unless it involves loss **3.130** of pay or privileges, although 'it may well be felt to be demeaning to and is clearly a serious step for any Commissioner suspended from duty'. Paragraph 32 provides:

> Its purpose is for when a Commissioner's attendance at the office, or undertaking of duties outside the office, would prejudice the ordinary conduct of the IPCC, its reputation, the investigation process or where it would be detrimental to the well-being of a complainant when that complainant is a fellow Commissioner or an IPCC employee. A Commissioner may be suspended by the Chair. Such suspension should be confirmed by the Home Office within two working days and reviewed every two weeks.

There is no further definition of either the process or the parties at the Home **3.131** Office that confirm the suspension. There is no associated Home Office material. It is not clear who is to conduct the review and whether, if this is the chair, this involves confirmation by the Home Office each time. The rights of, respectively, the Commissioner and the complainant in the process are not addressed.

The IPCC stages

'1. The preliminary examination'

This is the first of the 'IPCC stages'. In respect of complaints against Commission **3.132** members, it is conducted by the deputy chair; in respect of a complaint against the deputy chair, by the chair, and in respect of a complaint against the chair, by a Senior Civil Service (SCS) employee or by a Home Office appointee.

---

[64] September 2006 Commission document, para 23.
[65] Ibid, para 25.

3.133 The overview expresses the 'time expectation' for the preliminary examination as one week, and the purpose of it is defined as follows:

- Eliminate the clearly malicious, frivolous or repetitious and complaints about competence, process or outcome (of IPCC investigation into the police) [sic] which have been dressed up as misconduct complaints, leaving for consideration those which require further investigation to establish if they have substance or not
- Identify whether the complaint is, at face value, of serious or non-serious misconduct. Serious misconduct is conduct such that, if established, removal of the Commissioner from office could be construed under the Commissioners' Terms of Engagement

3.134 The detail of the process in the preliminary examination is covered at paras 1–7 of the September 2006 Commission document. Of particular relevance is the supposed distinction between misconduct and 'competence or process'. As rehearsed at para 7:

> . . . the [deputy chair] may also make a determination on whether the complaint is actually about competence or process, rather than misconduct, in the undertaking of the IPCC's role in relation to a complaint against the police. Competence/process complaints are NOT covered in what follows; but are subject to a different process framework.

3.135 The 'different process framework' is not defined. The distinction between misconduct and competence is not easy to understand or justify. There is no reason in principle why (gross) incompetence in the performance of duties should not amount to misconduct, although, by analogy with police officers, gross incompetence does fall under the 2008 Performance, rather than Conduct, Regulations.

3.136 The residual paragraphs in relation to the preliminary examination address:

- recording the complaint and outcome (para 1);
- disclosure of the complainant's details to the affected Commissioner (para 2, disclosed 'unless prejudicial to the well-being of the complainant');
- disclosure of the terms of the complaint to the affected Commissioner (para 4, presumption in favour of 'full disclosure of complainant's first account and any supporting statements' unless 'inimical to the collection of necessary evidence on the complaint');
- requests for, and timetable, for service of 'additional input' (para 6); and
- the deputy chair ending the process when material is not forthcoming to counter an initial suggestion that the complaint is 'frivolous, misplaced or repetitious' (para 7).

3.137 By para 3, if the deputy chair is conflicted, the chair will consider it, or refer it to a 'suitable independent party' to do so. The nature of such a party is not defined.

By para 5, the deputy chairman will 'propose to' the chairman whether the **3.138** complaint is serious or non-serious, 'and similarly advise the Commissioner in question of this recommendation'. Under the September 2006 Commission document, neither the Commissioner affected, nor the complainant, appear to enjoy any right to make representations on this central decision; nor do they enjoy any right of appeal. Under the May 2004 Commission document, however, the deputy chairman's determination may be referred to the chairman at the initiative of either complainant or Commissioner. The Commissioner may revise the original decision, but the basis of discretion (review/appeal) is not identified. The complaint file will be held with the Commissioner's personnel file for the currency of tenure.

All complaints identified by the chairman as non-serious are passed to a deputy **3.139** chair for attention on a geographical north/south basis.[66] The deputy chair can adopt, subject to reporting duties, 'any procedure that appears to them to be the most appropriate' to determine the complaint. It is to be assumed that this will be subject to the subsequent September 2006 Commission document.

The reporting duty is to record the outcome in the complaints file, and notify the **3.140** complainant and chair of the outcome. A ten-day timetable is anticipated for resolution under the May 2004 Commission document[67] and mirrored in the September 2006 Commission document.

'2A. Complaint investigation and findings'

This is the first part of the second of the 'IPCC stages' set out in the September **3.141** 2006 Commission document, which, of course, presupposes that the matter has progressed beyond the preliminary examination.

In the 'overview', the responsibility lies with the chairman for serious misconduct **3.142** and the deputy chairman for non-serious conduct. The 'time expectation' is two weeks, and the 'purpose' is 'to identify from the evidence presented whether the complaint has substance and the degree of misconduct involved, together with any mitigating factors'.

In cases progressing to the second stage that are judged to be 'trivial', the task **3.143** of investigation may be delegated or assigned 'appropriately' by the deputy chairman, although the chairman will consider the outcome if Commissioner culpability is identified.[68]

---

[66] May 2004 Commission document, para 10.
[67] Ibid, para 11.
[68] September 2006 Commission document, para 10.

3.144 The detailed provisions[69] provide that this stage 'is the major element in the process for all complaints of misconduct where there is no prima facie case for dismissing the complaint'.

3.145 The relevant paragraphs produce, even in serious cases, a non-adversarial, inquisitorial, investigative process with no right of 'cross-questioning' by the Commissioner or the complainant. In particular cases, it is wholly foreseeable that this will produce a sense of unfairness; in others, it will produce actual unfairness.

3.146 Whilst inquisitorial procedures lacking the right of cross-questioning, and even the right to legal representation, are not wholly uncommon in the context of commercial employment, no doubt to encourage (junior) employees to complain about misconduct by others, dismissed employees enjoy the right to bring claims for wrongful and unfair dismissal to an independent statutory employment tribunal, where such rights of disclosure and effective participation do exist. Appointed public officials, including the chair and ordinary members of the Commission, do not enjoy these employment rights.

3.147 Whilst it is unlikely that internal disciplinary proceedings engage the Human Rights Act 1998, in the context of inquests (another form of inquisitorial proceedings), the right to examine has been held to be important—particularly (but not exclusively), for interested persons who lack the right to address the court on the facts.[70]

3.148 By para 9, the appropriate party[71] will:

> . . . review all the evidence, interview parties as appropriate and allow the Commissioner being investigated full opportunity to respond to the allegations made, before concluding on the balance of probabilities whether the allegation has been established or not, and with what degree of culpability. It is expected that this will be done formally to a degree appropriate to the severity of the allegation, with investigation followed by suitable hearing. Evidence may be taken orally or in writing. Oral evidence will be transcribed by someone appointed for that purpose by the Chair/Deputy Chair. It will form part of the record of the investigation. The Chair/Deputy Chair will make a substantive and reasoned formal statement of findings and conclusions drawn from the evidence presented.

---

[69] Ibid, para 8.

[70] *R v HM Coroner at Hammersmith, ex p Peach* [1980] 1 QB 211, 219; *R v Southwark Coroner, ex p Hicks* [1987] 1 WLR 1624, 1629; *R (on the application of Paul and the Ritz Hotel Ltd) v Assistant Deputy Coroner of Inner West London* [2007] EWHC 2721 (Admin), 40(vi) and (vii) (substantive appeal to the Court of Appeal, relating to r 37 of the Coroners' Rules 1984, SI 1984/552, upheld: see [2007] EWCA Civ 1259).

[71] In serious or conflict cases, the chairman; in non-serious cases, the deputy chairman; if both conflicted, an independent person.

The extended meaning of 'balance of probabilities' (in other words, the civil **3.149** standard of proof) is considered in the context of the Police (Conduct) Regulations 2004 and 2008 at 5.52 and 8.105 *et seq.* There is no reason why any different principle should apply, and the presumed burden (there being no adversarial 'prosecutor', but rather a complainant in an inquisitorial investigation) is that a particular allegation must be proved rather than disproved.

By para 11, the limited rights of the parties are self-evident: **3.150**

> The Commissioner being investigated has a right to see the detail of the complaint and respond to it, as well as responding directly in his/her own defence. The Commissioner in question may be accompanied at any hearing by a Union representative, a fellow Commissioner or similar 'friend'. However, the accompanying person will not have representation rights as such at hearings. The role is confined to offering advice to the Commissioner in question. A Commissioner may seek legal support in connection with the investigation or review of a complaint assessed as serious: but neither Commissioner, Union representative, 'friend' nor legal support will have freedom to cross-question Complainant or other witnesses.

Although the procedure, particularly under para 11, provides discretion to the **3.151** party charged with the investigation, the complainant has no express right of participation in this stage at any point. The right to seek a 'review' of the outcome of the investigation arises under para 12. A dissatisfied Commissioner may 'ask' for a review, a complainant may 'request' one, or the chairman can initiate one. It is not clear whether the chairman is bound to order a review when asked or requested or whether he has discretion.

The complainant does not appear to have a specific right to see the 'substantive **3.152** and reasoned formal statement of findings and conclusions drawn from the evidence' required by para 9. It may be thought that this statement should routinely be disclosed to a complainant in order to make sense of the right to request a review. Under the review process, however, the complainant does not have the right to make representations to the reviewer. Read together, and literally, paras 9, 12, and 15 appear to promote disclosure to, and rights to make reasoned representations on review by, exclusively, the Commissioner.

'2B. Investigation review'

This is described in the overview to the September 2006 Commission document **3.153** as being undertaken by an independent person 'retained or appointed' by the chairman, at the instigation of either the affected Commissioner or the complainant, with a 'time expectation' of two weeks.

The purpose is described as to review evidence and the conclusions from it. **3.154** As the overview describes it, 'this is a process and quality review, not a re-hearing of the complaint. The Commissioner under investigation has, however, right of access to the independent reviewer to put his arguments for review'.

3.155 Further detail is added by paras 13–17. By para 13, the independent person appointed or retained by the chairman for this purpose will be 'appointed in advance' in the interests of 'timeliness and of openness'. This presumably means in advance of the preliminary examination.

3.156 To secure the purpose of the review ('. . . intended to ensure that due process has been observed, that evidence presented has been sufficient sufficiently robust for the purpose and that rational conclusions have been drawn from it': para 14), the reviewer may seek 'clarification' of evidence from the Commissioner or complainant concerned', but 'will not repeat the investigation process' and 'no distinctly new evidence will be taken by the reviewer' (para 15).

3.157 The Commissioner (although not apparently the complainant, even if the review is at the complainant's request) may make representations to the reviewer to the effect that 'insufficient weight has been placed on aspects of the rebuttal or on aspects of the original evidence presented' (para 15). The obstacle to new evidence arises in this context: in other words, the reviewer may seek 'clarification' (by implication, new evidence), but the affected Commissioner cannot submit new evidence unless invited by way of clarification.

3.158 By para 15, the reviewer's conclusions must be disclosed to the Commissioner concerned. There is no express right for the complainant to have such disclosure, although this may well not exclude discretion to disclose.[72] It may simply mean that there is no discretion as to disclosure to the affected Commissioner. In that para 17 expressly provides that a complainant has no avenue of appeal 'from any decision not to consider a complaint further or to uphold the complaint made following this review stage other than through due process of law' (not defined, but presumably judicial review), non-disclosure in particular cases may be particularly surprising.

3.159 On conclusion of any review—or before, if none is sought—where a complaint of personal misconduct has been upheld against a Commissioner, 'the chairman will either recommend sanctions to the Home Office or take such steps as are appropriate in the circumstances'.

3.160 The overview to the September 2006 Commission document states that it is only the third stage (the sanctions stage) that is the responsibility of the Home Office. Paragraph 2 of the May 2004 Commission document expressly provides that nothing in it shall be construed as restricting the powers of the Home Secretary under s 9 of, and Sch 2 to, the 2002 Act to make and terminate appointments to

---

[72] See, in the context of chief officer reviews under reg 40 of the Police (Conduct) Regulations 2004, SI 2004/645, the analysis of Mr Justice Burton in *R (IPCC) v Chief Constable of West Midlands* [2007] EWHC 2715 (Admin), [17]: '. . . the presence of a statement that he must let in (a) does not rule out any question of the fact that he may let in (b).'

the Commission. It is contended that the September 2006 Commission document, agreed unilaterally by the Commissioners, cannot override the s 9 power either.[73] If correct, the Home Secretary may exercise s 9 powers outside the procedures of the Commission documents.

'3A. Sanctions consideration' (for allegations of a serious nature)

This only arises where the 'IPCC process'—that is, stages 1 and 2 of the September 2006 Commission document—has substantiated serious misconduct—namely, that which may lead to dismissal. If non-serious, the overview states that 'such further steps as may be appropriate and applicable in these cases are for the Chair to determine'. The further steps are nowhere defined or considered.   **3.161**

In serious cases, by para 19, a Home Office appointee (although not the same appointee as conducted stage 2B) undertakes the process. His task is expected to be 'informed by a report and recommendations' from the IPCC chairman. The overview states that the 'time expectation' is two weeks.   **3.162**

The affected Commissioner has a right to make written representations and, either at the request, or with the consent, of the appointee, make representations in person. The Commissioner has a right to be legally represented at the 'sanctions consideration stage' (para 21), which is presumed to apply to the whole stage, rather than simply to the part of it covered in para 21 (which addresses the later role in the process of a Director General in the Home Office). The implication of the three stages is that the right to make representations applies only to sanctions in relation to the facts proved under stage 2B even if these are contentious. Put simply, it is mitigation, rather than defence.   **3.163**

The Home Secretary's appointee's report and conclusions are then sent to the appropriate Director General within the Home Office who, 'having considered any such representations, either in person or in writing, as appropriate', will make a recommendation to the Home Secretary (para 21). Neither the identity of those entitled to make representations, nor the material to be disclosed to them in order to do so in any meaningful way, is set out.   **3.164**

'3B. Sanctions decision'

Paragraph 15 of the May 2004 Commission document provides that if a serious complaint is made out, it will be referred to the Home Office in order for the Home Secretary to make a determination under para 2(6)(f) or (g) of Sch 2 to the 2002 Act. This is mirrored by para 22 of the September 2006 Commission   **3.165**

---

[73] For an illustration of the basic principle that guidance/protocols cannot displace statutory powers, see *R (Chief Constable of Somerset and Avon) v Police Appeals Tribunal* [2004] EWHC 220 (Admin), [29].

document, which simply provides that 'any decision to dismiss will be taken by the Home Secretary. There is no avenue of appeal from this decision, which is final and binding on all parties'.

3.166 It is assumed that loss of public office will attract the right of judicial review. Self-evidently, judicial review is not an appeal within the process.

The Commission staff

Statutory regulation

3.167 A complaint against a member of the Commission's staff is regulated by the IPCC (Staff Conduct) Regulations 2004,[74] in force from 1 April 2004. The enabling statutory provisions are ss 27 and 105(4) of the 2002 Act, the latter provision being the general power in the Secretary of State to make regulations under the Act by statutory instrument.

3.168 According to the IPCC Annual Report 2006–07, there were some 220 such complaints in 2006–07, an increase of some 150 per cent on the previous year, of which nineteen were upheld. It is not immediately obvious that this statistic is limited to staff as distinct from Commissioners.

3.169 Section 27 provides for the Secretary of State to regulate the manner in which cases in which allegations of misconduct are made against members of the Commission's staff, and cases in which there is otherwise an indication that there may have been misconduct by a member of the Commission's staff, are dealt with. By subs (4), the Secretary of State is bound to consult the Commission before issuing a regulation.

3.170 The 2004 Regulations provide for a familiar sequential approach to any allegation of misconduct relating to a member of Commission staff. Where an allegation comes within the s 27 criteria (reproduced as reg 2(2)), the first consideration is whether the allegation takes a form to which para (3) of reg 2 applies. If it does, the Commission 'shall' take the steps set out in reg 3.

3.171 Paragraph (3) of reg 2 is set out below. By reg 2(2), 'any other allegation' requires the Commission to 'take such action in relation to that allegation or indication as it thinks appropriate'. This is neither defined in the Regulations, nor subject to a specific right of review or appeal. In an appropriate case, including the classification of the allegation or indication as outside reg 2(3) (impliedly by the Commission), judicial review may lie. To a degree, these matters are answered in

---

[74] The Independent Police Complaints Commission (Staff Conduct) Regulations 2004, SI 2004/660.

the internal staff disciplinary and dismissal procedure, which is not a public document.

Paragraph (3) of reg 2 applies to any complaint that: **3.172**

(a) either—
    (i) has been made by or on behalf of a member of the public or a person serving with the police who has been adversely affected by the conduct complained of; or
    (ii) has been made by a member of the Commission or a member of the Commission's staff and in the view of the Commission should be recorded and dealt with as in regulation 3;
(b) concerns the conduct of a member of the Commission's staff in his capacity as such; and
(c) is in writing.

The limitations on the subject matter of complaint are self-evident. Additionally, **3.173** reg 2(4) provides that, for the purpose of para (3)(a)(i), a person is not directly affected by conduct by reason only of the fact that he witnessed it. The Regulations permit a person serving with the police to complain about the conduct of a member of Commission staff other than when the latter is acting as such, but such a complaint will fall outside the reg 3 procedures.

Further limitations are prescribed by regs 6 (dispensation from requirement to **3.174** investigate in particular circumstances, including inexcusable delay, impracticability of investigation, and repetition), 7 (withdrawn complaints), and 8 (postponement in circumstances wherein the complainant is also under investigation by the Commission 'until the conclusion of the investigation'). The 'conclusion of the investigation' is not defined for these purposes.

Remaining allegations and complaints against members of Commission staff **3.175** are subject to procedures set out in regs 3–5.

Regulation 3 prescribes the action to be taken in relation to a recordable com- **3.176** plaint—that is, one to which reg 2(3) applies. The Commission is required to cause a record to be made of the complaint, determine whether the complaint is a serious complaint, and, subject to its assessment of either prejudice to the investigation or the public interest, notify the complainant and the person complained about of the recording of the complaint and the notification.

By reg 3(3), a complaint is a serious complaint if it would, if proved, be likely to **3.177** result in a person involved being dismissed or required to resign. This mirrors, in different language, the test for gross misconduct under the Police (Conduct) Regulations 2008.

For complaints other than serious complaints, reg 4 provides that, unless it con- **3.178** cerns the conduct of the chief executive (see reg 5(1)), it shall be dealt with 'in accordance with internal procedures'. These internal procedures are not specifically defined, but may include the sanctions of dismissal or a requirement to resign (reg 4(2)).

3.179 The complainant does not appear to have any right to information in respect of a non-serious complaint, as determined by the Commission, under the Regulations. The Commission is clearly required to act reasonably and proportionately according to public law principles.

3.180 Regulation 5 provides for the determination of serious complaints against staff members of the Commission. The starting point is the appointment of a person, who may be a member of the Commission's staff, to investigate the complaint (reg 5(1)). There is no provision as to the status of this person in the Regulations.

3.181 Suspension of the person complained about pending resolution of the investigation is possible if 'necessary' either for the efficient carrying out of the Commission's functions, or in the public interest (reg 5(2); neither term is defined).

3.182 Other than internal documents, there is a complete absence of regulation of the procedure governing the investigation of a serious complaint, which contrasts markedly with the resolution of complaints made about, rather than by, police officers.

3.183 Regulation 5(3) simply provides, without more, that the person appointed to investigate under para (1) shall make a written report of the findings of the investigation and send it to the Commission. Regulation 5(4) provides that the Commission shall determine whether to take any disciplinary or other action as a result of those findings, and, if so, 'to proceed with such action to a proper conclusion'.

3.184 Participation of the complainant is apparently limited to reg 5(5), and is once again contingent on the uncertain test of public interest as determined by the Commission. The right created is that 'unless the Commission is of the opinion that it would be contrary to the public interest, the complainant shall be notified of the progress of the investigation and of any disciplinary action taken as a result of those findings'.

Internal procedures

3.185 These Regulations are supplemented by internal procedures—although the latter are not readily available to the public, there is a staff code of conduct, written in January 2004 and updated in December 2007. The staff disciplinary and dismissal procedure is applicable to all staff on contract, but not to secondees, who remain subject to their employer's disciplinary procedures.

3.186 The written procedure is complex and addresses the different parties responsible for each rank of employee. The decision-making matrix is as illustrated in Table 3.1.

Table 3.1 IPCC misconduct procedures: a summary table of the decision-making hierarchy

Employee	Authority to give oral warning	Authority to give first written warning	Authority to give final written warning	Authority to dismiss	Appeal against a warning	Appeal against dismissal
Chief executive (CE)	Commissioner	Commissioner	Commissioner	Commissioner	Appeal committee of Commission	Appeal committee of Commission
Director	CE	CE	CE	Commissioner	Appeal committee of Commission	Appeal committee of Commission
Regional director	Director of investigations	Director of investigations	Director of investigations	Director of investigations	CE	Appeal committee of Commission
Head of service	Director	Director	Director	Director	CE	Appeal committee of Commission
Other staff	Immediate line manager	Head of section/ group, team leader, or equivalent	Director	Director	Director or CE	Appeal committee of Commission

3.187 This book does not attempt a detailed rehearsal of the internal procedures. Certain features, however, attract comment.

3.188 Under the scheme, relevant managers are encouraged to distinguish between 'misconduct' (attracting some form of disciplinary process) and 'capability' (in relation to which other procedures must be followed before recourse to discipline). Capability may be either incapacity due to frequent absence on the ground of non-chronic illness, or due to 'poor or inadequate performance in undertaking the duties and responsibilities of the job'. The procedure says that 'the use of formal disciplinary procedures should be a last resort, rather than a first response to a potentially disciplinary matter'. This approach to discipline, and capability, is not always the experience of police officers under scrutiny by the IPCC. If, however, the complaint against the IPCC staff member is potentially gross misconduct, the disciplinary procedure commences at the investigation stage.

3.189 Assuming that the matter proceeds to a disciplinary panel, it consists of a manager, or, in serious cases (gross misconduct), a director, as chair and key decision maker, advised by a second person from either human resources or a qualified independent manager. The panel may be enlarged to up to four, including the director. There is discretion in the disciplinary panel as to what, if any, witnesses are called.

3.190 The affected member of staff will be entitled to a 'full explanation' of the case against him, and to 'be informed of' the content of any statements provided by witnesses. Whether this extends to paper copies of the material is not addressed. There is no express right for the affected party to question witnesses. The witnesses called on behalf of the affected staff member must relate to fact and not character (para 2.5(d)). The rights of the person making the complaint are not addressed at all. An appeal must be made in writing within ten working days.

3.191 Many of these procedures mirror the practices of private industry, and staff members, of course, have enforceable rights in employment law for constructive, unfair, and wrongful dismissal. The lack of any right to question the complaining party—particularly if a fellow staff member—promotes reporting of misconduct.

3.192 Given the sensitivity and importance of the work conducted by members of the Commission staff, and the resultant damage to careers and reputations of serving police officers if investigations are inadequate, and the probability of complaint from the police officer complained of or the party complaining (which probability will broadly correlate to the degree of public profile enjoyed by a particular investigation), the IPCC (Staff Conduct) Regulations 2004 and associated internal procedures appear to be inadequate for purpose. The complaining members of the public (including police officers) enjoy few rights.

Discretion is afforded at every stage of the process to the Commission, without **3.193** corresponding definition of the proper criteria affecting the exercise of discretion, the conduct of the investigation, or rights of participation to those affected by it.

It may be observed that the use of unpublished internal procedures to regulate **3.194** the determination of serious complaints against staff members is difficult to reconcile with the 'core belief' of 'openness' claimed by the Commission in the performance of its work to improve the complaints system.

G. Conclusion

The IPCC is progressively well established. Police forces are becoming more **3.195** familiar with the relationship and division of roles. The greatest tension tends to arise:

(i) in determining the form of an investigation under Sch 3 of the 2002 Act (namely independent; managed; supervised; or local); and
(ii) when it directs the fact and form of misconduct proceedings against the opinion of the affected officer's force.

These tensions are inevitable and probably healthy. That said, an obdurate insist- **3.196** ence on misconduct charges affects real officers, and the IPCC must be seen to adopt the intended change of culture from misconduct and punishment to one of performance and learning under the 2008 Performance and Conduct Regulations.

4

COMPLAINTS AND MISCONDUCT II:
OVERVIEW OF THE 2004 AND 2008
CONDUCT AND PERFORMANCE
REGULATIONS, AND ASSOCIATED
APPEALS

A. **Overview**	4.01	The structure of subsequent	
Introduction and the history of reform	4.01	associated chapters	4.15
The Taylor Review and		B. **Process Charts**	4.18
parliamentary intent	4.10		
Summary of central changes			
under the 2008 regime	4.14		

A. Overview

Introduction and the history of reform

The Regulations relating to police conduct and performance have undergone **4.01** four fundamental changes since 1985—in 1999,[1] 2003,[2] 2004,[3] and 2008. Certain of the provisions, such as notification requirements to the officer concerned once a matter is sent for investigation, have a pedigree extending back at least as far as the Police (Discipline) Regulations 1977.[4]

---

[1] The Police (Conduct) Regulations 1999, SI 1999/730, and the Police (Efficiency) Regulations 1999, SI 1999/732.

[2] When attendance considerations were added to the Police (Efficiency) Regulations 1999 by the Police (Efficiency) (Amendment) Regulations 2003, SI 2003/528.

[3] The Police (Conduct) Regulations 2004, SI 2004/645, reflecting the advent of the Independent Police Complaints Commission (IPCC).

[4] SI 1977/580.

4.02   The regime introduced by the quartet of 2008 Regulations—namely, the Police (Performance) Regulations 2008 (the 2008 Performance Regulations),[5] the Police (Conduct) Regulations 2008 (the 2008 Conduct Regulations),[6] the Police (Complaints and Misconduct) (Amendment) Regulations 2008,[7] and Police Appeals Tribunals Rules 2008 (the PAT Rules),[8] coupled with the associated Home Office Guidance[9]—is accordingly the latest in a series. It is also probably the most dramatic in terms of the intended reform of the management of police performance and misconduct.

4.03   Central as background to this reform process was the Police (Reform) Act 2002 Act (the 2002 Act), which introduced the extended role of the Independent Police Complaints Commission (IPCC) relative to its predecessor, the Police Complaints Authority (PCA), and, with it, a change of culture within the 2004 Conduct Regulations. All officers—both senior and non-senior—were brought within the same set of Conduct Regulations, and the right of review by a chief officer was introduced for non-senior officers. The 1999 Efficiency Regulations (as amended) and the PAT Rules, however, remained unchanged.

4.04   The 2008 reforms are more important in both purpose and detail than the 2004 changes. In relation to individual performance, the barely used 1999 Efficiency Regulations (which, ultimately, addressed both unsatisfactory performance and attendance) are replaced by the 2008 Performance Regulations.

4.05   As will be seen, the structure of these is not without difficulty—not least in terms of the introduction of internal appeals from the first and second stage meeting— but an intended change of culture lies behind it in terms of treating poor performance as a management, rather than misconduct, issue wherever possible. The 2008 Performance Regulations may take much conduct out of the conduct regime entirely if used appropriately. The final outcome of the unsatisfactory performance procedures (UPPs)—that is, the 'third stage meeting'—attracts the right of appeal to the police appeals tribunals.

4.06   The 2008 Conduct Regulations remove the chief officer's review, and introduce new concepts of 'misconduct' and 'gross misconduct'. Save for 'totting up' exceptions, only an allegation of gross misconduct will attract a hearing with legal representation. This places a far greater practical burden on local representatives and the appropriate authority charged with decision making under the process.

---

[5]   SI 2008/2862.

[6]   SI 2008/2864.

[7]   SI 2008/2866.

[8]   SI 2008/2863.

[9]   Home Office Guidance, *Police Officer Misconduct, Unsatisfactory Performance and Attendance Management Procedures*, issued pursuant to s 87 of the Police Act 1996.

Assuming that gross misconduct is established (the panel may alternatively find **4.07** the conduct not proved, or, even if proved, that it simply amounts to misconduct), the range of sanctions is radically altered so as to require a decision simply between dismissal and a form of written notice. The sanctions of requiring resignation or imposing a reduction in rank are removed entirely from the conduct regime. The procedural obligations on the accused officer in terms of identifying issues and providing material in advance are much increased.

The 2008 PAT Rules reflect an amendment to s 85 of the Police Act 1996 so as **4.08** to define the grounds of appeal, permit summary dismissal of an appeal by the chair, reduce the legal qualifying experience required of a chair, and permit sanction to be increased on appeal.

Given the new procedures and timescales, confidence in the new system will **4.09** only be retained if the respective 2008 Performance and Conduct Regulations are used as intended—that is, to promote a culture of learning and improvement for identified defects in professional performance, and restricting conduct matters to facts properly described as positive misconduct rather than merely deficient performance. Of course, performance that, by objective standards, is seriously deficient may properly amount to misconduct, but it is contended that this objective threshold between 'performance' and 'misconduct' is intended to be set high. This would reflect the process leading to the 2008 regime and the statements of intent associated with it.

The Taylor Review and parliamentary intent

The 2008 regime for police complaints and conduct matters came into force on **4.10** 1 December 2008. It reflects primarily recommendations made in the January 2005 *Review of Police Disciplinary Arrangements Report*[10] by a multi-agency committee chaired by William Taylor.[11] This report was, in turn, informed by the conclusion of the Morris Inquiry[12] published in December 2004.

The Taylor Review identified particular key recommendations. Most of these **4.11** are reflected in the new Regulations and changes to Sch 3 of the 2002 Act.

---

[10] Available online at <http://www.press.homeoffice.gov.uk>.

[11] William Taylor CBE QPM joined the Metropolitan Police Service (MPS) in 1965 and, via deputy chief constable at Thames Valley Police, rose to the rank of Assistant Commissioner, Specialist Operations, at the MPS. He was appointed Commissioner of the City of London Police in 1994, one of Her Majesty's Inspector of Constabulary (HMIC) for England and Wales in 1998, and, from 1 January 1999, Her Majesty's Chief Inspector of Constabulary (HMCIC) for Scotland, from which post he retired in August 2001.

[12] *The Report of the Morris Inquiry: An Independent Inquiry into Professional Standards and Employment Matters in the MPS*, 14 December 2004, available online at <http://www.mpa. gov.uk>.

In introducing the new Regulations to the First Parliamentary Delegated Sub-Committee,[13] the Home Office Minister made the following observations:

> First, the Taylor review found that the current system for dealing with police misconduct can be slow and disproportionate. It gives little or no encouragement to managers to deal swiftly and proportionately with low-level misconduct matters. Disciplinary hearings were seen as more akin to criminal court hearings and even low level misconduct matters were decided by three-person panels of more senior police officers. The new system ensures that police managers are given the responsibility and ability to deal with misconduct in a fair and proportionate manner at a local level. Time scales are built into the process to ensure timeliness in all misconduct and gross misconduct cases. An independent panel member appointed by the police authority will sit on gross misconduct cases to bring a public perspective to the holding of police officers to account.
>
> Secondly, The Taylor report proposed a new single code as the touchstone for individual behaviour and as a clear indication of organizational and peer expectations. Together with all stakeholders, we have produced the new standards of professional behaviour for police officers, which form part of the conduct regulations. The standards set out clear expectations of the behaviour that the public and colleagues expect of all police officers.
>
> The Taylor review also proposed that the misconduct procedures be based on the ACAS principles to modernize the system and make it easier for individual officers and the police service generally to learn lessons and improve the service to the public. A key point that emerged was the need to shift the emphasis and culture in police misconduct and unsatisfactory performance matters from blame and punishment to development and improvement. The change in the disciplinary procedures is seismic.

4.12 This ministerial statement should be read in the context of the core principles underpinning the reforms reflected in the Taylor Review. Ultimately, the Regulations and (where applicable) the associated Home Office Guidance are subject to ordinary principles of statutory interpretation—but the core Taylor Review recommendations may inform the process, particularly in terms of the intended change of culture.

4.13 The core Taylor Review recommendations can be summarized as follows:

(i) given the uniqueness of policing and the powers of police officers, the retention of a 'regulatory' as distinct from 'employment law' approach to police conduct issues—thought to be preferable because it would: (a) maintain parliamentary approval of police conduct arrangements; and (b) benefit

---

[13] Parliamentary Debates, House of Commons Official Report, First Delegated Legislation Committee, Mon 27 October 2008, available from HM Stationary Office.

from the experience of employment law; whilst (c) not being vulnerable to the vagaries and uncertainties of changes in employment law;

(ii) a regulatory framework that is simple, minimal, and not overly legalistic or adversarial, with the Advisory, Conciliation and Arbitration Service (ACAS) Code of Practice on Disciplinary and Grievance Procedures as the basis for regulation;

(iii) a new single code (incorporating ethics and conduct) for individual officer behaviour, and a clear indication of organization and peer expectations—the long-term intention being to have the same code for officers and staff;

(iv) an intention of encouraging a culture of learning and development for individuals and the organization;

(v) an open and transparent environment for handling police discipline with investigations, not needing to be centred on the criminal model, and with hearings being less adversarial and 'similarities with "military Courts Martial" avoided';

(vi) initial reports (whether from the public or internally generated) being formally assessed, with the full range of options available for responding (crime, gross misconduct, misconduct, unsatisfactory performance, etc);

(vii) conduct issues being separated into two distinct categories—namely, 'misconduct' and 'gross misconduct'—to 'promote proportionate handling, clarify the available outcomes and provide a better public understanding of the policing environment';

(viii) conduct matters to be dealt with 'at the lowest possible line management level. Misconduct should not rise above the BCU (or equivalent) level and gross misconduct should be reserved for the most serious behavioural issues. The latter are likely to be handled by professional standards departments';

(ix) a singular appeal mechanism;

(x) strict designated time limits, with consequences for any unreasonable failure to adhere to these;

(xi) mechanisms to ensure that matters that are properly the subject of capability and performance are not inappropriately managed as matters of conduct—in ACAS terms, distinguishing 'capability' from 'wilful misconduct', and in police terms, distinguishing 'performance' from 'misconduct'; and

(xii) a review of the unsatisfactory performance procedures to create a holistic management of public concerns about policing, whereby conduct and performance are viewed side by side.

Summary of central changes under the 2008 regime

4.14 The black-letter reforms to the 2008 regime, which are intended to effect the above policy reforms, can be summarized as follows:

(i) an attempt to harmonize public complaints and recordable conduct matters with internal conduct matters, the former to be addressed in an amended Sch 3 to the 2002 Act, effected by Sch 23 of the Criminal Justice and Immigration Act 2008, and the latter to be addressed by the 2008 Conduct Regulations. The effect is that the initial investigations are distinct, but similar[14]—but that those different systems 'converge' after the point at which the investigator writes the report on the investigation;[15]

(ii) the repeal of the old Code of Conduct and its replacement with the more purposive definitions of Standards of Professional Behaviour;

(iii) the creation of a formal and important distinction between 'misconduct' as 'a breach of the Standards of Professional Behaviour', and 'gross misconduct' as 'a breach of the Standards of Professional Behaviour so serious that dismissal would be justified';

(iv) the obligation on the 'appropriate authority' and/or IPCC (in recordable complaints and recordable conduct matters, etc) constantly to assess the conduct in question,[16] to determine whether it is:
   (a) misconduct or gross misconduct (requiring application of the 2008 Conduct Regulations); or
   (b) underperformance (requiring application of the 2008 Performance Regulations); or
   (c) suboptimal conduct (requiring only management action, as defined in reg 3(1) of the 2008 Conduct Regulations as meaning 'action or advice intended to improve the conduct of the officer concerned');

(v) the division of responses to alleged misconduct into either:
   (a) management action, which does not constitute 'misconduct proceedings'; and

---

[14] See Pt 3 of the 2008 Conduct Regulations and Pt 3 (in particular, paras 19A–19E) of Sch 3 of the 2002 Act. For example, for an internal conduct matter, the officer concerned receives a written notice of the investigation under reg 15 of the 2008 Conduct Regulations, but for a public complaint (which is certified as subject to the special requirements), receives a written notice under reg 14A of the Police (Complaints and Misconduct) Regulations 2004, SI 2004/643, as amended by reg 3 of the Police (Complaints and Misconduct) (Amendment) Regulations 2008, SI 2008/2866.

[15] See para 22 of Sch 3 of the 2002 Act, and reg 18 of the 2008 Conduct Regulations.

[16] See regs 12(1), (5), and 19(1) of the 2008 Conduct Regulations, which require an initial assessment of the conduct and a further assessment after the investigation report has been submitted, and which entitle the appropriate authority to revise its assessment at any time before the start of misconduct proceedings, which regime is replicated in Sch 3 matters.

(b) 'misconduct proceedings', which are defined to mean either a misconduct meeting or a misconduct hearing. A misconduct hearing deals with
allegations of gross misconduct, or allegations of misconduct in which
the officer has a live final written warning at the time of the assessment
under reg 12 of the 2008 Conduct Regulations (the so-called 'totting
up' process).

These distinctions between 'misconduct' and 'gross misconduct', and
'meeting' and 'hearing', are fundamental to the reforms, and an important
aspect of the attempt to achieve proportionality;

(vi) the outcomes[17] from the new 'meetings' and 'hearings' have been radically
reformed. The 'meeting' can either take no further action, or impose management advice, a written warning, or a final written warning. The 'hearing'
can, in addition to any of those lesser outcomes, impose dismissal, with or
without notice. Gone completely under the new regime are the sanctions of
reduction in rank, fine, reprimand, or caution (although, it will be noted,
that reduction in rank remains an available outcome under the Police
(Performance) Regulations 2008);

(vii) also gone from the 2008 regime are chief constable 'reviews'; instead, the
only appeal from the 2008 Conduct Regulations is to the police appeals
tribunals. New, however, is the appeal from the misconduct meeting to a
more senior officer or police staff member;

(viii) the misconduct meeting is presided over by a more senior officer or staff
member than the officer concerned—this being only one aspect of the
greater involvement of police staff in the new conduct regime. The three-
person panel for misconduct hearings will now always comprise one independent member appointed by the police authority and may be chaired by
a senior human resources professional rather than a chief officer. Indeed,
it is permissible for a gross misconduct panel to comprise only one police
officer, who might only be of superintending rank;

(ix) the listing of meetings or hearings is to be significantly expedited, with a
default time limit of thirty days (although this seems certain to be breached
routinely for gross misconduct hearings, given the need to secure the
attendance of so many personnel for these hearings);

(x) the treatment of live witnesses is also significantly different in that witnesses shall only be called if the person presiding (whether at the meeting
or hearing) considers it 'necessary in the interests of justice' that they attend;

---

[17] Formerly, 'sanctions' under reg 35 of the 2004 Conduct Regulations; now, 'disciplinary action'
under reg 35 of the 2008 Conduct Regulations.

(xi) the 2008 Conduct Regulations place greater emphasis on 'cards on the table', in that the officer concerned is obliged to identify his plea, the points of dispute, any mitigation, the points of law, and the witnesses much earlier in the process, with the potential risk of adverse inferences being drawn by the persons conducting the proceedings if he does not do so;

(xii) further, the person(s) presiding at the misconduct proceedings will be provided not only with the investigator's report (itself a new departure and more in line with civilian employment procedures), but also all of the other relevant documents. Panels presiding at a misconduct hearing constituted under the 2004 Conduct Regulations saw only in advance, as of right, the misconduct charges;

(xiii) what is recorded and for what period is amended by the Police (Amendment) Regulations 2008;[18]

(xiv) the procedures in terms of appeal to the police appeals tribunals have been significantly revised, and introduce a higher threshold for intervention by the tribunal on appeal, and the possibility of the sanction increasing.

The structure of subsequent associated chapters

4.15 Each of these Regulations, and the associated Home Office Guidance and PAT Rules, are considered in detail in subsequent chapters of this book, and reproduced in material part in the appendices. A flow chart reflecting the process is set out at Figure 4.0.

4.16 The Regulations and associated subjects are covered in the following order:

- Chapter 5—the Police (Performance) Regulations 2008;
- Chapter 6—the new Standards of Professional Behaviour, and the early decisions to be taken after the complaint, conduct matter, or death or serious injury (DSI) matter is drawn to the attention of the appropriate authority or IPCC;
- Chapter 7—investigations;
- Chapter 8—misconduct proceedings under the Police (Conduct) Regulations 2008;
- Chapter 9—proceedings under the Police (Conduct) Regulations 2004;
- Chapter 10—the 'fast track' or 'special cases' under each of the 2004 and 2008 Conduct Regulations, and paras 20A–20H of Sch 3 to the 2002 Act; and

---

[18] SI 2008/2865, amending reg 15 of the Police Regulations 2003, SI 2003/527 (as amended by the Police (Amendment) (No 2) Regulations 2006, SI 2006/3449, and the Police (Amendment) Regulations 2005, SI 2005/2834), reproduced at Appendix J.

- Chapter 11—chief officer reviews under the 2004 Conduct Regulations and appeals to the police appeals tribunals under each of the 2004 and 2008 Regulations.

Further, abuse of process (including the consequences of departure from the intended regulatory process) within these regimes is addressed in Chapter 12. Removal of probationers under reg 13 of the Police Regulations 2003,[19] and its relationship with misconduct proceedings, is addressed in Chapter 13. **4.17**

B. Process Charts

The resultant processes are far from straightforward. There are a number of variables that determine the appropriate process, and there is discretion within that process. The following process charts[20] attempt to reflect these in a manageable form. **4.18**

---

[19] SI 2003/527.
[20] Prepared by Inspector Mustaqa Patala of Lancashire Constabulary and reproduced by kind permission of his chief constable.

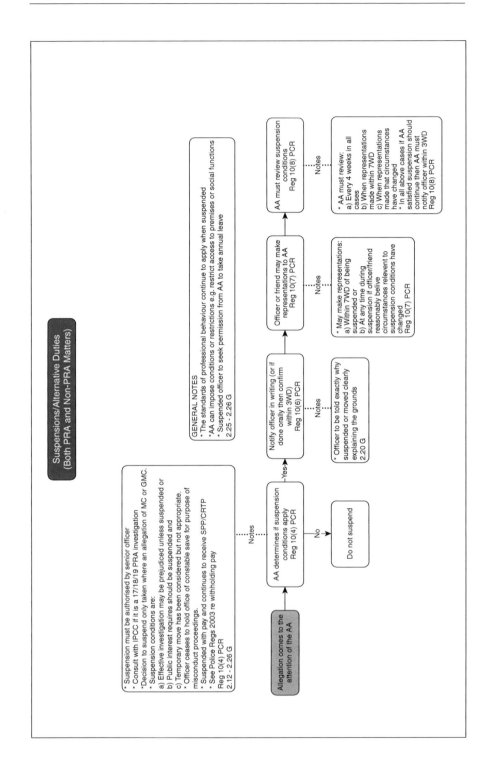

Suspensions/Alternative Duties
(Both PRA and Non-PRA Matters)

Allegation comes to the attention of the AA

* Suspension must be authorised by senior officer
* Consult with IPCC if it is a 17/18/19 PRA investigation
* Decision to suspend only taken where an allegation of MC or GMC.
* Suspension conditions are:
a) Effective investigation may be prejudiced unless suspended or
b) Public interest requires should be suspended and
c) Temporary move has been considered but not appropriate.
* Officer ceases to hold office of constable save for purpose of misconduct proceedings.
* Suspended with pay and continues to receive SPP/CRTP
* See Police Regs 2003 re witholding pay
Reg 10(4) PCR
2.12 - 2.26 G

Notes

AA determines if suspension conditions apply
Reg 10(4) PCR

No → Do not suspend

Yes →

Notify officer in writing (or if done orally then confirm within 3WD)
Reg 10(6) PCR

Notes

* Officer to be told exactly why suspended or moved clearly explaining the grounds
2.20 G

Officer or friend may make representations to AA
Reg 10(7) PCR

Notes

* May make representations:
a) Within 7WD of being suspended or
b) At any time during suspension if officer/friend reasonably belive circumstances relevent to suspension conditions have changed
Reg 10(7) PCR

AA must review suspension conditions
Reg 10(8) PCR

Notes

* AA must review:
a) Every 4 weeks in all cases
b) When representations made within 7WD
c) When representations made that circumstances have changed
* In all above cases if AA satisfied suspension should continue then AA must notify officer within 3WD
Reg 10(8) PCR

GENERAL NOTES
* The standards of professional behaviour continue to apply when suspended
* AA can impose conditions or restrictions e.g. restrict access to premises or social functions
* Suspended officer to seek permission from AA to take annual leave
2.25 - 2.26 G

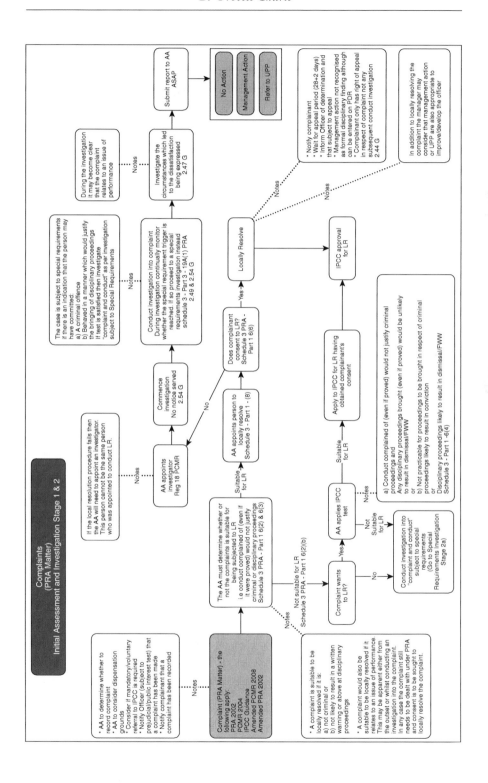

Complaints
(PRA Matter)
Initial Assessment and Investigation Stage 1 & 2

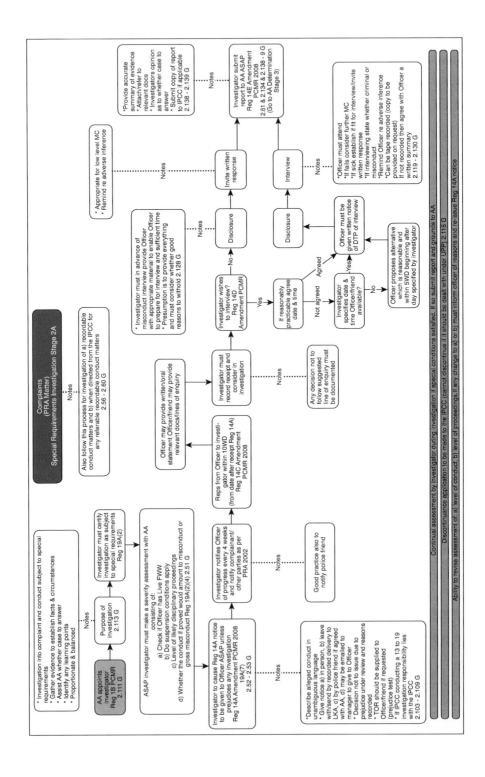

Complaints (PRA Matter)
Special Requirements Investigation Stage 2A

Notes

Also follow this process for investigation of a) recordable conduct matters and b) when directed from the IPCC for any referable recordable conduct matters
2.56 - 2.60 G

*Investigation into complaint and conduct subject to special requirements
*Gather evidence to establish facts & circumstances
*Assist AA whether case to answer
*Identify any learning points
*Proportionate & balanced

AA appoints investigator
Reg 1B PCMR
2.111 G

→ Purpose of investigation 2.113 G → Investigator must certify investigation as subject to special requirements Reg 19A(2)

Notes

ASAP investigator must make a severity assessment with AA consisting of:
a) Check if Officer has Live FWW
b) Do suspension conditions apply
c) Level of likely disciplinary proceedings
d) Whether the conduct if proved would amount to misconduct or gross misconduct Reg 19A(2)(4) 2.51 G

Investigator to cause Reg 14A notice to be given to Officer ASAP unless prejudices any investigation Reg 14A Amendment PCMR 2008 2.52 - 2.53 G

Notes

*Describe alleged conduct in unambiguous language
* Give notice a) in person, b) leave with/send by recorded delivery to LKA, c) by police friend if agreed with AA, d) may be emailed to manager to give to Officer
* Decision not to issue due to prejudice under review and reasons recorded
* TOR should be supplied to Officer/friend if requested (prejudice test)
* If IPCC conducting a 13 to 19 investigation responsibility lies with the IPCC
2.103 - 2.109 G

Investigator notifies Officer of progress every 4 weeks and notify complainant/ other parties as per PRA 2002

Notes

Good practice also to notify police friend

Reps from Officer to investigator within 10WD (from date after receipt Reg 14A) Reg 14C Amendment PCMR 2008

Officer may provide written/oral statement Officer/friend may provide relevant docs/lines of enquiry

Investigator must record receipt and consider in investigation

Notes

Any decision not to follow suggested line of enquiry must be documented

Investigator wishes to interview? Reg 14D Amendment PCMR

—No→ Disclosure → Invite written response

*Investigator must in advance of misconduct interview provide Officer with appropriate material to enable Officer to prepare for interview and sufficient time
* Presumption is to provide everything and must consider whether good reasons to withold 2.128 G

Notes

↓Yes

If reasonably practicable agree date & time

Agreed → Officer must be given written notice of DTP of interview → Disclosure → Interview

Not agreed↓

Investigator specifies date & time Officer/friend available? —Yes→

No↓

Officer proposes alternative which is reasonable and within 5WD beginning after day specified by investigator

Notes

*Officer must attend
*If fails consider further MC
*If sick establish if fit for interview/invite written response
*If interviewing state whether criminal or misconduct
*Remind Officer re adverse inference
*Can be tape recorded (copy to be provided on request)
If not recorded then agree with Officer a written summary
2.119 - 2.130 G

*Provide accurate summary of evidence
* Attach/refer to relevant docs
*Investigators opinion as to whether case to answer
* Submit copy of report to IPCC if applicable
2.138 - 2.139 G

Notes

* Appropriate for low level MC
* Remind re adverse inference

Investigator submit report to AA ASAP Reg 14E Amendment Reg PCMR 2008
2.61 & 2.134 & 2.138 - 9 G
(Go to AA Determination Stage 3)

Notes

Continual assessment by investigator during investigation. If so submit report and grounds to AA

Discontinuance application to be made to the IPCC (cannot discontinue if it should be dealt with under UPP) 2.115 G

Ability to revise assessment of: a) level of conduct, b) level of proceedings. If any change to a) or b) must inform officer of reasons and re-issue Reg 14A notice

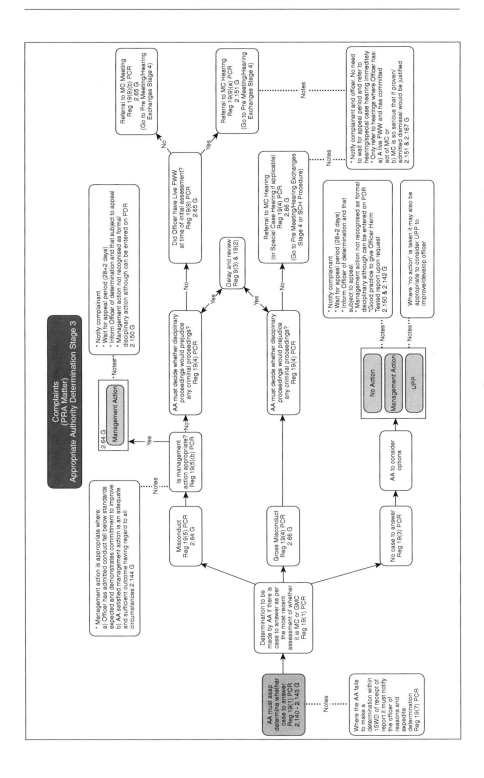

**Complaints
(PRA Matter)
Appropriate Authority Determination Stage 3**

Referral to MC Meeting
Reg 19(9)(b) PCR
2.65 G
(Go to Pre Meeting/Hearing
Exchanges Stage 4)

Referral to MC Hearing
Reg 19(9)(a) PCR
2.151 G
(Go to Pre Meeting/Hearing
Exchanges Stage 4)

Did Officer have Live FWW
at time of initial assessment?
Reg 19(9) PCR
2.65 G

* Notify complainant
* Wait for appeal period (28+2 days)
* Inform Officer of determination and that subject to appeal
* Management action not recognised as formal disciplinary action although can be entered on PDR
2.150 G

• Notes

2.64 G
Management Action

Is management action appropriate? Reg 19(5)(b) PCR

AA must decide whether disciplinary proceedings would prejudice any criminal proceedings? Reg 19(4) PCR

Delay and review Reg 9(3) & 19(2)

Referral to MC Hearing (or Special Case Hearing if applicable) Reg 19(4) PCR 2.66 G
(Go to Pre Meeting/Hearing Exchanges Stage 4 or SCH Procedure)

AA must decide whether disciplinary proceedings would prejudice any criminal proceedings? Reg 19(4) PCR

* Notify complainant and officer. No need to wait for appeal period and refer to hearing/special case hearing immediately
* Only refer to hearings where Officer has:
a) A live FWW and has committed act of MC or
b) MC is so serious that if proven/admitted dismissal would be justified
2.151 & 2.167 G

• Notes

* Management action is appropriate where:
a) Officer has admitted conduct fell below standards expected and demonstrates commitment to improve
b) AA satisfied management action is an adequate and sufficient outcome having regard to all circumstances 2.144 G

• Notes

Misconduct Reg 19(5) PCR 2.64 G

Gross Misconduct Reg 19(4) PCR 2.66 G

No case to answer Reg 19(3) PCR

AA to consider options

No Action

Management Action

UPP

* Notify complainant
* Wait for appeal period (28+2 days)
* Inform Officer of determination and that subject to appeal
* Management action not recognised as formal disciplinary although can be entered on PDR
*Good practice to give Officer Harm Tested report upon request
2.150 & 2.142 G

• Notes•

Where "no action" is taken it may also be appropriate to consider UPP to improve/develop officer

• Notes•

Determination to be made by AA if there is case to answer as per the most recent assessment of whether it is MC or GMC Reg 19(1) PCR

AA must asap determine whether case to answer Reg 19(1) PCR 2.140 - 2.143 G

• Notes

Where the AA fails to make a determination within 15WD of receipt of report it must notify the officer of reasons and expedite determination Reg 19(7) PCR

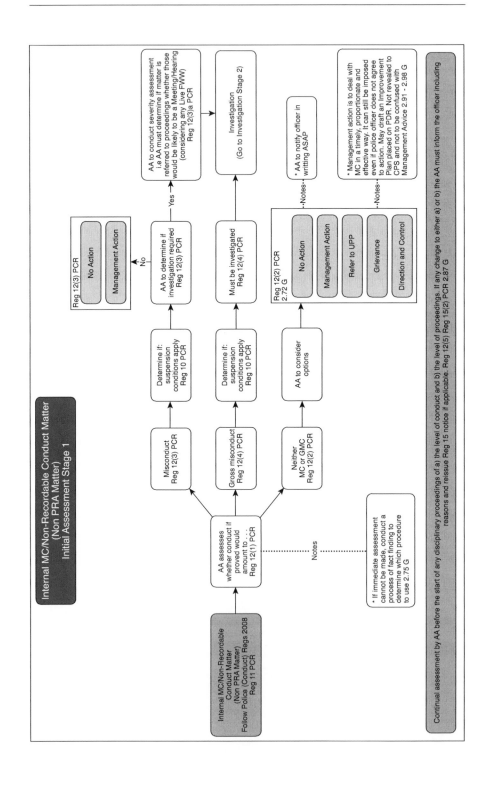

Internal MC/Non-Recordable Conduct Matter (Non PRA Matter) Initial Assessment Stage 1

Internal MC/Non-Recordable Conduct Matter (Non PRA Matter) Follow Police (Conduct) Regs 2008 Reg 11 PCR

AA assesses whether conduct if proved would amount to . . . Reg 12(1) PCR

Notes

* If immediate assessment cannot be made, conduct a process of fact finding to determine which procedure to use 2.75 G

Misconduct Reg 12(3) PCR

Gross misconduct Reg 12(4) PCR

Neither MC or GMC Reg 12(2) PCR

Determine if: suspension conditions apply Reg 10 PCR

Determine if: suspension conditions apply Reg 10 PCR

AA to consider options

AA to determine if investigation required Reg 12(3) PCR

Reg 12(3) PCR
- No Action
- Management Action

Must be investigated Reg 12(4) PCR

Reg 12(2) PCR 2.72 G
- No Action
- Management Action
- Refer to UPP
- Grievance
- Direction and Control

No

Yes

AA to conduct severity assessment i.e AA must determine if matter is referred to proceedings whether those would be likely to be a Meeting/Hearing (considering any Live FWW) Reg 12(3)a PCR

Investigation (Go to Investigation Stage 2)

Notes·····

* AA to notify officer in writing ASAP

·····Notes

* Management action is to deal with MC in a timely, proportionate and effective way. It can still be imposed even if police officer does not agree to action. May draft an Improvement Plan placed on PDR. Not revealed to CPS and not to be confused with Management Advice 2.91 - 2.98 G

Continual assessment by AA before the start of any disciplinary proceedings of a) the level of conduct and b) the level of proceedings. If any change to either a) or b) the AA must inform the officer including reasons and reissue Reg 15 notice if applicable. Reg 12(5) Reg 15(2) PCR 2.87 G

102

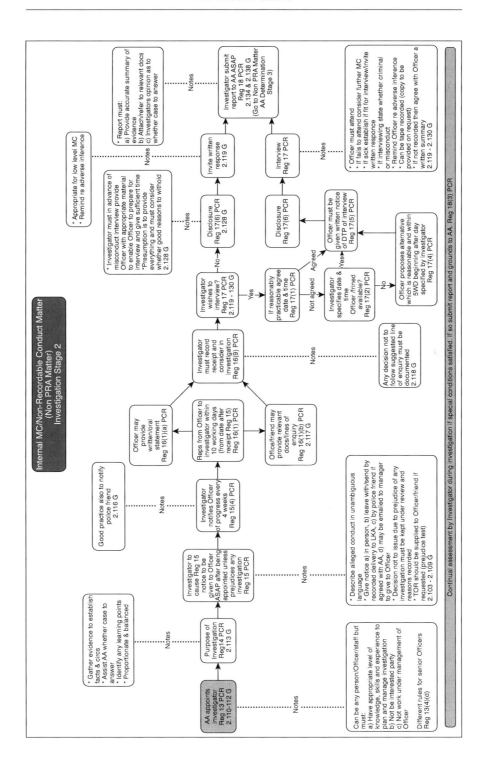

Internal MC/Non-Recordable Conduct Matter
(Non PRA Matter)
Investigation Stage 2

* Gather evidence to establish facts & circs
* Assist AA whether case to answer
* Identify any learning points
* Proportionate & balanced

Notes

AA appoints investigator
Reg 13 PCR
2.110-112 G

Purpose of Investigation
Reg14 PCR
2.113 G

Can be any person/Officer/staff but must:
a) Have appropriate level of knowledge, skills and experience to plan and manage investigation
b) Not be interested party
c) Not work under management of Officer

Different rules for senior Officers
Reg 13(4)(d)

Investigator to cause Reg 15 notice to be given to Officer ASAP after being appointed unless prejudices any investigation
Reg 15 PCR

Notes

* Describe alleged conduct in unambiguous language
* Give notice a) in person, b) leave with/send by recorded delivery to LKA, c) by police friend if agreed with AA, d) may be emailed to manager to give to Officer
* Decision not to issue due to prejudice of any investigation must be kept under review and reasons recorded
* TOR should be supplied to Officer/friend if requested (prejudice test)
2.103 - 2.109 G

Investigator notifies Officer of progress every 4 weeks
Reg 15(4) PCR

Good practice also to notify police friend
2.116 G

Notes

Officer may provide written/oral statement
Reg 16(1)(a) PCR

Reps from Officer to investigator within 10 working days (from date after receipt Reg 15)
Reg 16(1) PCR

Office/friend may provide relevant docs/lines of enquiry
Reg 16(1)(b) PCR
2.117 G

Investigator must record receipt and consider in investigation
Reg 16(9) PCR

Notes

Any decision not to follow suggested line of enquiry must be documented
2.118 G

Investigator wishes to interview?
Reg 17 PCR
2.119 - 130 G

— No →

Disclosure
Reg 17(6) PCR
2.128 G

Notes

* Investigator must in advance of misconduct interview provide Officer with appropriate material to enable Officer to prepare for interview and give sufficient time
* Presumption is to provide everything and must consider whether good reasons to withold
2.128 G

Invite written response
2.119 G

Notes

* Appropriate for low level MC
* Remind re adverse inference

* Report must:
a) Provide accurate summary of evidence
b) Attach/refer to relevant docs
c) Investigators opinion as to whether case to answer

Notes

Investigator submit report to AA ASAP
Reg 18 PCR
2.134 & 2.138 G
(Go to Non PRA Matter AA Determination Stage 3)

— Yes →

If reasonably practicable agree date & time
Reg 17(1) PCR

— Agreed →

Officer must be given written notice of DTP of interview
Reg 17(5) PCR

Disclosure
Reg 17(6) PCR

Interview
Reg 17 PCR

Notes

* Officer must attend
* If fails to attend consider further MC
* If sick establish if fit for interview/invite written response
* If interviewing state whether criminal or misconduct
* Remind Officer re adverse inference
* Can be tape recorded (copy to be provided on request)
* If not recorded then agree with Officer a written summary
2.119 - 130 G

— Not agreed →

Investigator specifies date & time
Officer /frined available?
Reg 17(2) PCR

— Yes →

(to Officer must be given written notice)

— No →

Officer proposes alternative which is reasonable and within 5WD beginning after day specified by investigator
Reg 17(4) PCR

Notes

Continual assessment by Investigator during investigation if special conditions satisfied. If so submit report and grounds to AA. Reg 18(3) PCR

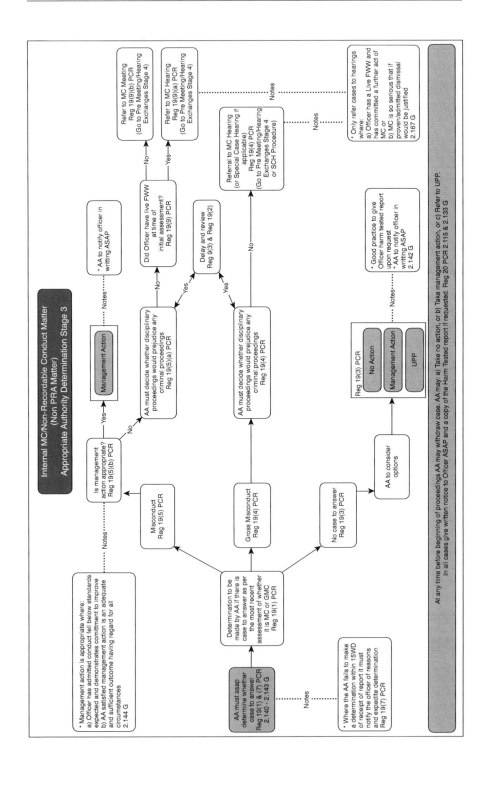

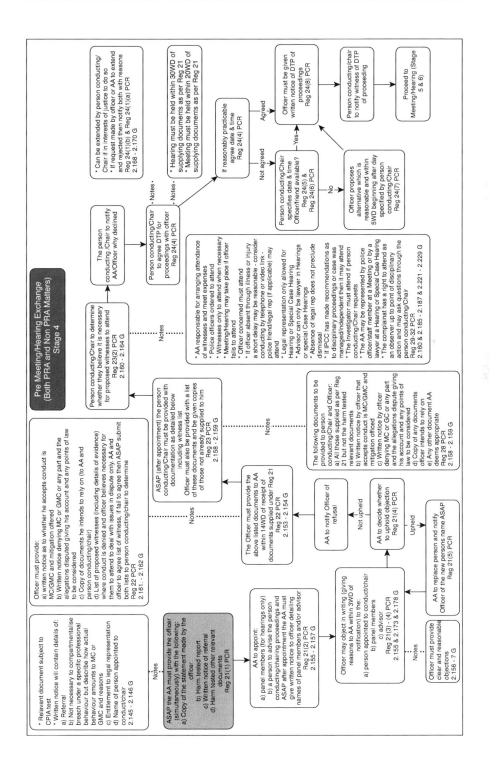

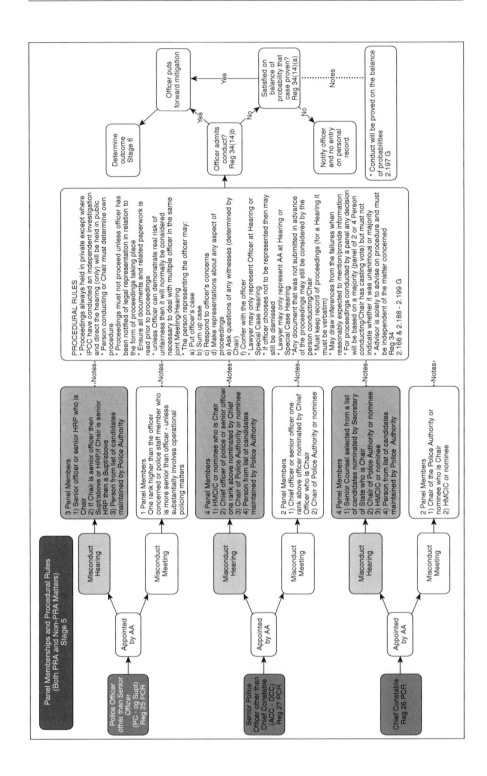

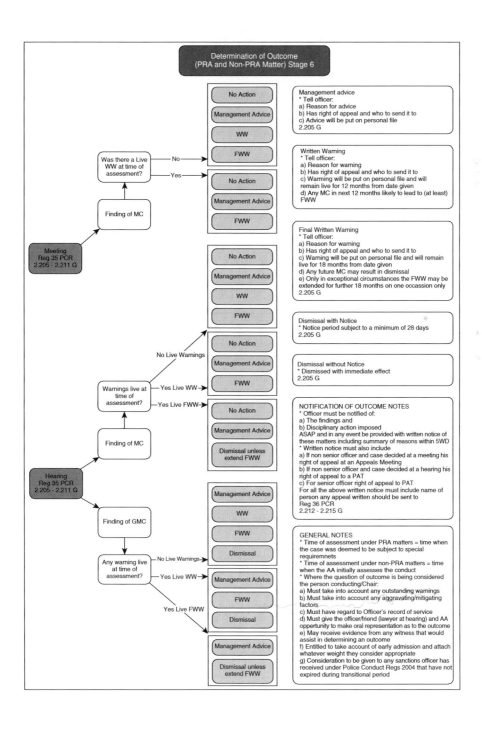

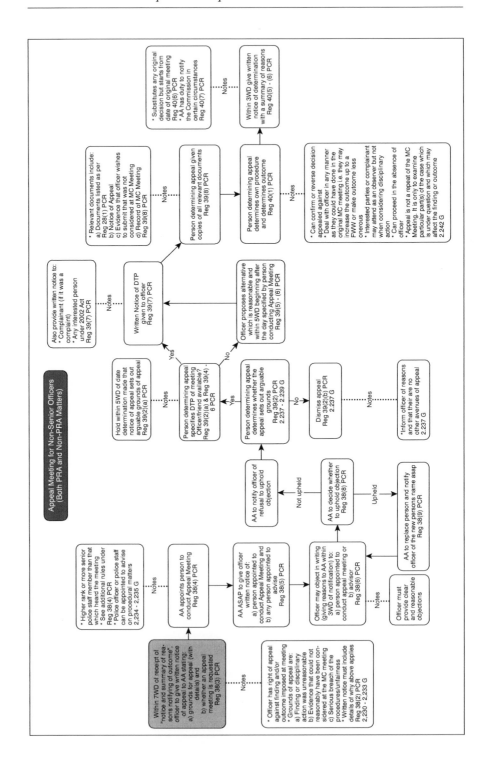

Appeal Meeting for Non-Senior Officers
(Both PRA and Non-PRA Matters)

Within 7WD of receipt of appeal "notice and summary of reasons notifying of outcome" officer to give written notice of appeal to AA stating:
a) grounds for appeal (with details) and
b) whether an appeal meeting is requested
Reg 38(3) PCR

Notes
* Officer has right of appeal against finding and/or outcome imposed at meeting
* Grounds of appeal are:
a) Finding or disciplinary action was unreasonable
b) Evidence that could not reasonably have been considered at the MC meeting
c) Serious breach of the procedures/unfairness
* Written notice must include details of why above applies
Reg 38(2) PCR
2.230 - 2.233 G

AA appoints person to conduct Appeal Meeting
Reg 38(4) PCR

Notes
* Higher rank or more senior police staff member than that which heard the meeting
* See additional rules under Reg 38(4) PCR
* Police officer or police staff can be appointed to advise on procedural matters
2.234 - 2.235 G

AA ASAP to give officer written notice of:
a) person appointed to conduct Appeal Meeting and
b) any person appointed to advise
Reg 38(5) PCR

Officer may object in writing (giving reasons to AA within 3WD of notification) to:
a) person appointed to conduct appeal meeting or
b) advisor
Reg 38(6) PCR

Notes
Officer must provide clear and reasonable objections

AA to decide whether to uphold objection
Reg 38(8) PCR

Upheld → AA to replace person and notify officer of the new persons name asap
Reg 38(9) PCR

Not upheld → AA to notify officer of refusal to uphold objection

Person determining appeal specifies DTP of meeting Officer/friend available?
Reg 39(2)(a) & Reg 39(4) - 6 PCR

Notes
Hold within 5WD of date determination made that notice of appeal sets out arguable grounds of appeal
Reg 39(2)(a) PCR

Person determining appeal determines whether the appeal sets out arguable grounds
Reg 39(2) PCR
2.237 - 2.239 G

Yes → Written Notice of DTP given to officer
Reg 39(7) PCR

No → Dismiss appeal
Reg 39(2)(b) PCR
2.237 G

Notes
*Inform officer of reasons and that their are no other avenues of appeal
2.242 G

Officer proposes alternative which is reasonable and within 5WD beginning after the day specified by person conducting Appeal Meeting
Reg 39(5) - (6) PCR

Also provide written notice to:
* Complainant (if it was a complaint)
* Any interested person under 2002 Act
Reg 39(7) PCR

Notes

Person determining appeal given copies of all relevant documents
Reg 39(8) PCR

* Relevant documents include:
a) Documents listed as per Reg 28(1) PCR
b) Notice of Appeal
c) Evidence that officer wishes to submit that was not considered at MC Meeting
d) Record of MC Meeting
Reg 39(8) PCR

Notes

Person determining appeal determines own procedure and determines outcome
Reg 40(1) PCR

Notes
* Can confirm or reverse decision appealed against
* Deal with officer in any manner as they could have done in the original MC meeting i.e. they may increase the outcome up to a FWW or make outcome less onerous
* Interested parties or complainant may attend as an observer but not when considering disciplinary action
* Can proceed in the absence of officer
* Appeal is not a repeat of the MC Meeting. It is only to examine particular part(s) of the case which is under question and which may affect the finding or outcome
2.242 G

* Substitutes any original decision but starts from date of original meeting
Reg 40(6) PCR
* AA has duty to notify the Commission in certain circumstances
Reg 40(7) PCR

Notes

Within 3WD give written notice of determination with a summary of reasons of determination
Reg 40(5) - (6) PCR

Notes

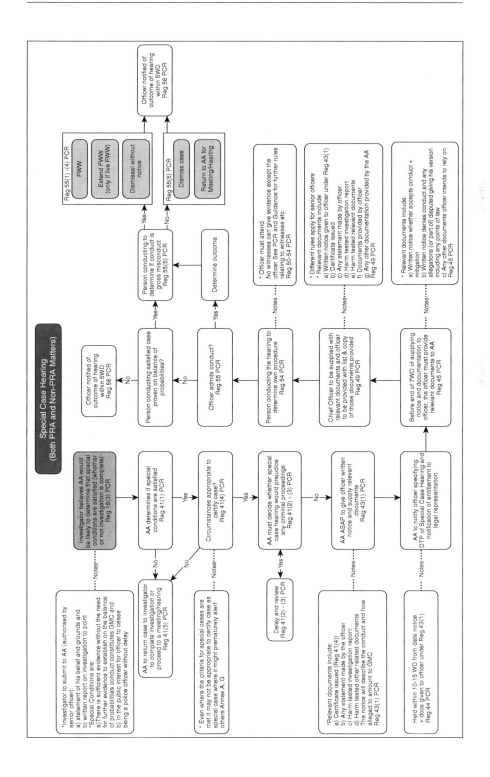

Special Case Hearing
(Both PRA and Non-PRA Matters)

Investigator believes AA would be likely to determine that special conditions are satisfied (whether or not investigation is complete)
Reg 18(3) PCR

Investigator to submit to AA (authorised by senior officer):
a) statement of his belief and grounds and
b) written report on investigation to point
Special Conditions are:
a)There is sufficient evidence without the need for further evidence to establish on the balance of probabilities conduct constitutes GMC and
b) In the public interest for officer to cease being a police officer without delay

AA determines if special conditions are satisfied
Reg 41(1) PCR

No → AA to return case to investigator to complete investigation or proceed to a meeting/hearing
Reg 41(5) PCR

Yes ↓

Circumstances appropriate to certify case?
Reg 41(4) PCR

Even where the criteria for special cases are met it may not be appropriate to certify case as special case where it might prematurely alert others Annex A, G

Yes ↓

AA must decide whether special case hearing would prejudice any criminal proceedings
Reg 41(2) - (3) PCR

No →

Yes → Delay and review
Reg 41(2) - (3) PCR

AA ASAP to give officer written notice and supply relevant documents
Reg 43(1) PCR

Relevant documents include:
a) Certificate issued (Reg 41(4))
b) Any statement made by the officer
c) Harm tested investigation report
d) Harm tested other related documents
The notice will describe the conduct and how alleged to amount to GMC
Reg 43(1) PCR

AA to notify officer specifying DTP of Special Case Hearing and notification of entitlement to legal representation

Held within 10-15 WD from date notice + docs given to officer under Reg 43(1)
Reg 44 PCR

Before end of 7WD of supplying notice and documentation to officer, the officer must provide relevant documents to AA
Reg 45 PCR

Relevant documents include:
a) Written notice whether accepts conduct + mitigation
b) Written notice denies conduct and any allegations (or part of) disputed giving his version including any points of law
c) Any other documents officer intends to rely on
Reg 45 PCR

Chief Officer to be supplied with relevant documents and officer to be provided with list & copy of those documents provided
Reg 49 PCR

* Different rules apply for senior officers
* Relevant documents include:
a) Written notice given to officer under Reg 43(1)
b) Certificate issued
c) Any statement made by officer
d) Harm tested investigation report
e) Harm tested relevant documents
f) Documents provided by officer
g) Any other documentation provided by the AA
Reg 49 PCR

Person conducting the hearing to determine own procedure
Reg 54 PCR

* Officer must attend
No witnesses can give evidence except the officer See PCR and Guidance for further rules relating to witnesses etc:
Reg 50-54 PCR

Officer admits conduct?
Reg 55 PCR

No →

Yes → Determine outcome

Person conducting satisfied case proven on balance of probabilities?

No →

Yes → Person conducting to determine if conduct is gross misconduct
Reg 55(5) PCR

Yes → Reg 55(1) -(4) PCR
- FWW
- Extend FWW (only if live FWW)
- Dismissal without notice

No → Reg 55(5) PCR
- Dismiss case
- Return to AA for Meeting/Hearing

Officer notified of outcome of hearing within 5WD
Reg 56 PCR

Officer notified of outcome of hearing within 5WD
Reg 56 PCR

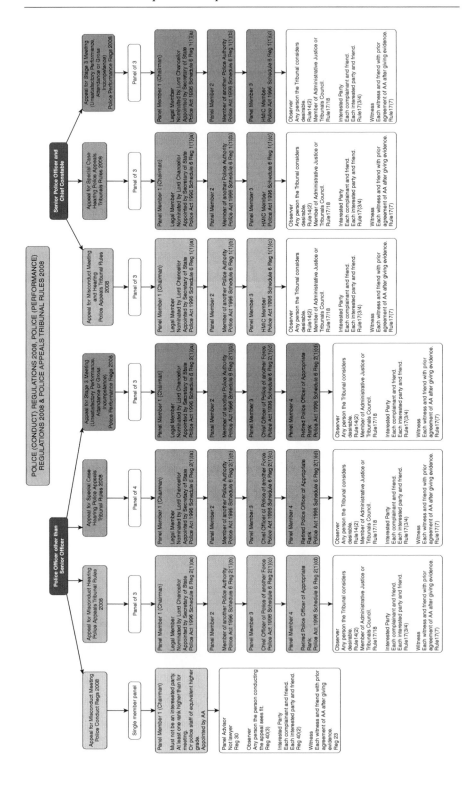

POLICE (CONDUCT) REGULATIONS 2008, POLICE (PERFORMANCE) REGULATIONS 2008 & POLICE APPEALS TRIBUNAL RULES 2008

110

5

THE POLICE (PERFORMANCE) REGULATIONS 2008

A.	**Overview**	5.01	Arrangement of the second-stage	
	Background	5.01	meeting (reg 20)	5.145
	The structure of the Regulations	5.23	Procedure at and after the	
B.	**Preliminaries**	5.34	second-stage meeting	
	Definitions	5.34	(regs 21 and 22)	5.148
	'Police friend'	5.46	Appeals against the finding	
	Procedure at meetings under the		and outcome of the second-stage	
	Regulations	5.49	meeting (regs 23–25)	5.151
	'Nominated persons' (reg 9)	5.54	E. **The Third Stage**	5.155
C.	**The First Stage**	5.57	Arrangement of the third-stage	
	Pre-regulatory action	5.59	meeting (reg 27)	5.160
	Unsatisfactory performance	5.63	Gross incompetence	
	Unsatisfactory attendance	5.71	(regs 28 and 29)	5.161
	Chapter 4 of the Home Office		Procedure on receipt	
	Guidance	5.80	of notice of the third-stage	
	Invoking the Regulations	5.92	meeting (reg 32)	5.167
	The circumstances in which a first-stage		The management of witnesses	
	meeting may be required (reg 12)	5.93	(reg 33)	5.174
	Arrangement of the first-stage		The timing and notice	
	meeting (reg 13)	5.96	of the third-stage meeting	
	Procedure at the first-stage meeting		(reg 34)	5.177
	(reg 14)	5.104	Panel members (regs 30 and 31)	5.178
	Procedure following the first-stage		Procedure at the third-stage	
	meeting (reg 15)	5.112	meeting (regs 35 and 36)	5.188
	Appeals against the finding and		The finding (reg 37)	5.190
	outcome of a first-stage meeting		Outcomes (reg 38)	5.194
	(regs 16–18)	5.123	Assessment of performance	
	The first-stage appeal meeting (reg 18)	5.131	or attendance following	
D.	**The Second Stage**	5.136	third-stage meetings (regs 39–41)	5.201
	The circumstances in which a		F. **Police Appeals**	
	second-stage meeting may be		**Tribunals**	5.208
	required (reg 19)	5.136	G. **Conclusion**	5.209

A. Overview

Background

5.01 The Police (Performance) Regulations 2008 (the 2008 Performance Regulations)[1] are made pursuant to the Secretary of State's powers under ss 50, 51, 84, and 85 of the Police Act 1996. They came into force on 1 December 2008, and do not apply if the unsatisfactory performance or attendance came to the attention of the line manager for the officer concerned before that date.[2] What is meant by 'came to the attention of' will doubtless cause debate in some cases.

5.02 They repeal the previous material Regulations—namely, the Police (Efficiency) Regulations 1999 (the 1999 Efficiency Regulations),[3] which dealt with performance, and the Police (Efficiency) (Amendment) Regulations 2003,[4] which imported attendance issues into the 1999 Efficiency Regulations. They also repealed the Police (Efficiency) (Amendment No 2) Regulations 2003,[5] which simply applied the 1999 Efficiency Regulations to the National Crime Squad (NCS).

5.03 The 1999 Efficiency Regulations (as amended) comprised twenty-two regulations spanning seven-and-a-half standard statutory instrument pages. The 2008 Performance Regulations comprise forty-one regulations and span twenty-nine standard statutory instrument pages.

5.04 Thus, in effect, the 2008 Performance Regulations supplant the 1999 Efficiency Regulations, as amended, and establish procedures for the taking of proceedings against police officers up to the rank of chief superintendent and special constables, in respect of unsatisfactory performance and unsatisfactory attendance.

5.05 The policy driver for the 2008 Performance Regulations was the so-called 'Taylor reform process'. It is intended by those responsible for the reforms that the 2008 Performance Regulations should be viewed as a complementary 'package' with the Police (Conduct) Regulations 2008 (the 2008 Conduct Regulations)[6] to address misconduct and/or performance (to include attendance) in the round. There is an intended change of culture from the threat of misconduct proceedings, with associated sanctions, to one of local monitoring directed at improving individual performance, based on learning. Whether the multiple layers of

---

[1] SI 2008/2862.
[2] Regulation 3(2).
[3] SI 1999/732.
[4] SI 2003/528.
[5] SI 2003/2600.
[6] SI 2008/2864.

appeal within the 2008 Performance Regulations promote this in practice will become clear over time.

As Pt 3 of the Home Office Guidance entitled *Police Officer Misconduct,* **5.06** *Unsatisfactory Performance and Attendance Management Procedures*, makes clear, the 2008 Performance Regulations have been prepared by the Home Office in consultation with the requisite statutory (and other) consultees.[7]

The 2008 Performance Regulations represent an attempt by the Home Office to **5.07** bring the management of unsatisfactory performance and attendance more into line with that which prevails in the non-police sector—that is, to make it more consistent with ordinary employer–employee relations, which are, in many cases, subject to the principles in the Advisory, Conciliation and Arbitration Service (ACAS) Code of Conduct.

Police officers are not employees for the purposes of the Employment Rights Act **5.08** 1996 and do not enjoy most of the rights therein, but are common law 'office holders'. By contrast, most employees—including, of course, police staff—are not subject to regulations, but instead to contracts of employment, many of which incorporate their own code of conduct and ACAS codes.

The 2008 Performance Regulations are to be read subject to chs 3 and 4 of the **5.09** Home Office Guidance, which is issued pursuant to s 87(1) Police Act 1996 and to which 'regard must be had'. The status of such guidance is addressed at 1.66 *et seq*. In general terms, as para (b) of the introduction to the Guidance states, 'whilst it is not necessary to follow its terms exactly in all cases, the guidance should not be departed from without good reason'.

Chapter 3 of the Guidance addresses unsatisfactory performance procedures **5.10** (UPPs). Paragraph 1.3 of the introduction provides further insight into the policy considerations underpinning the 2008 Performance Regulations:

> The underlying principle of the procedures is to provide a fair, open and proportionate method of dealing with performance and attendance issues and to encourage a culture of learning and development for individuals and the organization.

Paragraph 1.5 of the introduction to ch 3 of the Guidance makes clear that: **5.11**

> the primary aim of the procedures is to improve performance and attendance in the police service. It is envisaged that early intervention via management action should achieve the desired effect of improving and maintaining a police officer's performance or attendance to an acceptable level.

---

[7] Namely, the Association of Chief Police Officers (ACPO), the Police Federation of England and Wales (PFEW), the Police Superintendents' Association of England and Wales (PSAEW), the Chief Police Officers' Staff Association (CPOSA), the Association of Police Authorities (APA), Her Majesty's Inspectorate of Constabulary (HMIC), the Independent Police Complaints Commission (IPCC), and the National Policing Improvement Agency (NPIA).

5.12 The Guidance also makes clear that 'the procedures in the performance regulations are largely the same whether applied to unsatisfactory performance or attendance', although the precursor management issues, and Guidance obligations, in attendance cases (covered by ch 4 of the Guidance) are a little different.

5.13 One such precursor management obligation is set out as a 'key principle' in ch 4 of the Guidance—that is, that 'any decision to use the unsatisfactory performance procedures to deal with poor attendance should be taken only after all supportive approaches have been offered in line with force policy'. The 'key principles' also make clear that such policy should be 'well-publicised and accessible to all ', with 'ownership at . . . the chief officer level '. It is doubtful whether, in practice, this 'ownership' objective will be met.

5.14 It can be seen from the foregoing that the intention of the Home Office is to elevate the status and deployment of the 2008 Performance Regulations, and to tackle underperformance and poor attendance, it being well known (perhaps notorious) that the 1999 Efficiency Regulations were rarely invoked by forces. This is underscored by para 1.14 of ch 3 of the Guidance, which states that 'the importance of challenging unsatisfactory performance or attendance of individual police officers in the context of overall unit/force performance and the police officer's personal development should not be underestimated '. It is the experience of the authors that managerial failure to tackle underperformance is a major contributory factor to the high (and increasing) number of employment tribunals claims brought within the police service. Applicant officers routinely seek to bring their own failures, which have been poorly managed, under one of the six strands of discrimination that are a prerequisite to jurisdiction.

5.15 Furthermore, para 2.1 of ch 3 states:

> the performance of individual police officers is a key element in the delivery of a quality policing service. Police officers should know what standard of performance is required of them and be given appropriate support to attain that standard.

5.16 The final key principle in ch 4 is that 'where the UPPs are invoked, the primary aim is to improve attendance. However, one available outcome of the UPPs is termination of service'. In other words, if an officer does not achieve satisfactory attendance, then his or her career is likely to be over.

5.17 Chapter 4 of the Guidance further emphasizes the policy driver of harmonizing police and staff procedures. Paragraph 7 of ch 4 states:

> this guidance covers an attendance management policy as it relates to police officers, including Special Constables . . . while acknowledging the differing employment status of officers and staff, the principles of effective attendance management set out here are generally applicable to both officers and staff, and forces may chose to develop a single policy to cover both officers and staff.

It may be said that the Guidance is inevitably in tension between, on the one **5.18** hand, stressing the need for proportionality, confidentiality, and fairness (perhaps reflecting the aspirations of the various staff associations) and, on the other hand, stressing the importance of challenging underperformance and non-attendance (perhaps reflecting the concern of the Home Office to drive up performance within the police service, where, for example, sickness rates traditionally significantly exceed those in the private sector, and where underperformance by police officers is not always effectively tackled).

Nonetheless, it is clear that the underlying policy driver for these Regulations is to **5.19** tackle underperformance and non-attendance. For example, paras 1.17–1.19 of ch 3 of the Guidance is devoted to reminding management of the need for ongoing performance assessment and review.

Paragraph 1.17 provides that: **5.20**

> Every police officer should have some form of performance appraisal, or what is commonly referred to as a 'performance and development review' (PDR). The PDR should be the principal method by which the police officer's performance and attendance is monitored and assessed. It is the responsibility of the line manager to set objectives for his or her staff, and it is the responsibility of all police officers, with appropriate support from management, to ensure that they both understand and meet those objectives. Objectives set by the line manager should be specific, measurable, achievable, relevant, and time-related (SMART).

Paragraph 1.18 provides that: **5.21**

> The activities and behaviours expected of a police officer in order to achieve his or her objectives should be in accordance with the relevant national framework, which will form the basis of the police officer's role profile.

The line manager should point out any shortfall in performance or attendance **5.22** at the earliest opportunity, and consideration should be given as to whether this has arisen due to inadequate instruction, training, or supervision, or for some other reason. Again, in the experience of the authors, PDRs are often characterized by euphemism rather than constructive, evidence-based, criticism. This practice contributes to the difficulties that forces face in defending discrimination claims in employment tribunals, when the direct evidence of underperformance fails to accord with the more contemporaneous PDR. If para 1.17 of ch 3 of the Guidance were followed, with 'SMART' PDRs, the police service would find itself better able to defend many intrinsically unmeritorious claims.

The structure of the Regulations

The 2008 Performance Regulations set out what is essentially a three-stage proc- **5.23** ess of meetings ('first', 'second', and 'third'). Each meeting enjoys a right of appeal, the first two to a more senior manager. The ultimate point of appeal, from the third-stage meeting, is, as with the 2008 Conduct Regulations, to a police appeals tribunal. As with the Conduct Regulations, chief officer reviews (which were provided for by regs 19–22 of the 1999 Efficiency Regulations) have been abolished.

5.24   The 2008 Performance Regulations are divided into five parts:

- Pt 1, 'Preliminary' (regs 1–4);
- Pt 2, 'General' (regs 5–11);
- Pt 3, 'First stage' (regs 12–18);
- Pt 4, 'Second stage' (regs 19–25); and
- Pt 5, 'Third stage' (regs 26–41).

5.25   A meeting can be convened where the affected officer's line manager considers that his or her performance or attendance is unsatisfactory. The purpose of the meeting is to 'discuss the performance or attendance of the officer concerned'.

5.26   The Regulations do not envisage live witnesses at first or second-stage meetings. At third-stage meetings, witnesses will be heard only if the panel chair deems it to be 'necessary' for the witness to give evidence, in the interests of fairness.

5.27   Following representations by, or on behalf of, the officer concerned, the line manager either determines that his concerns were unfounded or otherwise require no further action, or issues a new instrument called a written improvement notice (WIN), which can be for a specified period of no longer than twelve months.

5.28   At the end of the 'specified' period of the WIN, or the end of the 'validity' period of the WIN (the validity period always being twelve months), the line manager (re)assesses the performance or attendance of the officer concerned for the specified or validity period of the WIN, and thereafter either takes no further action, or, if there has been insufficient improvement within the specified period or a failure to maintain a sufficient improvement during the balance of the validity period, invokes the second/third-stage meeting process, and so the process continues. The key obligation on the officer concerned is to improve sufficiently within the specified period of the WIN, and thereafter to maintain that improvement for the validity period. It will be seen that the WIN is, potentially, an extremely potent management tool.

5.29   The first and second-stage meetings are quasi-administrative, and are intended to reflect civilian-style management procedures. It is at—and only at—the third-stage meeting that there is a more formal three-person panel with the provision for witnesses, evidence, and so forth.

5.30   The maximum outcome at the first-stage meeting is a WIN. The maximum outcome at the second-stage meeting is a final WIN. The panel at the third-stage meeting has the power to dismiss the officer, reduce him in rank, extend the final WIN, issue a final WIN, or redeploy the officer to alternative duties. It is observed that, from 1 December 2008, reduction in rank is an outcome available only under the 2008 Performance Regulations.

Unlike the third (and final) stage 'inefficiency hearing' under the 1999 Efficiency **5.31** Regulations, there is no right to legal representation within the 2008 Performance Regulations, other than at third-stage gross incompetence meetings under the reg 28 'fast track' procedure, or at a police appeals tribunal under the Police Appeals Tribunals Rules 2008 (the PAT Rules).[8]

Regulation 28 provides for a fast-track procedure during which, if the appro- **5.32** priate authority considers that the performance of an officer constitutes gross incompetence, it may refer the officer directly to a third-stage meeting. Gross incompetence is defined in reg 4.

The interrelationship between the 2008 Performance Regulations and the **5.33** associated Home Office Guidance is laid out in Table 5.1.

B. Preliminaries

Definitions

Regulation 4 of the 2008 Performance Regulations identifies and defines con- **5.34** cepts that are new to the 2008 Regulations as compared with the previous 1999 regime. As is to be expected, in many respects, the new language reflects the 'civilianization' of the intended procedures. Certain concepts merit specific reference.

Gross incompetence 'and cognate expressions' is relevant to the reg 28 procedure, **5.35** and is defined as 'a serious inability or failure of a police officer to perform the duties of the role or rank he is currently undertaking to a satisfactory standard, to the extent that dismissal would be justified'.[9] The officer's attendance record is expressly precluded from being taken into account when considering gross incompetence.

The 2008 Performance Regulations (in common with the 2008 Conduct **5.36** Regulations) introduce the concept of the 'human resources professional' (HRP). An HRP is simply a police officer or police staff member who has specific responsibility for personnel matters relating to police officers. The HRP has an important role in the Performance Regulations in terms of advising line managers at meetings and, ultimately, in sitting on the panels for third-stage meetings.

Another important new concept is that of the 'interested party'—that is, someone **5.37** whose involvement in any of the roles delineated under the 2008 Performance

---

[8] SI 2008/2863. The police appeals tribunal is addressed in Chapter 11.
[9] See reg 4, 'Interpretation and delegation'.

Table 5.1 A summary of the Police (Performance) Regulations 2008

PPR 2008	Heading of regulation	Comment	Cross-reference: Home Office Guidance (ch 3)
Part 1: Preliminary			
1	*Citation, commencement and extent*	In force 1 December 2008	
2	*Application*	Regulations apply only to members of police forces of the rank of chief superintendent or below, and do not apply to probationers	*Scope* 1.8
3	*Revocation and transitional provisions*	Revokes the Police (Efficiency) Regulations 1999, SI 1999/732, and the two further sets of regulations amending them	
		Will still apply to unsatisfactory performance brought to line manager's attention before 1 December 2008	
4	*Interpretation and delegation*	Definitions of key terms, including 'unsatisfactory performance' as 'an ability or failure of a police officer to perform the duties of the role or rank he is currently undertaking to a satisfactory standard or level'	
		Appropriate authority (chief officer of the police force) can delegate any functions to member of at least the rank of chief inspector or someone of a similar level of seniority	
Part 2: General			
5	*Police friend*	Role of the police friend	*Principles* 1.15
		Police officers (other than special constables) can seek advice from their staff association, and all police officers can be advised and represented by their police friend in accordance with the principles described in the introduction section of the Home Office Guidance	
6	*Legal representation*	Right to legal representation only at third-stage meetings where the procedure has been initiated at this stage (ie gross incompetence cases)	*Principles* 1.15

(Continued)

No.	Provision	Description	Cross-reference	Para.
7	*Provision of notices or documents*	Manner in which a written notice or document is to be given to or supplied to a police officer		
8	*Procedure at meetings under these Regulations*	General provision about the procedure for meetings, including: possibility of proceeding in absentia, the role of the officer's representative, that the panel chair determines whether any question should or should not be put to a witness, the applicable standard of proof being the balance of probabilities, and the panel's right to consider any document regardless of prior disclosure to panel or officer	*Principles*	1.16
9	*Nominated person*	Senior manager may appoint another person to carry out the functions of a line manager or a second line manager under the Regulations		
10	*References to certain periods*	Appropriate authority can extend certain time limits specified in the Regulations if it is 'appropriate' to do so Such a period cannot be extended to a total length exceeding 12 months unless there are 'exceptional circumstances' Time periods (eg three working days) this will begin on the first working day following the day on which the particular action has taken place	*Introduction*	1.4
11	*Suspension of certain periods*	Certain periods specified in the Regulations shall not include any 'career break' taken by the officer	*The formal UPP process: improvement notice extensions and suspensions*	4.10

Part 3: First Stage

No.	Provision	Description	Cross-reference	Para.
12	*Circumstances in which a first stage meeting may be required*	Meeting required when the line manager considers that the performance or attendance of an officer is unsatisfactory A single complaint from a member of the public about a police officer's performance will not usually trigger the UPPs, which are designed to deal with a pattern of unsatisfactory performance (except where there is a single incident of gross incompetence)	*Sources of information* *Management action* *Performance issues: framework of action* *Attendance issues: action under the Police (Performance) Regulations*	1.21 1.28 2.4 3.20

Table 5.1 Cont.

PPR 2008	Heading of regulation	Comment	Cross-reference: Home Office Guidance (ch 3)	
13	*Arrangement of first stage meeting*	Requirements for written notice of meeting. Notice will set out, inter alia, the procedures to be followed and a summary of reasons why performance is considered unsatisfactory	*The first stage: preparation and purpose*	5.1
14	*Procedure at first stage meeting*	Provisions regarding the required and permitted attendance at the meeting and the procedure to be followed (concerns explained by line manager, officer given opportunity to respond, communication of findings)	*At the first stage meeting*	5.9
15	*Procedure following first stage meeting*	Requirements for written record of meeting and, if necessary, a written improvement notice (including explanation of appeal procedure). Officer entitled to submit written comments on any written record within seven working days after record received by him, provided that he has not exercised right to appeal (period can be extended on application if 'appropriate to do so')	*At the first stage meeting*	5.14
16	*Appeal against the finding and outcome of a first stage meeting*	Sets out: subject matter for appeal; grounds of appeal; requirement for written notice of appeal within seven working days of receipt of relevant documents (can be extended by second line manager if 'appropriate'); permitted grounds of appeal (exhaustive); required contents of notice of appeal; appeal hearing to take place within seven working days after receipt of notice of appeal or whenever 'necessary or expedient'	*First stage appeals* / *The first stage: appeal grounds*	5.26 / 5.28
17	*Arrangement of first stage appeal meeting*	Officer to receive written notice of the date of the meeting and the procedures to be followed, and informing him of his rights to receive advice from a staff association representative, and to be accompanied and represented by a police friend		5.32

No.	Entry	Subheading	Description	Ref.
18	*Procedure at first stage appeal meeting*	*At the first stage appeal meeting*	Provisions regarding the required and permitted attendance at the meeting and the procedure to be followed	5.33
			Finding may then be confirmed or reversed, and/or terms of the written notice may be confirmed or varied	
			The officer shall receive written notice of the decision and a written summary of the reasons 'as soon as practicable' after the meeting, and at least before the end of three working days	

Part 4: Second Stage

No.	Entry	Subheading	Description	Ref.
19	*Circumstances in which a second stage meeting may be required*	*Assessment of performance or attendance*	The officer will be required to attend a second meeting if, during specified periods, he has failed to improve his performance or attendance, or if he has failed to maintain such an improvement	5.19
		The second stage: preparation and purpose	Must concern unsatisfactory performance or attendance that is similar to, or connected with, unsatisfactory performance or attendance referred to in the written improvement notice	6.1
20	*Arrangement of second stage meeting*	*The second stage: preparation and purpose*	Officer to receive written notice of meeting and requirement on him to attend. Notice will set out, inter alia, the procedures to be followed and a summary of reasons why performance is considered unsatisfactory	6.1
21	*Procedure at second stage meeting*	*At the second stage meeting*	Provisions regarding the required and permitted attendance at the meeting, and the procedure to be followed (concerns explained by line manager, officer given opportunity to respond, communication of findings, and terms of required improvement in performance)	6.10
22	*Procedure following second stage meeting*	*Procedure following second stage meeting*	Requirements for written record of meeting and, if necessary, a final written improvement notice, including explanation of appeal procedure	6.15
			Officer entitled to submit written comments on any written record within seven working days after record received by him, provided that he has not exercised right to appeal (period can be extended on application if 'appropriate to do so')	

(Continued)

Table 5.1 Cont.

PPR 2008	Heading of regulation	Comment	Cross-reference: Home Office Guidance (ch 3)
23	*Appeal against the finding and outcome of a second stage meeting*	Sets out: subject matter for appeal; grounds of appeal; requirement of written notice of appeal within seven working days of receipt of relevant documents (can be extended if senior manger considers it 'appropriate'); permitted grounds of appeal (exhaustive); required contents of notice of appeal; second-stage appeal meeting to take place within seven working days after receipt of notice of appeal or whenever 'necessary or expedient'	*Second stage appeal* 6.26 *Appeal grounds* 6.28
24	*Arrangement of second stage appeal meeting*	Officer to receive written notice of the date of the meeting, the procedures to be followed, and the attendees, and informing him of his rights to receive advice from a staff association representative, and to be accompanied and represented by a police friend	
25	*Procedure at second stage appeal meeting*	Provisions regarding the required and permitted attendance at the meeting and the procedure to be followed (officer entitled to make representations personally and/or by police friend)	*At the second stage* 6.33 *appeal meeting*
		Possible findings include: conclusion that officer should not have been required to attend second-stage meeting; reversal or confirmation of finding made at second-stage meeting and/or confirmation or variation of terms of the written notice	
		Officer to receive written notice of decision, with summary of reasons	
Part 5: Third Stage			
26	*Assessment following second stage meeting*	Officer required to attend a third meeting following a second-stage meeting if, during specified periods, he has failed to improve his performance or attendance, or if he has failed to maintain such an improvement	*Assessment of* 6.20 *performance or attendance*
		Meeting must concern unsatisfactory performance or attendance that is similar to, or connected with, that referred to in the final written improvement notice	*The third stage:* 7.1 *preparation and purpose*

27	*Arrangement of a third stage meeting*	Officer to receive written notice of meeting and requirement on him to attend before a panel appointed by the appropriate authority	*The third stage: preparation and purpose*	7.1
		Notice will set out, inter alia, the procedures to be followed, a summary of reasons why the performance is considered unsatisfactory, the possible outcomes of the meeting, the possible attendees, and the officer's right to advice from a representative of his staff association, and to be accompanied by a police friend and to legal representation		
28	*Circumstances in which a third stage meeting may be required without a prior first or second stage meeting*	Even where an officer has not attended a first or second-stage meeting, he may be required to attend a third stage when the appropriate authority considers that performance constitutes 'gross incompetence'	*Initiation of procedures at stage three*	4.13
			Gross incompetence third stage meetings	7.8
29	*Arrangement of a third stage meeting without a prior first or second stage meeting*	Written notice should set out, inter alia, procedures to be followed, reasons why performance constitutes 'gross incompetence', possible outcomes of the meeting, possible attendees, the officer's right to advice from a representative of a staff association, and his rights to legal representation and to be accompanied by a police friend	*Initiation of procedures at stage three*	4.13
			Gross incompetence third stage meetings	7.8
30	*Appointment of panel members*	Meeting is conducted by a panel of three persons appointed by the chief officer of police in accordance with this regulation	*Panel membership and procedure*	7.16
		At least one panel member must be a police officer and one must be a human resources professional		
31	*Right of officer concerned to object to panel members*	Objection must be made in writing to the appropriate authority before the end of three working days of notification of constitution of panel	*Objection to panel members*	7.23

(Continued)

Table 5.1 Cont.

PPR 2008	Heading of regulation	Comment	Cross-reference: Home Office Guidance (ch 3)
32	*Procedure on receipt of notice of third stage meeting*	Within 14 days of receipt of written notice of meeting (unless extended), the officer shall provide written notice of whether he accepts that his performance, etc, was unsatisfactory or that he was grossly incompetent, and include any submissions in mitigation	*Procedure on receipt of notice of third stage meeting*	7.34
		Where he does not accept allegations or disputes them in part, he must provide written notice of the matter that he disputes and any arguments on points of law that he wishes to be put to the panel	
		Within three days after that, he must provide a list of witnesses	
33	*Witnesses*	Panel chair has ultimate control over witnesses to be called	*Witnesses and evidence*	7.36
34	*Timing and notice of third stage meeting*	Meeting shall take place within 30 working days after written notice of meeting (may be extended if panel chair 'considers that it would be in the interests of fairness to do so')	*Meeting dates and timeframes*	7.31
		Written notice of the date of the meeting must be given to the officer Officer may attend by video link if he has informed the panel chair in advance and the chair considers that there are reasonable grounds for doing so	
35	*Postponement and adjournment of a third stage meeting*	May adjourn meeting if panel chair considers it 'necessary or expedient'	*Postponement and adjournment of a third stage meeting*	7.50
36	*Procedure at a third stage meeting*	Sets out procedure for meeting, which is ultimately determined by the panel	*At the third stage meeting*	7.43

37	*Finding*	Makes provision for the decision of the panel, which must set out the panel's finding (should be based on a simple majority), its reasons, and any outcome ordered under reg 38	7.44
38	*Outcomes*	Finding of unsatisfactory performance or attendance under reg 26(2) or (4): dismissal with 28 days' notice; reduction in rank with immediate effect; extension of final written improvement notice (only in exceptional circumstances); redeployment Finding of gross incompetence under reg 28: dismissal with immediate effect; reduction in rank with immediate effect; issue of a final written improvement notice; redeployment Finding of unsatisfactory performance under reg 28: issue of a written importance notice	
39	*Assessment of performance or attendance following third stage meeting*	Where a written improvement notice has been issued under reg 38, performance will be assessed as if officer had received a written improvement notice under reg 15	7.63
40	*Assessment of improvement notices issued at the third stage*	Where a final written improvement notice has been issued/extended under reg 38 and there has not been sufficient improvement or maintenance thereof, officer required to attend another third-stage meeting	7.55
41	*Assessment of final and extended-final improvement notices issued at third stage*	Where an officer is required to attend another third-stage meeting, it shall be conducted by the same panel as the initial third-stage meeting An extension of the final written improvement notice is not available as a penalty in these circumstances	

Regulations 'could reasonably give rise to a concern as to whether he could act impartially'.

5.38 Whilst superficially this may appear to create a rod for management's back, the well-established principles as to judicial bias[10] must, to some extent, be qualified by the regulatory context. As will be seen, the 2008 Performance Regulations expressly provide that the affected officer's line manager (and other local decision makers) are an intrinsic part of the process. The mere fact that the line manager knows the affected officer will thus not ordinarily disqualify him if he is merely acting as such. As to this, similar principles to the chief officer acting as such in respect of chief officer reviews under the 2004 Conduct Regulations must apply (see 11.16–11.20).

5.39 In practice, it is contended that the line manager (or other relevant decision maker) will only be disqualified if it can be shown that there is either: (i) some 'personal' reason to justify the appearance of bias; or (ii) knowledge that the line manager is party to knowledge of matters of personal history about the affected officer that could be said to prejudice him in the approach to the actual evidence strictly forming part of the procedure. This will always be a matter of fact and degree. The threshold for this to be established may be affected by considerations of proportionality and the outcomes available at the particular stage.

5.40 'Line manager' unsurprisingly means the police officer or police staff member who has immediate supervisory responsibility for the officer concerned. Perhaps of greater interest is the explicit recognition given to non-police officers for management responsibility of the performance and attendance of officers. This is further evidence of the incremental movement towards 'civilianization' of the process.

5.41 A 'second line manager' is a person senior in rank to the first line manager, if a police officer, and someone who has supervisory responsibility for the line manager, if a staff member. A second line manager must be appointed by the appropriate authority for the purposes of these regulations.

5.42 A 'senior manager' is the supervisor of the second line manager, or a police officer or staff member nominated by the appropriate authority of at least the same rank or equivalent as the second line manager.

---

[10] The test for bias was set out by the House of Lords in *Porter v Magill* [2002] 2 AC 357, especially *per* Lord Hope at [102]–[103]. More recently, the Master of the Rolls restated the relevant law at [4]–[7] of *Howell and ors v Millais and ors* [2007] EWCA Civ 720. The relevant question is whether 'all the circumstances' of the case would 'lead a fair-minded and informed observer to conclude that there was a real possibility . . . that the tribunal was biased'. At [5], the Master of the Rolls summarized the principles that had been down by the Court of Appeal in *AWG Group v Morrison* [2006] EWCA Civ 6. Note, in particular, point (vi): 'In most cases, the answer, one way or the other will be obvious. But if in any case there is real ground for doubt, that doubt should be resolved in favour of recusal.'

Importantly, unsatisfactory performance or attendance is defined as 'an inability **5.43** or failure of a police officer to perform the duties of the role or rank he is currently undertaking to a satisfactory standard or level'. It is unclear what the difference is between 'standard' and 'level'. 'Inability' suggests 'cannot'; 'failure' suggests 'will not'. The distinction between 'role' and 'rank' is self-evident, and feeds into the later availability of an outcome at the third-stage meeting of redeployment or reduction in rank of the unsatisfactorily performing officer.

As with the 2008 Conduct Regulations, 'police staff member' means an employee **5.44** of a police authority who is under the direction and control of a chief officer of police.

Regulation 4(3) permits the appropriate authority to delegate any of its functions **5.45** under the Regulations to an officer of the rank of chief inspector or above, or a staff member of at least equivalent seniority in the opinion of the appropriate authority. Plainly, chief officers will wish to select their delegates with some care to promote effective implementation of the Regulations. Effectiveness includes maintaining the confidence of those subject to the Regulations.

'Police friend'

Regulation 5 provides that the officer concerned is entitled to choose a police **5.46** officer, police staff member, or person nominated by his staff association who is not otherwise involved to act as his 'police friend'. Regulation 5(3) entitles the police friend to perform his various functions within a reasonable amount of his duty time.

The police friend has the rights identified in reg 5(2)—that is, to advise the officer **5.47** concerned throughout, to represent him at meetings, to make representations to the appropriate authority concerning any aspect of the Regulations, and to accompany the officer concerned to any meeting that he is required to attend under the Regulations.

Other than where the officer concerned has the right to be legally represented and **5.48** so chooses (which right exists only for 'gross incompetence' third-stage meetings), he may only be represented at meetings under these Regulations by a police friend. Accordingly, the police friend is a significant player in these Regulations.

Procedure at meetings under the Regulations

Even if an officer chooses not to attend a meeting under the Regulations, or **5.49** appears at a third-stage meeting 'by video link or other means', he may nonetheless still be represented at the meeting by his police friend or (in gross incompetence cases only) relevant lawyer. Furthermore, by reg 8(2), meetings may be proceeded with and concluded in the absence of the officer concerned, whether or not he is represented.

5.50 Regulation 8(3) expressly identifies the entitlement of the police friend or lawyer representing the officer concerned to:

(a) address the meeting in order to do any or all of the following—
  (i) put the case of the officer concerned;
  (ii) sum up that case;
  (iii) respond on behalf of the officer concerned to any view expressed at the meeting;
  (iv) make representations concerning any aspect of proceedings under these Regulations; and
  (v) in the case of a third stage meeting only, subject to paragraph (7), ask questions of any witnesses;

[. . .]

5.51 Regulation 8(3)(b) explicitly provides that police friends or relevant lawyers may 'confer with the officer concerned'. This is not the only explicit provision within the Regulations that one might have thought was too obvious to require: for another example, the police friend or relevant lawyer 'may not answer any questions asked of the officer concerned during a meeting' (reg 8(6)).

5.52 The standard of proof for a finding of unsatisfactory performance or attendance, or gross incompetence, is the balance of probabilities (reg 8(8)(a)), although the officer concerned is entitled to consent to a finding of unsatisfactory performance, etc.[11] The meaning of the standard of proof is considered more extensively in relation to the 2008 Conduct Regulations at 8.105–8.108. Stated shortly, there is a single test that applies, but the inherent probability of an event remains a relevant consideration.

5.53 Documents that have not been supplied to the officer concerned or the panel pursuant to the Regulations may nonetheless be considered at a meeting (reg 8(9)), presumably subject to the usual application of natural justice.

'Nominated persons' (reg 9)

5.54 Cognisant perhaps of the radical nature of the proposition that a police sergeant conducts a first-stage meeting, and a police inspector conducts a second-stage meeting, reg 9 provides for the option of a more senior-ranking alternative. This may be directed, in part, at giving forces time to train their lower management to implement the 2008 Performance Regulations.

5.55 Regulation 9(1) provides that a senior manager may appoint a 'nominated person' to carry out any of the functions of the line manager or second line manager under the Regulations. The nominated person, whether officer or staff, must

---

[11] See also para 1.16 of Pt 3 of the Home Office Guidance.

be—in the opinion of the appropriate authority, which may presumably delegate that particular function itself to a chief inspector—of at least equivalent, if not greater, rank than the person whose functions he is carrying out.

Naturally, the nominated person can only act at the level of management that he **5.56** comes in to replace, and not thereafter at a higher level again. In other words, the progression of management from first line manager (or nominated person), then second line management (or more senior nominated person), is preserved.

C. The First Stage

It is convenient to examine the first-stage process set out in Pt 3 of the Regu-   **5.57** lations, including the appeal process, in some detail, because the second-stage process largely repeats the first stage.

The starting point is not, in fact, reg 1, which identifies the circumstances in   **5.58** which a first-stage meeting may be required; it is earlier, and to be found within ch 3 of the Home Office Guidance.

Pre-regulatory action

It is clear from chs 3 (and, indeed, 4) of the Guidance that before the 2008   **5.59** Performance Regulations are invoked, managers (as the noun implies) should first have actually *managed* an officer's performance or attendance. It is anticipated that this requirement will be unknown to many police supervisors.

Paragraph 1.24 of ch 3 of the Guidance reminds management that they may be   **5.60** 'alerted to unsatisfactory performance or attendance on the part of one of their police officers as a result of information from a member of the public. The information from a member of the public may take the form of a formal complaint', and that such cases 'must be dealt with in accordance with the established procedures for the handling of complaints'.

Furthermore, management is reminded, by para 1.25 of ch 3, that 'the outcome   **5.61** of an investigation into a complaint alleging misconduct' may be 'that an issue of unsatisfactory performance or attendance' is identified. In such cases:

> the outcome of the investigation may be that the appropriate authority will determine that there is no case to answer in respect of misconduct or gross misconduct but it may be appropriate to take action under the UPPs in order that the police officer may learn and improve his or her performance or attendance.

This is a vivid example of the theme rehearsed in the overview to this chapter (see   **5.62** 5.05 above) that the Home Office intends the Conduct and Performance Regulations to be viewed as a complementary package.

Unsatisfactory performance

5.63 The Home Office Guidance specifically outlines the necessary precursory management steps to invoking the Regulations for unsatisfactory performance. Paragraph 1.26 of ch 3 sets out the important point of principle that:

> A single complaint from a member of the public about a police officer's performance will not normally trigger the UPPs, which are designed to deal with a 'pattern' of unsatisfactory performance (except where there is a single incident of gross incompetence). However, where the complaint adds to existing indications of unsatisfactory performance, it may be appropriate to initiate the UPPs or, if the police officer is already subject to these, to continue to the next stage of the process.

5.64 It will be noted that, other than for a single incident of gross incompetence, the Regulations are designed to deal with a 'pattern' of unsatisfactory performance.

5.65 Paragraph 1.28 of ch 3 states that 'managers are expected to deal with unsatisfactory performance or attendance issues in the light of their knowledge of the individual and the circumstances giving rise to these concerns', and para 1.29 then sets out what it says are 'some generally well understood principles which should apply in such circumstances'. These include the following important obligations of management:

(a) the line manager must discuss any shortcoming (s) or concern (s) with the individual at the earliest possible opportunity. It would be quite wrong for the line manager to accumulate a list of concerns about the performance or attendance of an individual and delay telling him or her about them until the occasion of the police officer's annual or mid-term PDR meetings;

(b) the reason for dissatisfaction must be made clear to the individual as soon as possible and there must be a factual basis for discussing the issues i.e. the discussion must relate to specific incidents or omissions that have occurred;

(c) line managers should seek to establish whether there are any underlying reasons for the unsatisfactory performance or attendance. For example, in the context of performance, a failure to perform a task correctly may be because the individual was never told how to do it or was affected by personal circumstances. In that case it may be appropriate for the line manager to arrange further instruction or guidance;

(d) consideration should be given as to whether there is any health or welfare issue that is or may be affecting performance or attendance. If a police officer has or may have a disability within the scope of the Disability Discrimination Act this in particular needs to be taken fully into account and the requirements of that legislation complied with;

[...]

(g) depending on the circumstances, it may be appropriate to indicate to the police officer that if there is no, or insufficient, improvement, then the matter will be dealt with under the UPPs;

(h) line managers are expected to gather relevant evidence and keep a contemporaneous note of interactions with the police officer;

[...]

Paragraph 1.30 of ch 3 covers the position 'when a line manager first becomes   **5.66**
aware of some unsatisfactory aspect(s) of the police officer's performance or
attendance and is dealing with the issue as an integral part of normal line management responsibilities'. In other words, subject to gross incompetence under
reg 28, the above steps should be worked through by the line manager before the
Regulations are invoked.

The importance of line managers understanding and appreciating their pre-   **5.67**
regulatory management responsibilities cannot be overstated. A failure to do so is
likely to render the use of the Regulations thereafter more difficult and subject
to interminable (and possibly successful) challenge on grounds including
departure from the Guidance, management unfairness, that the officer was not
given the support to which he was entitled, and so forth. Such complaints may
endure through to the police appeals tribunal. The objective of promoting efficient and informed local resolution would thereby be defeated.

Accordingly, the advice contained in para 1.31 of ch 3 of the Guidance is of   **5.68**
fundamental evidential and procedural importance:

> Management action taken as a result of identifying unsatisfactory performance
> or attendance should be put on record which may be the police officer's PDR.
> In particular, the line manager should record the nature of the performance or
> attendance issue; the advice given and steps taken to address the problems identified.
> Placing matters on record is important to ensure continuity in circumstances
> where one or more members of the management chain may move on to other duties
> or the police officer concerned moves to new duties. It is also important to put on
> record when improvement has been made in his or her performance or attendance.

Paragraph 1.32 of ch 3 expresses the ambition that 'as a result of [such] management   **5.69**
action, performance or attendance will improve and continue to an acceptable
level', but para 1.33 then confirms that 'where there is no improvement, insufficient
improvement, or the improvement is not sustained over a reasonable period of time
. . . it will then be appropriate to use the UPPs'—that is, to proceed to reg 12.

Under the subheading 'Framework for action', para 2.4 of ch 3 states that there   **5.70**
is 'no single formula for determining the point at which a concern about a police
officer's performance should lead to formal procedures under the (performance
regulations) being taken' and the familiar formula that 'each case must be considered on its merits'. The Guidance does, however, then give the following guidance
by way of 'emphasis':

- the intention of performance management including formal action under the
  Police (Performance) Regulations is to improve performance;
- occasional lapses below acceptable standards should be dealt with in the course of
  normal management activity and should not involve the application of the UPPs,
  which are designed to cover either repeated failures to meet such standards or
  more serious cases of unsatisfactory performance;

- managers should be able to demonstrate that they have considered whether management action is appropriate before using the UPPs.

Unsatisfactory attendance

5.71   As to the precursory management steps that must be taken before invoking the 2008 Performance Regulations in respect of unsatisfactory attendance, Pt 3 of ch 3 again provides significant guidance.

5.72   Paragraph 3.1 of ch 3 makes clear that this part of the Guidance 'should be read in conjunction with the guidance on developing attendance management policies (see chapter 4)', and that 'all forces are required to have an attendance management policy in place. Failure to do so or to adhere to the terms of that policy will be taken into account under these procedures'. This again represents a challenge for forces and management therein, the failure to respond to which will be prayed in aid by officers made the subject of the Regulations.

5.73   The Guidance adds (reassuring sounding) words, reasserting the obligation upon management 'as far as is reasonably practicable' to provide 'a healthy and safe working environment for its police officers', but then proceeds to emphasize that 'the key objective of attendance management policies within forces and the appropriate use of the [2008 Performance Regulations] insofar as they relate to managing unsatisfactory attendance, is to encourage an attendance culture within forces'.

5.74   This is reinforced with guidance declaring that:

> managing sickness absence is vitally important both in terms of demonstrating a supportive attitude towards police officers and for the efficiency of the organisation. Managing attendance is about creating a culture where all parties take ownership of the policy and act reasonably in the operation of the scheme with managers being proactive in managing sickness.

5.75   Thereafter the 'primary aim' of the procedures is restated as being 'to improve attendance in the police service', which it is envisaged will, in most cases, be achieved by 'supportive action'. It is acknowledged that there 'may however be cases where it will be appropriate for managers to take formal action under the Performance Regulations'. Where attendance does not improve to acceptable levels or where there is no realistic prospect of a return to work in a reasonable time frame, then termination of service may be appropriate.

5.76   As with unsatisfactory performance, under the heading 'Framework for action', the Guidance provides that:

> Attendance management in the police service is intended to be a positive and supportive process to improve attendance. In all cases, the starting point is supportive action. Except where a police officer fails to co-operate, appropriate supportive action must be taken before formal action is taken under the Performance Regulations
> . . .

The practical consequence is the need for management first to take 'supportive **5.77** action' prior to instituting the regulatory procedures. Indeed, it is advanced by the Guidance as a necessary precondition of the implementation of the regulatory procedures. An affected officer has a legitimate expectation that the procedures in chs 3 and 4 of the Guidance will be followed. Less obvious is what, in any individual case, will discharge the obligation to provide supportive action.

As with unsatisfactory performance, the Guidance concludes (at para 3.11 of **5.78** ch 3) that 'There is no single formula for determining the point at which concern about a police officer's attendance should lead to formal procedures under the Performance Regulations being invoked. Each case must be considered on its merits'. It then gives the following guidance by way of 'emphasis':

- The intention of attendance management including formal action under the Police (Performance) Regulations is to improve attendance.
- Where police officers are injured or ill they should be treated fairly and compassionately.
- Managers should be able to demonstrate that they have acted reasonably in all actions taken at all stages of the attendance management process, including any action under the Police (Performance) Regulations.

Further detailed guidance is given in paras 3.12–3.23 of ch 3, including manage- **5.79** ment's obligation to monitor an officer's attendance, the role of the force's occupational health service, and the statutory obligations under the Disability Discrimination Act 1995 (as amended).

Chapter 4 of the Home Office Guidance

Chapter 4 of the Home Office Guidance is dedicated entirely to addressing attend- **5.80** ance management. It is intended to 'highlight the key principles that should guide police forces in developing good attendance management policies and practices'. The introduction identifies:

> a clear expectation that forces will have in place an attendance policy that meets the standards set out in this guidance. Failure to have or to follow such a policy could be taken into account when decisions are being made, or appeals decided under the UPPs.

As to the definition of 'unsatisfactory attendance' as 'the inability or failure **5.81** of a police officer to perform the duties of the role or rank he is currently undertaking to a satisfactory standard or level', ch 4 confirms that 'in this context [attendance management], this would be due to absence during agreed hours of duty', but goes on to say that, in the case of lateness, 'there will be a need to establish the reasons for the behaviour. Consideration should be given to whether the matter is properly dealt with under the attendance management policy or as an issue of personal misconduct'.

5.82   Chapter 4 identifies (in some detail) the key principles of good attendance management, of which perhaps the most important, from the perspective of compliance with the 2008 Performance Regulations, is the proposition that 'any decision to use the UPPs to deal with poor attendance should be taken only after all supportive approaches have been offered in line with force policy'. This merely underscores the importance of the force, at chief officer level, ensuring the design, implementation, and monitoring of an appropriate attendance management policy, because failure to do so will enable officers against whom the Regulations are invoked to complain of a departure from the Guidance.

5.83   Chapter 4 reiterates the duty on each force to:

> ensure it has in place formal policies and procedures setting out its approach to the management of attendance. These should be endorsed by chief officers. The policy should have clear aims and objectives. It is essential that these are communicated to all managers, officers and their representatives and steps taken to ensure that they are familiar with, and fully understand their responsibilities. Officers should have ready access to the policy and procedures.

5.84   Furthermore, the chief officers 'should appoint a named individual at a senior level who takes the lead on attendance issues' and 'the policy should set out clearly the force's expectations in respect of attendance management'.

5.85   The Guidance identifies the ingredients of effective attendance management policies, the desired outcomes of an attendance management procedure, and the features that an effective procedure should contain. It is prescriptive. It enjoins forces to take a 'pro-active and supportive approach to managing absence, identifying and tackling any barriers to good attendance'.

5.86   The Guidance then identifies the appropriate approach to short-term and long-term—that is, twenty-eight calendar days or more—absence, and emphasizes the importance of 'clear, locally published arrangements . . . to maintain contact with officers who are absent for extended periods'.

5.87   The Guidance further obliges management to facilitate a return to work, including by making the officer's medical practitioners:

> aware that the return to work can be phased, either by reducing hours at the start of the return or adjusting some of the tasks of the role to ensure no undue risk is placed on the officer concerned. Managers should ensure an appropriate 'risk assessment' is undertaken in such cases. Managers can be active in their support and encouragement for an early, safe return to work.

5.88   The Guidance enjoins the early involvement of occupational health to advise managers. Guidance is offered in relation to the effect of further reg 28 of the Police Regulations 2003[12] and its implications for sick pay. The Guidance sets out

---

[12] SI 2003/527.

a detailed prescription for return-to-work interviews and touches (lightly) upon the Disability Discrimination Act 1995, albeit without offering much guidance.

The Guidance also asserts the benefits of the use of recuperative duties to aid an **5.89** early return to work and explains the use of restricted duties. It confirms that there will be occasions:

> where the medical condition causing the absence will be very serious and potentially with a permanent effect. In such cases the issues of whether the officer is 'permanently disabled' within the definition used in ill-health retirement guidance, will need to be considered.

Finally, the Guidance gets to the UPPs and states that 'where supportive **5.90** approaches have failed to improve attendance to acceptable levels, and ill-health retirement is inappropriate, it may be necessary to use the UPPs', for which it refers the reader back to ch 3.

Thus, it can be seen that, taken together, chs 3 and 4 contain the Guidance on the **5.91** supportive approaches required by management prior to invoking the Regulations for unsatisfactory performance or attendance. Adherence to the Guidance is not simply a necessary precursor to invoking the Regulations, but, if followed, reflects many important statements of good management practice and policy that will promote standards of performance and attendance more generally.

Invoking the Regulations

Provided that management has properly discharged its various obligations of **5.92** 'supportive action', as set out in the Home Office Guidance, that it has properly evidenced the same, and that the officer concerned has failed sufficiently to improve his performance or attendance, then the situation may arise when management is entitled to invoke the Regulations.

The circumstances in which a first-stage meeting may be required (reg 12)

How, then, are the Regulations triggered? The answer lies in reg 12, which provides **5.93** that 'where the line manager for a police officer considers that the performance or attendance of that officer is unsatisfactory', he may 'require the officer concerned to attend a [first-stage meeting] to discuss the performance or attendance of the officer concerned'.

The line manager (or nominated person if reg 9 is relied upon by the appropriate **5.94** authority) will need to keep one eye on Pt 3 of the Regulations and the other on Pt 5 of ch 3 of the Home Office Guidance. The whole point about a regulated employment regime is that the Regulations are—at least, in substance, and preferably, in form—to be complied with.

Departures without good reason run the risk of causing difficulties for management, **5.95** not only within the regulated regime, but also, potentially, with employment tribunals, where regulatory departure may be relied upon as evidence of irregular or discrepant treatment, particularly if—as will mainly be the case in the context of the police service—a discrimination claim is alleged.[13] Furthermore, line managers need to adopt good record-keeping practices so that their actions pursuant to the Regulations are properly evidenced at all times as being rational and evidence-based.

Arrangement of the first-stage meeting (reg 13)

5.96 If the first line manager invokes the Regulations, then reg 13 obliges him 'as soon as reasonably practicable'[14] to send a notice to the officer concerned. The required content of the notice served on the affected officer is onerous. It must:

(a) require him to attend a first-stage meeting of the UPPs with the line manager;

(b) inform him of the procedures for determining the date and time of the meeting under paras (3)–(6) (see 5.101 below);

(c) summarize the reasons why his performance or attendance is considered to be unsatisfactory;

(d) inform him of the possible outcomes of the three stage meetings;

(e) inform him that a HRP or a police officer may attend the meeting to advise the line manager on the proceedings;

(f) inform him that, if he consents, any other person specified in the notice may attend the meeting;

(g) inform him that he may seek advice from a representative of his staff association;

(h) inform him that he may be accompanied and represented at the meeting by a police friend; and

(i) inform him that he must provide to the line manager in advance of the meeting a copy of any document on which he intends to rely at the meeting.

5.97 It is to be anticipated that most forces will introduce a standard form for the reg 13 notice, which can be suitably modified for the near identical notices required for second and third-stage meetings.

5.98 It is, of course, para (c) that requires the most careful thought by the line manager, because it obliges him to summarize the reasons why the officer's performance or attendance is considered to be unsatisfactory. Not only must this be clearly set out and evidence-based, but it must also—given the provisions of regs 19(6)

---

[13] On grounds of race, sex, religion or belief, sexual orientation, age, or disability.

[14] As to which phrase, see Chapter 7 on the case law surrounding reg 15 of the 2008 Conduct Regulations (the successor to reg 9, and, before that, reg 7), which may well be prayed in aid by those made the subject of the Performance Regulations and for similar reasons.

and 26(6)—stand the test of time. Put simply, management cannot 'switch horses mid-race' and subsequently rely upon a different contended basis of unsatisfactory performance or attendance not initially identified and particularized.

Regulations 19(6) and 26(6) provide that the relevant meeting must concern unsatisfactory performance or attendance 'which is similar to or connected with the unsatisfactory performance or attendance referred to in the written improvement notice'. This appears to permit, at most, additional (subsequent) evidence within the same species of complaint as identified in the original WIN; anything outside that would require the process to start from the beginning. The implications of this cannot be avoided by drafting generic, rather than specific, grounds.[15] **5.99**

In addition to service of the written notice, the line manager must also attach any document upon which he relied in arriving at the view that triggered the notice under reg 12—that is, any document that caused the line manager to consider the officer's performance or attendance to be unsatisfactory. Whilst an apparently innocuous obligation, the failure to discharge it will give the officer concerned forensic ammunition. This ammunition can be discharged to raise objections at the first-stage meeting and/or to mount a subsequent appeal under, for example, reg 16(4)(d) (that 'there was a serious breach of the procedures . . . or other unfairness . . .'). **5.100**

Subparagraphs (3)–(6) of reg 13 set out the (administratively cumbersome) process for fixing a date and time for the first-stage meeting, which is intended to be 'agreed' between the line manager and the officer concerned. It provides the officer concerned with a limited entitlement to postpone, provided that such postponement is reasonable and not more than five working days beyond the date specified originally by the line manager. **5.101**

Regulation 13(8) imposes an obligation upon the officer concerned 'in advance of the first stage meeting' to provide the line manager with a copy of any document on which he intends to rely at the meeting. **5.102**

Paragraph 5.4 of ch 3 of the Guidance expands on the issue of documentation and confirms that any 'document or other material that was not submitted in advance of the meeting may be considered at the meeting at the discretion of the line manager . . . to ensure fairness to all parties', but also states that 'the presumption should be that such documents or material will not be permitted unless it can be shown that they were not previously available to be submitted in advance'. **5.103**

---

[15] See (in the context of misconduct charges) *R (Wheeler) v AC House of the MPS* [2008] EWHC 439 (Admin), as to the significance of the failure to specify sufficiently in the charge the alleged failures in supervision behind a broadly worded misconduct charge.

Procedure at the first-stage meeting (reg 14)

5.104 The meeting is to be conducted by the line manager or the 'nominated person'. This will impose an alien process upon managers of sergeant and inspector rank who may well have no such so-called 'human resources' experience. Accordingly, reg 14(3) provides that an HRP or police officer 'may attend the meeting to advise the line manager on the proceedings'. Furthermore, any other person specified in the reg 13 notice may also—by consent of the officer concerned—attend.

5.105 Regulation 14(5) provides that the line manager shall, consistent with basic minimum procedural requirements of fairness:

(i) explain why the line manager considers that the performance or attendance of the officer concerned is unsatisfactory; and

(ii) provide the officer concerned and/or his police friend with an opportunity to make representations.

5.106 Paragraph 5.5 of ch 3 of the Guidance states that the purpose of the meeting is to hear the evidence of the unsatisfactory performance or attendance, and to give the police officer the opportunity to put forward his or her views, including identification of any factors that are affecting the police officer's performance or attendance and what the police officer considers can be done to address them. The reference to 'evidence' is somewhat misleading, because there appears—at least on the face of the Regulations—to be no provision for the calling of witnesses at the first (or, indeed, second) stage meeting. The language of reg 14 is of 'representations', with no specific reference either to witnesses or evidence.

5.107 Where, upon hearing such representations, the line manager finds that the performance or attendance of the police officer has been satisfactory during the period in question, he will inform the police officer that no further action will be taken.

5.108 Where, however, the line manager finds that the performance or attendance has been unsatisfactory, the line manager must (reg 14(6)) then inform the officer concerned:

(i) in what respect his performance or attendance is considered unsatisfactory;

(ii) of the improvement that is required in his performance or attendance;

(iii) that, if a sufficient improvement is not made within such reasonable period as the line manager shall specify (being a period not greater than twelve months), he may be required to attend a second-stage meeting in accordance with reg 18;

(iv) that he will receive a written improvement notice; and

(v) that if a sufficient improvement in his performance or attendance is not maintained during the validity period of such notice, he may be required to attend a second-stage meeting in accordance with reg 18.

The above represents merely the verbal adumbration of what thereafter (see 5.112 **5.109** *et seq* below) must be reduced to writing. It may accordingly be prudent for the line manager to adjourn for a short period before reading out the requisite findings. Indeed, there would be nothing to prevent the line manager from adjourning for a short period to complete a draft of the WIN and to use that as a scripted basis for his verbal address to the officer.

The line manager will need to give careful thought as to how best to particularize **5.110** the unsatisfactory performance or attendance and, consistent therewith, the precise improvement required. This will promote fairness to the affected officer (he will know what specific aspects of performance will be measured under the WIN), and a sloppily drafted WIN is more likely to give rise to appeal. Exploiting the latter is, no doubt, an attractive avenue for a habitually underperforming officer seeking to delay his likely progression to enforced removal from the force for as long as possible.

Paragraph 5.13 of ch 3 of the Guidance suggests that the specified period for **5.111** improvement 'would not normally exceed 3 months'. It might be said that, whilst the period must be fair and reasonable in all of the circumstances, to make it any longer than three months simply runs the risk, in certain cases, of delaying the inevitable, which cannot easily be said to be in the public interest.

Procedure following the first-stage meeting (reg 15)

The obligations upon the first line manager after the first-stage meeting continue **5.112** to be onerous. He must cause to be prepared two documents: a 'written record of the meeting' (whether or not he made a finding of unsatisfactory performance or attendance);[16] and a WIN (where there was a finding of unsatisfactory performance or attendance).

Furthermore, the line manager must send a copy of any written record that **5.113** has been compiled, and any WIN, to the officer concerned, together (where unsatisfactory performance or attendance has been found) with notice of his right to appeal under reg 16 and matters therein. As before, it might be expected that forces will introduce suitable standard forms for these rigorous notice provisions; a failure to do so runs the risk of line managers inadvertently failing in their regulatory obligations and thereby undermining their good intentions.

Regulation 15(3) specifies the requirements of the WIN. It shall: **5.114**

    (a) record the matters of which the officer concerned was informed (or would have been informed had he attended the meeting) [that is, the particulars of his unsatisfactory

---

[16] Although the record is not required if neither the officer nor a police friend attended the meeting.

performance or attendance, the improvement required of him, and the consequences
if sufficient improvement is not maintained during the validity period of the notice] . . .;

(b) state the period for which it is valid; and

(c) be signed and dated by the line manager.

5.115 It is important to notice that the validity period of the WIN is always twelve
months, even though the period for sufficient improvement specified in the
notice may be shorter (although it can be anything up to twelve months). The
significance of the validity period, as distinct from the reasonable period for
improvement specified in the WIN, is that if the line manager considers that,
notwithstanding sufficient improvement having been made within the reasonable
period specified under reg 14(6)(c), the officer has, during the validity period,
failed to maintain a sufficient improvement in his performance or attendance, the
line manager can invoke the second-stage process.

5.116 In other words, the officer concerned is at peril of proceeding to the second stage
under the Regulations either for failing sufficiently to improve his performance or
attendance during the reasonable period specified in the WIN, or for failing to
maintain a sufficient improvement in his performance or attendance during the
(potentially much longer) validity period of the WIN.

5.117 Given that the intention of the 2008 Performance Regulations was to introduce a
proportionate and swift regime to tackle underperformance and poor attendance,
it is perhaps a little surprising that the Regulations provide remarkably robust
rights of response and appeal on the part of the officer concerned. Thus it is that—
provided that he does not lodge an appeal under reg 16—the officer concerned is
entitled to submit written comments on any written record of the meeting that
the line manager serves upon him. This creates the vista of officers placing on the
record disputes of fact or disagreements with management, presumably to pray
the same in aid later in the process, should that become necessary or desirable.

5.118 The final—and unsurprising—obligation on the line manager after the first stage
meeting is to file together: (i) any written record of the meeting; (ii) the WIN;
and (iii) any written comments of the officer concerned lodged under the procedure identified at 5.117. This is because all such documents may be required if the
officer's case proceeds to the next stage.

5.119 Chapter 3 of the Home Office Guidance provides further advice as to the action
required by officer and management following the service of a WIN. Paragraph 5.18 provides that:

> Normally it will be appropriate to agree an action plan . . . setting out the actions
> which should assist the police officer to perform his or her duties to an acceptable
> standard. This may be agreed at the UPP meeting or at a later time specified by the
> line manager. It is expected that the police officer will co-operate with implementa-
> tion of the action plan and take responsibility for his or her own development or

improvement. Equally, the police officer's managers must ensure that any actions to support the police officer to improve are implemented.

Plainly, care must be taken by management to avoid the action plan conflicting **5.120** with the terms or spirit of the WIN, because any such conflict could be deployed by the officer concerned by way of challenge to any second-stage proceedings.

Paragraph 5.19 of ch 3 of the Guidance proceeds to state that it is: **5.121**

> Expected that the police officer's performance or attendance will be actively moni-tored against the improvement notice and, where applicable, the action plan by the line manager throughout the specified period of the improvement notice. The line manager should discuss with the police officer any concerns that the line manager has during this period as regards his or her performance or attendance and offer advice and guidance where appropriate.

In other words, the line manager is enjoined not simply to permit the officer con- **5.122** cerned to continue to perform or attend unsatisfactorily during the specified period of the WIN, but actively to manage the officer concerned, so as to achieve the necessary improvement required by the WIN and, presumably, to maintain that improvement during the validity period of the WIN.

Appeals against the finding and outcome of a first-stage meeting (regs 16–18)

The 1999 Efficiency Regulations contained no rights of appeal by the officer con- **5.123** cerned in respect of the first or second-stage 'interviews' (contrasting with the new language of 'meetings'). The 2008 Performance Regulations not only contain rights of appeal from both first and second-stage meetings, but also extensive rights of appeal. The practical consequence may be a greater propensity for bureaucracy and for a determined officer to protract proceedings, on merit or otherwise.

The entitlement to appeal under reg 16 exists only where the line manager made **5.124** a finding of unsatisfactory performance or attendance, in which case the officer concerned is entitled to appeal against that finding or any of the 'relevant terms' of the WIN.

The relevant terms of the WIN are defined by reg 16(3) as follows: **5.125**

(a) the respect in which the performance or attendance of the officer concerned is considered unsatisfactory;
(b) the improvement that is required in his performance or attendance;
(c) the length of the period specified by the line manager in accordance with regulation 14(6)(c) [ie at the first-stage meeting].

The officer concerned can accordingly appeal both against the finding that his **5.126** performance or attendance was unsatisfactory, and, even if he accepts that it was unsatisfactory or fails on that appeal, the particulars of that finding, the particulars of the improvement required, and the length of period in which he is required to achieve sufficient improvement.

5.127 Regulation 16(4) purports to limit the grounds for appealing any of the above four matters by identifying the 'only' grounds of appeal. In fact, on careful examination, it can be seen that the grounds could scarcely be more expansive. They are as follows:

(a) that the finding of unsatisfactory performance or attendance was unreasonable;

(b) that any of the relevant terms of the written improvement notice are unreasonable;

(c) that there is evidence that could not reasonably have been considered at the first stage meeting which could have materially affected the finding of unsatisfactory performance or attendance or any of the relevant terms of the written improvement notice;

(d) that there was a breach of the procedures set out in these Regulations or other unfairness which could have materially affected the finding of unsatisfactory performance or attendance or any of the relevant terms of the written improvement notice.

5.128 The officer concerned must launch his appeal with written notice to his second line manager within seven days of receipt of any written record of the first-stage meeting and any WIN, although the second line manager has the discretion to extend this time period 'if he is satisfied that it is appropriate to do so'. The officer's written notice of appeal must set out the grounds of the appeal and be accompanied by any evidence on which the officer relies (reg16(6)).

5.129 The first-stage appeal meeting is to be heard not later than seven days after the second line manager has received the officer's written notice of appeal, although, once again, this time limit may be extended by the second line manager if he considers it 'necessary or expedient' to permit such extension of time.

5.130 As soon as reasonably practicable after receipt of the officer's notice of appeal, the second line manager must send the officer concerned a written notice informing him:

(i) of the procedures for determining the date and time of the meeting (which are as for the first-stage meeting);

(ii) that an HRP or a police officer may attend the meeting to advise the second line manager on the proceedings;

(iii) that, if he consents, any other person specified in the notice may attend the meeting;

(iv) that he may seek advice from a representative of his staff association; and

(v) that he may be accompanied and represented at the meeting by a police friend.

The first-stage appeal meeting (reg 18)

5.131 The procedure at the first-stage appeal meeting is identical to that at the first-stage meeting other than that the second line manager conducts the meeting. The second line manager may, after considering representations, confirm or reverse the finding of unsatisfactory performance or attendance, or confirm or vary the relevant terms of the WIN appealed against.

5.132 In other words, the second line manager can quash the finding of unsatisfactory performance or attendance completely or, if such finding was justified or not appealed against, confirm or vary the relevant terms of the WIN. It follows that, for all practical purposes, a disgruntled officer concerned can institute a completely new hearing on appeal, albeit before his second line manager.

5.133 Whilst, however, reg 18(7) provides that the second line manager has only the powers that the first line manager had available to him at the first-stage meeting, it is to be noted that the power of the second line manager to vary the relevant terms of the WIN mean that he can, for example, increase the specified period and increase the improvement required. This may operate as a healthy disincentive to certain officers from appealing the outcomes from the first-stage meeting.

5.134 As soon as reasonably practicable after the conclusion of the first-stage appeal meeting, the officer concerned shall be given written notice of the second line manager's decision and a written summary of the reasons for that decision. The written notice of the decision must be provided within three working days of the appeal.

5.135 Where the second line manager has reversed the finding of unsatisfactory performance or attendance, or varied any of the relevant terms of the WIN, the decision of the second line manager shall take effect by way of substitution for the finding or the terms appealed against from the date of the first stage meeting.

D. The Second Stage

The circumstances in which a second-stage meeting may be required (reg 19)

5.136 The second stage of the process is commenced by the line manager assessing the sufficiency of the improvement of the officer's performance or attendance during the period specified on the WIN, and/or whether the officer has maintained that improvement during the validity period of the WIN. If insufficiency of improvement or maintenance of improvement is found by the line manager, then the second-stage meeting is convened.

5.137 The first duty on the line manager is, as soon as reasonably practicable after the period specified for improvement on the WIN has ended, to assess the performance of the officer concerned during that period, in consultation with the second line manager and/or an HRP, and notify the officer concerned in writing whether the line manager considers that there has been a sufficient improvement in performance or attendance during the specified period.

5.138 If the line manager considers that there has been sufficient improvement, he should, per para 5.21 of ch 3 of the Home Office Guidance, notify the officer in writing of this, and:

> . . . should also inform the police officer that whilst [his] performance or attendance . . . is now satisfactory, the improvement notice is valid for a period of 12 months . . . so that it is possible for the second stage of the procedures to be initiated if the performance or attendance of the police officer falls below an acceptable level within the remaining period.

5.139 Thus the Guidance clearly intends that the officer concerned is reminded that he remains in peril for the validity period of the WIN.

5.140 If, however, at the end of the period specified in the WIN, the line manager considers that there has been an insufficient improvement in performance or attendance, he shall, at the same time as he gives the officer notice of his assessment, also give notice in writing that he is required to attend a second-stage meeting to consider his performance or attendance (reg 19(2)).

5.141 The other trigger for the second-stage meeting is provided by reg 19(3) and (4)—that is, where the line manager considers that the officer concerned has, during the validity period of the WIN, failed to maintain a sufficient improvement in his performance or attendance.

5.142 Thus it can be seen that, to avoid the second stage of the process, the officer concerned needs both: (i) to improve his performance or attendance during the period specified in the WIN; and (ii) to maintain that improvement for the validity period of the WIN—that is, twelve months.

5.143 Whether commenced under reg 19(2) or (3), the line manager has to inform the officer concerned of the fact that the matter will proceed to a second-stage meeting and the senior manager has to direct the same.

5.144 As already identified, but importantly, reg 19(6) provides that the unsatisfactory performance or attendance that comprises the subject matter of the second-stage meeting must be 'similar to or connected with' the unsatisfactory performance or attendance referred to in the WIN. By implication, if this criterion is not met, the line manager will have no option but to invoke the first-stage meeting procedure under Pt 3 of the Regulations.

Arrangement of the second-stage meeting (reg 20)

5.145 The obligation to notify the officer concerned of all of the same matters that were required to be notified when arranging a first-stage meeting falls this time to the second line manager, who must, in the (elaborate) notice (again, presumably to be made the subject of a force specific standard form), identify that the line manager may also attend the meeting.

Just as with the notice of the first-stage meeting, the notice for the second-stage meeting must be accompanied by a copy of 'any document relied upon by the line manager when he formed the view' which triggered the second-stage meeting. **5.146**

Furthermore, the arrangements for fixing the date and time of the second-stage meeting mirror those at the first stage. **5.147**

Procedure at and after the second-stage meeting (regs 21 and 22)

The procedure at the second-stage meeting is identical to that at the first-stage meeting, except that it is the second line manager (or nominated person under reg 9) who conducts the meeting and, in the event of an adverse finding, that the WIN issued is to be a 'final' one. **5.148**

Similarly, the procedure following the second-stage meeting is identical to that following the first-stage meeting, other than, of course, that the regulatory obligations concerning the conduct of the meeting fall upon the second line manager. The validity period of the final WIN is also twelve months. **5.149**

The officer concerned enjoys the same rights to make representations on any written record of the second-stage meeting. **5.150**

Appeals against the finding and outcome of the second-stage meeting (regs 23–25)

The officer concerned enjoys identical rights of appeal from the second-stage meeting to those enjoyed from the first-stage meeting, with one enhancement: he may also appeal against the very decision of the line manager to require him to attend the second-stage meeting. **5.151**

The notice of appeal is to be served by the officer concerned on the senior manager, and it is the senior manager who must convene and conduct the second-stage appeal meeting. After considering representations, the senior manager can, as with the second line manager before him at the first-stage appeal meeting, confirm or reverse the finding of unsatisfactory performance or attendance, and confirm or vary the relevant terms of the final WIN. **5.152**

The senior manager also has the power, where the point is advanced, to make a finding that the officer concerned should not have been required to attend the second-stage meeting in the first place. **5.153**

The obligation on the senior manager after the second-stage appeal meeting reproduces that on the second line manager after the first-stage appeal meeting. **5.154**

E. The Third Stage

5.155 As soon as reasonably practicable after the date on which the period specified in the final WIN ends, the line manager of the officer concerned 'shall assess the perform-ance or attendance of the officer concerned during that period, in consultation with the second line manager or a human resources professional (or both)'.

5.156 If the line manager considers that there has been a sufficient improvement in performance or attendance, he shall notify the officer concerned of that in writing.

5.157 If, however, the line manager considers either that there has been an insufficient improvement by the officer concerned within the period specified by the final WIN, or that the officer concerned has, during the validity period of the final WIN following the expiry of the specified period, failed to maintain a sufficient improvement in his performance or attendance, the line manager shall, at the same time as he gives notice of his assessment to the officer concerned, also notify the officer concerned in writing that he is required to attend a third-stage meeting to consider his performance or attendance.

5.158 The third-stage meeting has the possibility of terminating the officer's career or reducing his rank. Thus the obligation on management fully to discharge the protective procedural aspects of the third-stage process are the greater.

5.159 The senior manager has the responsibility, once the written notice has gone to the officer concerned, to direct that a third-stage meeting be arranged under reg 27. Once again, any such third-stage meeting must concern unsatisfactory perfor-mance or attendance that is 'similar to or connected with' the unsatisfactory per-formance or attendance referred to in the final WIN.

Arrangement of the third-stage meeting (reg 27)

5.160 The senior manager is under the obligation 'as soon as reasonably practicable' to send a notice to the officer concerned that is in near-identical terms to the notices directing the officer to a first or second-stage meeting. Given the potential out-comes from a third-stage meeting, the senior manager must ensure substantial compliance with the notice requirements. He must also attach to the notice any document on which he relied in arriving at the view that triggered the notice for the third-stage meeting.

Gross incompetence (regs 28 and 29)

5.161 Before moving on to consider the procedure at a third-stage meeting, it is helpful to examine the other 'fast-track' route to such meetings under regs 28 and 29.

Regulation 28 applies where the appropriate authority considers that the performance of a police officer constitutes 'gross incompetence'. In such a case, the appropriate authority may inform the officer concerned in writing that he is required to attend a third-stage meeting to consider his performance. In effect, the officer concerned skips straight to the third (and final) stage of the process. There is no similar provision for grossly unsatisfactory attendance. **5.162**

It is the appropriate authority that directs that a third-stage meeting be arranged under reg 29. **5.163**

Under reg 29, the appropriate authority must provide the officer concerned with the usual written notice concerning the fact of, and outcomes possible, from the third-stage meeting, in terms that are nearly identical to the notices that must be served prior to a first or second-stage meeting. Of course, the notice will require the appropriate authority to summarize why the performance of the officer concerned is said to constitute gross incompetence. **5.164**

'Gross incompetence' is defined in reg 4 to mean: **5.165**

> a serious inability or failure of a police officer to perform the duties of the role or rank he is currently undertaking to a satisfactory standard or level, to the extent that dismissal would be justified, except that no account shall be taken of the attendance of a police officer when considering whether he has been grossly incompetent.

Paragraph 7.8 of ch 3 of the Home Office Guidance says that: **5.166**

> There may be exceptional circumstances where the appropriate authority considers the performance (not attendance) of the police officer to be so unsatisfactory as to warrant the procedures being initiated at the third stage. This could be as a result of a single incident of 'gross incompetence'. It is not envisaged that an appropriate authority would initiate the procedures at the third stage in respect of a series of acts over a period of time.

Procedure on receipt of notice of the third-stage meeting (reg 32)

The procedure leading up to, and at, the third-stage meeting is different from that which prevails for the first or second stages of the process. **5.167**

Within fourteen days of receipt of the notice of the third-stage meeting, the officer concerned must comply with various obligations, as follows. **5.168**

The officer concerned shall provide to the appropriate authority: **5.169**

(i) written notice of whether or not he accepts that his performance or attendance has been unsatisfactory, or that he has been grossly incompetent;

(ii) where he accepts that his performance or attendance has been unsatisfactory, or that he has been grossly incompetent, any written submission that he wishes to make in mitigation;

     (iii) where he does not accept that his performance or attendance has been unsatisfactory, or that he has been grossly incompetent, or where he disputes part of the matters referred to in the notice, written notice of:

        (a) the matters that he disputes and his account of the relevant events; and

        (b) any arguments on points of law that he wishes to be considered by the panel.

5.170   Furthermore, the officer concerned is obliged to provide the appropriate authority and the panel with a copy of any document on which he intends to rely at the third-stage meeting.

5.171   Where the officer concerned has proposed witnesses, he shall 'if reasonably practicable, agree a list of proposed witnesses with the senior manager'. Where agreement is not forthcoming, the officer concerned shall supply to the appropriate authority his list of proposed witnesses and their addresses.

5.172   In other words, the officer concerned attempts to agree the necessary witnesses with the senior manager and, failing that, supplies his proposed list to the appropriate authority. The latter can then submit its list of proposed witnesses to the chair. It is for the chair of the third-stage meeting panel to determine which, if any, witnesses will be called.

5.173   A 'proposed witness' is defined as 'a witness whose attendance at the third stage meeting the officer concerned or the appropriate authority (as the case may be) wishes to request of the panel chair'. As will be seen, either party has the opportunity to argue for the necessity of attendance of a particular witness. It is contended that the benefit of any doubt should be in favour of requiring attendance. This is proportionate to the available outcomes and may help to avoid appeals to a police appeals tribunal.

The management of witnesses (reg 33)

5.174   As soon as reasonably practicable after any list of proposed witnesses has been agreed or supplied (under reg 32), the appropriate authority shall supply that list to the panel chair together, in the case of a 'supplied' and not agreed list, with a list of its proposed witnesses. It becomes the duty of the panel chair to consider the list or lists of proposed witnesses (if any), and to determine which, if any, witnesses should attend the third-stage meeting.

5.175   Additionally, the panel chair may determine that witnesses not named in any list of proposed witnesses should attend the third-stage meeting.

5.176   Regulation 33(4) provides that no witnesses shall give evidence at a third-stage meeting unless the panel chair 'reasonably believes that it is necessary in the interests of fairness for the witness to do so', in which case, he shall, in the case of a police officer witness, order him to attend and, in the case of any other witness, cause him to be given notice that his attendance is necessary, and of the date, time, and place of the meeting.

The timing and notice of the third-stage meeting (reg 34)

This is provided for by reg 34. Subject to discretion in the chair, the objective is **5.177** to have the hearing not more than thirty working days after the service of the regs 27 or 29 notice.

Panel members (regs 30 and 31)

Regulation 30 specifies the composition of the panel, which is to be appointed by **5.178** the appropriate authority.

The panel comprises a chair and two other members. No panel member shall be **5.179** an interested party. The chair must be a senior officer or senior HRP. A 'senior human resources professional' means an HRP who, in the opinion of the appropriate authority, has sufficient seniority, skills, and experience to be a panel chair.

One panel member shall be either a police officer or an HRP of at least the rank **5.180** of superintendent, or (in the opinion of the appropriate authority) equivalent. The other panel member shall be either a police officer or a police staff member of at least the rank of superintendent, or (in the opinion of the appropriate authority) equivalent.

Furthermore, at least one panel member shall be a police officer and at least one **5.181** panel member shall be an HRP, and each panel member shall be of at least the same rank as, or (in the opinion of the appropriate authority) equivalent of, the officer concerned.

As soon as reasonably practicable after the panel members have been appointed, **5.182** the appropriate authority must notify the officer concerned of their names. The officer then has certain entitlements to object (see reg 31 at 5.184 below).

As soon as the appropriate authority has appointed the panel members, he shall **5.183** arrange for them and the officer concerned to receive copies of all documents that were available to those conducting the first and second-stage meetings, together with any material generated subsequently thereto.

Regulation 31(1) provides that the officer concerned may object to the appoint- **5.184** ment of any of the panel members. Such objection must be made in writing to the appropriate authority not later than three working days after receipt of the notification of the panel members to him and must set out the officer's grounds of objection.

5.185 Adjudication in relation to the objection is conducted by the appropriate authority, which must notify the officer concerned in writing whether it upholds or rejects an objection to any panel member. If the appropriate authority upholds an objection, it shall remove that member from the panel and shall appoint a new member to the panel.

5.186 If the appropriate authority appoints a new panel member, it must ensure that the reg 30 requirements for the composition of the panel are met.

5.187 As soon as reasonably practicable after any such (re)appointment, the appropriate authority shall notify in writing the officer concerned of the name of the new panel member. The officer may then object once more and the adjudication and/or reappointment process starts over again. There is no express prohibition on an application being made directly to the panel at the meeting itself.

Procedure at the third-stage meeting (regs 35 and 36)

5.188 Regulation 35 entitles the chair of the panel to adjourn meetings on their own volition or at the request of the officer concerned, in the interests of necessity or expedience. If he does so, he must keep everyone advised regarding why he has adjourned, in writing, and to when he has adjourned.

5.189 Regulation 36 makes detailed provision for the procedure at the third-stage meeting, including the following key provisions, which, individually and collectively, simply serve to demonstrate the importance of those conducting the meeting knowing what they are doing.

   (i) The procedure is to be determined by the panel chair, subject only to the regulations and natural justice.

   (ii) The meeting shall be held in private.

   (iii) An HRP, police officer, or relevant lawyer may attend the meeting to advise the panel on the proceedings. Where the officer concerned is a special constable, the appropriate authority shall appoint a special constable with sufficient seniority and experience to attend to advise the panel.

   (iv) As with the earlier stage meetings, it is the duty of the panel chair to provide the officer concerned and his friend with an opportunity to make representations.

   (v) A verbatim record of the meeting shall be taken and the officer is entitled to a copy of such record if he requests it.

The finding (reg 37)

5.190 After the meeting, the panel must make a finding as to whether the performance or attendance of the officer concerned during the period specified in the final

WIN or the validity period of the same has been satisfactory or not, or, in a reg 28 (gross incompetence) case, whether his performance constitutes gross incompetence, unsatisfactory performance, or neither. Panels should clearly distinguish finding from outcome.

Any finding or decision of the panel under regs 37 or 38 shall be based on a simple majority, but shall not indicate whether it was taken unanimously or by a majority. **5.191**

The panel shall reduce its decision to writing, and, where its finding has been adverse to the officer in any of the foregoing respects, it must give its reasons and any outcome under reg 38. The copy of its written decision must be sent to the officer concerned and his line manager as soon as practicable after the third-stage meeting, but in any event no later than three working days thereafter. **5.192**

The copy of the decision sent to the officer concerned shall be accompanied by a notice in writing setting out the circumstances in which a decision may be appealed to a police appeals tribunal under s 85 of the Police Act 1996. **5.193**

Outcomes (reg 38)

The outcomes (sanctions) available to the panel depend on whether the finding was in relation to unsatisfactory performance or attendance, or gross incompetence. **5.194**

As to a finding of unsatisfactory performance or attendance, the panel may order: **5.195**

(i) dismissal, subject to a minimum notice period of twenty-eight days;
(ii) reduction in rank with immediate effect;
(iii) redeployment to alternative duties (which may involve a reduction of rank) within the police force concerned.

If, however, the panel is satisfied that there are exceptional circumstances justifying it, it may order an extension of the final WIN. **5.196**

As to a finding of gross incompetence, the panel may order: **5.197**

(i) dismissal, subject to a minimum notice period of twenty-eight days;
(ii) dismissal with immediate effect;
(iii) reduction in rank with immediate effect;
(iv) the issue of a final WIN; or
(v) redeployment to alternative duties (which may involve a reduction of rank) within the police force concerned.

The panel may not order reduction in rank where the officer concerned is a special constable, or if the third-stage meeting relates to the attendance record of the officer concerned. **5.198**

5.199 If, on a gross incompetence case, the panel makes a finding of unsatisfactory performance, but not gross incompetence, it must order the issue of a WIN.

5.200 Regulation 38 makes detailed provision concerning the requirements of the WIN, or final WIN, issued by the third-stage panel.

Assessment of performance or attendance following third-stage meetings (regs 39–41)

5.201 Regulation 39 applies where a WIN has been issued under reg 38 and simply restarts the process at the second stage as if under reg 19.

5.202 Regulation 40 applies where a final WIN has been issued or extended under reg 38 and requires, as soon as reasonably practicable after the end of the reasonable period specified by the panel under reg 38 or at the end of the balance of the validity period, the panel to assess whether the officer has sufficiently improved or maintained the improvement, respectively, of his performance or attendance.

5.203 If the panel considers that there has been an insufficient improvement, or that the improvement has not been maintained during the validity period, the panel chair shall, at the same time as he gives notification of the panel's assessment, notify the officer concerned in writing that he is required to attend another third-stage meeting to consider his performance or attendance. In other words, the panel can, in effect, send the officer back to a third-stage meeting if his performance or attendance fails sufficiently to improve after it issued a final WIN at a third-stage meeting.

5.204 If the panel decides to send the matter back to a third-stage meeting, then the duty is on the appropriate authority to direct that a third-stage meeting be arranged under reg 27 and to notify the officer accordingly. As before, the unsatisfactory performance or attendance considered by the panel must be similar to, or connected with, that specified in the originating WIN.

5.205 Where any of the panel members are not able to continue to act 'second time around', the appropriate authority shall remove that member from the panel and appoint a new member to the panel, subject to the panel complying with the reg 30 requirements. The officer concerned continues to enjoy the same rights to object to the panel members under reg 31.

5.206 Regulation 41 provides that, where an officer is required to attend another third-stage meeting under reg 40, that meeting shall be conducted by the same panel as that which conducted the initial third-stage meeting (subject to any changes made thereto).

5.207 The reconvened panel has the same reg 38 outcomes available to it, other than that it cannot extend the final WIN.

F. Police Appeals Tribunals

Appeals from third-stage meetings are to police appeals tribunals (see reg 37(4) **5.208**
and s 85 of the Police Act 1996). Such appeals are dealt with in Chapter 11.

G. Conclusion

The intended change of culture from blame and sanction, to one of monitored **5.209**
performance, learning, and improvement, is strongly to be welcomed. What
remains to be seen is whether the 2008 Performance Regulations are over-
elaborate and protracted, with disproportionate administrative requirements
and rights of appeal before the third stage. The bureaucracy involved may deter
some (weak) supervisors from using the procedures effectively—or even at all.
Furthermore, the procedures will only work and bring the intended benefits to the
police service if chief officers both champion the procedures and support those
supervisors who deploy them.

The rights of appeal may serve to defeat the intended purpose of effecting **5.210**
targeted, immediate, and intrusive local management. A genuine officer that is
willing to listen to management, and is willing and capable of improving his
performance or attendance, will benefit from the new regime. Conversely,
difficult to manage or obdurate officers may exploit the procedures to their
advantage.

Properly understood and applied, the 2008 Performance Regulations contain **5.211**
mechanisms whereby police management can potentially significantly reduce the
volume of discrimination claims, by reliance upon a non-discriminatory regulatory regime that focuses on performance and attendance rather than race
or sex, etc. Furthermore, properly understood and intelligently applied, the
2008 Performance Regulations contain the real potential for driving up police
performance.

6

STANDARDS OF PROFESSIONAL BEHAVIOUR AND THE INITIAL HANDLING OF A REPORT

A. Overview	6.01	
B. The New Standards of Professional Behaviour	6.26	
Context: the commencement of the Police (Conduct) Regulations 2008	6.26	
Further guidance as to the Standards of Professional Behaviour in the Home Office Guidance	6.44	
C. Initial Handling: The Police Reform Act 2002, Sch 3, or the Police (Conduct) Regulations 2008	6.61	
The application of Sch 3 to the 2002 Act	6.64	
D. The Police Reform Act 2002, Pt 2: Complaints, Conduct Matters, and DSI Matters	6.71	
Complaints	6.72	
Conduct matters	6.76	
DSI matters	6.77	
A person serving with the police	6.80	
The application of Pt 2 to officers who have ceased to serve	6.81	
The exclusion from Sch 3 of direction and control matters	6.82	
Schedule 3 to the Police Reform Act 2002	6.83	
E. Police Reform Act 2002, Sch 3, Pt 1: The Handling of Complaints	6.85	
Local resolution (Sch 3, para 6)	6.100	
Appeals relating to local resolution (Sch 3, para 9)	6.116	
Dispensation by the IPCC	6.119	

F. Police Reform Act 2002, Sch 3, Pt 2: The Handling of Conduct Matters	6.125	
Civil proceedings involving a conduct matter	6.126	
The recording of conduct matters in other cases	6.128	
A conduct matter disclosed during DSI investigation	6.131	
Other mandatory referrals to the IPCC by the appropriate authority	6.132	
Discretionary referrals by the appropriate authority to the IPCC	6.133	
G. Police Reform Act 2002, Sch 3, Pt 2A: The Handling of DSI Matters	6.140	
H. Police Reform Act 2002, Sch 3: Miscellaneous Aspects	6.146	
Restrictions on proceedings	6.146	
Special cases (Sch 3, paras 20A–20I)	6.149	
The power of the IPCC to discontinue an investigation (Sch 3, para 21)	6.151	
I. Conclusion	6.157	

A. Overview

6.01 As Figure 4.1 demonstrated, the process applied to a particular allegation is subject to a number of variables. At its most simple level, contingent on the statutory
classification of the underlying event under Pt 3 of Sch 3 to the Police Reform Act
2002, the initial handling may be the responsibility (as 'appropriate authority') of
either the Independent Police Complaints Commission (IPCC), if under Sch 3,
or the affected officer's force, if not.

6.02 There are further distinctions between whether the allegation is a complaint, conduct, or death and serious injury (DSI) matter, and whether it must or may be
referred by the appropriate authority or police authority to the IPCC for one of a
number of forms of investigation. Decisions must be made as to the use of the local
resolution procedure. Subsequent processing of the matter requires decisions as
to the use of managerial action only, the Police (Performance) Regulations 2008[1]
(or their predecessor),[2] and the Police (Conduct) Regulations 2004[3] or 2008.[4]

6.03 Within each of these stages are statutory rights of appeal and challenge. On one
view, the whole framework is extraordinarily complicated given the straightforward objectives that it is said to promote. The 2008 regime, in particular, appears to
have added to, rather than reduced, the inherent complexity of the procedures.

6.04 The provisions of Pt 3 of Sch 3 to the 2002 Act must be read in conjunction with
the Police (Complaints and Misconduct) Regulations 2004,[5] and the statutory
guidance issued by the IPCC under s 22 of the 2002 Act. The 2004 Regulations
were amended in 2006[6]—introducing a third category of mandatory referral to the
IPCC (namely, that of DSI matters) and changing the referral requirement to the
end of the day following the day on which the duty arises, whether a working day
or not—and in 2008[7]—introducing regs 14A–14E as to written notices (reg 14A),
police friends (reg 14B), representations to the investigator (reg 14C), interviews
during investigation (reg 14D), and the report of the investigation (reg 14E).

6.05 Plainly, an allegation—a report—can come to the attention of the appropriate
authority in a number of ways, whether from the public (a third party may report a

---

[1] SI 2008/2862.
[2] The Police (Efficiency) Regulations 1999, SI 1999/732.
[3] SI 2004/645.
[4] SI 2008/2864.
[5] SI 2004/643.
[6] The Police (Complaints and Misconduct)(Amendment) Regulations 2006, SI 2006/1406,
in force 22 June 2006.
[7] The Police (Complaints and Misconduct)(Amendment) Regulations 2008, SI 2008/2866,
in force 1 December 2008.

matter provided that the qualifying complainant gives written permission), other police officers (s 37 of the 2002 Act, 'Disciplinary proceedings and protected disclosures', applies s 43K of the Employment Rights Act 1996 to reports after 1 April 2004), or the IPCC.

The conduct covered by Pt 2 of the 2002 Act is the conduct of those serving with the police.[8] A person is serving with the police if he is a member of a police force, an employee of a police authority who is under the direction and control of a chief officer, or a special constable who is under the direction and control of a chief officer.[9]   **6.06**

References in the 2002 Act to a member of the public do include references to those serving with the police, those who are members of the staff of the Serious Organised Crime Agency (SOCA), those who are members of the staff of the National Policing Improvement Agency (NPIA), and those who are persons engaged on relevant service, within the meaning of s 97(1)(a) or (d) of the 1996 Act (temporary service of various kinds).[10] Such persons, however, are not members of the public for the purposes of the 2002 Act if they are under the direction and control of the same chief officer as the person whose conduct is in question (s 29(4)(a)), or if they were on duty either: (i) at the time when the conduct is supposed to have taken place, in relation to him; or (ii) at the time when they were supposed to have been adversely affected by, or to have witnessed, the conduct (s 29(4)).   **6.07**

If the underlying event does not disclose a matter requiring a formal investigation, it may be addressed through the IPCC local resolution procedure, or, if it is a non-IPCC matter, through the local resolution procedure or investigation and line management within the relevant home force.   **6.08**

A very high proportion of complaints received are resolved through these mechanisms.[11] The IPCC local resolution procedure, arising under para 8 of   **6.09**

---

[8] Section 12(2) of the 2002 Act.
[9] Section 12(7) of the 2002 Act.
[10] Section 29(3) of the 2002 Act.
[11] According to IPCC data in its Annual Report 2007–08, there were 28,963 complaint cases recorded by police forces across England and Wales in the year ending 31 March 2008. In total, 48,280 individual allegations were made against police. For the first time since the IPCC was set up in 2004, a majority of police forces (twenty-four out of forty-three) saw decreases in the number of complaint cases that they recorded. One in eight police complaint cases involved an appeal to the IPCC. The IPCC completed 3,592 valid appeals during the year. Over 900 were against the non-recording of a complaint, over 400 were against the local resolution process, and 2,260 were against the outcome of a police investigation. More than one in four appeals (28 per cent) were upheld by the IPCC. One half of the appeals against the police service's decision not to record a complaint were upheld. Three in ten appeals relating to the way in which local resolution was handled were upheld. Fewer appeals were upheld about the outcome of a completed police investigation (19 per cent). Six out of ten complaints alleged either neglect of duty (24 per cent), rudeness and intolerance

Sch 3 of the 2002 Act, and reg 4(1) of the Police (Complaints and Misconduct) Regulations 2004,[12] is described in the IPCC publication *The Local Resolution Process*.[13]

6.10 To encourage transparency, early resolution, and the active cooperation of the officer concerned, evidence provided by the affected officer as part of the local resolution procedure may not be used in other proceedings 'except to the extent that it consists of an admission relating to a matter that has not been subjected to local resolution'.[14] By para 2.44 of the Home Office Guidance on Police Officer Misconduct, Unsatisfactory Performance and Attendance Management Procedures,[15] any management action taken as a result of local resolution may be recorded on the performance and development review of the officer concerned, the content of which may be admissible in subsequent unrelated disciplinary procedures.

6.11 The complainant has some rights of appeal within the local resolution procedure based on procedural failures, but, ultimately, not such as to affect any final determination on the substantive merits. In other words, in all practical senses, both the complainant and the officer concerned agree the form of dispute resolution, and, subject to material procedural failures, agree from the outset to be bound by the factual result.

6.12 The Home Office Guidance addresses line management resolution within the applicable Conduct Regulations, and the related topic of treating the underlying conduct within the 2008 Performance Regulations (or the 1999 Efficiency Regulations). These and other initial classification decisions and procedures are addressed within this chapter. The 2008 Performance Regulations were introduced in Chapter 4 and addressed directly in Chapter 5.

6.13 If, by reference to the gravity or nature of the underlying event, a 'formal' investigation is required, the investigating authority must serve a notice of investigation on the officer concerned as soon as reasonably practicable, subject to the legitimate consideration of the risk of prejudice to other pending inquiries. At this point, from the perspective of the officer concerned, there is convergence in the substance, if not the form, of the statutory processes.

(22 per cent), or common assault (14 per cent). There was a rise of almost one quarter in the number of complaints about stop and search, from 434 in 2006–07, to 536 in 2007–08. Nearly 20,000 of the 45,524 completed allegations were resolved at a local level, without the need for a formal investigation. Despite official support for the quick and informal process, there appears to be a general downward trend in the proportions of allegations finalized this way.

[12] SI 2004/643.
[13] Available online at <http://www.ipcc.gov.uk>.
[14] Schedule 3, para 8(3), to the 2002 Act.
[15] Issued pursuant to s 87(1) of the Police Act 1996.

The IPCC has four different forms of investigation under para 15(4) of Pt 3 of   **6.14**
Sch 3, with each form attracting specific provisions under Pt 3. These are: (a) by
the appropriate authority on its own behalf ('local', para 16); (b) by that authority
supervised by the IPCC ('supervised', para 17); (c) by that authority managed
by the IPCC ('managed', para 18); or (d) by the IPCC independently ('IPCC'
para 19). The IPCC determines which will apply at the outset (para 15(4))—but,
by para 15(5), this determination is subject to ongoing review and the form of
investigation may change if justified. The criteria used to determine the form of
investigation are addressed at 7.67–7.70.

The procedures under the applicable Conduct Regulations determine the rights   **6.15**
and obligations of the officer concerned from the point of service of the notice
of investigation—that is, respectively, a reg 9 notice under the 2004 Conduct
Regulations, a reg 14A notice under the 2004 Complaints and Misconduct
Regulations (if an IPCC investigation under Sch 3 to the 2002 Act), or a reg 15
notice under the 2008 Conduct Regulations.

The rights of the complainant are determined by whether the investigation is   **6.16**
under Pt 3 of Sch 3 to the 2002 Act, or simply conducted internally by the force.
An 'internal' investigation may be delegated to officers from an independent force
within the direction and control discretion of the chief constable.

If it is a Sch 3 investigation, the complainant enjoys statutory rights to be kept   **6.17**
informed of the progress of the investigation at defined intervals. What this means,
in practice, is developing over time. The statute and IPCC statutory guidance
emphasize that the process tends towards transparency, and further IPCC guidance is pending. Such disclosure must be balanced against the legitimate needs
of the investigation.[16] Some of the competing considerations are reflected in
R (Saunders)(Tucker) v IPCC and ors:[17] the once-confidential investigating officer's
report is now routinely disclosed to the complainant (subject to the 'harm' tests),
and forms an intrinsic part of the material provided to the officer concerned and
any tribunal in misconduct proceedings.

Similarly, for Sch 3 matters, the IPCC retains an active participatory role in the   **6.18**
conduct of investigations and misconduct proceedings within its Sch 3 statutory
role. It may, for example, require a force to bring misconduct charges, to order that
the misconduct hearing takes place in public, to perform the role of the presenting
officer, or to attend hearings and chief officer reviews (the latter restricted only to
the 2004 regime), and it has locus to challenge material decisions within this process

---

[16] *Reynolds v CC Sussex, with the IPCC as an interested party* [2008] EWHC 1240 (Admin); [27],
R (Reynolds) v IPCC [2008] EWCA Civ 1160, CA.
[17] [2008] EWHC 2372 (Admin).

by way of judicial review. It may (under para 20H(1) of Sch 3) 'recommend' that a matter be certified as a 'special case' under para 20B(3), and may ultimately direct that course if the recommendation is not accepted (para 20H(7)).

6.19 What the IPCC cannot do, of course, is determine the final outcome of any investigation conducted by the force on its own behalf, or any misconduct hearing or meeting. Neither can it determine questions of suspension and operational deployment pending resolution of an investigation, although there are circumstances in which it must be consulted by the appropriate authority.

6.20 Each of these aspects of the process is addressed sequentially by Chapters 6–9. The rights and obligations of the officer concerned are largely determined by the terms of the applicable Conduct Regulations. Proceedings under the 2008 Conduct Regulations are addressed in Chapter 8; those falling within the 2004 Conduct Regulations are tackled in Chapter 9.

6.21 It is contended that a misconduct panel under the 2004 Conduct Regulations is likely to refer to the 2008 Home Office Guidance for contemporary guidance on the application of those Regulations in order to reduce arbitrary and unfair avoidable distinctions. This may apply to considerations of disclosure and the approach to sanction, including the application of the controversial Annex N to the 2004 Home Office Guidance (a presumption of loss of office for drink-driving, abolished in the 2008 regime). A modern restatement, not otherwise in conflict with the language of the 2004 Conduct Regulations, will be a good and sufficient reason for departure if it promotes a truer and fairer result.

6.22 Fast-track or 'special cases' arise under both Sch 3 and other investigations, and the detailed procedures once so certified are within the applicable Conduct Regulations. These matters are addressed in Chapter 10.

6.23 There is further convergence at the point of chief officer's review (under the 2004 Conduct Regulations) and police appeals tribunals (addressed in Chapter 11). Arguments as to abuse of process (more neutrally, the consequences of regulatory departure and contentions that a fair hearing is impracticable) are addressed in Chapter 12.

6.24 A central consideration is that, under the 2008 regime, all decision making will have to reflect the new professional code applicable to all police officers—namely, the 'Standards of Professional Behaviour' set out in the Schedule to the 2008 Conduct Regulations. These are intended to provide a modern, purposive, set of benchmark criteria against which to measure contemporary standards of professional police conduct (see 6.26 *et seq* below).

6.25 Table 6.1 rehearses the prominent features of correspondence between the amended 2004 Complaints and Misconduct Regulations and Sch 3 of the 2002 Act.

Table 6.1 A summary of the Police (Complaints and Misconduct) Regulations 2004, as amended[18], and the Police Reform Act 2002, Sch 3, as amended

PCMR 2004, as amended	Heading of regulation	Comment	Cross-reference: Police Reform Act 2002 Sch 3
1	*Citation, commencement and interpretation*	In force 1 April 2004 concurrent with creation of the IPCC Amended by reg 3 of the Police (Complaints and Misconduct)(Amendment) Regulations 2008, SI 2008/2866, for reports on or after 1 December 2008	
2	*Reference of complaints to the Commission*	Specified complaints (as defined in the statutory guidance) Notification requirements (See reg 5A for DSI matters and 'next-day' referral obligation)	*Part 1* *Handling of complaints* *1 Duties to preserve evidence relating to complaints* *2 Initial handling and recording of complaints* *3 Failures to notify or record a complaint* *4 Reference of complaints to Commission* *5 Duties of Commission on references under paragraph 4* *6 Handling of complaints by the appropriate authority*

(*Continued*)

---

[18] SI 2004/643, in force 1 April 2004; the Police (Complaints and Misconduct)(Amendment) Regulations 2006, SI 2006/1406, in force 22 June 2006; the Police (Complaints and Misconduct)(Amendment) Regulations 2006, SI 2008/2866, in force 1 December 2008.

Table 6.1 *Cont.*

PCMR 2004, as amended	Heading of regulation	Comment	Cross-reference: Police Reform Act 2002 Sch 3
3	*Dispensation by the Commission*	Criteria for dispensation from requirements of Sch 3 (includes, in part, conduct matters)	*7 Dispensation by the Commission from requirements of Schedule* [See also Pt 3. paras 23 and 24]
4	*Local resolution of complaints*	'Appointed person'	*8 Local resolution of complaints* *9 Appeals relating to local resolution*
5	*Recording and reference of conduct matters*	Definitions of 'conduct matters' Amended by 2006 Regulations to insert duty to refer DSI matters and (reg 5A) the manner of referral of a DSI matter 'as the Commission specifies' and where directed not later than the end of the day following the direction, and in any other case not later than the end of the day following the day on which the matter first came to the attention of the appropriate authority	*Part 2* **Handling of conduct matters** *10 Conduct matters arising in civil proceedings* *11 Recording etc. of conduct matters in other cases* *12 Duties to preserve evidence relating to conduct matters* *13 Reference of conduct matters to the Commission* *14 Duties of Commission on references under paragraph 13* *Part 2A* **Handling of death and serious injury (DSI) matters** *14A Duty to record DSI matters* *14B Duty to preserve evidence relating to DSI matters* *14C Reference of DSI matters to the Commission* *14D Duties of Commission under paragraph 14C* [See also Pt 3, '21A Procedure where conduct matter is revealed during investigation of DSI matter']
5A	*Reference of death or serious injury*	Added by Police (Complaints and Misconduct) (Amendment) Regulations 2006, SI 2006/1406, reg 2(4) (22 June 2006)	See Pt 2A and Pt 3, para 21A

6 | Power of Commission to impose requirements in relation to an investigation which it is supervising | 'Any reasonable requirement' as appears 'necessary', subject to: (i) the consent of the DPP; and (ii) representations from the affected chief officer as to resources

Part 3
Investigations and subsequent proceedings
15 *Power of the Commission to determine the form of an investigation [15(4)(a) by the appropriate authority on its own behalf, (b) by that authority under the supervision of the Commission, (c) by that authority under the management of the Commission, or (d) by the Commission]*
16 *Investigations by the appropriate authority on its own behalf*
17 *Investigations supervised by the Commission*
18 *Investigations managed by the Commission*
19 *Investigations by the Commission itself*
19A *Special procedure where investigation relates to police officer or special constable*
19B *Assessment of seriousness of conduct under investigation*
19C *Duty to consider submissions from person whose conduct is being investigated*
19D *Interview of person whose conduct is being investigated*
19E *Duty to provide certain information to appropriate authority*
22 *Final reports on investigations: complaints, conduct matters and certain DSI matters*
23 *Action by the Commission in response to an investigation report*
24 *Action by the appropriate authority in response to an investigation report [under para 22(2) or (3)]*
24A *Final reports on investigations: other DSI matters*
24B *Action by the Commission in response to an investigation report under paragraph*
24A *(where such report indicates crime or misconduct)*
24C *Action by the Commission in response to an investigation report under paragraph*
24A *(where such report does not indicate crime or misconduct)*
27 *Duties with respect to disciplinary proceedings [duty of the appropriate authority to take the action required by the Commission's recommendation]*
Accelerated procedure in special cases
20A *Accelerated procedure in special cases*
20B *Investigations managed or carried out by Commission: action by appropriate authority*
20C *Investigations managed or carried out by Commission: action by Commission [re para 20B(6) notification]*

(Continued)

Table 6.1 *Cont.*

PCMR 2004, as amended	Heading of regulation	Comment	Cross-reference: Police Reform Act 2002 Sch 3
			20D *Investigations managed or carried out by Commission: action by Commission* [re para 20B(7) notification]
			20E *Other investigations: action by appropriate authority* [re investigations by appropriate authority on its own behalf, or supervised investigations, and statement and a special report submitted under para 20A(2) or (3)]
			20F *Other investigations: action by appropriate authority* [notification requirements if Commission certifies a case under para 20E(3)]
			['20G *Special cases: Director of Public Prosecutions*' repealed 1 December 2008, under the Criminal Justice and Immigration Act 2008 (Commencement No 4 and Saving Provision) Order 2008, SI 2008/2993, subject to art 3]
			20H *Special cases: recommendation or direction of Commission* [Commission may recommend certification under para 20B(3) and duty on appropriate authority to notify Commission whether it accepts the recommendation; if not, certification may be directed]
			20I *Special cases: recommendation or direction of Commission* [recommendation under para 20H: if appropriate authority fails to certify under para 20B(3) and to proceed accordingly, 'it shall be the duty of the Commission to determine what (if any) further steps to take under paragraph 20H']
7	*Power of Commission to discontinue an investigation*	May still require an investigation report	21 *Power of the Commission to discontinue an investigation*
8	*Appeals to the Commission: failures to notify or record a complaint*	Timetable	3

9	*Appeals to the Commission: local resolution*		*9 Appeals relating to local resolution*
10	*Appeals to the Commission with respect to an investigation*		*25 Appeals to the Commission with respect to an investigation* *26 Reviews and re-investigations following an appeal*
11	*Manner in which duties to provide information are to be performed*		*28 Information for complainant about disciplinary recommendations*
12	*Exceptions to the duty to keep the complainant informed and to provide information for other persons*		*28 Information for complainant about disciplinary recommendations*
13	*Meaning of "relative"*	Spouse, partner, parent, or adult child	
14	*Copies of complaints etc.*	Anonymity	
		Prejudicial to any criminal investigation or pending proceedings	
		Otherwise contrary to the public interest	
14A	*Written notices*	Introduced by the 2008 Amendment Regulations	
14B	*Police friend*	Introduced by the 2008 Amendment Regulations	

(Continued)

165

Table 6.1 *Cont.*

PCMR 2004, as amended	Heading of regulation	Comment	Cross-reference: Police Reform Act 2002 Sch 3
14C	*Representations to the investigator*	Introduced by the 2008 Amendment Regulations	
14D	*Interviews during investigation*	Introduced by the 2008 Amendment Regulations	
14E	*Report of investigation*	Introduced by the 2008 Amendment Rregulations	
15	*Withdrawn and discontinued complaints*		
16	*Circumstances in which an investigation or other procedure may be suspended*		20 *Restrictions on proceedings pending the conclusion of an investigation*
17	*Resumption of investigation after criminal proceedings*	If complainant does wish it to continue, then it does If not, then discretion whether to treat as a conduct matter	
18	*Appointment of persons to carry out investigations*	Qualifications of investigator	Paragraphs 16–19

19	*Combining and splitting investigations*	If 'more efficient and effective or is otherwise in the public interest'
20	*Relinquishing the Commission's supervision or management of an investigation*	
21	*Complaints against a person who has subsequently ceased to serve with the police*	Parts 2 and 2A of Sch 3 shall apply
22	*Complaints against a person whose identity is unascertained*	Parts 2 and 2A of Sch 3 shall apply
23	*Notification of actions and decisions*	Separate to where discipline recommended
24	*Keeping of records*	Every police authority and chief officer shall keep records 'in such form as the Commission shall determine' of every complaint or purported complaint, conduct matter recorded by it or him, and 'every exercise of a power or performance of a duty under Part 2 of the 2002 Act'

(Continued)

Table 6.1 *Cont.*

PCMR 2004, as amended	Heading of regulation	Comment	Cross-reference: Police Reform Act 2002 Sch 3
25	*Register to be kept by the Commission*	Commission shall establish and maintain a register of all information supplied to it by a police authority or chief officer under Pt 2 of the 2002 Act Limited disclosure (reg 25(2) incl '*necessary or conducive to the purpose of* . . . [a number of matters to demonstrate the thoroughness of the system]'	
26	*Delegation of powers and duties by chief officer*	Including local resolution: partly amended by 2006 Regulations	
27	*Manner and time limits of notifications*	Any notification in writing: exceptional circumstances outweigh time limits	
28	*Application to contracted-out staff*	Parts 2 and 2A applying to detention officer or escort officer only in so far as a complaint relates to, or another instance of misconduct involves, the carrying out of the designated function	

| 29 | | Revoked by Serious Organised Crime and Police Act 2005 (Consequential and Supplementary Amendments to Secondary Legislation) Order 2006, SI 2006/594, Sch. 1, para 43(1) (April 2006) |
| 30 | *Disciplinary proceedings for police staff* | Definition of disciplinary proceedings for police staff: *'any proceedings or management process during which the conduct of such a person is considered with a view to determining if sanction'* |

169

B. The New Standards of Professional Behaviour

Context: the commencement of the Police (Conduct) Regulations 2008

6.26 The 2008 Conduct Regulations are the latest in a line of police disciplinary regulations.[19] They came into force on 1 December 2008,[20] whereupon the predecessor Regulations were revoked. The 2008 Conduct Regulations apply only to allegations in respect of conduct by a police officer[21] that came to the attention of the appropriate authority on or after 1 December 2008.

6.27 Where an allegation was brought to the attention of the appropriate authority prior to 1 December 2008, the 2004 Conduct Regulations continue to apply. It would probably be an abuse—that is, a serious departure from the intended regulatory regime—to have deliberately delayed processing an allegation so that it came to the attention of an appropriate authority only after the date of commencement of the new Regulations.

6.28 The 2008 Conduct Regulations apply 'where an allegation comes to the attention of an appropriate authority which indicates that the conduct of a police officer may amount to misconduct or gross misconduct'.[22] The appropriate authority is defined as the police authority for a senior officer,[23] and, in all other cases, the chief officer of police of the police force concerned.

6.29 A 'senior officer' is defined as 'a member of a police force holding a rank above that of chief superintendent'[24]—that is, a chief officer, or an officer of Association of Chief Police Officers (ACPO) rank. The role of appropriate authority for non-senior officers is commonly attributed to the deputy chief constable of a force.

6.30 'Misconduct' is defined in reg 3(1) as a breach of the 'Standards of Professional Behaviour'. 'Gross misconduct' is defined in the same regulation as 'a breach of the Standards of Professional Behaviour so serious that dismissal would be justified'.

6.31 The 'Standards of Professional Behaviour' are defined by reg 3(1) as those contained in the (only) Schedule to the 2008 Conduct Regulations.

---

[19] Including the Police (Discipline) Regulations 1977, SI 1977/580; the Police (Discipline) Regulations 1985, SI 1985/518; the Police (Conduct) Regulations 1999, SI 1999/730; and the Police (Conduct) Regulations 2004, SI 2004/645.

[20] Regulation 1(1).

[21] Which, by reg 3(1), means a member of a police force or special constable of any rank (see also reg 3(2)).

[22] Regulation 5.

[23] Regulation 3(1).

[24] Ibid.

These Standards replace the old Code of Conduct as rehearsed in Sch 1 of the 2004 **6.32** Conduct Regulations. The major difference is that the Standards of Professional Behaviour are drafted in purposive—arguably, positively aspirational—language. Unhelpfully, however, the new Standards are not numbered. This would have been helpful for ease of reference and, in practice, for drafting particulars of alleged breaches.

Thus, whereas the old para 1 of Sch 1 ('Honesty and integrity') reads 'it is of para- **6.33** mount importance that the public has faith in the honesty and integrity of police officers. Officers should therefore be open and truthful in their dealings; avoid being improperly beholden to any person or institution; and discharge their duties with integrity', the equivalent replacement reads somewhat more directly 'police officers are honest, act with integrity and do not compromise or abuse their position'.

In substance, all of the former twelve paragraphs of the old Code of Conduct find **6.34** their way into the new regime—albeit that four of them are now subsumed within the Home Office Guidance.[25]

There are, however, 'new' elements in the Standards: **6.35**

(i) Under 'Orders and instructions' is stated 'police officers abide by police regulations, force policies and lawful orders'. This would seem to exclude any contended defence by an accused officer that he did not know that something was included in police regulations, or that a policy existed. Admittedly, whilst local force orders invariably mandated an obligation to maintain such knowledge, it is now explicitly an obligation for all police officers to ensure sufficient familiarity with police regulations and, perhaps more significantly, force policies.[26]

(ii) It is contended that the corollary of this—reflected in the Guidance, to an extent[27]—is the maintenance of efficient and tested systems of distribution of such policies to officers and staff. IPCC investigations have repeatedly demonstrated that merely having policies available on the force intranet does not promote widespread absorption by even diligent officers who must apply them. A force that is serious about ensuring knowledge of important operational policies will, in conjunction with any other training, distribute them directly and selectively to targeted officers by email, on an auditable 'received and read' basis.

---

[25] Namely, Sch 1, paras 8 ('Criminal offences'), 9 ('Property'), 10 ('Sobriety'), and 11 ('Appearance'). On merit, some of these were often within para 12—namely, 'General conduct'.
[26] Of particular significance, eg, in the context of custody duties, firearms operations, external business interests, domestic violence, safer neighbourhoods, and hate and race crimes.
[27] For example, para 1.7 of ch 1 of the Home Office Guidance 2008.

If an investigation demonstrates systematic failures in the effective distribution of relevant policies (and it is contended that simply having them available on a force intranet is not genuine and meaningful distribution unless the availability has been properly advertised to individual officers), it would be wrong, and probably arbitrary, to isolate individual officers for misconduct proceedings even if the resultant ignorance led to an adverse outcome.

(iii) The old 'General conduct' paragraph is now (more appropriately) entitled 'Discreditable conduct' and enjoins officers, whether on or off duty, to behave in a manner that does not 'discredit the police service or undermine public confidence in it'. No longer is the test conduct 'likely to bring discredit', and this may be argued to create difficulties for conduct that is, objectively, likely to bring discredit, but which does not, or did not, in event, bring such discredit.

This is contended to be an inherently weak argument. It would be surprising if culpability were only to arise on the contingency that conduct was discovered. The misconduct panel is concerned with the intrinsic quality of the conduct, rather than the manner, or risk, of detection. In any event, the prohibition of conduct that 'undermines public confidence' will probably cover any contended ambiguity once the conduct has been identified.

(iv) The tenth and final standard is entitled 'Challenging and reporting improper conduct',[28] and states 'police officers report, challenge or take action against the conduct of colleagues which has fallen below the standard of professional behaviour'. This would appear to make explicit (if this was needed) that it is not acceptable for police officers of any rank—but particularly of supervisory rank (see para 1.5 of the Guidance at 6.40 below)—to turn a blind eye to significant misconduct by fellow or subordinate officers. There is now—in a context of learning and development, as much as punishment—an explicit obligation to challenge and report such misconduct, where it is appropriate to do so.

6.36 Chapter 1 of the Home Office Guidance expands on the standard of professional behaviour. What it does not address is whether particular standards require a subjective failure—that is, a culpable mental element by the officer concerned—or a failure as determined by purely objective professional criteria, such as the test for dangerous driving. It is contended that, whilst certain offences necessarily require a wholly objective benchmark standard to be met, in order to amount to misconduct—still less gross misconduct—there is a mental (or subjective) element to others. It is surely the defining difference in most cases between 'performance' (arguably misconduct), on the one hand, and 'gross misconduct', on the other.

---

[28] Formerly subsumed in the final clause of para 6 ('Lawful orders'): '. . . officers should . . . oppose any improper behaviour, reporting it where appropriate.'

As applied to an allegation of dishonesty against a solicitor, the Administrative **6.37**
Court in *Bryant v Law Society*[29] agreed with the divisional court in *Donkin v Law
Society*[30] that character evidence was admissible at the fact-finding stage of the proceedings as going to credibility and propensity. This applies the two-stage objec-
tive/subjective *Twinsectra*[31] test to dishonesty. This, it is contended, is the appropriate
approach to allegations of lack of integrity or honesty by police officers.

Such considerations were live in *R (Wheeler) v AC House of the MPS*.[32] The Court **6.38**
addressed two material matters. At [1.11], it observed:

> If we leave out the reference to the benefit of hindsight, in circumstances where it is
> said that superiors of an officer were themselves at fault, it does seem to me that,
> using their professional knowledge and experience, a Panel, if the evidence justifies
> it, is entitled to come to the conclusion that an officer failed to do that which he obvi-
> ously should have done. However, it is most important that a disciplinary tribunal,
> such as the Panel in this case or the Assistant Commissioner, should be clear that they
> are not using the benefit of hindsight in departing from the standard applied by other
> officers at the time in question.

At [1.13] and [1.14], the practicality of performing the duties was held to have **6.39**
been relevant to take into consideration in determining whether a breach had
occurred. The original findings seemed to indicate:

> that Mr Wheeler was guilty as charged because he was in fact in the line of command,
> and without consideration of the question whether, having regard to his other duties,
> he was sensibly able to exercise supervision and whether his not doing so amounted
> to a clear breach of his duties.

> The unfairness of considering discipline charges when an officer was merely doing
> that which he had been trained to do in terms of practising rapid-response driving
> was commented on in *Milton (No 2)*.[33]

Paragraph 1.5 of the Guidance states: **6.40**

> Those entrusted to supervise and manage others are role models for delivering a
> professional, impartial and effective policing service. They have a particular respon-
> sibility to maintain standards of professional behaviour by demonstrating strong
> leadership and by dealing with conduct which has fallen below these standards in an
> appropriate way, such as by management action or the formal misconduct process.
> Above all else police managers should lead by example.

---

[29] [2007] EWHC 3043.
[30] [2007] EWHC 414.
[31] *Twinsectra Ltd v Yardley* [2002] 2 AC 164.
[32] [2008] EWHC 439 (Admin).
[33] *Milton v Crown Prosecution Service* [2007] EWHC 532, *per* Mr Justice Gross at [36(i)], where
he observed that, given the instructions given to the appellant by senior officers, he could not avoid
'expressing some surprise that there should have been (as we were told) disciplinary proceedings;
that, however, is not a matter for me'. See 15.146 *et seq.*

6.41 Such leadership will doubtless require, inter alia, supervisory and senior officers within forces to:

(i)   set their expectations as to conduct in particular areas of police operations, so that all officers within a force know exactly where they stand;

(ii) do so clearly and accessibly, so that officers cannot complain of ignorance or confusion on the matter; and

(iii) enforce breaches of such expectations, utilizing the 2008 Performance or Conduct Regulations where appropriate.

6.42 The combination of the setting of clear expectations, readily accessible to all officers and properly enforced,[34] will tend to minimize the opportunity for officers accused of misconduct to advance arguments premised on an assertion that the particular conduct complained of was simply representative of that accepted as falling within the margin of tolerance applied systematically to standards by a particular force.[35] The argument is probably fairly characterized as a species of the heading of 'breach of legitimate expectation' applied in judicial review proceedings.

6.43 Paragraph 1.7 of ch 1 of the Home Office Guidance recognizes that the police service has a responsibility to keep police officers informed of changes to police regulations, local policies, laws, and procedures, but also that police officers 'have a duty to keep themselves up to date on the basis of the information provided'.

Further guidance as to the Standards of Professional Behaviour in the Home Office Guidance

6.44 The Guidance tends to expand upon the intended meaning in the Schedule to the 2008 Conduct Regulations.

6.45 Under 'Honesty and integrity',[36] it seeks to offer guidance on, amongst other issues, gifts and gratuities offered to police officers, which, it states, 'must be declared in accordance with local force policy'. It must, therefore, be hoped that police forces will review and update their policies on such matters (including expenses) to ensure that they are clear, coherent, and readily understandable. This has not always been the case and officers of all ranks have found themselves caught out by conflicting interpretations on such matters.

6.46 Under 'Authority, respect and courtesy', the Guidance enjoins that, in exercising their duties, 'police officers never abuse their authority or the power entrusted to them'.

---

[34] See also 9.37–9.44.

[35] See, eg, the principles in *R v North and East Devon Health Authority, ex p Coughlan* [2001] 1 QB 213, 242.

[36] In *Bolt v Chief Constable of Merseyside Police* [2007] EWHC 2607 (Admin), at [26], Underhill J said: 'As para. 1 of the Code rightly emphasises, integrity is a fundamental requirement for a police officer. I should, frankly, be dismayed to think that such conduct was not of a kind which was normally thought to merit dismissal. . .'

Furthermore, police officers do not 'under any circumstances inflict, instigate or tolerate any act of inhuman or degrading treatment (as enshrined in Article 3 of the European Convention on Human Rights)', an injunction repeated under 'Use of force'. As already observed, whether each of these matters is wholly objective or partly subjective is a more difficult (and undecided) consideration, particularly when the allegation is such as 'abuse of authority' or 'lack of tolerance'.

Perhaps significantly (in the context of domestic violence and victims of, or vulnerable witnesses to, crime more generally), police officers are enjoined to 'recognise that some individuals who come into contact with the police . . . may be vulnerable and therefore may require additional support and assistance'. Many misconduct cases arise from implicit breaches of such an injunction. **6.47**

Under 'Equality and diversity', police officers are reminded to carry out their duties 'in accordance with current equality legislation'[37] and 'in accordance with Article 14 of the European Convention on Human Rights'—an onerous burden, if read literally, given the complexity of the applicable case law. These aspirations, however, doubtless reflect the origins of the Standards of Professional Behaviour in, amongst other documents, the European Convention on Human Rights (ECHR) and the Council of Europe's Code of Police Ethics.[38] **6.48**

Unsurprisingly, the Guidance reminds officers of the 'need to retain the confidence of all communities and therefore respect all individuals and their traditions, beliefs and lifestyles provided that such are compatible with the rule of law'. Police managers are reminded of their 'particular responsibility to support the promotion of equality and by their actions to set a positive example'. **6.49**

Under 'Use of force', officers are, again unsurprisingly, reminded of their need to justify all uses of force, whether by reference to s 3 of the Criminal Law Act 1967, s 117 of the Police and Criminal Evidence Act 1984, or common law.[39] To this list must be added the statutory definition of 'self-defence' under s 76 of the Criminal Justice and Immigration Act 2008 (see 15.90). **6.50**

Under 'Duties and responsibilities' is the injunction that police officers must 'ensure that accurate records are kept of the exercise of their duties and powers as required by relevant legislation, force policies and procedures'. Under this heading, para 9 of the old Code of Conduct ('Property') is subsumed in para 1.49 of the Guidance. **6.51**

---

[37] An onerous burden, given the volume and complexity of such legislation.

[38] Available online at <http://www.coe.int>.

[39] Paragraph 1.36 of the Home Office Guidance asserts that, under Art 2(2) of the ECHR, there is a 'stricter test for the use of lethal force'. This is wrong: see *R (Bennett) v HM Coroner for Inner South London* [2006] EWHC 196 (Admin), [25]. The 'absolute necessity' threshold in Art 2 is no different from the common law threshold for the use of lethal force: '. . .in truth, if any officer reasonably decides that he must use lethal force, it will inevitably be because it is absolutely necessary to do so. To kill when it is not absolutely necessary to do so is surely to act unreasonably.'

6.52   Under 'Confidentiality' is contained the additional injunction, not contained in the Standards of Professional Behaviour, that 'police officers never access or disclose any information that is not in the proper course of police duties and do not access information for personal reasons'. Misuse of police databases is one of the most common acts of police misconduct.

6.53   The Guidance also states that 'police officers who are unsure if they should access or disclose information always consult with their manager or department that deals with data protection or freedom of information before accessing or disclosing it'. Frequently, those officers who improperly access police databases are unable to show that they sought permission for their access, reported their access after doing so, or made a record of the same, thus tending to undermine their subsequent claims to bona fides. Equally, there is, of course, a danger of circularity of reasoning if the officer concerned contends that he had no doubt that his access was legitimate and therefore did not seek advice.

6.54   Under 'Fitness for duty', the Guidance makes clear that 'the use of illegal drugs will not be condoned', and that a 'self declaration made after a police officer is notified of the requirement to take a test for possible substance misuse cannot be used to frustrate action being taken for misconduct that may follow a positive test result'.

6.55   Under 'Discreditable conduct', there is welcome, if belated, recognition that the mere fact that the media reports the conduct of an officer is not the arbiter of whether that conduct breaches this aspect of the Standards. Although the wording does not refer to the test being a tendency or likelihood of bringing discredit upon the police service, the accompanying Guidance tends to resurrect the old 'likely to bring discredit' test. It should be remembered, however, that the Guidance cannot alter the meaning of the regulation.

6.56   More detailed guidance is also provided in relation to the public/private life dichotomy, with 'due regard' being required to the officer's right to a private life. That said, the very next paragraph of the Guidance (para 1.71) states that 'even when off duty, police officers do not behave in a manner that discredits the police service or undermines public confidence'.

6.57   Probably as a consequence of the number of misconduct cases involving officers abusing their business interests (registered or otherwise), the Guidance addresses the issue under 'Off-duty conduct', and specifically reminds officers of reg 7 of the Police Regulations 2003.[40]

6.58   Finally, under the heading 'Challenging and reporting improper conduct', the Guidance explains that police officers are 'expected to uphold the standards of professional behaviour in the police service by taking appropriate action if they

---

[40] SI 2003/527.

come across the conduct of a colleague which has fallen below these standards. They never ignore such conduct'.

If applied in practice, this could have a significant impact upon police officer **6.59** behaviour. It is the experience of both authors that many misconduct charges involve the latest manifestation of earlier patterns of questionable conduct known to other officers of concurrent or superior rank, but which, for a host of different (generally poor) reasons, have never been reported. Not infrequently, the failure to challenge or report such behaviour—particularly if borderline misconduct—leads to the professional demise of otherwise reasonable officers whose careers could, in all probability, have been saved by earlier challenge and proportionate management intervention. Equally, overzealous reporting of minor performance matters could be both demoralizing for a team and undermining of the margin of discretion for line managers.

Recognizing that junior officers may feel unable to challenge a colleague directly, **6.60** the Guidance requires them to report to a more senior officer—'preferably to a line manager'—or even, via a confidential reporting mechanism, to the police authority, or the IPCC. Further, as stated, the protected disclosure provisions of the Employment Rights Act 1996 apply by virtue of s 37 of the 2002 Act.

C. Initial Handling: The Police Reform Act 2002, Sch 3, or the Police (Conduct) Regulations 2008

It is important for all persons interested in the outcome of a report to be clear **6.61** under which statutory regime they are operating. In summary:

(i) the recording of complaints, conduct matters, and DSI matters are dealt with under Pts 1, 2, and 2A of Sch 3 to the 2002 Act, as are the considerations of whether a matter must be referred to the oversight of the IPCC (dealt with in this chapter);

(ii) assuming that the matter has proceeded this far—that is, that is has not been locally resolved—at the point where alleged misconduct is assessed and a formal investigation deemed necessary, then Pt 3 of Sch 3, and (coincidentally) Pt 3 of the 2008 Conduct Regulations apply (or the equivalent under the 2004 Conduct Regulations) (dealt with in Chapter 7).

If an investigation results in the decision to refer to misconduct proceedings, **6.62** then—contingent on the status of the officer and (primarily) when the report was made—either the 2004 Conduct Regulations or Pt 4 of the 2008 Conduct Regulations, coupled with the applicable Home Office Guidance, govern the mechanics of the misconduct proceedings (see Chapters 8, for more on the latter, and 9, for the former).

6.63   The remainder of this chapter addresses the process in the context of the 2008 Conduct Regulations. Distinctions with the 2004 Conduct Regulations are primarily concerned with the procedures following charge. It is necessary to distinguish the jurisdiction of the 2008 Conduct Regulations and that of Sch 3 to the 2002 Act, as amended.

The application of Sch 3 to the 2002 Act

6.64   Certain complaints or conduct matters (defined by s 12(1) and (2) of the 2002 Act), and all DSI matters (defined by s 12(2A)), start under Sch 3 of the 2002 Act. In those circumstances, the IPCC must determine the form of investigation under para 15(4) of Sch 3. Others will be investigated subject to the regime in Pt 3 of the 2008 Conduct Regulations. By reg 11, Pt 3 of the 2008 Conduct Regulations ('Investigations') does not apply to cases to which any of the para 15(4) forms of investigation apply—namely, paras 16 (local investigation), 17 (supervised investigation), 18 (managed investigation), or 19 (independent investigation).

6.65   Investigations to which paras 16–19 of Sch 3 of the 2002 Act apply are subject to the investigative regime in paras 19A–19E of that Schedule (so-called 'special requirements' cases), which must be read with regs 14A–14E of the 2004 Complaint and Misconduct Regulations, as amended. Special requirements under Sch 3 apply only to police officers and special constables, not to police staff.

6.66   The amendments to Sch 3 brought about by Sch 23 to the Criminal Justice and Immigration Act 2008, coupled with the Police (Complaints and Misconduct) (Amendment) Regulations 2008,[41] have the effect of bringing both investigative regimes into line with each other. As already observed, the underlying control of the process is reflected at different points, such as service of the (near-identical) notice of investigation under reg 14A if a Sch 3 investigation, but under reg 15 if not. A similar parallel regime is created for 'special cases' under Sch 3 within paras 20A–20I, which follows the scheme in Pt 5 of the 2008 Conduct Regulations.

6.67   There are differences: for example, the 2008 Conduct Regulations apply only to police officers and special constables,[42] whereas Sch 3 applies to all 'persons serving with the police'.[43]

6.68   Schedule 3 overlays various obligations on appropriate authorities (such as obtaining and preserving evidence, and questions of referral to the IPCC), and also gives the IPCC various rights to intervene and direct the appropriate authorities in relation to the handling of investigations and outcomes.

---

[41] SI 2008/2866.

[42] See the definition of 'police officer' in regs 5 and 3(1).

[43] Defined by s 12(7) of the 2002 Act to mean police officers, employees of police authorities who are under the direction and control of a chief officer, and special constables similarly under the chief officer's direction and control. See also s 29(3).

Final convergence of the 'parallel' regimes of the 2008 Conduct Regulations and **6.69**
paras 19A–19E of Sch 3 regime occurs at the point where the investigator's report
is completed: see para 22 of Sch 3 ('Final reports on investigations: complaints,
conduct matters and certain DSI matters'), and reg 18 of the 2008 Conduct
Regulations ('Report of investigation').

This convergence is reflected in reg 19(1) of the 2008 Conduct Regulations. **6.70**
Regulation 19 is the start of Pt 4 to the Regulations, and deals with the mechanisms for the promulgation of misconduct proceedings and applies to all matters,
whatever their statutory origin. That said, complaints and conduct matters that
proceed under Pt 4 of the Regulations, but which originated under Sch 3 of the
2002 Act, retain the IPCC's statutory overview, as reflected in paras 22–27 of Sch 3.

D. The Police Reform Act 2002, Pt 2: Complaints, Conduct Matters, and DSI Matters

Part 2 of the 2002 Act deals with public complaints against the police, conduct **6.71**
matters, DSI matters, and the creation of the IPCC.

Complaints

Part 2 of the 2002 Act defines a 'complaint' in s 12(1) as 'any complaint about the **6.72**
conduct of a person serving with the police' made by specified persons. Certain
exclusions (police officers, etc) from members of the public for these purposes
were reflected at 6.06 above. The qualifying specified persons are:

(a) a member of the public who claims to be the person in relation to whom the conduct took
   place;
(b) a member of the public not falling within paragraph (a) who claims to have been adversely
   affected by the conduct;
(c) a member of the public who claims to have witnessed the conduct;
(d) a person acting on behalf of a person falling within any of paragraphs (a) to (c).

By s 12(3) and (4) of the 2002 Act, the 'adversely affected' category does not **6.73**
include someone adversely affected merely because they have seen or heard the
alleged conduct or the alleged effects of the same, unless:

(a) it was only because the person in question was physically present, or sufficiently nearby,
   when the conduct took place or the effects occurred that he was able to see or hear the
   conduct or its effects; or
(b) the adverse effect is attributable to, or was aggravated by, the fact that the person in relation
   to whom the conduct took place was already known to the person claiming to have suffered
   the adverse effect.[44]

---

[44] Section 12(4) of the 2002 Act.

6.74 Under s 12(5), a member of the public is to be taken to have witnessed conduct if, and only if:

    (a) he acquired his knowledge of that conduct in a manner which would make him a competent witness capable of giving admissible evidence of that conduct in criminal proceedings;[45] or

    (b) he has in his possession or under his control anything which would in any such proceedings constitute admissible evidence of that conduct.

6.75 By s 12(6), a qualifying member of the public is not to be taken to have authorized another person to act on his behalf unless:

    (a) that other person is . . . designated . . . by the [IPCC] as a person through whom complaints may be made, or he is of a description of persons so designated; or

    (b) the other person has been given, and is able to produce, the written consent to his so acting of the person on whose behalf he acts.

Conduct matters

6.76 Section 12(2) of Pt 2 of the 2002 Act defines 'conduct matter' as any matter that is not, and has not been, the subject of a complaint, but in relation to which there is an indication that a person serving with the police may have:

    (a) committed a criminal offence; or

    (b) behaved in a manner which would justify the bringing of disciplinary proceedings.

DSI matters

6.77 Section 12(2A) of the 2002 Act[46] defines 'death or serious injury matter' ('DSI matter') as meaning 'any circumstances, other than those which are or have been the subject of a complaint or which amount to a conduct matter in or in consequence of which a person has died or has sustained serious injury', and:

    (i) at the time of the DSI, the person had been arrested by a person serving with the police and had not been released from that arrest, or was otherwise detained in the custody of a person serving with the police (s 12(2B)); or

    (ii) at, or before, the time of the DSI, the person had contact (of whatever kind, and whether direct or indirect) with a person serving with the police who was acting in the execution of his duties, and there is an indication that the contact may have caused (whether directly or indirectly), or contributed to, the DSI (s 12(2C).[47]

---

[45] If the witness could give evidence in criminal proceedings, then self-evidently he will be able to do so in misconduct proceedings.

[46] As inserted by Sch 12, para 3, of the Serious Organised Crime and Police Act 2005.

[47] Both as similarly inserted. The reach of the legislation to encompass as many situations as possible connected with the police can be seen.

DSI matters were introduced to Pt 2 of the 2002 Act when it became clear that **6.78** DSIs attributed to, or following contact with, the police could occur without anyone necessarily complaining so as to trigger the complaint procedure, or without there necessarily being evidence of a conduct matter so as to trigger the equivalent conduct procedure. The lacuna was filled by s 12(2A)–(2D) of the Act, introduced by Sch 12, para 3, of the Serious Organised Crime and Police Act 2005.

A person serving with the police is covered by the DSI matters although 'contact' **6.79** does not include contact that he has whilst acting in the execution of his duties—that is, when 'off duty', he may qualify as a member of the public suffering DSI for these purposes, but not if the qualifying injury is suffered when executing police duties. This makes sense, because serious injury suffered on duty would otherwise attract the provisions of Pt 2A, and, equally, there is no reason of public policy to exclude DSIs suffered by a member of a police force if that person was simply a member of the public when the event occurred.

A person serving with the police

A person is serving with the police for the purpose of Pt 2 of the 2002 Act if he **6.80** is a member of a police force (that is, a police officer), an employee of a police authority who is under the direction and control of a chief officer (that is, a civilian member of police staff, but not someone contracted in by a chief officer), or a special constable who is under the direction and control of a chief officer.[48]

The application of Pt 2 to officers who have ceased to serve

Regulation 21 of the 2004 Complaints and Misconduct Regulations provides **6.81** that, where a complaint or conduct matter relates to the conduct of a person who has ceased to be a person serving with the police since the time of the conduct in question, then Pt 2 of the Act applies in relation to such a person 'as if it did not include any requirement for an appropriate authority to determine whether disciplinary proceedings should be brought against a person whose conduct is the subject-matter of a report'. In other words, the investigation should continue even though, self-evidently, there will be no jurisdiction to take disciplinary action against the person no longer serving with the police. This is no doubt driven by the legitimate considerations of institutional learning and public accountability.

The exclusion from Sch 3 of direction and control matters

Section 13 provides that Sch 3 of the Act makes provision for the handling of **6.82** complaints, conduct, and DSI matters, and for the carrying out of investigations,

---

[48] Section 12(7) of the 2002 Act.

but is subject to s 14. Section 14(1) removes from the coverage of Sch 3 'so much of any complaint as relates to the direction and control of a police force' by the chief officer of police of that force, or a person carrying out those functions. (Direction and control has already been separately addressed at 1.04–1.10.)

Schedule 3 to the Police Reform Act 2002

6.83   It is to be noted that Sch 23 to the Criminal Justice and Immigration Act 2008 amended Sch 3 to the 2002 Act significantly. As Table 6.1 demonstrates, the first three parts of Sch 3 address the duties on the police to preserve evidence, to record complaints, and to refer matters to the IPCC. Part 1 of Sch 3 deals with the handling of complaints, Pt 2 deals with the handling of conduct matters, and Pt 2A deals with the handling of DSI matters.

6.84   It is necessary to address each Part separately.

E.   Police Reform Act 2002, Sch 3, Pt 1: The Handling of Complaints

6.85   Part 1 of Sch 3 to the 2002 Act sets out the following key duties.

  (i)   By para 1, where a complaint is made to a chief officer about the conduct of a person under his direction and control, or the chief officer becomes aware that such a complaint has been made to the IPCC or a police authority, the chief officer 'shall take all such steps as appear to him to be appropriate for the purposes of Part 2 of this Act for obtaining and preserving evidence relating to the conduct complained of '.

 (ii)   It follows that the chief officer must have in place adequate managerial systems to ensure that evidence is not lost, dissipated, or otherwise degraded once he is on notice as to a complaint. This is an obvious obligation to ensure the integrity of the complaints system—although it is one that, as a matter of experience, has not always been discharged effectively despite the seniority of the officer charged with the responsibility.

(iii)   The duty on the chief officer must be discharged as soon as practicable after the complaint is made or he becomes aware of it, and it is an ongoing duty. Furthermore, the chief officer is under a duty to take such specific steps for obtaining or preserving evidence as his police authority or the IPCC may direct.

6.86   Paragraph 2 imposes duties upon the IPCC, police authority, and chief officer to determine who is the appropriate authority, to ensure notification of the complaint to the person who is the appropriate authority, and to notify the complainant that the appropriate authority has been notified. It also requires that the appropriate authority (chief officer or police authority) record the complaint. This is presumably both to ensure an audit trail and to promote the collection of data for empirical purposes.

Paragraph 3 deals with the procedure where the chief officer or police authority **6.87** decides, in relation to anything that is or purports to be a complaint pursuant to para 2, not to take any action under para 2 for notifying or recording the whole, or any part, of what has been received. In such a situation, the police authority or chief officer must notify the complainant of:

   (i)   the decision to take no action;
  (ii)   the grounds on which the decision was made; and
 (iii)   his right to appeal against that decision under para 3.

The complainant's right of appeal lies to the IPCC, which, on receiving such an **6.88** appeal, shall:

   (i)   determine whether any action under para 2 should have been taken; and
  (ii)   if it finds in the complainant's favour, give directions to the police authority or chief officer as to the action to be taken for making a determination, or for notifying or recording what was received.

The police authority or chief officer is under a duty to comply with any such direc- **6.89** tions given. Paragraph 3(7) provides for the Secretary of State to make regulations concerning such appeals, and reg 8 of the 2004 Complaints and Misconduct Regulations makes such provision.

Paragraph 4 of Sch 3 deals with the important issue of reference of complaints **6.90** to the IPCC. There are two categories of referral: mandatory and discretionary.

Paragraph 4(1) of Sch 3 confirms that referral of a complaint to the IPCC is man- **6.91** datory when:

   (i)   the complaint alleges that the conduct complained of resulted in DSI;
  (ii)   the complaint is one specified in the regulations (reg 2(2) of the 2004 Complaints and Misconduct Regulations specifies complaints that allege conduct which constitutes the commission of a serious assault, a serious sexual offence, serious corruption, criminal or other misconduct aggravated by discriminatory behaviour, and complaints arising from the same incident as one resulting in DSI);[49]
 (iii)   the IPCC requires the appropriate authority to refer for its consideration. The IPCC thus retains ultimate control of referrals.

---

   [49] Appendix A of the IPCC's statutory guidance under s 22 of the 2002 Act provides further definition of serious injury, serious assault, 'assaults which as a general rule need not be referred to the IPCC', serious sexual offences, serious corruption, criminal offences and behaviour aggravated by discriminatory behaviour, and serious arrestable offences.

6.92 The discretionary referral of complaints arises where the appropriate authority considers it appropriate to refer by reason of (Sch 3, para 4(2)):

    (a) the gravity of the subject-matter of the complaint; or

    (b) any exceptional circumstances.

6.93 It follows that, when coupled with the IPCC's entitlement under para 4(1)(c) to 'call in' any complaint for referral, it would appear unlikely that many complaints of substantial public concern could fall into the discretionary category and not be referred.

6.94 Paragraph 4(3) contains a provision for police authorities whereby, if a reference under para 4(1) or (2) is neither made nor required to be made, a police authority may nonetheless refer a complaint to the IPCC if it is one in relation to which a chief officer of police maintained by that police authority is the appropriate authority, and the police authority considers that it would be appropriate to make a reference by reason of the gravity of the subject matter or any exceptional circumstances.

6.95 It would seem that this saving provision in para 4(3)[50] provides a 'fail-safe' whereby a police authority can ensure a referral to the IPCC even if the relevant chief officer, as appropriate authority, does not do so.

6.96 Referrals—most particularly, mandatory referrals—must be made within a specified timescale (see para 4(4) of Sch 3 and reg 2(3) of the 2004 Complaints and Misconduct Regulations). The reference to 'working' day was removed by the 2006 Amendment Regulations. Powers to refer are ongoing and irrespective of whether the complaint is already being investigated or has previously been referred. This is presumably to ensure the necessary ongoing review and reconsideration as circumstances change.

6.97 In this context, the person referring the complaint to the IPCC must also notify the complainant and (other than where to do so might prejudice the possible investigation) the person complained against.[51] One must assume that similar considerations that apply to withholding service of notices of investigation would apply here.

6.98 Paragraph 5 of Pt 1 of Sch 3 provides that, upon any referrals under para 4, the IPCC shall determine whether the complaint needs to be investigated. Guidance as to the exercise of this discretion is published on its website.[52] If the IPCC considers that an investigation is necessary, it must then determine the form that the investigation should take (see Pt 3 and para 15 of Sch 3, at 6.14 above).

---

[50] And see Sch 3, para13(3), for conduct matters.

[51] Schedule 3, para 4(6).

[52] See <www.ipcc.gov.uk>.

If the IPCC considers that investigation is not necessary, it may nonetheless **6.99** refer the matter back to the appropriate authority to be dealt with by it in accordance with para 6 (so-called 'local resolution'). In other words, the IPCC can decide that an investigation is unnecessary, but that the appropriate authority should consider whether local resolution is appropriate. If the IPCC makes a reference back to the appropriate authority for consideration of local resolution, it must, again, notify the complainant and the person complained against (with the same exemption for the latter if doing so might prejudice a future investigation).

Local resolution (Sch 3, para 6)

Local resolution was introduced in the overview to this chapter. It is an important **6.100** mechanism that tends to operate in the interests of all parties. The statutory context, and the practical rights and procedures, are well documented in IPCC literature. Local resolution considerations only arise where:

(i) a complaint has been recorded by the appropriate authority; and

(ii) the complaint has not been referred (because it did not need to be and/or was not, in the appropriate authority's discretion) or was referred to the IPCC (whether because it had to be or was), but was referred back under para 5(2) (as 'not the subject of paragraph 15 determination'—that is, not requiring investigation).

In other words, local resolution considerations only arise where the **6.101** complaint was not serious in the first place or, although apparently sufficiently serious for referral, was, for some reason, referred back by the IPCC. For all practical purposes, by whatever mechanism, local resolution only arises on less serious complaints.

Accordingly, in respect of any recorded complaint that has not been referred **6.102** to the IPCC, or which has been referred to the IPCC, but is then referred back (and subject only to the dispensation provisions of para 7—see 6.119 below), the appropriate authority must determine whether or not the complaint is 'suitable for being subjected to local resolution' (Sch 3, para 6(2)).

If the appropriate authority determines that the complaint is suitable for local **6.103** resolution, and the complainant consents to such, then the appropriate authority must make arrangements for the complaint to be locally resolved.

If, however, the appropriate authority determines that the complaint is not suit- **6.104** able for local resolution, or considers that it is suitable, but the complainant disagrees that it is so suitable, then the appropriate authority must make arrangements for the complaint to be investigated by the appropriate authority on its own behalf—that is, for an 'in-force' local investigation.

6.105 Paragraph 6(3) of Sch 3 provides the criteria for suitability for local resolution. A complaint is not suitable for local resolution unless either:

> (a) the appropriate authority is satisfied that the conduct complained of (even if it were proved) would not justify the bringing of any criminal or disciplinary proceedings;[53] or
>
> (b) the [IPCC], in a case falling within sub-paragraph (4), has approved the use of local resolution.

6.106 Paragraph 6(4) empowers the IPCC to approve the use of local resolution in the case of any complaint if, on an application by the appropriate authority, the IPCC is satisfied:

> (i) either that the conduct complained of, even if proved, would not justify the bringing of criminal proceedings and that any disciplinary proceedings that were justified would not result in a dismissal or final written warning;[54] or
>
> (ii) that it will not be practicable, even if the complaint is thoroughly investigated, for criminal proceeding successfully to be brought or disciplinary proceedings to be brought, which would be likely to result in dismissal or the giving of a final written warning.

6.107 Thus it can be seen that the IPCC is entitled to approve an application by the appropriate authority for local resolution, provided that:

> (i) the appropriate authority applies for local resolution; and
>
> (ii) criminal proceedings could not be justified or would not be practical even if thoroughly investigated, or where the likely disciplinary action in any disciplinary proceedings would not result in dismissal or final written warning, or it is not practicable even if the complaint is thoroughly investigated to bring disciplinary proceedings that would produce either of these outcomes.

6.108 Considerations of the effect of delay and the likely result of any disciplinary action, and the subsequent conduct and commitment to the force of the officer concerned, are clearly relevant. In other words, the IPCC can, and should, consider

---

[53] It is a little unclear whether the 'would not justify' test means that the appropriate authority considers that the complaint, even if proved, would not justify even 'management advice', ie the lowest formal disciplinary action under the 2008 Conduct Regulations, or whether the test is broader and reflects public interest and proportionality. To the extent that there is a difference, the authors adopt the second approach: the Home Office Guidance provides discretion in any case as to whether misconduct proceedings are proportionate and fair in all of the circumstances, including delay and probable sanction.

[54] Paragraph 6(4)(a)(ii) and (b)(ii) of Sch 3 to the 2002 Act have been amended by para 4 of Sch 23 to the Criminal Justice and Immigration Act 2008 to reflect the new, more limited, disciplinary sanctions available under the 2008 Conduct Regulations from 1 December 2008: see the Criminal Justice and Immigration Act 2008 (Commencement No 4 and Saving Provision) Order 2008, SI 2008/2993.

the quality and likely effect of mitigation in determining the likely practicable result of any disciplinary action.

The appropriate authority can only apply for local resolution once to the IPCC in respect of the same complaint. Before a complainant can give his consent for local resolution, he must have been informed of his rights of appeal under para 9—that is, of his right to appeal the conduct of the local resolution of that complaint (see 6.116 below). Presumably, giving this information to the complainant is intended to encourage local resolution because the complainant has the knowledge that he can appeal aspects of the process. **6.109**

Paragraph 8 of Sch 3 sets up the mechanism for local resolution, and provides that the arrangements by the appropriate authority may include the appointment of a person serving with the police who is under the direction and control of the chief officer to 'secure the local resolution of the complaint'. This person can thus be a police officer or member of police staff. **6.110**

The Secretary of State may, by regulation, provide for the procedures for local resolution. This was achieved by reg 4(1) of the 2004 Complaints and Misconduct Regulations, which provides that, subject to the regulation, 'any procedures which are approved by the Commission' will apply. Regulation 4 provides substantive provision as to recording, comments by affected parties, and provision of records, and by reg 4A, that any statement made by any person for local resolution purposes 'shall not be admissible in any subsequent criminal, civil or disciplinary proceedings except to the extent that it consists of an admission relating to a matter that has not been subjected to local resolution'. This is presumably to encourage a frank approach to the local resolution. **6.111**

Paragraph 5.3.7 of the IPCC statutory guidance contends that 'local resolution is an umbrella process that may work in a number of different ways'. As already stated, it has published a local resolution process, which must represent the approved procedure under reg 4(1).[55] **6.112**

Paragraph 8(4) of Sch 3 of the 2002 Act provides that if, after attempts at local resolution, it appears to the appropriate authority that local resolution is impossible or the matter is not suitable for such resolution, then the appropriate authority 'shall make arrangements for the complaint to be investigated'. **6.113**

Paragraph 8(5) of Sch 3 provides for the discontinuance of local resolution if the appropriate authority makes a determination under para 8(4), or if the IPCC notifies the appropriate authority that it requires the complaint to be referred to it under para 4 of Sch 3,[56] or if the complaint is otherwise so referred. The last two **6.114**

---

[55] Available online at <http://www.ipcc.gov.uk>.
[56] Schedule 3, para 8(5)(b).

scenarios could arise if it were to emerge that the complaint was more serious than originally appeared. The provision at para 8(5)(b) is another example of the IPCC retaining ultimate control of the public complaints process.

6.115 Finally, para 8(6) disqualifies from involvement in any subsequent investigation any person who participated in any attempt at local resolution.

Appeals relating to local resolution (Sch 3, para 9)

6.116 Paragraph 9(8) of Sch 3 to the 2002 Act provides that the Secretary of State may, by regulation, provide for the form, manner, and procedure for such appeals. These provisions are found in reg 9 of the 2004 Complaints and Misconduct Regulations. Paragraph 9(1) of Sch 3 provides that the complainant has the right of appeal to the IPCC 'against the conduct of the local resolution' of his complaint—but para 9(2) provides that it is only alleged contraventions of 'procedural requirements' that may be appealed.

6.117 Upon receipt of any such appeal, the IPCC must first given the person appealed against and the appropriate authority an opportunity to make representations about the issues raised in the appeal. Upon receipt of any such representations, the IPCC then determines whether there have been any contraventions of the procedural requirements.

6.118 If the IPCC determines in the complainant's favour:

(i) it shall give such directions as it considers appropriate to the appropriate authority 'as to the future handling of the complaint', and it shall be the duty of the appropriate authority to comply with any such directions;

(ii) where those directions state that the future handling of the complaint should include an investigation, then para 15 of Sch 3 ('Form of investigation') shall apply (see 6.14 above);

(iii) by para 9(7) of Sch 3 and, coincidentally, reg 9(7) of the 2004 Complaints and Misconduct Regulations, the IPCC is obliged to notify all concerned as to its determinations and directions under para 9.

Dispensation by the IPCC

6.119 If, in a case to which para 6 applies,[57] the appropriate authority considers that (i) it should handle the complaint otherwise than in accordance with the Schedule or should take no action in relation to it, and (ii) the complaint falls within a description of complaints specified in the regulations made by the Secretary of

---

[57] That is, where a complaint has been recorded by the appropriate authority, but the complaint has not been referred to the IPCC; or where it was referred to the IPCC, but was referred back to the appropriate authority.

State for the purposes of para 7, the appropriate authority may apply to the IPCC for permission to handle the complaint in whatever manner (if any) that the appropriate authority thinks fit.

The specified complaints are those set out in reg 3(2) of the 2004 Complaints and **6.120** Misconduct Regulations—that is, complaints in relation to which the appropriate authority considers that:

(i) more than twelve months have elapsed between the incident, or the latest incident giving rise to the complaint and the making of the complaint, and either that no good reason for the delay has been shown, or that injustice would be likely to be caused by the delay;

(ii) the matter is already the subject of a complaint;

(iii) the complaint discloses neither the name and address of the complainant, nor that of any other interested person, and it is not reasonably practicable to ascertain such a name or address;

(iv) the complaint is vexatious, oppressive, or otherwise an abuse of the procedures for dealing with complaints;[58]

(v) the complaint is repetitious;[59] or

(vi) it is not reasonably practicable[60] to complete the investigation of the complaint or any other procedures under Sch 3 to the 2002 Act.

Regulation 3(6) provides that any application by the appropriate authority under **6.121** para 7(1) of Sch 3 shall be in writing and accompanied by:

(i) a copy of the complaint;

(ii) the reasons for the application;

(iii) where the grounds for the application is one of 'repetition', a copy of the previous complaint and the record of any resolution, withdrawal, or dispensation of that complaint; and

(iv) copies of any other documents or material in the appropriate authority's possession that are relevant to the complaint.

Regulation 3(7) provides that the appropriate authority shall supply any further information requested by the IPCC for the purpose of considering any dispensation application made under para 7 of Sch 3.

Any dispensation application made by the appropriate authority under para 7 must **6.122** be notified to the complainant, and the IPCC must notify both the appropriate authority and the complaint of its dispensation decision. Pending the decision by

---

[58] By analogy, see r 3.4 of the Civil Procedure Rules 1998, as considered at para 3.4 *et seq* in *The White Book Service*, London: Sweet & Maxwell, and updated at <http://www.sweetandmaxwell.co.uk/whitebook>.

[59] Defined in reg 3(3) of the 2004 Complaints and Misconduct Regulations.

[60] Defined ibid.

the IPCC, the appropriate authority shall not take any action pursuant to Sch 3 in relation to the complaint.

6.123 If the IPCC gives the permission sought by the appropriate authority, then the latter may handle the complaint in whatever manner it thinks fit, including taking no action in relation to it. Conversely, if the IPCC rejects the appropriate authority's application under para 7 of Sch 3, it must refer the matter back to the appropriate authority for a decision under para 6(2) and the appropriate authority must make that determination. In practice, this will be as between local resolution or an in-force investigation.

6.124 A dispensation application can only be made to the IPCC once in respect of the same complaint. There are competing authorities as to whether a dispensation decision, once made and promulgated, is final or admits of further representations: see Chapter 7 n 82.

F. Police Reform Act 2002, Sch 3, Pt 2: The Handling of Conduct Matters

6.125 Part 2 of Sch 3 of the 2002 Act sets out further duties upon police authorities and chief officers in relation to the recording of conduct matters.

Civil proceedings involving a conduct matter

6.126 Paragraph 10 deals with the obligation to record conduct matters arising in civil proceedings. It requires that, where a police authority or chief officer receives notification that civil proceedings[61] have been brought by a member of the public against that authority or chief officer, or it otherwise appears that such proceedings are likely to be brought and that those proceedings involve, or would involve, a conduct matter,[62] then the police authority or chief officer shall determine whether it is the appropriate authority in relation to the conduct matter and shall:

(i) if it or he is not, notify the appropriate authority about the proceedings and the circumstances that constitute the apparent conduct matter (para 10(2)(b));

(ii) if it or he is the appropriate authority, record the matter (para 10(3)).

---

[61] For the purposes of para 10, civil proceedings involve a conduct matter if they relate to a conduct matter or are proceedings that relate to a matter in relation to which a conduct matter, or evidence of a conduct matter, is or may be relevant: see para 10(6).

[62] Defined in s 12(2) of the 2002 Act.

It can be seen that, as with public complaints, there is an obligation on the **6.127** appropriate authority to record conduct matters—again, presumably for statistical purposes. As with complaints, the Home Secretary shall provide regulations governing the timings of compliance with para 10.

The recording of conduct matters in other cases

Paragraph 11 deals with the obligation to record conduct matters arising in other **6.128** cases—that is, not from actual or intimated civil proceedings—in a like manner to para 10.

Paragraph 11(5) contains a final saving position for the IPCC, which may, if it **6.129** appears to it that any recordable conduct matter has not been recorded by the appropriate authority, direct the appropriate authority to record the matter and the appropriate authority must comply with such direction.

Upon recording the matter, the appropriate authority shall first determine **6.130** whether the matter is one that it is required to refer to the IPCC under para 13(1), or is one that it would be appropriate to refer under para 13(2). If it is not required to refer the matter to the IPCC and does not do so, the appropriate authority may deal with the matter in such manner as it may determine.

A conduct matter disclosed during DSI investigation

A conduct matter may be disclosed during the investigation of a DSI matter. **6.131** The procedure to be followed in such a case is prescribed by para 21A of Sch 3. In substance, a notification requirement arises as between the investigator and appropriate authority, and, if determined as such, the identified conduct matter is recorded under para 11 of Sch 3. By para 21A(6), the investigation then continues under the provisions of the Schedule and associated regulations (reg 5 of the 2008 Conduct Regulations) applicable to recorded conduct matters. This is a rights-led approach, designed to protect the legitimate interests of affected officers.

Other mandatory referrals to the IPCC by the appropriate authority

Paragraph 13(1) of Sch 3 sets out three situations in which referral by the **6.132** appropriate authority to the IPCC is mandatory. It can be seen that para 13(1) contains analogous provisions for conduct matters to those of para 4(1) for complaints. The mandatory situations are where:

(a) that matter relates to any incident or circumstances in or in consequence of which any person has died or suffered serious injury;

(b) that matter is of a description specified for the purposes of this sub-paragraph in regulations made by the Secretary of State [reg 5(2) and (3)(a) of the 2004 Complaints and Misconduct Regulations]; or

(c) the [IPCC] notifies the appropriate authority that it requires that matter to be referred to [it] for its consideration.

Discretionary referrals by the appropriate authority to the IPCC

6.133 Paragraph 13(2) of Sch 3 provides that, where the appropriate authority is not obliged to make a reference to the IPCC under para 13(1), it may nonetheless do so if it considers that it would be appropriate to do so by reason of the gravity of the matter or any exceptional circumstances. Again, para 13(2) provides analogous powers to the appropriate authority to conduct matters to those of para 4(2) for complaints matters.

6.134 As with para 4(3) for complaints, para 13(3) contains a saving provision for police authorities whereby, if a reference under para 13(1) or (2) is neither made nor required to be made, the police authority may nonetheless refer a conduct matter to the IPCC if it is one in relation to which a chief officer is the appropriate authority, and the police authority considers that it would be appropriate to refer by reason of the gravity of the subject matter or any exceptional circumstances.

6.135 It is difficult to be prescriptive as to when this discretion should be exercised. Anything in relation to which there is a strong public interest may qualify, such as a 'near miss' in custody, a fundamental mishandling of a vulnerable witness, or a suggestion of systematic failure. It is often in the interests of a force for an independent element to be introduced to any such investigation in terms of promoting public confidence.

6.136 As with referrals of complaints to the IPCC, Sch 3 provides for the police authority or chief officer to notify the person serving with the police whose conduct is the subject of the referral to be notified of the fact of the referral, unless to do so would prejudice a possible future investigation.[63]

6.137 Paragraph 12 of Sch 3 contains identical substantive duties upon appropriate authorities for obtaining and preserving evidence relating to conduct matter to those imposed by para 1 in relation to complaints.

6.138 Paragraph 14 of Sch 3 contains a like duty upon the IPCC in relation to conduct matters to that which para 5 does for complaints—that is, to determine whether the recordable conduct matter must be investigated. If not, the IPCC may refer the matter back to the appropriate authority to be dealt with by that authority as it sees fit. The reference back must be notified to the person to whose conduct the matter relates, subject to the exception where to do so might prejudice a possible future investigation.

6.139 Given the absence of a 'complainant' as such, Pt 2 of Sch 3 does not, inevitably, contain analogous provisions concerning rights of appeal against non-recording of conduct matters.

---

[63] Paragraph 13(6).

G. Police Reform Act 2002, Sch 3, Pt 2A:
The Handling of DSI Matters

Part 2A of Sch 3[64] sets out further duties upon police authorities and chief officers **6.140** in relation to the recording of DSI matters. It is considerably more straightforward in its drafting than Pts 1 and 2.

Paragraph 14A(1) requires that, where a DSI matter comes to the attention of the **6.141** appropriate authority, it shall be the duty of the appropriate authority to record the matter. The mandatory obligation to record presumably flows from the fact that the matter in question is intrinsically serious.

Paragraph 14A(2) contains the saving position for the IPCC, which may, if it **6.142** appears to it that any matter that has come to its attention is a DSI matter that has not been recorded by the appropriate authority, direct the appropriate authority to record the matter and the appropriate authority must comply with such direction.

Similarly, para 14B contains identical substantive duties upon appropriate author- **6.143** ities for obtaining and preserving evidence relating to DSI matters to those imposed by paras 1 and 12 in relation to complaints and conduct matters, respectively.

Paragraph 14C provides that it shall be the duty of the appropriate authority to **6.144** refer a DSI matter to the IPCC within a period provided for by regulations made by the Secretary of State. Thus, the very fact of the seriousness of the matter removes any discretion on the part of the appropriate authority: *all* DSI matters must be referred to the IPCC.

As with complaints and conduct matters, the IPCC must then determine whether **6.145** it is necessary for the DSI matter to be investigated and, if it determines that it is not, it may refer the DSI matter to the appropriate authority to be dealt with as it thinks fit.[65] Self-evidently, not all DSI matters will require investigations or investigations outside the force.

---

[64] Inserted by s 160 and Sch 12 of the Serious Organised Crime and Police Act 2005, and in force from 1 July 2005: see the Serious Organised Crime and Police Act 2005 (Commencement No 1, Transitional and Transitory Provisions) Order 2005, SI 2005/1521, art 3(1)(w).

[65] Paragraph 14D.

H. Police Reform Act 2002, Sch 3: Miscellaneous Aspects

Restrictions on proceedings

6.146 Paragraph 20 of Sch 3 prohibits the bringing of criminal or disciplinary proceedings until either the appropriate authority has certified the case to be a
'special case' (see 6.149 below), or a report on the investigation has been
submitted to the IPCC or appropriate authority under paras 22 or 24A
(final reports on Sch 3 investigations). This prohibition does not, however,
apply to criminal proceedings brought by the Director of Public Prosecutions
(DPP), in any case in which it appears to the DPP that there are exceptional
circumstances that make it undesirable to delay the bringing of such
proceedings.

6.147 The sequence of misconduct as against criminal proceedings is addressed by
reg 9 of the 2008 Conduct Regulations and the associated Home Office
Guidance, at paras 2.27 *et seq* and 2.35 *et seq*. It will be seen that, subject to
legitimate considerations of prejudice and fairness, the expectation is that
misconduct proceedings may occur before the criminal process is concluded.
Where the special case provisions are met, the risk of prejudice from the
perspective of the prosecution, but not the officer concerned, is necessarily
reduced.

6.148 In either event, it will be for the officer concerned to identify the specific unfairness of proceeding with misconduct charges before the resolution of a criminal
allegation. These arguments always reflect competing considerations and are
case-sensitive.

Special cases (Sch 3, paras 20A–20I)

6.149 Paragraph 20A deals with 'special cases' (more commonly known as 'fast-track'
cases). This paragraph is analogous to, and imports for complaints and recordable
conduct matters the same substantive provisions as provided for in Pt 5 of the
2008 Conduct Regulations.

6.150 As previously stated, the IPCC may (under para 20H(1) of Sch 3) 'recommend'
that a matter be certified as a 'special case' under para 20B(3), and may ultimately
direct that course if the recommendation is not accepted (para 20H(7)). The
process is considered in detail at 10.09–10.23.

The power of the IPCC to discontinue an investigation (Sch 3, para 21)

6.151 Paragraph 21 provides that if, at any time, it appears to the IPCC (whether on
application by the appropriate or otherwise) that a complaint or matter being

investigated (whether locally, supervised, or managed), is of a description specified in reg 7 of the 2004 Complaints and Misconduct Regulations, then the IPCC may, by order, require the discontinuance of the investigation.

Regulation 7(2) provides that the qualifying situations are those: **6.152**

(a) in which the complainant refuses to co-operate to the extent that the Commission considers that it is not reasonably practicable to continue the investigation;
(b) which the complainant has agreed may be subjected to local resolution;
(c) which the Commission considers is vexatious, oppressive or otherwise an abuse of the [Sch 3] procedures for dealing with complaints or conduct matters;
(d) which is repetitious, as defined in regulation 3(3); or
(e) which the Commission otherwise considers is such as to make it not reasonably practicable to proceed with the investigation.

Paragraph 21(2) provides that the IPCC shall not discontinue any para 19 (that   **6.153** is, IPCC) investigation except in cases authorized by regulations made by the Secretary of State. The relevant regulation is to be found in reg 7(3) of the 2004 Complaints and Misconduct Regulations, which provides that para 19 investigations may be discontinued where they fall within the provisions of reg 7(2) (see 6.152 above). In other words, exactly the same provisions apply for discontinuing IPCC investigations.

Regulation 7(4) provides that any application by an appropriate authority   **6.154** for permission to discontinue an investigation under para 21 shall be in writing, and accompanied by a copy of the complaint and a memorandum from the appropriate authority, summarizing the investigation to date and the reasons for the application. Regulation 7(5) provides that the appropriate authority shall:

(a) send the complainant a copy of any such application on the same day as the day on which the application is sent to the Commission[;]
(b) supply any further information requested by the Commission for the purpose of considering that application.

When the IPCC makes an order under para 21, it must give notice of discontinu-   **6.155** ance to:

(i) the appropriate authority;
(ii) every person entitled to be kept properly informed in relation to the subject matter of the investigation under s 21; and
(iii) where applicable, the complainant.

Where an investigation of a complaint, recordable conduct, or DSI matter is dis-   **6.156** continued pursuant to para 21, the IPCC may give the appropriate authority directions specified in reg 7(7) of the 2004 Complaints and Misconduct Regulations and may itself take such steps as described in regs 7(8) and (9). The appropriate authority must comply with any such directions.

I. Conclusion

6.157 Although the various regulatory provisions are expressed in mandatory language, on a proper examination, a high proportion of them are directory, rather than mandatory in effect—that is, breach of any requirement will not automatically vitiate proceedings. Each breach must be considered in its statutory context to determine the answer on the facts. More likely will be the requirement on the affected person—complainants and the officers concerned, particularly—to demonstrate practical unfairness and prejudice in consequence of regulatory departure.

6.158 Nonetheless, the initial handling does create certain fixed rights and other directory powers that generate strong legitimate expectations as to what procedures will be followed. Allowing for the rules as to exhausting inherent procedural remedies before challenging by way of judicial review, decision making within the administration of each stage of a public complaints system will invariably have a sufficient public quality to attract judicial review.

6.159 The same propositions apply to material rehearsed in Chapter 7, and, to a degree, within the administration of the associated Conduct Regulations in Chapters 8 and 9.

7

INVESTIGATIONS UNDER SCHEDULE 3 OF THE 2002 ACT AND THE 2008 CONDUCT REGULATIONS

A. **Overview of the Investigatory Regimes and the Police (Conduct) Regulations 2008** 7.01
The Police (Conduct) Regulations 2008 and the associated Home Office Guidance: a summary 7.05
Part 1: 'Preliminary' 7.07
　The harm test and the implied duty of disclosure (reg 4) 7.14
　Interpretation of the prescribed reg 4 'harm test' 7.31
Part 2: 'General' 7.35
　The status and role of a police friend (reg 6) 7.36
　Legal and other representation (reg 7) 7.46
　The effect of outstanding or possible criminal proceedings (reg 9) 7.50
　Suspension (reg 10) 7.55

B. **Determination of the Investigatory Regime** 7.63
Introduction 7.63
Forms of investigation 7.67
Independent investigations under para 19: additional points 7.71

C. **Assessment of Conduct** 7.74
Schedule 3 matters: 'severity assessment' 7.76
Assessment of conduct under Part 3 of the 2008 Conduct Regulations 7.83

D. **The Appointment of the Investigator** 7.91
The definition and the enhanced role of the investigator in the 2008 regime 7.91
The appointment of the investigator in Sch 3 investigations 7.96
Investigators under the 2008 Conduct Regulations 7.103
Investigators under paras 16–18 of Sch 3 to the 2002 Act 7.105

E. **The Purpose of the Investigation** 7.110

F. **Written Notices of Investigation** 7.113
The history and purpose of 'notices of investigation' 7.113
The content of notices of investigation 7.120
Matters specific to reg 15 notices 7.122

G. **Representations to the Investigator** 7.126
Schedule 3 matters 7.127
2008 Conduct Regulations 7.129

H. **Interviews** 7.134
Pre-interview procedures 7.137
Discretion as to interviews 7.144
Criminal and misconduct interviews as part of a single investigation 7.145
Application of the Regulation of Investigatory Powers Act 2000 (RIPA) 7.155

Admissibility of intercept evidence,
and directed or intrusive
surveillance, in misconduct
proceedings   7.155
Intercepted communications
under Pt 1 of RIPA and lawful
business monitoring   7.157
Directed and intrusive surveillance
under Pt II of RIPA   7.162
I. **The Report of the Investigation**   7.167
The 2008 Conduct Regulations   7.167
Investigation reports for Sch 3
investigations   7.169
Action by the IPCC in response to
an investigation report from a
managed or IPCC investigation
(Sch 3, para 23)   7.173
Notification requirements
on the IPCC   7.178
Procedures following the service of
a para 23(6) notification   7.179

Action by the IPCC in response to an
investigation report from a local or
supervised investigation
(Sch 3, para 24)   7.182
Final reports on other DSI matters
(Sch 3, paras 24A–24C)   7.186
Appeals to the IPCC in relation
to an investigation
(Sch 3, para 25)   7.189
Reviews and reinvestigations
following an appeal
(Sch 3, para 26)   7.196
The duties and IPCC powers of
recommendation and direction in
relation to disciplinary proceedings
(Sch 3, para 27)   7.198
Information for the complainant
about disciplinary recommendations
(Sch 3, para 28)   7.203
J. **Conclusion**   7.206

A. Overview of the Investigatory Regimes and the Police (Conduct) Regulations 2008

7.01   There are, effectively, parallel regimes for investigating complaints or conduct matters under Pt 3 of the Police (Conduct) Regulations 2008[1] and (coincidentally) Pt 3 of Sch 3 to the Police Reform Act 2002. Before reviewing them, it is helpful to take an overview of the regime. There is a high degree of integration between the respective provisions, and those of the Police (Performance) Regulations 2008.[2] From the perspective of the officer concerned, the practical point of convergence arises at the service of the notice of investigation under either reg 14A of the Police (Complaint and Misconduct) Regulations 2004[3] (Sch 3 investigations) or reg 15 of the 2008 Conduct Regulations (non-Sch 3 matters).

7.02   As will be seen, from the point of initial recording and handling, there is a formal point of convergence later than the service of written notices—namely, the decision following investigation to refer to misconduct proceedings under reg 19 of the 2008 Conduct Regulations. This can properly be said to be the point of

---

[1] SI 2008/2864.
[2] SI 2008/2862.
[3] SI 2004/643.

convergence for investigations under Sch 3 and those under the 2008 Conduct Regulations.

Similarly, the initial recording and handling of any matter (in certain cases, man- **7.03** datory under Sch 3) has consequences through to determination of the final outcome. Within these processes, of particular practical significance are the determination of which investigatory regime applies, the appointment of the investigator, the content of the notice of investigation, disclosure, interviews, and representations to the investigator during the process.

The conclusion of the investigation may result in misconduct proceedings, at **7.04** which point, as stated, the investigatory regimes converge under reg 19 of the 2008 Conduct Regulations. If so referred, the operative misconduct procedures under Pt 4 of the 2008 Conduct Regulations are then the same, other than that the Independent Police Complaints Commission (IPCC) has an enhanced role in misconduct proceedings that originate in investigations under paras 16–19 of Sch 3 of the 2002 Act in terms of its ability to recommend or direct proceedings. Furthermore, complainants have specific rights to attend and participate (see regs 31–34), and the IPCC has enhanced rights of attendance and participation in relation to misconduct proceedings that started under paras 16–19 of Sch 3.

The Police (Conduct) Regulations 2008 and the associated Home Office Guidance: a summary

The 2008 Conduct Regulations are conveniently set out in five Parts, as follows. **7.05**

(i) Part 1 ('Preliminary') deals with preliminary matters, including definitions and explanation of the new reg 4 'harm test' when considering matters of disclosure.

(ii) Part 2 ('General') deals with application, police friends, legal and other representation, the mechanisms for service of documents, the resolution of misconduct matters when criminal proceedings are outstanding, and the mechanisms and test for suspending an officer from duty.

(iii) Part 3 ('Investigations') deals with investigations for misconduct allegations that are not covered by paras 16–19 of Sch 3 to the 2002 Act—that is, one of the four forms of investigation determined by the IPCC under para 15(4) of Sch 3—from the moment of assessment of the conduct (an important concept under the 2008 Regulations), to the report of the investigation.

(iv) Part 4 ('Misconduct proceedings') represents the convergence of the investigatory regimes under Sch 3 and the 2008 Conduct Regulations, respectively, and takes the matter from the referral of a case to misconduct proceedings through to the outcome, including appeals from misconduct meetings— although not appeal from misconduct hearings, which, with the abolition of a chief officer's review, are now dealt with exclusively by the Police Appeals Tribunals Rules (PAT Rules) 2008.[4]

(v) Part 5 ('Fast track procedure for special cases') deals exclusively with special cases—that is, those considered appropriate for fast tracking.

7.06 The interrelationship with the associated Home Office Guidance on *Police Officer Misconduct, Unsatisfactory Performance and Attendance Management Procedures*[5] is reflected in Table 7.1, and, to a large extent, simply requires the practitioner to connect one set of mechanistic provisions with another. As already observed, however expressed, many of these regulatory provisions will be directory, rather than mandatory, in effect and breach will not automatically vitiate proceedings. This chapter seeks to identify and analyse the provisions that are anticipated to have a direct practical bearing on the conduct of matters in practice.

Part 1: 'Preliminary'

7.07 Regulations 1 ('Citation, commencement and extent') and 2 ('Revocation and transitional provisions') operate so as to apply the 2008 Conduct Regulations to conduct that came to the attention of the appropriate authority on or after 1 December 2008. Preceding matters are addressed by the Police (Conduct) Regulations 2004,[6] considered in outline at Chapter 9.

7.08 Regulation 3 ('Interpretation and delegation') sets out the key definitions and the entitlement of chief officers to delegate various functions under the Regulations. Regulation 3(5) provides that where the appropriate authority is a chief officer, he may, subject to reg 3(6), delegate any of his functions under the Regulations to a member of a police force of at least the rank of chief inspector, or a police staff member who, in the opinion of the chief officer, is of at least a similar level of seniority to a chief inspector. Regulation 3(6) provides a reservation that, where the appropriate authority delegates its functions under regs 10 ('Suspension') or 41 ('Referral to a special cases hearing'), 'the decisions shall be authorised by a senior officer'. It follows—and is certainly desirable—that, in relation to particularly sensitive decisions (suspension and fast tracking), a senior officer should have some meaningful involvement.

7.09 The important new definitions under the 2008 regime were addressed in part in preceding chapters. Regulation 3(1) provides an extensive list of definitions that, for the most part, are self-evident.

---

[4] SI 2008/2863.
[5] Issued under s 87(1) of the 2002 Act.
[6] SI 2004/645.

Table 7.1 A summary of the Police (Conduct) Regulations 2008 and the Home Office Guidance on *Police Officer Misconduct, Unsatisfactory Performance and Attendance Management Procedures*

PCR 2008	Heading of regulation	Comment	Cross-reference: Home Office Guidance, Introduction, and chs 1 and 2
Part 1			
1	*Citation, commencement and extent*	In force 1 December 2008	
2	*Revocation and transitional provisions*	Police (Conduct) Regulations 2004, SI 2004/645, revoked only for allegations brought to appropriate authority's attention after 1 December 2008	
3	*Interpretation and delegation*		*Definitions* 2.78
4	*The harm test*	Criteria to justify non-disclosure to affected officer	2.146
Part 2			
5	*Application*	Where allegation of misconduct or gross misconduct is brought to authority's attention	
6	*Police Friend*	Police friend may advise, represent, and accompany officer (cf reg 14A of the Police (Complaints and Misconduct) Regulations 2004, SI 2004/643)	*Police friend* Introduction p 8–9
7	*Legal and other representation*	Right to legal representation at misconduct hearing or special case hearing	
8	*Provision of notices or documents*	Criteria for service	

(Continued)

201

Table 7.1 *Cont.*

PCR 2008	Heading of regulation	Comment	Cross-reference: Home Office Guidance, Introduction, and chs 1 and 2
9	*Outstanding or possible criminal proceedings*	Postpone if hearing would prejudice criminal proceedings	*Conducting Investigations where there are possible or outstanding criminal proceedings* 2.27 *Misconduct action following criminal proceedings* 2.35
10	*Suspension*	Paid suspension permitted only when redeployment/ change of duties is not appropriate and investigation may be prejudiced or suspension is in the public interest	*Suspension, restricted or change of duty* 2.12
Part 3			
11	*Application of this Part*	Not applicable where Sch 3, paras 16–19, to the Police Reform Act 2002	
12	*Assessment of conduct*	Authority must investigate conduct, if proved, would be gross misconduct. Otherwise authority can investigate, take management action, or take no action	*Severity assessment* 2.51 *Investigation of conduct matters* 2.56 *Assessment of conduct (is the case one of misconduct?)* 2.70
13	*Appointment of investigator*	Criteria for investigators	*Appointment of investigator* 2.110
14	*Investigation*	Purpose of investigation	*Investigation* 2.113
15	*Written notices*	Form for notices	*Written notification to officer concerned* 2.103
16	*Representations to the investigator*	Officer has ten working days in which to provide statement and relevant documents	
17	*Interviews during investigation*	Form for interviews	*Interviews during investigation* 2.119
18	*Report of investigation*	Form for written report	*Investigation report and supporting documents* 2.138

Part 4

19	*Referral of case to misconduct proceedings*	Authority decides action on basis of written report	*Referring a matter to misconduct proceedings following investigation of a complaint or recordable conduct matter*	2.63
			Assessment of conduct (is the case one of misconduct?)	2.70
			Severity assessment (is the matter potentially misconduct or gross misconduct?)	2.82
			Dealing with misconduct	2.89
			Management action	2.91
			Taking further disciplinary proceedings	2.99
			Action prior to misconduct meetings/hearings	2.144
			Misconduct meetings/hearings	2.166
20	*Withdrawal of case*			
21	*Notice of referral to misconduct proceedings and panel membership*	Notice to officer as soon as practicable		
22	*Procedure on receipt of notice*	Officer has 14 days (unless exceptional extension granted) in which to provide notice of whether he accepts allegation and or mitigation.		
23	*Witnesses*	No witness shall give evidence unless necessary in the interests of justice	*Witnesses*	2.160
24	*Timing and notice of misconduct proceedings*	Twenty working days for misconduct meeting Thirtyworking days for misconduct hearing	*Timing for holdings meetings/hearings*	2.168
25	*Persons conducting misconduct proceedings: officers other than senior officers*	Panel needed of specific composition	*Misconduct hearing – non-senior officers (regulation 25)*	2.174

(Continued)

Table 7.1 *Cont.*

PCR 2008	Heading of regulation	Comment	Cross-reference: Home Office Guidance, Introduction, and chs 1 and 2	
26	*Persons conducting misconduct proceedings: chief constables etc.*	Panel needed of specific composition	*Misconduct meetings/hearings – senior officers (regulations 26 and 27)*	2.179
27	*Persons conducting misconduct proceedings: other senior officers*	Panel needed of specific composition	*Misconduct meetings/hearings – senior officers (regulations 26 and 27)*	2.179
28	*Documents to be supplied*	Documents to be given to person(s) conducting proceedings	*Documents for the meeting/hearing*	2.158
29	*Attendance of officer concerned at misconduct proceedings*	Officer to attend unless chair informed of reasonable grounds	*Meeting/hearing in absence of officer concerned*	2.185
30	*Participation of Commission and investigator at misconduct proceedings*	Commission/or its lawyers may attend if Sch 3, paras 18–19, to the 2002 Act applied, or if paras 16–17 applied and the Commission made a recommendation or direction to hold disciplinary proceedings	*IPCC direction and attendance at meetings/ hearings*	2.227
31	*Attendance of complainant or interested person at misconduct proceedings*	Complainant may attend proceedings, unless giving evidence, and ask questions of officer through the chair	*Attendance of complainant or interested person at misconduct proceedings*	2.221
32	*Attendance of others at misconduct proceedings*	Misconduct proceedings generally private		
33	*Exclusion from misconduct proceedings*	Chair can exclude anyone attending proceedings if information needs to be heard, but should not be disclosed under the harm test		
34	*Procedure at misconduct proceedings*	Chair shall broadly determine procedure	*Conduct of misconduct meeting/hearing*	

35	*Outcome of misconduct proceedings*	List of outcomes available	*Outcome of meetings/hearings* / *Outcomes available at misconduct meetings/hearings*	2.200 / 2.205
36	*Notification of outcome*	Officer must be notified of outcome and as soon as practicable, within no less than five working days	*Notification of the outcome* / *Expiry of warnings*	2.212 / 2.216
37	*Record of misconduct proceedings*	Verbatim record of proceedings must be kept and supplied to officer on request		
38	*Appeal from misconduct meeting: officers other than senior officers*	Right of appeal against outcomes / Grounds limited: disciplinary action unreasonable; fresh evidence; serious breach of procedures / Officer must notify authority within seven working days after receiving notification of outcome	*Right of appeal* / *Appeal following misconduct meeting – non-senior officers (regulations 38 to 40 of the Conduct Regulations)*	2.230 / 2.234
39	*Appeal meeting*	Will be held if person determining appeal determines that notice of appeal sets out arguable grounds of appeal	*Appeal following misconduct hearing – non-senior officers* / *Appeals against misconduct meetings/hearings – senior officers*	2.243 / 2.244
40	*Procedure and finding of the appeal*	Person determining the appeal shall broadly determine procedure / Finding: confirm or reverse decision; deal with officer in any manner that the chair of misconduct proceedings could have done so		
Part 5				
41	*Referral of case to special case hearing*	Authority, on receiving investigator's report, may certify case as a special case if it conforms to conditions of Sch 3, para 20A(7), to the 2002 Act	*Fast-track procedures (special cases)*	Annex A, 9–14

(Continued)

205

Table 7.1 *Cont.*

PCR 2008	Heading of regulation	Comment	Cross-reference: Home Office Guidance, Introduction, and chs 1 and 2
42	*Remission of case*	Authority may remit case to be dealt with under Pt 4 at any time until the beginning of the special case hearing	
43	*Notice of referral to special case hearing*	Officer must be notified of certification and referral, and notice must describe the conduct and how it amounts to gross misconduct	
44	*Notice of special case hearing*	Authority must notify the officer of hearing specifying a date for the hearing not less than ten and not more than 15 working days after s 43 notice	
45	*Procedure on receipt of notice*	Officer's response to s 43 notice and any supporting documents must be supplied to authority within seven working days	
46	*Person conducting special case hearing: officers other than senior officers*		
47	*Persons conducting special case hearing: chief constables etc.*		
48	*Persons conducting special case hearing: other senior officers*		

No.	Item	Description		Reference
49	*Documents to be supplied*	Documents to be supplied to person conducting special case hearing		
50	*Attendance of officer concerned at special case hearing*	Officer to attend unless chair informed of reasonable grounds	*Absence of police officer concerned at the hearing*	Annex A, 21
51	*Participation of Commission and investigator at special case hearing*	Commission/ or its lawyers may attend if Sch 3, paras 18–19, to the 2002 Act applied, or if paras 16–17 applied and the Commission made a recommendation or direction		
52	*Attendance of complainant and interested persons at special case hearing*	Complainant may attend proceedings	*Complaint cases*	Annex A, 5–7
53	*Attendance of others at special case hearing*	Hearings generally private / Commission-appointed person may attend		
54	*Procedure at special case hearing*	Chair will determine procedure	*Special case process*	Annex A, 9–14
55	*Outcome of special case hearing*	List of outcomes	*Outcome of special case hearing*	Annex A, 15–20
56	*Notification of outcome*	Officer must be notified of outcome as soon as practicable and no later than five working days after hearing		
57	*Record of special case hearing*	Verbatim record of hearing must be taken		

(Continued)

207

Table 7.1 *Cont.*

PCR 2008	Heading of regulation	Comment	Cross-reference: Home Office Guidance, Introduction, and chs 1 and 2
Part 6			
58	*Record of disciplinary proceedings*	Chief officer must keep a record of disciplinary proceedings brought against every officer	
Schedule			**Ch 1 Guidance on Standards of Professional Behaviour**
	Honesty and integrity		*Honesty and integrity* 1.12
	Authority, respect and courtesy		*Authority, respect and courtesy* 1.18
	Equality and diversity		*Equality and diversity* 1.26
	Use of force		*Use of force* 1.32
	Orders and instructions		*Orders and instructions* 1.38
	Duties and responsibilities		*Duties and responsibilities* 1.45
	Confidentiality		*Confidentiality* 1.50
	Fitness for duty		*Fitness for duty* 1.54
	Discreditable conduct		*Discreditable conduct* 1.60
	Challenging and reporting improper conduct		*Challenging and reporting improper conduct* 1.77

Certain of these definitions merit comment. Given the enhanced role of non-police officers—or 'police staff', as they are now most commonly known—in the process, 'human resources professional' (HRP) means a police officer or police staff member who has specific responsibility for personnel matters relating to members of a police force. 'Interested party' means a person whose appointment could reasonably give rise to a concern as to whether he could act impartially under the 2008 Conduct Regulations and is to be distinguished from 'interested person', which has the meaning given to it by s 21(5) of the 2002 Act. 'Management action' means 'action or advice intended to improve the conduct of the officer concerned', and is distinguished from 'management advice', which means 'management action imposed following misconduct proceedings or an appeal meeting'. Management advice is the 'lowest' form of formal disciplinary action/outcome under the 2008 regime. **7.10**

'Misconduct proceedings' covers a 'misconduct hearing'—that is, a hearing to which the officer concerned is referred under reg 19, and at which he may be dealt with by disciplinary action up to and including dismissal—and a 'misconduct meeting'—that is, a meeting at which the officer concerned is referred under reg 19, and at which he may be dealt with by disciplinary action up to and including a final written warning. **7.11**

Regulation 3(3) delineates the 'in force' periods for written warnings. A written warning shall remain in force for twelve months from the date on which it takes effect, and (subject to regs 35(6)(b)[7] and 55(2)(b)[8]), a final written warning shall remain in force for a period of eighteen months from the date on which it takes effect.[9] Under the Regulations, the existence of such written warnings may determine the form of misconduct proceedings and the required approach to outcome. Coupled with this, the Police (Amendment) Regulations 2008[10] make important changes to reg 15 of the Police Regulations 2003[11] in terms of the content of personal records. The new reg 15 provisions are set out at Appendix J. **7.12**

Finally, reg 3(7) and (8) provides that any proceedings under the 2008 Conduct Regulations are disciplinary proceedings for the purposes of s 87(5) of the Police Act 1996 (dealing with the applicability of Home Office Guidance) and s 29(1) of the 2002 Act (covering the interpretation of Pt 2 of the Act). **7.13**

---

[7] The entitlement of the person(s) conducting the proceedings to extend a final written warning on one occasion only for a period of eighteen months from the date on which it would otherwise expire: see reg 35(7) and (8).

[8] Analogous provision for the extension of final written warnings for special cases.

[9] Regulation 3(4) exempts from the time periods for written and final written warnings the time during which an officer is on a career break.

[10] SI 2008/2865.

[11] SI 2003/527.

The harm test and the implied duty of disclosure (reg 4)

7.14 Regulation 4 introduces specific criteria—'the harm test'—that are absent from predecessor Conduct Regulations as to the circumstances in which the appropriate authority will be justified in not providing disclosure to the officer concerned. The disclosure test relates to 'information in documents which are stated to be subject to the harm test under these Regulations'. Although reg 21(1)(c)(ii) mandates service (at notification of referral to misconduct proceedings) of material including 'any other relevant document gathered during the course of the investigation', it is contended that, when properly understood in terms of law, this obligation will cover any material held by the appropriate authority that is relevant applying the test under the Criminal Procedure and Investigations Act 1996 (CPIA), whether or not it was strictly 'gathered during the course of the investigation'.

7.15 Not only is the harm test new, but it also includes the implied acceptance—similarly lacking from previous misconduct procedures—of the nature and extent of the obligation on the appropriate authority to disclose relevant material at all. The lack of certainty as to this duty, and, in some cases, denial by the presenting side that any such duty existed, was the source of repeated and serious concern in practice. It produced a lack of consistency in approach between different police forces. To an extent, the differences may have been attributable to the different professional backgrounds of lawyers for the presenting side (often specializing in civil or employment law) and those defending (often specializing in criminal law). As professional regulation develops as a legal specialism in its own right, these distinctions are progressively reducing in practice.

7.16 By analogy with criminal proceedings—in which the police and the Crown Prosecution Service (CPS) are indivisibly 'the State' for the purposes of disclosure—the disclosure obligation is contended to cover all documents held by the appropriate authority and IPCC that become relevant to proceedings, whether or not they directly formed part of the immediate investigation. As with a criminal prosecutor, the presenting officer is under a positive duty to familiarize himself with the material in order to discharge his duty of disclosure. Under the CPIA, and self-evidently, this primary duty can neither be delegated within the investigation, nor to the misconduct tribunal.

7.17 In many cases, the disclosure obligation may, of course, only arise by way of reaction to the initiative of the accused officer in his required responses to the service of notices within the Regulations. The obligation to conduct a fair investigation does not require an investigator to search exhaustively for material that may assist the officer. Once directed to specific categories of material, however, the disclosure and harm tests must be applied.

7.18 The harm test recognizes that the appropriate authority has a duty of disclosure, and para 2.146 of the Home Office Guidance provides that relevance is to be determined under the provisions of the CPIA. The harm test only arises for application once a document (or other information known to or held by the appropriate authority) is relevant applying the CPIA test.

Disclosure under the Criminal Procedure and Investigations Act 1996. Para- **7.19** graph 2.146 of the Home Office Guidance provides simply that '. . . in determining which documents are relevant, the test to be applied will be that under the Criminal Procedure and Investigations Act 1996, namely whether any document or other material undermines the case against the police officer concerned or would assist the police officer's case'. This tends to oversimplify a substantial body of law relating to the nature of the CPIA disclosure obligation.

Given the express adoption of the CPIA test in the Guidance, case law in this **7.20** criminal context is directly applicable to determinations of relevance under the 2008 Conduct Regulations. If relevant, however, actual disclosure will be determined not by considerations of public interest immunity as in criminal proceedings, but by the wider harm test articulated in reg 4 of the 2008 Conduct Regulations, which includes considerations of proportionality within misconduct proceedings, and especially at misconduct meetings, which may produce a different outcome than if the same material were considered in criminal proceedings. The following analysis attempts no more than a statement of general principle.

The basic duty of disclosure under the CPIA is prescribed by s 3 of that Act. The **7.21** Home Office Guidance identifies the test to be applied to determine relevance as distinct from prescribing a procedure to be followed by the appropriate authority. In any event, s 3 of the CPIA provides as follows.

3 Initial duty of prosecutor to disclose

(1) The prosecutor must—
  (a) disclose to the accused any prosecution material which has not previously been disclosed to the accused and which might reasonably be considered capable of undermining the case for the prosecution against the accused or of assisting the case for the accused, or
  (b) give to the accused a written statement that there is no material of a description mentioned in paragraph (a)
(2) For the purposes of this section prosecution material is material—
  (a) which is in the prosecutor's possession, and came into his possession in connection with the case for the prosecution against the accused, or
  (b) which, in pursuance of a code operative under Part II, he has inspected in connection with the case for the prosecution against the accused.
(3) Where material consists of information which has been recorded in any form the prosecutor discloses it for the purposes of this section—
  (a) by securing that a copy is made of it and that the copy is given to the accused, or
  (b) if in the prosecutor's opinion that is not practicable or not desirable, by allowing the accused to inspect it at a reasonable time and a reasonable place or by taking steps to secure that he is allowed to do so;
  and a copy may be in such form as the prosecutor thinks fit and need not be in the same form as that in which the information has already been recorded.

(4) Where material consists of information which has not been recorded the prosecutor discloses it for the purposes of this section by securing that it is recorded in such form as he thinks fit and—

    (a) by securing that a copy is made of it and that the copy is given to the accused, or

    (b) if in the prosecutor's opinion that is not practicable or not desirable, by allowing the accused to inspect it at a reasonable time and a reasonable place or by taking steps to secure that he is allowed to do so.

(5) Where material does not consist of information the prosecutor discloses it for the purposes of this section by allowing the accused to inspect it at a reasonable time and a reasonable place or by taking steps to secure that he is allowed to do so.

(6) Material must not be disclosed under this section to the extent that the court, on an application by the prosecutor, concludes it is not in the public interest to disclose it and orders accordingly.

(7) Material must not be disclosed under this section to the extent that it is material the disclosure of which is prohibited by section 17 of the Regulation of Investigatory Powers Act 2000.

[. . .]

7.22 The duty of disclosure is a continuing one and must be kept under review (see s 7A of the CPIA), although the continuous nature of this duty is uncontentious in any context. In *R v H*,[12] which remains the leading authority in respect of s 3, it was held that, in determining whether material falls within s 3(1)(a), the parties' respective cases must be carefully, but not restrictively, analysed, to identify the specific facts that the prosecution sought to establish and the specific grounds on which the charges were disputed. The Attorney-General issued detailed guidelines[13] in April 2005 to supplement these statutory provisions.

7.23 **The Attorney-General's Guidelines on Disclosure of Information in Criminal Proceedings (April 2005).** The Attorney-General's Guidelines of April 2005 are instructive as to the underlying principles behind disclosure in the context of criminal proceedings. The Foreword provides that:

> Disclosure is one of the most important issues in the criminal justice system and the application of proper and fair disclosure is a vital component of a fair criminal justice system. The "golden rule" is that fairness requires full disclosure should be made of all material held by the prosecution that weakens its case or strengthens that of the defence.

7.24 Fair disclosure is defined in para 1 of these Guidelines as 'an inseparable part of a fair trial' and (in para 3) as 'designed to ensure that there is fair disclosure of material which may be relevant to an investigation and which does not form part of the prosecution case':

> [Disclosure] should assist the accused in the timely preparation and presentation of their case and assist the court to focus on all the relevant issues in the trial.

---

[12] [2004] 2 AC 134, HL.

[13] The Attorney-General's Guidelines on *Disclosure of Information in Criminal Proceedings* (April 2005), reproduced in Archbold (2009) *Criminal Pleading Evidence and Practice*, at [A242A]–[A257] and in *Blackstone's Criminal Practice* (2009) at Appendix 5.

Disclosure which does not meet these objectives risks preventing a fair trial taking place.

Equally, the Introduction states that the Guidelines are directed at 'ensuring that **7.25** a just and fair disclosure process is not abused so that it becomes unwieldy, bureaucratic and effectively unworkable', that 'a fair trial should not require consideration of irrelevant material and should not involve spurious applications or arguments which serve to divert the trial process from examining the real issues before the court' (para 2), and that 'fairness does recognise that there are other interests that need to be protected, including those of victims and witnesses who might otherwise be exposed to harm' and 'should also ensure that material is not disclosed which overburdens the participants in the trial process, diverts attention from the relevant issues, leads to unjustifiable delay, and is wasteful of resources' (para 6).

These are the competing considerations involved in achieving the single objective **7.26** of a fair hearing. Misconduct proceedings are self-evidently not criminal proceedings, and the full technical requirements of the CPIA do not apply. As the reg 4 harm test anticipates, proportionality may produce a different result where the sanction is a written warning rather than imprisonment. Subject to that, the underlying principles may legitimately be imported to misconduct proceedings and, applied appropriately, will go some considerable way to improving the confidence in the new regime. Effective loss of either rank (either through non-promotion, or at least gross compromise to operational deployment) or office for misconduct carries with it a significant loss of reputation and greatly diminished subsequent employment prospects. Furthermore, certain findings render an officer effectively non-operational in criminal investigations,[14] which is inevitably demoralizing for the officer concerned and unhelpful to those that must deploy him.

In any event, no better test for disclosure exists, and whatever test is applied should **7.27** be both identifiable and universal across police forces. Under the heading 'General principles', paras 10–14 are relevant from the Attorney-General's Guidelines.

10. Generally, material which can reasonably be considered capable of undermining the prosecution case against the accused or assisting the defence case will include anything that tends to show a fact inconsistent with the elements of the case that must be proved by the prosecution. Material can fulfil the disclosure test:

(a) by the use to be made of it in cross-examination; or
(b) by its capacity to support submissions that could lead to:
    (i) the exclusion of evidence; or
    (ii) a stay of proceedings; or

---

[14] See the 'real difficulty' identified by Collins J in *R (Chief Constable of Avon and Somerset) v Police Appeals Tribunal* [2004] EWHC 220 (Admin) at [32].

> (iii) a court or tribunal finding that any public authority had acted incompatibly with the accused's rights under the ECHR,[15] or
>
> (c) by its capacity to suggest an explanation or partial explanation of the accused's actions.
>
> 11. In deciding whether material may fall to be disclosed under paragraph 10, especially (b)(ii), prosecutors must consider whether disclosure is required in order for a proper application to be made. The purpose of this paragraph is not to allow enquiries to support speculative arguments or for the manufacture of defences.
>
> 12. Examples of material that might reasonably be considered capable of undermining the prosecution case or of assisting the case for the accused are:
>
> > i. Any material casting doubt upon the accuracy of any prosecution evidence.
> > ii. Any material which may point to another person, whether charged or not (including a co-accused) having involvement in the commission of the offence.
> > iii. Any material which may cast doubt upon the reliability of a confession.
> > iv. Any material that might go to the credibility of a prosecution witness.
> > v. Any material that might support a defence that is either raised by the defence or apparent from the prosecution papers.
> > vi. Any material which may have a bearing on the admissibility of any prosecution evidence.
>
> 13. It should also be borne in mind that while items of material viewed in isolation may not be reasonably considered to be capable of undermining the prosecution case or assisting the accused, several items together can have that effect.
>
> 14. Material relating to the accused's mental or physical health, intellectual capacity, or to any ill treatment which the accused may have suffered when in the investigator's custody is likely to fall within the test for disclosure set out in paragraph 8 above.

7.28 In police misconduct proceedings, the officer concerned should make specific requests in writing where appropriate in order to promote an informed disclosure decision by the presenting side. Responses from the investigator/appropriate authority should similarly be both reasoned and in writing. If the harm test has been applied, there should be specificity as to which criterion is said to justify non-disclosure of relevant material. Any contended failure to disclose may then be raised with the appropriate authority, persons conducting the misconduct proceedings, or a police appeals tribunal (or in associated judicial review proceedings) on a wholly unambiguous basis.

7.29 The inherent right of those conducting misconduct proceedings to set their own procedure under reg 34(1) allows for applications by the presenting side, based on certain of these heads of contended harm to be made *ex parte*. By para 40 of the

---

[15] Although Art 6 of the European Convention on Human Rights (ECHR) is not applicable to police misconduct proceedings: *Pellegrin v France* (2001) 31 EHRR 651, considered at 12.59.

Attorney-General's Guidelines, however, 'neutral material or material damaging to the defendant need not be disclosed and must not be brought to the attention of the court', and 'only in truly borderline cases should the prosecution seek a judicial ruling on the disclosability of material in its hands'.

By para 41, if 'prosecutors are satisfied that a fair trial cannot take place where **7.30** material which satisfies the disclosure test cannot be disclosed, and that this cannot or will not be remedied including by, for example, making formal admissions, amending the charges or presenting the case in a different way so as to ensure fairness or in other ways, they must not continue with the case'. The same principles may apply to misconduct proceedings.

Interpretation of the prescribed reg 4 'harm test'

It is in the above context that it is contended that the reg 4 criteria should be inter- **7.31** preted and applied. Some of the criteria—'interests of national security'; 'dispropor- tionate' to the misconduct alleged; 'necessary and proportionate for the protection and welfare of witnesses'; 'otherwise in the public interest'—are highly subjective and not elsewhere defined. They are liable to abuse if the nature and purpose of the CPIA disclosure obligations are either not understood or not applied in practice.

Where the presenting side has material that would, applying an approach broadly **7.32** similar to that of the prosecution under the CPIA and the Attorney-General's Guidelines of April 2005, qualify for disclosure, it is contended that any such material should ordinarily be disclosed in what are accusatory proceedings almost invariably held in private. In certain situations, the misconduct investigation will have been conducted concurrently with a criminal investigation. The disclosure obligation in either event bites on charge, meaning, in the context of misconduct, upon referral of the matter to misconduct proceedings.

This approach is relevance-driven, requires active cooperation from the officer **7.33** concerned to identify the real issues and legitimate areas of investigation, and allows for considerations of proportionality. As rehearsed, the test under s 3(1) of the CPIA is that, subject to non-disclosure based on public interest immunity, disclosure 'must' be made of any material held by the prosecution 'which might reasonably be considered capable of undermining the case for the prosecution against the accused or assisting the case for the accused '.

As a matter of first principle, this may include material that could reasonably lead **7.34** to identifiable and legitimate lines of inquiry by the defence.[16] It does not apply to

---

[16] And see *Compagnie Financiere du Pacific v Peruvian Guano Co* [1882] 11 QBD 55, 63, where Brett LJ said, in the context of civil proceedings: 'It seems to me that every document relates to the matter in question in the action, which not only would be evidence upon any issue, but also which, it is reasonable to suppose, contains information which may—not which must—either directly or

lines of inquiry that are manifestly speculative. It applies equally to material that may simply mitigate the outcome—that is, sanction—rather than go directly to a defence to a charge.[17] It includes material that might, realistically, demonstrate any inherent unfairness in the prosecutor's position or conduct (such as an arbitrary approach to which persons in equivalent positions were charged) and, as a corollary, which may promote an abuse of process argument by the officer concerned. If individual failings have occurred in the context of documented wider systemic failings by the force, these documents (or their effect) should be disclosed in a suitable form. If necessary, the relevant conclusions of otherwise confidential senior management reports may be summarized and disclosed as distinct from the original report.

Part 2: 'General'

7.35 Part 2 of the 2008 Conduct Regulations deals with a miscellany of important issues. As Table 7.1 demonstrates, this includes the status and role of a police friend (reg 6), legal and other representation (reg 7), provision of notices or documents (reg 8), outstanding or possible criminal proceedings (reg 9), and suspension (reg 10). Each of these is associated with additional detailed material in the Home Office Guidance. To a large extent, the provisions are both detailed and self-explanatory.

The status and role of a police friend (reg 6)

7.36 A 'police friend' has a well-established and important role in the performance and misconduct procedures. In the performance of that role, the practice and expectation has developed that, when acting as such, communication between the friend and the officer concerned will be privileged and confidential. To this extent—and subject to the exceptions to legal professional privilege that exist in law—it may be argued that the ordinary obligation to report misconduct under the performance standards must be taken to be suspended when the information has come to the police friend in his capacity as such.

7.37 This is unquestionably contentious, however, and has not been tested to any conclusion in court. It may not apply, for example, to knowledge of continuing misconduct, and certainly not to crime. Even this may be fact-sensitive and contingent on whether the friend was acting as agent of an instructed solicitor

---

indirectly enable the party requiring the affidavit either to advance his own case or to damage the case of his adversary. … a document can properly be said to contain information which may enable the party requiring the affidavit either to advance his own case or to damage the case of his adversary, if it is a document which may fairly lead him to a train of inquiry, which may have either of these two consequences …'

17 See para 58 of the Attorney-General's Guidelines (April 2005): 'in all cases the prosecutor must consider disclosing in the interests of justice any material, which is relevant to sentence (e.g. information which might mitigate the seriousness of the offence or assist the accused to lay blame in part upon a co-accused or another person.)'

at the time, thereby attracting the associated duties of confidentiality for privileged communication.

In any event, the qualifications to act as a police friend are rehearsed in reg 6(1). **7.38**
There are equivalent provisions under reg 14B of the 2004 Complaint and Misconduct Regulations, as amended.

The officer concerned is entitled to select a police officer, or staff member, or per- **7.39**
son nominated by his staff association, to act as his police friend, provided that such a person is not 'otherwise involved in the matter' (which necessarily must include any 'interested party' within reg 3(1)). The Regulations do not prescribe that the police friend be a member of the same force, and the Home Office Guidance anticipates that they may not. By reg 6(3), the chief officer of the friend's force shall permit him to use a reasonable amount of duty time for the purposes designated in reg 6(2).

Whilst (under the Guidance) an officer may decline to act as a friend, the provi- **7.40**
sions are silent as to whether a chief officer is entitled to refuse to permit a particular officer so to act as a matter of direction and control. Respect must, of course, be given to the principle that the officer concerned must be at liberty to select his own police friend. It is contended, however, that direction and control could extend to refusal in appropriate circumstances, given the wider operational obligations of a chief officer. Further, given that the Guidance anticipates that the police friend's own force will pay the reasonable expenses of that friend when acting as such for an officer in a different force, the necessity of the right of discretionary refusal on the same basis is promoted.

Regulation 6(2) sets out the entitlements of a police friend—that is, to advise the **7.41**
officer concerned throughout the proceedings, to represent the officer at such proceedings (unless he is legally represented), to make any relevant representations to the appropriate authority concerning any aspect of the proceedings, and to accompany the officer concerned to any interview, meeting, or hearing.

The Guidance materially adds to, and qualifies, these core procedural rights and **7.42**
duties. It provides (as did the predecessor Guidance) that the friend may, at any point, make representations 'that there are insufficient grounds upon which to base the case and/or that the correct procedures have not been followed, clearly setting out the reasons and submitting any supporting evidence'. This is an important right and should be exercised: (i) for the contention to be considered on merit; and (ii) in order to document and support the bases of any subsequent submissions at the substantive hearing or appeal therefrom.

Equally, the Guidance repeats earlier guidance in asserting that 'it is not the role of **7.43**
the police friend to conduct his or her own investigation into the matter', and highlighting the opportunity (obligation under the 2008 Conduct Regulations) set out

in para 2.117, by way of presumed alternative to investigation, to provide information to the investigator. The distinction between informed representation and investigation is more easily stated than applied, but tends to demonstrate the caution necessarily required when, for example, accessing police databases in the contended performance of the role as a police friend.

7.44 Whether such conduct is a 'police purpose' is contentious. Fairness and effective representation suggests that not every line of inquiry on behalf of a defendant officer should have to be filtered through a request to the appropriate authority or investigator. There is a distinction between accessing general force policies, etc, on the intranet, for this 'police purpose', and, for example, accessing the Police National Computer (PNC) for information about a particular witness. In that the investigating side has access to these records, however, equality of arms will often require that consent is given to the police friend to access classes of documents without having to disclose specifics or the result to the appropriate authority.

7.45 On any view, the 2008 regime is intended, in the words of a member of Parliament on the relevant parliamentary committee,[18] to reduce the probability of an affected officer getting 'lawyered up' until that is absolutely justified by reference to the available outcome (sanction). Whilst this policy objective is wholly consistent with the intended cultural shift under the 2008 regime, the corollary is to place a greatly increased premium on the effective performance of the police friend in the vast majority of investigations. Police friends are, ultimately, neither lawyers nor trained advocates, and should not substitute for the same in serious or complex situations.

Legal and other representation (reg 7)

7.46 Consistent with the philosophy of proportionate action—and broadly seeking to mirror civilian Advisory, Conciliation and Arbitration Service (ACAS) procedures—the right to direct participation by a lawyer in the process is heavily circumscribed by the regulations. Regulation 7(1) establishes the entitlement of the officer concerned to be legally represented by a 'relevant lawyer'[19] at a misconduct hearing or special case hearing. It follows that no legal representation is permitted at misconduct meetings. Similarly, police friends, but not lawyers, are entitled to attend purely misconduct interviews (see also reg 17). There is, however, a right to legal representation at a misconduct hearing and before the police appeals tribunals.

7.47 The appropriate authority may be represented at misconduct proceedings, special case hearings, and appeal meetings by a police officer or staff member of the police

---

[18] David Ruffley MP, House of Commons Official Report of the First Delegated Legislation Committee, 27 October 2008, available from HM Stationery Office.
[19] As defined in reg 3(1).

force concerned, or, for parity, a relevant lawyer where the officer concerned is also so entitled. The rights of participation and attendance, respectively, by others, including the IPCC, the complainant, and other interested persons, at misconduct proceedings are addressed by regs 30 and 31 (see 8.66–8.85). Simple attendance (as distinct from participation) of others is addressed by regs 32–34.

Regulation 7(5) provides that the appropriate authority may appoint a person to **7.48** advise the person or persons conducting the misconduct meeting or hearing, respectively, a special case hearing, or an appeal meeting, although that person may not be a 'relevant lawyer' at the misconduct or appeal meeting, but only the special case hearing. Again, this is consistent with lawyers only being present at hearings, whether ordinary or special case variants. It is good and accepted practice for such an 'advisory' lawyer to place on the record a summary of legal advice provided to the misconduct panel. Doing so allows the officer's representative to make any submissions on any legal advice given. Any such advice or opinion obviously should not extend to matters of pure fact rather than law. The lawyer cannot—and must not appear to—become the decision maker.

Nothing in the Regulations can, of course, prevent the officer concerned, or his **7.49** police friend, from obtaining legal advice or representation outside these parameters. It follows that indirect participation by lawyers for the officer subject to proceedings—through advice, or drafting material for the relevant decision maker or tribunal—is perfectly legitimate. Lawyers are not precluded from sending letters on behalf of the police friend at any stage of the process, and the investigator or presenting side could hardly object to such involvement, not least because they are likely, in many cases, to be the beneficiary of legal advice obtained through the force solicitor.

The effect of outstanding or possible criminal proceedings (reg 9)

Regulation 9(1) requires those with responsibility for promulgating misconduct **7.50** proceedings to 'proceed without delay'. A strong (and justifiable) perception of endemic delay in the conduct of misconduct proceedings probably explains the prescriptive timetables for resolution in the 2008 regime. In practice, the aspirations of the 2008 Conduct Regulations in this respect are unlikely to be met unless a high proportion of matters formerly addressed as misconduct are assessed as suitable for resolution under the 2008 Performance Regulations. Even then, the rights of appeal at each stage militate against early final resolution in disputed cases.

One factor that may lawfully delay the referral of a case to misconduct proceed- **7.51** ings or a special case hearing is where the appropriate authority decides that such proceedings 'would prejudice any criminal proceedings' (reg 9(2)) and that, for the duration of that period, no such proceedings shall take place (reg 9(3)). The competing considerations are obvious, but are resolved in practice by the necessity of avoiding compromise to the criminal proceedings. The Home Office Guidance addresses the situation at paras 2.27–2.34.

7.52 In particular circumstances, a defendant officer may argue that it is unfair to require misconduct proceedings to conclude before the resolution of an outstanding criminal matter. This is more obviously the case if he is the defendant in the criminal proceedings. Evidence given at a misconduct hearing, although not on oath, may be relevant to and admissible in the criminal matter. This is without prejudice to the operation of the special case procedures in qualifying circumstances.

7.53 Equally, the appropriate authority has a positive duty under reg 9(4), in relation to the deployment of a witness in misconduct proceedings 'who is or may be a witness in any criminal proceedings', to consult the relevant prosecutor before making its decision under reg 9(2)—that is, before deciding whether misconduct proceedings would prejudice any criminal proceedings. 'Relevant prosecutor' is defined by reg 9(5).

7.54 It can be seen that, for obvious reasons of public policy—namely, according primacy to criminal rather than misconduct proceedings—the appropriate authority cannot refer a case to misconduct proceedings until satisfied that such proceedings would not prejudice any criminal proceedings.

Suspension (reg 10)

7.55 Few executive decisions are more likely to demoralize a serving police officer (and his family and colleagues) than suspension from duties. It is common experience that officers who are suspended for prolonged periods of time never return to policing, even when exonerated of all material allegations, whether criminal or misconduct. Many subject to prolonged suspensions are driven to medical retirement, thus imposing a continuing financial burden on their force.

7.56 Such suspension—probably any suspension—has an unquantifiable personal and professional cost in relation to the officer. As a matter of fundamental principle, therefore, suspension should be used as a genuine last resort and only when compelling reasons prevail. Equally, even the inappropriate 'defensive' use of restricted duties will be both demoralizing and humiliating for an officer whose integrity is not in dispute.

7.57 In this context, it is contended that, in applying any test as to 'public confidence', the appropriate authority must recognize the public interest in avoiding suspension or the use of restricted duties pending the resolution of an investigation wherever possible. 'Public confidence', whilst a subjective concept, cannot be taken to mean the confidence of either an ill-informed member of the public or one who is closely associated with the alleged victim of an officer's conduct. The unmerited suspension of groups of officers for years, largely at the initiative of campaigning groups following controversial police-related deaths, demonstrates the need for strong and objective decision making at senior-officer level.

It is contended that the test should be strictly objective and led by the continued **7.58** competence of a particular officer to perform particular policing duties. In particular, it should not reflect considerations of inaccurate, and emotional, media coverage of an event.[20] The days of competent and experienced officers whose underlying integrity is not challenged spending years on suspension should be over.

To a degree, the 2008 Conduct Regulations and associated Home Office Guidance **7.59** reflect a greater maturity and institutional confidence as to these matters than hitherto existed. Regulation 10, which provides the power of the appropriate authority to suspend, on full pay,[21] the officer concerned from his office and membership of the force, provides a de facto presumption against suspension unless the 'suspension conditions' apply:

    (a) having considered temporary redeployment to alternative duties or an alternative location as an alternative to suspension, the appropriate authority has determined that such redeployment is not appropriate in all the circumstances of the case; and

    (b) it appears to the appropriate authority that either—

        (i) the effective investigation of the case may be prejudiced unless the officer concerned is so suspended; or

        (ii) having regard to the nature of the allegation and any other relevant considerations, the public interest requires that he should be so suspended.

It follows that, under the 2008 regime, temporary redeployment must be excluded **7.60** as a possibility before the 'old' test is applied. Paragraph 2.13 of the Home Office Guidance unequivocally states that 'a temporary move to a new location or role must always be considered first as an alternative to suspension'.

The power to suspend arises from the time at which the Regulations first apply **7.61** to the officer concerned (under reg 5), up until it is decided that the officer concerned shall not be referred to misconduct proceedings, or such proceedings have concluded.[22] The power is within the discretion of the appropriate authority and not the IPCC, although there is a duty of consultation as to either suspension or resumption of duties pending resolution of proceedings in supervised, managed, or independent investigations under paras 15(4) and 17–19 of Sch 3 to the 2002 Act.

---

[20] For judicial recognition of the problem, see, eg, *R (Bennett) v HM Coroner for Inner London South* [2006] EWHC 196 (Admin), at [28].

[21] To include any special priority payments or competency-related threshold payments that were in force at the time of the suspension: see para 2.15 of the Home Office Guidance. Note, however, the provisions of para 1 to Sch 2 to the Police Regulations 2003, providing for withholding of pay when a suspended officer is in prison or has absented himself from duty and whose whereabouts are unknown to the chief officer.

[22] Regulation 10(5).

7.62 There are other detailed provisions as to the giving of reasons for suspension:

- reasons for the suspension shall be notified to the officer in writing (reg 10(6));

- the officer concerned or his police friend may make representations to the appropriate authority within seven days of suspension, and any time thereafter 'if he reasonably believes that circumstances relevant to the suspension conditions have changed' (reg 10(7));

- the appropriate authority must review the suspension conditions on receipt of any such representations from the officer concerned; and if there has been no previous review, within four weeks of the suspension taking effect; on being notified of an apparent change of circumstances; and in any event every four weeks from the date of any previous review (reg 10(8)); and

- within three working days of any such review, the appropriate authority must notify the officer in writing of the reasons for the continuing suspension (reg 10(9)).

B. Determination of the Investigatory Regime

Introduction

7.63 From 1 December 2008, investigations into complaints or conduct matters reported on or after that date will take place under either Pt 3 of the 2008 Conduct Regulations or Pt 3 of Sch 3 to the 2002 Act. Regulation 11 of the 2008 Conduct Regulations expressly disapplies Pt 3 of the 2008 Conduct Regulations ('Investigations') to any investigation to which paras 16–19 of Sch 3 to the 2002 Act apply. This obviously includes investigations determined by the IPCC under para 15(4) of Sch 3 as suitable for 'local' investigation (that is, by the appropriate authority). Thus the same investigator in a force may be wearing one of two statutory hats.

7.64 Part 3 of Sch 3 covers investigations of complaints and recordable conduct, and death and serious injury (DSI) matters. Subject to the Sch 3 jurisdiction of the IPCC, by reg 5, Par t 3 of the 2008 Conduct Regulations covers investigations 'where an allegation comes to the attention of an appropriate authority which indicates that the conduct of a police officer may amount to misconduct or gross misconduct'.

7.65 Those responsible for the 2008 regime sought to harmonize these largely parallel regimes. In terms of the conduct of investigations, this chapter examines the key stages, highlighting the commonality of themes:

(i) assessment of conduct ('severity assessment');
(ii) the appointment of investigator;
(iii) investigation;
(iv) written notices;

(v)   interviews; and

(vi) investigation reports.

From whatever statutory origin, there are a number of points of convergence: for **7.66**
example, service of the notice of investigation, the investigation report, and referral of a case to misconduct proceedings. To a large extent, from the perspective
of the officer under investigation, the rights and procedures are coterminous.
From the perspective of a complainant, there are differences in the obligations
owed by the investigator and, more generally, in terms of disclosure of information.
If the matter progresses to misconduct proceedings, whilst the rights of the
complainant and officer are effectively identical, the power of direction and rights
of participation by the IPCC differ according to which investigative regime
applies.

Forms of investigation

The forms of investigation under para 15(4) of Sch 3 to the 2002 Act were intro- **7.67**
duced in Chapter 6. Further guidance as to the exercise of discretion in this determination is reflected in the IPCC statutory guidance issued under s 22 of the
2002 Act. This is presently under review and revisions are anticipated in 2009.

Paragraph 5.6.9 of the IPCC Guidance provides (reversing the order in para 15(4) **7.68**
of Sch 3) that:

(i)   an investigation will be conducted independently by the IPCC under
      para 19 of Sch 3 for 'incidents that cause the greatest level of public concern,
      have the greatest potential to impact on communities or have serious impli-
      cations for the reputation of the police service';

(ii) a managed investigation under para 18 is 'conducted by the police under the
      direction and control of the IPCC, when an incident, or a complaint or
      allegation of misconduct, is of such significance and probable public con-
      cern that the investigation of it needs to be under the direction and control
      of the IPCC but does not need an independent investigation';

(iii) a supervised investigation under para 17 is appropriate 'when the IPCC decides
      that an incident or a complaint or allegation of misconduct is of less significance
      and probable public concern than for an independent or managed investiga-
      tion but oversight by the Commission is appropriate', and

(iv) a 'local' investigation by the appropriate authority under para 16 'is appro-
      priate where the IPCC concludes that none of the factors identified in terms
      of seriousness of the case or public interest exist and that the police have the
      necessary resources and experience to carry out an investigation without
      external assistance'.

The IPCC's statutory guidance provides that the managed form of investigation **7.69**
is distinguished from the supervised by reference to the managing role of the

IPCC regional director or investigator. Another distinction—and probably the corollary of the embedded managerial role of IPCC in managed investigations—is that the complainant has a right of appeal against local or supervised investigations, but not other forms.

7.70 Each form of investigation requires terms of reference and an investigation plan, which (certainly for the non-local forms of investigation) are either written, or must be agreed, by the IPCC (under para 5.6.11 of the IPCC guidance). These terms of reference will reflect the 'principles of investigation of serious incidents' (para 5.6.10: 'the starting point is to investigate the incident, not the assumption that someone is to blame'). The terms of reference certainly, and 'main points of the investigation' plan probably, will be 'shared' with the complainant. They are organic and subject to review as the investigation proceeds.

Independent investigations under para 19: additional points

7.71 Independent investigations under para 19 require the IPCC to designate appropriate staff to the investigation. Special provision is made for investigations into the Commissioner or Deputy Commissioner of the Metropolitan Police Service (MPS).

7.72 Significantly, para 19(4) provides that a member of the IPCC's staff who is designated to undertake an IPCC investigation, and who is not a constable seconded to the IPCC under s 97(8) of the Police Act 1996, 'shall, for the purposes of the carrying out of the investigation and all purposes connected with it, have all those powers and privileges throughout England and Wales'. They do not become police officers for other defined statutory purposes, however: they assume the powers and privileges, but not the office.

7.73 Paragraph 19(7) provides that references in this context to the powers and privileges of a constable:

(i) are references to any power or privilege conferred by or under any enactment (including one passed after the passing of the 2002 Act) on a constable; and

(ii) shall have effect as if every such power were exercisable, and every such privilege existed, throughout England and Wales, and the adjacent United Kingdom waters.

C. Assessment of Conduct

7.74 For matters covered by either Pt 3 of Sch 3 to the 2002 Act or Pt 3 of the 2008 Conduct Regulations, there is a new and important obligation—namely, that of assessing the alleged misconduct in question.

The policy driver for this assessment was the desire to avoid all allegations of **7.75** police misconduct being subjected to the same degree of investigation regardless of the intrinsic gravity of the allegation in question. An early assessment of seriousness is required in order to promote a proportionate response. Whilst the resultant investigation may require review contingent on the evidence collected,[23] if applied effectively, these 'assessments', or 'severity assessments', should operate in the interests of all parties. Delay in processing low-level alleged misconduct was endemic and manifestly not in the public interest in any respect.

Schedule 3 matters: 'severity assessment'

Paragraph 5 of Sch 23 to the Criminal Justice and Immigration Act 2008[24] **7.76** (in force 1 December 2008) inserts after para 19 of Sch 3 to the 2002 Act new paras 19A–19E, dealing with so-called 'special requirements'. The purpose of these new paragraphs is to bring the investigation of recordable complaints, conduct matters, and DSI matters into line with the equivalent provisions within Pt 3 of the 2008 Conduct Regulations.

Paragraph 19A provides that paras 19B–19E 'apply to investigations of complaints **7.77** or recordable conduct matters in cases where the person concerned [ie the subject of complaint or referral] is a member of a police force or a special constable'. Paragraph 19B ('Assessment of seriousness of conduct under investigation') replicates the assessment required to be performed by the appropriate authority under reg 12 of the 2008 Conduct Regulations. Guidance as to the assessment of conduct under the Regulations (not applicable to Sch 3 investigations) is provided additionally in the Home Office Guidance at paras 2.51–2.55. The IPCC statutory guidance addresses the assessment for Sch 3 matters.

For Sch 3 matters, para 19B(1) deals with complaint investigations and provides **7.78** that if it appears to the investigator that there is an indication that the person being investigated may have committed a criminal offence or behaved in a manner that would justify the bringing of disciplinary proceedings, the investigator must certify the investigation as one subject to 'special requirements'.

The significance of the 'special requirements' certification is that it then requires the **7.79** investigator, as soon as reasonably practicable after certifying, to make a 'severity assessment' in relation to the person being investigated. The investigator of a

---

[23] See reg 12(5) and Sch 3, para 19B(9) and (10).

[24] The Criminal Justice and Immigration Act 2008 (Commencement No 3 and Transitional Provisions) Order 2008, SI 2008/2712, art 2 and Sch 1, para 17(b); the Criminal Justice and Immigration Act 2008 (Commencement No 4 and Saving Provision) Order 2008, SI 2008/2993, art 2(1)(i)(ii).

recordable conduct matter similarly must make such a severity assessment. Paragraph 19B(4) defines 'severity assessment' as meaning an assessment as to:

(a) whether the conduct, if proved, would amount to misconduct or gross misconduct, and

(b) if the conduct were to become the subject of disciplinary proceedings, the form which those proceedings would be likely to take.

7.80 Any such assessment is only to be made after consultation with the appropriate authority (para 19B(5)). It is contended that, in determining the probable outcome, consideration may be given at the assessment stage to the officer's professional record and the likely quality of mitigation, since this may affect the form of misconduct proceedings.

7.81 Paragraph 19B(9) and (10) allows for the investigator to revise the severity assessment, but oblige him then to issue further notification of the prescribed information to the person being investigated. Once the severity assessment has been made under para 19B, the investigator of the complaint or recordable conduct matter must notify the person being investigated in specified terms (analogous to reg 15 of the 2008 Conduct Regulations), as rehearsed in reg 14A of the 2004 Complaint and Misconduct Regulations, as amended, and (in so far as different) as to the effect of paras 19C, 19C(2), and 19D of Sch 3.

7.82 The obligation to give the notification to the person being investigated does not apply 'for so long as the person investigating the complaint or matters consider that giving the notification might prejudice the investigation or any other investigation (including, in particular, a criminal investigation)'—that is, an entitlement to withhold analogous to that provided for by reg 15(3) of the 2008 Conduct Regulations.

Assessment of conduct under Part 3 of the 2008 Conduct Regulations

7.83 By analogy with para 19B of Sch 3 to the 2002 Act, reg 12 introduces the duty on the appropriate authority to make a series of determinations at fixed points in the process. The underlying objective is the promotion of proportionate investigations and outcomes, and is reflected in reg 12(2)–(4), grading cases from 'no misconduct', to 'simple misconduct', and finally 'gross misconduct', with different options available for each once so assessed.

7.84 The first assessment (reg 12(1)) is to 'assess whether the conduct which is the subject matter of the allegation, if proved, would amount to misconduct or gross misconduct or neither'. If it would amount to gross misconduct, then investigation is mandatory under reg 12(4).

7.85 Where the appropriate authority assesses that the conduct, if proved, would amount neither to misconduct nor to gross misconduct, it may (reg 12(2)), either: (i) take no action; or (ii) take 'management action' against (as distinct from giving 'management advice' to) the officer concerned; or (iii) refer the matter to be dealt with under the 2008 Performance Regulations. If any of these decisions are taken, the officer must be notified in writing as soon as practicable (reg 12(6)). This process reflects the complementary nature of the 2008 Conduct Regulations and the 2008 Performance Regulations, which are intended to apply as a coherent single package in the context of a philosophy of learning and development, rather than blame and punishment.

Where the appropriate authority assesses that the conduct, if proved, would **7.86** amount to simple misconduct as distinct from gross misconduct, by reg 12(3), 'it shall determine whether or not it is necessary for the matter to be investigated'—that is, a formal investigation may not be proportionate ('necessary') even when a proven allegation would represent simple misconduct. Examples might be alleged rudeness to the public or the officer's personal appearance. In those circumstances, the appropriate authority may (reg 12(3)(b)) either take no action, or take only management action.

If the appropriate authority assesses that an investigation is required, then it will **7.87** be investigated (see reg 13 *et seq*) and (reg 13(a)) it must then determine additionally whether, if the matter were referred to misconduct proceedings, those would be likely to be a misconduct meeting or hearing. The form of proceedings will necessarily be the latter if, at the time of the assessment, the officer concerned is the subject of a 'live' final written warning, by reason of the effect of reg 19(9)(a), or was reduced in rank under the 2004 Conduct Regulations in the eighteen months prior to the assessment of conduct (reg 19(9)(b)).

The significance of the reg 12 determination is that it informs the content of the **7.88** subsequent reg 15 notice of investigation (see 7.120 *et seq* below). By this notice, the officer is effectively notified at the point of investigation that the initial assessment will lead to misconduct proceedings—and consequently the range of outcomes—of the type articulated in the notice.

As every assessment under reg 12 is subject to revision under reg 12(5) at any **7.89** point 'before the start of misconduct proceedings',[25] this should ameliorate some of the damaging uncertainty inherent in being the subject of investigation. The necessity of a well-informed initial assessment is self-evident in this context. Revision upwards to gross misconduct (and, with it, the procedures and powers of a misconduct hearing) will invariably require genuinely significant fresh evidence to have emerged if it is to be justified within the intended regulatory framework. No different principle applies to severity assessments under Sch 3. The potential for unfairness is otherwise acute.

---

[25] '"Misconduct proceedings" means a misconduct meeting or misconduct hearing': reg 3(1).

7.90 Demonstrably, this discretion is helpful, and driven by the desire for proportionality and effective management. It is—perfectly sensibly—only where the appropriate authority determines that the conduct, if proved, would amount to gross misconduct that investigation of the matter is mandatory.

D. The Appointment of the Investigator

The definition and the enhanced role of the investigator in the 2008 regime

7.91 The investigator of any allegation of misconduct or crime in any context performs an important forensic role, and must, of course, act impartially, proportionately, and strictly objectively. The primary duty is to establish facts. These basic features are reflected in statute, regulations, and associated Home Office Guidance, and should be uncontentious—but the documented history of police investigations 'into their own' is unhappily littered with contrary examples.

7.92 Within the 2008 regime, the investigator of any matter referred for investigation plays an enhanced role. As set out, he has a role in determining whether the special requirements apply (although the decision is strictly that of the appropriate authority), in making the severity assessment (likewise), and in determining the form of the reg 14A/15 notice of investigation. He has a role in addressing any representations made by the officer concerned during the investigation and is likely to be central to the disclosure process. Additionally, in every case that proceeds that far, his investigation report is not simply material upon which discretion is exercised as to the fact and form of misconduct proceedings, but is an intrinsic part of the material submitted to the persons conducting the misconduct proceedings.

7.93 This transparency is new to the 2008 regime and requires a wholly revised approach to the form and content of the report of the 'investigating officer' (IO). Unlike the presumed confidentiality of the 'IO's report' under previous Conduct Regulations,[26] when it was used as an internal report only and rarely disclosed to the misconduct panel or the officer concerned, the investigator's report must now be written with the defined statutory duties and recipients in mind. Under the 2008 regime, it is a different beast, with the same name, but from a related species.

7.94 What is required is set out in detail at 7.167–7.172 below. In summary, it must provide an 'accurate summary of the evidence', attach or refer to any relevant

---

[26] Particularly before the implementation of the 2002 Act: see *R (Green) v Police Complaints Authority* [2004] 1 WLR 725, considered at 3.30. See also *Taylor v Anderton* [1995] 1 WLR 447, which now appears to be largely ignored in practice.

documents, and 'indicate the investigator's opinion as to whether there is a case to answer for misconduct or gross misconduct'.

The important point to make is that reasons for the opinion are not required for inclusion. The necessity of including 'the opinion' as to the defined matters is a corollary of the requisite formality within the Regulations that such an assessment has, in fact, been made by a qualified investigator applying the statutory test. It is contended that, beyond including the formality of the opinion, reasons for it should perhaps be included only with extreme circumspection. The reasoning behind the concluded 'opinion' is not (or, at least, should not be) admissible in misconduct proceedings and may be highly prejudicial. It will certainly be perceived as such by officers the subject of allegations. The opinion is better perceived as a form of certification that the regulatory process has been followed, than as a licence to include other irrelevant subjective assertions.   **7.95**

The appointment of the investigator in Sch 3 investigations

There are some differences as to the process of appointment, qualifications, and powers of direction over the investigator arising from the different forms of investigation that may be determined by the IPCC under Sch 3.   **7.96**

Once a complaint, conduct matter, or DSI matter has been determined by the IPCC as suitable for a local investigation under para 16 of Sch 3 to the 2002 Act, it is the duty of the appropriate authority to appoint a person (defined in para 16(3), but who need not be a police officer) to investigate the complaint or matter.   **7.97**

On notification that the IPCC has determined that the investigation must be supervised, the appropriate authority must appoint a person (defined in para 17(2)) to investigate the complaint or matter. Paragraph 17(3)–(5) provides the IPCC with an apparent power to veto the appropriate authority's choice of investigator. Once again, specific provision is made (see subparas (6) and (6A)) for supervised investigations into chief officers.   **7.98**

Importantly, for supervised investigations, the investigator 'shall comply with all such requirements in relation to the carrying out of that investigation as may, in accordance with regulations made for the purposes of this sub-paragraph by the Secretary of State, be imposed by the Commission in relation to that investigation'. The relevant regulations are the 2004 Complaints and Misconduct Regulations, reg 6 of which identifies the requirements that may be imposed on the investigator during a supervised investigation to be 'any reasonable requirements as to the conduct of the investigation as appear to [the IPCC] to be necessary'.   **7.99**

Some idea of the type of requirements that will be imposed is derived from para 5.6.9 of the IPCC statutory guidance, which speaks of the IPCC being able   **7.100** to agree the terms of reference and investigation plan with the force, and for regular reviews of the investigation.

7.101 Two limitations only are placed on the exercise of this discretion by the IPCC, as follows.

(i) In situations in which the possibility of criminal proceedings arise, the IPCC is prohibited from imposing any requirement relating to the obtaining or preservation of evidence of a criminal offence 'without first obtaining the consent of the Director of Public Prosecutions to the imposition thereof '.

(ii) It is prohibited from imposing any requirement 'relating to the resources to be made available by a chief officer for the purposes of an investigation without first consulting him and having regard to any representations he may make'.

7.102 The latter limitation is self-evidently to prevent the IPCC from imposing—at least without prior consultation—financial or other requirements that the chief officer may, reasonably, regard to be disproportionate or impracticable.

Investigators under the 2008 Conduct Regulations

7.103 The equivalent provision under the 2008 Conduct Regulations is reg 13, where, when the matter is to be investigated pursuant to the reg 12 determination, the appropriate authority has the duty to appoint 'a person to investigate the matter'.[27] The very language of reg 13(2) illustrates that the person no longer needs to be a police officer. Many forces' professional standards departments recruit recently retired police officers—often former detectives—to undertake investigations, which has a dual benefit of ensuring experience and—very often by reason of retirement—greater detachment.

7.104 Regulation 13(4) stipulates the necessary qualifications for the investigator: he must have the an appropriate level of knowledge, skills, and experience to plan and manage the investigation;[28] he must not be an interested party—that is, a person whose appointment could reasonably give rise to a concern as to whether he could act impartially under the 2008 Conduct Regulations; he must not work, directly or indirectly, under the management of the officer concerned;[29] and, in the case of investigations into senior officers—that is, officers of Association of

---

[27] If the officer concerned is the Commissioner of Police of the Metropolis or his Deputy, the appropriate authority must notify the Secretary of State, who will appoint the investigator.

[28] In effect, replicating the provisions of reg 18(1)(a) of the 2004 Complaints and Misconduct Regulations, which apply to recordable complaints and conduct matters. The respective provisions, whilst perhaps appearing to state the obvious, may reflect a historic perception that this benchmark was not always met in practice.

[29] This disqualification would appear to be too obvious to need stating, although it is odd that the equivalent disqualification for those supervising the officer concerned, past or present, is not present.

Chief Police Officers (ACPO) level—the investigator cannot be either the chief officer or member of the same force (in the MPS, 'serving in the same division') as that senior officer.

Investigators under paras 16–18 of Sch 3 to the 2002 Act

For investigations within paras 16–18 of Sch 3 (local, supervised, and managed), **7.105** reg 18 of the 2004 Complaints and Misconduct Regulations provides similar qualification criteria.

Given that the investigator will often be conducting investigations into very seri- **7.106** ous misconduct (possibly criminal in substance), and where the public interest may be significant, one might have thought that the police service would invest in appointing only investigators of the highest quality and experience of substantial investigations. When this expectation has not been met, historically, the adverse consequences for the police forces and affected officers in terms of cost, morale, and publicity have invariably been acute.

Express criteria of this sort, however, facilitate meaningful representations by **7.107** affected parties if the criteria are contended not to have been fulfilled. There ought to be little scope for dispute as to what does and what does not qualify or disqualify a person from investigating. Whether a particular prior relationship (short of a 'management' relationship) disqualifies is always a question of fact and degree.

In certain situations, investigators need to liaise closely with those responsible **7.108** for parallel criminal proceedings. The conduct investigation may cover the same factual background, or may simply arise in the context of a criminal investigation into the conduct of a member of the public. In the latter context, cross-disclosure considerations will arise.

The necessity of clear decision making is at its most acute in this context in respect **7.109** of interviews under caution of the officer concerned (see 7.145–7.154). Paragraph 2.112 of the Home Office Guidance provides that the force's professional standards department 'should be consulted before an investigation is commenced to ensure that there are no other matters that need to be considered prior to any investigation', which is self-evidently sound advice.

E. The Purpose of the Investigation

Regulation 14 of the 2008 Conduct Regulations provides that the purpose of the **7.110** investigation is: (i) to gather evidence to establish the facts and circumstances of the alleged misconduct or gross misconduct; and (ii) to assist the appropriate authority to establish whether there is a case to answer in respect of the same.

These criteria are directed at promoting a thorough and efficiently focused investigation into clearly defined matters. Paragraph 2.114 of the Home Office Guidance reflects the fact that that these obvious objectives were not always matched in practice:

> A frequent criticism of previous misconduct investigations was that they were lengthy, disproportionate and not always focussed on the relevant issue(s). It is therefore crucial that any investigation is kept proportionate to ensure that an overly lengthy investigation does not lead to grounds for challenge.

7.111 Paragraph 1.113 of the Guidance adds a further purpose to the investigation— that is, to 'identify any learning for the individual or the organisation'. This is an extension of the intended wider guardianship function of the IPCC, and directed at feeding lessons from identified failures into improved policing practice, locally and nationally. For the same reason, investigations do not end simply because misconduct proceedings against a particular officer—for example, through the expiry of a fixed-term appointment (FTA)[30]—are impossible.

7.112 All investigations require written terms of reference. These are disclosed to the complainant and the officer under investigation. Both such parties may make representations to the investigator as to the parameters set, and the terms are subject to continuing review.

F. Written Notices of Investigation

The history and purpose of 'notices of investigation'

7.113 The required 'notices of investigation' (under reg 14A of the 2004 Complaints and Misconduct Regulations for Sch 3 investigations and reg 15 of the 2008 Conduct Regulations in relation to non-Sch 3 investigations) have a pedigree going back at least to the Police (Discipline) Regulations 1977,[31] in which they were required under reg 7. Under the 2004 Conduct Regulations, they became known as 'the reg 9'.

7.114 In *R v Chief Constable of Merseyside Police, ex p Calveley and ors*,[32] the Master of the Rolls described (at 432D–G) the primary purpose of the Regulation as being:

> to put the officer on notice that a complaint has been made and to give him a very early opportunity to put forward a denial, which in some cases might even take the form of an alibi, or an explanation and to collect evidence in support of that denial or explanation.

---

[30] See *Surrey Police Authority v Beckett* [2001] EWCA Civ 1253, CA.
[31] SI 1977/580.
[32] [1986] 1 QB 424.

The obligation to serve a notice of investigation bites on the appointment of the **7.115** investigator. The essential purpose of the notice is to enable the affected officer at the first practicable opportunity to take the initiative in defence of the allegation, and, in particular, to reduce the adverse evidential and forensic consequences that delayed notification could bring. It enables him—if he so elects—to direct the attention of the investigator to lines of inquiry that may otherwise not arise.

The notice requirement was described in *Calveley* as directory, rather than **7.116** mandatory, in the sense that breach did not, of itself, vitiate disciplinary proceedings, but also as 'an essential protection for officers facing disciplinary charges'. The Court of Appeal in *R v Chief Constable of the Merseyside Police, ex p Merrill*[33] distinguished the consequence of breach from 'abuse of process' and held that:

> The Chief Constable had no need to concern himself with "abuse of process." As a judicial tribunal, he had a discretionary power to dismiss the charge without hearing the full evidence if he was satisfied that, whatever the evidence might reveal, it would be unfair to proceed further. "Unfairness" in this context is a general concept which comprehends prejudice to the accused, but can also extend to a significant departure from the intended and prescribed framework of disciplinary proceedings or a combination of both.

The consequences of regulatory departure are considered in greater detail at 12.49– **7.117** 12.54. An argument that *Merrill* was superseded by the subsequent leading authority as to the consequences of delay in the criminal context—*Attorney-General's Reference No 1 of 1990*[34]—was rejected by the Administrative Court in *R (Wilkinson and ors) v Chief Constable of West Yorkshire*,[35] in which the Court held that 'there is at least one very real distinction between the ordinary criminal cases and disciplinary proceedings brought against police officers under the 1985 regulations, and that is the fact of both the spirit and the letter of the regulations themselves'.[36]

Under *Merrill*, a deliberate and unjustifiable failure to serve a notice will still attract **7.118** discretion in the misconduct panel to act on the basis of resultant unfairness 'whatever the evidence might reveal' as to the merits of the underlying allegation. Additionally, *Wilkinson* indorsed (at [56]) the principle in *Merrill* that whilst:

> 'the ultimate quest, having regard to the risk of prejudice, was to determine whether a fair trial can be held', the 'delay may be so great and so unjustifiable as to give rise to injustice to an accused, requiring a stay or a dismissal of proceedings, even in the absence of specific prejudice.'

There is nothing in the 2008 regime that alters the 'spirit and letter' of the **7.119** Regulations so far as the form of the notice of investigation is concerned from that

---

[33] [1989] 1 WLR 1077.
[34] [1992] 1 QB 630.
[35] [2002] EWHC 2353 (Admin).
[36] Ibid, at [55] *per* Davis J.

which has applied since at least 1977. It is a fundamental obligation on the investigator to serve it as soon as practicable after appointment,[37] allowing only for non-service where to serve 'might prejudice the investigation or any other investigation' (particularly a criminal one).

The content of notices of investigation

7.120   Under either of regs 14A or 15, the obligation is on the investigator to give written notice of eight matters. These are not set out in exactly the same sequence in the two regulations (paras (b) and (c) are reversed in the reg 14A(1) requirements arising under para 19B(7) of Sch 3), but they are identical in effect, save for necessary changes of language to reflect the identity of the investigator and appropriate authority.

7.121   The requirements (with annotations added), as rehearsed in reg 15(1) (which may be the most common form of notice in practice), are that the officer concerned is to be given a notice:

> (a) describing the conduct that is the subject matter of the allegation and how that conduct is alleged to fall below the Standards of Professional Behaviour;[38]
>
> (b) of the appropriate authority's assessment of whether that conduct, if proved, would amount to misconduct or gross misconduct;[39]
>
> (c) that there is to be an investigation into the matter[40] and the identity of the investigator;[41]
>
> (d) of whether, if the matter were to be referred to misconduct proceedings, those would be likely to be a misconduct meeting or a misconduct hearing and the reason for this;[42]
>
> (e) that if the likely form of any misconduct proceedings to be held changes, further notice (with reasons) will be given;[43]

---

[37] As to which, see *Calveley* (at 432D–G); Donaldson MR in *Merrill* (at 1086E–H) gave as an 'obvious example' of where it would be justified in withholding service of the notice the situation of a complaint of a systematic taking of bribes, 'when the investigating officer might reasonably wish to set a trap as part of the investigation which would be prejudiced by the giving of the notice'. He made clear, however, that non-service of the notice could only be justified 'for so long as is necessary to avoid such prejudice'.

[38] The equivalent of the former obligation to describe 'the nature of the report, complaint or allegation'.

[39] This is an important feature of the new regime, because it enables the officer concerned to understand, from the very outset, the appropriate authority's assessment of the seriousness, or otherwise, of the allegation. This, in turn, is intended to assist the officer concerned to adopt a realistic stance, if he knows that he is facing nothing more than, for example, a written warning.

[40] Part of the notice obligations under reg 9 of the 2004 Conduct Regulations.

[41] A new obligation: previously, there has been no obligation to identify the investigator in the written notice.

[42] As set out, gross misconduct, if proved, will necessarily proceed to a misconduct hearing; conversely, simple misconduct, if proved, may not even proceed to a misconduct meeting. The purpose of this obligation is similar to that for element (b)—namely, to enable the officer concerned to understand the likely forum for any potential misconduct proceedings.

[43] In other words, if upon further investigation it becomes clear that contrary to initial impressions, the allegation will not amount to gross misconduct, the officer concerned must be told as much.

(f) informing him that he has the right to seek advice from his staff association or any other body and of the effect of regulation 6(1);[44]

(g) of the effect of regulations 7(1) to (3)[45] and 16[46]; and

(h) informing him that whilst he does not have to say anything it may harm his case if he does not mention when interviewed or when providing any information under regulations 16(1) or 22(2) or (3) something which he later relies on in any misconduct proceedings or special case hearing or at an appeal meeting or appeal hearing.[47]

Matters specific to reg 15 notices

Part 3 of the 2008 Conduct Regulations, of which reg 15 forms a part, does not apply to Sch 3 investigations—that is, those attracting a notice under reg 14A(1) of the 2004 Complaints and Misconduct Regulations. Strictly, the following matters are not directly applicable to investigations pursuant to a reg 14A notice. It is to be anticipated, however, that equivalent procedures will be followed in Sch 3 investigations. There is, after all, no distinction in content or purpose, or as to methods of service, and the two regimes should, so far as possible, mirror each other in application from the perspective of the affected officer.   **7.122**

A standard template is provided for reg 15 notices at Annex E to ch 2 of the Home Office Guidance. Paragraph 2.104 of the Guidance states that the notice of investigation 'should clearly describe in unambiguous language the particulars of the conduct that it is alleged fell below the standards expected of a police officer'.   **7.123**

Additionally, para 2.105 suggests that the terms of reference of the investigation (or that part relating to the officer concerned) should (subject to there being no sufficient risk of prejudice to that or any other investigation) 'be supplied to the police officer and to his or her police friend on request, and they should both be informed if the terms of reference change'. If the investigation is, or may be, criminal in nature, this test may have to be applied with caution: it is not, after all, a duty owed to other criminal suspects. Regulation 15(4) obliges the investigator to keep the officer concerned notified of the progress of the investigation.   **7.124**

Regulation 15(2) contains the important obligation on the appropriate authority, if it revises its assessment of the misconduct or its determination of the likely form of any subsequent misconduct proceedings, to give the officer concerned further   **7.125**

---

[44] See above: this simply identifies who may act as a police friend.

[45] Regulation 7 deals with rights to legal representation.

[46] See below: reg 16 identifies certain rights of the officer concerned to make representations to the investigator.

[47] This amounts to a warning of the possibility of the person(s) conducting any misconduct proceedings to draw an adverse inference in relation to something advanced at those proceedings that was not, but could reasonably have been, advanced either under the (discretionary) provision of reg 16, or the (mandatory) provisions of reg 22(2) and (3) (which concerns the disclosure and other obligations on the officer concerned after he has received notice of referral to misconduct proceedings).

written notice of the new assessment of the misconduct and the form of any sub-sequent misconduct proceedings. This may, of course, be an assessment up to gross misconduct or down to simple misconduct, with associated consequences as to the form of the misconduct proceedings. As observed at 7.89 above, to revise upwards to gross misconduct will invariably require material fresh evidence to have emerged.

G. Representations to the Investigator

7.126 As part of the new 'cards on the table' approach enjoined by the Taylor reforms, under either investigatory regime there is a continuing right to make representations to the investigator.

Schedule 3 matters

7.127 For Sch 3 matters, once the reg 14A notice has been served on the person concerned, para 19C defines the nature of the 'duty to consider submissions from person whose conduct is being investigated'. Paragraph 19C applies to a complaint that is subject to the special requirements or an investigation of a recordable conduct matter. Paragraph 19C(2) provides that if, before the expiry of the time limit notified under para 19B(7), the person concerned provides the investigator with a relevant statement or document or any person of a prescribed prescription, then the investigator must consider the statement or document.

7.128 The possibility of an adverse inference from a failure to respond to the reg 14A(h) element of the notice of investigation is a parallel of reg 15(1)(h) of the 2008 Conduct Regulations. Adverse inferences are addressed in detail at 8.89 *et seq*.

2008 Conduct Regulations

7.129 Regulation 16(1) of the 2008 Conduct Regulations provides that, before the end of ten working days starting with the first working day after notice is given under reg 15(1) (unless the period is extended by the investigator),[48] the officer concerned 'may provide a written or oral statement relating to any matter under investigation to the investigator', and the officer concerned or his police friend 'may provide any relevant documents to the investigator'.

7.130 It is not mandatory for an officer to respond to the notice of investigation in this sense under either investigatory regime. If he does not make any such statement or provide any such document, he does so at peril of the warning given

---

[48] Which, presumably, it might be in a case of complexity or for some other compelling reason: eg the officer was on holiday when the notice was served on his police friend.

under reg 15(1)(h), that an incomplete or misleading statement or disclosure of documents 'may harm his case'. As with any adverse inference of this nature, whether or not it arises will be a question of fact and degree.

Regulation 16(2) of the 2008 Conduct Regulations requires the investigator to 'consider any such statement or document' and to make a record of having received either. This must be read in conjunction with para 2.118 of the Home Office Guidance, which emphasizes that the investigator's said duty is intended to ensure that 'the investigation is as fair as possible' and to 'enable a fair and balanced investigation report to be prepared'. **7.131**

For the avoidance of any possible doubt, reg 16(3) defines 'relevant document' to mean 'a document relating to any matter under investigation' and to include a document 'containing suggestions as to lines of inquiry to be pursued or witnessed to be interviewed'. Implicitly, therefore, officers who are the subject of written notices under reg 15 are entitled to suggest lines of inquiry or relevant witnesses to the investigator. Any investigator would, quite apart from the explicit obligation under reg 16(2), ignore such representations as his peril. **7.132**

The policy behind reg 16 (and, by analogy, para 19C of Sch 3 to the 2002 Act) is explained in para 2.117 of the Home Office Guidance—that is, that 'the police officer or his or her police friend, acting on the police officer concerned's instructions, is encouraged to suggest at an early stage any line of enquiry that would assist the investigation and to pass to the investigator any material they consider relevant to the enquiry'. The promotion of an iterative process involving all of the relevant parties—with repeated opportunities to define the direction and content of investigation—is consistent with the objective of the investigation producing the correct assessment of the conduct in question after the evidence has been captured. If this is the result, then certain investigations that would otherwise have resulted in misconduct proceedings may not now do so. **7.133**

H. Interviews

History demonstrates that the quality of interview of one police officer by another is not always of the requisite standard. There is doubtless a menu of contributory factors. Some interviewing officers—possibly (and paradoxically) in an attempt to appear wholly professional and objective—appear to lose these qualities when presented with a police officer interviewee. Too often, there is a lack of clarity as to the factual and legal basis of an interview for criminal conduct. Many interviewers appear not to understand the requirements of offences, such as perverting the course of justice, manslaughter, and (particularly) misconduct in public office. A criminal interview is often used defensively when the interviewer does not have grounds to justify it and cannot do so when invited to articulate them. **7.134**

7.135 An additional basis for confused thinking by investigators contaminated the process when the criminal caution was (for all practical purposes) introduced to misconduct interviews by the 2004 Conduct Regulations. Despite a common form of caution, there is, and must be, a clear separation between interviews relating to suspected criminal conduct and those for misconduct purposes. The interrelationship between criminal and misconduct interviews in this context is considered at 7.145–7.54 below.

7.136 The investigatory regimes provide specific procedures for purely misconduct interviews. Conversely, ordinary criminal rules of procedure apply to criminal interviews.

Pre-interview procedures

7.137 Regulation 17 of the 2008 Conduct Regulations and reg 14D of the 2004 Complaints and Misconduct Regulations (for Sch 3 investigations) provide only that the investigator 'shall, if reasonably practicable, agree a date and time for the interview with the officer concerned', and, where no agreement is achieved, that the investigator 'shall specify a date and time for the interview'.

7.138 Both regs 17 and 14D condescend to even greater micromanagement of the process: where a date and time has been specified by the investigator, and the officer concerned or his police friend is unavailable and the officer concerned (or presumably his friend on his behalf) proposes an alternative date that is reasonable and within five working days of the original date specified by the investigator, then the interview 'shall be postponed to the time proposed by the officer concerned'. Once the date and time of the interview has been so fixed, the investigator must ensure that the officer or person concerned is given written notice of the date, time, and place for the interview.[49]

7.139 The probable justification for these notice requirements lies in the role of the police friend and in providing sufficient opportunity for the officer concerned to obtain legal advice before interview. The officer is entitled to be accompanied by a police friend, but not a legal representative, at a purely misconduct interview. Prior to the interview, the investigator must provide the officer or person concerned 'with such information as the investigator considers appropriate in the circumstances of the case to enable the officer concerned to prepare for the interview'.[50]

7.140 The discharge of this last obligation will invariably impact upon any subsequent attempt by the presenting side to rely upon the 'adverse inference' provisions

---

[49] See reg 17(5) of the 2008 Conduct Regulations and reg 14D(5) of the 2004 Complaints and Misconduct Regulations.
[50] Regulation 17(6) of the 2008 Conduct Regulations and reg 14D(6) of the 2004 Complaints and Misconduct Regulations.

of reg 15(1)(h) of the 2008 Conduct Regulations or reg 14A(h) of the 2004 Complaints and Misconduct Regulations, in that, if the investigator does not provide appropriate pre-interview disclosure, the officer or person concerned, if referred to misconduct proceedings, will have greater scope for justifying silence or reticence in interview. Paragraphs 2.127–2.128 of the Home Office Guidance provide further commentary on this aspect of the regulation.

Regulation 17(7) of the 2008 Conduct Regulations and reg 14D(7) of the 2004 **7.141** Complaints and Misconduct Regulations provide that the officer or person concerned 'shall attend the interview'. This appears to create a duty and, correspondingly, the possibility of misconduct arising by the very fact of missing an interview.

In the context of these notification and disclosure requirements, reg 17(8) of the **7.142** 2008 Conduct Regulations and reg 14D(8) of the 2004 Complaints and Misconduct Regulations provide that, during the interview, the police friend may not answer any questions asked of the officer or person concerned. By the date of interview, there should be few, if any, surprises (beyond those justified strategically by the wider investigation) as to what is raised and the interviewee should have had enough time to prepare. This does not prevent the interviewee from seeking to suspend the interview to obtain advice. The police friend may make procedural representations during the interview: this does not amount to 'answering questions'.

There is nothing procedurally to prevent the officer concerned from submitting **7.143** a prepared statement. Whether an adverse inference then arises from a decision not to answer questions will be a matter of fact and degree at any subsequent misconduct proceedings. More perhaps than ordinary defendants, however, police officers—particularly senior officers—who decline to be interviewed may well risk appearing 'unprofessional' in the minds of the misconduct panel.

Discretion as to interviews

Paragraphs 2.119–2.130 of the Home Office Guidance provide further insight into **7.144** the policy behind the interview provisions. It is made clear that it will not always be necessary to conduct a formal interview, particularly when dealing with 'low-level misconduct' in relation to which 'it may be more appropriate, proportionate and timely to request a written account from the police officer'. Sick officers (and others) may be invited to provide a written response to the allegations within a specified period 'and may be sent the questions that the investigator wishes to be answered'.

Criminal and misconduct interviews as part of a single investigation

An investigation may cover suspected criminal conduct by the officer concerned. **7.145** This may overlap, to an extent, with the misconduct investigation. The identity of the investigator may be the same. The necessity of separation is never more acute than at the point of interview. Although the subject matter of the interview and words of the caution preceding it are common, criminal and misconduct proceedings are different, and should remain so.

7.146 The differences, whilst obvious, have become confused in practice. A criminal caution is only necessary when the investigator has a suspicion on reasonable grounds that the officer concerned may have committed a criminal offence. Far too many interviews with police officers are conducted under criminal caution when there is, in reality, no objective basis for such suspicion, and the investigator is often (embarrassingly) unable to articulate one. Such justification as has been provided habitually demonstrates an ignorance of the elements of the criminal offence in question.

7.147 Applied in this context, the criminal caution is thus used defensively, but inappropriately, by the investigator. This has particularly been the case in Sch 3 investigations following critical incidents such as deaths in custody. It is unfair to the officer concerned, and gives the false and unjustified impression to friends or family of the injured or deceased person that there is an objective basis to suspect criminal conduct. This sets the climate afterwards and negatively affects all aspects of the procedure (particularly for evidence at any subsequent inquest), and interested persons' perception of, and confidence in, the procedure.

7.148 Assuming that there is an objective basis to suspect criminal conduct, then the officer is entitled to be represented at a criminal interview by a lawyer. If the interview is restricted to criminal matters under investigation, the pre-interview misconduct procedures will not apply. It is contended that, in so far as the misconduct investigation covers the same ground, there should be no separate misconduct interview, or element of interview, until the criminal process is concluded. Whether a misconduct interview is then required is case-sensitive.

7.149 If the officer elects to answer 'no comment' in the criminal interview, he may be re-interviewed under the misconduct procedures at the conclusion of the criminal process, and the adverse inference provisions will apply for misconduct purposes from silence (if any) at the re-interview rather than the original criminal interview. This is 'cleaner' in terms of determining whether an adverse inference arises (it avoids the wholly legitimate contention that there are many good reasons not to answer questions in a criminal context that may not apply equally to the misconduct context), and protects the interests of both the investigator and the affected officer in the misconduct process.

7.150 If, however, the officer concerned elects to answer questions during the criminal interview, those answers may be used in subsequent misconduct proceedings: see *R (Pamplin) v The Law Society*,[51] in which it was held that *Woolgar v Chief*

---

[51] [2001] EWHC Admin 300.

Constable of Sussex Police[52] (confirming the confidentiality of criminal interviews) did not prevent disclosure of such a criminal interview by the investigator to those responsible for the professional regulation of the party under investigation. The court held (at [16]–[17]):

> ... Indeed, the rationale of the case of *Woolgar* is flatly against the proposition that it is a precondition to disclosure, in the circumstances under scrutiny, being legal, that notice should be given to the person affected.

> 17. I take the ratio of the decision of the Court of Appeal from page 36 of the judgment, in the penultimate paragraph on the page, which reads as follows:

> "Even if there is no request from the regulatory body, it seems to me that if the police come into possession of confidential information which, in their reasonable view, in the interests of public health or safety, should be considered by a professional or regulatory body, then the police are free to pass that information to the relevant regulatory body for its consideration."

Woolgar was concerned with the conduct of a nurse, and *Pamplin* with that of **7.151** a solicitor's clerk. In the policing context, the reference to health and safety is unnecessary: what is required is material relevant to the maintenance of professional standards in any context. It follows that the practice of inviting an officer to 'adopt' the criminal interview for discipline purposes at the end of the interview is unnecessary: as a matter of first principle, the criminal interview answers are admissible without such consent.

It would, however, be a clear abuse of process—a deliberate and unjustifiable **7.152** departure from the intended Regulations—for an interviewer to characterize conduct as criminal simply in order to avoid the specific notification and other procedural requirements attaching to purely misconduct investigations. Prima facie, avoiding these requirements prejudices the officer. Interviewers must accordingly be able to articulate at interview the objective basis of suspicion of criminal conduct if such an abuse of process application is to be resisted. If it is contended that giving reasons to the interviewee may prejudice the investigation in some way, the interviewer should make a contemporaneous and unassailable record before interview of the full reasoning justifying the contended conclusion that a criminal caution is appropriate and necessary. Simply rehearsing the conclusion would clearly be insufficient for these purposes.

Consistent with this procedural separation, para 2.124 of the Home Office **7.153** Guidance contains the important injunction to investigators and interviewers alike that, where the matter to be investigated involves both criminal and misconduct allegations, 'it should be made clear to the police officer concerned at the

---

[52] [2000] 1 WLR 25, CA.

start of the interview whether he or she is being interviewed in respect of the criminal or misconduct allegations'.

7.154 Paragraph 2.125 identifies that this may be achieved 'by conducting two separate interviews', and that conducting separate criminal and misconduct interviews 'does not prevent the responses given in respect of the criminal interview being used in the misconduct investigation and therefore a separate misconduct interview may not be required'. The Guidance proceeds to warn against misconduct interviews not under (presumably) criminal caution being subject to inadmissibility rulings in criminal proceedings. In truth, only rarely should misconduct interviews form part of any criminal case unless they represent an intrinsic part of the criminal offence, such as an attempt to pervert the course of justice.

Application of the Regulation of Investigatory Powers Act 2000 (RIPA)

Admissibility of intercept evidence, and directed or intrusive surveillance, in misconduct proceedings

7.155 Many misconduct proceedings (particularly hearings) will have started life as criminal investigations during which either: (i) communications have been intercepted under Pt 1 of the Regulation of Investigatory Powers Act 2000 (RIPA); or (ii) directed or intrusive surveillance has been carried out under Pt II. RIPA, the Codes issued under s 71 of the Act and associated case law provides an extensive body of authority as to the limits of admissibility of such material, and the (highly) limited extent to which the affected officer may seek to challenge the lawfulness of the authorisation.[53] A comprehensive consideration of this case law is beyond the scope of this book.

7.156 In general terms, however, the legal position as to admissibility of material under Pts I and II of the Act in misconduct proceedings is contended to be relatively straightforward—that is, material that is admissible in criminal proceedings will certainly be admissible in misconduct proceedings—but the converse (particularly in terms of Pt II) is not inevitably the case, given the more liberal admissibility rules in misconduct proceedings as compared with criminal proceedings. There is no general principle of law that either limits the use of admissible evidence to any one set of legal proceedings or to use against the narrow subject of the authorization.

Intercepted communications under Pt 1 of RIPA and lawful business monitoring

7.157 The statutory regimes in terms of intercepted communications and directed or intrusive surveillance are prescriptive, and apply equally to each form of legal proceedings in which evidence may be sought to be admitted. Challenges to authorizations similarly have to follow the intended statutory regime, including

---

[53] See *R v H; R v C* [2004] 2AC 134, HL, and *R v GS* [2005] EWCA Crim 887, CA.

the Codes of Practice issued under s 71 of the Act and, where applicable, complaints to the Interception of Communications Commissioner (Pt I RIPA) or the Surveillance Commissioner (Pt II RIPA) and through the statutory Investigatory Powers Tribunal.

Expressed broadly, in terms of intercept material under Pt 1, under s 17 disclosure **7.158** of the content of intercept material is not admissible in any proceedings unless it is an exception under s 18, (including (by s 18(4)) anything made lawful by virtue of ss 1(5)(c), 3, or 4.)[54]

Section 4 ('Power to provide for lawful interception') provides for a wide range **7.159** of specific circumstances in which such interception will be lawful including by subs (2), the power invested in the Secretary of State to make regulations authorizing any such conduct as described in the regulations 'as appears to him to constitute a legitimate practice reasonably required for the purpose, in connection with the carrying on of any business, of monitoring or keeping a record of—

> (a) communications by means of which transactions are entered into in the course of that business; or
> (b) other communications relating to that business or taking place in the course of its being carried on.

Section 4(7) defines 'a business' to include 'references to any activities of a govern- **7.160** ment department, of any public authority or of any person or office holder on whom functions are conferred by or under any enactment'. The Telecommunications (Lawful Business Practice)(Interception of Communications) Regulations 2000[55] were made pursuant to s 4. They are far-reaching in effect when applied to policing. According to the Explanatory Note (a fair summary, although not part of the Regulations):

> "The interception has to be by or with the consent of a person carrying on a business (which includes the activities of government departments, public authorities and others exercising statutory functions) for purposes relevant to that person's business and using that business's own telecommunication system", and "Interceptions are authorised for – monitoring or recording communications –
>
> • to establish the existence of facts, to ascertain compliance with regulatory or self-regulatory practices or procedures or to ascertain or demonstrate standards which are or ought to be achieved (quality control and training);
> • in the interests of national security (in which case only certain specified public officials may make the interception);
> • to prevent or detect crime;
> • to investigate or detect unauthorised use of telecommunication systems, or
> • to secure, or as an inherent part of, effective system operation;

---

[54] As to the application of s 18, see the preliminary ruling of McCombe J in *Raissi v Commissioner of Police of the Metropolis* [2007] EWHC 2842.
[55] SI 2699/2000.

- monitoring received communications to determine whether they are business or personal communications;
- monitoring communications made to anonymous telephone helplines.

Interceptions are authorised only if the controller of the telecommunications system on which they are effected has made all reasonable efforts to inform potential users that interceptions may be made.

The Regulations do not authorise interceptions to which the persons making and receiving the communications have consented: they are not prohibited by the Act."

7.161 In marked contrast to RIPA authorizations, the interception need only be made by the 'system controller' (defined by reg 2(d) as meaning, in relation to any telecommunication system, 'a person with a right to control its operation or use') and the evidence captured may, of course, reflect the activities of either police officers or other civilian employees. It follows that, assuming that the regulatory conditions are satisfied and that the interception was not otherwise an abuse of process (for example, made not for the regulatory purpose, but simply to avoid RIPA), intercepted communications under this regime will be admissible in evidence.

Directed and intrusive surveillance under Pt II of RIPA

7.162 The emphasis under Pt II of RIPA in terms of directed and intrusive surveillance is somewhat different. The purpose of authorization under Pt II is to ensure the admissibility of such evidence under s 78 of the Police and Criminal Evidence Act 1984 (PACE) and compliance with the Human Rights Act 1998 (HRA),[56] and in particular to establish that the surveillance is 'in accordance with the law' for the purpose of Art 8(2) of the European Convention on Human Rights (ECHR).[57] RIPA does not make covert surveillance unlawful, nor does it oblige an investigative body to obtain authorization before it carries out surveillance. The absence of the appropriate authorization does not necessarily render the surveillance unlawful.[58] However, covert surveillance will often engage the Art 8(1) right to private life[59] and, absent a RIPA authorization, the surveillance *may* not meet the requirement of Article 8(2) that the interference be 'in accordance with the law'. This requirement would be satisfied by operating within the RIPA regime. However, surveillance conducted in accordance with a code of sufficient precision and clarity *might* satisfy the Article 8(2) requirement. An example is the Employment Practices Data Protection Code issued by the Information Commissioner issued

---

[56] See para 1.8 of the Code of Practice issued under RIPA, s 71.

[57] See RIPA, s 27(1), and para 3 of the Explanatory Notes to the Act. Prior to RIPA, the UK was found to be in breach of Art 8 by the ECtHR because of the absence of a clear law regulating surveillance: *Khan v UK* (2001) 31 EHRR 45.

[58] See RIPA, s 80, and para 180 of the Explanatory Notes.

[59] Not all surveillance will, of course, engage Art 8, eg general surveillance of the public in non-specific crime prevention measures, such as routine use of closed-circuit television (CCTV): *Friedl v Austria* (1995) 21 EHRR 83.

under s 51 of the Data Protection Act 1998. Part 3 deals with 'monitoring at work' and offers guidance on the justifications for surveillance, the form it might take, and the level at which authorization should be obtained.

C v Police and Secretary of State for the Home Department[60] concerned an applica- **7.163**
tion to the Investigatory Powers Tribunal by a retired police officer who was the beneficiary of an enhanced injury on duty award under the Police Pension Regulations 1987.[61] He was made subject to surveillance to test the extent of his disability, in relation to which no RIPA authority was sought and when he was the subject of neither criminal nor misconduct proceedings. Although the case was concerned with the jurisdiction of the Tribunal to hear the complaint, the main question considered was whether the applicant was the target of 'directed' surveillance, as defined by s 26 of RIPA, and, in particular, whether the surveillance was for a 'specific investigation' or a 'specific operation' under s 26(2)(a).

The Tribunal found that the surveillance undertaken, despite being covert and for **7.164**
the purpose of obtaining private information about the applicant, was not directed surveillance within the meaning of s 26, because of the contextual interpretative limitations placed on the terms 'specific investigation' and 'specific operation'. The Tribunal distinguished an 'ordinary function' of a public authority (the police force's relationship with its staff) from a 'core function' (police preventing and detecting crime), and concluded that the surveillance in question was the former variant and thus not covered by RIPA. Accordingly, the Tribunal declined jurisdiction to hear the case. The result of *C v Police* is that authorizations for directed surveillance under Part II of RIPA may not be sought for internal misconduct investigations, save where the officer is being investigated for criminal conduct.

Accordingly, since RIPA authorization cannot be obtained for most 'misconduct **7.165**
only' investigations, the questions that will need to be addressed in each case when considering surveillance and/or its product will include the following:

(i) Is Art 8 engaged at all? This will require analysis of the facts, and questions such as whether the surveillance is covert, its purpose, the nature of the activity surveilled, and whether the person surveilled had any reasonable expectation of privacy.

(ii) If Article 8 is engaged, is the surveillance 'in accordance with law'? Although RIPA cannot be relied upon, the Force might be able to rely on the Employment Practices Code.

---

[60] IPT/03/02H.
[61] SI 1987/257.

(iii) If Article 8 is engaged and the surveillance was 'in accordance with law', was it *necessary* in a democratic society in pursuit of one of the legitimate aims listed in Article 8(2) and *proportionate* to that aim? The answer will be fact-sensitive. It will depend on the purpose for which the surveillance operation was mounted and whether the level of intrusion into the target's private life was justified by the seriousness of suspected misconduct. If gross misconduct is being alleged at a misconduct hearing, it will not be difficult to identify a legitimate aim under Art 8(2), nor will it be difficult to establish that the proposed use of the material is proportionate.

(iv) If Article 8 has been breached, will the evidence obtained in breach of Article 8 be admissible in misconduct proceedings? The answer will, again, be fact-sensitive. If those who undertook the surveillance did so in good faith (that is, reasonably believing it to be proportionate) for proper purposes (investigating gross misconduct), and if there is nothing inherently unfair about the surveillance product, most panels are likely to conclude that the product should be admissible in the public interest, having regard to the purpose of gross misconduct hearings.[62] If, however, there has been deliberate abuse (for example, to record covertly privileged communications), even where the product of the intercept is not shown to have been used by the investigators, maintenance of the rule of law may require that proceedings are stayed as an abuse of process.[63]

7.166 To meet such challenges to admissibility—and, in particular, to address assertions of bad faith or abuse of process—those authorizing covert surveillance are well advised to follow the Employment Practices Code (unless and until the RIPA regime is amended) and to maintain clear contemporaneous records of both the fact and bases of decision making in these respects.

I. The Report of the Investigation

The 2008 Conduct Regulations

7.167 On completion of his investigation, the investigator shall, as soon as practicable, submit a written report on his investigation to the appropriate authority. Regulation 18(2)[64] provides that the report shall: (i) provide an accurate summary of the evidence; (ii) attach or refer to any relevant documents; and (iii) indicate the investigator's opinion as to whether there is a case to answer for misconduct or

---

[62] And see, by analogy with civil proceedings, *Jones v Warwick University* [2003] EWCA Civ 151.

[63] See *R v Grant and ors* [2005] EWCA Crim 1089, [2006] QB 60, [2005] 3 WLR.437, [2005] 2 Cr.App R. 28, [2005] Crim LR 955.

[64] See also reg 14E of the 2004 Complaints and Misconduct Regulations.

gross misconduct. The contended purpose of certifying compliance with objective procedures rather than importing inadmissible subjective opinion was addressed at 7.94–7.95 above.

Regulation 18(3) places an ongoing obligation on the investigator to submit a report to the appropriate authority if, at any time, he believes that the appropriate authority 'would, on consideration of the matter, be likely to determine that the special conditions are satisfied'. These relate to referral as a special case for fast tracking (see Chapter 10). **7.168**

Investigation reports for Sch 3 investigations

The position for Sch 3 matters is more complicated. The starting point is para 22 ('Final Reports on complaints, conduct matters and certain DSI matters'), which is analogous to reg 18 of the 2008 Conduct Regulations. It applies on the completion of an investigation of a complaint or a conduct matter, at which point: **7.169**

(i) the local investigator under para 16 of Sch 3 submits his report on the investigation to the appropriate authority;

(ii) the supervised or managed investigator under paras 17 and 18, respectively, submits his report to the IPCC and sends a copy of the same to the appropriate authority; and

(iii) the IPCC investigator under para 19 submits his report to the IPCC (meaning a commissioner).

Paragraph 22(7) provides for the Secretary of State, by regulations, to make provisions requiring a report on investigations within para 19C(1)(a)[65] or (b)[66] to include specified matters and to be accompanied by specified documents. **7.170**

Regulation 14E of the 2004 Complaints and Misconduct Regulations (which emulates reg 18(2) of the 2008 Conduct Regulations) requires that the said investigator's report shall: (i) provide an accurate summary of the evidence; (ii) attach or refer to any relevant documents; and (iii) indicate the investigator's opinion as to whether there is a case to answer in respect of misconduct or gross misconduct, or whether there is no case to answer. **7.171**

The investigator shall provide the appropriate authority with copies of such further documents or other items in his possession as the authority may request, provided that the appropriate authority: (i) considers such documents or items to be of relevance to the investigation; and (ii) requires a copy to comply with any **7.172**

---

[65] That is, a complaint certified under para 19B(1) as subject to special requirements.
[66] Recordable conduct matter.

obligation under ss 50(3)[67] or 51(2A)[68] of the Police Act 1996, and/or ensuring that any such person receives a fair hearing at any disciplinary proceedings.

Action by the IPCC in response to an investigation report from a managed or IPCC investigation (Sch 3, para 23)

7.173 Paragraph 23 of Sch 3 to the 2002 Act applies where an investigation report for a managed or IPCC investigation is submitted to the IPCC under para 22(3) or (5), respectively. If it appears that the appropriate authority has not already received a copy of the report, the IPCC shall send it one.

7.174 More significantly, on receipt of the report, the IPCC shall determine whether:

    (i)   the report indicates that a criminal offence may have been committed by a person to whose conduct the investigation related (para 23(2A), 'the first condition'); and

    (ii) the circumstances are such that, in the opinion of the IPCC, it is appropriate for the matters dealt with in the report to be considered by the Director of Public Prosecutions (DPP) (para 23(2B)(a)), *or* any matters dealt with in the report fall within any prescribed category of matters (para 23(2B)(b), 'the second condition').

7.175 If the IPCC determines that the first and second conditions are satisfied, then it must notify the DPP of that determination, send him a copy of the report, and notify the appropriate authority and complainant, and every person entitled to be kept properly informed under s 21 of the 2002 Act.

7.176 Paragraph 23(2B)(a) represents a significant departure from the old regime,[69] in that it is no longer always mandatory for any report that merely 'may' disclose a criminal offence to be sent to the DPP unless it is in a prescribed category. Such references produce inevitable (and routinely extended) delay to the disposition of misconduct proceedings. The obvious adverse consequences of setting the threshold for referral too low (thereby removing discretion) are increasingly recognized by the IPCC. The IPCC should develop greater confidence in not referring matters where the prospects of a prosecution arising are remote.

---

[67] Procedures for disciplinary proceedings for police officers.

[68] Procedures for disciplinary proceedings for special constables.

[69] See para 23(2)(b) and (c), before the amendments under Sch 23 to the Criminal Justice and Immigration Act 2008, which effectively obliged the IPCC to notify the DPP if a criminal offence *'may have been committed'* and to send him a copy of the report, and which, read with the old para 23(6)(b) of Sch 3, held up the further consideration misconduct proceedings until the DPP had notified the IPCC that no further action was to be taken in the criminal jurisdiction.

The prescribed matters are yet to be provided for in regulations.[70]   **7.177**

Notification requirements on the IPCC

Once the DPP has decided whether to take criminal proceedings arising from the   **7.178**
report, he must notify the IPCC (para 23(3)). At the same time as the IPCC is
deciding whether it must send the report to the DPP, it must also notify the appropriate authority that it must, in accordance with regulations under ss 50 or 51 of
the Police Act 1996—that is, the 2008 Conduct Regulations—determine whether
any person identified in the report has a case to answer in respect of misconduct
or gross misconduct, and what action, if any, the appropriate authority will take
(para 23(6)).

Procedures following the service of a para 23(6) notification

Upon receipt of a notification under para 23(6),[71] the appropriate authority   **7.179**
must make the para 23(6) determinations and submit a memorandum to the
IPCC that: (i) sets out its determinations; and (ii) if it has decided against misconduct proceedings against any person to whose conduct the investigation related,
sets outs its reasons. Perhaps unsurprisingly, the obligation to give reasons to the
IPCC applies only when the appropriate authority decides against misconduct
proceedings.

On receipt of the appropriate authority's para 23(7) memorandum,[72] the IPCC   **7.180**
must: (i) consider whether the appropriate authority's determinations are
appropriate; (ii) determine whether or not, in the light of these considerations, to
make recommendations under para 27 (see 7.198 below); and (iii) make such
recommendations (if any) under para 27 as it thinks fit.[73]

On making the para 23(8) determination, the IPCC shall notify the complainant   **7.181**
and/or every person entitled to be kept properly informed, pursuant to s 21 of the
2002 Act. Such notification must set out: (i) the 'findings' of the report; (ii) the
IPCC's determination under para 23(8)(b) (that is, whether to make recommendations under para 27); and (iii) the action that the appropriate authority is to be
recommended to take as a consequence of the para 23(8)(b) determination. The
regulations applicable to keeping a complainant properly informed in s 20(5)–(7)
of the 2002 Act apply in relation to para 23(9).

---

[70] These are anticipated to include intrinsically sensitive cases such as police shootings.
[71] The para 23(6) notification should be expressed as such to reflect its significance.
[72] Which, as for the IPCC under para 23(6), the appropriate authority would do well to identify
as such, to avoid confusion.
[73] Paragraph 27 empowers the IPCC, in effect, to overrule the appropriate authority by way,
initially, of recommendation.

Action by the IPCC in response to an investigation report from a local or supervised investigation (Sch 3, para 24)

7.182 Paragraph 24 of Sch 3 applies where an investigation report for a local or supervised investigation (under paras 16 and 17, respectively) is submitted to the appropriate authority under para 22(2) or (3), respectively. A very similar process as that for managed and IPCC investigations then follows, and the language of para 24(2A) and (2B) is identical to the equivalent under para 23 already set out (see 7.173 *et seq* above), except that the determination is made by the appropriate authority as distinct from the IPCC.

7.183 Furthermore, for a supervised (but not local) investigation relating to a recordable conduct matter, the appropriate authority must notify the IPCC of its decision as to whether to refer the same to the DPP (para 24(5A)), and, if the appropriate authority's determination is against sending the matter to the DPP, the IPCC may review that determination and direct the appropriate authority to send a copy of the report to the DPP (para 24(5B). The appropriate authority must comply with any such direction from the IPCC (para 24(5C)).

7.184 Once the DPP has decided whether to take criminal proceedings arising from the report, he must notify the appropriate authority (para 24(3)), and the appropriate authority is under a duty to notify the complainant and every person entitled to be kept properly informed under s 21 of the 2002 Act of the DPP's decision. At the same time as the appropriate authority is deciding whether it must send the report to the DPP, it must also determine, in accordance with regulations under ss 50 or 51 of the Police Act 1996 (that is, the 2008 Conduct Regulations), whether any person identified in the report has a case to answer in respect of misconduct or gross misconduct, and what action, if any, the appropriate authority will take (para 24(6)).[74]

7.185 Upon making its determinations under para 24(6), the appropriate authority must give notification to the complainant, and every person entitled to be kept properly informed in relation to the complaint under s 21 of the 2002 Act, of the findings of the report, its determination under para 24(6) (that is, whether to take misconduct proceedings), and the complainant's right of appeal under para 25.

Final reports on other DSI matters (Sch 3, paras 24A–24C)

7.186 Paragraph 24A applies on the completion of an investigation of a DSI matter in which neither the IPCC nor appropriate authority has made a determination under para 21A(2) or (4) (relating to the investigator's duty of referral to IPCC or appropriate authority, as specified, of potential criminal conduct or misconduct

---

[74] There is a possible, as yet unresolved, distinction between para 24(6)(a)(ii) and (6)(b).

disclosed prior to the conclusion of investigation into the DSI matter). In such cases, the investigator shall submit a report on the investigation to the IPCC and send a copy of the same to the appropriate authority. Upon receipt of the report, the IPCC must determine whether the report indicates that a person serving with the police may have committed a criminal offence or behaved in a manner that would justify the bringing of disciplinary proceedings. This is effectively a procedural backstop.

If the IPCC determines either question in the affirmative, it shall notify the appropriate authority and, if it appears that the appropriate authority has not already been sent a copy of the report, send a copy to that authority (para 24B(1)). Upon receipt of such a determination by the IPCC, the appropriate authority shall record the matter under para 11 as a conduct matter, and the person investigating the DSI matter shall then investigate the conduct matter as if appointed or designated to do so. The other provisions of Sch 3 then apply in relation to that matter accordingly. **7.187**

If the IPCC determines both para 24A(4) questions in the negative, it shall make such recommendations or give such advice under s 10(1)(e) (if any) as it considers necessary or desirable. **7.188**

Appeals to the IPCC in relation to an investigation (Sch 3, para 25)

Paragraph 25 applies only to local and supervised investigations. It provides the complainant with rights of appeal to the IPCC. The appeal process is rehearsed in the IPCC procedure,[75] issued in the context of the timetable and rights prescribed by reg 10 of the 2004 Complaints and Misconduct Regulations,[76] and the terms of the statutory guidance issued by the IPCC under s 22 of the 2002 Act. **7.189**

The statutory grounds for appeal by the complainant are: **7.190**

  (i) a right to appeal on the grounds that he has not been provided with adequate information about:
     (a) the findings of the investigation; or
     (b) any determination of the appropriate authority relating to the taking or not taking of action in respect of any matters dealt with in the report;
  (ii) a right to appeal against 'the findings of the investigation';

---

[75] Available online at <http://www.ipcc.gov.uk>.
[76] Paragraph 25(13) provides for the Secretary of State to make regulations for dealing with the form, manner, timescales, and procedures to be adopted for such appeals.

(iii) a right of appeal against any determination by the appropriate authority that a person to whose conduct the investigation related has or has not a case to answer in respect of misconduct or gross misconduct;

(iv) a right of appeal against any determination by the appropriate authority relating to the taking or not taking of action in respect of any matters dealt with in the report;[77] and

(v) a right of appeal against any determination by the appropriate authority under para 24(2)(a) not to send the report to the DPP (in relation only to local and supervised investigations).

7.191 The IPCC has the duty to notify the appropriate authority, every person entitled to be kept properly informed in relation to the complaint under s 21 of the 2002 Act, and the person complained against of any appeal brought under para 25(2) of Sch 3 to the Act.

7.192 On the bringing of an appeal, the IPCC may require to see a copy of any local investigation report, and require the appropriate authority to submit a memorandum to it that sets out:

(i) whether the appropriate authority has determined that a person to whose conduct the investigation relates has a disciplinary case to answer;

(ii) what action (if any) the appropriate authority had determined that it is required to, or will, take in respect of the matters dealt with in the report;

(iii) its reasons for not taking disciplinary proceedings; and

(iv) its reasons for not sending the report to the DPP.

7.193 On appeal, the IPCC must determine the following matters and has the associated powers:

(i) whether the complainant has been provided with adequate information about the matters mentioned in para 25(2)(a)—if the IPCC determines, on appeal, that the complainant has not been provided with adequate information, it shall give the appropriate authority all such directions as it considers appropriate for securing that the complainant is properly informed (although this power is subject to the overriding provision in s 20(5) of the 2002 Act);[78]

(ii) whether the findings of the investigation need to be reconsidered—if it determines that the findings of the investigation need to be reconsidered,

---

[77] This would appear to relate to matters beyond the taking of disciplinary action and to cover matters such as recommendations as to corporate issues set out in the report.

[78] Paragraph 25(6).

it shall either review those findings without an immediate further investigation, or direct that the complaint be reinvestigated;[79]

(iii) whether the appropriate authority has made an appropriate determination in respect of whether persons have a case to answer and an appropriate determination in relation to what (disciplinary) action it will take—if, on appeal, it determines that the appropriate authority is not proposing to take action in consequence of the report that the IPCC considers appropriate, it shall determine whether or not to make recommendations under para 27 and to make any such recommendation under that paragraph that it thinks fit;[80] and

(iv) whether the first and second conditions (delineating whether the report is sent to the DPP) are satisfied—if, on appeal, it determines that the first and second conditions are satisfied in respect of the investigation report, it shall direct the appropriate authority to notify the DPP of its determination and send the DPP a copy of the report.[81]

The IPCC must give notification of any determinations under para 25 to the appropriate authority, complainant, every person entitled to be kept properly informed under s 21, and, except where to do so might prejudice any proposed review or reinvestigation of the complaint, the person complained against (para 25(10)).[82] Similarly, the IPCC must give notification to the same persons of any directions given to the appropriate authority under para 25. **7.194**

Finally, the appropriate authority is under a duty to comply with any such directions.[83] **7.195**

Reviews and reinvestigations following an appeal (Sch 3, para 26)

On a review under para 25(8)(a) of the findings of the investigation, the IPCC is entitled under para 26(1) to: **7.196**

(a) uphold the findings in whole or in part;

---

[79] Ibid, (8).

[80] Ibid, (9).

[81] Ibid, (9A).

[82] Ibid, (3); see also reg 23(2) of the 2004 Complaints and Misconduct Regulations. Importantly, once the para 25 appeal decision has been made and promulgated there is no power to vary it by reason of further representation. The alternative approach would promote unacceptable uncertainty given the statutory context: *R (Dennis) v IPCC* (2008) EWHC (Admin) 1158, ((40)). At (38)–(40) the court identified that the decided authorities *(R Wilkinson) v Police Complaints Authority* (2004) EWHC 678 and *R v Police Complaints Authority ex p Hanratty*, 25 July 1995) are apparently in conflict as to whether a decision to dispense with an investigation was similarly final. See also *R (Deborah Clare) v Independent Police Complaints Commission* (2005) EWHC 1108 (Admin) for requirement of effective service of decision.

[83] Ibid, (12).

>   (b) give the appropriate authority such directions—
>
>   (i) as to the carrying out by the appropriate authority of its own review of the findings,
>
>   (ii) as to the information to be provided to the complainant, and
>
>   (iii) generally as to the handling of the matter in the future,
>
>   as the Commission thinks fit;
>
>   (c) to direct that the complaint be re-investigated.

7.197 Where the IPCC directs a reinvestigation, it must make a determination as to the form of the same and, in this regard, para 15(3)–(7) of Sch 3 apply. As usual, the IPCC is obliged to notify the appropriate authority, complainant, every person entitled to be kept properly informed, and (save for the standard reservation) the person complained against, of any determinations or directions made under para 26.

The duties and IPCC powers of recommendation and direction in relation to disciplinary proceedings (Sch 3, para 27)

7.198 Paragraph 27 applies where the appropriate authority:

>   (a) has given, or is required to give, notification under paragraph 24(7) of the action it is proposing to take in relation to the matters dealt with in any report of the investigation; or
>
>   (b) has submitted, or is required to submit, a memorandum to the [IPCC] under paragraphs 23 [IPCC or managed investigation] or 25 [appeals] setting out the action that it is proposing to take in relation to those matters.

7.199 It shall be the duty of the appropriate authority to take the action that has been, or is required to be, notified, or is required to be set out in the memorandum, and, whether that action consists of or includes the bringing of disciplinary proceedings, to secure that those proceedings, once brought, are proceeded with to a proper conclusion. Whether para 27 applies by virtue of the appropriate authority's obligation to submit a memorandum under paras 23 or 25, the IPCC may make a recommendation to the appropriate authority in respect of any person serving with the police:

>   (i) that the person has a disciplinary case to answer;
>
>   (ii) that disciplinary proceedings of the form specified in the recommendation are brought against that person;[84] and
>
>   (iii) that any disciplinary proceedings brought against that person are modified so as to deal with such aspects of that conduct as may be so specified.[85]

---

[84] Which appears to reflect the power of the IPCC to recommend the form of disciplinary proceedings, ie whether managerial, performance, or misconduct, and if misconduct, whether a misconduct meeting or hearing.

[85] Which appears to reflect the power of the IPCC to recommend which Standards of Professional Behaviour have been breached and how.

Upon receipt of any such recommendation, it is the duty of the appropriate **7.200**
authority to notify the IPCC whether it accepts the recommendation and, if it
does, to set out in the notification the steps that it is proposing to take to give effect
to the same. If, however, the appropriate authority does not take steps to secure
that full effect is given to any IPPC recommendation, the IPCC may direct
the appropriate authority to take steps for that purpose and it shall be the duty of
the appropriate authority to comply with the direction. Any such direction
(para 27(4)) from the IPCC must be accompanied by reasons.

It will therefore be seen that the IPCC retains the 'whip hand' in terms of the **7.201**
bringing and form of disciplinary proceedings. Thus it is that para 27(7) provides
that, where disciplinary proceedings are brought in accordance with any IPPC
recommendation or direction, it shall be the duty of the appropriate authority to
ensure that such proceedings are proceeded with to a proper conclusion. This can,
and does, create tensions with the appropriate authority. Furthermore, the appropriate authority is under a duty to keep the IPCC notified of progress with regards
to disciplinary proceedings arising from paras 23 or 25.

These important powers of recommendation and direction are matched in terms **7.202**
of increased rights of participation for both the IPCC and complainant in the
misconduct proceedings themselves (see 8.66–8.85).

Information for the complainant about disciplinary recommendations (Sch 3, para 28)

Where the IPCC makes a para 27 recommendation in relation to a complaint **7.203**
investigation and the appropriate authority notifies the IPCC that its recommendation has been accepted, the IPCC must notify the complainant and every person entitled to be kept properly informed of that fact, and of the steps that have
been, or are to be taken, by the appropriate authority to give effect to the
recommendation.

Where the IPCC makes a para 27 recommendation in relation to a complaint **7.204**
investigation and the appropriate authority notifies the IPCC that its recommendation has not been accepted, in whole or in part, or the appropriate authority
fails to give full effect to any such recommendations, it is the duty of the IPCC to
determine what, if any, further steps to take under para 27 (for example, to give
directions).

It shall be the duty of the IPCC to notify the complainant and every person **7.205**
entitled to be kept properly informed:

(i) of any determination that it may make not to take any further steps in
relation to the appropriate authority's decision not to act upon a para 27
recommendation; and

(ii) where the IPCC determines under para 27 to take further steps, the outcome of the taking of those steps.

J. Conclusion

7.206 The above provisions are obviously fundamental to the scheme of investigation of complaints against, and alleged misconduct by, police officers. They create a heightened expectation that allegations will be dealt with proportionately. The rights of different interested persons are better defined than under previous regulatory arrangements. Equally, there is an expectation embedded in the process of greater disclosure by, and communication between, the officer concerned, the investigator, and the presenting officer, respectively. Experience alone will determine whether these legitimate objectives are met in practice. The required change of culture is significant and must be made equally by all parties if the process is to work as intended.

7.207 Under the 2008 Conduct Regulations, these cultural changes find equal reflection in the procedures governing the conduct of misconduct proceedings. These aspects are considered next, in Chapter 8.

8

MISCONDUCT PROCEEDINGS UNDER THE POLICE (CONDUCT) REGULATIONS 2008

A. **Referral of Case**	8.01	
The referral of the case to misconduct		
proceedings	8.07	
Withdrawal of the case	8.18	
Disclosure of the investigator's report		
to the officer concerned	8.21	
Notice of referral to misconduct		
proceedings and panel		
membership: reg 21	8.23	
Form of written notice and		
particularity of 'charge'	8.25	
The identity of, and objection to,		
panel members	8.31	
B. **Procedure on Receipt of Notice**	8.35	
C. **Witnesses**	8.40	
The timing and notice of misconduct		
proceedings	8.45	
Persons conducting misconduct		
proceedings for non-senior officers:		
reg 25	8.51	
The constitution of the panel:		
misconduct meetings for		
non-senior officers	8.52	
The constitution of the panel:		
misconduct hearings for		
non-senior officers	8.53	
Constitution of panels, etc,		
in relation to senior officers	8.58	
Documents to be supplied: reg 28	8.61	
D. **Rights of Attendance and**		
Participation in Misconduct		
Proceedings	8.66	
The nature of 'private' misconduct		
proceedings	8.66	

The officer concerned	8.67	
The IPCC	8.68	
The investigator	8.69	
Hearings in public	8.70	
Complainants and interested persons	8.76	
E. **Procedure at Misconduct**		
Proceedings	8.86	
The power of the chair to		
determine the procedure at		
misconduct proceedings	8.86	
Adverse inferences	8.89	
The questioning of witnesses	8.96	
The prescribed task of the person		
conducting or chairing the		
proceedings	8.104	
The burden and standard of proof	8.105	
The relevance of previous good		
character to fact finding	8.109	
Majority findings	8.111	
F. **Outcomes**	8.112	
Mitigation	8.125	
The approach to outcomes	8.129	
Notification of outcomes	8.138	
G. **Appeals from Misconduct**		
Proceedings	8.142	
Appeals against the outcome		
of a misconduct meeting	8.143	
Appeals from the outcomes		
of misconduct hearings	8.155	

A. Referral of Case

8.01 Part 4 of the Police (Conduct) Regulations 2008[1] sets out the procedures to be followed once a decision has been taken to refer a case for misconduct proceedings—that is, a misconduct meeting or hearing. This Part applies whatever the origins of the case. In other words, Sch 3 to the Police Reform Act 2002 and the 2008 Conduct Regulations formally converge from this point and hereinafter (for the purposes of the procedures to be followed), although, as will be seen, some distinctions remain within the process if the referral to misconduct proceedings arose from an investigation under any of paras 16–19 of Sch 3 to the 2002 Act.

8.02 Part 4 of the 2008 Conduct Regulations sets out procedures that are markedly different from those of their 2004 predecessor.[2] In summary, the fundamental distinctions include:

(i) the bifurcation into meetings and hearings;

(ii) the obligation on the officer concerned to show his evidential hand or risk an adverse inference being drawn by the person(s) conducting the proceedings;

(iii) the enhanced role of the person conducting or chairing the proceedings to determine the necessity of attendance by witnesses;

(iv) the enhanced role of non-police officers (that is, police staff), who may adjudicate at meetings and at hearings—at a hearing, it is possible for the chair to be a senior human resources professional (HRP) and one of the 'wing' members must be an 'independent' member appointed from a list held by the police authority; and

(v) the radically different menu of available 'outcomes' (formerly known as 'sanctions').

8.03 Other aspects have not changed and misconduct hearings, in particular, may not, in practice, appear as different as the authors of the new regime may have anticipated or hoped. The basic sequence of events—namely, an opening of the facts by the presenting officer (which will invariably be a qualified lawyer in gross misconduct cases), the calling only of contentious and important witnesses (whose attendance, if available, will surely inevitably be 'necessary' in practice in the interests of justice), evidence from the defendant officer, and closing addresses as necessary by each side—will remain the pattern for misconduct hearings.

---

[1] SI 2008/2864.
[2] The Police (Conduct) Regulations 2004, SI 2004/645.

Good practice from the history of previous misconduct hearings should be **8.04** adopted and encouraged. This includes: the use of written opening notes (with opportunity for principled objection before service on the panel); agreed indexed and paginated bundles of relevant documents; the exclusion of contentious evidence by agreement in advance between the parties, where possible, to avoid inherently prejudicial applications to the panel; the use and cross-service of written skeleton arguments on points of law; the calling of all of the available important, but properly contentious, witnesses of fact; the discretionary use of written closing arguments; and any legal adviser to the tribunal placing matters of advice on the record for reasons of transparency.

Few, if any, participants in the process—including panel members—would **8.05** instinctively regard any of these as other than the minimum requirements of good and acceptable modern tribunal practice to promote a fair hearing for all participants. It promotes confidence in the outcome, as well as ordered and transparent decision making. Most would recoil from the fairness of an adverse finding in a case in which the central disputed witnesses, whilst available, had not been called in evidence—particularly where that was coupled with the exercise by the appropriate authority of its new right to make representations as to outcome. The obligation on the appropriate authority and his agent, the presenting officer, to act both impartially and judicially in this context is acute, especially given the apparent default setting of the misconduct panel having the right to see, in advance, the investigator's report, statements of evidence, and relevant exhibits.

In any event, the Pt 4 convergence starts with referral of the case under any form **8.06** of investigation to misconduct proceedings under reg 19.

The referral of the case to misconduct proceedings

Regulation 19 provides that (subject to special cases and the requirements of **8.07** para 6 of Sch 3 of the 2002 Act), the appropriate authority shall, upon receipt of the investigator's written report, 'as soon as practicable determine whether the officer concerned has a case to answer in respect of misconduct or gross misconduct'. The investigator's report results from either reg 18 of the 2008 Conduct Regulations ('Report of investigation'),[3] or para 22 of Sch 3 to the 2002 Act (for investigations under paras 16–19 of the same, producing a 'Final report on investigation').[4]

---

[3] Which will be investigations of recordable, but non-referable, conduct matters, which come into the system via para 11(3)(b) of Sch 3 to the 2002 Act.

[4] In relation to complaints subject to the special requirements, or conduct or DSI matters, which, in turn, requires the appropriate authority to make a determination under para 23(7) of Sch 3 (managed and IPCC investigation) or para 24(6) of Sch 3 (local or supervised investigation).

8.08 Where any disciplinary proceedings have been delayed by the application of reg 9(3),[5] as soon as practicable after the appropriate authority considers that such proceedings would not longer prejudice any criminal proceedings, it shall (again, subject to special case considerations) make a further determination as to whether the officer concerned has a case to answer.[6]

8.09 Where the appropriate authority determines that there is no case to answer, it may either: (i) take no disciplinary action against the officer concerned; or (ii) take management action against the officer concerned; or (iii) refer the matter to be dealt with under the Police (Performance) Regulations 2008.[7]

8.10 The inclusion of the last 'performance' option tends to reinforce the parliamentary intention that the 2008 Performance Regulations and the 2008 Conduct Regulations should be viewed as a single complementary package. This is reinforced by paras 2.131–2.137 of the Home Office Guidance on *Police Officer Misconduct, Unsatisfactory Performance and Attendance Management Procedures*[8] under the subheading 'Moving between misconduct and UPP'.[9] The Guidance stresses the importance of the regime being sufficiently flexible to accommodate switches from the Conduct to the Performance Regulations.

8.11 Where the appropriate authority determines that there is a case to answer in respect of misconduct, it may refer the case to misconduct proceedings or take management action against the officer concerned.[10] The latter option is another manifestation of the reformers' laudable pursuit of proportionality.

8.12 Where management action is opted for, the officer concerned must be given notice of this as soon as practicable.[11] Paragraph 2.144 of the Guidance requires the appropriate authority to determine whether a misconduct case to answer 'can be dealt with by means of immediate management action without the need to refer the case to a misconduct meeting', and gives as an example of appropriate use the context when 'the police officer concerned has accepted that his or her conduct fell below the standards expected of a police officer and demonstrates a commitment to improve his or her conduct in the future and to learn from that particular case'.

8.13 It follows that the presumed misconduct need not result in disciplinary proceedings if, in the considered opinion of the appropriate authority, such proceedings

---

[5] 'For any period during which the appropriate authority considers any misconduct proceedings or special case proceedings would prejudice any criminal proceedings, no such misconduct or special case proceedings shall take place.'
[6] Regulation 19(2).
[7] SI 2008/2862.
[8] Issued under s 87(1) of the 2002 Act.
[9] Unsatisfactory performance procedures.
[10] Regulation 19(5).
[11] Ibid, (8).

would not be proportionate or appropriate. This discretionary 'get-out' clause may avoid some of the adverse consequences of the near inevitability of misconduct proceedings on a literal application of the 2004 Conduct Regulations. In practice, of course, written warnings were often negotiated and accepted to avoid this, but the new provision lends legitimacy to the previous pragmatism.

Whether the form of proceedings is a meeting or hearing is determined addition- **8.14** ally by whether the officer concerned had a 'live' final written warning in force at the date of the original assessment (respectively, under reg 12(1) of the 2008 Conduct Regulations or reg 14A of the Police (Complaints and Misconduct) Regulations 2004,[12] as amended) (reg 19(9)(a)), or had been reduced in rank under the 2004 Conduct Regulations in the eighteen-month period preceding the date of assessment (reg 19(9)(b)). If so, the form of proceedings must be a misconduct hearing.

Where the appropriate authority determines that there is a case to answer for **8.15** gross misconduct, it shall, subject only to reg 9(3) considerations (prejudice to other investigations, etc), refer the case to a misconduct hearing.[13]

Thus it can be seen that there is a commonality of approach between the early **8.16** assessment of a case (whether under reg 12 of the 2008 Conduct Regulations or para 19B(10) of Sch 3 to the 2002 Act) and the equivalent assessment after receipt by the appropriate authority of the investigator's report under both regimes. Where the appropriate authority has accepted an IPCC recommendation under para 27(3)[14] of Sch 3, or has a duty under para 27(4)[15] of Sch 3 to comply with an IPCC direction, then it shall, again subject only to reg 9(3), refer the case to the nominated form of misconduct proceedings.

Where the appropriate authority fails to determine, on receipt of the investigator's **8.17** report, whether there is a case to answer, and fails to decide what action to take under reg 19(5) within fifteen working days after receipt of the report, it must notify the officer concerned of the reason for this.

Withdrawal of the case

Regulation 20 of the 2008 Conduct Regulations provides the appropriate authority **8.18** with the power 'at any time before the beginning of the misconduct proceedings' (defined in reg 3 to mean the misconduct meeting or hearing) to withdraw

---

[12] SI 2004/643.
[13] Regulation 19(4).
[14] Recommendation as to disciplinary proceedings by the IPCC in Sch 3 investigations.
[15] Direction as to disciplinary proceedings by the IPCC in Sch 3 investigations.

the case. This does not prevent any person(s) conducting any meeting or hearing from dismissing any misconduct proceedings at any point once they have started those proceedings. It is contended that the appropriate authority may elect to offer no further evidence on a charge, or specifics of charge, once misconduct proceedings have started, because this is not technically 'withdrawing' the case in the procedural sense used in reg 20.

8.19 Regulation 20(2) empowers the appropriate authority, on withdrawing proceedings, to take no further action against the officer concerned, to take management action, or to refer the matter to be dealt with under the 2008 Performance Regulations (another regulatory reinforcement of the policy drive to treat the 2008 Conduct Regulations and 2008 Performance Regulations as a complementary package).

8.20 Where the appropriate authority withdraws the proceedings, the officer concerned must be given written notice of the same, together with notice of any management or other action that may be taken—for example, referral of the matters to be dealt with under the 2008 Performance Regulations.

Disclosure of the investigator's report to the officer concerned

8.21 More generally, the officer concerned is also entitled, subject to the harm test, to a copy of the investigator's report (or such parts of the report as relate to him). Paragraph 2.142 of the Home Office Guidance describes providing the report to the officer as 'good practice'. This is presumably to maximize the sense of transparency and fairness to the officer concerned, and to assist in any learning or development that may be available.

8.22 Regulation 20 does not apply to cases under paras 16–19 of Sch 3 to the 2002 Act, where the equivalent provision is under reg 7 of the 2004 Complaints and Misconduct Regulations.

Notice of referral to misconduct proceedings and panel membership: reg 21

8.23 Where a case is referred to misconduct proceedings, the appropriate authority must provide the officer concerned, as soon as practicable, with three tranches of material, as follows:

(i) a written notice of referral;
(ii) a copy of any statement that the officer may have made to the investigator during the course of the investigation; and
(iii) subject to the reg 4 harm test, a copy of the investigator's report (together with any document attached to, or referred to, in the report that relates to him) and 'any other relevant document gathered during the course of the investigation'.

The second requirement is probably uncontentious. The third—that is, disclo- **8.24**
sure of documents 'gathered during the course of the investigation'—is contended
to represent the minimum rights of disclosure under the Criminal Procedure and
Investigations Act 1996 (CPIA) test. Disclosure was addressed at 7.14–7.34.

Form of written notice and particularity of 'charge'

As to the form of written notice, this raises some central practical issues as to the **8.25**
particularization of allegations. The written notice must reflect:

(i)   the fact of the referral;
(ii) the conduct that is alleged to be misconduct or gross misconduct;[16]
(iii) the name of the person appointed to conduct the misconduct meeting or
      chair the misconduct hearing (and the officer's entitlement to object to such
      person); and
(iv) the officer's rights to representation under reg 7.

This written notice plainly includes the concept of the 'charge', although neither **8.26**
the 2008 Conduct Regulations nor the Home Office Guidance ever use the term.
The position under the 2004 Conduct Regulations was somewhat clearer and
associated with the reg 21 procedure to promote agreement of a separate statement of facts when the charge was admitted. Plainly, the framing of the allegation
must be done with sufficient particularity to ensure that there is absolute clarity
as to what the officer is alleged to have done wrong, which of the Standards of
Professional Behaviour he is said to have breached, and why.[17]

Failure to particularize supervisory failures in this sense was held to be fatal to **8.27**
charges alleging supervisory failures in *R (Wheeler) v AC House of the Metropolitan
Police*.[18] The same principle applies to any charge. The court referred (at [1.7]):

> to the vagueness of the charges in the hope that in future charges will be more focused
> and more specific. It is sufficient if a charge is particularised subsequent to its being
> first formulated, but certainly it should be sufficiently particularised well before the
> hearing so that the respondent to disciplinary charges knows not just what it is
> alleged he failed to do, but in what respects he failed, so that he can then see whether
> or not, consistent with his other duties, he could or should have done that which it
> is alleged he should have done.

Paragraph 2.149 of the Home Office Guidance provides that 'it is necessary **8.28**
to describe the particulars of the actual behaviour of the police officer that is

---

[16] In professional disciplinary proceedings, there can be little objection to the promulgation
of charges concerning disparate matters: see *Reza v GMC* [1991] 12 AC 181, HL. Accordingly,
attempts at 'severance' of charges will face an uphill struggle unless the grounds are compelling.
[17] The rule against duplicity of charges has little application in professional disciplinary proceedings: see *Gee v GMC* [1987] 1 WLR 564.
[18] [2008] EWHC 439 (Admin).

considered to amount to misconduct or gross misconduct and the reasons it is thought the behaviour amounts to such' but does not—perhaps unhelpfully— articulate any prescribed recommended forms of charge.

8.29 Demonstrably, the 'charge' should be sufficiently particularized to meet the objections made by the court in *Wheeler*. There is legitimate scope for argument as to what is required in the charge between, on the one hand, a form of particularized indictment on the criminal model and, on the other, a form of pleading from the civil jurisdiction. The important ingredient, on either model, is absolute clarity as to what it is said the officer either did do or alternatively omitted to do, and why that is a breach of the Standards of Professional Behaviour.

8.30 In practice, the officer concerned may often be prepared to admit the particulars (or some of them), but on a basis of fact different from that advanced by the appropriate authority. Pleading contentious matters in the charge may sometimes obstruct this process. In such a situation, the panel may, if resolution of the basis of plea is required (sometimes, the dispute of fact is not sufficiently material to affect the outcome), admit evidence and/or hear submissions on the face of the served documents to resolve the matter. This scenario is common and amounts to a procedure analogous to a so-called *Newton* hearing[19] in criminal proceedings.

The identity of, and objection to, panel members

8.31 The appropriate authority also has the obligation, as soon as practicable, to give the officer concerned written notice of the identity of the person appointed under reg 7(5) to advise the person(s) conducting the misconduct proceedings and, where those proceedings are to be conducted by a panel, the identity of the 'wing' members of the same.[20] Again, this notice must advise the officer concerned of his entitlement to object to those persons.

8.32 Regulation 21 set out the procedures whereby the officer concerned may object to any person appointed thereunder to conduct (including chair) his misconduct proceedings or to advise at the same. The objection must be made in writing to the appropriate authority within three days of the officer receiving the notice of the persons' names and must set out the grounds for objection.

8.33 It is for the appropriate authority to adjudicate upon the objection and such adjudication will presumably follow the principles of actual or apparent bias identified in cases reflected at 11.16–11.20. Regulation 3 of the 2008 Conduct Regulations refers to 'a person whose involvement in a role could reasonably give

---

[19] *R v Newton* (1982) 77 Cr App R 13, CA. Resolution of disputed issues of fact following a guilty plea for the purpose of determining the basis of sentence is a well-established and approved part of criminal procedure.

[20] Regulation 21(2).

rise to a concern as to whether he could act impartially under these regulations'. Simple membership of the same force will not create this risk: the association will probably have to be personal and imply some form of adverse prior knowledge about the officer whose conduct is in question. Mere professional acquaintance will not be a sufficient basis for objection.[21]

If the appropriate authority upholds the objection, then the person in question **8.34** will be replaced and a substitute appointed by the appropriate authority. This process may be repeated if the officer concerned can identify proper (*per* para 2.156 of the Home Office Guidance, 'compelling') ground for objection. In smaller forces, it may not be difficult to identify such grounds, and thus appointments under reg 25 may need to go to outside forces. This is permissible, given that there is no stipulation that the person conducting the meeting, or persons conducing the hearing, need be from the same force as the officer concerned. Indeed, it is probably desirable if the proceedings have to resolve considerations of alleged systemic failures by the affected officer's home force.

B. Procedure on Receipt of Notice

Regulation 22 marks one the of the most significant reforms in the 2008 Conduct **8.35** Regulations in that it imposes upon the officer concerned significantly enhanced obligations of disclosure, both in terms of documents on which he may rely, but also substantively in terms of showing his hand. Adverse inferences may arise at misconduct proceedings if disclosure is not made as prescribed.

Within fourteen working days of the officer concerned receiving the documents **8.36** to which he is entitled under reg 21(1) (which period may be extended by the person conducting or chairing the misconduct proceedings),[22] the officer concerned 'shall comply with paragraphs (2) and (3)'. Regulation 22(2) obliges the officer concerned to provide to the appropriate authority:

(i) written notice of whether or not he accepts that his conduct amounts to misconduct or gross misconduct (an officer charged with gross misconduct may thereby accept that he has committed misconduct, but not gross misconduct);

(ii) where he accepts that he has committed misconduct or gross misconduct, 'any written submission he wishes to make in mitigation' (it appears to

---

[21] See Sullivan J in *R (Bird) v Chief Constable of Avon and Somerset*, CO/2425/00, 10 July 2000.

[22] The 2008 Conduct Regulations necessarily suffer from the wordiness born of needing to refer each time to 'person conducting the proceedings' to cover meetings, and person 'chairing the proceedings' to cover hearings.

follow that he may chose not to submit a written submission, but to advance any mitigation verbally at the misconduct proceedings);

(iii) where he denies any misconduct, or disputes part of the case against him, written notice of:

(a) the allegations that he disputes and his account of the relevant events;

(b) any arguments on points of law that he wishes to be considered by those conducting any misconduct proceedings.

8.37 Regulation 22(3) obliges the officer concerned at the same time to provide the appropriate authority with a copy of any document on which he intends to rely at the misconduct proceedings. This is another new and important obligation on the officer concerned. In effect, he must give disclosure of documents on which he proposes to rely. On one view, it promotes case management generally and a review of merits by the appropriate authority specifically, and is no different in species than disclosure in civil proceedings. On another (and leaving aside the reality of observing the identified time limits in practice), it is an obligation not matched in degree in criminal proceedings, notwithstanding the common adversarial quality of each form of proceeding and the obligations to provide 'defence statements' under the CPIA.

8.38 The risk to the officer concerned in not complying with these obligations is clear from reg 34(10)–(12)—that is, the entitlement of those conducting the proceedings to draw such inferences 'as appear proper' from the failure. If service of material reflects the exercise of discretion by the representatives of the officer concerned as distinct from the officer himself, it is contended that, in practice, little, if any, weight may attach in practice to most breaches of reg 22. Reliance on such advice will not, however, assist the officer concerned (as with the advice to answer 'no comment' in interview) if the hearing panel concludes that it is no more than a 'convenient smokescreen' for his decision.

8.39 In either event, the standard directions in criminal proceedings as to the approach to adverse inferences will apply (see 8.89 *et seq* below). The adverse inference cannot become the main evidence to prove any allegation: it is the quality of direct evidence that should be determinative.

C. Witnesses

8.40 Paragraph 2.160 of the Home Office Guidance states that 'generally speaking misconduct meetings and hearings will be conducted without witnesses'. This proposition seems inherently unlikely in respect of contested misconduct hearings, and not consonant with the 2008 Conduct Regulations, which explicitly envisage witnesses, where they are necessary. Witnesses are inevitable when there is a contentious piece of material evidence that comes from a witness or witnesses. A witness's testimony can reasonably be characterized as 'material' if it may have a significant (that is, more than minimal) impact upon either finding or outcome. The attendance of such a witness will invariably be 'necessary' to achieve a fair hearing. Distinctions between misconduct meetings and hearings may legitimately arise, however, as to the form of questioning of witnesses and, perhaps, even as to their necessity, although this may be to confuse proportionality with fairness.

Regulation 22(4) ('Procedure on receipt of notice') requires that, three working **8.41** days after the officer concerned has complied with reg 22(2) (the response obligations addressed at 8.35–8.39 above), 'the appropriate authority and the officer concerned shall each supply to the other a list of proposed witnesses or give notice that they did not have any proposed witnesses' and any such list must include brief details of the evidence that the witness is able to adduce.

Regulation 22(5) requires the officer concerned, if reasonably practicable, to agree **8.42** a list of proposed witnesses with the appropriate authority. If the officer concerned has failed to respond under reg 22, the appropriate authority will presumably still have to produce the requisite list for such agreement as the basis on which it intends to prove its case.

Regulation 23 prescribes the mechanism for resolving whether any witness is **8.43** actually to be called. The appropriate authority has the obligation to supply either the list agreed under reg 22(5) or, where no such list is agreed, the lists supplied by both parties under reg 22(4), to the person conducting or chairing the proceedings. The obligation is then on that person to determine 'which, if any, witness should attend the misconduct proceedings'. Regulation 23(3) provides the crucial test—that is, that 'no witness shall give evidence at misconduct proceedings unless the person conducting or chairing those proceedings reasonably believes that it is necessary for the witness to do so in the interests of justice'. That there is such a test is unremarkable as a matter of case management.

As already stated, however, police officer confidence in misconduct proceedings **8.44** (part of any assessment of the interests of justice, and a concept that otherwise can be rendered meaningless) will only be maintained if every available contentious witness is called who is material to the allegations. Any findings adverse to the officer concerned following receipt of such evidence will prove more resilient on appeal. These factors, taken together, promote the interests of all participants in misconduct proceedings and directly correspond with the instinctive approach of most of them.

The timing and notice of misconduct proceedings

The timescales envisaged by the 2008 Conduct Regulations are unquestionably **8.45** tight. So long as fair and effective representation is not compromised, there can be no objection to this. In theory, a misconduct meeting must take place within twenty working days after provision of the documents to the officer under reg 21(1), and a misconduct hearing must take place within thirty workings days of the same.

8.46 There is no doubt that the timescale for the meeting is an appropriate one; indeed, if such meetings routinely take longer than four weeks to convene, the system will probably be failing. The idea, however, that a serious misconduct allegation, which will likely end an officer's career if proven and which will include counsel acting for both sides, can be convened within thirty working days is, perhaps, optimistic. History shows that it is the recruitment of senior officers to populate the panels that can generate significant delay and, if the spirit of the new 2008 Conduct Regulations is to be made to work, senior officers and senior HRPs will need to prioritize such matters.

8.47 Paragraph (2) of reg 24 builds in discretion on the part of the persons conducting or chairing the proceedings to extend the timescales where it would be 'in the interests of justice to do so'. The appropriate authority may have had months (often with counsel instructed) to prepare for service of the reg 21 notice. It is contended that the defendant officer must be given proportionate time in which to respond and prepare. The instruction of competent defence counsel at the last minute for such important proceedings is often easier said than done. It is observed, additionally, that an ordinary criminal practitioner will lack the necessary expertise for police misconduct proceedings and that the principle of equality of arms should prevail.

8.48 Either the officer concerned or the appropriate authority can, of course, make an application for further time. The person conducting the proceedings is, however, obliged to give reasons for their decisions (either for or against an extension of time) to both the appropriate authority and the officer concerned. Paragraph 2.170 of the Home Office Guidance states that:

> In order to maintain confidence in the misconduct procedures it is important that the misconduct meetings/hearings are held as soon as practicable and extensions to the timescales should be an exception rather than the rule. To that end, managers appointed to conduct or chair misconduct meetings/hearings are to ensure that a robust stance is taken in managing the process whilst ensuring the fairness of the proceedings. Extensions may be appropriate for example if the case is particularly complex. It will not normally be considered appropriate to extend the timescale on the grounds that the police officer concerned wishes to be represented by a particular lawyer.

8.49 Obviously, 'counsel's convenience' is only one of a number of relevant considerations. Equally, misconduct proceedings should not be fixed around the convenience of (pre-instructed) counsel for the appropriate authority, with the defendant officer left to find an equivalent at thirty working days' notice.

Furthermore, where an officer was represented at criminal proceedings by a particular legal team, the fairness and benefits of continuity of representation will generally militate in favour of reasonable extensions of time periods. As is so often with the case, the application of discretion will be partly an instinctive reaction as to what is fair, and always a matter of fact and degree.

The procedure for fixing the date of the proceedings is set out in reg 24(4)–(8). **8.50** The person conducting or chairing the proceedings has the duty of agreeing a date and time with the officer concerned, if reasonably practicable. Where no date and time is so agreed, the person conducting or chairing the proceedings shall specify a date and time. Where, however, the officer concerned or his police friend will not be available at the specified time, and the officer concerned proposes an alternative that is reasonable and, in any event, within five working days starting on the day after the originally specified date, then the person conducting or chairing the proceedings must postpone the proceedings accordingly.[23] Once the date and time has been agreed or specified, the officer concerned must be given written notice of the date, time, and place of the proceedings.

Persons conducting misconduct proceedings for non-senior officers: reg 25

The composition of the adjudicatory body for meetings and hearings is, unsur- **8.51** prisingly, different, although the appropriate authority appoints both.

The constitution of the panel: misconduct meetings for non-senior officers

The misconduct meeting is conducted by a person who is not an interested party **8.52** (as defined in reg 3) and who is: (i) for police officers, another officer of at last one rank higher than the officer concerned; and (ii) for special constables, an officer of at least the rank of sergeant or a senior HRP. A further alternative person to conduct the misconduct meetings for police officers or special constable is, unless the case substantially involves operational policing matters, a police staff member who is, in the appropriate authority's opinion, more senior than the officer concerned.

The constitution of the panel: misconduct hearings for non-senior officers

As can be seen, the role of police staff members under the 2008 Conduct **8.53** Regulations is much enhanced as compared with that under the 2004 Conduct Regulations, in which their role was virtually non-existent.

---

[23] Whilst no doubt directed at promoting 'fairness', it is difficult to understand why, in a disciplined profession, the person conducting the proceedings is not entitled simply to stipulate the date and time, having regard to all relevant factors.

8.54   A misconduct hearing is conducted by a panel of three persons, comprising:

(i)   a senior (that is, chief) officer or senior HRP in the chair;

(ii)   a person selected from a list of candidates maintained by a police authority for the purposes of these Regulations; and

(iii)   if the chair is a senior officer, either another police officer of at least superintendent rank, or a HRP; if the chair is a senior HRP, a police officer of at least the rank of superintendent.

8.55   Thus it will be noted that the panel for misconduct hearings under the 2008 Conduct Regulations:

- will always have a police authority-appointed member—that is, at least one lay member (as compared with the 2004 regime, under which such a member only appeared when the case was one to which paras 16–19 of Sch 3 to the 2002 Act applied);

- will always include at least one police officer of at least the rank of superintendent, but may have only one police officer sitting on it (as compared with the 2004 regime, under which at least two police officers would always preside);

- will always have at least one HRP on it (under the 2004 regime, a HRP never sat on the panel, unless the police authority-nominated person for cases covered by paras 16–19 of Sch 3 to the 2002 Act was such coincidentally);

- may be chaired by a non-police officer (which could not happen under the 2004 regime); and

- may be populated by two chief officers, including the chief constable (which never happened under the 2004 Regulations).

8.56   Regulation 25(5) defines 'senior human resources professional' to mean a HRP who, in the opinion of the appropriate authority, has sufficient seniority, skills, and experience to conduct the hearing or meeting.

8.57   It remains, of course, to be seen how enthusiastic appropriate authorities will be to appoint HRPs to sit on panels for misconduct hearings. But it seems certain that the universal inclusion of a non-police officer on panels for such hearings will mark a change in the nature and feel of such hearings.

Constitution of panels, etc, in relation to senior officers

8.58   The constitution of panels for senior officers—that is, those of Association of Chief Police Officer (ACPO) rank—is addressed by regs 26 and 27.

8.59   In summary, reg 26 provides for the constitution of panels for misconduct proceedings against: a chief constable; the Commissioner, Deputy Commissioner, or Assistant Commissioner of the Metropolitan Police Service (MPS); and the Commissioner of the City of London police force. A misconduct meeting is chaired by the chair of the police authority (or nominee), sitting with HM Chief Inspector of Constabulary (HMCIC) or an inspector of constabulary nominated by him. For a misconduct hearing, these two persons are supplemented by a barrister on the list maintained by the Secretary of State (who is the chair) and a person on the list maintained for the purposes of the Regulations by the police authority.

In summary, reg 27 provides for the constitution of panels for misconduct **8.60** proceedings against 'other' senior (ACPO) officers. For a misconduct meeting, this requires an officer of suitable, more senior, rank from the home force, who is the chair, and the chair of the police authority (or nominee). If a misconduct hearing, these persons are supplemented by HMCIC or an inspector of constabulary nominated by him, and a person on the list maintained for the purposes of the Regulations by the police authority.

Documents to be supplied: reg 28

Regulation 28 identifies the documents to be supplied by the appropriate **8.61** authority (presumably a function that it will delegate to its professional standards department, or equivalent) to the persons conducting the meeting or hearing. They are to be contrasted with the 2004 Conduct Regulations, under which, in contested cases, the panel only received as of right a copy of the charge.[24] Under the 2008 Regulations, the panel receives copies of the documents provided to the officer concerned under reg 21(1) (that is, the 'charge', the investigator's report, and the disclosed investigation documents), and those provided by the officer concerned under reg 22(2) (that is, the intended plea, mitigation, his account, any points of law) and (3) (any documents on which he intends to rely).

Additionally, and more controversially, in a case disputed on any basis, the appro- **8.62** priate authority receives (reg 28(1)(c)) 'any other documents that, in the opinion of the appropriate authority, should be considered at the misconduct proceedings'. Although the officer concerned is entitled to a list of the same documents (having already been provided with them or having provided them himself) and a copy of any that he has not already received 'prior to the hearing' (not defined), the discretion is with the appropriate authority. Clearly, it would be good practice—and would minimize the risk of fatal or material prejudice—for the parties to seek to agree a list of such documents before submission to the panel.

Those presenting the case against officers in misconduct proceedings would **8.63** do well to ensure that the documentation necessary for such hearings is well ordered—that is, paginated, indexed, and logically presented. Furthermore, care

---

[24] See reg 22 of the 2004 Conduct Regulations.

should be taken by the 'presenting side'[25] not to introduce any controversial or sensitive documents to the panel without the consent of the officer concerned or, where he is legally represented, his legal team. Similarly, caution should apply as to the provision of the investigator's report if it contains inadmissible opinion evidence, or evidence of a highly contentious nature. The content of the investigator's report—and, specifically, the contended purpose of certification in terms of the reference to 'opinion'—was addressed at 7.93–7.95.

8.64 Any investigator whose approach lacks objectivity in this sense, or who, as a minimum, fails to appreciate the prejudice that may be caused by including otherwise inadmissible opinion evidence, will quite reasonably face the allegation in questioning that he has not reproduced in practice the qualities of experience and judgement that were a prerequisite to appointment. Resolution (or even rehearsal) of collateral issues of this kind undermines confidence in the outcome of any proceedings, and does not promote the substantive merits of the same.

8.65 If a document must be provided to the misconduct panel on an *ex parte* basis (for example, a claim of public interest immunity), then appropriate notice should be given to the officer concerned. Nothing is more undermining to perceptions of fairness than failing to do this, particularly if any member of the panel knows the investigation team. Such applications should be wholly exceptional in practice. For the most part (consistent with the ordinary principles of disclosure at para 41 of the Attorney-General's Guidelines on *Disclosure in Criminal Proceedings*),[26] the appropriate authority should seek to advance its case without reliance on such material.

D. Rights of Attendance and Participation in Misconduct Proceedings

The nature of 'private' misconduct proceedings

8.66 Regulations 29–33 delineate who may, or must, attend misconduct proceedings. In fact, subject to explicit provision to the contrary, misconduct proceedings 'shall be in private'—but there is a significant amount of explicit provision to the contrary, as follows.

---

[25] Not a term, in fact, used in either the 2008 Conduct Regulations or the Home Office Guidance, but one that is bound to continue to be used in practice in an adversarial context. The express nature and duties of a presenting officer are, under the 2004 Conduct Regulations, considered at 9.94.
[26] See 7.30.

The officer concerned

The officer concerned must attend, although provision is made for him to participate by video link 'or other means' if there are good reasons for his doing so.
Even if the officer concerned does not attend, his police friend and lawyer (if it is
a hearing) may participate.[27] Unsurprisingly, and necessarily, proceedings may
be conducted and concluded in the absence of the officer concerned, whether or
not he is represented.

8.67

The IPCC

In any case in which paras 18 or 19 of Sch 3 to the 2002 Act applied, or paras 16
or 17 of the same Schedule applied and the IPCC made a recommendation
(under para 27(3)) or direction (under para 27(4)(a)), the IPCC may attend the
proceedings 'to make representations'. Whilst the nature of these is not delineated, reg 30(2) provides that, where the IPCC does attend, it may instruct a lawyer
to represent it at misconduct hearings. If so, the complainant or any interested
person, and the officer concerned, must be notified.

8.68

The investigator

The investigator (or a nominee)[28] shall also attend the proceedings 'on the request
of the person conducting or chairing those proceedings to answer questions'. The
officer concerned may require him to address the content of the investigation
report and any alleged failures in the investigation, which serves to demonstrate
the value of most representations to the investigator during the investigation
being both made and answered in writing. This may generate more, rather than
less, correspondence than under the 2004 Conduct Regulations, doubtless an
unintended consequence of providing the investigator's report to the misconduct
tribunal. Such correspondence can quickly become attritional, unless each party
adopts a constructive approach.

8.69

Hearings in public

Where a misconduct hearing arises from a case under para 19 of Sch 3 to the 2002
Act (that is, an investigation by the IPCC itself) and the IPCC considers
that 'because of the gravity of the case or other exceptional circumstances it would
be in the public interest to do so', the IPCC may 'direct that the whole or part of
the misconduct hearing be held in public'.[29] The only limitation on this discretion

8.70

---

[27] See reg 29.
[28] Defined by reg 30(4).
[29] Regulation 32(5).

(other than the explicit need for 'gravity or other exceptional circumstances') is that the IPCC must, before so directing,[30] consult with the appropriate authority, officer concerned, complainant or interested person, and any witnesses.

8.71 At the time of going to print, the IPCC had only directed one such public hearing under the 2004 regime (where similar provision exists)—namely, alleged misconduct by police under the relevant force domestic violence policy preceding the (potentially avoidable) murder of Colette Lynch in Warwickshire. Not only was the murder particularly shocking, but the evidence also tended to disclose chronic failures by the force in implementing its domestic violence policy (relying substantially on distributing the policy by intranet) and significant errors by mental health professionals in managing the murderer in the community. Even with an inquest to follow, the merits of transparency were obvious. An officer from an outside force chaired the hearing, with an independent member also sitting.

8.72 Addressed generally, following a public hearing of the evidence, a misconduct panel may feel more, rather than less, able to impose sanctions on merit below those demanded publicly by, or on behalf of, the complainant. The reasons for a decision, and the evidence to justify it, are public. Uninformed media criticism may be addressed on merit by, or on behalf of, the officer concerned or the complainant from a reliable and documented premise, especially if the statement of findings is made public.

8.73 The IPCC publishes additional criteria as to such recommendations,[31] which largely reflect the matters rehearsed in reg 32(5). The central consideration is determining whether the public interest—perhaps exceptionally—requires a public hearing. A public hearing ultimately does no more than mirror the practices operating in other professional disciplinary contexts, such as the General Medical Council (GMC) and the Law Society, which routinely hold disciplinary hearings in this manner.

8.74 Subject to resourcing implications (the cost of the hearing itself falls to the local police rather than the profession as a whole), public hearings arising from investigations of acute public concern should become a more familiar part of the police misconduct landscape.

8.75 As can be seen, in totality, the 2008 Conduct Regulations provide significant scope for IPCC oversight and control of many aspects of police misconduct proceedings.

---

[30] Ibid, (6) requires the persons conducting the hearing to comply with such a direction.
[31] Available online at <http://www.ipcc.gov.uk>.

Complainants and interested persons

Regulation 31 deals with the attendance of complainants or interested persons **8.76** (as defined by s 29 of the 2002 Act, and reg 3 of the 2004 Complaints and Misconduct Regulations), and applies only to misconduct proceedings arising from a conduct matter to which paras 16–19 of Sch 3 applied, or the investigation of a complaint that was certified as subject to special requirements under para 19B(1)(a) of Sch 3 (that is, complaints that were not subject to local resolution or the 2008 Conduct Regulations).

In the above situation, the appropriate authority is obliged to notify the com- **8.77** plainant or interested person of the date, time, and place of the misconduct proceedings. Subject, then, only to the discretion of the person conducting or chairing the proceedings to impose conditions (including exclusion from the proceedings), the complainant or any interested person 'may attend the misconduct proceedings as an observer up to but not including the point at which the person conducting or chairing those proceedings considers the question of disciplinary action'.

This entitlement was introduced by Sch 3 to the 2002 Act in April 2004. It is **8.78** somewhat curious that the 2008 regime maintains the exclusion of the complainants or interested persons at the point when an officer may be dismissed. This is not mirrored in other professional disciplinary proceedings with a qualifying public interest. Transparency apparently does not extend in police misconduct to hearing the reasons for outcome (sanction) as they are given (instead, they will doubtless be relayed formally afterwards). The contended justification for this, in most cases, is elusive. In practice, the officer concerned is invariably asked if he objects to the continued presence of the complainant for this stage. This can—given the politics of the situation—be in the category of an offer made that the officer concerned will feel unable to refuse.

Subject to exemptions and the discretion of the person conducting or chairing **8.79** the proceedings, the complainant or any interested person may be accompanied at the proceedings by one other person and, if they have a special need, by one further person to 'accommodate that need'. 'Special need' is defined by reg 31(7) as existing if the opinion of the person conducting or chairing the proceedings is that the person 'has a disability or learning difficulty, or does not have sufficient knowledge of English to fully participate in or understand the misconduct proceedings'.

One explicit limitation on the attendance of the complainant or interested per- **8.80** son, or their companion, is when the complainant or interested person is to give evidence at misconduct proceedings. In such a case, very sensibly, the complainant on interested person and any person permitted to accompany them 'shall not be allowed to attend the proceedings before he gives his evidence'.[32] Self-evidently, this is directed at reducing the risk that evidence will be affected by reports of the evidence of other witnesses, or at least at minimizing the risk of that suggestion (with or without justification) being made. In that the same witness may have had access to the investigation report, the protections provided may be more theoretical than real.

8.81 The complainant or interested person may request the person conducting or chairing the proceedings to put questions to the officer concerned (but not, apparently, other witnesses, which must be taken to be a deliberate drafting policy), and the person conducting or chairing the proceedings has discretion to do so (although it must be hoped that the person 'presenting' the case will more than adequately do so in respect of any legitimate questions that the complainant or interested person might have).

8.82 Regulation 32(8) provides the person conducting or chairing the proceedings with an overriding discretion to 'impose such conditions as he sees fit relating to the attendance' of persons at misconduct proceedings 'in order to facilitate the proper conduct of the proceedings'. That discretion applies to the attendance of complainants and interested persons under reg 31, and 'others' under reg 32.

8.83 Furthermore, reg 32(3) provides that, subject to any contrary decision by the person conducting or chairing the misconduct proceedings, a witness other than a complainant, interested person, or the officer concerned shall only attend the proceedings for the purpose of giving their evidence. The person conducting or chairing the proceedings would appear to have discretion under reg 34 to permit witnesses to attend beyond the giving of their evidence.

8.84 The person conducting or chairing the misconduct proceedings has a discretion to permit a witness 'to be accompanied at those proceedings by one other person'—presumably to ensure the welfare of the witness.[33]

8.85 Finally, reg 33 requires the person conducting or chairing the misconduct proceedings to exclude attendees to prevent them from receiving information that, under the harm test, they ought not. The exclusion prevails only whilst that evidence is being given.

---

[32] Regulation 31(5).
[33] Regulation 32(4).

F. Procedure at Misconduct Proceedings

The power of the chair to determine the procedure at misconduct proceedings

As with the 2004 Conduct Regulations, by reg 34(1) of the 2008 Conduct **8.86**
Regulations, 'the person conducting or chairing the misconduct proceedings shall
determine the procedure at those proceedings'. Obviously, that discretion is subject to the other regulations, the Home Office Guidance, and the proper application of established minimum procedural standards applicable in professional
misconduct proceedings (a working definition of the otherwise subjective concepts of 'interests of justice' or 'natural justice'). As with other disciplinary regulations worded in mandatory language ('shall', 'must', etc), given the statutory
context, many, in law, will be directory rather than mandatory in effect, meaning
that breach will not automatically vitiate proceedings.

Regulation 34 prohibits proceedings from starting unless the officer concerned **8.87**
has been notified of his rights to representation under reg 7(1)–(3). Paragraphs (3)
and (4) make provision for adjournments where apparently 'necessary or expedient', although proceedings shall not 'except in exceptional circumstances, be
adjourned solely to allow the complainant or any witness or interested person to
attend'. Paragraphs (5)–(8) provide discretion as to the admission of evidence and
the rights of the person representing the officer concerned (reg 34(5)).

Where there are specific rights in the regulation itself, there is no discretion. **8.88**
In other respects, reg 34 provides a wide discretion on the part of the person conducting or chairing the proceedings to admit documents, subject to the usual
penalties or caveats that must necessarily follow from late service. The discretion
extends to all aspects of case management and the range of orders that may arise
either at a directions hearing or during the resumed substantive hearing. It is an
inherent power to regulate matters within the terms of the Regulations, associated
Guidance and natural justice.

Adverse inferences

In this context, reg 34(10) and (12), read in conjunction, provides the entitlement **8.89**
of the person conducting or chairing the proceedings to draw such inferences
'as appear proper' from the failure of the officer concerned:

(i) on being questioned by an investigator any time after he was given written
notice under reg 15(1) of the 2008 Conduct Regulations or reg 14A of the
2004 Complaints and Misconduct Regulations; or

(ii) in submitting any information, or by not submitting any information at all,
under regs 16(1) or 22(2) or (3), or para 19C of Sch 3 to the 2002 Act;

to mention any fact relied on in his case at the misconduct proceedings, 'being a fact which in the circumstances existing at the time,[34] the officer concerned could reasonably have been expected to mention when so questioned or when providing such information'.

8.90 The possibility of an adverse inference under (ii) above is a significant departure from previous regulations, although may be said to be a logical extension of it. It is this provision, of course, which gives reg 22(2) and (3) its 'bite'. Officers—and their representatives—who fail to grasp the significance of breach of the provision do so at their own professional risk.

8.91 If documents are under consideration for service without a concluded decision as to actual reliance having been taken one way or the other, the officer concerned should communicate this in writing at the time to the investigator/appropriate authority, to avoid the possibility of an unfair adverse inference arising subsequently. Such correspondence may be subject to disclosure on the issue of adverse inference, and, accordingly, should not become either litigious or attritional. It need not ordinarily identify the precise material under consideration.

8.92 Whether an adverse inference arises is a matter of discretion and should reflect a relatively complex legal direction. In the criminal context[35]—on which the adverse inference regulations are modelled directly—the direction for a jury where the question of an adverse inference arises are available from the Judicial Studies Board (JSB).[36] It may be adapted for each of the relevant situations under the 2004 and 2008 Conduct Regulations.

8.93 The guidance includes the proposition that consideration of adverse inferences should be discussed with counsel before any direction arises. This would be good practice for any misconduct panel. Specific submissions should be invited from the presenting side as to whether—and, if so, on what basis—an adverse inference is invited. This may then be addressed on merit by the defending side. The matter may then be addressed in appropriate terms—minimizing the risk of material misdirection—by the panel in its final determination of the charge.

8.94 The JSB direction includes the following essential matters for determination in this context:

(i)   to consider whether an adverse direction should be given at all;
(ii) to identify the precise fact or facts to which the direction should relate; and
(iii) to identify the permissible inferences.

---

[34] That is, of the written notice or obligations under the delineated regulations.
[35] Section 34 of the Criminal Justice and Public Order Act 1994 (defendant's failure to mention facts when questioned or charged).
[36] Practice Direction [1995] 2 Cr App R 192, available online at <http://www.jsboard.co.uk>.

If an adverse inference (meaning a conclusion adverse to the acceptance of the **8.95**
case of the officer concerned) may arise, the following direction arises. Clearly,
the terms of this direction are relevant to determining whether it arises on the facts
at all. Adverse inferences do not reverse the burden of proof and only become
relevant in so far as the officer concerned has a case to answer based on other
evidence. The recommended direction is based on a series of statutory provisions
and authorities,[37] and is associated in its original form with some seventeen
additional notes. These are excluded, but may, of course, be relevant. With this
editing, it provides:

1. Before his interview(s) the defendant was cautioned. He was first told that he
   need not say anything. It was therefore his right to remain silent. However, he
   was also told that it might harm his defence if he did not mention when
   questioned something which he later relied on in court; and that anything he did
   say might be given in evidence.
2. As part of his defence, the defendant has relied upon (here specify the facts to
   which this direction applies). But [the prosecution says] [he admits] that he
   failed to mention these facts when he was interviewed about the offence(s).
   [If you are sure that is so, this/This] failure may count against him. This is
   because you may draw the conclusion from his failure that he [had no answer
   then/had no answer that he then believed would stand up to scrutiny/has since
   invented his account/has since tailored his account to fit the prosecution's case/
   (here refer to any other reasonable inferences contended for]. If you do draw that
   conclusion, you must not convict him wholly or mainly on the strength of it;
   but you may take it into account as some additional support for the prosecution's
   case and when deciding whether his [evidence/case] about these facts is true.
3. However, you may draw such a conclusion against him only if you think it is a
   fair and proper conclusion, and you are satisfied about three things: first, that
   when he was interviewed he could reasonably have been expected to mention
   the facts on which he now relies; second, that the only sensible explanation for
   his failure to do so is that he had no answer at the time or none that would stand
   up to scrutiny; third, that apart from his failure to mention those facts, the
   prosecution's case against him is so strong that it clearly calls for an answer
   by him.
4. (Add, if appropriate) The defence invite you not to draw any conclusion from
   the defendant's silence, on the basis of the following evidence (here set out the
   evidence). If you [accept this evidence and] think this amounts to a reason why
   you should not draw any conclusion from his silence, do not do so. Otherwise,
   subject to what I have said, you may do so.
5. (Where legal advice to remain silent is relied upon, add the following to or
   instead of paragraph 4 as appropriate:) The defendant has given evidence that he
   did not answer questions on the advice of his solicitor/legal representative. If you

---

[37] Sections 34 and 38(3) of the Criminal Justice and Public Order Act 1994, and the five
'essentials' listed in *R v Cowan* [1996] 1 Cr App R 1, 7 DG, to the extent that they have been applied
to s 34 cases: *R v Argent* [1997] 2 Cr App R 27; *Murray v UK* (1996) 22 EHRR 29; and *Condron v
UK* (2001) 31 EHRR 1, [2000] Crim LR 679.

accept the evidence that he was so advised, this is obviously an important consideration: but it does not automatically prevent you from drawing any conclusion from his silence. Bear in mind that a person given legal advice has the choice whether to accept or reject it; and that the defendant was warned that any failure to mention facts which he relied on at his trial might harm his defence. Take into account also (here set out the circumstances relevant to the particular case, which may include the age of the defendant, the nature of and/or reasons for the advice given, and the complexity or otherwise of the facts in which he relied at the trial). Having done so, decide whether the defendant could reasonably have been expected to mention the facts on which he now relies. If, for example, you considered that he had or may have had an answer to give, but genuinely relied on the legal advice to remain silent, you should not draw any conclusion against him. But if, for example, you were sure that the defendant had no answer, and merely latched onto the legal advice as a convenient shield behind which to hide, you would be entitled to draw a conclusion against him, subject to the direction I have given you.

The questioning of witnesses

8.96 Regulation 34(5)(v) provides a right for the representative of the officer concerned to 'ask questions of any witness' in misconduct proceedings, subject only to reg 34(8)—namely, that 'whether any question should or should not be put to a witness shall be determined by the person conducting or chairing the misconduct proceedings'. On the face of the regulation, therefore, the situation is straightforward and familiar: the person representing the officer (and presumably, if not represented, the officer himself) may question the witness subject only to discretion in the chair as to whether a question asked by that person of that witness should or should not be put.

8.97 It is contended that the reg 34(8) discretion is directed at the intrinsic merits of the question rather than restricting the rights of the representative to ask questions directly of the witness. After all, the process of questioning the witness is often central to the fairness of the proceedings and the endeavour to get to the truth. This applies equally to questioning of the officer concerned by the presenting side.

8.98 Paragraph 2.194 of the Home Office Guidance provides as follows and, it is contended, tends to alter the meaning of reg 34(5)(v) and (8). It provides:

> Where a witness(es) does attend to give evidence then any questions to that witness should be made through the person conducting the meeting or in the case of a misconduct hearing the chair. This does not prevent the person conducting the meeting or the chair in a misconduct hearing allowing questions to be asked directly if they feel that is appropriate. It is for the person(s) conducting the meeting/hearing to control the proceedings and focus on the issues to ensure a fair meeting/hearing.

8.99 The subtle, but significant, change of emphasis is as between an expectation that the representative will question witnesses directly, subject to the reg 34(8) control of individual questions by that questioner, to a presumption that questions will ordinarily be asked of witnesses through the chair. If the two are—as they appear to be—in conflict, that conflict must, as a matter of law, be resolved by applying the regulation itself rather than the Guidance. The Guidance cannot alter the meaning of the regulation.[38]

Questioning of witnesses indirectly through the chair has its origins in internal **8.100** disciplinary proceedings in the private sector. It addresses the risk that employees may otherwise be reluctant to complain about a colleague's conduct: in other words, at low-level ('inquisitorial') meetings conducted without lawyers, it necessarily depersonalizes the process. Additionally, of course, the subject of internal disciplinary proceedings in the private sector will often have the right to claim unfair or wrongful dismissal at the employment tribunal—a right (absent a claim within one of the statutory heads of employment discrimination) not enjoyed by police officers and whose rights at the police appeals tribunals are heavily circumscribed.

Further, in practice, effective questioning of contentious witnesses will only be **8.101** possible (and is only desirable) if conducted by the instructed advocate. The chair does not have instructions—he should not be seen, through questioning, to have formed an opinion—and it places him in an invidious position generally. The officer concerned will have no confidence in the process. Furthermore, questioning by the chair in misconduct hearings is unlikely, most of the time, to be as effective forensically for reasons that are self-evident.

Such questioning through the chair may, however, become necessary in excep- **8.102** tional circumstances if a particular questioner is undermining the fair conduct of proceedings, the duty of fairness extending to the legitimate interests of the witness. Questioning that amounts to intimidation would fall within this category.

It is contended that the appropriate starting point for the regulation of ques- **8.103** tioning is as provided for in reg 34. This will invariably apply at a misconduct hearing. Questions through the chair may be more appropriate at a misconduct meeting where the conduct in issue involves the immediate professional colleagues of the officer concerned, and direct questioning would, for some reason, be inappropriate or deter the witness from giving evidence. This should again be regarded as an exceptional step.

---

[38] See *R (Chief Constable of Somerset and Avon) v Police Appeals Tribunal* [2004] EWHC 220 (Admin), see generally at 1.66 *et seq* and considered further at 8.131 below in the context of 'outcomes'.

The prescribed task of the person conducting or chairing the proceedings

8.104 Regulation 34(13) requires the adjudicators to 'review the facts of the case' and decide whether the conduct of the officer concerned amounts, at a misconduct meeting, to misconduct, or, at a misconduct hearing, to misconduct or gross misconduct. Persons conducting or chairing proceedings would do well, in their decisions, to distinguish finding from outcome, even though, very often, the same facts will be relevant to both issues.

The burden and standard of proof

8.105 Regulation 34(14) provides that the standard of proof is (as with the Police (Conduct) Regulations 1999 and the 2004 Conduct Regulations[39]) the balance of probabilities. Although para 2.197 of the Home Office Guidance (published in December 2008) provides, inter alia, that 'the more serious the allegation of misconduct that is made or the more serious the consequences for the individual which flow from a finding against him or her, the more persuasive (cogent) the evidence will need to be in order to meet that standard', this implied concept of a sliding scale (reflected in the previous Guidance at para 3.81) is now unequivocally wrong when applied to police misconduct proceedings.

8.106 A series of decided cases appear to resolve the approach to the meaning of the civil standard of proof—the balance of probabilities—particularly as applied to misconduct proceedings. In *R (IPCC) v AC Hayman*,[40] Mitting J reviewed *In re H*,[41] *In re B*,[42] and *In re Doherty*,[43] before concluding[44] that Lord Carswell's dicta, in the last sentence of [28] in *In Re B*, 'laid down the true proposition of law'—that is, that 'They do not require a different standard of proof or especially cogent standard of evidence, merely appropriately careful consideration by the tribunal before it is satisfied of the matter which has to be established'.

8.107 Mitting J continued (at [20]) that:

> Of course in disciplinary proceedings the tribunal must look with the greatest care at accusations which potentially give rise to serious consequences. But in determining whether or not they occurred, it applies a single unvarying standard, the balance of probabilities. If satisfied it is more likely than not that the facts occurred, then it must find them proved and draw appropriate conclusions as to sanction.

---

[39] SI 1999/730 and SI 2004/645 respectively.
[40] [2008] EWHC 2191 (Admin).
[41] [1996] AC 563, HL.
[42] [2008] UKHL 35.
[43] [2008] UKHL 33.
[44] Ibid, at [19].

It appears to follow that references in the Home Office Guidance to an 'increased **8.108** cogency' of evidence where the allegation is a serious one have little or no useful place in the binary determination of fact that the misconduct panel must make. References to percentages—'51 per cent'—are equally unhelpful in practice. Quite simply, either the presenting side has produced evidence that makes it more likely than not that a thing happened, or it has not. The inherent probability or improbability of the thing happening (such as corrupt activity by an officer with compelling previous positive good character, where a reasonable alternative explanation for evidence exists) is merely one factor in answering the question. A panel will, of course, require cogent evidence to prove that which is otherwise inherently improbable.

The relevance of previous good character to fact finding

A corollary of this approach to the standard of proof is that the officer concerned **8.109** should be permitted to call evidence of character where to do so may be relevant to either: (i) his credibility; or (ii) propensity, which includes the inherent probability or improbability of his having done the thing alleged. A similar principle was held to apply on the determination of an allegation of dishonesty made against a solicitor in *Donkin v Law Society*.[45] Failure to admit such evidence at the misconduct tribunal was considered (at [25]) a 'significant legal error' justifying a redetermination.

It is not permissible to call character evidence at the fact-finding stage, rather than **8.110** as to sanction, if the only purpose is to downgrade what would otherwise be serious professional misconduct to some lesser form of misconduct.[46] In other words, it must be directly relevant to the determination of the charge, as rehearsed at 8.104 above.

Majority findings

Regulation 34(15) provides that any decision of a misconduct panel shall be **8.111** based on a majority. Where there is a panel of two or four, the chair will have the casting vote if necessary. In either event, it shall not indicate whether it was taken unanimously or by a majority. These are familiar and uncontentious provisions: the tribunal produces a single decision, and it is irrelevant in law whether it was unanimous or not as between members of the tribunal.

---

[45] [2007] EWHC 414 (Admin).
[46] See *R (Campbell) v GMC* [2006] 1 WLR 3488, CA.

F. Outcomes

8.112 The available 'outcomes' (the preferred new language for 'sanctions') are very different from those available under the 2004 Conduct Regulations, and are now prescribed by regs 35–37. Gone completely are the sanctions of requirement to resign, reduction in rank, fine, reprimand, and caution. The replacements tend to prevent a middle-range outcome, and will routinely present misconduct hearings with a wholly invidious choice. The removal of the power to reduce rank, in particular, will be keenly felt in respect of supervisory failures.

8.113 In any event, the new outcomes are:

    (i) at a misconduct meeting, management advice, written warning, or final written warning;[47] and

    (ii) at a misconduct hearing, all of the above, plus dismissal with or without notice.[48]

8.114 It is to be noted that, at a misconduct meeting, the person conducting the meeting need not start at management advice as the first outcome: it is permissible to go straight in at a final written warning, dependent, of course, upon the severity of the misconduct.[49] Furthermore, at a misconduct meeting or hearing, if only simple misconduct is proven, the person or persons conducting the proceedings may simply record a finding of misconduct, but take no further action. This might occur where, for example, the mere burden of the proceedings themselves has acted as a form of sanction for that misconduct, such that no further sanction is necessary, or where the officer's subsequent conduct demonstrates particular professionalism.

8.115 If dismissal with notice is imposed, the minimum notice is twenty-eight days (reg 35(3)).

8.116 If, at a misconduct hearing, the finding after consideration of the evidence is one of misconduct, but not gross misconduct, then the panel may not impose dismissal (of either variant) unless the officer was the subject of a final written warning on the date of the assessment (see reg 12(1) of the 2008 Conduct Regulations, or reg14A of the 2004 Complaints and Misconduct Regulations).

---

[47] Regulation 35(2)(a).
[48] Ibid, (b).
[49] Regulation 15 of the Police Regulations 2003, SI 2003/527, as amended by SI 2006/3449 and 2005/2834, in respect of the 2004 Conduct Regulations, and reg 2 of the Police (Amendment) Regulations 2008, SI 2008/2865 (see Appendix J) (with associated paras 2.216–2.219 of the Home Office Guidance), in respect of the 2008 Performance Regulations and Conduct Regulations, addresses the expiry of written warnings.

In other words, the clear policy on outcomes is that dismissal can only be imposed **8.117** for gross misconduct, or for misconduct where the 'totting up' of earlier misconduct takes effect in relation to an officer already on a final written warning. This seems fair and proportionate.

There are three other important nuances to the determination of the outcome. **8.118**

Firstly, where, at the date of assessment of the conduct, the officer concerned **8.119** had a written warning in force, a further written warning shall not be given by way of outcome from misconduct meeting or hearing. In other words, if the misconduct is sufficiently serious to justify a written warning, it will be a 'final' variant of the same.[50]

Secondly, where the officer concerned had a final written warning in force on the **8.120** date of the assessment, he shall not receive a written warning or final written warning save that, in exceptional circumstances, the final written warning may be extended.[51]

Again, this would appear to indicate that an officer on a final written warning **8.121** can expect, if the misconduct is proven, to be dismissed (with or without notice), but that the persons conducting the proceedings may, in exceptional circumstances, extend a final written warning, albeit that this can only occur once.[52] Some assistance is provided by para 2.210 of the Home Office Guidance, which states that 'if a further act of misconduct comes before a misconduct hearing after an extension has been imposed, unless it is sufficiently minor to justify management advice, the police officer will be dismissed'.

Paragraph 2.211 of the Guidance provides that the requisite 'exceptional **8.122** circumstances':

> may include where the misconduct which is subject of the latest hearing pre-dates the misconduct for which the police officer received his or her original final written warning, or the misconduct in the latest case is significantly less serious than the conduct that led to the current final written warning being given.

The extension of the final written warning is for eighteen months from the date **8.123** on which it would otherwise expire.[53]

Thirdly, where (at a misconduct hearing) there is a finding of gross misconduct **8.124** and the outcome determined is one of dismissal, 'the dismissal shall be without notice'.[54] This presumably reflects the philosophy that an officer who is guilty of

---

[50] Regulation 35(5).
[51] Ibid, (6).
[52] Ibid, (8).
[53] Ibid, (7).
[54] Ibid, (9).

gross misconduct and in respect of whom dismissal is justified should not be in the police service a day longer than necessary.

Mitigation

8.125 Regulation 35(10) identifies the factors to which the person(s) conducting the proceedings must regard in determining the outcome, as follows.

(i) They 'shall have regard to the record of police service of the officer concerned as shown on his personal record' (reg 35(10)(a)). It is thus important that police forces ensure the accuracy of officers' personal records. Regulation 15 of the Police Regulations 2003,[55] as amended, regulates the period for which matters form part of the officer's formal 'written record'. Paragraph 2.44 of the Home Office Guidance provides that management action arising from local resolution of a complaint, whilst not a disciplinary outcome, may be recorded on the officer's professional and development review (PDR). This would presumably extend by analogy to any management action on the PDR.

(ii) They 'may receive evidence from any witness whose evidence would, in his or their opinion, assist them in determining the question' (reg 35(10)(b)). This provision is obviously directed at character testimonials and the quality of performance since the proven misconduct, although there is discretion for the persons conducting the hearing (in particular) to decline to hear such evidence in circumstances under which, for example, no amount of good character evidence could possibly affect the inevitable outcome of dismissal without notice. That said, in most cases, a misconduct hearing panel would do well to admit such evidence before moving to dismiss without notice, for the sake of the appearance of fairness.

(iii) They 'shall give . . . the officer concerned, his police friend or, at a misconduct hearing, his relevant lawyer . . . an opportunity to make oral or written representations before any such question is determined' (reg 35(10)(c)). This is the obvious entitlement of the officer concerned, by himself or his friend or lawyer, to advance mitigation.

8.126 In an important departure, mirroring the practice in other professional disciplinary contexts, the same opportunity to make representations on outcome is now afforded to the appropriate authority or the person appointed to represent the appropriate authority.[56] Whether this extends to the IPCC is an interesting point. It is not the appropriate authority under regs 35(10) and 7(4), but, in qualifying

---

[55] SI 2003/527.
[56] Reg 35(10)(c)(ii).

investigations, may, under reg 30(1), 'attend the misconduct proceedings to make representations', which representations are not elsewhere defined.

It is entirely foreseeable that the appropriate authority and the IPCC will disagree **8.127** as to outcome in particular cases, and it would difficult to justify compelling an appropriate authority positively to promote an outcome with which it does not genuinely agree. This may exceptionally justify separate representations by the IPCC as to outcome.

The Home Office Guidance encourages that regard be had to 'any aggravating **8.128** or mitigating factors' (para 2.201) and to the significance, if any, of an early admission (para 2.202). That real credit should be given for early admissions of fact, particularly where such was not inevitable on the available evidence, is probably obvious.

The approach to outcomes

Under the 2008 regime, outcomes remain very much a matter of professional **8.129** judgement for the misconduct panel. There is little in the Home Office Guidance to direct thinking. The philosophy of the 2008 regime is to emphasize a culture of learning and development over that of blame and punishment. Unlike, for example, proceedings before the GMC, there is no formal guidance on indicative sanction or 'fitness to practice', or any substantial body of decided cases to promote analysis. In reality, given the range of conduct involved, a prescriptive approach is impossible.

History demonstrates that the exercise of professional discretion is the better **8.130** approach. Application of Annex N to the 2004 Guidance (prescribing dismissal as the sanction for drink-driving) was inconsistent to the point of arbitrariness, and often perceived as operating against the public interest when it resulted in the removal of otherwise outstanding police officers.

Certain findings will, other than wholly exceptionally, admit of only one con- **8.131** clusion—namely, dismissal. In that misconduct findings may be disclosed to defendants in criminal proceedings, certain misconduct findings will render an officer effectively non-operational. This was recognized to be a relevant consideration by the Administrative Court in *R (Chief Constable of Somerset and Avon) v Police Appeals Tribunal*[57] at [32]–[34]. Similarly, in the legal and medical contexts, it has been held that the respective misconduct panels were properly concerned with the reputation of the profession as a whole, and the fortunes of the individual practitioner are of less importance.[58]

---

[57] [2004] EWHC 220 (Admin).
[58] See *Bolton v Law Society* [1994] 1 WLR 512, 517–19, as applied in *GMC v Fatnani and Raschid* [2007] EWCA Civ 46, CA. See also *Law Society v Salsbury* [2008] EWCA Civ 1285 for a post-HRA

8.132   Set against that is the legitimate consideration of personal mitigation, particularly if the breach established is one of basic competence—that is, if the breach reflects a simple objective failure to meet standards, or an isolated mistake with serious consequences. Few, if any, officers will complete thirty years' service without committing a mistake. If there is no deliberation, or pattern of misconduct, and the officer is capable of retraining, dismissal will often be unfair and disproportionate. It is not in the public interest for otherwise commendable careers to end in consequence of an isolated piece of misconduct that is solely attributable to poor decision making or judgement, and from which an otherwise competent professional person has learnt lessons.

8.133   These considerations were reflected by the Privy Council[59] in *Bijl v The GMC*.[60] The Council (notably Lords Hoffman, Mackay of Clashfern, and Clyde) considered a finding of serious professional misconduct, and the associated sanction of erasure from the register of medical practitioners. There was no appeal against the finding of serious professional misconduct. At [13] of the decision, the Privy Council stated:

> The Committee was rightly concerned with public confidence in the profession and its procedures for dealing with doctors who lapse from professional standards. But this should not be carried to the extent of feeling it necessary to sacrifice the career of an otherwise competent and useful doctor who presents no danger to the public in order to satisfy a demand for blame and punishment. As was said in *A Commitment to Quality, A Quest for Excellence,* a recent statement on behalf of the Government, the medical profession and the National Health Service: "The Government, the medical profession and the NHS pledge . . . without lessening commitment to safety and public accountability of services, to recognise that honest failure should not be responded to primarily by blame and retribution but by learning and by a drive to reduce risks for future patients.

8.134   The Privy Council agreed (at [14]) that Doctor Bijl's conduct was 'a serious lapse which they describe as the appellant abandoning his patient when her condition was still serious', but noted that the doctor was 'clearly determined never to make that mistake again'. It set out that his two proven failures:

> involved serious errors of judgment, but neither involved any allegation against his practical skills as a doctor such as might be difficult to improve at a later stage of his career. He has had a serious lesson which on the evidence available should prevent a

---

restatement of the principles in *Bolton*. In *Redgrave v Commissioner of Police of the Metropolis* [2003] 1 WLR 1136, Simon Brown LJ, at [33], confirmed that the purpose of professional disciplinary proceedings was the protection of the public and the maintenance of the reputation of the profession.

[59]   Disciplinary matters were, at that time, addressed in the first instance by the Professional Conduct Committee of the GMC. An appeal lay to the Board of the Privy Council under s 40 of the Medical Act 1983.

[60]   Appeal No 78 of 2000.

repetition of these errors of judgment, were he to be allowed to practise in the future, particularly if he does so under conditions intended to avoid such repetition.

There is no reason of public policy why these principles should not apply to police **8.135** officers of proven integrity in respect of isolated poor decision making or lack of judgement. It appears consistent with the underlying purpose of the 2008 regime. This is not to challenge that certain officers must, of course, be dismissed for gross misconduct, in situations such as gratuitous and unprovoked violence, flagrant and self-interested dishonesty, or concerted attempts to pervert the course of justice.

In determining considerations of deterrence and public confidence, a sophisti- **8.136** cated, rather than crude, approach is required. In *Walker v Royal College of Veterinary Surgeons*,[61] Lord Mance, having reviewed the guidance given by Lord Bingham in *Bolton v Law Society*,[62] went on to say:

> The reputation of and confidence in the profession of veterinary surgeons is impor-
> tant in a manner which bears an analogy to, even if it is not precisely the same as,
> that described by Sir Thomas Bingham in *Bolton v Law Society* but it is not to say
> that it would be correct to bracket all cases of knowingly inaccurate veterinary
> certification into a single group and to treat them as equivalently serious. That would
> not be right when considering how far an offender needs to be deprived of the oppor-
> tunity to practice in order to prevent re-offending, or what sanction is necessary to
> maintain or restore public confidence in the profession. Deterrence is an important
> consideration, but it must be deterrence in the light of the particular circumstances
> of the offence to which any deterrent sentence is directed.

Each of the preceding authorities confirms the principle additionally that these **8.137** competing considerations are matters for the expert professional discretion of the panel, and only exceptionally will a challenge succeed by way of judicial review to a properly reasoned decision. As to the appellate rather than review jurisdiction of police appeals tribunals, see 11.54–11.60.

Notification of outcomes

Regulation 36 delineates the procedures for notification of outcome and is to be **8.138** read in conjunction with paras 2.212–2.215 of the Home Office Guidance. In substance, the officer concerned is to be informed of the finding and any disciplinary action imposed as soon as practicable, and, in any event, shall be provided with written notice of these matters and a summary of the reasons within five working days of beginning with the first working day after the conclusion of the misconduct proceedings.[63]

---

[61] Privy Council Appeal No 16 of 2007.
[62] [1994] 1 WLR 512.
[63] Regulation 36(1).

8.139 Where there was a finding of misconduct or gross misconduct, the written notice shall include notice of the right of appeal (under reg 38) from the misconduct meeting, or notice of the right to appeal to a police appeals tribunal from a misconduct hearing.[64] The name of the person to whom any appeal should be sent must be included in the notice.[65]

8.140 Finally, reg 37 provides that a 'record of the misconduct proceedings shall be taken and in the case of a misconduct hearing that record shall be verbatim'. Thus misconduct hearings must (as ever) be tape-recorded (unless a force wishes to invest in a team of stenographers).

8.141 The officer is entitled, on request, to a copy of the record of the proceedings reg 37(2). This is a strange, apparently absolute, entitlement, because it would seem to apply even to an officer dismissed without notice for gross misconduct who does not appeal the finding or outcome. He would then be in a position to publicize the same to the media, which would seem to be highly undesirable, particularly if vulnerable witnesses, etc, may have given evidence against him. If such a risk were to arise, it may be that this directory requirement would be disapplied by the appropriate authority applying a de facto harm test, and that such non-compliance would not vitiate the concluded misconduct proceedings.

G. Appeals from Misconduct Proceedings

8.142 Regulation 38 provides the entitlement of (non-senior) police officers to appeal against contested findings, or disciplinary actions imposed, at misconduct meetings. There is no equivalent of the chief officer's review under the 2004 Conduct Regulations, and it follows that the only appeal from a misconduct hearing is to the police appeals tribunals.

Appeals against the outcome of a misconduct meeting

8.143 These are prescribed by regs 38–40 of the 2008 Conduct Regulations. The only grounds of appeal against the findings of a misconduct meeting are outlined at reg 38(2) as that:

(a) the finding or disciplinary action was unreasonable;

(b) there is evidence that could not reasonably have been considered at the misconduct meeting which could have materially affected the finding or decision on disciplinary action; or

(c) there was a serious breach of the procedures set out in these Regulations or other unfairness which could have materially affected the finding or decision on disciplinary action.

---

[64] Regulation 36(2).
[65] Ibid, (3).

It must be observed that the scope for appeal is, despite the use of the word 'only' **8.144** in para (2), extensive, and it must be hoped that management within the police service will be able to avoid excessive appeals from misconduct meetings, which were, after all, intended to be relatively summary and informal events.

To launch an appeal, the officer concerned gives written notice to the appropriate **8.145** authority within seven working days after the day of receipt by him of the notice of the findings and outcome (although this period can be extended), and the officer's notice must contain his grounds of appeal and an indication of whether a meeting is requested.[66]

The appeal is determined by a person (officer or staff member) of at least one rank **8.146** higher (or deemed rank higher for police staff) than the person who conducted the misconduct meeting, appointed by the appropriate authority.[67] The appropriate authority has the duty, as soon as practicable, to give the appellant written notice of the identity of the person appointed to determine the appeal and of the person appointed to advise that person, and of his right to object to such persons. As with reg 21(3), the officer concerned has the entitlement to object to the persons who will determine or advise upon his appeal, as to which (somewhat laborious) procedure, see reg 38(6)–(12).

The procedure for the appeal meeting is governed by reg 39 and obviously only **8.147** applies where the officer concerned has sought a meeting for the resolution of his appeal. The person appointed to determine the appeal must first determine whether the notice of appeal sets out 'arguable grounds of appeal'.[68] If he determines that it does not, 'he shall dismiss the appeal', thus hopefully swiftly extinguishing trivial or frivolous appeals.

If, however, he determines that the notice of appeal contains arguable grounds, **8.148** then he shall hold a meeting with the officer concerned, the fixing of which date is the subject of the usual procedure (as to which, see reg 39(4)–(6)).

Written notice of the date, time, and place of the appeal meeting is to be given to **8.149** the officer concerned and:

(i) the complainant, where the misconduct was certified as subject to the special requirements under para 19B(1) of Sch 3 to the 2002 Act;
(ii) any interested person, where the misconduct meeting arose from a conduct matter to which paras 16–19 of Sch 3 applied.[69]

---

[66] Regulation 38(3).
[67] Ibid, (4).
[68] Regulation 39(2).
[69] Ibid, (7).

8.150   Prior to the appeal meeting, the appropriate authority must supply the person determining the appeal with a copy of the documents provided to the person who held the misconduct meeting, the notice of appeal, the record of the misconduct meeting, and any 'new' evidence that the officer concerned wishes to submit in support of his appeal.[70] The procedure for the appeal is delineated in reg 40 and, as with all misconduct proceedings, the person conducting the appeal determines the procedure.

8.151   Any complainant or interested person who has received notice of the appeal meeting may attend the appeal meeting as an observer up to, but not including, the determination of disciplinary action,[71] although there remains discretion on the part of the person determining the appeal to impose reasonable conditions in relation to such attendance 'in order to facilitate the proper conduct of the appeal meeting'.[72]

8.152   The person conducting the appeal meeting may[73] confirm or reverse the decision (on finding or outcome) appealed against, or deal with the officer concerned in any manner in which the person conducting the misconduct meeting could have dealt with him under reg 35.[74] Thus it will be seen that the person conducting the meeting may increase the outcome to the maximum available at a misconduct meeting—namely, a final written warning. This may act as a deterrent to frivolous appeals.

8.153   The officer concerned is to be given written notice of the outcome of the appeal, with a summary of the reasons, within three working days starting on the day after the determination of the appeal (which may be a determination after a meeting or not).[75] The decision of the person determining the appeal takes effect by way of substitution for the decision of the person conducting the original meeting and as from the date of the written notice of the outcome of that meeting.[76]

8.154   In cases to which paras 18 or 19 of Sch 3 applied, or paras 16 and 17 applied and the IPPC made a recommendation or direction,[77] the appropriate authority is under an obligation to given the IPCC written notice of the determination of the

---

[70] Regulation 39(8).
[71] Regulation 40(2).
[72] Ibid, (3).
[73] Ibid, (4)(b).
[74] Ibid, (4).
[75] Ibid, (5).
[76] Ibid, (6).
[77] Under para 27(3) and 27(4)(a) of Sch3 to the 2002 Act, respectively.

appeal with a summary of reasons.[78] This is consonant with the policy that the IPCC should retain maximum oversight of misconduct proceedings with which it has had dealings.

Appeals from the outcomes of misconduct hearings

As stated, appeals from misconduct hearings are dealt with by the Police Appeals **8.155** Tribunal Rules (PAT Rules) 2008[79] and are addressed in Chapter 11.

---

[78] Regulation 40(7).
[79] SI 2008/2863.

9

THE POLICE (CONDUCT) REGULATIONS 2004

A. **Overview**	9.01	
The Police (Conduct) Regulations 2004 and the application of Home Office Guidance	9.01	
The purpose of proceedings under the 2004 Conduct Regulations	9.07	
The relationship between the 2004 and 2008 Home Office Guidance	9.12	
The application of the 2004 Conduct Regulations	9.16	
B. **The Structure, Purpose, and Application of the Regulations and the Home Office Guidance**	9.22	
The structure and purpose	9.22	
Application	9.25	
The Code of Conduct	9.32	
C. **General Points and Procedural Challenges**	9.45	
D. **Non-senior Officers**	9.54	
Initial handling: informal resolution outside misconduct procedures	9.54	
Local resolution and the role of a 'friend'	9.59	
Words of advice and written warnings as part of local resolution	9.63	

Formal investigation: notifications and the duties of disclosure	9.69
Notice of investigation under reg 9: service	9.74
The investigation and use of criminal interviews	9.79
The investigating officer's report and procedure on its receipt	9.80
Withdrawal of a case	9.82
Autrefois acquit	9.83
Joint hearings and legal representation at joint hearings	9.85
Disclosure and drafting charges (reg 14)	9.87
Drafting charges under reg 14	9.90
The role of the presenting officer	9.94
Other procedural steps before a hearing	9.97
Witness notification and attendance	9.98
Officers conducting the hearing	9.101
Procedure at the hearing	9.106
Sanctions	9.111
Reviews and appeals	9.114
E. **Senior Officers Under the 2004 Conduct Regulations**	9.115
F. **Conclusion**	9.117

A. Overview

The Police (Conduct) Regulations 2004 and the application of Home Office Guidance

9.01 The Police (Conduct) Regulations 2004[1] are reproduced as Appendix C and came into force on 1 April 2004. They revoked equivalent predecessor provisions as set out in reg 2—in particular, the Police (Conduct) Regulations 1999[2] and the Police (Conduct) (Senior Officers) Regulations 1999.[3] The 2004 Conduct Regulations are supplemented by detailed Home Office Guidance on *Police Unsatisfactory Performance Complaints and Misconduct Procedures* issued under s 87 of the Police Act 1996. The interrelationship between the 2004 Regulations and the Guidance is set out in Table 9.1.

9.02 In that reports, complaints, etc (excluding those relating to special constables), received after 1 December 2008 will be addressed under the 2008 regime, misconduct proceedings under the 2004 Conduct Regulations should become somewhat exceptional by 2010. Those that arise will typically reflect delay pending resolution of related criminal proceedings or the product of particularly complex investigations.

9.03 Many of the matters of general application are addressed more fully in Chapters 6–8—specifically: (i) in relation to the application of Sch 3 of the Police Reform Act 2002 from 1 April 2004; and (ii) general procedural points applicable to misconduct proceedings under either set of Conduct Regulations. It follows that the treatment of the 2004 Conduct Regulations is somewhat less extensive. Headline themes are highlighted for reference. There are many features in common (or at least with a high degree of practical equivalence), starting with the association of the Conduct Regulations with Home Office Guidance.

9.04 As with the 2008 regime, the power invested, under s 87 of the 1996 Act, in the Home Secretary to issue guidance to police authorities, chief officers of police, and other members of police forces concerning the discharge of their functions under these Regulations requires that 'they shall have regard to any such guidance in the discharge of their functions'. 'Having regard to' means what it says: guidance is just that. It is not a straightjacket.

9.05 It is fundamental that the Guidance cannot alter the rules of statutory interpretation in respect of the core regulatory provisions.[4] The Home Secretary

---

[1] SI 2004/645.
[2] SI 1999/730.
[3] SI 1999/731.
[4] See, inter alia, *R (Chief Constable of Somerset and Avon) v Police Appeals Tribunal* [2004] EWHC 220 (Admin), considered in detail at 11.54 *et seq*.

thus could not issue guidance to the police appeals tribunals under this power. More generally, where the statutory provision and the Home Office Guidance cannot be reconciled, the former must take precedence.

Paragraph (c) of the Introduction to the Guidance reflects the primary purposes **9.06** of the misconduct procedures and the discretion of a misconduct panel to depart from the Guidance for cause. It provides:

> The guidance on the individual procedures is designed to further the twin aims of being fair to the individual officer and of arriving at a correct assessment of the matter in question. The procedures are intended as means to this end, not as ends in themselves. Thus, a departure from the procedures described in this guidance will be justified if – and only if – it can be shown that it led to a truer and fairer result than observing them would have done.

The purpose of proceedings under the 2004 Conduct Regulations

Neither the Regulations nor the Guidance are exhaustive of the obligations of the **9.07** presenting side. The accused officer naturally would point to the para (a) expectation in the Introduction that procedures are 'designed to accord with the principles of natural justice and the basic principles of fairness'. To some extent, these 'international' concepts simply mean what one believes them to, but they are applied here in the context of a highly mature legal system. Equally, 'the correct assessment of the matter in question' is fact, rather than process, driven, and neutral as between presenting and defending sides.

Article 6 of the European Convention on Human Rights (ECHR)—the right to **9.08** a fair trial within a reasonable time—has no direct application to misconduct proceedings.[5] This reference to basic principles of fairness has particular significance to considerations of disclosure of material to the officer concerned that are defined by regs 14(1) (disclosure obligations to affected officer when giving notice to refer a case to a hearing) and 21 (documents to be supplied to the officer concerned). It is contended that the disclosure obligations articulated in respect of the Police (Conduct) Regulations 2008[6]—that is, under the Criminal Procedure and Investigations Act 1996 (CPIA), subject to the harm test[7]—should be applied by the appropriate authority identically in all future misconduct proceedings. Arbitrary distinctions will otherwise arise in practice between regimes running concurrently in time.

The corollary, however, is that the procedures are not simply designed to be fair to **9.09** the officer concerned, any more than the sole purpose of criminal proceedings is

---

[5] See *Pellegrin v France* (2001) 31 EHRR 651, considered at 7.27 and 12.59–12.60.
[6] SI 2008/2864.
[7] See 7.14–7.34.

to be fair to the defendant. Fairness to the accused is a minimum procedural obligation, but there is a legitimate public interest in the procedures establishing the truth of an allegation and, assuming that a breach of the code is proved, the appropriate sanction. This is no more than a reflection in the effective regulation of particular professions that directly affect the public. These objectives are consistent and concurrent with each other, rather than in competition.

9.10 The public interest in protecting the integrity of the process means that, in exceptional circumstances, deliberate manipulation of procedures would represent an abuse of process by the presenting side such as to require the proceedings to end at the initiative of the tribunal. Such an order—concerned as it is with ensuring respect for the rule of law—arises without reference to the underlying guilt of the accused party.

9.11 More generally, however, the different purpose of misconduct proceedings relative to those in the criminal context was rehearsed unambiguously in *R (Redgrave) v Commissioner of Police of the Metropolis*.[8]

The relationship between the 2004 and 2008 Home Office Guidance

9.12 As rehearsed in its Introduction, departure from the Home Office Guidance is justified if there is good reason, and if to do so would produce a truer and fairer result. The Guidance applicable to the 2004 Conduct Regulations evolved over time to reflect amendments—most notably to the criteria for pursuing a misconduct hearing following criminal proceedings (para 3.40) and the meaning of 'standard of proof' (para 3.81). As to the latter, the 2004 Guidance (and the 2008 equivalent) is now discordant with the law as to the meaning of standard of proof in misconduct proceedings,[9] and, as such, this would represent a good reason to depart from it.

9.13 More generally, it is contended that, unless the Home Office Guidance is clearly specific to the procedures in the 2004 Conduct Regulations, the terms of the 2008 Guidance may be relevant to how the 2004 Conduct Regulations should be applied. The 2008 Guidance is a modern restatement of the underlying purpose of misconduct proceedings, and for points of fundamental principle—including the interpretation of the Code of Conduct, disclosure, joint hearings, legal representation, the admissibility of evidence of good and bad character, standards of proof, case management, and the appropriate approach to sanction—there is every reason to seek to promote a consistent approach across the two sets of Conduct Regulations, so long as consistent with the actual language of the 2004 Conduct Regulations.

---

[8] [2003] EWCA Civ 04.
[9] See *R (IPCC) v AC Hayman* [2008] EWHC 2191 (Admin), and discussion at 8.106–8.108.

Certain of the Guidance, however, is clearly directly relevant to only one or other of the 2004 or 2008 regimes, and misconduct panels will have to ensure that any particular provision is properly understood in the context of the wider regulatory regime to which it relates. **9.14**

Application of the ordinary principles of statutory interpretation means, in somewhat simple terms, that where the 2004 Conduct Regulations prescribe a particular procedure—such as the extent of an affected officer's obligation (or not) to provide details of his case in advance of the hearing, and what material is provided to the misconduct panel in advance—these must be applied according to the ordinary meaning of the statutory language of the relevant Conduct Regulations. There are some genuine differences between the respective Regulations—such as disclosure obligations on the officer concerned—and these differences continue through the process of review and appeal from the misconduct hearing. Such regulatory differences must be respected. **9.15**

The application of the 2004 Conduct Regulations

The Conduct Regulations essentially apply to all police officers, including special constables and student officers during probation. Embedded within the Regulations and associated Home Office Guidance are procedural distinctions reflecting the status of the accused officer as a senior officer (over the rank of chief superintendent), other officers (sworn constables up to, and including, the rank of chief superintendent), and probationers. The position of probationers is considered in greater detail in Chapter 13. Clearly, in terms of volume, the vast majority of conduct addressed by the Regulations in practice relates to non-senior officers. **9.16**

This chapter is directed at the initial management of investigations to the point of sanction when the 2004 Conduct Regulations apply. Certain investigations will be handled initially by the Independent Police Complaints Commission (IPCC) under Sch 3 to the 2002 Act and the associated statutory guidance issued by the IPCC under s 22 of the Act. As set out in Chapters 5–8, in a Sch 3 investigation, the IPCC has rights and duties, and these are similarly reflected within the 2004 Conduct Regulations, as amended. The complainant in an IPCC investigation has rights, including rights of appeal against decisions as to charge, which do not arise in wholly internal ('local') investigations. **9.17**

As with the 2008 regime, the 2004 Conduct Regulations apply once a decision has been taken to refer the matter to a formal investigation rather than address it 'informally' through management action up to, and including, a formal written warning. Once a formal investigation begins, a duty arises on the relevant investigator to serve a notice of investigation under reg 9 of the 2004 Conduct Regulations (the equivalent to reg 15 of the 2008 Conduct Regulations). **9.18**

9.19 Where applicable, 'special' or 'fast track cases' are addressed in Chapter 10; chief officer reviews and appeals to the police appeals tribunals, in Chapter 11; 'abuse of process'—including the consequences of regulatory departure—is addressed in Chapter 12. Discretionary removal of probationers under the Police Regulations 2003[10] is addressed at Chapter 13.

9.20 Common—but fundamental—principles of general application to the conduct Regulations of 2004 and 2008 are analysed in the context of the 2008 Regulations. This includes points such as the appropriate test for disclosure, the meaning of the 'applicable civil standard of proof', and what minimum requirements may apply within the discretion of the misconduct tribunal to determine its own procedure.

9.21 Within the 2004 Conduct Regulations, it would perhaps have been more convenient and straightforward to introduce separate sections of the Regulations discretely to cover standard of proof and special cases, and/or senior and non-senior officers. As it is, the single set of Regulations has to be deconstructed at each stage for the purposes of interpretation. For ease of analysis, the relevant procedures applicable under the Regulations to senior and non-senior officers, respectively, are separated within this chapter.

B. The Structure, Purpose, and Application of the Regulations and the Home Office Guidance

The structure and purpose

9.22 The 2004 Conduct Regulations consist of forty-five regulations and two Schedules. Schedule 1 sets out the 'Code of Conduct' (hence the shorthand language invariably employed of 'breach of Code 5', etc) and some associated notes. Schedule 2 sets out provisions applicable to special cases.

9.23 The Home Office Guidance consists of six sections and associated appendices, and additionally some thirteen annexes. Section 1 is directed at unsatisfactory performance procedures (UPPs) under the 1999 Police (Efficiency) Regulations which are not further considered in this work. The relevant Police (Efficiency) Regulations 1999[11] were rarely used in practice and accordingly are not further analysed.

9.24 The relevant association between the 2004 Conduct Regulations and the Home Office Guidance is summarized in Table 9.1.

---

[10] SI 2003/527.
[11] SI 1999/732.

Table 9.1 A summary of the Police (Conduct) Regulations 2004 and associated Home Office Guidance on *Police Unsatisfactory Performance Complaints and Misconduct Procedures*

PCR 2004	Heading of regulation	Comment	Cross-reference: Home Office Guidance, ch 3 Chapter 3, Misconduct Procedures	
1	Citation, commencement and extent	In force 1 April 2004 Revoked from 1 December 2008	*I. RECEIPT OF AND ACTION ON INFORMATION*	
			General	3.1
			Fast track procedures (special cases)	3.7
			Complaints cases	3.8
			Non-complaint cases	3.10
2	Revocations and transitional provisions			
3	Interpretation			
4	Suspension	Suspension permitted only where: investigation may be prejudiced or in the public interest Suspension only permitted given prior approval of Commission	*II. FORMAL INVESTIGATION* *Suspension and removal from normal duties*	3.20
5	Suspension—urgent cases	In urgent cases, suspension permitted with immediate effect in relation to senior officers		
6	Conduct of investigations where there are outstanding criminal proceedings	Proceedings (except suspension) shall not take place where there are outstanding criminal proceedings except in exceptional cases	*Timings of investigations*	3.35
			Criminal proceedings	
			Civil proceedings	3.37

(*Continued*)

Table 9.1 *Cont.*

PCR 2004	Heading of regulation	Comment	Cross-reference: Home Office Guidance, ch 3
			Chapter 3, Misconduct Procedures
7	*Appointment of supervising officer*	Criteria for appointment	
8	*Appointment of investigating officer*	Criteria for appointment	*The investigating officer* 3.20
9	*Notice of investigation*	Written notice of investigation shall be given to the officer as soon as is practicable	*Notification of investigation* 3.21 *Interviews* 3.24
10	*Investigating officer's report*	Written report must be prepared as soon as reasonably practicable on the case	*III. INVESTIGATION REPORTS*
11	*Procedure on receipt of investigating officer's report*	Authority may refer case to a hearing on receipt of the report	*Consideration of investigation* 3.24 *report* *Action on investigation report* 3.28 *Complaints cases* 3.40 3.42
12	*Withdrawal of case*	Authority/supervising officer may direct that the case be withdrawn at any time before the start of the hearing	
13	*Sanction without hearing and notice of proceedings: senior officers*	If senior officer accepts misconduct, authority may impose sanction under reg 35 without a hearing	
14	*Notice of decision to refer case to a hearing*	Officer to be given notice that a decision to refer the case to a hearing will take place as soon as practicable At least 21 days before the date of the hearing, officer to be supplied with any relevant statement or document from the investigation	

15	*Limitation on sanctions: officers other than senior officers*	No sanction under reg 35 can be imposed on an officer who is not a senior officer unless the case has been referred to a hearing		
16	*Notice of hearing*	Authority shall ensure that, at least 21 days in advance of the hearing, the officer is notified of the date of the hearing	*Notifying the officer concerned*	3.46
17	*Legal representation*	Right to elect to be legally represented Right extends to special constable Amended by the Serious Organised Crime and Police Act 2005 (Consequential and Supplementary Amendments to Secondary Legislation) Order 2006, SI 2006/594, in force 1 April 2006	*Legal representation*	3.50
18	*Procedure on receipt of notice*	Response to notification and documents supplied to be returned by the officer within 14 days		
19	*Persons conducting the hearing: officers other than senior officers*	Hearing shall be heard by three police officers who are not interested parties	*Appointment of case officer* *Appointment of officers to take hearing*	3.43 3.54
20	*Person conducting the hearing: senior officers*	Hearing shall be heard by one person appointed from an approved list		
21	*Documents to be supplied to the officer concerned*	Where the officer accepts the misconduct, a summary of the facts is to be supplied to the officer at least 14 days before the hearing The officer has seven days in which to respond		
22	*Documents to be supplied to tribunal or to persons conducting the hearing*	A copy of the notice given under reg 14 and a copy of the summary of the facts given under reg 22	*Documents for the hearing*	3.52

(Continued)

Table 9.1 *Cont.*

PCR 2004	Heading of regulation	Comment	Cross-reference: Home Office Guidance, ch 3 Chapter 3, Misconduct Procedures	
23	*Representation: officers other than senior officers*	Officer will be represented by an appointed police officer unless officer has elected to be legally represented under reg 18, or wishes to represent himself or choose his own police officer representative	*Appointment of presenting officer*	3.44
24	*Representation: senior officers*	Senior officer will be represented by an independent solicitor or counsel		
25	*Participation by the Independent Police Complaints Commission*	Commission may present the case where the Commission has given a direction	*IPCC recommendation/direction*	3.45
26	*Conduct of hearing*	Adjournments permitted where necessary or expeditious. Decisions of the officers conducting the case taken by a simple majority	*IV. FORMAL HEARINGS* *Purpose and conduct of hearing*	3.57
27	*Procedure at hearing*	Tribunal may determine its own procedure	*Joint hearings* *Documents for the hearing* *Witnesses* *The 'friend'*	3.49 3.52 3.55 3.56
28	*Attendance of officer concerned at hearing*	Officer shall attend the hearing. Hearing may take place in officer's absence. Hearing may be adjourned where the authority is informed that the officer is/will be ill or unavoidably absent	*Presence of officer concerned* *Attendance at hearing – ill health*	3.67 3.68
29	*Attendance of complainant and interested persons at hearing*	Complainant or interested party may attend hearing except where they are to give evidence		

30	*Attendance of others at hearing*	Generally the hearing is to be private
		Members of the Commission may attend
31	*Exclusion of public from hearing*	Public may be excluded where any person may in giving evidence disclose to the public information that is not in the public interest to be disclosed
32	*Statements in lieu of oral evidence*	Documents may be adduced in evidence even if they have not been disclosed with the consent of the officer and the tribunal
		Questions of admissibility and whether questions may be put are determined by the tribunal
33	*Remission of cases: officers other than senior officers*	Where presiding officer is an interested party or the officer was not informed of his right to be represented, the case may be remitted to another officer of equivalent rank
34	*Record of hearing*	Verbatim record of proceedings shall be made. A transcript of the record will be provided to the officer after he has lodged notice of an appeal
		Amended by SI 2006/594
35	*Sanctions*	List of sanctions available: dismissal, requirement to resign; reduction in rank; fine; (in case of special constable) suspension from duties; reprimand; caution
36	*Personal record to be considered before sanction imposed*	Tribunal shall have regard to the record of the officer

V. OUTCOME OF HEARINGS

Burden and standard of proof	3.69
Range of sanctions	3.71
Drink driving convictions	3.79
No further action	3.80
Adjourned hearing	3.82

(Continued)

Table 9.1 *Cont.*

PCR 2004	Heading of regulation	Comment	Cross-reference: Home Office Guidance, ch 3 Chapter 3, Misconduct Procedures
37	*Notification of finding*	Non-senior officer: informed orally of the decision at the hearing and written notification within three days Senior officer: written notification as soon as possible	*Notifications of decision* 3.81
38	*Copy of report and decision to be sent to the Secretary of State*		
39	*Expenses of hearing*	In case of a senior officer, expenses met from the police fund	
40	*Request for a review: officers other than senior officers*	Review of sanction by chief officer/Assistant Commissioner can be requested within 14 days of receipt of written summary of reasons given	*Chief constable's review* 3.83
41	*Conduct of the review*	Reviewing officer shall hold a meeting with the officer	
42	*Finding of the review*	Officer informed on finding within three days of review Reviewing officer may confirm, overturn, or reduce sanction, but may not increase the sanction	
43	*Hearing of review in absence of chief officer*	Review conducted by deputy/assistant chief constable where chief constable an interested party	
44	*Record of conduct proceedings*	Chief officer must keep a record of all conduct proceedings	*Misconduct books* 3.86 *Records of police officers* 3.87 *fingerprints*

45 Special cases	Regulations apply, suitably adapted by Sch 2 to special cases (see **Chapter 10**)	Fast-track procedures (special cases) 3.7 *APPENDIX – FAST-TRACK PROCEDURES (SPECIAL CASES)*

Annexes

A Appointment of investigating officer from another force
B Notification of investigation to officer concerned
C Formal warnings in complaints cases
D Legal representation
E Officers appointed to conduct hearings
F Evidence at hearings
G Witnesses
H Other persons who may attend hearings
J Ill health
K Roles of HMIC and police authorities
L Officers seconded under section 97
M Forms
N Drink drive convictions

Schedules

1

1 Honesty and integrity
2 Fairness and impartiality
3 Politeness and tolerance
4 Use of force and abuse of authority
5 Performance of duties
6 Lawful orders
7 Confidentiality
8 Criminal offences
9 Property
10 Sobriety
11 Appearance
12 General conduct

2	Special cases (see **Chapter 10**)	Fast-track procedures (special cases) *APPENDIX – FAST-TRACK PROCEDURES (SPECIAL CASES)*

Application

9.25 Interpretation is addressed by reg 3. Certain investigations fall outside the Regulations and within Sch 3 to the 2002 Act—that is, one of the four forms of investigation determined by the IPCC under para 15 of the Schedule. In terms of initial handling and investigation, points of general principle were reflected in Chapters 6 and 7, and this chapter avoids repetition.

9.26 As stated, the 2004 Conduct Regulations apply to all police officers, which include all members of a police force and special constables. Excluded are permanent senior and non-senior members of the National Criminal Intelligence Service (NCIS).

9.27 'Senior officer' is defined (reg 3(2)) to cover a chief constable, a deputy chief constable, or an assistant chief constable, or, in the case of the City of London and Metropolitan police forces, a member of the force in question of, or above, the rank of commander. Misconduct proceedings are to be distinguished from the power of police authorities to require senior officers to retire or resign on the grounds of efficiency or effectiveness,[12] or equivalent powers,[13] invested in the Home Secretary to require a police authority to exercise these powers in relation to the Commissioner of Police of the Metropolis or Deputy Commissioner or any chief constable.

9.28 'Officer other than a senior officer' means a police officer below the rank of senior officer, including (reg 3(3)(a)) a special constable. By reg 3(3)(b), any special constable of a rank or grade equivalent to, or above, the rank of chief superintendent shall be treated as if he were a chief superintendent. This produces the result that no special constable is treated as a senior officer in these misconduct proceedings.

9.29 In respect of members of a police force other than special constables, the Regulations apply to any report, complaint, or allegation received on or after 1 April 2004, regardless of when the conduct in question occurred (reg 3(3)(a)).

9.30 In respect of special constables, even if the relevant report, complaint, or allegation was received after 1 April 2004, the Regulations do not apply if the conduct complained of 'occurred or commenced' before that date (reg 3(3)(b)).

9.31 The 'appropriate standard' means the standard set out in the Code of Conduct, and 'conduct matter' means any matter that is not, and has not been, the subject of a complaint, but in the case of which there is an indication (whether from the

---

[12] Sections 9E–9G, 11, and 12 of the Police Act 1996, as amended by ss 30–32 of the Police (Reform) Act 2002 (see Chapter 2).

[13] Section 42 of the Police Act 1996, as amended, considered at 2.12.

circumstances or otherwise) that a person serving with the police may have: (a) committed a criminal offence; or (b) behaved in a manner that would justify the bringing of disciplinary proceedings.

The Code of Conduct

The Code of Conduct (Sch 1 to the Regulations) prescribes a single code that **9.32** is applicable to all officers. There is no further definition of terms in the 2004 Home Office Guidance. This contrasts with the approach under the 2008 Guidance, in which the entirety of ch 1 is dedicated to 'Guidance on Standards of Professional Behaviour'. This 2008 Guidance may be persuasive in the context of interpretation of the Code of Conduct in Sch 1 of the 2004 Conduct Regulations.

It may be said that the Code is directed at the maintenance of objective standards **9.33** of professional conduct. This was addressed at 6.36–6.42. Note (c) to the Code provides that:

> Police behaviour, whether on or off duty, affects public confidence in the police service. Any conduct which brings or is likely to bring discredit to the police service may be the subject of sanction. Accordingly, any allegation of conduct which could, if proved, bring or be likely to bring discredit to the police service should be investigated in order to establish whether or not a breach of the Code has occurred and whether formal disciplinary action is appropriate. No investigation is required where the conduct, if proved, would not bring or would not be likely to bring, discredit to the police service.

This is the threshold test under the 2004 Conduct Regulations—no investigation **9.34** is required if the matter if proved is unlikely to bring 'discredit' on the police[14]— but one that applies equally to off-duty conduct. The equivalent paragraph under the 1999 Conduct Regulations provided that it applied to off-duty conduct if it 'was serious enough to indicate that an officer is not fit to be a police officer', and that such off-duty conduct 'will be measured against the generally accepted standards of the day'. As to the first limb, the change of language in 2004 was arguably intended to include a more extensive range of off-duty conduct in the legitimate coverage of misconduct proceedings. Whether this was either desirable or occurred in practice is a moot point.

As observed, there is surprisingly little direct guidance as to the meaning of the **9.35** matters expressed in the Code. The general proposition must be that the Performance and Conduct Regulations are directed at the maintenance of minimum objective standards of professional conduct. Equally, if proved, these are positive misconduct findings as distinct from managerial decisions simply

---

[14] As to 'likely to bring discredit', see 6.35.

providing an objective basis for retraining or advice. Certain breaches (sobriety, appearance, reporting criminal conduct) readily lend themselves to such a purely objective interpretation. Others do not and appear to import a subjective element in relation to the defendant officer's state of mind.

9.36 Obvious amongst these—certainly in practice, if not in strict theory—are alleged breaches of Code 1: namely, that an officer has acted without honesty or integrity. It may be observed that it is possible for an officer to lack honesty by objective standards. In practice, this would only be evidence in support of an allegation that he or she subjectively acted dishonestly for the purposes of a misconduct finding. The appropriate test is contended to be the two-stage objective/subjective *Twinsectra*[15] formula, as approved in *Bryant v Law Society*.[16]

9.37 Others are more difficult in terms of the relevance of subjective considerations. An example is Code 5, described as 'Performance of duties'. If left at that, an objective test may have been readily assumed. Code 5 is defined, however, as requiring an officer to be 'conscientious and diligent' in the performance of his or her duties. So what of an officer's incompetent, but subjectively 'conscientious', best effort?

9.38 As was discussed at 6.36–6.39, in practice, assuming (i) 'practicability' of performance, and (ii) applying the force standards at the time of the misconduct alleged, Code 5 is used as a charge where there is a failure to meet the minimum objective professional benchmark of performance: failure to meet such a benchmark presupposes a lack of 'conscientious or diligent' performance. The same principle applies to considerations of careless driving and in other professions, including medicine. An individual's incompetent best may still properly—and necessarily—amount to culpable 'misconduct' in this narrow sense.

9.39 Public confidence in the maintenance of professional standards requires this benchmark approach to Code 5. Subjective considerations may affect sanction. By analogy, a Fitness to Practice Panel at the General Medical Council (GMC) first determines the question of what facts are proved (by admission or evidence); then whether, on the basis of the facts proved, the practitioner's fitness to practice is impaired; and, if impaired, what sanction should then be imposed. Helpfully, but wholly unlike police misconduct, there is a well-documented set of indicative sanctions to assist the decision-making process at the sanction stage.[17]

9.40 Other elements in the Code are less straightforward to apply. Code 4 covers 'Use of force and abuse of authority'. Approached from first principles, the

---

[15] *Twinsectra v Yardley* [2002] 2 AC 164.
[16] [2007] EWHC 3043.
[17] See the GMC's Indicative Sanctions Guidance for Fitness to Practice Panels.

reasonableness of the use of force may be approached objectively, even where it is accepted that a particular officer did no more than he subjectively considered necessary. 'Abuse' of authority, however, may be said to imply a knowing (or at least, subjectively reckless) abuse of power by the officer in question.

A wholly subjective approach to both use of force and abuse of authority is, **9.41** however, implied by the language of the Code ('officers must never knowingly use more force than is reasonable, nor should they abuse their authority'). A subjective approach to 'abuse of authority' arises by analogy with what must be proved for the mental element of the criminal offence of misconduct in public office.[18] In such situations, it is contended that the better charge is under Code 5—that is, conduct judged by purely objective standards and mitigated for the purpose of sanction by the subjective belief of the officer concerned.

Similar reasoning may be said to apply to Code 12—that is, 'General conduct'. **9.42** This is better described (as it is in the 2008 Conduct Regulations) as 'discreditable conduct' and is particularized as behaviour that is 'likely to bring discredit on the police service'. This must mean likely as and when known by a member of the public. The fact that conduct was not likely to be discovered is of little, if any, significance in this sense. It is the intrinsic nature of the conduct that matters, as distinct from the probability of discovery.

As a matter of degree—certainly when applied to the performance of duties, **9.43** as distinct from off-duty conduct—this is often used in practice to denote con- duct that is positively discreditable, rather than simply not meeting the minimum objective standard. This may, of course, arise from the simple degree of failure inherent in conduct, but is better used in circumstances in which the duty breached is particularly sensitive in terms of the elusive concept of 'public confidence' and/ or the subjective deliberation of the officer concerned.

Misconduct tribunals are required to balance the role that misconduct charges **9.44** perform in the maintenance of professional standards with the corollary that the allegation is one of professional misconduct. To this extent, underperformance is to be distinguished from knowing misconduct in terms of framing charges. Lesser forms of intervention (the UPPs) to address performance are available (if wholly underused) under the 1999 Efficiency Regulations, and, for this reason, are actively promoted under the intended new culture of the 2008 regime of performance and misconduct (see Chapter 4).

---

[18] See *Attorney-General's Reference No 3 of 2003* [2005] QB 73, considered at 15.12 *et seq.*

C. General Points and Procedural Challenges

9.45 Paragraph 3.6 of the Home Office Guidance provides that, in respect of initial handling and investigative procedures, it only applies to those cases that fall outside the Police Reform Act 2002—that is, those matters that are not public complaints (s 12 of the Act) or recordable conduct matters (paras 10 and 11 of Sch 3 to the Act). These are handled by the IPCC pursuant to the 2002 Act and associated statutory guidance.[19] Similar exceptions occur within the Regulations in respect of complaint or conduct matters to which paras 16, 17, 18, or 19 of Sch 3 to the 2002 Act apply. The initial handling of Sch 3 investigations is considered in detail in Chapter 6.

9.46 By para 6 of Sch 1 to the 2004 Conduct Regulations, police officers are under a positive duty to report suspected breaches of the Code of Conduct by other officers: 'Officers should support their colleagues in the execution of their lawful duties, and oppose any improper behaviour, reporting it where appropriate.' This element is expressed even more positively in the 'Standards of Professional Behaviour' under the 2008 regime.[20]

9.47 Equally, the misconduct procedures are not available as a vehicle with which to litigate management complaints. This is the proper role of grievance procedures.

9.48 One continuing 'right' embedded in the Guidance is worth consideration from the outset. Forms of discretion are built into the process at each stage. The Guidance appears to provide a right in the officer concerned to challenge the exercise of discretion by a particular decision maker at any stage, including the formal misconduct hearing. The right is rehearsed at paras 3.10 and 3.11:

> 3.10. At any stage of a case, up to and including a formal hearing, the officer concerned may submit that there are insufficient grounds upon which to base the case and/or that the correct procedures have not been followed. It will be for the officer responsible for the relevant stage of the case to consider any such submission and determine how best to respond to it, bearing in mind the need to ensure fairness to the officer concerned.
>
> 3.11. In cases where it is clear that there will need to be legal arguments based, say, on the way the force or police authority/service authority have applied the procedures, consideration should be given to holding a preliminary hearing. If the case is one in which the officer concerned has elected to be represented, the force may decide to appoint a lawyer to present its case. For reasons of effectiveness and economy, though, the force may consider that their own need for a lawyer could be confined to the legal argument stage.

---

[19] Addressed at 3.79, and 6.128–6.130.
[20] Addressed at 9.32–9.44 above.

Apart from fundamental points as to abuse of process—broadly, either that a **9.49** fair hearing is, for some practical reason, impossible, or (wholly exceptionally) that the presenting side has acted in a way that is in deliberate breach of procedures to a degree that makes it unconscionable for the proceedings to continue— this would cover matters such as decisions to refer to a misconduct panel, the decision as to a full powers panel (which, of course, may be challenged either way), and the form of charge.

What test is applied to the exercise of these discretionary matters is less obvious. **9.50** The tests applied by the Administrative Court in judicial review are well known, but arguably set too high where the original decision maker is concerned to review the exercise of discretion by another within a regulated internal process. Intervention need not imply criticism of the original decision maker, but rather a different opinion within a recognized spectrum. Equally, the misconduct panel should be slow to operate routinely as a route of appeal rather than 'review' of procedural decisions.

Working tests to apply to a particular decision under challenge might be that **9.51** the original decision maker has clearly applied the wrong test, or has produced a result that is contrary to the intended purpose of the misconduct procedures, or that the decision (for example, as to the need for a full powers board) may be changed without criticism so as to produce a fairer and sufficiently proportionate result.

Regulation 27 (procedure at hearing) provides that the relevant tribunal shall **9.52** determine its own procedure and (reg 27(2)) 'shall review the facts of the case and decide whether or not the conduct of the officer concerned met the appropriate standard'. If not (reg 27(7)), it 'shall decide whether it would be reasonable to impose any, and if so which, sanction'.

This is sometimes contended to exhaust the function of the misconduct panel so **9.53** as to exclude the categories of challenge reflected at 9.48–9.51 above. Subject to the caution already expressed, the preferred view is that the Home Office Guidance, in this context, applies rather than contradicts the Regulations and is therefore consistent with it.

D. Non-senior Officers

Initial handling: informal resolution outside misconduct procedures

The Conduct Regulations themselves say little as to the initial handling of the **9.54** generality of qualifying complaints. Specific matters that are addressed include provisions as to the conduct of misconduct investigations where there are outstanding criminal proceedings (reg 6: other than the exercise of the power to suspend under regs 4 or 5, proceedings under the Regulations shall not take place unless the appropriate authority believes that, in the exceptional circumstances of the case, it would be appropriate for them to do so) and specific provision as to special cases (Sch 2 to the 2004 Conduct Regulations).

9.55 The obligation to serve a written notice of investigation under reg 9 is on the investigating officer. The determination of an allegation does not, however, inevitably reach the stage of appointing an investigating officer.

9.56 The investigating officer is appointed by the supervising officer, who in turn 'may' be appointed by the chief officer under reg 7 if a qualifying report, complaint, or allegation is received that indicates that the conduct of a police officer did not meet the required standard. By reg 7(3), the supervising officer shall be:

    (a) of at least the rank of chief inspector and at least one rank above that of the officer concerned;

    (b) a member of, or a special constable appointed for the area of, the same force as the officer concerned; and

    (c) not an interested party.

9.57 The Home Office Guidance allows for a matter to be addressed without the appointment of a supervising officer. By para 3.6:

> it is an essential part of effective line management that managers should be aware of the conduct and performance of the individuals they manage. It is an integral part of a line manager's normal responsibilities to decide how to respond to any information which gives rise to concerns about an individual's conduct or performance.

9.58 The discretion as to 'informal resolution' (meaning resolution without formal misconduct proceedings) in non-public complaints cases is reflected at paras 3.13–3.18 of the Guidance. It is essentially discretion led by the intrinsic gravity of allegation as to whether or not 'local inquiries' are sufficient. Local inquiries are those not involving the intervention of the relevant professional standards department.

Local resolution and the role of a 'friend'

9.59 By paras 3.8, 3.9, and 3.15, the Home Office Guidance anticipates that the officer concerned will have the benefit of a police 'friend' throughout the process, and access to legal advice as necessary. The unresolved complexities of the legal status of a police friend, in terms particularly of confidential conversations and legal professional privilege, were addressed at 7.36 *et seq*.

9.60 The role of a 'friend' is addressed in detail in the introduction to the 2008 Guidance. This asserts that it is not the role of the police friend to conduct his or her own investigation into the matter. The distinction between defending a charge and investigation may be more elusive in practice. It also demonstrates the importance of disclosure by the presenting side, which, under the 2008 Guidance (para 2.146), is expressly according to the principles under the CPIA (see 7.14–7.34).

The 2004 Guidance anticipates (para 3.14) that, under the local procedure, 'the **9.61** officer concerned will be informed of the details of the allegation or information that gives cause for concern and be given a full opportunity to respond to the allegation or information and to offer an explanation'. This notification is purely under the Guidance and, accordingly, technically distinct from the reg 9 notice. The reg 9 notice requirements are less extensive than the equivalent under the 2008 regime, but so is the corresponding nature of the duty in terms of response. This is contended to be a paradigm of when the 2008 Guidance cannot alter the meaning of the 2004 Conduct Regulations.

Whether failure to respond as part of the purely informal process may subse- **9.62** quently attract an adverse inference is less clear. The better course is to invite such an inference only as part of the formal reg 9 process if that arises. If the matter can be dealt with informally, then no formal reg 9 notice is required. If that is not possible, then the possibility of an adverse inference will arise only once it is served. This mirrors the approach to representations made during the local resolution process in IPCC investigations.

Words of advice and written warnings as part of local resolution

Words of advice and/or other management action may be given even when the **9.63** alleged misconduct is not admitted by the affected officer. There is no appeal from the giving of words of advice. Clearly, as non-admitted and non-recorded conduct, the weight to be attached to such a unilateral decision in any subsequent hearing (such as, for example, similar fact evidence for allegedly repetitive conduct) is heavily qualified.

A written warning (which is recorded and valid for twelve months from the **9.64** date on which it is administered) is given by a superintendent or above and requires the affected officer to admit the relevant failure. The terms of such a warning are properly the subject of negotiation. On any future investigation, if there are two valid written warnings recorded, the matter must be referred to a formal hearing. The regulation and the language of para 3.16 of the Home Office Guidance appears to make the date on which the officer admits a failure the relevant date, as distinct from the date of the failure itself.

Regulation 15 of the Police Regulations 2003[21] expunges written warnings **9.65** from an officer's record after a fixed period. So it is that, whilst management advice

---

[21] The Police (Amendment) Regulations 2008, SI 2008/2865, reproduced at Appendix J, amended these for proceedings after 1 December 2008.

(a lesser sanction) or management action (not a disciplinary outcome at all) on the officer's personal development record may be raised at the sanction stage of proceedings, a written warning may not be if it has been expunged through passage of time to the date of hearing. This is despite the fact that a written warning requires the conduct to have been admitted.

9.66 Equally anomalously, the same written warning may have been the trigger for a mandatory referral to a formal hearing under reg 11. The same appears to apply to the amended reg 15 under the Police (Amendment) Regulations 2008.[22] However surprising in effect, this is contended to be what the regulation actually says and it must be applied as such.

9.67 If the conduct is not admitted for the purpose of a written warning, there is a choice between doing nothing, imposing words of advice, or referral to a formal hearing.

9.68 Once it is clear that formal misconduct proceedings are required, the 'informal' process must cease and a supervising officer must be appointed. Assuming that an investigating officer is then appointed under reg 8 (itself a discretionary step), a more formal process commences. This starts with the service of the reg 9 notice of investigation.

Formal investigation: notifications and the duties of disclosure

9.69 Following a qualifying allegation, there are various points in the regulatory process at which the affected officer is entitled to notice of an event and associated service of identified material. The Regulations prescribe the minimum obligations, but are supplemented, to a degree, by the Home Office Guidance and, at the actual misconduct hearing, the discretion in the tribunal to set its own procedure subject to any specific other regulations.

9.70 Subject to the Guidance, the first regulation giving the affected officer any right to information is reg 9—the so-called 'notice of investigation'. This notice (known as a 'Reg 9') has been a part of the misconduct regime from at least 1977, and survives as reg 15 in the 2008 Conduct Regulations.

9.71 If the matter is referred to a hearing, the affected officer becomes entitled under reg 14(1) to notice of this fact and all any relevant material obtained during the course of the investigation.

9.72 If the alleged conduct is subsequently admitted, the affected officer is entitled under reg 21 to a statement of facts prepared by the presenting side and to respond to it.

---

[22] SI 2008/2865: see Appendix J.

These duties are considered briefly in turn. They are contingent on the appoint- **9.73**
ment and roles of a supervising officer under reg 7, and an investigating officer
under reg 8.

Notice of investigation under reg 9: service

As stated the reg 9 notice has a pedigree going back at least to the Police **9.74**
(Discipline) Regulations 1977[23] (in which it was reg 7) and is reproduced with
some significant revisions (particularly as to the likely form of misconduct
proceedings, and hence maximum outcome) in reg 15 of the 2008 Conduct
Regulations.

In relation to a non-senior officer, and matters outside paras 17–19 of Sch 3 to the **9.75**
2002 Act matters (that is, those handled by the IPCC), the chief officer has
discretion under reg 7(1) as to the appointment of a suitably qualified supervising
officer, and that officer has discretion as to the appointment of an investigating
officer under reg 8(1).

Regulation 8 contains further provision as to the status of the investigating **9.76**
officer. 'Interested party' is not defined, but must take its meaning from the
statutory context. Mere professional knowledge of the officer under investigation
will not disqualify an investigator from so acting. It is assumed by the Regulations that the investigating officer will ordinarily be from the same force.
Considerations of bias[24] may apply, subject to the limited decisions actually
taken by the supervising and investigating officers. Neither is the ultimate tribunal of fact, and there are procedural rights to challenge decisions throughout
the process.

The reg 9 notice obligations bite on the appointment of the investigating officer, **9.77**
whether by the IPCC as investigator directly under reg 9, or through regs 8 and 9.
The essential purpose of the notice is to enable the affected officer, at the first
practicable opportunity, to take the initiative in defence of the allegation, and
in particular to reduce the adverse evidential consequences that delayed notification would bring. It enables him—if he so elects—to direct the attention of the
investigation to lines of inquiry that may otherwise not arise.

The nature and effect of the reg 9 notice was considered at 7.113 *et seq* and is **9.78**
addressed further (in the context of wider principles of regulatory departure)
at 12.51–12.54. The terms of the notice differ in detail from the equivalent
forms under the 2008 regime as described, most particularly as to there being

---

[23] SI 1977/580.
[24] See 11.16–11.20.

no indication in a reg 9 notice of the likely level of misconduct proceeding that will result.

The investigation and use of criminal interviews

9.79   At the investigation and interview stage, it is contended that, in practice, there is little distinction with the 2008 regime. Regulations 7 and 8 reflect appointments, and the qualification for appointment, of supervisory and investigation officers, respectively. In respect of non-senior officers, the investigation report is submitted to the supervising officer, who then (reg 11) has discretion as to whether to refer the matter to a hearing. The approach to the conduct and sequence of criminal and misconduct interviews, in particular, was considered at 7.134–7.154. The same principles are contended to apply to the 2004 regime.

The investigating officer's report and procedure on its receipt

9.80   Unlike the arrangement under the 2008 Conduct Regulations, under the 2004 regime, the investigating officer's report is not part of the material provided to the misconduct panel; neither is it a document to which the officer concerned is entitled as of right—although, of course, original evidential material reflected within it may be subject to disclosure. Under reg 10, there is a duty to prepare the report as soon as practicably possible.

9.81   Once completed, discretion arises as to whether misconduct proceedings result. Under reg 11, the matter must be referred to a hearing if the officer concerned has had two written warnings about his conduct in the previous twelve months and 'has in a statement under regulation 9 admitted that his conduct failed to meet the appropriate standard'. Regulation 11 provides for further investigation and that 'where a case is not referred to a hearing no reference shall be made to it on the officer concerned's personal record'. Whether this would prevent management advice arising from the same facts to be so recorded is a more difficult question, because 'it' under reg 11(7) does appear to relate to 'the case' rather than the non-referral.

Withdrawal of a case

9.82   Subject to the Sch 3 powers of direction of the IPCC, a case may be withdrawn 'at any time before the beginning of the hearing' (reg 12(1)). This does not prevent the presenting side from offering no further evidence once the hearing has started, because, rather than technically withdrawing the case, this simply produces an inevitable 'not proved' outcome delivered by the relevant misconduct panel.

Autrefois acquit

9.83   An important consideration that routinely arises in practice is the bringing of misconduct proceedings following acquittal on particular criminal charges.

Given the different purposes of the proceedings, the different standards of proof and rules as to admissibility of evidence, and the different elements of particular charges, a previous acquittal frequently does not operate as any form of bar to misconduct charges. This was the focus of the leading case of *Redgrave*.[25]

With those general propositions made, a previous acquittal is often directly relevant to the exercise of the wider discretion as to whether misconduct charges are necessary. Paragraph 3.40 of the Home Office Guidance provides some useful advice as to how the obvious competing considerations may be resolved. It is self-explanatory in content: **9.84**

> A previous acquittal in criminal proceedings in respect of an allegation which is the subject of disciplinary proceedings is a relevant factor which should be taken into account in deciding whether to continue with those proceedings. Relevant factors in deciding whether to proceed with disciplinary proceedings include the following, non-exhaustive, list:
> (a) Whether the allegation is in substance the same as that which was determined during criminal proceedings;
> (b) Whether the acquittal was the result of a substantive decision on the merits of the charge (whether by the judge or jury) after the hearing of evidence;
> (c) Whether significant further evidence is available to the tribunal, either because it was excluded from consideration in criminal proceedings or because it has become available since.

> Each case will fall to be determined on its merits and an overly-prescriptive formula should not be adopted.

> It may further be unfair to proceed with disciplinary proceedings in circumstances where there has been a substantial delay in hearing disciplinary proceedings by virtue of the prior criminal proceedings.

> Regard should be had in this respect to such factors as:
> • the impact of the delay on the officer (including the impact on his health and his career);
> • whether the delay has prejudiced his defence in any disciplinary proceedings;
> • whether there will be a further substantial delay whilst disciplinary proceedings are heard (including the impact of that delay).

Joint hearings and legal representation at joint hearings

The Home Office Guidance outlines (para 3.49) when it is appropriate to hold a joint hearing for two or more officers accused of misconduct arising out of the same incident. The presumption is that separate hearings will be held unless this can be done without prejudice to the defendant officer. The 2008 Guidance (para 2.182–2.184) tends to reverse this presumption. The difference is probably **9.85**

---

[25] *Redgrave v Commissioner of Police of the Metropolis* [2003] EWCA Civ 4; [2003] 1 WLR 1136.

academic, because, in practice and for a whole range of very good reasons, a single hearing covering a common factual background is desirable. As with the criminal jurisdiction, there will still be some cases in which separate hearings are appropriate notwithstanding a common factual background.

9.86 Associated with this, Annex D to the Guidance provides (although the Regulations appear not to) that if a joint hearing is held and an accused officer does not qualify for legal representation (that is, if it is not a full powers board under reg 17), but others do so qualify, the right to legal representation should be extended. This is obviously sensible, although appears necessarily to involve interpreting reg 17 as not exhaustive of the right to legal representation and a generous interpretation of the misconduct panel's power to determine its own procedure under reg 27(1).

Disclosure and drafting charges (reg 14)

9.87 Regulation 14 is a central provision. It provides as follows.

14 Notice of decision to refer case to a hearing

(1) Where a case is to be referred to a hearing, as soon as practicable the officer concerned shall be given written notice of the decision to refer the case to a hearing, and at least 21 days before the date of the hearing he shall be supplied with copies of—
   (a) any statement he may have made to the investigating officer; and
   (b) any relevant statement, document or other material in each case obtained during the course of the investigation.
(2) The notice given under paragraph (1) shall specify the conduct of the officer concerned which it is alleged failed to meet the appropriate standard and the paragraph of the Code of Conduct in respect of which the appropriate standard is alleged not to have been met.

9.88 The disclosure obligation under reg 14(1)(b) is broad and covers 'any' relevant statement, document, or other material in each case obtained during the course of the investigation. The key word is 'relevant', which must mean relevant to the matters set out in reg 14(2). The regulation does not limit this to matters relied on by the presenting side.

9.89 The disclosure obligation arises at the point at which the decision is taken to refer the matter to a hearing. It is not contingent on whether or not the officer concerned admits the conduct. The disclosure obligation is contended to be identical to that considered under the 2008 regime at 7.14 *et seq* (and see 9.95 below).

Drafting charges under reg 14

9.90 The obligation on the presenting side is to draft a charge that sufficiently particularizes the matters set out at reg 14(2). It is not required to draft an extensive statement of facts, but should particularize the conduct sufficiently to identify the substance of the complaint. A lack of particularity as to alleged supervisory failures was a legitimate ground for judicial review in *R (Wheeler) v AC House of the MPS*.[26] The Court referred (at [1.7]):

> . . . to the vagueness of the charges in the hope that in future charges will be more focused and more specific. It is sufficient if a charge is particularised subsequent to its being first formulated, but certainly it should be sufficiently particularised well before the hearing so that the respondent to disciplinary charges knows not just what it is alleged he failed to do, but in what respects he failed, so that he can then see whether or not, consistent with his other duties, he could or should have done that which it is alleged he should have done.

A statement of facts only becomes necessary if the affected officer indicates (under regs 18 and 21) that he accepts what is set out in the reg 14 notice. If he does so, a statement of facts under reg 21 is prepared and the associated procedure is followed. If not, then reg 21(3) expressly provides that no statement of facts will be prepared. **9.91**

To this extent, the practice of drafting extensive facts as part of the charge is apparently contrary to the 2004 Conduct Regulations. Certainly, in practice, it may be counterproductive in terms of promoting a bare acceptance by the affected officer that his conduct was in breach of the Code of Conduct. In criminal terms, what is required under reg 14 is a sufficiently particularized indictment, rather than a case summary. The factual basis of any admitted charge so particularized is addressed in reg 21. **9.92**

If the charge is contended to lack sufficient particularity, this may be raised directly with the presenting side and, if not resolved, directly with the misconduct panel. If the reg 21 statement cannot be agreed, then the misconduct panel should have the points of disagreement identified and determine a procedure to resolve them if it deems such resolution necessary. In all of this, the presenting officer is under a duty to act fairly and constructively, especially because the summary of facts and any response by the officer concerned must be supplied to the panel under reg 22(b). In practice, the process is usually conducted 'informally', and the original summary and the officer's response are not provided as such without consent. **9.93**

The role of the presenting officer

Where the Home Office Guidance makes clear[27] that 'the presenting officer's role is to help the officers taking the hearing to establish the facts of the case; he or she will not act as a prosecutor', this is contended to impose a greater rather than lesser **9.94**

---

[26] [2008] EWHC 439 (Admin).
[27] At para 3.50.

expectation of transparency in assisting the process of establishing the truth of a situation. This will include, for example, calling witnesses that go to the central facts even if they do not assist him, unless there is some positive reason to justify that the evidence is unworthy of belief. The duty is well established in the criminal context.[28]

9.95 The role is that of presenting (or making available to the defendant officer to present) all potentially relevant evidence that may reasonably bear on an issue. It is contended that the appropriate approach to disclosure (namely, applying the CPIA) is resolved rather than created by the 2008 Guidance (considered at 7.14 *et seq*) and that there should be a common approach under both sets of Regulations. The proceedings are such that career-ending adverse findings may result. The process is sufficiently flexible to accommodate considerations of public interest immunity.

9.96 Similarly, under reg 4 of the 2008 Conduct Regulations, a specific 'harm test' is introduced. This may be said to apply the considerations already rehearsed. It may properly be used as a template for the approach to discretion under the 2004 Conduct Regulations in the absence of express alternative provisions.

Other procedural steps before a hearing

9.97 The minimum requirements are essentially self-evident from the Regulations. Regulation 16 requires notification of the time, date, and place of the hearing at least twenty-one days before the hearing. Regulation 17 addresses legal representation.

Witness notification and attendance

9.98 Regulation 18 addresses 'Procedure on receipt of notice'. It has been, and remains, an important point of distinction with the 2008 Conduct Regulations. The officer concerned is required (upon notice that the last of the reg 14 documents has been supplied) to indicate whether: (i) he admits that his conduct did not meet the appropriate standard; (ii) where entitled under reg 17, whether he wishes to be legally represented (the right to legal representation for the presenting side under regs 23 or 25(2)(a) is contingent on this); and (iii) to notify whether he intends to call any witnesses 'to relevant facts' (but, importantly, neither who nor which), and the names and addresses of witnesses 'whose attendance he wishes to be secured' (but not those whose attendance he will secure himself).

---

[28] See *R v Russell-Jones (Kenneth)* [1995] 3 All ER 239, [1995] I Cr App R 538.

Additionally, by reg 18(2), if the witness whose attendance is to be secured is a **9.99** police officer, that officer 'shall be ordered to attend' (subject to such a request amounting to an abuse of process, this appears to be an absolute right), and, if not a police officer, the supervising officer must give due date and notice that attendance is required to the witness.

More importantly, subject to argument at any pre-hearing review, the officer **9.100** concerned is not required to filter his witness requirements through the misconduct panel applying a test of necessity. Obviously, the officer concerned may be required (as with criminal proceedings) to justify the attendance of a witness and the panel has discretion as to what procedure it follows. Paragraph (3) reiterates that nothing in the regulation requires the hearing to be adjourned simply for witness non-attendance. This is unremarkable and fact-specific in terms of the practical consequences.

Officers conducting the hearing

In relation to non-senior defendant officers, the basic position is addressed by **9.101** reg 19 in detailed terms. The chief officer makes appointments in investigations other than those arising under paras 17–19 of Sch 3 to the 2002 Act. Unless the power of remission is exercised under reg 33, and subject to some necessary qualifications in terms of rank for the City of London or Metropolitan police, the panel consists of three police officers of at least superintendent rank, presided over by an officer of at least the rank of assistant chief constable.

The qualifying Sch 3 investigation cases substitute one of the officers of at least **9.102** superintendent rank with a person selected by the police authority for the force concerned from a list maintained by that authority (see reg 19(5)).

It is to be observed that the chief officer may appoint officers from outside his own **9.103** force on this basis. Sometimes, this is done to promote public confidence in the outcome (for example, where the misconduct alleged reflects badly on the senior management of the home force, or resolution of the matter is otherwise 'political'). On other occasions, it has been done at the request of the officer concerned when the test for 'interested parties' is not met, but the conduct of the defence involves criticism of the home force that can only be seen to be fairly considered by a wholly independent panel.

By reg 22, prior to the hearing, the misconduct panel is supplied, as of right, with **9.104** very limited documentation indeed: namely, a copy of the notice (but not the material) under reg 14—that is, the reg 14(2) notice specifying the conduct that it is alleged failed to meet the appropriate standard—and, where such failure is admitted only, the statement of facts and any response under reg 21.

The contrast with reg 28 of the 2008 Conduct Regulations is clear. Apart from all **9.105** the relevant documents under regs 21, 22, and 45 (itself extensive, and including the investigating officer's report), by reg 28(1)(c), in contested cases under the 2008 Conduct Regulations the appropriate authority may supply in advance, as of right rather than by consent, 'any other documents that, in the opinion of the appropriate authority, should be considered at the misconduct proceedings'. As already observed, this discretion is open to abuse. Under the 2004 Conduct Regulations, it simply does not exist: documents supplied in advance for case management purposes must reflect the consent of the officer concerned.

Procedure at the hearing

9.106 Procedure at the hearing is addressed by reg 27. The narrow purpose of the procedure is as stated in para (2): those conducting the hearing 'shall review the facts of the case and decide whether or not the conduct of the officer concerned met the appropriate standard'. If the officer concerned admits the failure, this is evidence from which the panel may find that it did not meet the standard expected; otherwise, it must be proved to the civil standard.

9.107 If the standard is not met, by reg 27(7), the panel must then decide 'whether it is reasonable to impose any sanction, and if so which'.

9.108 The wide discretion afforded under reg 27(1) in terms of determining the appropriate procedure is reproduced in the 2008 Conduct Regulations. It is contended that no different principle arises as to its application. A hearing should be conducted according to contemporary standards of case management, which will involve directions as to the use of written documents for either side at each stage of the process. There is no reason in principle why opening and closing arguments cannot be reduced to writing, and it is often good practice and of assistance to the panel to do so.

9.109 Case management principles are addressed in Chapter 8, including the appropriate approach to adverse inferences (see 8.89 *et seq*), and the admissibility and use of hearsay evidence. Other regulations address, in a straightforward manner, considerations as to the attendance of the officer (reg 28), the attendance of the complainant and interested persons at the hearing (reg 29), the attendance of others at the hearing (reg 30), the exclusion of the public from the hearing in the public interest (reg 31), and statements in lieu of evidence (reg 32).

9.110 Remission of cases is addressed by reg 33. It must arise when a presiding officer appointed is an interested person otherwise than in his capacity as such (which is usually, of course, ascertained before appointment), or where the presiding officer in a hearing initially conducted with limited powers (that is, no reg 17 notice) determines that it should be a 'full powers' panel. In the latter situation, the presiding officer to whom it is so remitted shall not be given any indication of the initial presider's assessment of the case, or of the sanction that might be imposed. There is residual discretion (reg 33(5)) to remit at any point outside these contexts if 'considered appropriate'.

Sanctions

The range of sanctions is rehearsed at reg 35(2):   **9.111**

    (a) dismissal from the force;
    (b) requirement to resign from the force as an alternative to dismissal taking effect either forthwith or on such date as may be specified in the decision;
    (c) reduction in rank;
    (d) fine;
    (e) in the case of a special constable only, suspension from all or from operational duties only for a limited period of up to three months;
    (f) reprimand;
    (g) caution.

The maximum fine is effectively up to thirteen days' pay, which may only be   **9.112**
deducted at the rate of one day's pay per week.[29] The misconduct panel has no power itself to impose any other sanction as part of the misconduct procedure. This does not prevent the outcome resulting in management action (for example, as to immediate operational deployment, or retraining), as determined by the line management of the office concerned.

A misconduct panel would be justified in considering the philosophy of learning   **9.113**
and development over blame and punishment under the 2008 regime in the approach to sanction in future under the 2004 Conduct Regulations. Obviously, certain conduct will only merit dismissal under either.

Reviews and appeals

Any sanction may be made subject of a chief officer's review under reg 40 (see   **9.114**
Chapter 11). The only qualifying sanction for the purpose of an application to the police appeals tribunals is reduction in rank or above.

E. Senior Officers Under the 2004 Conduct Regulations

In reality, there are now very few proceedings under the 2004 Conduct Regulations   **9.115**
pending against senior officers,[30] and those that arise in future are likely to be few in number. For that reason only the central points of distinction with the conduct of proceedings against non-senior officers under the same Regulations

---

[29] This is expressed in more complicated language in reg 35(6).
[30] Who often seem to negotiate early retirements with their police authorities rather than face the rigours of a disciplinary process.

are rehearsed. It is emphasized that investigations under Sch 3 to the 2002 Act are not directly reflected in this analysis.

9.116 The central distinctive features of the applicable procedures are:

(i) the appropriate authority is the police authority in the force area (reg 3(1));

(ii) suspension must be notified and justified to the IPCC (reg 4(3)), which power may be exercised until the IPCC 'decide otherwise' (reg 4(5)(d));

(iii) suspension with immediate effect may be ordered by the chief officer (reg 5(1)(b)), subject to the provisions of reg 5(3);

(iv) no supervising officer to the investigation is appointed (reg 7);

(v) when appointed, the investigating officer is appointed by the appropriate authority (reg 8(6)), subject to the qualifications in reg 8(8)—that is, not the chief officer, and (other than the Metropolitan Police Service (MPS)), not in the same force, if the MPS is not in the same division;

(vi) the appropriate authority effectively performs the role of the supervising officer in terms of receipt, and action in respect, of the investigation report under regs 10–12;

(vii) if the senior officer accepts that his conduct did not meet the appropriate standard, the appropriate authority may impose one of the available sanctions under reg 35 without the need for a hearing (reg 13(1));

(viii) in any other case, whether or not the breach is admitted, the appropriate authority effectively has a residual discretion as to whether to refer the matter to a misconduct hearing (reg 13(4));

(ix) the persons conducting the hearing are defined by reg 20 (a single person maintained on a list of persons selected and maintained by the appropriate authority from a list of persons nominated by the Lord Chancellor, advised by one or more 'assessors' on 'matters pertaining to the police') and certain persons are disqualified from acting as assessors (reg 20(2)(a)–(c));

(x) subject to the right under reg 25 of the IPCC to present matters covered by a power of direction under para 27(4)(a) of Sch 3 to the 2002 Act, the case is presented by an independent solicitor as mentioned in reg 14(4), or some other independent solicitor or counsel (reg 24(1)). In either event the senior officer may be represented;

(xi) the reg 33 powers of remission do not apply;

(xii) at the conclusion of the hearing, by reg 27(8), the tribunal must 'as soon as possible' submit a 'report' to the appropriate authority, with a copy to the officer concerned, setting out:
(a) whether the conduct of the senior officer met the appropriate standard;
(b) if not, any recommendation as to sanction within reg 35(3); and

    (c) 'any other matter arising out of the hearing which it desires to bring to the notice of the appropriate authority';

(xiii) on receipt of the reg 27(8) report, under reg 35(3), the appropriate authority shall decide whether to dismiss the case, or:

    (a) to record that the conduct failed to meet the appropriate standard, but to take no further action; or

    (b) to record a finding and impose a sanction;

(xiv) the available sanctions (reg 35(4)) are:

    (a) dismissal;

    (b) requirement to resign as an alternative to dismissal taking effect either forthwith or on such date as may be specified in the recommendation or decision;

    (c) fine (calculated as for non senior officer); or

    (d) reprimand.

(xv) these matters must be notified in writing (reg 37(2) and a copy of the report of the tribunal and the decision of the appropriate authority (which, by implication, may—perhaps exceptionally and only with reasoned justification—be different) sent to the Secretary of State;

(xvi) with the notification of the appropriate authority decision must be notification of the right to appeal to the police appeals tribunals (reg 37(3)(a)). This represents the senior officer's only right of appeal. The provisions as to chief officer's reviews do not apply.

F. Conclusion

It will be seen that there are some significant differences as between the 2004 and 2008 regimes for non-senior officers. The 2008 regime is intended to reduce the proportion of reports of underperformance and positive misconduct that result in misconduct proceedings—particularly of a form that may end in loss of office. **9.117**

In practice, as applied to senior officers, a high proportion of reports were 'negotiated' away by the appropriate authority, tending, at times, to demoralize those non-senior officers to whom such pragmatism was not extended. Senior officers are subject to a much more similar procedure to non-senior officers under the 2008 regime and the relative treatment of officers of different ranks will require review. **9.118**

10

SPECIAL ('FAST-TRACK') CASES UNDER THE POLICE (CONDUCT) REGULATIONS 2004 AND 2008

A. Overview	10.01	
B. The Role of the Independent Police Complaints Commission (IPCC) and Crown Prosecution Service (CPS)	10.09	
Providing information to the affected officer and the complainant in Sch 3 cases	10.24	
C. Special Cases Under the 2004 Conduct Regulations	10.43	
Criteria for special cases under the 2004 Conduct Regulations	10.48	
The procedure for consideration in advance of the hearing	10.54	
The procedure for the hearing (paras 17–27 of the Appendix		

to ch 3 of the Home Office Guidance)	10.64	
Chief constable's review, special constables, and non-senior officers	10.70	
Appeal to the police appeals tribunals from a fast-track review	10.75	
D. Special Cases Under the 2008 Conduct Regulations	10.77	
Pre-hearing procedures	10.83	
Procedure following the decision to certify and refer to a special-case hearing	10.87	
Procedure at the special-case hearing	10.98	
Outcomes and notification	10.108	
E. Conclusion	10.110	

A. Overview

There is no conceptual difficulty with the need for a so-called 'special case' or 'fast-track' procedure. It is in the public interest that a police force be able to dismiss an officer where there is an overwhelming and unanswerable case of sufficiently serious criminal or gross misconduct without the need, for example, to await the outcome of criminal proceedings against him or others. Obviously, the regulations must—and do, quite sensibly—address the overlap with criminal proceedings. **10.01**

Aside from substantially compressing the timetable, which is already relatively tight (in theory) even for standard cases, the important effect of the special case **10.02** procedures is to take live witnesses out of the picture entirely, with the exception of the accused officer under the Police (Conduct) Regulations 2008.[1]

10.03 If, however, use of the procedures is not limited in practice to genuinely special (exceptional) cases, it is likely to generate significant injustice. The rights of the accused officer are heavily circumscribed at the special case hearing, and it is an unsatisfactory remedy to have to pursue an appeal to the police appeals tribunals. The delay and expense inherent in such an appeal does not serve the interests of either the officer or the force.

10.04 The use of the special case procedure under the Police (Conduct) Regulations 2004[2] was, in practice, limited to cases involving unanswerable proof of serious criminal conduct by the police officer: in terms, where the officer was caught 'red-handed'. This was consistent with the language of the 2004 Regulations and the associated 2004 Home Office Guidance on *Police Unsatisfactory Performance Complaints and Misconduct Procedures*, as amended. The 2008 Home Office Guidance—although not the 2008 Conduct Regulations—is still, following several revisions in drafting, expressed in language that is designed to limit their use to 'incontrovertible evidence' cases.

10.05 As with other guidance, the obligation is simply to 'have regard to' it. The Home Office Guidance is easy to change relative to statutory instruments. The application of it is also more flexible, as reflected in the introductory paragraphs to the 2004 and 2008 Guidance. There is discretion to depart from the Guidance where to do so would lead to a 'truer and fairer result', although the tribunal should not do so 'without good reason'. The 2004 and 2008 Conduct Regulations identify the decision maker at each stage, some bare criteria for use, and basic procedural matters. The Guidance adds detail to both sets of Regulations in respect of the purpose and use of the applicable special case procedures, and its importance is accordingly particularly high.

10.06 The obvious potential mischief is that it will always be tempting for an appropriate authority, chief officer, or the Independent Police Complaints Commission (IPCC) to invoke the special-case procedure where a police officer is suspected of misconduct justifying dismissal. There is almost invariably an arguable case on paper—but the accused officer has very limited rights in that procedure and the timetable is very short. Unless the criteria for invoking the procedure are narrowly interpreted, according to intended purpose, there is no doubt that, at some point, an affected officer will suffer unfair consequences.

---

[1] SI 2008/2864.
[2] SI 2004/645.

In that a constable (although not special constable) may appeal a qualifying **10.07** sanction to the police appeals tribunals, which retain discretion to admit oral evidence, using the procedure inappropriately produces no long-term advantage.

The relatively straightforward procedures under each of the 2004 and 2008 **10.08** Regulations are complicated by the provisions under the Police Reform Act 2002 in relation to the IPCC.

B. The Role of the Independent Police Complaints Commission (IPCC) and Crown Prosecution Service (CPS)

The context for the majority of special cases—that is, an investigation into seri- **10.09** ous crime or gross misconduct by serving police officers—will usually reflect the involvement of the IPCC and the Crown Prosecution Service (CPS). The IPCC was created, and the relevant provisions of the 2002 Act came into force, on 1 April 2004. Transitional arrangements have been addressed at 3.22–3.40.

Powers of direction in these respects, both as to certifying a matter as a special **10.10** case and the timing of any such proceedings, are addressed in Pt 3 of Sch 3 to the 2002 Act, and in particular paras 20 (general restrictions on criminal or disciplinary proceedings pending the conclusion of an investigation), 20A–L ('Accelerated procedure in special cases'; especially 20H, 'Special cases: recommendation or direction of Commission'), and 27 (duties and powers of direction with respect to disciplinary proceedings, covering both standard and special cases).

Paragraphs 20A, B, D(2), E, and G are amended by paras 6–10 of Sch 23 to the **10.11** Criminal Justice and Immigration Act 2008. These provisions substitute various statutory references with that of the person 'investigating the complaint or matter' and largely remove the notification obligations in relation to the Director of Public Prosecutions (DPP).

Although the procedures provide for a series of reports and recommendations **10.12** by, and to, the IPCC and the appropriate authority, ultimately, the IPCC has a power of direction covering discipline charges in respect of three of the four forms of investigation (that is, managed, supervised, or independent) set out in para 15(4) of Pt 3 of Sch 3 to the 2002 Act. If the powers of direction under para 27(4)(a) of that Act are used, reg 25(1) of the 2004 Conduct Regulations permits the IPCC, as distinct from the appropriate authority or supervising officer, to present the case.

Different considerations may apply if an appropriate authority is investigating the **10.13** matter for itself.

10.14 Paragraph 20H applies to investigations 'where the appropriate authority has submitted, or is required to submit, a memorandum to the Commission under paragraph 20B(7)', in which case, the Commission may make a recommendation to the appropriate authority that it should certify the case under para 20B(3). Paragraph 20B(7) effectively applies to investigations managed or carried out by the Commission.

10.15 Under para 20I(2) of Pt 3 of Sch 3 to the 2002 Act, where, in the case of an investigation of a complaint, the appropriate authority (i) notifies the Commission that it does not accept the recommendation made by the Commission under para 20H, or (ii) fails to certify the case under para 20B(3) and to proceed accordingly, 'it shall be the duty of the Commission to determine what (if any) further steps to take under paragraph 20H'.

10.16 As rehearsed below, the further steps under para 20H(7), for qualifying investigations, include the power to direct the appropriate authority to certify, and a duty on the appropriate authority to comply with the direction and proceed accordingly.

10.17 In any event, the special conditions required for invoking the special-case procedure are the same (para 20A(7) and (8)), and the appropriate authority is required in the first instance, in any case, to determine whether it is satisfied (para 20B(2)). If so, unless it considers that the circumstances are such as to make it inappropriate to do so, it shall certify it as such under reg 11 (para 20B(3)(a)), and notify the IPCC (para 20B(6)) and (before the amendments under the 2008 Act, which removes the requirement) the DPP, sending the latter a copy of the report (para 20B(5)).

10.18 By para 20G(1), on receiving a copy of a special report under paras 20B(5) or 20E(5) (investigations by appropriate authority on its own behalf), the DPP may request the appropriate authority not to bring disciplinary proceedings without his prior agreement, if the DPP considers that bringing such proceedings might prejudice any future criminal proceedings. This provision is removed by the amendments under the 2008 Act.

10.19 If, however, the appropriate authority determines either that the special conditions are not satisfied, or that, although satisfied, the circumstances are such as to make it inappropriate at present to bring disciplinary proceedings, it is required to send a reasoned memorandum to the IPCC (para 20B(7) and (8)). The IPCC must then consider whether to make a recommendation under para 20H.

10.20 If no such recommendation is made, that determination is notified to the appropriate authority (and those appointed in managed investigations (para 18), and designated to investigate in an IPCC independent investigation (para 19)).

By para 20H(1), where the appropriate authority has submitted, or is required to **10.21** submit, a memorandum to the Commission under para 20B(7), the Commission may make a recommendation to the appropriate authority that it should certify the case under para 20B(3). Paragraph 20H(6) provides that it shall be the duty of the appropriate authority to notify the Commission whether it accepts the recommendation, and, if it does, to certify the case and proceed accordingly.

If the recommendation is not accepted, the IPCC has a duty to determine **10.22** what further steps (if any) to take under para 20H (see para 20I(2)). There is a power of direction, and if, after the Commission has made a recommendation, the appropriate authority does not certify the case, the IPCC may direct the appropriate authority so to certify it, and it shall be the duty of the appropriate authority to comply with the direction and proceed accordingly (para 20H(7)).

The direction can extend to setting out the steps to be taken by the appropriate **10.23** authority in order to give effect to the recommendation (para 27(5)). Where the Commission gives the appropriate authority a direction, it shall supply the appropriate authority with a statement of its reasons for doing so (para 27(6)).

Providing information to the affected officer and the complainant in Sch 3 cases

Section 20 of the 2002 Act provides the statutory duty on the IPCC to keep the **10.24** complainant informed about the progress of the investigation, any provisional findings of the person carrying out the investigation, whether any report has been submitted under para 22 of Sch 3 to the 2002 Act, the action (if any) that is taken in respect of the matters dealt with in any such report, and the outcome of any such action. These duties are qualified by regulations[3] reflecting the public interest considerations in respect of disclosure at s 20(6)–(9).

The duty to provide this information to other persons is provided for in s 21: **10.25** whomever else it does involve, it includes neither the officer under investigation nor his representative.

Most of the stages under Sch 3 to the 2002 Act are accordingly coupled with **10.26** notification obligations relating to the complainant, whether the matter is a standard or a special case. Part 3 is no different in this respect. The more interesting consideration is that relating to the extent of what must be disclosed at each relevant stage. In general terms, it may be observed that the obligations to notify complainants, and the extent of what must be disclosed, are more extensive than those in respect of affected police officers. This can produce an unfair disparity in the context of high-profile investigations such as those following a death in

---

[3] Police (Complaints and Misconduct) Regulations 2004, SI 2004/643, reg 12.

custody, particularly when the implied duty of confidence is breached (see
R (Saunders) v IPCC and ors).[4]

10.27   The disclosure obligations in terms of the affected officer are essentially prescribed
by the applicable notification requirements within the Conduct Regulations.

10.28   In terms of the accelerated procedure under Pt 3 of Sch 3, if the appropriate
authority certifies the matter as a special case under para 20B(6), it is required
(under para 20C) to give a notification in the case of a complaint to the complainant, and to every person entitled to be kept properly informed in relation to
the complaint under s 21, and, in the case of a recordable conduct matter, to every
person entitled to be kept properly informed in relation to that matter under
that section.

10.29   Paragraph 20B applies only to managed, supervised, and independent investigations (that is, those coming within para 20A(3)), in which the investigator
must submit a statement of, and the grounds for, belief that the matter is a special
case, and a written report of the investigation to that point. This is the 'special
report' referred to for notification requirements.

10.30   If the matter is investigated by an appropriate authority on its own behalf,
identical duties arise under para 20E and, if certified as a special case under
para 20E(3), para 20F(2). Under these provisions, it is simply a 'report', as distinct
from 'special report', that is produced.

10.31   The notification required is one setting out the findings of the special report or
report, the appropriate authority's determination under para 20E(2), and the
action that the appropriate authority is required to take as a consequence of that
determination.

10.32   It would appear that notification of the 'findings of the special report/report' does
not necessarily mean providing the report itself. Paragraph 20C(4), and the
equivalent para 20F(4), provide that, subject to any other regulations:

> the Commission shall be entitled (notwithstanding any obligation of secrecy
> imposed by any rule of law or otherwise) to discharge the duty to give a person
> mentioned in sub-paragraph (1) notification of the findings of the special report by
> sending that person a copy of that report.

10.33   This is not an easy provision to interpret. It appears to permit the notification to
be made by sending the special report, although not requiring notification in this
manner. It appears to permit notification 'notwithstanding'[5] any obligation of
secrecy imposed by any rule of law or otherwise.

---

[4]   [2008] EWHC 2372 (Admin); [74]-[83].
[5]   The *Shorter Oxford English Dictionary* meaning being 'in spite of, without regard to or
prevention by'.

The resolution of this probably lies in regulations issued pursuant to s 20 of the **10.34** 2002 Act. Section 20(1) and (2) imposes the duty on the IPCC (or appropriate authority, if investigating on its own behalf) to keep the complainant (and others within s 21) informed of the matters listed in s 20(4). Paragraph 20C(3) of Pt 3 of Sch 3 provides that s 20(5)–(7) shall have effect in respect of the notification requirements on the IPCC. The same applies to the notification requirements under ss 20F (following certification by the appropriate authority under s 20E(3)) and 20H (recommendation by the IPCC to the appropriate authority to certify a case).

Section 20(5) provides that the duties imposed in respect of providing informa- **10.35** tion shall be performed, and shall have effect subject to such exceptions, as the Secretary of State may, by regulation, provide.

The applicable regulations are the Police (Complaints and Misconduct) Reg- **10.36** ulations 2004.[6] Regulation 12 provides a common set of criteria for exceptions to the duty to keep the complainant informed and to provide information for other persons in respect of the duties mentioned in ss 20(1) and (2) (duty to keep the complainant informed), and 21(6) and (7) (duty to provide information for other persons) of the 2002 Act, and in paras 23(9) and 24(7) of Sch 3 to that Act (action by the Commission or appropriate authority in response to an investigation report).

By reg 12(3) of the 2004 Complaints and Misconduct Regulations, the party **10.37** responsible for providing information is required to consider whether the non-disclosure is justified where (and these appear to be disjunctive criteria):

(a) that information is relevant to, or may be used in, any actual or prospective disciplinary proceedings;
(b) the disclosure of that information may lead to the contamination of the evidence of witnesses during such proceedings;
(c) the disclosure of that information may prejudice the welfare or safety of any third party;
(d) that information constitutes criminal intelligence.

There must be a 'real risk' of the disclosure of the information having a 'signifi- **10.38** cant' effect. 'Significant' is not defined and is not a straightforward word to define. In the context of the meaning of 'significant risk' in respect of sentencing for dangerous offenders under ss 224–229 of the Criminal Justice Act 2003, the Court of Appeal held, in *R v Lang*,[7] that it should be given a dictionary definition—that is, 'a higher threshold than mere possibility of occurrence', which 'can be taken to mean noteworthy, of considerable amount or importance'.

---

[6] SI 2004/643.
[7] *R v Lang and ors* [2005] EWCA Crim 2864, [2006] 2 Cr App R(S) 3, at [6], [7], [16], and [17].

10.39 Conversely, in the joined cases of *R v Stephens; R v Mujuru*,[8] the Court of Appeal held that the expression 'significant risk', when used in the context of the offence of causing or allowing the death of a child under s 5 of the Domestic Violence, Crimes and Disorder Act 2004, did not require this approach. The jury needed no direction on the meaning of the expression in the context of a test as to significant risk of serious harm to a child.

10.40 In the particular context, it is likely that a 'significant' risk of an adverse effect may appropriately be a low hurdle. A different approach properly applied in *Lang*, in which the consequence was a mandatory sentence. These matters were considered by the Administrative Court in *R (Saunders) v IPCC and ors*,[9] considered in greater detail at 14.91–14.93 below. Greater disclosure may be appropriate in inquest related proceedings if the recipient is a properly interested person, but, as always, the exercise of discretion is fact-sensitive.

10.41 There are other duties to provide basic information consistent with s 21 of the 2002 Act within Sch 3. These do not generate more extensive disclosure obligations than those already addressed, and are within reg 12 of the 2004 Complaints and Misconduct Regulations.

10.42 It is predicted that the IPCC will publish guidance as to the discharge of its statutory disclosure obligations in this and other contexts.

C. Special Cases Under the 2004 Conduct Regulations

10.43 The relevant provisions are reg 45, Pts 1 ('Conditions') and 2 ('Special cases: modifications [to the preceding regulations]') of Sch 2 to the 2004 Conduct Regulations, and the Appendix to ch 3 of the Home Office Guidance. This material is reproduced in full at Appendices C and I. It is, accordingly, not repeated extensively in this chapter. The references to paragraph numbers relating to the Home Office Guidance in this part of this chapter refer to the appendix to ch 3 unless the contrary is indicated.

10.44 The structure of the Regulations is somewhat clumsy, in that, rather than simply defining a discrete, self-contained, procedure for special cases, Pt 2 of Sch 2 of the 2004 Conduct Regulations provides a series of detailed 'modifications' to the preceding regulations in respect of standard cases. This requires cross-referencing for each such modification.

---

8   [2007] EWCA Crim 1249.
9   [2008] EWHC 2372 (Admin).

The Home Office Guidance, in relation to special cases, is divided into a num- **10.45**
ber of subheadings: (i) procedure for consideration in advance of hearing
(paras 10–16); (ii) procedure for the hearing (paras 17–27); (iii) chief constable's
review, special constables and non-senior officers (paras 28–38); and (iv) appeals
to the police appeals tribunals (paras 39–41). The primary features of each are
considered in turn.

The procedure at any hearing very largely speaks for itself from the terms of the **10.46**
modified Regulations and the associated Home Office Guidance. It is essentially
a paper exercise in terms of evidence coupled with oral submissions at the substantive hearing. Accordingly, the most important considerations are the process,
and criteria, by which a matter is determined to fall within the special-case
criteria.

Although not reflected in the modified Regulations, according to the Guidance **10.47**
(para 5), once the process has started, it may, at any time, be converted back
into a standard case, or a standard case may be converted into a fast-track case,
but 'on only one occasion either way'. This is presumed to mean one transfer per
investigation once it has been formally classified—that is, by the issue of a fast-
track notice (see reg 14, as modified, and para 11 of the Guidance)—as distinct
from considered for classification, under one head or the other.

Criteria for special cases under the 2004 Conduct Regulations

Regulation 45 is essentially an enabling regulation. The conditions that must be **10.48**
satisfied are prescribed by Pt 1 of Sch 2 of the 2004 Conduct Regulations,
as follows.

Conditions

(1) The conditions referred to in regulation 45 are—
   (a) the report, complaint or allegation indicates that the conduct of the officer concerned is
       of a serious nature and that an imprisonable offence may have been committed by the
       officer concerned; and
   (b) the conduct is such that, were the case to be referred to a hearing under regulation 11 and
       the tribunal or officers conducting that hearing were to find that the conduct failed to
       meet the appropriate standard, they would in the opinion of the appropriate officer or
       appropriate authority be likely to impose the sanction specified in regulation 35(2)(a)
       or (4)(a) (dismissal from the force); and
   (c) the report, complaint or allegation is supported by written statements, documents or
       other material which is, in the opinion of the appropriate officer or appropriate authority,
       sufficient without further evidence to establish on the balance of probabilities that the
       conduct of the officer concerned did not meet the appropriate standard; and
   (d) the appropriate officer or appropriate authority is of the opinion that it is in the public
       interest for the officer concerned to cease to be a member of a police force, or to be a
       special constable, without delay.
(2) In this paragraph an "imprisonable offence" means an offence which is punishable with
    imprisonment in the case of a person aged 21 or over.

10.49 Importantly, however, these provisions (which have a threshold that the allegation is supported, on paper, by material that is, in the opinion of the decision maker, 'sufficient without further evidence' to prove it) are supplemented by the terms of the Home Office Guidance. Conceptually, there would be very few allegations of serious misconduct that would not otherwise meet the test. On one view, and consistent with the two-stage (evidential sufficiency and public interest) approach taken in the Code for Crown Prosecutors,[10] any investigation into a serious offence should only result in a discipline charge if it is more likely than not that the charge will be proved. If the evidence is not sufficient without further evidence to provide a realistic prospect of the matter being proved, then there should be no charge.

10.50 Further, and self-evidently, it will always be in the public interest for such an officer to be removed without delay: what the qualification in para 1(d) is presumed to refer to is the necessity of waiting for proceedings affecting others (and possibly the officer himself), or sensitive investigations, to conclude before material is disclosed under the procedure to the accused officer. This discretion is reflected at para 3 of the Guidance.

10.51 Paragraph 2 of the Guidance sets the threshold test in more specific, and purposive, terms than the Regulations. It provides:

> In almost all circumstances, the procedures set out in the main part of section 3 will be applied. However, in a small number of cases, and only exceptionally, it will be appropriate to use the fast track procedures. They are designed to deal with cases of gross misconduct where an officer has been caught 'red handed' committing a serious crime, either as a single incident (for instance, a serious assault) or, more likely, after a long-running inquiry which uncovers serious apparent wrongdoing by a police officer (for instance, corruption).

10.52 It is observed that this test is unlikely to be satisfied when: (i) the officer concerned denies the allegation; and (ii) the proof of the allegation is, to any material degree, contingent on the reliability or accuracy of any witness or witnesses. For example, it is almost inevitably unsuitable for a disputed case of assault (that is, where there are competing versions of events, and a claim of self-defence), or a matter contingent on a disputed allegation of dishonesty or lack of integrity that is dependent on reported conversations rather than simply reflecting incontrovertible documentary proof.

10.53 The point is reinforced by reference to the procedure governing the admissibility of evidence at the hearing. The modified reg 15 ('no witness shall be called by either party to the case'), and paras 4–6 and 20 of the Guidance, are unambiguous

---

[10] Available online at <http://www.cps.gov.uk>.

that there will be no oral witness testimony at the fast-track hearing, including from the officer concerned. This makes it unrealistic to advance certain defences.

The procedure for consideration in advance of the hearing

A decision to fast track may be made at any stage during an inquiry into a report, **10.54** allegation, or complaint. In respect of a non-senior officer, the matter is referred by the head of professional standards to the chief officer (the appropriate officer) responsible to the chief constable—or Commissioner of the Metropolitan Police Service (MPS)—for complaints and discipline for consideration of invoking the procedure. In the case of a senior officer, the investigating officer will submit the case to the police authority or service authority. Where the matter is within any of the forms of an IPCC investigation, there is an extra layer of complication (see 10.09–10.42 above).

There is no express provision at this stage for the accused officer to challenge, **10.55** or have any role in, the determination that the matter be dealt with as a special case. It is contended that such an argument may be advanced at the hearing itself (see 10.65 below).

Regulation 12 of the Conduct Regulations is modified (by para 2 of Pt 2 of Sch 2) **10.56** to provide that 'at any time before the beginning of the hearing the appropriate authority (in the case of a senior officer) or appropriate officer (in the case of an officer other than a senior officer) may direct that the case be returned to the investigating officer or supervising officer, as the case may be'. This at least permits representations to be made on behalf of the accused officer as to the appropriateness of the procedure.

A decision to fast track a case attracts some formality. The appropriate officer **10.57** making the decision must give written notice, referred to as a 'fast-track notice' in the Home Office Guidance. Regulation 14 is substituted. In respect of a non-senior officer, an 'interview' is arranged at which the accused officer is served with the formal documents and copies of 'any relevant statement, document or other material obtained during the course of the investigation', and at which the process is explained. This may represent difficulties if the investigation is sensitive, and there is no express equivalent of the 'harm' test as rehearsed in reg 4 of the 2008 Conduct Regulations. There are provisions for alternative service if the affected officer does not attend this so-called interview. In the case of a senior officer, the written notice and copy document shall be given to the officer concerned by an independent solicitor instructed by the appropriate authority to this effect.

In terms of the notional timetable, reg 16 is amended to require the fixing of a **10.58** date for the hearing, which shall be not less than twenty-one and not more than twenty-eight days from the date on which notice is given under reg 14, and shall ensure that the officer concerned is forthwith notified of the time, date, and place of the hearing. Regulation 18, as modified, provides that the officer concerned should signify his or her intention to admit or deny the alleged breach of the Code of Conduct within fourteen days' notice under reg 14. By para 16 of the Guidance, however, this is expressed as not later than two weeks prior to the date of the hearing.

10.59 The modified reg 26 provides that the tribunal or the officer conducting the hearing may adjourn if it appears necessary or expedient to do so, but: (a) shall not exercise the power to adjourn more than once; and (b) shall not adjourn for longer than a period of one week or, on application by the officer concerned, an aggregated period of four weeks.

10.60 Paragraph 25 of the Guidance reproduces this, and adds:

> If either time expires and the hearing does not proceed, the case is to be referred back to the professional standards/complaints and discipline department or, in the case of a senior officer, the police authority/service authority, for standard track procedures to be applied or resumed (which is likely to await the outcome of criminal proceedings).

10.61 This provision is vulnerable to an argument that it alters the meaning of the regulation and, in any event, is overprescriptive as to consequences in terms of an adjournment. The answer may lie in the fact that this is guidance only, and departure from it may be justified with good reason to promote the objectives of the Conduct Regulations.

10.62 The written decision must be given within twenty-four hours after the conclusion of the hearing (para 22).

10.63 In respect of a senior officer, the tribunal may only recommend the outcome and/ or sanction that it considers appropriate to the relevant police authority. The police authority may dismiss the case, or direct that it be returned to the investigating officer, or take any of the action in reg 35(2) or (3). If either proved or admitted, para 23 of the Guidance anticipates that 'it is likely that the most severe punishment of dismissal will normally be appropriate'.

The procedure for the hearing (paras 17–27 of the Appendix to ch 3 of the Home Office Guidance)

10.64 By para 17 of the Home Office Guidance, the fast-track hearing for special constables and non-senior officers is presided over by the chief constable (or the Assistant Commissioner in the MPS), or, if that person is not 'appropriate' (not defined, but presumably disqualified by either bias or unavailability), by the chief constable of another force. The chief constable is provided with the papers seven days prior to the hearing. A fast-track hearing for a senior officer is presided over by a tribunal as specified at reg 20 (see also para 3.62 of the Guidance).

It is contended that the potential for an accused officer to challenge the use of the **10.65** fast-track procedure arises as a necessary implication of the range of orders open to the chief constable under para 20 of the Appendix to ch 3 of the Guidance. The chief constable has no power to hear oral testimony, but must invite submissions 'as to why the officer concerned should not be found to have breached the Code as alleged on the basis of the evidence provided'.

After hearing such submissions, he can either: **10.66**

(a) find that the conduct has not been proved; or

(b) decide that the matter requires further inquiry or testing of the evidence, and refer it back for standard-track proceedings (which is likely to await the outcome of criminal proceedings) to the stage of the appointment of the investigating officer; or

(c) decide that the conduct has been proved.

It is contended that the submissions on behalf of the accused officer must be **10.67** capable of addressing each of these outcomes. This is an appropriate, and logical, reading down of the right to make submissions as to why the officer should not be found to have breached the Code. Given that the likely alternative in most cases to a finding under (b) will be a finding that the matter is proved, followed by dismissal, this is fair to the accused officer and the force. It is consistent with the range of orders open on a review of a fast-track hearing, which includes a decision (para 36(b)) that the case should not have been fast tracked.

There is no threshold test under para 20(b). It is contended that the test should **10.68** be that there is a 'real possibility' that further enquiry or testing evidence could affect either the finding or sanction. If the test is set higher than that—that is, as 'more likely than not' to produce a different outcome—it is probable that avoidable chief constable's reviews and appeals to the police appeals tribunals will result.

Equally, if set too low—that is, as a 'remote' rather than 'real' possibility of a **10.69** different outcome on further enquiry or testing—the legitimate purpose of the procedure, particularly given the nature of the right of appeal to the police appeals tribunal, would be lost. The police authority should not remain liable to pay an officer, who will invariably be suspended from duty, from limited public resources based on a remote possibility of a different outcome.

Chief constable's review, special constables, and non-senior officers

The review by the chief constable afforded by the standard-track procedures **10.70** is replicated in the fast-track procedures by a review conducted by a chief constable from another force. An Assistant Commissioner from the MPS can undertake a review for another force. The review may concern either the finding that the Code of Conduct had been breached or the level of sanction imposed, or both. The affected officer's chief constable will be similarly bound by the 'recommendation' of the appointed chief constable.[11]

10.71 The process of the review should be as described in ch 4 of the Home Office Guidance (addressed in Chapter 11). Under para 30 of the Appendix to ch 3, a written notice must be served within fourteen days of receipt of written notification of the decisions of the original hearing, and should state whether a meeting is required.

10.72 The officer should be provided 'without delay' with 'access to such parts of the recording or verbatim notes of the hearing as are necessary to establish the specific grounds for the request for the review'. 'Access to' and 'necessary' qualify the expectation that a full set of papers and transcript is available as a right of the affected officer. Given the sensitive background to many of these cases, this is not intrinsically surprising. Although, in practice, this discretion may be filtered in the first instance through the force solicitor, ultimately, it must be a decision for the chief constable conducting the review.

10.73 The review should be carried out within thirty days of the written notification of the original decision (para 31), and, if a meeting is required, seven days' written notice should be given to the officer (para 34). There is discretion in the chief officer 'and the officer concerned' as to who may attend in addition to those who are entitled to be present under para 34. Those entitled to be present include the complainant. The meaning of 'and the officer concerned' in this context is unclear. The consent of the officer concerned is not required at a review, and the list of those entitled to be present does not exclude the possibility of others.[12]

10.74 There are four possible decisions (set out in para 36) and associated outcomes (para 37). If the outcome is a sanction that qualifies for an appeal to the police appeals tribunals, this must be notified in the decision. The combined effect is as follows:

(i) that the conduct had not been proved to the required standard—in which case, the earlier decision will be quashed and the officer concerned reinstated; or

(ii) that the case should not have been fast tracked—in which case, the outcome will be quashed and the case referred back to the officer's force professional standards, or complaints and discipline, department for consideration of standard tracking the matter; or

---

[11] See *R (Bolt) v Chief Constable of Merseyside Police (with Chief Constable of North Wales Police as an interested party)* [2007] EWHC 2607 (Admin) at [22]–[24].

[12] See *R (IPCC) v Chief Constable of the West Midlands Police (Howarth)* [2007] EWHC 2715 (Admin).

(iii) that the conduct was proved, but the sanction imposed was too severe—in which case, the reviewing officer will substitute another, less severe, sanction, which can include no further action; or

(iv) that the decision was correct.

Appeal to the police appeals tribunals from a fast-track review

This is set out at paras 39–41 of the Appendix to ch 3 of the Home Office **10.75** Guidance. It is available to those officers (but not special constables) who have been dismissed, required to resign, or reduced in rank. The matter is addressed at ch 5 of the Guidance and in more detail at 11.45 *et seq*. Differences for senior officers are set out at paras 3.98–3.101 of the Guidance and at 11.61.

There are few special provisions relative to a straightforward appeal. The police **10.76** appeals tribunals, accordingly, have discretion to receive oral evidence. By para 40, the right of appeal is to a tribunal set up by the affected police officer's own police authority. An officer may defer exercising the right to appeal until four weeks after the conclusion of criminal proceedings or a CPS decision not to bring criminal proceedings. An extension may be granted at the discretion of the police authority.

D. Special Cases Under the 2008 Conduct Regulations

The relevant provisions are set out in Pt 5 of the 2008 Conduct Regulations— **10.77** namely, regs 41–57. The revocation of the 2004 Conduct Regulations and transitional arrangements are as set out at reg 2. They are associated with detailed guidance in Appendix A to the 2008 Home Office Guidance. This material is reproduced in full at Appendices G and I. It is, accordingly, not repeated extensively in this chapter. References to paragraph numbers relating to the Home Office Guidance in this part of this chapter refer to Appendix A of the 2008 Guidance unless otherwise stated.

Given the common purposes, there is a significant degree of overlap with the pro- **10.78** cedures under the 2004 Conduct Regulations. Equally, there are differences— particularly as to the expectation under the 2008 procedures that the accused officer will submit a detailed written response, and evidence, in relation to the allegation, and may be asked questions as to his account at the hearing. The possibility of oral evidence from the affected officer somewhat changes the character of the hearing. Additionally, as with ordinary misconduct hearings, the right to a chief constable's review is abolished. The right of appeal to the police appeals tribunals is preserved by reg 58.

The bare criteria for a matter to qualify as a special case are somewhat buried in the **10.79** interpretation section (reg 3) of the 2008 Conduct Regulations. By reg 3(2)(c), the special conditions are that: (i) there is sufficient, in the form of written statements or other documents, without the need for further evidence, whether written or oral, to establish on the balance of probabilities that the conduct of the officer concerned constitutes gross misconduct; and (ii) it is in the public interest for the officer concerned to cease to be a police officer without delay. By reg 3(1), 'gross misconduct' means a breach of the Standards of Professional Behaviour that is so serious that dismissal would be justified.

10.80 In practice, (ii) will only apply if use of the special-case procedure would not tend to compromise a criminal investigation or trial. The threshold under (i) is no different from that used to justify any gross misconduct allegation, which obviously generated the unwelcome possibility that the special-case procedure could be used routinely rather than exceptionally. The protection against this outcome (and it is suggested this protection should have been incorporated into the Regulations, rather than simply the relatively easily amended Guidance) is found in para 2 of Annex A to the Guidance. Having rehearsed the special conditions, it adds:

> These procedures are therefore designed to deal with cases where the evidence is incontrovertible in the form of statements, documents or other material (eg CCTV) and is therefore sufficient without further evidence to prove gross misconduct and it is in the public interest, if the case is found or admitted for the police officer to cease to be a member of the police service forthwith.

10.81 It may be observed that there is nothing intrinsic to the Regulations to justify the assertion that 'these procedures are therefore designed ...', etc. The assertion as to 'design' no doubt reflects the history of special-case procedures, and detailed statutory consultation prior to the publication of the 2008 Home Office Guidance. It is an important qualification as to intended use given the language of the Conduct Regulations. The points rehearsed at 10.48–10.52 apply equally here.

10.82 As with the procedure under the 2004 Conduct Regulations, the Guidance spells out that the special-case procedures can only be used if the appropriate authority certifies the case as a special case, having determined that the 'special conditions' are satisfied, or if the IPCC has given a direction under para 20H(7) of Sch 3 to the 2002 Act.

Pre-hearing procedures

10.83 The procedures to determine the referral (or not) of a matter as a special case are found within reg 41, and paras 9 and 10 of Annex A to the Guidance. The decision is activated by an investigator's report under reg 18(3). For non-senior officers, the decision must be certified by a senior officer—that is, holding a rank above that of chief superintendent (see reg 3). For senior officers, the decision and certification is by the police authority. If certifying and referring may compromise criminal proceedings, the decision may be delayed (reg 41(2) and (3)). Further, the matter may be referred back to the investigator, if the investigation is found to be incomplete, in order to complete the investigation (reg 41(5)).

There are essentially three options in any other context—that is: (i) to certify as a **10.84** special case and refer it to a special-case hearing; (ii) to determine that the special conditions are not satisfied; or (iii) to determine that, although the special conditions are satisfied, the circumstances are such as to make certification inappropriate. This appears to mean inappropriate for reasons other than compromising a criminal investigation by virtue of regs 9(3), and 41(2) and (3).

In relation to either (ii) or (iii), the matter thereafter proceeds under the ordinary **10.85** procedures of Pt 4 of the 2008 Conduct Regulations.

Regulation 42 permits the appropriate authority (other than in a case in which the **10.86** IPCC has given a direction under para 20H(7) of Sch 3 to the 2002 Act) to direct that the case be dealt with under Pt 4 'at any time before the beginning of the special case hearing' if it considers that the special conditions are no longer satisfied. It clearly permits the affected officer to make representations as to the certification as a special case, either directly or as part of the required written submissions within the procedure.

Procedure following the decision to certify and refer to a special-case hearing

Under reg 43, the officer affected thereafter becomes entitled to a copy of the **10.87** certificate under reg 41(1), any statement that he may have made to the investigator during the course of the investigation, and, subject to the harm test under reg 4: (i) the investigator's report or such parts of that report as relate to him (together with any document attached to or referred to in that report 'as it relates to him'); and (ii) any other relevant document gathered during the course of the investigation. The notice shall 'describe' the conduct that is the subject matter of the case and how that conduct is alleged to amount to gross misconduct. It is observed that the Home Office Guidance does not reproduce these matters accurately, and the Regulations must take precedence.

The definition of relevance for disclosure purposes is left to the appropriate **10.88** authority: reg 43(3) defines 'relevant document' as a document that, in the opinion of the appropriate authority, is relevant to the affected officer's case. This must, as a matter of basic fairness, mean documents within the possession of, or otherwise available to, the appropriate authority that are, or may be, relevant to defence of the charge, as well as its proof.

The affected officer assumes extended obligations under the 2008 Conduct **10.89** Regulations, mirroring the pattern for ordinary cases under Pt 4. The critical obligations arise under reg 45, as follows.

Procedure on receipt of notice

(1) Within 7 working days of the date on which the written notice and documents to be supplied to the officer concerned under regulation 43(1) are so supplied, the officer concerned shall provide to the appropriate authority—

    (a) written notice of whether or not he accepts that his conduct amounts to gross misconduct;

    (b) where he accepts that his conduct amounts to gross misconduct, any written submission he wishes to make in mitigation;

    (c) where he does not accept that his conduct amounts to gross misconduct, written notice of—

        (i) the allegations he disputes and his account of the relevant events; and

        (ii) any arguments on points of law he wishes to be considered by the person or persons conducting the special case hearing.

(2) At the same time, the officer concerned shall provide the appropriate authority and the person conducting or chairing the special case hearing with a copy of any document he intends to rely on at the hearing.

10.90 This timetable is obviously short in the extreme. No suggested sanction for failing to meet it is provided in either the Regulations or associated Home Office Guidance. Paragraph 12 of the related Guidance provides, additionally, that the date of the hearing ('meeting') will be not less than ten working days and not more than fifteen working days from the date on which the special case certificate and other documents are served.

10.91 There is no reason why these written arguments of law should not address the certification and referral of the matter under the special-case procedure. The appropriate authority is then at liberty to remit the case to Pt 4 where appropriate under reg 42.

10.92 Whether the special-case hearing has power to do this is more difficult and addressed at 10.98 *et seq* and 10.108 *et seq* below. There is no express equivalent of the 2004 power, however, to decide that the matter requires further inquiry or testing of the evidence, and refer it back for standard-track proceedings (which is likely to await the outcome of criminal proceedings) to the stage of the appointment of the investigating officer.

10.93 The Regulations thereafter address procedural matters preceding the substantive hearing. The documents to be supplied to any person conducting the hearing (reg 49) include all of the documents identified to date, and any others that the appropriate authority finds should be considered. These must all be supplied to the affected officer 'prior to the hearing'. Late service, as ever, runs the risk of an application to exclude evidence or to adjourn.

10.94 There is no provision at this point for service of documents withheld from the officer under the reg 4 harm test. It is presumed that the procedure for such harmful documents is within the discretion of the hearing to set its own procedure under reg 54(1). There will be circumstances in which the appropriate authority would wish the tribunal, but not the accused officer, to see certain sensitive material. Whether this can be achieved fairly in any individual case will be contingent on the precise context. Self-evidently, however, if such material is relied on in evidence, the circumstances will have to be exceptional to justify admissibility without disclosure.

There is no obligation on the appropriate authority to respond to material pro- **10.95**
vided by the affected officer under reg 45. It is contended that, in most cases, a written response would be good practice and a formal written opening note is becoming standard practice.

Other regulations address the attendance of the officer concerned (reg 50), the **10.96**
participation of the IPCC and investigator (reg 51, including the power in the person chairing the hearing to require the attendance of the investigator under reg 51(3) 'to answer questions'), the attendance of the complainant and interested persons at special-case hearing (reg 52, which is limited to investigations under paras 16–19 of Sch 3 to the 2002 Act, or as certified under para 19B(1) of that Sch—that is, assessment of seriousness of conduct—with observer status only and no right to attend for mitigation or sanction), and attendance of others as nominated by the IPCC in limited qualifying circumstances (reg 53).

The detail and effect of these matters are largely self-evident from the Regulations. **10.97**
The material consideration in the majority of special cases is the procedure at the hearing itself.

Procedure at the special-case hearing

Regulation 53(1) provides that, subject to reg 52, the special-case hearing shall be **10.98**
in private. The provision as to the IPCC directing that the whole, or part, of misconduct hearing may be in public under reg 32(5) appears to be limited to a misconduct hearing under Pt 4, as distinct from a special-case hearing under Pt 5. 'Misconduct hearing' and 'special-case hearing' have specific and different definitions under reg 2.

The critical procedural provisions are set out in reg 54. There is considerable **10.99**
discretion built in as to the procedure generally ('subject to these regulations', the person chairing 'shall determine the procedure'—reg 54(1)), adjournments (not other than exceptionally solely to permit the complainant or any interested person to attend, but otherwise where necessary or expedient—reg 54(3) and (4)), and admission of additional documents not served in advance (reg 54(9)).

In a change from the 2004 special-case procedure, by reg 54(5), although there **10.100**
will be no other oral evidence, the officer concerned is permitted to give evidence.

This may be to promote a fuller inquiry and restrict avoidable appeals to the police appeals tribunals. Perhaps unnecessarily, reg 54(8) adds that 'the police friend or relevant lawyer of the officer concerned may not answer any questions asked of the officer concerned during the special case hearing'. This must be read down as applying to questions of fact (that is, evidence), as distinct from matters of law.

10.101 The additional rationale for these changes may lie in the availability of the adverse inference from silence when questioned, reflected in reg 54(10) and (11). Without the opportunity for the affected officer to explain his earlier silence on a particular issue, it would be arguably unfair in any case to draw an adverse inference. Whether it is drawn is another matter entirely: an officer interviewed in criminal proceedings may well be justified in remaining silent for that purpose and it may be unfair to draw an adverse inference from it in misconduct proceedings. Interviews and adverse inferences are addressed at 7.134 *et seq* and 8.86 *et seq*.

10.102 Regulation 54(6) permits the person representing the officer concerned to address the hearing in order to do any or all of the following:

   (i)   to put the case of the officer concerned;

   (ii) to sum up that case;

   (iii) to respond on behalf of the officer concerned to any view expressed at the proceedings; and

   (iv) to make representations concerning any aspect of proceedings under the Regulations.

10.103 The only express power given to those conducting the special-case hearing is (reg 54(13)) to review the facts of the case and decide whether or not the conduct of the officer concerned amounts to gross misconduct. If it is not found to amount to gross misconduct, the options appear to be (reg 55(5)) either to dismiss the case or to return it to the appropriate authority to deal with under Pt 4. This presumably means to deal with as an allegation not amounting to gross misconduct under the Regulations, and para 17 of the associated Home Office Guidance suggests that the referring back to standard procedures 'may be because the person(s) conducting the hearing consider that the conduct is misconduct rather than gross misconduct'. Given the terms of the regulation, it is difficult to see what wider meaning it can have.

10.104 What is not addressed is the wholly foreseeable situation whereby the special-case hearing decides, notwithstanding questions asked of the investigator and/or affected officer, that either: (i) further enquiry would be beneficial; or (ii) whilst the matter would amount to gross misconduct if proved, the Pt 5 procedure is inappropriate (that is, the evidence is not incontrovertible and live oral testimony is required from a witness other than the officer).

As has been said, the power of the appropriate authority to remit under reg 42(1) **10.105** applies only to any time before the beginning of the special-case hearing. Paragraph 18 of the Guidance overlooks this language, and provides that:

> there is power under regulation 42 for the appropriate authority to remit the case to be dealt with under the standard procedures at any time. This might be because he, she or it considers that a particular witness whose evidence is crucial to the case and is disputed must be called to give oral testimony.

Taken at its highest, this appears to be a presumed power in the appropriate **10.106** authority, rather than a discretion enjoyed by those conducting the special-case hearing. It is unlikely that accused officers will regard the appropriate authority as having an unbiased and objective opinion on this point. It is not, however, easy to read down the language of the Regulations to import the power, either in the appropriate authority or, still less, those conducting the hearing.

Faced with such a scenario, the special-case hearing faces an invidious choice **10.107** between finding a matter proved (whilst believing that relevant oral evidence should be heard), dismissing it (believing gross misconduct proved, but to be fair procedurally), or reverting to Pt 4 as a misconduct allegation. In practice, assuming an adverse finding and a qualifying resultant sanction, the likely outcome is an appeal to the police appeals tribunals, coupled with an application to hear the additional oral evidence.

Outcomes and notification

These are addressed by regs 55–58 of the 2008 Conduct Regulations, and cover **10.108** outcome of the special-case hearing (reg 55), notification of outcome (reg 56), the record of special-case hearing (reg 57—a verbatim record to be supplied on request to the officer), and the record of disciplinary proceedings (Pt 6, reg 58).

The available sanctions are a final written warning, an extension of a final written **10.109** warning, or dismissal without notice. Only the latter attracts the right to appeal to the police appeals tribunals. There is no chief constable's review under the 2008 Regulations. Under reg 55(8), there appears to be no provision to receive oral evidence as to character before sanction is determined.

E. Conclusion

It will be seen that the special-case procedures, whilst necessary, are somewhat **10.110** unsatisfactory in execution. Certain of the flaws inherent in the 2004 special-case procedures (particularly the lack of oral evidence from the affected officer) have been remedied.

10.111 The 2008 procedures generate different difficulties. The special conditions criteria are dangerously close to those justifying a gross misconduct charge. The lack of express power in the special-case hearing (or even in the appropriate authority once it has begun) to remit a case that would clearly amount to gross misconduct to the Pt 4 procedure to reflect the necessity of either further enquiry or oral evidence from a party other than the officer is a genuine flaw, with foreseeable practical consequences.

10.112 The potential unfairness of these and other features of the new scheme is compounded by the restricted rights of appeal following an adverse outcome. Chief officer reviews are abolished and, as is addressed in Chapter 11, the Police Appeals Tribunals Rules (PAT Rules) 2008[13] significantly restrict the bases for appeal. One can expect the Administrative Court to be kept busy for a period of time if the procedures are misused by appropriate authorities.

---

[13] SI 2008/2863.

11

CHIEF OFFICER REVIEWS, INTERNAL APPEALS, AND POLICE APPEALS TRIBUNALS

A. Overview	11.01	Limitation periods	11.62
B. Chief Officer's Review Under		Procedure on notice of appeal	11.64
the 2004 Conduct Regulations	11.08	Procedure at the hearing	11.66
Chief officer reviews: core provisions		Attendance and power to compel	
under the 2004 Conduct Regulations		witness attendance	11.67
and the Home Office Guidance	11.10	The statement of the tribunal's	
The officer conducting the review	11.12	determination and record of	
Who may attend	11.21	proceedings	11.70
The scope of the review	11.26	Appeals under the 2008 PAT	
Interpretation of chief officer review		Rules	11.72
provisions by the Administrative		The nature of the jurisdiction	
Court	11.33	exercised by the police appeals	
The right to participate		tribunals under the 2008	
in the hearing	11.38	PAT Rules	11.75
The outcome of the review	11.39	Notice of appeal, the procedure	
C. Senior Officer Appeals	11.44	on receipt of notice, and time	
D. The Police Appeals Tribunals	11.45	limits	11.87
Statutory basis	11.45	Review of appeal and dismissal	
Common features: Police Act 1996,		on the papers	11.99
s 85 and Sch 6	11.49	Determination without	
Appeals under the 1999 PAT		a hearing	11.101
Rules	11.54	The procedure for determining	
The nature of the jurisdiction		the hearing	11.102
exercised by the police appeals		The statement of the tribunal's	
tribunals under the 1999 PAT		determination	11.109
Rules	11.54	E. Conclusion	11.112
Respondent	11.61		

A. Overview

11.01 It is relatively straightforward to identify the right of review or appeal under any particular set of Conduct or Performance Regulations. Less straightforward is the nature of discretion exercised by a particular review or appellate body, which varies, and is less easy to define than the appellate jurisdiction exercised in civil or criminal proceedings. The nature of the discretion differs significantly for the police appeals tribunals as between matters determined under the Police Appeals Tribunals Rules (PAT Rules) 1999[1] from those under the PAT Rules 2008.[2]

11.02 The officer's right of 'review' by a chief constable from a qualifying finding at a misconduct hearing under reg 40 of the Police (Conduct) Regulations 2004[3] was new, ill-defined, and did not work satisfactorily for any party in practice. It is not reproduced under the Police (Conduct) Regulations 2008.[4] The relatively short provisions covering such reviews, intended to create a flexible and fast remedy for clear error, generated at least four substantive applications for judicial review as to purpose and effect.

11.03 Such wholly internal reviews tended to demonstrate the tensions inherent in any consideration of one senior officer's decision by another senior officer from the same force. It is not easy to overrule a working colleague. The Police (Performance) Regulations 2008[5] considered in Chapter 5 create a series of internal appeals that run the same risk.

11.04 The 2008 PAT Rules extend the jurisdiction of the police appeals tribunals to include certain matters of performance under the 2008 Performance Regulations, and to act as the only review or appeal tribunal from qualifying findings under the 2008 Conduct Regulations. Section 85 of the Police Act 1996 is amended, and the resultant 2008 PAT Rules create a right for an appeal to be dismissed by the chair without the necessity of a full tribunal, permit sanction to be increased, and (subject to interpretation) introduce a higher threshold for intervention (by defining—and thereby restricting—the grounds of appeal) by the tribunals than existed under the 1999 PAT Rules.

---

[1] SI 1999/818, as amended by the Police Appeals Tribunals (Amendment) Rules 2003, SI 2003/2597, and the Serious Organised Crime and Police Act 2005 (Consequential and Supplementary Amendments to Secondary Legislation) Order 2006, SI 2006/594.
[2] SI 2008/2863, in force 1 December 2008.
[3] SI 2004/645.
[4] SI 2008/2864.
[5] SI 2008/2862.

The changes reduce the qualifying legal experience required of a chair to bring it **11.05**
in line with other tribunals covered by the Administrative Justice and Tribunals
Council.[6]

The practical effect is that the 2004 Conduct Regulations provide for a chief **11.06**
officer's review from any finding or sanction under those regulations at the initiative of the affected officer. The Police (Efficiency) Regulations 1999,[7] and 2004
Conduct Regulations, generate rights of appeal that are determined under the
1999 PAT Rules. The 2008 Performance Regulations and 2008 Conduct
Regulations generate rights of appeal that will be determined under the 2008
PAT Rules. The 2008 PAT Rules do not create any right for the presenting side to
appeal an outcome to the tribunals. Section 85 of the 1996 Act continues to
restrict this right to the affected officer.

These matters are reflected in Table 11.1. **11.07**

B. Chief Officer's Review Under the 2004 Conduct Regulations

Regulation 40 of the 2004 Conduct Regulations introduced the right for an **11.08**
officer (other than a senior officer) to seek a review by a chief officer of any finding
or sanction under reg 35. The rights of senior officers are addressed at 11.44
below, but effectively are restricted to the rights of appeal to a police appeals
tribunals.

The chief officer review is effectively abolished under the 2008 Conduct **11.09**
Regulations. Both the Morris Inquiry[8] (14 December 2004) and the Taylor
Review of Police Disciplinary Arrangements Report[9] (January 2005) raised concerns
as to reviews. The nature and purpose of the review was not settled with any
precision until a series of cases at the Administrative Court in 2007 and 2008.
In practice, there was a wholly unsatisfactory lack of certainty as to both procedure and substance. As to the latter, the critical question is what test a chief
officer applies on review before intervening. As will be seen, this question, although
now answered, continues to permit flexibility in approach dependent on
context.

---

[6] Formerly, the Council of Tribunals.
[7] SI 1999/732.
[8] *The Report of the Morris Inquiry: An Independent Inquiry into Professional Standards and Employment Matters in the MPS*, available online at <http://www.mpa.gov.uk>.
[9] Available online at <http://www.press.homeoffice.gov.uk>.

Table 11.1 Summary of rights review and appeal under efficiency, performance, and misconduct regulations 1999–2008

Officer	Applicable regulations	Chief officer review?	Qualifying outcome	Applicable PAT Rules
Senior officer (ie above rank of chief superintendent)	Police (Conduct) Regulations 2004 SI 2004/645	No	Dismissal, requirement to resign, or reduction in rank	1999
	Police (Conduct) Regulations 2008 SI 2008/2864	No	Finding of misconduct or gross misconduct, and any associated disciplinary action, made at a misconduct meeting, misconduct hearing, or special case hearing	2008
Non-senior officers	Police (Efficiency) Regulations 1999 SI 1999/732	No	Dismissal, requirement to resign, or reduction in rank	1999
	Police (Conduct) Regulations 2004 SI 2004/645	Yes	Dismissal, requirement to resign, or reduction in rank	1999
	Police (Performance) Regulations 2008 SI 2008/2862	No	From third-stage meeting under reg 26: dismissal or reduction in rank	2008
			From third-stage meeting under reg 28: (a) dismissal with or without notice; (b) reduction in rank; (c) redeployment to alternative duties; (d) the issue of a final written improvement notice; or (e) the extension of a final written improvement notice	
	Police (Conduct) Regulations 2008 SI 2008/2864	No	Finding of misconduct or gross misconduct, and any associated disciplinary action, at a misconduct meeting, hearing, or special case hearing	2008

Chief officer reviews: core provisions under the 2004 Conduct Regulations and the Home Office Guidance

The basic provisions are regs 40 (request for a review, officers other than senior **11.10** officers), 41 (conduct of the review), 42 (finding of the review), and 43 (hearing in the absence of chief officer). These regulations are supplemented by the associated Home Office Guidance—in particular, ch 4. In this context, the detailed provisions are found in the Guidance.

The Regulations themselves are silent as to the purpose of a review or the test to **11.11** be applied. Procedurally, a request for a review must be made to the reviewing officer in writing within fourteen days of receipt of the written summary of reasons given in accordance with reg 37(1), unless this period is extended by the reviewing officer. The request for a review 'shall state the grounds on which the review is requested and whether a meeting is requested'.

The officer conducting the review

In most cases, the review is conducted by a chief officer (defined in s 29 of the **11.12** Police Reform Act 2002 as the chief officer of police of any police force), or, in respect of a member of the Metropolitan Police Service (MPS) or a special constable appointed for the Metropolitan police district, the Assistant Commissioner.

By reg 43(1), where the chief officer is an interested party or the circumstances in **11.13** s 12A(1) or (2) of the 1996 Act—that is, forces with assistant chief constables—or s 54(1) of the Police Act 1997—that is, deputy director-general of the National Crime Squad (NCS)—apply, the review shall be conducted by the deputy chief constable or assistant chief constable designated under s 12A(2) of the 1996 Act, or, in the case of members of the NCS, by the deputy director-general of that squad. By reg 43(2), where the deputy chief constable or designated assistant chief constable is absent or an interested party, the review shall be conducted by the chief officer of another force who has agreed to act in that capacity.

As to the meaning of 'interested party', this is not defined in the 2002 Act. **11.14** Regulation 33 of the 2004 Conduct Regulations (remission of cases) speaks of the presiding officer as 'an interested party otherwise than in his capacity as such'. Paragraph 4.10 of the Home Office Guidance provides that the reviewing officer 'must have had no previous involvement in the case under review, and nor must he or she have any detailed knowledge of the case prior to the request for a review'. The 'case under review' must be taken to include any involvement in either the misconduct investigation or any associated wider criminal investigation. It is observed that the Guidance speaks of 'detailed knowledge'. This is not defined.

These provisions are supplemented by para 4.11 of the Guidance, which disquali- **11.15** fies the designated deputy if he has 'previously been involved in the case' or 'has overall responsibility for complaints and discipline matters'. If this is the case, the matter is reviewed by another chief constable or, in relation to the MPS, another Assistant Commissioner. That officer makes 'recommendations', which are binding on the home force[10] (see 11.41–11.42 below).

11.16 More generally, as was addressed in the context of the performance meetings at 5.38–5.39, 'bias' must be taken to mean bias as applied in the particular context of police misconduct proceedings. It is observed that the 2008 Conduct Regulations specifically provide[11] that 'interested party' means 'a person whose involvement in the role could reasonably give rise to a concern as to whether he could act impartially under these regulations'.

11.17 The formulations as to judicial bias in *Porter v Magill*[12] and *AWG Group v Morrison*[13] are plainly relevant: '. . . having ascertained all the circumstances bearing on the suggestion that the judge was (or would be) biased, the court must ask "whether those circumstances would lead a fair-minded and informed observer to conclude that there was a real possibility . . . that the tribunal was biased".' The direction and control function of the chief officer under s 10 of the 1996 Act means, however, that this test is qualified—and more restricted—in its application by the fact that the 'circumstances bearing on the suggestion of bias' include his statutory role.

11.18 In the context of a chief officer determining disciplinary proceedings whilst concurrently the defendant to employment proceedings, the Court of Appeal in *R v Chief Constable of Merseyside Police, ex p Bennion*,[14] held that:

> The requirements of judicial impartiality which would be understood to apply to any judge should not be assumed inexorably to apply to a Chief Constable conducting disciplinary proceedings in accordance with his operational responsibilities. It could not be accepted, therefore, that in every case where a police officer is proceeding against the Chief Constable in the employment tribunal, the Chief Constable must disqualify himself, on grounds that he would be sitting as a judge in his own cause, from adjudicating in any disciplinary proceedings where the outcome would have any bearing on the proceedings before the tribunal . . . where there is no disqualifying personal interest, a Chief Constable is vested with a statutory responsibility to hear disciplinary proceedings against an officer, with a discretion to remit the case. Notwithstanding his general interest in the outcome of every disciplinary hearing, it is normally appropriate and thought to be in the best interests of the force as a whole for the Chief Constable to adjudicate in disciplinary matters.

---

[10] *R (Bolt) v Chief Constable of Merseyside Police* [2007] EWHC 2607 (QB).
[11] Police (Conduct) Regulations 2008, SI 2008/2864, reg 3.
[12] [2002] 2 AC 357, 494, HL, [102]–[103].
[13] [2006] 1 All ER 967, *per* Mummery LJ at [7].
[14] [2001] EWCA Civ 638, [2001] IRLR 442, [2002] ICR 136.

This case concerned the obligation under reg 14(1) of the Police (Discipline) **11.19**
Regulations 1985[15] to remit determination of a charge to a different chief officer
if the chief officer concerned was interested in the case 'otherwise than in his
capacity as such' (reg 14(2)). This, it is contended, does not provide a distinction
with a difference in terms of the subsequent interpretation of the Conduct
Regulations, and, indeed, is reproduced at reg 33 of the 2004 Conduct Regulations. The fundamental operational responsibilities of a chief officer under the
1996 Act are identical. The chief officer is accountable to (amongst others) the
police authority and the Independent Police Complaints Commission (IPCC),
and the affected officer has a statutory right of appeal to the police appeals
tribunals.

In practice, it creates a high threshold for a chief officer to disqualify himself at the **11.20**
application of the affected officer. Remission to an outside chief officer is more
likely—and often occurs at the initiative of the affected officer's force—to preserve the confidence of the complainant (and the public) in the process. Remission
also promotes confidence when a particular complaint has attracted public
criticism of the force, and accused officers perceive that determination of allegations against them by a chief officer may be unfairly (if subconsciously) affected
by considerations of adverse publicity and force reputation, as distinct from the
legitimate consideration of public confidence.

Who may attend

By reg 41 of the 2004 Conduct Regulations, the reviewing officer shall hold a **11.21**
'meeting' with the officer concerned if requested to do so. Where a meeting is
held, the officer concerned may be accompanied by another police officer and,
in a case in which reg 17 applies, by counsel or a solicitor. In terms of outcome,
reg 42(2) provides that the reviewing officer may 'confirm or overturn' the decision of the hearing, or he may impose a different sanction, which is specified in
reg 35(2), but he may not impose a sanction greater than that imposed at the
hearing.

In terms of those that may attend, it was contended by the affected officer, **11.22**
and (based on legal advice) the chief officer conducting the review, in *R (IPCC) v
Chief Constable of the West Midlands Police (re Howarth)*,[16] that the criteria were

---

[15] SI 1985/518.

[16] [2007] EWHC 2715 (Admin). The Chief Constable of West Midlands Police was acting
as reviewing officer on behalf of the Chief Constable of the Derbyshire Constabulary. This followed the appointment of an external chief officer to determine the original misconduct hearing,
which related to a series of fundamental errors in the investigation into the murder of Tania Moore.
This was primarily to ensure the proceedings appeared independent of matters of force reputation,
from the perspective both of the deceased's family and the officers subject to misconduct charges.

exhaustive of those entitled to attend and that there was, accordingly, no power to permit attendance of either the IPCC or the complainant. This was rejected by the court, which found both that regulatory language permitted it, and that the Home Office Guidance was within the principle of *Laker Airways Limited v Department of Trade*.[17] Mr Justice Burton concluded ([39]):

> I am entirely satisfied that the claimant is correct in concluding that there is no bar on the attendance of other parties than the officer. The matter remains at the discretion of the reviewing officer. It is suggested by the defendant and the third interested party that this in some way foresees the possibility that there will be positively more people present, at what is described as a meeting than there were at the hearing. I have no doubt at all that sensible reviewing officers will seek to limit the numbers of people present, but will exercise their discretion so that no more people are present, and possibly less in terms of overall numbers, than were at the hearing, and indeed will exercise the discretion consistently with the approach of the Regulations towards the hearings and the appeals. But that the reviewing officer does have a discretion, I am entirely certain.

11.23   Further, 'attendance' extended, even in the absence of provision in either the Regulations or the associated Guidance, to the right of participation in argument as to the merits of the review.[18] This is at the discretion of the reviewing officer.

11.24   In considering arguments as to costs, however, the court appeared to reject an implied suggestion on behalf of the IPCC that his ruling created a legitimate expectation in every case that the IPCC would be entitled to attend. Exclusion would be subject to challenge on familiar grounds of *Wednesbury* unreasonableness. In practice, the point is likely, in future, to be academic. There will seldom be good reason to exclude either the IPCC (particularly following an independent, managed, or supervised investigation) or proportionate attendance by, or on behalf of, a complainant.

11.25   It may be observed that the officer seeking the review appears to have little to lose by seeking a review. The position is not this straightforward in practice. Even allowing for the notionally tight timetable in which to determine a review,

---

[17]   [1977] QB 643, HL, at 699C: '… the Secretary of State can give guidance by way of explanation or amplification of, or supplement to, the general objectives: but not so as to reverse or contradict them …'

[18]   At [27]: 'I am entirely clear that there is a role for others than the officer at the review hearing at the discretion of the reviewing officer. It has been suggested to me that the review is only a review and not an appeal and, for example, evidence would not be led at such a meeting. But that is not so say that argument may not be run on a review, such as a case that the decision at the hearing was flawed for some reason or other; flawed in law, flawed because of a lack of disclosure, flawed because of some misconduct or alleged misconduct of one side, or even of the presiding officer. It is in this context that it is important for there to be at least the opportunity for inter partes argument at the review meeting if the reviewing officer considers that it might be necessary'.

the officer affected may suffer management action (for example, in allocation of duties or entitlement to selection for specialist posts) outside the Conduct Regulations, and adverse comment by the chief officer on review could be a relevant consideration.

The scope of the review

The Regulations themselves do not provide any guidance as to the conduct of the **11.26** review meeting, save that one must be held if requested, and that there is an entitlement for the affected officer to be accompanied and/or legally represented. There is also no guidance as to the appropriate test to be applied by the reviewing officer in either confirming or overturning the original decision.

Paragraph 4.2 of the Home Office Guidance defines the 'scope' of the review as to **11.27** 'provide the opportunity for a Chief Constable to take quick action to rectify clear errors or inconsistencies in process or determination by the earlier hearing'. Paragraph 4.8 provides that 'where a personal hearing takes place, this will not amount to a fresh re-hearing of the case. Rather it will be an opportunity for the officer concerned to state his grounds for seeking a review of the hearings decisions in person, and will allow the Chief Constable to question the officer concerned about those grounds or any other relevant points'. Paragraph 4.12 provides that the task of the chief constable conducting the review will be to determine whether the original hearing was 'conducted fairly and whether the outcome decided upon appears to have been justified and appropriate to the nature of the case'.

These provisions have been considered by the Administrative Court (see 11.33– **11.28** 11.43 below).

The character of the review also derives its flavour most directly from the Guidance **11.29** rather than from the Regulations. The scope of the review impacts upon the approach of the chief officer conducting it to intervention, and the nature and extent of participation by others.

In procedural terms, the Guidance confirms that the written request must be with **11.30** the chief officer within fourteen days, subject to extension in 'exceptional circum-stances'. The officer will be given 'access' to such parts of the recording as are 'necessary' to establish specific grounds of review (para 4.3). This implies that the review will not ordinarily wait for a full transcript.

The request is made to the chief officer, whose office must copy it to the case/ **11.31** presenting or personnel officer. This officer obtains the account of the original presiding officer in response to the written grounds, and returns the whole to the chief officer. According to the Guidance, no further action is expected of the pre-senting officer 'unless the request for a review contains important new statements whose accuracy needs to be checked' (para 4.5). The objective is for the presiding officer's account to be with the chief officer within one week of the written request for a review, with the review 'dealt with' within a week of this (para 4.6).

11.32 This timetable is rarely met in practice. Paragraph 4.16 of the Guidance adds that the 'aim' is to complete the review within four weeks of the written notice, and in no case any later than thirty days after the original hearing in an unsatisfactory performance case and sixty days in a misconduct case. The presiding officer's account is served on the officer seeking a review. The chief constable can seek 'extra information' from the presiding officer (and, inferentially from the approach in *Howarth*, others)[19] either before or during the hearing.

The interpretation of chief officer review provisions by the Administrative Court

11.33 It has already been set out (see 11.21–11.25 above) that the Administrative Court read into these provisions discretion invested in the reviewing officer to permit others to attend and participate in the review. It is contended that, if the presenting side intends to make positive assertions at the review meeting, as distinct from merely answering questions, good practice demands service of such submissions in advance and in writing.

11.34 The appropriate scope of the review was considered in detail in *R (IPCC) v Hayman*,[20] which also informed the reasoning of the court in *Howarth*[21] and *Bolt*.[22] The court held that the Regulations and the Home Office Guidance, read together with the statutory right of appeal to the police appeals tribunals, meant that a review is intended 'to be far less extensive in its scope than an appeal under section 85 of the Act' (that is, the appeal to the tribunals). The key conclusions of Mr Justice Wyn Williams were rehearsed at [35] and [36]:

> 35. In these circumstances it would be wrong of me to "re-write" the guidance in this judgment in my own words or put a gloss upon one or more aspects of the guidance. The reviewing officer's obligation is to have proper regard to the guidance as written. That said it does seem to me that the following emerges clearly from the guidance and cannot sensibly be contradicted. First, a review provides an opportunity "to take quick action to rectify clear errors or inconsistencies in process or determination by the earlier hearing." Secondly, a personal hearing "will not amount to a fresh re-hearing of the case." Thirdly the task of the reviewing officer is to determine

---

[19] *R (IPCC) v Chief Constable of the West Midlands Police (re Howarth)* [2007] EWHC 2715 (Admin), see 11.22 above.

[20] [2007] EWHC 2136 (Admin).

[21] *R (IPCC) v Chief Constable of the West Midlands Police (re Howarth)* [2007] EWHC 2715 (Admin).

[22] *R (Bolt) v Chief Constable of Merseyside Police* [2007] EWHC 2607 (QB).

"whether the original hearing was conducted fairly and whether the outcome decided upon appears to have been justified and appropriate to the nature of the case." In my judgment the use of the word "appears" is deliberate and it militates against the notion of an in-depth re-appraisal of the issues before the panel. Fourthly, the review must be conducted fairly which, obviously must mean fairly both to the officer seeking the review and to those who have laid the disciplinary charge against him.

36. It should not be thought, however, that a reviewing officer who embarks upon a detailed re-appraisal of the evidence at the hearing or who, in effect, turns a review into a re-hearing necessarily acts beyond his powers. To repeat he is given the express power of "overturning" the decision of the panel and it may be that circumstances will arise in which it is not just permissible but desirable that a review should be a much more detailed process than is contemplated by the guidance. It is neither desirable nor possible for me to lay down what the circumstances might be which would justify a departure from the guidance. If such a departure does take place, however, it will be necessary for the reviewing office to explain why and to identify clearly the "good reason" which justifies a departure from the approach set out in the guidance.

This creates an interesting balance for the chief officer concerned. On the one hand, the review is not a re-hearing and is intended to rectify clear errors within a short period of the original decision. On the other hand, the officer seeking a review will frequently be justified in contending that it is only on a detailed consideration of the evidence that the clear error may be so identified. This approach was indorsed by the Administrative Court in *R (Woodhams) v AC Ghaffur*.[23] The chief officer must also make a prediction as to the probable result at any subsequent tribunal, which does conduct a full appeal on merits, albeit taking into account the professional judgments of the professional misconduct panel and review. **11.35**

If the reviewing chief officer reasonably concludes that the tribunal may, on a more extensive consideration of the evidence than is required on review, allow an appeal—particularly if this reinstates the appellant officer following a requirement to resign or dismissal—then it is difficult to see the public interest in delaying that finding to the tribunal. Intervention on this basis is a reasonable extension of the duties of direction and control under s 10 of the 1996 Act. **11.36**

Equally, the reviewing officer may well conclude—particularly in cases involving competence rather than integrity—that loss of office, whilst not a 'clear error' in judicial review terms, is disproportionate or, whilst 'justified', is not 'appropriate' to the individual circumstances, particularly for uncharacteristic failures of performance. Such an outcome reflects no criticism of the original panel. Delay to reinstatement is expensive and reduces the likely effectiveness on return of the affected officer. **11.37**

---

[23] CO/6155/2008.

The right to participate in the hearing

11.38 As has been set out (see 11.21–11.25 above), beyond those entitled to attend as of right, the reviewing officer has discretion in terms of attendance and participation.

The outcome of the review

11.39 The extent of the reviewing officer's duty to give reasons in determining whether the original outcome was justified and appropriate was addressed in *R (Wheeler) v AC House of the MPS*.[24] This judicial review was primarily concerned with the vagueness of charges in respect of a supervising officer, but the nature of the obligation on the reviewing officer was described (at [1.16]) as follows:

> Nor is it to be expected of the reviewer that he goes through all the evidence that was given below where a transcript is available. What he must do is address the substantial points made on behalf of the person seeking review. His reasons need not be elaborate or long, and certainly should not be analysed as if they were a judgment of a judge of the Administrative Court, but it should appear from them that he was conscious of the substantial issues raised by the disciplined person, and explain why or on what basis he has concluded that the review should uphold the decision of the Panel.

11.40 The same reasoning would inevitably apply if the decision of the original panel were not upheld.

11.41 Where the reviewing officer is from a different force, para 4.11 of the Home Office Guidance provides that the chief officer conducting the review 'will consider the case and make a recommendation as to whether to uphold or vary the decisions of the hearing to the Chief Constable of the officer concerned, who will remain responsible for the implementation of the decision'.

11.42 This 'recommendation' is binding on the requesting chief officer, notwithstanding his direction and control function under s 10 of the 1996 Act. If he is unhappy with the recommendation, the remedy lies in judicial review.[25] The court rejected the claim that the requirement to retain an officer in whom the chief officer had no confidence undermined the latter's role or statutory duties:

> The fact that a chief constable has ultimate responsibility for the conduct of his force does not mean that he must have untrammelled power to hire and fire. There are other circumstances in which, as here, a decision as to who should be a member of his force rests with someone other than himself – most obviously where a panel declines to recommend dismissal or where, if it does so, the decision is overturned by the Police Appeals Tribunal.

---

[24] [2008] EWHC 439 (Admin).
[25] See *R (Bolt) v the Chief Constable of Merseyside Police, with the Chief Constable of North Wales Police as an interested party* [2007] EWHC 2607 (QB).

In either event, the officer conducting the review is required (reg 42(1)) to inform **11.43** the affected officer of the finding of the review within three days of the completion of the review. Where the affected officer remains dismissed, required to resign, or reduced in rank, he shall be notified in writing of his right of appeal to the police appeals tribunals (reg 42(4)). In a case in which the IPCC has made a direction to an appropriate authority under para 27(4) of Sch 3 to the 2002 Act, the reviewing officer is required to notify the Commission of the outcome of the review, and provide the Commission with a written record of the reasons for his determination (reg 42(5)).

C. Senior Officer Appeals

The 2004 Conduct Regulations revoked the Police (Conduct)(Senior Officers) **11.44** Regulations 1999.[26] As has been stated, there is no chief officer's review for such officers. The right of appeal is accordingly directly to the police appeals tribunals, whether under the 1999 or 2008 PAT Rules.

D. The Police Appeals Tribunals

Statutory basis

The statutory basis of the police appeals tribunals derives from s 85 of, and Sch 6 **11.45** to, the 1996 Act (the latter as amended by para 11 of Sch 22 to the Criminal Justice and Immigration Act 2008). These set certain constitutional rights and parameters, summarized below, which are common to any police appeals tribunal. Of real practical significance, however, is the detail of rules issued under the 1996 Act, because these provide the basis on which a tribunal must exercise its discretion.

The relevant rules are the 1999 and 2008 PAT Rules. They are sufficiently differ- **11.46** ent to be regarded as separate regimes arising from the same statutory origin.

The police appeals tribunal exercises a difficult jurisdiction in the sense that if it **11.47** reinstates an appellant officer, it will invariably be against the original judgment of the senior officers (including chief officers) from the respondent's force. The chair of the tribunal is not a police officer, and is not responsible for the direction and control of the force. Equally, appellant officers have restricted rights in employment terms, limited in simple terms to claims of victimization and

---

[26] SI 1999/731, as amended by the Greater London Authority Act 1999 (Consequential Amendments) (Police) Order 2000, SI 2000/1549, the Criminal Justice and Police Act 2001 (Consequential Amendments) (Police Ranks) Regulations 2001, SI 2001/3888, and the Police (Conduct) (Senior Officers) (Amendment) Regulations 2003, SI 2003/2596.

discrimination but not unfair dismissal. The police appeals tribunal introduces a necessary independent element to the most serious sanctions (and procedural safeguards for other outcomes) imposed on serving police officers, including loss of office.

11.48 These tensions were reflected both in the approaches both of police appeals tribunals under the 1999 PAT Rules and that of the Administrative Court to the nature of their jurisdiction. The 2008 PAT Rules introduce a more rigid set of criteria for appeal. Subject to how the statutory language is interpreted, it may be that a higher threshold has been set for intervention by the tribunals. Coupled with the abolition of the chief officer's review, this places much more weight on the quality and fairness of the original misconduct or special case hearing.

Common features: Police Act 1996, s 85 and Sch 6

11.49 Section 85 of the 1996 Act, whilst essentially an enabling Act, defines the core powers of the police appeals tribunal. In order to permit certain changes in the 2008 PAT Rules, however, it had to be amended.[27] It merits reproduction in the original and amended forms. The amended form is set out in the context of the 2008 PAT Rules at 11.72 below. The original form provides the statutory basis for the 1999 PAT Rules, and reads (in relevant part) as follows.

85 Appeals against dismissal etc

(1) A member of a police force who is dismissed, required to resign or reduced in rank by a decision taken in proceedings under regulations made in accordance with section 50(3) may appeal to a police appeals tribunal against the decision except where he has a right of appeal to some other person; and in that case he may appeal to a police appeals tribunal from any decision of that other person as a result of which he is dismissed, required to resign or reduced in rank.

(2) Where a police appeals tribunal allows an appeal it may, if it considers that it is appropriate to do so, make an order dealing with the appellant in a way—

    (a) which appears to the tribunal to be less severe than the way in which he was dealt with by the decision appealed against, and

    (b) in which he could have been dealt with by the person who made that decision.

(3) The Secretary of State may make rules as to the procedure on appeals to police appeals tribunals under this section.

11.50 A number of important features emerge from these bare provisions. The right to an appeal is contingent on sanction, rather than the nature of the charge giving rise to sanction. Hence an officer may have no right of appeal against a finding that he has, for example, acted with a lack of integrity, however damaging this may be professionally. The right of appeal is the officer's, and there is no equivalent for the presenting side. Under the 1999 PAT Rules, sanction may not be increased, although it may under the 2008 PAT Rules. The detailed rules are by the

---

[27] Criminal Justice and Immigration Act 2008, Sch 22, para 8.

mechanism of statutory instrument, and allow for the power to compel witness attendance.

Schedule 6 of the 1996 Act addresses other framework matters. Aside from **11.51** matters that are to be addressed under the Rules, there are some central matters, as follows:

(i) the constitution and appointment of the tribunal, which differs as between appeals by senior officer (para 1) and non-senior officers (para 2)—in either case, the chair must have qualifying legal experience and has a casting, or second, vote where necessary, and the tribunal will include a police authority member, and another member with defined senior policing qualifications (these provisions are amended in detail by para 11(2) and (3) of Sch 22 to the Criminal Justice and Immigration Act 2008 for appeals under the 2008 Regulations);

(ii) the right to determine a matter without a hearing following written and, where requested, oral representation (para 6(1)), and the right for each side to be legally represented (para 6(2)) (para 6 is abolished by para 11(2) and (3) of Sch 22 to the 2008 Act);

(iii) the substituting effect of any appeal that is allowed from the date of the original determination (para 7(1)) and the fact that the reinstated officer shall, 'for the purpose of reckoning service for pension and, to such extent (if any) as may be determined by the order, for the purpose of pay, be deemed to have served in the force or in his rank continuously from the date of the original decision to the date of his reinstatement' (the backdating effect of decision is preserved by para 11(5) and (3) of Sch 22 to the 2008 Act, although express reference to pay is removed and, if the sanction is increased by the police appeals tribunal, the practical consequence is not addressed); and

(iv) costs (para 9(1))—an appellant 'shall pay the whole of his own costs unless the police appeals tribunal directs that the whole or any part of his costs are to be defrayed out of the police fund of the relevant police authority' (not amended under Sch 22 to the 2008 Act).

It can be seen that the stakes can be quite high in financial terms for each side, **11.52** although the appellant officer never becomes liable for costs other than his own. Notwithstanding the theoretical timetables, in practice, a police appeals tribunal may not determine an appeal for months, sometimes years, after the original event. The officer will be entitled to appropriate compensation if successful. In theory, this may be reduced by sums earned in substitution by the reinstated officer during the relevant period. Paragraph 7(1) of Sch 6 requires the tribunal to 'deal with' any period covered by suspension immediately preceding the original decision. What this actually means in practice is unclear.

11.53 As can be seen, subject to these core elements, the material procedures are delegated to the Rules.

Appeals under the 1999 PAT Rules

The nature of the jurisdiction exercised by the police appeals tribunals under the 1999 PAT Rules

11.54 This is fundamental to understanding the approach to discretion exercised at each stage of the process. The leading case on the point is *R (Chief Constable of Somerset and Avon) v Police Appeals Tribunal*.[28] It was contended, on behalf of the chief constable, following the decision of the police appeals tribunal to substitute a financial penalty for the original requirement to resign, that the discretion of the tribunal was that of 'review' (in the judicial sense, rather than the chief officer review sense) rather than appeal, and that, accordingly, the original decision should only have been varied if it was such that no reasonable tribunal could reasonably have imposed it. The appellant relied on the language of para 5.24 of the relevant Home Office Guidance.

11.55 The court rejected this approach and found (at [24]) that guidance issued under s 87 of the 1996 Act—the Home Office Guidance—did not apply to the police appeals tribunal, and was restricted in its application to police authorities, chief officers of police, and other members of police forces concerning the discharge of their functions under regulations made under s 50. The police appeals tribunal was an independent tribunal that took over the function formerly (and unsatisfactorily) performed by the Secretary of State under s 103 of the Police and Criminal Evidence Act 1984 (PACE) and it would be 'surprising' if the Guidance were to extend to its function.

11.56 In terms of the approach to such appeals under the 1999 PAT Rules, the court held (at [26]):

> There is nothing in the statutory framework which indicates the way in which the tribunal must approach its task. It is, in terms, an appeal. It is an appeal to an expert tribunal. In those circumstances one would expect that that tribunal, particularly where it can hear fresh evidence and consider all matters that are put before it (and it has the power to substitute in the case of sanctions any that could have been imposed by the tribunal from which it is hearing the appeal), has a full power to reconsider and exercise its own judgment as to what the appropriate outcome should be.

11.57 At [28] of the judgment, the court added:

> Nonetheless, it seems to me that when Parliament confers a right of appeal to a specialist tribunal such as the Police Appeals Tribunal, it is inherent in that that the powers of the tribunal are to consider all matters put before it, in the form of fresh

---

[28] [2004] EWHC 220 (Admin).

evidence or fresh submissions or whatever, and to reach its own conclusions upon the matter. Of course, it will have regard to the decision of the body from whom the appeal is brought. It will have regard to the views of the chief constable, and it will no doubt be slow to differ from those views unless it is persuaded that they were, in its view, wrong, but if it is so persuaded then it has an obligation to apply what it believes to be the correct result.

It is observed that this language has been replaced in the 2008 PAT Rules with **11.58** that of establishing that a finding was 'unreasonable'. Whether, and to what extent, this affects the approach of the police appeals tribunals in practice remains to be seen. It is arguable that the Rules cannot revise the fundamental nature of the s 85 appeal to one amounting to judicial review.

A less deferential approach to intervention on appeal is reflected in *Walker v Royal* **11.59** *College of Veterinary Surgeons*.[29] The appeal to the Privy Council followed the removal of Dr Walker's name from the register after a finding of providing false certifications on two separate and similar occasions. The Board reminded itself of the approach indicated by the Privy Council in *Ghosh v GMC*.[30] Lord Millett said that, although the Board's jurisdiction is appellate rather than supervisory, it is 'incumbent on the appellant to demonstrate some error has occurred in the proceedings before the committee or in its decision, but that is true of most appellate processes', that 'the Board will accord an appropriate measure of respect' to the judgment of a professional disciplinary committee on, inter alia, 'the measures necessary to maintain professional standards and provide adequate protection to the public', but that 'it will not defer to the committee's judgment more than is warranted by the circumstances' and that it is, on this basis, open to the appellate Board 'to decide whether the sanction of erasure was appropriate or necessary in the public interest or was excessive and disproportionate'.

This approach appears apposite to that required of a police appeals tribunal on **11.60** appeal under either of the applicable Rules.

Respondent

By r 4, the respondent on an appeal by a senior officer shall be a person designated **11.61** for the purpose by the relevant police authority, and for any other officer, it shall be the chief officer of that force.

Limitation periods

The notice of appeal in standard cases must be within twenty-one days of the **11.62** date on which the decision appealed against was notified to the appellant within the relevant regulations (r 5(1)). In fast-track/special cases under reg 39 of the

---

[29] Privy Council Appeal No 16 of 2007, 21 November 2007, reasons given 3 April 2008.
[30] [2001] 1 WLR 1915.

2004 Conduct Regulations, and appeals under reg 25 of the Police (Conduct) (Senior Officer) Regulations 1999,[31] this time is extended to twenty-eight days from the conclusion of any criminal proceedings in which the appellant is charged with an offence in respect of the conduct to which the decision appealed against related, or a decision that no such criminal proceedings will be instituted or taken over by the Director of Public Prosecutions (DPP) has been communicated to the appellant (r 5(2)).

11.63 In either event, the notice of appeal shall be given in writing to the relevant police authority and a copy of the notice shall be sent to the respondent (r 5(3)). At this point, r 6 prescribes a series of important procedural events, with a timetable for compliance. Rule 7 provides for the procedure governing extension of time limits within rr 5 and 6, with the initial application being made to the police authority and, if refused, a right of appeal (within fourteen days of the written decision refusing extension) to the chair of the police appeals tribunal.

Procedure on notice of appeal

11.64 Rule 6 provides for a detailed timetable and procedure for exchange of documents and written arguments. In summary:

(i)   'as soon as practicable' after the notice of appeal, the respondent shall provide to the police authority a copy of the report of the person who made the decision appealed against, the transcript of the original hearing, and any documents 'made available to' the person conducting the original hearing (r 6(1));

(ii)   the appellant shall be provided with the transcript at the same time (r 6(2));

(iii)   the appellant shall, within twenty-eight days of the service of the transcript, submit to the police authority: (a) a statement of the grounds of appeal; (b) any supporting documents; and (c) either written representations as to a request for a hearing other than on the papers under para 6 of Sch 6 to the 1996 Act, or a written request for an oral hearing to make representations as to a hearing other than on the papers, although, in either case, the right to make oral representations to the chair remains (r 6(3));

(iv)   all of the r 6(3) documents must be copied to members of the tribunal and the respondent 'as soon as practicable' (r 6(4));

(v)   the respondent must provide to the police authority and appellant within twenty-one days of service of these matters a written statement of his response to these matters (r 6(5) and (6));

(vi)   all of these documents must be copied to the members of the tribunal as soon as practicable.

---

[31] SI 1999/731.

The police appeals tribunal is entitled to determine the appeal 'without a **11.65** hearing'—that is, on the basis of written representations and the original evidence. It may determine that a full re-hearing is necessary in the circumstances of the appeal, or that only particular elements need be dealt with in this way. Under para 6 of Sch 6 to the 1996 Act, the appellant has the right to request a full hearing, and is entitled to make oral representations to the chair on this point (r 6(5)(c)). This decision may accordingly be made by the chair rather than the full tribunal. Rules 8 and 9 (procedure at hearing, and hearing in private) apply to such applications (r 6(8)).

Procedure at the hearing

Where a case is to be determined at a hearing, the procedure is covered by rr 8 and 9. **11.66** There are few exceptions to the broad point that the procedure at a hearing shall be determined by the tribunal (r 9(4)). Evidence at the hearing, as distinct from procedure, is addressed by r 10. Under r 8(1), the chair must cause the parties to be given to be given notice of the date of the hearing of not less than twenty-eight days, or such shorter period as may, with the agreement of both parties, be determined, before the hearing begins.

Attendance and power to compel witness attendance

The hearing is covered by s 250(2) and (3) of the Local Government Act 1972[32] **11.67** ('Powers in relation to local inquiries', including power to issue witness summons, etc). It may proceed in the absence of either party, or be adjourned, where 'it appears just and proper to do so' (r 8(3)) and beyond those entitled to attend (including a member of the Administrative Justice and Tribunals Council) has discretion to allow or exclude others (r 9). The attendance and participation of a complainant is specifically addressed by r 12, including the right to ask questions of the appellant officer (r 12(4)).

Written statements may be admitted under the principles of r 11. **11.68**

---

[32] '(2) For the purpose of any such local inquiry, the person appointed to hold the inquiry may by summons require any person to attend, at a time and place stated in the summons, to give evidence or to produce any documents in his custody or under his control which relate to any matter in question at the inquiry, and may take evidence on oath, and for that purpose administer oaths, … Provided that—(a) no person shall be required, in obedience to such summons, to attend to give evidence or to produce any such documents, unless the necessary expenses of his attendance are paid or tendered to him; and (b) nothing in this section shall empower the person holding the inquiry to require the production of the title, or of any instrument relating to the title, of any land not being the property of a local authority. (3) Every person who refuses or deliberately fails to attend in obedience to a summons issued under this section, or to give evidence, or who deliberately alters, suppresses, conceals, destroys, or refuses to produce any book or other document which he is required or is liable to be required to produce for the purposes of this section, shall be liable on summary conviction to a fine not exceeding [level 3 on the standard scale] or to imprisonment for a term not exceeding six months, or to both.'

11.69 Under r 10, the sequence of evidence at the hearing follows the pattern of a familiar appeal, reinforcing the sense that it is an appeal by way of re-hearing, albeit qualified by the service of the totality of material before the original panel and the principles in R (Chief Constable of Somerset and Avon) v Police Appeals Tribunal.[33] Rule 10(1) provides that unless the tribunal determines otherwise, the evidence given by the respondent shall be given first (this sequence is reversed under the 2008 PAT Rules). Evidence is (unlike at the original hearing) given on oath (r 10(2)), and all witnesses giving evidence at the hearing shall be subject to examination and cross-examination (r 10(3)).

The statement of the tribunal's determination and record of proceedings

11.70 The notification requirements are as rehearsed in r 13. A written decision with reasons is required (r 13(1)), which shall be submitted within a reasonable period of the determination of the appeal to the relevant police authority (non-senior officers) or the Secretary of State (senior officers). This must be copied to the appellant and respondent as soon as practicable by the police authority (r 13(3)). If the matter arose from a complaint, the authority 'shall notify the complainant of the outcome' (r 13(4)). The different language suggests that the complainant is not entitled as of right to the tribunal's written statement and order.

11.71 By r 10(5), a verbatim record of the evidence given at the hearing shall be taken and kept for a period of not less than seven years from the date of the end of the hearing, unless the chairman of the tribunal requests that a transcription of the record be made.

Appeals under the 2008 PAT Rules

11.72 The starting point is the revised terms of s 85 of the 1996 Act.[34] The amendments are as follows:

PART i—AMENDMENTS TO THE POLICE ACT 1996

Appeals against dismissal etc.

8. (1) Section 85 (appeals against dismissal etc.) is amended as follows.
(2) For subsections (1) and (2) substitute—
   "(1) The Secretary of State shall by rules make provision specifying the cases in which a member of a police force or a special constable may appeal to a police appeals tribunal.
   (2) A police appeals tribunal may, on the determination of an appeal under this section, make an order dealing with the appellant in any way in which he could have been dealt with by the person who made the decision appealed against."

---

[33] [2004] EWHC 220 (Admin)—see 11.54 above.
[34] Criminal Justice and Immigration Act 2008, Sch 22, para 8.

(3) For subsection (4) substitute—

"(4) Rules made under this section may, in particular, make provision—

    (a) for enabling a police appeals tribunal, in such circumstances as are specified in the rules, to determine a case without a hearing;

    (b) for the appellant or the respondent to be entitled, in a case where there is a hearing, to be represented—

        (i) by a relevant lawyer within the meaning of section 84,

        or

        (ii) by a person who falls within any description of persons prescribed by the rules;

    (c) for enabling a police appeals tribunal to require any person to attend a hearing to give evidence or to produce documents, and rules made in pursuance of paragraph (c) may apply subsections (2) and (3) of section 250 of the Local Government Act 1972 with such modifications as may be set out in the rules.

    (4A) Rules under this section may make different provision for different cases and circumstances."

11.73 Whilst it may be observed that many of the changes do not appear to favour the appellant's prospects, including the availability of all sanctions available to the original decision maker (in other words, introducing the possibility of sanction increasing), and the power to dismiss an appeal without a hearing (effectively summary dismissal), the Act is not amended so as to give any other interested party—the presenting officer, the complainant, or the IPCC, even in cases in which it directed charges and/or presented the evidence—a right of appeal against the original decision.

11.74 The practical significance of the amendment to s 85 becomes apparent when the 2008 PAT Rules are considered in greater detail. The 2008 Rules are reproduced in full at Appendix H. They came into force on 1 December 2008, but do not apply (r 2(2)) to appeals against decisions under the 1999 Efficiency Regulations or the 2004 Conduct Regulations.

The nature of the jurisdiction exercised by the police appeals tribunals under the 2008 PAT Rules

11.75 Although Annex C to the 2008 Home Office Guidance purports to provide guidance as to appeals to police appeals tribunals, the status of this guidance is questionable. Section 87 of the 1996 Act, as amended by para 9 of Sch 22 to the Criminal Justice and Immigration Act 2008, does not give power to issue guidance to the tribunal. As applied to the 2004 Regulations, the Administrative Court confirmed this principle in terms in R (Chief Constable of Somerset and Avon) v Police Appeals Tribunal.[35] The 2008 PAT Rules are, accordingly, considered without reference to this Guidance.

11.76 Unlike the 1999 PAT Rules, the 2008 PAT Rules purport to define 'the circumstances in which a police officer may appeal to a tribunal'. The detailed provisions

---

[35] [2004] EWHC 220 (Admin).

are set out in rr 4 (qualifying findings arising under the 2008 Conduct Regulations) and 5 (qualifying findings following a third-stage meeting under the 2008 Performance Regulations).

11.77 In relation to a qualifying appeal under the 2008 Conduct Regulations, an officer may appeal a finding of gross misconduct (save where that was admitted, r 4(3)) and/or the disciplinary action imposed.

11.78 The grounds of appeal are, however, restricted. Rule 4(4) provides that:

    (4) The grounds of appeal under this rule are—
        (a) that the finding or disciplinary action imposed was unreasonable; or
        (b) that there is evidence that could not reasonably have been considered at the original hearing which could have materially affected the finding or decision on disciplinary action; or
        (c) that there was a breach of the procedures set out in the Conduct Regulations, the Police (Complaints and Misconduct) Regulations 2004, Schedule 3 to the Police Reform Act 2002 or other unfairness which could have materially affected the finding or decision on disciplinary action.

11.79 The language of 'unreasonable' may appear to import considerations of how the discretion afforded to decision makers under familiar administrative law principles is approached. So-called *Wednesbury* unreasonableness—that is, broadly, whether the decision was so unreasonable that no reasonable decision maker, applying its mind to all of the relevant considerations, could have come to it—is a high test.

11.80 It is contended that the strict public law definition may not, however, be the appropriate test for the tribunals to apply in this statutory context. Unlike the Administrative Court, the police appeals tribunal is an expert appellate tribunal exercising a jurisdiction as such. The test as to what is unreasonable must take its meaning from that context. As considered at 11.56–11.60, the relationship between an expert specialist appellate statutory tribunal and the original misconduct panel is different from that between an expert tribunal and the Administrative Court. 'Unreasonable' remains a significant hurdle on any view.

11.81 In terms of appeals arising under the 2008 Performance Regulations (assuming that the officer has not admitted the relevant unsatisfactory performance or attendance, in which event, that finding may not be appealed), there are detailed provisions under r 5 as to when an appeal may arise.

11.82 By r 5(4), if the relevant finding (unsatisfactory performance or attendance) followed a third-stage meeting under reg 26 of the 2008 Performance Regulations, the officer may appeal the outcomes of either dismissal or reduction in rank.

11.83 By r 5(5), if a finding of gross incompetence or unsatisfactory performance arose under the provisions of reg 28 of the 2008 Performance Regulations (that is, the third-stage meeting was the first hearing), the officer may appeal the outcomes of dismissal, reduction in rank, redeployment to alternative duties, the issue of a final written improvement notice (WIN), or the issue of a WIN.

That the police appeals tribunals should be concerned with the lower levels of **11.84** outcome (redeployment, etc) is perhaps surprising. Outside the Performance Regulations, chief officers have power to redeploy as part of the direction and control of the force under s 10 of the 1996 Act. WINs are fundamentally managerial, except that they are part of the performance regime.

In any event, the grounds of appeal are prescribed by r 5(6), as follows: **11.85**

(6) The grounds of appeal under this rule are—
    (a) that the finding or outcome imposed was unreasonable; or
    (b) that there is evidence that could not reasonably have been considered at the original hearing which could have materially affected the finding or decision on the outcome; or
    (c) that there was a breach of the procedures set out in the Performance Regulations or other unfairness which could have materially affected the finding or decision on the outcome; or
    (d) that, where the police officer was required to attend the third stage meeting under regulation 26 of the Performance Regulations, he should not have been required to attend that meeting as it did not, in accordance with regulation 26(6) or 40(9) of those Regulations, concern unsatisfactory performance or attendance similar to or connected with the unsatisfactory performance or attendance referred to in the final written improvement notice.

Subject to the meaning of 'reasonableness', these provisions appear relatively **11.86** clear, although the threshold for intervention will only become apparent in practice. Given the new power invested in the police appeals tribunals to increase the sanction (or 'outcome'), it may be that affected police officers will be circumspect in their approach to appealing fundamentally management outcomes.

Notice of appeal, the procedure on receipt of notice, and time limits

In summary, rr 6 and 7 make provision for the giving of a notice of appeal. **11.87** Rule 9 sets out the procedure on receipt of this notice, including the provision of documents. Under r 10, time periods under r 9 may be extended on application.

Within the relevant rules are some important provisions. The basic rule is that **11.88** written notice of appeal must be served before the end of ten working days, beginning with the first working day after the day on which the written copy of the relevant decision was supplied (r 6(1)). It must be made in writing to the police authority (r 6(2)). If the appellant officer requires a transcript of the original hearing, he must request one (r 6(3)).

Discretion to extend this period is given, under r 7, to the chair of the police appeals **11.89** tribunal and is subject to considerations of what was reasonably practicable.

If the limit is not extended under this discretion, then the chair may dismiss the appeal (r 7(4)) regardless of the intrinsic merit of the grounds of appeal.

11.90 Aside from formalities of service, the procedure on notice of appeal under r 9 is prescriptive as to what each party must provide to the tribunal. The respondent (defined under r 8) must, as soon as practicable and in any event within fifteen working days following receipt of the written appeal, supply the police authority with documents and a transcript (if requested), as set out in r 9(2). The transcript must be provided at the same time to the appellant.

11.91 Within twenty working days of receipt of the transcript where requested (r 9(6) (a)), or thirty-five working days after giving notice of appeal to the police authority (r 9(6)(b)), the appellant must provide to the police authority the material rehearsed at r 9(4).

11.92 No doubt in order to permit consideration by the tribunal on the papers under r 11, this must include:

    (a) a statement of the relevant decision and his grounds of appeal;
    (b) any supporting documents;
    (c) where the appellant is permitted to adduce witness evidence—
        (i) a list of any proposed witnesses;
        (ii) a witness statement from each proposed witness; and
    (d) if he consents to the appeal being determined without a hearing, notice in writing that he so consents.

11.93 Importantly, by r 9(5)(a), an appellant is only permitted to adduce witness evidence where he is relying on the ground of appeal set out in rr 4(4)(b) or 5(6)(b), and by r 9(5)(b), a 'proposed witness' is a person:

    (i) whom the appellant wishes to call to give evidence at the hearing;
    (ii) whose evidence was not and could not reasonably have been considered at the original hearing; and
    (iii) whose evidence could have materially affected the relevant decision.

11.94 This sets a premium on preparation for the original hearing. It may be more readily applied to special cases (fast-track hearings), although the evidential test to defeat the original finding as unreasonable remains formidable.

11.95 This material must be provided by the authority to the respondent as soon as practicable (r 9(7)). By r 9(8), the respondent then has twenty working days in which to supply the police authority with:

    (a) a statement of his response to the appeal;
    (b) any supporting documents;
    (c) where the respondent is permitted to adduce witness evidence—
        (i) a list of any proposed witnesses;
        (ii) a witness statement from each proposed witness; and
    (d) if he consents to the appeal being determined without a hearing, notice that he so consents.

By r 9(9), however, the respondent's rights are contingent on the appellant relying **11.96** on grounds of appeal under rr 4(4)(b) or 5(6)(b), and the terms of that reliance. A 'proposed witness' for the respondent must be a person whom the respondent wishes to call at the hearing and whose evidence is relevant to all, or part, of the evidence relied on by the appellant for the purposes of rr 4(4)(b) or 5(6)(b).

Rule 9(10) requires the respondent to give the appellant a copy of the documents **11.97** under r 9(8)(a)(c) and (d), but only a list of the documents under r 9(8)(b). The reason for this distinction is not clear. The police authority is required to copy all of the material to the chair upon receipt (r 9(10)).

This produces the unhappy consequence that the chair may be considering **11.98** documents in exercising discretion under r 11 that are not seen by the appellant. There is, however, power to request documents at any time from the chair under r 13. Reasons for non-disclosure following such a request must be given by the relevant party in writing (r 13(3)). The rules are silent as to what then happens, although this may be the circumstance envisaged by r 11(2)(b), considered at 11.99 below. At the hearing itself, the tribunal has power to regulate its own procedure and to require production (and disclosure) of documents.

Review of appeal and dismissal on the papers

Rule 11 imports an important new power in the chair—and the exercise of the **11.99** power is simply that of the chair, not of the full tribunal—to dismiss an appeal upon receipt of all of the above documentation where it has (r 11(2)(a)) 'no real prospect of success', and (r 11(2)(b)) there is no other compelling reason why the appeal should proceed. It is perhaps difficult to conceive of circumstances under r 11(2)(b), other than those already rehearsed.

If the chair considers that the appeal should be dismissed, before making that **11.100** determination final he must give the parties notice in writing of that view and the reasons for it. The parties thereafter have ten working days following receipt to respond in writing, after which the determination is made. As with extensions of time limits, there is no appeal from this within the Rules. The remedy—if any— must lie in judicial review.

Determination without a hearing

If the appeal is not dismissed under r 11, and in a departure from the 1999 PAT **11.101** Rules, the only circumstance in which a hearing may be avoided under the 2008 PAT Rules is if the appellant consents (see r 12). The procedure is then determined under rr 13–21.

The procedure for determining the hearing

Certain of the rules require no analysis. The power to request disclosure of **11.102** documents under r 13 applies following the provision of documents under r 9(4) or (8). The tribunal retains powers under s 250(2) and (3) of the Local Government Act 1972 (see 11.67 above).

11.103 Absent agreement, the chair must give at least twenty working days' notice of the date of the hearing (r 14(1)). The chair determines which witnesses are to give evidence (r 14(2)) and no witness shall give evidence unless the chair 'reasonably believes' that it is 'necessary' for the witness to do so. There is an obvious premium in the relevant party articulating in their written grounds why this necessity is said to be established. The chair assumes the responsibility of notifying such witnesses.

11.104 Legal and other representation is addressed in r 15. Either side may be legally represented. If represented by a lawyer, the appellant has the right to be accompanied by a police friend. The police friend must be given duty time for these purposes.

11.105 Rule 16 prescribes the procedure at the hearing. Subject to the Rules, it is determined by the tribunal (r 16(1)) and it may proceed in the absence of either party (r 16(2)). Importantly, by r 16(3), 'unless the tribunal determines otherwise the evidence adduced by the appellant shall be given first'. Whilst unusual at first sight, this is consistent with the prior provision of transcripts of the original hearing, and the fact that the appeal is on limited grounds and is not intended as a re-hearing.

11.106 Under r 17, there is power to admit statements in lieu of oral evidence. Those who may attend the otherwise private hearing (r 18(1)) are prescribed by rr 19 (attendance of complainant) and 20 (the IPCC).

11.107 No one in the capacity of complainant or interested party (or someone accompanying the same) may attend before they have given evidence. The complainant may ask questions of the appellant (although not, it seems by implication, other witnesses unless this arises under r 16(1)) through the chair (r 19(6)). The IPCC must be given notice of a specified appeal[36] and may attend as an observer in relation to the same. Parties may be excluded or attend on set conditions at the discretion of the chair (r 21).

11.108 These provisions should be read in the context of the approach of the Administrative Court to provisions as to the meaning of 'in private', in the context of the conduct of chief officer reviews under the 2004 Conduct Regulations, see 11.21–11.25 above.

---

[36] Under r 3, 'specified appeal' means an appeal in which the relevant decision arose from a complaint or conduct matter to which one of paras 17–19 of Sch 3 to the 2002 Act (investigations) applied.

The statement of the tribunal's determination

Under r 22(1), the tribunal shall determine whether the ground(s) of appeal **11.109** have been made out. As to the appropriate test, see 11.80 *et seq* above. There is no standard of proof applicable to this, which is a corollary of the test for the grounds of appeal under rr 4 and 5, respectively. The chair must prepare a written statement of the determination and the reasons for it (r 22(3)), which must be served as soon as practicably possible on all relevant parties under r 22(4)–(6). The appellant must be served with it within three working days of determination.

Not set out expressly in the rules is the effect of the amendment to s 85 of the 1996 **11.110** Act achieved by para 8 of Sch 22 to the Criminal Justice and Immigration Act 2008. Subsections (1) and (2) (set out at 11.49 above) are substituted. Paragraph 8(2)(2) contains the critical amendment, and provides:

> A police appeals tribunal may, on a determination on an appeal under this section, make an order dealing with the appellant on any way in which he could have been dealt with by the person who made the decision appealed against.

The effect of this is clear. An officer's outcome—or sanction—may be increased **11.111** rather than simply maintained or reduced. How this discretion will be applied in practice is a moot point. In that para 7 of Sch 6 to the 1996 Act, as amended by para 11(5) of Sch 22 to the Criminal Justice and Immigration Act 2008, provides that the resultant order under s 85(2) of the 1996 Act shall take effect by way of substitution for the decision appealed against, and from the date of that decision, there may be some practical implications in terms of pension calculations if the sanction is increased to loss of office.

E. Conclusion

These rights of review and appeal provide much by way of procedure and less by **11.112** way of practical application. The range of matters that may be referred to the police appeals tribunals is increased under the 2008 PAT Rules although the grounds of appeal are more restrictive. The power of summary dismissal is coupled with a new right to a hearing, assuming that the matter has not been dismissed. It remains the case that only the affected officer may appeal, although a more proactive role for the respondent is anticipated once such an appeal is attempted.

It is contended that whilst the tribunal should respect the findings of the orig- **11.113** inal panel, it should not define its jurisdiction in terms identical to that of the Administrative Court. A finding may be unreasonable if it simply fails to reflect the weight of material before a particular tribunal. This does not imply that the decision was so unreasonable that the original hearing could not have made it. There is no reason of public policy why the meaning of 'unreasonable' in the particular statutory context needs to mirror that applied in public law proceedings.

12

ABUSE OF PROCESS

A. Overview   12.01
B. The Police as a Regulated
    Profession   12.08
    The primacy of regulations   12.08
    Examples of consequences of failing to
        follow the regulatory framework   12.17
    The timing and availability
        of judicial review   12.24
C. Jurisdiction   12.27
    Ex p Bennett and executive
        unlawfulness   12.27

The practicability of a fair hearing
    and regulatory departure   12.36
Exceptional remedy   12.45
Burden   12.47
D. Regulatory Departure   12.49
E. Delay   12.55
F. 'Fair Hearing Impossible'   12.57
G. Article 6 of the European
    Convention on Human Rights
    (ECHR)   12.59
H. Conclusion   12.65

A. Overview

'Abuse of process' is a much-used term within misconduct investigations and **12.01** proceedings—but use does not always evidence understanding. This may, in part, be attributable to it representing something of an umbrella term covering a number of fundamentally different legal principles. The common feature, apart from the umbrella term, is the outcome sought by the affected officer—that is, a stay of some, or all, of the proceedings against him.

In absolute summary, whilst abuse of process should not be reduced to hard-edged **12.02** categories, it generally reflects one of two situations:

(i) a submission that a fair hearing—that is, the determination of the charge in question—is, for some practical reason, not possible (typically the consequences of delay or 'missing' evidence, and such prejudice not necessarily reflecting any fault on the part of the investigating or presenting side); or

(ii) a finding that there has been deliberate executive unlawfulness (unconscionable behaviour) by the investigating/presenting side in the conduct of the matter, such that the continuation of proceedings, regardless of the guilt of the accused officer, would be wrong if the necessary integrity and reputation of the regulatory process is to be preserved.

12.03 With that said, whilst the second category of abuse (in shorthand, the *Bennett*[1] category, directed at preserving the integrity of the rule of law) should be wholly exceptional in practice, it is, to some extent, qualified—to the advantage of the officer concerned—by the broader discretion arising from *Merrill*,[2] as applied in *Wilkinson*,[3] protecting officers against a 'significant departure from the intended regulatory framework' without the need to establish an abuse of process as such. This was first addressed at 7.113–7.119 and appears to remain a valid approach.

12.04 The *Merrill/ Wilkinson* heading of regulatory departure—although expressly not an application of abuse of process as such—is probably best characterized as an application of the first category of abuse, because it usually requires not simply a departure from the intended regulatory framework, but practical irredeemable prejudice arising as a result to a degree that makes continuation of the proceedings unfair.

12.05 A deliberate and unconscionable departure by the investigating/presenting side from the prescribed and intended regulatory protections, however, would come within the second category (that is, the *Bennett* type) of abuse of process.

12.06 More generally, the relevant principles are, to a large extent, imported from criminal proceedings. In the context of professional misconduct proceedings, however, some additional principles arise that, in the most general terms, may be said to restrict the contexts in which applications will be successful. This reflects the distinctions between the purposes of criminal and professional disciplinary proceedings, respectively, as rehearsed in authorities including *Redgrave*[4] and *Council for the Regulation of Healthcare Professionals v General Medical Council and Saluja*.[5]

12.07 An important point of principle is that the approach to abuse of process arguments must reflect the nature of the police as a regulated profession. As such, the intended regulatory regime should be followed, although a reasoned and justifiable departure where discretion exists within it will not contravene this principle. The nature of a regulated profession leads into further consideration of the principles underpinning abuse of process in the context of police misconduct proceedings.

---

[1] *R v Horseferry Road Magistrates' Court, ex p Bennett* [1994] 1 AC 42, HL.
[2] *R v Chief Constable of Merseyside Police, ex p Merrill* [1989] 1 WLR 1077.
[3] *R (Wilkinson and ors) v Chief Constable of West Yorkshire* [2002] EWHC 2353 Admin.
[4] *R (on the application of Redgrave) v Commissioner of the Police of the Metropolis* [2003] EWCA Civ 04.
[5] [2006] EWHC 2784 (Admin), [2007] 1 WLR 3094.

B. The Police as a Regulated Profession

The primacy of regulations

Police officers serve in a regulated profession. The terms of 'employment' (of **12.08** course, police officers are office holders, not 'employees', other than when deemed to be employees for specific purposes or policy objectives)[6] are governed by regulations that include:

  (i) the Police Regulations 2003,[7] as amended, which are the main overarching regulations dealing with 'terms and conditions', including restrictions on police officers' private lives, sick pay, and so forth;
 (ii) the respective Police (Performance) and Police (Conduct) Regulations, concerning misconduct, performance, and attendance; and
(iii) the Police Pension Regulations 2006,[8] addressing matters such as compulsory retirement on grounds of age (reg 19), efficiency of the force (reg 20), or permanent disability (reg 21).

Indeed, so far as the authors can discern, a serving police officer in England and **12.09** Wales can only be dismissed or otherwise compulsorily required to retire pursuant to the above regulations and the routes set out therein. Those regulations accordingly provide the protections for the officers concerned and must, as a matter of 'due process', be adhered to.

It is to be noted that, during the Taylor reform process, the reformers elected not **12.10** to go down the route of making police officers ordinary employees by removing the unique status of the office of constable. Instead, it was determined by all of the stakeholders to that process—including the Association of Chief Police Officers (ACPO), the Superintendents' Association, and the Police Federation—that the police should remain a regulated profession.

It is therefore a little surprising just how frequently senior police officers apparently forget that, when Parliament lays down regulations, it does so with the expectation that they be adhered to. Not to do so is, prima facie, a departure from the intended and prescribed framework for dealing with police employment, conduct, performance, or whatever other situation is embraced by the applicable regulation. The power of direction and control cannot extend to ignoring the prescribed regulatory framework. **12.11**

---

  [6] For example, vicarious liability and employment rights.
  [7] SI 2003/527.
  [8] SI 2006/3415 (replacing A18–A20 of the Police Pensions Regulations 1987, SI 1987/257); see also Police Pensions (Amendment) Regulations 2006/740.

12.12 Officers and staff who operate in professional standards departments have the task of investigating allegations of criminality or misconduct against police officers. This they do pursuant to the statutory regimes that govern criminal investigations, including the Police and Criminal Evidence Act 1984 (PACE), the Criminal Procedure and Investigations Act 1996 (CPIA), and the Regulation of Investigatory Powers Act 2000 (RIPA). Self-evidently, the investigation of police officers is an acutely challenging task, given the advanced forensic knowledge of many of those subject to investigation, and the reluctance, in some contexts, of fellow officers to provide evidence against colleagues.

12.13 These investigative challenges are compounded by the additional burden of the regulatory overlay, which is the subject of this book—principally, the provisions of Sch 3 to the Police Reform Act 2002 (with associated duties to complainants), and the associated Conduct Regulations and statutory guidance. As can be seen from preceding chapters, these provisions are complex and burdensome, and contain numerous traps and pitfalls for the underinformed investigator.

12.14 Whilst many resultant assertions of regulatory departure (or abuse of process) ultimately come to nothing because they fail to identify either any sufficient deliberation by the investigating officer (or his team) or resultant significant practical unfairness to the officer concerned, such applications can be used to (sometimes effectively) distract the focus from the intrinsic merits of the conduct under investigation.

12.15 It is contended that most such applications could be avoided if those in the police service charged with the (admittedly difficult) task of investigating police officers had a better appreciation of their precise regulatory obligations and, perhaps to a lesser extent, a better understanding of good investigative practice—a topic for a different book. Whilst experienced in pure criminal investigations, many, if not most, professional standards operatives are given little if any training in the applicable regulations or guidance. Such ignorance, when and where demonstrated, inevitably undermines confidence in the competence and conclusions of the investigation more generally, and hence may indirectly affect the outcome.

12.16 At the date of publication, it remains the case that neither ACPO nor the National Policing Improvement Agency (NPIA) have any nationally accredited or credible training programme for professional standards department operatives. Similarly, most chief officers discharging the function of 'appropriate authority' under the regulatory regime appear to have, despite its obvious importance, little, or no, training for the role. The inevitable corollary is that chief officers have repeatedly found themselves criticized by the Administrative Court for their doubtless well-intentioned, but nonetheless fundamentally misdirected, decisions in this regulatory context.[9] This observation could also be made in respect of those populating misconduct panels.

---

[9] A pithy example being Wilkie J's criticisms of the Deputy Chief Constable of Greater Manchester Police in *Coghlan v GMP* [2004] EWHC 2801 (Admin), at [54]–[62] and [67]. The deputy chief

Examples of consequences of failing to follow the regulatory framework

An example of the restrictions placed on managerial discretion by the imposition   **12.17**
of a regulatory regime is to be found in the case of *O'Leary v Chief Constable of
Merseyside Police*.[10] The chief constable had reprimanded the officer concerned
under reg 24 of the Police (Discipline) Regulations 1985[11] for admitted discreditable conduct, and simultaneously announced that he was removing any restriction on his deployment. The assistant chief constable subsequently sought to
re-impose a restriction on the officer's deployment in the light of the reprimand
that the chief constable had just imposed.

The officer concerned (who was subsequently sent to prison for corruption on   **12.18**
unrelated matters several years later) sought judicial review to challenge the
decision of the assistant chief constable on the grounds that: (i) the decision
amounted to an abuse of discretion, and was contrary to a legitimate expectation
arising from the earlier decision of the chief constable; and (ii) the lack of opportunity to make representations to the assistant chief constable before the subsequent decision was procedurally unfair.

Perhaps unsurprisingly, Maurice Kay J found (at [13]) that: **12.19**

> In the course of discharging his statutory responsibility in disciplinary proceedings
> the chief constable made a clear representation which, on the basis of the principle
> expounded in *Coughlan*[12] gave rise to a legitimate expectation on the part of the
> claimant that his future deployment would be considered on the merits, free from
> any prior restriction. In my judgment, when the chief constable directed that the
> decision be "superceded", he unlawfully frustrated that legitimate expectation. I am
> not persuaded that the supercession can be justified or excused by characterising it as
> an operational[13] rather than a disciplinary matter.

The claimant succeeded additionally on the second ground. The court found that   **12.20**
there was:

> procedural unfairness in procuring a change of mind on the part of the chief consta-
> ble on the basis of a report that was not disclosed to the claimant. The chief consta-
> ble, having come to a decision at the end of a fair hearing, then proceeded to alter a
> part of it [namely the removal of restriction on deployment] to the detriment of the
> claimant on the basis of a report which contained errors and in relation to which the
> claimant was not given the opportunity to make a representation. Again, I do not

---

constable had overlooked paras 3.18–3.20 of the December 2002 Home Office Guidance in determining the question of whether a suspended officer accused of corruption should be permitted to
retire—an oversight found to have rendered unlawful his decision to permit the retirement of the
accused officer.

[10] [2001] EWHC Admin 57.

[11] SI 1985/518, which regulation identified the available sanctions (from dismissal to caution)
in the light of a finding of a breach of the Code of Conduct.

[12] *R v North and East Devon Health Authority, ex p Coughlan* [2002] 2 WLR 622.

[13] Namely, as a direction and control matter, under s 10 of the Police Act 1996.

think that this can be justified by seeking to identify the report as an operational rather than a disciplinary matter. It was too closely connected with the disciplinary hearing.

12.21 Two lessons for chief officers emerge. Firstly, comments in sanction hearings (or what will now be called 'outcome' hearings) should be restricted to the minimum necessary to convey and justify the outcome, and, secondly, care must be taken not to impose measures beyond those available under the regulations. The range of outcomes under the regulations, as such, is defined in the regulations.

12.22 The practical implications of managing within a regulated profession are further illustrated in *Hodgson v South Wales Police*.[14] The force was found to have acted without procedural fairness when considering an A19 compulsory retirement. The case echoed criticism of the chief officers in North Wales Police in *Evans*[15] relating to the procedures followed to dispense with the services of probationary officer under reg 13 of the Police Regulations 2003, considered further in Chapter 13.

12.23 Such criticism is likely only to increase under the more complex 2008 regime where there are materially more decisions within the statutory and regulatory framework for chief officers, senior officers, and professional standards operatives to make, and where such decisions, by reason of their public law quality, are theoretically susceptible to judicial review.[16]

The timing and availability of judicial review

12.24 Applying ordinary and well-established principles in judicial review, the officer concerned will generally be obliged first (and where possible) to exhaust his local (alternative) remedies within the regulations before resorting to judicial review. These local remedies include the rights of appeal to a police appeals tribunal. In *Wilkinson v Chief Constable of West Yorkshire Police*,[17] the court rehearsed that the 'principle is that the power to grant judicial review would ordinarily not be exercised where there are alternative remedies open unless there are exceptional circumstances'.[18]

12.25 At [45], Davis J explained why, in the circumstances of the application, it was appropriate to grant judicial review despite the existence of alternative regulatory remedies—that is, the desirability of avoiding the 'cost, uncertainty and delay and stress of a contested substantive hearing of very great length before the correctness of the preliminary ruling could be challenged on appeal to the appeals tribunal'.

---

[14] [2008] EWHC 1183 (Admin).

[15] *Chief Constable of the North Wales Police v Evans* [1982] 1 WLR 1155.

[16] As in, eg, *Hodgson v South Wales Police* [2008] EWHC 1183 (Admin)—see [23]–[31] reviewing other relevant authorities on susceptibility.

[17] [2002] EWHC 2353 (Admin), *per* Davis J at [40].

[18] Following Donaldson MR in *R v Chief Constable of Merseyside Police, ex p Merrill* [1989] 1 WLR 1077 at 1088C–1088D.

Stated shortly, if the point taken is of this character, judicial review may represent **12.26** a more efficient remedy for all parties than exhausting rights through the appeals tribunal. In practice, such applications remain somewhat exceptional, but will be more readily justified where both sides agree that the issue is one of fundamental principle in the sense described in *Merrill* and *Wilkinson*. The decision must, of course, have the requisite 'public' quality to qualify for judicial review. Many internal managerial decisions will not. In *Tucker v the National Crime Squad*,[19] the Court of Appeal found (at [22]):

> The present case is not about dismissal. The impugned decision did not affect the Appellant's status as a Detective Inspector. While it is true that the NCS performs an important public function, as do police forces generally, that does not mean that every decision personal to an individual officer engages public law remedies. There is a line over which the courts cannot go. It is impermissible to trespass into the management of police forces generally or the NCS in particular.

C. Jurisdiction

Ex p Bennett and executive unlawfulness

In *R v Horseferry Road Magistrates' Court, ex p Bennett*,[20] Lord Lowry advanced **12.27** various definitions (at 73H–74C), and approved previous international authority in stating that 'the court is entitled to protect its process from abuse'. At 76C–76E, he made clear that this jurisdiction was not restricted to the trial process itself, but included matters antecedent to it—namely, investigative impropriety.

The decision in *Bennett* was concerned with a flagrant and deliberate failure by **12.28** state authorities to follow the law to the disadvantage of the accused. The court was not bound to tolerate such deliberate executive unlawfulness and could protect itself from this abuse by imposing a stay of proceedings. This category of deliberation by investigating authorities may be thought to be exceptional. It operates regardless of the guilt of the accused and is directed at maintenance of the integrity of the rule of law.

There was no suggestion that the accused could not have a fair trial in practical **12.29** terms. Their Lordships emphasized the court's jurisdiction 'to oversee executive action and to refuse to countenance behaviour that threatens either basic human rights or the rule of law'.[21]

---

[19] [2003] EWCA Civ 57, at [11]–[51].
[20] [1994] 1 AC 42, HL.
[21] *Per* Lord Griffiths, at 61H–62C. See also 64B–64D.

12.30   At 67F–67H, Lord Bridge said:

> There is, I think, no principle more basic to any proper system of law than the main-
> tenance of the rule of law itself. When it is shown that the law enforcement agency
> responsible for bringing a prosecution has only been enabled to do so by participat-
> ing in violation of international law and of the laws of another state in order to secure
> the presence of the accused within the territorial jurisdiction of the court, I think
> that respect for the rule of law demands that the court take cognizance of that
> circumstance.

12.31   At 70E–70F, Lord Oliver of Aylmerton (although disagreeing in the result) said:

> It is, of course, not in dispute that the court has a power to prevent the abuse of its
> own process and that must, I would accept, include power to investigate the bona
> fides of the charge which it is called upon to try and to decline to entertain a charge
> instituted in bad faith or oppressively . . .

12.32   At 74F–74H, Lord Lowry said:

> . . . a court has a discretion to stay any criminal proceedings on the ground that to try
> those proceedings will amount to an abuse of its own process either (1) because it will
> be impossible (usually by reason of delay) to give the accused a fair trial or (2) because
> it offends the court's sense of justice and propriety to be asked to try the accused in
> the circumstances of the particular case.

12.33   Such dicta have been applied regularly in the criminal jurisdiction. In *R v Latif*,[22]
Lord Steyn set out (at 112G–112H):

> The court has a discretion: it has to perform a balancing exercise. If the court con-
> cludes that a fair trial is not possible, it will stay the proceedings. This is not what the
> present case is concerned with. It is plain that a fair trial was possible and that such a
> trial took place. In this case the issue is whether, despite the fact that a fair trial was
> possible, the judge ought to have stayed the criminal proceedings on broader consid-
> erations of the integrity of the criminal justice system. The law is settled. Weighing
> countervailing considerations of policy and justice, it is for the judge in the exercise
> of his discretion to decide whether there has been an abuse of process, which amounts
> to an affront to the public conscience and requires the criminal proceedings to be
> stayed: *Reg. v. Horseferry Road Magistrates' court, ex parte Bennett.*

12.34   In *A v Secretary of State for the Home Department*,[23] Lord Bingham rehearses an
authoritative and convenient analysis of abuse of process under this head, including reference to *R (Mullen) v Secretary of State for the Home Department*.[24] The
appellant had been subject to a fair trial, and convicted and sentenced to thirty
years' imprisonment for terrorism before the circumstances of the State's involvement in his illegal abduction was known. Notwithstanding presumed guilt, his
conviction was quashed. Similar, if more complex, factual issues in the context of

---

22   [1996] 1 WLR 104.
23   [2006] 2 AC 221, at [19]–[22].
24   [2000] QB 529, CA.

the legitimate boundaries of state entrapment are rehearsed in *Attorney-General's Reference (No 3 of 2000) (Looseley)*.[25]

Similarly, the civil courts have always recognized the existence of a jurisdiction to strike out claims as abusing the process of the court.[26] Rule 3.4(2) of the Civil Procedure Rules explicitly empowers the civil courts to strike out any proceeding that is 'an abuse of the court's process or is otherwise likely to obstruct the just disposal of the proceedings'. Paragraph 3.4.3 of the 2009 edition of the White Book rehearses that 'the categories of abuse of process are many and not closed', and reflects Lord Bingham's formulation that it involves 'using that process for a purpose or in a way significantly different from its ordinary and proper use.'[27] **12.35**

The practicability of a fair hearing and regulatory departure

In practice, the real and legitimate concern of any tribunal is to ensure a fair hearing for the accused, whilst remembering that it is not the role of the tribunal to exercise disciplinary powers over the investigators or presenting side. It must, however, end proceedings if the accused is simply unable to receive a fair hearing in practical terms. **12.36**

As already observed (see 12.01–12.02 above), the reality in the modern regulatory tribunal is that proceedings will only be stopped, without the evidence against the accused having first been tested, if the accused can show one of two situations: (i) practical prejudice to a fair determination however so caused; or (ii) *Bennett*-type executive unlawfulness. To these must be added considerations of regulatory departure following *Merrill* and *Wilkinson* (see 7.113–7.119), which may fairly be characterized as free-standing, although something of a hybrid of the other categories. **12.37**

The matter was explicitly dealt with by the Master of the Rolls in the police discipline case of *R v Chief Constable of Merseyside Police, ex p Merrill*,[28] in which Lord Donaldson MR said, at 1085 F–1085G, in relation to the 1985 Discipline Regulations, that: **12.38**

> The Chief Constable had no need to concern himself with "abuse of process." As a judicial tribunal, he had a discretionary power to dismiss the charge without hearing the full evidence if he was satisfied that, whatever the evidence might reveal, it would be unfair to proceed further. "Unfairness" in this context is a general concept which comprehends prejudice to the accused, but can also extend to a significant departure from the intended and prescribed framework of disciplinary proceedings or a combination of both.

---

[25] *R v Looseley; Attorney-General's Reference (No 3 of 2000)* [2002] 1 Cr App R 29, [2001] 1 WLR 2060, HL.

[26] See, eg, Lord Bingham of Cornhill in *Attorney General v Barker* [2000] 1 FLR 759.

[27] Waller LJ (ed) (2009) *The White Book*, London: Sweet & Maxwell; citing Lord Bingham in *Attorney General v Barker*, ibid.

[28] [1989] 1 WLR 1077, CA.

12.39   In *Redgrave v Commissioner of Police of the Metropolis*,[29] Moses J reviewed supposed differences in approach 'in considering the protean concept of unfairness'[30] and concluded that the correct approach to applications to dismiss (or stay) charges without hearing the evidence 'is to consider whether a fair or just hearing is possible in the light of such inexcusable delay and serious prejudice as the officer may establish'.

12.40   He continued with the important dictum that 'if disciplinary boards or others conducting disciplinary hearings focus on the concept of the possibility of a fair hearing, they will, in my view, be following the guidance given both by ex parte Merrill and Attorney-General's Reference (No 1 of 1990)'.

12.41   Judicial reviews from other regulatory jurisdictions have confirmed the existence in the jurisdiction of the professionally regulated to challenge misconduct charges without the evidence being heard, including *Council for the Regulation of Healthcare Professionals v GMC and Saluja*,[31] *Varma v GMC*,[32] a General Medical Council (GMC) case, and *Johnson and Maggs v PCC of Nursing and Midwifery Council*,[33] a midwifery case.

12.42   In *Saluja*, an appeal from the decision of the 'fitness to practise' panel of the GMC to stay proceedings as an abuse, the judge derived the following principles from a review of authorities in the case of regulatory and disciplinary proceedings:

   (i)   To impose a stay of proceedings is exceptional;
   (ii) Both domestic and European authority make plain that the position so far as abuse of power by a non-state agency such as a regulator is different to that of the executive's misuse of state power;
   (iii) There is no state involvement where disciplinary proceedings are brought. Such proceedings are brought against a professional person by his regulator in order to protect the public, uphold professional standards and maintain confidence in the profession, and are to a significant degree different to a criminal prosecution and any alleged misuse of power by the state's agents; and
   (iv) Even if the doctor's rights under either Articles 6 or 8 had been infringed it was merely a matter to be taken into account when deciding whether there had been an abuse of process.

12.43   This approach, which reflects earlier authorities including *R v GMC, ex p Toth*[34] and *R (Gibson) v GMC*,[35] is echoed in *Redgrave*.[36] At [38] (when explaining the

---

[29]   [2002] EWHC 1074 (Admin).
[30]   Those differences having been considered previously by Sedley J in *R v Chief Constable of Devon and Cornwall Constabulary, ex p Hay* [1996] 2 All ER 711.
[31]   [2006] EWHC 2784 (Admin).
[32]   [2008] EWHC 753 (Admin).
[33]   [2008] EWHC 885 (Admin).
[34]   [2000] 1 WLR 2209.
[35]   [2004] EWHC 2781 (Admin).
[36]   [2003] EWCA Civ 04.

non-applicability of the protection against double jeopardy to statutory regulatory proceedings), Simon Brown LJ said that the 'character and purpose' of professional regulatory proceedings was 'entirely different' from that of criminal proceedings.

These authorities consistently demonstrate that public confidence in the regulation of professional conduct requires that a complaint should, in the absence of some special or sufficient reason, be investigated in disciplinary proceedings and that only a very clear case of manifest unfairness in the conduct of proceedings will justify a stay on any basis. Professional misconduct proceedings represent the last available mechanism with which to remove a potentially unfit professional from practice. Equally, whilst it is not in the public interest for (for example) dishonest or violent police officers to be retained in office, removal must reflect a fair hearing and the integrity of the process must be protected. These are competing considerations for the determining misconduct panel. **12.44**

Exceptional remedy

Consistent with this, the courts have repeatedly emphasized that the trial process itself is equipped to deal with most contended categories of abuse. There is power to exclude evidence if it has been obtained improperly. The exceptional quality of a permanent stay is reflected in *Attorney-General's Reference (No1 of 1990)*:[37] **12.45**

> Stays imposed on the grounds of delay or for any other reason should only be employed in exceptional circumstances . . . In principle, therefore, even where the delay can be said to be unjustifiable, the imposition of a permanent stay should be the exception rather than the rule.

This echoes the observation of Lord Morris of Borth-y-Gest in *Connelly v DPP*[38] that 'generally speaking a prosecutor has as much right as a defendant to demand a verdict of a jury on an outstanding indictment, and where either demands a verdict a judge has no jurisdiction to stand in the way of it', and, more recently, Lord Steyn's observations in *Latif*[39] that: **12.46**

> the judge must weigh in the balance the public interest in ensuring that those that are charged with grave crimes should be tried and the competing public interest in not conveying the impression that the court will adopt the approach that the end justifies any means.

---

[37] [1992] 1 QB 630, 643G–643H.
[38] [1964] AC 1254, 1304, HL.
[39] *R v Latif* [1996] 1 WLR 104, 113A—see 12.33 above.

Burden

12.47 Where the basis for the application to halt the misconduct proceedings without hearing the evidence is that the officer concerned cannot receive a fair hearing, then the burden is on him to prove that he cannot have a fair hearing.[40] Obviously, unconscionable conduct, rather than practical unfairness, must be established in *Bennett*-type applications.

12.48 This chapter will now examine the three main practical circumstances in which applications to stay proceedings are made in the specific context of police misconduct proceedings—namely, regulatory departure, delay, and the generic heading of 'fair hearing impossible'.

D. Regulatory Departure

12.49 The investigation and presentation of police complaints or conduct matters are governed by statute and, more directly, regulation—in particular, the Police (Conduct) Regulations 2008[41] and the near-identical provisions within Sch 3 to the 2002 Act. They are therefore regulatory proceedings.

12.50 It follows that those responsible for their investigation and presentation must strive to adhere to the Regulations and the associated Home Office Guidance on *Police Officer Misconduct, Unsatisfactory Performance and Attendance Management Procedures*.[42] It also follows that any departure from the 'the intended and prescribed framework of disciplinary proceedings'[43] gives rise to the possibility of complaint by the officer concerned.

12.51 The most common (and certainly most litigated) species of abuse of process arguments brought in the police disciplinary regime over the years has been that complaining that the notice of investigation (whether under reg 7 of the 1985 Discipline Regulations, or reg 9 of the Police (Conduct) Regulations 1999[44] or 2004,[45] and now reg 15 of the 2008 Conduct Regulations, or reg 14E of the Police (Complaints and Misconduct) Regulations 2004)[46] was not served 'as soon

---

[40] See *Attorney-General's Ref (No 1 of 1990)* [1992] 1 QB 630, 644A–644B, and *per* Moses J in *Redgrave v Commissioner of Police of the Metropolis* [2002] EWHC 1074 (Admin), who stated at [38] that 'the burden clearly lies upon the police officer asserting such prejudice to establish it'.

[41] SI 2008/2864.

[42] The Guidance is statutory in its origin—see s 87(1) of the Police Act 1996.

[43] *R v Chief Constable of Merseyside Police, ex p Merrill* [1989] 1 WLR 1077, 1085G.

[44] SI 1999/730.

[45] SI 2004/645.

[46] SI 2004/643.

as practicable'. This remains the injunction on the investigator in the 2008 regime.

Notices of investigation—directory, rather than mandatory, in effect, so that a **12.52** breach does not automatically vitiate proceedings—in this sense were considered at 7.113–7.119 and that analysis is not repeated here. The point of general application is perhaps *R v Chief Constable of the Merseyside Police, ex p Calveley*[47] (434G–435A):

> . . . a police officer's submission to police disciplinary procedures is not uncondi-
> tional. He agrees to and is bound by these procedures taking them as a whole. Just as
> his right of appeal is constrained by the requirement that he give prompt notice of
> appeal, so he is not to be put in peril in respect of disciplinary, as contrasted with
> criminal, proceedings unless there is substantial compliance with the police discipli-
> nary regulations. That has not occurred in this case. Whether in all the circumstances
> the Chief Constable, and the Secretary of State on appeal, is to be regarded as being
> without jurisdiction to hear and determine the charges which are not processed in
> accordance with the statutory scheme or whether, in natural justice, the Chief
> Constable and the Secretary of State would, if they directed themselves correctly in
> law, be bound to rule in favour of the applicants on the preliminary point, is perhaps
> only of academic interest. The substance of the matter is that, against the back-
> ground of the requirement of regulation 7 that the applicants be informed of the
> complaint and given an opportunity to reply within days rather than weeks, the
> applicants had no formal notice of the complaints for well over two years. This is so
> serious a departure from the police disciplinary procedure that, in my judgment, the
> court should, in the exercise of its discretion, grant judicial review and set aside the
> determination of the Chief Constable.

Thus can be seen the development of the proposition that if the accused officer is **12.53** to succeed on a reg 14A/15 argument, or in respect of any other departure from the intended regulatory framework, in modern practice, he must show not only prejudice, but prejudice such as to render a fair hearing of the matter (or part of the allegation) impossible.

The new misconduct regime, under the 2008 Conduct Regulations and the paral- **12.54** lel regime in Sch 3 of the 2002 Act, contains a large number of critical decisions to be taken by the appropriate authority (for example, the initial assessment or whether to refer to misconduct proceedings), or the investigator (the written notice or the content of the written report), or the person conducting or chairing the proceedings (whether to permit witnesses and which documents to permit the officer concerned to see). It is, accordingly, not difficult to anticipate arguments based on regulatory departure in this context.

---

[47] [1986] QB 424, CA. The House of Lords subsequently dismissed various contended causes of action brought by the affected officers for damages: see [1989] AC 1228.

E. Delay

12.55 Any consideration of the law on delay and its management at misconduct proceedings must start with the *Attorney-General's Reference (No 1 of 1990)*,[48] from which the following principles may be derived.

(i) Stays imposed on the ground of delay should be employed only in exceptional circumstances. That general observation is, however, to be viewed against the backdrop of new Conduct Regulations, which require serious expedition in the investigative and presenting phases.

(ii) Flowing from the first point, even where the delay can be said to be unjustifiable, the imposition of a permanent stay should be the exception, rather than the rule.

(iii) More rare still should be cases in which a stay can properly be imposed in the absence of any fault on the part of the complainant or prosecution/investigator.

(iv) Delay due merely to the complexity of the case or contributed to by the actions of the officer concerned (for example, by going sick at critical stages of the investigation) should never be the foundation for a stay.

(v) No stay on the grounds of delay should be imposed unless the officer concerned shows, on the balance of probabilities, that, owing to the delay (and no other causes), he will suffer serious prejudice to the extent that no fair hearing can be held.

(vi) In assessing the existence of prejudice, the power of the misconduct panel to regulate its procedures and admissibility of evidence should be borne in mind (see reg 34 of the 2008 Conduct Regulations).

12.56 It is worth observing that, in the criminal jurisdiction, many historic allegations of serious sexual abuse are now tried even in the absence of corroboration. The trial process is presumed able to address the practical consequences.

F. 'Fair Hearing Impossible'

12.57 Where, for whatever reason, a fair hearing (meaning a reasoned determination of the allegation) is simply no longer possible, the person conducting or chairing the misconduct proceedings should dismiss the charges without hearing the evidence.

---

[48] [1992] 1 QB 630, 643G–644D.

This may include the loss of key evidence (or memory) through delay, or error in failing to secure key exhibits.

As stated above, the burden is on the officer concerned to demonstrate, on the **12.58** balance of probabilities, that he cannot have a fair hearing. To surmount such a hurdle, he will generally need to show something such as the destruction of key (potentially) exculpatory evidence, or the death or disappearance of a key witness. As to the investigator's role in the preservation of relevant evidence, see *Ebrahim v Feltham Magistrates Court, sub nom Mouat v DPP*.[49] Each case will be wholly fact-sensitive.

G. Article 6 of the European Convention on Human Rights (ECHR)

It is well established that police misconduct proceedings are not protected by **12.59** Art 6 of the European Convention on Human Rights (ECHR), because they involve the conduct of those involved in 'direct or indirect participation in the exercise of powers conferred by public law and duties designed to safeguard the general interests of the State or of other public authorities'.[50]

This 'functional criterion' excluding the application of Art 6 would cease to apply **12.60** to disputes following retirement, such as in respect of pension rights, because 'the special relationship of trust and loyalty binding them to the State has ceased to exist and the employee can no longer wield a portion of the State's sovereign power'.

This approach has been confirmed in two English cases. In *Lee v UK*,[51] the appli- **12.61** cant was a police sergeant who was suspended from duty for his failure to cooperate with an internal investigation into allegations that a police officer had been supplying steroids. It was alleged that Lee had attempted to pervert the course of justice and had deliberately withheld information. No criminal charges were brought on the advice of the Crown Prosecution Service (CPS) that there was insufficient evidence, but, twenty days before the officer was due to retire on grounds of ill health, he was charged with disciplinary proceedings for having allegedly failed to provide a statement for the purposes of the investigation into the drug allegations. He was subsequently found guilty of neglect of duty at those disciplinary proceedings and reprimanded. An appeal was dismissed.

Lee sought to bring an application to the European Court of Human Rights **12.62** alleging a breach of Art 6 on the basis that he had been denied legal assistance,

---

[49] [2001] 2 Cr App R 23.
[50] See *Pellegrin v France* (2001) 31 EHRR 651, at [66]–[67].
[51] App no 53429/99, 16 May 2000; [2000] Police Law Reports 170.

and that the disciplinary proceedings were unfair and were a disguised attempt to resurrect a criminal charge. Lee's application was declared inadmissible because the disciplinary proceedings taken against him did not involve the determination of a 'criminal charge' within the meaning of Art 6(1).

12.63 In *R (Whitehead and Daglish) v Chief Constable Avon and Somerset*,[52] Richards J explicitly referred to *Lee*, and seemingly disposed of the argument that Art 6 applies to police disciplinary proceedings at [26] and [27] of his judgment. At [27], he stated that he regarded the decision in *Lee* as 'clear' and saw no reason why he should not give full effect to it. In his judgment, 'disciplinary proceedings of the present kind are not criminal proceedings within Article 6 of the Convention. That being so the claimants' argument necessarily fails'.

12.64 Whether the non-applicability of Art 6 to police misconduct proceedings makes any substantive difference to the rights of officers concerned is a matter for debate. In practical terms, the test is one of fairness and practicability even without Art 6.

H. Conclusion

12.65 More could be written about abuse of process. In practice, in what is a heavily fact-specific area, the officer concerned will usually need to establish what practical unfairness genuinely exists to prevent a fair determination of an allegation.

12.66 In criminal proceedings, a practice direction of national application requires notice of application at least twenty-one days before the application is determined. This approach—that is, a written application on notice to the presenting side well before the substantive hearing—is manifestly within the duty of the officer concerned under reg 22(2) of the 2008 Conduct Regulations. Many applications will be avoidable if the obligation to serve a written notice of investigation has been served as required as soon as practicable by the investigating officer and if that notice is properly drafted. Furthermore, closer adherence more generally to the regulatory obligations coupled with good investigative practices will also help to reduce the volume of 'unfairness' applications.

---

[52] [2001] EWHC (Admin) 433.

13

PROBATIONERS

A. Overview	13.01	Conclusions from the case law	13.23
B. Regulation 13 of the Police		Procedure	13.24
Regulations 2003	13.03	C. Conclusion	13.26
Decided authorities	13.14		

A. Overview

As has been set out, there are only a limited number of bases on which a police **13.01** constable of any rank may be compelled to lose office. Not every police recruit will pass the training programme and graduate to the office. Subject to that type of failure, the chief officer has discretion to dispense with the services of a probationer for reasons not restricted to proven acts of misconduct or incompetence.

This is an important and probably necessary power, given the long-term conse- **13.02** quences of managing those officers who are of the wrong character or temperament to hold the office of constable. Equally, the necessary discretion to remove must not be exercised in an arbitrary manner and is not an appropriate substitute for misconduct proceedings if the alleged basis for dispensation is a specific disputed misconduct allegation. These competing considerations are reflected in the legislation and limited number of associated decided authorities.

B. Regulation 13 of the Police Regulations 2003

Regulation 13(1) of the Police Regulations 2003[1] provides as follows: **13.03**

> Subject to the provisions of this regulation, during his period of probation in the force the services of a constable may be dispensed with at any time if the chief officer considers that he is not fitted, physically or mentally, to perform the duties of his office, or that he is not likely to become an efficient or well conducted constable.

---

[1] SI 2003/527.

13.04 It will be seen that there are two bases upon which the chief constable can dispense with the probationer's services—that is, if he considers that the probationer is either (i) not 'fitted', 'physically or mentally', to perform the duties of his office; or (ii) is 'not likely' to become an 'efficient or well-conducted constable'.

13.05 These terms are nowhere defined and are, to a degree, somewhat subjective. 'Not likely' is clearly a lower hurdle than 'not capable'. Any chief constable would doubtless contend that he or she is well able to identify and define the requirements (mental or otherwise) to perform the duties of a constable and/or to become an efficient and well-conducted constable. These requirements presumably include (although plainly are not limited to) common sense, good judgement, and self-control.

13.06 There is little difficulty if there are objective reasons to question a probationer's integrity or emotional maturity. Of greater challenge is ill-judged—but lawful— off-duty conduct, or a 'sense'—unsupported by more than experience or instinct— that a particular probationer is not of the calibre to be appointed constable.

13.07 At first blush, one might have thought that by introducing reg 13 (and its identical predecessors), Parliament intended to provide chief constables with a summary form of 'dismissal' for those who had not accrued the full rights and entitlements of constables. Used appropriately, it is a filter that operates in the wider public interest. Indeed, it seems arguable that the existence of reg 13, with its heading 'Discharge of probationer', suggests that a probationer has attenuated rights as compared with those of a 'full' constable who, after all, can only be dismissed pursuant to the regime set out under the Conduct or Performance Regulations.

13.08 The only requirement in deploying reg 13 would be—as in any 'employment' situation—that the employer acts with procedural and substantive fairness. Considerations of proportionality and fairness affect the exercise of discretion in this context, just as they do for any employer in a non-policing context determining the outcome of a probationary period. It is probably an area in which the courts will be slow to interfere with the reasoned exercise of discretion by the chief constable: this is a classic part of the management of direction and control of a force under s 10 of the Police Act 1996. As with any exercise of discretion, however, an unreasoned decision will appear arbitrary and attract challenge.

13.09 Difficulties have arisen, however, in the history of the application of reg 13 and its predecessors. This is reflected both in the decided authorities and in the drafting of the 2004 Home Office Guidance on *Police Unsatisfactory Performance Complaints and Misconduct Procedures*. The language of the 2008 Guidance should be considered for matters arising after 1 December 2008.

Paragraph (e) of the 2004 Guidance states as follows: **13.10**

> Whilst probationers are not subject to the procedures for dealing with unsatisfactory performance (since there are separately established procedures for dealing with the performance of probationers), they are subject to the misconduct procedures. The provision for a chief officer to dispense with the services of a constable during his or her probationary period should not be used as an alternative means of dismissing a probationer who should properly face misconduct proceedings. When misconduct proceedings are appropriate and justified, they should be brought; where they are not brought, a probationer should not be left with the impression that he or she has been suspected of misconduct and been given no chance to defend him or herself.

This wording reflects the approach of the courts that, in disputed cases of specific   **13.11** acts of misconduct, the disciplinary (that is, conduct) regulations should be invoked rather than the more summary reg 13.

The position may be subject to slight revision in that para 2.11 of the 2008   **13.12** Guidance states as follows:

> The chief officer has discretion whether to use the misconduct procedures or the procedures set out at Regulation 13 of the Police Regulations 2003 (discharge of probationer) as the most appropriate means of dealing with a misconduct matter. In exercising this discretion due regard should be had to whether the student police officer admits to the conduct or not. Where the misconduct in question is not admitted by the student police officer then, in most, if not all cases the matter will fall to be determined under the misconduct procedures. If the Regulation 13 procedure is used, the student police officer should be given a fair hearing (i.e. an opportunity to comment and present mitigation) under that procedure.

The chief constable will have to identify in disputed misconduct cases why the   **13.13** misconduct procedures are not being used. Regulation 13 is, of course, wider than situations contingent on proof of specific acts amounting to misconduct under the Code of Conduct.

Decided authorities

Three cases have been commonly interpreted as requiring that reg 13 should not   **13.14** be used as a means of 'circumnavigating' the Conduct Regulations.

In *Chief Constable of North Wales v Evans*,[2] the House of Lords found that the chief   **13.15** constable had not acted fairly in that he had failed to put to the probationer the key allegations that led to the concerns about him. The primary basis of the dispensation (in fact, the probationer resigned as an alternative) was related to a possible breach of a tenancy agreement (keeping dogs in a council property until arrangements could be made to rehouse them). Whether such conduct meets the

---

² [1982] 1 WLR 1155.

reg 13 test (it is hard to see that it could be a misconduct offence) is intrinsically subjective.

13.16 It is to be observed that the procedural unfairness found to have occurred did not lead to an order of reinstatement. The Lords referred to this being an order that 'might border on usurpation of the powers of the chief constable'. Although arguably less deference has been given to this consideration in recent history,[3] it is still highly relevant. A declaration that dispensation under reg 13 was not justified may permit an applicant to apply to a different force without prejudice.

13.17 In *Carroll v West Midlands Police*,[4] the dismissed probationer explicitly relied upon the equivalent predecessor of para (e) to the Introduction to the 2004 Guidance to argue that he should have been subject to misconduct proceedings rather than reg 13 discharge proceedings. This failure, he contended, was both *Wednesbury* unreasonable and unfair.

13.18 The Court of Appeal agreed with both of these propositions. It observed that the lower (divisional) court had found the claimant probationer's evidence on crucial disputes more reliable than his accusers. Thus, had the probationer been placed before a misconduct panel, he might well have been acquitted. In those circumstances, it is therefore perhaps unsurprising that the Court was disinclined to find for the chief constable.

13.19 The authority is more valuable for the underlying approach of the Court. McCowan LJ concluded[5] that 'prima facie, therefore, there should have been disciplinary proceedings concerning the allegations, since the appellant denied them and made serious allegations of conspiracy against his accusers'. Lord Justice Rose observed[6] that 'the fundamental flaw in the fairness of the Chief Constable's decision was that he assumed facts to be established which were and had been, virtually from the outset, disputed by the appellant, notably on the basis that other officers were conspiring against him', and Balcombe LJ found,[7] in relation to the key two allegations, that:

> there were disputed issues of fact . . . Mr Carroll had not himself made any significant admission as to the relevant facts. In my judgment, in failing to give Mr Carroll the opportunity to deal with those contested issues of fact by the means of a disciplinary hearing the Chief Constable broke the duty of fairness which, of course, is recognised by [the Home Office Guidance].

---

[3] See the series of cases determined under reg 40 of the Police (Conduct) Regulations 2004, SI 2004/645, regarding chief officer reviews.
[4] Unreported, 10 May 1994, CA.
[5] Transcript p 14.
[6] Transcript p 15.
[7] Transcript p 17.

It is, however, noteworthy that the Court of Appeal did not suggest that fairness   **13.20**
could *only* be achieved by formal misconduct proceedings.

In *Farmer v British Transport Police*,[8] whilst the Court of Appeal again recognized   **13.21**
that a probationer should ordinarily be dismissed under the equivalent of reg 13
for misconduct only when the misconduct is admitted, nonetheless the Court
found that 'where the offence is admitted, there will be many cases where it would
be contrary to good administration to go by the disciplinary route. The probationary period is there to discover and deal with fundamental unsuitability of outlook
or temperament or behaviour. Each of these might manifest themselves in misconduct, but would in most cases be more appropriately resolved in the probationer's dismissal procedure concerned as it is not so much with the individual
charges as with fundamental questions about whether the probationary police
constable is fitted to peform the testing duties required of the police'.

In giving the judgment of the Court, Henry LJ concluded (with emphasis added)   **13.22**
as follows:

> . . . the cases of *Evans* and *Carroll* each show that, in what I might call mainstream
> policing,[9] where the Police Regulations apply, *it has never been suggested that there is*
> *no discretion to proceed by the probationary dismissal procedures where misconduct such*
> *as might be prosecuted under the disciplinary process is charged* . . . In conclusion, there
> are two separate dismissal procedures which govern probationers.[10] The decision
> which to use is a decision for the employing force. Where the facts a founding the
> complaint are not admitted, in most if not all cases the decision is likely to be that
> the question whether the charge is proved or not proved be decided under the
> disciplinary procedures.

Farmer was followed in *R (Khan) v Chief Constable of Lancashire*.[11] In this case a
probationer police constable had engaged in sexual conduct with an intoxicated
female student he had met in a nightclub. The conduct involved another male
and was video- recorded. The student alledged rape but no prosecution resulted.
The chief constable dispensed with the probationer under regulation 13, an
approach endorsed by the Administrative Court. The dispensation was based on
the incontrovertible facts and associated findings as to the probationer's lack of
judgement and conduct towards a vulnerable young woman for sexual gratifica-
tion. The Court did not accept that a disciplinary body would have been better
placed to assess the primary facts.

---

[8] Unreported, 30 July 1999, CA.
[9] *Farmer* was a British Transport Police case.
[10] That is, reg 13 (dispensation) or the Conduct Regulations (requirement to resign or
dismissal).
[11] [2009] EWHC 472 (Admin).

Similarly the Court (applying *Sunday Times v United Kingdom*[12] and *Pay v United Kingdom*[13]) rejected arguments that regulation 13 or the application of it on the facts was in breach of Article 8 of the European Convention on Human Rights (any interference with the private rights of Article 8(1) must be prescribed by law). An employee owed his employer a duty of loyalty and discretion which could be breached by private conduct.

Conclusions from the case law

13.23   The following key points emerge.

(i)   First and foremost, the probationer must be treated fairly, both procedurally and substantively. 'Procedural fairness' requires adherence to internal procedures and application of the rules of natural justice in terms of the procedure. 'Substantive fairness' means weighing the evidence in a fair and even-handed manner.

(ii) If there is no dispute on the material facts upon which the chief constable proposes to base his decision, then it is difficult to see why it would be unfair to utilize the reg 13 provisions.

(iii) If the material facts *are* disputed, then the effect of para (e) of the Introduction to the 2004 Home Office Guidance requires, ordinarily, *but not always*, misconduct rather than reg 13 proceedings. Under para 2.11 of the 2008 Guidance: '[W]here the misconduct in question is not admitted by the student police officer then, in most, if not all cases the matter will fall to be determined under the misconduct procedures.'

(iv) This assumes that the conduct could qualify as a misconduct offence. If not, then reg 13 appears appropriate.

(v)   Both versions of the Guidance, and *Farmer*, seem to recognize that there remains discretion in exceptional cases to utilize the reg 13 discharge route, notwithstanding that the 'concerns' about the probationer are in the nature of allegations of misconduct.

Procedure

13.24   If a chief constable determines that he has before him a case in which he wishes to apply the reg 13 procedure, he must ensure that procedural and substantive fairness is afforded. In particular, he would be well advised to ensure that the following steps have been taken.

---

[12]   [1979] 2 EHRR 245.

[13]   [2009] IRLR 139. A probation officer was dismissed because of his private activities in merchandising products connected with bondage and sado-masochism. This was upheld by the European Court of Human Rights.

(i) Internal force polices should both exist and be followed (the probationer has a legitimate expectation that they will).

(ii) The probationer should be advised in writing what the concerns are under reg 13 and supporting documentation should be provided to him or her.

(iii) If the allegation amounts to a specific allegation of misconduct, the reasons for proceeding by way of reg 13 rather than through misconduct proceedings should be set out in writing.

(iv) The probationer should be given an opportunity to make representations (verbal or written) about the concerns, including the use of reg 13, with a right to appeal to a more senior officer. It is standard practice for the reg 13 procedure to be instigated by the divisional commander, who sends a recommendation to the deputy chief constable—or equivalent in the Metropolitan Police Service (MPS)—who may also hold a meeting with the probationer, before sending the matter to the chief constable for a final decision;

(v) If practicable, the chief constable should hold a meeting with the probationer concerned. His final decision should be promulgated to the probationer, in writing, with reasons being given for the decision to dispense with his services. The reasons should be specific and factual, rather than simply rehearsing that one or more of the tests under reg 13 have been met.

In relation to (v) above, a reg 13 decision is susceptible to challenge by way **13.25** of judicial review. Accordingly, the chief constable should himself be satisfied that the dispensation letter:

(i) identifies with precision the factors upon which he relies;

(ii) relies only upon those facts that are admitted or incontrovertible (findings as to mental health are to be avoided unless supported by expert evidence; questions of maturity, attitude and temperament do not require expert evidence);

(iii) identifies with precision which limbs of reg 13 are relied upon;

(iv) faithfully reflects his views as to the personal qualities that he expects of his officers—it is, after all, the responsibility of a chief constable to determine what is or is not acceptable within his force.

C. Conclusion

It is clear that the use of reg 13 will be justified only in exceptional circumstances **13.26** if the matter is an allegation of misconduct in relation to which the facts are in dispute. Considerations of mental suitability to graduate to the office of constable do not amount to misconduct. Of course, if the facts on which such an assessment is made are in dispute, a fair procedure must be adopted to resolve any dispute.

13.27 The language of the 2008 Home Office Guidance is not so different from that of its 2004 predecessor as to suggest a significant change of culture between these provisions. The probationer may be said to have, and to require, rights that are proportionate with the personal investment involved in joining the police and the associated negative consequences if removed under reg 13. Equally, a chief constable must be afforded some discretion in the selection of those recruited to serve as part of the force. To this extent, graduation from probationer to constable should be seen as a privilege, not as a right.

14

INQUESTS

A. **Overview** 14.01
  Introduction 14.01
  Coronial law, policing, and the
    engagement of Art 2 of
    the ECHR 14.14
B. **The Nature and Purpose
  of an Inquest** 14.25
  Statutory purpose: statutory
    provisions 14.28
  Jamieson and *Middleton* inquests:
    general observations 14.33
  Inquests distinguished from other
    forms of proceeding 14.37
C. **The Duty to Hold, and the
  Timing of, an Inquest** 14.43
  The duty to hold an inquest (s 8(1)) 14.47
  Summoning a jury (s 8(3) and (4)) 14.52
  Inquests and criminal
    proceedings (s 16) 14.59
  Inquests following a public inquiry 14.68
  The scope of the inquest if resumed 14.71
  Challenging decisions regarding
    resumption or the conduct of an
    inquest 14.74
D. **The Scope of the Inquest:
  Jamieson, *Middleton*, and Art 2** 14.77
  Introduction and central conclusions
    in *Jamieson* 14.77
  Article 2 and *Middleton* 14.84
  Subsequent developments in the
    context of Art 2 inquests 14.87

Participation, *Amin*, and
  disclosure 14.89
Middleton, narrative verdicts,
  and restrictions on narrative
  verdicts 14.95
Rule 43 and the Coroners
  (Amendment) Rules 2008 14.105
E. **Fundamental Points
  of Procedure** 14.110
  Qualification as an interested
    person 14.110
  The funding of interested persons 14.112
    Police officers 14.112
    Relatives of the deceased 14.116
  Anonymity 14.127
  Presence in court for other witnesses
    and the privilege against
    self-incrimination 14.142
  Witness summons and the
    admissibility of disputed
    evidence 14.147
F. **Verdicts** 14.153
  Withdrawing a verdict from the
    jury: *Galbraith* and *Douglas-
    Williams* 14.156
  Leaving verdicts at inquests 14.162
  Unlawful killing and the lethal
    use of firearms 14.168
  Challenging decisions as
    to verdicts 14.179
G. **Conclusion** 14.180

A. Overview

Introduction

14.01 A significant area of growth in recent years has been the scale and expectations attaching to inquests in connection with police conduct. This, in part, reflects a general momentum towards greater public accountability by the police when they are associated in any way with a death. More specifically, it reflects the investigative obligation on the State under Art 2 of the European Convention on Human Rights (ECHR), as to which the Human Rights Act 1998 (HRA) created enforceable rights for deaths occurring after 2 October 2000.

14.02 It is widely recognized that these greatly enhanced expectations have not been matched by additional resources, or the necessary changes in law and procedure. In relation to the law, there has been a series of detailed national reports into the adequacy of existing arrangements. These include the Home Office's *Death Certification and Investigation in England Wales and Northern Ireland: Report of the Fundamental Review* (the Luce Report),[1] *The Third Report of the Shipman Inquiry on Death Certification and Investigation,*[2] and the Home Office Position Paper responding to these reports, *Reforming the Coroner and Death Certification Service.*[3]

14.03 In June 2006, this process finally culminated in a draft Coroners Bill.[4] The respective Secretary and Ministers of State stated, in the Foreword, that the proposed reforms:

> . . . will address weaknesses that have become increasingly evident over the last 20 years. The coroners' system at present is fragmented, non-accountable, variable in its processes and its quality, ineffective in part, archaic in its statutory basis, and very much dependent on the good people working in, or resourcing it, at present for its continued ability to respond to the demands we place upon it.

14.04 On 27 March 2008, the Ministry of Justice published[5] changes resulting from consultation indicating that the Bill would be introduced in Parliament 'as soon as Parliamentary time allowed'. The Coroners Bill did not find a place in the Queen's Speech in 2007. At the time of writing, it (retitled 'the Coroners and Justice Bill',[6] and curiously now including matters relating to criminal, rather than coronial, law) forms part of the intended parliamentary timetable for 2009.

---

[1] Cm 5831, 4 June 2003.
[2] Cm 5854, 14 July 2003.
[3] Cm 6159, 11 March 2004.
[4] Cm 6849.
[5] Available online at <http://www.justice.gov.uk>.
[6] HC 185.

The original omission led the normally reserved Coroners' Society of England **14.05**
and Wales (CSEW) to issue a statement[7] expressing 'disappointment' that the
'legislative planners have not understood the need for significant reform to the law
and structure in which coroners have to deliver our services', commenting that,
despite much scrutiny, 'the system has in the main been neglected' and 'a perception of a postcode lottery given the varying resources available to coroners', and
highlighting 'basic examples of essential legal changes' that would not become
law. No informed practitioner would disagree.

It remains to be seen whether the Bill will become law in the foreseeable future. **14.06**
Pending reform, the existing arrangements satisfy nobody.

Coroners (funded as they are by local authorities) often simply lack the resources **14.07**
to conduct the inquest in a satisfactory manner. By way of example, one archaic
mandatory obligation is to hold the inquest within the coroner's geographical
jurisdiction. Finding and resourcing appropriate accommodation for a substantial hearing with multiple interested persons is invariably easier said than done.

The quality of training received has generated comment in more than one **14.08**
judicial review[8] that a senior judicial figure is required to conduct complex and
contentious hearings. Whilst certain inquests have been conducted by High
Court or senior Crown Court judges sitting as deputy coroners, this is not always
practicable. The coroner's summing up at an inquest is equally, if not more,
demanding than the obligation on a senior judge trying an allegation of homicide
in the Crown Court, yet the training and experience is widely divergent.

Families of the deceased face genuine obstacles in obtaining public funding for **14.09**
their representation (see 14.116–14.126 below). This can produce the wholly
unsatisfactory result of public (or other agency) funding for all interested persons
(including police officers) except the family of the deceased. Many—including
the authors of this book—are not persuaded by the legal fiction that the coroner
will make full inquiry of all relevant matters that would have been raised by representatives of the family of the deceased. If this is the case, why is there any right to
representation of any interested person at any time? That is not to say that the

---

[7] 6 November 2007, available online at <http://www.coronersociety.org.uk>.
[8] See Mr Justice Leveson in *R (Sharman) v Her Majesty's Coroner for Inner North London* [2005]
EWHC 857 (Admin) at [58]: 'This was always going to be a highly sensitive and difficult inquest to
conduct. All deserved better from the system and it is sufficient if I add my weight to the call to
implement the change recommended by [ch 9, para 8(c) of the Luce Report, to the effect that
exceptionally complex or contentious inquests should be conducted by a senior Crown Court or
High Court judge]. Without any disrespect to the Coroner, this extremely difficult case would have
benefited from judicial oversight at a higher level.' These observations were adopted by the Court of
Appeal: [2005] EWCA Civ 967, [38].

coroner will not attempt it, but rather to recognize that the family of the deceased may lack confidence that the objective sought will be achieved to its satisfaction.

14.10　Equally unsatisfactory, from the perspective of the affected police officers, is that the procedures at an inquest resemble that of a criminal trial without any of the legal protections and safeguards associated with such a trial. The theoretically inquisitorial process does not appear as such in practice. There is invariably a sense of the deceased's family's representatives prosecuting, through the inquest, an allegation of unlawful killing or neglect. As is now explicitly recognized by higher courts,[9] the prohibition on naming any party as criminally liable under r 42 of the Coroners Rules 1984[10] is no protection whatsoever from public censure when the inevitable logic of a verdict of unlawful killing is that a particular person is responsible and guilty to the criminal standard of manslaughter or murder. Legal niceties are lost between the courtroom and the next day's newspaper coverage.

14.11　These difficulties are compounded by the delay—often measured in years—before the substantive inquest takes place. This delay and associated uncertainty is positively harmful to all interested persons. Additionally, few high-profile police-related inquests in recent history have escaped judicial review proceedings. Verdicts of unlawful killing by the police (including inquests into the well-publicized deaths of Roger Sylvester and Harry Stanley) have consistently been overturned by higher courts on the basis of insufficient evidence and/or material misdirection by the coroner to the jury.

14.12　An indicator of the unreliability of such a verdict is that no successful prosecution has followed a verdict of unlawful killing at an inquest relating to the police. This, in turn, unfairly undermines the confidence of the deceased's family in the prosecuting authorities.

14.13　Similarly, the attempted use of juries to determine wider questions of system and policy (as distinct from narrow specific questions of fact) is legitimately criticized.[11] As is subsequently set out (see 14.99 below), it is contended that any recommendations in these respects are properly for the coroner under r 43 of the Coroners Rules 1984. Pending further progress with the Bill, secondary legislation[12] has strengthened the provisions in respect of r 43 and the momentum away from wider policy and system findings by juries is likely to be increased (see 14.105 below).

---

⁹ See 14.168–14.170 below.
¹⁰ SI 1984/552.
¹¹ See Pill LJ in *R (Sacker) v West Yorkshire Coroner* [2003] 2 All ER 278, [24]–[27], CA; *R (Scholes) v Secretary of State for the Home Department* [2006] EWCA Civ 1343, CA.
¹² The Coroners (Amendment) Rules 2008, SI 2008/1652, in force 17 July 2008.

Coronial law, policing, and the engagement of Art 2 of the ECHR

Coronial law is a significant topic in its own right and this chapter is directed only **14.14** at issues that routinely arise in a policing context.

There are a number of familiar policing scenarios. The police may simply have **14.15** played an uncontroversial part in a wider narrative of events preceding a death. A death may follow from interaction with other State agencies—in particular, those providing emergency medical care—generating legitimate considerations as to the quality of protocols governing responsibilities between the two. Where a death is attributable to the (unlawful) actions of a third party, however, Art 2(1) of the ECHR ('Everyone's right to life shall be protected by law . . .') may still be engaged. The European Court of Human Rights (EctHR) held, in *Osman v UK*,[13] as follows.

(i) The first sentence of Art 2(1) enjoins the State not only to refrain from the intentional and unlawful taking of life, but also to take appropriate steps to safeguard the lives of those within its jurisdiction. The State's obligation in this respect extends beyond its primary duty to secure the right to life by putting in place effective criminal law provisions to deter the commission of offences against the person, backed up by law-enforcement machinery for the prevention, suppression, and sanctioning of breaches of such provisions. Article 2 may also imply, in certain well-defined circumstances, a positive obligation on the authorities to take preventive operational measures to protect an individual whose life is at risk from the criminal acts of another individual.

(ii) Bearing in mind the difficulties involved in policing modern societies, the unpredictability of human conduct and the operational choices that must be made in terms of priorities and resources, such an obligation must be interpreted in a way that does not impose an impossible or disproportionate burden on the authorities. Accordingly, not every claimed risk to life can entail for the authorities a Convention requirement to take operational measures to prevent that risk from materializing. Another relevant consideration is the need to ensure that the police exercise their powers to control and prevent crime in a manner that fully respects the due process and other guarantees that legitimately place restraints on the scope of their action to investigate crime and bring offenders to justice, including the guarantees contained in Arts 5 and 8 of the Convention.

(iii) Where there is an allegation that the authorities have violated their positive obligation to protect the right to life in the context of their abovementioned

---

[13] (1998) 29 EHRR 245, at [115] and [116].

duty to prevent and suppress offences against the person, it must be established to the Court's satisfaction that the authorities knew, or ought to have known, at the time of the existence of a real and immediate risk to the life of an identified individual or individuals from the criminal acts of a third party and that they failed to take measures within the scope of their powers that, judged reasonably, might have been expected to avoid that risk. The Court does not accept that the failure to perceive the risk to life in the circumstances known at the time or to take preventive measures to avoid that risk must be tantamount to gross negligence or wilful disregard of the duty to protect life. Such a rigid standard must be considered to be incompatible with the requirements of Art 1 of the Convention and the obligations of contracting States under that Article to secure the practical and effective protection of the rights and freedoms laid down therein, including Art 2. For the Court, and having regard to the nature of the right protected by Art 2, a right fundamental in the scheme of the Convention, it is sufficient for an applicant to show that the authorities did not do all that could be reasonably expected of them to avoid a real and immediate risk to life of which they have or ought to have knowledge. This is a question that can only be answered in the light of all if the circumstances of any particular case.

14.16 Even more controversially, a member of the public may die following direct contact with the police—in particular, following restraint. Statistics in respect of this are maintained by the Independent Police Complaints Commission (IPCC).[14] Every year, there are inevitably a number of deaths in custody; every year, a number of members of the public are likely to be killed by dedicated police firearms units. Each such event may, or may not, involve any culpability on the part of the police officers involved. Each attracts an exhaustive investigation and frequently multiple sets of proceedings in different tribunals. Resolution of these is measured in years.

14.17 The fact that some deaths are an almost inevitable consequence of the duties performed by the police is often overlooked. The tragedy experienced by individual families may easily be overtaken by the stampede of those with a wider social or political agenda in respect of the police that, of necessity, requires a vehicle for promotion.

14.18 Equally, however, there is no question but that it is in the public interest, and that of all those personally involved in or affected by a death, for there to be a

---

[14] Available online at <http://www.ipcc.gov.uk >. In 2006–07, there were thirty-six road traffic fatalities, one fatal police shooting (out of over 18,000 authorized deployments of firearms), twenty-seven deaths in or following police custody, and eighteen deaths during or following other police contact.

comprehensive independent investigation in public into each such death. By that means, culpability may either be identified or excluded, and systems of policing may be improved.

The vehicle of inquiry into such deaths has historically been the Coroner's Court. **14.19** In qualifying circumstances, a death may give rise to criminal allegations and other forms of investigation or public inquiry. Self-evidently, the relationship between associated investigations and coronial proceedings must be regulated. What material must be disclosed to the coroner from the misconduct investigation is less than straightforward (see 14.89–14.94 below).

There is an inevitable overlap with the functions and role of the IPCC in such **14.20** cases, because the IPCC will invariably act concurrently as the investigating agency for the coroner and report directly to him. The IPCC has a statutory responsibility[15] under ss 20 and 21 of the Police Reform Act 2002 to keep certain persons informed as to the progress of the IPCC investigation. There is no published guidance as to what the discharge of this obligation may involve in any particular investigation. The IPCC must obviously not act so as to risk compromise to the investigation,[16] and there is, accordingly, no statutory right for the family to receive copies of actual evidence.

Interested persons at an inquest receive material at the discretion of the coroner. **14.21** In that the IPCC will have the original material, it is for the coroner in each individual case to determine what the interested persons may receive and when. Evidence necessarily must be provided in sufficient time for interested persons to prepare it if effective participation is to be achieved.[17] The disclosure test is what, in the coroner's opinion, is relevant to the purposes of the inquest and nothing else (see 14.92 below).

---

[15] Police Reform Act 2002, s 20(2) and (4). Section 20(4) provides that the matters of which the complainant must be kept properly informed are: (a) the progress of the investigation; (b) any provisional findings of the person carrying out the investigation; (c) whether any report has been submitted under para 22 of Sch 3; (d) the action (if any) that is taken in respect of the matters dealt with in any such report; and (e) the outcome of any such action.

[16] *Reynolds v CC Sussex, with the IPCC as an interested party* [2008] EWHC 1240 (Admin), [27]; *R (Reynolds) v IPCC* [2008] EWCA Civ 1160, CA: *R (Saunders)(Tucker) v IPCC and ors* [2008] EWHC 2372 (Admin)

[17] *R (Coker) v HM Coroner for Inner South District of Greater London* [2006] EWHC 614 (Admin), [16]. See also *R (Bentley) v HM Coroner for Avon* [2001] EWHC 170 (contemporary standards of disclosure), *Howlett v HM Coroner for the County of Devon and Mr and Mrs Holcroft* [2006] EWHC 2570 (disapproving delaying disclosure until the hearing), and *R (Smith) v Oxford Assistant Deputy Coroner and ors* [2008] 3 WLR 1284 (cost of copying may have to be met by the interested person, but refusal to disclose at least by inspection 'may be difficult to justify in an Article 2 case', *per* Collins J at [37]).

14.22 The extent of family involvement in the investigation may be directly relevant to the question of whether the Art 2 investigative obligation has been discharged before the coroner determines the form of a particular inquest.

14.23 This chapter cannot seek to provide more than an outline of the essential features of coronial proceedings as applied to deaths involving contact with the police. Fundamental to the conduct of inquest proceedings is an understanding as to the particular nature and purpose of an inquest. Although it is easily stated that inquest proceedings are inquisitorial (that is, fact-finding, with interested 'persons' not 'parties'), those appearing at them in whatever capacity continue to be surprised by the practical consequences in terms of rights of participation and procedures. Assumptions in these respects imported from adversarial proceedings are usually misplaced.

14.24 With all that said, the essential parameters of the existing arrangements, as applicable particularly to police-related proceedings, may be rehearsed.

B. The Nature and Purpose of an Inquest

14.25 The statutory purpose of an inquest is defined by reference to s 11 of the Coroners Act 1988 and r 36 of the Coroners Rules 1984. The 1988 Act was a consolidating piece of legislation relating substantially to Acts of 1860 and 1887.

14.26 The end result of an inquest is the completion of an inquisition, which sets out the particulars required by the statute. The form of inquisition is similarly determined by statute,[18] although recent developments in the interpretation of the law have affected what is recorded in terms of the circumstances of the death. Used appropriately, it provides an important source document as to empirical analysis of causes of death nationally.

14.27 It is emphasized that the inquest may legitimately hear evidence that extends beyond the scope of anything that may be required or permitted in the verdict.[19] This may represent an element of discharging the investigative obligation under Art 2. The process of investigation of issues in evidence may lead to recommendations under r 43 by the coroner in the absence of any particular finding in the verdict.

---

[18] Form 22 in Sch 4, pursuant to r 60 of the Coroners Rules 1984.
[19] See *R v Inner West London Coroner, ex p Dallaglio* [1994] 4 All ER 139, CA; *R (Takoushis) v Inner North London Coroner and anor* [2006] 1 WLR 461, [2005] EWCA Civ 1440, CA.

Statutory purpose: statutory provisions

There is a common obligation on the tribunal (coroner or jury) to give the verdict **14.28** and certify it by an inquisition, and to inquire of, and find, the particulars required by the Births and Deaths Registration Act 1953.[20] Additionally, in material part, s 11 of the 1988 Act provides as follows:

(2) The coroner shall, at the first sitting of the inquest, examine on oath concerning the death all persons who tender evidence as to the facts of the death and all persons having knowledge of those facts whom he considers it expedient to examine.

[. . .]

(5) An inquisition—

   (a) shall be in writing under the hand of the coroner and, in the case of an inquest held with a jury, under the hands of the jurors who concur in the verdict;

   (b) shall set out, so far as such particulars have been proved—

      (i) who the deceased was; and

      (ii) how, when and where the deceased came by his death, and

   (c) shall be in such form as may be prescribed in rules made in accordance with Part 1 of Schedule 1 to the Constitutional Reform Act 2005.[21]

(6) At a coroner's inquest into the death of a person who came by his death by murder, manslaughter, corporate manslaughter or infanticide, the purpose of the proceedings shall not include the finding of any person guilty of the murder, manslaughter, corporate manslaughter or infanticide; and accordingly a coroner's inquisition shall in no case charge a person with any of those offences.

Rules 36 and 42 of the Coroners Rules 1984 provide as follows: **14.29**

36 Matters to be ascertained at inquest

(1) The proceedings and evidence at an inquest shall be directed solely to ascertaining the following matters, namely—

   (a) who the deceased was;

   (b) how, when and where the deceased came by his death;

   (c) the particulars for the time being required by the Registration Acts to be registered concerning the death.

(2) Neither the coroner nor the jury shall express any opinion on any other matters.

[. . .]

42 Verdict

No verdict shall be framed in such a way as to appear to determine any question of—

   (a) criminal liability on the part of a named person, or

   (b) civil liability.

These provisions are deceptively straightforward—in particular, as to the legiti- **14.30** mate scope of findings as to 'how' the deceased came by his death. Often, the direct answer to 'how' will be immediately obvious: for example, following a fatal

---

[20] Coroners Act 1988, s 11(3) (jury) and (4) (coroner without jury).

[21] Section 11(5)(c) is as substituted by the Constitutional Reform Act 2005, s 12(2), Sch 1, Pt 2, paras 19 and 20, in force 3 April 2006: see the Constitutional Reform Act 2005 (Commencement No 5) Order 2006, SI 2006/1014, art 2(a), Sch 1, para 7.

shooting by the police or a suicide by hanging in a cell. As set out below, (see 14.33 *et seq*) following *Middleton*,[22] for qualifying inquests, the language of 'how' has been extended from a narrow meaning (following *Jamieson*)[23] of 'by what means' to be 'by what means and in what circumstances' surrounding these self-evident facts, albeit consistent with the prohibition within r 42.

14.31 It will be seen that s 11(6) prohibits certain forms of verdict. Historically, the Coroner's Court returned such verdicts and these operated as a committal for trial. It remains the case that no findings of civil liability may be made (and, in practice, this prohibits language implying the same, such as 'negligently', although the use of the expression 'serious failure' was approved by the Administrative Court in *R (Smith) v Oxford Assistant Deputy Coroner and others* [2008] 3 WLR 1284), and nor must there be a finding of criminal liability 'on the part of named person'. This permits a so-called short-form verdict of unlawful killing so long as no person is named. It additionally permits a narrative verdict of unreasonable use of force in appropriate circumstances, and subject to considerations of lawful use of force and standards of proof.

14.32 It will be seen that s 11(6) prohibits a verdict of corporate manslaughter. This was inserted by the Corporate Manslaughter and Corporate Homicide Act 2007.[24]

Jamieson and *Middleton* inquests: general observations

14.33 The core statutory provisions affecting the nature and procedures at an inquest have not changed since 1988. The fundamentals are rehearsed below (see 14.43 *et seq*). In that statutory context, there is a broad, temporally defined distinction between an inquest conducted under the principles of the leading Court of Appeal case of *R v HM Coroner for North Humberside and Scunthorpe, ex p Jamieson*[25] and any inquest conducted under the principles set out by the House of Lords a decade later in *R (Middleton) v West Somerset Coroner and anor*.[26] Other decided cases plainly promote interpretation of these leading authorities.

14.34 At the most basic level of analysis, the expectations made, and conduct, of an inquest will vary according to whether the death in question occurred before or after the implementation of the HRA. It is now clear that deaths occurring before

---

[22] *R (Middleton) v West Somerset Coroner and anor* [2004] 2 AC 182, HL.

[23] *R v HM Coroner for North Humberside and Scunthorpe, ex p Jamieson* [1995] QB 1, [1994] 3 WLR 82, [1994] 3 All ER 972, CA.

[24] Section 26, Sch 2, paras 1(1) and (2)(a), effective from 6 April 2008 under the Corporate Manslaughter and Corporate Homicide Act 2007 (Commencement No 1) Order 2008, SI 2008/401, art 2(1).

[25] [1995] QB 1, [1994] 3 WLR 82, [1994] 3 All ER 972, CA.

[26] [2004] 2 AC 182, HL.

2 October 2000 are not subject to the Art 2 investigative obligation[27] and, in substance, will be approached according to the principles of *Jamieson*. For deaths after that date, the material obligations are rehearsed in *Middleton*—particularly as to the more extensive form of a narrative verdict. The details as to these differing obligations are considered below.

The extent to which there is a genuinely hard distinction in practice is somewhat **14.35** more contentious. It has always been open to an inquest to hear evidence extending beyond that required strictly to complete the particulars of the final inquisition (see 14.77 *et seq*).

Further, what is required to discharge the Art 2 investigative obligation in any given **14.36** context involves a degree of flexibility, reflecting considerations such as whether other investigations or hearings (including criminal proceedings) have already met the obligation. *Middleton* allows for flexibility as to the requirements of an extended narrative verdict. As will be seen, even a *Middleton* narrative verdict may in appropriate circumstances be no more extensive than the *Jamieson*-style, short, neutral statement, but should address the central factual issues surrounding the death.[28]

Inquests distinguished from other forms of proceeding

An inquest is an investigation on behalf of the State into a qualifying death for **14.37** limited statutory purposes. It is, accordingly, fundamentally inquisitorial in nature, although properly interested persons have a right to participate. Points of procedure within the Coroners Rules 1984 are reflected at 14.42 below. It is similar in species to a public inquiry, and wholly different in species to adversarial proceedings such as those that occur in a criminal, civil, or disciplinary context. With some limits under the Rules, the coroner has a wide discretion as to how the statutory purpose is achieved and may conduct pre-inquest hearings to determine relevant matters.[29]

The corollary of this is that each witness is called by the coroner and at his discre- **14.38** tion. There are no parties, only interested persons. Interested persons simply have the right to ask questions that the coroner determines are relevant to the purpose of the inquest. The coroner asks questions of each witness first. By r 21, if the interested person is represented and is a witness, his representative asks questions of that interested person last.

By r 40, interested persons cannot address the coroner 'on the facts', which (as **14.39** addressed below) is contended to mean that they cannot seek to promote a

---

[27] See *In re McKerr* [2004] UKHL 12, [2004] 1 WLR 807, [2004] 2 All ER 409, HL (NI); *R (on the application of Hurst) v Commissioner of Police of The Metropolis* [2007] UKHL 13, HL.

[28] See 14.95–14.104 below.

[29] See *R (Coker) v HM Coroner for Inner South District of Greater London* [2006] EWHC 614 (Admin).

particular factual verdict with the tribunal in the manner of a closing submission. Submitting arguments to the coroner (although not the jury) as to what verdicts on the evidence may arise—including the appropriate central issues for a narrative verdict, but short of which verdict should actually be returned—is contended to be a matter of law requiring a ruling, as distinct from a prohibited address on the facts. This is consistent with observations from Lord Bingham in *Middleton* at [36] set out at 14.86 below.

14.40 These basic points of purpose and distinction have been recognized and emphasized judicially, and affect every aspect of procedure at the inquest. Lord Bingham confirmed the distinctions in *R v Davis*.[30] In addressing the use of anonymous witnesses in criminal proceedings, he expressly distinguished for that purpose inquest proceedings:

> 21. The House has approved the admission of anonymous written statements by a coroner conducting an inquest: see *R v HM Attorney-General for Northern Ireland, Ex p Devine* [1992] 1 WLR 262. But, as Lord Lane CJ pointed out in the transcript of his judgment of the court in *R v South London Coroner, Ex p Thompson*, reported in part at (1982) 126 SJ 625, an inquest is an inquisitorial process of investigation, quite unlike a criminal trial; there is no indictment, no prosecution, no defence, no trial; the procedures and rules of evidence suitable for a trial are unsuitable for an inquest: see *R v HM Coroner for North Humberside and Scunthorpe, Ex p Jamieson* [1995] QB 1, 17. Above all, there is no accused liable to be convicted and punished in that proceeding.

14.41 In *Jamieson*, Lord Bingham (as Sir Thomas Bingham MR) rehearsed additional observations from Lord Lane in *R v South London Coroner, ex p Thompson*[31] including the proposition that an inquest is a 'fact-finding exercise and not a method of apportioning guilt', and concluding that 'the function of an inquest is to seek out and record as many of the facts concerning the death as the public interest requires'.

14.42 What is required in practice will depend on considerations under Art 2, and the applicability of *Middleton* and *Amin*.[32] The shorthand distinction between inquisitorial and adversarial proceedings is not wholly hard-edged. This is not simply a matter of perception for the interested persons. In *Middleton*, Lord Bingham characterized the 'hybrid' quality of proceedings:

> 26. The Coroners Rules 1984 have effect as if made under section 32 of the 1988 Act, which gives the Lord Chancellor, with the concurrence of the Secretary of State, a wide power to make rules for regulating the practice and procedure at inquests and to prescribe forms for use in connection with inquests. The 1984 Rules prescribe a hybrid procedure, not purely inquisitorial or purely adversarial. On the one hand,

---

[30] [2008] UKHL 36, HL, *per* Lord Bingham.
[31] (1982) 126 SJ 625.
[32] *R (Amin) v Secretary of State for the Home Department* [2003] UKHL 51, [2003] 3 WLR 1169, HL.

notice of the inquest must be given to the next-of-kin of the deceased and a widely defined group of other interested parties (rule 19), who are entitled to examine witnesses either in person or by an authorised advocate (rule 20); witnesses are privileged against self-incrimination; notice must be given to, and attendance facilitated of, persons whose conduct is likely to be called into question (rules 24 and 25). On the other hand, the coroner calls and first examines all witnesses, the representative of a witness questioning him last (rule 21); no person is allowed to address the coroner or the jury as to the facts (rule 40); and there is no particularised charge or complaint as in criminal or civil proceedings. In addition to examining the witnesses the coroner (rule 41) sums up the evidence to the jury and directs them as to the law, drawing their attention to rules 36(2) and 42. Rule 43 provides:

> "A coroner who believes that action should be taken to prevent the recurrence of fatalities similar to that in respect of which the inquest is being held may announce at the inquest that he is reporting the matter in writing to the person or authority who may have power to take such action and he may report the matter accordingly."

C. The Duty to Hold, and the Timing of, an Inquest

The duty on a coroner to hold an inquest is prescribed by ss 8 and 16 of the 1988 Act. In material part, s 8 provides as follows. **14.43**

8 Duty to hold inquest

(1) Where a coroner is informed that the body of a person ("the deceased") is lying within his district and there is reasonable cause to suspect that the deceased—
   (a) has died a violent or an unnatural death;
   (b) has died a sudden death of which the cause is unknown; or
   (c) has died in prison or in such a place or in such circumstances as to require an inquest under any other Act,
   then, whether the cause of death arose within his district or not, the coroner shall as soon as practicable hold an inquest into the death of the deceased either with or, subject to subsection (3) below, without a jury.

(2) [This section specified the number of jurors as between seven and eleven.]

(3) If it appears to a coroner, either before he proceeds to hold an inquest or in the course of an inquest begun without a jury, that there is reason to suspect—
   (a) that the death occurred in prison or in such a place or in such circumstances as to require an inquest under any other Act;
   (b) that the death occurred while the deceased was in police custody, or resulted from an injury caused by a police officer in the purported execution of his duty;
   (c) that the death was caused by an accident, poisoning or disease notice of which is required to be given under any Act to a government department, to any inspector or other officer of a government department or to an inspector appointed under section 19 of the Health and Safety at Work etc Act 1974; or
   (d) that the death occurred in circumstances the continuance or possible recurrence of which is prejudicial to the health or safety of the public or any section of the public,
   he shall proceed to summon a jury in the manner required by subsection (2) above.

(4) If it appears to a coroner, before he proceeds to hold an inquest, on resuming an inquest begun with a jury after the inquest has been adjourned and the jury discharged or in the course of an inquest begun without a jury, that there is any reason for summoning a jury, he may proceed to summon a jury in the manner required by subsection (2) above.

14.44 Leaving aside considerations of jurisdiction in terms of where the body lies, the section prescribes a two-stage test once the coroner has been informed of a death under s 8(1).

14.45 The first stage is to determine, under s 8(1), whether an inquest is required. If not, the ordinary certification requirements will be followed without an inquest being held. Section 19 of the Act allows for a post-mortem to determine whether an inquest is required.

14.46 Assuming that an inquest is necessary, the second part of the test (s 8(3) and (4)) is as to whether the inquest must sit with a jury.

The duty to hold an inquest (s 8(1))

14.47 The meaning of 'violent and unnatural death' was considered in detail by the Divisional Court (Laws LJ) in *R (Canning) v Northampton Coroner*,[33] applying the test in *R (Touche) v Inner North London Coroner*[34] that a death was unnatural if there was reason to suspect that there was a gross failure to provide basic medical attention and that the need for such attention was obvious at the time. In *Touche*, Simon Brown LJ also stated obiter that unnatural deaths might include 'cases involving a wholly unsuspected death from natural causes which should not have occurred but for some human failure'.

14.48 In *Canning*, the court found that the s 8(1) discretion could only be challenged on the grounds of *Wednesbury* unreasonableness.

14.49 It may be that many deaths in a policing context will satisfy the s 8(1) test, but it does not automatically follow that every death in custody will meet the test. If the certified cause of death is coronary failure, or a prisoner dying in his sleep in the cells, and the *Touche* test is not otherwise met (for example, ignoring a known risk identified in the risk assessment on admission to custody), then the death will be neither an unnatural one nor a sudden death where the cause is unknown.

14.50 The application of the test as to a sudden death where the cause is unknown is usefully demonstrated in *R (Kasperowicz) v Plymouth Coroner*.[35] This reflected the death of an 88-year-old woman at home, twenty-five days after discharge from hospital, in relation to which no doctor was willing to certify the cause of death and the family objected to an autopsy on religious grounds. The court upheld the decision of the coroner to order a post-mortem, not least because s 19 of the 1988 Act permits it in order to ascertain whether or not an inquest is necessary.

---

[33] [2005] EWHC 3125 (Admin), DC.
[34] [2001] QB 1206, [43].
[35] [2005] EWCA Civ 44.

'Sudden' was held to mean 'a proper ascertainment of the cause of every uncertified death'.[36]

Self-evidently, the coroner's decision in this respect must reflect the evidence available at the time. Invariably, an inquest may be opened and adjourned pending further investigation. Following investigation, the coroner must determine the scope of the inquest. **14.51**

Summoning a jury (s 8(3) and (4))

If s 8(1) is satisfied, decisions arise under s 8(3) or (4). If one or more of the s 8(3) criteria are met, then the coroner has no discretion as to summoning a jury. By contrast, s 8(4) is discretionary. These subsections are reproduced at 14.43. **14.52**

Each such case is fact-specific. In the policing context, the applicable provision is often s 8(3)(b). The relevant test is again in the language of suspicion, rather than belief that one of the applicable criteria is met. Section 8(3)(d), in particular, imports subjective considerations in any given context.[37] **14.53**

Section 8(3)(d) was relied on by the Administrative Court[38] to justify the resumption of the inquests into the deaths of Diana, Princess of Wales, and Dodi al Fayed with a jury because the circumstances leading up to the fatal collision 'were very unusual and had additional features to those found in a more usual kind of road traffic accident' (at [37]). The additional features essentially related to the pursuit of the vehicle by press photographers and there was a real likelihood of recurrence of such conduct in relation to other celebrities. **14.54**

In applying and distinguishing decided authorities,[39] the court observed (at [32]) in relation to s 8(3)(d) that: **14.55**

> For the provision to apply, the circumstances need not 'cause the death' . . . The prospect of recurrence required for the section to be applicable is low; it is the possibility of recurrence and not any higher chance. For the section to apply, only a section of the public needs to be at risk from recurrence.

The court also found (at [42]) that the logical approach was to determine the scope of the inquest before exercising the discretions under s 8(3)(d) and (4). The actual decision reflected the finding under s 8(3)(d), although observations were made by the court as to submissions under s 8(4). **14.56**

---

[36] *Per* Sedley LJ at [10]. The extent of the autopsy required could be proportionate to the circumstances.

[37] For a detailed application of s 8(3)(d) in the context of alleged system failures, see *R (Takoushis) v Inner North London Coroner* [2006] 1 WLR 461, [2005] EWCA Civ 1440, CA.

[38] *Paul and ors v Deputy Coroner of the Queen's Household and Assistant Deputy Coroner for Surrey (Baroness Elizabeth Butler-Sloss)* [2007] EWHC 408, (Admin), at [30]–[46].

[39] Specifically, *R v HM Coroner at Hammersmith, ex p Peach (No 1 and 2)* [1980] 1 QB 211, CA.

14.57   Assuming that s 8(3) was not met, the discretion under s 8(4):

   (i)   properly took into account the ability of a coroner sitting alone to provide more extensive reasons than a jury (at [43]);

   (ii)   should have taken into account (but not be determined by) the opinions of the deceased's family (at [44]); and

   (iii) allowed that it was relevant to consider whether the facts of the case bore any resemblance to the types of situation covered by the mandatory provisions under s 8(3) (at [45]), in which context, the court observed that 'by examining the policy considerations behind the mandatory provisions it might be possible to find guidance as to the manner in which the discretion should be exercised'.

14.58   These observations are clearly of general application in the context of inquests, albeit that many would question the practical value at considerable public expense of the Diana inquest. Once s 8(1) and (3)(d) was met, however, there was no discretion as to resuming the inquest with a jury. The discretion not to resume an inquest arises in circumstances defined by ss 16 and 17 of the 1988 Act.

Inquests and criminal proceedings (s 16)

14.59   Section 16 is rehearsed below in material part. Certain of the offences defined under s 16(1) came into force on 24 September 2007, as appointed under the Road Safety Act 2006, s 61(1).

> **16 Adjournment of inquest in [event of criminal proceedings]**
>
> (1) If on an inquest into a death the coroner before the conclusion of the inquest—
>   (a) is informed by the designated officer for a magistrates' court under section 17(1) below that some person has been charged before a magistrates' court with—
>   (i) the murder, manslaughter, corporate manslaughter or infanticide of the deceased;
>   (ii) an offence under section 1, 2B, 3ZB or 3A of the Road Traffic Act 1988 (dangerous driving, careless driving, unlicensed, disqualified or uninsured drivers or careless driving when under the influence of drink or drugs) committed by causing the death of the deceased; . . .
>   (iii) an offence under section 2(1) of the Suicide Act 1961 consisting of aiding, abetting, counselling or procuring the suicide of the deceased; or
>   [(iv an offence under section 5 of the Domestic Violence, Crime and Victims Act 2004 (causing or allowing the death of a child or vulnerable adult); or
>   (b) is informed by the Director of Public Prosecutions that some person has been sent for trial for an offence (whether or not involving the death of a person other than the deceased) alleged to have been committed in circumstances connected with the death of the deceased, not being an offence within paragraph (a) above, and is requested by the Director to adjourn the inquest,
>   then, subject to subsection (2) below, the coroner shall, in the absence of reason to the contrary, adjourn the inquest until after the conclusion of the relevant criminal proceedings and, if a jury has been summoned, may, if he thinks fit, discharge them.
> (2) The coroner—
>   (a) need not adjourn the inquest in a case within subsection (1)(a) above if, before he has done so, the Director of Public Prosecutions notifies him that adjournment is unnecessary; and

    (b) may in any case resume the adjourned inquest before the conclusion of the relevant crimi-
          nal proceedings if notified by the Director that it is open to him to do so.

(3) After the conclusion of the relevant criminal proceedings, or on being notified under para-
      graph (b) of subsection (2) above before their conclusion, the coroner may, subject to the fol-
      lowing provisions of this section, resume the adjourned inquest if in his opinion there is
      sufficient cause to do so.

[. . .]

(7) Where a coroner resumes an inquest which has been adjourned in compliance with subsec-
      tion (1) above—
    (a) the finding of the inquest as to the cause of death must not be inconsistent with the out-
          come of the relevant criminal proceedings;
    (b) the coroner shall supply to the registrar of deaths after the termination of the inquest a
          certificate under his hand stating the result of the relevant criminal proceedings; and
    (c) the provisions of section 11(7) above shall not apply in relation to that inquest.

These provisions are, to a degree, self-explanatory in terms of respective duties and **14.60**
responsibilities. Coroners effectively have to wait before exercising discretion as to
resumption until relevant criminal proceedings are concluded. Strictly, the obligation only arises once a person has been sent for trial. In practice, the inquest will
not resume until the coroner has received notification as to the outcome of any
criminal or IPCC investigation.

In the policing context, the central practical issue is the exercise of discretion **14.61**
under s 16(3). The statutory language could hardly define a wider discretion: the
coroner 'may' (subject to the limitations on verdict set out) resume the adjourned
inquest 'if in his opinion there is sufficient cause to do so'.

Section 16(3) obviously must take its meaning from the intended scope of any **14.62**
resumed inquest and the jurisprudence as to the Art 2 obligation when it is
engaged. The nature of the criminal proceedings is also directly relevant. If there
was a guilty plea and hence no critical scrutiny of witnesses, or no consideration
of systemic failures by State agencies in failing to prevent a murder, or no direct
evidence as to particular elements of causation, then these matters are capable
of remedy through an inquest and may reasonably provide sufficient cause
to resume.

The point is made by reference to *R v Inner West London Coroner, ex p Dallaglio*,[40] **14.63**
a decision closely following *Jamieson*, each of which involved Sir Thomas
Bingham MR. The circumstances related to the sinking of the pleasure steamer,
The Marchioness, on the River Thames. The captain of the barge responsible
(Captain Henderson) was prosecuted. The first trial took place in April 1991, a
year after the inquest had been halted on the intervention of the Director of Public
Prosecutions (DPP). The jury was unable to agree. He was retried in July 1991,

---

[40] [1994] 4 All ER 139, CA.

but, again, the jury disagreed. In the usual way, the prosecution then decided to proceed no further and a 'not guilty' verdict was entered. In neither trial did he give evidence.

14.64 The Court (*per* Simon Brown LJ) held:

> Although there must inevitably be formidable difficulties in resuming these inquests now, nearly five years after the disaster, and although no one could pretend that such a proceeding would be a satisfactory alternative to the public inquiry so long denied these applicants, I for my part am not prepared to say that a fresh coroner would be bound to refuse a resumption. The decision to be made under s 16(3) is of a highly discretionary character and in no way circumscribed by a need to find exceptional circumstances, only 'sufficient cause'. The coroner states that 'only rarely' are inquests resumed after criminal proceedings but, of course, the section itself expressly envisages, rather than discourages, such a course.
>
> Given that many of the survivors and eye witnesses have still to give their full evidence, and none of the rescue services and those who engaged them; indeed that despite the plethora of other proceedings, some only of the potential witnesses have yet given full evidence and that for the most part directed to issues other than would properly arise at an inquest hearing, it might perhaps still be worth holding one. Many, indeed, were the reasons suggested by the applicants' counsel for allowing a resumption. I confess to finding few as persuasive or eloquent as a letter from two grieving parents, Mr and Mrs Garnham, in response to the coroner's circular of 3 July 1992:
>
> > 'Personally [we] want this inquest to continue, hoping at least some of the questions not yet answered can be. The main question being HOW was it possible for 51 young and healthy people to die in the middle of London on a Saturday on a very busy river even at that time of night, what happened to rescue and emergency services, that so many had to lose their lives, much of this rescue remains a mystery. Perhaps you can find the answer for us.'
>
> I, therefore, would reject [the] futility argument. And I would do so with some relief. As Bingham LJ pointed out in a natural justice context in *R v Chief Constable of the Thames Valley Police, ex p Cotton* [1990] IRLR 344 at 352:
>
> > 'This is a field in which appearances are generally thought to matter.'

14.65 *Hurst*[41] (which was primarily concerned with whether the HRA applied to the conduct of inquests into deaths before it became law) reinforces the purposes of an inquest under Art 2 in relation to deaths when it is engaged. Article 2 is likely to promote resumption, rather than the opposite, as is the obligation on affected persons to respond to r 43 recommendations following the Coroners (Amendment) Rules 2008.[42]

14.66 Although the point is not believed to have arisen in practice, if the circumstances of a particular death attract the investigative obligation under Art 2 as defined

---

[41] [2007] UKHL 13.
[42] SI 2008/1652, in force 17 July 2008.

in *Middleton*, and/or the earlier proceedings have not afforded sufficient participation by the family of the deceased (see *Amin*),[43] and the inquest is the vehicle to discharge the Art 2 obligation, even within this wide discretion it may be very difficult to resist resumption of an inquest. The appropriate scope of the resultant inquest is another matter (see 14.71 below).

If, however, the Art 2 investigative obligation is either not engaged or has been **14.67** met, it is contended that it does not follow automatically that the discretion must be exercised against resumption. As will be set out, Art 2 prescribes minimum standards, rather than exhaustive ones. The coroner is exercising his discretion in the context of his statutory powers and the statutory purposes of an inquest, rather than simply by reference to Art 2. Whilst the fact that resumption is not required to meet Art 2 is obviously a relevant consideration, it cannot, accordingly, be determinative. It is contended that a coroner may reasonably conclude that there is a sufficient basis to resume within the exercise of his statutory discretion even when this is not necessary under Art 2.

Inquests following a public inquiry

This relatively unusual situation is addressed by s 17A of the 1988 Act.[44] A quali- **14.68** fying public inquiry of which notice is given to the coroner is defined by reference to subs (1) as: (a) a public inquiry conducted or chaired by a judge held into the events surrounding the death; and in which (b) the Lord Chancellor considers that the cause of death is likely to be adequately investigated by the inquiry.

In those circumstances, by s 17A(4), a coroner may only resume an inquest that **14.69** has been adjourned in compliance with subs (1) if, in his opinion, there is 'exceptional reason' for doing so. He shall not do so:

(a) before the end of the period of 28 days beginning with the day on which the findings of the public inquiry are published; or
(b) if the Lord Chancellor notifies the coroner that this paragraph applies, before the end of the period of 28 days beginning with the day on which the public inquiry is concluded.

By s 17A(5), where a coroner resumes an inquest that has been adjourned in com- **14.70** pliance with subs (1):

(a) the provisions of section 8(3) above shall not apply in relation to that inquest; and
(b) if he summons a jury (but not where he resumes without a jury, or with the same jury as before the adjournment), he shall proceed in all respects as if the inquest had not previously begun and the provisions of this Act shall apply accordingly as if the resumed inquest were a fresh inquest.

---

[43] [2003] UKHL 51, [2003] 3 WLR 1169.
[44] As inserted by s 71(1) of the Access to Justice Act 1999.

The scope of the inquest if resumed

14.71 The observations of Lord Bingham in *Amin*[45] as to the conduct and scope of an inquest if it follows on from other concluded inquiries merit rehearsal. He observed:

> 39. I cannot accept the submission of [the Secretary of State] that any further inquiry is unlikely to unearth new and significant facts. The papers before the House raise questions which any legal representative of the family would properly wish to pursue and the discovery of further new facts of significance may well be probable. But it is true that there are factual areas—for example, the killing itself, and the cause of death—which have already been fully explored and of which little or no further examination is required. Many of the factual findings made by Mr Butt and the CRE can no doubt be taken as read. It will be very important for the investigator to take a firm grip on the inquiry so as to concentrate the evidence and focus the cross-examination on issues justifying further exploration. Reliance should be placed on written statements and submissions so far as may properly be done at a hearing required to be held in public. All those professionally engaged, for any party, should bear in mind their professional duty to ensure that the investigation of this tragic and unnecessary death is conducted in a focused and disciplined way.

14.72 The advantage of applying these words to inquests resumed after other exhaustive independent investigation and public scrutiny is obvious. Many inquests appear to cover well-trodden ground with no obvious advantage—particularly given the prohibition on any verdict inconsistent with that at a criminal trial.

14.73 In practice, repetition is almost invariably extensive. If the factual background is contentious, interested persons inevitably adopt diametrically opposed positions on core factual issues following earlier inquiries, including acquittals at trial. The different standards of proof applicable between criminal and most findings at an inquest mean that acquittal does not strictly prove more than that certain conduct was not proved to a criminal standard, although there are restrictions on the verdict available at an inquest in those circumstances. The evidence heard by an inquest jury is different from that at a criminal trial and there is no provision in the Rules for interested persons to agree facts or make admissions.

Challenging decisions regarding resumption or the conduct of an inquest

14.74 Qualifying persons may challenge decisions of coroners by way of judicial review. Such challenges are not uncommon. It is also not uncommon for the coroner to be unrepresented at the substantive application in consequence of the implications in costs if any challenge to his discretion succeeds. Submissions in support of the coroner are usually made in writing, and oral submissions adopting the

---

[45] [2003] UKHL 51, [2003] 3 WLR 1169.

same are routinely made by interested persons who appear at the judicial review in the capacity of interested parties.

Section 13 of the 1988 Act provides a power in the Attorney-General to apply to the High Court to order an inquest or a new inquest. If, on such an application, the High Court is satisfied as respects a coroner either (a) that he refuses or neglects to hold an inquest which ought to be held, or (b) where an inquest has been held by him, that (whether by reason of fraud, rejection of evidence, irregularity of proceedings, insufficiency of inquiry, the discovery of new facts or evidence, or otherwise) it is necessary or desirable in the interests of justice that another inquest should be held, it may so order.

14.75

Plainly, an interested person must persuade the Attorney-General to apply and the exercise of that discretion by the Attorney-General is itself a decision that may attract judicial review. A case illustrating the exercise of discretion under s 13 is *Clayton v South Yorkshire Coroner*.[46] Whilst the court accepted that aspects of the procedure at the inquest were materially irregular (particularly the timing and form of direction as to majority verdicts, when coupled with a so-called *Watson* direction as to 'give and take' when deliberating), it declined to order a fresh inquest, because there was no evidence to contradict the accounts of police officers as to the circumstances of restraint preceding a cardiac arrest. It was common ground that if the officers' accounts were accurate, restraint was lawful. It followed that no different verdict[47] could arise at a fresh inquest based on mere assertions, rather than actual evidence as to the police officers' conduct.

14.76

D. The Scope of the Inquest: *Jamieson, Middleton*, and Art 2

Introduction and central conclusions in *Jamieson*

The Court of Appeal's judgment in *Jamieson* provides the framework for inquests conducted in relation to deaths preceding the HRA. Lord Bingham suggested in *Middleton* (at [27]) that the earlier decision provided 'an orthodox analysis of the Act and the Rules and an accurate, if uncritical, compilation of judicial authority as it then stood'. He observed that, 'remarkably', neither the Court of Appeal nor counsel made reference to the ECHR.

14.77

---

[46] [2005] EWHC 1196 Admin, DC. See also *R v Inner South London Coroner, ex p Kendall* [1988] 1 WLR 1186, 1193–1194 (it is not appropriate for a fresh inquest to be ordered if that would achieve little or no practical benefit).

[47] The deceased suffered a cardiac arrest following restraint by the police. The evidence established that his heart was severely compromised by an unlawful stabbing a year before and that this injury was causative of fatal arrhythmia. The jury was accordingly considering a number of verdicts, including unlawful killing based on the stabbing, rather than the allegedly unlawful conduct of the police. In the event, it returned an open verdict.

14.78 In practice, the majority of inquests relating to the police in the future will relate to deaths following the implementation of the HRA. To this extent, it is sufficient to rehearse the central propositions in *Jamieson* that apply to inquests before that date. *Jamieson* was narrowly concerned with the verdicts of neglect and lack of care, but the following propositions are of general application.

14.79 Following a review of authority, the Court set out the following.

General conclusions

This long survey of the relevant statutory and judicial authority permits certain conclusions to be stated.

(1) An inquest is a fact-finding inquiry conducted by a coroner, with or without a jury, to establish reliable answers to four important but limited factual questions. The first of these relates to the identity of the deceased, the second to the place of his death, the third to the time of death. In most cases these questions are not hard to answer but in a minority of cases the answer may be problematical. The fourth question, and that to which evidence and inquiry are most often and most closely directed, relates to how the deceased came by his death. Rule 36 requires that the proceedings and evidence shall be directed solely to ascertaining these matters and forbids any expression of opinion on any other matter.

(2) Both in s 11(5)(b)(ii) of the 1988 Act and in r 36(1)(b) of the 1984 rules, 'how' is to be understood as meaning 'by what means'. It is noteworthy that the task is not to ascertain how the deceased died, which might raise general and far-reaching issues, but 'how ... the deceased came by his death', a more limited question directed to the means by which the deceased came by his death.

(3) It is not the function of a coroner or his jury to determine, or appear to determine, any question of criminal or civil liability, to apportion guilt or attribute blame. This principle is expressed in r 42 of the 1984 rules. The rule does, however, treat criminal and civil liability differently: whereas a verdict must not be framed so as to appear to determine any question of criminal liability *on the part of a named person*, thereby legitimating a verdict of unlawful killing provided no one is named, the prohibition on returning a verdict so as to appear to determine any question of civil liability is unqualified, applying whether anyone is named or not.

(4) This prohibition in the rules is fortified by considerations of fairness. Our law accords a defendant accused of crime or a party alleged to have committed a civil wrong certain safeguards rightly regarded as essential to the fairness of the proceedings, among them a clear statement in writing of the alleged wrongdoing, a right to call any relevant and admissible evidence and a right to address factual submissions to the tribunal of fact. These rights are not granted—and the last is expressly denied by the rules—to a party whose conduct may be impugned by evidence given at an inquest.

(5) It may be accepted that in case of conflict the statutory duty to ascertain how the deceased came by his death must prevail over the prohibition in r 42. But the scope for conflict is small. Rule 42 applies, and applies only, to the verdict. Plainly the coroner and the jury may explore facts bearing on criminal and civil liability. But the verdict may not appear to determine any question of criminal liability on the part of a named person nor any question of civil liability.

(6) There can be no objection to a verdict which incorporates a brief, neutral, factual statement: 'the deceased was drowned when his sailing dinghy capsized in heavy seas', 'the deceased was killed when his car was run down by an express train on a level crossing', 'the deceased died from crush injuries sustained when gates were opened at Hillsborough Stadium'. But such verdict must be factual, expressing no judgment or opinion, and it is not the jury's function to prepare detailed factual statements.

[(7)–(12) These points of conclusion relate specifically to neglect and lack of care as verdicts.]

(13) It is for the coroner alone to make reports with a view to preventing the recurrence of a fatality. That is the effect of rr 36(2) and 43.

(14) It is the duty of the coroner as the public official responsible for the conduct of inquests, whether he is sitting with a jury or without, to ensure that the relevant facts are fully, fairly and fearlessly investigated. He is bound to recognise the acute public concern rightly aroused where deaths occur in custody. He must ensure that the relevant facts are exposed to public scrutiny, particularly if there is evidence of foul play, abuse or inhumanity. He fails in his duty if his investigation is superficial, slipshod or perfunctory. But the responsibility is his. He must set the bounds of the inquiry. He must rule on the procedure to be followed. His decisions, like those of any other judicial officer, must be respected unless and until they are varied or overruled.

These clear statements of principle require little by way of attempted amplification. **14.80** In practice, point of conclusion (6) defines what is referred to as a *Jamieson* narrative verdict.

The tension produced by the neutrality of the narrative suggested and s 8(3)(d) of **14.81** the 1988 Act was addressed in *Dallaglio*.[48] The scope of the inquest verdict produced on a narrow reading of *Jamieson* was agreed to be difficult to reconcile with the legislative policy underlying the subsection.

The Court (which notably was presided over by Sir Thomas Bingham MR, who **14.82** gave judgment in *Jamieson*) adopted the analysis of Morland J in *R v HM Coroner for Western District of East Sussex, ex p Homberg*[49] that '. . . rule 36 should not be so interpreted as to defeat the purpose of section 8(3)(d) . . . If "the proceedings and evidence" are narrowly confined, the answers to the "how" question will not serve the purpose of the section, the prevention or reduction of the risk of future injuries in similar circumstances', and resolved the tension by reference to point (14) of the conclusions set out above in *Jamieson*. The Court in *Dallaglio* concluded (at 155):

That, of course, was a s 8(3)(a) case, but its adaptability to a s 8(3)(d) context is obvious. It is, in short, for the individual coroner to recognise and resolve the tension existing between ss 8(3) and 11(5)(b) of the 1988 Act and r 36. The inquiry is almost bound to stretch wider than strictly required for the purposes of a verdict.

---

48 [1994] 4 All ER 139, CA.
49 (1994) 158 JP 357, 381.

How much wider is pre-eminently a matter for the coroner whose rulings upon the question will only exceptionally be susceptible to judicial review.

14.83 As will be seen, the form of narrative required may not be determined wholly by reference to the rights engaged by the HRA. *Middleton* expressly anticipates that a *Jamieson* narrative may be sufficient in particular circumstances even when Art 2 is engaged. The Administrative Court in *R (Longfield Care Homes) v HM Coroner for Blackburn*[50] did not limit the necessity of a narrative verdict to Art 2 cases.

Article 2 and *Middleton*

14.84 By Art 1 of the ECHR, member States bound themselves to secure to everyone within their respective jurisdictions the rights and freedoms defined in Pt 1 of the Convention. The first of those rights, expressed in Art 2, is the right to life and —in para 1 —provides: 'Everyone's right to life shall be protected by law. No one shall be deprived of his life intentionally save for in the execution of a sentence of a court following his conviction of a crime for which this penalty is fixed by law.'

14.85 Lord Bingham set out a summary of the underlying principles flowing from this basic provision in *Middleton* and the questions for consideration for the Court. These merit reproduction:

> 2. The European Court of Human Rights has repeatedly interpreted article 2 of the European Convention as imposing on member states substantive obligations not to take life without justification and also to establish a framework of laws, precautions, procedures and means of enforcement which will, to the greatest extent reasonably practicable, protect life. See, for example, *LCB v United Kingdom* (1998) 27 EHRR 212, para 36; *Osman v United Kingdom* (1998) 29 EHRR 245; *Powell v United Kingdom* (App No 45305/99, unreported 4 May 2000), 16–17; *Keenan v United Kingdom* (2001) 33 EHRR 913, paras 88–90; *Edwards v United Kingdom* (2002) 35 EHRR 487, para 54; *Calvelli and Ciglio v Italy* (App No 32967/96, unreported, 17 January 2002); *Öneryildiz v Turkey* (App No 48939/99, unreported, 18 June 2002).
>
> 3. The European Court has also interpreted article 2 as imposing on member states a procedural obligation to initiate an effective public investigation by an independent official body into any death occurring in circumstances in which it appears that one or other of the foregoing substantive obligations has been, or may have been, violated and it appears that agents of the state are, or may be, in some way implicated. See, for example, *Taylor v United Kingdom* (1994) 79-A DR 127, 137; *McCann v United Kingdom* (1995) 21 EHRR 97, para 161; *Powell v United Kingdom, supra* p 17; *Salman v Turkey* (2000) 34 EHRR 425, para 104; *Sieminska v Poland* (App No 37602/97, unreported, 29 March 2001); *Jordan v United Kingdom* (2001) 37 EHRR 52, para 105; *Edwards v United Kingdom, supra,* para 69; *Öneryildiz v Turkey, supra,* paras 90-91; *Mastromatteo v Italy* (App No 37703/97, unreported, 24 October 2002).
>
> 4. The scope of the state's substantive obligations has been the subject of previous decisions such as *Osman* and *Keenan* but is not in issue in this appeal. Nor does any

---

[50] [2004] EWHC 2467 (Admin), [29].

issue arise about participation in the official investigation by the family or next of kin of the deceased, as recently considered by the House in *R (Amin) v Secretary of State for the Home Department* [2003] UKHL 51, [2003] 3 WLR 1169. The issue here concerns not the conduct of the investigation itself but its culmination. It is, or may be, necessary to consider three questions.

(1) What, if anything, does the Convention require (by way of verdict, judgment, findings or recommendations) of a properly conducted official investigation into a death involving, or possibly involving, a violation of article 2?

(2) Does the regime for holding inquests established by the Coroners Act 1988 and the Coroners Rules 1984 (SI 1984/552), as hitherto understood and followed in England and Wales, meet those requirements of the Convention?

(3) If not, can the current regime governing the conduct of inquests in England and Wales be revised so as to do so, and if so how?

The Court resolved the questions in the following way: **14.86**

29. How far, then, does the current regime for conducting inquests in England and Wales match up to the investigative obligation imposed by article 2?

30. In some cases the state's procedural obligation may be discharged by criminal proceedings. This is most likely to be so where a defendant pleads not guilty and the trial involves a full exploration of the facts surrounding the death. It is unlikely to be so if the defendant's plea of guilty is accepted (as in *Edwards*), or the issue at trial is the mental state of the defendant (as in *Amin*), because in such cases the wider issues will probably not be explored.

31. In some other cases, short verdicts in the traditional form will enable the jury to express their conclusion on the central issue canvassed at the inquest. *McCann* has already been given as an example: see paragraph 14 above. The same would be true if the central issue at the inquest were whether the deceased had taken his own life or been killed by another: by choosing between verdicts of suicide and unlawful killing, the jury would make clear its factual conclusion. But it is plain that in other cases a strict *Ex p Jamieson* approach will not meet what has been identified above as the Convention requirement. In *Keenan* the inquest verdict of death by misadventure and the certification of asphyxiation by hanging as the cause of death did not express the jury's conclusion on the events leading up to the death. Similarly, verdicts of unlawful killing in *Edwards* and *Amin*, although plainly justified, would not have enabled the jury to express any conclusion on what would undoubtedly have been the major issue at any inquest, the procedures which led in each case to the deceased and his killer sharing a cell.

32. The conclusion is inescapable that there are some cases in which the current regime for conducting inquests in England and Wales, as hitherto understood and followed, does not meet the requirements of the Convention. This is a conclusion rightly reached by the judge in this case (see paragraph 44 below) and by the Court of Appeal both in the present case (see paragraph 44 below) and in cases such as *R (Davies) v HM Deputy Coroner for Birmingham* [2003] EWCA Civ 1739 (2 December 2003, unreported), paragraph 71.

33. Question (3) Can the current regime governing the conduct of inquests in England and Wales be revised so as to meet the requirements of the Convention, and if so, how?

34. Counsel for the Secretary of State rightly suggested that the House should propose no greater revision of the existing regime than is necessary to secure compliance

with the Convention, even if it were (contrary to his main submission) to reach the conclusion just expressed. The warning is salutary. There has recently been published "Death Certification and Investigation in England, Wales and Northern Ireland: The Report of a Fundamental Review" (June 2003, Cm 5831). Decisions have yet to be made on whether, and how, to give effect to the recommendations. Those decisions, when made, will doubtless take account of policy, administrative and financial considerations which are not the concern of the House sitting judicially. It is correct that the scheme enacted by and under the authority of Parliament should be respected save to the extent that a change of interpretation (authorised by section 3 of the Human Rights Act 1998) is required to honour the international obligations of the United Kingdom expressed in the Convention.

35. Only one change is in our opinion needed: to interpret "how" in section 11(5) (b)(ii) of the Act and rule 36 (1)(b) of the Rules in the broader sense previously rejected, namely as meaning not simply "by what means" but "by what means and in what circumstances".

36. This will not require a change of approach in some cases, where a traditional short form verdict will be quite satisfactory, but it will call for a change of approach in others (paragraphs 30–31 above). In the latter class of case it must be for the coroner, in the exercise of his discretion, to decide how best, in the particular case, to elicit the jury's conclusion on the central issue or issues. This may be done by inviting a form of verdict expanded beyond those suggested in form 22 of Schedule 4 to the Rules. It may be done, and has (even if very rarely) been done, by inviting a narrative form of verdict in which the jury's factual conclusions are briefly summarised. It may be done by inviting the jury's answer to factual questions put by the coroner. If the coroner invites either a narrative verdict or answers to questions, he may find it helpful to direct the jury with reference to some of the matters to which a sheriff will have regard in making his determination under section 6 of the Fatal Accidents and Sudden Deaths Inquiry (Scotland) Act 1976: where and when the death took place; the cause or causes of such death; the defects in the system which contributed to the death; and any other factors which are relevant to the circumstances of the death. It would be open to parties appearing or represented at the inquest to make submissions to the coroner on the means of eliciting the jury's factual conclusions and on any questions to be put, but the choice must be that of the coroner and his decision should not be disturbed by the courts unless strong grounds are shown.

37. The prohibition in rule 36(2) of the expression of opinion on matters not comprised within sub-rule (1) must continue to be respected. But it must be read with reference to the broader interpretation of "how" in section 11(5)(b)(ii) and rule 36(1) and does not preclude conclusions of fact as opposed to expressions of opinion. However the jury's factual conclusion is conveyed, rule 42 should not be infringed. Thus there must be no finding of criminal liability on the part of a named person. Nor must the verdict appear to determine any question of civil liability. Acts or omissions may be recorded, but expressions suggestive of civil liability, in particular "neglect" or "carelessness" and related expressions, should be avoided. Self-neglect and neglect should continue to be treated as terms of art. A verdict such as that suggested in paragraph 45 below ("The deceased took his own life, in part because the risk of his doing so was not recognised and appropriate precautions were not taken to prevent him doing so") embodies a judgmental conclusion of a factual nature, directly relating to the circumstances of the death. It does not identify any individual

nor does it address any issue of criminal or civil liability. It does not therefore infringe either rule 36(2) or rule 42.

38. The power of juries to attach riders of censure or blame was abolished on the recommendation of the Report of the Departmental Committee on Coroners under the chairmanship of Lord Wright (Cmd 5070, 1936). It has not been reintroduced. Juries do not enjoy the power conferred on Scottish sheriffs by the 1976 Act to determine the reasonable precautions, if any, whereby the death might have been avoided (section 6(1)(c)). Under the 1984 Rules, the power is reserved to the coroner to make an appropriate report where he believes that action should be taken to prevent the recurrence of fatalities similar to that in respect of which the inquest is being held. Compliance with the Convention does not require that this power be exercisable by the jury, although a coroner's exercise of it may well be influenced by the factual conclusions of the jury. In England and Wales, as in Scotland, the making of recommendations is entrusted to an experienced professional, not a jury. In the ordinary way, the procedural obligation under article 2 will be most effectively discharged if the coroner announces publicly not only his intention to report any matter but also the substance of the report, neutrally expressed, which he intends to make.

Subsequent developments in the context of Art 2 inquests

Although an extensive rehearsal, these passages are central to any understanding **14.87** of modern coronial proceedings involving the police and Art 2. When Art 2 is engaged—and quite possibly even when not (see 14.95 below)—the form of verdict in practice will reflect the *Middleton* principles. Subject to that, it appears that Art 2 must, of course, be engaged on the facts: not every narrative of events involving a death and the police will engage Art 2. It must potentially have been the responsibility of agents of the State (see 14.15 above).

In this context, a useful analysis of the present position in relation to deaths in **14.88** custody was set out by the Court of Appeal (Sir Anthony Clarke MR) in *R (D) v Secretary of State for the Home Department and Inquest:*[51]

> 9. It is common ground that the following principles apply to a case of a death in custody:
>
> i) The purposes of the investigation are those stated by Lord Bingham in *R (Amin) v Secretary of State for the Home Department* [2003] UKHL 51, [2004] 1 AC 632, at paragraph 31, namely
> "to ensure so far as possible that the full facts are brought to light; that culpable and discreditable conduct is exposed and brought to public notice; that suspicion of deliberate wrongdoing (if unjustified) is allayed; that dangerous practices and procedures are rectified; and that those who have lost their relative may at least have the satisfaction of knowing that lessons learned from his death may save the lives of others".

---

[51] [2006] EWCA Civ 143, CA.

ii) The Convention does not adopt a prescriptive approach to the form of the investigation. So long as minimum standards are met, it is for the state to decide the most effective method of investigating: see eg *Edwards v United Kingdom* (2002) 35 EHRR 487, 511 at paragraph 69 and *Amin* per Lord Bingham at paragraph 31, Lord Slynn at paragraph 42 and Lord Hope at paragraph 63.

iii) The minimum requirements were stated in *Jordan v United Kingdom* (2001) EHRR 52 at paragraphs 106–109, *Edwards* at paragraphs 69–73 and in *Amin* at paragraph 25. They are these:

a) the authorities must act of their own motion;

b) the investigation must be independent;

c) the investigation must be effective in the sense that it must be conducted in a manner that does not undermine its ability to establish the relevant facts;

d) the investigation must be reasonably prompt;

e) there must be a "sufficient element of public scrutiny of the investigation or its results to secure accountability in practice as well as in theory; the degree of public scrutiny required may well vary from case to case": see Jordan at paragraph 109 and Edwards at paragraph 73; and

f) there must be involvement of the next of kin "to the extent necessary to safeguard his or her legitimate interests": see Jordan at paragraph 109 and Edwards at paragraph 73.

10. It is we think accepted that, as Mr Pannick put it in his skeleton argument, even the minimum requirements involve a degree of flexibility: see *Goodson v HM Coroner for Bedfordshire* [2004] EWHC Admin 2931 at paragraph 68.

Participation, *Amin*, and disclosure

14.89 As to participation by the family, reference should be made to *Amin*[52] and *Jordan*.[53] Participation need not extend to the right to question witnesses. It is the participation by the family in the totality of the State's investigations that is contended to be material, as distinct from at any one stage.

14.90 Each person with control of evidence must exercise discretion according to his or her statutory duties. Hence the IPCC must exercise discretion under ss 20(1)(2) and (4) (duty to keep complainant informed), and 21(6) and (7) (duty to provide information to other interested persons) of the 2002 Act, consistent with that statutory duty alone. It should be remembered that the police do not routinely release evidential material to relatives of the deceased during homicide investigations. The IPCC is acting in the capacity of the investigating officer in this sense.

14.91 Apart from the minimum obligations set out in ss 20 and 21,[54] there is an implied discretion[55] as to what should be provided. There is limited statutory assistance on

---

[52] *R (Amin) v Secretary of State for the Home Department* [2003] UKHL 51, [2004] 1 AC 632.
[53] *Jordan v United Kingdom* (2001) EHRR 52.
[54] See n 16 above.
[55] *R (Reynolds) v IPCC* [2008] EWCA Civ 1160, CA, appealing *Reynolds v CC Sussex, with the IPCC as an interested party* [2008] EWHC 1240 (Admin).

the point. Consistent with the language of these sections, reg 11(2)(a) of the Police (Complaints and Misconduct) Regulations 2004[56] speaks of '*the progress of the investigation*' and reg 11(2)(b) 'of any provisional findings of the person carrying out the investigation as frequently as the Commission determines to be appropriate in order for the complainant to be kept properly informed'. Regulation 12 provides exceptions to this duty. Paragraph 5.5.1 of the statutory guidance issued by the IPCC speaks of transparency 'subject to assessing the risk of any prejudice to the investigation'. Each investigation is different. It is contended not to be the statutory purpose of the IPCC to provide material simply to facilitate consideration of a civil action.

The competing principles were reflected in *R (Saunders) v IPCC and ors*.[57] **14.92** The sister of the deceased claimed that the extent of disclosure by the IPCC was inadequate. In submissions, it was conceded that the duty did not extend to witness statements. Without resolving the specific complaint, Underhill J set out (at [81]) that it was 'part of the policy of the Act that the Commission should be as open as is reasonably possible in the communication of information to interested persons', and (at [82]):

> . . . The judgment of what information requires to be disclosed can in the nature of things only be made by the body conducting the investigation (here, the Commission), though of course subject to the intervention of the Court where that judgment is exercised irrationally or otherwise unlawfully. Although I shall not try to specify all the factors which fall to be taken into account in making that judgment (apart from the 'harm' test under reg. 12), one important consideration in the case of witness evidence will be whether the evidence is in a sufficiently coherent and settled form for it to be reliably communicated, either in the form of the statement itself or by a summary which gives its gist.

Home Office Circular 31/2002 ('Guidance to the police on pre-inquest disclosure') **14.93** sets out the extent and timing of disclosure by the police in relation to the extended definition of a death in custody, and promotes transparency of disclosure by the police through the coroner after any IPCC or Crown Prosecution Service (CPS) decision. It provides for familiar duties of confidentiality for those receiving such material (para 13), and suggests that other interested persons ('including the family of the deceased') 'who have in their possession material about the death not otherwise disclosed to the police or the Coroner, should at the same time bring it to the attention of the Coroner and offer to provide similar pre-inquest disclosure to other interested persons' (para 14). Whilst reflecting consultation with groups such as Liberty and Inquest, it is contended that this non-statutory Circular

---

[56] SI 2004/643.
[57] [2008] EWHC 2372 (Admin).

cannot create an enforceable obligation against interested persons. At most, it creates a legitimate expectation as to the approach of police forces.

14.94 The material provided to the coroner will be released to interested persons at the discretion of the coroner under the terms of the 1988 Act, consistent with the Art 2 obligation to ensure that there is adequate participation by the family. Obviously, such material must be disclosed equally to other interested persons. The timing of disclosure must promote the Art 2 objective.[58] Principles as to disclosure of sensitive material by the police to the coroner are addressed in *Re Maddison*[59] and *McCaughey and anor, re application for judicial review*.[60] For an application of the different approach to material simply going to credibility, see *Musumeci v AG of New South Wales*,[61] in which the Supreme Court of New South Wales upheld the exercise of discretion in the particular case against releasing material that may simply have affected credibility.

Middleton, narrative verdicts, and restrictions on narrative verdicts

14.95 The headline effect of *Middleton* was to extend the possible scope of a narrative verdict to include in what circumstances the death occurred. The court suggested that the original verdict in *Amin* did not permit the jury to return a verdict on the 'major issue' at the inquest—that is, the procedures that led in each case to the deceased and his killer sharing a cell. The approved narrative in *Middleton* at [37] is notable, however, for its brevity: '. . . the deceased took his own life, in part because the risk of his doing so was not recognised and appropriate precautions were not taken to prevent him doing so.'

14.96 It is important to note the qualifications set out at [37] of the decision. These limitations should be borne in mind if suggested questions for the jury to answer are drafted. Without hearing legal argument, the court in *R (Clayton) v The Coroner for South Yorkshire (East District) and ors*[62] doubted the utility of an illustrative three-page questionnaire introduced by the applicant.

---

[58] See *R (Coker) v HM Coroner for Inner South District of Greater London* [2006] EWHC 614 (Admin), [16]. See also *R (Bentley) v HM Coroner for Avon* [2001] EWHC 170 (contemporary standards of disclosure), *Howlett v HM Coroner for the County of Devon and Mr and Mrs Holcroft* [2006] EWHC 2570 (disapproving delaying disclosure until the hearing), and *R (Smith) v Oxford Assistant Deputy Coroner and ors* [2008] 3 WLR 1284 (cost of copying may have to be met by the interested person, but refusal to disclose at least by inspection 'may be difficult to justify in an Article 2 case', *per* Collins J at [37]).

[59] The Times, 28 November 2002, DC.

[60] [2004] NIQB 2 (20 January 2004). This included unredacted intelligence reports that may have attracted public interest immunity in criminal proceedings and a police report for the DPP. The coroner would obviously have to exercise discretion as to the form in which such material was admitted, if it was relevant.

[61] [2002] NSWSC 425.

[62] [2005] EWHC 1196 Admin, DC.

Mitting J appeared to extend the scope of the obligation to return a narrative to **14.97** non-Art 2 inquests in *R (on the application of Longfield Care Homes) v HM Coroner for Blackburn*.[63] At [29], he set out that:

> *Middleton* was concerned with a death in custody in which Article 2 of the European Convention on Human Rights was engaged. This factor led the House of Lords to conclude that the restrictive approach to the law as stated in *Jamieson*, that an inquest was only concerned with how death occurred and not with how and in what circumstances it occurred, could no longer be supported. But the comments made by the House are not restricted to verdicts in cases of death where the State may have had a hand and are of general application.

Some may question the last sentence as a fair reading of *Middleton*. In any event, **14.98** and applying *Middleton*, Mitting J found that, in cases in which the death results from more than one cause of different types, a narrative verdict is often required. The draft narrative that he gave on the facts read: 'Mrs Hall died of bronchopneumonia resulting from dementia. Her death was probably accelerated by a short time by the effect on her pneumonia of injuries sustained when she fell through an unattended open window, which lacked an opening restrictor, in the lounge of Longfield Residential Home on 16 April 2003.' He expressed no finding as to neglect (there had been a misdirection as to this), and saw no purpose in a fresh inquest to determine the issue.

Consistent with [38] of *Middleton* is the disapproval of narrative verdicts to express **14.99** conclusions on matters of wider system or resourcing. This is reflected most directly in the judgment of Pill LJ in *Scholes v Secretary of State for the Home Department*,[64] who observed:

> 69. Having regard to the issue raised on the judicial review, I am doubtful as to the appropriateness of them being dealt with, insofar as they were, by a Coroner's jury. However clearly and conscientiously the questions are drafted, the jury cannot be expected to give answers to questions of resources and policy which could provide reliable guides to an improvement in conditions. For example, while criticism of documentation and communication was appropriate, the "failure in the system", alleged on behalf of the appellant, went much further than that. For the jury to say that it was "policy" not to place young offenders in [local authority secure children's homes] and to state, "that there were no budgetary constraints" is difficult to reconcile with the evidence given. The negative answer to the question "any failure of the system [was] a gross failure" may be tenable but its value is questionable in the search for improvement.
>
> 70. I make these points not to criticise the jury but respectfully to question the value, as a way of discharging Article 2 duties, in present circumstances, of questions such as these put to the jury. As a fact finding tribunal, the jury is well established and valued for its part in the administration of justice in England and Wales. As such, it operated effectively in this case. Questions on factual issues will sometimes

---

[63] [2004] EWHC 2467 (Admin).
[64] [2006] EWCA Civ 1343, CA.

be helpful. However, the value of a jury's views as a tool for assessing and improving procedures is in my view limited in circumstances where further investigation of policies and administrative procedures, as distinct from facts, is required. Reliance on a jury's contribution by way of answering a questionnaire, however well intentioned, may be inappropriate. Some of the jury's answers in the present case illustrate the limitations of the procedure. I should wish to repeat the reservations I expressed in *Sacker v West Yorkshire Coroner* [2003] 2 All ER 278, at paragraphs 24 to 27.

14.100 Also disapproved was a suggested verdict purporting to find a breach of Art 2: see *R (Commissioner of Police of the Metropolis) v South London Coroner*,[65] in which the court observed (at [16]), in response to a suggestion on behalf of the family that the jury be asked to consider a verdict that 'the deceased died as a result of a violation of his right to life contrary to Article 2 of the European Convention on Human Rights', that it was 'most surprising that, as the law currently stands at all events, it can be said that a jury should ever be invited to consider so arcane and so quasi-legal, as well as so emotive, a verdict'.

14.101 In terms of which facts need to be addressed, guidance is obtained from a wealth of authorities that the inquest must address issues relevant only to matters under the 1988 Act, as qualified by *Middleton*. Whether the questions addressed in narrative must be limited to those concerning cause of death is contentious: on one view, if this were the case, the narrative would, in effect, be pre-*Middleton*; on another, the ECtHR has held that the Art 2 obligation was discharged where there was a full investigation into the death that culminates in a decision (including a decision as a matter of law by the coroner) as to whether the use of lethal force was legally justified, even when not associated with a narrative element.[66]

14.102 An extended approach to narrative verdicts was indorsed by the Administrative Court in *R (Cash) v HM Coroner for the County of Northamptonshire*.[67] Keith J quashed the inquisition and ordered a new inquest in circumstances in which the direction to, and applied by, the jury produced:

> . . . a narrative that added nothing of significance to anyone's knowledge of the circumstances surrounding Mr Cash's death. It certainly cast no light on the core factual issues which the inquest had addressed: whether the police had needed to restrain Mr Cash at all; if so, whether it would have been sufficient for the police officers to have held his arms without taking him to the ground . . .

14.103 A competing view, limiting narrative findings as to the circumstances directly affecting the cause of death, is reflected in *R (Pekkelo) v HM Coroner for Central Kent*.[68] In terms of Convention law, it is arguable that the Strasbourg

---

[65] [2003] EWHC 1829 (Admin).
[66] See *Bubbins v UK* (2005) 41 EHRR 458, [153], reflecting a similar approach in *Jordan v UK* (2001) 37 EHRR 52.
[67] [2007] EWHC 1354 (Admin).
[68] 1 Inquest LR 119, [2006] EWHC 1265 Admin.

Courts have not interpreted the investigative obligation as requiring findings to be made as to matters that were not causally relevant to death.[69] It may be contended that the ambit of the investigative obligation should not extend beyond this Strasbourg jurisprudence.[70] Some resolution arose in *R (Lewis) v HM Coroner for the Mid and North Division of the County of Shropshire.*[71] The Administrative Court held that as a matter of discretion a Coroner was entitled to limit narrative questions to matters that directly caused death.

On either view of these authorities, it is clear that well-drafted questions directly **14.104** relating to the circumstances of the death are desirable and legitimate when necessary.[72] A challenge to the decision of the coroner simply to leave 'closed' narrative questions, without the opportunity to add additional observations or findings, failed in the currency of the inquest into the death of Jean Charles de Menezes.[73] The questions can, and should, be incorporated into any direction to the jury to avoid an unstructured essay contravening the Coroners Rules 1984. Good practice in criminal trials promotes the use of written directions of law to the jury and no lesser standard should apply to inquests.[74]

Rule 43 and the Coroners (Amendment) Rules 2008

All of the proceedings considered previously—in particular, *Middleton* (especially **14.105** at [38]), *Sacker,*[75] and *Scholes*[76]—were decided under a previous version of r 43.[77] This essentially permitted the coroner to report a matter to a relevant body in order to reduce the possibility of a death recurring in similar circumstances. In particular circumstances, such a report may have produced improvements, but the power was manifestly somewhat limited.

This was remedied, from 17 July 2008, by the Coroners (Amendment) Rules **14.106** 2008.[78] The coroner has power to give a copy of the report to the Lord Chancellor (who may publish it), and to interested persons and to any other person who may

---

[69] See *Jordan v UK* (2001) 37 EHRR 52, [105] and [107]; *Powell v UK* (2000) EHRR CD 362, 364; *McCann v UK* (1996) 21 EHRR 97.

[70] See *N v Home Secretary* [2005] 2 AC 296, 305H–306H.

[71] [2009] EWHC 661 (Admin).

[72] See *Middleton* at [36].

[73] *R (Maria Otone de Menezes) v the Assistant Deputy Coroner for Inner South London,* [2008] EWHC 3356 (Admin) 3 December 2008.

[74] See *R (Clayton) v The Coroner for South Yorkshire (East District) and ors* [2005] EWHC 1196 (Admin); *Sharman v HM Coroner for Inner North London and anor* [2005] EWCA Civ 967, [34].

[75] *Sacker v West Yorkshire Coroner* [2003] 2 All ER 278.

[76] *Scholes v Secretary of State for the Home Department* [2006] EWCA Civ 1343, CA.

[77] '43 Prevention of similar fatalities   A coroner who believes that action should be taken to prevent the recurrence of fatalities similar to that in respect of which the inquest is being held may announce at the inquest that he is reporting the matter in writing to the person or authority who may have power to take such action and he may report the matter accordingly.'

[78] SI 2008/1652.

have an interest. By r 43A, the person to whom the report is made is required to give the coroner a written response to it within fifty-six days, subject to extension under r 43B. Provision is also made for a copy of the report, or a summary of it, to be given to the Lord Chancellor, interested persons, and any other person who may have an interest.

14.107 This represents a significant improvement in terms of accountability for those affected by r 43 recommendations. The response of the affected party, and the government's response to any particular issue, is likely to become public. This extended power further reduces the desirability of juries being asked to return verdicts addressing more than identified and specific questions of fact.

14.108 Overall, however, it will be seen that the narrative verdict is in the ascendant and may avoid the necessity of emotive findings expressed in terms as unlawful killing. Narrative verdicts, however, are subject to the need for clear direction and control. Core factual issues relevant to the broad circumstances of the death need to be identified and addressed. Given the need for jurors to agree—whether unanimously or by a majority (see s 12(2) and 14.153 below)—the inquisition as a whole, however, and to sign it following receipt of a verdict, overcomplicated narrative questions may operate in practice against the effective return of any verdict if the required agreement cannot be reached on each question.

14.109 Where findings may be adverse to interested persons, there is a compelling need for clear (preferably agreed) written directions of law, including relating to the full meaning of the standard of proof. As to the latter, it is contended that the directions as to inherent improbability and cogency of evidence that apply in civil proceedings should apply to inquest verdicts.[79] Questions of policy, and of wider resourcing and systems, are for the coroner under r 43.

E. Fundamental Points of Procedure

Qualification as an interested person

14.110 'Interested persons' are defined by r 20(2) of the Coroners Rules 1984. It will be seen that this may produce a significant number of interested persons as of right, with others at the discretion of the coroner. Rule 20(2) provides as follows:

(2) Each of the following persons shall have the rights conferred by paragraph (1):—

    (a) a parent, child, spouse, civil partner, partner[80] and any personal representative of the deceased;

    (b) any beneficiary under a policy of insurance issued on the life of the deceased;

---

[79] See analysis of civil standard of proof at 8.105–8.108.

[80] 'Partner' was inserted by the Coroners (Amendment) Rules 2005, SI 2005/420, r 5, in force 1 June 2005 (see r 1(1)); 'civil partner', by the Civil Partnership Act 2004 (Amendments to

(c) the insurer who issued such a policy of insurance;

(d) any person whose act or omission or that of his agent or servant may in the opinion of the coroner have caused, or contributed to, the death of the deceased;

(e) any person appointed by a trade union to which the deceased at the time of his death belonged, if the death of the deceased may have been caused by an injury received in the course of his employment or by an industrial disease;

(f) an inspector appointed by, or a representative of, an enforcing authority, or any person appointed by a government department to attend the inquest;

(g) the chief officer of police;

(h) any other person who, in the opinion of the coroner, is a properly interested person.

In *R v Greater London District Coroner, ex p Driscoll*,[81] an interested person needed **14.111** to have more than an 'idle curiosity' and to have 'a genuine desire to participate more than by the mere giving of evidence in the determination of how, when and where the deceased came by his death'. Campaigning or pressure groups have not, as yet, been granted interested person status.

The funding of interested persons

Police officers

The funding of interested persons at what are often extended proceedings is **14.112** another matter. In terms of police officers falling within r 20(2)(d), the funding of legal representation is governed by Home Office Circular 43/2001. After setting out the statutory basis of such funding, the document concludes (para 11) that:

> . . . police officers must be confident that Police Authorities will provide financial support for officers in legal proceedings where they have acted in good faith and have exercised their judgement reasonably. Police Authorities will need to decide each case on its own merits, but subject to that there should be a strong presumption in favour of payment where these criteria are met.

A failure to follow this Circular would almost certainly attract judicial review. **14.113** The costs of representation at an inquest are considerable and there is no power to recover the costs from any interested person or the court. The arrangements between the Police Federation of England and Wales (PFEW) and its members are such that an officer falling outside the Circular may expect to have his costs met by the Federation. The same applies to superintendents and officers of Association of Chief Police Officers (ACPO) rank.

It is important to recognize that the Circular will often result in the police author- **14.114** ity funding individual officers and the force separately. The funding relates to the individual officer who may be affected by the proceedings and who qualifies in his

---

Subordinate Legislation) Order 2005, SI 2005/2114, art 2(1), Sch 1, para 4, in force 5 December 2005 (see art 1).

[81] (1995) 159 JP 45.

own right as an interested person. Without falling outside the Circular, such an officer may be subject to a reg 14A or 15 notice. There will often be a material difference of approach between the interests of the force (particularly in terms of policy and training) and the individual officer. It is only where there is no possibility of such a conflict that funding of the individual officer could reasonably be refused.

14.115 Equally, the test for conflict between individual police officers with interested person status is subtly different from that which may exist in adversarial proceedings. The officers are witnesses, rather than defendants. A simple conflict of recollection or observation between police officer witnesses does not produce a conflict such that different representation is required. Of course, if there is a material conflict such that the inescapable conclusion is that one witness is lying, different issues will arise. As ever, these are fundamentally questions of fact and degree.

Relatives of the deceased

14.116 The situation for relatives of the deceased is less straightforward and satisfactory. Funding is means-tested, effectively on a 'whole family' basis, and determined by the Legal Services Commission (LSC). A distinction is drawn between 'legal help' surrounding the inquest and advocacy services at the inquest itself. Where a family has to fund the matter itself, there is no provision to recover costs in connection with the inquest. This is a corollary of the inquisitorial nature of the proceedings. The family may, however, apply to recover costs of the inquest in any related civil action on an *inter partes* basis if such costs were reasonably incurred in pursuit of the civil claim. This indirect recovery (that is, not from the LSC) is obviously uncertain at the date of the inquest.

14.117 Funding of representation at inquests is governed by the Access to Justice Act 1999, which established the LSC and the Community Legal Services Fund (CLSF, also known as 'Legal Aid'). Advocacy services before coroners are among the categories of service generally excluded from funding (see s 6 and Sch 2 of the 1999 Act), but that is subject to the possibility of funding in specified circumstances under s 6(8). The LSC can only make a recommendation to the relevant Minister in this respect, save for limited categories of case, including deaths in custody, where the discretion (applying the same test) is devolved back to the LSC.

14.118 The LSC Manual, which has undergone a series of revisions, includes guidance from the Lord Chancellor (now the Minister for Legal Aid at the Ministry of Justice). At any one time, it will be necessary to consider the latest draft. The categories of case reflected at 14.117 are included. Basic principles remain relatively consistent, however.

14.119 Funding of representation for advocacy (as distinct from so-called 'legal help') is, and will remain, 'exceptional'. 'Legal help' includes assistance preparing for an inquest, drafting questions and written submissions, and the funding of a solicitor to act as a 'McKenzie friend' (that is, a friend who sits next to the family member during the inquest, but who does not perform any advocacy services).

The reason that such funding remains exceptional is the contention within the **14.120** Manual that 'for most inquests where the Article 2 obligation arises, the coroner will be able to carry out an effective investigation into the death, without the need for advocacy'. The exceptional categories provided for in the Manual adopt the following basic criteria:

- that there is a 'significant wider public interest' (SWPI), as defined by the Funding Code guidance, in the applicant being legally represented at the inquest; or
- funded representation for the family is likely to be necessary for the coroner to carry out an effective investigation into the death, as required by Art 2.

A series of authorities demonstrate the practical application of these tests, which **14.121** should be read in the context of the highly detailed guidance in the Manual. What is clear is that the mere fact that Art 2 is engaged does not produce either a SWPI, or (given the presumption of competence in the coroner) a right to funded advocacy at the inquest. The fact that an advocate may assist the hearing does not, of itself, produce the required necessity.

The high-water mark for families is *R (Khan) v the Secretary of State for Health*.[82] **14.122** This complex, 'sad and disturbing', case related to potentially criminal medical negligence causing death, which engaged Art 2. The deceased's family had played no part in the various State and internal investigations. It was 'remarkably' excluded (at [99]) from the hospital trust's investigation completely. The Court found (at [86]) that the investigative obligation under Art 2 had not been met and that the holding of an inquest would not discharge that obligation if the family could not play an effective part itself. Given the complexity of the history, it found as a fact (at [96]), in an 'exceptional' case (at [99]), that the second of the two criteria was met.

Even in *Khan*, however, the statutory means test[83] appeared likely to defeat fund- **14.123** ing for representation. Mr Khan was barely above the means test, and had a wife and four children to support. The Court observed (at [98]):

> If the legal aid route is the state's preferred route towards fulfilling its Article 2 obliga-
> tions in a case like this, it seems to us at present seriously open to question whether a
> provision which requires someone like Mr Khan to fund the entire cost of his lawyer's
> appearance at the inquest into his daughter's death entirely out of his own pocket in

---

[82] [2003] EWCA Civ 1129, CA.
[83] Then under reg 5(6) of the Community Legal Service (Funding) Regulations 2000, SI 2000/516.

a case as serious and as complex as this (without any possibility of reimbursement by the state) is compatible with the requirements of the Convention.

14.124 Many would sympathize with this view and there has been some limited softening of the means test. In substance, however, the strict primary test as to funding advocacy services continues to apply. In *R (on the application of Challender) v Legal Services Commission*,[84] the court observed that there was:

> nothing in the cases post-dating *Khan* to support a broader approach than that expressed in *Khan* itself when it was said that in the overwhelming majority of cases the coroner can conduct an effective judicial investigation himself and that only in exceptional cases will Article 2 require legal representation for the family of the deceased.

14.125 Similar sentiments were expressed by the Court of Appeal in *Minister for Legal Aid v R (Main)*,[85] an inquest following a collision between a train and a car on a level crossing, which killed five. Allowing for the recognized variables in the decision-making process (the alleged extent of involvement by the State in the death, the complexity, the degree to which matters were disputed, etc), as a point of general principle, it observed:

> 43. We return to the starting point that in relation to a discretionary spending decision the court should be particularly careful before reaching a conclusion of *Wednesbury* unreasonableness. In our view, the Minister was entitled rationally to conclude that full legal representation of the family was not required in order for the coroner properly to investigate the relevant public safety issues, even though such representation may have assisted him to do so, and that there was insufficient public benefit from such representation to cause her in her discretion to authorise such expenditure.

14.126 For advocacy services (as distinct from legal help), the LSC considers the available resources of the extended family, rather than the single applicant, before exercising discretion as to funding. The net result of all this is that obtaining funding for families at Art 2 inquests remains deeply challenging and uncertain, and that any judicial review of a Minister's discretion in this respect faces formidable obstacles. It would be unfortunate if an unintended consequence of the more extensive (and correspondingly expensive) Art 2 inquests was that the family of the deceased were to be less, rather than more, likely to receive State funding for advocacy services.

Anonymity

14.127 Deaths relating to the conduct of the police are frequently controversial. Some will involve a deceased person with links to organized crime and the possibility of retributive violence. Others will involve the shooting dead of a member of the

---

[84] [2004] EWHC 924 (Admin).
[85] [2007] EWCA Civ 1147, CA.

public by authorised firearms officers. Others involve the conduct of covert officers. Some—such as the death of Jean Charles de Menezes at Stockwell underground station—involve a combination of these factors.

An inquest is fundamentally an inquiry held in public as to the circumstances of **14.128** a death. Equally, there are compelling reasons for certain police officer or other witnesses to be granted anonymity when giving their evidence. This may relate to real or perceived physical risks associated their identity becoming known (that is, the threat of retributive action, whether in connection with the particular death or earlier covert duties), or simply that to identify a particular police officer would render him non-operational in any existing future covert capacity. Covert officers are highly trained and, self-evidently, it is not in the public interest for them to lose operational status simply in consequence of appearing as a witness at an inquest.

As recognized by the House of Lords in *R v Davis*,[86] the fundamentally different **14.129** nature of inquest and criminal proceedings justifies greater latitude in granting anonymity at an inquest (see 14.40).

As *Van Colle v Chief Constable of Hertfordshire*[87] confirmed, there is a duty of care **14.130** owed by State authorities (including investigating authorities such as the IPCC) to witnesses and employees to take all reasonable steps to prevent harm. *Osman v UK*[88] remains good law. It follows that there is an obligation on the investigating authorities to anonymize witness names that may reasonably require it, pending any determination by the coroner, before the names are made public or released to interested persons.

Equally, an affected police officer should be quick to claim anonymity at the out- **14.131** set of the investigation pending such judicial determination. It is too late afterwards.

Aside from legitimate considerations as to operational effectiveness, more diffi- **14.132** cult issues arise in the context of perceived risk of retributive violence. If there is an objectively supported risk of serious harm to the officer or his family if anonymity is not granted, the situation is relatively straightforward. The difficulty arises when either: (i) it is not possible to quantify the objective risk; or (ii) the quantified objective risk is less serious than the affected officer's subjective assessment of that risk.

---

[86] [2008] UKHL 36, *per* Lord Bingham.
[87] [2008] UKHL 50, overturning the Court of Appeal ([2007] EWCA Civ 325, [2007] 2 Cr App R 32) on the facts.
[88] (1998) 29 EHRR 245, [115].

14.133   Such an officer and his family may suffer significant psychological harm if an identity is disclosed in that context. The risk of harm may be limited to the consequences to the officer's children if his occupation and role were to become known.

14.134   These competing considerations are reflected in a series of decided authorities including *R v Lord Saville, ex p A*,[89] *R (A) v Lord Saville*,[90] *Bennett v Officers A and B*,[91] and *Re Officer L*.[92] There is a distinction between the narrow considerations under Art 2 and a broader common law test based on subjective considerations unique to the particular witness.

14.135   In *Re Officer L*, the House of Lords (NI) set out a concise summary of the relevant legal principles. In terms of the Art 2 obligation, it adopted the classic rehearsal at [115] and [116] of *Osman*[93] to the effect that:

> For the court and having regard to the nature of the right protected by Article 2, a right fundamental in the scheme of the Convention, it is sufficient for an applicant to show that the authorities did not do all that could be reasonably expected of them to avoid a real and immediate risk to life of which they have or ought to have knowledge. This is a question which can only be answered in the light of all the circumstances of any particular case.

14.136   Further, it added (at [20]) that:

> Two matters have become clear in the subsequent development of the case-law. First, this positive obligation arises only when the risk is "real and immediate". The wording of this test has been the subject of some critical discussion, but its meaning has been aptly summarised in Northern Ireland by Weatherup J in *Re W's Application* [2004] NIQB 67, where he said that:
>
> ". . . a real risk is one that is objectively verified and an immediate risk is one that is present and continuing."
>
> It is in my opinion clear that the criterion is and should be one that is not readily satisfied: in other words, the threshold is high.

14.137   The Lords then rehearsed the nature and relevance of subjective fears, and the basis of the common law test. At [22], they set out:

> The principles which apply to a tribunal's common law duty of fairness towards the persons whom it proposes to call to give evidence before it are distinct and in some respects different from those which govern a decision made in respect of an article 2 risk. They entail consideration of concerns other than the risk to life, although as the Court of Appeal said in paragraph 8 of its judgment in the *Widgery Soldiers* case, an allegation of unfairness which involves a risk to the lives of witnesses is pre-eminently one that the court must consider with the most anxious scrutiny. Subjective fears,

---

[89]   [2000] 1 WLR 1855.
[90]   [2002] 1 WLR 1249.
[91]   [2004] EWCA Civ 1439.
[92]   [2007] 4 All ER 965, [2007] 1 WLR 2135, [2007] UKHL 36.
[93]   (1998) 29 EHRR 245.

even if not well founded, can be taken into account, as the Court of Appeal said in the earlier case of *R v Lord Saville of Newdigate, ex p A* [2000] 1 WLR 1855. It is unfair and wrong that witnesses should be avoidably subjected to fears arising from giving evidence, the more so if that has an adverse impact on their health. It is possible to envisage a range of other matters which could make for unfairness in relation of witnesses. Whether it is necessary to require witnesses to give evidence without anonymity is to be determined, as the tribunal correctly apprehended, by balancing a number of factors which need to be weighed in order to reach a determination.

At [29], the Lords reconciled the practical relationship between the Art 2 consideration of anonymity and that which is decided by reference to the common law principles, Lord Hoffman having stated (at [28]) that: **14.138**

> I think that it is possible, however, to conduct the exercise basically as a single test, which is obviously desirable in the interests of simplicity. This could be done by approaching it as a single decision under the common law, having regard in the process to the requirements of Article 2.

At [29], the Lords rehearsed this single (as distinct from two-part) decision as follows: **14.139**

> . . . the exercise to be carried out by the tribunal faced with a request for anonymity should be the application of the common law test, with an excursion, if the facts require it, into the territory of Article 2. Such an excursion would only be necessary if the tribunal found that, viewed objectively, a risk to the witness's life would be created or materially increased if they gave evidence without anonymity. If so, it should decide whether that increased risk would amount to a real and immediate risk to life. If it would, then the tribunal would ordinarily have little difficulty in determining that it would be reasonable in all the circumstances to give the witnesses a degree of anonymity. That would then conclude the exercise, for that anonymity would be required by Article 2 and it would be unnecessary for the tribunal to give further consideration to the matter. If there would not be a real and immediate threat to the witness's life, then Article 2 would drop out of consideration and the tribunal would continue to decide the matter as one governed by the common law principles. In coming to that decision the existence of subjective fears can be taken into account, on the basis which I earlier discussed (see paragraph 22). For the same reasons as those which I have set out in paragraph 20, however, I would not regard it as essential in every case to commence consideration of the issue by seeking to identify such subjective fears.

The net result of this is a broad-textured discretion that legitimately seeks to reflect: (i) operational considerations; (ii) objective Art 2 grounds under *Osman*; and (iii) subjective considerations in relation to a particular witness, including the perception of risk by that witness. There is demonstrably greater latitude to grant anonymity in inquisitorial proceedings. In a particular—perhaps extreme—case, the operational sensitivity may arguably be such as to justify screening from the jury, as well as the public. In each case, a detailed risk assessment is prepared by the police to support the application. **14.140**

14.141 It will be a question of fact and degree in each case as to whether, and to what extent, other protective measures may apply, including the use of screens. For example, in the inquest into the death of Simon Murden (shot by an authorised police firearms team), the two officers directly responsible for the shooting were granted anonymity and followed proceedings through a live link to a secure room in the court building. A similar procedure was adopted at the inquest into the death of Jean Charles de Menezes.

Presence in court for other witnesses and the privilege against self-incrimination

14.142 The general rule (and another manifestation of the intended inquisitorial nature of proceedings) is that any witness is generally permitted to be present for the whole of the evidence, including that preceding his own.

14.143 The coroner has discretion to prevent a witness being present for the evidence of others. Circumstances include that in which there is likely to be a conflict or a witness whose account needs to be tested in isolation from other witnesses.[94]

14.144 As to self-incrimination, the situation is covered by r 22. This provides as follows.

> **22 Self-incrimination**
>
> (1) No witness at an inquest shall be obliged to answer any question tending to incriminate himself.
> (2) Where it appears to the coroner that a witness has been asked such a question, the coroner shall inform the witness that he may refuse to answer.

14.145 It is to be noted that the privilege appears to extend to any criminal offence, including misconduct in public office. Whether it extends to matters that may solely implicate a police officer in misconduct, rather than criminal, matters is a more difficult question. It is certainly good practice for the relevant decision makers to have made clear the liability or not of any police officer to future criminal or misconduct proceedings before the inquest resumes.

14.146 Rule 22(2) anticipates a question-by-question approach to self-incrimination. There is no reason, in practice, however, for a coroner to decline to permit extensive questioning of a witness who has made clear that the privilege will be claimed (and will be granted) for a whole class or series of questions on the same facts. To require or permit every question to be asked within such a defined class would not promote the conduct of the inquest. It is contended to be within his presumption power to make orders within *R (Coker) v Inner London South Coroner*.[95]

---

[94] See *R v Surrey Coroner, ex p Campbell* [1982] QB 661, 676.
[95] [2006] EWHC 614 (Admin).

Witness summons and the admissibility of disputed evidence

The coroner has power under s 10(2) and (4) of the 1988 Act to issue a witness **14.147** summons to secure the attendance of a witness to give relevant evidence. Subject to the fact that all evidence is only admissible at the discretion of the coroner (the interested persons may only invite the coroner to call a witness), r 37 provides for the admission of documentary evidence relevant to the purposes of the inquest from any living person that, in his opinion, is unlikely to be disputed, unless a person who, in the opinion of the coroner, is within r 20(2) objects to the documentary evidence being admitted.

By r 37(2), documentary evidence so objected to may be admitted if, in the opin- **14.148** ion of the coroner, the maker of the document is unable to give oral evidence within a reasonable period.

Rule 37(5) addresses witnesses that are deceased. **14.149**

The application of these rules (and the residue of r 37 provides for procedural **14.150** matters that must be followed in their application) was considered in detail in *R (Paul and the Ritz Hotel) v Assistant Deputy Coroner of Inner West London* (the Diana/al Fayed inquest).[96] The core issue was the admissibility of witness statements from photographer members of the paparazzi that had followed the deceased before the fatal accident. These witnesses were in France and able, but unwilling, to travel to the UK to give evidence during the inquest.

Following an extensive review of authority, the court was critical of the quality of **14.151** drafting of r 37, but found that it defined exhaustively the discretion of the coroner to admit documentary evidence. There was no separate common law power that could be relied on. A witness who was able, but unwilling, to come to give evidence was outside r 37(2). Such evidence could only be given by calling a witness as to what was set out in the document.

In practical terms, this means that a suitable witness (such as the person to whom **14.152** the statement was made) must be called to prove the document. At the inquest into the death of Jean Charles de Menezes, certain evidence was introduced under this heading through an IPCC investigator.

F. Verdicts

The chapter has already considered the emergence and legitimate parameters of **14.153** narrative verdicts, and the necessity of clear agreed written directions of law. It is not intended to review other technical verdicts in any detail. By s 12(2) of the

---

[96] [2007] EWHC 2721 (Admin); [2007] EWCA Civ 1259, CA.

1988 Act, majority verdicts are permissible so long as the number in the minority is not more than two (that is, any number between five and nine in the majority, and up to two in the minority, is acceptable).

14.154 The standard of proof applicable to any verdict is not constant. Verdicts of either unlawful killing (or a narrative finding amounting to unlawful use of force causing death) and suicide require proof to the criminal standard of each of the requisite elements. For a verdict of suicide, there must be clear evidence of the requisite intention, which will include evidence of an appreciation that the fatal act was likely to be fatal.[97]

14.155 As already contended,[98] there is no reason, in principle, why findings within a verdict to the civil standard should not be made according to a full exposition of the meaning of the civil standard. In general terms, the more serious the misconduct alleged, the less inherently probable it is.

Withdrawing a verdict from the jury: *Galbraith* and *Douglas-Williams*

14.156 As a simple proposition before a verdict can be regarded as lawful, there has to be sufficient evidence to support it as a matter of law. This applies equally to the criminal and coronial jurisdictions. If there is insufficient evidence, the verdict should be withdrawn as a possibility from the jury.

14.157 In the criminal context, the law is well established from the test laid down in *R v Galbraith*.[99] The Court was concerned to decide between two schools of thought: (i) that the judge should stop the case if, in his view, it would be unsafe (alternatively 'unsafe or unsatisfactory') for the jury to convict; and (ii) that he should do so only if there is no evidence on which a jury properly directly could properly convict.

14.158 The second of these schools of thought was preferred and the test formulated as follows.

(i) If there is no evidence that the crime alleged has been committed by the defendant there is no difficulty—the judge will stop the case.

---

[97] Whilst no longer a crime, there is a presumption against suicide and it must be strictly proved. Suicide 'is voluntarily doing an act for the purpose of destroying one's own life while one is conscious of what one is doing, and in order to arrive at a verdict of suicide there must be evidence that the deceased intended the consequences of the act'. The mere fact that accident is not established does not mean to say that suicide is established: *R v Cardiff City Coroner, ex p Thomas* [1970] 1 WLR 1475, 1478, QBD. See also *R v City of London Coroner, ex p Barber* [1975] 1 WLR 1310 (*per* Lord Widgery, 'the possibility of suicide may be there for all to see, but it must not be presumed merely because it seems on the face of it to be a likely explanation').

[98] See 14.109 above.

[99] [1981] 2 All ER 1060, (1981) 73 Cr App R 124, CA.

(ii) The difficulty arises where there is some evidence, but it is of a tenuous character—for example, because of inherent weakness or vagueness or because it is inconsistent with other evidence.

   (a) Where the judge concludes that the prosecution evidence, taken at its highest, is such that a jury properly directed could not properly convict on it, it is his duty, on a submission being made, to stop the case.

   (b) Where, however, the prosecution evidence is such that its strength or weakness depends on the view to be taken of a witness's reliability, or other matters that are, generally speaking, within the province of the jury and in which, on one possible view of the facts, there is evidence on which the jury could properly come to the conclusion that the defendant is guilty, then the judge should allow the matter to be tried by the jury.

The Court observed that borderline cases could be left to the discretion of the judge. Each such case turns on its own facts and the court must consider the totality of the evidence in making an assessment. **14.159**

Although frequently elevated to a point of principle, the first-instance decision in *R v Shippey*[100] is no more than an application of the basic test. It concerned an allegation of rape, in relation to which the sole evidence was that of the complainant, and which evidence was said to be seriously internally inconsistent and contradictory. In those circumstances, the court was entitled to consider the whole of the account. For an application of the test the other way—that is, where a witness was contradictory in some respects, but otherwise supported by forensic evidence—see *R v Lesley*.[101] **14.160**

More recently, in *R v Hedgcock and ors*,[102] the Court of Appeal considered the approach to inferences at the close of the prosecution case and concluded (at [21]) that 'if at the close of the Crown's case the trial judge concludes that a reasonable jury could not reject all realistic explanations that would be consistent with innocence, then it would be his duty to stop the case'. To many observers, this comes close to usurping the function of the jury. **14.161**

Leaving verdicts at inquests

The proper approach at an inquest represents a qualified application of *Galbraith*. Whilst the test fundamentally remains one of evidential sufficiency, unlike a criminal **14.162**

---

[100] [1988] Crim LR 767.

[101] [1996] 1 Cr App R 39, CA.

[102] [2007] EWCA Crim 3486, CA. The decision (quashing convictions for an internet dialogue-based conspiracy to rape children because the evidence did not justify the rejection of the possibility of fantasy, rather than an intention to carry out the admitted agreement to rape) is controversial on the facts.

trial, in which the verdict is either 'guilty' or 'not guilty', an inquest may have a range of highly technical verdicts open to it at the close of the evidence. The obvious question is whether a coroner is required to leave each such hypothetical verdict to a jury in each and every case simply because the evidence may technically support it.

14.163 The short answer is 'no'. This subtle difference of approach emerged in *R (on the application of Douglas-Williams) v Inner South London Coroner*:[103]

> The strength of the evidence is not the only consideration and, in relation to wider issues, the coroner has a broader discretion. If it appears there are circumstances which, in a particular situation, mean in the judgment of the coroner, acting reasonably and fairly, it is not in the interests of justice that a particular verdict be left to the jury, he need not leave that verdict. He, for example, need not leave all possible verdicts just because there is technically evidence to support them. It is sufficient if he leaves those verdicts which realistically reflect the thrust of the evidence as a whole. To leave all possible verdicts could in some situations merely confuse and overburden the jury and if that is the coroner's conclusion he can not be criticised if he does not leave a particular verdict.

14.164 In *R (Bennett) v HM Coroner for Inner South London*,[104] Collins J interpreted this (at [32]) as applicable to a situation in which a verdict was perhaps unnecessary or undesirable, but that 'one has to consider the propriety of not leaving a particular verdict in the circumstances and on the facts of any given case'. The Court of Appeal[105] agreed (at [27]) that there was 'some (if small) distinction' from criminal proceedings in the application of the *Galbraith* test, but stated (at [31]) that:

> the question is an evidential one and that considerations as to whether an inquest is a satisfactory form of process in identifying whether criminal conduct has taken place or as to whether some evidence might or might not have been admissible at a criminal trial, are irrelevant.

14.165 The significance of this approach is reduced in the context of narrative verdicts, because well-formulated questions will avoid the necessity of the type of technical verdict that the Court was considering.

14.166 It follows that, applied to the policing context and particularly to that of the possibility of unlawful killing, *Douglas-Williams* is really of little assistance. If—applying *Galbraith*—the evidence supports a verdict of unlawful killing (or, for example, neglect, as used in coronial proceedings), then the verdict should be left to the jury, assuming that it cannot better be addressed by a narrative. As to sufficiency of evidence for a verdict of unlawful killing, see 15.100.

---

[103] [1999] 1 All ER 344, (1999) 162 JP 751, CA.
[104] [2006] EWHC 196 (Admin).
[105] *R (Bennett) v HM Coroner for Inner South London* [2007] EWHC Civ 617, CA.

Importantly, and additionally, however, the courts have produced detailed guid- **14.167**
ance as to the proper approach of the coroner if unlawful killing is to be left in the
context of use of force by police officers.

Unlawful killing and the lethal use of firearms

The elements of unlawful killing and self-defence are considered respectively at **14.168**
15.75 *et seq* and 15.88 *et seq*. No lesser standard of direction or proof applies to
the verdict in inquest proceedings.[106] As to self-defence, once in force, s 76 of the
Criminal Justice and Immigration Act 2008 defines the relevant considerations.
Section 76 is set out at 15.90.

Verdicts of unlawful killing applied to the actions of police officers, even when not **14.169**
strictly named in the verdict itself, are intrinsically controversial. The point was
first made by the Collins J in the Administrative Court in *R (Anderson and ors) v
HM Coroner for Inner North London*[107] and repeated in connection with the judicial review arising from the decision of the coroner not to leave the verdict of
unlawful killing at the inquest into the death of Derek Bennett. In the latter:[108]

> While the coroner's rules make it clear that any verdict, including of course unlawful
> killing, cannot identify any individual or individuals, in a case such as this - indeed
> in many if not most cases where police action has caused a death - there will be
> only one or a very few identifiable persons responsible. They are thus branded, and
> some organs of the media do not help by describing such a verdict in terms which
> convey that that person or those persons have been found guilty of murder. I am
> bound to say that I seriously wonder whether the time has not come to abolish the
> verdict of unlawful killing altogether. If the court or jury is not satisfied that the
> killing was lawful, it can say so, and others can then investigate, or will have
> before investigated, whether there is sufficient evidence to justify any criminal
> proceedings.

Similar sentiments have been rehearsed by the Administrative Court and the **14.170**
Court of Appeal in respect of the inquest verdict following the death of Harry
Stanley (*Sharman*). In *Anderson and ors*, the court found that the coroner could
not have been criticized if he had declined to leave the verdict of unlawful killing.
Having done so, the summing-up was so deficient that the verdict was quashed
but there was no purpose in a fresh inquest. In *Sharman*, the verdict was quashed
and should not have been left to the jury. In *Bennett*, the coroner's decision not
to leave the verdict of unlawful killing was upheld. The consistent theme is the

---

[106] See *Sharman v HM Coroner for Inner North London* [2005] EWCA Civ 967, CA, at [34].
[107] [2004] EWHC 2729 (Admin), quashing the verdict of unlawful killing in relation to the
death of Roger Sylvester. The deceased has suffered a cardiac arrest whilst delirious and under
restraint, pending medical assessment under s 136 of the Mental Health Act 1983.
[108] [2006] EWHC 196 (Admin).

necessity of directions of law that closely follow the actual evidence and articulate exactly what must be proved.

14.171 In summary, the statutory defence set out in s 3 of the Criminal Law Act 1977 permits 'such force as is reasonable in the circumstances in the prevention of crime or in effecting or assisting in the lawful arrest of offenders or suspected offenders or of persons unlawfully at large' and extends to providing a defence if reasonable force is used in self-defence or the defence of another. In the context of the criminal law, that defence (evaluated according to the subjective belief of the person seeking to rely on it, even if mistaken) must be negatived by the Crown to the criminal standard.

14.172 This applies equally to the use of force to restrain during a lawful arrest and the deliberate act of shooting. In *Bennett*,[109] the Administrative Court found that the domestic law was wholly consistent in this respect with the Art 2 jurisprudence as to 'absolute necessity' and the contrary was not argued on appeal. It also rejected a contention that a different test applied to agents of the State using force from that which applied to others using self-defence.

14.173 The *Galbraith* test is always difficult to apply in the context of self-defence where lethal force has been used. This was recognized in terms by the Court of Appeal in *Sharman*.[110] It observed (at [11]):

> It will be seen that that rubric is very difficult to apply to a case such as the present where the issue is self defence. Of course the issue is not, as it is at the end of the prosecution case in a criminal trial, whether there is some evidence to support the prosecution's positive case. The issue is rather, whether there is sufficient evidence to suggest that the prosecution will succeed in negativing self defence.

14.174 The Court went on to observe that the test was 'more helpfully' stated in the context of an inquest:

> . . . in the more generalised form that was suggested in an inquest context by Lord Woolf, Master of the Rolls, in *ex parte Palmer* in 1997. He said at page 19 of his judgment that the test that he would apply is: "Is this a case where it would be safe for the jury to come to the conclusion that there had been an unlawful killing?" That, in this case, means that the question is whether it would be safe for the jury to come to the conclusion that the defence of self defence had been disproved beyond reasonable doubt.

14.175 Applying this test, the Court of Appeal, through *Sharman* and *Bennett*, has made it most unlikely that a verdict of unlawful killing will follow in the context of a spontaneous shooting when the police officers concerned are reacting to a

---

[109] [2006] EWHC 196 (Admin), concluding at [25].
[110] [2005] EWCA Civ 967, CA.

member of the public who is believed to be armed. The absence of an honest belief must be established to the criminal standard.

In *Sharman*,[111] a legal direction that appeared to associate any finding that the **14.176** police officers concerned had lied about aspects of their evidence with an automatic conclusion of unlawful killing was emphatically rejected. The Court had to consider the totality of the objective evidence surrounding the shooting before any such verdict could follow. On the facts, even if it found that the officers had lied, no reasonable jury properly directed in law could have concluded that the absence of honest belief as to the threat posed by the deceased was established to the criminal standard.

The same approach is contended to apply to the use of force in restraint, particu- **14.177** larly when the member of the public concerned is demonstrating acute behavioural disturbance and appropriate risk management is attempted. Although less spontaneous in nature, a finding equivalent to manslaughter in such circumstances would require compelling evidence that an intrinsically demanding, but necessary, policing activity was being conducted, in knowing and deliberate breach of police training as to the risks associated with the activity and/or the observed effect of restraint on the particular member of the public.

Cardiac failure associated with such restraint is often sudden and unexpected, and **14.178** may reflect an underlying (drug-induced) cardiomyopathy even in an outwardly fit young adult. Deaths associated with restraint are statistically very rare and hindsight is deployed disproportionately at inquests in this context. Liability to a criminal finding should only arise in exceptional circumstances.

Challenging decisions as to verdicts

The coroner's ruling as to the available verdicts and form of verdicts is obviously **14.179** of fundamental importance to all interested persons. Although intrinsically a decision within a broad discretion,[112] it is nonetheless susceptible to judicial review. The Administrative Court and Court of Appeal have repeatedly stated that intervention by way of judicial review while the inquest is in progress (particularly when a jury is involved) will arise only in 'the most exceptional circumstances'.[113]

---

[111] Ibid, at [15], [18]–[24], [28], and [34]–[36].
[112] See *Middleton* at [36].
[113] *R v HM Coroner for East Kent, ex p Spooner (The Herald of Free Enterprise)* (1988) 152 JP 115, approved in *R v HM Coroner for Inner North London, ex p Diesa Koto* (1993) 157 JP 857, 859G, *per* Lloyd LJ; see also *R v HM Coroner for Exeter and East Devon, ex p Palmer* [1997] EWCA 2951; *R (Khan) v HM Coroner for West Hertfordshire* [2002] EWHC 302 (Admin); *R (Craik) v HM Coroner for Wiltshire* [2004] EWHC 2653 (Admin).

G. Conclusion

14.180 It will be seen that inquest proceedings represent the most open form of public accountability for the police relating to the performance of their duties, including systems of work, but that they are, at the same time, the least satisfactory for all interested persons.

14.181 As and when the Coroners and Justice Bill is enacted, some of the most unsatisfactory features of existing arrangements may be addressed—and that date cannot arrive soon enough for participants in the existing system. More radical reform—such as removing juries entirely—has been resisted. It is hoped that the statutory changes, including the associated new Coroners Rules, will not come to represent a missed opportunity.

15

POLICE-RELATED CRIMINAL OFFENCES

A. Overview	15.01	Unlawful and dangerous act	
Common issues	15.01	manslaughter	15.91
The relationship with misconduct		Gross negligence manslaughter	15.96
charges	15.08	The application of basic	
B. Misconduct in Public Office	15.10	principles to the performance	
A summary of the elements	15.15	of police duties	15.102
'1. A public officer acting as such		Conclusions regarding	
(paragraph 54)'	15.20	gross negligence	
'Public office'	15.22	manslaughter	15.111
'Acting as such'	15.39	Corporate manslaughter	15.114
'2. Wilfully neglects to perform		The offence	15.118
his duty and/or wilfully		Conclusions regarding	
misconducts himself		corporate manslaughter	15.126
(paragraphs 28, 30, 45 and 55)'	15.45	**D. Driving-related Offences**	15.128
'Wilful neglect'	15.51	The law	15.133
Recklessness	15.58	Section 87 exemption	15.138
The tort of misfeasance		The application of the exemption	
in public office	15.62	to police response drivers	15.141
'3. To such a degree as to amount		*Milton*	15.146
to an abuse of the public's trust		Dangerous driving	15.149
in the office holder (paragraphs 46		The relevance of expert	
and 56 to 59)'	15.66	driving ability	15.153
'4. Without reasonable excuse		Speed as a basis	
or justification (paragraph 60)'	15.70	of dangerousness	15.155
Conclusions in relation		The meaning and application	
to misconduct in public office	15.73	of the police purpose	
C. Unlawful Killing	15.75	exemption	15.156
Introduction	15.75	A summary of the liability of the	
An overview of the forms		police driver and the associated	
of homicide	15.78	duty of other road users	15.159
The duty of care	15.81	**E. Conclusions**	15.163
Causation	15.84		
Self-defence and reasonable use			
of force in the performance			
of a legal duty	15.88		

A. Overview

Common issues

15.01 Police officers are liable to prosecution in relation to the unlawful performance of duty. The most common of the relevant offences in practice are considered in this chapter.

15.02 In certain respects, the underlying principles are straightforward and represent no more than an ordinary application of the criminal law. For example, the use of force to effect an arrest, to restrain, or to conduct a search must, as with the use of force in self-defence, be reasonable in all of the circumstances believed to exist by the officer using the force. A so-called *Palmer*[1] direction relating to how this issue is approached will apply. This has application to potential charges of assault and, assuming that causation is proved, to manslaughter. If a death results, whether or not criminal charges follow, these matters invariably become relevant at an inquest.

15.03 Police duties other than those involving the use of force equally generate considerations of criminal conduct. These include driving-related offences arising from accidents—many fatal—caused typically by rapid-response vehicles. Self-evidently, specific legal issues arise in relation to the correct approach to liability of a police officer when using a response vehicle. These matters are considered in detail at 15.128 *et seq* below. Many police officers (as with members of the public) have been protected in the past by the disproportionate differential between causing death by dangerous driving, attracting a maximum sentence of fourteen years' imprisonment and (assuming that the officer concerned is not under the influence of either drink or drugs), simply careless driving, attracting a maximum penalty of a level four fine at the magistrates' court. The new offence of causing death by careless driving (in force from 18 August 2008) will extend the possibility of prosecution (and a term of imprisonment of up to five years) to a much wider range of conduct by reactive police officers.

15.04 As was demonstrated by the successful prosecution of the Metropolitan Police Service (MPS) in relation to the operation that resulted in the death of Jean Charles de Menezes, police forces may become liable under health and safety legislation directed at safe systems of work for employees and those affected by the

---

[1] *Palmer v R* [1971] AC 814, PC, followed by the Court of Appeal in *R v McInnes* (1971) 55 Cr App R 551 and, as applied to soldiers and police officers, by the House of Lords in *R v Clegg* [1995] 1 AC 482, HL (there is no special rule in relation to either). This common law meaning of 'reasonable force' has been set out in statutory form in the Criminal Justice and Immigration Act 2008, s 76 ('Reasonable force for purposes of self-defence etc'), which received Royal Assent on 8 May 2008. See 15.90 below.

systems of work. The personal liability of chief officers was removed following the prosecution of the Commissioner of the MPS in 2006. The liable legal personality is now the office of Commissioner.

Of greater application, in practice, is the common law offence of misconduct in public office. This offence, which has its origins in the sixteenth century, was rarely used in practice against police officers until the last ten years. For a number of reasons—including simply wider knowledge on the part of prosecuting authorities of the existence of the offence, and greater political momentum to make police officers publicly accountable for their conduct—recent history has seen an exponential growth in the number of prosecutions. **15.05**

This momentum may be slowed, or even reversed, by the limited conviction rate in such trials, which may, in part, be attributed to a lack of comprehension on the part of prosecuting authorities of the detailed elements of the offence that must be proved. Juries have also shown reluctance to criminalize officers that have simply done their best in difficult circumstances. On a proper understanding of the requirements of the offence, such police officers often should not have been prosecuted in the first place. The distinction between incompetence (or mistakes) and serious criminality has too frequently been overlooked in this context. **15.06**

Aspects of these offences are considered in this chapter, with an emphasis on misconduct in public office, manslaughter, and driving-related offending. Unlawful killing is also considered in Chapter 14 in the context of inquest verdicts, and the substantive and investigative requirements of Art 2 of the European Convention on Human Rights (ECHR). The possibility in future of liability of police forces for the offence of corporate manslaughter is addressed. This work does not attempt a comprehensive analysis of the law of homicide beyond this. **15.07**

The relationship with misconduct charges

Depending on the factual circumstances, an officer may be liable to misconduct proceedings following acquittal. This is particularly relevant following acquittal of a charge of misconduct in public office, because the matters that must be proved differ significantly as between the criminal and misconduct charge. Equally, there may be circumstances under which the underlying misconduct is effectively the same and, subject to considerations of the different standards of proof, subsequent misconduct charges would be inappropriate. **15.08**

The limited extent to which the principle of double jeopardy applies generally as between criminal and internal misconduct proceedings was reflected in *Redgrave v Commissioner of Police of the Metropolis*.[2] Additional guidance arises in the Home **15.09**

---

[2] [2003] 1 WLR 1136, [2003] EWCA Civ 4, CA.

Office Guidance on *Police Unsatisfactory Performance Complaints and Misconduct Procedures* for each of the Police (Conduct) Regulations 2004[3] and 2008[4] (see ch 3, para 3.40, of the 2004 Guidance and ch 2, paras 2.35–2.40, of the 2008 Guidance). These rehearse a number of criteria by which the decision regarding misconduct charges in a particular case is taken, and may include considerations other than simply whether a charge would be proved, such as delay from the incident, likely penalty, etc.

B. Misconduct in Public Office

15.10 As a common law, rather than statutory, offence, the definition of the elements of misconduct in public office requires consideration of case law. There is no general rule that common law offences are less certain in definition than statutory offences, and it may be thought that, after several centuries of evolution, the elements of any given common law offence would be well established and easily applied. This is not true of misconduct in public office.

15.11 On any view, it is a serious criminal offence. It is triable only on indictment and carries an unlimited prison sentence. There is no statutory guideline as to sentence, although the statutory guideline as to 'seriousness'[5] applies to all criminal offences.

15.12 Uncertainty as to the meaning and the requirements of the offence culminated in the detailed analysis of the Court of Appeal in *Attorney General's Reference No 3 of 2003*.[6] Whilst the offence applies not only to police officers, but also to anyone that holds public office, the *Attorney General's Reference* arose in a policing context—that is, alleged failures by police officers in their treatment of Christopher Alder preceding his death in custody. Whilst a more extended historical analysis is possible,[7] for most practical purposes, this single authority, properly understood, is sufficient, although this is not to say that definitional arguments have been eliminated.

15.13 The recurrent difficulty in practice is that the detail of the opinion of the Court of Appeal is repeatedly overlooked at the point at which a decision is taken

---

[3] SI 2004/645.

[4] SI 2008/2864.

[5] Sentencing Guidelines Council Guideline, *Overarching Principles: Seriousness*, 16 December 2004, available online at <http:www.sentencing-guidelines.gov.uk>, issued under the provisions of s 170(9) of the Criminal Justice Act 2003. By virtue of s 172 of the Act, every court must have regard to a relevant guideline.

[6] [2005] QB 73, [2004] 2 Cr App R 23, [2004] 3 WLR 451, [2004] EWCA Crim 868.

[7] See, eg, Nicholls, C., Daniel, T., Polaine, M., and Hatchard, J. (2006) *Corruption and the Misuse of Public Office*, Oxford: OUP, ch 3.

to prosecute. This applies particularly to the mental element of the offence—'wilful neglect'—and to the circumstances in which liability will arise if culpability is contended to be contingent on the exercise of discretion. As will be seen, even determining to whom the offence applies (that is, answering the question of who within the police service holds public office) is not without difficulty.

The elements of the offence may usefully be considered in turn and in detail. **15.14**

A summary of the elements

It is emphasized that any summary risks a significant oversimplification of the **15.15** requirements of the offence. Liability to conviction is invariably determined only after a detailed consideration of the elements of the offence, as distinct from applying any summary of the detail. With that said, the analyses of different courts, including that in the *Attorney General's Reference*, promote a summary as a starting point and these summaries may usefully be rehearsed as background.

In the *Attorney General's Reference*, the Court of Appeal expressed its conclusions **15.16** at [61] of the opinion, with original cross-referencing as to other directly relevant paragraphs:

> The circumstances in which the offence may be committed are broad and the conduct which may give rise to it is diverse. A summary of its elements must be considered on the basis of the contents of the preceding paragraphs. The elements of the offence of misconduct in a public office are:
>
> 1. A public officer acting as such (paragraph 54).
> 2. Wilfully neglects to perform his duty and/or wilfully misconducts himself (paragraphs 28, 30, 45 and 55).
> 3. To such a degree as to amount to an abuse of the public's trust in the office holder (paragraphs 46 and 56 to 59).
> 4. Without reasonable excuse or justification (paragraph 60).
>
> As with other criminal charges, it will be for the judge to decide whether there is evidence capable of establishing guilt of the offence and, if so, for the jury to decide whether the offence is proved.

In producing this analysis, the Court had considered—and, to a significant extent, **15.17** adopted—the reasoning of Sir Anthony Mason NPJ in the Court of Final Appeal in Hong Kong in *Shum Kwok Sher v Hong Kong Special Administrative Region*,[8] in which the question arose whether the common law offence of misconduct in a public office was so imprecise as to be unconstitutional under the Basic Law. The Court held that the offence was not arbitrary, or imprecise, or vague enough to violate the relevant requirements.

---

[8] [2002] 5 HKCSAR 381.

15.18 More recently, in the same court, the same judge has perfected his definition of the elements of the offence so as to reflect the analysis of the Court of Appeal in the *Attorney General's Reference*. In *Sin Kam Wah and anor v Hong Kong Special Administrative Region*[9] (involving a senior superintendent of police responsible for policing organized crime and vice accepting the gratuitous sexual services of women whom he knew were under the control of the second defendant, a beneficial owner and de facto operator of nightclubs and prostitutes offering 'hostess services'), the judge stated at [45] and [46] (without any need for greater analysis than it reflecting the *Attorney General's Reference*) that the offence is committed where:

1. A public official;
2. In the course of or in relation to his public office;
3. Wilfully misconducts himself; by act or omission, for example by wilfully neglecting or failing to perform his duty;
4. Without reasonable excuse or justification; and
5. Where such conduct is serious, not trivial, having regard to the responsibilities of the office and the office holder, the importance of the public objects which they serve and the nature and extent of the departure from those responsibilities.

The misconduct must be deliberate rather than accidental in the sense that the official either knew that his conduct was unlawful or wilfully disregarded the risk that his conduct was unlawful. Wilful misconduct which is without reasonable justification or excuse is culpable.

15.19 Plainly, however useful, the Court of Final Appeal in Hong Kong does not provide more than persuasive authority for courts in England and Wales. The structure of the more extensive reasoning in the *Attorney General's Reference* is accordingly adopted for the purpose of analysis.

'1. A public officer acting as such (paragraph 54)'

15.20 This may be thought to be straightforward. In practice, it is not. Paragraph 54 of the opinion simply states as follows:

Roderick Evans J [the trial judge] rightly acknowledged the "great variety of circumstances" in which the offence of misconduct in a public office may be charged. It is clear from the authorities that the defendant must be a public officer acting as such. In the absence of submissions on those ingredients, which may in some circumstances present problems of definition, we do not propose to elaborate on them.

15.21 Self-evidently, there are, within this single element, two matters that must be proved: (i) that the defendant held public office; and (ii) that the allegation

---

[9] [2005] 2 HKLRD 375, 391.

relates to his exercise of that public office. Each of these may be contentious in any given case.

'Public office'

Police constables   It is well established that the office of constable is a public **15.22** office for these purposes. Early authorities often involved police constables. In *Crowther's Case*,[10] prosecution followed where an officer had failed to make a 'hue and cry' after being informed of a burglary. In *Mackally's Case*,[11] a constable who failed to act in accordance with his duty to the Crown was criminally liable, and in *R v Dytham*,[12] a constable who failed to intervene in a brutal assault in the street because he was going off duty was liable for his omission.

Less certain is the status of anyone engaged in police-related work who does not **15.23** hold the office of constable. This category will include designated persons under s 38 of the Police Reform Act 2002, civilian employees under the direction and control of the chief officer who are not so designated, and third parties (that is, those not employed directly by the police authority) subcontracted to perform aspects of the functions of a police force. In the modern policing environment, in which civilians and third parties are now used to perform traditional policing duties, is public office to be determined by function or paymaster?

Persons designated under s 38 of the 2002 Act: community support officers, 15.24 investigating officers, detention officers, escort officers, and staff custody officers   Section 38 ('Police powers for police authority employees') provides:

(1) the chief officer of police of any police force may designate any person who—
    (a) is employed by the police authority maintaining that force, and
    (b) is under the direction and control of that chief officer,
    as an officer of one or more of the descriptions specified in subsection (2).
(2) The description of officers are as follows—
    (a) community support officer;
    (b) investigating officer;
    (c) detention officer;
    (d) escort officer;
    (e) staff custody officer.
[...]
(4) A chief officer of police or a Director General shall not designate a person under this section unless he is satisfied that that person—
    (a) is a suitable person to carry out the functions for the purposes of which he is designated;
    (b) is capable of effectively carrying out those functions; and

---

[10] (1600) Cro Eliz 654.
[11] (1611) 9 Co Rep 656.
[12] [1979] QB 722.

(c) has received adequate training in the carrying out of those functions and in the exercise and performance of the powers and duties to be conferred [or imposed] on him by virtue of the designation.

15.25   As will be seen, such 'designated officers' almost certainly hold public office (and there has been at least one prosecution of such a designated detention officer[13] at which public office was accepted by the defence), but what of those who fulfil s 38(1) but are not designated under s 38(2)?

15.26   **Contracted-out staff under s 39 of the 2002 Act: detention and escort officers**   Section 39 of the 2002 Act makes provision for 'Police powers for contracted out staff', applicable (subs (1)) if a police authority has entered into a contract with a person ('the contractor') for the provision of services relating to the detention or escort of persons who have been arrested or are otherwise in custody. In that context (subs (2)), the chief officer may designate any person who is an employee of the contractor as either, or both, of (subs (2)(a)) a detention officer, or (subs(2)(b)) an escort officer. By subs (3), a person designated under this section shall have the powers and duties conferred or imposed on him by the designation.

15.27   The residue of s 39 makes detailed provision as to the qualifications required of such contracted-out detention and escort officers, the functions that they may legitimately perform, the handling of complaints arising from the performance of such functions, and the power of the Secretary of State to make regulations in respect of such complaints. The Independent Police Complaints Commission (IPCC) has a role in the investigation of qualifying complaints against such parties.[14]

15.28   These provisions came into force at different dates on either 1 October 2002 or 1 April 2003.[15] They were not considered in the *Attorney General's Reference*, and, to that extent, the submission reflected in the opinion at [62] (to the effect that there is an unfairness and illogicality if those holding a public office, such as

---

[13] *R v Green*, Southwark Crown Court, 7 January 2008.

[14] In relation to the disapplication of Pt 2 of the 2002 Act to a complaint received, or a conduct matter that comes to the attention of an appropriate authority, about conduct by a person designated under subs (2) above, which occurred before 1 April 2004, see the Independent Police Complaints Commission (Transitional Provisions) Order 2004, SI 2004/671, art 3.

[15] Subsections (1)–(8), (11)(c), (12), and (13) in force 1 April 2003: see the Police Reform Act 2002 (Commencement No 4) Order 2003, SI 2003/808, art 2(b). Subsections (9), (10), and (11) (a), (b), and (d) in force 1 October 2002: see the Police Reform Act 2002 (Commencement No 1) Order 2002, SI 2002/2306, art 2(d)(i). Subsection (11), paras (a) and (b) substituted by the Police and Justice Act 2006, s 6(1), Sch 4, para 13, and in force 1 April 2007: see the Police and Justice Act 2006 (Commencement No 2, Transitional and Saving Provisions) Order 2007, SI 2007/709, art 3(d). See further, in relation to the British Transport Police (BTP) in England and Wales, the Railways and Transport Safety Act 2003, ss 28 and 77(3).

police officers, are to be liable to a sanction not applicable to those in private employment who do similar work) may have proceeded on a false premise.

In terms of those falling within either of ss 38 or 39 of the 2002 Act, it is con- **15.29**
tended that the functions performed are within public office. The function is identical to that historically performed by police constables, and those perform- ing them must be designated as fit for purpose by the chief officer. Members of the public may complain about performance and such complaints are within the jurisdiction of the IPCC. As will be seen, such an approach to classifying such parties as holders of public office is also wholly consistent with the evolving function-led approach in case law. It avoids arbitrary distinctions between those performing identical functions.

Non-designated staff performing police-related functions   As to those per- **15.30**
forming police-related functions outside designation under ss 38 and 39 (whether as employees under the direction and control of the police authority or chief officer, and/or as contracted-out staff performing the same functions), the posi- tion is contended to be far less clear. At one level, everyone employed in whatever capacity by, or on behalf of, a police force is performing a function in which the public has an interest, and is likely to be paid ultimately from public funds. It would be surprising if each such person were liable to prosecution as the holder of public office. Any organization, whether public or not, requires internal admin- istrative staff, and such parties cannot sensibly be contended to hold public office.

The existing definitions, however, produce no clear answer, and the resolution **15.31**
of the uncertainty may lie as much in policy and/or practice as in legal theory. There is no obvious reason why the offence is not used for a far greater range of potential defendants in other occupations in which the public has an equal inter- est, but, in practice, it is not. If a function-led approach gains currency, the failure in practice to prosecute individuals in other professions—including medicine, law, and politics[16]—will become increasingly difficult to justify. If the distinction between appointed public office and private employment is not pivotal, then prosecution policy should be consistent across public service professions.

A review of the decided authorities—which are largely historic—suggests an **15.32**
approach that is function-led and not contingent on either payment or source of payment. As has been rehearsed, the relevant English authorities on this point were not considered in detail in the *Attorney General's Reference*. Earlier definitions of the offence (including the on-duty police constable omitting to act so as to

---

[16] Although it is established that members of Parliament hold public office: see *R v Currie and ors* (1992), unreported, Central Criminal Court; *R v Boston* (1923) 33 CLR 386 (the High Court of Australia); *Rao and ors v State of India* [1999] 3 LRC 297 (the Supreme Court of India).

prevent a serious assault in *Dytham*)[17] were reflected in the 1996 appeal of *R v Bowden*,[18] which, in turn, adopted the reasoning of the Court of Appeal in *R v Bembridge*[19] some two centuries before.

15.33   *Bowden* concerned a maintenance manager employed by a local authority, who arranged for otherwise unauthorized work to be carried out at his partner's house. The key to whether or not his duty involved the exercise of public office involved a broadly worded test as to 'an office of trust concerning the public' and 'that this is true by whomever and in whatever way the officer is appointed'. The Court held that 'a public office is correctly defined as embracing "everyone who is appointed to discharge a public duty, and receives compensation in whatever form whether from the Crown or otherwise"', adopting the definition in *Henly v Lyme Corporation*,[20] and that 'in no case has it been laid down that the offence is limited to officers or agents of the Crown'. His conviction was upheld.

15.34   In *Lancaster and Worrall*,[21] the Court held that the 'nature of the office is immaterial as long as it is for the public good', and similarly, in *R v Whitaker*,[22] an army officer who accepted a corrupt payment in respect of granting a tenancy of a regimental canteen was found to have held public office. A 'public office holder' was defined as 'an officer who discharges any duty in the discharge of which the public are interested, more clearly so if he is paid out of a fund provided by the public'.

15.35   International jurisprudence also promotes a function-led approach. In *R v Boston*,[23] the High Court of Australia was considering whether the functions and duties of a member of Parliament (MP) meant that it was a public office. By a majority, the Court held that it did, because a MP has 'duties to perform which would constitute in law an office', and that such duties were those 'appertaining to the position that he fills, a position of no transient or temporary existence, a position forming a recognised place in the constitutional machinery of government'.[24] Hirst J found that the core element was whether or not there is an obligation to discharge a duty in which the public is interested and that 'the application and the principle is not confined to public servants in the narrow sense under direct orders of the Crown'.[25]

15.36   A similar approach to MPs was adopted more recently by the Supreme Court of India in *Rao and ors v State of India*,[26] although the Court's finding of a separate

---

17 [1979] QB 722, 725–8.
18 [1996] 1 Cr App R 104, [1996] 1 WLR 98, CA.
19 (1783) 3 Doug 327, CA.
20 (1828) 5 Bing 91.
21 (1890) 16 Cox CC 739.
22 [1914] 3 KB 1283, [1914] 10 Cr App R 245, CA.
23 (1923) 33 CLR 386.
24 Ibid, 402.
25 Ibid, 411.
26 [1999] 3 LRC 297.

requirement for the office to have an existence independent of the office holder is questionable in the context of modern practices in political and other public service contexts.[27]

Conclusion regarding 'public office' The various formulations are not pro-   **15.37**
ductive of a hard-edged definition. A function-led approach is emerging. Applied to a policing context, the nearer the function of a particular party comes to operational policing—or, at least, the functions traditionally performed by police constables—the more probable it is that such a party will qualify as a holder of public office. Such a conclusion is further promoted by a chief officer having direction and control over and/or a power of designation in respect of the relevant person, as well as by the applicable machinery to determine complaints.

Outside such parties, determining whether someone holds public office may be   **15.38**
contingent on factors including whether or not the person in question is res-
ponsible for the allocation and use of police authority (or other public) funds (see *Whitaker* and *Bowden*), and whether a particular role is essentially policing (that is, public) or administrative (that is, wholly internal) in nature.

'Acting as such'

The conduct must reflect the public officer acting as such. However reprehen-   **15.39**
sible conduct may be, the gravamen of the offence lies in abusing the trust placed by the public in the office holder in the exercise of public office. Applied to police constables, conduct that is off-duty and which has no nexus with police duties will not qualify. Equally, in the performance of police duties, there is a positive duty to act. The offence may be committed by omission as much as by positive action.

The boundary as to what is an exercise of office is not completely hard-edged.   **15.40**
For example, police officers routinely meet and address the legitimate demands of vulnerable witnesses: can liability extend to off-duty conduct towards or with such a vulnerable party?

The answer to this is always going to be fact-specific, but the short answer is   **15.41**
contended to be 'yes'. Firstly, police officers must be aware that such victims of crime are vulnerable at the point of reporting serious crime. Secondly, any personal relationship is likely—or at least liable—to compromise the police investigation, and with it, the public interest in the investigation of crime. Thirdly, the public would reasonably expect a police officer (especially one who is trained in this regard) not to risk taking advantage of the potential vulnerability of the witness. The obligation to act professionally as a police officer invariably would

---

[27] See Nicholls et al, *Corruption and the Misuse of Public Office*, [3.47].

exclude any private relationship until the potential for an abuse of trust as documented above was eliminated. The concepts of 'on' and 'off' duty would have no application to such a context.

15.42 Other contexts generate considerations of fact and degree. For example, to what extent may police constables use information obtained in that capacity to promote their private interests when off duty? What is the extent of a police constable's duty to act to prevent crime when off duty? The answer is contended to be that off-duty conduct may be an exercise of office in this sense (the public office of constable does not end when the officer is off duty), but that the failure must represent serious misconduct before an omission to intervene becomes culpable. As will be seen, the potential consequences of failing to act are relevant to such a question.

15.43 In *Sin Kam Wah*,[28] it was argued that the knowing receipt of sexual services by the (off-duty) senior superintendent from prostitutes under the de facto management control of his host was not conduct in, or in relation to, his office. This was rejected on the basis that, to constitute the offence:

> . . . wilful misconduct which has a relevant relationship with a defendant's public office is enough. Thus, misconduct otherwise than in the performance of the defendant's public duties may nevertheless have such a relationship with his public office as to bring that office into disrepute, in circumstances where the misconduct is both culpable and serious and not trivial.[29]

15.44 On the facts of the case, the Court had no doubt that the 'necessary relationship' existed. Equally, it is likely that if the senior superintendent had simply visited prostitutes as a client in his private capacity when off duty, without the wider relationship with their manager, this would not, of itself, have represented an exercise of public office. It would almost inevitably have justified removal from the police force—and possibly prosecution, if such conduct were intrinsically unlawful—but not prosecution for the specific offence of misconduct in public office. These are the sorts of distinction that may arise in practice.

'2. Wilfully neglects to perform his duty and/or wilfully misconducts himself (paragraphs 28, 30, 45 and 55)'

15.45 This element of the offence has produced more confusion than others. This reflects the language of earlier authorities, and the concurrent, but separate, developments in decided authorities as to the meaning of 'wilful neglect' and 'recklessness'. Each has now essentially been resolved.

---

[28] [2005] 2 HKLRD 375. See 15.18 above.
[29] Ibid, at [47].

Following the *Attorney General's Reference*, what is now clear is that, before a **15.46**
police officer is guilty of misconduct in public office, he will have to be proved to
have had a state of mind that constitutes wilful neglect of the public duty that he
is said to have failed to perform. It follows that a constable who is wholly ignorant
of the duty (even if he should have appreciated it), or who has made an honest
mistake (albeit incompetently) in the performance of that duty (for example, as to
the assessment of risk), will not be culpable in this subjective sense, although
such conduct may represent a breach of the objective standards set for the
purposes of certain breaches of the Code of Conduct under the applicable Conduct
Regulations.

To some extent, this represents the common law coming full circle. In *R v Borron*,[30] **15.47**
a magistrate was indicted for the offence. Abbott CJ stated (at 434):

> ... They [magistrates] are indeed, like every other subject of this kingdom, answer-
> able to the law for the faithful and upright discharge of their trust and duties. But,
> whenever they have been challenged upon this head, either by way of indictment, or
> application to this Court for a criminal information, the question has always been,
> not whether the act done might, upon full and mature investigation, be found strictly
> right, but from what motive it had proceeded; whether from a dishonest, oppressive,
> or corrupt motive, under which description, fear and favour may generally be
> included, or from mistake or error. In the former case, alone, they have become the
> objects of punishment. To punish as a criminal any person who, in the gratuitous
> exercise of a public trust, may have fallen into error or mistake belongs only to the
> despotic ruler of an enslaved people, and is wholly abhorrent from the jurisprudence
> of this kingdom.

The force of this reasoning is too often overlooked in respect of the prosecution **15.48**
of police officers for this offence, and, even now, it may be that the formulation in
terms of wilful neglect is still not wholly applied in practice where serious
objective failures in police performance are identified.

The Court of Appeal specifically considered the meanings of 'recklessness', 'wilful **15.49**
neglect', and 'wilful misconduct' in the *Attorney General's Reference* at [11]–[30].
As has been set out in rehearsing the elements of the offence, the Court additionally identified specific paragraphs in this context from the opinion as a whole.
These are rehearsed for ease of reference in full, as follows.

> 28. In *Graham v Teesdale & Anr* [1981] 81 LGR 117, Webster J considered the
> meaning of the expression "wilful misconduct" in section 161 of the Local
> Government Act 1972. The case was concerned with the audit of local authority
> accounts by a district auditor. Webster J stated, at page 123, that wilful misconduct
> means "deliberately doing something which is wrong knowing it to be wrong or
> with reckless indifference as to whether it is wrong or not". That statutory con-
> struction has been approved by the Court of Appeal and the House of Lords in

---

[30] (1820) 3 B&Ald 432.

Lloyd v McMahon [1987] AC 625 and *Porter v Magill* [2002] AC 357 (per Lord Bingham of Cornhill at page 464, giving the references in *Lloyd*). We regard that direction as helpful in present circumstances, considering as we do that the concept of wilful misconduct is apt to the offence of misconduct in public office (see *Dytham* below). A *G* direction upon the meaning of reckless would of course need to be incorporated.

[. . .]

30. The issue which was perceived to have caused the problem at trial, and the principal question perceived to have resulted from the judge's ruling, has, in our view, been resolved by the decision in *G*. There must be an awareness of the duty to act or a subjective recklessness as to the existence of the duty. The recklessness test will apply to the question whether in particular circumstances a duty arises at all as well as to the conduct of the defendant if it does. The subjective test applies both to reckless indifference to the legality of the act or omission and in relation to the consequences of the act or omission.

[. . .]

45. We share, with respect, counsels' difficulty in understanding, upon the first qualification, the need for conduct to be both wilful and intentional. The need for both was considered important by Sir Anthony Mason and also by Bokhary PJ. The explanation may be in the reference to "the intent to do an act or refrain from doing an act" so that the conduct must be deliberate rather than accidental. The judge was also underlining what he had said earlier, at paragraph 82, that "mere inadvertence is not enough". Having cited the two limbs of the test in *Sheppard* as disjunctive, it is unlikely that Sir Anthony Mason would require intent as distinct from recklessness in relation to advertence to the consequences. If there is a difference, we adopt the approach in *G*, which in any event binds us. The decision of the Final Court of Appeal in *Shum Kwok Sher* of course precedes that decision.

[. . .]

55. There must be a breach of duty by the officer. It may consist of an act of commission or one of omission. The conduct must be wilful, in the sense already considered.

15.50 To this may be added some additional analysis. Three specific elements may be addressed: (i) the meaning of 'wilful neglect'; coupled with (ii) in this context, the meaning of 'recklessness', and (iii) relevant principles as to the mental element of the crime that arise from the associated tort of misfeasance on public office.

'Wilful neglect'

15.51 The Shorter Oxford English Dictionary defines 'wilful' as 'of an action etc,: done on purpose; deliberate; intentional'. This has been, and remains, a useful starting point for analysis.

15.52 The expression 'wilful neglect' is used in the statutory context of s 1 of the Children and Young Persons Act 1933, directed at criminal liability for an adult with responsibility for a child that 'wilfully neglects him in a manner likely to cause him unnecessary suffering or injury to health'. The Court of Appeal in the *Attorney*

General's Reference found the expression 'wilful neglect' apposite to the basis of liability for the offence of misconduct in public office, and adopted the meaning of the expression as defined by the House of Lords in relation to the s 1 offence under the 1933 Act in *R v Sheppard*.[31] It will be seen that it is relatively straightforward to extrapolate from the role of parents with duties to a child to that of a police constable performing public duties—particularly, for example, custody or investigative duties.

In *Sheppard*, the House of Lords allowed an appeal against conviction by **15.53** parents who failed to seek medical assistance for their child. The majority found unacceptable an objective test of fault—that is, whether a reasonable parent, with knowledge of the facts known to the parents in the case, would appreciate that failure to have the child medically examined was likely to cause unnecessary suffering or injury to health. The proposition that wilfulness followed automatically from their undoubted failure was rejected.

The respective Law Lords formulated the test in different language, but the **15.54** practical effect is largely the same. The formulation of Lord Diplock is found at [21] of the *Attorney General's Reference*. In terms of the speeches of Lord Edmund-Davies and Lord Keith of Kinkel, the Court of Appeal set out the following.

22. Lord Edmund-Davies accepted, at p 412A, the proposition that "the requirement of wilfulness means, or should mean, that a parent who omits to call in the doctor to his child is not guilty of the offence if he does not know that the child needs assistance" and continued (at 412C):

"But to that must be added that a parent reckless about the state of his child's health, not caring whether or not he is at risk, cannot be heard to say that he never gave the matter a thought and was therefore not wilful in not calling in a doctor. In such circumstances recklessness constitutes mens rea no less than positive awareness of the risk involved in failure to act."

23. However, this paragraph, cited with approval by Lord Steyn in *G*, is followed (412F) by the comment that "the stronger the objective indications of neglect, the more difficult for defendants to repel the conclusion that they *must* have known of the plight of the children in their charge, or at least that they had been recklessly regardless of their welfare."

24. The third member of the majority, Lord Keith of Kinkel, stated, at p 418:

"I turn now to consider the meaning of the adverb "wilfully" which governs and qualifies "neglects" and all the other verbs in section 1(1). This is a word which ordinarily carries a perjorative sense. It is used here to describe the mental element, which, in addition to the fact of neglect, must be proved in order to establish an offence under the sub-section. The primary meaning of "wilful" is "deliberate". So a parent who knows that his child needs medical care and deliberately, that is by conscious decision, refrains from calling a doctor, is guilty under the subsection. As a matter of

---

[31] [1981] AC 394, HL.

general principle, recklessness is to be equiparated with deliberation. A parent who fails to provide medical care which his child needs because he does not care whether it is needed or not is reckless of his child's welfare. He too is guilty of an offence. But a parent who has genuinely failed to appreciate that his child needs medical care, through personal inadequacy or stupidity or both, is not guilty."

15.55 The relevance of this to the criminal liability of a police constable is obvious, and in particular to any allegation of misconduct based on simple objective incompetence or stupidity. It is consistent with what Lord Steyn referred to (at [55] of *R v G*[32]) as '. . . the general tendency in modern times of our criminal law. The shift is towards adopting a subjective approach. It is generally necessary to look at the matter in the light of how it would have appeared to the defendant'.

15.56 In the context—which is a common one—of the potential liability of escorting or custody officers in relation to the welfare of prisoners in their care, a custody officer who genuinely does not appreciate that a prisoner needs care—even through personal inadequacy, or stupidity, or both—is not guilty of wilful misconduct. He is, however, at risk of an accusation of recklessness as to this fact if he does nothing to determine the nature of the risk in an individual case. An officer cannot close his mind to risk, but if he is either assured by other custody staff (expressly, or by implication), misled as to facts, or makes honest, but mistaken, assumptions about whether a prisoner is in a medically vulnerable state, then the element of wilfulness is less likely to be established. Even if mistaken, his state of mind will be genuine, rather than reckless.

15.57 Further, it is contended that if the failure to determine the nature of the risk in an individual case is itself a mistake (that is, an oversight or inadvertence, even if serious), then wilful neglect will similarly not be established. The central test is subjective—that is, what is the knowledge or belief of the public officer actually proved to have been, rather than the objective question of what he should have known or believed.

Recklessness

15.58 Consistent with this, and as part of any direction as to wilful neglect, is the subsequent House of Lords authority of *G*.[33] Although the case was concerned with the definition of recklessness in s 1 of the Criminal Damage Act 1971, general principles were laid down. It was established that a defendant could not be culpable under the criminal law of doing something involving a risk of injury to another or damage to property if he genuinely did not perceive the risk.

---

[32] [2003] UKHL 50.
[33] Ibid.

At [32], Lord Bingham stated that it was a 'salutary principle that conviction of **15.59**
serious crime should depend on proof not simply that the defendant caused
(by act or omission) an injurious result to another but that his state of mind when
so acting was culpable', and that:

> The most obviously culpable state of mind is no doubt an intention to cause the
> injurious result, but knowing disregard of an appreciated and unacceptable risk of
> causing an injurious result or a deliberate closing of the mind to such risk would be
> readily accepted as culpable also. It is clearly blameworthy to take an obvious and
> significant risk of causing injury to another. But it is not clearly blameworthy to do
> something involving a risk of injury to another if (for reasons other than self-induced
> intoxication: *R v Majewski* ([1977] AC 443) one genuinely does not perceive the
> risk. Such a person may fairly be accused of stupidity or lack of imagination, but
> neither of those failings should expose him to conviction of serious crime or the risk
> of punishment.

Lord Bingham's conclusion, at [41], was as follows. **15.60**

> A person acts recklessly within the meaning of section 1 of the Criminal Damage Act
> 1971 with respect to – (i) a circumstance when he is aware of a risk that it exists or
> will exist; (ii) a result when he is aware of a risk that it will occur; and it is, in the
> circumstances known to him, unreasonable to take the risk.

In certain contexts (for example, corruption), the application of recklessness **15.61**
as to consequences may be a distraction. In practice, an accused officer will not be
able to argue that he closed his mind to the public harm caused by such corrupt
payments. What any decision maker (investigator, prosecutor, defence lawyer,
or judge) must focus on is the evidence supportive of a culpable state of mind in
any individual case. Objective failures of performance may be sufficient for a
discipline charge, but not for criminal liability.

The tort of misfeasance in public office

The Court of Appeal in the *Attorney General's Reference* referred to the tort of **15.62**
misfeasance in public office, and, in particular, to the comprehensive analysis
that it received from the House of Lords in *Three Rivers District Council v Governor &
Company of the Bank of England (No 3)*.[34] Whilst there were purposive differences
between the two, the Court of Appeal found (at [48]) that 'the approach
in Three Rivers to the mental element appears to us, however, to be consistent
with that we find appropriate to the criminal offence', and (at [53]):

> In so far as comparisons between the criminal offence and the tort are relevant, and
> in particular the required mental element and the extent of the required departure

---

[34] [2003] 2 AC 1, HL. It was claimed (unsuccessfully on the facts) that the Bank was liable to
former depositors with The Bank of Credit and Commerce International for the tort of misfeasance
in public office because of the Bank's failure in its responsibilities for supervising banking activities
in the UK.

from proper standards, the approach in *Three Rivers* appears to us to be consistent with that in the criminal cases and in our conclusions. Neither the mental element associated with the misconduct, nor the threshold of misconduct should be set lower for the crime than for the tort.

15.63 The necessity of subjective recklessness in the tort has been emphasized in a number of subsequent cases.[35] Applied to the mental element of the crime, this raises some important considerations in terms of culpability of police officers or those in public office related to policing. Whilst the mental element inherent in the tort (particularly as to bad faith) is not favoured for incorporation routinely as an element of the direction to the jury in the criminal case (although the motive with which an officer may be relevant), the approval of the mental element of the tort is nevertheless significant.

15.64 Of particular relevance is liability where the public officer has discretion in the performance of his duties. As rehearsed by the Court of Appeal, the following principle applies:

> 52. Lord Millett referred, at page 235B, to the core concept [of the tort of misfeasance in public office] as being abuse of power and stated, at page 237C:
>
> "In conformity with the character of the tort, the failure to act must be deliberate, not negligent or inadvertent or arising from a misunderstanding of the legal position. In my opinion, a failure to act can amount to misfeasance in public office only where (i) the circumstances are such that the discretion whether to act can only be exercised in one way so that there is effectively a duty to act; (ii) the official appreciates this but nevertheless makes a conscious decision not to act; and (iii) he does so with intent to injure the plaintiff or in the knowledge that such injury will be the natural and probable consequence of his failure to act."

15.65 These requirements are fundamental and of general application, and must, of course, be read with the requirement as to seriousness. They are easily overlooked within the body and structure of the opinion of the Court of Appeal in the *Attorney General's Reference*. If a police officer is said to have made a wrong decision as an exercise of discretion, he will only be liable to prosecution if the criteria rehearsed above are satisfied, although element (iii) probably has to be read down to make allowance for the distinctions between the tort and the crime, and the wider conclusions as to wilful neglect and recklessness.

'3. To such a degree as to amount to an abuse of the public's trust in the office holder (paragraphs 46 and 56 to 59)'

15.66 These are important additional threshold requirements before the offence is established. As with any threshold, there is a degree of subjectivity involved in the

---

[35] *Stockwell v Society of Lloyd's* [2007] EWCA Civ 390; *London Borough of Southwark v Dennett* [2007] EWCA Civ 1091; *Carter and ors v Chief Constable of the Cumbria Police* [2008] EWHC 1072 (QB).

application of the law. Whilst Widgery J in *R v Llewellyn-Jones*[36] observed that identifying this threshold in context of misconduct in public office 'puts no heavier burden upon [a jury] than when in more familiar contexts they are called upon to consider whether driving is dangerous or a publication is obscene or a place of public resort is a disorderly house', and a similar approach is taken in respect of the capacity of a jury to determine whether negligence is criminal,[37] 'seriousness', in the context of police misconduct, is arguably somewhat more subjective and contentious than determining these matters.

The threshold is, in any event, clearly intended, as a matter of social policy and practicality, to restrict the offence to genuinely serious misconduct. To this extent, there is an obligation on trial judges to take a robust view—without, of course, usurping the function of the jury—based on experience, of what conduct legitimately may be included. Not every alleged piece of misconduct satisfies this criterion, and a judge is entitled to rule that, in a particular case, no reasonable jury properly directed as to the history and nature of the offence could conclude that the alleged misconduct was sufficiently serious. This discretion is no different from that articulated in respect of gross negligence manslaughter (see 15.100 below). Acquittal does not ordinarily prevent charges under the Conduct Regulations directed at objective standards of performance.   **15.67**

As with preceding elements, the specific paragraphs identified by the Court of Appeal for reference within its opinion are rehearsed below.   **15.68**

> 45. Where we have, with respect, found Sir Anthony Mason's judgment valuable is in his approval of the general test in *Dytham* and his reference, at paragraph 86, to a second qualification. Having considered the authorities, we agree that the misconduct complained of must be serious misconduct. Whether it is of a sufficiently serious nature will depend on the factors stated by Sir Anthony Mason along with the seriousness of the consequences which may follow from an act or omission. An act or omission which may have as its consequence a death, viewed in terms of the need for maintenance of public standards to be marked and the public interest to be asserted, is likely to be more serious than one which would cause a trivial injury. This factor is likely to have less significance where, as in *Shum Kwok Sher*, the allegation is of corruption where the judgment upon the conduct may not vary directly in proportion to the amount of money involved.
>
> [. . .]
>
> 56. The approach in *Three Rivers* also demonstrates the many-faceted nature of the tort, as of the crime. It supports the view expressed in the criminal cases, from *Borron* to *Shum Kwok Sher*, that there must be a serious departure from proper standards before the criminal offence is committed; and a departure not merely negligent but amounting to an affront to the standing of the public office held. The threshold is a

---

[36] [1967] 1 QB 429, CA.
[37] *R v Adomako* [1995] AC 171, 187C and 187E, HL.

high one requiring conduct so far below acceptable standards as to amount to an abuse of the public's trust in the office holder. A mistake, even a serious one, will not suffice. The motive with which a public officer acts may be relevant to the decision whether the public's trust is abused by the conduct. As Abbott CJ illustrated in *Borron*, a failure to insist upon a high threshold, a failure to confine the test of misconduct as now proposed, would place a constraint upon the conduct of public officers in the proper performance of their duties which would be contrary to the public interest.

57. As Lord Widgery CJ put it in *Dytham*, the leading modern criminal case: the element of culpability "must be of such a degree that the misconduct impugned is calculated to injure the public interest so as to call for condemnation and punishment". The constitutional context has changed but the rationale for the offence remains that stated by Lord Mansfield in *Bembridge*: those who hold public office carry out their duties for the benefit of the public as a whole and, if they abuse their office, there is a breach of the public's trust. By way of example, the failure of the constable in *Dytham* to act, in the absence of a justification or excuse, crossed the threshold for this offence.

58. It will normally be necessary to consider the likely consequences of the breach in deciding whether the conduct falls so far below the standard of conduct to be expected of the officer as to constitute the offence. The conduct cannot be considered in a vacuum: the consequences likely to follow from it, viewed subjectively as in *G*, will often influence the decision as to whether the conduct amounted to an abuse of the public's trust in the officer. A default where the consequences are likely to be trivial may not possess the criminal quality required; a similar default where the damage to the public or members of the public is likely to be great may do so. In a case like the present, for example, was the death or serious injury of the man arrested the likely consequence, viewed subjectively, of inaction, or was it merely an uncomfortable night? There will be some conduct which possesses the criminal quality even if serious consequences are unlikely but it is always necessary to assess the conduct in the circumstances in which it occurs.

59. The consequences of some conduct, such as corrupt conduct, may be obvious; the likely consequences of other conduct of public officers will be less clear but it is impossible to gauge the seriousness of defaulting conduct without considering the circumstances in which the conduct occurs and its likely consequences. The whole should be considered in the context of the nature of the office and, as Sir Anthony Mason stated in *Shum Kwok Sher*, the responsibilities of the office and office holder.

15.69   These propositions do not require detailed analysis: fundamentally, even a serious mistake is not a basis for criminal liability so long as it is in an honest (genuine) attempt to discharge the public office held. The whole context matters and the likely consequences, viewed subjectively as in *G*, will invariably be relevant.

'4. Without reasonable excuse or justification (paragraph 60)'

15.70   Paragraph 60 simply provides: 'The failure to meet standards must occur without justification or excuse, a further requirement, though not one which has been the subject of detailed submissions'.

Assuming that the other elements have been proved, it may be difficult con- **15.71** ceptually to identify (still less to define) what could ever constitute a reasonable excuse or justification. It is probably a matter of fact for the jury, rather than a matter of law. The corollary is that, subject to legal direction as to the other elements, the court may not be able to rule that a particular matter was incapable of amounting to a reasonable justification or excuse.

It is contended that matters capable of amounting to a reasonable justification **15.72** or excuse might include a junior officer claiming that he was bullied or coerced into particular misconduct by a senior officer (although short of duress), or an officer doing his honest best against a background of wholly inadequate practical resources or training. There may well be an overlap in individual cases in this sense with the requirement to prove serious misconduct that is calculated to 'offend the public conscience'. These are not matters that have attracted further judicial determination.

Conclusions in relation to misconduct in public office

Used appropriately, misconduct in public office is an important and necessary **15.73** criminal offence. It has the flexibility to cover conduct not caught by other substantive criminal offences, and is, in any event, directly and specifically related to the question of public confidence in the discharge of duties by public officers.

Given the wide range of conduct to which it may apply, it is obviously appropriate **15.74** for the prosecuting authorities both to understand the detailed requirements of the offence and to adopt a consistent policy nationally as to when it is used. Police officers may well be justified in a perception that it is used against them in inappropriate circumstances, and, more generally, to a degree that is not matched in the approach of the prosecuting authorities to other public officers, or those performing functions in which the public has an interest.

C. Unlawful Killing

Introduction

This work does not attempt any definitive analysis of the law of homicide. The **15.75** basic elements that must be proved are rehearsed for reference. Particular issues are identified that are relevant to the liability of police officers in this general context.

Police officers owe a duty of care to a class of individuals in consequence of their **15.76** office and, within that class, fatalities almost inevitably occur. Self-evidently, there is no limit to the circumstances in which a death may result from contact with police officers. Liability is often contended to arise following a fatal shooting (where, if the force used is not reasonable, the logical finding is that the death represents murder), or in the context of restraint causing (as that concept is defined) death. Additionally, and as considered at 15.128 *et seq* below, liability arises for causing death by dangerous or, in the future, careless driving.

15.77   The Corporate Manslaughter and Corporate Homicide Act 2007 came into force on 6 April 2008.[38] This creates a new offence of corporate manslaughter (corporate homicide in Scotland) under s 1 of the Act and extends this liability to police forces. As will be seen, the provisions extending liability to deaths of persons within places including custody areas were not brought into force by the Commencement Order. When these provisions do come into force—which will probably be consequential on the first death in custody in relation to which they should have been available and were not—they will make police forces liable to prosecution and a fine if the offence is proved. The 2007 Act is considered at 15.114–15.127 below.

An overview of the forms of homicide

15.78   Murder is unlawful killing with intent to kill or cause grievous bodily harm. Voluntary manslaughter occurs when all of the elements of murder are present, including intent to kill or cause grievous bodily harm, but the crime is reduced to manslaughter by reason of: (i) provocation; (ii) diminished responsibility; or (iii) death being caused in pursuance of a suicide pact. These defences are not considered further in the context of this book.

15.79   Involuntary manslaughter is unlawful killing without intent to kill or cause grievous bodily harm. Apart from specific intent, the elements of the offence are the same, and hence law as to reasonable force and causation, etc, applies.

15.80   There are two categories of involuntary manslaughter: (i) unlawful and dangerous act manslaughter; and (ii) gross negligence manslaughter. The elements of each of these categories are considered below. The common elements of duty of care and causation are addressed first. The existence of a duty of care is always relevant to gross negligence manslaughter.

The duty of care

15.81   Defining when a duty of care is owed by a police officer is a matter of some legal complexity. Certain situations are well established, such as the duty owed to those in police detention and to other road users. As to the latter, the police are given a margin of discretion in the performance of duties to reflect the public interest in the effective performance of emergency vehicles.

---

[38] The Corporate Manslaughter and Corporate Homicide Act 2007 (Commencement No 1) Order 2008, SI 2008/401.

Aside from situations in which the assumption of a duty of care is uncontentious, **15.82**
the law has developed such that considerations of public policy determine whether
a duty of care exists. Mere forseeability of harm as a consequence of negligent
police performance does not create a duty of care. Without such a duty existing,
the negligent performance of police duties will not attract either civil or criminal
liability. Competing considerations of public interest arise and resolution of
these in any particular context is inherently somewhat subjective. These policy
considerations are reflected in the exclusions from duties of care rehearsed in
s 2 of the 2007 Act, considered at 15.127 below.

From an extensive body of law, certain basic principles emerge in relation to when **15.83**
a duty of care will be held to exist.

(i) In order to establish liability in negligence, three conditions must be satisfied:
   (a) the existence of a duty of care;
   (b) a breach of that duty; and
   (c) that the breach caused injury.

(ii) Applied to gross negligence manslaughter, another condition must be met—
   that is, that the breach of duty, given the risk of *death*, must be 'gross'.

(iii) In novel contexts, whether in a policing environment or not (that is, those in
   which the duty of care is contentious), the court will apply the three-stage
   test to the existence of a duty rehearsed in *Caparo Industries Plc v Dickman*.[39]
   The claimant of a duty must establish:
   (a) that the harm suffered was reasonably foreseeable;[40]
   (b) that there was sufficient 'proximity' between him or herself and the
       defendant; and
   (c) that it is 'fair, just, and reasonable' to impose a duty of care on the
       defendant.

(iv) Determining the third *Caparo* element is essentially a question of public
   policy 'not susceptible of any precise definition' and ultimately driven by
   pragmatism.[41]

---

[39] [1990] 2 AC 605, HL.
[40] Itself a question of fact: see, eg, *McNern v Commissioner of Police of the Metropolis* [2000] Pol
LR 117, CA.
[41] *Caparo Industries Plc v Dickman* [1990] 2 AC 605, 617–618, HL. More recently, in *R v Evans
(Gemma)* [2009] EWCA Crim 650; [2009] WLR (D) 118, the Court of Appeal held that, for the
purposes of gross negligence manslaughter, when a person had created or contributed to the creation
of a state of affairs which he knew or ought to have known had become life threatening to another
person, a consequent duty would normally arise on him to act by taking reasonable steps to save
another's life. Further, the existence or otherwise of such a duty of care was a question of law, whereas
the question whether the facts established the existence of the duty was for the jury. If the existence
of the duty was in dispute, the jury should be directed that if particular facts were established then
in law a duty would arise but if other facts were present the duty would be negatived.

(v) Applied to the policing context, the leading authority remains *Hill v Chief Constable of West Yorkshire*,[42] as considered in particular in *Van Colle v Chief Constable of Hertfordshire Police*.[43]

(vi) In *Hill*, the claim by a relative of one of the victims of the 'Yorkshire Ripper' for negligently failing to arrest Peter Sutcliffe earlier and so prevent the murder failed because:

    (a) a duty to protect an individual against the criminal acts of a third party would normally only arise in special circumstances and thus the police owed no general duty to protect the victims of crime; and

    (b) in terms of public policy, to impose such a duty would not be fair and reasonable, because it might lead to police officers acting in a defensive manner with a view to potential liability and because it might divert resources from combating crime to defending civil claims.

(vii) This core principle was upheld in *Van Colle* in terms of protecting prosecution witnesses subject to specific and identified threats. Per Lord Phillips at [97]: '[I]n the absence of special circumstances the police owe no common law duty of care to protect individuals against harm caused by criminals'.

(viii) The existence of duty has, however, been held to arise in specific operational contexts: for example, *Knightley v Johns*[44] (police liable to a police motorcyclist directed the wrong way down a one-way tunnel after an accident); *Rigby v Chief Constable of Northamptonshire*[45] (police liable for the manner in which dangerous equipment was used to end a siege); and *AG v Hartwell*[46] (police force liable for acts of an officer with a firearm, where the issue of that firearm to that officer, given his character, was negligent).

(ix) There are many other examples of when the duty has been held not to exist.[47] In general terms, the ordinary, public policy-driven, exclusion of a duty of care will apply to investigative and policy considerations, and will only be avoided when a specific operation creates a sufficient proximity between the police and identifiable categories of person who may be directly affected. Although not binding, the existence of a duty of care in the conduct of an

---

[42] [1989] 1 AC 53, HL.

[43] [2008] 3 All ER 977, HL.

[44] [1982] 1 WLR 349.

[45] [1985] 1 WLR 1242.

[46] [2004] 1 WLR 1273, PC.

[47] See *Alexandrou v Oxford* [1993] 4 All ER 328 (no duty to prevent crime even after summoned to a scene); *Calveley v Chief Constable of Merseyside Police* [1989] AC 1228 (chief officer not liable for failing to pursue complaint of misconduct); *Heagren v Chief Constable of Norfolk* [1997] EWCA Civ 2044, CA (no duty on the facts to make reasonable inquiry as to reliability of intelligence before initiating armed search); *Brooks v Commissioner of Police of the Metropolis* [2005] 1 WLR 1495, HL (no duty to provide support and assistance to vulnerable witness); *Elguzouli-Daf v Commissioner of Police of the Metropolis* [1995] QB 335 (CPS owes no duty of care to those it prosecutes for reasons of public policy as rehearsed in *Hill v Chief Constable of West Yorkshire* [1989] 1 AC 53, HL).

armed raid at a specific address was conceded in *Ashley v Chief Constable of Sussex Police*.[48]

Causation

The relevant conduct must have caused death—that is, it must have killed the deceased. This has a specific meaning in the context of homicide. With one exception,[49] any act that is a 'significant' or 'substantial' cause of death renders the author responsible for that death if the other elements of murder are proved. **15.84**

In law, it is enough that the relevant act contributed 'significantly' to the death; it need not be the sole or principal cause.[50] On a charge of causing death by dangerous driving, the driving, if dangerous, must be a 'substantial' cause of death, indicating that it must be something more than minimally contributing[51] to the death. The same approach has been approved in other cases of homicide.[52] Although this may appear to be a low threshold, establishing causation in many policing contexts, including restraint or pursuit, is often extremely difficult. **15.85**

Where there is an issue as to whether death was caused by some supervening event, such as medical negligence, the duty on the prosecution is to prove that the accused's act contributed significantly to the death, rather than to establish that the supervening event was not a significant cause of death.[53] **15.86**

Circumstances may arise where the intervention of a third person may be regarded as the sole cause of the victim's death so as to avoid criminal liability. Neither a reasonable act performed for the purpose of self-defence, nor anything done in the execution of legal duty, qualifies as such an intervening act.[54] **15.87**

Self-defence and reasonable use of force in the performance of a legal duty

Police officers are regularly required to use force in the execution of their duties. At common law, and under statutory powers including s 3 of the Criminal Law Act 1967 and s 117 of the Police and Criminal Evidence Act 1984 (PACE), reasonable force may be used. There are no special rules applicable to either **15.88**

---

[48] [2008] 3 All ER 573.

[49] Namely, the taking away of a man's life by perjury, which is not, in law, murder or manslaughter: *R v Daniel* (1754) 1 Leach 44, (1754) 1 East PC 333.

[50] *R v Pitts* (1842) C & Mar 248; *R v Curley (James)* [1909] 2 Cr App R 96,109, CA.

[51] *R v Hennigan* [1971] 55 Cr App R 262, CA.

[52] *R v Cato* [1976] 62 Cr App R 41, 46, CA, in which the manslaughter resulted from an injection of heroin.

[53] *R v Mellor (Gavin Thomas)*, The Times, 29 February 1996, CA.

[54] *R v Pagett* (1983) 76 Cr App R 279, CA. A conviction for manslaughter was upheld in circumstances under which the appellant used the deceased as a shield whilst firing at the police, who responded with lethal force.

soldiers or police officers, and whether or not force is reasonable will always involve considerations as to the honest (if mistaken) belief of the author.

15.89 There is now a statutory test for reasonable force set out in s 76 of the Criminal Justice and Immigration Act 2008. When in force, the statutory test will reflect the series of relevant subjective considerations (honest, but mistaken, belief of the author; instinctive reaction as 'strong' (but not determinative) evidence that force was reasonable, etc) behind the ultimately objective finding as to whether the force used was reasonable in all of the circumstances. It will always be a question of fact what a trained police officer will honestly and instinctively believe is necessary, and what is objectively proportionate in the circumstances from such a trained officer.

15.90 Section 76 provides as follows.

76 Reasonable force for purposes of self-defence etc.

(1) This section applies where in proceedings for an offence—
  (a) an issue arises as to whether a person charged with the offence ("D") is entitled to rely on a defence within subsection (2), and
  (b) the question arises whether the degree of force used by D against a person ("V") was reasonable in the circumstances.
(2) The defences are—
  (a) the common law defence of self-defence; and
  (b) the defences provided by section 3(1) of the Criminal Law Act 1967 (c. 58) or section 3(1) of the Criminal Law Act (Northern Ireland) 1967 (c. 18 (N.I.)) (use of force in prevention of crime or making arrest).
(3) The question whether the degree of force used by D was reasonable in the circumstances is to be decided by reference to the circumstances as D believed them to be, and subsections (4) to (8) also apply in connection with deciding that question.
(4) If D claims to have held a particular belief as regards the existence of any circumstances—
  (a) the reasonableness or otherwise of that belief is relevant to the question whether D genuinely held it; but
  (b) if it is determined that D did genuinely hold it, D is entitled to rely on it for the purposes of subsection (3), whether or not—
    (i) it was mistaken, or
    (ii) (if it was mistaken) the mistake was a reasonable one to have made.
(5) But subsection (4)(b) does not enable D to rely on any mistaken belief attributable to intoxication that was voluntarily induced.
(6) The degree of force used by D is not to be regarded as having been reasonable in the circumstances as D believed them to be if it was disproportionate in those circumstances.
(7) In deciding the question mentioned in subsection (3) the following considerations are to be taken into account (so far as relevant in the circumstances of the case)—
  (a) that a person acting for a legitimate purpose may not be able to weigh to a nicety the exact measure of any necessary action; and
  (b) that evidence of a person's having only done what the person honestly and instinctively thought was necessary for a legitimate purpose constitutes strong evidence that only reasonable action was taken by that person for that purpose.
(8) Subsection (7) is not to be read as preventing other matters from being taken into account where they are relevant to deciding the question mentioned in subsection (3).
(9) This section is intended to clarify the operation of the existing defences mentioned in subsection (2).

(10) In this section—
    (a) "legitimate purpose" means—
        (i) the purpose of self-defence under the common law, or
        (ii) the prevention of crime or effecting or assisting in the lawful arrest of persons mentioned in the provisions referred to in subsection (2)(b);
    (b) references to self-defence include acting in defence of another person; and
    (c) references to the degree of force used are to the type and amount of force used.

Unlawful and dangerous act manslaughter

15.91 The basic statement of the law originates with *DPP v Newbury*,[55] in which the House of Lords approved the dictum in *R v Larkin*[56] that:

> Where the act which a person is engaged in performing is unlawful, then if at the same time it is a dangerous act, that is, an act which is likely to injure another person, and quite inadvertently the doer of the act causes the death of that other person by that act, then he is guilty of manslaughter.

15.92 The act causing death must be intrinsically unlawful. An act that is otherwise lawful, such as driving a car, does not become unlawful for these purposes if it contravenes the criminal law simply in consequence of the manner of its execution, such as speeding.[57] This form of manslaughter distinguishes between acts of commission likely to cause harm resulting in death (which may attract liability) and acts of omission.[58] There is no general principle of English law that requires, in the absence of a duty of care, a person to act so as to help another.

15.93 If there is a duty of care, however, (as was clearly the case in *R v Lowe*[59] as between parent and child in a prosecution of the former for both manslaughter and wilful neglect under s 1 of the Children and Young Persons Act 1933), liability for a death may arise on the same facts on the basis of gross negligence manslaughter. This covers so-called 'motor manslaughter'. As will be seen, however, gross negligence manslaughter, unlike unlawful and dangerous act manslaughter, requires consideration of whether an obvious and serious risk of death existed.

15.94 The mental element that must be proved in respect of unlawful and dangerous act manslaughter is that in relation to the unlawful act, as distinct from establishing that the actor knew that the act was unlawful and dangerous. The prosecution must prove additionally that the unlawful act was such that 'all sober and reasonable people would inevitably recognise must subject the other person to, at least, the risk of some harm resulting therefrom, albeit not serious harm'.[60]

---

[55] [1977] AC 500, 506 and 507, HL.
[56] (1942) 29 Cr App R 18, 23, CA.
[57] *Andrews v DPP* [1937] AC 576.
[58] *R v Lowe* [1973] QB 702, 709, (1973) 57 Cr App R 365, 371, CA.
[59] Ibid.
[60] *R v Church* [1966] 1 QB 59, (1966) 49 Cr App R 206, CA, approved in *DPP v Newbury* [1977] AC 500, 510, HL.

15.95 In a policing context, the issue for any allegation of unlawful and dangerous act manslaughter is invariably whether the particular force used was reasonable. As is set out in respect of inquest verdicts in respect of fatal shootings, the momentum is towards the courts requiring positive evidence that an officer believed otherwise than that the force was reasonable and necessary before any liability may arise where the allegation involves the use of force on duty. The reasoning in the context of the lethal use of firearms may extend to restraint situations. Quite separate is the question of liability for gross negligence manslaughter.

Gross negligence manslaughter

15.96 The leading authorities in respect of gross negligence manslaughter are *R v Adomako*[61] and *R v Misra*.[62] In terms of the former, the elements of the offence were defined as follows:[63]

> . . . the ordinary principles of the law of negligence apply to ascertain whether or not the defendant has been in breach of a duty of care towards the victim who has died. If such of duty is established the next question is whether that breach of duty caused the death of the victim. If so, the jury must go on to consider whether that breach of duty should be characterised as gross negligence and therefore as a crime. This will depend on the seriousness of the breach of duty committed by the defendant in all the circumstances in which the defendant was placed when it occurred. The jury will have to consider whether the extent to which the defendant's conduct departed from the proper standard of care incumbent upon him, involving as it must have done a risk of death to the patient, was such that it should be judged criminal.

15.97 *Misra* held (at [62]) that there was sufficient certainty in this definition since the question for the jury was not a disjunctive (circular) one involving determination of whether the negligence was gross, and, additionally, whether it was a crime, but a single one as to whether the conduct was grossly negligent and consequentially a crime. See also fn 41, above.

15.98 It is emphasized that it is the risk of death rather than any lesser consequence that is relevant.[64] Additionally, the negligence must, given the risk of death, be 'gross'. In *Misra*, the trial judge suggested that 'mistakes, even very serious mistakes, and errors of judgment, even very serious errors of judgment, and the like are nowhere near enough for a crime as serious as manslaughter to be committed', and that the test was whether, given the proven standard expected of 'a reasonably competent and careful senior house officer', the alleged conduct fell so far below 'the standard' that it was something 'truly exceptionally bad, and which showed such an indifference to an obviously serious risk to the life of [the deceased] and such a

---

[61] [1995] 1 AC 171.
[62] [2005] 1 Cr App R 21, CA.
[63] [1995] 1 AC 171, 187.
[64] *Misra* at [52].

depature from the standard to be expected' to amount to the very serious crime of manslaughter.

This was described on appeal as 'fair and balanced', and the approach of the **15.99** Court of Appeal (at [26]) suggests that, in the context of professional standards and obligations, the conduct must be 'truly exceptionally bad', and showing such a 'high degree of indifference to an obvious and serious risk to the patient's life' as to justify conviction for manslaughter.

Although *Adomako* suggests[65] that the question of gross negligence is 'supremely **15.100** a jury question', it is also a matter of law whether particular conduct is reasonably capable of meeting this test and a judge is justified in withdrawing the matter from the jury for insufficiency of evidence, as in *R (Da Silva) v DPP*.[66] Richards LJ stated (at [A33]):

> The fact that, if the case is left to them, this issue is pre-eminently a question for the jury to decide does not, in our view, preclude a judge from taking it away from them on a submission of no case to answer, if in his judgment no jury properly directed could convict on the evidence led. Equally, it does not prevent a prosecutor faced with the evidential test under the [Code for Crown Prosecutors] from making the type of assessment that the [Crown Prosecutor] made in this case as to the probability of the jury convicting.

The law touching gross negligence manslaughter was reviewed in *R (Rowley) v* **15.101** *Director of Public Prosecution*.[67] At [30] *et seq*, Kennedy LJ dealt with the question whether subjective recklessness and the defendant's state of mind were relevant to the question of gross negligence manslaughter. The following propositions emerge.

(i) Evidence of the defendant's state of mind is not a prerequisite to a conviction for manslaughter by gross negligence, but a defendant who is subjectively reckless in regard to a risk of death provides a strong indication that his negligence was criminal ([30]–[33]).

(ii) The state of mind of a defendant may be taken into account in the defendant's favour when considering whether his conduct amounts to a criminal offence ([33]–[34], and [38] *et seq*). Thus absence of subjective recklessness and awareness of risk is a factor that can weigh in favour of a defendant.

---

65 [1995] 1 AC 171, 187B–187E, HL.
66 [2006] EWHC 3204 (Admin). This related to the appeal by relatives of Jean Charles de Menezes against the decision of the DPP against prosecution of any police officer involved in events preceding his death.
67 [2003] EWHC 693 (Admin), [22]–[40].

The application of basic principles to the performance of police duties

15.102 The principles inherent in these leading cases were reflected in the ruling of Mrs Justice Dobbs in the prosecution of three police officers for gross negligence manslaughter at the Hull Crown Court, culminating in a ruling at the close of the prosecution case on 19 April 2005.[68] Her ruling was important and, significantly, was not subsequently referred to the Court of Appeal by the prosecution by way of an Attorney General's Reference under ss 35–36 of the Criminal Justice Act 1988.

15.103 The core allegation was that a custody sergeant and two escorting officers had been criminally negligent in leaving a chronic heroin addict by the side of a road at a force border some distance from her home address, in cold conditions and without money, on her release from custody. The deceased was found a month later in an adjacent field and had died from hypothermia. The evidence tended to prove that she had walked from the roadside into the field.

15.104 Whilst there were submissions as to causation (unbeknown to the officers, the deceased was released with procyclidine, a prescription drug, which may have induced a rapid deterioration in her condition on release so as to cause disorientation), the judge ruled that there was no case to answer. This ruling was on the basis that the prosecution had not proved the requisite standard of care applicable in the circumstances to the discharge of the admitted duty of care.

15.105 Based on authorities including *Adomako* and *Misra*, the elements of the offence were characterized by the judge as follows:

> In order to establish the offence alleged there must be evidence such that a reasonable jury, properly directed, could be sure of the following: that the defendant owed the deceased a duty of care; that there was an established standard of care; that there was a breach of that duty of care; that the defendant's conduct fell so far below the standard to be expected of a reasonably competent and careful officer in whatever category he was working that it was something truly exceptionally bad and that it showed an indifference to an obvious and serious risk to the life of the deceased; and that the breach of care caused the death of the deceased.

15.106 No evidence, expert or otherwise, was called as to the standard of care expected from a custody officer releasing a prisoner, or from an escorting officer dropping such a released prisoner away from a police station. The prosecution contended that the standard of care would have been met by leaving the deceased at her home address—albeit that the address was used habitually by the deceased and others for the systematic abuse of heroin and other unlawful drugs.

15.107 The prosecution submitted that the duty and standard of care on the police officer who has assumed responsibility for another is as set out in *Kirkham v*

---

[68] *R v Hickinbottom and ors*, unreported, 19 April 2005, Hull Crown Court.

Chief Constable of Manchester[69] (sic)—that is, to take all reasonable steps to avoid acts or omissions that he could reasonably foresee would be likely to harm the deceased—and that the standard of care was 'no more than a conventional general standard of behaviour, no more than the position to be envisaged by any member of the public'. Reliance was placed, by analogy, on the competence of a jury to determine the quality or standard of driving where negligence was alleged, without the need for additional evidence as to driving standards.

This was rejected by the judge. She stated that *Adomako* expressly, and *Kirkham* implicitly, required all of the circumstances to be considered when considering breach of duty. The judge set out the following principle in respect of alleged negligence by professional persons: **15.108**

> In my view, where a professional person is charged with an offence of this kind, an allegation made against them in relation to their conduct during the course of their job, it will be necessary in most cases for the jury to have evidence, whether one calls it expert or not, of the standards applicable within that job, whether it be common practice, guidance, rules or the like. It is not for the jury to determine what police officers should do in certain situations, but for them to determine in the light of what is accepted behaviour within the profession whether they fell below those standards and, if they did, whether the extent was so bad as to be criminal.
>
> As pointed out by leading counsel for the first defendant, even in road traffic cases, which are said to be within the experience of juries, there is a standard, namely the Highway Code. I have said that in most cases some such evidence is required, but in a few cases it may be blatantly obvious. This, in my view, is not such a case.

The judge rehearsed a number of matters (including the quality of the initial risk assessment, whether and when a doctor should have been called, whether there was an obligation to make arrangements for transport to the home address some 25 miles away in a different force area) as to which there were 'important unanswered questions and a lack of evidence', which meant that the jury would not be in a position to assess properly all of the circumstances of the case.[70] She concluded: **15.109**

> The consequence of this lack of evidence is that the jury has no benchmark against which to judge: (a) whether in all the circumstances there has been a breach of duty of care; and (b) if so, whether that breach was so serious as to be criminal.

15.110

In the particular case, there was, accordingly, no case to answer. The underlying approach of the judge is, however, of general application to allegations of negligence, including gross negligence manslaughter, against operational police officers. Save for 'blatant' situations, the professional benchmark of performance will need to be established as a comparator of the standard of care before a

---

[69] *Kirkham v Chief Constable of Greater Manchester Police* [1990] 2 QB 283, 289B and 293H–294B, CA.
[70] In fact, there was neither a published guideline nor training in Humberside Police in relation to the release of prisoners.

breach of duty is proved. The approach of Mrs Justice Dobbs is vindicated in the test for 'gross breach' under s 8 of the Corporate Manslaughter and Corporate Homicide Act 2007 (set out at 15.125 below), which makes express provision for reference to health and safety guidance and training.

Conclusions regarding gross negligence manslaughter

15.111 On any view, the degree of negligence must be 'very high'[71] before criminal liability may reasonably arise. To this extent, Lord Atkin's words in *Andrews v DPP*[72] are still instructive. In the course of citing *R v Bateman*,[73] and in the context of how a jury should approach the question of whether proven negligence was a crime, he said:

> . . . whatever epithet be used and whether epithets, such as 'culpable,' 'criminal,' 'gross,' 'wicked,' 'clear,' facts must be such that, in the opinion of the jury, the negligence of the accused went beyond a mere matter of compensation between subjects and showed such disregard for life and the safety of others as to amount to a crime against the State and conduct deserving punishment.

15.112 Whilst *Adomako* confirms that this question of criminal negligence (assuming the existence of a duty of care and causation, and that the conduct is capable in law of amounting to at least negligence) is 'supremely' a jury question, and while *Misra* confirmed that it is the risk of death rather than that of serious injury that is relevant, the observation as to 'disregard for human life' remains a powerful indicator of what level of negligence should attract prosecution.

15.113 A prosecution should not proceed on the simple basis that negligence is proved and that the criminality of that negligence is a jury matter. Applying the Code for Crown Prosecutors,[74] it must be more likely than not that criminal negligence will be proved to the requisite criminal standard before a person (including a police force) is charged. The court may rule as a matter of law that the proven conduct cannot satisfy this test.[75]

Corporate manslaughter

15.114 Following well-documented years of debate, a new offence of corporate manslaughter (corporate homicide in Scotland) was created by the Corporate Manslaughter and Corporate Homicide Act 2007. It came into force on 6 April 2008.[76] Whilst a relatively short Act—comprising only twenty-eight sections

---

[71] *Per* Phillimore LJ in *R v Lowe* [1973] 57 Cr App R 365, 370.
[72] (1937) 26 Cr App R 35, [1937] AC 576.
[73] (1925) 19 Cr App R 8.
[74] Available online at <http://www.cps.gov.uk>.
[75] See *R (Da Silva) v DPP* [2006] EWHC 3204 (Admin).
[76] The Corporate Manslaughter and Corporate Homicide Act 2007 (Commencement No 1) Order 2008, SI 2008/401.

and two Schedules—the sections are detailed and only an outline of the applicable provisions is attempted.

Whilst police forces are defined as organizations to which the offence relates, **15.115** the 2007 Act excludes certain operations and activity entirely from the scope of potential liability (s 5), and the provisions extending the relevant duty of care to deaths in custody (s 2(1)(d)) was excluded from the provisions brought into force by the Commencement Order. This reflected considerations of political expediency in the passage of the Bill. The same criterion will doubtless determine when the subsection is brought into force. In other words, the provision is likely to come into force following the first well-publicized catastrophic failure in a custody system that leads to an avoidable death.

It follows that much, but not all, of the potential exposure of police forces to **15.116** liability for this offence is thereby presently excluded. By s 18, there is no individual liability for the offence as an aider, abettor, etc, under common law, or for a person encouraging or assisting crime under Pt 2 of the Serious Crime Act 2007. Forces remain subject to health and safety legislation (s 19), as defined in s 25 ('Interpretation').[77]

The application to police forces is qualified by s 13. By s 13(1), a police force **15.117** means:

    (a) a police force within the meaning of—
        (i) the Police Act 1996 (c 16), or
        (ii) the Police (Scotland) Act 1967 (c 77);
    (b) the Police Service of Northern Ireland;
    (c) the Police Service of Northern Ireland Reserve;
    (d) the British Transport Police Force;
    (e) the Civil Nuclear Constabulary; and
    (f) the Ministry of Defence Police.

The offence

In unusually direct statutory language, 'the offence' is defined in s 1 of the Act. In **15.118** relevant part, it provides as follows.

1 The offence

(1) An organisation to which this section applies is guilty of an offence if the way in which its activities are managed or organised—
    (a) causes a person's death, and
    (b) amounts to a gross breach of a relevant duty of care owed by the organisation to the deceased.

---

[77] Section 25 provides that 'health and safety legislation' means any statutory provision dealing with health and safety matters, including, in particular, provision contained in the Health and Safety at Work etc Act 1974 or the Health and Safety at Work (Northern Ireland) Order 1978, SI 1978/1039.

(2) The organisations to which this section applies are—

    (a) a corporation;

    (b) a department or other body listed in Schedule 1;

    (c) a police force;

    (d) a partnership, or a trade union or employers' association, that is an employer.

(3) An organisation is guilty of an offence under this section only if the way in which its activities are managed or organised by its senior management is a substantial element in the breach referred to in subsection (1).

(4) For the purposes of this Act—

    (a) "relevant duty of care" has the meaning given by section 2, read with sections 3 to 7;

    (b) a breach of a duty of care by an organisation is a "gross" breach if the conduct alleged to amount to a breach of that duty falls far below what can reasonably be expected of the organisation in the circumstances;

    (c) "senior management", in relation to an organisation, means the persons who play significant roles in—

       (i) the making of decisions about how the whole or a substantial part of its activities are to be managed or organised, or

       (ii) the actual managing or organising of the whole or a substantial part of those activities.

15.119 The meaning of the 'relevant duty of care' is defined in s 2. As applied to police forces, reference should be made to s 13(2) (relating to members of police forces etc to be treated as employed by that force). Section 2 provides as follows.

2 Meaning of "relevant duty of care"

(1) A "relevant duty of care", in relation to an organisation, means any of the following duties owed by it under the law of negligence—

    (a) a duty owed to its employees or to other persons working for the organisation or performing services for it;

    (b) a duty owed as occupier of premises;

    (c) a duty owed in connection with—

       (i) the supply by the organisation of goods or services (whether for consideration or not),

       (ii) the carrying on by the organisation of any construction or maintenance operations,

       (iii) the carrying on by the organisation of any other activity on a commercial basis, or

       (iv) the use or keeping by the organisation of any plant, vehicle or other thing;

    [(d) a duty owed to a person who, by reason of being a person within subsection (2), is someone for whose safety the organisation is responsible.

(2) A person is within this subsection if—

    (a) he is detained at a custodial institution or in a custody area at a court or police station;

    (b) he is detained at a removal centre or short-term holding facility;

    (c) he is being transported in a vehicle, or being held in any premises, in pursuance of prison escort arrangements or immigration escort arrangements;

    (d) he is living in secure accommodation in which he has been placed;

    (e) he is a detained patient.] *Not in force*

(3) Subsection (1) is subject to sections 3 to 7.

15.120 Section 3 excludes from the relevant duty of care certain 'public policy decisions, exclusively public functions and statutory inspections', while s 4 specifies military activities, s 5 specifies policing and law enforcement activities, s 6 specifies emergency responses, essentially by the fire and medical services, and s 7 specifies child protection and probation functions.

As can be seen, the provisions under s 2(1)(d) represent an important exclusion of **15.121** liability for police forces. Section 5 is in force and provides as follows.

5 Policing and law enforcement

(1) Any duty of care owed by a public authority in respect of—
   (a) operations within subsection (2),
   (b) activities carried on in preparation for, or directly in support of, such operations, or
   (c) training of a hazardous nature, or training carried out in a hazardous way, which it is considered needs to be carried out, or carried out in that way, in order to improve or maintain the effectiveness of officers or employees of the public authority with respect to such operations,
   is not a "relevant duty of care".
(2) Operations are within this subsection if—
   (a) they are operations for dealing with terrorism, civil unrest or serious disorder,
   (b) they involve the carrying on of policing or law-enforcement activities, and
   (c) officers or employees of the public authority in question come under attack, or face the threat of attack or violent resistance, in the course of the operations.
(3) Any duty of care owed by a public authority in respect of other policing or law-enforcement activities is not a "relevant duty of care" unless it falls within section 2(1)(a), (b) or (d).
(4) In this section "policing or law-enforcement activities" includes—
   (a) activities carried on in the exercise of functions that are—
      (i) functions of police forces, or
      (ii) functions of the same or a similar nature exercisable by public authorities other than police forces;
   (b) activities carried on in the exercise of functions of constables employed by a public authority;
   (c) activities carried on in the exercise of functions exercisable under Chapter 4 of Part 2 of the Serious Organised Crime and Police Act 2005 (c 15) (protection of witnesses and other persons);
   (d) activities carried on to enforce any provision contained in or made under the Immigration Acts.

Subsection (4) is of interest, because it appears to be inclusionary, rather than **15.122** an exhaustive definition of what is included in policing or law-enforcement activities.

As to specific operations (terrorism, civil unrest, or serious disorder, which terms **15.123** are not defined), s 5(2) imposes conjunctive requirements limiting the extent of the exemption from the relevant duty of care. It is a matter of opinion whether, for example, the circumstances of the fatal shooting of Jean Charles de Menezes in Stockwell would have met the s 5(2) exemption—particularly s 5(2)(c).

In theory, activities or operations outside these criteria may come within the defi- **15.124** nition of the offence. Importantly, however, by s 5(3), 'in respect of other policing or law-enforcement activities', a duty of care has to fall within s 2(1)(a), (b), or (d) before it is a relevant duty of care. As matters stand, it follows that the only relevant duty for the purpose of the liability of a qualifying police force is: (i) a duty owed to its employees or to other persons working for the organization or performing services for it; or (ii) a duty owed as occupier of premises.

15.125 The test for 'gross breach' is defined by s 8 of the Act. To a degree, it may be seen that the language reflects the reasoning in the common law context of gross negligence manslaughter. There may well be cross-fertilization in time. In any event, s 8 provides as follows.

8 Factors for jury
(1) This section applies where—
　(a) it is established that an organisation owed a relevant duty of care to a person, and
　(b) it falls to the jury to decide whether there was a gross breach of that duty.
(2) The jury must consider whether the evidence shows that the organisation failed to comply with any health and safety legislation that relates to the alleged breach, and if so—
　(a) how serious that failure was;
　(b) how much of a risk of death it posed.
(3) The jury may also—
　(a) consider the extent to which the evidence shows that there were attitudes, policies, systems or accepted practices within the organisation that were likely to have encouraged any such failure as is mentioned in subsection (2), or to have produced tolerance of it;
　(b) have regard to any health and safety guidance that relates to the alleged breach.
(4) This section does not prevent the jury from having regard to any other matters they consider relevant.
(5) In this section "health and safety guidance" means any code, guidance, manual or similar publication that is concerned with health and safety matters and is made or issued (under a statutory provision or otherwise) by an authority responsible for the enforcement of any health and safety legislation.

Conclusions regarding corporate manslaughter

15.126 Pending the coming into force of s 2(1)(d) (liability for deaths in custody), it is not anticipated that prosecution of police forces under this Act will arise with any regularity. Even when applied to deaths in custody, there are considerable challenges to any prosecution.

15.127 The new offence may affect the conduct of inquests by the relevant police forces, and it will be more necessary than ever for forces to demonstrate systems of work and training that are alert to, and address effectively, the well-documented risks to vulnerable persons affected by policing, including police officers and other employees. It may not, for example, be sufficient to rely on training through distributing materials on the intranet if that is not coupled with systems to ensure that affected staff have both read, and are applying, the relevant training materials.

D. Driving-related Offences

Death and serious injury (DSI) caused by the driving of police officers when **15.128**
performing operational duties is a matter of legitimate public concern. In 2007,
the IPCC published an extensive report entitled *Police Road Traffic Incidents:*
A Study of Cases Involving Serious and Fatal Injuries,[78] which was laid before
Parliament by the Home Secretary pursuant to s 11(5)(b) of the 2002 Act.

The context for the report was the alarming fact that approximately forty people **15.129**
die each year in road traffic incidents involving the police, with the majority
of deaths being the result of a police pursuit. Although no official figures existed,
the report's estimate (based on different surveys) was that there were between
11,000 and 19,000 police pursuits in England and Wales during 2005 and 2006,
and that between one and eleven pursuits out of every thousand lead to a death.
There were between three and four million immediate responses per year, and a
fatality rate of 1/150,000 for all emergency police responses.

There is clearly a balance to be struck between public safety and the competing **15.130**
public interest in ensuring a rapid and effective response to an emergency situation. Ultimately, it is the responsibility of the response driver to drive safely in any
given set of road conditions. Few, if any, emergencies will justify a response
that creates a real risk of causing serious injury or death to other members of the
public, including any person being pursued by the police. Each such situation
will be fact-specific.

More generally, driving offences have attracted review and reform to reflect **15.131**
public concern. The Road Safety Act 2006, when in force, creates a new offence
of causing death by careless or inconsiderate driving (s 20), increases the penalty
for careless driving from a level four fine to level five (s 23), provides a definition
of the meaning of 'careless or inconsiderate driving' (s 30), and makes provision
for alternative verdicts following acquittal on a charge of manslaughter (s 33).

In terms of prosecution and sentencing policy, the Crown Prosecution Service **15.132**
(CPS) has published a detailed report (*Prosecuting Bad Driving: A Consultation on*
CPS Policy and Practice—Response to Consultation),[79] and the Sentencing
Guidelines Council (SGC) has produced a consultation guideline (*Causing Death*
by Driving),[80] which one may expect to evolve into a statutory guideline in the
latter part of 2008.

---

[78] IPCC Research and Statistics Series: Paper 7, available online at <http://www.ipcc.gov.uk>.
[79] Available online at <http://www.cps.gov.uk>.
[80] Available online at <http://www.sentencing-guidelines.gov.uk>.

The law

15.133 It is useful to rehearse the basic statutory provisions that relate to the offences and definitions relating to careless and dangerous driving, and the terms of the statutory exemption when a vehicle is driven for a police purpose.

15.134 The offences are found in ss 1–3 of the Road Traffic Act 1988, as amended by ss 1 (offences of dangerous driving) and 2 (careless, and inconsiderate, driving) of the Road Traffic Act 1991. As amended, the 1988 Act provides as follows.

1 Causing death by dangerous driving

A person who causes the death of another person by driving a mechanically propelled vehicle dangerously on a road or other public place is guilty of an offence.

2 Dangerous driving

A person who drives a mechanically propelled vehicle dangerously on a road or other public place is guilty of an offence.

2A Meaning of dangerous driving

(1) For the purposes of sections 1 and 2 above a person is to be regarded as driving dangerously if (and, subject to subsection (2) below, only if)—
   (a) the way he drives falls far below what would be expected of a competent and careful driver, and
   (b) it would be obvious to a competent and careful driver that driving in that way would be dangerous.
(2) A person is also to be regarded as driving dangerously for the purposes of sections 1 and 2 above if it would be obvious to a competent and careful driver that driving the vehicle in its current state would be dangerous.
(3) In subsections (1) and (2) above "dangerous" refers to danger either of injury to any person or of serious damage to property; and in determining for the purposes of those subsections what would be expected of, or obvious to, a competent and careful driver in a particular case, regard shall be had not only to the circumstances of which he could be expected to be aware but also to any circumstances shown to have been within the knowledge of the accused.
(4) In determining for the purposes of subsection (2) above the state of a vehicle, regard may be had to anything attached to or carried on or in it and to the manner in which it is attached or carried.

3 Careless, and inconsiderate, driving

If a person drives a mechanically propelled vehicle on a road or other public place without due care and attention, or without reasonable consideration for other persons using the road or place, he is guilty of an offence.

15.135 As has been stated, to this must be added the new offence of causing death by careless or inconsiderate driving introduced by s 20 of the Road Safety Act 2006.[81] This inserts the new offence as s 2B into the 1988 Act.

---

[81] In force 18 August 2008 under the Road Safety Act 2006 (Commencement No 4) Order 2008, SI 2008/1918.

Importantly, careless driving is also defined under the 2006 Act, which (by s 30) **15.136**
adds s 3ZA to the 1988 Act.[82]

3ZA Meaning of careless, or inconsiderate, driving
(1) This section has effect for the purposes of sections 2B and 3 above and section 3A below.
(2) A person is to be regarded as driving without due care and attention if (and only if) the way he
drives falls below what would be expected of a competent and careful driver.
(3) In determining for the purposes of subsection (2) above what would be expected of a careful
and competent driver in a particular case, regard shall be had not only to the circumstances of
which he could be expected to be aware but also to any circumstances shown to have been
within the knowledge of the accused.
(4) A person is to be regarded as driving without reasonable consideration for other persons only
if those persons are inconvenienced by his driving.

As will be seen (see 15.141 *et seq* below), the extended definition under subs (3) is **15.137**
important in the context of the liability of a trained police driver. Subsection (4)
appears to exclude simple risk to property if no person is inconvenienced and
removes liability on the basis of the hypothetical bystander. A charge of driving
without due care and attention (rather than without reasonable consideration for
other persons) may arise on those facts.

Section 87 exemption

These provisions take effect in respect of police driving subject to s 87 of the Road **15.138**
Traffic Regulations Act 1984 and regs 15(2) and 33(2) of the Traffic Signs
Regulations and General Directions 1994.[83] Section 87 will be substituted by s 19
of the Road Safety Act 2006 when that section is brought into force. Although
there is no material difference in respect of the basic exemption, the Secretary
of State becomes empowered to issue regulations as to the content of the courses
of training to satisfy s 87(3).

Section 87, as presently in force, provides as follows. **15.139**

87 Exemptions from speed limits
(1) No statutory provision imposing a speed limit on motor vehicles shall apply to any vehicle
on an occasion when it is being used for fire and rescue authority, ambulance or police purposes,
if the observance of that provision would be likely to hinder the use of the vehicle for the
purpose for which it is being used on that occasion.
(2) Subsection (1) above applies in relation to a vehicle being used—
(a) for Serious Organised Crime Agency purposes, or
(b) for training persons to drive vehicles for use for Serious Organised Crime Agency purposes,
as it applies in relation to a vehicle being used for police purposes.

---

[82] Appointment (for certain purposes) 24 September 2007: see the Road Safety Act 2006
(Commencement No 2) Order 2007, SI 2007/2472, art 2(h). Section 61 applies the provisions to
driving after the date of the Commencement Order.
[83] SI 1994/1519.

(3) But (except where it is being used for training the person by whom it is being driven) subsection (1) above does not apply in relation to a vehicle by virtue of subsection (2) above unless it is being driven by a person who has been trained in driving vehicles at high speeds.

15.140 As amended under s 19 of the 2006 Act, it provides as follows.

87 Exemptions from speed limits

(1) No statutory provision imposing a speed limit on motor vehicles shall apply to any vehicle on an occasion when—
  (a) it is being used for fire and rescue authority purposes or for or in connection with the exercise of any function of a relevant authority as defined in section 6 of the Fire (Scotland) Act 2005, for ambulance purposes or for police or Serious Organised Crime Agency purposes,
  (b) it is being used for other prescribed purposes in such circumstances as may be prescribed, or
  (c) it is being used for training persons to drive vehicles for use for any of the purposes mentioned in paragraph (a) or (b) above,
  if the observance of that provision would be likely to hinder the use of the vehicle for the purpose for which it is being used on that occasion.
(2) Subsection (1) above does not apply unless the vehicle is being driven by a person who—
  (a) has satisfactorily completed a course of training in the driving of vehicles at high speed provided in accordance with regulations under this section, or
  (b) is driving the vehicle as part of such a course.
(3) The Secretary of State may by regulations make provision about courses of training in the driving of vehicles at high speed.

The application of the exemption to police response drivers

15.141 Some basic points emerge from the statutory provisions. The basic effect is to exempt emergency services vehicles on duty from the criminal process arising from contravention of the statutory provisions relating to speed limits, keep left signs, and traffic lights. This applies only when the vehicle is being used for a relevant emergency purpose and when driven by a person trained in driving vehicles at high speed, or who is driving the vehicle in the course of such training. It follows that the untrained driver of an ordinary police patrol (or squad) car will not be exempt.

15.142 Similarly, the exemption is not to any liability for careless or dangerous driving. These offences may logically be committed notwithstanding the exemption.

15.143 In determining negligence (breach of duty), the courts take into account the fact that a police driver may have had little time for considered reflection and may have been driving in difficult conditions.[84] The relationship between speed and dangerous (or, in the civil context, negligent) driving has been considered in a number of authorities.

---

[84] *Marshall v Osmond* [1983] QB 1034, CA.

The general position is concisely stated by the Court of Appeal in *Keyse v The*   **15.144**
Commissioner of Police of the Metropolis and Scutts,[85] an appeal arising from the
death of a schoolboy when hit by a 'highly conspicuous' police response car when
the former was crossing a road at night. The basic propositions of law were stated
as follows:

> 24. When judged in relation to speed restrictions, speed alone is not decisive of the
> question of negligence. It is sometimes plainly dangerous to drive at the permitted
> maximum, and equally, driving in excess of the limit, even if liable to result in pros-
> ecution for speeding, is not necessarily, and invariably, negligent. Emergency services
> vehicles on duty are expressly exempted from the criminal process arising from con-
> travention of the statutory provisions relating to speed limits, keep left signs, and
> traffic lights (section 87 of the Road Traffic Regulations Act 1984 and Regulation
> 15(2) and 33(2) of the Traffic Signs Regulations and General Directions 1994).
> None of these provisions sanctions negligent driving, or indemnifies the negligent
> driver of a vehicle on emergency duty against civil liability. The duty of the driver to
> take care remains undiminished.

The application of these provisions was subject of detailed judicial scrutiny in   **15.145**
DPP v Milton (No 1)[86] in 2006 and *Milton v the CPS (No 2)*[87] in 2007. These
appeals by way of case stated arose in the context of 'eye-wateringly' fast driving by
a trained police driver, and resolved the important linked issues of: (i) the objective test to be applied to dangerous driving given the terms of the s 87 exemption;
and (ii) whether the objectively determinable competence of a trained police
driver was a relevant circumstance under s 2A(3) of the 1988 Act, as amended.

Milton

The facts of *Milton* were somewhat unusual. On the evening of 4 December 2003,   **15.146**
PC Milton, who was a Grade I advanced police driver with the West Mercia
Constabulary, came on duty to find that he had been assigned to drive an unmarked
Vauxhall Vectra, with which he was unfamiliar. In accordance with the advice that
he had been given during his training as an advanced driver, he took the opportunity during his tour of duty to familiarize himself with the vehicle's handling
characteristics. In the early hours of the morning of 5 December, he drove on the
M54 motorway at an average speed of 148 mph; he drove on the A5 trunk road at
an average speed of 114 mph; and he drove within a built-up area at an average
speed of over 60 mph.

This driving involved overtaking other vehicles and driving through (or at least   **15.147**
across) various road junctions. Road and weather conditions were otherwise good.

---

[85] [2001] EWCA Civ 715, CA.
[86] [2006] EWHC 242 (Admin), *per* Hallett LJ and Owen J.
[87] [2007] EWHC 532 (Admin), *per* Smith LJ and Gross J.

He was charged with dangerous driving and offences of exceeding different speed limits. The findings of the magistrates' court generated two appeals by way of case stated.

15.148 From these authorities, various propositions emerge, as follows.

Dangerous driving

15.149 Applying *R v Collins (Lezlie)*[88] and *Attorney General's Reference (No 4 of 2000)*,[89] the test for dangerous driving under s 2A(1) is wholly objective (*Milton (No 1)*, at [10], [15], [24], and [38]; *Milton (No 2)*, at [8], [9], [25], and [34(iv)]).

15.150 The driver's subjective belief as to the safety of his driving is irrelevant to this objective test (*Collins*; *Milton (No 1)*).

15.151 'Obvious' requires more than that the danger would have been foreseeable to the competent and careful driver. The situation must be one in which the competent and careful driver would say that the danger was plain for all to see (*Collins*, at 445C-E; *Milton (No 1)*, at [24] and [38]).

15.152 The opinion of expert witnesses as to whether or not the respondent was driving dangerously was inadmissible and should have played no part in the district judge's deliberations (*Milton (No 1)*, at [53]);

The relevance of expert driving ability

15.153 The fact that the driver is a trained (in *Milton*, a Grade I advanced) police driver is a circumstance to which regard must be had pursuant to s 2A(3). The weight to be attached to such a circumstance is entirely a matter for the fact-finder. On the one hand, the fact-finder might conclude that the driving was thoroughly dangerous, regardless of the skill of the individual driver; on the other hand, he might conclude that, whereas for a driver of ordinary skill, such driving would have been dangerous, for a man of exceptional skill, it was not. Such a thought process does not offend against the requirement that the test for dangerous driving is objective. It simply refines the objective test by reference to existing circumstances. This brings into account objective facts favourable to the driver just as those unfavourable to him may be relevant (*Milton (No 2)*, at [27] and [34(iv)], applying *R v Woodward*[90] (alcohol) and *R v Marison*[91] (hypoglcaemia)).

---

[88] [1997] RTR 439, CA. A Grade I advanced police driver had driven very fast in pursuit of a stolen car. He crossed a junction at high speed and collided with another vehicle, causing two deaths. He gave evidence that he believed that the police were controlling traffic at that junction and that it was safe for him to cross it at speed. The Court of Appeal held that his belief about the safety of what he was doing was irrelevant to the issue.

[89] [2001] 2 Cr App R 417, 412, CA.

[90] [1995] RTR 130, CA.

[91] [1997] RTR 457, CA.

Objective evidence of this nature, favourable or unfavourable, will only excep- **15.154**
tionally be admissible and still less often determinative of the objective test under
the following circumstances.

> It will, in my view, only be the extremes of 'special skill' and 'almost complete lack of
> experience' that will be such as could affect the mind of the decision maker. The mere
> fact that a driver has driven for 30 years without an accident will not be relevant; nor
> will evidence that a driver does not drive frequently.[92]

> Having regard to the objective test of "driving dangerously", there will, in the nature
> of things, be relatively very few circumstances known to the accused capable of hav-
> ing a bearing on the competent and careful driver's consideration of the driving in
> question. It is likely that there will be fewer still which do in fact serve to alter the
> result to which the court would otherwise have come, though that is a matter for the
> tribunal of fact. The subjective views of the accused are irrelevant, for the reasons
> given in [*Milton (No 1)*]. It is therefore inherently likely that only circumstances
> known to the driver and capable of objective proof, will need to be taken into
> consideration.[93]

Speed as a basis of dangerousness

Speed alone is not sufficient for dangerous or negligent driving—'it has to be a **15.155**
question of speed in the context of all the circumstances'—and is always a matter
of fact and degree (*Milton (No 1)*, at [56] and [59]; *Keyse*, at [24] and [30]).

The meaning and application of the police purpose exemption

As to what is within a 'police purpose' under s 87, the guidance of the Court of **15.156**
Appeal in *Aitken v Yarwood*[94] applies. The police purposes exemption was held to
apply to a police officer who, having broken down en route to court, felt that he
had to speed to arrive there in time. At 333, Winn J, with whom the other members of the Court agreed, observed as follows:

> On the other hand, it is, I think, equally clear that it cannot have been the intention
> of the legislature when enacting these words, to make it the sole criterion whether or
> not at the material point of time a police purpose, taking that as the example, was
> then actually being performed; it is a necessary extension of the immunity granted
> that if a particular use is essential for the performance of a police purpose, although
> it does not of itself constitute an act of performance of that purpose, that the immu-
> nity should extend that far.

> It would be dangerous, in my judgment, to state any instances or examples by way of
> illustration, since inevitably when any such suggested instance came under the
> microscope in a trial, it would be found that any reference here made to it would tend
> rather to mislead than to assist a court concerned with deciding the instant
> problem.

---

[92] *Milton (No 2)*, *per* Smith LJ at [28].
[93] Ibid, *per* Gross J at [34(vii)].
[94] [1965] 1 QB 327, CA.

15.157 Lord Parker CJ, in agreeing with Winn J, observed at 334:

> On the findings of the justices, it seems to me an inevitable conclusion that the use of that vehicle at that time was an integral and necessary part of the purpose to be achieved, namely, to give evidence at 10 o'clock in the magistrates' court.

15.158 Whether speeds significantly in excess of the speed limit qualify as a police purpose is a matter of fact and degree, and requires the exemption to be considered for each offence separately. Applied to *Milton*, the following approach was set out in *Milton (No 1)* by Hallett LJ:

> 58. In my view, the same considerations may not apply to driving at 90 miles per hour in a built-up area, as apply to driving at 150 miles per hour on a motorway. It will, of course, depend on the instructions given and the findings of fact made. Familiarising oneself with a vehicle and honing one's skills does not necessarily involve driving at 90 miles per hour through residential streets, if that is what they were. Nor does it necessarily involve driving at 150 miles per hour. Thus, as it seems to me, the judge is obliged to make his findings of fact and then relate them to the individual offence charged and found proved.
>
> 59. I decline to find, as Mr Lawson appeared to invite us to do, that a police officer who drives at excessive speeds as are involved here could not possibly come within the exemption, save when he is in hot pursuit of a dangerous criminal. It is a matter of fact and degree for the tribunal of fact.

A summary of the liability of the police driver and the associated duty of other road users

15.159 In general terms, it follows that the obligation on a police officer to drive safely—that is, to take reasonable care in all of the circumstances—is identical to that of any other road user. Part of the consideration of what is safe (or what is reasonable care) is the circumstance that other road users (including pedestrians) may legitimately be expected by the responding police driver to react appropriately to an emergency vehicle responding as such. This, of course, demands both that the emergency vehicle is identifiable and that the road user or pedestrian may take avoiding action. If children may be present, the risk assessment is inevitably affected.

15.160 The tension was reflected in the reasoning of the Court of Appeal in *Keyse* in allowing the appeal of the Commissioner against the original finding of liability. The Court found that the motorist's duty to take reasonable care is too obvious to require authority. Whether the driving in any particular case fell short of the requisite standard is a question of fact.

15.161 In terms of liability, the Court (Judge LJ) found:

> 29. In my judgment, even in an emergency, a driver is required to drive reasonably carefully in all the circumstances. One significant feature of such cases where the vehicle in question is deployed by one of the emergency services, is that the driver is

normally entitled to assume that other road users will not ignore the unmistakable evidence of its approach, and where appropriate, temporarily at any rate, will use the road accordingly. Pedestrians can usually be expected to follow the relevant advice in the Highway Code. . .depending on all the circumstances, the speed at which such a vehicle may reasonably be driven is likely to be faster either than that of a vehicle not being deployed in an emergency, or a vehicle, in an emergency, which does not or cannot highlight that it is being used for such a purpose . . .

[. . .]

31. . . . in my judgment, although drivers should allow for the unexpected when they are at the wheel of a car, it would inhibit the valuable work done for the community as a whole, if drivers in the emergency services were not allowed to drive their vehicles on the basis that pedestrians would recognise their warning lights and sirens and give them proper priority by keeping out of their paths.

Although to a degree fact-specific, these observations reflect some important **15.162** points of principle in terms of the liability of response drivers. If driving is not negligent, it is unlikely that it will be either without due care or attention or, still less, dangerous.

E. Conclusions

These offences demonstrate that those engaged in operational policing are **15.163** necessarily subject to the criminal law in the performance of duties. In any civilized country, the exercise of power must be lawful. Additional criminality arises when those engaged in policing misuse data to which they have obtained access in their capacity as such.

Equally clearly demonstrated is the competing public interest in not criminal- **15.164** izing the performance of police duties until the manner of performance represents a serious breach of standards. Operational policing would be compromised if a perception were to emerge that genuine human error routinely attracted prosecution. The courts have consistently recognized where the balance between the competing considerations should lie, and it is for the prosecuting authorities and, where appropriate, trial judges, to ensure that these matters are reflected consistently in practice.

APPENDICES

A. A Table of Force Statistics   501

B. The Police Appeals Tribunals Rules 1999, SI 1999/818   504

C. The Police (Conduct) Regulations 2004, SI 2004/645   510

D. The Police (Complaints and Misconduct) Regulations 2004,
    SI 2004/643, as amended   532

E. The Police Reform Act 2002, Schedule 3, Part 1   554

F. The Police (Performance) Regulations 2008, SI 2008/2862   587

G. The Police (Conduct) Regulations 2008, SI 2008/2864   613

H. The Police Appeals Tribunals Rules 2008, SI 2008/2863   646

I. Home Office Guidance (2008) *Police Officer Misconduct, Unsatisfactory
    Performance and Attendance Management Procedures*   656

J. The Police (Amendment) Regulations 2008, SI 2008/2865   749

APPENDIX A

A Table of Force Statistics

Police Act 1996, Sch 1

Police areas with force names and numbers of officers and staff[1]

Force	All constables	ACPO rank	Police staff[2]	PCSOs	Designated officers[3]
Avon and Somerset Constabulary	3,407	5	2,289	377	0
Bedfordshire Police	1, 207	3	724	120	37
Cambridgeshire Constabulary	1,379	3	892	197	25
Cheshire Constabulary	2,181	4	1,406	231	11
Cleveland Police	1,692	3	701	170	0
Cumbria Constabulary	1,246	4	773	99	33
Derbyshire Constabulary	2,095	4	1,266	166	47
Devon and Cornwall Constabulary	3,529	5	2,147	354	0
Dorset Police	1,518	3	959	151	53
Durham Constabulary	1,632	3	816	162	0
Essex Police	3,385	5	1,986	436	70
Gloucestershire Constabulary	1,353	4	700	162	56
Greater Manchester	8,034	5	3,534	773	159
Hampshire Constabulary	3,912	5	2,430	324	99

[1] Figures taken from Home Office Statistical Bulletin 08/08, *Police Service Strength England and Wales*, 31 March 2008 (2nd edn).

[2] Police staff comprises non-officer police employees, excluding police community support officers (PCSOs), traffic wardens, and designated officers.

[3] Designated officers are persons employed by the police authority who have been chosen by chief officers to exercise specified powers that would otherwise only be available to police officers. Designated officers were introduced under the Police Reform Act 2002, which enables the appropriate designation of skilled police staff to one or more of four roles: PCSO; investigation officer; detention officer; escort officer. The figures shown exclude PCSOs.

Force	All constables	ACPO rank	Police staff[2]	PCSOs	Designated officers[3]
Hertfordshire Constabulary	2,162	4	1,490	246	92
Humberside	2,243	3	1,313	318	83
Kent Police	3,718	5	2,337	377	170
Lancashire Constabulary	3,675	4	1,927	400	0
Leicestershire Constabulary	2,241	4	1,142	212	39
Lincolnshire Police	1,201	3	760	165	4
City of London Police	830	3	299	46	0
Merseyside Police	4,477	6	2,203	407	0
Metropolitan Police Service	31,460	36	14,085	4,247	200
Norfolk Constabulary	1,578	4	1,053	274	44
Northamptonshire Police	1,309	4	1,024	159	0
Northumbria Police	3,983	4	1,863	254	144
North Yorkshire Police	1,581	4	1,079	180	0
Nottinghamshire Police	2,369	3	1,372	259	89
South Yorkshire Police	3,201	5	2,038	334	0
Staffordshire Police	2,269	4	1,309	209	45
Suffolk Constabulary	1,319	3	814	140	38
Surrey Police	1,944	4	1,808	211	179
Sussex Police	3,075	3	1,974	372	20
Thames Valley	4,186	4	2,772	521	0
Warwickshire Police	1,036	4	629	133	0
West Mercia Constabulary	2,486	5	1,647	272	0
West Midlands Police	8,412	7	3,436	748	0
West Yorkshire Police	5,822	6	3,247	757	0
Wiltshire Constabulary	1,210	3	879	147	0
Dyfed Powys Police	1,194	1	625	73	25
Gwent Police	1,487	3	855	139	0
North Wales Police	1,579	3	774	159	37

Force	All constables	ACPO rank	Police staff[2]	PCSOs	Designated officers[3]
South Wales Police	3,244	4	1,575	327	115
Total (43 forces)	141,861	202	76,952	15,808	1,914

The Police Appeals Tribunals Rules 1999, SI 1999/818

STATUTORY INSTRUMENTS

1999 No. 818

POLICE

Police (Conduct) Regulation 2004

Made	*13th March 1999*
Laid before Parliament	*22nd March 1999*
Coming into force	*1st April 1999*

The Secretary of State, in exercise of the powers conferred on him by section 85 of the Police Act 1996[1] and after consultation with the Council on Tribunals in accordance with section 8 of the Tribunals and Inquiries Act 1992[2], hereby makes the following Rules:

Citation and commencement

1. These Rules may be cited as the Police Appeals Tribunals Rules 1999 and shall come into force on 1st April 1999.

Revocations and transitional provisions

2. - (1) Subject to paragraph (2), the Police (Appeals) Rules 1985[3] (hereinafter called "the 1985 Rules") are hereby revoked.

(2) In relation to an appeal against a decision made in accordance with the Police (Discipline) Regulations 1985[4] or the Police (Discipline) (Senior Officers) Regulations 1985[5]-

(a) nothing in these Rules shall apply, and

(b) the 1985 Rules shall continue to have effect.

Interpretation

3. - (1) In these Rules, unless the context otherwise requires-

"the Act" means the Police Act 1996;

"original hearing" means the conduct hearing or inefficiency hearing at the conclusion of which the appellant was found to have failed to meet the appropriate standard or, as the case may be, the appellant's performance was found to have been unsatisfactory;

"tribunal" in relation to a case means the police appeals tribunal appointed to determine that case.

(2) In these Rules, any expression which appears also in the Police (Conduct) Regulations 1999[6] or the Police (Efficiency) Regulations 1999[7] shall, unless the contrary intention appears, have the same meaning as in those Regulations.

The respondent

4. - (1) The respondent on an appeal by a senior officer shall be a person designated for the purpose by the relevant police authority.

(2) The respondent on an appeal by a member of a police force who is not a senior officer shall be the chief officer of that force.

Notice of appeal

5. - (1) Subject to rule 7 and paragraph (2), the time within which notice of an appeal under section 85 of the Act shall be given is 21 days from the date on which the decision appealed against was notified to the appellant in pursuance of regulations made in accordance with section 50(3) of the Act.

(2) In a case to which regulation 39 of the Police (Conduct) Regulations 1999 or regulation 25 of the Police (Conduct) (Senior Officers) Regulations 1999[8] applies where the decision appealed against was given in pursuance of those Regulations as modified by Part II of Schedule 2 or, as the case may be, by Part II of the Schedule to those Regulations, the time within which notice of an appeal under section 85 of the Act shall be given is 28 days from-

(a) the conclusion of any criminal proceedings in which the appellant is charged with an offence in respect of the conduct to which the decision appealed against related; or

(b) a decision that no such criminal proceedings will be instituted or taken over by the Director of Public Prosecutions has been communicated to the appellant.

(3) The notice of appeal shall be given in writing to the relevant police authority and a copy of the notice shall be sent to the respondent.

Procedure on notice of appeal

6. - (1) As soon as practicable after receipt of a copy of the notice of appeal, the respondent shall provide to the relevant police authority-

(a) a copy of the report of the person who made the decision appealed against;

(b) the transcript of the proceedings at the original hearing; and

(c) any documents which were made available to the person conducting the original hearing.

(2) A copy of the transcript mentioned in paragraph (1)(b) shall at the same time be sent to the appellant.

(3) Subject to rule 7, the appellant shall, within 28 days of the date on which he receives a copy of the transcript mentioned in paragraph (1)(b), submit to the relevant police authority-

(a) a statement of the grounds of appeal;

(b) any supporting documents; and

(c) either-

   (i) any written representations which the appellant wishes to make under paragraph 6 of Schedule 6 to the Act or, as the case may be, any request to make oral representations under that paragraph; or

   (ii) a statement that he does not wish to make any such representations as are mentioned in paragraph (i):

Provided that, in a case where the appellant submits a statement under sub-paragraph (c)(ii), nothing in this paragraph shall prevent representations under paragraph 6 of Schedule 6 to the Act being made by him to the chairman of the tribunal.

(4) The documents submitted to the police authority under paragraph (3) shall, as soon as practicable, be copied to the members of the tribunal and to the respondent.

(5) The respondent shall, not later than 21 days from the date on which he receives the copy documents sent to him under paragraph (4), submit to the relevant police authority-

(a) a statement of his response to the appeal;

(b) any supporting documents; and

(c) either-
    (i) any written representations which the respondent wishes to make under paragraph 6 of Schedule 6 to the Act or, as the case may be, any request to make oral representations under that paragraph; or
    (ii) a statement that he does not wish to make any such representations as are mentioned in paragraph (i):
Provided that, in a case where the respondent submits a statement under sub-paragraph (c)(ii), nothing in this paragraph shall prevent representations under paragraph 6 of Schedule 6 to the Act being made by him to the chairman of the tribunal.

(6) The respondent shall at the same time send a copy of the documents referred to in paragraph (5)(a) and (c) to the appellant, together with a list of the documents (if any) referred to in paragraph (5)(b).

(7) The documents submitted to the police authority under paragraph (5) shall, as soon as practicable, be copied to the members of the tribunal.

(8) So far as applicable, rules 8 and 9 shall apply in relation to the hearing of any oral representations under paragraph 6 of Schedule 6 to the Act as they apply in relation to the hearing of an appeal under section 85 of the Act; and the appellant and the respondent shall be entitled to be represented at the hearing of such oral representations as if it were the hearing of such an appeal.

Extensions of time limits

7. - (1) The relevant police authority may extend the period referred to in rule 5(1) or (2) or 6(3) in any case where the authority is satisfied, on the application of the appellant, that by reason of the special circumstances of the case it is just to do so; and in such a case rules 5 and 6 shall have effect as if for that period there were substituted such extended period as the authority may specify.

(2) Where the relevant police authority refuses an application by the appellant under paragraph (1), it shall give the appellant notice in writing of the reasons for the decision and of the right of appeal conferred by paragraph (3).

(3) An appellant whose application under paragraph (1) is refused may, not later than 14 days after receiving notice under paragraph (2), appeal in writing to the chairman of the tribunal against the decision of the relevant police authority.

(4) The chairman may, on such an appeal, make any decision which the relevant police authority had power to make under paragraph (1); and, where he extends the period referred to in rule 5(1) or (2) or 6(3), rules 5 and 6 shall have effect as if for that period there were substituted such extended period as the chairman may specify.

Procedure at hearing

8. - (1) Where a case is to be determined at a hearing, the chairman of the tribunal shall cause the appellant and the respondent to be given notice of the date of the hearing not less than 28 days, or such shorter period as may with the agreement of both parties be determined, before the hearing begins.

(2) Subsections (2) and (3) of section 250 of the Local Government Act 1972[9] (powers in relation to local inquiries) shall apply to the hearing as if-
    (a) references to a local inquiry were references to a hearing held under Schedule 6 to the Act;
    (b) references to the person appointed to hold the inquiry, or to the person holding the inquiry, were references to the chairman of the tribunal; and
    (c) references to that section were references to this rule.

(3) The tribunal may proceed with the hearing in the absence of either party, whether represented or not, if it appears to be just and proper to do so, and may adjourn it from time to time as may appear necessary for the due hearing of the case.

(4) Subject to these Rules, the procedure at a hearing shall be determined by the tribunal.

Hearing to be in private

9. - (1) Subject to paragraph (3) and rule 12, the hearing shall be held in private:
Provided that it shall be within the discretion of the tribunal to allow such person or persons as it considers desirable to attend the whole or such part of the hearing as it may think fit.

(2) Notwithstanding that the tribunal has allowed a person to attend the hearing, where it appears to the tribunal that a witness may in giving evidence disclose information which, in the public interest, ought not to be disclosed to a member of the public, the tribunal shall require any member of the public present to withdraw while that evidence is given.

(3) A member of the Council on Tribunals shall be entitled to attend the hearing.

Evidence at hearing

10. - (1) Unless the tribunal otherwise determines, the evidence adduced by the respondent shall be given first.

(2) All oral evidence given at the hearing shall be given on oath.

(3) All witnesses giving evidence at the hearing shall be subject to examination and cross-examination.

(4) Any question as to whether any evidence is admissible, or whether any question should or should not be put to a witness, shall be determined by the tribunal.

(5) A verbatim record of the evidence given at the hearing shall be taken and kept for a period of not less than seven years from the date of the end of the hearing unless the chairman of the tribunal requests that a transcription of the record be made.

Statements in lieu of oral evidence

11. - (1) Subject to the provisions of this rule, the tribunal may admit evidence by way of a written statement made by a person, notwithstanding that he may not be called as a witness, so, however, that evidence shall not be admissible under this rule if it would not have been admissible had it been given orally.

(2) For the purposes of this rule, a written statement purporting to be made and signed by a person and witnessed by another person shall be presumed to have been made by that person unless the contrary be shown.

(3) Nothing in this rule shall prejudice the admission of written evidence which would be admissible apart from the provisions of this rule.

Attendance of complainant at hearing

12. - (1) This rule shall apply in relation to a hearing where the decision appealed against arose from a complaint and the appeal is not against sanction only.

(2) The chairman of the tribunal shall cause notice of the date of the hearing to be sent to the complainant, at the same time as such notice is sent to the appellant and the respondent in pursuance of rule 8(1).

(3) Notwithstanding anything in rule 9(1) but subject to paragraph (5), the tribunal shall allow the complainant to attend the hearing while witnesses are being examined, or cross-examined, on the facts alleged and, if the tribunal considers it appropriate so to do on account of the age of the complainant, or otherwise, shall allow him to be accompanied by a personal friend or relative who is not to be called as a witness at the inquiry:
Provided that-
  (a) where the complainant is to be called as a witness at the hearing he and any person allowed to accompany him shall not be allowed to attend before he gives his evidence; and

(b) where it appears to the tribunal that a witness may in giving evidence disclose information which, in the public interest, ought not to be disclosed to a member of the public, it shall require the complainant and any person allowed to accompany him to withdraw while that evidence is given.

(4) Where the appellant gives evidence, then, after the person representing the respondent has had an opportunity of cross-examining him, the chairman of the tribunal shall put to him any questions which the complainant requests should be so put and might have been properly so put by way of cross-examination and, at his discretion, may allow the complainant himself to put such questions to the appellant.

(5) Subject as aforesaid, the complainant and any person allowed to accompany him shall neither intervene in, nor interrupt the hearing; and if he or such a person should behave in a disorderly or abusive manner, or otherwise misconduct himself, the chairman of the tribunal may exclude him from the remainder of the hearing.

Statement of tribunal's determination

13. - (1) The chairman of the tribunal shall prepare a written statement of the tribunal's determination of the appeal and of the reasons for the decision.

(2) The statement prepared under paragraph (1) and a record of any order made under section 85(2) of the Act shall be submitted to the relevant police authority and, in the case of an appeal by a senior officer, to the Secretary of State within a reasonable period after the determination of the appeal.

(3) The relevant police authority shall, as soon as practicable, copy the statement and any record of an order submitted to it under paragraph (2) to the appellant and the respondent.

(4) In a case where the decision appealed against arose from a complaint, the relevant police authority shall notify the complainant of the outcome of the appeal.

Jack Straw

One of Her Majesty's Principal Secretaries of State

Home Office

13th March 1999

EXPLANATORY NOTE

(This Note is Not Part of the Rules)

These Rules make provision as to the procedure on appeals to police appeals tribunals under section 85 of the Police Act 1996 ("the Act").

Rule 2 revokes, with transitional provisions, the Police (Appeals) Rules 1985 and rule 3 provides for the interpretation of these Rules. Rule 4 prescribes who shall be the respondent to an appeal and rules 5 and 6 provide for the notice of appeal to be given in writing within the prescribed period and for the procedure on such notice being given. Rule 7 allows for the extension of prescribed time limits.

Rules 8 to 11 provide for the procedure to be followed, and for the evidence to be given, at a hearing held to determine an appeal and rule 12 makes provision for the attendance of the complainant in a case arising from a complaint by a member of the public. Rule 13 requires a written statement of the tribunal's determination to be prepared.

[1] 1996 c. 16.

[2] 1992 c. 53; Schedule 1 (which specifies the tribunals to which the consultation requirement applies) was amended by paragraph 46 of Schedule 7 to the Police Act 1996.

[3] S.I. 1985/576.

[4] S.I. 1985/518, as amended by S.I. 1991/1673, S.I. 1995/1475 and S.I. 1995/2517.

[5] S.I. 1985/519.

[6] S.I. 1999/730.

[7] S.I. 1999/732.

[8] S.I. 1999/731.

[9] 1972 c. 70.

APPENDIX C

The Police (Conduct) Regulations 2004, SI 2004/645

STATUTORY INSTRUMENTS

2004 No. 645

POLICE, ENGLAND AND WALES

Police (Conduct) Regulations 2004

Made	*8th March 2004*
Laid before Parliament	*11th March 2004*
Coming into force	*1st April 2004*

The Secretary of State, in exercise of the powers conferred on him by sections 50 and 51 of the Police Act 1996[1] and section 81 of the Police Act 1997[2], and after supplying a draft of these Regulations to the Police Advisory Board for England and Wales and taking into consideration their representations in accordance with section 63(3) of that Act[3], hereby makes the following Regulations:

1 Citation and commencement

These Regulations may be cited as the Police (Conduct) Regulations 2004 and shall come into force on 1st April 2004.

2 Revocations and transitional provisions

(1) The provisions set out in paragraph (2) are hereby revoked.
(2) Those provisions are -
    (a) regulation 2 of the Special Constables Regulations 1965[4] (suspension).
    (b) the Police (Conduct) Regulations 1999[5];
    (c) the Police (Conduct) (Senior Officers) Regulations 1999[6];
    (d) articles 11 and 12 of the Greater London Authority Act 1999 (Consequential Amendments) (Police) Order 2000[7];
    (e) regulations 5 and 6 of the Criminal Justice and Police Act 2001 (Consequential Amendments) (Police Ranks) Regulations 2001[8];
    (f) the Police (Conduct) (Amendment) Regulations 2003[9];
    (g) the Police (Conduct) (Senior Officers) (Amendment) Regulations 2003[10].
(3) Where a report, complaint or allegation -
    (a) was received before 1st April 2004 in respect of conduct by a member of a police force or a special constable; or
    (b) has been or is received on or after 1st April 2004 in respect of conduct by a special constable which occurred or commenced before 1st April 2004,
    nothing in these Regulations shall apply, and the provisions mentioned in paragraph (2) shall, as far as applicable, continue to have effect.

3 Interpretation

(1) In these Regulations -

"appropriate authority" means -

(a) where the officer concerned is a senior officer of any police force, the police authority for the force's area;

(b) [. . .]

(c) in any other case, the chief officer of the police officer's force;

"appropriate officer" means -

(a) where the officer concerned is a member of the metropolitan police force or the City of London police force or a special constable appointed for the area of one of those forces, a police officer of at least the rank of commander in that police force;

(b) in any other case, a police officer of at least the rank of assistant chief constable;

"appropriate standard" means the standard set out in the Code of Conduct;

"conduct matter" means any matter which is not and has not been the subject of a complaint but in the case of which there is an indication (whether from the circumstances or otherwise) that a person serving with the police may have -

(a) committed a criminal offence; or

(b) behaved in a manner which would justify the bringing of disciplinary proceedings.

"Code of Conduct" means the code of conduct contained in Schedule 1;

"the Commission" means the Independent Police Complaints Commission;

"the officer concerned" means the police officer in relation to whose conduct there has been a report, complaint or allegation;

"officer other than a senior officer" means a police officer below the rank of senior officer;

"police officer" means a member of a police force or a special constable;

"senior officer" means a chief constable, a deputy chief constable or an assistant chief constable or, in the case of the City of London and metropolitan police forces, a member of the force in question of or above the rank of commander;

"supervising officer" means a police officer appointed under regulation 7 to supervise the investigation of a case;

"the 1996 Act" means the Police Act 1996; and

"the 2002 Act" means the Police Reform Act 2002[11].

(2) [. . .]

(3) In the following regulations -

(a) a reference to an officer other than a senior officer shall include a reference to a special constable, regardless of the rank or grade he holds;

(b) any special constable of a rank or grade equivalent to or above the rank of chief superintendent shall be treated as if he were a chief superintendent.

Amendment

Para (1): in definition "appropriate authority" para (b) revoked by SI 2006/594, art 2, Schedule, para 44(1), (2)(a), date in force 1 April 2006 except in relation to anything that occurred, or is alleged to have occurred, before that date: see SI 2006/594, arts 1, 2, Schedule, para 44(3). Para (2) revoked by SI 2006/594, art 2, Schedule, para 44(1), (2)(b) on same basis (arts 1, 2, Schedule, para 44(3).

4 Suspension

(1) Where it appears to the appropriate authority, on receiving a report, complaint or allegation which indicates that the conduct of a police officer does not meet the appropriate standard, that the officer concerned ought to be suspended from his office as constable and (in the case of a member of a force) from membership of the force, the appropriate authority may, subject to the following provisions of this regulation, so suspend him.

(2) The appropriate authority shall not so suspend a police officer unless it appears to it that either of the following conditions ("the suspension conditions") is satisfied -

    (a) that the effective investigation of the matter may be prejudiced unless the officer concerned is so suspended;

    (b) that the public interest, having regard to the nature of the report, complaint or allegation, and any other relevant considerations, requires that he should be so suspended.

(3) If the appropriate authority determines that a senior officer ought to be suspended under this regulation, it shall forthwith notify the Commission of its decision and of the suspension condition appearing to it to justify its decision.

(4) If, upon being so notified of the decision of the appropriate authority, the Commission is satisfied that the suspension condition in question is fulfilled, it shall as soon as practicable notify its approval of the suspension of the senior officer concerned to the appropriate authority; and the suspension of the officer shall not have effect unless the approval of the Commission is so given.

(5) The appropriate authority concerned may exercise the power to suspend the officer concerned under this regulation at any time, subject to paragraphs (3) and (4), from the time of the receipt of the report, complaint or allegation until -

    (a) it is decided that the conduct of the officer concerned shall not be the subject of proceedings under regulation 11;

    (b) the notification of a finding that the conduct of the officer concerned did not fail to meet the appropriate standard;

    (c) a sanction has been imposed under regulation 35 and, in the case of an officer other than a senior officer, either the officer concerned has not requested a review within the period specified in regulation 40 or any such review has been completed;

    (d) in the case of a senior officer, the Commission decide otherwise;

    (e) in the case of a senior officer, a notification that, in spite of a finding that the conduct of the officer failed to meet the appropriate standard, no sanction should be imposed.

(6) Where the officer concerned is suspended under this regulation, he shall remain suspended until there occurs any of the events mentioned in paragraph (5)(a) to (e), or until the appropriate authority decides he shall cease to be suspended, whichever first occurs.

(7) Where the officer concerned who is suspended is required to resign under regulation 35, he shall remain suspended until the requirement to resign takes effect.

(8) Where the appropriate authority is a chief officer, he may delegate his powers under this regulation -

    (a) where the officer concerned is a member of the City of London or metropolitan police force or is a special constable appointed for the area of one of those forces, to an officer of at least the rank of commander,

    (b) in any other case, to an officer of at least the rank of assistant chief constable.

5 Suspension -urgent cases

(1) Subject to paragraph (2), in cases of urgency, the like power of suspension as under regulation 4(1) and (2) may be exercised with immediate effect -

    (a) in relation to a chief officer, by the police authority; and

    (b) in relation to any other senior officer, by the chief officer concerned.

(2) Where a senior officer has been suspended under paragraph (1), the police authority or, as the case may be, the chief officer shall notify the Commission forthwith.

(3) The suspension of a senior officer under this regulation shall cease to have effect -

    (a) at the expiry of 24 hours from its imposition unless within that period the Commission has notified the appropriate authority of its approval of it, or

    (b) if earlier, when any of the events mentioned in regulation 4(5)(a) to (e) occurs.

6 Conduct of investigations where there are outstanding criminal proceedings

Where there are criminal proceedings outstanding against the officer concerned, proceedings under these Regulations, other than the exercise of the power to suspend under regulation 4 or 5, shall not take place unless the appropriate authority believes that in the exceptional circumstances of the case it would be appropriate for them to do so.

7 Appointment of supervising officer

(1) Subject to paragraph (2), where a report, complaint or allegation is received by the chief officer which indicates that the conduct of a police officer (other than a senior officer) did not meet the appropriate standard, the case may be referred by him to a police officer, who satisfies the conditions in paragraph (3), to supervise the investigation of the case.

(2) Paragraph (1) shall not apply where the case arises from a complaint or conduct matter to which paragraph 17, 18 or 19 of Schedule 3 to the 2002 Act applies.

(3) The supervising officer shall be -

    (a) of at least the rank of chief inspector and at least one rank above that of the officer concerned;

    (b) a member of, or a special constable appointed for the area of, the same force as the officer concerned; and

    (c) not an interested party.

8 Appointment of investigating officer

(1) A supervising officer may appoint an investigating officer to investigate the case.

(2) Where an appropriate authority receives a report, complaint or allegation which indicates that the conduct of a senior officer did not meet the appropriate standard, it shall take the steps set out in paragraph (4).

(3) Paragraphs (1) and (2) shall not apply where the case arises from a complaint or conduct matter to which paragraph 16, 17, 18 or 19 of Schedule 3 to the 2002 Act applies.

(4) In the case of a senior officer, unless the appropriate authority decides, in the light of such preliminary enquiries as it may make, that no proceedings under regulation 14 need be taken, it shall refer the matter to an investigating officer who shall cause it to be investigated.

(5) If the matter concerns the conduct of the Commissioner of Police of the Metropolis or the Deputy Commissioner of Police of the Metropolis -

    (a) the appropriate authority shall notify the Secretary of State; and

    (b) the Secretary of State shall appoint a person (whether a police officer or not) as the investigating officer.

(6) In any other case which concerns the conduct of a senior officer, the investigating officer shall be appointed by the appropriate authority.

(7) In a case which concerns the conduct of an officer other than a senior officer, the investigating officer shall be -

    (a) a member of the same police force as the officer concerned or, if the chief officer of some other force is requested and agrees to provide an investigating officer, a member of that other force;

    (b) of at least the rank of sergeant;

    (c) if the officer concerned is a superintendent or chief superintendent and -

        (i) if the investigating officer is a member of the City of London or metropolitan police force, of at least the rank of commander;

        (ii) if the investigating officer is a member of any other force, of at least the rank of assistant chief constable.

(8) In a case which concerns the conduct of a senior officer, neither -

    (a) the chief officer concerned; nor

    (b) in a case where the person who is the subject of the investigation is a senior officer in a force other than the metropolitan police force, a member of the same force as that person; nor

    (c) in case where the person who is the subject of the investigation is a senior officer in the metropolitan police force, a person serving in the same division as that person;

    shall be appointed as the investigating officer for the purposes of paragraph (5) or (6).

(9) An investigating officer shall be -

    (a) other than in a case falling within paragraph (5), of at least the same rank as the officer concerned; and

    (b) not an interested party.

(10) A reference in this regulation to a member of a police force shall include a reference to a special constable appointed for the area of that force.

9 Notice of investigation

The investigating officer shall as soon as is practicable (without prejudicing his own or any other investigation of the matter) cause the officer concerned to be given written notice -

    (a) that there is to be an investigation in to the case;

    (b) of the nature of the report, complaint or allegation;

    (c) informing him that he is not obliged to say anything concerning the matter, but that it may harm his defence if he does not mention when questioned or when providing a written response something which he later relies on in any subsequent proceedings under these Regulations;

    (d) informing him that he may, if he so desires, make a written or oral statement concerning the matter to the investigating officer or to the appropriate authority and that if he makes such a statement it may be used in any subsequent proceedings under these Regulations;

    (e) informing him that he has the right to seek advice from his staff association or any other body; and

    (f) informing him that he has the right to be accompanied by a police officer, who shall not be an interested party, to any meeting, interview or hearing.

10 Investigating officer's report

(1) At the end of his investigation the investigating officer shall as soon as practicable submit a written report on the case -

    (a) if the case concerns a senior officer, to the appropriate authority;

    (b) in any other case, to the supervising officer; and

    (c) if the Commission is managing or supervising the investigation, to the Commission.

(2) If at any time during his investigation it appears to the investigating officer that the case is one in respect of which the conditions specified in Part 1 of Schedule 2 are likely to be satisfied, he shall, whether or not the investigation is at an end, submit to the appropriate authority (in the case of a senior officer) or supervising officer (in any other case) -

    (a) a statement of his belief that the case may be one to which regulation 45 applies and the grounds for that belief; and

    (b) a written report on the case so far as it has then been investigated.

11 Procedure on receipt of investigating officer's report

(1) Subject to paragraphs (2) and (4) to (6), on receipt of the investigating officer's report the appropriate authority (in the case of a senior officer) or supervising officer (in any other case) may refer the case to a hearing.

(2) Where -

    (a) the appropriate authority has a duty to take action, secure that disciplinary proceedings are proceeded with or to comply with a direction under paragraph 27 of Schedule 3 to the 2002 Act; or

(b) the officer concerned has received two written warnings about his conduct within the previous twelve months and has in a statement made under regulation 9 admitted that his conduct failed to meet the appropriate standard,

the appropriate authority (in the case of a senior officer) or supervising officer (in any other case) shall refer the case to a hearing.

(3) If the appropriate authority or supervising officer decides that no proceedings under regulation 14 need be taken, they shall so inform the officer concerned in writing as soon as possible.

(4) Where the appropriate authority, on receipt of a report submitted by the investigating officer under regulation 10(2), is of the opinion that the case is one in respect of which the conditions specified in Part 1 of Schedule 2 are likely to be satisfied, it shall take the steps set out in paragraph (6).

(5) Where the supervising officer, on receipt of a report submitted by the investigating officer under regulation 10(2), is of the opinion that the case is one in respect of which the conditions specified in Part 1 of Schedule 2 are likely to be satisfied, he shall refer the case to the appropriate officer who take the steps set out in paragraph (6).

(6) Those steps are -

(a) if the conditions specified in Part 1 of Schedule 2 are not satisfied, return the case to the investigating officer or supervising officer as the case may be to complete the investigation (if necessary);

(b) if the conditions specified in Part 1 of Schedule 2 are satisfied -

(i) certify the case as a special case and refer it to a hearing, and notify the officer concerned accordingly; or

(ii) if the circumstances are such as, in his opinion, make such certification inappropriate, return the case to the investigating officer or supervising officer as the case may be.

(7) Where a case is not referred to a hearing no reference to it shall be made on the officer concerned's personal record.

(8) Proceedings at or in connection with a hearing to which a case is referred under this regulation shall, for the purposes of section 29(1) of the 2002 Act (interpretation of Part 2), be disciplinary proceedings.

12 Withdrawal of case

(1) At any time before the beginning of the hearing the appropriate authority (in the case of a senior officer) or the supervising officer (in any other case) may direct that the case be withdrawn, unless the appropriate authority has a duty to proceed under paragraph 27 of Schedule 3 to the 2002 Act.

(2) Where a direction is given under paragraph (1), the appropriate authority or supervising officer shall, as soon as possible, cause the officer concerned to be served with a written notice of the direction and the case shall be treated as if it had not been referred to a hearing.

13 Sanction without hearing and notice of proceedings: senior officers

(1) If a senior officer accepts that his conduct did not meet the appropriate standard, the appropriate authority may impose a sanction under regulation 35 without the case being dealt with in accordance with regulation 13(3) and (4) and regulations 14 to 34.

(2) Notwithstanding that the senior officer concerned accepts that his conduct did not meet the appropriate standard, the appropriate authority may, after considering the report of the investigation, deal with the matter according to the appropriate authority's discretion if it is satisfied that it does not justify the imposition of any sanction under these Regulations.

(3) If the senior officer concerned -

(a) accepts that his conduct did not meet the appropriate standard but the appropriate authority does not proceed as mentioned in paragraph (1) or (2); or

(b) does not accept that his conduct failed to meet the appropriate standard but the appropriate authority, after taking into account any statement he may have made, is not satisfied that his conduct did meet the appropriate standard,

then the appropriate authority shall refer the case to a hearing.

(4) Notwithstanding that a case is one to which this regulation applies by virtue of paragraph (3)(b), if, after considering the report of the investigation, the appropriate authority is satisfied that the conduct in question, even if found to have failed to meet the appropriate standard, would not justify the imposition of any sanction under these Regulations, the case need not be referred to a hearing and the matter may be dealt with according to the appropriate authority's discretion.

14 Notice of decision to refer case to a hearing

(1) Where a case is to be referred to a hearing, as soon as practicable the officer concerned shall be given written notice of the decision to refer the case to a hearing, and at least 21 days before the date of the hearing he shall be supplied with copies of -
(a) any statement he may have made to the investigating officer; and
(b) any relevant statement, document or other material in each case obtained during the course of the investigation.

(2) The notice given under paragraph (1) shall specify the conduct of the officer concerned which it is alleged failed to meet the appropriate standard and the paragraph of the Code of Conduct in respect of which the appropriate standard is alleged not to have been met.

(3) In this regulation, any reference to a copy of a statement shall, where it was not made in writing, be construed as a reference to a copy of an account thereof.

(4) In the case of a senior officer, the notice mentioned in paragraph (1) shall be given to that officer by an independent solicitor instructed by the appropriate authority to this effect.

(5) The reference in paragraph (4) to an independent solicitor is a reference to a solicitor who is not a member, officer or servant of the appropriate authority or of any local authority which appoints any member of the appropriate authority.

15 Limitation on sanctions: officers other than senior officers

No sanction may be imposed under regulation 35 on a police officer who is not a senior officer unless the case has been referred to a hearing.

16 Notice of hearing

(1) The appropriate authority (in the case of a senior officer) or the supervising officer (in any other case) shall ensure that at least 21 days in advance the officer concerned is notified of the time, date and place of the hearing.

(2) In a case to which this paragraph applies the hearing may, if the appropriate authority or supervising officer considers it appropriate in the circumstances, take place before the expiry of the 21 days referred to in paragraph (1).

(3) Paragraph (2) applies where the officer concerned is given a written notice under regulation 14(1) of a decision to refer the case to a hearing and -
(a) at the time he receives such a notice he is detained in pursuance of the sentence of a court in a prison or other institution to which the Prison Act 1952[12] applies, or has received a suspended sentence of imprisonment; and
(b) having been supplied under regulation 14 with the documents therein mentioned he does not elect to be legally represented at the hearing.

17 Legal representation

(1) If a supervising officer is of the opinion that the hearing should have available the sanctions of dismissal, requirement to resign or reduction in rank, he shall cause the officer concerned to be given notice in writing, at the same time as he is given notice of the decision to refer the

case to a hearing under regulation 14, of the opportunity to elect to be legally represented at the hearing and of the effect of section 84(1) to (3) of the 1996 Act or of paragraphs (3) to (5) of this regulation, as appropriate.

(2) If an appropriate authority is of the opinion that the sanctions of dismissal or requirement to resign should be available, it shall cause the senior officer concerned to be given notice in writing, at the same time as he is given notice of the decision to refer the case to a hearing under regulation 14, of the opportunity to elect to be legally represented at the hearing.

(3) A special constable [. . .] may not be dismissed, required to resign or reduced in rank by a decision taken in proceedings under these regulations unless he has been given an opportunity to elect to be legally represented at any hearing held in the course of those proceedings.

(4) Where a special constable [. . .] makes an election to which paragraph (3) refers, he may be represented at the hearing, at his option, either by counsel or by a solicitor.

(5) Except in a case where a special constable [. . .] has been given an opportunity to elect to be legally represented and has so elected, he may be represented at the hearing only by another police officer.

Amendment

Para (3)–(5): words omitted revoked by SI 2006/594, art 2, Schedule, para 44(1), (2)(c)-(e) date in force 1 April 2006 except in relation to anything that occurred, or is alleged to have occurred, before that date: see SI 2006/594, arts 1, 2, Schedule, paras 44 (1), (2)(d), 2(e) and (3).

18 Procedure on receipt of notice

(1) The officer concerned shall be invited to state in writing, within 14 days of the date on which he is notified that the last of the documents required by regulation 14(1) to be supplied to him has been so supplied -
  (a) whether or not he accepts that his conduct did not meet the appropriate standard;
  (b) in a case where regulation 17 applies, whether he wishes to be legally represented at the hearing;
  (c) whether he proposes to call any witnesses to relevant facts at the hearing and the names and addresses of any such witnesses whose attendance he wishes to be secured.

(2) Any witness whose attendance the officer concerned wishes to be secured who is a member of a police force shall be ordered to attend at the hearing of the case, and the appropriate authority (in the case of a senior officer) or supervising officer (in any other case), where so requested, shall cause any other such witnesses to be given due notice that their attendance is desired and of the time and place of the hearing.

(3) Nothing in this regulation shall require a hearing to be adjourned where a witness is unable or unwilling to attend the hearing.

19 Persons conducting the hearing: officers other than senior officers

(1) Subject to paragraph (5), where a case concerning an officer other than a senior officer is referred to a hearing it shall be heard by three police officers appointed by the chief officer concerned who shall not be interested parties.

(2) Subject to regulation 33, one such officer shall be of at least the rank of assistant chief constable or, where the officer concerned is a member of the City of London or metropolitan police force, of at least the rank of commander, who shall be the presiding officer.

(3) Subject to paragraph (4), the presiding officer shall be assisted by two police officers of at least the rank of superintendent.

(4) Where the officer concerned is a superintendent or a chief superintendent, the presiding officer shall be assisted by two officers of the rank of assistant chief constable or, if the assisting officers are members of the City of London or metropolitan police force, of at least the rank of commander, who shall, unless the officer concerned is a member of the metropolitan police force, be from a different force or forces from the officer concerned.

(5) In a case where the hearing arises from a complaint or conduct matter which has been the subject of an investigation under paragraph 17, 18 or 19 of Schedule 3 to the 2002 Act, paragraph (3) shall not apply and the presiding officer shall be assisted by two persons of whom one is a police officer of at least the rank of superintendent (or, if the officer concerned is a superintendent or chief superintendent, of at least the rank of an assisting officer under paragraph (4)) and the other is a person selected by the police authority for the force concerned from a list of candidates maintained by that authority.

(6) A reference in this regulation to a member of a police force shall include a reference to a special constable appointed for the area of that force.

20 Person conducting the hearing: senior officers

(1) Where a case concerning a senior officer is referred to a hearing it shall be heard by a tribunal consisting of a single person selected and appointed by the appropriate authority from a list of persons nominated by the Lord Chancellor.

(2) To assist the tribunal on matters pertaining to the police there shall also be appointed by the appropriate authority one or more assessors selected by that authority with the approval of the tribunal one of whom is or has been a chief officer of police, so, however, that there shall not be so appointed -

    (a) a person who is one of Her Majesty's inspectors of constabulary;

    (b) the chief officer or former chief officer of any force under whom the senior officer concerned has served as a senior officer in the previous five years;

    (c) a member, officer or servant of the appropriate authority or of any local authority which appoints any member of the appropriate authority.

21 Documents to be supplied to the officer concerned

(1) Where the officer concerned -

    (a) is not a senior officer, or

    (b) is a senior officer and the appropriate authority does not proceed as mentioned in regulation 13(1) or (2),

and he accepts, in accordance with regulation 18, that his conduct fell short of the appropriate standard a summary of the facts of the case shall be prepared, a copy of which shall be supplied to the officer concerned at least 14 days before the hearing.

(2) If the officer concerned does not agree with the summary of facts he may submit a response within 7 days of receipt of the summary.

(3) Where the officer concerned does not accept that his conduct fell short of the appropriate standard no summary of facts shall be prepared.

22 Documents to be supplied to tribunal or to persons conducting the hearing

There shall be supplied to tribunal or, as the case may be, to the persons conducting the hearing -

    (a) a copy of the notice given under regulation 14; and

    (b) a copy of any summary of facts prepared under regulation 21, and of any response from the officer concerned.

23 Representation: officers other than senior officers

(1) In the case of an officer other than a senior officer, unless the officer concerned has given notice in accordance with regulation 18 that he wishes to be legally represented, the supervising officer shall appoint a police officer to present the case.

(2) If the officer has given such notice, the supervising officer may either appoint a police officer to present the case or may instruct an independent solicitor or counsel to present the case.

(3) The officer concerned may conduct his case either in person or by a police officer selected by him or, if he has given notice in accordance with regulation 18 that he wishes to be legally represented, by counsel or a solicitor.

(4) This regulation has effect subject to the provisions of regulation 25.

24 Representation: senior officers

(1) In the case of a senior officer, the case shall be presented -
    (a) by the independent solicitor mentioned in regulation 14(4); or
    (b) by some other independent solicitor or counsel.
(2) In paragraph (1)(b), "independent solicitor" has the same meaning as in regulation 14.
(3) The senior officer concerned may conduct his case either in person or by a representative.
(4) This regulation has effect subject to the provisions of regulation 25.

25 Participation by the Independent Police Complaints Commission

(1) In any case where the Commission has given a direction under paragraph 27(4)(a) of Schedule 3 to the 2002 Act, the Commission may itself present the case.
(2) If the case concerns -
    (a) a senior officer; or
    (b) an officer other than a senior officer and that officer has given notice in accordance with regulation 18 that he wishes to be legally represented,
the Commission may instruct an independent solicitor or counsel to present the case.
(3) Where the Commission decides to present the case or to instruct an independent solicitor or counsel under paragraph (1) -
    (a) it shall notify -
        (i) the appropriate authority or supervising officer as the case may be;
        (ii) the complainant; and
        (iii) any interested person under section 21(5) of the 2002 Act,
    of its decision and the reasons for that decision;
    (b) the appropriate authority or supervising officer shall notify the officer concerned of the Commission's participation; and
    (c) neither the appropriate authority or supervising officer, nor any solicitor or counsel instructed by either of them, shall present the case.

26 Conduct of hearing

(1) The tribunal or officers conducting the hearing may from time to time adjourn the hearing if it appears to them to be necessary or expedient to do so for the due hearing of the case.
(2) Where the case concerns an officer other than a senior officer, any decision of the officers conducting the hearing shall be based on a simple majority, but shall not indicate whether it was taken unanimously or by a majority.

27 Procedure at hearing

(1) Subject to the provisions of these Regulations, the tribunal or as the case may be the officers conducting the hearing shall determine their own procedure.
(2) The tribunal or officers conducting the hearing shall review the facts of the case and decide whether or not the conduct of the officer concerned met the appropriate standard.
(3) The tribunal or officers conducting the hearing shall not find that the conduct of the officer concerned failed to meet the appropriate standard unless the conduct is -
    (a) admitted by the officer concerned; or
    (b) proved by the person presenting the case on the balance of probabilities,
to have failed to meet that standard.
(4) Where evidence is given at a hearing that the officer concerned, at any time after he was given written notice under regulation 9, on being questioned by an investigating officer failed to mention orally or in writing any fact relied on in his defence at that hearing, being a fact which in the circumstances existing at the time the officer concerned could reasonably have been

expected to mention when so questioned or when making a statement under regulation 9(d), paragraph (5) applies.

(5) Where this paragraph applies, the tribunal or officers conducting the hearing may draw such inferences from the failure as appear proper.

(6) Paragraph (5) does not apply in relation to a failure to mention a fact if the failure occurred before this regulation was brought into force.

(7) Where the case concerns an officer other than a senior officer, if the officers conducting the hearing decide that the conduct of the officer concerned did not meet the appropriate standard, they shall decide whether it would be reasonable to impose any, and if so which, sanction.

(8) Where the case concerns a senior officer, the tribunal shall, as soon as possible after the hearing, submit a report to the appropriate authority, together with a copy to the senior officer concerned, setting out -

(a) the finding of the tribunal under paragraph (2);

(b) if that finding was that the conduct of the senior officer concerned failed to meet the appropriate standard, a recommendation as to any sanction which, subject to regulation 35(3), in its opinion should be imposed; and

(c) any other matter arising out of the hearing which it desires to bring to the notice of the appropriate authority.

28 Attendance of officer concerned at hearing

(1) The officer concerned shall attend the hearing.

(2) If the officer concerned fails to attend the hearing it may be proceeded with and concluded in his absence.

(3) Where the officer concerned informs the tribunal or presiding officer in advance that he is unable to attend due to ill-health or some other unavoidable reason, the hearing may be adjourned.

(4) Where, because of the absence of the officer concerned, it is impossible to comply with any procedure set out in these Regulations, that procedure shall be dispensed with.

29 Attendance of complainant and interested persons at hearing

(1) This regulation shall apply in the case of a complaint or a conduct matter which falls under Part 2 of the 2002 Act.

(2) Notwithstanding anything in regulation 30(1), but subject to the following provisions of these Regulations, a complainant or interested person shall be entitled to attend the hearing up to and including the point at which the hearing decides whether the conduct of the officer concerned met the appropriate standard.

(3) A complainant and interested person may each nominate and be accompanied by up to three other persons (or such higher number as the tribunal or presiding officer shall permit).

(4) Where a complainant or interested person, or any person allowed to accompany him, is to be called as a witness at the hearing, he and any person allowed to accompany him shall not be allowed to attend before he gives his evidence.

(5) Where the officer concerned gives evidence, then, after the presenting officer has had an opportunity of cross-examining him, the tribunal or presiding officer shall put to him any questions which the complainant or interested person requests should be so put and might have been properly so put by the presenting officer or, at the tribunal or presiding officer's discretion, may allow the complainant or interested person to put such questions to the officer concerned.

(6) In this regulation a reference to the complainant is a reference to the originator of the complaint notwithstanding that it was transmitted to the chief officer concerned or appropriate authority by some other person or by the Commission or some other body.

(7) In this regulation a reference to an interested person has meaning given by section 21(5) of the 2002 Act.

30 Attendance of others at hearing

(1) Subject to regulation 29 and the following provisions of this regulation, the hearing shall be in private.

(2) Any member of the Commission shall be entitled to attend the hearing in a case to which regulation 29 applies or which arises from a complaint or conduct matter to which paragraph 17, 18 or 19 of Schedule 3 to the 2002 Act applies.

(3) The officer concerned may be accompanied at the hearing by another police officer and, at the discretion of the tribunal or presiding officer as the case may be, by any other person (or, in a case where the complainant or an interested person is accompanied by a greater number of persons, by that number of persons).

(4) The tribunal or presiding officer may allow witnesses to be accompanied at the hearing by a relative or friend.

(5) Where a case arises from a complaint or conduct matter which has been investigated under paragraph 19 of Schedule 3 to the 2002 Act and the Commission considers that because of its gravity or other exceptional circumstances it would be in the public interest to do so, the Commission may, having consulted the appropriate authority, the officer concerned, the complainant and any witnesses, direct that the whole or part of the hearing will be held in public.

(6) A direction under paragraph (5), together with the reasons for that direction, shall be notified within five days to the persons consulted under that paragraph.

(7) Subject as aforesaid, no person allowed to attend shall either intervene in, or interrupt, the hearing; and if he behaves in a disorderly or abusive manner, or otherwise misconducts himself, the tribunal or presiding officer may exclude him from the remainder of the hearing.

(8) The tribunal or presiding officer may impose such conditions as he sees fit relating to the attendance of persons at the hearing under regulation 29 and this regulation.

31 Exclusion of public from hearing

Where it appears to the tribunal or presiding officer that any person may, in giving evidence, disclose information which, in the public interest, ought not to be disclosed to a member of the public he shall require any member of the public including the complainant and any person allowed to accompany the complainant or any witness to withdraw while the evidence is given.

32 Statements in lieu of oral evidence

(1) Any question as to whether any evidence is admissible, or whether any question should or should not be put to a witness, shall be determined by the tribunal or presiding officer.

(2) With the consent of the officer concerned the tribunal or presiding officer may allow any document to be adduced in evidence during the hearing notwithstanding that a copy thereof has not been supplied to the officer concerned in accordance with regulation 14(1).

33 Remission of cases: officers other than senior officers

(1) The hearing of the case -
    (a) shall, in the circumstances mentioned in paragraph (2); or
    (b) may, in the circumstances mentioned in paragraph (5),
    be remitted by the presiding officer concerned to a police officer of equivalent rank in the force concerned or to a police officer of equivalent rank in another force who, at the presiding officer's request, has agreed to act as the presiding officer in the matter.

(2) A case shall be so remitted if -
    (a) the presiding officer is an interested party otherwise than in his capacity as such; or

(b) there would not, because the officer concerned was not given notice under regulation 17 of the opportunity to elect to be legally represented at the hearing, be available on a finding against him any of the sanctions referred to in that regulation, and it appears to the presiding officer concerned that those sanctions ought to be so available and that accordingly it would be desirable for there to be another hearing at which the officer concerned could, if he so wished, be so represented.

(3) Where a case is remitted to another police officer under paragraph (2)(b) notice in writing shall be served on the officer concerned inviting him to elect, within 14 days of the receipt thereof, to be legally represented at the hearing before that officer.

(4) An officer remitting a case under paragraph (2)(b) shall not give to the officer to whom the case has been remitted any indication of his assessment of the case or of the sanction which might be imposed.

(5) A case not falling within paragraph (2) may be remitted by the presiding officer in accordance with paragraph (1) if, either before or during the hearing, the presiding officer concerned considers remission appropriate.

34 Record of hearing

(1) A verbatim record of the proceedings at the hearing shall be taken and, if the officer concerned so requests within the time limit for any appeal and after he has lodged notice of appeal in accordance with rules made under section 85 of the 1996 Act [. . .], a transcript of the record or a copy thereof shall be supplied to him by the tribunal or presiding officer.

(2) In a case which relates to a senior officer, a transcript of the record shall be made and sent to the appropriate authority.

Amendment

Para (1): words omitted revoked by SI 2006/594, art 2, Schedule, para 44(1), (2)(f) date in force 1 April 2006 except in relation to anything that occurred, or is alleged to have occurred, before that date: see SI 2006/594, arts 1, 2, Schedule, para 44(3).

35 Sanctions

(1) Subject to section 84(1) of the 1996 Act, the persons conducting the hearing in the case of an officer other than a senior officer may -
   (a) record a finding that the conduct of the officer concerned failed to meet the appropriate standard but take no further action; or
   (b) impose any of the sanctions in paragraph (2).

(2) Those sanctions are -
   (a) dismissal from the force;
   (b) requirement to resign from the force as an alternative to dismissal taking effect either forthwith or on such date as may be specified in the decision;
   (c) reduction in rank;
   (d) fine;
   (e) in the case of a special constable only, suspension from all or from operational duties only for a period of up to three months;
   (f) reprimand;
   (g) caution.

(3) On receipt of the report of a tribunal under regulation 27(8), the appropriate authority shall decide whether to dismiss the case or -
   (a) to record a finding that the conduct of the senior officer concerned failed to meet the appropriate standard but to take no further action; or
   (b) to record such a finding and impose a sanction.

(4) The sanctions which may be imposed on a senior officer under paragraph (3) are -
  (a) dismissal from the force;
  (b) requirement to resign from the force as an alternative to dismissal taking effect either forthwith or on such date as may be specified in the recommendation or decision;
  (c) fine;
  (d) reprimand.

(5) Any sanction imposed under paragraph (1) or (3), except a requirement to resign, shall have immediate effect.

(6) A fine imposed under paragraph (1) or (3) shall be such that, if it were recovered by way of deductions from the pay of the officer concerned during the period of thirteen weeks following the imposition of the sanction, the aggregate sum which might be so deducted in respect of any one week (whether on account of one or more fines) would not exceed one seventh of his weekly pay.

36 Personal record to be considered before sanction imposed

(1) Where the question of the sanction to be imposed is being considered, the tribunal or persons conducting the hearing -
  (a) shall have regard to the record of police service of the officer concerned as shown on his personal record and may receive evidence from any witness whose evidence would, in their opinion, assist them in determining the question; and
  (b) the officer concerned, or his representative, shall be afforded an opportunity to make oral or, if appropriate, written representations as respects the question or to adduce evidence relevant thereto.

(2) Regulation 32(1) shall apply to proceedings at which such evidence as is referred to in paragraph (1)(a) or (b) of this regulation or such oral representations as are referred to in paragraph (1)(b) of this regulation is given or are made as it applies to the proceedings before the persons conducting the hearing or the tribunal.

37 Notification of finding

(1) In the case of an officer other than a senior officer, the officer concerned shall be informed orally of the finding and of any sanction imposed at the conclusion of the hearing, and shall be provided with a written notification and summary of the reasons within three days.

(2) In the case of a senior officer, the officer concerned shall, as soon as possible after the appropriate authority has taken its decision under regulation 35(3), be provided with a written notification of the finding and of any sanction imposed.

(3) A written notification under this regulation shall include -
  (a) in a case where the officer concerned is a member of a police force, notification of the right to appeal to a Police Appeals Tribunal; and
  (b) in the case of an officer other than a senior officer, notification of the right to request a review.

38 Copy of report and decision to be sent to the Secretary of State

In the case of a senior officer, a copy of the report of the tribunal together with the decision of the appropriate authority shall be sent by the appropriate authority to the Secretary of State.

39 Expenses of hearing

(1) In the case of a senior officer, all the expenses of a hearing under these Regulations, including the costs of the senior officer concerned, shall be defrayed out of the police fund [. . .]

(2) Any costs payable under this regulation shall be subject to taxation in such manner as the Secretary of State may direct.

Amendment

Para (1): words omitted revoked by SI 2006/594, art 2, Schedule, para 44(1), (2)(g) date in force 1 April 2006 except in relation to anything that occurred, or is alleged to have occurred, before that date: see SI 2006/594, arts 1, 2, Schedule, para 44(3).

40 Request for a review: officers other than senior officers

(1) Where -
    (a) a sanction is imposed on an officer other than a senior officer under regulation 35(1), or
    (b) the persons conducting a hearing decide that the conduct of an officer other than a senior officer failed to meet the appropriate standard but decide not to impose a sanction,
the officer concerned shall be entitled to request the chief officer of the force concerned or, where the officer concerned is a member of the metropolitan police force or is a special constable appointed for the metropolitan police district, the Assistant Commissioner ("the reviewing officer"), to review the finding or the sanction (if any) imposed or both the finding and the sanction.

(2) A request for a review must be made to the reviewing officer in writing within 14 days of receipt of the written summary of reasons given in accordance with regulation 37(1) unless this period is extended by the reviewing officer.

(3) The request for a review shall state the grounds on which the review is requested and whether a meeting is requested.

41 Conduct of the review

(1) The reviewing officer shall hold a meeting with the officer concerned if requested to do so.

(2) Where a meeting is held the officer concerned may be accompanied by another police officer and, in a case where regulation 17 applies, by counsel or a solicitor.

42 Finding of the review

(1) The officer concerned shall be informed of the finding of the reviewing officer in writing within three days of completion of the review.

(2) The reviewing officer may confirm or overturn the decision of the hearing or he may impose a different sanction which is specified in regulation 35(2) but he may not impose a sanction greater than that imposed at the hearing.

(3) The decision of the reviewing officer shall take effect by way of substitution for the decision of the hearing and as from the date of that hearing.

(4) Where as a result of the decision of the reviewing officer an officer who is a member of a police force is dismissed, required to resign or reduced in rank he shall be notified in writing of his right of appeal to a Police Appeals Tribunal.

(5) In a case where the Commission has made a direction to an appropriate authority under paragraph 27(4) of Schedule 3 to the 2002 Act, the reviewing officer shall notify the Commission of the outcome of the review and provide the Commission with a written record of the reasons for his determination.

43 Hearing of review in absence of chief officer

(1) Subject to paragraphs (2) to (4), where the chief officer is an interested party or the circumstances in section 12A(1) or (2) of the 1996 Act[] or [. . .] apply, the review shall be conducted by the deputy chief constable or assistant chief constable designated under section 12A(2) of the 1996 Act [...]

(2) Where the deputy chief constable or designated assistant chief constable is absent or an interested party, the review shall be conducted by the chief officer of another force who has agreed to act in that capacity.

(3) Where the officer concerned is a member of the metropolitan police force, or is a special constable appointed for the metropolitan police district, the review shall be conducted by an Assistant Commissioner who is not an interested party.

(4) Where the officer concerned is a member of the City of London police force, or is a special constable appointed for the area of that force, the review shall be conducted by the Commissioner or, if he is absent or an interested party, by the chief officer of another force who has agreed to act in that capacity or an Assistant Commissioner of the metropolitan police force who has agreed to act in that capacity.

Amendment

Para (1): first words omitted revoked by SI 2006/594, art 2, Schedule, para 44(1), (2)(h)(i); final words omitted revoked by SI 2006/594, art 2, Schedule, para 44(1), (2)(h)(ii) date in force 1 April 2006 except in relation to anything that occurred, or is alleged to have occurred, before that date: see SI 2006/594, arts 1, 2, Schedule, para 44(3).

44 Record of conduct proceedings

(1) Subject to paragraph (2), the chief officer concerned shall cause a record to be kept in which shall be entered the case brought against every officer concerned, together with the finding thereon and a record of the decision in any further proceedings in connection therewith.

(2) Where the officer concerned is a chief officer, the appropriate authority shall cause for such a record to be kept.

45 Special cases

(1) This regulation applies to any case in which a report, complaint or allegation is made which indicates that the conduct of a police officer did not meet the appropriate standard and in respect of which the conditions specified in Part 1 of Schedule 2 are satisfied and the appropriate authority or appropriate officer has issued a certificate under regulation 11(6)(b)(i).

(2) In the application of these Regulations to a case to which this regulation applies, regulations 12 to 43 shall, subject to paragraph (3), have effect subject to the modifications specified in Part 2 of Schedule 2.

(3) Where the case is one to which this regulation applies but has been returned to the supervising officer or appropriate authority in pursuance of any provision of these Regulations as modified by Part 2 of Schedule 2, the provisions referred to in paragraph (2) shall thereafter have effect in relation to the case without modification.

(4) In Part 2 of Schedule 2, any reference to a provision in these Regulations shall, unless the contrary intention appears, be construed as a reference to that provision as modified by that Part.

Hazel Blears

Minister of State

Home Office

8th March 2004

Schedule 1

Regulation 3

Code of Conduct

Honesty and integrity

1. It is of paramount importance that the public has faith in the honesty and integrity of police officers. Officers should therefore be open and truthful in their dealings; avoid being improperly beholden to any person or institution; and discharge their duties with integrity.

Fairness and impartiality

2. Police officers have a particular responsibility to act with fairness and impartiality in all their dealings with the public and their colleagues.

Politeness and tolerance

3. Officers should treat members of the public and colleagues with courtesy and respect, avoiding abusive or deriding attitudes or behaviour. In particular, officers must avoid: favouritism of an individual or group; all forms of harassment, victimisation or unreasonable discrimination; and overbearing conduct to a colleague, particularly to one junior in rank or service.

Use of force and abuse of authority

4. Officers must never knowingly use more force than is reasonable, nor should they abuse their authority.

Performance of duties

5. Officers should be conscientious and diligent in the performance of their duties. Officers should attend work promptly when rostered for duty. If absent through sickness or injury, they should avoid activities likely to retard their return to duty.

Lawful orders

6. The police service is a disciplined body. Unless there is good and sufficient cause to do otherwise, officers must obey all lawful orders and abide by the provisions of legislation applicable to the police. Officers should support their colleagues in the execution of their lawful duties, and oppose any improper behaviour, reporting it where appropriate.

Confidentiality

7. Information which comes into the possession of the police should be treated as confidential. It should not be used for personal benefit and nor should it be divulged to other parties except in the proper course of police duty. Similarly, officers should respect, as confidential, information about force policy and operations unless authorised to disclose it in the course of their duties.

Criminal offences

8. Officers must report any proceedings for a criminal offence taken against them. Conviction of a criminal offence or the administration of a caution may of itself result in further action being taken.

Property

9. Officers must exercise reasonable care to prevent loss or damage to property (excluding their own personal property but including police property).

Sobriety

10. Whilst on duty officers must be sober. Officers should not consume alcohol when on duty unless specifically authorised to do so or it becomes necessary for the proper discharge of police duty.

Appearance

11. Unless on duties which dictate otherwise, officers should always be well turned out, clean and tidy whilst on duty in uniform or in plain clothes.

General conduct

12. Whether on or off duty, police officers should not behave in a way which is likely to bring discredit upon the police service.

Notes

(a) The primary duties of those who hold the office of constable are the protection of life and property, the preservation of the Queen's peace, and the prevention and detection of criminal offences. To fulfil these duties they are granted extraordinary powers; the public and the police service therefore have the right to expect the highest standards of conduct from them.

(b) This Code sets out the principles which guide police officers' conduct. It does not seek to restrict officers' discretion: rather it aims to define the parameters of conduct within which that discretion should be exercised. However, it is important to note that any breach of the principles in this Code may result in action being taken by the organisation, which, in serious cases, could involve dismissal.

(c) Police behaviour, whether on or off duty, affects public confidence in the police service. Any conduct which brings or is likely to bring discredit to the police service may be the subject of sanction. Accordingly, any allegation of conduct which could, if proved, bring or be likely to bring discredit to the police service should be investigated in order to establish whether or not a breach of the Code has occurred and whether formal disciplinary action is appropriate. No investigation is required where the conduct, if proved, would not bring or would not be likely to bring, discredit to the police service.

SCHEDULE 2

Regulation 45

SPECIAL CASES

PART 1

CONDITIONS

1. - (1) The conditions referred to in regulation 45 are -
(a) the report, complaint or allegation indicates that the conduct of the officer concerned is of a serious nature and that an imprisonable offence may have been committed by the officer concerned; and
(b) the conduct is such that, were the case to be referred to a hearing under regulation 11 and the tribunal or officers conducting that hearing were to find that the conduct failed to meet the appropriate standard, they would in the opinion of the appropriate officer or appropriate authority be likely to impose the sanction specified in regulation 35(2)(a) or (4)(a) (dismissal from the force); and
(c) the report, complaint or allegation is supported by written statements, documents or other material which is, in the opinion of the appropriate officer or appropriate authority,

sufficient without further evidence to establish on the balance of probabilities that the conduct of the officer concerned did not meet the appropriate standard; and

(d) the appropriate officer or appropriate authority is of the opinion that it is in the public interest for the officer concerned to cease to be a member of a police force, or to be a special constable, without delay.

(2) In this paragraph an "imprisonable offence" means an offence which is punishable with imprisonment in the case of a person aged 21 or over.

PART 2

MODIFICATIONS

2. For regulation 12 there shall be substituted the following regulation -

"**12.** At any time before the beginning of the hearing the appropriate authority (in the case of a senior officer) or appropriate officer (in the case of an officer other than a senior officer) may direct that the case be returned to the investigating officer or supervising officer, as the case may be.".

3. For regulation 14 there shall be substituted the following regulation -

"**14.** - (1) The appropriate authority or the appropriate officer, as the case may be, shall ensure that, as soon as practicable, the officer concerned is given written notice of the decision to refer the case to a hearing and supplied with copies of -

(a) the certificate issued under regulation 11(6)(b)(i);

(b) any statement he may have made to the investigating officer; and

(c) any relevant statement, document or other material obtained during the course of the investigation.

(2) The notice given under paragraph (1) shall specify the conduct of the officer concerned which it is alleged failed to meet the appropriate standard and the paragraph of the Code of Conduct in respect of which the appropriate standard is alleged not to have been met.

(3) In this regulation any reference to a copy of a statement shall, where it was not made in writing, be construed as a reference to a copy of an account thereof.

(4) In the case of an officer who is not a senior officer, the officer concerned shall be invited to an interview with the appropriate officer at which he shall be given the notice mentioned in paragraph (1), but if the officer concerned fails or is unable to attend that interview, the notice and copy document referred to in that paragraph shall be -

(a) delivered to the officer concerned personally, or

(b) left with some person at, or sent by recorded delivery to, the address at which he is residing.

(5) In the case of a senior officer, if the appropriate authority does not proceed as mentioned in regulation 13(1) or (2), the notice mentioned in paragraph (1) shall be given to that officer by an independent solicitor instructed by the appropriate authority to this effect.

(6) The reference in paragraph (5) to an independent solicitor is a reference to a solicitor who is not a member, officer or servant of the appropriate authority or of any local authority which appoints any member of the appropriate authority".

4. For regulations 16 and 17 there shall be substituted the following regulations -

"**16.** The appropriate authority or, as the case may be, the appropriate officer shall fix a date for the hearing which shall be not less than 21 and not more than 28 days from the date on which notice is given under regulation 14 and shall ensure that the officer concerned is forthwith notified of the time, date and place of the hearing.

17. The appropriate officer shall cause the officer concerned to be given notice in writing, at the same time as he is given notice of the hearing under regulation 16, of the opportunity to elect to be legally represented at the hearing and of the effect of section 84(1) to (3) of the 1996 Act, or of paragraphs (3) to (5) of this regulation, as appropriate.".

5. In regulation 18 (procedure on receipt) -
    (a) in paragraph (1), for the words from "on which he is notified" to the end there shall be substituted the words

"on which he receives the documents referred to in regulation 14 -

    (a) whether or not he accepts that his conduct did not meet the appropriate standard; and
    (b) whether he wishes to be legally represented at the hearing"; and
    (b) paragraphs (2) and (3) shall be omitted.

6. For regulation 19 there shall be substituted the following regulation -

"**19.** - (1) Subject to paragraph (2), a case which is referred to a hearing under regulation 11(6)(b)(i) shall be heard -

(a) in the case of the metropolitan police force, by an Assistant Commissioner;
(b) in any other case, by the chief officer concerned.

(2) Where the chief officer concerned is an interested party, the case shall be heard by the chief officer of another force who has agreed to act in that capacity".

7. Regulation 21 shall be omitted.
8. In regulation 22 (documents to be supplied to officers conducting the hearing), for "persons" there shall be substituted "officer" and for paragraphs (a) and (b) there shall be substituted the words "a copy of the notice given, and of any documents provided to the officer concerned, under regulation 14".
9. In regulation 23 (representation), in paragraphs (1) and (2) for "supervising" there shall be substituted "appropriate".
10. For regulation 26 (conduct of hearing) there shall be substituted the following regulation -

"**26.** The tribunal or the officer conducting the hearing may adjourn if it appears to him to be necessary or expedient to do so; but

(a) shall not exercise the power to adjourn more than once; and
(b) shall not adjourn for longer than a period of one week or, on application by the officer concerned, four weeks".

11. In regulation 27 (procedure at hearing) -
(a) for "officers" wherever occurring there shall be substituted "officer"; and
(b) for "their" in paragraph (1) there shall be substituted "his".

12. In regulation 29 (attendance of complainant and interested persons at hearing) -
(a) paragraphs (4) and (5) shall be omitted; and
(b) for the words "presiding officer" wherever they occur there shall be substituted "officer conducting the hearing".

13. In regulation 30 (attendance of others at hearing) -
(a) paragraphs (4) to (6) shall be omitted;
(b) for "presiding officer" there shall be substituted "officer conducting the hearing"; and
(c) in paragraph (7) the words "Subject as aforesaid" shall be omitted.

14. Regulation 31 (exclusion of public from hearing) shall be omitted.

15. In regulation 32 (statements in lieu of oral evidence) -
(a) in paragraph (1), the words ", or whether any question should or should not be put to a witness," shall be omitted;
(b) in paragraph (2), for "14(1)" there shall be substituted "14(1) or (4)";
(c) for the words "presiding officer" wherever they occur there shall be substituted "officer conducting the hearing"; and

(d) at the end there shall be added the following paragraph -

"(3) No witnesses shall be called by either party to the case.".

16. In regulation 33 (remission of cases) -
    (a) paragraphs (2)(b), (3) and (4) shall be omitted;
    (b) for the words "presiding officer" wherever they occur there shall be substituted "officer conducting the hearing"; and
    (c) at the end there shall be added the following paragraph -

"(6) The officer conducting the hearing may return the case to the supervising officer if, either before or during the hearing, the officer conducting the hearing considers it appropriate to do so".

17. In regulation 34 (record of hearing) for "presiding officer" there shall be substituted "officer conducting the hearing".

18. In regulation 35 (sanctions) -
    (a) in paragraph (1), for "persons" there shall be substituted "officer";
    (b) in paragraph (3), after the words "dismiss the case or" insert "direct that it is to be returned to the investigating officer or".

19. In regulation 36 (personal record to be considered before sanction imposed) -
    (a) for "persons" there shall be substituted "officer";
    (b) in paragraph (1)(a) for the words "may receive evidence from any witness whose evidence" there shall be substituted "may admit such documentary evidence as"; and
    (c) in paragraph (1)(b) after the word "adduce" there shall be inserted "documentary".

20 In regulation 37(1) (notification of finding) for "three days" there shall be substituted "24 hours".

21 In regulation 40 (request for a review) -
    (a) in paragraph (1)(b) for "persons" substitute "officer", and for "decide", in both places where it appears, substitute "decides";
    (b) in paragraph (1) for the words from "chief officer" to the end there shall be substituted "chief officer concerned to refer the case to the chief officer of another force who has agreed to act in that capacity ("the reviewing officer") to review the finding or the sanction (if any) imposed or both the finding and the sanction"; and
    (c) in paragraph (2), for the words "reviewing officer" in the first place where they occur there shall be substituted "chief officer concerned" and the words from "unless" to the end shall be omitted.

22. In regulation 42 (finding of the review) -
    (a) in paragraph (1), for "three days" there shall be substituted "24 hours"; and
    (b) at the end there shall be added the following paragraph -

"(6) Where the reviewing officer considers that the officer conducting the hearing should have returned the case to the supervising officer under regulation 33(6), he shall so return the case and the case shall thereafter be deemed to have been returned under that paragraph".

23. Regulation 43 shall be omitted.

EXPLANATORY NOTE

(This Note is not Part of the Regulations)

These Regulations make provision, under sections 50 and 51 of the Police Act 1996 and section 81 of the Police Act 1997, with respect to the conduct of members of police forces and special constables and the maintenance of discipline and establish procedures for cases in which police officers may be dealt with by dismissal, requirement to resign, reduction in rank, fine, reprimand or caution.

The Regulations revoke the Police (Conduct) Regulations 1999 and the Police (Conduct) (Senior Officers) Regulations 1999, and replace them with a single set of provisions. In certain respects the procedures which apply to senior officers (those of or above the rank of assistant chief constable or commander) continue to differ from those which apply to other officers. For these purposes, special constables are treated as if they are not senior officers, regardless of the actual rank or grade they have.

Regulation 5 enables an appropriate authority (as defined in regulation 3) to suspend an officer in respect of whose conduct a report, complaint or allegation has indicated failure to meet the appropriate standard.

Regulation 7 provides for the appointment of a supervising officer (in the case of officers other than senior officers only) and regulation 8 provides for the appointment of an investigating officer whose report may lead to a hearing. Regulations 9 to 22 deal with the preliminary stages prior to a hearing and regulations 23 to 32 with representation, procedure and attendance at the hearing. Regulation 33 allows (and in certain cases requires) a hearing to be remitted to another presiding officer (in the case of officers other than senior officers only). Regulation 34 requires a record to be kept and regulations 35 and 36 deal with the imposition of sanctions.

Regulations 37 to 43 deal with the procedure following a hearing, including, in the case of officers other than senior officers, review at the request of the officer concerned by the chief officer of his force or another senior officer. Regulation 44 requires a record book to be kept recording proceedings under the Regulations.

Schedule 1 sets out the Code of Conduct which represents the appropriate standard for officers, and regulation 45 and Schedule 2 provide for the Regulations to be modified in the case of special cases of serious conduct of a criminal nature.

Notes:

[1] 1996 c. 16; the power in section 50 is extended by section 84 of the Police Act 1996, and the powers in section 50 and 51 are extended by section 36 of the Police Reform Act 2002 (c. 30).

[2] 1997 c. 50; as amended by section 89(2) of the Police Reform Act 2002.

[3] Section 63(3) was amended by section 134(1) of, and paragraphs 72 and 83(1) and (3) of Schedule 9 to, the Police Act 1997 (c. 50) and by sections 90(5), 91(5) and 107(1) of, and paragraph 17 of Schedule 7 to, the Police Reform Act 2002.

[4] S.I. 1965/536; by virtue of section 17 of the Interpretation Act 1978 (c. 30) these Regulations have effect as if made under section 51 of the Police Act 1996.

[5] S.I. 1999/730; as amended by S.I. 2000/1549, 2001/3888 and 2003/2599.

[6] S.I. 1999/731; as amended by S.I. 2000/1549, 2001/3888 and 2003/2596.

[7] S.I. 2000/1549.

[8] S.I. 2001/3888.

[9] S.I. 2003/2599.

[10] S.I. 2003/3596.

[11] N2002 c. 30.

[12] 1952 c. 52.

[13] Section 12A was inserted by section 124(2) of the Criminal Justice and Police Act 2001 (c. 16).

The Police (Complaints and Misconduct) Regulations 2004, SI 2004/643[1]

STATUTORY INSTRUMENTS

2004 No. 643

POLICE, ENGLAND AND WALES

Police (Complaints and Misconduct) Regulations 2004

Made	*8th March 2004*
Laid before Parliament	*11th March 2004*
Coming into force	*1st April 2004*

Whereas the Secretary of State, has consulted, in accordance with sections 24 and 39(11) of the Police Reform Act 2002[1], the Independent Police Complaints Commission, persons whom he considers to represent the interests of police authorities, persons whom he considers to represent the interests of chief officers of police and such other persons as he thinks fit;

And whereas the Secretary of State has supplied a draft of these Regulations to the Police Advisory Board for England and Wales and has taken into consideration their representations in accordance with section 63(3)(d) of the Police Act 1996[2];

Now, therefore, the Secretary of State, in exercise of the powers conferred on him by sections 39(1) and 83(1) to (2A) of the Police Act 1997[3], and sections 13, 20(5), 21(10) and (12), 23, 29(1), 39(9) and 105(4) and (5) of, and paragraphs 3(7), 4(1)(b) and (4), 7(1) and (3), 8(2), 9(8), 11(2)(c), 13(4), 23(11), 24(9) and 25(13) of Schedule 3 to, the Police Reform Act 2002, hereby makes the following Regulations:

Citation, commencement and interpretation

1. - (1) These Regulations may be cited as the Police (Complaints and Misconduct) Regulations 2004 and shall come into force on 1st April 2004.

(2) In these Regulations–

"the 2002 Act" means the Police Reform Act 2002[4];

"bank holiday" means a day which is a bank holiday under the Banking and Financial Dealings Act 1971 in England and Wales.

"the Commission" means the Independent Police Complaints Commission;

["a relevant offence" means—

(a) an offence for which the sentence is fixed by law,

---

[1] With amendments arising under the Police (Complaints and Misconduct) (Amendment) Regulations 2006, SI 2006/1406, and the Police (Complaints and Misconduct)(Amendment) Regulations 2008, SI 2008/2866.

(b) an offence for which a person of 18 years or over (not previously convicted) may be sentenced to imprisonment for a term of seven years (or might be so sentenced but for the restrictions imposed by section 33 of the Magistrates' Courts Act 1980;]²

"working day" means any day other than a Saturday or Sunday or a day which is a bank holiday or public holiday in England and Wales.

Amendments to the Regulations introduced by the Police (Complaints and Misconduct) (Amendment) Regulations 2008, SI 2008/2866, reg 3, in relation only to allegations in respect of conduct by a person concerned that comes to the attention of either the appropriate authority or the Commission on or after 1 December 2008, are as follows.

[**3.**—(1) The 2004 Regulations shall be amended as follows.

(2) In regulation 1(2) (citation, commencement and interpretation) the following definitions are inserted in the appropriate alphabetical places—

""Conduct Regulations" means the Police (Conduct) Regulations 2008( );

"appeal hearing" has the same meaning as in the Conduct Regulations;

"appeal meeting" has the same meaning as in the Conduct Regulations;

"investigator" means a person appointed or designated to investigate under paragraph 16, 17, 18 or 19 of Schedule 3 to the 2002 Act (investigations);

"misconduct hearing" has the same meaning as in the Conduct Regulations;

"misconduct meeting" has the same meaning as in the Conduct Regulations;

"misconduct proceedings" means a misconduct meeting or misconduct hearing;

"police friend" means a person chosen by the person concerned in accordance with regulation 14B;

"police officer" means a member of a police force or special constable;

"police staff member" means an employee of a police authority who is under the direction and control of a chief officer of police;

"special case hearing" has the same meaning as in the Conduct Regulations;

"Standards of Professional Behaviour" has the same meaning as in the Conduct Regulations;".]

Reference of complaints to the Commission

2. - (1) For the purposes of paragraph 4(1)(b) of Schedule 3 to the 2002 Act (reference to the Commission of any complaint of a specified description), the complaints set out in paragraph (2) are hereby specified.

(2) Those complaints are–

(a) any complaints not falling within paragraph 4(1)(a) of that Schedule but alleging conduct which constitutes–

(i) a serious assault, as defined in guidance issued by the Commission;

(ii) a serious sexual offence, as defined in guidance issued by the Commission;

(iii) serious corruption, as defined in guidance issued by the Commission;

(iv) a criminal offence or behaviour which is liable to lead to a disciplinary sanction and whichineithercasewasaggravatedbydiscriminatorybehaviouronthegroundsofa person'srace,sex,religion,orotherstatusidentifiedinguidancebytheCommission;

[(v) a relevant offence, or]³

---

² Definition inserted by the Serious Organised Crime and Police Act 2005 (Powers of Arrest) (Consequential Amendments) Order 2005, SI 2005/3389. art 26(2), 1 January 2006.

³ Substituted by SI 2005/3389, art 26(3), 1 January 2006.

(b) complaints which arise from the same incident as one in which any conduct falling within sub-paragraph (a) or within paragraph 4(1)(a) of Schedule 3 to the 2002 Act is alleged.

(3) Where a complaint is required to be referred to the Commission under sub-paragraph (1)(a) or (b) of paragraph 4 of Schedule 3 to the 2002 Act, notification of the complaint shall be given to the Commission–

(a) not later than the end of the [. . .]2 day following the day on which it first becomes clear to the appropriate authority that the complaint is one to which that sub-paragraph applies, and

(b) in such manner as the Commission specifies.

(4) Where a complaint is required to be referred to the Commission under sub-paragraph (1)(c) of paragraph 4 of Schedule 3 to the 2002 Act, notification of the complaint shall be given to the Commission–

(a) not later than the end of the [. . .][4] day following the day on which the Commission notifies the appropriate authority that the complaint is to be referred, and

(b) in such manner as the Commission specifies.

Dispensation by the Commission

3. - (1) For the purposes of paragraph 7 of Schedule 3 to the 2002 Act (dispensation by the Commission from requirements of Schedule 3) the complaints set out in paragraph (2) are hereby specified–

(2) Those complaints are complaints where the appropriate authority considers that–

(a) more than 12 months have elapsed between the incident, or the latest incident, giving rise to the complaint and the making of the complaint and either that no good reason for the delay has been shown or that injustice would be likely to be caused by the delay;

(b) the matter is already the subject of a complaint;

(c) the complaint discloses neither the name and address of the complainant nor that of any other interested person and it is not reasonably practicable to ascertain such a name or address;

(d) the complaint is vexatious, oppressive or otherwise an abuse of the procedures for dealing with complaints;

(e) the complaint is repetitious; or

(f) it is not reasonably practicable to complete the investigation of the complaint or any other procedures under Schedule 3 to the 2002 Act.

(3) For the purposes of paragraph (2)(e) a complaint is repetitious if, and only if–

(a) it is substantially the same as a previous complaint (whether made by or on behalf of the same or a different complainant), or it concerns substantially the same conduct as a previous conduct matter;

(b) it contains no fresh allegations which significantly affect the account of the conduct complained of;

(c) no fresh evidence, being evidence which was not reasonably available at the time the previous complaint was made, is tendered in support of it; and

(d) as respects the previous complaint or conduct matter, either–

(i) the requirements of paragraph 23(7) or 24(6) of Schedule 3 to the 2002 Act (determination by the appropriate authority of what action to take) were complied with;

[4] Word repealed by the Police (Complaints and Misconduct) (Amendment) Regulations 2006, SI 2006/1406, reg 2(2), 22 June 2006.

      (ii) the complaint was locally resolved in accordance with the provisions of paragraph 8 of that Schedule;

      (iii) the Commission gave the appropriate authority a direction under regulation 7(7)(b) (requirement to dispense with the requirements of Part 2 of the 2002 Act);

      (iv) the complainant gave such notification that he withdrew the complaint as is mentioned in regulation 15(1)(a); or

      (v) the Commission, under paragraph 7 of Schedule 3 to the 2002 Act, gave the appropriate authority permission to handle the complaint in whatever way it saw fit.

(4) For the purposes of paragraph (2)(f) it is not reasonably practicable to complete the investigation of a complaint or any other procedures under Schedule 3 to the 2002 Act if, and only if–

    (a) it is not reasonably practicable to communicate with the complainant or a person acting on his behalf; or

    (b) it is not reasonably practicable to complete a satisfactory investigation in consequence of–

      (i) a refusal or failure, on the part of the complainant, to make a statement or afford other reasonable assistance for the purposes of the investigation; or

      (ii) the lapse of time since the event or events forming the subject-matter of the complaint.

(5) In this regulation any reference to action not being reasonably practicable shall include a reference to action which it does not appear reasonably practicable to take within a period which is reasonable in all the circumstances of the case.

(6) An application under paragraph 7(1) of Schedule 3 to the 2002 Act for permission to handle a complaint in whatever manner (if any) an authority thinks fit shall be in writing and shall be accompanied by–

    (a) a copy of the complaint;

    (b) an explanation of the appropriate authority's reasons for making the application;

    (c) in a case falling within paragraph (2)(e), the previous complaint and a copy of the record of any resolution, withdrawal or dispensation of that complaint;

    (d) copies of any other documents or material in the possession of the appropriate authority which are relevant to the complaint.

(7) The appropriate authority shall supply any further information requested by the Commission for the purpose of considering an application by that authority made under paragraph 7 of Schedule 3 to the 2002 Act.

Local resolution of complaints

4. - (1) The procedures that are to be available for dealing with a complaint which is to be subjected to local resolution are, subject to the provisions of this regulation, any procedures which are approved by the Commission.

(2) Where it appears to the appointed person that the complaint had in fact already been satisfactorily dealt with at the time it was brought to his notice, he may, subject to any representation by the complainant, treat it as having been locally resolved.

(3) The appointed person shall as soon as practicable give the complainant and the person complained against an opportunity to comment on the complaint.

(4) The appointed person shall not, for the purpose of locally resolving a complaint, tender on behalf of the person complained against an apology for his conduct unless the person complained against has admitted the conduct in question and has agreed to the apology.

(5) Where the person complained against chooses not to comment on the complaint, the appointed person shall record this fact in writing.

(6) Where a complaint has been dealt with by way of local resolution a record shall be made as soon as practicable of the outcome of the procedure and the person complained against shall be sent a copy of that record.

(7) A complainant shall be entitled to obtain a copy of that record from the appropriate authority if he applies for such a copy not later than the end of three months from the day on which–

    (a) the local resolution of his complaint was achieved; or

    (b) for whatever other reason, it was determined that the complaint should no longer be subject to that procedure.

(8) An appropriate authority shall provide a copy of any such record as soon as practicable after it has received such an application.

(9) In this regulation, " the appointed person" means a person appointed under paragraph 8(1) of Schedule 3 to the 2002 Act to secure the local resolution of a complaint.

Recording and reference of conduct matters

5. - (1) For the purposes of paragraph 11(2)(c) of Schedule 3 to the 2002 Act (recording etc. of conduct matters), the following descriptions of conduct are hereby specified–

    (a) a serious assault, as defined in guidance issued by the Commission;

    (b) a serious sexual offence, as defined in guidance issued by the Commission;

    (c) serious corruption, as defined in guidance issued by the Commission;

    (d) a criminal offence or behaviour which is liable to lead to a disciplinary sanction and which in either case was aggravated by discriminatory behaviour on the grounds of a person's race, sex, religion, or other status identified in guidance by the Commission;

    [(e) a relevant offence;]⁵

    (f) conduct whose gravity or other exceptional circumstances make it appropriate to record the matter in which the conduct is involved; or

    (g) conduct which is alleged to have taken place in the same incident as one in which conduct within sub-paragraphs (a) to (e) is alleged.

(2) For the purposes of paragraph 13(1)(b) of Schedule 3 to the 2002 Act (reference of recordable conduct matters to the Commission) any matter which relates to conduct falling within paragraph (1)(a) to (e) or (g) of this regulation is hereby specified.

(3) Any conduct matter which is required to be referred to the Commission shall be referred in such manner as the Commission specifies and–

    (a) if the matter falls within sub-paragraph (1)(a) or (b) of paragraph 13 of Schedule 3 to the 2002 Act, not later than the end of the [. . .]⁶ day following the day on which it first becomes clear to the appropriate authority that the conduct matter is one to which that sub-paragraph applies, and

    (b) if the matter falls within sub-paragraph (1)(c) of that paragraph, not later than the end of the [. . .]2 day following the day on which the Commission notifies the appropriate authority that the conduct matter is to be referred.

[Reference of Death or Serious Injury (DSI) matters

5A. - Any DSI matter which is required to be referred to the Commission shall be referred in such manner as the Commission specifies and—

    (a) in a case where the Commission directs that the matter be referred to it, not later than the end of the day following the day on which the Commission so directs;

    (b) in any other case, not later than the end of the day following the day on which the matter first comes to the attention of the appropriate authority.]⁷

Power of Commission to impose requirements in relation to an investigation which it is supervising

6. - (1) For the purposes of paragraph 17(7) of Schedule 3 to the 2002 Act (investigations supervised by the Commission) the requirements which may be imposed by the Commission on a

---

⁵ Substituted by SI 2005/3389, art 26(4), 1 January 2006.
⁶ Word repealed by SI 2006/1406, reg 2(3), 22 June 2006.
⁷ Added by SI 2006/1406, reg 2(4), 22 June 2006.

˙person appointed to investigate a complaint [, recordable conduct matter or DSI matter]1 are, subject to paragraphs (2) and (3), any reasonable requirements as to the conduct of the investigation as appear to it to be necessary.

(2) Where at any stage of an investigation of a complaint [, recordable conduct matter or DSI matter]⁸ the possibility of criminal proceedings arises, the Commission shall not, under paragraph (1), impose any requirement relating to the obtaining or preservation of evidence of a criminal offence without first obtaining the consent of the Director of Public Prosecutions to the imposition thereof.

(3) The Commission shall not, under paragraph (1), impose any requirement relating to the resources to be made available by a chief officer for the purposes of an investigation without first consulting him and having regard to any representations he may make.

Power of the Commission to discontinue an investigation

7. - (1) For the purposes of paragraph 21(1) of Schedule 3 to the 2002 Act (discontinuance of investigations) the descriptions of complaint or matter set out in paragraph (2) of this regulation are hereby specified.

(2) Those descriptions are any complaint or matter–
(a) in which the complainant refuses to co-operate to the extent that the Commission considers that it is not reasonably practicable to continue the investigation;
(b) which the complainant has agreed may be subjected to local resolution;
(c) which the Commission considers is vexatious, oppressive or otherwise an abuse of the procedures for dealing with complaints [, conduct matters or DSI matters]⁹;
(d) which is repetitious, as defined in regulation 3(3); or
(e) which the Commission otherwise considers is such as to make it not reasonably practicable to proceed with the investigation.

(3) For the purposes of paragraph 21(2) of Schedule 3 to the 2002 Act the cases in which the Commission is authorised to discontinue an investigation that is being carried out in accordance with paragraph 19 of that Schedule are any cases where the complaint [, conduct matter or DSI matter]¹⁰ under investigation falls within paragraph (2) of this regulation.

(4) Any application by an appropriate authority to the Commission for an order that it discontinue an investigation shall be in writing and shall be accompanied by–
(a) a copy of the complaint, and
(b) a memorandum from the appropriate authority containing a summary of the investigation undertaken so far and explaining the reasons for the application to discontinue the investigation.

(5) The appropriate authority shall–
(a) send the complainant a copy of any such application on the same day as the day on which the application is sent to the Commission
(b) supply any further information requested by the Commission for the purpose of considering that application.

(6) The Commission shall not require the discontinuance of an investigation in a case where there has been no application to do so by the appropriate authority unless it has consulted with that authority.

---

⁸ Words substituted by SI 2006/1406, reg 2(5), 22 June 2006.
⁹ Words substituted by SI 2006/1406, reg 2(6)(a), 22 June 2006.
¹⁰ Words substituted by SI 2006/1406, reg 2(6)(b), 22 June 2006.

(7) A direction given to an appropriate authority by the Commission under paragraph 21(4)(a) of Schedule 3 to the 2002 Act may–

    (a) require the appropriate authority to produce an investigation report on the discontinued investigation under paragraph 22 of that Schedule and to take any subsequent steps under that Schedule;

    (b) where the investigation concerned a complaint, require the appropriate authority to dispense with the requirements of Part 2 of the 2002 Act as respects that complaint;

    (c) in a case within paragraph (1)(b) require the appropriate authority to subject the complaint to local resolution;

    (d) direct the appropriate authority to handle the matter in whatever manner (if any) that authority thinks fit.

(8) The steps set out in paragraph (9) are hereby specified for the purposes of paragraph 21(4)(b) of Schedule 3 to the 2002 Act (steps that may be taken by the Commission when an investigation is discontinued).

(9) Those steps are–

    (a) to produce an investigation report on the discontinued investigation and take any subsequent steps under that Schedule;

    (b) where the investigation concerned a complaint, to dispense with the requirements of Part 2 of the 2002 Act as respects that complaint;

    (c) to handle the matter in whatever manner it thinks fit.

Appeals to the Commission: failures to notify or record a complaint

8. - (1) An appeal under paragraph 3 of Schedule 3 to the 2002 Act against any failure referred to in paragraph 3(3) (failure by a police authority or chief officer to determine who is the appropriate authority or to notify or record anything under paragraph 2) shall be made within 28 days of the date on which notification of that failure is made or sent to the complainant under paragraph 3(2) of that Schedule.

(2) Any such appeal shall be made in writing and shall state–

    (a) details of the complaint;

    (b) the date on which the complaint was made;

    (c) the name of the police force or police authority which gave notification of the failure;

    (d) the grounds for the appeal; and

    (e) the date on which the complainant was notified of the determination or of the failure to record the complaint.

(3) Where the Commission receives such an appeal it shall–

    (a) notify the police authority or chief officer concerned of the appeal, and

    (b) request any information from any person which it considers necessary to dispose of the appeal.

(4) Where the Commission receives an appeal which fails to comply with one or more of the requirements mentioned in paragraph (2), it may decide to proceed as if those requirements had been complied with.

(5) A police authority or chief officer shall supply to the Commission any information requested under paragraph (3)(b).

(6) The Commission shall determine the outcome of the appeal as soon as practicable.

(7) The Commission shall notify the complainant and the police authority or chief officer concerned of the reasons for its determination.

(8) The Commission may extend the time period mentioned in paragraph (1) in any case where it is satisfied that by reason of the special circumstances of the case it is just to do so.

Appeals to the Commission: local resolution

9. - (1) Any appeal under paragraph 9 of Schedule 3 to the 2002 Act (appeal by a complainant whose complaint has been subjected to local resolution against the conduct of the local resolution) shall be made within 28 days of the date on which the alleged contravention of the procedural requirements occurred.

(2) Any such appeal shall be made in writing and shall state–

   (a) details of the complaint;

   (b) the date on which the complaint was made;

   (c) the grounds for the appeal; and

   (d) the date on which the complainant was notified of the outcome of that local resolution.

(3) Where the Commission receives such an appeal it shall request any information from any person which it considers necessary to dispose of the appeal.

(4) Where the Commission receives an appeal which fails to comply with one or more of the requirements mentioned in paragraph (2), it may decide to proceed as if those requirements had been complied with.

(5) The appropriate authority shall supply to the Commission any further information requested of it under paragraph (3).

(6) The Commission shall determine the outcome of the appeal as soon as practicable.

(7) The Commission shall notify the complainant, the appropriate authority and the person complained against of the reasons for its determination.

(8) The Commission shall notify the complainant and the person complained against of any direction it gives to the appropriate authority as to the future handling of the complaint.

(9) The Commission may extend the time period mentioned in paragraph (1) in any case where it is satisfied that by reason of the special circumstances of the case it is just to do so.

Appeals to the Commission with respect to an investigation

10. - (1) Any appeal made by a complainant under paragraph 25(2) of Schedule 3 to the 2002 Act shall be made within 28 days of the date on which the appropriate authority sends a notification to the complainant of its determination under paragraph 24(7) of that Schedule as to what action (if any) it will take in respect of the matters dealt with in the investigation report.

(2) Any such appeal shall be in writing and shall state–

   (a) details of the complaint;

   (b) the date on which the complaint was made;

   (c) the grounds for the appeal; and

   (d) the date on which the complainant received notification under paragraph 24(7) of Schedule 3.

(3) Where the Commission receives such an appeal it shall request any information from any person which it considers necessary to dispose of the appeal.

(4) Where the Commission receives an appeal which fails to comply with one or more of the requirements mentioned in paragraph (2), it may decide to proceed as if those requirements had been complied with.

(5) The appropriate authority shall supply to the Commission any further information requested of it under paragraph (3).

(6) The Commission shall determine the outcome of the appeal as soon as practicable.

(7) The Commission shall notify the complainant and the appropriate authority of the reasons for its determination.

(8) The Commission may extend the time period mentioned in paragraph (1) in any case where it is satisfied that by reason of the special circumstances of the case it is just to do so.

Manner in which duties to provide information are to be performed

11. - (1) For the purposes of sections 20(5) and 21(10) of the 2002 Act (duties to keep complainant and other persons informed), the manner in which the Commission or, as the case may be, an appropriate authority shall perform the duties imposed by those sections are as follows.

(2) The Commission, in a case falling within section 20(1) or 21(6) of the 2002 Act (investigation of a complaint [, conduct matter or DSI matter][1] by or under the management of the Commission), shall inform the complainant or, as the case may be, the interested party–

  (a) of the progress of the investigation promptly and in any event–

    (i) if there has been no previous notification, within four weeks of the start of the investigation; and

    (ii) in any other case, within four weeks of the previous notification;

  (b) of any provisional findings of the person carrying out the investigation as frequently as the Commission determines to be appropriate in order for the complainant to be kept properly informed.

(3) An appropriate authority, in a case falling within section 20(2) or 21(7) of the 2002 Act (investigation of a complaint [, conduct matter or DSI matter][11] by an appropriate authority), shall inform the complainant or the interested party (as the case may be)–

  (a) of the progress of the investigation promptly and in any event–

    (i) if there has been no previous notification, within four weeks of the start of the investigation; and

    (ii) in any other case, within four weeks of the previous notification.

  (b) of any provisional findings of the person carrying out the investigation as frequently as the appropriate authority determine to be appropriate in order for the complainant to be kept properly informed.

(4) When an investigation has been completed, each complainant and interested person shall be notified–

  (a) of the date on which the final report under paragraph 22 of Schedule 3 to the 2002 Act is likely to be submitted;

  (b) of the date on which the notification under paragraph 23(9) or 24(7) of that Schedule is likely to be given.

(5) In performing the duties imposed by section 20(1) and (2) and section 21(6) and (7) of the 2002 Act, and by paragraphs 23(9) and 24(7) of Schedule 3 to that Act, the Commission or, as the case may be, the appropriate authority shall determine whether it is appropriate to offer, or to accede to a request for, a meeting with a complainant or, as the case may be, an interested person.

(6) As soon as practicable after any such meeting the Commission or, as the case may be, the appropriate authority shall send to the complainant or interested person a written record of the meeting and an account of how any concerns of that person will be addressed.

(7) As soon as practicable after any misconduct hearing or other action that is taken in respect of the matters dealt with in any report submitted under paragraph 22 of Schedule 3 to the 2002 Act, the Commission or, as the case may be, an appropriate authority shall notify any complainant and interested person of the outcome of that hearing or action, including the fact and outcome of any appeal against the findings of or sanctions imposed by such a hearing.

(8) Subject to paragraphs (5) and (9) any notification under this regulation shall be made in writing.

(9) If the Commission or, as the case may be, the appropriate authority, considers that an investigation has made minimal or no progress since the previous notification, then the next notification

---

[11] Words substituted by SI 2006/1406, reg 2(7), 22 June 2006.

may be made by any means that in the opinion of the Commission or, as the case may be, the appropriate authority is suitable.

Exceptions to the duty to keep the complainant informed and to provide information for other persons

12. - (1) Subject to paragraph (2), the duties mentioned in section 20(1) and (2) (duty to keep the complainant informed) and section 21(6) and (7) (duty to provide information for other persons) of the 2002 Act and in paragraphs 23(9) and 24(7) of Schedule 3 to that Act (action by the Commission or appropriate authority in response to an investigation report) shall not apply in circumstances where in the opinion of the Commission, or, as the case may be, of the appropriate authority, the non-disclosure of information is necessary for the purpose of–
    (a) preventing the premature or inappropriate disclosure of information that is relevant to, or may be used in, any actual or prospective criminal proceedings;
    (b) preventing the disclosure of information in any circumstances in which its non-disclosure–
        (i) is in the interests of national security;
        (ii) is for the purposes of the prevention or detection of crime, or the apprehension or prosecution of offenders;
        (iii) is required on proportionality grounds; or
        (iv) is otherwise necessary in the public interest.
(2) The Commission or, as the case may be, the appropriate authority shall not conclude that the non-disclosure of information is necessary under paragraph (1) unless it is satisfied that–
    (a) there is a real risk of the disclosure of that information causing an adverse effect; and
    (b) that adverse effect would be significant.
(3) Without prejudice to the generality of paragraph (1), the Commission or, as the case may be, the appropriate authority shall consider whether the non-disclosure of information is justified under that paragraph in circumstances where–
    (a) that information is relevant to, or may be used in, any actual or prospective disciplinary proceedings;
    (b) the disclosure of that information may lead to the contamination of the evidence of witnesses during such proceedings;
    (c) the disclosure of that information may prejudice the welfare or safety of any third party;
    (d) that information constitutes criminal intelligence.

Meaning of "relative"

13. - For the purposes of section 21(12) of the 2002 Act (meaning of " relative"), the description of person that is hereby prescribed is any spouse, partner, parent or adult child.

Copies of complaints etc.

14. - (1) Where a complaint is recorded under paragraph 2(6) of Schedule 3 to the 2002 Act, the appropriate authority shall–
    (a) supply to the complainant a copy of the record made of that complaint; and
    (b) subject to paragraphs (2) to (4), supply to the person complained against a copy of the complaint.
(2) A copy of a complaint supplied under this regulation may be in a form which keeps anonymous the identity of the complainant or of any other person.
(3) An appropriate authority may decide not to supply such a copy of a complaint if it is of the opinion that to do so–
    (a) might prejudice any criminal investigation or pending proceedings, or
    (b) would otherwise be contrary to the public interest.
(4) Where an appropriate authority decides not to supply such a copy, it shall keep that decision under regular review.

[Written notices[12]

14A. - (1) For the purposes of paragraph 19B(7) of Schedule 3 to the 2002 Act (assessment of seriousness of conduct under investigation) the notification given by the investigator to the person concerned must be in writing and state—

(a) the conduct that is the subject matter of the allegation and how that conduct is alleged to fall below the Standards of Professional Behaviour;

(b) that there is to be an investigation into the matter and the identity of the investigator;

(c) the investigator's assessment of whether that conduct, if proved, would amount to misconduct or gross misconduct;

(d) whether, if the matter were to be referred to misconduct proceedings, those would be likely to be a misconduct meeting or a misconduct hearing;

(e) that if the likely form of any misconduct proceedings to be held changes, further notice (with reasons) will be given;

(f) that he has the right to seek advice from his staff association or any other body and of the effect of regulation 14B(1);

(g) the effect of regulation 14C and paragraph 19C of Schedule 3 to the 2002 Act (duty to consider submissions from person whose conduct is being investigated) and regulations 7(1) to (3) of the Conduct Regulations (legal or other representation); and

(h) that whilst he does not have to say anything it may harm his case if he does not mention when interviewed or when providing any information under regulation 14C or regulation 22(2) or (3) of the Conduct Regulations (procedure on receipt of notice of referral to misconduct proceedings) something which he later relies on in any misconduct proceedings, special case hearing, an appeal meeting or appeal hearing.

(2) For the purposes of paragraph 19B(10) of Schedule 3 to the 2002 Act (assessment of seriousness of conduct under investigation), if following service of the notice under paragraph (1), the investigator revises his assessment of the conduct in accordance with paragraph 19B(9) of Schedule 3 to the 2002 Act or his determination of the likely form of any misconduct proceedings to be taken, the investigator shall as soon as practicable, give the person concerned further written notice of—

(a) the assessment of whether the conduct, if proved, would amount to misconduct or gross misconduct as the case may be and the reason for that assessment;

(b) whether, if the case were to be referred to misconduct proceedings, those would be likely to be a misconduct meeting or a misconduct hearing and the reason for this.

(3) The notice whether given in accordance with paragraph (1) or (2) shall be—

(a) given to the person concerned in person;

(b) left with some person at, or sent by recorded delivery to, the person concerned's last known address; or

(c) given to him in person by his police friend where the police friend has agreed with the appropriate authority to deliver the notice.

Police friend

14B. - (1) Where the person concerned is a police officer he may choose—

(a) a police officer;

(b) a police staff member; or

---

[12] Regulations 14A–14E inserted by the Police (Complaints and Misconduct)(Amendment) Regulations 2008, SI 2008/2866, reg 3(3), 1 December 2008. By reg 2, these provisions apply only to allegations in respect of conduct by a person concerned that comes to the attention of either the appropriate authority or the Commission, on or after 1 December 2008.

(c) where the officer concerned is a member of a police force, a person nominated by his staff association,

who is not otherwise involved in the matter to act as his police friend.

(2) Where the person concerned is a police staff member he may choose—

(a) a person employed by a trade union of which he is an official within the meaning of sections 1 and 119 of the Trade Union and Labour Relations (Consolidation) Act 1992 (meaning of trade union);[13]

(b) an official of a trade union (within that meaning) whom the union has reasonably certified in writing as having experience of, or as having received training in, acting as a police staff member's companion at disciplinary proceedings;

(c) a police officer;

(d) a police staff member; or

(e) any other person nominated by the person concerned and approved by the chief officer of the force in which a police staff member is serving,

who is not otherwise involved in the matter to act as his police friend.

(3) A police friend may—

(a) provide any relevant document to the investigator in accordance with paragraph 19C(2)(b) of Schedule 3 to the 2002 Act (power to prescribe persons who may provide submissions to the investigator);

(b) accompany the officer concerned to any interview conducted under regulation 14D;

(c) advise the person concerned throughout proceedings under these Regulations; and

(d) make representations to the Commission concerning any aspect of the proceedings under these Regulations.

(4) Where a police friend is a police officer or a police staff member, the chief officer of police of the force of which the police friend is a member shall permit him to use a reasonable amount of duty time for the purposes referred to in paragraph (3).

(5) The reference in paragraph (4) to the force of which the police friend is a member shall include a reference to the force maintained for the police area for which a special constable is appointed and the force in which a police staff member is serving.

Representations to the investigator

14C. - For the purposes of paragraph 19B(7)(c) of Schedule 3 to the 2002 Act (time limits for providing documents to the investigator), the person concerned or police friend shall have 10 working days starting with the day after which the notice is given under regulation 14A(1) (unless this period is extended by the investigator) to provide any relevant statement or relevant document as the case may be.

Interviews during investigation

14D. - (1) For the purposes of paragraph 19D(1) of Schedule 3 to the 2002 Act (interview of person whose conduct is being investigated), where an investigator wishes to interview the person concerned as part of his investigation, he shall, if reasonably practicable, agree a date and time for the interview with the person concerned.

(2) Where no date and time is agreed under paragraph (1), the investigator shall specify a date and time for the interview.

(3) Where a date and time is specified under paragraph (2) and—

(a) the person concerned or his police friend will not be available at that time; and

(b) the person concerned proposes an alternative time which satisfies subsection (4),

the interview shall be postponed to the time proposed by the person concerned.

---

[13] To which Act which there are amendments not relevant to these Regulations.

(4) An alternative time must—
    (a) be reasonable; and
    (b) fall before the end of the period of 5 working days beginning with the first working day after the day specified by the investigator.

(5) The person concerned shall be given written notice of the date, time and place of the interview.

(6) The investigator shall, in advance of the interview, provide the person concerned with such information as the investigator considers appropriate in the circumstances of the case to enable the person concerned to prepare for the interview.

(7) The person concerned shall attend the interview.

(8) A police friend may not answer any questions asked of the person concerned during the interview.

Report of investigation

14E. - (1) For the purposes of paragraph 22(7) of Schedule 3 to the 2002 Act (final reports on investigations), on completion of an investigation the investigator's report shall—
    (a) provide an accurate summary of the evidence;
    (b) attach or refer to any relevant documents; and
    (c) indicate the investigator's opinion as to whether there is a case to answer in respect of misconduct or gross misconduct or whether there is no case to answer."

(2) In regulation 18 (appointment of persons to carry out investigations)—
    (a) In paragraph (1)(a) for "conduct the investigation and to manage the resources that will be required during that process" substitute "manage the investigation";
    (b) For paragraph (1)(b) substitute the following sub–paragraph—

        "(b) if he is a person whose involvement in the role could reasonably give rise to a concern as to whether he could act impartially under these Regulations";

    (c) For paragraph (1)(d) substitute the following sub–paragraph—
    "(d) in a case where the officer concerned is a senior officer, if he is—
        (i) the chief officer of police of the police force concerned;
        (ii) a member of the same force as the officer concerned, or where the officer concerned is a member of the Metropolitan Police Force, serving in the same division as the officer concerned.";

    (d) Omit paragraph (2);
    (e) In paragraph (3)(a) for "senior police officer" substitute "senior officer";
    (f) In paragraph (3)(b) omit "(other than in paragraph (1)(d))" and after "special constable" insert "appointed for the area of that force and a police staff member serving in that force;".]

Withdrawn and discontinued complaints

15. - (1) If an appropriate authority receives from a complainant notification in writing signed by him or by his solicitor or other authorised agent on his behalf to the effect either–
    (a) that he withdraws the complaint, or
    (b) that he does not wish any further steps to be taken in consequence of the complaint,
then the appropriate authority shall forthwith record the withdrawal or the fact that the complainant does not wish any further steps to be taken, as the case may be, and subject to the following provisions of this regulation, the provisions of Part 2 of the 2002 Act shall cease to apply in respect of that complaint.

(2) Where a complainant gives such notification as is mentioned in paragraph (1) to the Commission but, so far as is apparent to the Commission, has not sent that notification to the appropriate authority, then–
    (a) the Commission shall send a copy of the notification to the appropriate authority;

    (b) that appropriate authority shall record the withdrawal or the fact that the complainant does not wish any further steps to be taken, as the case may be; and

    (c) subject to the following provisions of this regulation, the provisions of Part 2 of the 2002 Act shall cease to apply in respect of that complaint.

(3) Where a complainant gives such notification as is mentioned in paragraph (1) to an appropriate authority, or where the appropriate authority receives a copy of a notification under paragraph (2), and it relates to a complaint–

    (a) which was referred to the Commission under paragraph 4(1) of Schedule 3 to the 2002 Act and which has not been referred back to the appropriate authority under paragraph 5(2) of that Schedule;

    (b) which the appropriate authority knows is currently the subject of an appeal to the Commission under paragraph 3, 9 or 25 of that Schedule; or

    (c) which was notified to the appropriate authority by the Commission under paragraph 2(1) of that Schedule,

then the appropriate authority shall notify the Commission that it has recorded the withdrawal of the complaint or the fact that the complainant does not wish any further steps to be taken, as the case may be.

(4) In a case falling within paragraph (3)(b) or (c), the appropriate authority shall also–

    (a) determine whether it is in the public interest for the complaint to be treated as a recordable conduct matter; and

    (b) notify the Commission of its determination and the reasons for that determination.

(5) In a case falling within paragraph (3)(a), the Commission shall determine whether it is in the public interest for the complaint to be treated as a recordable conduct matter, and shall notify the appropriate authority of its decision.

(6) Where a determination is made that a complaint is to be treated as a recordable conduct matter, then the provisions of Part 2 of Schedule 3 to the 2002 Act shall apply to that matter.

(7) Where a complainant gives such notification as is mentioned in paragraph (1) to an appropriate authority, or where the appropriate authority receives a copy of a notification under paragraph (2), and that notification relates to a complaint which does not fall within any of sub-paragraphs (a) to (c) of paragraph (3), then–

    (a) the appropriate authority shall determine whether it is in the public interest for the complaint to be treated as a recordable conduct matter;

    (b) if the complaint is to be treated as a recordable conduct matter, the provisions of Part 2 of Schedule 3 to the 2002 Act shall apply to that matter;

    (c) if the complaint is not to be treated as a recordable conduct matter, the provisions of Part 2 of the 2002 Act shall cease to apply in respect of that complaint.

(8) In a case where–

    (a) a complaint has been subjected to an investigation by the appropriate authority on its own behalf;

    (b) the complaint is currently subject to an appeal to the Commission under paragraph 25 of Schedule 3 to the Act; and

    (c) the appropriate authority has notified the Commission under paragraph (4)(b) that it has determined that the complaint is not to be treated as a recordable conduct matter,

the Commission shall consider whether it is in the public interest for that determination to be reversed, and if so it shall instruct the appropriate authority to reverse the decision.

(9) Where a complainant indicates that he wishes to withdraw the complaint or that he does not wish any further steps to be taken in consequence of the complaint, but he fails to provide a notification to that effect in writing signed by him or on his behalf, then–

    (a) in the case of an indication received by the appropriate authority, the authority shall take the steps set out in paragraph (10);

(b) in the case of an indication received by the Commission, the Commission shall refer the matter to the appropriate authority which shall take the steps set out in paragraph (10).

(10) Those steps are–

    (a) the appropriate authority shall write to the complainant to ascertain whether he wishes to withdraw his complaint or does not wish any further steps to be taken in consequence of the complaint;

    (b) if the complainant indicates that he wishes to withdraw his complaint or does not wish any further steps to be taken in consequence of the complaint, or if he fails to reply within 21 days, the appropriate authority shall treat the indication as though it had been received in writing signed by the complainant;

    (c) if the complainant indicates that he does not wish to withdraw his complaint, or that he does wish further steps to be taken in consequence of the complaint, the appropriate authority shall start or resume the investigation as the case may be.

(11) The appropriate authority shall notify the person complained against if–

    (a) it records the withdrawal of a complaint or the fact that the complainant does not wish any further steps to be taken;

    (b) it determines that a complaint shall be treated as a recordable conduct matter;

    (c) the Commission determines that a complaint shall be treated as a recordable conduct matter;

    (d) the Commission instructs it to reverse a decision not to treat a complaint as a recordable conduct matter;

    (e) the provisions of Part 2 of the 2002 Act cease to apply in respect of a complaint.

(12) But nothing in paragraph (11) shall require the appropriate authority to make a notification if it has previously decided under regulation 14(3) not to notify the person complained against of the complaint because it is of the opinion that that might prejudice any criminal investigation or pending proceedings or would be contrary to the public interest.

Circumstances in which an investigation or other procedure may be suspended

16. - (1) The Commission may suspend any investigation or other procedure under Part 2 of the 2002 Act which would, if it were to continue, prejudice any criminal proceedings.

(2) An appropriate authority may, subject to paragraph (3), suspend any investigation or other procedure under Part 2 of the 2002 Act which would, if it were to continue, prejudice any criminal investigation or proceedings.

(3) The Commission may direct that any investigation or other procedure under Part 2 of the 2002 Act which is liable to be suspended under paragraph (2) shall continue if it is of the view that it is in the public interest to make such a direction.

(4) The Commission shall consult the appropriate authority before making such a direction.

Resumption of investigation after criminal proceedings

17. - (1) Where the whole or part of the investigation of a complaint has been suspended until the conclusion of criminal proceedings, and the complainant has failed to indicate after the conclusion of those proceedings that he wishes the investigation to start or be resumed, the Commission or, as the case may be, appropriate authority shall take the steps set out in paragraph (2).

(2) The Commission or appropriate authority shall take all reasonable steps to contact the complainant to ascertain whether he wants the investigation to start or be resumed as the case may be.

(3) If the complainant indicates that he does wish the investigation to start or be resumed, the Commission or appropriate authority shall start or resume the investigation as the case may be.

(4) If the complainant indicates that he does not want the investigation to start or be resumed, or if he fails to reply within 21 days to a letter sent to him by the Commission or appropriate

authority, the Commission or appropriate authority as the case may be shall determine whether it is in the public interest for the complaint to be treated as a recordable conduct matter.

(5) If the Commission or appropriate authority determines that it is not in the public interest for the complaint to be treated as a recordable conduct matter, the provisions of Part 2 of the 2002 Act shall cease to apply to the complaint.

(6) If the Commission or appropriate authority determines that it is in the public interest for the complaint to be treated as a recordable conduct matter, the provisions of Part 2 of Schedule 3 to the 2002 Act shall apply to the matter.

(7) The Commission or appropriate authority shall notify the person complained against if paragraph (5) or (6) applies.

(8) But nothing in paragraph (7) shall require the Commission or appropriate authority to make a notification if it is of the opinion that that might prejudice any criminal investigation or pending proceedings or would be contrary to the public interest.

Appointment of persons to carry out investigations

18. - (1) No person shall be appointed to carry out an investigation under paragraph 16, 17 or 18 of Schedule 3 to the 2002 Act (investigation by the appropriate authority on its own behalf, supervised and managed investigations)–

(a) unless he has an appropriate level of knowledge, skills and experience to plan and conduct the investigation and to manage the resources that will be required during that process;

(b) if he has any social, financial or other connection, whether or not within the work environment, with the person whose conduct is being investigated which could, on an objective appraisal of the material facts, give rise to a legitimate fear as to whether that investigation can be carried out impartially;

(c) if he works, directly or indirectly, under the management of the person whose conduct is being investigated;

(d) in a case where the person who is the subject of the investigation is a senior police officer and is a member of a force other than the metropolitan police force, if he is a member of the same force as that person.

(2) No member of a police force shall be appointed to carry out an investigation under paragraph 16, 17 or 18 of Schedule 3 to the 2002 Act in a case where the person who is the subject of the investigation is also a member of a police force, unless the officer so appointed is–

(a) of at least the rank of sergeant;

(b) if the officer under investigation is a superintendent or chief superintendent and–

(i) if the investigating officer is a member of the City of London or metropolitan police force, of at least the rank of commander;

(ii) if the investigating officer is a member of any other force, of at least the rank of assistant chief constable;

(c) of at least the same rank as the officer concerned.

(3) In this regulation–

(a) " senior police officer" means a chief constable, a deputy chief constable or an assistant chief constable or, in the case of the City of London police force, a member of that force of or above the rank of commander;

(b) any reference (other than in paragraph (1)(d)) to a member of a police force shall include a reference to a special constable;

(c) any reference to an officer of a particular rank shall include a reference to a special constable of an equivalent rank or grade.

Combining and splitting investigations

19. - (1) An appropriate authority which is carrying out an investigation on its own behalf may–

(a) combine that investigation with another such investigation; or

(b) split that investigation into two or more such separate investigations if it considers that it is more efficient and effective, or is otherwise in the public interest, to do so.

(2) Subject to paragraph (3), where the Commission is supervising, managing or carrying out an investigation, it may–

    (a) combine that investigation with another investigation; or

    (b) split that investigation into two or more separate investigations,

    if it considers that it is more efficient and effective, or is otherwise in the public interest, to do so.

(3) The Commission shall not take any action under paragraph (2) in relation to a supervised or managed investigation except after consultation with the appropriate authority.

(4) Nothing in this regulation shall prevent the Commission from determining that–

    (a) where an investigation is split into two or more separate investigations, those investigations may take different forms;

    (b) two or more separate investigations which take different forms (including an investigation being carried out by the appropriate authority on its own behalf) may be combined into a single investigation.

Relinquishing the Commission's supervision or management of an investigation

20. - (1) This regulation applies where the Commission–

    (a) relinquishes the management of an investigation in favour of a supervised investigation or an investigation by the appropriate authority on its own behalf, or

    (b) relinquishes the supervision of an investigation in favour of an investigation by the appropriate authority on its own behalf.

(2) Where this regulation applies, the Commission–

    (a) shall notify the appropriate authority, the complainant [, any interested person within the meaning of section 21 of the 2002 Act][14] and the person complained against of its decision, and the reasons for that decision; and

    (b) shall send to the appropriate authority any documentation and evidence gathered during its investigations as will assist the appropriate authority to carry out its functions under Part 2 of the 2002 Act.

(3) But nothing in paragraph (2)(a) shall require the Commission to make a notification to the person complained against if it is of the opinion that that might prejudice any criminal investigation or pending proceedings or would be contrary to the public interest.

Complaints against a person who has subsequently ceased to serve with the police

21. - Where a complaint or conduct matter relates to the conduct of a person who has ceased to be a person serving with the police since the time of the conduct, then Part 2 of the 2002 Act shall apply in relation to such a person as if it did not include any requirement for an appropriate authority to determine whether disciplinary proceedings should be brought against a person whose conduct is the subject-matter of a report.

Complaints against a person whose identity is unascertained

22. - (1) Where a complaint or conduct matter relates to the conduct of a person whose identity is unascertained at the time at which the complaint is made or the conduct matter is recorded, or whose identity is not ascertained during or subsequent to, the investigation of the complaint or recordable conduct matter, then Part 2 of the 2002 Act and these Regulations shall apply in relation to such a person as if it did not include–

    (a) any requirement for the person complained against to be given a notification or an opportunity to make representations;

---

[14] Words inserted by SI 2006/1406, reg 2(8), 22 June 2006.

    (b) any requirement for the Commission or the appropriate authority to determine whether a criminal offence may have been committed by the person whose conduct has been the subject-matter of an investigation, or to take any action in relation to such a determination;

    (c) any requirement for an appropriate authority to determine whether disciplinary proceedings should be brought against a person whose conduct is the subject-matter of a report.

(2) Where the identity of such a person is subsequently ascertained, the Commission and appropriate authority shall take such action in accordance with Part 2 of the 2002 Act and these Regulations as they see fit, regardless of any previous action taken under that Part as modified above.

Notification of actions and decisions

23. - (1) So far as not covered by paragraph 23(9) and (10) and paragraph 25(10) and (11) of Schedule 3 to the 2002 Act (notifications by the Commission in relation to recommending disciplinary proceedings), where the Commission takes any action or decisions in consequence of it having received a memorandum under paragraph 23(7) or paragraph 25(3) of that Schedule, it shall notify such action or decisions, together with an explanation of its reasons for having taken them, to–

    (a) the appropriate authority;

    (b) the complainant and any other interested person within the meaning of section 21(5) of the 2002 Act;

    (c) subject to paragraph (3), the person complained against.

(2) Without prejudice to the generality of paragraph (1), the Commission shall include in any notification under that paragraph a statement as to whether it intends to bring and conduct, or otherwise participate or intervene in, any disciplinary proceedings.

(3) The Commission may decide not to give such a notification and explanation to the person complained against if it is of the opinion that that notification might prejudice any criminal investigation, pending proceedings, or review of the complaint.

Keeping of records

24. - Every police authority and chief officer shall keep records, in such form as the Commission shall determine, of–

    (a) every complaint and purported complaint that is made to it or him;

    (b) every conduct matter recorded by it or him under paragraph 10(3) of Schedule 3 to the 2002 Act;

    [(ab) every DSI matter recorded by it or him under paragraph 14A[15] of Schedule 3 to the 2002 Act;][16]

    (c) every exercise of a power or performance of a duty under Part 2 of the 2002 Act.

Register to be kept by the Commission

25. - (1) The Commission shall establish and maintain a register of all information supplied to it by a police authority or chief officer under Part 2 of the 2002 Act.

(2) Subject to paragraph (3), the Commission may publish or otherwise disclose to any person any information held on the register provided that the publication or disclosure is necessary for or conducive to the purpose of–

    (a) learning lessons from the handling of, or demonstrating the thoroughness and effectiveness of local resolutions, of investigations by the Commission, or of managed or supervised investigations;

---

[15] Paragraph 14A was inserted by s 160 of, and para 12 of Sch 12 to, the Serious Organised Crime and Police Act 2005.

[16] Added by SI 2006/1406, reg 2(9), 22 June 2006.

(b) raising public awareness of the complaints system; or

(c) improving the complaints system.

(3) Information may not be published or disclosed in circumstances where in the opinion of the Commission the non-disclosure of information is necessary for the purposes mentioned in regulation 12(1)(a) and (b).

Delegation of powers and duties by chief officer

26. - (1) Subject to paragraphs (3) and (4), a chief officer may delegate all or any of the powers or duties conferred or imposed on him by or under Part 2 of the 2002 Act to such an officer as is mentioned in paragraph (2).

(2) Those powers or duties may be delegated–

(a) in the City of London police force, to an assistant commissioner or a commander of that force;

(b) in the metropolitan police force, to an assistant commissioner, a deputy assistant commissioner or a commander of that force;

(c) in any other police force, to a deputy chief constable or an assistant chief constable of that force.

(3) A chief officer may delegate all or any of his powers or duties in relation to the local resolution of complaints under Part 2 of the 2002 Act to any person serving with the police.

(4) A chief officer shall not, in any particular case, delegate any power or duty under paragraph (1) to an officer who has acted as investigating officer in that case, or who has acted in relation to it in pursuance of an attempt to resolve it by way of local resolution.

[. . .]¹⁷

Manner and time limits of notifications

27. - (1) Any notification to be given under these Regulations shall–

(a) unless otherwise specified in these Regulations or determined in guidance issued by the Commission, be given in writing;

(b) unless otherwise specified in these Regulations, be made within such period as the Commission may determine in guidance.

(2) No time limit mentioned in these Regulations or determined by the Commission shall apply in any case where exceptional circumstances prevent that time limit being complied with.

Application to contracted-out staff

28. - (1) Subject to paragraph (2), Part 2 of the 2002 Act and these Regulations shall apply in relation to a detention officer or escort officer as they apply in relation to a person serving with the police.

(2) Paragraph (1) applies only insofar as a complaint relates to, or another instance of misconduct involves, the carrying out of functions for the purposes of which any power or duty is conferred or imposed by a designation under section 39(2) of the 2002 Act (police powers for contracted-out staff).

(3) References in Part 2 of the 2002 Act to a person who is under the direction and control of a chief officer shall include references to a detention officer or escort officer who has been so designated by that chief officer.

(4) In this regulation, "detention officer" means a person designated under section 39(2)(a) of the 2002 Act and "escort officer" means a person designated under section 39(2)(b) of that Act.

29. - [. . .]¹⁸

Disciplinary proceedings for police staff

---

¹⁷ Revoked by SI 2006/1406, reg 2(10), 22 June 2006.
¹⁸ Revoked by SI 2006/594, Sch 1, para 43(1), 1 April 2006.

30. - In relation to a person serving with the police who is not a member of a police force or a special constable, for the purposes of Part 2 of the 2002 Act, "disciplinary proceedings" means any proceedings or management process during which the conduct of such a person is considered in order to determine whether a sanction or punitive measure is to be imposed against him in relation to that conduct.

Hazel Blears
Minister of State
Home Office
8th March 2004

EXPLANATORY NOTE

(This Note is Not Part of the Regulations)

These Regulations set out the process to be followed under Part 2 of the Police Reform Act 2002 ("the Act") in relation to complaints against persons serving with the police and misconduct by such persons.

Regulation 2 sets out descriptions of complaint which must be referred by the appropriate authority (the police authority, in the case of a complaint against an officer above the rank of chief superintendent, or the chief officer in any other case) to the Independent Police Complaints Commission ("the Commission").

Regulation 3 prescribes categories of complaints which the Commission may permit an appropriate authority to handle in whatever manner the authority thinks fit. These categories include complaints that were unreported for over a year old, complaints that are anonymous, vexatious, repetitious or have already been investigated, and complaints that cannot reasonably practicably be investigated.

Regulation 4 sets out procedural requirements which are to be met when complaints are subjected to a local resolution procedure.

Regulation 5 sets out descriptions of conduct by persons serving with the police which must be recorded by an appropriate authority and referred to the Commission. These include assaults causing actual bodily harm, serious corruption, misconduct aggravated by discriminatory behaviour, serious arrestable offences, and other grave or exceptional conduct.

Regulation 6 allows the Commission to specify the requirements which it can impose on a person conducting an investigation which is supervised by the Commission.

Regulation 7 sets out descriptions of complaints or conduct matters into which an investigation can be discontinued by order of the Commission. These include investigations where the complainant refuses to co-operate or agrees to the local resolution procedure, and complaints that are vexatious, repetitious or cannot reasonably practicably be investigated. The procedural consequences of a discontinuance are also set out.

Regulations 8 to 10 set out the procedures to be followed if an appeal is made to the Commission against a failure to record a complaint, against the conduct of the local resolution of a complaint or in relation to the investigation of a complaint.

Regulation 11 sets out the duties imposed on the Commission and on appropriate authorities to keep complainants and other interested persons informed about the investigation of a complaint or conduct matter.

Regulation 12 sets out the exceptions to those duties.

Regulation 13 defines the word "relative" for the purposes of identifying the persons who are to be regarded as interested persons and accordingly must, if they have indicated that they so consent, be kept informed about the handling of a complaint or conduct matter.

Regulation 14 requires an appropriate authority to supply a complainant with a copy of the record made of his complaint, and (subject to exceptions) to supply to a person complained against a copy of that complaint.

Regulation 15 sets out the procedure to be followed if a complainant withdraws his complaint or indicates that he does not wish any further steps to be taken as a result of his complaint. This procedure includes a requirement on the appropriate authority or Commission to consider whether the subject-matter of the complaint should be treated as a recordable conduct matter, in which case it can continue to be subject to an investigation.

Regulation 16 allows the Commission to direct an investigation to be suspended while another investigation or procedure takes place.

Regulation 17 sets out the procedure to be followed if the investigation of a complaint has been suspended until the conclusion of criminal proceedings. In these circumstances an appropriate authority need not resume the investigation if the complainant fails to indicate that he wishes this to happen.

Regulation 18 imposes requirements and restrictions on the categories of persons who may carry out investigations of complaints and conduct matters.

Regulation 19 provides for the combining of more than one investigation into a single investigation, and for the splitting of a single investigation into two or more separate investigations.

Regulation 20 sets out the procedure to be followed if the Commission relinquishes control of an investigation that it has been supervising or managing.

Regulation 21 explains how the Regulations apply if a complaint is made against a person who subsequently ceases to serve with the police.

Regulation 22 explains how the Regulations apply if a complaint is made against a person serving with the police whose identity is not ascertained.

Regulation 23 imposes requirements on the Commission to inform interested parties of any steps it takes in relation to disciplinary proceedings or criminal prosecution, when an investigation is completed.

Regulation 24 requires police authorities and chief officers to keep records relating to complaints and conduct matters.

Regulation 25 requires the Commission to keep a register of the information which it receives from police authorities and chief officers, and sets out the circumstances in which information stored on that register can be disclosed.

Regulation 26 gives chief officers power to delegate functions conferred on them by the Act. This is without prejudice to the power of a police chief at common law to delegate powers to suitable officers for whom the chief officer is answerable.

Regulation 27 provides that the timescale and manner in which various notifications must be made under the Act can be determined by the Commission in guidance.

Regulation 28 provides that Part 2 of the Act and these Regulations apply to contracted-out staff designated as detention officers or escort officers in the carrying out of their functions.

Regulation 29 provides that Part 2 of the Act and these Regulations apply to members of the National Criminal Intelligence Service and the National Crime Squad.

Regulation 30 identifies the proceedings which are to constitute disciplinary proceedings for police staff for the purposes of the definition of "disciplinary proceedings" in section 29(1) of the Act.

Notes:

[1] 2002 c. 30.

[2] 1996 c. 16; section 63(3)(d) was inserted by section 107 of, and paragraph 17 of Schedule 7 to, the 2002 Act.

[3] 1997 c. 50; sections 39(1) and 83(1) to (2A) were substituted by section 25 of the 2002 Act.

[4] 1971 c. 80.

[. . .]

The Police Reform Act 2002, Schedule 3, Part 1

SCHEDULE 3
HANDLING OF COMPLAINTS AND CONDUCT MATTERS ETC.

PART 1
HANDLING OF COMPLAINTS

1 Duties to preserve evidence relating to complaints

(1) Where a complaint is made about the conduct of a chief officer, it shall be the duty of the police authority maintaining his force to secure that all such steps as are appropriate for the purposes of Part 2 of this Act are taken, both initially and from time to time after that, for obtaining and preserving evidence relating to the conduct complained of.

(2) Where—

    (a) a complaint is made to a chief officer about the conduct of a person under his direction and control, or

    (b) a chief officer becomes aware that a complaint about the conduct of a person under his direction or control has been made to the Commission or to a police authority,

the chief officer shall take all such steps as appear to him to be appropriate for the purposes of Part 2 of this Act for obtaining and preserving evidence relating to the conduct complained of.

(3) The chief officer's duty under sub-paragraph (2) must be performed as soon as practicable after the complaint is made or, as the case may be, he becomes aware of it.

(4) After that, he shall be under a duty, until he is satisfied that it is no longer necessary to do so, to continue to take the steps from time to time appearing to him to be appropriate for the purposes of Part 2 of this Act for obtaining and preserving evidence relating to the conduct complained of.

(5) It shall be the duty of a police authority to comply with all such directions as may be given to it by the Commission in relation to the performance of its duty under sub-paragraph (1).

(6) It shall be the duty of a chief officer to take all such specific steps for obtaining or preserving evidence relating to any conduct that is the subject-matter of a complaint as he may be directed to take for the purposes of this paragraph by the police authority maintaining his force or by the Commission.

2 Initial handling and recording of complaints

(1) Where a complaint is made to the Commission—

    (a) it shall ascertain whether the complainant is content for the police authority or chief officer who is the appropriate authority to be notified of the complaint; and

    (b) it shall give notification of the complaint to the appropriate authority if, and only if, the complainant is so content.

(2) Where a complaint is made to a police authority, it shall—

    (a) determine whether or not it is itself the appropriate authority; and

    (b) if it determines that it is not, give notification of the complaint to the person who is.

(3) Where a complaint is made to a chief officer, he shall—
   (a) determine whether or not he is himself the appropriate authority; and
   (b) if he determines that he is not, give notification of the complaint to the person who is.

(4) Where the Commission—
   (a) is prevented by sub-paragraph (1)(b) from notifying any complaint to the appropriate authority, and
   (b) considers that it is in the public interest for the subject-matter of the complaint to be brought to the attention of the appropriate authority and recorded under paragraph 11,
   the Commission may bring that matter to the appropriate authority's attention under that paragraph as if it were a recordable conduct matter, and (if it does so) the following provisions of this Schedule shall have effect accordingly as if it were such a matter.

(5) Where the Commission, a police authority or a chief officer gives notification of a complaint under any of sub-paragraphs (1) to (3) or the Commission brings any matter to the appropriate authority's attention under sub-paragraph (4), the person who gave the notification or, as the case may be, the Commission shall notify the complainant—
   (a) that the notification has been given and of what it contained; or
   (b) that the matter has been brought to the appropriate authority's attention to be dealt with otherwise than as a complaint.

(6) Where—
   (a) a police authority determines, in the case of any complaint made to the authority, that it is itself the appropriate authority,
   (b) a chief officer determines, in the case of any complaint made to that chief officer, that he is himself the appropriate authority, or
   (c) a complaint is notified to a police authority or chief officer under this paragraph,
   the authority or chief officer shall record the complaint.

(7) Nothing in this paragraph shall require the notification or recording by any person of any complaint about any conduct if—
   (a) that person is satisfied that the subject-matter of the complaint has been, or is already being, dealt with by means of criminal or disciplinary proceedings against the person whose conduct it was; or
   (b) the complaint has been withdrawn.

3 Failures to notify or record a complaint

(1) This paragraph applies where anything which is or purports to be a complaint in relation to which paragraph 2 has effect is received by a police authority or chief officer (whether in consequence of having been made directly or of a notification under that paragraph).

(2) If the police authority or chief officer decides not to take action under paragraph 2 for notifying or recording the whole or any part of what has been received, the authority or chief officer shall notify the complainant of the following matters—
   (a) the decision to take no action and, if that decision relates to only part of what was received, the part in question;
   (b) the grounds on which the decision was made; and
   (c) that complainant's right to appeal against that decision under this paragraph.

(3) The complainant shall have a right of appeal to the Commission against any failure by the police authority or chief officer to make a determination under paragraph 2 or to notify or record anything under that paragraph.

(4) On an appeal under this paragraph, the Commission shall—
   (a) determine whether any action under paragraph 2 should have been taken in the case in question; and
   (b) if the Commission finds in the complainant's favour, give such directions as the Commission considers appropriate to the police authority or chief officer as to the action to be taken for making a determination, or for notifying or recording what was received;

and it shall be the duty of a police authority or chief officer to comply with any directions given under paragraph (b).

(5) Directions under sub-paragraph (4)(b) may require action taken in pursuance of the directions to be treated as taken in accordance with any such provision of paragraph 2 as may be specified in the direction.

(6) The Commission—

    (a) shall give notification both to the police authority or, as the case may be, the chief officer and to the complainant of any determination made by it under this paragraph; and

    (b) shall give notification to the complainant of any direction given by it under this paragraph to the police authority or chief officer.

(7) The Secretary of State may by regulations make provision—

    (a) for the form and manner in which appeals under this paragraph are to be brought;

    (b) for the period within which any such appeal must be brought; and

    (c) for the procedure to be followed by the Commission when dealing with or disposing of any such appeal.

4 Reference of complaints to the Commission

(1) It shall be the duty of the appropriate authority to refer a complaint to the Commission if—

    (a) the complaint is one alleging that the conduct complained of has resulted in death or serious injury;

    (b) the complaint is of a description specified for the purposes of this sub-paragraph in regulations made by the Secretary of State; or

    (c) the Commission notifies the appropriate authority that it requires the complaint in question to be referred to the Commission for its consideration.

(2) In a case where there is no obligation under sub-paragraph (1) to make a reference, the appropriate authority may refer a complaint to the Commission if that authority considers that it would be appropriate to do so so by reason of—

    (a) the gravity of the subject-matter of the complaint; or

    (b) any exceptional circumstances.

(3) In a case in which a reference under sub-paragraph (1) or (2) is neither made nor required to be made, a police authority may refer a complaint to the Commission if—

    (a) it is one in relation to which the chief officer of police of the police force maintained by that authority is the appropriate authority; and

    (b) the police authority considers that it would be appropriate to do so reason of—

        (i) the gravity of the subject-matter of the complaint; or

        (ii) any exceptional circumstances.

(4) Where there is an obligation under this paragraph to refer a complaint to the Commission, it must be so referred within such period as may be provided for by regulations made by the Secretary of State.

(5) Subject to sub-paragraph (7), the following powers—

    (a) the power of the Commission by virtue of sub-paragraph (1)(c) to require a complaint to be referred to it, and

    (b) the power of a police authority or chief officer to refer a complaint to the Commission under sub-paragraph (2) or (3), shall each be exercisable at any time irrespective of whether the complaint is already being investigated by any person or has already been considered by the Commission.

(6) A police authority or chief officer which refers a complaint to the Commission under this paragraph shall give a notification of the making of the reference—

    (a) to the complainant, and

    (b) except in a case where it appears to that authority or chief officer that to do so might prejudice a possible future investigation of the complaint, to the person complained against.

(7) A complaint that has already been referred to the Commission under this paragraph on a previous occasion—

  (a) shall not be required to be referred again under this paragraph unless the Commission so directs; and

  (b) shall not be referred in exercise of any power conferred by this paragraph unless the Commission consents.

5 Duties of Commission on references under paragraph 4

(1) It shall be the duty of the Commission in the case of every complaint referred to it by a police authority or chief officer, to determine whether or not it is necessary for the complaint to be investigated.

(2) Where the Commission determines under this paragraph that it is not necessary for a complaint to be investigated, it may, if it thinks fit, refer the complaint back to the appropriate authority to be dealt with by that authority in accordance with paragraph 6.

(3) Where the Commission refers a complaint back under sub-paragraph (2), it shall give a notification of the making of the reference back—

  (a) to the complainant, and

  (b) except in a case where it appears to the Commission that to do so might prejudice a possible future investigation of the complaint, to the person complained against.

6 Handling of complaints by the appropriate authority

(1) This paragraph applies where a complaint has been recorded by the appropriate authority unless the complaint—

  (a) is one which has been, or must be, referred to the Commission under paragraph 4; and

  (b) is not for the time being either referred back to the authority under paragraph 5 or the subject of a determination under paragraph 15.

(2) Subject to paragraph 7, the appropriate authority shall determine whether or not the complaint is suitable for being subjected to local resolution, and—

  (a) if it determines that it is so suitable and the complainant consents, it shall make arrangements for it to be so subjected; and

  (b) in any other case, it shall make arrangements for the complaint to be investigated by that authority on its own behalf.

(3) A determination that a complaint is suitable for being subjected to local resolution shall not be made unless either—

  (a) the appropriate authority is satisfied that the conduct complained of (even if it were proved) would not justify the bringing of any criminal or disciplinary proceedings; or

  (b) the Commission, in a case falling within sub-paragraph (4), has approved the use of local resolution.

(4) The Commission may approve the use of local resolution in the case of any complaint if, on an application by the appropriate authority, the Commission is satisfied—

  (a) that the following two conditions are fulfilled—

    (i) that the conduct complained of (even if it were proved) would not justify the bringing of any criminal proceedings; and

    (ii) that any disciplinary proceedings the bringing of which would be justified in respect of that conduct (even if it were proved) would be unlikely to result in a dismissal [or the giving of a final written warning];[1]

  or

---

[1] Words substituted by the Criminal Justice and Immigration Act 2008 (CJIA), Sch 23, para 4, in force 1 December 2008, under the Criminal Justice and Immigration Act 2008 (Commencement No 4 and Saving Provision) Order 2008, SI 2008/2993, subject to savings specified at art 3.

    (b) that it will not be practicable (even if the complaint is thoroughly investigated) for either of the following to be brought—
        (i) criminal proceedings in respect of the conduct to which it relates that would be likely to result in a conviction; or
        (ii) disciplinary proceedings in respect of that conduct that would be likely to result in a dismissal [or the giving of a final written warning.][2]

(5) No more than one application may be made to the Commission for the purposes of sub-paragraph (4) in respect of the same complaint.

(6) Before a complainant can give his consent for the purposes of this paragraph to the local resolution of his complaint he must have been informed of his rights of appeal under paragraph 9.

(7) A consent given for the purposes of this paragraph shall not be capable of being withdrawn at any time after the procedure for the local resolution of the complaint has been begun.

7 Dispensation by the Commission from requirements of Schedule

(1) If, in a case in which paragraph 6 applies, the appropriate authority considers—
    (a) that it should handle the complaint otherwise than in accordance with this Schedule or should take no action in relation to it, and
    (b) that the complaint falls within a description of complaints specified in regulations made by the Secretary of State for the purposes of this paragraph,
the appropriate authority may apply to the Commission, in accordance with the regulations, for permission to handle the complaint in whatever manner (if any) that authority thinks fit.

(2) The appropriate authority shall notify the complainant about the making of the application under this paragraph.

(3) Where such an application is made to the Commission, it shall, in accordance with regulations made by the Secretary of State—
    (a) consider the application and determine whether to grant the permission applied for; and
    (b) notify its decision to the appropriate authority and the complainant.

(4) Where an application is made under this paragraph in respect of any complaint, the appropriate authority shall not, while the application is being considered by the Commission, take any action in accordance with the provisions of this Schedule (other than under paragraph 1) in relation to that complaint.

(5) Where the Commission gives permission under this paragraph to handle the complaint in whatever manner (if any) the appropriate authority thinks fit, the authority—
    (a) shall not be required by virtue of any of the provisions of this Schedule (other than paragraph 1) to take any action in relation to the complaint; but
    (b) may handle the complaint in whatever manner it thinks fit, or take no action in relation to the complaint, and for the purposes of handling the complaint may take any step that it could have taken, or would have been required to take, but for the permission.

(6) Where the Commission determines that no permission should be granted under this paragraph—
    (a) it shall refer the matter back to the appropriate authority for the making of a determination under paragraph 6(2); and
    (b) the authority shall then make that determination.

(7) No more than one application may be made to the Commission under this paragraph in respect of the same complaint.

---

[2] Ibid.

8 Local resolution of complaints

(1) The arrangements made by the appropriate authority for subjecting any complaint to local resolution may include the appointment of a person who—
   (a) is serving with the police, and
   (b) is under the direction and control of the chief officer of police of the relevant force, to secure the local resolution of the complaint.

(2) The Secretary of State may by regulations make provision—
   (a) for the different descriptions of procedures that are to be available for dealing with a complaint where it is decided it is to be subjected to local resolution;
   (b) for requiring a person complained against in a case in which the complaint is subjected to local resolution to be given an opportunity of commenting, in such manner as may be provided for in the regulations, on the complaint;
   (c) for requiring that, on the making of an application in accordance with the regulations, a record of the outcome of any procedure for the local resolution of any complaint is to be given to the complainant.

(3) A statement made by any person for the purposes of the local resolution of any complaint shall not be admissible in any subsequent criminal, civil or disciplinary proceedings except to the extent that it consists of an admission relating to a matter that has not been subjected to local resolution.

(4) If, after attempts have been made to resolve a complaint using local resolution, it appears to the appropriate authority—
   (a) that the resolution of the complaint in that manner is impossible, or
   (b) that the complaint is, for any other reason, not suitable for such resolution,
   it shall make arrangements for the complaint to be investigated by that authority on its own behalf.

(5) The local resolution of any complaint shall be discontinued if—
   (a) any arrangements are made under sub-paragraph (4);
   (b) the Commission notifies the appropriate authority that it requires the complaint to be referred to the Commission under paragraph 4; or (c) the complaint is so referred otherwise than in pursuance of such a notification.

(6) A person who has participated in any attempt to resolve a complaint using local resolution shall be disqualified for appointment under any provision of this Schedule to investigate that complaint, or to assist with the carrying out of the investigation of that complaint.

9 Appeals relating to local resolution

(1) Subject to sub-paragraph (2), a complainant whose complaint has been subjected to local resolution shall have a right of appeal to the Commission against the conduct of the local resolution of that complaint.

(2) The only matter that shall fall to be determined on an appeal under this paragraph is whether there have been any contraventions of the procedural requirements relating to the local resolution of the complaint.

(3) Where an appeal is brought under this paragraph, it shall be the duty of the Commission to give both—
   (a) the person complained against, and
   (b) the appropriate authority,
   an opportunity of making representations about the matters to which the appeal relates.

(4) On an appeal under this paragraph, the Commission shall determine whether there have been any contraventions of the procedural requirements relating to the local resolution of the complaint.

(5) Where the Commission finds in the complainant's favour on an appeal under this paragraph—
   (a) it shall give such directions as the Commission considers appropriate to the appropriate authority as to the future handling of the complaint; and

(b) it shall be the duty of the appropriate authority to comply with any directions given to it under this sub-paragraph.

(6) Where the Commission determines for the purposes of sub-paragraph (5) that the future handling of the complaint should include an investigation, paragraph 15 shall apply as it applies in the case of a determination mentioned in sub-paragraph (1) of that paragraph.

(7) The Commission—

    (a) shall give notification to the appropriate authority, to the complainant and to the person complained against of any determination made by it under this paragraph; and

    (b) shall give notification to the complainant and to the person complained against of any direction given by it under this paragraph to the appropriate authority.

(8) The Secretary of State may by regulations make provision—

    (a) for the form and manner in which appeals under this paragraph are to be brought;

    (b) for the period within which any such appeal must be brought; and

    (c) for the procedure to be followed by the Commission when dealing with or disposing of any such appeal.

Part 2
Handling of Conduct Matters

10 Conduct matters arising in civil proceedings

(1) This paragraph applies where—

    (a) a police authority or chief officer has received notification (whether or not under this paragraph) that civil proceedings relating to any matter have been brought by a member of the public against that authority or chief officer, or it otherwise appears to a police authority or chief officer that such proceedings are likely to be so brought; and

    (b) it appears to that authority or chief officer (whether at the time of the notification or at any time subsequently) that those proceedings involve or would involve a conduct matter.

(2) The authority or chief officer—

    (a) shall consider whether it or, as the case may be, he is the appropriate authority in relation to the conduct matter in question; and

    (b) if it or he is not, shall notify the person who is the appropriate authority about the proceedings, or the proposal to bring them, and about the circumstances that make it appear as mentioned in sub-paragraph (1)(b).

(3) Where a police authority or chief officer determines for the purposes of this paragraph that it or, as the case may be, he is the appropriate authority in relation to any conduct matter, it or he shall record that matter.

(4) Where the appropriate authority records any matter under this paragraph it—

    (a) shall first determine whether the matter is one which it is required to refer to the Commission under paragraph 13 or is one which it would be appropriate to so refer; and

    (b) if it is not required so to refer the matter and does not do so, may deal with the matter in such other manner (if any) as it may determine.

(5) Nothing in sub-paragraph (3) shall require the appropriate authority to record any conduct matter if it is satisfied that the matter has been, or is already being, dealt with by means of criminal or disciplinary proceedings against the person to whose conduct the matter relates.

(6) For the purposes of this paragraph civil proceedings involve a conduct matter if—

    (a) they relate to such a matter; or

    (b) they are proceedings that relate to a matter in relation to which a conduct matter, or evidence of a conduct matter, is or may be relevant. (7) The Secretary of State may by regulations provide for the times at which, or the periods within which, any requirement of this paragraph is to be complied with; and the period from which any such period is to run shall be such time as may be specified in those regulations or as may be determined in a manner set out in the regulations.

11 Recording etc. of conduct matters in other cases

(1) Where—

    (a) a conduct matter comes (otherwise than as mentioned in paragraph 10) to the attention of the police authority or chief officer who is the appropriate authority in relation to that matter, and

    (b) it appears to the appropriate authority that the conduct involved in that matter falls within sub-paragraph (2),

    it shall be the duty of the appropriate authority to record that matter.

(2) Conduct falls within this sub-paragraph if (assuming it to have taken place)—

    (a) it appears to have resulted in the death of any person or in serious injury to any person;

    (b) a member of the public has been adversely affected by it; or

    (c) it is of a description specified for the purposes of this sub-paragraph in regulations made by the Secretary of State.

(3) Where the appropriate authority records any matter under this paragraph it—

    (a) shall first determine whether the matter is one which it is required to refer to the Commission under paragraph 13 or is one which it would be appropriate to so refer; and

    (b) if it is not required so to refer the matter and does not do so, may deal with the matter in such other manner (if any) as it may determine.

(4) Nothing in sub-paragraph (1) shall require the appropriate authority to record any conduct matter if it is satisfied that the matter has been, or is already being, dealt with by means of criminal or disciplinary proceedings against the person to whose conduct the matter relates.

(5) If it appears to the Commission—

    (a) that any matter that has come to its attention is a recordable conduct matter, but

    (b) that that matter has not been recorded by the appropriate authority,

    the Commission may direct the appropriate authority to record that matter; and it shall be the duty of that authority to comply with the direction.

12 Duties to preserve evidence relating to conduct matters

(1) Where a recordable conduct matter that relates to the conduct of a chief officer comes to the attention of the police authority maintaining his force, it shall be the duty of that authority to secure that all such steps as are appropriate for the purposes of Part 2 of this Act are taken, both initially and from time to time after that, for obtaining and preserving evidence relating to that matter.

(2) Where a chief officer becomes aware of any recordable conduct matter relating to the conduct of a person under his direction and control, it shall be his duty to take all such steps as appear to him to be appropriate for the purposes of Part 2 of this Act for obtaining and preserving evidence relating to that matter.

(3) The chief officer's duty under sub-paragraph (2) must be performed as soon as practicable after he becomes aware of the matter in question.

(4) After that, he shall be under a duty, until he is satisfied that it is no longer necessary to do so, to continue to take the steps from time to time appearing to him to be appropriate for the purposes of Part 2 of this Act for obtaining and preserving evidence relating to the matter.

(5) It shall be the duty of a police authority to comply with all such directions as may be given to it by the Commission in relation to the performance of any duty imposed on it by virtue of sub-paragraph (1).

(6) It shall be the duty of the chief officer to take all such specific steps for obtaining or preserving evidence relating to any recordable conduct matter as he may be directed to take for the purposes of this paragraph by the police authority maintaining his force or by the Commission.

13 Reference of conduct matters to the Commission

(1) It shall be the duty of a police authority or a chief officer to refer a recordable conduct matter to the Commission if, in a case (whether or not falling within paragraph 10) in which the authority or chief officer is the appropriate authority—

(a) that matter relates to any incident or circumstances in or in consequence of which any person has died or suffered serious injury;

(b) that matter is of a description specified for the purposes of this sub-paragraph in regulations made by the Secretary of State; or

(c) the Commission notifies the appropriate authority that it requires that matter to be referred to the Commission for its consideration.

(2) In any case where there is no obligation under sub-paragraph (1) to make a reference, the appropriate authority may refer a recordable conduct matter to the Commission if that authority considers that it would be appropriate to do so by reason of—

(a) the gravity of the matter; or

(b) any exceptional circumstances.

(3) In a case in which a reference under sub-paragraph (1) or (2) is neither made nor required to be made, a police authority maintaining any police force may refer any recordable conduct matter to the Commission if—

(a) it is one in relation to which the chief officer of police of that force is the appropriate authority; and

(b) the police authority considers that it would be appropriate to do so by reason of—

(i) the gravity of the matter; or

(ii) any exceptional circumstances.

(4) Where there is an obligation under this paragraph to refer any matter to the Commission, it must be so referred within such period as may be provided for by regulations made by the Secretary of State.

(5) Subject to sub-paragraph (7), the following powers—

(a) the power of the Commission by virtue of sub-paragraph (1)(c) to require a matter to be referred to it, and

(b) the power of a police authority or chief officer to refer any matter to the Commission under sub-paragraph (2) or (3),

shall each be exercisable at any time irrespective of whether the matter is already being investigated by any person or has already been considered by the Commission.

(6) Where—

(a) a police authority or chief officer refers a matter to the Commission under this paragraph, and

(b) that authority or chief officer does not consider that to do so might prejudice a possible future investigation of that matter,

that authority or chief officer shall give a notification of the making of the reference to the person to whose conduct that matter relates.

(7) A matter that has already been referred to the Commission under this paragraph on a previous occasion—

(a) shall not be required to be referred again under this paragraph unless the Commission so directs; and

(b) shall not be referred in exercise of any power conferred by this paragraph unless the Commission consents.

14 Duties of Commission on references under paragraph 13

(1) It shall be the duty of the Commission, in the case of every recordable conduct matter referred to it by a police authority or chief officer under paragraph 13, to determine whether or not it is necessary for the matter to be investigated.

(2) Where the Commission determines under this paragraph that it is not necessary for a record-able conduct matter to be investigated, it may if it thinks fit refer the matter back to the appropriate authority to be dealt with by that authority in such manner (if any) as that authority may determine.

(3) Where—
  (a) the Commission refers a matter back to the appropriate authority under this paragraph, and
  (b) the Commission does not consider that to do so might prejudice a possible future investiga-tion of that matter,
  the Commission shall give a notification of the making of the reference to the person to whose conduct that matter relates.

[14A Duty to record DSI matters

(1) Where a DSI matter comes to the attention of the police authority or chief officer who is the appropriate authority in relation to that matter, it shall be the duty of the appropriate authority to record that matter.

(2) If it appears to the Commission—
  (a) that any matter that has come to its attention is a DSI matter, but
  (b) that that matter has not been recorded by the appropriate authority,
  the Commission may direct the appropriate authority to record that matter; and it shall be the duty of that authority to comply with the direction.

14B Duty to preserve evidence relating to DSI matters

(1) Where—
  (a) a DSI matter comes to the attention of a police authority, and
  (b) the relevant officer in relation to that matter is the chief officer of the force maintained by that authority,
  it shall be the duty of that authority to secure that all such steps as are appropriate for the purposes of Part 2 of this Act are taken, both initially and from time to time after that, for obtaining and preserving evidence relating to that matter.

(2) Where—
  (a) a chief officer becomes aware of a DSI matter, and
  (b) the relevant officer in relation to that matter is a person under his direction and control,
  it shall be his duty to take all such steps as appear to him to be appropriate for the purposes of Part 2 of this Act for obtaining and preserving evidence relating to that matter.

(3) The chief officer's duty under sub-paragraph (2) must be performed as soon as practicable after he becomes aware of the matter in question.

(4) After that, he shall be under a duty, until he is satisfied that it is no longer necessary to do so, to continue to take the steps from time to time appearing to him to be appropriate for the purposes of Part 2 of this Act for obtaining and preserving evidence relating to the matter.

(5) It shall be the duty of a police authority to comply with all such directions as may be given to it by the Commission in relation to the performance of any duty imposed on it by virtue of sub-paragraph (1).

(6) It shall be the duty of the chief officer to take all such specific steps for obtaining or preserving evidence relating to any DSI matter as he may be directed to take for the purposes of this paragraph by the police authority maintaining his force or by the Commission.

14C Reference of DSI matters to the Commission

(1) It shall be the duty of the appropriate authority to refer a DSI matter to the Commission.

(2) The appropriate authority must do so within such period as may be provided for by regulations made by the Secretary of State.

(3) A matter that has already been referred to the Commission under this paragraph on a previous occasion shall not be required to be referred again under this paragraph unless the Commission so directs.

14D Duties of Commission on references under paragraph 14C

(1) It shall be the duty of the Commission, in the case of every DSI matter referred to it by a police authority or a chief officer, to determine whether or not it is necessary for the matter to be investigated.
(2) Where the Commission determines under this paragraph that it is not necessary for a DSI matter to be investigated, it may if it thinks fit refer the matter back to the appropriate authority to be dealt with by that authority in such manner (if any) as that authority may determine.][3]

PART 3

INVESTIGATIONS AND SUBSEQUENT PROCEEDINGS

15 Power of the Commission to determine the form of an investigation

(1) This paragraph applies where—
  (a) a complaint [,recordable conduct matter or DSI matter][4] is referred to the Commission; and
  (b) the Commission determines that it is necessary for the complaint or matter to be investigated.
(2) It shall be the duty of the Commission to determine the form which the investigation should take.
(3) In making a determination under sub-paragraph (2) the Commission shall have regard to the following factors—
  (a) the seriousness of the case; and
  (b) the public interest.
(4) The only forms which the investigation may take in accordance with a determination made under this paragraph are—
  (a) an investigation by the appropriate authority on its own behalf;
  (b) an investigation by that authority under the supervision of the Commission;
  (c) an investigation by that authority under the management of the Commission;
  (d) an investigation by the Commission.
(5) The Commission may at any time make a further determination under this paragraph to replace an earlier one.
(6) Where a determination under this paragraph replaces an earlier determination under this paragraph, or relates to a complaint or matter in relation to which the appropriate authority has already begun an investigation on its own behalf, the Commission may give—
  (a) the appropriate authority, and
  (b) any person previously appointed to carry out the investigation,
  such directions as it considers appropriate for the purpose of giving effect to the new determination.
(7) It shall be the duty of a person to whom a direction is given under sub-paragraph (6) to comply with it.

---

[3] Inserted by the Serious Organised Crime and Police Act 2005 (SOCPA), Sch 12, para 12, in force 1 July 2005.
[4] Words substituted by SOCPA, Sch 12, para 13.

(8) The Commission shall notify the appropriate authority of any determination that it makes under this paragraph in relation to a particular complaint [,recordable conduct matter or DSI matter].⁵

16 Investigations by the appropriate authority on its own behalf

(1) This paragraph applies if the appropriate authority is required by virtue of—

  (a) any determination made by that authority under paragraph 6(2) (whether following the recording of a complaint or on a reference back under paragraph 5(2)) or under paragraph 8(4), or

  (b) any determination made by the Commission under paragraph 15,

  to make arrangements for a complaint [, recordable conduct matter or DSI matter]⁶ to be investigated by the appropriate authority on its own behalf.

(2) This paragraph also applies if—

  (a) a determination falls to be made by that authority under paragraph 10(4)(b), 11(3)(b) or 14(2) in relation to any recordable conduct matter [or under paragraph 14D(2) in relation to any DSI matter];⁷ and

  (b) the appropriate authority determine that it is necessary for the matter to be investigated by the authority on its own behalf.

(3) Subject to sub-paragraph (4) [or (5)],⁸ it shall be the duty of the appropriate authority to appoint—

  (a) a person serving with the police (whether under the direction and control of the chief officer of police of the relevant force or of the chief officer of another force), [. . .]⁹

  [(b) a member of the staff of the Serious Organised Crime Agency,[or]¹⁰]¹¹

  [(c) a member of the staff of the National Policing Improvement Agency who is a constable,]¹²

  to investigate the complaint or matter.

(4) The person appointed under this paragraph to investigate any complaint or [conduct matter]¹³—

  (a) in the case of an investigation relating to any conduct of a chief officer, must not be a person under that chief officer's direction and control; and

  (b) in the case of an investigation relating to any conduct of the Commissioner of Police of the Metropolis or of the Deputy Commissioner of Police of the Metropolis, must be the person nominated by the Secretary of State for appointment under this paragraph.

[(5) The person appointed under this paragraph to investigate any DSI matter—

  (a) in relation to which the relevant officer is a chief officer, must not be a person under that chief officer's direction and control;

  (b) in relation to which the relevant officer is the Commissioner of Police of the Metropolis or the Deputy Commissioner of Police of the Metropolis, must be the person nominated by the Secretary of State for appointment under this paragraph.]¹⁴

---

⁵ Ibid.

⁶ Words substituted by SOCPA, Sch 12, para 14(2).

⁷ Words inserted by SOCPA, Sch 12, para 14(3).

⁸ Words inserted by SOCPA, Sch 12, para 14(4).

⁹ Inserted by the Police and Justice Act 2006 (PJA), Sch 1(7), para 89(2), in force 1 April 2007.

¹⁰ Ibid.

¹¹ Substituted by SOCPA, Sch 2, para 11(2).

¹² Inserted by PJA, Sch 1(7), para 89(2).

¹³ Word substituted by SOCPA, Sch 12, para 14(5).

¹⁴ Inserted by SOCPA, Sch 12, para 14(6).

17 **Investigations supervised by the Commission**

(1) This paragraph applies where the Commission has determined that it should supervise the investigation by the appropriate authority of any complaint [, recordable conduct matter or DSI matter].[15]

(2) On being given notice of that determination, the appropriate authority shall, if it has not already done so, appoint—

(a) a person serving with the police (whether under the direction and control of the chief officer of police of the relevant force or of the chief officer of another force), [. . .][16]

[(b) a member of the staff of the Serious Organised Crime Agency,[or][17]][18]

[(c) a member of the staff of the National Policing Improvement Agency who is a constable,][19]

to investigate the complaint or matter.

(3) The Commission may require that no appointment is made under sub-paragraph (2) unless it has given notice to the appropriate authority that it approves the person whom that authority proposes to appoint.

(4) Where a person has already been appointed to investigate the complaint or matter, or is selected under this sub-paragraph for appointment, and the Commission is not satisfied with that person, the Commission may require the appropriate authority, as soon as reasonably practicable after being required to do so—

(a) to select another person falling within sub-paragraph (2)(a) [, (b) or (c)][20] to investigate the complaint or matter; and

(b) to notify the Commission of the person selected.

(5) Where a selection made in pursuance of a requirement under sub-paragraph (4) has been notified to the Commission, the appropriate authority shall appoint that person to investigate the complaint or matter if, but only if, the Commission notifies the authority that it approves the appointment of that person.

(6) A person appointed under this paragraph to investigate any complaint or [conduct matter][21]—

(a) in the case of an investigation relating to any conduct of a chief officer, must not be a person under that chief officer's direction and control; and

(b) in the case of an investigation relating to any conduct of the Commissioner of Police of the Metropolis or of the Deputy Commissioner of Police of the Metropolis, must be the person nominated by the Secretary of State for appointment under this paragraph.

[(6A) The person appointed under this paragraph to investigate any DSI matter—

(a) in relation to which the relevant officer is a chief officer, must not be a person under that chief officer's direction and control;

(b) in relation to which the relevant officer is the Commissioner of Police of the Metropolis or the Deputy Commissioner of Police of the Metropolis, must be the person nominated by the Secretary of State for appointment under this paragraph.][22]

(7) The person appointed to investigate the complaint or matter shall comply with all such requirements in relation to the carrying out of that investigation as may, in accordance with regulations made for the purposes of this sub-paragraph by the Secretary of State, be imposed by the Commission in relation to that investigation.

---

15 Words substituted by SOCPA, Sch 12, para 15(2).
16 Inserted by PJA, Sch 1(7), para 89(3), in force 1 April 2007.
17 Ibid.
18 Substituted by SOCPA, Sch 2, para 11(3).
19 Inserted by PJA, Sch 1(7), para 89(3).
20 Words substituted by PJA, Sch 1(7), para 89(4).
21 Word substituted by SOCPA, Sch 12, para 15(3).
22 Inserted by SOCPA, Sch 12, para 15(4).

18 Investigations managed by the Commission

(1) This paragraph applies where the Commission has determined that it should manage the investigation by the appropriate authority of any complaint [, recordable conduct matter or DSI matter].[23]

(2) [Sub-paragraphs (2) to (6A) of paragraph 17][24] shall apply as they apply in the case of an investigation which the Commission has determined is one that it should supervise.

(3) The person appointed to investigate the complaint or matter shall, in relation to that investigation, be under the direction and control of the Commission.

19 Investigations by the Commission itself

(1) This paragraph applies where the Commission has determined that it should itself carry out the investigation of a complaint [, recordable conduct matter or DSI matter].[25]

(2) The Commission shall designate both—

    (a) a member of the Commission's staff to take charge of the investigation on behalf of the Commission, and

    (b) all such other members of the Commission's staff as are required by the Commission to assist him.

(3) The person designated under sub-paragraph (2) to be the person to take charge of an investigation relating to any conduct of the Commissioner of Police of the Metropolis or of the Deputy Commissioner of Police of the Metropolis must be the person nominated by the Secretary of State to be so designated under that sub-paragraph.

[(3A) The person designated under sub-paragraph (2) to be the person to take charge of an investigation of a DSI matter in relation to which the relevant officer is the Commissioner of Police of the Metropolis or the Deputy Commissioner of Police of the Metropolis must be the person nominated by the Secretary of State to be so designated under that sub-paragraph.][26]

(4) A member of the Commission's staff who—

    (a) is designated under sub-paragraph (2) in relation to any investigation, but

    (b) does not already, by virtue of section 97(8) of the 1996 Act, have all the powers and privileges of a constable throughout England and Wales and the adjacent United Kingdom waters,

shall, for the purposes of the carrying out of the investigation and all purposes connected with it, have all those powers and privileges throughout England and Wales and those waters.

(5) A member of the Commission's staff who is not a constable shall not, as a result of sub-paragraph (4), be treated as being in police service for the purposes of—

    (a) section 280 of the Trade Union and Labour Relations (Consolidation) Act 1992 (c. 52) (person in police service excluded from definitions of " worker" and " employee"); or

    (b) section 200 of the Employment Rights Act 1996 (c. 18) (certain provisions of that Act not to apply to persons in police service).

(6) The Secretary of State may by order provide that such provisions of the 1984 Act relating to investigations of offences conducted by police officers as may be specified in the order shall apply, subject to such modifications as may be so specified, to investigations of offences conducted by virtue of this paragraph by members of the Commission's staff designated under sub-paragraph (2).

---

[23] Words substituted by SOCPA, Sch 12, para 16(2).
[24] Word substituted by SOCPA, Sch 12, para 16(3).
[25] Words substituted by SOCPA, Sch 12, para 17(2).
[26] Inserted by SOCPA, Sch 12, para 17(3).

(7) References in this paragraph to the powers and privileges of a constable—

    (a) are references to any power or privilege conferred by or under any enactment (including one passed after the passing of this Act) on a constable; and

    (b) shall have effect as if every such power were exercisable, and every such privilege existed, throughout England and Wales and the adjacent United Kingdom waters (whether or not that is the case apart from this sub-paragraph).

(8) In this paragraph "United Kingdom waters" means the sea and other waters within the seaward limits of the United Kingdom's territorial sea.

[19A Special procedure where investigation relates to police officer or special constable

Paragraphs 19B to 19E apply to investigations of complaints or recordable conduct matters in cases where the person concerned (see paragraph 19B(11)) is a member of a police force or a special constable.

19B Assessment of seriousness of conduct under investigation

(1) If, during the course of an investigation of a complaint, it appears to the person investigating that there is an indication that a person to whose conduct the investigation relates may have—

    (a) committed a criminal offence, or

    (b) behaved in a manner which would justify the bringing of disciplinary proceedings,

the person investigating must certify the investigation as one subject to special requirements.

(2) If the person investigating a complaint certifies the investigation as one subject to special requirements, the person must, as soon as is reasonably practicable after doing so, make a severity assessment in relation to the conduct of the person concerned to which the investigation relates.

(3) The person investigating a recordable conduct matter must make a severity assessment in relation to the conduct to which the investigation relates—

    (a) as soon as is reasonably practicable after his appointment or designation, or

    (b) in the case of a matter recorded in accordance with paragraph 21A(5) or 24B(2), as soon as is reasonably practicable after it is so recorded.

(4) For the purposes of this paragraph a "severity assessment", in relation to conduct, means an assessment as to—

    (a) whether the conduct, if proved, would amount to misconduct or gross misconduct, and

    (b) if the conduct were to become the subject of disciplinary proceedings, the form which those proceedings would be likely to take.

(5) An assessment under this paragraph may only be made after consultation with the appropriate authority.

(6) On completing an assessment under this paragraph, the person investigating the complaint or matter must give a notification to the person concerned that complies with sub-paragraph (7).

(7) The notification must—

    (a) give the prescribed information about the results of the assessment;

    (b) give the prescribed information about the effect of paragraph 19C and of regulations under paragraph 19D;

    (c) set out the prescribed time limits for providing the person investigating the complaint or matter with relevant statements and relevant documents respectively for the purposes of paragraph 19C(2);

    (d) give such other information as may be prescribed.

(8) Sub-paragraph (6) does not apply for so long as the person investigating the complaint or matter considers that giving the notification might prejudice—

    (a) the investigation, or

    (b) any other investigation (including, in particular, a criminal investigation).

(9) Where the person investigating a complaint or matter has made a severity assessment and considers it appropriate to do so, the person may revise the assessment.

(10) On revising a severity assessment, the person investigating the complaint or matter must notify the prescribed information about the revised assessment to the person concerned.

(11) In this paragraph and paragraphs 19C to 19E—

" the person concerned" —

(a) in relation to an investigation of a complaint, means the person in respect of whom it appears to the person investigating that there is the indication mentioned in paragraph 19B(1);

(b) in relation to an investigation of a recordable conduct matter, means the person to whose conduct the investigation relates;

" relevant document" —

(a) means a document relating to any complaint or matter under investigation, and

(b) includes such a document containing suggestions as to lines of inquiry to be pursued or witnesses to be interviewed;

" relevant statement" means an oral or written statement relating to any complaint or matter under investigation.

19C Duty to consider submissions from person whose conduct is being investigated

(1) This paragraph applies to—

(a) an investigation of a complaint that has been certified under paragraph 19B(1) as one subject to special requirements, or

(b) an investigation of a recordable conduct matter.

(2) If before the expiry of the appropriate time limit notified in pursuance of paragraph 19B(7)(c)—

(a) the person concerned provides the person investigating the complaint or matter with a relevant statement or a relevant document, or

(b) any person of a prescribed description provides that person with a relevant document,

that person must consider the statement or document.

19D Interview of person whose conduct is being investigated

(1) The Secretary of State may by regulations make provision as to the procedure to be followed in connection with any interview of the person concerned which is held during the course of an investigation within paragraph 19C(1)(a) or (b) by the person investigating the complaint or matter.

(2) Regulations under this paragraph may, in particular, make provision—

(a) for determining how the time at which an interview is to be held is to be agreed or decided,

(b) about the information that must be provided to the person being interviewed,

(c) for enabling that person to be accompanied at the interview by a person of a prescribed description.

19E Duty to provide certain information to appropriate authority

(1) This paragraph applies during the course of an investigation within paragraph 19C(1)(a) or (b).

(2) The person investigating the complaint or matter must supply the appropriate authority with such information in that person's possession as the authority may reasonably request for the purpose mentioned in sub-paragraph (3).

(3) That purpose is determining, in accordance with regulations under section 50 or 51 of the 1996 Act, whether the person concerned should be, or should remain, suspended—
   (a) from office as constable, and
   (b) where that person is a member of a police force, from membership of that force.]²⁷

20 Restrictions on proceedings pending the conclusion of an investigation

(1) No criminal or disciplinary proceedings shall be brought in relation to any matter which is the subject of an investigation in accordance with the provisions of this Schedule [until—
   (a) the appropriate authority has certified the case as a special case under paragraph 20B(3) or 20E(3), or
   (b) a report on that investigation has been submitted to the Commission or to the appropriate authority under paragraph 22 or 24A.]²⁸

(2) Nothing in this paragraph shall prevent the bringing of criminal or disciplinary proceedings in respect of any conduct at any time after the discontinuance of the investigation in accordance with the provisions of this Schedule which relates to that conduct.

(3) The restrictions imposed by this paragraph in relation to the bringing of criminal proceedings shall not apply to the bringing of criminal proceedings by the Director of Public Prosecutions in any case in which it appears to him that there are exceptional circumstances which make it undesirable to delay the bringing of such proceedings.

[20A

(1) If, at any time before the completion of his investigation, [the person investigating]²⁹ a complaint or recordable conduct matter believes that the appropriate authority would, on consideration of the matter, be likely to consider that the special conditions are satisfied, he shall proceed in accordance with the following provisions of this paragraph.

(2) If the person was appointed under paragraph 16, he shall submit to the appropriate authority—
   (a) a statement of his belief and the grounds for it; and
   (b) a written report on his investigation to that point;
   and if he was appointed following a determination made by the Commission under paragraph 15 he shall send a copy of the statement and the report to the Commission.

(3) If the person was appointed under paragraph 17 or 18 or designated under paragraph 19, he shall submit to the appropriate authority—
   (a) a statement of his belief and the grounds for it; and
   (b) a written report on his investigation to that point;
   and shall send a copy of the statement and the report to the Commission.

(4) A person submitting a report under this paragraph shall not be prevented by any obligation of secrecy imposed by any rule of law or otherwise from including all such matters in his report as he thinks fit.

(5) A statement and report may be submitted under this paragraph whether or not a previous statement and report have been submitted; but a second or subsequent statement and report may be submitted only if the person submitting them has grounds to believe that the appropriate authority will reach a different determination under paragraph 20B(2) or 20E(2).

---

²⁷ Inserted by CJIA, Sch 23, para 5, in force 3 November 2008 in relation to the power to make regulations, subject to savings and transitional provisions specified in SI 2008/2721, art 4, and in force 1 December 2008 subject to savings specified in SI 2008/2993, art 3 otherwise.
²⁸ Paragraph 20(1)(a) inserted and existing text renumbered as para 20(1)(b) by SOCPA, Sch 11, para 2.
²⁹ Words substituted by CJIA, Sch 23, para 6(2), in force 1 December 2008 under SI 2008/2993, subject to savings specified at art 3.

(6) After submitting a report under this paragraph, the person [investigating][30] the complaint or recordable conduct matter shall continue his investigation to such extent as he considers appropriate.

(7) The special conditions are that—

    [(a) there is sufficient evidence, in the form of written statements or other documents, to establish on the balance of probabilities that conduct to which the investigation relates constitutes gross misconduct;][31]

    (c) it is in the public interest for the person whose conduct [it is][32] to cease to be a member of a police force, or to be a special constable, without delay.

[. . .][33]

(9) In paragraphs 20B to 20H " special report" means a report submitted under this paragraph.

20B

(1) This paragraph applies where—

    (a) a statement and special report on an investigation carried out under the management of the Commission, or

    (b) a statement and special report on an investigation carried out by a person designated by the Commission,

are submitted to the appropriate authority under paragraph 20A(3).

(2) The appropriate authority shall determine whether the special conditions are satisfied.

[(3) If the appropriate authority determines that the special conditions are satisfied then, unless it considers that the circumstances are such as to make it inappropriate to do so, it shall—

    (a) certify the case as a special case for the purposes of regulations under section 50(3) or 51(2A) of the 1996 Act; and

    (b) take such steps as are required by those regulations in relation to a case so certified.][34]

[. . .][35]

(6) The appropriate authority shall notify the Commission of a certification under sub-paragraph (3).

(7) If the appropriate authority determines—

    (a) that the special conditions are not satisfied, or

    (b) that, although those conditions are satisfied, the circumstances are such as to make it inappropriate at present to bring disciplinary proceedings,

it shall submit to the Commission a memorandum under this sub-paragraph.

(8) The memorandum required to be submitted under sub-paragraph (7) is one which—

    (a) notifies the Commission of its determination that those conditions are not satisfied or (as the case may be) that they are so satisfied but the circumstances are such as to make it inappropriate at present to bring disciplinary proceedings; and

    (b) (in either case) sets out its reasons for so determining.

(9) In this paragraph "special conditions" has the meaning given by paragraph 20A(7).

---

[30] Words substituted by CJIA, Sch 23, para 6(3).
[31] Schedule 3, para 20A(7)(a) substituted for Sch 3, para 20A(7)(a) and (b) by CJIA, Sch 23, para 6(4)(a).
[32] Words substituted by CJIA c 4 Sch 23 para 6(4)(b) (December 1, 2008: substitution has effect on December 1, 2008 as SI 2008/2993 subject to savings specified in SI 2008/2993 art.3)
[33] Repealed by CJIA, Sch 28(8), para 1.
[34] Schedule 3, para 20B(3) substituted for Sch 3, para 20B(3) and (4) by CJIA, Sch 23, para 7(2).
[35] Repealed by CJIA, Sch 28(8), para 1.

20C

(1) On receipt of a notification under paragraph 20B(6), the Commission shall give a notification—
  (a) in the case of a complaint, to the complainant and to every person entitled to be kept properly informed in relation to the complaint under section 21; and
  (b) in the case of a recordable conduct matter, to every person entitled to be kept properly informed in relation to that matter under that section.

(2) The notification required by sub-paragraph (1) is one setting out—
  (a) the findings of the special report;
  (b) the appropriate authority's determination under paragraph 20B(2); and
  (c) the action that the appropriate authority is required to take as a consequence of that determination.

(3) Subsections (5) to (7) of section 20 shall have effect in relation to the duties imposed on the Commission by sub-paragraph (1) as they have effect in relation to the duties imposed on the Commission by that section.

(4) Except so far as may be otherwise provided by regulations made by virtue of sub-paragraph (3), the Commission shall be entitled (notwithstanding any obligation of secrecy imposed by any rule of law or otherwise) to discharge the duty to give a person mentioned in sub-paragraph (1) notification of the findings of the special report by sending that person a copy of that report.

20D

(1) On receipt of a memorandum under paragraph 20B(7), the Commission shall—
  (a) consider the memorandum;
  (b) determine, in the light of that consideration, whether or not to make a recommendation under paragraph 20H; and
  (c) if it thinks fit to do so, make a recommendation under that paragraph.

(2) If the Commission determines not to make a recommendation under paragraph 20H, it shall notify the appropriate authority and the person [investigating the complaint or matter]³⁶ of its determination.

20E

(1) This paragraph applies where—
  (a) a statement and a special report on an investigation carried out by an appropriate authority on its own behalf, or
  (b) a statement and a special report on an investigation carried out under the supervision of the Commission,
  are submitted to the appropriate authority under paragraph 20A(2) or (3).

(2) The appropriate authority shall determine whether the special conditions are satisfied.

[(3) If the appropriate authority determines that the special conditions are satisfied then, unless it considers that the circumstances are such as to make it inappropriate to do so, it shall—
  (a) certify the case as a special case for the purposes of regulations under section 50(3) or 51(2A) of the 1996 Act; and
  (b) take such steps as are required by those regulations in relation to a case so certified.]³⁷
[...]³⁸

(6) Where the statement and report were required under paragraph 20A(2) to be copied to the Commission, the appropriate authority shall notify the Commission of a certification under sub-paragraph (3).

---

³⁶ Words substituted by CJIA, Sch 23, para 8.
³⁷ Schedule 3, para 20E(3), substituted for Sch 3, para 20E(3) and (4) by CJIA, Sch 23, para 9(2).
³⁸ Repealed by CJIA, Sch 28(8), para 1.

(7) If the appropriate authority determines—
  (a) that the special conditions are not satisfied, or
  (b) that, although those conditions are satisfied, the circumstances are such as to make it inappropriate at present to bring disciplinary proceedings,
  it shall notify the person [investigating the complaint or matter]³⁹ of its determination.
(8) In this paragraph "special conditions" has the meaning given by paragraph 20A(7).

20F

(1) If the appropriate authority certifies a case under paragraph 20E(3), it shall give a notification—
  (a) in the case of a complaint, to the complainant and to every person entitled to be kept properly informed in relation to the complaint under section 21; and
  (b) in the case of a recordable conduct matter, to every person entitled to be kept properly informed in relation to that matter under that section.
(2) The notification required by sub-paragraph (1) is one setting out—
  (a) the findings of the report;
  (b) the authority's determination under paragraph 20E(2); and
  (c) the action that the authority is required to take in consequence of that determination.
(3) Subsections (5) to (7) of section 20 shall have effect in relation to the duties imposed on the appropriate authority by sub-paragraph (1) as they have effect in relation to the duties imposed on the appropriate authority by that section.
(4) Except so far as may be otherwise provided by regulations made by virtue of sub-paragraph (3), the appropriate authority shall be entitled (notwithstanding any obligation of secrecy imposed by any rule of law or otherwise) to discharge the duty to give a person mentioned in sub-paragraph (1) notification of the findings of the special report by sending that person a copy of that report.

[. . .]⁴⁰

20H

(1) Where the appropriate authority has submitted, or is required to submit, a memorandum to the Commission under paragraph 20B(7), the Commission may make a recommendation to the appropriate authority that it should certify the case under paragraph 20B(3).
(2) If the Commission determines to make a recommendation under this paragraph, it shall give a notification—
  (a) in the case of a complaint, to the complainant and to every person entitled to be kept properly informed in relation to the complaint under section 21; and
  (b) in the case of a recordable conduct matter, to every person entitled to be kept properly informed in relation to that matter under that section.
(3) The notification required by sub-paragraph (2) is one setting out—
  (a) the findings of the special report; and
  (b) the Commission's recommendation under this paragraph.
(4) Subsections (5) to (7) of section 20 shall have effect in relation to the duties imposed on the Commission by sub-paragraph (2) as they have effect in relation to the duties imposed on the Commission by that section.
(5) Except so far as may be otherwise provided by regulations made by virtue of sub-paragraph (4), the Commission shall be entitled (notwithstanding any obligation of secrecy imposed by any rule of law or otherwise) to discharge the duty to give a person mentioned in sub-paragraph (2) notification of the findings of the special report by sending that person a copy of the report.

---

³⁹ Words substituted by CJIA, Sch 23, para 9(4).
⁴⁰ Paragraph 20G repealed by CJIA, Sch 28(8), para 1.

(6) It shall be the duty of the appropriate authority to notify the Commission whether it accepts the recommendation and (if it does) to certify the case and proceed accordingly.

(7) If, after the Commission has made a recommendation under this paragraph, the appropriate authority does not certify the case under paragraph 20B(3)—

(a) the Commission may direct the appropriate authority so to certify it; and

(b) it shall be the duty of the appropriate authority to comply with the direction and proceed accordingly.

(8) Where the Commission gives the appropriate authority a direction under this paragraph, it shall supply the appropriate authority with a statement of its reasons for doing so.

(9) The Commission may at any time withdraw a direction given under this paragraph.

(10) The appropriate authority shall keep the Commission informed of whatever action it takes in response to a recommendation or direction.

20I

(1) Where—

(a) the Commission makes a recommendation under paragraph 20H in the case of an investigation of a complaint, and

(b) the appropriate authority notifies the Commission that the recommendation has been accepted,

the Commission shall notify the complainant and every person entitled to be kept properly informed in relation to the complaint under section 21 of that fact and of the steps that have been, or are to be, taken by the appropriate authority to give effect to it.

(2) Where in the case of an investigation of a complaint the appropriate authority—

(a) notifies the Commission that it does not accept the recommendation made by the Commission under paragraph 20H, or

(b) fails to certify the case under paragraph 20B(3) and to proceed accordingly,

it shall be the duty of the Commission to determine what (if any) further steps to take under paragraph 20H.

(3) It shall be the duty of the Commission to notify the complainant and every person entitled to be kept properly informed in relation to the complaint under section 21—

(a) of any determination under sub-paragraph (2) not to take further steps under paragraph 20H; and

(b) where it determines under that sub-paragraph to take further steps under that paragraph, of the outcome of the taking of those steps.][41]

21 Power of the Commission to discontinue an investigation

(1) If it any time appears to the Commission (whether on an application by the appropriate authority or otherwise) that a complaint or matter that is being investigated—

(a) by the appropriate authority on its own behalf, or

(b) under the supervision or management of the Commission,

is of a description of complaint or matter specified in regulations made by the Secretary of State for the purposes of this sub-paragraph, the Commission may by order require the discontinuance of the investigation.

(2) The Commission shall not discontinue any investigation that is being carried out in accordance with paragraph 19 except in such cases as may be authorised by regulations made by the Secretary of State.

---

[41] Inserted by SOCPA, Sch 11, para 3.

(3) Where the Commission makes an order under this paragraph or discontinues an investigation being carried out in accordance with paragraph 19, it shall give notification of the discontinuance—
   (a) to the appropriate authority;
   (b) to every person entitled to be kept properly informed in relation to the subject matter of the investigation under section 21; and
   (c) in a case where the investigation that is discontinued is an investigation of a complaint, to the complainant.

(4) Where an investigation of a complaint [, recordable conduct matter or DSI matter]⁴² matter is discontinued in accordance with this paragraph—
   (a) the Commission may give the appropriate authority directions to do any such things as it is authorised to direct by regulations made by the Secretary of State;
   (b) the Commission may itself take any such steps of a description specified in regulations so made as it considers appropriate for purposes connected with the discontinuance of the investigation; and
   (c) subject to the preceding paragraphs, neither the appropriate authority nor the Commission shall take any further action in accordance with the provisions of this Schedule in relation to that complaint or matter.

(5) The appropriate authority shall comply with any directions given to it under sub-paragraph (4).

[21A Procedure where conduct matter is revealed during investigation of DSI matter

(1) If during the course of an investigation of a DSI matter it appears to a person appointed under paragraph 18 or designated under paragraph 19 that there is an indication that a person serving with the police ("the person whose conduct is in question") may have—
   (a) committed a criminal offence, or
   (b) behaved in a manner which would justify the bringing of disciplinary proceedings,
   he shall make a submission to that effect to the Commission.

(2) If, after considering a submission under sub-paragraph (1), the Commission determines that there is such an indication, it shall—
   (a) notify the appropriate authority in relation to the DSI matter and (if different) the appropriate authority in relation to the person whose conduct is in question of its determination; and
   (b) send to it (or each of them) a copy of the submission under sub-paragraph (1).

(3) If during the course of an investigation of a DSI matter it appears to a person appointed under paragraph 16 or 17 that there is an indication that a person serving with the police ("the person whose conduct is in question") may have—
   (a) committed a criminal offence, or
   (b) behaved in a manner which would justify the bringing of disciplinary proceedings,
   he shall make a submission to that effect to the appropriate authority in relation to the DSI matter.

(4) If, after considering a submission under sub-paragraph (3), the appropriate authority determines that there is such an indication, it shall—
   (a) if it is not the appropriate authority in relation to the person whose conduct is in question, notify that other authority of its determination and send to that authority a copy of the submission under sub-paragraph (3); and
   (b) notify the Commission of its determination and send to it a copy of the submission under sub-paragraph (3).

---

⁴² Words substituted by SOCPA, Sch 12, para 19.

(5) Where the appropriate authority in relation to the person whose conduct is in question—

    (a) is notified of a determination by the Commission under sub-paragraph (2),

    (b) (in a case where it is also the appropriate authority in relation to the DSI matter) makes a determination under sub-paragraph (4), or

    (c) (in a case where it is not the appropriate authority in relation to the DSI matter) is notified by that other authority of a determination by it under sub-paragraph (4),

it shall record the matter under paragraph 11 as a conduct matter [. . .]⁴³

[(6) Where a DSI matter is recorded under paragraph 11 as a conduct matter by virtue of sub-paragraph (5)—

    (a) the person investigating the DSI matter shall (subject to any determination made by the Commission under paragraph 15(5)) continue the investigation as if appointed or designated to investigate the conduct matter, and

    (b) the other provisions of this Schedule shall apply in relation to that matter accordingly.]⁴⁴]⁴⁵

[22 **Final reports on investigations: complaints, conduct matters and certain DSI matters**

(1) This paragraph applies on the completion of an investigation of—

    (a) a complaint,[or]⁴⁶

    (b) a conduct matter [...]⁴⁷

(2) A person appointed under paragraph 16 shall submit a report on his investigation to the appropriate authority.

(3) A person appointed under paragraph 17 or 18 shall—

    (a) submit a report on his investigation to the Commission; and

    (b) send a copy of that report to the appropriate authority.

(4) In relation to [a matter that was formerly a DSI matter but has been recorded as a conduct matter in pursuance of paragraph 21A(5)],⁴⁸ the references in sub-paragraphs (2) and (3) of this paragraph to the appropriate authority are references to—

    (a) the appropriate authority in relation to the DSI matter; and

    (b) (where different) the appropriate authority in relation to the person whose conduct is in question.

(5) A person designated under paragraph 19 as the person in charge of an investigation by the Commission itself shall submit a report on it to the Commission.

(6) A person submitting a report under this paragraph shall not be prevented by any obligation of secrecy imposed by any rule of law or otherwise from including all such matters in his report as he thinks fit.

[(7) The Secretary of State may by regulations make provision requiring a report on an investigation within paragraph 19C(1)(a) or (b)—

    (a) to include such matters as are specified in the regulations;

    (b) to be accompanied by such documents or other items as are so specified.

(8) A person who has submitted a report under this paragraph on an investigation within paragraph 19C(1)(a) or (b) must supply the appropriate authority with such copies of further documents or other items in that person's possession as the authority may request.

---

⁴³ Words repealed by CJIA, Sch 28(8), para 1.
⁴⁴ Inserted by CJIA, Sch 23, para 11(3).
⁴⁵ Inserted by SOCPA, Sch 12, para 20.
⁴⁶ Word inserted by CJIA, Sch 23, para 12(2)(a).
⁴⁷ Substituted by CJIA, Sch 28(8), para 1.
⁴⁸ Words substituted by CJIA, Sch 23, para 12(3).

(9) The appropriate authority may only make a request under sub-paragraph (8) in respect of a copy of a document or other item if the authority—

    (a) considers that the document or item is of relevance to the investigation, and

    (b) requires a copy of the document or the item for either or both of the purposes mentioned in sub-paragraph (10).

(10) Those purposes are—

    (a) complying with any obligation under regulations under section 50(3) or 51(2A) of the 1996 Act which the authority has in relation to any person to whose conduct the investigation related;

    (b) ensuring that any such person receives a fair hearing at any disciplinary proceedings in respect of any such conduct of his.][49]][50]

23 Action by the Commission in response to an investigation report

(1) This paragraph applies where—

    (a) a report on an investigation carried out under the management of the Commission is submitted to it under [sub-paragraph (3) of paragraph 22];[51] or

    (b) a report on an investigation carried out by a person designated by the Commission is submitted to it under [sub-paragraph (5)][52] of that paragraph.

(2) On receipt of the report, the Commission—

    (a) if it appears that the appropriate authority has not already been sent a copy of the report, shall send a copy of the report to that authority;

    [(b) shall determine whether the conditions set out in sub-paragraphs (2A) and (2B) are satisfied in respect of the report;][53]

    (c) if it determines that [those conditions are so satisfied],[54] shall notify the Director of Public Prosecutions of the determination and send him a copy of the report; and

    (d) shall notify the appropriate authority [and the persons mentioned in sub-paragraph (5)][55] of its determination under paragraph (b) and of any action taken by it under paragraph (c).

[(2A) The first condition is that the report indicates that a criminal offence may have been committed by a person to whose conduct the investigation related.

(2B) The second condition is that—

    (a) the circumstances are such that, in the opinion of the Commission, it is appropriate for the matters dealt with in the report to be considered by the Director of Public Prosecutions, or

    (b) any matters dealt with in the report fall within any prescribed category of matters.][56]

(3) The Director of Public Prosecutions shall notify the Commission of any decision of his to take, or not to take, action in respect of the matters dealt with in any report a copy of which has been sent to him under sub-paragraph (2)(c).

(4) It shall be the duty of the Commission to notify the persons mentioned in sub-paragraph (5) if criminal proceedings are brought against any person by the Director of Public Prosecutions in respect of any matters dealt with in a report copied to him under sub-paragraph (2)(c).

---

[49] Inserted by CJIA, Sch 23, para 12(4), in force 3 November 2008 in relation to the power to make regulations subject to savings and transitional provisions specified in SI 2008/2721, art 4, and 1 December 2008 subject to savings specified in SI 2008/2993, art 3, otherwise.

[50] Substituted by SOCPA, Sch 12, para 21.

[51] Word substituted by SOCPA, Sch 12, para 22(2)(a).

[52] Word substituted by SOCPA, Sch 12, para 22(2)(b).

[53] Substituted by CJIA, Sch 23, para 13(2)(a).

[54] Words substituted by CJIA, Sch 23, para 13(2)(b).

[55] Words inserted by CJIA, Sch 23, para 13(2)(c).

[56] Inserted by CJIA, Sch 23, para 13(3).

(5) [The]⁵⁷ persons are—

    (a) in the case of a complaint, the complainant and every person entitled to be kept properly informed in relation to the complaint under section 21; and

    (b) in the case of a recordable conduct matter, every person entitled to be kept properly informed in relation to that matter under that section.

[(6) On receipt of the report, the Commission shall also notify the appropriate authority that it must—

    (a) in accordance with regulations under section 50 or 51 of the 1996 Act, determine—

        (i) whether any person to whose conduct the investigation related has a case to answer in respect of misconduct or gross misconduct or has no case to answer, and

        (ii) what action (if any) the authority is required to, or will in its discretion, take in respect of the matters dealt with in the report, and

    (b) determine what other action (if any) the authority will in its discretion take in respect of those matters.

(7) On receipt of a notification under sub-paragraph (6) the appropriate authority shall make those determinations and submit a memorandum to the Commission which—

    (a) sets out the determinations the authority has made, and

    (b) if the appropriate authority has decided in relation to any person to whose conduct the investigation related that disciplinary proceedings should not be brought against that person, sets out its reasons for so deciding.]⁵⁸

(8) On receipt of a memorandum under sub-paragraph (7), the Commission shall—

    (a) consider the memorandum and whether the appropriate authority [has made the determinations under sub-paragraph (6)(a)]⁵⁹ that the Commission considers appropriate in respect of the matters dealt with in the report;

    (b) determine, in the light of its consideration of those matters, whether or not to make recommendations under paragraph 27; and

    (c) make such recommendations (if any) under that paragraph as it thinks fit.

(9) On the making of a determination under sub-paragraph (8)(b) the Commission shall give a notification—

    (a) in the case of a complaint, to the complainant and to every person entitled to be kept properly informed in relation to the complaint under section 21; and

    (b) in the case of a recordable conduct matter, to every person entitled to be kept properly informed in relation to that matter under that section.

(10) The notification required by sub-paragraph (9) is one setting out—

    (a) the findings of the report;

    (b) the Commission's determination under sub-paragraph (8)(b); and

    (c) the action which the appropriate authority is to be recommended to take as a consequence of the determination.

(11) Subsections (5) to (7) of section 20 shall have effect in relation to the duties imposed on the Commission by sub-paragraph (9) of this paragraph as they have effect in relation to the duties imposed on the Commission by that section.

(12) Except so far as may be otherwise provided by regulations made by virtue of sub-paragraph (11), the Commission shall be entitled (notwithstanding any obligation of secrecy imposed by any rule of law or otherwise) to discharge the duty to give a person mentioned in sub-paragraph (9) notification of the findings of the report by sending that person a copy of the report.

---

⁵⁷ Word substituted by CJIA, Sch 23, para 13(4).
⁵⁸ Substituted by CJIA, Sch 23, para 13(5).
⁵⁹ Words substituted by CJIA, Sch 23, para 13(6).

[(13) In relation to a DSI matter in respect of which a determination has been made under paragraph 21A(2) or (4), the references in this paragraph to the appropriate authority are references to the appropriate authority in relation to the person whose conduct is in question.][60]

24 Action by the appropriate authority in response to an investigation report

(1) This paragraph applies where—
  (a) a report of an investigation is submitted to the appropriate authority in accordance with [paragraph 22(2)];[61] or
  (b) a copy of a report on an investigation carried out under the supervision of the Commission is sent to the appropriate authority in accordance with [paragraph 22(3)].[62]

(2) On receipt of the report or (as the case may be) of the copy, the appropriate authority—
  [(a) shall determine whether the conditions set out in sub-paragraphs (2A) and (2B) are satisfied in respect of the report;][63]
  (b) if it determines that [those conditions are so satisfied],[64] shall notify the Director of Public Prosecutions of the determination and send him a copy of the report [; and][65]
  [(c) shall notify the persons mentioned in subparagraph (5) of its determination under paragraph (a) and of any action taken by it under paragraph (b).][66]

[(2A) The first condition is that the report indicates that a criminal offence may have been committed by a person to whose conduct the investigation related.

(2B) The second condition is that—
  (a) the circumstances are such that, in the opinion of the appropriate authority, it is appropriate for the matters dealt with in the report to be considered by the Director of Public Prosecutions, or
  (b) any matters dealt with in the report fall within any prescribed category of matters.][67]

(3) The Director of Public Prosecutions shall notify the appropriate authority of any decision of his to take, or not to take, action in respect of the matters dealt with in any report a copy of which has been sent to him under sub-paragraph (2).

(4) It shall be the duty of the appropriate authority to notify the persons mentioned in sub-paragraph (5) if criminal proceedings are brought against any person by the Director of Public Prosecutions in respect of any matters dealt with in a report copied to him under sub-paragraph (2)(b).

(5) [The][68] persons are—
  (a) in the case of a complaint, the complainant and every person entitled to be kept properly informed in relation to the complaint under section 21; and
  (b) in the case of a recordable conduct matter, every person entitled to be kept properly informed in relation to that matter under that section.

[(5A) In the case of a report falling within sub-paragraph (1)(b) which relates to a recordable conduct matter, the appropriate authority shall also notify the Commission of its determination under sub-paragraph (2)(a).

---

60 Inserted by SOCPA, Sch 12, para 22(3).
61 Word substituted by SOCPA, Sch 12, para 23(2)(a).
62 Word substituted by SOCPA, Sch 12, para 23(2)(b).
63 Substituted by CJIA, Sch 23, para 14(2)(a).
64 Words substituted by CJIA, Sch 23, para 14(2)(b).
65 Inserted by CJIA, Sch 23, para 14(2)(c).
66 Ibid.
67 Inserted by CJIA, Sch 23, para 14(3).
68 Word substituted by CJIA, Sch 23, para 14(4).

(5B) On receipt of such a notification that the appropriate authority has determined that the conditions in sub-paragraphs (2A) and (2B) are not satisfied in respect of the report, the Commission—

(a) shall make its own determination as to whether those conditions are so satisfied, and

(b) if it determines that they are so satisfied, shall direct the appropriate authority to notify the Director of Public Prosecutions of the Commission's determination and to send the Director a copy of the report.

(5C) It shall be the duty of the appropriate authority to comply with any direction given to it under sub-paragraph (5B).][69]

[(6) On receipt of the report or (as the case may be) copy, the appropriate authority shall also—

(a) in accordance with regulations under section 50 or 51 of the 1996 Act, determine—

(i) whether any person to whose conduct the investigation related has a case to answer in respect of misconduct or gross misconduct or has no case to answer, and

(ii) what action (if any) the authority is required to, or will in its discretion, take in respect of the matters dealt with in the report, and

(b) determine what other action (if any) the authority will in its discretion take in respect of those matters.][70]

(7) On the making of [the determinations][71] under sub-paragraph (6) the appropriate authority shall give a notification—

(a) in the case of a complaint, to the complainant and to every person entitled to be kept properly informed in relation to the complaint under section 21; and

(b) in the case of a recordable conduct matter, to every person entitled to be kept properly informed in relation to that matter under that section.

(8) The notification required by sub-paragraph (7) is one setting out—

(a) the findings of the report;

[(b) the determinations the authority has made under subparagraph (6); and][72]

(d) the complainant's right of appeal under paragraph 25.

(9) Subsections (5) to (7) of section 20 shall have effect in relation to the duties imposed on the appropriate authority by sub-paragraph (7) of this paragraph as they have effect in relation to the duties imposed on the appropriate authority by that section.

(10) Except so far as may be otherwise provided by regulations made by virtue of sub-paragraph (9), the appropriate authority shall be entitled (notwithstanding any obligation of secrecy imposed by any rule of law or otherwise) to discharge the duty to give a person mentioned in sub-paragraph (7) notification of the findings of the report by sending that person a copy of the report.

[(11) In relation to a DSI matter in respect of which a determination has been made under paragraph 21A(2) or (4), the references in this paragraph to the appropriate authority are references to the appropriate authority in relation to the person whose conduct is in question.][73]

[24A

(1) This paragraph applies on the completion of an investigation of a DSI matter in respect of which neither the Commission nor the appropriate authority has made a determination under paragraph 21A(2) or (4).

---

[69] Inserted by CJIA, Sch 23, para 14(5).
[70] Substituted by CJIA, Sch 23, para 14(6).
[71] Words substituted by CJIA, Sch 23, para 14(7).
[72] Schedule 3, para 24(8)(b), substituted for Sch 3, para 24(8)(b) and (c) by CJIA, Sch 23, para 14(8).
[73] Inserted by SOCPA, Sch 12, para 23(3).

(2) [The person investigating]⁷⁴ shall—
    (a) submit a report on the investigation to the Commission; and
    (b) send a copy of that report to the appropriate authority.

(3) A person submitting a report under this paragraph shall not be prevented by any obligation of secrecy imposed by any rule of law or otherwise from including all such matters in his report as he thinks fit.

(4) On receipt of the report, the Commission shall determine whether the report indicates that a person serving with the police may have—
    (a) committed a criminal offence, or
    (b) behaved in a manner which would justify the bringing of disciplinary proceedings.

24B

(1) If the Commission determines under paragraph 24A(4) that the report indicates that a person serving with the police may have—
    (a) committed a criminal offence, or
    (b) behaved in a manner which would justify the bringing of disciplinary proceedings,
    it shall notify the appropriate authority in relation to the person whose conduct is in question of its determination and, if it appears that that authority has not already been sent a copy of the report, send a copy of the report to that authority.

(2) Where the appropriate authority in relation to the person whose conduct is in question is notified of a determination by the Commission under sub-paragraph (1), it shall record the matter under paragraph 11 as a conduct matter [. . .].⁷⁵

[(3) Where a DSI matter is recorded under paragraph 11 as a conduct matter by virtue of sub-paragraph (2)—
    (a) the person investigating the DSI matter shall (subject to any determination made by the Commission under paragraph 15(5)) investigate the conduct matter as if appointed or designated to do so, and
    (b) the other provisions of this Schedule shall apply in relation to that matter accordingly.]⁷⁶

24C

(1) If the Commission determines under paragraph 24A(4) that there is no indication in the report that a person serving with the police may have—
    (a) committed a criminal offence, or
    (b) behaved in a manner which would justify the bringing of disciplinary proceedings,
    it shall make such recommendations or give such advice under section 10(1)(e) (if any) as it considers necessary or desirable.

(2) Sub-paragraph (1) does not affect any power of the Commission to make recommendations or give advice under section 10(1)(e) in other cases (whether arising under this Schedule or otherwise).]⁷⁷

25 Appeals to the Commission with respect to an investigation

(1) This paragraph applies where a complaint has been subjected to—
    (a) an investigation by the appropriate authority on its own behalf; or
    (b) an investigation under the supervision of the Commission.

---

⁷⁴ Words substituted by CJIA, Sch 23, para 15.
⁷⁵ Words repealed by CJIA, Sch 28(8), para 1.
⁷⁶ Inserted by CJIA, Sch 23, para 16(3).
⁷⁷ Inserted by SOCPA, Sch 12, para 24.

(2) The complainant shall have the following rights of appeal to the Commission—

    (a) a right to appeal on the grounds that he has not been provided with adequate information—

        (i) about the findings of the investigation; or

        [(ii) about any determination of the appropriate authority relating to the taking (or not taking) of action in respect of any matters dealt with in the report on the investigation;]⁷⁸

    (b) a right to appeal against the findings of the investigation; [. . .]⁷⁹

    [(ba) a right of appeal against any determination by the appropriate authority that a person to whose conduct the investigation related has a case to answer in respect of misconduct or gross misconduct or has no case to answer;

    (c) a right of appeal against any determination by the appropriate authority relating to the taking (or not taking) of action in respect of any matters dealt with in the report; and

    (d) a right of appeal against any determination by the appropriate authority under paragraph 24(2)(a) as a result of which it is not required to send the Director of Public Prosecutions a copy of the report;]⁸⁰

and it shall be the duty of the Commission to notify the appropriate authority, every person entitled to be kept properly informed in relation to the complaint under section 21 and the person complained against of any appeal brought under this paragraph.

[(2A) In sub-paragraph (2)—

    (a) references to the findings of an investigation do not include a reference to findings on a report submitted under paragraph 20A; and

    (b) references to the report of an investigation do not include a reference to a report submitted under that paragraph.]⁸¹

(3) On the bringing of an appeal under this paragraph, the Commission may require the appropriate authority to submit a memorandum to the Commission which—

    [(za) sets out whether the appropriate authority has determined that a person to whose conduct the investigation related has a case to answer in respect of misconduct or gross misconduct or has no case to answer;]⁸²

    [(a) sets out what action (if any) the authority has determined that it is required to or will, in its discretion, take in respect of the matters dealt with in the report;]⁸³

    (c) if the appropriate authority has decided in relation to [a person to whose conduct the investigation related]⁸⁴ that disciplinary proceedings should not be brought against that person, sets out its reasons for so deciding; [and]⁸̲

    [(d) if the appropriate authority made a determination under paragraph 24(2)(a) as a result of which it is not required to send the Director of Public Prosecutions a copy of the report, sets out the reasons for that determination;]⁸⁵

and it shall be the duty of the appropriate authority to comply with any requirement under this sub-paragraph.

(4) Where the Commission so requires on the bringing of any appeal under this paragraph in the case of an investigation by the appropriate authority on its own behalf, the appropriate authority shall provide the Commission with a copy of the report of the investigation.

---

⁷⁸ Substituted by CJIA, Sch 23, para 17(2)(a).
⁷⁹ Word repealed by CJIA, Sch 28(8), para 1.
⁸⁰ Schedule 3, para 25(2)(ba)–(d) substituted for Sch 3, para 25(2)(c), by CJIA, Sch 23, para 17(2)(b).
⁸¹ Inserted by SOCPA, Sch 11, para 4.
⁸² Inserted by CJIA, Sch 23, para 17(3)(a).
⁸³ Schedule 3, para 25(3)(a), substituted for Sch 3, para 25(3)(a) and (b), by CJIA, Sch 23, para 17(3)(b).
⁸⁴ Words substituted by CJIA, Sch 23, para 17(3)(c).
⁸⁵ Inserted by CJIA, Sch 23, para 17(3)(d).

(5) On an appéal under this paragraph, the Commission shall determine [such of the following as it considers appropriate in the circumstances][86]—

   (a) whether the complainant has been provided with adequate information about the matters mentioned in sub-paragraph (2)(a);

   (b) whether the findings of the investigation need to be reconsidered; [. . .][87]

   [(c) whether the appropriate authority—

      (i) has made such a determination as is mentioned in sub-paragraph (3)(za) that the Commission considers to be appropriate in respect of the matters dealt with in the report, and

      (ii) has determined that it is required to or will, in its discretion, take the action (if any) that the Commission considers to be so appropriate; and

   (d) whether the conditions set out in paragraph 24(2A) and (2B) are satisfied in respect of the report.][88]

(6) If, on an appeal under this paragraph, the Commission determines that the complainant has not been provided with adequate information about any matter, the Commission shall give the appropriate authority all such directions as the Commission considers appropriate for securing that the complainant is properly informed.

(7) Nothing in sub-paragraph (6) shall authorise the Commission to require the disclosure of any information the disclosure of which to the appellant has been or is capable of being withheld by virtue of regulations made under section 20(5).

(8) If, on an appeal under this paragraph, the Commission determines that the findings of the investigation need to be reconsidered, it shall either—

   (a) review those findings without an immediate further investigation; or

   (b) direct that the complaint be re-investigated.

(9) If, on an appeal under this paragraph, the Commission determines that the appropriate authority [has not made a determination as to whether there is a case for a person to whose conduct the investigation related to answer that the Commission considers appropriate or has not determined that it is required to or will, in its discretion, take the action in respect of the matters dealt with in][89] the report that the Commission considers appropriate, the Commission shall—

   (a) determine, in the light of that determination, whether or not to make recommendations under paragraph 27; and

   (b) make such recommendations (if any) under that paragraph as it thinks fit.

[(9A) If, on an appeal under this paragraph, the Commission determines that the conditions set out paragraph 24(2A) and (2B) are satisfied in respect of the report, it shall direct the appropriate authority—

   (a) to notify the Director of Public Prosecutions of the Commission's determination, and

   (b) to send the Director a copy of the report.][90]

(10) The Commission shall give notification of any determination under this paragraph—

   (a) to the appropriate authority,

   (b) to the complainant;

   (c) to every person entitled to be kept properly informed in relation to the complaint under section 21; and

   (d) except in a case where it appears to the Commission that to do so might prejudice any proposed review or re-investigation of the complaint, to the person complained against.

---

[86] Words inserted by CJIA, Sch 23, para 17(4)(a).
[87] Word repealed by CJIA, Sch 28(8), para 1.
[88] Schedule 3, para 25(5)(c) and (d), substituted for Sch 3, para 25(5)(c), by CJIA, Sch 23, para 17(4)(b).
[89] Words substituted by CJIA, Sch 23, para 17(5).
[90] Inserted by CJIA, Sch 23, para 17(6).

(11) The Commission shall also give notification of any directions given to the appropriate authority under this paragraph—
  (a) to the complainant;
  (b) to every person entitled to be kept properly informed in relation to the complaint under section 21; and
  (c) except in a case where it appears to the Commission that to do so might prejudice any proposed review or re-investigation of the complaint, to the person complained against.
(12) It shall be the duty of the appropriate authority to comply with any directions given to it under this paragraph.
(13) The Secretary of State may by regulations make provision—
  (a) for the form and manner in which appeals under this paragraph are to be brought;
  (b) for the period within which any such appeal must be brought; and
  (c) for the procedure to be followed by the Commission when dealing with or disposing of any such appeal.

26 Reviews and re-investigations following an appeal

(1) On a review under paragraph 25(8)(a) of the findings of an investigation the powers of the Commission shall be, according to its determination on that review, to do one or more of the following—
  (a) to uphold the findings in whole or in part;
  (b) to give the appropriate authority such directions—
      (i) as to the carrying out by the appropriate authority of its own review of the findings,
      (ii) as to the information to be provided to the complainant, and
      (iii) generally as to the handling of the matter in future,
    as the Commission thinks fit;
  (c) to direct that the complaint be re-investigated.
(2) Where the Commission directs under paragraph 25 or sub-paragraph (1) that a complaint be re-investigated, it shall make a determination of the form that the re-investigation should take.
(3) Sub-paragraphs (3) to (7) of paragraph 15 shall apply in relation to a determination under sub-paragraph (2) as they apply in the case of a determination under that paragraph.
(4) The other provisions of this Schedule (including this paragraph) shall apply in relation to any re-investigation in pursuance of a direction under paragraph 25(8) or sub-paragraph (1) of this paragraph as they apply in relation to any investigation in pursuance of a determination under paragraph 15.
(5) The Commission shall give notification of any determination made by it under this paragraph—
  (a) to the appropriate authority;
  (b) to the complainant;
  (c) to every person entitled to be kept properly informed in relation to the complaint under section 21; and
  (d) except in a case where it appears to the Commission that to do so might prejudice any proposed re-investigation of the complaint, to the person complained against.
(6) The Commission shall also give notification of any directions given to the appropriate authority under this paragraph—
  (a) to the complainant;
  (b) to every person entitled to be kept properly informed in relation to the complaint under section; and
  (c) except in a case where it appears to the Commission that to do so might prejudice any proposed review or re-investigation of the complaint, to the person complained against.

27 Duties with respect to disciplinary proceedings

(1) This paragraph applies where, in the case of any investigation, the appropriate authority—

    (a) has given, or is required to give, a notification under paragraph 24(7) of the action it is [required to or will, in its discretion,][91] take in relation to the matters dealt with in any report of the investigation; or

    (b) has submitted, or is required to submit, a memorandum to the Commission under paragraph 23 or 25 setting out the action that it is [required to or will, in its discretion,][92] take in relation to those matters.

(2) Subject to paragraph 20 and to any recommendations or directions under the following provisions of this paragraph, it shall be the duty of the appropriate authority—

    (a) to take the action which has been or is required to be notified or, as the case may be, which is or is required to be set out in the memorandum; and

    (b) in a case where that action consists of or includes the bringing of disciplinary proceedings, to secure that those proceedings, once brought, are proceeded with to a proper conclusion.

(3) Where this paragraph applies by virtue of sub-paragraph (1)(b), the Commission may make a recommendation to the appropriate authority in respect of any person serving with the police—

    [(za) that the person has a case to answer in respect of misconduct or gross misconduct or has no case to answer in relation to his conduct to which the investigation related;][93]

    [(a) that disciplinary proceedings of the form specified in the recommendation are brought against that person in respect of his conduct to which the investigation related;][94]

    (b) that any disciplinary proceedings brought against that person are modified so as to [deal with such aspects of that conduct][95] as may be so specified;

    and it shall be the duty of the appropriate authority to notify the Commission whether it accepts the recommendation and (if it does) to set out in the notification the steps that it is proposing to take to give effect to it.

(4) If, after the Commission has made a recommendation under this paragraph, the appropriate authority does not take steps to secure that full effect is given to the recommendation—

    (a) the Commission may direct the appropriate authority to take steps for that purpose; and

    (b) it shall be the duty of the appropriate authority to comply with the direction.

(5) A direction under sub-paragraph (4) may, to such extent as the Commission thinks fit, set out the steps to be taken by the appropriate authority in order to give effect to the recommendation.

(6) Where the Commission gives the appropriate authority a direction under this paragraph, it shall supply the appropriate authority with a statement of its reasons for doing so.

(7) Where disciplinary proceedings have been brought in accordance with a recommendation or direction under this paragraph, it shall be the duty of the authority to ensure that they are proceeded with to a proper conclusion.

(8) The Commission may at any time withdraw a direction given under this paragraph; and sub-paragraph (7) shall not impose any obligation in relation to any time after the withdrawal of the direction.

---

[91] Words substituted by CJIA, Sch 23, para 18(2).
[92] Ibid.
[93] Inserted by CJIA, Sch 23, para 18(3)(a).
[94] Substituted by CJIA, Sch 23, para 18(3)(b).
[95] Words substituted by CJIA, Sch 23, para 18(3)(c).

(9) The appropriate authority shall keep the Commission informed—

    (a) in a case in which this paragraph applies by virtue of sub-paragraph (1)(b), of whatever action it takes in pursuance of its duty under sub-paragraph (2); and

    (b) in every case of a recommendation or direction under this paragraph, of whatever action it takes in response to that recommendation or direction.

28 Information for complainant about disciplinary recommendations

(1) Where—

    (a) the Commission makes recommendations under paragraph 27 in the case of an investigation of a complaint, and

    (b) the appropriate authority notify the Commission that the recommendations have been accepted,

the Commission shall notify the complainant and every person entitled to be kept properly informed in relation to the complaint under section 21 of that fact and of the steps that have been, or are to be taken, by the appropriate authority to give effect to it.

(2) Where in the case of an investigation of a complaint the appropriate authority—

    (a) notify the Commission that it does not (either in whole or in part) accept recommendations made by the Commission under paragraph 27, or

    (b) fails to take steps to give full effect to any such recommendations,

it shall be the duty of the Commission to determine what if any further steps to take under that paragraph.

(3) It shall be the duty of the Commission to notify the complainant and every person entitled to be kept properly informed in relation to the complaint under section 21—

    (a) of any determination under sub-paragraph (2) not to take further steps under paragraph 27; and

    (b) where they determine under that sub-paragraph to take further steps under that paragraph, of the outcome of the taking of those steps.

[29 Minor definitions

In this Part of this Schedule—

"gross misconduct" means a breach of the Standards of Professional Behaviour that is so serious as to justify dismissal;

"misconduct" means a breach of the Standards of Professional Behaviour;

"the person investigating" , in relation to a complaint, recordable conduct matter or DSI matter, means the person appointed or designated to investigate that complaint or matter;

"prescribed" means prescribed by regulations made by the Secretary of State;

"the Standards of Professional Behaviour" means the standards so described in, and established by, regulations made by the Secretary of State.][96]

---

[96] Inserted by CJIA, Sch 23, para 19, in force 3 November 2008 in relation to the power to make regulations subject to savings and transitional provisions specified in SI 2008/2721, art 4, and 1 December 2008 subject to savings specified in SI 2008/2993, art 3, otherwise.

The Police (Performance) Regulations 2008, SI 2008/2862

STATUTORY INSTRUMENTS

2008 No. 2862

POLICE, ENGLAND AND WALES

The Police (Performance) Regulations 2008

Made	*5th November 2008*
Laid before Parliament	
Coming into force	*1st December 2008*

The Secretary of State makes the following Regulations in exercise of the powers conferred by sections 50, 51 and 84 of the Police Act [1].

In accordance with section 63(3)[2] of that Act, she has supplied the Police Advisory Board for England and Wales with a draft of these Regulations and has taken into consideration the representations of that Board.

In accordance with section 84(9)[3] of that Act, a draft of these Regulations was laid before Parliament and approved by a resolution of each House of Parliament.

PART 1
PRELIMINARY

Citation, commencement and extent

1.—(1) These Regulations may be cited as the Police (Performance) Regulations 2008 and shall come into force on 1st December 2008.

(2) These Regulations extend to England and Wales.

Application

2. These Regulations shall not apply in relation to—
   (a) a member of a police force above the rank of chief superintendent;
   (b) an officer of the rank of constable who has not completed his period of probation.

Revocation and transitional provisions

3.—(1) Subject to paragraph (2), the following Regulations are revoked—
   (a) the Police (Efficiency) Regulations 1999[4];
   (b) the Police (Efficiency) (Amendment) Regulations 2003[5]; and
   (c) the Police (Efficiency) (Amendment No.2) Regulations 2003[6].

(2) Where unsatisfactory performance or attendance by a police officer came to the attention of the line manager for such officer before 1st December 2008, nothing in these Regulations shall apply and the Regulations mentioned in paragraph (1) shall continue to have effect.

Interpretation and delegation

4.—(1) In these Regulations—

"the 1996 Act" means the Police Act 1996;

"the Police Regulations" means the Police Regulations 2003[7];

"appropriate authority" means the chief officer of police of the police force concerned;

"bank holiday" means a day which is a bank holiday under the Banking and Financial Dealings Act 1971[8] in England and Wales;

"document" means anything in which information of any description is recorded and includes any recording of a visual image or images;

"first stage appeal meeting" has the meaning assigned to it by regulation 16;

"first stage meeting" has the meaning assigned to it by regulation 12;

"gross incompetence" and cognate expressions mean a serious inability or serious failure of a police officer to perform the duties of his rank or the role he is currently undertaking to a satisfactory standard or level, to the extent that dismissal would be justified, except that no account shall be taken of the attendance of a police officer when considering whether he has been grossly incompetent;

"human resources professional" means a police officer or police staff member who has specific responsibility for personnel matters relating to members of a police force;

"interested party" means a person whose appointment could reasonably give rise to a concern as to whether he could act impartially under these Regulations;

"line manager" means the police officer or the police staff member who, in either case, has immediate supervisory responsibility for the officer concerned;

"nominated person" means a person appointed by the senior manager in accordance with regulation 9;

"officer concerned" means the police officer in respect of whom proceedings under these Regulations are, or are proposed to be, taken;

"panel" means a panel appointed by the appropriate authority in accordance with regulation 30 subject to any change to the membership of that panel in accordance with regulation 31 and to the provisions of regulations 40 and 41;

"panel chair" means the chair of the panel;

"police force concerned" means—

(a) where the officer concerned is a member of a police force, the police force of which he is a member; and

(b) where the officer concerned is a special constable, the police force maintained for the police area for which he is appointed;

"police friend" means a person chosen by the officer concerned in accordance with regulation 5;

"police officer" means a member of a police force or a special constable;

"police staff member" means an employee of a police authority who is under the direction and control of a chief officer of police;

"proposed witness" means a witness whose attendance at a third stage meeting the officer concerned or the appropriate authority (as the case may be) wishes to request of the panel chair;

"relevant lawyer" has the same meaning as in section 84(4) of the 1996 Act, subject to the provisions of paragraph 35 of Schedule 27 to the Criminal Justice and Immigration Act 2008;

"relevant terms of the final written improvement notice" has the meaning assigned to it by regulation 23;

"relevant terms of the written improvement notice" has the meaning assigned to it by regulation 16;

"second line manager" means the person appointed by the appropriate authority to act as the second line manager for the purposes of these Regulations in relation to the officer concerned and who is either—

(a) a member of the police force concerned having supervisory responsibility for the line manager and who (in a case where the line manager is a member of the force) is senior in rank to the line manager, or

(b) a police staff member who has supervisory responsibility for the line manager;

"second stage appeal meeting" has the meaning assigned to it by regulation 23;

"second stage meeting" has the meaning assigned to it by regulation 19;

"senior manager" means—

(a) the police officer or police staff member who is for the time being the supervisor of the person who is, in relation to the officer concerned, the second line manager; or

(b) in the absence of such supervisor, the police officer or police staff member nominated by the appropriate authority to carry out any of the functions of such supervisor under these Regulations, being of at least the same rank (or equivalent) as the person who is, in relation to the officer concerned, the second line manager;

"senior officer" means a member of a police force holding a rank above that of chief superintendent;

"staff association" means—

(a) in relation to a member of a police force of the rank of chief inspector or below, the Police Federation of England and Wales; and

(b) in relation to a member of a police force of the rank of superintendent or chief superintendent, the Police Superintendents' Association of England and Wales;

"third stage meeting" has the meaning assigned to it by regulations 26 and 28;

"unsatisfactory performance procedures" means the procedures set out in these Regulations;

"validity period" has the meaning assigned to it by regulations 15(4), 22(4), 38(6)(d) and (7)(c); and

"working day" means any day other than a Saturday or a Sunday or a day which is a bank holiday or a public holiday in England and Wales.

(2) In these Regulations—

(a) references to—

(i) unsatisfactory performance or attendance;

(ii) the performance or attendance of an officer being unsatisfactory,

mean an inability or failure of a police officer to perform the duties of the role or rank he is currently undertaking to a satisfactory standard or level;

(b) "unsatisfactory performance or attendance" may be construed as a reference to unsatisfactory performance and attendance;

(c) "performance or attendance" may be construed as a reference to performance and attendance.

(3) The appropriate authority may, subject to paragraph (4), delegate any of its functions under these Regulations to—

(a) a member of a police force of at least the rank of chief inspector; or

(b) a police staff member who, in the opinion of the appropriate authority is of at least a similar level of seniority to a chief inspector.

(4) Where the appropriate authority delegates its functions under regulation 28, the decisions shall be authorised by a senior officer.

(5) Any proceedings under these Regulations are disciplinary proceedings for the purposes of section 87 of the 1996 Act (guidance concerning disciplinary proceedings)[9].

PART 2

GENERAL

Police friend

5.—(1) The officer concerned may choose—

    (a) a police officer;

    (b) a police staff member; or

    (c) where the officer concerned is a member of a police force, a person nominated by his staff association,

who is not otherwise involved in the matter, to act as his police friend.

(2) A police friend may—

    (a) advise the officer concerned throughout the proceedings under these Regulations;

    (b) unless the officer concerned has the right to be legally represented under regulation 6 and chooses to be so represented, represent the officer concerned at a meeting under these Regulations;

    (c) make representations to the appropriate authority concerning any aspect of the proceedings under these Regulations; and

    (d) accompany the officer concerned to any meeting which the officer concerned is required to attend under these Regulations.

(3) Where a police friend is a police officer or a police staff member, the chief officer of police of the force of which the police friend is a member shall permit him to use a reasonable amount of duty time for the purposes referred to in paragraph (2).

(4) The reference in paragraph (3) to the force of which the police friend is a member shall include a reference to the force maintained for the police area for which a special constable is appointed and the force in which a police staff member is serving.

Legal representation

6.—(1) Where a police officer is required to attend a third stage meeting under regulation 28, he has the right to be legally represented at such meeting by a relevant lawyer of his choice.

(2) If such an officer chooses not to be legally represented—

    (a) such meeting may take place and he may be dismissed or receive any other outcome under regulation 38(2) or (5) without his being legally represented; and

    (b) the panel conducting such meeting may nevertheless be advised by a relevant lawyer at the meeting in accordance with regulation 36(4).

(3) Except in a case where the officer concerned has the right to be legally represented and chooses to be so represented, he may be represented at a meeting under these Regulations only by a police friend.

(4) A third stage meeting under regulation 28 shall not take place unless the officer concerned has been notified in writing of the effect of this regulation.

Provision of notices or documents

7. Where any written notice or document is to be given or supplied to the officer concerned under these Regulations, it shall be—

    (a) given to him in person; or

    (b) left with some person at, or sent by recorded delivery to, his last known address.

Procedure at meetings under these Regulations

8.—(1) Where the officer concerned does not attend a meeting under these Regulations or where the officer concerned participates in a third stage meeting by video link or other means under regulation 34(9), he may nonetheless be represented at that meeting by his–

    (a) police friend; or

    (b) where the officer is required to attend the third stage meeting under regulation 28, his relevant lawyer.

(2) Where the officer concerned does not attend a meeting under these Regulations or participate in a third stage meeting by video link or other means under regulation 34(9), the meeting may be proceeded with and concluded in the absence of the officer concerned whether or not he is so represented.

(3) During any meeting under these Regulations, the person representing the officer concerned may—

    (a) address the meeting in order to do any or all of the following–

        (i) put the case of the officer concerned;

        (ii) sum up that case;

        (iii) respond on behalf of the officer concerned to any view expressed at the meeting;

        (iv) make representations concerning any aspect of proceedings under these Regulations; and

        (v) in the case of a third stage meeting only, subject to paragraph (7), ask questions of any witnesses;

    (b) confer with the officer concerned.

(4) Where the person representing the officer concerned is a relevant lawyer, the police friend of the officer concerned may also confer with the officer concerned.

(5) Where the officer concerned is participating in a third stage meeting by video link or other means in accordance with regulation 34(9), the person representing the officer or (if different) his police friend (or both) may also participate in the third stage meeting by such means together with the officer concerned.

(6) The police friend or relevant lawyer of the officer concerned may not answer any questions asked of the officer concerned during a meeting.

(7) Whether any question should or should not be put to a witness at a third stage meeting shall be determined by the panel chair.

(8) At any meeting under these Regulations, the person or the panel conducting the meeting shall not make a finding of unsatisfactory performance or attendance or gross incompetence unless—

    (a) he is or they are satisfied on the balance of probabilities that there has been unsatisfactory performance or attendance or gross incompetence; or

    (b) the officer concerned consents to such a finding.

(9) The person conducting or chairing a meeting under these Regulations may allow any document to be considered at that meeting notwithstanding that a copy of it has not been—

    (a) supplied to him by the officer concerned in accordance with regulation 13(8), 16(6)(b), 20(8), 23(6)(b) or 32(3);

    (b) supplied to the officer concerned in accordance with regulation 13(2), 20(2), 27(2) or 29(2); or

    (c) made available to each panel member or given to the officer concerned under regulation 30(11).

Nominated persons

9.—(1) A senior manager may appoint another person (a "nominated person") to carry out any of the functions of the line manager or the second line manager in these Regulations.

(2) Where a person is appointed to carry out any of the functions of the line manager under paragraph (1) he may not also be appointed to carry out any of the functions of the second line manager under that paragraph.

(3) Where a person is appointed to carry out any of the functions of the second line manager under paragraph (1) he may not also be appointed to carry out any of the functions of the line manager under that paragraph.

(4) A nominated person shall be a member of the police force concerned or a police staff member in the police force concerned and shall be, in the opinion of the appropriate authority, of at least the same or equivalent rank or grade as the person whose functions he is carrying out.

(5) Where a nominated person is appointed by the senior manager, references in these Regulations to a line manager or a second line manager, as the case may be, shall be construed as references to the nominated person, in relation to the functions which the nominated person has been appointed to carry out.

References to certain periods

10.—(1) The appropriate authority may, on the application of the officer concerned or otherwise, extend the period specified in accordance with any of the regulations mentioned in paragraph (2) if it is satisfied that it is appropriate to do so.

(2) The regulations mentioned in this paragraph are—
   (a) regulation 14(6)(c);
   (b) regulation 21(6)(c); and
   (c) regulation 38(6)(c) and (7)(a).

(3) Unless the appropriate authority is satisfied that there are exceptional circumstances making it appropriate, any such period may not be extended if the extension would result in the total length of that period exceeding 12 months.

(4) Where an extension is granted under paragraph (1) to a period specified under a regulation mentioned in paragraph (2), any reference in these Regulations to such period shall be construed as a reference to that period as so extended.

Suspension of certain periods

11.—(1) Any reference in these Regulations to a period mentioned in paragraph (2) shall not include any time the officer concerned is taking a career break under regulation 33(12) of the Police Regulations (leave) and the determination of the Secretary of State made under that regulation.

(2) The periods mentioned in this paragraph are—
   (a) a period specified in accordance with regulation 14(6)(c);
   (b) the validity period of a written improvement notice;
   (c) a period specified in accordance with regulation 21(6)(c);
   (d) the validity period of a final written improvement notice;
   (e) a period specified under regulation 38(6)(c) or (7)(a);
   (f) the validity period of a final written improvement notice extended under regulation 38.

PART 3

FIRST STAGE

Circumstances in which a first stage meeting may be required

12. Where the line manager for a police officer considers that the performance or attendance of that officer is unsatisfactory, he may require the officer concerned to attend a meeting (in these Regulations referred to as a first stage meeting) to discuss the performance or attendance of the officer concerned.

Arrangement of first stage meeting

13.—(1) If the line manager wishes to require a police officer to attend a first stage meeting, he shall give a notice in writing to the officer concerned—
   (a) requiring him to attend a first stage meeting of the unsatisfactory performance procedures with the line manager;

   (b) informing him of the procedures for determining the date and time of the meeting under paragraphs (3) to (6);
   (c) summarising the reasons why his performance or attendance is considered unsatisfactory;
   (d) informing him of the possible outcomes of a first stage meeting, a second stage meeting and a third stage meeting;
   (e) informing him that a human resources professional or a police officer may attend the meeting to advise the line manager on the proceedings;
   (f) informing him that, if he consents, any other person specified in the notice may attend the meeting;
   (g) where the officer concerned is a member of a police force, informing him that he may seek advice from a representative of his staff association;
   (h) informing him that he may be accompanied and represented at the meeting by a police friend; and
   (i) informing him that he must provide to the line manager in advance of the meeting a copy of any document he intends to rely on at the meeting.
(2) Such notice shall be accompanied by a copy of any document relied upon by the line manager when coming to his view mentioned in regulation 12 that the performance or attendance of the officer concerned is unsatisfactory.
(3) The line manager shall, if reasonably practicable, agree a date and time for the meeting with the officer concerned.
(4) Where no date and time is agreed under paragraph (3), the line manager shall specify a date and time for the meeting.
(5) Where a date and time is specified under paragraph (4) and—
   (a) the officer concerned or his police friend will not be available at that time; and
   (b) the officer concerned proposes an alternative time which satisfies paragraph (6),
   the meeting must be postponed to the time proposed by the officer concerned.
(6) An alternative time must—
   (a) be reasonable; and
   (b) fall before the end of five working days beginning with the first working day after the day specified by the line manager under paragraph (4).
(7) The line manager shall give to the officer concerned a notice in writing of the date and time of the first stage meeting determined in accordance with paragraphs (3) to (6) and of the place of the meeting.
(8) In advance of the first stage meeting, the officer concerned shall provide the line manager with a copy of any document he intends to rely on at the meeting.

Procedure at first stage meeting

14.—(1) The following provisions of this regulation apply to the procedure to be followed at the first stage meeting.
(2) The meeting shall be conducted by the line manager.
(3) A human resources professional or a police officer may attend the meeting to advise the line manager on the proceedings.
(4) Any other person specified in the notice referred to in regulation 13(1) may attend the meeting if the officer concerned consents to such attendance.
(5) The line manager shall—
   (a) explain to the officer concerned the reasons why the line manager considers that the performance or attendance of the officer concerned is unsatisfactory;
   (b) provide the officer concerned with an opportunity to make representations in response;
   (c) provide his police friend (if he has one) with an opportunity to address the meeting in accordance with regulation 8(3)(a).

(6) If, after considering any representations made in accordance with paragraph (5)(b) or (c), the line manager finds that the performance or attendance of the officer concerned has been unsatisfactory, he shall—

    (a) inform the officer concerned in what respect his performance or attendance is considered unsatisfactory;

    (b) inform the officer concerned of the improvement that is required in his performance or attendance;

    (c) inform the officer concerned that, if a sufficient improvement is not made within such reasonable period as the line manager shall specify (being a period not greater than 12 months), he may be required to attend a second stage meeting in accordance with regulation 19 and the line manager shall specify the date on which this period ends;

    (d) inform the officer concerned that he will receive a written improvement notice; and

    (e) inform the officer concerned that if the sufficient improvement referred to in sub-paragraph (c) is not maintained during any part of the validity period of such notice remaining after the expiry of the period specified in accordance with sub-paragraph (c), he may be required to attend a second stage meeting in accordance with regulation 19.

(7) The line manager may, if he considers it appropriate, recommend that the officer concerned seeks assistance in relation to any matter affecting his health or welfare.

(8) The line manager may postpone or adjourn the meeting to a specified later time or date if it appears to him necessary or expedient to do so.

Procedure following first stage meeting

15.—(1) The line manager shall, as soon as reasonably practicable after the date of the conclusion of the first stage meeting—

    (a) cause to be prepared a written record of the meeting; and

    (b) where he found at the meeting that the performance or attendance of the officer concerned has been unsatisfactory, cause to be prepared a written improvement notice.

(2) Where the officer concerned has failed to attend a first stage meeting, if the line manager finds that the performance or attendance of the officer has been unsatisfactory, he shall as soon as reasonably practicable—

    (a) cause to be prepared a written improvement notice; and

    (b) if the police friend of the officer concerned attended the meeting, cause to be prepared a written record of the meeting.

(3) A written improvement notice shall—

    (a) record the matters of which the officer concerned was informed (or would have been informed had he attended the meeting) under sub-paragraphs (a) to (c) and (e) of regulation 14(6);

    (b) state the period for which it is valid; and

    (c) be signed and dated by the line manager.

(4) A written improvement notice shall be valid for a period of twelve months from the date of the notice (the "validity period").

(5) The line manager shall give a copy of any written record and any written improvement notice to the officer concerned as soon as reasonably practicable after they have been prepared.

(6) Where the line manager found that the performance or attendance of the officer concerned has been unsatisfactory and has caused to be prepared a written improvement notice, he shall, at the same time as supplying the documents mentioned in paragraph (5), notify the officer concerned in writing of the matters set out in regulation 16, of the name of the person to whom a written notice of appeal must be given under that regulation, of his entitlements under paragraphs (7) and (8) and of the effect of paragraph (9).

(7) Subject to paragraphs (8) and (9), the officer concerned shall be entitled to submit written comments on any written record to the line manager before the end of 7 working days

beginning with the first working day after the day on which the copy is received by the officer concerned.

(8) The line manager may, on the application of the officer concerned, extend the period specified in paragraph (7) if he is satisfied that it is appropriate to do so.

(9) The officer concerned shall not be entitled to submit written comments on the written record if he has exercised his right to appeal under regulation 16.

(10) The line manager shall ensure that any written record, any written improvement notice and any written comments of the officer concerned on the written record are retained together and filed.

Appeal against the finding and outcome of a first stage meeting

16.—(1) This regulation applies where, at the first stage meeting, the line manager found that the performance or attendance of the officer concerned has been unsatisfactory.

(2) Where this regulation applies, the officer concerned may appeal against–

(a) such finding; or

(b) any of the matters specified in paragraph (3) and recorded in the written improvement notice (in these Regulations referred to as the relevant terms of the written improvement notice),

or both.

(3) The matters specified in this paragraph are—

(a) the respect in which the performance or attendance of the officer concerned is considered unsatisfactory;

(b) the improvement that is required in his performance or attendance;

(c) the length of the period specified by the line manager in accordance with regulation 14(6)(c).

(4) The only grounds of appeal under this regulation are—

(a) that the finding of unsatisfactory performance or attendance was unreasonable;

(b) that any of the relevant terms of the written improvement notice are unreasonable;

(c) that there is evidence that could not reasonably have been considered at the first stage meeting which could have materially affected the finding of unsatisfactory performance or attendance or any of the relevant terms of the written improvement notice;

(d) that there was a breach of the procedures set out in these Regulations or other unfairness which could have materially affected the finding of unsatisfactory performance or attendance or any of the relevant terms of the written improvement notice.

(5) Any appeal shall be commenced by the officer concerned giving written notice of appeal to the second line manager before the end of 7 working days beginning with the first working day after receipt of the documents referred to in regulation 15(5).

(6) Such notification must–

(a) set out the grounds of appeal of the officer concerned; and

(b) be accompanied by any evidence on which the officer concerned relies.

(7) The second line manager may, on the application of the officer concerned, extend the period specified in paragraph (5) if he is satisfied that it is appropriate to do so.

(8) Subject to paragraph (9), the meeting at which the appeal will be heard (referred to in these Regulations as the first stage appeal meeting) shall take place before the end of 7 working days beginning with the first working day after the day on which the notification under paragraph (5) is received by the second line manager.

(9) A first stage appeal meeting may take place after the period of 7 working days referred to in paragraph (8) if the second line manager considers it necessary or expedient, in which case he shall notify the officer concerned of his reasons in writing.

Arrangement of first stage appeal meeting

17.—(1) As soon as reasonably practicable after receipt by the second line manager of the notification of appeal referred to in regulation 16(5), the second line manager shall give a notice in writing to the officer concerned—

    (a) informing him of the procedures for determining the date and time of the meeting under paragraphs (2) to (5);

    (b) informing him that a human resources professional or a police officer may attend the meeting to advise the second line manager on the proceedings;

    (c) informing him that, if he consents, any other person specified in the notice may attend the meeting;

    (d) where the officer concerned is a member of a police force, informing him that he may seek advice from a representative of his staff association; and

    (e) informing him that he may be accompanied and represented at the meeting by a police friend.

(2) The second line manager shall, if reasonably practicable, agree a date and time for the meeting with the officer concerned.

(3) Where no date and time is agreed under paragraph (2), the second line manager shall specify a date and time for the meeting.

(4) Where a date and time is specified under paragraph (3) and—

    (a) the officer concerned or his police friend will not be available at that time; and

    (b) the officer concerned proposes an alternative time which satisfies paragraph (5),

the meeting must be postponed to the time proposed by the officer concerned.

(5) An alternative time must—

    (a) be reasonable; and

    (b) fall before the end of five working days beginning with the first working day after the day specified by the second line manager under paragraph (3).

(6) The second line manager shall give to the officer concerned a notice in writing of the date and time of the first stage appeal meeting determined in accordance with paragraphs (2) to (5) and of the place of the meeting.

Procedure at first stage appeal meeting

18.—(1) The following provisions of this regulation apply to the procedure to be followed at a first stage appeal meeting.

(2) The meeting shall be conducted by the second line manager.

(3) A human resources professional or a police officer may attend the meeting to advise the second line manager on the proceedings.

(4) Any other person specified in the notice referred to in regulation 17(1) may attend the meeting if the officer concerned consents to such attendance.

(5) The second line manager shall—

    (a) provide the officer concerned with an opportunity to make representations; and

    (b) provide his police friend (if he has one) with an opportunity to address the meeting in accordance with regulation 8(3)(a).

(6) After considering any representations made in accordance with paragraph (5), the second line manager may—

    (a) confirm or reverse the finding of unsatisfactory performance or attendance;

    (b) confirm or vary the relevant terms of the written improvement notice appealed against.

(7) Where the second line manager has reversed the finding of unsatisfactory performance or attendance, he shall also revoke the written improvement notice.

(8) The second line manager may postpone or adjourn the meeting to a specified later time or date if it appears to him necessary or expedient to do so.

(9) As soon as reasonably practicable after the conclusion of the meeting, the officer concerned shall be given written notice of the second line manager's decision and a written summary of the reasons for that decision, but in any event, the officer concerned shall be given written notice of the decision before the end of three working days beginning with the first working day after the conclusion of the meeting.

(10) Where the second line manager has—

(a) reversed the finding of unsatisfactory performance or attendance and revoked the written improvement notice; or

(b) varied any of the relevant terms of the written improvement notice,

the decision of the second line manager shall take effect by way of substitution for the finding, the written improvement notice issued or the relevant terms of the written improvement notice appealed against from the date of the first stage meeting.

PART 4
SECOND STAGE

Circumstances in which a second stage meeting may be required

19.—(1) Where a police officer has received a written improvement notice, as soon as reasonably practicable after the date on which the period specified in accordance with regulation 14(6)(c) ends—

(a) the line manager shall assess the performance or attendance of the officer concerned during that period, in consultation with the second line manager or a human resources professional (or both); and

(b) the line manager shall notify the officer concerned in writing whether the line manager considers that there has been a sufficient improvement in performance or attendance during that period.

(2) If the line manager considers that there has not been a sufficient improvement, he shall, at the same time as he gives notification under paragraph (1)(b), also notify the officer concerned in writing that he is required to attend a meeting (in these Regulations referred to as a second stage meeting) to consider his performance or attendance.

(3) Where—

(a) the officer concerned has not been required to attend a second stage meeting under paragraph (2), or

(b) the officer concerned has been required to attend a second stage meeting under paragraph (2) but the second line manager did not make a finding of unsatisfactory performance or attendance at that meeting,

the officer concerned may be required to attend a second stage meeting under paragraph (4).

(4) If the line manager considers that the officer concerned has failed to maintain a sufficient improvement in his performance or attendance during any part of the validity period of the written improvement notice remaining after the expiry of the period specified in accordance with regulation 14(6)(c), he shall notify the officer concerned in writing of the matters set out in paragraph (5).

(5) Those matters are—

(a) that he is of the view mentioned in paragraph (4); and

(b) that the officer concerned is required to attend a meeting (in these Regulations referred to as a second stage meeting) to consider his performance or attendance.

(6) Any second stage meeting which a police officer is required to attend must concern unsatisfactory performance or attendance which is similar to or connected with the unsatisfactory performance or attendance referred to in the written improvement notice.

Arrangement of second stage meeting

20.—(1) Where the line manager requires the officer concerned to attend a second stage meeting, the second line manager shall as soon as reasonably practicable give a notice in writing to the officer concerned—

(a) referring to the requirement on the officer concerned to attend a second stage meeting of the unsatisfactory performance procedures with the second line manager;

(b) informing him of the procedures for determining the date and time of the meeting under paragraphs (3) to (6);

(c) summarising the reasons why his performance or attendance is considered unsatisfactory;

(d) informing him of the possible outcomes of a second stage meeting and a third stage meeting;

(e) informing him that the line manager may attend the meeting;

(f) informing him that a human resources professional or a police officer may attend the meeting to advise the second line manager on the proceedings;

(g) informing him that, if he consents, any other person specified in the notice may attend the meeting;

(h) where the officer concerned is a member of a police force, informing him that he may seek advice from a representative of his staff association;

(i) informing him that he may be accompanied and represented at the meeting by a police friend; and

(j) informing him that he must provide to the second line manager in advance of the meeting a copy of any document he intends to rely on at the meeting.

(2) Such notice shall be accompanied by a copy of any document relied upon by the line manager when he formed the view referred to in regulation 19(2) or (4), as the case may be.

(3) The second line manager shall, if reasonably practicable, agree a date and time for the meeting with the officer concerned.

(4) Where no date and time is agreed under paragraph (3), the second line manager shall specify a date and time for the meeting.

(5) Where a date and time is specified under paragraph (4) and—

(a) the officer concerned or his police friend will not be available at that time; and

(b) the officer concerned proposes an alternative time which satisfies paragraph (6),

the meeting must be postponed to the time proposed by the officer concerned.

(6) An alternative time must—

(a) be reasonable; and

(b) fall before the end of five working days beginning with the first working day after the day specified by the second line manager under paragraph (4).

(7) The second line manager shall give to the officer concerned a notice in writing of the date and time of the second stage meeting determined in accordance with paragraphs (3) to (6) and of the place of the meeting.

(8) In advance of the second stage meeting, the officer concerned shall provide the second line manager with a copy of any document he intends to rely on at the meeting.

Procedure at second stage meeting

21.—(1) The following provisions of this regulation shall apply to the procedure to be followed at the second stage meeting.

(2) The meeting shall be conducted by the second line manager and may be attended by the line manager.

(3) A human resources professional or a police officer may attend the meeting to advise the second line manager on the proceedings.

(4) Any other person specified in the notice referred to in regulation 20(1) may attend the meeting if the officer concerned consents to such attendance.

(5) The second line manager shall—
  (a) explain to the officer concerned the reasons why he has been required to attend the meeting;
  (b) provide the officer concerned with an opportunity to make representations in response;
  (c) provide his police friend (if he has one) with an opportunity to address the meeting in accordance with regulation 8(3)(a).

(6) If, after considering any representations made under paragraph (5)(b) or (c), the second line manager finds that the performance or attendance of the officer concerned has been unsatisfactory during the period specified in accordance with regulation 14(6)(c) or during any part of the validity period of the written improvement notice remaining after the expiry of such period, he shall—
  (a) inform the officer concerned in what respect his performance or attendance is considered unsatisfactory;
  (b) inform the officer concerned of the improvement that is required in his performance or attendance;
  (c) inform the officer concerned that, if a sufficient improvement is not made within such reasonable period as the second line manager shall specify (being a period not greater than 12 months), he may be required to attend a third stage meeting in accordance with regulation 26 and the second line manager shall specify the date on which this period ends;
  (d) inform the officer concerned that he will receive a final written improvement notice; and
  (e) inform the officer concerned that if the sufficient improvement referred to in sub-paragraph (c) is not maintained during any part of the validity period of such notice remaining after the expiry of the period specified in accordance with sub-paragraph (c), he may be required to attend a third stage meeting in accordance with regulation 26.

(7) The second line manager may, if he considers it appropriate, recommend that the officer concerned seeks assistance in relation to any matter affecting his health or welfare.

(8) The second line manager may postpone or adjourn the meeting to a specified later time or date if it appears to him necessary or expedient to do so.

Procedure following second stage meeting

22.—(1) The second line manager shall, as soon as reasonably practicable after the date of the conclusion of the second stage meeting—
  (a) cause to be prepared a written record of the meeting; and
  (b) where he made a finding at the meeting as set out in regulation 21(6), cause to be prepared a final written improvement notice.

(2) Where the officer concerned has failed to attend a second stage meeting, if the second line manager makes a finding as set out in regulation 21(6), he shall as soon as reasonably practicable—
  (a) cause to be prepared a final written improvement notice; and
  (b) if the police friend of the officer concerned attended the meeting, cause to be prepared a written record of the meeting.

(3) A final written improvement notice shall—
  (a) record the matters of which the officer concerned was informed (or would have been informed had he attended the meeting) under sub-paragraphs (a) to (c) and (e) of regulation 21(6);
  (b) state the period for which it is valid; and
  (c) be signed and dated by the second line manager.

(4) A final written improvement notice shall be valid for a period of twelve months from the date of the notice (the "validity period").

(5) The second line manager shall give a copy of any written record and any final written improvement notice to the officer concerned as soon as reasonably practicable after they have been prepared.

(6) Where the second line manager made a finding as set out in regulation 21(6) and has caused to be prepared a final written improvement notice, he shall, at the same time as supplying the documents mentioned in paragraph (5), notify the officer concerned in writing of the matters set out in regulation 23, of the name of the person to whom a written notice of appeal must be given under that regulation, of his entitlements under paragraphs (7) and (8) and of the effect of paragraph (9).

(7) Subject to paragraphs (8) and (9), the officer concerned shall be entitled to submit written comments on the written record to the second line manager before the end of 7 working days beginning with the first working day after the day on which the copy is received by the officer concerned.

(8) The second line manager may, on the application of the officer concerned, extend the period specified in paragraph (7) if he is satisfied that it is appropriate to do so.

(9) The officer concerned shall not be entitled to submit written comments on the written record if he has exercised his right to appeal under regulation 23.

(10) The second line manager shall ensure that any written record, any final written improvement notice and any written comments of the officer concerned on the written record are retained together and filed.

Appeal against the finding and outcome of a second stage meeting

23.—(1) This regulation applies where, at the second stage meeting, the second line manager found that the performance or attendance of the officer concerned has been unsatisfactory as set out in regulation 21(6).

(2) Where this regulation applies, the officer concerned may appeal against one or more of the following—
   (a) such finding;
   (b) any of the matters specified in paragraph (3) and recorded in the final written improvement notice (in these Regulations referred to as the relevant terms of the final written improvement notice);
   (c) the decision of the line manager to require the officer concerned to attend the second stage meeting.

(3) The matters specified in this paragraph are—
   (a) the respect in which the performance or attendance of the officer concerned is considered unsatisfactory;
   (b) the improvement that is required in his performance or attendance;
   (c) the length of the period specified by the second line manager in accordance with regulation 21(6)(c).

(4) The only grounds of appeal under this regulation are–
   (a) that, in relation to an appeal under paragraph (2)(c), the officer concerned should not have been required to attend the second stage meeting as the meeting did not, in accordance with regulation 19(6), concern unsatisfactory performance or attendance which is similar to or connected with the unsatisfactory performance or attendance referred to in the written improvement notice;
   (b) that the finding of unsatisfactory performance or attendance was unreasonable;
   (c) that any of the relevant terms of the final written improvement notice are unreasonable;
   (d) that there is evidence that could not reasonably have been considered at the second stage meeting which could have materially affected the finding of unsatisfactory performance or attendance or any of the relevant terms of the final written improvement notice;

(e) that there was a breach of the procedures set out in these Regulations or other unfairness which could have materially affected the finding of unsatisfactory performance or attendance or any of the relevant terms of the final written improvement notice.

(5) An appeal shall be commenced by the officer concerned giving written notice of appeal to the senior manager before the end of 7 working days beginning with the first working day after receipt of the documents referred to in regulation 22(5).

(6) Such notice must–

    (a) set out the grounds of appeal of the officer concerned; and

    (b) be accompanied by any evidence on which the officer concerned relies.

(7) The senior manager may, on the application of the officer concerned, extend the period specified in paragraph (5) if he is satisfied that it is appropriate to do so.

(8) Subject to paragraph (9), the meeting at which the appeal will be heard (referred to in these Regulations as a second stage appeal meeting) shall take place before the end of 7 working days beginning with the first working day after the day on which the notification under paragraph (5) is received by the senior manager.

(9) A second stage appeal meeting may take place after the period of 7 working days referred to in paragraph (8) if the senior manager considers it necessary or expedient, in which case he shall notify the officer concerned of his reasons in writing.

Arrangement of second stage appeal meeting

24.—(1) As soon as reasonably practicable after receipt by the senior manager of the notice of appeal referred to in regulation 23(5), the senior manager shall give a notice in writing to the officer concerned—

    (a) informing him of the procedures for determining the date and time of the meeting under paragraphs (2) to (5);

    (b) informing him that a human resources professional or a police officer may attend the meeting to advise the senior manager on the proceedings;

    (c) informing him that, if he consents, any other person specified in the notice may attend the meeting;

    (d) where the officer concerned is a member of a police force, informing him that he may seek advice from a representative of his staff association; and

    (e) informing him that he may be accompanied and represented at the meeting by a police friend.

(2) The senior manager shall, if reasonably practicable, agree a date and time for the meeting with the officer concerned.

(3) Where no date and time is agreed under paragraph (2), the senior manager shall specify a date and time for the meeting.

(4) Where a date and time is specified under paragraph (3) and—

    (a) the officer concerned or his police friend will not be available at that time; and

    (b) the officer concerned proposes an alternative time which satisfies paragraph (5),

the meeting must be postponed to the time proposed by the officer concerned.

(5) An alternative time must—

    (a) be reasonable; and

    (b) fall before the end of five working days beginning with the first working day after the day specified by the senior manager under paragraph (3).

(6) The senior manager shall give to the officer concerned a notice in writing of the date and time of the second stage appeal meeting determined in accordance with paragraphs (2) to (5) and of the place of the meeting.

Procedure at second stage appeal meeting

25.—(1) The following provisions of this regulation apply to the procedure to be followed at a second stage appeal meeting.

(2) The meeting shall be conducted by the senior manager.

(3) A human resources professional or a police officer may attend the meeting to advise the senior manager on the proceedings.

(4) Any other person specified in the notice referred to in regulation 24(1) may attend the meeting if the officer concerned consents to such attendance.

(5) The senior manager shall—

    (a) provide the officer concerned with an opportunity to make representations; and

    (b) provide his police friend (if he has one) with an opportunity to address the meeting in accordance with regulation 8(3)(a).

(6) After considering any representations made in accordance with paragraph (5), the senior manager may—

    (a) in an appeal under regulation 23(2)(c), make a finding that the officer concerned should not have been required to attend the second stage meeting and reverse the finding made at that meeting;

    (b) confirm or reverse the finding of unsatisfactory performance or attendance made at the second stage meeting;

    (c) confirm or vary the relevant terms of the final written improvement notice appealed against.

(7) Where the senior manager has reversed the finding of unsatisfactory performance or attendance made at the second stage meeting, the senior manager shall also revoke the final written improvement notice.

(8) The senior manager may postpone or adjourn the meeting to a specified later time or date if it appears to him necessary or expedient to do so.

(9) As soon as reasonably practicable after the conclusion of the meeting, the officer concerned shall be given written notice of the senior manager's decision and a written summary of the reasons for that decision but in any event, the officer concerned shall be given written notice of the decision before the end of three working days beginning with the first working day after the conclusion of the meeting.

(10) Where the senior manager has—

    (a) reversed the finding made as set out in regulation 21(6) and revoked the final written improvement notice; or

    (b) varied any of the relevant terms of the final written improvement notice,

    the decision of the senior manager shall take effect by way of substitution for the finding, the final written improvement notice issued or the relevant terms of the final written improvement notice appealed against from the date of the second stage meeting.

PART 5

THIRD STAGE

Assessment following second stage meeting

26.—(1) Where a police officer has received a final written improvement notice, as soon as reasonably practicable after the date on which the period specified in accordance with regulation 21(6)(c) ends—

    (a) the line manager shall assess the performance or attendance of the officer concerned during that period, in consultation with the second line manager or a human resources professional (or both); and

    (b) the line manager shall notify the officer concerned in writing whether the line manager considers that there has been a sufficient improvement in performance or attendance during that period.

(2) If the line manager considers that there has not been a sufficient improvement, he shall, at the same time as he gives notification under paragraph (1)(b), also notify the officer concerned

in writing that he is required to attend a meeting (in these Regulations referred to as a third stage meeting) to consider his performance or attendance.

(3) Where—
   (a) the officer concerned has not been required to attend a third stage meeting under paragraph (2), or
   (b) the officer concerned has been required to attend a third stage meeting under paragraph (2) but the panel did not make a finding of unsatisfactory performance or attendance at that meeting,
   the officer concerned may be required to attend a third stage meeting under paragraph (4).

(4) If the line manager considers that the officer concerned has failed to maintain a sufficient improvement in his performance or attendance during any part of the validity period of the final written improvement notice remaining after the expiry of the period specified in accordance with regulation 21(6)(c), he shall notify the officer concerned in writing of the matters set out in paragraph (5).

(5) Those matters are—
   (a) that he is of the view mentioned in paragraph (4); and
   (b) that the officer concerned is required to attend a meeting (in these Regulations referred to as a third stage meeting) to consider his performance or attendance.

(6) Subject to regulation 28, any third stage meeting which a police officer is required to attend must concern unsatisfactory performance or attendance which is similar to or connected with the unsatisfactory performance or attendance referred to in the final written improvement notice.

Arrangement of a third stage meeting

27.—(1) Where the line manager requires the officer concerned to attend a third stage meeting, the senior manager shall as soon as reasonably practicable give a notice in writing to the officer concerned—
   (a) referring to the requirement on the officer concerned to attend a third stage meeting of the unsatisfactory performance procedures with a panel appointed by the appropriate authority;
   (b) informing him of the procedures for determining the date and time of the meeting under regulation 34;
   (c) summarising the reasons why his performance or attendance is considered unsatisfactory;
   (d) informing him of the possible outcomes of the meeting;
   (e) informing him that a human resources professional and a police officer may attend the meeting to advise the panel on the proceedings;
   (f) informing him that a relevant lawyer may attend the meeting to advise the panel on the proceedings and on any question of law that may arise at the meeting;
   (g) where the officer concerned is a special constable, informing him that a special constable shall attend the meeting to advise the panel;
   (h) informing him that, if he consents, any other person specified in the notice may attend the meeting;
   (i) where the officer concerned is a member of a police force, informing him that he may seek advice from a representative of his staff association; and
   (j) informing him that he may be accompanied and represented at the meeting by a police friend.

(2) Such notice shall be accompanied by a copy of any document relied upon by the line manager when he formed the view referred to in regulation 26(2) or (4), as the case may be.

(3) A third stage meeting under this regulation shall not take place unless the officer concerned has been notified of his right to representation under paragraph (1)(j).

Circumstances in which a third stage meeting may be required without a prior first or second stage meeting

28.—(1) This regulation applies where the appropriate authority considers that the performance of a police officer constitutes gross incompetence.

(2) Where this regulation applies, the appropriate authority may inform the officer concerned in writing that he is required to attend a meeting to consider his performance.

(3) Such meeting shall be referred to in these Regulations as a third stage meeting, notwithstanding that the officer concerned has not attended a first stage meeting or a second stage meeting in respect of such performance.

Arrangement of a third stage meeting without a prior first or second stage meeting

29.—(1) Where the appropriate authority has informed the officer concerned under regulation 28(2) that he is required to attend a third stage meeting, the appropriate authority shall as soon as reasonably practicable give to the officer concerned a notice in writing—

(a) referring to the requirement on the officer concerned to attend a third stage meeting of the unsatisfactory performance procedures with a panel appointed by the appropriate authority;

(b) informing him of the procedures for determining the date and time of the meeting under regulation 34;

(c) summarising the reasons why his performance is considered to constitute gross incompetence;

(d) informing him of the possible outcomes of the meeting;

(e) informing him that a human resources professional and a police officer may attend the meeting to advise the panel on the proceedings;

(f) informing him that a relevant lawyer may attend the meeting to advise the panel on the proceedings and on any question of law that may arise at the meeting;

(g) where the officer concerned is a special constable, informing him that a special constable shall attend the meeting to act as an advisor to the panel;

(h) informing him that, if he consents, any other person specified in the notice may attend the meeting;

(i) where the officer concerned is a member of a police force, informing him that he may seek advice from a representative of his staff association;

(j) informing him of the effect of regulation 6; and

(k) informing him that he may be accompanied at the meeting by a police friend.

(2) Such notice shall be accompanied by a copy of any document relied upon by the appropriate authority when it formed the view referred to in regulation 28(1).

Appointment of panel members

30.—(1) The third stage meeting shall be conducted by a panel, which shall comprise a panel chair and two other members.

(2) The panel shall be appointed by the appropriate authority.

(3) The panel chair shall be a senior officer or a senior human resources professional.

(4) One panel member shall be either a police officer or a human resources professional of at least the rank of superintendent or (in the opinion of the appropriate authority) equivalent.

(5) The other panel member shall be either a police officer or a police staff member of at least the rank of superintendent or (in the opinion of the appropriate authority) equivalent.

(6) At least one panel member shall be a police officer.

(7) At least one panel member shall be a human resources professional.

(8) Each panel member shall be of at least the same rank as or (in the opinion of the appropriate authority) equivalent of the officer concerned.

(9) No panel member shall be an interested party.

(10) As soon as reasonably practicable after the panel members have been appointed, the appropriate authority shall notify in writing the officer concerned of their names.

(11) As soon as the appropriate authority has appointed the panel members, the appropriate authority shall arrange for a copy of any document—

    (a) which was available to the line manager in relation to any first stage meeting;

    (b) which was available to the second line manager in relation to any second stage meeting; or

    (c) which was prepared or submitted under regulation 15, 18, 22, 25, 26, 27, 28 or 29 as the case may be,

to be made available to each panel member; and a copy of any such document shall be given to the officer concerned.

(12) For the purposes of this regulation, a "senior human resources professional" means a human resources professional who, in the opinion of the appropriate authority, has sufficient seniority, skills and experience to be a panel chair.

Right of officer concerned to object to panel members

31.—(1) The officer concerned may object to the appointment of any of the panel members.

(2) Any such objection must be made in writing to the appropriate authority before the end of 3 working days beginning with the first working day after receipt of the notification referred to in regulation 30(10) and must set out the grounds of objection of the officer concerned.

(3) The appropriate authority shall notify the officer concerned in writing whether it upholds or rejects an objection to any panel member.

(4) If the appropriate authority upholds an objection, the appropriate authority shall remove that member from the panel and shall appoint a new member to the panel.

(5) If the appropriate authority appoints a new panel member under paragraph (4), it must ensure that the requirements for the composition of the panel in regulation 30 continue to be met.

(6) As soon as reasonably practicable after any such appointment, the appropriate authority shall notify in writing the officer concerned of the name of the new panel member.

(7) The officer concerned may object to the appointment of a panel member appointed under paragraph (4).

(8) Any such objection must be made in accordance with paragraph (2), provided that it must be made before the end of 3 working days beginning with the first working day after receipt of the notification referred to in paragraph (6); and the appropriate authority shall comply with paragraphs (3) to (6) in relation to the objection, but paragraph (7) shall not apply.

Procedure on receipt of notice of third stage meeting

32.—(1) Before the end of—

    (a) 14 working days beginning with the first working day after the date on which a notice has been given to the officer concerned under regulation 27 or 29; or

    (b) where that period is extended by the panel chair for exceptional circumstances, such extended period,

the officer concerned shall comply with paragraphs (2) and (3).

(2) The officer concerned shall provide to the appropriate authority—

    (a) written notice of whether or not he accepts that his performance or attendance has been unsatisfactory or that he has been grossly incompetent, as the case may be;

    (b) where he accepts that his performance or attendance has been unsatisfactory or that he has been grossly incompetent, any written submission he wishes to make in mitigation;

    (c) where he does not accept that his performance or attendance has been unsatisfactory or that he has been grossly incompetent, or where he disputes all or part of the matters referred to in the notice given under regulation 27 or 29, written notice of—

        (i) the matters he disputes and his account of the relevant events; and

        (ii) any arguments on points of law he wishes to be considered by the panel.

(3) The officer concerned shall provide the appropriate authority and the panel with a copy of any document he intends to rely on at the third stage meeting.

(4) Before the end of 3 working days beginning with the first working day after the date on which the officer concerned has complied with paragraph (2), the senior manager and the officer concerned shall each supply to the other a list of proposed witnesses or give notice that they do not have any proposed witnesses; and any list of proposed witnesses shall include brief details of the evidence that each witness is able to adduce and their address.

(5) Where there are proposed witnesses, the officer concerned shall, if reasonably practicable, agree a list of proposed witnesses with the senior manager.

(6) Where no list of proposed witnesses is agreed under paragraph (4), the officer concerned shall supply to the appropriate authority his list of proposed witnesses.

Witnesses

33.—(1) As soon as reasonably practicable after any list of proposed witnesses has been—
    (a) agreed under regulation 32(5); or
    (b) supplied under regulation 32(6),
the appropriate authority shall supply that list to the panel chair together, in the latter case, with a list of its proposed witnesses.

(2) The panel chair shall—
    (a) consider the list or lists of proposed witnesses; and
    (b) subject to paragraph (3), determine which, if any, witnesses should attend the third stage meeting.

(3) The panel chair may determine that witnesses not named in any list of proposed witnesses should attend the third stage meeting.

(4) No witness shall give evidence at a third stage meeting unless the panel chair reasonably believes that it is necessary in the interests of fairness for the witness to do so, in which case he shall—
    (a) where the witness is a police officer, cause that person to be ordered to attend the third stage meeting; and
    (b) in any other case, cause the witness to be given notice that his attendance is necessary and of the date, time and place of the meeting.

Timing and notice of third stage meeting

34.—(1) Subject to paragraphs (2) and (6) and regulation 35, the third stage meeting shall take place before the end of 30 working days beginning with the first working day after the day on which a notice has been given to the officer concerned under regulation 27 or 29.

(2) The panel chair may extend the time period specified in paragraph (1) where he considers that it would be in the interests of fairness to do so.

(3) Where the panel chair extends the time period under paragraph (2), he shall provide written notification of his reasons for so doing to the appropriate authority and the officer concerned.

(4) The panel chair shall, if reasonably practicable, agree a date and time for the third stage meeting with the officer concerned.

(5) Where no date and time is agreed under paragraph (4), the panel chair shall specify a date and time for the third stage meeting.

(6) Where a date and time is specified under paragraph (5) and—
    (a) the officer concerned or his police friend will not be available at that time; and
    (b) the officer concerned proposes an alternative time which satisfies subsection (7),
the third stage meeting shall be postponed to the time proposed by the officer concerned.

(7) An alternative time must—
    (a) be reasonable; and
    (b) fall before the end of 5 working days beginning with the first working day after the day specified by the panel chair.

(8) The panel chair shall give to the officer concerned a notice in writing of the date and time of the third stage meeting determined in accordance with this regulation and of the place of the meeting.

(9) Where the officer concerned informs the panel chair in advance that he is unable to attend the third stage meeting on grounds which the panel chair considers reasonable, the panel chair may allow the officer concerned to participate in the meeting by video link or other means.

Postponement and adjournment of a third stage meeting

35.—(1) If the panel chair considers it necessary or expedient, he may direct that the third stage meeting take place at a different time to that specified in the notice given under regulation 34.

(2) Such direction may specify a time which falls after the period of 30 working days referred to in regulation 34(1).

(3) Where the panel chair makes a direction under paragraph (1) he shall notify in writing the officer concerned, the other panel members and the appropriate authority of his reasons and the revised time and place for the meeting.

Procedure at a third stage meeting

36.—(1) Subject to the provisions of this regulation, the procedure at the third stage meeting shall be such as the panel chair may determine.

(2) The third stage meeting shall be held in private.

(3) A human resources professional and a police officer may attend the meeting to advise the panel on the proceedings.

(4) A relevant lawyer may attend the meeting to advise the panel on the proceedings and on any question of law that may arise at the meeting.

(5) Where the officer concerned is a special constable, the appropriate authority shall appoint a special constable with sufficient seniority and experience to act as an adviser to the panel, who shall attend the meeting.

(6) Any other person specified in the notice referred to in regulation 27(1) or 29(1) may attend the meeting if the officer concerned consents to such attendance.

(7) Where the officer concerned is required to attend a third stage meeting under regulation 26, the panel chair shall—
   (a) provide the officer concerned with an opportunity to make representations in relation to the matters referred to in the notice given under regulation 27;
   (b) provide his police friend (if he has one) with an opportunity to address the meeting in relation to such matters in accordance with regulation 8(3)(a).

(8) Where the officer concerned is required to attend a third stage meeting under regulation 28, the panel chair shall—
   (a) provide the officer concerned with an opportunity to make representations in relation to the matters referred to in the notice given under regulation 29;
   (b) provide the person representing the officer with an opportunity to address the meeting in relation to such matters in accordance with regulation 8(3)(a).

(9) The panel chair may adjourn the meeting to a specified later time or date if it appears to him necessary or expedient to do so.

(10) A verbatim record of the meeting shall be taken; and the officer concerned shall, on request, be supplied with a copy of such record.

Finding

37.—(1) Following the third stage meeting, the panel shall make a finding whether—
   (a) in a case falling within regulation 26(2), the performance or attendance of the officer concerned during the period specified in accordance with regulation 21(6)(c) has been satisfactory or not;

(b) in a case falling within regulation 26(4), the performance or attendance of the officer concerned during any part of the validity period of the final written improvement notice remaining after the expiry of the period specified in accordance with regulation 21(6)(c) has been satisfactory or not; or

(c) in a case falling within regulation 28, the performance of the officer concerned constitutes gross incompetence, unsatisfactory performance or neither.

(2) The panel shall prepare (or shall cause to be prepared) their decision in writing which shall state the finding and, where they have found—

(a) in a case falling within regulation 26(2) or (4), that the performance or attendance of the officer concerned has been unsatisfactory; or

(b) in a case falling within regulation 28, that his performance constitutes gross incompetence or unsatisfactory performance,

their reasons as well as any outcome which they order under regulation 38.

(3) As soon as reasonably practicable after the conclusion of the meeting, the panel chair shall give a written copy of the decision to—

(a) the officer concerned; and

(b) the line manager,

but in any event, the officer concerned shall be given written notice of the finding before the end of three working days beginning with the first working day after the conclusion of the meeting.

(4) Where the panel have made a finding of unsatisfactory performance or attendance or gross incompetence, the copy of the decision given to the officer concerned shall be accompanied by a notice in writing setting out the circumstances in which and the timeframe within which a police officer may appeal to a police appeals tribunal under the Police Appeals Tribunals Rules 2008[10].

(5) Any finding or decision of the panel under this regulation or regulation 38 shall be based on a simple majority but shall not indicate whether it was taken unanimously or by a majority.

Outcomes

38.—(1) If the panel make a finding that, in a case falling within regulation 26(2) or (4), the performance or attendance of the officer concerned has been unsatisfactory they may, subject to paragraph (4), order—

(a) one of the outcomes mentioned in paragraph (3)(a), (c) or (f); or

(b) where the panel are satisfied that there are exceptional circumstances which justify it, the outcome mentioned in paragraph (3)(d).

(2) If the panel make a finding that, in a case falling within regulation 28, the performance of the officer concerned constitutes gross incompetence, they may order one of the outcomes mentioned in paragraph (3)(b), (c), (e) or (f).

(3) The outcomes mentioned in this paragraph are:

(a) dismissal of the officer concerned with notice, the period of such notice to be decided by the panel, subject to a minimum period of 28 days;

(b) dismissal of the officer concerned with immediate effect;

(c) reduction in rank of the officer concerned with immediate effect;

(d) an extension of the final written improvement notice;

(e) the issue of a final written improvement notice;

(f) redeployment to alternative duties (which may involve a reduction of rank) within the police force concerned.

(4) The panel may not order the outcome mentioned in paragraph (3)(c) where–

(a) the officer concerned is a special constable; or

(b) the third stage meeting relates to the attendance of the officer concerned.

(5) If the panel make a finding, in a case falling within regulation 28, of unsatisfactory performance, they shall order the issue of a written improvement notice.

(6) A written improvement notice or a final written improvement notice issued under this regulation shall—

(a) state in what respect the performance or attendance of the officer concerned (as the case may be) is considered unsatisfactory or grossly incompetent;

(b) state the improvement that is required in his performance or attendance;

(c) state that, if a sufficient improvement is not made within such reasonable period as the panel shall specify (being a period not greater than 12 months), the officer concerned may be required to attend a second stage meeting (in the case of a written improvement notice) or another third stage meeting (in the case of a final written improvement notice) and state the date on which this period ends;

(d) state that it shall be valid for a period of twelve months from the date of the notice (the "validity period");

(e) state that, if the sufficient improvement referred to in sub-paragraph (c) is not maintained during any part of the validity period remaining after the expiry of the period specified in accordance with sub-paragraph (c), he may be required to attend a second stage meeting (in the case of a written improvement notice) or another third stage meeting (in the case of a final written improvement notice); and

(f) be signed and dated by the panel chair.

(7) Where the panel orders an extension of the final written improvement notice—

(a) the notice shall be amended—

(i) to state that if the officer concerned does not make a sufficient improvement within such reasonable period as the panel shall specify (being a period not greater than 12 months) he may be required to attend another third stage meeting; and

(ii) to state the date on which this period ends;

(b) the panel may vary any of the other matters recorded in the notice;

(c) the notice shall be valid for a further period of twelve months from the date of the extension (the "validity period") and shall state the date on which it expires.

Assessment of performance or attendance following third stage meeting

39.—(1) This regulation applies where a written improvement notice has been issued under regulation 38.

(2) Where this regulation applies, the performance of the officer concerned shall be assessed under regulation 19 as if he had received a written improvement notice under regulation 15.

(3) Where, as a result of such assessment, the officer concerned is required to attend a second stage meeting, these Regulations shall have effect as if he had been required to attend that meeting under regulation 19; and—

(a) references to the period specified in accordance with regulation 14(6)(c) shall be construed as references to the period specified under regulation 38(6)(c); and

(b) references to the validity period of the written improvement notice shall be construed as references to the validity period of the written improvement notice issued under regulation 38.

(4) Where a police officer is required to attend such a second stage meeting, that meeting must concern unsatisfactory performance which is similar to or connected with the unsatisfactory performance referred to in the written improvement notice.

40.—(1) This regulation applies where a final written improvement notice has been issued or extended under regulation 38.

(2) Where this regulation applies, as soon as reasonably practicable after the reasonable period specified by the panel under regulation 38(6)(c) or (7)(a) ends—

(a) the panel shall assess the performance or attendance of the officer concerned (as the case may be) during that period; and

(b) the panel chair shall notify the officer concerned in writing whether the panel considers that there has been a sufficient improvement in performance or attendance during that period.

(3) If the panel considers that there has not been a sufficient improvement, the panel chair shall, at the same time as he gives notification under paragraph (2)(b), also notify the officer concerned in writing that he is required to attend another third stage meeting to consider his performance or attendance.

(4) Where—

(a) the officer concerned has not been required to attend a third stage meeting under paragraph (3), or

(b) the officer concerned has been required to attend a third stage meeting under paragraph (3) but the panel did not make a finding of unsatisfactory performance or attendance at that meeting,

the officer concerned may be required to attend a third stage meeting under paragraph (5).

(5) If the panel considers that the officer concerned has failed to maintain a sufficient improvement in his performance or attendance during any part of the validity period of the final written improvement notice remaining after the expiry of the period specified in accordance with regulation 38(6)(c) or (7)(a), the panel chair shall notify the officer concerned in writing of the matters set out in paragraph (6).

(6) Those matters are—

(a) that the panel is of the view mentioned in paragraph (5); and

(b) that the officer concerned is required to attend another third stage meeting to consider his performance or attendance.

(7) In a case falling within paragraph (3) or (5), the appropriate authority shall give the officer concerned the notice referred to in regulation 27.

(8) Where the officer concerned is required to attend a third stage meeting under this regulation, these Regulations shall have effect as if the case fell within regulation 26(2) or (4) as the case may be and—

(a) references to the period specified in accordance with regulation 21(6)(c) shall be construed as references to the period specified under regulation 38(6)(c) or (7)(a), as the case may be; and

(b) references to the validity period of the final written improvement notice shall be construed as references to the validity period mentioned in regulation 38(6)(c) or (7)(c), as the case may be.

(9) Any third stage meeting which a police officer is required to attend under this regulation must concern unsatisfactory performance or attendance which is similar to or connected with the unsatisfactory performance or attendance referred to in the final written improvement notice issued or extended under regulation 38.

(10) References in this regulation to the panel are references to the panel that conducted the initial third stage meeting, subject to paragraph (11).

(11) Where any of the panel members are not able to continue to act as such, the appropriate authority shall remove that member from the panel and shall appoint a new member to the panel.

(12) If the appropriate authority appoints a new panel member under paragraph (11), it must ensure that the requirements for the composition of the panel in regulation 30 continue to be met.

(13) As soon as reasonably practicable after any such appointment, the appropriate authority shall notify in writing the officer concerned of the name of the new panel member.

(14) The officer concerned may object to the appointment of a panel member appointed under paragraph (11).

(15) Any such objection must be made in accordance with regulation 31(2), provided that it must be made before the end of 3 working days beginning with the first working day after receipt of the notification referred to in paragraph (13); and the appropriate authority shall comply with regulation 31(3) to (6) in relation to the objection but paragraph (7) of that regulation shall not apply.

41.—(1) Where an officer is required to attend another third stage meeting under regulation 40—

(a) that meeting shall be conducted by the same panel as conducted the initial third stage meeting (subject to any change in that panel under regulation 40);

(b) the officer concerned shall not have the right to object to panel members under regulation 31, except in accordance with regulation 40;

(c) subject to paragraph (2), regulations 32 to 38 shall apply to, or in relation to, that meeting.

(2) Following that third stage meeting, the panel may not order the outcome mentioned in regulation 38(3)(d).

Home Office

Minister of State

Explanatory Note

(This Note is not Part of the Regulations)

These Regulations establish procedures for proceedings in respect of unsatisfactory performance or attendance of members of police forces of the rank of chief superintendent or below (excluding probationers) and special constables.

Part 1 deals with preliminary matters. Regulation 3 revokes the Police (Efficiency) Regulations 1999 and the two further sets of regulations which amended those regulations. However, such regulations shall continue to have effect in respect of unsatisfactory performance or attendance which came to the attention of a line manager before the coming into force of these Regulations. Regulation 4 provides definitions of terms used in these Regulations and makes provision in relation to the delegation of functions of the chief officer of police under these Regulations.

Part 2 deals with general matters. Regulations 5 and 6 make provision about the role of a police friend under these Regulations and the right to legal representation. Regulation 7 provides for the manner in which a written notice or document is to be given to or supplied to a police officer. Regulation 8 contains general provision about the procedure for meetings held in accordance with the Regulations. Regulation 9 makes provision for a senior manager to appoint someone to carry out functions of a line manager or a second line manager under the Regulations. Regulations 10 and 11 make provision about extensions and suspensions of certain periods specified in the Regulations.

Part 3 deals with the first stage of the procedures under the Regulations. It makes provision about the circumstances in which a first stage meeting may be required, the arrangement of such a meeting and the procedures to be followed at and subsequent to the meeting. If the outcome of the meeting is a finding of unsatisfactory performance or attendance, the police officer will be issued with a written improvement notice under regulation 15. Regulations 16 to 18 make provision for the officer to appeal against such a finding and/or particular terms of the notice.

Part 4 makes similar provision in respect of the second stage of the procedures. A police officer can be required to attend a second stage meeting following a first stage meeting if, during specified periods, he has failed to improve his performance or attendance, or if he has failed to maintain such an improvement. If the outcome of the second stage meeting is a finding of unsatisfactory performance or attendance, the police officer will be issued with a final written improvement notice under regulation 22. Regulations 23 to 25 make provision for the officer to appeal against such a finding and/or particular terms of the notice.

Part 5 makes provision in respect of the third stage of the procedures. A police officer can be required to attend a third stage meeting following a second stage meeting if, during specified periods, he has failed to improve his performance or attendance, or if he has failed to maintain such an improvement. A police officer can also be required to attend a third stage meeting, even where he has not attended a first or second stage meeting, if the appropriate authority considers that the performance of the officer constitutes gross incompetence. A third stage meeting is conducted by a panel of three persons appointed by the chief officer of police in accordance with regulation 30. Regulation 31 gives the police officer the right to object to any of the panel members. Regulations 32 to 36 deal with procedural matters relating to the third stage meeting, witnesses and the timing of the meeting. Regulation 37 makes provision for the decision of the panel following the third stage meeting, which must set out the panel's finding, its reasons and any outcome ordered under regulation 38. Regulations 39 to 41 make provision for the performance or attendance of the officer to be assessed following the third stage meeting where the panel have ordered the issue of a written improvement notice, or the issue or extension of a final written improvement notice. In such a case, the officer concerned may be required to attend a further meeting under these Regulations in connection with his performance or attendance.

These Regulations were laid before Parliament in draft as they are Regulations under section 84 of the Police Act 1996 coming into force at a time that is the earliest time at which any Regulations under section 84 are to come into force after the commencement of paragraph 7 of Schedule 22 to the Criminal Justice and Immigration Act 2008 (see section 84(8) of the Police Act 1996).

Notes:

[1] 1996 c.16. Section 50 was amended by paragraph 95 of Schedule 27 to the Greater London Authority Act 1999 (c.29) and section 125 of the Criminal Justice and Police Act 2001 (c.16). It is also amended by paragraph 3 of Schedule 22 to the Criminal Justice and Immigration Act 2008 (c.4). Section 51 was amended by section 128 of the Police Act 1997 (c.50) and section 35 of the Police Reform Act 2002 (c.30). It is also amended by paragraph 4 of Schedule 22 to the Criminal Justice and Immigration Act 2008. Section 84 was amended by section 125 of the Criminal Justice and Police Act 2001 and paragraph 119 of Schedule 21 to the Legal Services Act 2007 (c.29). It is also amended by paragraph 7 of Schedule 22 to the Criminal Justice and Immigration Act 2008.

[2] Relevant amendments to section 63 were made by paragraph 78 of Schedule 4 to the Serious Organised Crime and Police Act 2005 (c. 15). Section 63 is also amended by paragraph 6 of Schedule 22 to the Criminal Justice and Immigration Act 2008.

[3] Section 84(9) is inserted by paragraph 7 of Schedule 22 to the Criminal Justice and Immigration A[c]t 2008.

[4] S.I. 1999/732.

[5] S.I. 2003/528.

[6] S.I. 2003/2600.

[7] S.I. 2003/527. The relevant amending instrument is S.I. 2006/3449.

[8] 1971 c.80.

[9] Section 87 was amended by paragraph 18 of Schedule 7 to the Police Reform Act 2002. It is also amended by paragraph 9 of Schedule 22 to the Criminal Justice and Immigration Act 2008.

[10] S.I. 2008/2863.

APPENDIX G

The Police (Conduct) Regulations 2008, SI 2008/2864

STATUTORY INSTRUMENTS

2008 No. 2864

POLICE, ENGLAND AND WALES

The Police (Conduct) Regulations 2008

Made	*5th November 2008*
Laid before Parliament	
Coming into force	*1st December 2008*

The Secretary of State makes the following Regulations in exercise of the powers conferred by sections 50, 51 and 84 of the Police Act 1996[1].

In accordance with section 63(3)[2] of that Act, she has supplied the Police Advisory Board for England and Wales with a draft of these Regulations and has taken into consideration the representations of that Board.

In accordance with section 84(9)[3] of that Act, a draft of these Regulations was laid before Parliament and approved by a resolution of each House of Parliament.

PART 1
PRELIMINARY

Citation, commencement and extent

1.—(1) These Regulations may be cited as the Police (Conduct) Regulations 2008 and shall come into force on 1st December 2008.
(2) These Regulations extend to England and Wales.

Revocation and transitional provisions

2.—(1) Subject to paragraph (2), the Police (Conduct) Regulations 2004[4] are revoked.
(2) Where an allegation in respect of conduct by a police officer came to the attention of an appropriate authority before 1st December 2008 nothing in these Regulations shall apply and the Police (Conduct) Regulations 2004 shall continue to have effect.

Interpretation and delegation

3.—(1) In these Regulations—
"the 1996 Act" means the Police Act 1996;
"the 2002 Act" means the Police Reform Act 2002[5];
"the Police Regulations" means the Police Regulations 2003[6];
"the Complaints Regulations" means the Police (Complaints and Misconduct) Regulations 2004[7];
"the Performance Regulations" means the Police (Performance) Regulations 2008[8];
"allegation" means an allegation relating to a complaint or conduct matter;

"appropriate authority" means—
- (a) where the officer concerned is a senior officer of any police force, the police authority for the force's area;
- (b) in any other case, the chief officer of police of the police force concerned;

"appeal hearing" means an appeal to a police appeals tribunal in accordance with the Police Appeals Tribunals Rules 2008[9];

"appeal meeting" means a meeting held in accordance with regulation 39 following a misconduct meeting;

"bank holiday" means a day which is a bank holiday under the Banking and Financial Dealings Act 1971[10] in England and Wales;

"complainant" means the person referred to at section 12(1)(a) to (c) (as the case may be) of the 2002 Act (complaints, matters and persons to which Part 2 applies);

"complaint" has the meaning given to it by section 12(1) of the 2002 Act;

"conduct" includes acts, omissions and statements (whether actual, alleged or inferred);

"conduct matter" has the meaning given to it by section 12(2) of the 2002 Act;

"the Commission" means the Independent Police Complaints Commission established under section 9 of the 2002 Act (the Independent Police Complaints Commission);

"criminal proceedings" means—
- (a) any prospective criminal proceedings; or
- (b) all criminal proceedings brought which have not been brought to a conclusion (apart from the bringing and determination of any appeal other than an appeal against conviction to the Crown Court);

"disciplinary action" means, in order of seriousness starting with the least serious action—
- (a) management advice;
- (b) a written warning;
- (c) a final written warning;
- (d) an extension to a final written warning as described in regulation 35(6)(b);
- (e) dismissal with notice; or
- (f) dismissal without notice.

"disciplinary proceedings" means, other than in paragraph (7) or (8) of this regulation, any proceedings under these Regulations and any appeal from misconduct proceedings or a special case hearing dealt with under the Police Appeals Tribunals Rules 2008;

"document" means anything in which information of any description is recorded and includes any recording of a visual image or images;

"gross misconduct" means a breach of the Standards of Professional Behaviour so serious that dismissal would be justified;

"harm test" has the meaning given to it in regulation 4;

"HMCIC" means Her Majesty's Chief Inspector of Constabulary appointed under section 54(1) of the 1996 Act (appointment and functions of inspectors of constabulary);

"human resources professional" means a police officer or police staff member who has specific responsibility for personnel matters relating to members of a police force;

"informant" means a person who provides information to an investigation on the basis that his identity is not disclosed during the course of the disciplinary proceedings;

"interested party" means a person whose appointment could reasonably give rise to a concern as to whether he could act impartially under these Regulations;

"interested person" has the meaning given to it by section 21(5) of the 2002 Act (duty to provide information to other persons);

"investigator" means a person—
- (a) appointed under regulation 13; or

(b) appointed or designated under paragraph 16, 17, 18 or 19 of Schedule 3 (handling of complaints and conduct matters) to the 2002 Act (investigations),

as the case may be;

"management action" means action or advice intended to improve the conduct of the officer concerned;

"management advice" means management action imposed following misconduct proceedings or an appeal meeting;

"misconduct" means a breach of the Standards of Professional Behaviour;

"misconduct hearing" means a hearing to which the officer concerned is referred under regulation 19 and at which he may be dealt with by disciplinary action up to and including dismissal;

"misconduct meeting" means a meeting to which the officer concerned is referred under regulation 19 and at which he may be dealt with by disciplinary action up to and including a final written warning;

"misconduct proceedings" means a misconduct meeting or misconduct hearing;

"the officer concerned" means the police officer in relation to whose conduct there has been an allegation;

"personal record" means a personal record kept under regulation 15 of the Police Regulations (contents of personal records);

"police force concerned" means—

    (a) where the officer concerned is a member of a police force, the police force of which he is a member; and

    (b) where the officer concerned is a special constable, the police force maintained for the police area for which he is appointed;

"police friend" means a person chosen by the officer concerned in accordance with regulation 6;

"police officer" means a member of a police force or special constable;

"police staff member" means an employee of a police authority who is under the direction and control of a chief officer of police;

"proposed witness" means a witness whose attendance at the misconduct proceedings the officer concerned or the appropriate authority (as the case may be) wishes to request of the person conducting or chairing those proceedings;

"relevant lawyer" has the same meaning as in section 84(4) of the 1996 Act, subject to the provisions of paragraph 35 of Schedule 27 to the Criminal Justice and Immigration Act 2008;

"senior officer" means a member of a police force holding a rank above that of chief superintendent;

"special case hearing" means a hearing to which the officer concerned is referred under regulation 41 after the case has been certified as a special case;

"special case proceedings" means the referral of a case to a special case hearing and any proceedings at or in connection with such a hearing;

"staff association" means—

    (a) in relation to a member of a police force of the rank of chief inspector or below, the Police Federation of England and Wales;

    (b) in relation to a member of a police force of the rank of superintendent or chief superintendent, the Police Superintendents' Association of England and Wales; and

    (c) in relation to a member of a police force who is a senior officer, the Chief Police Officers' Staff Association;

"Standards of Professional Behaviour" means the standards of professional behaviour contained in the Schedule; and

"working day" means any day other than a Saturday or Sunday or a day which is a bank holiday or a public holiday in England and Wales.

(2) In these Regulations—

    (a) a reference to an officer other than a senior officer shall include a reference to a special constable, regardless of his level of seniority;

    (b) a reference to a copy of a statement shall, where it was not made in writing, be construed as a reference to a copy of an account of that statement;

    (c) the "special conditions" are that—

        (i) there is sufficient evidence, in the form of written statements or other documents, without the need for further evidence, whether written or oral, to establish on the balance of probabilities that the conduct of the officer concerned constitutes gross misconduct; and

        (ii) it is in the public interest for the officer concerned to cease to be a police officer without delay.

(3) For the purposes of these Regulations—

    (a) a written warning shall remain in force for a period of 12 months from the date on which it takes effect; and

    (b) subject to regulations 35(6)(b) and 55(2)(b), a final written warning shall remain in force for a period of 18 months from the date on which it takes effect.

(4) The reference to the period of—

    (a) 12 months in paragraph (3)(a); and

    (b) 18 months in paragraph (3)(b) and regulations 35(7) and 55(3),

shall not include any time when the officer concerned is taking a career break (under regulation 33(12) of the Police Regulations (leave) and the determination of the Secretary of State made under that regulation).

(5) Where the appropriate authority is a chief officer of police, he may, subject to paragraph (6), delegate any of his functions under these Regulations to a—

    (a) member of a police force of at least the rank of chief inspector; or

    (b) police staff member who, in the opinion of the chief officer is of at least a similar level of seniority to a chief inspector.

(6) Where the appropriate authority delegates its functions under regulation 10 or 41, the decisions shall be authorised by a senior officer.

(7) Any proceedings under these Regulations are disciplinary proceedings for the purposes of section 87(5) of the 1996 Act (guidance concerning disciplinary proceedings)[11].

(8) Any proceedings under these Regulations are disciplinary proceedings for the purposes of section 29(1) of the 2002 Act (interpretation of Part 2).

The harm test

4. Information in documents which are stated to be subject to the harm test under these Regulations shall not be supplied to the officer concerned in so far as the appropriate authority considers that preventing disclosure to him is—

    (a) necessary for the purpose of preventing the premature or inappropriate disclosure of information that is relevant to, or may be used in, any criminal proceedings;

    (b) necessary in the interests of national security;

    (c) necessary for the purpose of the prevention or detection of crime, or the apprehension or prosecution of offenders;

    (d) necessary for the purpose of the prevention or detection of misconduct by other police officers or police staff members or their apprehension for such matters;

    (e) justified on the grounds that providing the information would involve disproportionate effort in comparison to the seriousness of the allegations against the officer concerned;

    (f) necessary and proportionate for the protection of the welfare and safety of any informant or witness; or

    (g) otherwise in the public interest.

PART 2

GENERAL

Application

5. These Regulations apply where an allegation comes to the attention of an appropriate authority which indicates that the conduct of a police officer may amount to misconduct or gross misconduct.

Police friend

6.—(1) The officer concerned may choose—
- (a) a police officer;
- (b) a police staff member; or
- (c) where the officer concerned is a member of a police force, a person nominated by his staff association,

who is not otherwise involved in the matter, to act as his police friend.

(2) A police friend may—
- (a) advise the officer concerned throughout the proceedings under these Regulations;
- (b) unless the officer concerned has the right to be legally represented and chooses to be so represented, represent the officer concerned at the misconduct proceedings or special case hearing or appeal meeting;
- (c) make representations to the appropriate authority concerning any aspect of the proceedings under these Regulations; and
- (d) accompany the officer concerned to any interview, meeting or hearing which forms part of any proceedings under these Regulations.

(3) Where a police friend is a police officer or a police staff member, the chief officer of police of the force of which the police friend is a member shall permit him to use a reasonable amount of duty time for the purposes referred to in paragraph (2).

(4) The reference in paragraph (3) to the force of which the police friend is a member shall include a reference to the force maintained for the police area for which a special constable is appointed and the force in which a police staff member is serving.

Legal and other representation

7.—(1) The officer concerned has the right to be legally represented, by a relevant lawyer of his choice, at a misconduct hearing or a special case hearing.

(2) If the officer concerned chooses not to be legally represented at such a hearing he may be dismissed or receive any other outcome under regulation 35 or 55 without his being so represented.

(3) Except in a case where the officer concerned has the right to be legally represented and chooses to be so represented, he may be represented at misconduct proceedings or a special case hearing or an appeal meeting only by a police friend.

(4) The appropriate authority may be represented at misconduct proceedings or a special case hearing or an appeal meeting by—
- (a) a police officer or police staff member of the police force concerned; or
- (b) at a misconduct hearing or a special case hearing only, a relevant lawyer (whether or not the officer concerned chooses to be legally represented).

(5) Subject to paragraph (6), the appropriate authority may appoint a person to advise the person or persons conducting the misconduct proceedings or special case hearing or appeal meeting.

(6) At a misconduct meeting or an appeal meeting, the person appointed under paragraph (5) shall not be a relevant lawyer.

Provision of notices or documents

8. Where any written notice or document is to be given or supplied to the officer concerned under these Regulations, it shall be—
    (a) given to him in person;
    (b) left with some person at, or sent by recorded delivery to, his last known address; or
    (c) in respect of a written notice under regulation 15(1), given to him in person by his police friend where the police friend has agreed with the appropriate authority to deliver the notice.

Outstanding or possible criminal proceedings

9.—(1) Subject to the provisions of this regulation, proceedings under these Regulations shall proceed without delay.

(2) Before referring a case to misconduct proceedings or a special case hearing, the appropriate authority shall decide whether misconduct proceedings or special case proceedings would prejudice any criminal proceedings.

(3) For any period during which the appropriate authority considers any misconduct proceedings or special case proceedings would prejudice any criminal proceedings, no such misconduct or special case proceedings shall take place.

(4) Where a witness who is or may be a witness in any criminal proceedings is to be or may be asked to attend misconduct proceedings, the appropriate authority shall consult the relevant prosecutor (and when doing so must inform him of the names and addresses of all such witnesses) before making its decision under paragraph (2).

(5) For the purposes of this regulation "relevant prosecutor" means the Director of Public Prosecutions or any other person who has or is likely to have responsibility for the criminal proceedings.

Suspension

10.—(1) The appropriate authority may, subject to the provisions of this regulation, suspend the officer concerned from his office as constable and (in the case of a member of a police force) from membership of the force.

(2) An officer concerned who is suspended under this regulation remains a police officer for the purposes of these Regulations.

(3) A suspension under this regulation shall be with pay.

(4) The appropriate authority shall not suspend a police officer under this regulation unless the following conditions ("the suspension conditions") are satisfied—
    (a) having considered temporary redeployment to alternative duties or an alternative location as an alternative to suspension, the appropriate authority has determined that such redeployment is not appropriate in all the circumstances of the case; and
    (b) it appears to the appropriate authority that either—
        (i) the effective investigation of the case may be prejudiced unless the officer concerned is so suspended; or
        (ii) having regard to the nature of the allegation and any other relevant considerations, the public interest requires that he should be so suspended.

(5) The appropriate authority may exercise the power to suspend the officer concerned under this regulation at any time from the date on which these Regulations first apply to the officer concerned in accordance with regulation 5 until—
    (a) it is decided that the conduct of the officer concerned shall not be referred to misconduct proceedings or a special case hearing; or
    (b) such proceedings have concluded.

(6)   The appropriate authority may suspend the officer concerned with effect from the date and time of notification which shall be given either—

    (a)   in writing with a summary of the reasons; or

    (b)   orally, in which case the appropriate authority shall confirm the suspension in writing with a summary of the reasons before the end of 3 working days beginning with the first working day after the suspension.

(7)   The officer concerned (or his police friend) may make representations against his suspension to the appropriate authority—

    (a)   before the end of 7 working days beginning with the first working day after his being suspended;

    (b)   at any time during the suspension if he reasonably believes that circumstances relevant to the suspension conditions have changed.

(8)   The appropriate authority shall review the suspension conditions—

    (a)   on receipt of any representations under paragraph (7)(a);

    (b)   if there has been no previous review, before the end of 4 weeks beginning with the first working day after the suspension;

    (c)   in any other case—

        (i)   on being notified that circumstances relevant to the suspension conditions may have changed (whether by means of representations made under paragraph (7)(b) or otherwise); or

        (ii)   before the end of 4 weeks beginning with the day after the previous review.

(9)   Where, following a review under paragraph (8), the suspension conditions remain satisfied and the appropriate authority decides the suspension should continue, it shall, before the end of 3 working days beginning with the day after the review, so notify the officer concerned in writing with a summary of the reasons.

(10)   Subject to paragraph (12), where the officer concerned is suspended under this regulation, he shall remain so suspended until whichever of the following occurs first—

    (a)   the suspension conditions are no longer satisfied;

    (b)   either of the events mentioned in paragraph (5)(a) and, subject to paragraph (11), (5)(b).

(11)   Where an officer concerned who is suspended is dismissed with notice under regulation 35 he shall remain suspended until the end of the notice period.

(12)   In a case to which paragraph 17, 18 or 19 of Schedule 3 to the 2002 Act (investigations) applies, the appropriate authority must consult with the Commission—

    (a)   in deciding whether or not to suspend the officer concerned under this regulation; and

    (b)   before a suspension under this regulation is brought to an end by virtue of paragraph (10)(a).

Part 3
Investigations

Application of this Part

11.   This Part shall not apply to a case to which paragraph 16, 17, 18 or 19 of Schedule 3 to the 2002 Act (investigations) applies.

Assessment of conduct

12.—(1)   Subject to paragraph (6) the appropriate authority shall assess whether the conduct which is the subject matter of the allegation, if proved, would amount to misconduct or gross misconduct or neither.

(2) Where the appropriate authority assesses that the conduct, if proved, would amount to neither misconduct nor gross misconduct, it may—

    (a) take no action;

    (b) take management action against the officer concerned; or

    (c) refer the matter to be dealt with under the Performance Regulations.

(3) Where the appropriate authority assesses that the conduct, if proved, would amount to misconduct, it shall determine whether or not it is necessary for the matter to be investigated and—

    (a) if so, the matter shall be investigated and the appropriate authority shall further determine whether, if the matter were to be referred to misconduct proceedings, those would be likely to be a misconduct meeting or a misconduct hearing;

    (b) if not, the appropriate authority may—

        (i) take no action; or

        (ii) take management action against the officer concerned.

(4) Where the appropriate authority determines that the conduct, if proved, would amount to gross misconduct, the matter shall be investigated.

(5) At any time before the start of misconduct proceedings, the appropriate authority may revise its assessment of the conduct under paragraph (1) if it considers it appropriate to do so.

(6) Where the appropriate authority decides under this regulation to take no action, take management action or to refer the matter to be dealt with under the Performance Regulations, it shall so notify the officer concerned in writing as soon as practicable.

Appointment of investigator

13.—(1) This regulation applies where the matter is to be investigated in accordance with regulation 12.

(2) The appropriate authority shall, subject to paragraph (3), appoint a person to investigate the matter.

(3) If the officer concerned is the Commissioner of Police of the Metropolis or the Deputy Commissioner of Police of the Metropolis—

    (a) the appropriate authority shall notify the Secretary of State; and

    (b) the Secretary of State shall appoint a person to investigate the matter.

(4) No person shall be appointed to investigate the matter under this regulation—

    (a) unless he has an appropriate level of knowledge, skills and experience to plan and manage the investigation;

    (b) if he is an interested party;

    (c) if he works, directly or indirectly, under the management of the officer concerned; or

    (d) in a case where the officer concerned is a senior officer, if he is—

        (i) the chief officer of police of the police force concerned; or

        (ii) a member of the same police force as the officer concerned, or where the officer concerned is a member of the metropolitan police force, serving in the same division as the officer concerned.

(5) The reference in paragraph (4)(d)(ii) to a member of the police force shall include a reference to a special constable appointed for the area of that force and a police staff member serving in that force.

Investigation

14. The purpose of the investigation is to—

    (a) gather evidence to establish the facts and circumstances of the alleged misconduct or gross misconduct; and

    (b) assist the appropriate authority to establish whether there is a case to answer in respect of misconduct or gross misconduct or whether there is no case to answer.

Written notices

15.—(1) The investigator shall as soon as is reasonably practicable after being appointed, and subject to paragraph (3), cause the officer concerned to be given written notice—

   (a) describing the conduct that is the subject matter of the allegation and how that conduct is alleged to fall below the Standards of Professional Behaviour;

   (b) of the appropriate authority's assessment of whether that conduct, if proved, would amount to misconduct or gross misconduct;

   (c) that there is to be an investigation into the matter and the identity of the investigator;

   (d) of whether, if the matter were to be referred to misconduct proceedings, those would be likely to be a misconduct meeting or a misconduct hearing and the reason for this;

   (e) that if the likely form of any misconduct proceedings to be held changes, further notice (with reasons) will be given;

   (f) informing him that he has the right to seek advice from his staff association or any other body and of the effect of regulation 6(1);

   (g) of the effect of regulations 7(1) to (3) and 16; and

   (h) informing him that whilst he does not have to say anything it may harm his case if he does not mention when interviewed or when providing any information under regulations 16(1) or 22(2) or (3) something which he later relies on in any misconduct proceedings or special case hearing or at an appeal meeting or appeal hearing.

(2) If following service of the notice under paragraph (1), the appropriate authority revises its assessment of the conduct in accordance with regulation 12(5) or its determination of the likely form of any misconduct proceedings to be taken, the appropriate authority shall, as soon as practicable, give the officer concerned further written notice of—

   (a) the assessment of whether the conduct, if proved, would amount to misconduct or gross misconduct as the case may be and the reason for that assessment; and

   (b) whether, if the case were to be referred to misconduct proceedings, those would be likely to be a misconduct meeting or a misconduct hearing and the reason for this.

(3) The requirement to give a written notice to the officer concerned under paragraph (1) does not apply for so long as the investigator considers that giving such a notice might prejudice the investigation or any other investigation (including, in particular, a criminal investigation).

(4) Once a written notice has been given in accordance with paragraph (1), the investigator shall notify the officer concerned of the progress of the investigation—

   (a) if there has been no previous notification following the supply of the written notice under paragraph (1), before the end of 4 weeks beginning with the first working day after the start of the investigation; and

   (b) in any other case, before the end of 4 weeks beginning with the first working day after the previous notification.

Representations to the investigator

16.—(1) Before the end of 10 working days starting with the first working day after which the notice is given under regulation 15(1), (unless this period is extended by the investigator)—

   (a) the officer concerned may provide a written or oral statement relating to any matter under investigation to the investigator; and

   (b) the officer concerned or his police friend may provide any relevant documents to the investigator.

(2) The investigator shall, as part of his investigation, consider any such statement or document and shall make a record of having received it.

(3) In this regulation "relevant document"—

   (a) means a document relating to any matter under investigation, and

   (b) includes such a document containing suggestions as to lines of inquiry to be pursued or witnesses to be interviewed.

Interviews during investigation

17.—(1) Where an investigator wishes to interview the officer concerned as part of his investigation, he shall, if reasonably practicable, agree a date and time for the interview with the officer concerned.

(2) Where no date and time is agreed under paragraph (1), the investigator shall specify a date and time for the interview.

(3) Where a date and time is specified under paragraph (2) and—

(a) the officer concerned or his police friend will not be available at that time; and

(b) the officer concerned proposes an alternative time which satisfies subsection (4),

the interview shall be postponed to the time proposed by the officer concerned.

(4) An alternative time must—

(a) be reasonable; and

(b) fall before the end of the period of 5 working days beginning with the first working day after the day specified by the investigator.

(5) The officer concerned shall be given written notice of the date, time and place of the interview.

(6) The investigator shall, in advance of the interview, provide the officer concerned with such information as the investigator considers appropriate in the circumstances of the case to enable the officer concerned to prepare for the interview.

(7) The officer concerned shall attend the interview.

(8) A police friend may not answer any questions asked of the officer concerned during the interview.

Report of investigation

18.—(1) On completion of his investigation the investigator shall as soon as practicable submit a written report on his investigation to the appropriate authority.

(2) The written report shall—

(a) provide an accurate summary of the evidence;

(b) attach or refer to any relevant documents; and

(c) indicate the investigator's opinion as to whether there is a case to answer in respect of misconduct or gross misconduct or whether there is no case to answer.

(3) If at any time during his investigation the investigator believes that the appropriate authority would, on consideration of the matter, be likely to determine that the special conditions are satisfied, he shall, whether or not the investigation is complete, submit to the appropriate authority—

(a) a statement of his belief and the grounds for it; and

(b) a written report on his investigation to that point.

PART 4

MISCONDUCT PROCEEDINGS

Referral of case to misconduct proceedings

19.—(1) Subject to regulation 41 and paragraph (6)—

(a) on receipt of the investigator's written report; and

(b) in the case of such a report submitted under paragraph 22 of Schedule 3 to the 2002 Act (final reports on investigations), in making a determination under paragraph 23(7) or 24(6) of Schedule 3 to the 2002 Act (action in response to an investigation report) as to what action to take in respect of matters dealt with in that report,

the appropriate authority shall, as soon as practicable, determine whether the officer concerned has a case to answer in respect of misconduct or gross misconduct or whether there is no case to answer.

(2) Subject to paragraph (6), in a case where the disciplinary proceedings have been delayed by virtue of regulation 9(3), as soon as practicable after the appropriate authority considers that such proceedings would no longer prejudice any criminal proceedings, it shall, subject to regulation 41(3), make a further determination as to whether the officer concerned has a case to answer in respect of misconduct or gross misconduct or whether there is no case to answer.

(3) Where the appropriate authority determines there is no case to answer, it may—
    (a) take no further disciplinary action against the officer concerned;
    (b) take management action against the officer concerned; or
    (c) refer the matter to be dealt with under the Performance Regulations.

(4) Where the appropriate authority determines that there is a case to answer in respect of gross misconduct, it shall, subject to regulation 9(3) and paragraph (2), refer the case to a misconduct hearing.

(5) Where the appropriate authority determines that there is a case to answer in respect of misconduct, it may—
    (a) subject to regulation 9(3) and paragraph (2), refer the case to misconduct proceedings; or
    (b) take management action against the officer concerned.

(6) Where the appropriate authority—
    (a) accepts a recommendation under paragraph 27(3) of Schedule 3 to the 2002 Act (duties with respect to disciplinary proceedings) that proceedings are brought at a misconduct meeting or a misconduct hearing; or
    (b) has a duty under paragraph 27(4) (duties with respect to disciplinary proceedings) of that Schedule to comply with a direction to give effect to such a recommendation,
it shall, subject to regulation 9(3), refer the case to such a meeting or hearing.

(7) Where the appropriate authority fails to—
    (a) make the determination referred to in paragraph (1); and
    (b) where appropriate, decide what action to take under paragraph (5),
before the end of 15 working days beginning with the first working day after receipt of the investigator's written report, it shall notify the officer concerned of the reason for this.

(8) Where under paragraph (5) the appropriate authority determines to take management action, it shall give the officer concerned written notice of this as soon as practicable.

(9) Where the appropriate authority determines under paragraph (5) to refer the case to misconduct proceedings—
    (a) where the officer concerned had a final written warning in force at the date of the assessment of conduct under regulation 12(1) of these Regulations or regulation 14A of the Complaints Regulations[12] (as the case may be), those proceedings shall be a misconduct hearing;
    (b) where the officer concerned has been reduced in rank under the Police (Conduct) Regulations 2004 less than 18 months prior to the assessment of conduct under regulation 12(1) of these Regulations or regulation 14A of the Complaints Regulations (as the case may be), those proceedings shall be a misconduct hearing; and
    (c) in all other cases those proceedings shall be a misconduct meeting.

Withdrawal of case

20.—(1) Subject to paragraph (3), at any time before the beginning of the misconduct proceedings, the appropriate authority may direct that the case be withdrawn.

(2) Where a direction is given under paragraph (1)—
    (a) the appropriate authority may—
        (i) take no further action against the officer concerned;
        (ii) take management action against the officer concerned; or
        (iii) refer the matter to be dealt with under the Performance Regulations; and

    (b) the appropriate authority shall as soon as practicable give the officer concerned—

        (i) written notice of the direction, indicating whether any action will be taken under paragraph (2)(a); and

        (ii) where the investigation has been completed, on request and subject to the harm test, a copy of the investigator's report or such parts of that report as relate to the officer concerned.

(3) This regulation shall not apply to a case to which paragraph 16, 17, 18 or 19 of Schedule 3 to the 2002 Act (investigations) applies.

Notice of referral to misconduct proceedings and panel membership

21.—(1) Where a case is referred to misconduct proceedings, the appropriate authority shall as soon as practicable give the officer concerned—

    (a) written notice of—

        (i) the referral;

        (ii) the conduct that is the subject matter of the case and how that conduct is alleged to amount to misconduct or gross misconduct as the case may be;

        (iii) the name of the person appointed to (in the case of a misconduct meeting for an officer other than a senior officer) conduct or (in any other case) chair the misconduct proceedings and of the effect of paragraphs (3) to (6) of this regulation; and

        (iv) the effect of regulation 7(1) to (3) in relation to the form of misconduct proceedings to which the case is being referred;

    (b) a copy of any statement he may have made to the investigator during the course of the investigation; and

    (c) subject to the harm test, a copy of —

        (i) the investigator's report or such parts of that report as relate to him (together with any document attached to or referred to in that report as relates to him); and

        (ii) any other relevant document gathered during the course of the investigation.

(2) As soon as practicable after—

    (a) any person has been appointed under regulation 7(5) to advise the person or persons conducting the misconduct proceedings; and

    (b) where the misconduct proceedings are to be conducted by a panel, the person or persons comprising that panel (other than the chair) have been determined,

the appropriate authority shall give the officer concerned written notice of the names of such persons and of the effect of paragraphs (3) to (6) of this regulation.

(3) The officer concerned may object to any person whom he is notified under this regulation is to—

    (a) conduct (including chair) his misconduct proceedings; or

    (b) advise the person or persons conducting those proceedings.

(4) Any such objection must be made in writing to the appropriate authority before the end of 3 working days beginning with the first working day after the officer concerned is given notice of the person's name and must set out the grounds of objection of the officer concerned.

(5) The appropriate authority shall notify the officer concerned in writing whether it upholds or rejects an objection to any panel member or to any person appointed under regulation 7(5) to advise the person or persons conducting the misconduct proceedings.

(6) If the appropriate authority upholds the objection, the person to whom the officer concerned objects shall be replaced (in accordance with regulations 7(5) and (6) or 25 to 27 as appropriate).

(7) As soon as reasonably practicable after any such appointment, the appropriate authority shall notify in writing the officer concerned of the name of the new panel member, or the adviser to the person or persons conducting the misconduct proceedings, as the case may be.

(8) The officer concerned may object to the appointment of a person appointed under paragraph (6).

(9) Any such objection must be made in accordance with paragraph (4), provided that it must be made before the end of 3 working days beginning with the first working day after receipt of the notification referred to in paragraph (7); and the appropriate authority shall comply with paragraphs (5) to (7) in relation to that objection.

(10) In this regulation "relevant document" means a document which, in the opinion of the appropriate authority, is relevant to the case the officer concerned has to answer.

Procedure on receipt of notice

22.—(1) Before the end of—
- (a) 14 working days beginning with the first working day after the documents have been supplied to the officer concerned under regulation 21(1); or
- (b) where that period is extended by the person conducting or chairing the misconduct proceedings for exceptional circumstances, such extended period,
the officer concerned shall comply with paragraphs (2) and (3).

(2) The officer concerned shall provide to the appropriate authority—
- (a) written notice of whether or not he accepts that his conduct amounts to misconduct or gross misconduct as the case may be;
- (b) where he accepts that his conduct amounts to misconduct or gross misconduct as the case may be, any written submission he wishes to make in mitigation; and
- (c) where he does not accept that his conduct amounts to misconduct or gross misconduct as the case may be, or he disputes part of the case against him, written notice of—
  - (i) the allegations he disputes and his account of the relevant events; and
  - (ii) any arguments on points of law he wishes to be considered by the person or persons conducting the misconduct proceedings.

(3) The officer concerned shall provide the appropriate authority with a copy of any document he intends to rely on at the misconduct proceedings.

(4) Before the end of 3 working days beginning with the first working day after the date on which the officer concerned has complied with paragraph (2), the appropriate authority and the officer concerned shall each supply to the other a list of proposed witnesses or give notice that they do not have any proposed witnesses; and any list of proposed witnesses shall include brief details of the evidence that each witness is able to adduce and their address.

(5) Where there are proposed witnesses, the officer concerned shall, if reasonably practicable, agree a list of proposed witnesses with the appropriate authority.

Witnesses

23.—(1) As soon as practicable after any list of proposed witnesses has been—
- (a) agreed under regulation 22(5); or
- (b) where there is no agreement under regulation 22(4), supplied under regulation 22(4),
the appropriate authority shall supply that list to the person conducting or chairing the misconduct proceedings.

(2) The person conducting or chairing the misconduct proceedings shall—
- (a) consider the list or lists of proposed witnesses; and
- (b) subject to paragraph (3), determine which, if any, witnesses should attend the misconduct proceedings.

(3) No witness shall give evidence at misconduct proceedings unless the person conducting or chairing those proceedings reasonably believes that it is necessary for the witness to do so in the interests of justice, in which case he shall—
- (a) where the witness is a police officer, cause that person to be ordered to attend the misconduct proceedings; and

(b) in any other case, cause the witness to be given notice that his attendance is necessary and of the date, time and place of the proceedings.

Timing and notice of misconduct proceedings

24.—(1) Subject to paragraphs (2) and (6), the misconduct proceedings shall take place—

    (a) in the case of a misconduct meeting, before the end of 20 working days; or

    (b) in the case of a misconduct hearing, before the end of 30 working days,

beginning with the first working day after the documents have been supplied to the officer concerned under regulation 21(1).

(2) The person conducting or chairing the misconduct proceedings may extend the period specified in paragraph (1) where he considers that it would be in the interests of justice to do so.

(3) Where the person conducting or chairing the misconduct proceedings decides to extend the period under paragraph (2), or decides not to do so following representations from the officer concerned or the appropriate authority, he shall provide written notification of his reasons for that decision to the appropriate authority and the officer concerned.

(4) The person conducting or chairing the misconduct proceedings shall, if reasonably practicable, agree a date and time for the misconduct proceedings with the officer concerned.

(5) Where no date and time is agreed under paragraph (4), the person conducting or chairing the misconduct proceedings shall specify a date and time for those proceedings.

(6) Where a date and time is specified under paragraph (5) and—

    (a) the officer concerned or his police friend will not be available at that time; and

    (b) the officer concerned proposes an alternative time which satisfies subsection (7),

the misconduct proceedings shall be postponed to the time proposed by the officer concerned.

(7) An alternative time must—

    (a) be reasonable; and

    (b) fall before the end of 5 working days beginning with the first working day after the day specified by the person conducting or chairing the misconduct proceedings.

(8) The officer concerned shall be given written notice of the date, time and place of the misconduct proceedings.

Persons conducting misconduct proceedings: officers other than senior officers

25.—(1) This regulation applies where the officer concerned is an officer other than a senior officer.

(2) The misconduct meeting shall be conducted by a person appointed by the appropriate authority who is not an interested party and who satisfies paragraph (3).

(3) The person shall—

    (a) where—

        (i) the officer concerned is a member of a police force, be another member of a police force of at least one rank higher than the officer concerned;

        (ii) the officer concerned is a special constable, be a member of a police force of the rank of sergeant or above or a senior human resources professional; or

    (b) unless the case substantially involves operational policing matters, be a police staff member who, in the opinion of the appropriate authority, is more senior than the officer concerned.

(4) Where the case is referred to a misconduct hearing, that hearing shall be conducted by a panel of three persons appointed by the appropriate authority, comprising—

    (a) a senior officer or a senior human resources professional, who shall be the chair;

    (b) where—

        (i) the chair is a senior officer, a member of a police force of the rank of superintendent or above or a human resources professional;

    (ii) the chair is a senior human resources professional, a member of a police force of the rank of superintendent or above; and

(c) a person selected by the appropriate authority from a list of candidates maintained by a police authority for the purposes of these Regulations.

(5) For the purposes of this regulation, a "senior human resources professional" means a human resources professional who, in the opinion of the appropriate authority, has sufficient seniority, skills and experience to conduct the misconduct hearing or misconduct meeting as the case may be.

Persons conducting misconduct proceedings: chief constables etc.

26.—(1) Where the officer concerned is—

(a) a chief constable;

(b) in the case of the metropolitan police force—

    (i) the commissioner;

    (ii) the deputy commissioner; or

    (iii) an assistant commissioner; or

(c) in the case of the City of London police force, the commissioner,

the misconduct proceedings shall be conducted by a panel of persons as specified in paragraph (2) or (3) as appropriate, appointed by the appropriate authority.

(2) For a misconduct meeting, those persons are—

(a) the chair of the police authority for the police force concerned, or another member of that police authority nominated by him, who shall chair the meeting; and

(b) HMCIC or an inspector of constabulary nominated by him.

(3) For a misconduct hearing, those persons are—

(a) a barrister selected by the appropriate authority from a list of candidates nominated by the Secretary of State for the purposes of these Regulations, who shall be the chair;

(b) the chair of the police authority for the police force concerned, or another member of that police authority nominated by him;

(c) HMCIC or an inspector of constabulary nominated by him; and

(d) a person selected by the appropriate authority from a list of candidates maintained by a police authority for the purposes of these Regulations.

Persons conducting misconduct proceedings: other senior officers

27.—(1) Where the officer concerned is a senior officer other than one mentioned in regulation 26(1), the misconduct proceedings shall be conducted by a panel of persons as specified in paragraph (2) or (3) as appropriate, appointed by the appropriate authority.

(2) For a misconduct meeting, those persons are—

(a) (i) where the officer concerned is a member of the Metropolitan Police Force, an assistant commissioner or a senior officer of at least one rank above that of the officer concerned nominated by an assistant commissioner, who shall be the chair; or

    (ii) any other case, the chief officer of police of the police force concerned or a senior officer of at least one rank above that of the officer concerned nominated by that chief officer of police, who shall be the chair; and

(b) the chair of the police authority for the police force concerned or another member of that police authority nominated by him.

(3) For a misconduct hearing, those persons are—

(a) HMCIC or an inspector of constabulary nominated by him, who shall be the chair;

(b) the chief officer of police of the police force concerned or a senior officer of at least one rank above that of the officer concerned nominated by that chief officer of police;

(c) the chair of the police authority for the police force concerned or another member of that police authority nominated by him; and

(d) a person selected by the appropriate authority from a list of candidates maintained by a police authority for the purposes of these Regulations.

Documents to be supplied

28.—(1) Prior to the misconduct proceedings the appropriate authority shall supply the person or persons conducting the misconduct proceedings with a copy of—

(a) the documents given to the officer concerned under regulation 21(1)(a) to (c)(ii);

(b) the documents provided by the officer concerned under—

(i) regulation 22(2) and (3); and

(ii) where paragraph (2) applies, regulation 45; and

(c) where the officer concerned does not accept that his conduct amounts to misconduct or gross misconduct as the case may be or where he disputes any part of the case against him, any other documents that, in the opinion of the appropriate authority, should be considered at the misconduct proceedings.

(2) This paragraph applies where the appropriate authority has directed, in accordance with regulation 42(1), that the case be dealt with under this Part.

(3) Prior to the misconduct proceedings the officer concerned shall be supplied with a list of the documents supplied under paragraph (1) and a copy of any such document of which he has not already been supplied with a copy.

Attendance of officer concerned at misconduct proceedings

29.—(1) Subject to paragraph (2), the officer concerned shall attend the misconduct proceedings.

(2) Where the officer concerned informs the person conducting or chairing the misconduct proceedings in advance that he is unable to attend on grounds which the person conducting or chairing those proceedings considers reasonable, that person may allow the officer concerned to participate in the proceedings by video link or other means.

(3) Where the officer concerned is allowed to and does so participate in the misconduct proceedings or where the officer concerned does not attend the misconduct proceedings—

(a) he may nonetheless be represented at those proceedings by his—

(i) police friend; or

(ii) in the case of a misconduct hearing, his relevant lawyer (in which case the police friend may also attend); and

(b) the proceedings may be proceeded with and concluded in the absence of the officer concerned whether or not he is so represented.

(4) Where the officer concerned is represented in accordance with paragraph (3), the person representing the officer concerned or his police friend (if different), or both, may participate using the video link or other means where such means are also used by the officer concerned.

Participation of Commission and investigator at misconduct proceedings

30.—(1) In any case where—

(a) paragraph 18 or 19 of Schedule 3 to the 2002 Act (managed and independent investigations) applied; or

(b) paragraph 16 or 17 of Schedule 3 to the 2002 Act (investigations by the appropriate authority or supervised investigations) applied and the Commission—

(i) made a recommendation under paragraph 27(3) of that Schedule (duties with respect to disciplinary proceedings) which the appropriate authority accepted; or

(ii) gave a direction under paragraph 27(4)(a) of that Schedule (duties with respect to disciplinary proceedings),

the Commission may attend the misconduct proceedings to make representations.

(2) Where the Commission so attends the misconduct proceedings—

(a) if it is a misconduct hearing it may instruct a relevant lawyer to represent it;

(b) it shall notify the complainant or any interested person prior to those proceedings; and

(c) the person conducting or chairing the misconduct proceedings shall notify the officer concerned prior to the those proceedings.

(3) The investigator or a nominated person shall attend the misconduct proceedings on the request of the person conducting or chairing those proceedings to answer questions.

(4) For the purposes of this regulation, a "nominated person" is a person who, in the opinion of—

(a) the appropriate authority; or

(b) in a case to which paragraph 18 or 19 of Schedule 3 to the 2002 Act (managed and independent investigations) applied, the Commission,

has sufficient knowledge of the investigation of the case to be able to assist the person or persons conducting the misconduct proceedings.

Attendance of complainant or interested person at misconduct proceedings

31.—(1) This regulation shall apply in the case of misconduct proceedings arising from—

(a) a conduct matter to which paragraph 16, 17, 18 or 19 of Schedule 3 to the 2002 Act (investigations) applied; or

(b) the investigation of a complaint which was certified as subject to special requirements under paragraph 19B(1)[13] of that Schedule (assessment of seriousness of conduct).

(2) The appropriate authority shall notify the complainant or any interested person of the date, time and place of the misconduct proceedings.

(3) Subject to the provisions of this regulation, regulation 33 and any conditions imposed under regulation 32(8), the complainant or any interested person may attend the misconduct proceedings as an observer up to but not including the point at which the person conducting or chairing those proceedings considers the question of disciplinary action.

(4) Subject to paragraph (5), regulation 33 and any conditions imposed under regulation 32(8), a complainant or interested person may be accompanied by one other person, and if the complainant or interested person has a special need, by one further person to accommodate that need.

(5) Where a complainant or interested person, or any person accompanying him, is to give evidence as a witness at the misconduct proceedings, he and any person allowed to accompany him shall not be allowed to attend the proceedings before he gives his evidence.

(6) The person conducting or chairing the misconduct proceedings may, at his discretion, put any questions to the officer concerned that the complainant or interested person may request be put to him.

(7) For the purposes of this regulation, a person has a special need if, in the opinion of the person conducting or chairing the misconduct proceedings, he has a disability or learning difficulty, or does not have sufficient knowledge of English, to fully participate in or understand the misconduct proceedings.

Attendance of others at misconduct proceedings

32.—(1) Subject to regulation 31 and the provisions of this regulation, the misconduct proceedings shall be in private.

(2) A person nominated by the Commission may, as an observer, attend misconduct proceedings which arise from a case to which—

(a) paragraph 17, 18 or 19 of Schedule 3 to the 2002 Act (supervised, managed and independent investigations) applied; or

(b) paragraph 16 of Schedule 3 to the 2002 Act (investigations by the appropriate authority) applied and in relation to which the Commission—

(i) made a recommendation under paragraph 27(3) of that Schedule (duties with respect to disciplinary proceedings) which the appropriate authority accepted; or

(ii) gave a direction under paragraph 27(4)(a) of that Schedule (duties with respect to disciplinary proceedings).

(3) Subject to any contrary decision by the person conducting or chairing the misconduct proceedings, a witness other than a complainant, interested person or the officer concerned, shall only attend the misconduct proceedings for the purpose of giving their evidence.

(4) The person conducting or chairing the misconduct proceedings may, at his discretion, permit a witness in the misconduct proceedings to be accompanied at those proceedings by one other person.

(5) Where a misconduct hearing arises from a case to which paragraph 19 of Schedule 3 to the 2002 Act (investigations by the Commission) applied and the Commission considers that because of the gravity of the case or other exceptional circumstances it would be in the public interest to do so, the Commission may, having consulted with—

(a) the appropriate authority;

(b) the officer concerned;

(c) the complainant or interested person; and

(d) any witnesses,

direct that the whole or part of the misconduct hearing be held in public.

(6) It shall be the duty of the persons conducting the misconduct hearing to comply with a direction given under paragraph (5).

(7) A direction under paragraph (5), together with the reasons for it, shall be notified as soon as practicable, and in any event before the end of 5 working days beginning with the first working day after the decision was taken, to the persons consulted under that paragraph.

(8) The person conducting or chairing the misconduct proceedings may impose such conditions as he sees fit relating to the attendance under regulation 31 or this regulation of persons at the misconduct proceedings (including circumstances in which they may be excluded) in order to facilitate the proper conduct of the proceedings.

Exclusion from misconduct proceedings

33. Where it appears to the person conducting or chairing the misconduct proceedings that any person may, in giving evidence, disclose information which, under the harm test, ought not to be disclosed to any person attending the proceedings, he shall require such attendees to withdraw while the evidence is given.

Procedure at misconduct proceedings

34.—(1) Subject to these Regulations, the person conducting or chairing the misconduct proceedings shall determine the procedure at those proceedings.

(2) The misconduct proceedings shall not proceed unless the officer concerned has been notified of the effect of regulation 7(1) to (3) in relation to the form of misconduct proceedings taking place.

(3) Subject to paragraph (4), the person conducting or chairing the misconduct proceedings may from time to time adjourn the proceedings if it appears to him to be necessary or expedient to do so.

(4) The misconduct proceedings shall not, except in exceptional circumstances, be adjourned solely to allow the complainant or any witness or interested person to attend.

(5) The person representing the officer concerned may—

(a) address the proceedings in order to do any or all of the following—

(i) put the case of the officer concerned;

(ii) sum up that case;

(iii) respond on behalf of the officer concerned to any view expressed at the proceedings;

(iv) make representations concerning any aspect of proceedings under these Regulations; and

(v) subject to paragraph (8), ask questions of any witnesses; and

(b) confer with the officer concerned.

(6) Where (at a misconduct hearing) the person representing the officer concerned is a relevant lawyer, the police friend of the officer concerned may also confer with the officer concerned.

(7) The police friend or relevant lawyer of the officer concerned may not answer any questions asked of the officer concerned during the misconduct proceedings.

(8) Whether any question should or should not be put to a witness shall be determined by the person conducting or chairing the misconduct proceedings.

(9) The person conducting or chairing the misconduct proceedings may allow any document to be considered at those proceedings notwithstanding that a copy of it has not been supplied—
    (a) by the officer concerned to the appropriate authority in accordance with regulation 22(3); or
    (b) to the officer concerned in accordance with regulation 21(1).

(10) Where evidence is given or considered at the misconduct proceedings that the officer concerned—
    (a) on being questioned by an investigator at any time after he was given written notice under regulation 15(1) of these Regulations or regulation 14A of the Complaints Regulations; or
    (b) in submitting any information or by not submitting any information at all under paragraph 19C of Schedule 3 to the 2002 Act or regulation 16(1) or 22(2) or (3) (or, where paragraph (11) applies, regulation 45),
failed to mention any fact relied on in his case at the misconduct proceedings, being a fact which in the circumstances existing at the time, the officer concerned could reasonably have been expected to mention when so questioned or when providing such information, paragraph (12) applies.

(11) This paragraph applies where the appropriate authority has directed, in accordance with regulation 42(1), that the case be dealt with under this Part.

(12) Where this paragraph applies, the person or persons conducting the misconduct proceedings may draw such inferences from the failure as appear proper.

(13) The person or persons conducting the misconduct proceedings shall review the facts of the case and decide whether the conduct of the officer concerned amounts—
    (a) in the case of a misconduct meeting, to misconduct or not; or
    (b) in the case of a misconduct hearing, to misconduct, gross misconduct or neither.

(14) The person or persons conducting the misconduct proceedings shall not find that the conduct of the officer concerned amounts to misconduct or gross misconduct unless—
    (a) he is or they are satisfied on the balance of probabilities that this is the case; or
    (b) the officer concerned admits it is the case.

(15) At misconduct proceedings conducted by a panel, any decision shall be based on a majority (with, where there is a panel of two or four, the chair having the casting vote if necessary) but shall not indicate whether it was taken unanimously or by a majority.

Outcome of misconduct proceedings

35.—(1) Subject to the provisions of this regulation, the person or persons conducting the misconduct proceedings may—
    (a) impose any of the disciplinary action in paragraph (2)(a) or (b) or (6)(b) as appropriate; or
    (b) where he or they find the conduct amounts to misconduct but not gross misconduct following a misconduct meeting or hearing, record a finding of misconduct but take no further action.

(2) The disciplinary action is—
    (a) at a misconduct meeting—
        (i) management advice;
        (ii) written warning; or
        (iii) final written warning;

    (b) at a misconduct hearing—
        (i) management advice;
        (ii) written warning;
        (iii) final written warning;
        (iv) dismissal with notice; or
        (v) dismissal without notice.

(3) The disciplinary action referred to in paragraph (2) shall have effect from the date on which it is notified to the officer concerned and in the case of dismissal with notice, the person or persons conducting the misconduct hearing shall decide the period of notice to be given, subject to a minimum period of 28 days.

(4) Where the person or persons conducting the misconduct proceedings finds that the conduct of the officer concerned amounts to misconduct but not gross misconduct following a misconduct hearing, unless the officer concerned had a final written warning in force on the date of the assessment of the conduct under regulation 12(1) of these Regulations or regulation 14A of the Complaints Regulations (as the case may be), the officer concerned may not be dismissed whether with or without notice.

(5) Where the officer concerned had a written warning in force on the date of the assessment of the conduct under regulation 12(1) of these Regulations or regulation 14A of the Complaints Regulations (as the case may be), a written warning shall not be given.

(6) Where the officer concerned had a final written warning in force on the date of the assessment of the conduct under regulation 12(1) of these Regulations or regulation 14A of the Complaints Regulations (as the case may be)—
    (a) neither a written warning nor a final written warning shall be given; but
    (b) subject to paragraph (8), in exceptional circumstances, the final written warning may be extended.

(7) Where a final written warning is extended under paragraph (6)(b), that warning shall remain in force for a period of 18 months from the date on which it would otherwise expire.

(8) A final written warning may be extended on one occasion only.

(9) Where there is a finding of gross misconduct and the persons conducting the misconduct hearing decide that the officer concerned shall be dismissed, the dismissal shall be without notice.

(10) Where the question of disciplinary action is being considered, the person or persons conducting the misconduct proceedings—
    (a) shall have regard to the record of police service of the officer concerned as shown on his personal record;
    (b) may receive evidence from any witness whose evidence would, in his or their opinion, assist him or them in determining the question; and
    (c) shall give—
        (i) the officer concerned, his police friend or, at a misconduct hearing, his relevant lawyer; and
        (ii) the appropriate authority or person appointed to represent the appropriate authority in accordance with regulation 7(4);
    an opportunity to make oral or written representations before any such question is determined.

Notification of outcome

36.—(1) The officer concerned shall be informed of—
    (a) the finding of the person or persons conducting the misconduct proceedings; and
    (b) any disciplinary action imposed,
as soon as practicable and in any event shall be provided with written notice of these matters and a summary of the reasons before the end of 5 working days beginning with the first working day after the conclusion of the misconduct proceedings.

(2) Where there was a finding of misconduct or gross misconduct a written notice under this regulation shall include—
    (a) where the officer concerned is an officer other than a senior officer—
        (i) if the case was decided at a misconduct meeting, notice of his right of appeal under regulation 38; or
        (ii) if the case was decided at a misconduct hearing, notice of his right of appeal to a police appeals tribunal;
    (b) where the officer concerned is a senior officer, notice of his right of appeal to a police appeals tribunal.
(3) In all cases referred to in paragraph (2) a written notice under this regulation shall include the name of the person to whom an appeal should be sent.

Record of misconduct proceedings

37.—(1) A record of the misconduct proceedings shall be taken and in the case of a misconduct hearing that record shall be verbatim.
(2) The officer concerned shall, on request, be supplied with a copy of the record of the proceedings at the misconduct proceedings.

Appeal from misconduct meeting: officers other than senior officers

38.—(1) Where the officer concerned is an officer, other than a senior officer, whose case was decided at a misconduct meeting, he may, subject to the provisions of this regulation, appeal—
    (a) if he admitted his conduct amounted to misconduct, against any disciplinary action imposed under regulation 35; or
    (b) if (after he denied misconduct) the person conducting the misconduct meeting found that his conduct amounted to misconduct, against that finding or any disciplinary action imposed under regulation 35.
(2) The only grounds of appeal under this regulation are that—
    (a) the finding or disciplinary action imposed was unreasonable;
    (b) there is evidence that could not reasonably have been considered at the misconduct meeting which could have materially affected the finding or decision on disciplinary action; or
    (c) there was a serious breach of the procedures set out in these Regulations or other unfairness which could have materially affected the finding or decision on disciplinary action.
(3) An appeal under this regulation shall be commenced by the officer concerned giving written notice of appeal to the appropriate authority—
    (a) before the end of 7 working days beginning with the first working day after the written notice and summary of reasons is given under regulation 36 (unless this period is extended by the appropriate authority for exceptional circumstances); and
    (b) stating the grounds of appeal and whether a meeting is requested.
(4) An appeal under this regulation shall be determined—
    (a) where the person who conducted the misconduct meeting was a member of a police force, by—
        (i) a member of a police force of at least one rank higher than that person; or
        (ii) unless the case substantially involves operational policing matters, a police staff member who, in the opinion of the appropriate authority, is more senior than that person;
    (b) where the person who conducted the misconduct meeting was a police staff member, by—
        (i) a member of a police force who, in the opinion of the appropriate authority is more senior than that person; or
        (ii) a more senior police staff member,
    who is not an interested party, appointed by the appropriate authority.

(5) The appropriate authority shall as soon as practicable give the officer concerned written notice of—

(a) the name of the person appointed to determine the appeal under paragraph (4);

(b) the name of any person appointed under regulation 7(5) to advise the person determining the appeal; and

(c) the effect of paragraphs (6) to (9) of this regulation.

(6) The officer concerned may object to any person whom he is notified under this regulation is to—

(a) determine the appeal; or

(b) advise the person determining the appeal.

(7) Any such objection must be made in writing to the appropriate authority before the end of 3 working days beginning with the first working day after the officer concerned is given notice of the person's name and must set out the grounds of objection of the officer concerned.

(8) The appropriate authority shall notify the officer concerned in writing whether it upholds or rejects an objection to the person appointed to conduct the appeal meeting or to any person appointed under regulation 7(5) to advise the person conducting the appeal meeting.

(9) If the appropriate authority upholds the objection, the person to whom the officer concerned objects shall be replaced (in accordance with regulation 7(5) or (6) or paragraph (4) as appropriate).

(10) As soon as reasonably practicable after any such appointment, the appropriate authority shall notify in writing the officer concerned of the name of the new person appointed to determine the appeal or the advisor to the person determining the appeal as the case may be.

(11) The officer concerned may object to the appointment of a person appointed under regulation (9).

(12) Any such objection must be made in accordance with paragraph (7), provided that it must be made before the end of 3 working days beginning with the first working day after the officer concerned is given the notice referred to in paragraph (10); and the appropriate authority shall comply with paragraphs (8) to (10) in relation to that objection.

Appeal meeting

39.—(1) This regulation applies where the officer concerned requests a meeting in his written notice of appeal under regulation 38(3).

(2) The person determining the appeal shall determine whether the notice of appeal sets out arguable grounds of appeal and—

(a) if he determines that it does he shall hold an appeal meeting with the officer concerned, subject to paragraphs (3) and (5), before the end of 5 working days beginning with the first working day after that determination; and

(b) if he determines that it does not, he shall dismiss the appeal.

(3) The person determining the appeal may extend the time period specified in paragraph (2)(a) where he considers that it would be in the interests of justice to do so.

(4) The person determining the appeal shall specify a date and time for the appeal meeting.

(5) Where—

(a) the officer concerned or his police friend will not be available at that time; and

(b) the officer concerned proposes an alternative time which satisfies subsection (6),

the appeal meeting shall be postponed to the time proposed by the officer concerned.

(6) An alternative time must—

(a) be reasonable; and

(b) fall before the end of 5 working days beginning with the first working day after the day specified by the person determining the appeal.

(7) Written notice of the date, time and place of the appeal meeting shall be given to—

(a) the officer concerned;

    (b) where the misconduct meeting arose from a complaint which was certified as subject to special requirements under paragraph 19B(1) of Schedule 3 to the 2002 Act (assessment of seriousness of conduct), the complainant; and

    (c) where the misconduct meeting arose from a conduct matter to which paragraph 16, 17, 18 or 19 of Schedule 3 to the 2002 Act (investigations) applied, any interested person.

(8) Prior to the appeal meeting the appropriate authority shall supply the person determining the appeal with a copy of—

    (a) the documents given to the person who held the misconduct meeting as specified in regulation 28(1);

    (b) the notice of appeal given by the officer concerned under regulation 38(3);

    (c) the record of the misconduct meeting taken under regulation 37(1); and

    (d) any evidence of a kind referred to in regulation 38(2)(b) that the officer concerned wishes to submit in support of his appeal.

Procedure and finding of the appeal

40.—(1) Subject to the provisions of this regulation, the person determining the appeal shall determine the procedure at the appeal meeting.

(2) Subject to paragraph (3), any interested person or complainant given notice of the appeal meeting under regulation 39(7) may attend the appeal meeting as an observer up to but not including the point at which the person determining the appeal considers the question of disciplinary action.

(3) The person determining the appeal may impose such conditions as he sees fit relating to the attendance of persons under paragraph (2) at the appeal meeting (including circumstances in which they may be excluded) in order to facilitate the proper conduct of the appeal meeting.

(4) The person determining the appeal may—

    (a) confirm or reverse the decision appealed against;

    (b) deal with the officer concerned in any manner in which the person conducting the misconduct meeting could have dealt with him under regulation 35.

(5) Before the end of 3 working days beginning with the first working day after the determination of the appeal, the officer concerned shall be given written notice of that determination with a summary of the reasons.

(6) The decision of the person determining the appeal shall take effect by way of substitution for the decision of the person conducting the misconduct meeting and as from the date of the written notice of the outcome of that meeting.

(7) In a case where—

    (a) paragraph 18 or 19 of Schedule 3 to the 2002 Act applied (managed and independent investigations); or

    (b) paragraph 16 or 17 of Schedule 3 to the 2002 Act (investigation by appropriate authority and supervised investigations) applied and the Commission—

        (i) made a recommendation under paragraph 27(3) of that Schedule (duties with respect to disciplinary proceedings) which the appropriate authority accepted; or

        (ii) gave a direction to the appropriate authority under paragraph 27(4) of that Schedule (duties with respect to disciplinary proceedings),

the appropriate authority shall give the Commission written notice of the determination of the appeal with a summary of the reasons.

PART 5
FAST TRACK PROCEDURE FOR SPECIAL CASES

Referral of case to special case hearing

41.—(1) On receipt of a statement submitted by the investigator under regulation 18(3), the appropriate authority shall determine whether the special conditions are satisfied.

(2) In a case where special case proceedings have been delayed by virtue of regulation 9(3), as soon as practicable after the appropriate authority considers that such proceedings would no longer prejudice any criminal proceedings, it shall make a further determination as to whether the special conditions are satisfied.

(3) In a case where disciplinary proceedings have been delayed by virtue of regulation 9(3), the appropriate authority may, as soon as practicable after it considers that such proceedings would no longer prejudice any criminal proceedings, determine whether the special conditions are satisfied.

(4) Where the appropriate authority determines that the special conditions are satisfied, unless it considers that the circumstances are such as to make it inappropriate to do so, it shall certify the case as a special case and, subject to regulation 9(3) and paragraph (2), refer it to a special case hearing.

(5) Where the appropriate authority determines—

(a) that the special conditions are not satisfied; or

(b) that, although those conditions are satisfied, the circumstances are such as to make such certification inappropriate,

it shall, if the investigation was incomplete, return the case to the investigator to complete the investigation or, in any other case, proceed in accordance with Part 4.

(6) Where the appropriate authority is to proceed in accordance with Part 4, regulation 19(1) shall be read as if the following are omitted—

(a) the words "regulation 41 and"; and

(b) sub-paragraphs (a) and (b).

Remission of case

42.—(1) Subject to paragraph (4), at any time after the case has been referred to a special case hearing but before the beginning of that hearing the appropriate authority may direct that the case be dealt with under Part 4 if it considers that the special conditions are no longer satisfied.

(2) Where a direction is made under paragraph (1) the officer concerned shall be notified before the end of 3 working days beginning with the first working day after that direction is made and the appropriate authority shall proceed in accordance with Part 4.

(3) Where the appropriate authority is to proceed in accordance with Part 4, regulation 19(1) shall be read as if the following are omitted—

(a) the words "regulation 41 and"; and

(b) sub-paragraphs (a) and (b).

(4) Paragraph (1) shall not apply to a case where the Commission has given a direction under paragraph 20H(7) of Schedule 3 to the 2002 Act[14] (special cases: recommendation or direction of Commission).

Notice of referral to special case hearing

43.—(1) Where a case is certified as a special case and referred to a special case hearing, the appropriate authority shall as soon as practicable give the officer concerned written notice of these matters and shall supply him with a copy of—

(a) the certificate issued under regulation 41(4);

(b) any statement he may have made to the investigator during the course of the investigation; and

(c) subject to the harm test—

(i) the investigator's report or such parts of that report as relate to him (together with any document attached to or referred to in that report as relates to him); and

(ii) any other relevant document gathered during the course of the investigation.

(2) The notice given under paragraph (1) shall describe the conduct that is the subject matter of the case and how that conduct is alleged to amount to gross misconduct.

(3) For the purposes of this regulation "relevant document" means a document which, in the opinion of the appropriate authority, is relevant to the case of the officer concerned.

Notice of special case hearing

44. The appropriate authority shall specify a date for the special case hearing which shall be not less than 10 and not more than 15 working days after the date on which notice is given under regulation 43(1) and shall immediately notify the officer concerned of—

(a) the date, time and place of that hearing; and

(b) the effect of regulation 7(1) to (3) in relation to a special case hearing.

Procedure on receipt of notice

45.—(1) Before the end of 7 working days beginning with the first working day after the written notice given to the officer concerned under regulation 43(1), the officer concerned shall provide to the appropriate authority—

(a) written notice of whether or not he accepts that his conduct amounts to gross misconduct;

(b) where he accepts that his conduct amounts to gross misconduct, any written submission he wishes to make in mitigation;

(c) where he does not accept that his conduct amounts to gross misconduct, written notice of—

(i) the allegations he disputes and his account of the relevant events; and

(ii) any arguments on points of law he wishes to be considered by the person or persons conducting the special case hearing.

(2) Within the same time period, the officer concerned shall provide the appropriate authority with a copy of any document he intends to rely on at the hearing.

Person conducting special case hearing: officers other than senior officers

46.—(1) This regulation applies where the officer concerned is an officer other than a senior officer.

(2) The special case hearing shall be conducted by—

(a) where the police force concerned is the metropolitan police force, an assistant commissioner; or

(b) in any other case, subject to paragraph (3), the chief officer of police of the police force concerned.

(3) Where the chief officer of police of the police force concerned is an interested party or is unavailable, the special case hearing shall be conducted by the chief officer of police of another police force or an assistant commissioner of the metropolitan police force.

Persons conducting special case hearing: chief constables etc.

47.—(1) This regulation applies where the officer concerned is—

(a) a chief constable;

(b) in the case of the metropolitan police force—

(i) the commissioner;

(ii) the deputy commissioner; or

(iii) an assistant commissioner; or

(c) in the case of the City of London police force, the commissioner.

(2) The special case hearing shall be conducted by a panel of four persons appointed by the appropriate authority, comprising—

(a) a counsel selected by the appropriate authority from a list of candidates nominated by the Lord Chancellor for the purposes of these Regulations, who shall be the chair;

(b) the chair of the police authority for the police force concerned or another member of that police authority nominated by him;

(c) HMCIC or an inspector of constabulary nominated by him; and

(d) a person selected by the appropriate authority from a list of candidates maintained by a police authority for the purposes of these Regulations.

Persons conducting special case hearing: other senior officers

48. Where the officer concerned is a senior officer other than an officer mentioned in regulation 47(1), the special case hearing shall be conducted by a panel of four persons appointed by the appropriate authority, comprising—

(a) HMCIC or an inspector of constabulary nominated by him, who shall be the chair;

(b) the chief officer of police of the police force concerned or a senior officer of at least one rank above that of the officer concerned, nominated by that chief officer of police;

(c) the chair of the police authority for the police force concerned or another member of that police authority nominated by him; and

(d) a person selected by the appropriate authority from a list of candidates maintained by a police authority for the purposes of these Regulations.

Documents to be supplied

49.—(1) Prior to the hearing the appropriate authority shall supply the person or persons conducting the special case hearing with a copy of—

(a) the notice given to the officer concerned under regulation 43(1);

(b) the other documents given to the officer concerned under regulation 43(1)(a) to (c)(ii);

(c) the documents provided by the officer concerned under—

(i) regulation 45; and

(ii) where paragraph (2) applies, regulation 22(2) and (3);

(d) where the officer concerned does not accept that his conduct amounts to gross misconduct, any other documents that, in the opinion of the appropriate authority, should be considered at the hearing.

(2) This paragraph applies where the case was certified as a special case following a determination made under regulation 41(3).

(3) Prior to the hearing the officer concerned shall be supplied with a list of the documents supplied under paragraph (1) and a copy of any of such document of which he has not already been supplied with a copy.

Attendance of officer concerned at special case hearing

50.—(1) Subject to paragraph (2), the officer concerned shall attend the special case hearing.

(2) Where the officer concerned informs the person conducting or chairing the special case hearing in advance that he is unable to attend on grounds which the person conducting or chairing the hearing considers reasonable, that person may allow the officer concerned to participate in the hearing by video link or other means.

(3) Where the officer concerned is allowed to and does so participate in the special case hearing, or where the officer concerned does not attend the special case hearing—

(a) he may nonetheless be represented at that hearing by his—

(i) police friend; or

(ii) relevant lawyer (in which case the police friend may also attend); and

(b) the hearing may be proceeded with and concluded in the absence of the officer concerned whether or not he is so represented.

(4) Where the officer concerned is represented in accordance with paragraph (3), the person representing the officer concerned or his police friend (if different), or both, may participate using the video link or other means where such means are also used by the officer concerned.

Participation of Commission and investigator at special case hearing

51.—(1) In any case where—

(a) paragraph 18 or 19 of Schedule 3 to the 2002 Act (managed and independent investigations) applied; or

(b) paragraph 16 or 17 of Schedule 3 to the 2002 Act (investigations by the appropriate authority and supervised investigations) applied and the Commission—

   (i) made a recommendation under paragraph 20H(1) of that Schedule (special cases: recommendation or direction of Commission) which the appropriate authority accepted; or

   (ii) gave a direction under paragraph 20H(7) of that Schedule (special cases: recommendation or direction of Commission),

the Commission may attend the special case hearing to make representations.

(2) Where the Commission intends to attend the special case hearing—

(a) it may instruct a relevant lawyer to represent it;

(b) it shall notify the complainant or any interested person prior to the hearing; and

(c) the person conducting or chairing the special case hearing shall notify the officer concerned prior to the hearing.

(3) The investigator or a nominated person shall attend the special case hearing on the request of the person conducting or chairing the hearing to answer questions.

(4) For the purposes of this regulation, a "nominated person" is a person who, in the opinion of—

(a) the appropriate authority; or

(b) in a case to which paragraph 18 or 19 of Schedule 3 to the 2002 Act (managed and independent investigations) applied, the Commission,

has sufficient knowledge of the investigation of the case to be able to assist the person or persons conducting the special case hearing.

Attendance of complainant and interested persons at special case hearing

52.—(1) This regulation shall apply in the case of a special case hearing arising from a—

(a) conduct matter to which paragraph 16, 17, 18 or 19 of Schedule 3 to the 2002 Act (investigations) applied; or

(b) complaint which was certified as subject to special requirements under paragraph 19B(1) of that Schedule (assessment of seriousness of conduct).

(2) The appropriate authority shall notify the complainant or any interested person of the date, time and place of the special case hearing.

(3) Subject to any conditions imposed under regulation 53(3), the complainant or any interested person may—

(a) attend the special case hearing as an observer up to but not including the point at which the person conducting or chairing the hearing considers the question of disciplinary action; and

(b) be accompanied by one other person, and if the complainant or interested person has a special need, by one further person to accommodate that need.

(4) For the purposes of this regulation, a person has a special need if, in the opinion of the person conducting or chairing the special case hearing, he has a disability or learning difficulty, or does not have sufficient knowledge of English, to participate in or understand the special case hearing.

Attendance of others at special case hearing

53.—(1) Subject to regulation 52 and this regulation, the special case hearing shall be in private.

(2) A person nominated by the Commission may attend a special case hearing which arises from a case to which—

(a) paragraph 17, 18 or 19 of Schedule 3 to the 2002 Act (supervised, managed and independent investigations) applied; or

   (b) paragraph 16 of Schedule 3 to the 2002 Act (investigations by the appropriate authority) applied and in relation to which the Commission—

      (i) made a recommendation under paragraph 20H(1) of that Schedule (special cases: recommendation or direction of Commission) which the appropriate authority accepted; or

      (ii) gave a direction under paragraph 20H(7) of that Schedule (special cases: recommendation or direction of Commission).

(3) The person conducting or chairing the special case hearing may impose such conditions as he sees fit relating to the attendance of persons under regulation 52 or this regulation at the special case hearing (including circumstances in which they may be excluded) in order to facilitate the proper conduct of the hearing.

Procedure at special case hearing

54.—(1) Subject to these Regulations, the person conducting or chairing the special case hearing shall determine the procedure.

(2) The special case hearing shall not proceed unless the officer concerned has been notified of the effect of regulation 7(1) to (3) in relation to a special case hearing.

(3) Subject to paragraph (4), the person conducting or chairing the special case hearing may from time to time adjourn the hearing if it appears to him to be necessary or expedient to do so.

(4) The special case hearing shall not, except in exceptional circumstances, be adjourned solely to allow the complainant or any interested person to attend.

(5) No witnesses other than the officer concerned shall give evidence at the special case hearing.

(6) The person representing the officer concerned may—

   (a) address the hearing in order to do any or all of the following—

      (i) put the case of the officer concerned;

      (ii) sum up that case;

      (iii) respond on behalf of the officer concerned to any view expressed at the proceedings; and

      (iv) make representations concerning any aspect of proceedings under these Regulations; and

   (b) if the officer concerned is present at the proceedings or is participating in them by video link or other means in accordance with regulation 50(2), confer with the officer concerned.

(7) Where the person representing the officer concerned is a relevant lawyer, the police friend of the officer concerned may also confer with the officer concerned in the circumstances mentioned at paragraph (6)(b).

(8) The police friend or relevant lawyer of the officer concerned may not answer any questions asked of the officer concerned during the special case hearing.

(9) The person conducting or chairing the special case hearing may allow any document to be considered at the hearing notwithstanding that a copy of it has not been supplied—

   (a) by the officer concerned to the appropriate authority in accordance with regulation 45(2); or

   (b) to the officer concerned in accordance with regulation 43(1).

(10) Where evidence is given or considered at the special case hearing that the officer concerned—

   (a) on being questioned by an investigator, at any time after he was given written notice under regulation 15(1) of these Regulations or regulation 14A of the Complaints Regulations; or

   (b) in submitting any information or by not submitting any information at all under regulation 45 (or, where paragraph (12) applies, paragraph 19C of Schedule 3 to the 2002 Act or regulation 16(1) or 22(2) or (3)), failed to mention any fact relied on in his case at the special case hearing, being a fact which in the circumstances existing at the time, the officer concerned could reasonably have been expected to mention when so questioned or when providing such information, paragraph (11) applies.

(11) Where this paragraph applies, the person or persons conducting the special case hearing may draw such inferences from the failure as appear proper.

(12) This paragraph applies where the case was certified as a special case following a determination made under regulation 41(3).

(13) The person or persons conducting the special case hearing shall review the facts of the case and decide whether or not the conduct of the officer concerned amounts to gross misconduct.

(14) The person or persons conducting the special case hearing shall not find that the conduct of the officer concerned amounts to gross misconduct unless—

(a) he is or they are satisfied on the balance of probabilities that this is the case; or

(b) the officer concerned admits it is the case.

(15) At a special case hearing conducted by a panel, any decision shall be based on a majority (with the chair having the casting vote if necessary), but shall not indicate whether it was taken unanimously or by a majority.

Outcome of special case hearing

55.—(1) Where the person or persons conducting the special case hearing find that the conduct of the officer concerned amounts to gross misconduct, he or they shall impose disciplinary action, which may be—

(a) subject to paragraphs (2) and (3), a final written warning;

(b) extension of a final written warning in accordance with paragraph (2); or

(c) dismissal without notice.

(2) Where the officer concerned had a final written warning in force on the date of the assessment of the conduct under regulation 12(1) of these Regulations or regulation 14A of the Complaints Regulations (as the case may be)—

(a) a final written warning shall not be given; but

(b) subject to paragraph (4), in exceptional circumstances, the final written warning may be extended.

(3) Where a final written warning is extended under paragraph (2), that warning shall remain in force for a period of 18 months from the date on which it would otherwise expire.

(4) A final written warning may be extended on one occasion only.

(5) Where the person or persons conducting the special case hearing find that the conduct of the officer concerned does not amount to gross misconduct, he or they may—

(a) dismiss the case; or

(b) return the case to the appropriate authority to deal with in accordance with Part 4 at a misconduct meeting or, if the officer concerned had a final written warning in force at the date of the assessment of conduct under regulation 12(1) of these Regulations or regulation 14A of the Complaints Regulations (as the case may be), at a misconduct hearing .

(6) Where the case is returned to the appropriate authority under paragraph (5)(b), the appropriate authority shall proceed in accordance with Part 4, subject to regulation 19(1) being read as if the following are omitted—

(a) the words "regulation 41 and"; and

(b) sub-paragraphs (a) and (b).

(7) Except in the case of extending a final written warning, the disciplinary action shall have effect from the date on which it is notified to the officer concerned.

(8) Where the question of disciplinary action is being considered, the person or persons conducting the special case hearing—

(a) shall have regard to the record of police service of the officer concerned as shown on his personal record;

(b) may consider such documentary evidence as would, in his or their opinion, assist him or them in determining the question; and

(c) shall give—

    (i) the officer concerned; and

    (ii) his police friend or his relevant lawyer,

    an opportunity to make oral or written representations.

Notification of outcome

56.—(1) The officer concerned shall be informed of—

    (a) the finding; and

    (b) any disciplinary action imposed under regulation 55(1) or any action taken under regulation 55(5) as the case may be,

as soon as practicable and in any event shall be provided with written notice of these matters and a summary of the reasons before the end of 5 working days beginning with the first working day after the conclusion of the special case hearing.

(2) A written notice under this regulation shall include notice of the right of the officer concerned to an appeal hearing.

Record of special case hearing

57.—(1) A verbatim record of the proceedings at the special case hearing shall be taken.

(2) The officer concerned shall, on request, be supplied with a copy of the record of the proceedings at the special case hearing.

PART 6

RECORD KEEPING

Record of disciplinary proceedings

58.—(1) Subject to paragraph (2), the chief officer of police of the police force concerned shall cause a record to be kept of disciplinary proceedings and special case proceedings brought against every officer concerned, together with the finding and decision on disciplinary action and the decision in any appeal by the officer concerned.

(2) Where the officer concerned is a chief officer of police, the police authority of the police force concerned shall cause such a record to be kept.

Home Office   Minister of State

SCHEDULE

Regulation 3

STANDARDS OF PROFESSIONAL BEHAVIOUR

Honesty and Integrity

Police officers are honest, act with integrity and do not compromise or abuse their position.

Authority, Respect and Courtesy

Police officers act with self-control and tolerance, treating members of the public and colleagues with respect and courtesy.

Police officers do not abuse their powers or authority and respect the rights of all individuals.

Equality and Diversity

Police officers act with fairness and impartiality. They do not discriminate unlawfully or unfairly.

Use of Force

Police officers only use force to the extent that it is necessary, proportionate and reasonable in all the circumstances.

Orders and Instructions

Police officers only give and carry out lawful orders and instructions.

Police officers abide by police regulations, force policies and lawful orders.

Duties and Responsibilities

Police officers are diligent in the exercise of their duties and responsibilities.

Confidentiality

Police officers treat information with respect and access or disclose it only in the proper course of police duties.

Fitness for Duty

Police officers when on duty or presenting themselves for duty are fit to carry out their responsibilities.

Discreditable Conduct

Police officers behave in a manner which does not discredit the police service or undermine public confidence in it, whether on or off duty.

Police officers report any action taken against them for a criminal offence, any conditions imposed on them by a court or the receipt of any penalty notice.

Challenging and Reporting Improper Conduct

Police officers report, challenge or take action against the conduct of colleagues which has fallen below the Standards of Professional Behaviour.

EXPLANATORY NOTE

(This note is not part of the Regulations)

These Regulations were laid before Parliament in draft as they are Regulations under section 84 of the Police Act 1996 coming into force at a time that is the earliest time at which any Regulations under section 84 are to come into force after the commencement of paragraph 7 of Schedule 22 to the Criminal Justice and Immigration Act 2008 (see section 84(8) of the Police Act 1996).

The Regulations establish procedures for the taking of disciplinary proceedings in respect of the conduct of members of police forces and special constables ("police officers"). They apply to all police officers, although for senior officers (a police officer above the rank of chief superintendent), the persons dealing with some of the proceedings differ. For the purposes of these Regulations, special constables are treated as if they are non-senior officers regardless of their actual level of seniority. These Regulations also make provision in relation to the representation of police officers by a police friend and by a lawyer at proceedings at which the officer concerned may be dismissed.

These Regulations apply where an allegation comes to the attention of an appropriate authority (as defined in regulation 3) which indicates that the conduct of a police officer may amount to misconduct or gross misconduct (as defined in regulation 3). This includes an allegation contained within a complaint or conduct matter referred to the Independent Police Complaints Commission ("IPCC") in accordance with the Police Reform Act 2002 ("the 2002 Act"), except that Part 3 of these Regulations (Investigations) does not apply in such cases as Schedule 3 to the 2002 Act deals with the investigation of such cases.

Part 1 deals with preliminary matters. Regulation 2 revokes the Police (Conduct) Regulations 2004 save in relation to proceedings outstanding at 1st December 2008. Regulation 3 provides definitions of terms used in these Regulations, including the 'special conditions' which trigger the fast track procedure set out in Part 5; makes provision in relation to the delegation of the functions of a chief officer of police under these Regulations and provides that guidance may be issued under section 87(5) of the Police Act 1996 (guidance) in respect of any of the procedures in these Regulations. Regulation 4 sets out the harm test, which mirrors provisions in the Police (Complaints and Misconduct) Regulations 2004, placing restrictions on the disclosure of information to the officer concerned in the public interest.

Part 2 deals with general matters. Regulations 6 and 7 make provision about the role of a police friend under these Regulations and the right to legal representation. Regulation 9 provides that disciplinary or special case proceedings should proceed notwithstanding any criminal proceedings unless the appropriate authority considers they would prejudice such criminal proceedings. Regulation 10 makes provision in relation to the suspension of a police officer.

Part 3 deals with the investigation of conduct allegations other than those dealt with under Schedule 3 to the 2002 Act. Regulation 12 provides that the appropriate authority must make a preliminary assessment as to whether the conduct, if proved, would amount to misconduct, gross misconduct or neither, and sets out what action must or may be taken as a consequence of that assessment. Regulation 13 deals with the appointment of an investigator who, subject to conditions, may be a police officer, a police staff member or any other person. Regulation 14 sets out the purpose of the investigation. Regulation 15 provides for notice to be given to the officer concerned that there is to be an investigation and describes what must be set out in that notice. Regulation 16 provides that the investigator shall consider any suggestions as to lines of inquiry made by the officer concerned within the given time limit. Regulation 17 deals with interviews and regulation 18 with the investigation report.

Part 4 relates to misconduct proceedings. Regulation 19 provides that on receipt of the investigator's report (under these Regulations or Schedule 3 to the 2002 Act) the appropriate authority must determine whether or not there is a case to answer in respect of misconduct or gross misconduct, and makes provision about the referral of a case to a misconduct meeting or misconduct hearing. Regulation 21 provides that notice must be given to the officer concerned of the referral of their case to misconduct proceedings and provides that he may object to the persons appointed to deal with his case. Regulation 22 sets out the information the officer concerned must and may provide on receipt of such notice. Regulation 23 provides that the person conducting or chairing the misconduct proceedings will decide whether any witnesses will attend the proceedings, and that a witness may only attend where he reasonably believes this to be necessary. Regulations 25 to 27 set out the person(s) who will conduct the misconduct proceedings. Regulations 29 to 33 deal with who shall and may attend those proceedings. Regulation 34 covers the procedure at the proceedings and regulation 35 deals with outcomes. At a misconduct meeting the disciplinary action that may be imposed is management advice, a written warning or a final written warning. Such action is also available at a misconduct hearing, along with dismissal with or without notice or, in exceptional circumstances, the extension of a final written warning. The Police Appeals Tribunals Rules 2008 set out separately the right of appeal to a police appeals tribunal from misconduct proceedings but regulations 38 to 40 deal with an appeal by a non senior officer from a misconduct meeting.

Part 5 deals with the procedures for special case hearings for those cases where there is written or documentary evidence to establish gross misconduct on the balance of probabilities and it is in the public interest for the officer concerned to cease to be a police officer without delay. Procedures for these cases are fast tracked and there are no witnesses at the hearing other than the officer concerned. Regulation 58 requires a record to be kept of all proceedings under these Regulations and appeals.

The Schedule sets out the standards of professional behaviour expected of police officers, breach of which constitutes misconduct and a breach of which so serious that dismissal would be justified, constitutes gross misconduct.

Notes:

[1] 1996 c.16, Section 50 was amended by paragraph 95 of Schedule 27 to the Greater London Authority Act 1999 (c.29) and section 125 of the Criminal Justice and Police Act 2001 (c.16). It is also amended by paragraph 3 of Schedule 22 to the Criminal Justice and Immigration Act 2008 (c.4). Section 51 was amended by section 128 of the Police Act 1997 (c.50) and section 35 of the Police Reform Act 2002 (c.30). It is also amended by paragraph 4 of Schedule 22 to the Criminal Justice and Immigration Act 2008 (c. 4). Section 84 was amended by section 125 of the Criminal Justice and Police Act 2001 and paragraph 119 of Schedule 21 to the Legal Services Act 2007 (c.29). It is also amended by paragraph 7 of Schedule 22 to the Criminal Justice and Immigration Act 2008 (c. 4).

[2] Relevant amendments to section 63 were made by paragraph 78 of Schedule 4 to the Serious Organised Crime and Police Act 2005 (c. 15). Section 63 is also amended by paragraph 6 of Schedule 22 to the Criminal Justice and Immigration Act 2008 (c.4).

[3] Section 84(9) is inserted by paragraph 7 of Schedule 22 to the Criminal Justice and Immigration Act 2008 (c.4).

[4] S.I. 2004/645, as amended by S.I. 2006/594.

[5] 2002 c.30, as amended by section 160 of and Schedule 12 to the Serious Organised Crime and Police Act 2005 (c.15), section 1 of and Schedule 1 to the Police and Justice Act 2006 (c. 48) and section 127 of and Schedule 23 to the Criminal Justice and Immigration Act 2008 (c.4).

[6] S.I.2003/527, as amended by S.I.2005/2834 and S.I.2006/3449.

[7] S.I. 2004/643, as amended by S.I. 2008/2866.

[8] S.I. 2008/2862.

[9] S.I. 2008/2863.

[10] 1971 c.80.

[11] Section 87 of the 1996 Act was amended by section 107(1) of and paragraph 18 of Schedule 7 to the 2002 Act.

[12] Regulation 14A was inserted into S.I. 2004/642 by S.I. 2008/2866.

[13] Paragraph 19B was inserted into the 2002 Act by paragraph 5 of Schedule 23 to the Criminal Justice and Immigration Act 2008 (c. 4).

[14] Paragraph 20H of the 2002 Act was inserted by section 159 of and paragraphs 1 and 3 of Schedule 11 to the Serious Organised Crime and Police Act 2005 (c. 15).

The Police Appeals Tribunals Rules 2008, SI 2008/2863

STATUTORY INSTRUMENTS

2008 No. 2863

Police, England and Wales

The Police Appeals Tribunals Rules 2008

Made   *2008*

Laid before Parliament

Coming into force   *1st December 2008*

The Secretary of State makes the following Rules in exercise of the powers conferred by section 85 of the Police Act 1996[1].

In accordance with section 63(3) of that Act[2], the Secretary of State has supplied the Police Advisory Board for England and Wales with a draft of these Rules and has taken into consideration the representations of that Board.

In accordance with paragraph 24 of Schedule 7 to the Tribunals. Courts and Enforcement Act 2007[3], the Secretary of State has consulted the Administrative Justice and Tribunals Council.

In accordance with section 85(5A) of the Police Act 1996, a draft of these Rules was laid before Parliament and approved by a resolution of each House of Parliament.

Citation, commencement and extent

1.—(1) These Rules may be cited as the Police Appeals Tribunals Rules 2008 and shall come into force on 1st December 2008.

(2) These Rules extend to England and Wales.

Revocation and transitional provisions

2.—(1) Subject to paragraph (2), the following are revoked—
  (a) the Police Appeals Tribunals Rules 1999[4], and
  (b) paragraph 19 of the Schedule to the Serious Organised Crime and Police Act 2005 (Consequential and Supplementary Amendments to Secondary Legislation) Order 2006[5].

(2) In relation to an appeal under section 85 of the 1996 Act against a decision made in accordance with the Police (Efficiency) Regulations 1999[6] or the Police (Conduct) Regulations 2004[7], nothing in these Rules shall have effect and the provisions mentioned in paragraph (1) shall continue to have effect.

Interpretation

3.—(1) In these Rules—
  "appellant" means a police officer who has given a notice of appeal in accordance with rule 6 or 7;

"chair" for the purposes of rules 6 to 11 means a chairman appointed under Schedule 6 to the 1996 Act[8]; and for the purposes of rules 12 to 22 means the chairman of the tribunal;

"Conduct Regulations" means the Police (Conduct) Regulations 2008[9];

"IPCC" means the Independent Police Complaints Commission;

"original hearing" means—

> (a) the misconduct meeting, misconduct hearing or special case hearing under the Conduct Regulations; or
>
> (b) the third stage meeting under the Performance Regulations,
>
> at or following which the relevant decision was made;

"panel" includes a person who conducted a special case hearing under the Conduct Regulations;

"Performance Regulations" means the Police (Performance) Regulations 2008[10];

"relevant decision" means the finding, disciplinary action or outcome which may be appealed or is being appealed to a tribunal in accordance with rule 4 or 5, and related expressions shall be construed accordingly;

"relevant police authority" means the police authority which maintains—

> (a) the police force of which a police officer who wishes to appeal to a tribunal, or the appellant, is a member, or
>
> (b) the police force for the police area for which a police officer who wishes to appeal to a tribunal, or the appellant, is appointed as a special constable,
>
> as the case may be;

"relevant police force" means—

> (a) where the appellant is a member of a police force, the police force of which he is a member; and
>
> (b) where the appellant is a special constable, the police force maintained for the police area for which he is appointed;

"respondent" has the meaning given by rule 8;

"specified appeal" means an appeal where the relevant decision arose from a complaint or conduct matter to which paragraph 17, 18 or 19 of Schedule 3 to the 2002 Act (investigations) [11] applied; and

"tribunal" for the purposes of rules 3 to 11, means a police appeals tribunal appointed under Schedule 6 to the 1996 Act; and for the purposes of rules 12 to 22, means, in relation to an appeal, the police appeals tribunal appointed under Schedule 6 to the 1996 Act to determine that appeal.

(2) In these Rules, any expression which is also used in the Conduct Regulations or the Performance Regulations shall, unless that expression is given a different meaning in paragraph (1), have the same meaning as in those Regulations.

(3) Where any written notice or document is to be given or supplied to the appellant under these Rules, it shall be—

(a) given to him in person; or

(b) left with some person at, or sent by recorded delivery to, his last known address.

Circumstances in which a police officer may appeal to a tribunal

4.—(1) Subject to paragraph (3), a police officer to whom paragraph (2) applies may appeal to a tribunal in reliance on one or more of the grounds of appeal referred to in paragraph (4) against—

(a) the finding referred to in paragraph (2)(a), (b) or (c) made under the Conduct Regulations; or

(b) the disciplinary action, if any, imposed under the Conduct Regulations in consequence of that finding,

or both.

(2) This paragraph applies to—
    (a) an officer other than a senior officer against whom a finding of misconduct or gross misconduct has been made at a misconduct hearing; or
    (b) a senior officer against whom a finding of misconduct or gross misconduct has been made at a misconduct meeting or a misconduct hearing; or
    (c) an officer against whom a finding of gross misconduct has been made at a special case hearing.

(3) A police officer may not appeal to a tribunal against the finding referred to in paragraph (2)(a), (b) or (c) where that finding was made following acceptance by the officer that his conduct amounted to misconduct or gross misconduct (as the case may be).

(4) The grounds of appeal under this rule are—
    (a) that the finding or disciplinary action imposed was unreasonable; or
    (b) that there is evidence that could not reasonably have been considered at the original hearing which could have materially affected the finding or decision on disciplinary action; or
    (c) that there was a breach of the procedures set out in the Conduct Regulations, the Police (Complaints and Misconduct) Regulations 2004[12], Schedule 3 to the Police Reform Act 2002[13] or other unfairness which could have materially affected the finding or decision on disciplinary action.

5.—(1) Subject to paragraph (3), a police officer to whom paragraph (2) applies may appeal to a tribunal in reliance on one or more of the grounds of appeal referred to in paragraph (6) against—
    (a) a finding referred to in paragraph (2) made under the Performance Regulations; or
    (b) an outcome which is imposed under the Performance Regulations as a consequence of such a finding and is mentioned in paragraph (4) or (5),
    or both.

(2) This paragraph applies to a police officer against whom a finding of unsatisfactory performance or attendance or gross incompetence has been made at a third stage meeting.

(3) A police officer may not appeal to a tribunal against a finding referred to in paragraph (2) where that finding was made following acceptance by the officer that his performance or attendance has been unsatisfactory or that he has been grossly incompetent (as the case may be).

(4) Where there has been a finding of unsatisfactory performance or attendance following a third stage meeting which the police officer was required to attend under regulation 26 of the Performance Regulations, he may appeal against the following outcomes—
    (a) dismissal with notice,
    (b) reduction in rank.

(5) Where there has been a finding of gross incompetence or unsatisfactory performance following a third stage meeting which the police officer was required to attend under regulation 28 of the Performance Regulations, he may appeal against the following outcomes—
    (a) dismissal without notice,
    (b) reduction in rank,
    (c) redeployment to alternative duties,
    (d) the issue of a final written improvement notice,
    (e) the issue of a written improvement notice.

(6) The grounds of appeal under this rule are—
    (a) that the finding or outcome imposed was unreasonable; or
    (b) that there is evidence that could not reasonably have been considered at the original hearing which could have materially affected the finding or decision on the outcome; or
    (c) that there was a breach of the procedures set out in the Performance Regulations or other unfairness which could have materially affected the finding or decision on the outcome; or

(d) that, where the police officer was required to attend the third stage meeting under regulation 26 of the Performance Regulations, he should not have been required to attend that meeting as it did not, in accordance with regulation 26(6) or 40(9) of those Regulations, concern unsatisfactory performance or attendance similar to or connected with the unsatisfactory performance or attendance referred to in the final written improvement notice.

Notice of appeal

6.—(1) Subject to rule 7, a police officer who wishes to appeal to a tribunal shall give notice of the appeal before the end of 10 working days beginning with the first working day after the day on which he is supplied with a written copy of the relevant decision.

(2) The notice of appeal shall be given in writing to the relevant police authority.

(3) The officer may request a transcript of the proceedings (or part of the proceedings) at the original hearing in his notice of appeal.

7.—(1) This rule applies where a police officer who wishes to appeal to a tribunal wishes to give notice of the appeal after the end of the period mentioned in rule 6(1).

(2) A police officer may give notice of the appeal within a reasonable time after the end of such period and the notice shall be accompanied by the reasons why it was not served within such period and the reasons for the officer's view that it has been served within a reasonable time after such period.

(3) Upon receipt, the relevant police authority shall supply a copy of the notice and the reasons to the chair who shall determine—

(a) whether it was reasonably practicable for the notice to be given within the period mentioned in rule 6(1); and

(b) whether the notice has been given within a reasonable time after the end of such period.

(4) If the chair determines either that it was reasonably practicable for the notice to be given within such period or that the notice has not been given within a reasonable time after the end of such period, the appeal shall be dismissed.

(5) Where the appeal is not dismissed under paragraph (4), the appeal shall proceed and the chair shall give directions for the application of rule 9 to the appeal.

The respondent

8.—(1) Where the appellant is a senior officer, the respondent shall be a person designated by the relevant police authority.

(2) Where the appellant is any other police officer, the respondent shall be the chief officer of police of the relevant police force.

Procedure on notice of appeal

9.—(1) As soon as reasonably practicable, the relevant police authority shall supply a copy of the notice of appeal—

(a) to the respondent; and

(b) where the appeal is a specified appeal, to the IPCC.

(2) As soon as reasonably practicable after receipt of a copy of the notice of appeal, and in any event before the end of 15 working days beginning with the first working day after the day of such receipt, the respondent shall supply to the relevant police authority—

(a) a copy of the relevant decision made at or following the original hearing provided under regulation 36 or 56 of the Conduct Regulations or regulation 37(3) of the Performance Regulations;

(b) any documents which were made available to the panel conducting the original hearing; and

(c) a copy of any transcript requested under rule 6(3).

(3) A copy of any such transcript shall at the same time be given to the appellant.

(4) The appellant shall supply the following documents to the relevant police authority in accordance with paragraph (6)—

    (a) a statement of the relevant decision and his grounds of appeal;

    (b) any supporting documents;

    (c) where the appellant is permitted to adduce witness evidence—

        (i) a list of any proposed witnesses;

        (ii) a witness statement from each proposed witness; and

    (d) if he consents to the appeal being determined without a hearing, notice in writing that he so consents.

(5) For the purposes of paragraph (4)(c)—

    (a) an appellant is only permitted to adduce witness evidence where he is relying on the ground of appeal set out in rule 4(4)(b) or 5(6)(b);

    (b) a "proposed witness" is a person—

        (i) whom the appellant wishes to call to give evidence at the hearing;

        (ii) whose evidence was not and could not reasonably have been considered at the original hearing; and

        (iii) whose evidence could have materially affected the relevant decision.

(6) The appellant shall supply the documents mentioned in paragraph (4) before the end of—

    (a) 20 working days beginning with the first working day after the day on which he is supplied with a copy of the transcript under paragraph (3); or

    (b) where no transcript has been requested under rule 6(3), 35 working days beginning with the first working day after the day on which he gave notice of the appeal to the relevant police authority.

(7) The relevant police authority shall give a copy of the documents supplied under paragraph (4) to the respondent as soon as practicable following receipt.

(8) The respondent shall, before the end of 20 working days beginning with the first working day after the day on which he receives the documents given to him under paragraph (7), supply to the relevant police authority—

    (a) a statement of his response to the appeal;

    (b) any supporting documents;

    (c) where the respondent is permitted to adduce witness evidence—

        (i) a list of any proposed witnesses;

        (ii) a witness statement from each proposed witness; and

    (d) if he consents to the appeal being determined without a hearing, notice that he so consents.

(9) For the purposes of paragraph (8)(c)—

    (a) a respondent is only permitted to adduce witness evidence where the appellant is relying on the ground of appeal set out in rule 4(4)(b) or 5(6)(b);

    (b) a "proposed witness" is a person—

        (i) whom the respondent wishes to call to give evidence at the hearing; and

        (ii) whose evidence is relevant to all or part of the evidence on which the appellant is relying for the purposes of rule 4(4)(b) or 5(6)(b).

(10) The respondent shall at the same time as supplying the documents referred to in paragraph (8), give the appellant a copy of the documents referred to in paragraph (8)(a), (c) and (d), together with a list of the documents (if any) supplied under paragraph (8)(b).

(11) On receipt of the documents supplied under paragraph (8), the relevant police authority shall give to the chair a copy of the documents supplied under paragraphs (4) and (8).

Extensions of time limits

10.—(1) The appellant or the respondent may apply to the relevant police authority for an extension of a relevant period.

(2) Any such application shall set out the period of the required extension and the reasons for the application.

(3) As soon as practicable after receipt of an application under paragraph (1), the relevant police authority shall—

(a) give a copy of the application to the other party (being the appellant or the respondent as the case may be); and

(b) ask that other party whether he consents to the application.

(4) If the other party consents to the application, the relevant period shall be extended in accordance with the application and rule 9 shall have effect as if for that period there were substituted the extended period.

(5) If the other party does not consent to the application, the application shall be referred to the chair who shall determine whether the relevant period should be extended and if so by how long; and where he extends the relevant period, rule 9 shall have effect as if for that period there were substituted the extended period.

(6) In this rule, "relevant period" means, in relation to an application by the appellant, the period referred to in rule 9(6)(a) or (b) and, in relation to an application by the respondent, the period referred to in rule 9(2) or (8).

Review of appeal

11.—(1) Upon receipt of the documents mentioned in rule 9(4) and (8), the chair shall determine whether the appeal should be dismissed under paragraph (2).

(2) An appeal shall be dismissed under this paragraph if the chair considers that—

(a) the appeal has no real prospect of success; and

(b) there is no other compelling reason why the appeal should proceed.

(3) If the chair considers that the appeal should be dismissed under paragraph (2), before making his determination, he shall give the appellant and the respondent notice in writing of his view together with the reasons for that view.

(4) The appellant and the respondent may make written representations in response to the chair before the end of 10 working days beginning with the first working day after the day of receipt of such notification; and the chair shall consider any such representations before making his determination.

(5) The chair shall give the appellant, the respondent and the relevant police authority notice in writing of his determination.

(6) Where the chair determines that the appeal should be dismissed under paragraph (2)—

(a) the notification under paragraph (5) shall include the reasons for the determination; and

(b) the appeal shall be dismissed.

Determination of an appeal

12.—(1) Where an appeal has not been dismissed under rule 11, the chair shall determine whether the appeal should be dealt with at a hearing.

(2) The chair may determine that the appeal shall be dealt with without a hearing, but only if the appellant has so consented.

(3) Where the appeal is to be dealt with at a hearing, rules 13 to 21 shall apply and the chair shall give the appellant and the respondent his name and contact address.

Power to request disclosure of documents

13.—(1) At any time following the provision of the documents mentioned in rule 9(4) and (8), the appellant or the respondent (the "requesting party") may apply to the chair for disclosure of any document by the other party which is relevant to the appeal.

(2) The chair may request the disclosure of any such document by the other party and where it is disclosed, a copy shall be given to the chair and to the requesting party.

(3) Where a party does not comply with a request to disclose under paragraph (2), he shall give the chair and the requesting party his reasons for non-disclosure in writing.

Notice of the hearing

14.—(1) The chair shall cause the appellant and the respondent to be given written notice of the date, time and place of the hearing at least 20 working days, or such shorter period as may with the agreement of both parties be determined, before the date of the hearing.

(2) Where—

(a) the appellant is relying on the ground of appeal set out in rule 4(4)(b) or 5(6)(b); and

(b) either the appellant or the respondent (or both) have proposed witnesses under rule 9,

the chair shall determine which, if any, witnesses shall give evidence at the hearing.

(3) No witness shall give evidence at the hearing unless the chair reasonably believes that it is necessary for the witness to do so, in which case the chair shall—

(a) where the witness is a police officer, cause that person to be ordered to attend the hearing; and

(b) in any other case, cause the witness to be given notice that his attendance is necessary and of the date, time and place of the hearing.

Legal and other representation

15.—(1) The appellant has the right to be represented at a hearing by a relevant lawyer or a police friend.

(2) Where the appellant is represented at the hearing by a relevant lawyer, he may also be accompanied at the hearing by a police friend.

(3) If an appellant chooses not to be represented, the hearing may take place and the appeal may be determined without him being represented.

(4) The respondent has the right to be represented at a hearing by a relevant lawyer or by an officer of the police force or by the chief executive or other officer or employee of the relevant police authority.

(5) Where a police friend is a police officer or a police staff member, the chief officer of police of the force of which the police friend is a member shall permit him to use a reasonable amount of duty time for the purposes referred to in this rule.

(6) The reference in paragraph (5) to the force of which the police friend is a member shall include a reference to the force maintained for the police area for which a special constable is appointed and the force in which a police staff member is serving.

Procedure and oral evidence at hearing

16.—(1) Subject to these Rules, the procedure at a hearing shall be determined by the tribunal.

(2) The tribunal may proceed with the hearing in the absence of either party, whether represented or not, if it appears to be just and proper to do so, and may adjourn it from time to time if it appears necessary to do so.

(3) Unless the tribunal determines otherwise, the evidence adduced by the appellant shall be given first.

(4) Witnesses giving evidence at the hearing may be subject to questioning and cross-questioning.

(5) Any question as to whether any evidence is admissible, or whether any question should or should not be put to a witness, shall be determined by the tribunal.

(6) A verbatim record of the evidence given at the hearing shall be taken; and the relevant police authority shall keep such record for a period of not less than two years from the date of the end of the hearing.

Statements in lieu of oral evidence

17.—(1) Subject to the provisions of this rule, the tribunal may admit as evidence a witness statement of a proposed witness supplied under rule 9(4) or (8), notwithstanding that he is not to be called as a witness at the hearing.

(2) Evidence shall not be admissible under this rule if it would not have been admissible had it been given orally.

(3) For the purposes of this rule, a written statement purporting to be made and signed by a person and witnessed by another person shall be presumed to have been made by that person unless the contrary be shown.

(4) Nothing in this rule shall prejudice the admission of written evidence which would be admissible apart from the provisions of this rule.

Hearing to be in private

18.—(1) Subject to paragraph (2) and rules 19 and 20, the hearing shall be held in private.

(2) The tribunal may allow a person to attend all or part of the hearing as an observer for the purposes of training.

Attendance of complainant at hearing

19.—(1) This rule shall apply in relation to a hearing where the relevant decision arose from a complaint which was certified as subject to special requirements under paragraph 19A(1) of Schedule 3 to the 2002 Act (assessment of seriousness of conduct)[14].

(2) The chair shall cause notice of the date, time and place of the hearing to be given to the complainant or any interested person at the same time as such notice is given to the appellant and the respondent under rule 14(1).

(3) Subject to the provisions of this rule and rule 21, the complainant or any interested person (or both) may attend the hearing as an observer.

(4) Subject to the provisions of this rule and rule 21, a complainant or interested person may be accompanied by one other person, and if the complainant or interested person has a special need, by one further person to accommodate that need.

(5) Where—

   (a) a complainant,

   (b) an interested person, or

   (c) any person accompanying a complainant or an interested person

is a proposed witness (of either party) and is to give evidence at the hearing, none of the persons mentioned in subparagraphs (a) to (c) shall be allowed to attend the hearing before that evidence is given.

(6) The chair may, at his discretion, put any questions to the appellant that the complainant or interested person request be put to him.

Attendance of IPCC at hearing

20.—(1) This rule shall apply to a specified appeal.

(2) The chair shall cause notice of the date, time and place of the hearing to be given to the IPCC at the same time as such notice is given to the appellant and the respondent under rule 14(1).

(3) The IPCC may attend the hearing as an observer.

Exclusion from hearing

21.—(1) On the application of the appellant or the respondent or otherwise, the chair may require any observer to withdraw from all or any part of the hearing.

(2) The chair may impose such conditions as he sees fit relating to the attendance of an observer (or any person accompanying a complainant or interested person) at the hearing in order to facilitate the proper conduct of the hearing.

Statement of tribunal's determination

22.—(1) The tribunal shall determine whether the ground or grounds of appeal on which the appellant relies have been made out.

(2) The determination of the tribunal shall be based on a simple majority but shall not indicate whether it was taken unanimously or by a majority.

(3) The chair shall prepare a written statement of the tribunal's determination of the appeal and of the reasons for the decision.

(4) As soon as reasonably practicable after the determination of the appeal the chair shall cause the appellant, the respondent and the police authority to be given a copy of such statement; but, in any event, the appellant shall be given written notice of the decision of the tribunal before the end of 3 working days beginning with the first working day after the day on which the appeal is determined.

(5) Where the relevant decision arose from a complaint which was certified as subject to special requirements under paragraph 19A(1) of Schedule 3 to the 2002 Act (assessment of seriousness of conduct) the relevant police authority shall notify the complainant and any interested party of the decision of the tribunal.

(6) Where the appeal is a specified appeal, the relevant police authority shall notify the Independent Police Complaints Commission of the decision of the tribunal.

Home Office   Minister of State

EXPLANATORY NOTE

(This Note is not Part of the Rules)

These Rules set out the circumstances in which a member of a police force or a special constable may appeal to a police appeals tribunal. They also set out the procedures governing such an appeal.

Rule 2 deals with revocations and transitional provisions. Rule 3 deals with interpretation and provides that any expression which is also used in the Police (Conduct) Regulations 2008 or the Police (Performance) Regulations 2008 shall have the same meaning as in those Regulations, unless it is given a different meaning in rule 3(1).

A police officer may appeal to a police appeals tribunal following proceedings under the Police (Conduct) Regulations 2008 or the Police (Performance) Regulations 2008 in the circumstances set out in rules 4 and 5. Those rules set out the matters that may be appealed and the grounds of appeal.

Rules 6 and 7 make provision for the giving of a notice of appeal. Rule 9 sets out the procedure on receipt of this notice, including the provision of documents. Under rule 10, time periods under rule 9 may be extended on application.

Under rule 11, the chair must review each appeal that is brought and consider whether it should be dismissed in accordance with rule 11(2). If he is of the view that it should be dismissed, he must give the parties an opportunity to make written representations, before making his final decision.

Under rule 12, an appeal may be determined with or without a hearing. However, it can only be determined without a hearing if the appellant has consented to this.

Rules 13 to 21 apply where an appeal is to be dealt with at a hearing and set out a power for the chair to request the disclosure of documents, the procedure and entitlement to legal representation, provide for evidence and for the hearing to be in private, subject to rules 18 to 21.

Rule 22 deals with the determination of the appeal by the tribunal and the provision of a written statement of the determination.

These Rules were laid before Parliament in draft as they are the first Rules made under section 85 of the Police Act 1996 after the commencement of paragraph 8 of Schedule 22 to the Criminal Justice and Immigration Act 2008 (see section 85(5A) of the Police Act 1996).

Notes:

[1] 1996 c.16. Section 85 is amended by paragraph 8 of Schedule 22 to the Criminal Justice and Immigration Act 2008 (c.4).

[2] Section 63 was amended by Schedule 8 to the Police Reform Act 2002 (c.30), paragraph 78(3) of Schedule 4 to the Serious Organised Crime and Police Act 2005 (c.15), paragraph 68(3) of Schedule 1 to the Police and Justice Act 2006 (c.48) and paragraph 6 of Schedule 22 to the Criminal Justice and Immigration Act 2008.

[3] 2007 (c. 15). Police Appeals Tribunals are a "listed tribunal" for the purposes of Schedule 7 to the Tribunals, Courts and Enforcement Act 2007, under S.I. 2007/2951.

[4] S.I. 1999/818.

[5] S.I. 2006/594.

[6] S.I. 1999/732 as amended by S.I. 2003/528 and S.I. 2003/2600.

[7] S.I. 2004/645 as amended by S.I. 2006/549.

[8] Schedule 6 was amended by paragraph 107 of Schedule 27 to the Greater London Authority Act 1999 (c.29), by section 125 of the Criminal Justice and Police Act 2001 (c.16) and by paragraph 19 of Schedule 2 to the Police and Justice Act 2006. It is also amended by paragraph 27 of Schedule 10 to the Tribunals, Courts and Enforcement Act 2007, and by paragraph 11 of Schedule 22 to the Criminal Justice and Immigration Act 2008.

[9] S.I. 2008/2864.

[10] S.I. 2008/2862.

[11] Paragraph 17 was amended by paragraph 11(3) of Schedule 2 to and paragraph 15 of Schedule 12 to the Serious Organised Crime and Police Act 2005, paragraph 89 of Schedule 1 to the Police and Justice Act 2006. Paragraph 18 was amended by paragraph 16 of Schedule 12 to the Serious Organised Crime and Police Act 2005. Paragraph 19 was amended by paragraph 17 of Schedule 12 to the Serious Organised Crime and Police Act 2005.

[12] S.I. 2004/643, as amended by S.I. 2205/3389, 2006/594, 2006/1406, and 2008/2866.

[13] Schedule 3 was amended by paragraph 11 of Schedule 2, Schedule 11 and paragraphs 11 to 24 of Schedule 12 to the Serious Organised Crime and Police Act 2005 and by paragraph 89 of Schedule 1 to the Police and Justice Act 2006. It is also amended by paragraphs 3 to 19 of Schedule 23 and part 8 of Schedule 28 to the Criminal Justice and Immigration Act 2008.

[14] 2002 c.30. Paragraph 19A was inserted into the 2002 Act by paragraph 5 of Schedule 23 to the Criminal Justice and Immigration Act 2008 (c.4).

Home Office Guidance (2008) *Police Officer Misconduct, Unsatisfactory Performance and Attendance Management Procedures*

INTRODUCTION

(a) This guidance covers the Standards of Professional Behaviour for police officers, including special constables, and sets out the procedures for dealing with misconduct, unsatisfactory performance and attendance and for appeals to the Police Appeals Tribunal. The procedures described in this guidance are designed to accord with the principles of natural justice and the basic principles of fairness, and should be administered accordingly.

(b) The guidance is issued by the Secretary of State in accordance with the provisions of section 87(1) of the Police Act 1996. As such, those who are responsible for administering the procedures described in this guidance are reminded that they are required to take its provisions fully into account when discharging their functions. Whilst it is not necessary to follow its terms exactly in all cases, the guidance should not be departed from without good reason. This guidance is not a definitive interpretation of the relevant legislation. Interpretation is ultimately a matter for the courts. Where examples are given in this guidance they are not intended to be exclusive or exhaustive.

(c) The guidance on the individual procedures is designed to further the aims of being fair to the individual police officer and of arriving at a correct assessment of the matter in question and providing confidence in the system.

(d) The misconduct procedures set out in this guidance apply to all police officers, including special constables.

(e) The unsatisfactory performance procedures described in this guidance apply to all police officers (except student police officers in their probationary period) up to and including the rank of Chief Superintendent and all special constables. These unsatisfactory performance procedures do not apply to senior officers.

(f) The Police (Promotions) Regulations 1996 make provision for the chief officer of police, where he or she considers that a person, who is on probation in the rank of sergeant, is unlikely to perform the duties of that rank satisfactorily, to reduce the sergeant to the rank of constable. It is therefore important that in such cases the Promotion Regulations are used and not the Conduct or Performance Regulations.

(g) Guidance on dealing with issues of misconduct or unsatisfactory performance regarding police officers on secondment under section 97 of the Police Act 1996 can be found at Annex D.

Delegated authority

(h) Where reference is made to 'the appropriate authority' and the appropriate authority is a chief officer of police, he or she may delegate any of his or her functions to a police officer of at least the rank of chief inspector or a police staff member who is, in the opinion of the chief officer, of at least a similar level of seniority to a chief inspector.

(i) However any decision regarding the suspension of a police officer, a decision whether to refer a misconduct matter to a special case hearing or in the case of the Performance Regulations the decision to refer a matter direct to a stage 3 meeting for gross incompetence, shall be authorised by a senior officer.

(j) The misconduct and performance procedures are designed to be dealt with at the lowest appropriate managerial level having regard to all the circumstances of the particular matter.

Glossary

(k) Throughout the guidance the following terms will be used: -
  (a) "2002 Act" means the Police Reform Act 2002
  (b) "Conduct Regulations" means the Police (Conduct) Regulations 2008
  (c) "Performance Regulations" means the Police (Performance) Regulations 2008
  (d) "Complaint Regulations" means the Police (Complaint and Misconduct) Regulations 2004 as amended by the Police (Complaint and Misconduct) (Amendment) Regulations 2008
  (e) "IPCC statutory guidance" means the Independent Police Complaints Commission Statutory Guidance 'Making the new complaints system work better'
  (f) "misconduct proceedings" means misconduct meeting or misconduct hearing
  (g) The Conduct Regulations and the Performance Regulations use the term 'relevant lawyer'. 'Relevant lawyer' includes a solicitor or barrister and therefore these terms are used throughout this guidance.
  (h) "Appropriate authority" means: -
    • Where the officer concerned is a senior officer of any police force, the police authority for the force's area;
    • In any other case, the chief officer of police of the police force concerned.

Police Friend

Police officers have the right to consult with, and be accompanied by, a police friend at any interview during an investigation into misconduct and at all stages of the misconduct or performance proceedings.

The police officer concerned may choose a police officer, a police staff member or (where the police officer is a member of a police force) a person nominated by the police officer's staff association to act as his or her police friend. A person approached to be a police friend is entitled to decline to act as such.

A police friend cannot be appointed to act as such if he or she has had some involvement in that particular case e.g. he or she is a witness etc.

The police friend can:

• Advise the police officer concerned throughout the proceedings under the Police (Conduct) Regulations 2008 or Police (Performance) Regulations 2008.
• Unless the police officer concerned has the right to be legally represented and chooses to be so represented, represent the police officer concerned at the misconduct proceedings, performance proceedings, appeal meeting, a special case hearing or at a Police Appeals Tribunal.
• Make representations to the appropriate authority concerning any aspect of the proceedings under the Conduct or Performance Regulations; and
• Accompany the police officer concerned to any interview, meeting or hearing which forms part of any proceedings under the Conduct or Performance Regulations.

It is good practice to allow the police friend to participate as fully as possible, but at an interview, meeting or hearing the police friend is not there to answer questions on the police officer's behalf. It is for the police officer concerned to speak for himself or herself when asked questions.

A police friend who has agreed to accompany a police officer is entitled to take a reasonable amount of duty time to fulfil his or her responsibilities as a police friend and should be considered to be on duty when attending interviews, meetings or hearings.

Subject to any timescales set out in the Conduct or Performance Regulations, at any stage of a case, up to and including a misconduct meeting or hearing or an unsatisfactory performance meeting, the police officer concerned or his or her police friend may submit that there are insufficient grounds upon which to base the case and/or that the correct procedures have not been followed, clearly setting out the reasons and submitting any supporting evidence. It will be for the person responsible for the relevant stage of the case to consider any such submission and determine how best to respond to it, bearing in mind the need to ensure fairness to the police officer concerned.

At a misconduct meeting, hearing or special case hearing under the Conduct Regulations or the Performance Regulations where the police friend attends, he or she may –

   i) put the police officer concerned's case
   ii) sum up that case
  iii) respond on the police officer concerned's behalf to any view expressed at the meeting
  iv) make representations concerning any aspect of the proceedings
   v) confer with the police officer concerned
  vi) in a misconduct meeting or hearing, ask questions of any witness, subject to the discretion of the person(s) conducting that hearing.

A police officer is entitled to be legally represented at a misconduct hearing or special case hearing (in cases that fall to be dealt with under the Conduct Regulations) or a 3rd stage Performance meeting (for dealing with an issue of gross incompetence under the Performance Regulations). Where he or she decides to be so represented, the police friend can also attend and may consult with the police officer concerned, but will not carry out functions i)-iv) and vi) described above.

Where a police officer is arrested or interviewed in connection with a criminal offence committed whilst off duty that has no connection with his or her role as a serving police officer, then the police friend has no right to attend the criminal interview(s) of that police officer.

It is not the role of the police friend to conduct his or her own investigation into the matter. (See paragraph 2.117 regarding the opportunity to provide information to the investigator)

Where a police friend is acting as such for a colleague from another force, then the appropriate authority for the police friend should pay the reasonable expenses of the police friend.

CHAPTER 1
GUIDANCE ON STANDARDS OF PROFESSIONAL BEHAVIOUR

Introduction

1.1 Public confidence in the police is crucial in a system that rests on the principle of policing by consent. Public confidence in the police depends on police officers demonstrating the highest level of personal and professional standards of behaviour. The standards set out below reflect the expectations that the police service and the public have of how police officers should behave. They are not intended to describe every situation but rather to set a framework which everyone can easily understand. They enable everybody to know what type of conduct by a police officer is acceptable and what is unacceptable. The standards should be read and applied having regard to this guidance.

1.2 The standards of professional behaviour also reflect relevant principles enshrined in the European Convention on Human Rights and the Council of Europe Code of Police Ethics. They apply to police officers of all ranks from Chief Constable to Constable, Special Constables and to those subject to suspension.

1.3 The standards set out below do not restrict police officers' discretion; rather they define the parameters of conduct within which that discretion should be exercised. A breach of these high standards may damage confidence in the police service and could lead to action for misconduct, which in serious cases could involve dismissal.

1.4 The public have the right to expect the police service to protect them by upholding the law and providing a professional police service. Police officers have the right to a working environment free of harassment or discrimination from others within the service.

1.5 Those entrusted to supervise and manage others are role models for delivering a professional, impartial and effective policing service. They have a particular responsibility to maintain standards of professional behaviour by demonstrating strong leadership and by dealing with conduct which has fallen below these standards in an appropriate way, such as by management action or the formal misconduct process. Above all else police managers should lead by example.

1.6 In carrying out their duties in accordance with these standards, police officers have the right to receive the full support of the police service. It is recognised that the ability of police officers to carry out their duties to the highest professional standards may depend on the provision of appropriate training, equipment and management support.

1.7 The police service has a responsibility to keep police officers informed of changes to police regulations, local policies, laws and procedures. Police officers have a duty to keep themselves up to date on the basis of the information provided.

1.8 Where these Standards of Professional Behaviour are being applied in any decision or misconduct meeting/hearing, they shall be applied in a reasonable, transparent, objective and proportionate manner. Due regard shall be paid to the nature and circumstances of a police officer's conduct, including whether his or her actions or omissions were reasonable at the time of the conduct under scrutiny.

1.9 This guidance gives examples to help police officers interpret the standards expected in a consistent way. They are not intended to be an exclusive or exhaustive list.

1.10 Where the misconduct procedure is being applied, it is important to identify the actual behaviour that is alleged to have fallen below the standard expected of a police officer, with clear particulars describing that behaviour.

1.11 It should be remembered that the unsatisfactory performance procedures exist to deal with unsatisfactory performance, attendance and issues of capability.

Honesty and Integrity

1.12 Police officers are honest, act with integrity and do not compromise or abuse their position.

1.13 Police officers act with integrity and are open and truthful in their dealings with the public and their colleagues, so that confidence in the police service is secured and maintained.

1.14 Police officers do not knowingly make any false, misleading or inaccurate oral or written statements or entries in any record or document kept or made in connection with any police activity.

1.15 Police officers never accept any gift or gratuity that could compromise their impartiality. During the course of their duties police officers may be offered hospitality (e.g. refreshments) and this may be acceptable as part of their role. However, police officers always consider carefully the motivation of the person offering a gift or gratuity of any type and the risk of becoming improperly beholden to a person or organisation.

1.16 It is not anticipated that inexpensive gifts would compromise the integrity of a police officer, such as those from conferences (e.g. promotional products) or discounts aimed at the entire police force (e.g. advertised discounts through police publications). However, all gifts and gratuities must be declared in accordance with local force policy where authorisation may be required from a manager, Chief Officer or Police Authority to accept a gift or hospitality. If a police officer is in any doubt then they should seek advice from their manager.

1.17 Police officers never use their position or warrant card to gain an unauthorised advantage (financial or otherwise) that could give rise to the impression that the police officer is abusing his or her position. A warrant card is only to confirm identity or to express authority.

Authority, Respect and Courtesy

1.18 Police officers act with self-control and tolerance, treating members of the public and colleagues with respect and courtesy.

1.19 Police officers do not abuse their powers or authority and respect the rights of all individuals.

1.20 In exercising their duties, police officers never abuse their authority or the powers entrusted to them. Police officers are well placed to protect individuals and groups within society. They have been given important powers and responsibilities due to the complex and difficult situations they deal with. The public have the right to expect that such powers are used professionally, impartially and with integrity, irrespective of an individual's status.

1.21 Police officers do not harass or bully colleagues or members of the public. Challenging conduct or unsatisfactory performance or attendance in an appropriate manner would not constitute bullying.

1.22 Police officers do not, under any circumstances inflict, instigate or tolerate any act of inhuman or degrading treatment (as enshrined in Article 3 of the European Convention on Human Rights).

1.23 Police officers, recognise that some individuals who come into contact with the police, such as victims, witnesses or suspects, may be vulnerable and therefore may require additional support and assistance.

1.24 Police officers use appropriate language and behaviour in their dealings with their colleagues and the public. They do not use any language or behave in a way that is offensive or is likely to cause offence.

1.25 Like all professionals, police officers have special knowledge and experience that many others do not possess (for example what may or may not constitute an offence). Police officers do not take unfair advantage of the inequality that arises from a member of the public being ill-equipped to make an informed judgement about a matter in respect of which he or she does not have the special knowledge of the police officer.

Equality and Diversity

1.26 Police officers act with fairness and impartiality. They do not discriminate unlawfully or unfairly.

1.27 Police officers carry out their duties with fairness and impartiality and in accordance with current equality legislation. In protecting others' human rights, they act in accordance with Article 14 of the European Convention on Human Rights.

1.28 Police officers need to retain the confidence of all communities and therefore respect all individuals and their traditions, beliefs and lifestyles provided that such are compatible with the rule of law. In particular police officers do not discriminate unlawfully or unfairly when exercising any of their duties, discretion or authority.

1.29 Police officers pay due regard to the need to eliminate unlawful discrimination and promote equality of opportunity and good relations between persons of different groups.

1.30 Police managers have a particular responsibility to support the promotion of equality and by their actions to set a positive example.

1.31 Different treatment of individuals which has an objective justification may not amount to discrimination.

Use of Force

1.32 Police officers only use force to the extent that it is necessary, proportionate and reasonable in all the circumstances.

1.33 There will be occasions when police officers may need to use force in carrying out their duties, for example to effect an arrest or prevent harm to others.

1.34 It is for the police officer to justify his or her use of force but when assessing whether this was necessary, proportionate and reasonable all of the circumstances should be taken into account and especially the situation which the police officer faced at the time. Police officers use force only if other means are or may be ineffective in achieving the intended result.

1.35 As far as it is reasonable in the circumstances police officers act in accordance with their training in the use of force to decide what force may be necessary, proportionate and reasonable. Section 3 of the Criminal Law Act 1967, section 117 of the Police and Criminal Evidence Act 1984 and common law make it clear that force may only be used when it is reasonable in the circumstances.

1.36 Article 2 (2) of the European Convention on Human Rights provides a stricter test for the use of lethal force. The use of such force must be no more than is absolutely necessary: (a) in defence of any person from unlawful violence; (b) in order to effect a lawful arrest or to prevent the escape of a person lawfully detained; or (c) in action lawfully undertaken to quell a riot or insurrection.

1.37 Police officers respect everyone's right to life (as enshrined in Article 2 of the European Convention on Human Rights) and do not, under any circumstances, inflict, instigate or tolerate any act of torture, inhuman or degrading treatment or punishment (Article 3).

Orders and Instructions

1.38 Police officers only give and carry out lawful orders and instructions.

1.39 Police officers abide by police regulations, force policies and lawful orders.

1.40 The police service is a disciplined body and therefore any decision not to follow an order or instruction will need to be fully justified.

1.41 There may however be instances when failure to follow an order or instruction does not amount to misconduct. This may be for example where the police officer reasonably believed that a lawful order was in fact unlawful or where a police officer had good and sufficient reason not to comply having regard to all the circumstances and possible consequences.

1.42 Police officers do not give orders or instructions which they do not reasonably believe are lawful.

1.43 Police officers, to the best of their ability, support their colleagues in the execution of their lawful duty.

1.44 Police officers abide by police regulations and force policies and accept the restrictions on their private lives as described in Schedule 1 to the Police Regulations 2003 (as amended) and determinations made under those Regulations.

Duties and Responsibilities

1.45 Police officers are diligent in the exercise of their duties and responsibilities.

1.46 Police officers do not neglect their duties or responsibilities.

1.47 When deciding if a police officer has neglected his or her duties all of the circumstances should be taken into account. Police officers have wide discretion and may have to prioritise the demands on their time and resources. This may involve leaving a task to do a different one, which in their judgement is more important. This is accepted and in many cases essential for good policing.

1.48 Police officers ensure that accurate records are kept of the exercise of their duties and powers as required by relevant legislation, force policies and procedures.

1.49 In carrying out their duties police officers have a responsibility to exercise reasonable care to prevent loss of life or loss or damage to the property of others (including police property).

Confidentiality

1.50 Police officers treat information with respect and access or disclose it only in the proper course of police duties.

1.51 The police service shares information with other agencies and the public as part of its legitimate policing business. Police officers never access or disclose any information that is not in the proper course of police duties and do not access information for personal reasons. Police officers who are unsure if they should access or disclose information always consult with their manager or department that deals with data protection or freedom of information before accessing or disclosing it.

1.52 Police officers do not provide information to third parties who are not entitled to it. This includes for example, requests from family or friends, approaches by private investigators and unauthorised disclosure to the media.

1.53 Where a police officer provides any reference in a private as opposed to professional capacity, then he or she will make this clear to the intended recipient and will emphasise that it is being provided in a private capacity and no police information has been accessed or disclosed in giving such a reference.

Fitness for Duty

1.54 Police officers when on duty or presenting themselves for duty are fit to carry out their duties and responsibilities.

1.55 Police officers do not make themselves unfit or impaired for duty as a result of drinking alcohol, using an illegal drug or using a substance for non-medical purposes or intentionally misusing a prescription drug.

1.56 Police officers who present themselves to their force with a drink or drugs misuse problem will be supported if they demonstrate an intention to address the problem and take steps to overcome it. However, the use of illegal drugs will not be condoned. A self declaration made after a police officer is notified of the requirement to take a test for possible substance misuse cannot be used to frustrate action being taken for misconduct that may follow a positive test result.

1.57 Police officers who are aware of any health concerns that may impair their ability to perform their duties should seek guidance from the occupational health department and if appropriate reasonable adjustments can be made.

1.58 A police officer who is unexpectedly called to attend for duty and considers that he or she is not fit to perform such duty should say that this is the case.

1.59 Police officers when absent from duty, on account of sickness or injury, do not engage in activities that are likely to impair their return to duty. Police officers will engage with the force medical officer or other member of the occupational health team if required and follow any advice given unless there are reasonable grounds not to do so.

Discreditable Conduct

1.60 Police officers behave in a manner which does not discredit the police service or undermine public confidence, whether on or off duty.

1.61 Police officers report any action taken against them for a criminal offence, conditions imposed by a court or the receipt of any penalty notice.

1.62 Discredit can be brought on the police service by an act itself or because public confidence in the police is undermined. In general, it should be the actual underlying conduct of the police officer that is considered under the misconduct procedures, whether the conduct occurred on or off duty. However where a police officer has been convicted of a criminal offence that alone may lead to misconduct action irrespective of the nature of the conduct itself. In all cases it must be clearly articulated how the conduct or conviction discredits the police service.

1.63 In the interests of fairness, consistency and reasonableness the test is not solely about media coverage but has regard to all the circumstances.

1.64 Police officers are required to report as soon as reasonably practicable to their force any occasion in the UK or elsewhere where they have been subject to arrest, a summons for an offence, a penalty notice for disorder, an endorsable fixed penalty notice for a road traffic offence, or a charge or caution for an offence by any enforcement agency.

1.65 They must also report as soon as reasonably practicable all convictions and sentences and conditions imposed by any court, whether criminal or civil (excluding matrimonial proceedings (but including non-molestation orders or occupation orders)). 'Conditions imposed by a court' would include, for example, the issue of an Anti-Social Behaviour Order, a restraining order, or a bind-over.

1.66 A police officer being subject to any of these measures could discredit the police service and may result in action being taken for misconduct against him or her depending on the circumstances of the particular matter.

1.67 Police officers do not purchase or consume alcohol when on duty, unless specifically authorised to do so or it becomes necessary for the proper discharge of a particular police duty.

1.68 Police officers on duty whether in uniform or in plain-clothes, display a positive image of the police service in the standard of their appearance which is appropriate to their operational role.

1.69 Police officers attend punctually when rostered for duty or other commitment (e.g. attendance at court).

Off-duty conduct

1.70 Police officers have some restrictions on their private life. These restrictions are laid down in the Police Regulations 2003 (as described in paragraph 1.44). These restrictions have to be balanced against the right to a private life. Therefore, in considering whether a police officer has acted in a way which falls below these standards while off-duty, due regard should be given to that balance and any action should be proportionate taking into account all of the circumstances.

1.71 Even when off duty, police officers do not behave in a manner that discredits the police service or undermines public confidence.

1.72 In determining whether a police officer's off-duty conduct discredits the police service, the test is not whether the police officer discredits herself or himself but the police service as a whole.

1.73 Police officers are particularly aware of the image that they portray when representing the police service in an official capacity even though they may be off-duty (e.g. at a conference).

1.74 When police officers produce their warrant card (other than for identification purposes only) or act in a way to suggest that they are acting in their capacity as a police officer (e.g. declaring that they are a police officer) they are demonstrating that they are exercising their authority and have therefore put themselves on duty and will act in a way which conforms to these standards. For example, during a dispute with a neighbour a police officer who decides to produce a warrant card would be considered to be on duty.

1.75 An approved business interest should always be carried out in a way that does not compromise or give the impression of compromising the police officer's impartiality and is not incompatible with membership of a police force (as set out in Regulation 7 of Police Regulations 2003)

1.76 All forms of management action and formal outcomes for misconduct are available in response to off-duty conduct

Challenging and Reporting Improper Conduct

1.77 Police officers report, challenge or take action against the conduct of colleagues which has fallen below the standards of professional behaviour expected.

1.78 Police officers are expected to uphold the standards of professional behaviour in the police service by taking appropriate action if they come across the conduct of a colleague which has fallen below these standards. They never ignore such conduct.

1.79 Police officers who in the circumstances feel they cannot challenge a colleague directly, for example if they are a more junior rank and are not confident, report their concerns, preferably to a line manager. If they do not feel able to approach a line manager with their concerns, they may report the matter through the force's confidential reporting mechanism, or to the Police Authority or Independent Police Complaints Commission (IPCC).

1.80 Police officers are supported by the police service if they report conduct by a police officer which has fallen below the standards expected unless such a report is found to be malicious or otherwise made in bad faith.

1.81 It is accepted that the circumstances may make immediate action difficult but police managers are expected to challenge or take action as soon as possible.

1.82 It is accepted however that it will not always be necessary to report a police officer's conduct if the matter has been dealt with appropriately by a manager in the police service.

CHAPTER 2

GUIDANCE ON POLICE OFFICER MISCONDUCT PROCEDURES

2. General

2.1 This procedure applies to all police officers (including special constables) and underpins the Standards of Professional Behaviour which set out the high standards of behaviour that the police service and the public expect of police officers. Any failure to meet these standards may undermine the important work of the police service and public confidence in it.

2.2 This guidance applies to the handling of misconduct cases that have come to the notice of the appropriate authority on or after the 1st December 2008 and the previous Home Office guidance will apply to cases being dealt with under the Police (Conduct) Regulations 2004.

2.3 The misconduct procedures aim to provide a fair, open and proportionate method of dealing with alleged misconduct. The procedures are intended to encourage a culture of learning and development for individuals and/ or the organisation.

2.4 Disciplinary action has a part, when circumstances require this, but improvement will always be an integral dimension of any outcome (even in the case where an individual has been dismissed there can be learning opportunities for the Police Service).

2.5 The misconduct procedure has been prepared by the Home Office in consultation with the Association of Chief Police Officers (ACPO), the Police Federation of England and Wales (PFEW), the Police Superintendents' Association of England and Wales (PSAEW), the Chief Police Officers' Staff Association (CPOSA), the Association of Police Authorities (APA), Her Majesty's Inspectorate of Constabulary (HMIC) and the Independent Police Complaints Commission (IPCC).

2.6 The police misconduct procedures are designed to reflect what is considered to be best practice in other fields of employment while recognising that police officers have a special status as holders of the Office of Constable. The Police Service is committed to ensuring that the procedure is applied fairly to everyone.

2.7 It is important that managers understand their responsibility to respond to, and deal promptly, and effectively with, unsatisfactory behaviour and complaints about police conduct from members of the public and/or colleagues. It is a key responsibility of all managers to understand and apply the procedure in a fair, proportionate and timely manner.

2.8 The police service will support any manager who has exercised his or her judgement reasonably and adhered to the guidance provided.

2.9 Where the conduct is linked to a complaint, recordable conduct matter or death or serious injury matter (as defined in section 12 of, and paragraph 11 of Schedule 3 to, the 2002 Act) the appropriate authority is required to follow the provisions in the Police Reform Act 2002 (the "2002 Act"), the accompanying Police (Complaints and Misconduct) Regulations 2004[1] (the "Complaint Regulations") and the IPCC statutory guidance which set out how complaints by members of the public are to be dealt with.

2.10 The misconduct procedures should not be used as a means of dealing with unsatisfactory performance (see assessment stage at paragraph 2.71). The unsatisfactory performance procedures (see chapter 3) exist to deal with issues of individual unsatisfactory performance and attendance.

---

[1] As amended by the Police (Complaints and Misconduct) (Amendment) Regulations 2008, SI 2008/2866.

Student Officers

2.11 Student police officers (probationary constables) are not subject to the procedures for dealing with unsatisfactory performance, since there are separately established procedures for dealing with the performance of student police officers. However, student police officers are subject to the misconduct procedures. The chief officer has discretion whether to use the misconduct procedures or the procedures set out at Regulation 13 of the Police Regulations 2003 (Discharge of probationer) as the most appropriate means of dealing with a misconduct matter. In exercising this discretion due regard should be had to whether the student police officer admits to the conduct or not. Where the misconduct in question is not admitted by the student police officer then, in most, if not all cases the matter will fall to be determined under the misconduct procedures. If the Regulation 13 procedure is used, the student police officer should be given a fair hearing (i.e. an opportunity to comment and present mitigation) under that procedure.

Suspension, restricted or change of duty

2.12 The decision to suspend a police officer will only be taken where there is an allegation of misconduct/gross misconduct and:

- An effective investigation may be prejudiced unless the police officer is suspended; or
- The public interest, having regard to the nature of the allegation and any other relevant considerations, requires that the police officer should be suspended; and
- A temporary move to a new location or role has been considered but is not appropriate in the circumstances.

2.13 A temporary move to a new location or role must always be considered first as an alternative to suspension.

2.14 While suspended, a police officer ceases to hold the office of constable and, in the case of a member of a police force, ceases to be a member of a police force, save for the purposes of the misconduct proceedings.

2.15 Where it is decided that the police officer will be suspended from duty or moved to alternative duties, this will be with pay. The rate of any pay will be that which applied to the police officer at the time of suspension. Therefore if the police officer concerned was in receipt of a Special Priority Payment or a Competency Related Threshold Payment at the time of his or her suspension or temporary move to a new location or role as an alternative to suspension, those payments will continue to apply. This is subject to Schedule 2 to the Police Regulations 2003.

2.16 Paragraph 1 of Schedule 2 to the Police Regulations 2003 provide for pay to be withheld when a police officer who is suspended: -

(i) is detained in pursuance of a sentence of a court in a prison or other institution to which the Prison Act 1952 applies, or is in custody (whether in prison or elsewhere) between conviction by a court and sentence, or

(ii) has absented him or herself from duty and whose whereabouts are unknown to the chief officer (or an assistant chief officer acting as chief officer) or in the case of a senior officer the police authority.

2.17 The police officer or his or her police friend may make representations against the initial decision to suspend (within 7 working days beginning with the first working day after being suspended) and at any time during the course of the suspension if they believe the circumstances have changed and that the suspension is no longer appropriate.

2.18 Suspension is not a formal misconduct outcome and does not suggest any prejudgement.

2.19 The period of suspension should be as short as possible and any investigation into the conduct of a suspended police officer should be made a priority.

2.20 The police officer should be told exactly why he or she is being suspended, or being moved to other duties and this should be confirmed in writing. If suspension is on public interest grounds, it should be clearly explained, so far as possible, what those grounds are.

2.21 The use of suspension must be reviewed at least every 4 weeks, and sooner where facts have become known which suggest that suspension is no longer appropriate. In cases where the suspension has been reviewed and a decision has been made to continue that suspension, the police officer must be informed in writing of the reasons why.

2.22 Suspension must be authorised by a senior officer although the decision can be communicated to the police officer by an appropriate manager. The relevant Police Authority is responsible for dealing with the suspension of a senior officer.

2.23 In cases where the IPCC are supervising, managing or independently investigating a matter, the appropriate authority will consult with the IPCC before making a decision whether to suspend or not. It is the appropriate authority's decision whether to suspend a police officer or not. The appropriate authority must also consult the IPCC before making the decision to allow a police officer to resume his or her duties following suspension (unless the suspension ends because there will be no misconduct or special case proceedings or because these have concluded) in cases where the IPCC are supervising, managing or independently investigating a case involving that police officer.

2.24 In cases where the 2002 Act applies, the investigator will be responsible for ensuring that the appropriate authority is supplied with sufficient information to enable it to effectively review the need for continuing the suspension.

2.25 The Standards of Professional Behaviour continue to apply to police officers who are suspended from duty. The appropriate authority can impose such conditions or restrictions on the police officer concerned as are reasonable in the circumstances e.g. restricting access to police premises or police social functions.

2.26 Police officers who are suspended from duty are still allowed to take their annual leave entitlement in the normal way whilst so suspended, providing they seek permission from the appropriate authority. The appropriate authority should not unreasonably withhold permission to annual leave. Any annual leave not taken by the police officer concerned within a year will still be subject to the rules governing the maximum number of days that may be carried over.

Conducting investigations where there are possible or outstanding criminal proceedings

2.27 Where there are possible or outstanding criminal proceedings against a police officer, these will not normally delay the misconduct proceedings. They will only delay proceedings under the Conduct Regulations where the appropriate authority considers such action would prejudice the outcome of the criminal case. The presumption is that action for misconduct should be taken prior to, or in parallel with, any criminal proceedings. Where it is determined that prejudice to the outcome of the criminal case would result, then this decision shall be kept under regular review to avoid any unreasonable delay to the misconduct proceedings.

2.28 Where potential prejudice is identified, the proceedings under the Conduct Regulations will proceed as normal up until the referral of a case to misconduct proceedings or a special case hearing. So the matter will be investigated under the Conduct Regulations or Complaint Regulations and the investigation report submitted. The appropriate authority will then decide whether there is a case to answer in respect of misconduct or gross misconduct or neither. Where the decision is made that the matter amounts to misconduct and that management action is appropriate, then this can be taken without the need to refer the matter to misconduct proceedings. In other cases where there is a case to answer, no referral to misconduct proceedings or a special case hearing will take place if this would prejudice the criminal proceedings.

2.29 As soon as it appears to the appropriate authority that there is no longer any potential prejudice (because, for example, a witness is no longer going to be called, the trial has concluded or any other circumstances change), the appropriate authority must take action. Where misconduct proceedings were delayed, the appropriate authority shall make a determination whether to continue with the misconduct proceedings. This determination will include consideration as to whether the special conditions exist for using the fast track procedures (see Annex A).

2.30 The appropriate authority should always consider whether in proceeding with a misconduct meeting or hearing in advance of any potential criminal trial, there is a real risk of prejudice to that trial. If there is any doubt then advice should be sought from the Crown Prosecution Service (CPS) or other prosecuting authority.

2.31 In a case where a witness is to appear at a misconduct meeting or hearing and is also a witness or potentially a witness at the criminal trial then the appropriate authority must first consult with the CPS (or other prosecuting authority). Having carefully considered the views of the CPS the appropriate authority must then decide whether it would prejudice a criminal trial if the misconduct meeting or hearing proceeds.

2.32 It is important to note that a misconduct meeting/hearing is concerned with whether the police officer concerned breached the Standards of Professional Behaviour and not whether the police officer has or has not committed a criminal offence.

2.33 The decision as to when to proceed with a misconduct meeting/hearing rests with the appropriate authority.

2.34 At the end of a misconduct meeting/hearing, where there are also outstanding or possible criminal proceedings involving the police officer concerned, the CPS or other prosecuting authority shall (as soon as practicable) be informed of the outcome of the meeting/hearing.

Misconduct action following criminal proceedings

2.35 Subject to the guidance above, where misconduct proceedings have not been taken prior to criminal proceedings and the police officer is acquitted, consideration will then need to be given as to whether instigating misconduct proceedings or a special case hearing is a reasonable exercise of discretion in the light of the acquittal.

2.36 A previous acquittal in criminal proceedings in respect of an allegation which is the subject of misconduct or special case proceedings is a relevant factor which should be taken into account in deciding whether to continue with those proceedings.

2.37 Relevant factors in deciding whether to proceed with disciplinary or special case proceedings include the following, non-exhaustive, list:

(a) Whether the allegation is in substance the same as that which was determined during criminal proceedings;

(b) Whether the acquittal was the result of a substantive decision on the merits of the charge (whether by the judge or jury) after the hearing of evidence; and

(c) Whether significant further evidence is available to the misconduct meeting/hearing, either because it was excluded from consideration in criminal proceedings or because it has become available since.

2.38 Each case will fall to be determined on its merits and an overly-prescriptive formula should not be adopted.

2.39 It may further be unfair to proceed with misconduct proceedings in circumstances where there has been a substantial delay in hearing disciplinary or special case proceedings by virtue of the prior criminal proceedings.

2.40 Regard should be had in this respect to such factors as:

• the impact of the delay on the police officer (including the impact on his or her health and career);

• whether the delay has prejudiced his or her case in any disciplinary or special case proceedings; and

- whether there will be a further substantial delay whilst disciplinary or special case proceedings are heard (including the impact on the police officer of that delay).

Fast track procedures (special cases)

2.41 Guidance on dealing with special cases where the fast track procedures can be used can be found at Annex A.

Link between Misconduct Procedures and complaints, conduct matters and Death or Serious Injury cases to which the Police Reform Act 2002 (the 2002 Act) applies

2.42 The 2002 Act and the Complaint Regulations set out how complaints, conduct matters and death or serious injury (DSI) matters must be handled. All other cases are dealt with solely under the Conduct Regulations.

2.43 The 2002 Act and the Complaint Regulations also set out the matters that are required to be referred to the Independent Police Complaints Commission (IPCC).

Complaints – Local Resolution

2.44 The 2002 Act, Complaint Regulations and IPCC statutory guidance set out when complaints are suitable for Local Resolution and these procedures will continue to apply. It may be appropriate in dealing with a complaint using Local Resolution for a manager to take management action in addition and this is perfectly acceptable. However this will not be considered as formal disciplinary action although it does not prevent a manager from making a note of the action taken and recording this on the police officer's PDR (if appropriate). (See paragraph 2.96)

Complaints – Investigation

2.45 Where a complaint about the conduct of a police officer or special constable is not suitable to be resolved using the Local Resolution procedure or that procedure fails then the matter will need to be investigated under the provisions of the 2002 Act and the Complaint Regulations.

2.46 The investigation into the complaint must be proportionate having regard to the nature of the allegation and any likely outcome (see also IPCC statutory guidance).

2.47 An investigation into a complaint is not automatically an investigation into whether a police officer or a special constable has breached the standards of professional behaviour but rather an investigation into the circumstances that led to the dissatisfaction being expressed by the complainant of the actions of one or more persons serving with the police.

2.48 The 2002 Act and the Complaint Regulations set how the investigator shall be appointed to investigate the complaint and in addition set out: -

  i) When a complaint is subject of special requirements (see paragraph 2.49);
 ii) when a severity assessment must be made;
iii) the information required to be notified to the police officer concerned;
 iv) the duty of the investigator to consider relevant statements and documents;
  v) arrangements for interviewing the person whose conduct is being investigated; and
 vi) the matters to be included in the investigation report.

Special requirements

2.49 If, during an investigation into a complaint, it appears to the person investigating that there is an indication that a person to whose conduct the investigation relates may have –

a) committed a criminal offence, or
b) behaved in a manner which would justify the bringing of disciplinary proceedings,

the person investigating (the investigator) must certify the investigation as one subject to special requirements (paragraph 19A of Schedule 3 to the 2002 Act). Conduct matters, by definition, are subject to the special requirements.

2.50 Where the person investigating does not consider that the conduct subject of the investigation either amounts to a criminal offence or (even if proven or admitted) would (in the investigator's judgement) be referred to a misconduct meeting or hearing, the matter will not be subject of the special requirements and no Regulation 14A (Complaint Regulations) notice will be served on the police officer concerned and no severity assessment will be required. If the person investigating the complaint does certify the investigation as one subject of special requirements, the investigator must, as soon as is reasonably practicable after doing so, make a severity assessment in relation to the conduct (see below).

Severity assessment

2.51 The severity assessment means an assessment as to –

a) whether the conduct of the police officer concerned, if proved, would amount to misconduct or gross misconduct, and

b) if misconduct, the form (i.e. misconduct meeting or hearing) which disciplinary proceedings would be likely to take if the conduct were to become subject of such proceedings.

2.52 The severity assessment may only be made after consultation with the appropriate authority. The investigator shall ensure that a written notice is provided to the police officer concerned informing him or her that his or her conduct is being investigated unless the person investigating the complaint considers that giving the notification might prejudice –

a) the investigation, or

b) any other investigation (including, in particular, a criminal investigation).

(See paragraph 2.103 regarding written notices).

2.53 The written notice may indicate that although the conduct would amount to misconduct rather than gross misconduct, the fact that the police officer concerned has an outstanding live final written warning will mean that should the matter proceed to misconduct proceedings, those proceedings would take the form of a misconduct hearing.

2.54 Where the person investigating the complaint determines that the special requirements are not met (as there is no indication that the matter amounts to a criminal offence or the matter would not justify referring the matter to misconduct proceedings) then there is no requirement for a severity assessment and therefore no requirement to serve a written notice on the police officer concerned.

2.55 If, during the course of the investigation the investigator determines that the severity assessment should change due to the initial assessment being incorrect or new information being found that affects the original assessment, then a fresh assessment can be made and the police officer concerned informed accordingly. Considerable care should be taken in making the severity assessment or revising the assessment in order to avoid any unfairness to the police officer concerned. All decisions in determining or revising the severity assessment should be documented with reasons for the decision.

Investigation of Conduct matters

2.56 A conduct matter is defined in the Police Reform Act 2002 as: -

'any matter which is not and has not been the subject of a complaint but in the case of which there is an indication (whether from the circumstances or otherwise) that a person serving with the police may have-

a) committed a criminal offence; or

b) behaved in a manner which would justify the bringing of disciplinary proceedings'.

2.57 Paragraphs 10 and 11 of Schedule 3 to the 2002 Act and regulation 5 of the Complaint Regulations set out the conduct matters that are required to be recorded by the appropriate authority (recordable conduct matters).

2.58 Paragraph 13 of Schedule 3 to the 2002 Act and regulation 5 to the Complaint Regulations set out the categories of recordable conduct matters that are required to be referred to the IPCC.

2.59 Conduct matters that are not required to be recorded or referred to the IPCC may be dealt with by the appropriate authority. Where the appropriate authority determines that these conduct matters should be investigated, then this will be conducted under the provisions of the Conduct Regulations.

2.60 Recordable conduct matters are subject to the special requirements mentioned at paragraph 2.49 above and therefore the person investigating the matter will be required to undertake a severity assessment (see paragraphs 2.51 to 2.55 above) and comply with the special requirements.

**Investigation report following complaint (subject of special requirements)/
recordable conduct matter investigations.**

2.61 At the conclusion of an investigation into a complaint where the matter has been subject to the special requirements or constitutes a recordable conduct matter, the investigator, in addition to setting out his or her conclusions on the facts of the matter, will indicate whether he or she determines on the facts of the case that there is a case to answer in respect of misconduct or gross misconduct or that there is no case to answer.

2.62 The action that an appropriate authority proposes or does not propose to take in response to an investigation of a complaint may be subject to an appeal by a complainant. The IPCC also has the power in certain cases to recommend and direct that particular misconduct proceedings are held in respect of complaint and recordable conduct investigations (see further paragraph 2.150).

**Referring a matter to misconduct proceedings following investigation of a complaint
(subject of special requirements) or a recordable conduct matter.**

2.63 Where, following the investigation into a complaint subject to the special requirements or a recordable conduct matter, it is determined that there is a case to answer in respect of misconduct or gross misconduct then the appropriate authority will determine whether the matter should be referred to a misconduct meeting or hearing.

2.64 Where the appropriate authority determines that there is a case to answer in respect of misconduct but not gross misconduct it may determine that management action is an appropriate and proportionate response to the misconduct.

2.65 Where it is determined that there is a case to answer in respect of misconduct and management action is not appropriate, the appropriate authority shall refer the matter to a misconduct meeting (unless the police officer concerned has an outstanding final written warning which was live when the severity assessment was made, in which case the matter will be referred to a misconduct hearing).

2.66 In cases where there is a case to answer in respect of gross misconduct then the matter shall be referred to a misconduct hearing (or if the special conditions are satisfied a special case (fast track) hearing).

2.67 Referral to misconduct proceedings and the procedures to be followed thereafter are made under Part 4 (and Part 5 if appropriate) of the Conduct Regulations (regulation 19 onwards).

Death or Serious Injury matters (DSI)

2.68 Where there is an investigation into a death or serious injury case (DSI), where there is no complaint or indication of any conduct matter, then the investigation will focus on the circumstances of the incident (see also IPCC statutory guidance).

2.69 However, where during the course of the investigation into the DSI matter there is an indication that a person serving with the police may have committed a criminal offence or behaved in a manner that would justify the bringing of disciplinary proceedings then the DSI matter will be reclassified as a recordable conduct matter (or complaint if appropriate) and dealt with accordingly.

Misconduct Procedures

Assessment of conduct – (Is the case one of misconduct?)

2.70 Where an allegation is made against the conduct of a police officer or special constable, being a matter that does not involve a complaint, a recordable conduct matter or a death or serious injury (see paragraph 2.42 above), the matter will be dealt with under the Conduct Regulations from the outset. However, in the same way as described in paragraph 2.51 above, the appropriate authority must formally assess whether the conduct alleged, if proved, would amount to misconduct or gross misconduct.

2.71 The assessment may determine that the conduct alleged amounts to an allegation of unsatisfactory performance rather than one of misconduct. In such circumstances the matter should be referred to be dealt with under the UPPs. (See chapter 3).

2.72 The assessment may determine that the matter is more suitable to be dealt with through the grievance procedure or may be an issue of direction and control (see HO Circular 19/2005). In such cases the procedures for dealing with such matters should be used.

2.73 The purpose of the initial assessment is to:

• Ensure a timely response to an allegation or an issue relating to conduct
• Identify the police officer subject to the allegation and to eliminate those not involved.
• Ensure that the most appropriate procedures are used.

2.74 The assessment should be made by the appropriate authority (see delegation of authority in the Introduction section and glossary definition). The person making the assessment should always consider consulting the Professional Standards Department (PSD) or Human Resources Department for assistance.

2.75 If it is not possible to make an immediate assessment a process of fact finding should be conducted but only to the extent that it is necessary to determine which procedure should be used. It is perfectly acceptable to ask questions to seek to establish which police officers may have been involved in a particular incident and therefore to eliminate those police officers who are not involved.

2.76 A formal investigation into a particular police officer's conduct affords the police officer certain safeguards in the interests of fairness such as the service of a notice informing the police officer that his or her conduct is subject to investigation and notifying the police officer of his or her right to consult with a police friend. The initial assessment and in particular fact finding should therefore not go so far as to undermine these safeguards.

2.77 Even if the person making the assessment has decided that the matter is not potentially one of misconduct he or she should consider whether there are any developmental or organisational issues which may need to be addressed by the individual (e.g. through management action) or the organisation.

Definitions

2.78 For the purposes of making the assessment and any decision on the seriousness of the conduct the following definitions will be applied:-

Misconduct

2.79 Misconduct is a breach of the Standards of Professional Behaviour (see chapter 1).

Gross Misconduct

2.80 Gross misconduct means a breach of the Standards of Professional Behaviour so serious that dismissal would be justified.

Unsatisfactory Performance/Attendance

2.81 Unsatisfactory performance or unsatisfactory attendance mean an inability or failure of a police officer to perform the duties of the role or rank he or she is currently undertaking to a satisfactory standard or level (see chapter 3).

Severity assessment – Is the matter potentially misconduct or gross misconduct?

2.82 The purpose of assessing whether a matter is potentially misconduct or gross misconduct is to:

- Allow the police officer subject to the misconduct procedures to have an early indication of the possible outcome if the allegation is proven or admitted.
- Give an indication of how the matter should be handled (for example, locally or by the force Professional Standards Department).

2.83 Where an allegation is made which indicates that the conduct of a police officer did not meet the standards set out in the Standards of Professional Behaviour, the appropriate authority must decide whether, if proven or admitted, the allegation would amount to misconduct or gross misconduct.

2.84 Where it is determined that the conduct, if proved, would constitute misconduct, it must further be determined whether it is necessary for the matter to be investigated or whether management action is the appropriate and proportionate response to the allegation. If the appropriate authority decides to take no action or management action, this should be notified to the police officer concerned.

2.85 Where it is determined that the conduct if proved, would constitute gross misconduct then the matter will be investigated (unless the assessment is subsequently changed to misconduct in which case, if appropriate, no further investigation may be required).

2.86 The assessment will also determine whether, if the matter was referred to misconduct proceedings, those proceedings would be likely to be a misconduct meeting (for cases of misconduct) or a misconduct hearing (for cases of gross misconduct or if the police officer concerned has a live final written warning at the time of the assessment and there is a further allegation of misconduct).

2.87 If the initial assessment has been made incorrectly or if new evidence emerges, then a fresh assessment can be made. The matter may be moved up to a level of gross misconduct or down to a level of misconduct. In the interests of fairness to the police officer, where a further severity assessment is made which alters the original assessment then the police officer will be informed and will be provided with the reasons for the change in the assessment.

2.88 The same principle applies where the initial assessment suggests that the matter is one of misconduct or gross misconduct but subsequent investigation reveals that it is not, and may be, for example, one of unsatisfactory performance. In such cases the police officer will be informed that the matter is now not being considered as a matter of misconduct.

Dealing with misconduct

2.89 Unless there are good reasons to take no action, there are two ways by which line managers can deal with matters which have been assessed as potential misconduct:

- Management action
- Disciplinary action for misconduct – where it is felt that the matter should be investigated

2.90 A decision on which action will be appropriate will be made on the basis of the information available following the severity assessment.

Management action

2.91 The purpose of management action is to:

- Deal with misconduct in a timely, proportionate and effective way that will command the confidence of staff, police officers, the police service and the public.

- Identify any underlying causes or welfare considerations.
- Improve conduct and to prevent a similar situation arising in the future.

2.92 When appropriate, managers in the police service are expected and encouraged to intervene at the earliest opportunity to prevent misconduct occurring and to deal with cases of misconduct in a proportionate and timely way through management action. Even if the police officer does not agree to the management action it can still be imposed by the manager providing such action is reasonable and proportionate.

2.93 Management action may include:

- Pointing out how the behaviour fell short of the expectations set out in the Standards of Professional Behaviour
- Identifying expectations for future conduct.
- Establishing an improvement plan.
- Addressing any underlying causes of misconduct.

2.94 The police officer may in some cases be advised that any future misconduct even if it is of the same type, could be dealt with by disciplinary action rather than management action.

2.95 The manager may draft an improvement plan with the police officer. This should include timescales for improvement in the conduct. A written record should be made of any improvement action and placed on the police officer's PDR. Any such note should be agreed as an accurate record with the police officer concerned and copied to him or her. Where the police officer does not agree with the record then his or her comments will be recorded and kept with the record. Managers should ensure that any improvement plan recorded on the police officer's PDR is regularly reviewed and comment made as to the improvement or otherwise of the police officer.

2.96 Management action is not a disciplinary outcome but is considered to be part of the normal managerial responsibility of managers in the police service. Management action is always available, including during or after the process of resolving a complaint using Local Resolution. Management action does not have to be revealed to the CPS as it does not constitute a disciplinary outcome.

2.97 Where an appropriate manager decides at the severity assessment that management action is the most appropriate and proportionate way to deal with an issue of misconduct, there will be no requirement to conduct a formal investigation and therefore no requirement to give a written notice to the police officer concerned in accordance with the provisions in the Conduct Regulations. Where at a later stage, either following the investigation or on withdrawal of the case (under regulation 20 of the Conduct Regulations or Regulation 7 of the Complaint Regulations), an appropriate manager decides to take management action, written notice of this will be given to the police officer as soon as possible.

2.98 Management action is not to be confused with management advice. Management advice is a disciplinary outcome that can only be imposed following a misconduct meeting or hearing.

Taking further disciplinary proceedings

2.99 Where it is felt that management action is not appropriate to deal with the alleged breach of the Standards of Professional Behaviour then an investigation into the alleged misconduct may be necessary. Where in cases of potential misconduct, management action is not considered appropriate, there will be an investigation under the Conduct Regulations and in cases where the allegation amounts to one of gross misconduct, then the matter will always be investigated.

2.100 The purpose of taking further disciplinary proceedings is to:

- Establish the facts underlying the allegation.
- Deal with cases of misconduct in a timely, proportionate, fair and effective way such as will command the confidence of the police service and the public.
- Identify any underlying causes or welfare considerations.
- Identify any learning opportunities for the individual or the organisation.

2.101 The guidance set out above deals with the requirements for severity assessments to be conducted in cases to which the 2002 Act applies and those cases dealt with under the Conduct Regulations.

2.102 The following provisions apply to both types of cases with the requirements set out in either the Complaint Regulations for cases being dealt with under the 2002 Act or the Conduct Regulations for other cases. Once cases have been referred to misconduct proceedings, in all cases, the relevant regulations are the Conduct Regulations (Regulation 19 onwards).

Written notification to officer concerned

2.103 Written notification will be given to the police officer concerned by the investigator appointed to investigate the case, advising him or her that his or her conduct is under investigation – either under Regulation 15 of the Conduct Regulations or under Regulation 14A of the Complaint Regulations (in the case of complaints subject to special requirements (see paragraph 2.49) and recordable conduct investigations). (A standard notice template is found at Annex E) The notice will:

- Inform the police officer that there is to be an investigation of his or her potential breach of the Standards of Professional Behaviour and inform the police officer of the name of the investigator who will investigate the matter.
- Describe the conduct that is the subject of the investigation and how that conduct is alleged to have fallen below the Standards of Professional Behaviour
- Inform the police officer concerned of the appropriate authority's (or investigator's in a matter dealt with under the 2002 Act) assessment of whether the conduct alleged, if proved, would amount to misconduct or gross misconduct
- Inform the police officer of whether, if the case were to be referred to misconduct proceedings, those would be likely to be a misconduct meeting or misconduct hearing
- Inform the police officer that if the likely form of any misconduct proceedings changes the police officer will be notified of this together with the reasons for that change
- Inform the police officer of his or her right to seek advice from his or her staff association or any other body and who the police officer may choose to act as his or her police friend.
- Inform the police officer that if his or her case is referred to a misconduct hearing or special case hearing, he or she has the right to be legally represented by a relevant lawyer. If the police officer elects not to be so represented then he or she may be represented by a police friend. The notice will also make clear that if he or she elects not to be legally represented then he or she may be dismissed or receive any other disciplinary outcome without being so represented.
- Inform the police officer that he or she may provide, within 10 working days of receipt of the notice (unless this period is extended by the investigator) a written or oral statement relating to any matter under investigation and he or she (or his or her police friend) may provide any relevant documents to the investigator within this time.
- Inform the police officer that whilst he or she does not have to say anything, it may harm his or her case if he or she does not mention when interviewed or when providing any information within the relevant time limits something which he or she later relies on in any misconduct proceedings or special case hearing or at an appeal meeting or Police Appeals Tribunal.

2.104 The notice should clearly describe in unambiguous language the particulars of the conduct that it is alleged fell below the standards expected of a police officer.

2.105 The terms of reference for the investigation, or the part of the terms of reference for the investigation relating to the individual's conduct, should, subject to there being no prejudice to that or any other investigation, be supplied to the police officer and to his or her police friend on request, and they should both be informed if the terms of reference change.

2.106 The written notification may be provided to a manager (including by e mail) to give to the police officer concerned or where appropriate and with the agreement of the police friend the notice may be given to the police friend to give to the police officer concerned. In both cases the notice must be given to the police officer in person. Alternatively, the notice can be posted by recorded delivery to his or her last known address. The responsibility for ensuring that the notice is served rests with the investigator (in cases dealt with under the 2002 Act) or the appropriate authority. (In both cases it is the investigator who must cause the officer concerned to be given the written notice. Therefore whilst the appropriate authority may do it, the responsibility for ensuring that the notice is served rests with the investigator).

2.107 The investigator should ensure that the police officer subject to investigation shall, as soon as practicable, be provided with this written notification unless to do so would prejudice the investigation or any other investigation (including a criminal one). Any decision not to inform the police officer will be recorded and kept under regular review in order to avoid unreasonable delay in notifying the police officer concerned.

2.108 Where the IPCC is conducting an independent or managed investigation then the responsibility for ensuring that the police officer is provided with the written notification (as soon as practicable) rests with the investigator appointed or designated to conduct that investigation.

2.109 In the interests of fairness, care must be taken when an incident is being investigated to ensure that the notification is given to the police officer as soon as practicable after an investigator is appointed.(subject to any prejudice to that or any other investigation).

Appointment of investigator

2.110 Where the appropriate authority has assessed the allegation as being one of misconduct or gross misconduct and in the case of misconduct, has determined that the matter is not suitable for immediate management action then the appropriate authority will appoint an investigator. In cases being dealt with under the Conduct Regulations the investigator can be a police officer, police staff member or some other person and should be the most appropriate person having regard to all of the circumstances and the requirements set out in regulation 13 of the Conduct Regulations.

2.111 In cases falling under paragraphs 17 or 18 of Schedule 3 to the Police Reform Act 2002 the appropriate authority must follow the appropriate provisions regarding the approval of the investigator by the IPCC. The appropriate authority will also need to ensure that an investigator appointed under paragraphs 16, 17 or 18 of the 2002 Act has the necessary skills and experience as set out in regulation 18 of the Complaint Regulations.[2] (See IPCC Statutory Guidance). Cases falling under paragraph 19 of Schedule 3 shall be investigated by the Commission's own staff subject to Secretary of State having the power to nominate that person in the circumstances set out in paragraph 19(3) and (3A) of that Schedule.

2.112 The force Professional Standards Department should be consulted before an investigation is commenced to ensure that there are no other matters that need to be considered prior to any investigation (for example other investigations that may be ongoing into the conduct of the police officer concerned, or outstanding written warnings that are still live).

Investigation

2.113 The purpose of an investigation is to:
- Gather evidence to establish the facts and circumstances of the alleged misconduct
- Assist the appropriate authority to establish on the balance of probabilities, based on the evidence and taking into account all of the circumstances, whether there is a case to answer in respect of either misconduct or gross misconduct or that there is no case to answer.
- Identify any learning for the individual or the organisation.

---

[2] As amended by the Police (Complaints and Misconduct) (Amendment) Regulations 2008, SI 2008/2866.

2.114 In cases which are not being managed or dealt with by the IPCC, the appropriate authority should ensure that a proportionate and balanced investigation is carried out as soon as possible after any alleged misconduct comes to the appropriate authority's attention and that the investigation is carried out as quickly as possible allowing for the complexity of the case. A frequent criticism of previous misconduct investigations was that they were lengthy, disproportionate and not always focussed on the relevant issue(s).It is therefore crucial that any investigation is kept proportionate to ensure that an overly lengthy investigation does not lead to grounds for challenge. Where the investigation identifies that the issue is one of performance rather than misconduct, the police officer should be informed as soon as possible that the matter is now being treated as an issue of performance.

2.115 In cases which do not fall under the 2002 Act, the appropriate authority can discontinue an investigation if there is a change in circumstances which makes it appropriate to do so. Similarly, in cases which do fall under the 2002 Act, the appropriate authority can apply to the IPCC to discontinue an investigation (see paragraph 21 of Schedule 3 to the 2002 Act, paragraph 7 of the Complaint Regulations and the IPCC statutory guidance).

2.116 The investigator must ensure that the police officer is kept informed of the progress of the investigation. It is also good practice to keep the police friend informed of progress at the same time. The investigator is required to notify the police officer of the progress of the investigation at least every 4 weeks from the start of the investigation. The requirement under the Police Reform Act 2002 to keep the complainant or an interested person informed will also apply in relevant cases (See Regulation 11 of the Complaint Regulations and the IPCC Statutory Guidance).

2.117 The police officer or his or her police friend, acting on the police officer concerned's instructions, is encouraged to suggest at an early stage any line of enquiry that would assist the investigation and to pass to the investigator any material they consider relevant to the enquiry. (See regulation 16 of the Conduct Regulations and paragraph 19C of Schedule 3 to the 2002 Act and Regulation 14C of the Complaint Regulations).

2.118 The investigator (under the Conduct Regulations or the 2002 Act) has a duty to consider the suggestions submitted to him or her. The investigator should consider and document reasons for following or not following any submissions made by the police officer or his or her police friend with a view to ensuring that the investigation is as fair as possible. The suggestions may involve a further suggested line of investigation or further examination of a particular witness. The purpose is to enable a fair and balanced investigation report to be prepared and where appropriate made available for consideration at a misconduct meeting/hearing and to negate the need (except where necessary) for witnesses to attend a meeting/hearing.

Interviews during investigation

2.119 It will not always be necessary to conduct a formal interview with the police officer subject to the investigation. In some cases, particularly involving low level misconduct cases, it may be more appropriate, proportionate and timely to request a written account from the police officer.

2.120 Where a formal interview is felt to be necessary, the investigator should try and agree a time and date for the interview with the police officer concerned and his or her police friend if appropriate. The police officer will be given written notice of the date, time and place of the interview. The police officer must attend the interview when required to do so and it may be a further misconduct matter to fail to attend.

2.121 If the police officer concerned or his or her police friend is not available at the date or time specified by the investigator, the police officer may propose an alternative time. Provided that the alternative time is reasonable and falls within a period of 5 working days beginning with the first working day after that proposed by the investigator the interview must be postponed to that time.

2.122 Where a police officer is on certificated sick leave, the investigator should seek to establish when the police officer will be fit for interview. It may be that the police officer is not fit for ordinary police duty but is perfectly capable of being interviewed. Alternatively the police officer concerned may be invited to provide a written response to the allegations within a specified period and may be sent the questions that the investigator wishes to be answered.

2.123 It is important that there is a balance between the welfare of the police officer concerned and the need for the investigation to progress as quickly as possible in the interests of justice, the police service and the police officer subject to investigation.

2.124 Where a police officer is alleged or appears to have committed a criminal offence a normal criminal investigation will take place, with the police officer being cautioned in accordance with the PACE Code of Practice. Where the matter to be investigated involves both criminal and misconduct allegations, it should be made clear to the police officer concerned at the start of the interview whether he or she is being interviewed in respect of the criminal or misconduct allegations.

2.125 This may be achieved by conducting two separate interviews, although this does not prevent the responses given in respect of the criminal interview being used in the misconduct investigation and therefore a separate misconduct interview may not be required.

2.126 Care should be taken when conducting a misconduct interview where the police officer is also subject of a criminal investigation in respect of the same behaviour, as anything said by the police officer concerned in the misconduct interview when not under caution and used in the criminal investigation could be subject to an inadmissibility ruling by the court at any subsequent trial. If necessary, appropriate legal advice should be obtained.

2.127 At the beginning of a misconduct interview or when asking a police officer to provide a written response to an allegation, the police officer shall be reminded of the warning contained in regulation 15(1)(h) of the Conduct Regulations (or regulation 14A(1)(h) of the Complaint Regulations 2008 for cases dealt with under the 2002 Act) namely informing the police officer that whilst he or she does not have to say anything it may harm his or her case if he or she does not mention when interviewed or providing a written response something which he or she later relies on in any misconduct proceedings or special case hearing or appeal meeting or appeal hearing.

2.128 Prior to an interview with a police officer who is the subject of a misconduct investigation, the investigator must ensure that the police officer is provided with sufficient information and time to prepare for the interview. The information provided should always include full details of the allegations made against the police officer including the relevant date(s) and place(s) of the alleged misconduct (if known). The investigator should consider whether there are good reasons for withholding certain evidence obtained prior to the interview and if there are no such reasons then the police officer should normally be provided with all the relevant evidence obtained. The police officer will then have the opportunity to provide his or her version of the events together with any supporting evidence he or she may wish to provide. The police officer will be reminded that failure to provide any account or response to any questions at this stage of the investigation may lead to an adverse inference being drawn at a later stage.

2.129 Interviews do not have to be electronically recorded but if they are then the person being interviewed shall be given a copy upon request. If the interview is not electronically recorded then a written record or summary of the discussion must be given to the person being interviewed. The police officer concerned should be given the opportunity to check and sign that he or she agrees with the summary as an accurate record of what was said and should sign and return a copy to the investigator. Where a police officer refuses or fails to exercise his or her right to agree and sign a copy then this will be noted by the investigator. The police officer may make a note of the changes he or she wants to make to the record and a copy of this will be given to the person(s) conducting the hearing/meeting along with the investigator's account of the record.

2.130 Other than for a joint criminal/misconduct investigation interview it will not be necessary for criminal style witness statements to be taken. In misconduct investigations an agreed and signed written record of the information supplied will be sufficient.

Moving between Misconduct and UPP

2.131 It may not be apparent at the outset of an investigation whether the matter is one of misconduct or unsatisfactory performance or attendance. It should be established as soon as possible which procedure is the more appropriate. In some cases it may be that it is not clear which procedure should be used until there has been some investigation of the matter.

2.132 Assessing a matter as misconduct or a matter of performance or attendance is an important distinction to make. It is normally possible to distinguish between matters of unsatisfactory performance or attendance by a particular police officer and that of personal misconduct.

2.133 A matter that appears initially to relate to misconduct may, on investigation, turn out to be a matter relating to unsatisfactory performance or attendance and should be transferred to the unsatisfactory performance procedure (UPP), if appropriate, at the earliest opportunity. This can be done at any time before a misconduct meeting or hearing, in relation to a matter not dealt with under the 2002 Act, by withdrawing the case against the police officer concerned under regulation 20 of the Conduct Regulations and referring the matter to be dealt with under the UPPs. The police officer concerned shall be informed that the matter is no longer being investigated as a misconduct case.

2.134 It may be that the outcome of an investigation into an allegation is that an issue of unsatisfactory performance or attendance has been identified against one or more police officers who were the subject of the investigation rather than any issue of misconduct. In such cases the outcome of the allegation may be that the appropriate authority will determine that there is no case to answer in respect of misconduct or gross misconduct but it may be appropriate to take action under the UPPs in order that the police officer concerned may learn and improve his or her performance.

2.135 There may be very rare occasions when the matter proceeds under the misconduct procedure to a misconduct meeting or hearing and the person(s) conducting the proceedings find that the conduct of the police officer amounts to unsatisfactory performance or attendance as opposed to one of misconduct. In such cases, a finding on the facts of the case by the person(s) conducting the meeting or hearing can be used for the purposes of the UPPs. The person(s) conducting the meeting/hearing should in such cases make a finding that the conduct did not amount to misconduct and refer the matter to the appropriate authority.

2.136 The appropriate authority in such cases should then decide if taking action against the police officer concerned using the UPPs is a fair and reasonable exercise of discretion taking into account all of the circumstances of the case and in particular the same principles set out at paragraphs 2.39 and 2.40.

2.137 Material gathered under the UPP should not be used for the purposes of the misconduct procedure if this means that the safeguards for police officers provided in the misconduct procedure, such as provision for formal notification, are thereby undermined.

Investigation report and supporting documents

2.138 At the conclusion of the investigation the investigator must as soon as practicable submit his or her report of the investigation setting out an accurate summary of the evidence that has been gathered (regulation 18 of the Conduct Regulations or regulation 14E of the Complaint Regulations). The report shall also attach or refer to any relevant documents. It will also include a recommendation whether in the opinion of the investigator there is a case to answer in respect of misconduct or gross misconduct or whether there is no case to answer.

2.139 In cases where the investigation was conducted under paragraphs, 16 (local), 17 (supervised), 18 (managed) or 19 (independent) of Schedule 3 to the 2002 Act then the investigator will submit his or her report with recommendations in accordance with paragraph 22 of schedule 3 to the 2002 Act.

2.140 The appropriate authority shall make a decision based on the report. The appropriate authority shall determine whether there is a case to answer in respect of misconduct or gross misconduct or that there is no case of misconduct to answer (regulation 19 of Conduct Regulations).

2.141 If it is decided that there is no case of misconduct to answer then management action may still be appropriate. In matters involving a complaint, where the complaint was subject to a local or supervised investigation under the 2002 Act, the decision of the appropriate authority may be subject to an appeal by the complainant to the IPCC (see IPCC Statutory Guidance). Similarly in cases where an investigation into a complaint, recordable conduct matter or death or serious injury matter has been conducted under paragraph 18 (managed) or 19 (independent) of Schedule 3 to the 2002 Act, the IPCC has the power to make recommendations and give directions as to whether there is a case to answer.

2.142 If no further action is to be taken then it is good practice that the investigation report or part of the investigation report that is relevant to the police officer should be given, subject to the harm test, to the police officer on request.

2.143 The investigation report will also highlight any learning opportunities for either an individual or the organisation.

Action prior to misconduct meetings/hearings

2.144 In cases where it is decided that there is a misconduct case to answer, the appropriate authority will need to determine whether the matter can be dealt with by means of immediate management action without the need to refer the case to a misconduct meeting. This will be particularly appropriate in cases where the police officer concerned has accepted that his or her conduct fell below the standards expected of a police officer and demonstrates a commitment to improve his or her conduct in the future and to learn from that particular case. In addition the appropriate authority will need to be satisfied that this is the case and that management action is an adequate and sufficient outcome having regard to all the circumstances of the case.

2.145 Where the appropriate authority consider that there is a case to answer in respect of misconduct and that management action would not be appropriate or sufficient (for example because the police officer has a live Superintendent's warning issued under the previous procedures or the misconduct is serious enough to justify a written warning being given) then a misconduct meeting/hearing should be arranged and the police officer shall, subject to the harm test, be given a copy of the investigation report (or the part of the report which is relevant to him or her), any other relevant documents gathered during the course of the investigation and a copy of his statement to the investigator.

2.146 In determining which documents are relevant, the test to be applied will be that under the Criminal Procedure and Investigations Act 1996, namely whether any document or other material undermines the case against the police officer concerned or would assist the police officer's case.

2.147 Where a determination has been made that the conduct amounts to gross misconduct then the case shall be referred to a misconduct hearing (or special case hearing if appropriate).

2.148 The appropriate authority will also provide the police officer with a notice containing the matters discussed at regulation 21(1)(a) of the Conduct Regulations, including the particulars of the behaviour that is alleged to have fallen below the standards in the Standards of Professional Behaviour.

2.149 It is necessary to describe the particulars of the actual behaviour of the police officer that is considered to amount to misconduct or gross misconduct and the reasons it is thought the behaviour amounts to such.

2.150 It is important to note that in cases where the misconduct to be considered was identified as a direct result of a complaint, then any decision by the appropriate authority to hold or not to hold a particular misconduct proceeding may be subject to an appeal by the complainant. The appropriate authority, having made its decision on the outcome of the investigation into the complaint and whether there is a case to answer in respect of misconduct or gross misconduct will notify the complainant of its determination and inform the complainant of their right of appeal. The police officer subject of the investigation into his or her conduct should be informed of the determination of the appropriate authority but also informed that the appropriate authority's decision could be subject of an appeal by the complainant to the IPCC. The appropriate authority should then wait until either the 28 + 2 days[3] period that the complainant may appeal has elapsed or an appeal has been received and decided by the IPCC before serving the written notice described in paragraph 2.148 confirming how the proceedings are to be dealt with.

2.151 There is no requirement to wait until the period the complainant has to appeal has elapsed in cases where the appropriate authority has determined that the case should be dealt with at a misconduct hearing or a special case hearing.

2.152 No final decision can be taken by the appropriate authority in the case of a recordable conduct matter where the IPCC are considering whether to recommend or direct that an appropriate authority take particular misconduct proceedings unless the appropriate authority intends to refer the matter to a misconduct hearing or special case hearing. Therefore, the written notice should not be provided until the appropriate authority has heard from the IPCC.

2.153 Within 14 working days (unless this period is extended by the person(s) conducting the misconduct meeting/hearing for exceptional circumstances) beginning with the first working day after being supplied with the investigator's report and relevant documents and written notice described in paragraph 2.148, the police officer will be required to submit in writing: -

• whether or not he or she accepts that the behaviour described in the particulars amounts to misconduct or gross misconduct as the case may be
• where he or she accepts that his or her conduct amounts to misconduct or gross misconduct as the case may be, any written submission he or she wishes to make in mitigation
• where he or she does not accept that his or her conduct amounts to misconduct or gross misconduct as the case may be, or he or she disputes part of the case, written notice of the particulars of the allegation(s) he or she disputes and his or her account of the relevant events and any arguments on points of law he or she wishes the person(s) conducting the meeting or hearing to consider.

2.154 The police officer concerned will also (within the same time limit) provide the appropriate authority and the person(s) conducting the misconduct meeting or hearing with a copy of any document he or she intends to rely on at the misconduct proceedings. If such documents involve submissions on points of law then the person(s) conducting or chairing a meeting/hearing may take legal advice in advance of the meeting/hearing. In addition, at a misconduct hearing the persons conducting that hearing have the right to have relevant lawyer available to them for advice at the hearing.

2.155 The police officer shall be informed of the name of the person(s) holding the meeting/hearing together with the name of any person appointed to advise the person(s) conducting the meeting/hearing as soon as reasonably practicable after they have been appointed. The police officer may object to any person hearing or advising at a misconduct meeting or hearing within 3 working days starting with the first working day after he or she was notified of the person's name. In doing so the police officer concerned will need to set out clear and reasonable objections as to why a particular person(s) should not conduct or advise at the meeting/hearing.

---

[3] The statutory period for a complainant to appeal is twenty-eight days. The two extra days are, however, provided for the IPCC to process and inform the appropriate authority that an appeal has been received.

2.156 If the police officer concerned submits a compelling reason why such a person should not be involved in the meeting/hearing, a replacement should be found and the police officer will be notified of the name of the replacement and the police officer concerned will have the same right to object to that person.

2.157 The police officer concerned may object to a person(s) conducting a misconduct meeting or hearing or advising at such proceedings if, for example, the person(s) have been involved in the case in a way that would make it difficult to make an objective and impartial assessment of the facts of the case.

Documents for the meeting/hearing

2.158 The person(s) conducting the misconduct meeting/hearing shall be supplied (in accordance with regulation 28) with: -

- A copy of the notice supplied to the police officer that set out the fact that the case was to be referred to a misconduct meeting/hearing and details of the alleged misconduct etc.
- A copy of the investigator's report or such parts of the report that relate to the police officer concerned, any other relevant document gathered during the course of the investigation and a copy of any statement the officer.
- The notice provided by the police officer setting out whether or not the police officer accepts that his or her conduct amounts to misconduct or gross misconduct, any submission he or she wishes to make in mitigation where the conduct is accepted, and where he or she does not accept that the alleged conduct amounts to misconduct or gross misconduct or he or she disputes part of the case, the allegations he or she disputes and his or her account of the relevant events; any arguments on points of law submitted by the police officer concerned as well as any documents he intends to rely on at the meeting/hearing, submitted under regulation 22 of the Conduct Regulations.
- Where the police officer concerned does not accept that the alleged conduct amounts to misconduct or gross misconduct as the case may be or where he or she disputes any part of the case, any other documents that in the opinion of the appropriate authority should be considered at the meeting/hearing.
- Any other documents that the person(s) conducting the meeting/hearing request that are relevant to the case

2.159 The documents for the meeting/hearing should be given to the person(s) conducting the meeting/hearing as soon as practicable after he, she or they have been appointed to conduct the meeting/hearing.

Witnesses

2.160 Generally speaking misconduct meetings and hearings will be conducted without witnesses. A witness will only be required to attend a misconduct meeting/hearing if the person conducting or chairing the meeting/hearing reasonably believes his or her attendance is necessary to resolve disputed issues in that case. The appropriate authority should meet the reasonable expenses of any witnesses.

2.161 The appropriate authority and the officer concerned shall inform each other of any witnesses they wish to attend including brief details of eth evidence that person can provide and their addresses. They should attempt to agree which witness (es) are necessary to deal with the issue(s) in dispute.

2.162 The appropriate authority shall supply the person(s) conducting the proceedings with a list of the witnesses agreed between the parties or where there is no agreement, the lists provided by both the officer and the appropriate authority. The person conducting a misconduct meeting or the chair of a misconduct hearing will decide whether to allow such witnesses. The person conducting or chairing the misconduct proceedings may also decide that a witness other than one on such lists should be required to attend (if their attendance is considered necessary).

2.163 Where the person conducting a misconduct meeting or the chair of a misconduct hearing rejects the request for a particular witness(es) to attend it is good practice for the reasons for refusing to allow the attendance of the witness(es) to be given to the police officer concerned and the appropriate authority.

2.164 Whilst the person conducting the misconduct meeting or the chair of a misconduct hearing will decide whether a particular witness(es) are required, the appropriate authority will be responsible for arranging the attendance of any witness.

2.165 In special cases (fast track) no witnesses, other than the officer concerned, will provide evidence at the hearing. (See Annex A)

Misconduct meetings/hearings

Types of misconduct proceedings

2.166 There are two types of misconduct proceedings:

- A *Misconduct Meeting* for cases where there is a case to answer in respect of misconduct and where the maximum outcome would be a final written warning.
- A *Misconduct Hearing* for cases where there is a case to answer in respect of gross misconduct or where the police officer has a live final written warning and there is a case to answer in respect of a further act of misconduct. The maximum outcome at this hearing would be dismissal from the police service without notice.

2.167 It is important that misconduct hearings are only used for those matters where the police officer has a live final written warning and has potentially committed a further act of misconduct that warrants misconduct proceedings or the misconduct alleged is so serious that it is genuinely considered that if proven or admitted dismissal from the police service would be justified.

Timing for holding meetings/hearings

2.168 A misconduct meeting shall take place not later than 20 working days beginning with the first working day after the date on which the documents and material for the meeting have been supplied to the police officer under Regulation 21 of the Conduct Regulations. Misconduct hearings shall take place not later than 30 working days beginning with the first working day after the date the documents for the hearing have been supplied to the police officer concerned.

2.169 The time limit for holding a misconduct meeting or a misconduct hearing can be extended if in the interests of justice the person conducting or chairing the misconduct proceedings considers it appropriate to extend beyond that period. Any decision to extend or not to extend the time limit for a meeting/hearing and the reasons for it will be documented by that person and communicated to the appropriate authority and the police officer concerned. It is also good practice to inform the police friend of the police officer concerned (if applicable).

2.170 In order to maintain confidence in the misconduct procedures it is important that the misconduct meetings/hearings are held as soon as practicable and extensions to the timescales should be an exception rather than the rule. To that end, managers appointed to conduct or chair misconduct meetings/hearings are to ensure that a robust stance is taken in managing the process whilst ensuring the fairness of the proceedings. Extensions may be appropriate for example if the case is particularly complex. It will not normally be considered appropriate to extend the timescale on the grounds that the police officer concerned wishes to be represented by a particular lawyer.

Purpose of misconduct meeting/hearing

2.171 The purpose of a formal misconduct meeting/hearing is to:

- Give the police officer a fair opportunity to make his or her case having considered the investigation report including supporting documents and to put forward any factors the police officer wishes to be considered in mitigation (in addition to the submission which must be sent in advance to the person(s) conducting or chairing the meeting/hearing for his, her or their consideration).

- Decide if the conduct of the police officer fell below the standards set out in the Standards of Professional Behaviour based on the balance of probabilities and having regard to all of the evidence and circumstances.
- Consider what the outcome should be if misconduct is proven or admitted. Consideration will be given to any live written warnings or final written warnings (and any previous disciplinary outcomes that have not expired[4]) and any early admission of the conduct by the police officer.

Person(s) appointed to hold misconduct meetings/hearings

Misconduct meeting - Non senior officers (regulation 25)

2.172 A misconduct meeting for non senior officers (police officers up to and including the rank of Chief Superintendent and all special constables) will be heard by:

a) a police officer (or other member of a police force) of at least one rank above the police officer concerned. However, in the case of a special constable, the member of the police force must be a sergeant or above or a senior human resources professional; or

b) a police staff member who, in the opinion of the appropriate authority, is a grade above that of the police officer concerned. A police staff manager must not be appointed to conduct a misconduct meeting if the case substantially involves operational policing matters.

2.173 An appropriate manager (whether a police officer or police staff manager) may also be appointed as an adviser to the person appointed to hold the meeting if the appropriate authority considers it appropriate in the circumstances. The adviser's role is solely to advise on the procedure to be adopted and not as a decision maker. The manager appointed to conduct the meeting and (where appropriate) the adviser must be sufficiently independent in relation to the matter concerned (for example without any previous involvement in the matter) as to avoid any suggestion of unfairness.

Misconduct hearing - Non senior officers (regulation 25)

2174 A misconduct hearing for non senior officers will consist of a 3 person panel.

2.175 The chair will be either a senior officer or a senior Human Resources Professional. A senior Human Resources Professional means a human resources professional who in the opinion of the appropriate authority has sufficient seniority, skills and experience to conduct the misconduct hearing.

2.176 Where the senior Human Resources Professional is the chair then he or she will be accompanied by an independent member (appointed from the list held by the police authority) and a police officer of the rank of superintendent or above.

2.177 Where the senior officer is the chair then he or she will be accompanied by an independent member (appointed from the list held by the police authority) and a police officer of the rank of superintendent or above or a Human Resources Professional who is considered by the appropriate authority to be of sufficient grade to sit on the panel. The grade required for the Human Resources professional will depend on the rank of the police officer concerned.

2.178 The appropriate authority may appoint a person to advise the persons conducting the misconduct hearing and the adviser may be a relevant lawyer if required.

Misconduct meetings/hearings - Senior officers (regulations 26 and 27)

2.179 The persons who will hear misconduct meetings/hearings for senior officers are set out at Annex B.

---

[4] See reg 15 of the Police Regulations 2003, SI 2003/527.

Misconduct Hearings in Public

2.180 Where a misconduct hearing (not misconduct meetings) arises from a case where the IPCC have conducted an independent investigation (in accordance with paragraph 19 of Schedule 3 to the 2002 Act) and the IPCC considers that because of its gravity or other exceptional circumstances it would be in the public interest to do so, the IPCC may, having consulted with the appropriate authority, the police officer concerned, the complainant and any witnesses, direct that the whole or part of the misconduct hearing will be held in public.

2.181 The IPCC have published criteria for deciding when such cases will be held in public and a copy of this is available from the IPCC or the IPCC website at www.ipcc.gov.uk.

Joint meetings/hearings

2.182 Cases may arise where two or more police officers are to appear before a misconduct meeting or hearing in relation to apparent failures to meet the standards set out in the Standards of Professional Behaviour stemming from the same incident. In such cases, each police officer may have played a different part and any alleged misconduct may be different for each police officer involved. It will normally be considered necessary to deal with all the matters together in order to disentangle the various strands of action, and therefore a single meeting/hearing will normally be appropriate.

2.183 A police officer may request a separate meeting/hearing if he or she can demonstrate that there would be a real risk of unfairness to that police officer if his or her case was dealt with in a joint meeting/hearing. It is for the person conducting the meeting or the chair of a misconduct hearing to decide if a separate meeting or hearing is appropriate.

2.184 Where a joint meeting/hearing is held it will be the duty of the person(s) conducting the meeting/hearing to consider the case against each police officer and where a breach of the Standards of Professional Behaviour is found or admitted, to deal with each police officer's mitigation and circumstances individually and decide on the outcome accordingly. The person(s) conducting the meeting/hearing have the discretion to exclude the other officer(s) subject of the meeting/hearing if he, she or they determine it appropriate to do so e.g. when hearing each of the officers' mitigation.

Meeting/hearing in absence of officer concerned

2.185 It is in the interests of fairness to ensure that the misconduct meeting/hearing is held as soon as possible. A meeting/hearing may take place if the police officer fails to attend.

2.186 In cases where the police officer is absent (for example through illness or injury) a short delay may be reasonable to allow him or her to attend. If this is not possible or any delay is considered not appropriate in the circumstances then the person(s) conducting the meeting/hearing may allow the police officer to participate by telephone or video link. In these circumstances a police friend will always be permitted to attend the meeting/hearing to represent the police officer in the normal way (and in the case of a misconduct hearing the police officer's legal representative where appointed).

2.187 If a police officer is detained in prison or other institution by order of a court, there is no requirement on the appropriate authority to have the officer concerned produced for the purposes of the misconduct meeting/hearing.

Conduct of misconduct meeting/hearing

2.188 It will be for the person(s) conducting the meeting/hearing to determine the course of the meeting/hearing in accordance with the principles of natural justice and fairness.

2.189 The person(s) conducting the meeting/hearing will have read the investigator's report together with any account given by the police officer concerned during the investigation or when submitting his or her response under regulation 22 of the Conduct Regulations. The person(s) conducting the meeting/hearing will also have had the opportunity to read the relevant documents attached to the investigator's report.

2.190 Any document or other material that was not submitted in advance of the meeting/hearing by the appropriate authority or the police officer concerned may still be considered at the meeting/hearing at the discretion of the person(s) conducting the meeting/hearing. However the presumption should be that such documents will not be permitted unless it can be shown that they were not previously available to be submitted in advance.

2.191 Where any such document or other material is permitted to be considered, a short adjournment may be necessary to enable the appropriate authority or police officer concerned, as the case may be, to read or consider the document or other material and consider its implications.

2.192 Material that will be allowed, although not submitted in advance, will include mitigation where the police officer concerned denied the conduct alleged but the person(s) conducting the meeting/hearing found that the conduct had amounted to misconduct or gross misconduct and are to decide on outcome.

2.193 Where there is evidence at the meeting or hearing that the police officer concerned, at any time after being given written notice under regulation 15 of the Conduct Regulations (or regulation 14A of the Complaint Regulations), failed to mention when interviewed or when making representations to the investigator or under regulation 22 of the Conduct Regulations, any fact relied on in his or her defence at the meeting/hearing, being a fact which in the circumstances existing at the time the police officer concerned could reasonably have been expected to mention when questioned or providing a written response, the person(s) conducting the meeting/hearing may draw such inferences from this failure as appear appropriate.

2.194 Where a witness (es) does attend to give evidence then any questions to that witness should be made through the person conducting the meeting or in the case of a misconduct hearing the chair. This does not prevent the person conducting the meeting or the chair in a misconduct hearing allowing questions to be asked directly if they feel that is appropriate. It is for the person(s) conducting the meeting/hearing to control the proceedings and focus on the issues to ensure a fair meeting/hearing.

2.195 The person(s) conducting misconduct meetings/hearings will consider the facts of the case and will decide (on the balance of probabilities) whether the police officer's conduct amounted to misconduct, gross misconduct (in the case of a misconduct hearing) or neither. Where proceedings are conducted by a panel any decision shall be based on a majority (the chair having the casting vote where there is a panel of 2 or 4) if necessary. If the meeting decides that the police officer's conduct did not fall below the standards expected then as soon as reasonably practicable (and no later than 5 working days beginning with the first working day after the meeting or hearing) the police officer shall be informed and no entry will be made on his or her personal record.

2.196 A record of the proceedings at the meeting/hearing must be taken. In the case of a misconduct hearing this will be by means of a verbatim record whether by tape recording or any other recording method.

Standard of proof

2.197 In deciding matters of fact the misconduct meeting/hearing must apply the standard of proof required in civil cases, that is, the balance of probabilities. Conduct will be proved on the balance of probabilities if the person(s) conducting the meeting/hearing is/are satisfied by the evidence that it is more likely than not that the conduct occurred. The more serious the allegation of misconduct that is made or the more serious the consequences for the individual which flow from a finding against him or her, the more persuasive (cogent) the evidence will need to be in order to meet that standard.

2.198 Misconduct meeting/hearings should bear in mind the fact that police officers may be required to deal with some people who may have a particular motive for making false or misleading allegations against the police officer.

2.199 Therefore in making a decision whether the alleged conduct of a police officer is found or not, the person(s) conducting the misconduct meeting/hearing will need to exercise reasonable judgement having regard to all the circumstances of the case.

Outcomes of meetings/hearings

2.200 If the person(s) conducting the misconduct meeting/hearing find that the police officer's conduct did fail to meet the Standards of Professional Behaviour, then the person(s) conducting the meeting/hearing will then determine the most appropriate outcome.

2.201 In considering the question of outcome the person(s) conducting the meeting/hearing will need to take into account any previous written warnings (imposed under the Police (Conduct) Regulations 2008 but not Superintendent's warnings issued under the previous procedures) that were live at the time of the initial assessment of the conduct in question, any aggravating or mitigating factors and have regard to the police officer's record of service, including any previous disciplinary outcomes that have not been expunged in accordance with Regulation 15 of the Police Regulations 2003.[5] The person(s) conducting the meeting/hearing may (only if deemed necessary and at the person(s) conducting the meeting/hearings discretion) receive evidence from any witness whose evidence would in their opinion assist them in this regard.

2.202 The person(s) conducting the meeting/hearing are also entitled to take account of any early admission of the conduct on behalf of the police officer concerned and attach whatever weight to this as he, she or they consider appropriate in the circumstances of the case.

2.203 In addition, the police officer concerned and his or her 'police friend' (or where appropriate legal representative) will be given the opportunity to make representations on the question of the most appropriate outcome of the case.

2.204 The appropriate authority also has the opportunity to make representations as to the most appropriate outcome.

Outcomes available at misconduct meetings/hearings

2.205 The person(s) conducting the meeting/hearing may record a finding that the conduct of the police officer concerned amounted to misconduct and take no further action or impose one of the following outcomes:

a) Management advice
The police officer will be told:

- The reason for the advice
- That he or she has a right of appeal and the name of the person to whom the appeal should be sent.

b) Written warning
The police officer will be told:

- The reason for the warning.
- That he or she has a right to appeal and the name of the person to whom the appeal should be sent.
- That the warning will be put on his or her personal file and will remain live for twelve months from the date the warning is given. This means that any misconduct in the next 12 months is likely to lead to (at least) a final written warning.

c) Final written warning
The police officer will be told:

- The reason for the warning.
- That any future misconduct may result in dismissal

---

[5] As amended by the Police (Amendment) Regulations 2008, SI 2008/2865.

- That he or she has a right to appeal and the name of the person to whom the appeal should be sent.
- That the final written warning will be put on his or her personal file and will remain live for eighteen months from the date the warning is given. This means that only in exceptional circumstances will further misconduct (that justifies more than management advice) not result in dismissal. (In exceptional circumstances only, the final written warning may be extended for a further 18 months on one occasion only.)

At a misconduct hearing, in addition to the outcomes available at a), b) and c) above the persons conducting the hearing will also have available the outcomes of:

d) Dismissal with notice

The notice period will be determined by the persons conducting the meeting subject to a minimum of 28 days.

e) Dismissal without notice

Dismissal without notice will mean that the police officer is dismissed from the police service with immediate effect.

2.206 Where the persons conducting a misconduct hearing find that the police officer's conduct amounted to gross misconduct and decide that the police officer should be dismissed from the police service, then that dismissal will be without notice. Where a police officer appears before a misconduct hearing for an alleged act of gross misconduct, and the person(s) conducting the hearing find that the conduct amounts to misconduct rather than gross misconduct, then (unless the police officer already has a live final written warning) the disciplinary outcomes available to the panel are those that are available at a misconduct meeting only.

2.207 Where a case is referred to a misconduct meeting and the police officer concerned has a live written warning[6] and the police officer either admits or is found at the meeting to have committed a further act of misconduct, then the person conducting the misconduct meeting cannot impose another written warning. The person conducting the meeting will need to decide whether to take no action, give management advice or if he or she determines that either type of written warning is appropriate shall impose a final written warning.

2.208 Where a case is referred to a misconduct hearing on the grounds that the police officer concerned has a live final written warning and at the hearing the police officer either admits or is found to have committed a further act of misconduct, then the persons conducting the misconduct hearing cannot impose another written or a final written warning.

2.209 The persons conducting the hearing may give management advice. However if the persons conducting the hearing determine that the misconduct admitted or found should attract a further written or final written warning they will dismiss the police officer unless they are satisfied that there are exceptional circumstances that warrant the police officer concerned remaining in the police service.

2.210 Where the persons conducting the misconduct hearing determine that such exceptional circumstances exist, they will extend the current final written warning that the police officer has for a further 18 months from the date the warning would otherwise expire (so that the original final written warning will last for 36 months in total). An extension to a final written warning can only be given on one occasion. In other words, if a further act of misconduct comes before a misconduct hearing after an extension has been imposed, unless it is sufficiently minor to justify management advice, the police officer will be dismissed.

---

[6] A written warning or final written warning is live if, at the time that the latest allegation of misconduct was assessed—under reg 12 of the Police (Conduct) Regulations 2008, SI 2008/222864, or para 19B of the Police Reform Act 2002—the officer concerned had an outstanding written warning or final written warning that had not expired.

2.211 The exceptional circumstances may include where the misconduct which is subject of the latest hearing pre-dates the misconduct for which the police officer received his or her original final written warning or the misconduct in the latest case is significantly less serious than the conduct that led to the current final written warning being given.

Notification of the outcome

2.212 In all cases the police officer will be informed in writing of the outcome of the misconduct meeting/hearing. This will be done as soon as practicable and in any case within 5 working days beginning with the first working day after the conclusion of the misconduct meeting/hearing.

2.213 The notification in the case of a misconduct meeting will include notification to the police officer concerned of his or her right to appeal against the finding and/or outcome and the name of the person to whom any appeal should be sent.

2.214 In the case of a police officer who has attended a misconduct hearing, the notification will include his or her right of appeal to a Police Appeals Tribunal against any finding and/or outcome imposed.

2.215 In cases involving a complainant, where the complaint was subject of a local or supervised investigation the appropriate authority will be responsible for informing the complainant of the outcome. In cases managed or independently investigated by the IPCC, the IPCC will be responsible for informing the complainant of the outcome.

Expiry of Warnings

2.216 Notification of written warnings issued, including the date issued and expiry date will be recorded on the police officer's personal record, along with a copy of the written notification of the outcome and a summary of the matter.

2.217 Where a police officer has a live written warning and transfers from one force to another, then the live warning will transfer with the police officer and will remain live until the expiry of the warning and should be referred to as part of any reference before the police officer transfers.

2.218 Where a police officer who has a live written warning or final written warning takes a career break in accordance with Police Regulations then any time on such a break will not count towards the 12 months (in the case of a written warning) or 18 months (in the case of a final written warning) or 36 months (in the case of an extended final written warning) that the warning is live.

2.219 For example if a police officer has a written warning that has been live for six months and then goes on a career break for 12 months and then returns to the force, he or she will still have six months before the written warning expires on rejoining the force.

Special Priority Payment/Competency Related Threshold Payment

2.220 A finding or admission of misconduct at a misconduct meeting or hearing will not automatically result in the removal of a police officer's special priority payment or competency related threshold payment. Where a police officer has received a written warning or a final written warning this may trigger a review of the appropriateness of that police officer continuing to receive such payments. However the misconduct is to be considered alongside the other criteria for receiving the payments in reaching a decision as to whether it is appropriate and justified to remove such payments.

Attendance of complainant or interested person at misconduct proceedings

2.221 Where a misconduct meeting/hearing is being held as a direct result of a public complaint, the complainant or interested person will have the right to attend the meeting/hearing as an observer up until the point at which disciplinary action is considered (in addition to attending as a witness if required to do so). This right is subject to the right of the chair or person conducting the proceedings to exclude or impose conditions on the complainant's or interested party's attendance to facilitate the proper conduct of proceedings and to exclude them while evidence is being given, the disclosure of which to them would be contrary to the harm test. He or she may be accompanied by one other person and, if they have a special need, one further person to accommodate that need e.g. an interpreter, sign language expert etc.). The appropriate authority will therefore be responsible for notifying the complainant or interested person of the date, time and place of the misconduct meeting/hearing.

2.222 The misconduct meeting/hearing shall not be delayed solely in order to facilitate a complainant or interested person attending the meeting/hearing, although consideration will need to be given to whether the complainant or interested person is also a witness in the matter.

2.223 The complainant or interested person may at the discretion of the person conducting or chairing the meeting/hearing put questions through the person conducting or chairing the meeting or hearing. [Note: Complainants will not be permitted to put questions to the police officer in a special case hearing. See Annex A]

2. 224 Where the complainant is required to attend a meeting/hearing to give evidence, he or she will not be permitted to be present in the meeting/hearing before giving his or her evidence. Any person accompanying the complainant and/or the person assisting the complainant due to a special need will not be permitted to be present in the meeting/hearing before the complainant has given evidence (if applicable).

2.225 A complainant and any person accompanying the complainant will be permitted to remain in the meeting/hearing up to and including any finding by the person(s) conducting the meeting/hearing, after having given evidence (if appropriate). The complainant and any person accompanying the complainant will not be permitted to remain in the meeting/hearing whilst character references or mitigation are being given or the decision of the panel as to the outcome. However, the appropriate authority will have a duty to inform the complainant of the outcome of any misconduct meeting/hearing whether the complainant attends or not.

2.226 The person(s) conducting a misconduct meeting/hearing will have the discretion to allow a witness (who is not a complainant or interested person) who has attended and given evidence at the meeting/hearing to remain or to ask him or her to leave the proceedings after giving his or her evidence.

IPCC direction and attendance at meetings/hearings

2.227 Where the IPCC exercises its power (under paragraph 27 of Schedule 3 to the 2002 Act) to direct an appropriate authority to hold a misconduct meeting/hearing, this will also include a direction as to whether the proceedings will be a misconduct meeting or hearing. In making such a direction the IPCC will have regard to the severity assessment that has been made in the case and been notified to the police officer concerned.

2.228 Where a misconduct meeting/hearing is to be held following: -

- an investigation managed or independently investigated by the IPCC; or
- a local or supervised investigation where the IPCC has made a recommendation under paragraph 27(3) of Schedule 3 of Police Reform Act 2002 that misconduct proceedings should be taken and the recommendation has been accepted by the appropriate authority; or
- the IPCC has given a direction under paragraph 27(4) of that Schedule that misconduct proceedings shall be taken then the Commission may attend the misconduct meeting/hearing to make representations. Such representations may be an explanation why the IPCC has directed particular misconduct proceedings to be brought or to comment on the investigation.

2.229 Where the Commission is to attend a misconduct hearing, it may instruct a relevant lawyer to represent it.

Right of appeal

2.230 A police officer has a right of appeal against the finding and/or the outcome imposed at a misconduct meeting.

2.231 The appeal is commenced by the police officer concerned giving written notice of appeal to the appropriate authority, clearly setting out the grounds for the appeal within 7 working days beginning with the first working day after the receipt of the notification of the outcome of the misconduct meeting(unless this period is extended by the appropriate authority for exceptional circumstances).

2.232 The police officer has the right to be accompanied by a police friend.

2.233 The police officer concerned may only appeal on the grounds that: -

a) the finding or disciplinary action imposed was unreasonable;
b) there is evidence that could not reasonably have been considered at the misconduct meeting which could have materially affected the finding or decision on disciplinary action; or
c) there was a serious breach of the procedures set out in the regulations or other unfairness which could have materially affected the finding or decision on disciplinary action.

Appeal following misconduct meeting – non senior officers (regulations 38 to 40 of the Conduct Regulations)

2.234 An appeal against the finding and/or the outcome from a misconduct meeting will be heard by a member of the police service of a higher rank or a police staff manager who is considered to be of a higher grade than the person who conducted the misconduct meeting. A police staff manager should not be appointed to conduct the appeal if the case substantially involves operational policing matters.

2. 235 A police officer or police staff member may be present to advise the person conducting the appeal on procedural matters.

2.236 The person determining the appeal will be provided with the following documents: -

a) The notice of appeal from the police officer concerned setting out his or her grounds of appeal.
b) The record of the original misconduct meeting
c) The documents that were given to the person who held the original misconduct meeting.
d) Any evidence that the police officer concerned wishes to submit in support of his or her appeal that was not considered at the misconduct meeting.

2.237 The person appointed to deal with the appeal must first decide whether the notice of appeal sets out arguable grounds of appeal. If he or she determines that there are no arguable grounds then he or she shall dismiss the appeal and inform the police officer concerned accordingly setting out his or her reasons.

2.238 Where the person appointed to hear the appeal determines that there are arguable grounds of appeal and the police officer concerned has requested to be present at the appeal meeting, the person appointed to conduct the proceedings will hold a meeting with the police officer concerned. Where the police officer fails to attend the meeting, the person conducting the appeal may proceed in the absence of the police officer concerned.

2.239 The person conducting the appeal may consider:

• Whether the finding of the original misconduct meeting was unreasonable having regard to all the evidence considered or if the finding could now be in doubt due to evidence which has emerged since the meeting.
• Any outcome imposed by the misconduct meeting which may be considered as too severe or too lenient having regard to all the circumstances of the case.

- Whether the finding or outcome could be unsafe due to procedural unfairness and prejudice to the police officer (although the person conducting the appeal must also take into account whether the unfairness or prejudice could have materially influenced the outcome).

2.240 The person determining the appeal may confirm or reverse the decision appealed against. Where the person determining the appeal decides that the original disciplinary action imposed was too lenient then he or she may increase the outcome up to a maximum of a final written warning.

2.241 An appeal is not a repeat of the misconduct meeting. It is to examine a particular part(s) of the misconduct case which is under question and which may affect the finding or the outcome.

2.242 The appeal will normally be heard within 5 working days beginning with the working day after the determination that the officer concerned has arguable grounds of appeal. If the police officer concerned or his or her police friend is not available at the date or time specified by the person conducting the appeal, the police officer may propose an alternative time. Provided that the alternative time is reasonable and falls within a period of 5 working days beginning with the first working day after that proposed by the person conducting the appeal the appeal must be postponed to that time. Similarly, the officer concerned can object to the person appointed to conduct the appeal in the same way as he or she could for the original misconduct meeting.

Appeal following misconduct hearing – non senior officers

2.243 Where a police officer has appeared before a misconduct hearing then any appeal against the finding or outcome is to the Police Appeals Tribunal (see Annex C). The police officer should be informed that the Police Appeals Tribunal can increase any outcome imposed as well as reduce or overturn the decision of the misconduct hearing or special case hearing.

Appeals against misconduct meetings/hearings – senior officers

2. 244 Senior officers have the right to appeal against the finding and/or outcome of a misconduct meeting or hearing. The appeal in both cases will be made to the Police Appeals Tribunal. The police officer should be informed that the Police Appeal Tribunal can increase any outcome imposed as well as reduce or overturn the decision of the misconduct hearing or special case hearing.

CHAPTER 3
GUIDANCE ON UNSATISFACTORY PERFORMANCE AND
ATTENDANCE PROCEDURES (UPPs)

1. General

Introduction

1.1 The formal procedures to deal with unsatisfactory performance and attendance are set out in the Police (Performance) Regulations 2008 and are referred to in this guidance as UPPs.

1.2 The purpose of this guidance is to help managers to decide how and when to use the formal procedures in the Police (Performance) Regulations 2008 to manage unsatisfactory performance or unsatisfactory attendance on the part of police officers. Guidance focussing specifically on attendance management can be found at Paragraph 3.1.

1.3 The underlying principle of the procedures is to provide a fair, open and proportionate method of dealing with performance and attendance issues and to encourage a culture of learning and development for individuals and the organisation.

1.4 The procedures in the Police (Performance) Regulations 2008 are largely the same whether applied to unsatisfactory performance or attendance (the differences that do exist are set out clearly in this guidance). However the issues that arise in attendance cases may be different from those in performance cases. This guidance therefore contains separate sections dealing with performance and attendance before a section on the procedures. Where reference is made to time periods (e.g. 3 working days) this will begin on the first working day following the day on which the particular action has taken place.

1.5 The primary aim of the procedures is to improve poor performance and attendance in the police service. It is envisaged that early intervention via management action should achieve the desired effect of improving and maintaining a police officer's performance or attendance to an acceptable level.

1.6 There will, however, be cases where it will be appropriate for managers to take formal action under the procedures. At the conclusion of proceedings under the Regulations, one possible outcome is that a police officer's service may be terminated.

1.7 The UPPs have been prepared by the Home Office in consultation with the Association of Chief Police Officers (ACPO), the Police Federation of England and Wales (PFEW), the Police Superintendents' Association of England and Wales (PSAEW), the Chief Police Officers Staff Association (CPOSA), the Association of Police Authorities (APA), Her Majesty's Inspectorate of Constabulary (HMIC), the Independent Police Complaints Commission (IPCC) and the National Policing Improvement Agency (NPIA).

Scope

1.8 The procedures apply to police officers up to and including the rank of chief superintendent.

1.9 The procedures apply to all special constables. However, given the nature of special constables as unpaid volunteers, cases where the procedures are initiated for special constables may be limited to those where the special constable either contests that his or her performance or attendance is unsatisfactory or agrees that it is unsatisfactory but expresses a desire to continue with his or her special constable duties. In other cases the special constable may choose to resign from his or her role as a special constable. In setting meeting dates and establishing panels, regard should be had to the nature of special constables as volunteers who may have other work or personal commitments.

1.10 The procedures do not apply to student police officers during their probationary period. The procedures governing performance and attendance issues in respect of police students are determined locally by each force. These procedures are underpinned by regulation 13 of the Police Regulations 2003.

Principles

1.11 Performance and attendance management in the police service are intended to be positive and supportive processes, with the aim being to improve performance or attendance.

1.12 All unsatisfactory performance and attendance matters should be handled in a timely manner while maintaining confidence in the process. UPPs should be applied fairly in both a non-discriminatory and non-adversarial way and matters must be handled in the strictest confidence.

1.13 Where the UPPs are used, line managers in the police service and others involved in the process must act in a way which an objective observer would consider reasonable. At all times, the requirements of the Police (Performance) Regulations 2008 must be complied with.

1.14 The importance of challenging unsatisfactory performance or attendance of individual police officers in the context of overall unit/ force performance and the police officer's personal development should not be underestimated. Dealing sensitively and appropriately with unsatisfactory performance or attendance issues does not constitute bullying. If a police officer believes that he or she is being unfairly treated, he or she may have available the avenues of appeal that exist at each stage of the UPPs.

1.15 A police officer may seek legal advice at any time although legal representation is confined to third stage meetings where the procedure has been initiated at this stage (see paragraph 7.8 on "gross incompetence"). Police officers other than special constables can seek advice from their staff association and all police officers can be advised and represented by their police friend in accordance with the principles described in the introduction section of the guidance.

1.16 In deciding matters of fact the person(s) conducting the UPP meeting must apply the standard of proof required in civil cases, that is, the balance of probabilities. Unsatisfactory performance or attendance will be proved on the balance of probabilities if the person(s) conducting the meeting is/are satisfied by the evidence that it is more likely than not that the performance or attendance of the police officer is unsatisfactory. The more serious the allegation of poor performance that is made or the more serious the consequences for the individual which flow from a finding against him or her, the more persuasive (cogent) the evidence will need to be in order to meet that standard.

Ongoing performance assessment and review

1.17 Every police officer should have some form of performance appraisal, or what is commonly referred to as a "performance and development review" (PDR). The PDR should be the principal method by which the police officer's performance and attendance is monitored and assessed. It is the responsibility of the line manager to set objectives for his or her staff and it is the responsibility of all police officers, with appropriate support from management, to ensure that they both understand and meet those objectives. Objectives set by the line manager should be specific, measurable, achievable, relevant and time-related (SMART).

1.18 The activities and behaviours expected of a police officer in order to achieve his or her objectives should be in accordance with the relevant national framework which will form the basis of the police officer's role profile.

1.19 Any shortfall in performance or attendance should be pointed out at the earliest opportunity by the line manager and consideration given as to whether this is due to inadequate instruction, training, supervision or some other reason.

1.20 For national guidance on PDR implementation and improvement see:

   http://www.skillsforjustice.com/websitefiles/PDRguide.pdf

Sources of information

1.21 Unsatisfactory performance or attendance will often be identified by the immediate line manager of the police officer as part of his or her normal management responsibilities.

1.22 Where the police officer currently works to a manager who has no line management responsibility for him or her, it is the responsibility of that manager to inform the police officer's line manager of any performance or attendance issues he or she has identified.

1.23 Line managers may be police officers or police staff members.

1.24 It is also possible that line managers may be alerted to unsatisfactory performance or attendance on the part of one of their police officers as a result of information from a member of the public. The information from a member of the public may take the form of a formal complaint. Such cases must be dealt with in accordance with the established procedures for the handling of complaints.[7] Appropriate use of the Local Resolution procedure offers an opportunity to deal speedily with a complainant's concerns and to address any performance issues.

1.25 It may be that the outcome of an investigation into a complaint alleging misconduct is that an issue of unsatisfactory performance or attendance has been identified involving one or more police officers. In such cases the outcome of the investigation may be that the appropriate authority will determine that there is no case to answer in respect of misconduct or gross misconduct but it may be appropriate to take action under the UPPs in order that the police officer may learn and improve his or her performance or attendance.

1.26 A single complaint from a member of the public about a police officer's performance will not normally trigger the UPPs, which are designed to deal with a pattern of unsatisfactory performance (except where there is a single incident of gross incompetence). However, where the complaint adds to existing indications of unsatisfactory performance, it may be appropriate to initiate the UPPs or, if the police officer is already subject to these, to continue to the next stage of the process.

1.27 Whilst the unsatisfactory performance and attendance procedures are internal management procedures, it may be necessary at times to inform public complainants of action taken with respect to the police officer to whom the complaint relates. In explaining the outcome of a complaint a force may inform the complainant that the police officer may be subject to the statutory procedures for improving his or her performance.

Management action

1.28 Managers are expected to deal with unsatisfactory performance or attendance issues in the light of their knowledge of the individual and the circumstances giving rise to these concerns.

1.29 There are, however, some generally well understood principles which should apply in such circumstances:

(a) the line manager must discuss any shortcoming (s) or concern (s) with the individual at the earliest possible opportunity. It would be quite wrong for the line manager to accumulate a list of concerns about the performance or attendance of an individual and delay telling him or her about them until the occasion of the police officer's annual or mid-term PDR meetings;

(b) the reason for dissatisfaction must be made clear to the individual as soon as possible and there must be a factual basis for discussing the issues i.e. the discussion must relate to specific incidents or omissions that have occurred;

(c) line managers should seek to establish whether there are any underlying reasons for the unsatisfactory performance or attendance . For example, in the context of performance, a failure to perform a task correctly may be because the individual was never told how to do it or was

---

[7] Available online at <http://statguidance.ipcc.gov.uk>.

affected by personal circumstances. In that case it may be appropriate for the line manager to arrange further instruction or guidance;

(d) consideration should be given as to whether there is any health or welfare issue that is or may be affecting performance or attendance. If a police officer has or may have a disability within the scope of the Disability Discrimination Act this in particular needs to be taken fully into account and the requirements of that legislation complied with;

(e) in cases where the difficulty appears to stem from a personality clash with a colleague or line manager, or where for other reasons a change of duties might be appropriate, the police officer's line management may, in consultation with the appropriate HR adviser, consider re-deployment if this provides an opportunity for the police officer to improve his or her performance or attendance. Where a police officer is re-deployed in this way, the police officer and his or her new line management should be informed of the reasons for the move and of the assessment of his or her performance or attendance in the previous role;

(f) the line manager must make it clear to the police officer that he or she is available to give further advice and guidance if needed;

(g) depending on the circumstances, it may be appropriate to indicate to the police officer that if there is no, or insufficient, improvement, then the matter will be dealt with under the UPPs;

(h) line managers are expected to gather relevant evidence and keep a contemporaneous note of interactions with the police officer;

(i) challenging unsatisfactory performance or attendance in an appropriate manner does not constitute bullying. In considering whether action constitutes bullying, forces should have regard to their local policy on bullying.

1.30 The principles outlined above cover the position when a line manager first becomes aware of some unsatisfactory aspect(s) of the police officer's performance or attendance and is dealing with the issue as an integral part of normal line management responsibilities.

1.31 Management action taken as a result of identifying unsatisfactory performance or attendance should be put on record which may be the police officer's PDR. In particular, the line manager should record the nature of the performance or attendance issue; the advice given and steps taken to address the problems identified. Placing matters on record is important to ensure continuity in circumstances where one or more members of the management chain may move on to other duties or the police officer concerned moves to new duties. It is also important to put on record when improvement has been made in his or her performance or attendance.

1.32 Ideally, as a result of management action, performance or attendance will improve and continue to an acceptable level.

1.33 Where there is no improvement, insufficient improvement, or the improvement is not sustained over a reasonable period of time (preferably agreed between the line manager and the police officer), it will then be appropriate to use the UPPs.

1.34 The period of time agreed or determined by the line manager for the police officer concerned to improve his or her performance or attendance prior to using the UPPs must be sufficient to provide a reasonable opportunity for the desired improvement or attendance to take place and must be time limited.

1.35 This period may be extended if, due to some unforeseen circumstance (e.g. certified sickness absence in the context of performance issues) the police officer is unable to demonstrate whether or not the required improvement has been achieved.

2. Performance Issues

Introduction

2.1 The performance of individual police officers is a key element in the delivery of a quality policing service. Police officers should know what standard of performance is required of them and be given appropriate support to attain that standard.

2.2 Performance management is an integral part of a line manager's responsibilities. Managers should let a police officer know when he or she is doing well or, if the circumstances arise, when there are the first signs that there is a need for improvement in his or her performance. An essential part of effective line management is that managers should be aware of the contribution being made to meeting the aims and objectives of the team by each of the individuals they manage.

"Unsatisfactory performance"

2.3 Unsatisfactory performance (or attendance) is defined in Regulation 4 of the Police (Performance) Regulations 2008 as:

> "an inability or failure of a police officer to perform the duties of the role or rank he [or she] is currently undertaking to a satisfactory standard or level."

Framework for action

2.4 There is no single formula for determining the point at which a concern about a police officer's performance should lead to formal procedures under the Police (Performance) Regulations being taken. Each case must be considered on its merits. However the following points need to be emphasised:

- the intention of performance management including formal action under the Police (Performance) Regulations is to improve performance;
- occasional lapses below acceptable standards should be dealt with in the course of normal management activity and should not involve the application of the UPPs, which are designed to cover either repeated failures to meet such standards or more serious cases of unsatisfactory performance ;
- managers should be able to demonstrate that they have considered whether management action is appropriate before using the UPPs.

3. Attendance Issues

Introduction

3.1 This part of the guidance should be read in conjunction with the guidance on developing attendance management policies (see chapter 4). All forces are required to have an attendance management policy in place. Failure to do so or to adhere to the terms of that policy could be taken into account under these procedures.

3.2 The Police Service is committed to providing, as far as is reasonably practicable, a healthy and safe working environment for its police officers. It recognises that the health and welfare of police officers is a key element in the delivery of quality services, as well as in maintaining career satisfaction and staff morale.

3.3 The key objective of attendance management policies within forces and the appropriate use of the Police (Performance) Regulations 2008 insofar as they relate to managing unsatisfactory attendance, is to encourage an attendance culture within forces.

3.4 Managing sickness absence is vitally important both in terms of demonstrating a supportive attitude towards police officers and for the efficiency of the organisation. Managing attendance is about creating a culture where all parties take ownership of the policy and act reasonably in the operation of the scheme with managers being proactive in managing sickness.

3.5 The primary aim of the procedures is to improve attendance in the police service. It is envisaged that supportive action will in most cases achieve the desired effect of improving and maintaining a police officer's attendance to an acceptable level.

3.6 There may however be cases where it will be appropriate for managers to take formal action under the Performance Regulations. At the conclusion of procedures under the Regulations, termination of service is a possible outcome.

3.7 Where the UPPs are used in relation to attendance matters, such matters will normally relate to periods of sickness absence such that the ability of the police officer to perform his or her duties is compromised.

3.8 Other forms of absence not related to genuine sickness would normally be dealt with under the misconduct procedures e.g. where a police officer's absence is unauthorised.

Framework for action

3.9 Attendance management in the police service is intended to be a positive and supportive process to improve attendance. In all cases, the starting point is supportive action. Except where a police officer fails to co-operate, appropriate supportive action must be taken before formal action is taken under the Performance Regulations. A failure by a police officer to co-operate will not prevent formal action being taken or continued.

3.10 If supportive action is taken, the police officer co-operates and the attendance improves and is maintained at a satisfactory level, then there will be no need to take formal action under the Performance Regulations.

3.11 There is no single formula for determining the point at which concern about a police officer's attendance should lead to formal procedures under the Performance Regulations being invoked. Each case must be considered on its merits. However the following points need to be emphasised:

- The intention of attendance management including formal action under the Police (Performance) Regulations is to improve attendance.
- Where police officers are injured or ill they should be treated fairly and compassionately.
- Managers should be able to demonstrate that they have acted reasonably in all actions taken at all stages of the attendance management process, including any action under the Police (Performance) Regulations.
- In cases where a decision is made at a third stage meeting to impose an outcome, including dismissal from the service, then in most cases the police officer will have the right to appeal to a police appeals tribunal.

Monitoring attendance

3.12 All forces must ensure that arrangements are in place for the effective monitoring of sickness absences (and the reasons for them).

3.13 It is the responsibility of line managers, in conjunction with the force's Human Resources (HR) department if necessary, to monitor a police officer's attendance. A formal record of a police officer's period of illness will be kept in accordance with Regulation 15 of The Police Regulations 2003.

3.14 HR managers should be consulted when line managers are deciding whether it might be appropriate to use the UPPs in relation to unsatisfactory attendance.

Occupational health

3.15 The force Occupational Health Service is an essential part of effective attendance management and should be involved as soon as any concerns about a police officer's attendance are identified.

3.16 Where action is taken under the UPPs in respect of a police officer's attendance, the police officer may be referred to the Occupational Health Service for up to date information and advice at any stage within the procedure in accordance with force policy. This should enable the force to make an informed decision about a police officer's attendance. Where police officers do not attend appointments or otherwise fail to co-operate with the force's Occupational Health Service, an assessment will be made on the information available.

3.17 The role of the Force's Occupational Health Service is to advise on medical issues affecting a police officer's performance and attendance. Where the force has concerns about a police officer's health and the effect it has on his or her work and attendance, it may decide to seek medical advice on a range of issues, including but not limited to:

(i) the nature and extent of the police officer's medical problems;

(ii) when the medical problem is likely to be resolved;

(iii) whether the police officer will be fit to carry out his/her duties on his or her return to work;

(iv) the duties that the police officer may be fit to undertake;

(v) whether the police officer is a disabled person within the meaning of the Disability Discrimination Act;

(vi) whether there are any adjustments or adaptations to the work, equipment or workplace that might assist in improving attendance;

(vii) the likelihood of the illness recurring or of some other illness emerging;

(viii) any concerns raised by the police officer about their health and/or working environment;

(ix) whether the police officer may be permanently disabled.

Disability Discrimination Act 1995 (as amended) (DDA) and other statutory obligations

3.18 In any unsatisfactory attendance case it is essential that managers and the force ensure compliance with their obligations under the Disability Discrimination Act. (See Home Office circular 063/2003):

http://www.knowledgenetwork.gov.uk/HO/circular.nsf/1cc4f3413a62d1de80256c5b0051 01e4/5bab74ebdf5db31880256dff00575887?OpenDocument

3.19 Compliance with other statutory obligations including the Data Protection Act 1998 must also be ensured.

Action under the Police (Performance) Regulations 2008

3.20 Formal action under the Performance Regulations may be taken in cases of both unacceptable levels of persistent short-term absences and long-term absences due to sickness and/or injury. It should however be noted that it is not possible to be prescriptive about all circumstances where action under the Regulations may be appropriate.

3.21 In deciding whether to take action under the procedures managers must treat each case on its merits and consider all of the pertinent facts available to them, including:

(i) the nature of the illness, injury or condition

(ii) the likelihood of the illness, injury or condition (or some other related illness, injury or condition) recurring;

(iii) the pattern and length of absence(s) and the period of good health between them;

(iv) the need for the work to be done i.e. what impact on the force's performance and workload is the absence having;

(v) the extent to which a police officer has co-operated with supportive management action;

(vi) whether the police officer was made aware, in the earlier supportive action, that unless an improvement was made, action under the Performance Regulations might be used;

(vii) whether the selected medical practitioner (SMP) has been asked by the Police Authority to consider the issue of permanent disablement and/or the Police Authority is considering medical retirement;

(viii) the impact of the Disability Discrimination Act.

3.22 Action under the Police (Performance) Regulations 2008 should not normally be invoked unless:

(i) earlier supportive action was offered but the police officer either declined it or failed to co-operate and as a result there has not been the necessary improvement in the police officer's performance or attendance; and/or

(ii) the police officer is absent due to long-term sickness and, notwithstanding supportive management action having been taken, there is no realistic prospect of return to work in a reasonable timeframe.

3.23 Whether it is appropriate to take formal action in any particular case will depend on the known merits and facts of that case.

4. The UPP Process

Stages

4.1 There are potentially three stages to the UPPs, each of which involves a different meeting composition and possible outcomes.

4.2 A line manager can ask a HR professional or police officer (who should have experience of UPPs and be independent of the line management chain) to attend a UPP meeting to advise him or her on the proceedings at the first stage meeting. A line manager may also obtain such advice prior to a first stage meeting if he or she is in any doubt about the process. The second line manager may also have an advisor (as above) in respect of the second stage meeting. For stage three meetings, an HR professional, police officer, counsel or solicitor may attend the meeting to advise the panel on the proceedings.

Improvement notices and action plans

4.3 At the first and second stages, if it is found that the police officer's performance or attendance is unsatisfactory, an improvement notice will be issued. Improvement notices require a police officer to improve on his or her performance or attendance and must state:

- in what respect the police officer's performance or attendance is considered unsatisfactory;
- the improvement in performance or attendance required to bring the police officer to an acceptable standard;
- a "specified period" (see paragraph 4.5, below) within which improvement is expected to be made; and
- the "validity period" (see paragraph 4.6, below) of the written improvement notice.

4.4 The improvement notice should also inform the police officer of the possible consequences if improvement is not made or maintained within the period specified by the appropriate manager or panel (as applicable) or within the 12 month validity period, i.e. that he or she may be required to attend the next stage of the procedures.

4.5 The "specified period" of an improvement notice is a period specified by the manager conducting the meeting (having considered any representations made by or on behalf of the police officer) within which the police officer must improve his or her performance or attendance. It is expected that the specified period for improvement would not normally exceed 3 months. However, depending on the nature and circumstances of the matter, it may be appropriate to specify a longer or shorter period for improvement (but which should not exceed 12 months).

4.6 The "validity period" of an improvement notice describes the period of 12 months from the date of the notice within which performance or attendance must be maintained (assuming improvement is made during the specified period). If the improvement is not maintained within this period then the next stage of the procedures may be used (see also paragraph 4.12).

4.7 Improvement notices must be accompanied by the written record of the meeting and a notice informing the police officer of his or her right to appeal against the finding or terms of the improvement notice (or both of these). Following a second stage meeting, that documentation must also inform the police officer of his or her right to appeal against the decision to require him or her to attend the meeting. Any such appeal can only be made on the ground that the meeting did not concern unsatisfactory performance or attendance which was similar to or connected with that referred to in the written improvement notice.

4.8 Written improvement notices must be signed and dated by the person responsible for issuing the notice e.g. in the case of an improvement notice issued following a second stage meeting, by the second line manager.

4.9 An improvement notice would normally be followed by an action plan. An action plan describes what action(s) the police officer should take which should help him or her achieve and maintain the improvement required and would normally be formulated and agreed by both the police officer (and his or her police friend if desired) and his or her line manager. In particular, the action plan should:

• identify any weaknesses which may be the cause of unsatisfactory performance or attendance;
• describe what steps the police officer must take to improve performance and/or attendance and what support is available from the organisation e.g. training and support;
• specify a period within which actions identified should be followed up; and
• set a date (s) for a staged review (s) of the police officer's performance or attendance.

Improvement notice extensions and suspensions

4.10 On the application of the police officer or otherwise (e.g. on the application of his or her line manager), the appropriate authority may extend the "specified" period if it considers it appropriate to do so. This provision is intended to deal with situations that were not foreseen at the time of the issue of the improvement notice. For example, where the police officer has not had sufficient time to improve due to an emergency deployment to other duties.

4.11 In setting an extension to the specified period, consideration should be given to any known periods of extended absence from the police officer's normal role e.g. if the police officer is going to be on long periods of pre-planned holiday leave, study leave, or is due to undergo an operation. The extension should not lead to the improvement period exceeding 12 months unless the appropriate authority is satisfied that there are exceptional circumstances making this appropriate. These circumstances should be recorded.

4.12 The period for improvement under an improvement notice and the validity period of an improvement notice do not include any time that the police officer is taking a career break. For example, if a police officer is issued with an improvement notice with a specified period of 3 months and then takes career leave two months into the notice, whenever the police officer returns, he or she will have one month left of the 3 month specified period and ten months of the validity period of the notice.

Initiation of procedures at stage three

4.13 In very limited circumstances, explained in more detail in paragraph 7.8, it is possible to commence the UPPs at the third stage. This is to allow for cases of a degree of severity such that initiation at this stage is the only appropriate option.

4.14 In these cases only the police officer is entitled to choose to be legally represented by counsel or a solicitor.

Multiple instances of unsatisfactory performance

4.15 A police officer can move to a later stage of the UPPs only in relation to unsatisfactory performance or attendance that is similar to or connected with the unsatisfactory performance or attendance referred to in any previous written improvement notice. Where failings relate to different forms of unsatisfactory performance or attendance it will be necessary to commence the UPPs at the first stage (unless the failing constitutes gross incompetence). If more than one UPP is commenced, then, given that the procedures will relate to different failings and will have been identified at different times, the finding and outcome of each should be without prejudice to the other(s).

4.16 However, there may be circumstances where procedures have been initiated for a particular failing and an additional failing comes to light prior to the first stage meeting. In such circumstances it is possible to consolidate the two issues at the first stage meeting provided that there is sufficient time prior to the meeting to comply with the notification requirements explained in more detail below. If this is not possible, the first stage meeting should either be rearranged to a date which allows the requirements to be met or a separate first stage meeting should be held in relation to the additional matter.

5. The First Stage

Preparation and purpose

5.1 Having considered the use of management action (see paragraph 1.28), where a line manager considers that a police officer's performance or attendance is unsatisfactory and decides that the UPPs are the most appropriate way of addressing the matter(s), he or she will notify the police officer in writing that he or she is required to attend a first stage meeting and include in that notification the following details:

- details of the procedures for determining the date and time of the meeting (see paragraph 5.7);
- a summary of the reasons why the line manager considers the police officer's performance or attendance unsatisfactory;
- the possible outcomes of a first stage, second stage and third stage meeting;
- that a human resources professional or a police officer (who should have experience of UPPs and be independent from the line management chain) may attend the meeting to advise the line manager on the proceedings;
- that if the police officer agrees, any other person specified in the notice may attend the meeting;
- that prior to the meeting the police officer must provide the line manager with any documentation he or she intends to rely on in the meeting; and,
- the police officer's rights i.e. his or her right to seek advice from a representative of his or her staff association (in the case of a member of the police force) and to be accompanied and represented at the meeting by a police friend.

5.2 The notice shall be accompanied by copies of related documentation relied upon by the line manager in support of the view that the police officer's performance or attendance is unsatisfactory.

5.3 In advance of the meeting, the police officer shall provide the line manager with any documents on which he or she intends to rely in support of his or her case.

5.4 Any document or other material that was not submitted in advance of the meeting may be considered at the meeting at the discretion of the line manager. The purpose of allowing this discretion is to ensure fairness to all parties. However the presumption should be that such documents or material will not be permitted unless it can be shown that they were not previously available to be submitted in advance. Where such a document or other material is permitted to be considered, a short adjournment may be necessary to enable the line manager or the police officer, as the case may be, to read or consider the document or other material and consider its implications. The length of the adjournment will depend upon the case. A longer adjournment may be necessary if the material in question is complex.

5.5 The purpose of the meeting is to hear the evidence of the unsatisfactory performance or attendance and to give the police officer the opportunity to put forward his or her views. It will also be an opportunity to hear of any factors that are affecting the police officer's performance or attendance and what the police officer considers can be done to address them.

5.6 The line manager should explain that there are potentially three stages to the procedures and that the maximum outcome of a stage one meeting is an improvement notice and the maximum outcome of a stage two meeting is a final improvement notice. The line manager will also explain that if the procedure is followed to the final stage, dismissal, a reduction in rank (in the case of a member of a police force and in performance cases only), redeployment to alternative duties or an extended improvement notice (in exceptional circumstances) are possible outcomes.

5.7 Wherever possible, the meeting date and time should be agreed between the line manager and the police officer. However, where agreement cannot be reached the line manager must specify a time and date. If the police officer or his or her police friend is not available at the date or time specified by the line manager, the police officer may propose an alternative time. Provided that the alternative time is reasonable and falls within a period of 5 working days beginning with the first working day after that specified by the line manager, the meeting must be postponed to that time.

5.8 Once the date for the meeting is fixed, the line manager should send to the police officer a notice in writing of the date, time and place of the first stage meeting.

At the First Stage meeting

5.9 At the first stage meeting the line manager will:

(a) explain to the police officer the reasons why the line manager considers that the performance or attendance of the police officer is unsatisfactory;
(b) provide the police officer with the opportunity to make representations in response;
(c) provide his or her police friend (if he or she has one) with an opportunity to make representations (see Role of Police Friend);
(d) listen to what the police officer (and/or his or her police friend) has to say, ask questions and comment as appropriate.

5.10 The line manager may adjourn the meeting at any time if he or she considers it is necessary or expedient to do so. An adjournment may be appropriate where information which needs to be checked by the line manager emerges during the course of the meeting or the manager decides that he or she wishes to adjourn the meeting whilst he or she makes a decision.

5.11 Where the line manager finds that the performance or attendance of the police officer has been satisfactory during the period in question, he or she will inform the police officer that no further action will be taken.

5.12 Where having considered any representations by either the police officer and/ or his or her police friend, the line manager finds that the performance or attendance of the police officer has been unsatisfactory he or she shall:

(a) inform the police officer in what respect (s) his or her performance or attendance is considered unsatisfactory;
(b) inform him or her of the improvement that is required in his or her performance or attendance;
(c) inform the police officer that, if a sufficient improvement is not made within the period specified by the line manager, he or she may be required to attend a second stage meeting.
(d) inform the police officer that he or she will receive a written improvement notice.
(e) inform the police officer that if the sufficient improvement in his or her performance or attendance is not maintained during the validity period of such notice he or she may be required to attend a second stage meeting.

5.13 It is expected that the specified period for improvement would not normally exceed 3 months. However, depending on the nature and circumstances of the matter, it may be appropriate to specify a longer or shorter period for improvement (but which should not exceed 12 months).In determining the specified period of an improvement notice, consideration should also be given to any periods of known extended absence from the police officer's normal role.

Procedure following the First Stage meeting

5.14 As soon as reasonably practicable, following the meeting, the line manager shall cause to be prepared a written record of the meeting and, where he or she found at the meeting that the performance or attendance of the police officer was unsatisfactory, a written improvement notice. The written record and any improvement notice shall be sent to the officer as soon as reasonably practicable after they have been prepared. The written record supplied to the police officer should comprise a summary of the proceedings at that meeting.

5.15 Any written improvement notice must set out the information conveyed to the police officer in paragraph 5.12, state the period for which it is valid and be signed and dated by the line manager. Any improvement notice must be accompanied by a notice informing the police officer of his or her right to appeal and the name of the person to whom the appeal should be sent. The notice must also inform the police officer of his or her right to submit written comments on the written record of the meeting and of the procedure for doing so.

5.16 The police officer may submit written comments on the written record not later than the end of 7 working days after the date that he or she received it (unless an extension has been granted by the line manager following an application by the police officer). Any written comments provided by the police officer should be retained with the note. However, if the police officer has exercised his or her right to appeal against the finding or outcome of the first stage meeting, the police officer may not submit comments on the written record.

5.17 It is the responsibility of the line manager to ensure that the written record, written improvement notice and any written comments of the police officer regarding the written record are retained together and filed in accordance with force policies.

5.18 Normally it will be appropriate to agree an action plan (see paragraph 4.9) setting out the actions which should assist the police officer to perform his or her duties to an acceptable standard. This may be agreed at the UPP meeting or at a later time specified by the line manager. It is expected that the police officer will co-operate with implementation of the action plan and take responsibility for his or her own development or improvement. Equally, the police officer's managers must ensure that any actions to support the police officer to improve are implemented.

Assessment of Performance or Attendance

5.19 It is expected that the police officer's performance or attendance will be actively monitored against the improvement notice and, where applicable, the action plan by the line manager throughout the specified period of the improvement notice. The line manager should discuss with the police officer any concerns that the line manager has during this period as regards his or her performance or attendance and offer advice and guidance where appropriate.

5.20 As soon as reasonably practicable after the specified period of the improvement notice comes to an end, the line manager, in consultation with the second line manager or an HR professional (or both), must formally assess the performance or attendance of the police officer during that period.

5.21 If the line manager considers that the police officer's performance or attendance is satisfactory, the line manager should notify the police officer in writing of this. The notification should also inform the police officer that whilst the performance or attendance of the police officer is now satisfactory, the improvement notice is valid for a period of 12 months from the date printed on the notice so that it is possible for the second stage of the procedures to be initiated if the performance or attendance of the police officer falls below an acceptable level within the remaining period.

5.22 If the line manager considers that the police officer's performance or attendance is still unsatisfactory, the line manager should notify the police officer in writing of this. The line manager must also notify the police officer that he or she is required to attend a second stage meeting to consider these ongoing performance or attendance issues.

5.23 If the police officer has improved his or her performance or attendance to an acceptable standard within the specified improvement period, but then fails to maintain that standard within the 12 month validity period, it is open to the line manager to initiate stage two of the procedures.

5.24 In such circumstances the line manager must notify the police officer in writing of his or her view that the police officer's performance or attendance is unsatisfactory as the police officer has failed to maintain the improvement and that as a consequence the police officer is required to attend a second stage meeting to discuss his or her failure to maintain a satisfactory standard of performance or attendance.

5.25 Where an officer is required to attend a second stage meeting and at that meeting it is found that the officer has improved, he or she can still be required to attend another second stage meeting if he or she does not maintain his or her improvement within the 12 months that the improvement notice is valid.

First Stage appeals

5.26 A police officer has a right of appeal against the finding and the terms of the improvement notice imposed at stage one of the UPPs. However, any finding and outcome of this first stage meeting will continue to apply up to the date that the appeal is determined. Therefore where the police officer contests the finding or outcome, he or she should continue to follow the terms of the improvement notice and any accompanying action plan pending the determination of the appeal.

5.27 Any appeal should be made in writing to the second line manager within 7 working days following the day of the receipt of the improvement notice and written record of the meeting (unless the period is extended by the second line manager following an application by the police officer). The notice of appeal must clearly set out the grounds and evidence for the appeal.

Appeal grounds

5.28 The grounds for appeal are:

- that the finding of unsatisfactory performance or attendance is unreasonable;
- that any of the terms of the improvement notice are unreasonable;
- that there is evidence that could not reasonably have been considered at the first stage meeting which could have materially affected the finding of unsatisfactory performance or attendance or any of the terms of the written improvement notice;
- that there was a breach of the procedures set out in the Police (Performance) Regulations or other unfairness which could have materially affected the finding of unsatisfactory performance or attendance or the terms of the improvement notice.

5.29 On the basis of the above grounds of appeal, the police officer may appeal against the finding of unsatisfactory performance or attendance or the terms of the written improvement notice, those being:

- the respect in which the police officer's performance or attendance is considered unsatisfactory;
- the improvement which is required of the police officer; and/ or
- the length of the period specified for improvement by the line manager at the first stage meeting.

5.30 The police officer has the right to be accompanied and represented by a police friend at the first stage appeal meeting.

5.31 Wherever possible, the meeting date and time should be agreed between the second line manager and the police officer. However, where agreement cannot be reached the second line manager must specify a time and date. If the police officer or his or her police friend is not available at the date or time specified by the second line manager, the police officer may propose an alternative time. Provided that the alternative time is reasonable and falls within a period of 5 working days beginning with the first working day after that specified by the second line manager, the meeting must be postponed to that time.

5.32 Once a date for the meeting is fixed, the second line manager should send to the police officer a notice in writing of the date, time and place of the first stage appeal meeting together with the information required to be provided under Regulation 17 of the Performance Regulations.

At the first stage appeal meeting

5.33 At this meeting the second line manager will:

- provide the police officer with the opportunity to make representations;
- provide his or her police friend (if he or she has one) with an opportunity to make representations (see Role of Police Friend).

222

5.34 Having considered any representations by either the police officer and/ or his or her police friend, the second line manager may:

- confirm or reverse the finding of unsatisfactory performance or attendance;
- endorse or vary the terms of the improvement notice appealed against.

5.35 The second line manager may deal with the police officer in any manner in which the line manager could have dealt with him or her at the first stage meeting. Where the second line manager has reversed the finding of unsatisfactory performance or attendance he or she must also revoke the written improvement notice.

5.36 Within 3 working days of the day following the conclusion of the appeal meeting, the police officer will be given written notice of the second line manager's decision. If the second line manager is in a position to send a written summary of the reasons for that decision, then this may also accompany the written notice of the decision.

5.37 However, where the second line manager sends only the written notice of the decision to the police officer, as soon as reasonably practicable after the conclusion of the meeting, he or she will send a written summary of reasons for that decision.

5.38 Any decision made that changes the finding or outcome of the first stage meeting will take effect by way of substitution for the finding or terms appealed against and as from the date of the first stage meeting.

6. The second stage

Preparation and purpose

6.1 Initiation of the second stage must be for matters similar to or connected with the unsatisfactory performance or attendance referred to in the improvement notice issued at the first stage.

6.2 Where, at the end of the period specified in an improvement notice, the line manager finds that the police officer's performance or attendance has not improved to an acceptable standard during that period or that the police officer has not maintained an acceptable level of performance or attendance during the validity period of the notice, then the second line manager will notify the police officer in writing that he or she is required to attend a second stage meeting. The notification will state:

- the details of the procedures for determining the date and time of the meeting (see paragraph 6.8);
- a summary of the reasons why the line manager considers the police officer's performance or attendance unsatisfactory;
- the possible outcomes of a second stage and third stage meeting;
- that the line manager may attend the meeting;
- that a human resources professional or a police officer (who should have experience of UPPs and be independent from the line management chain) may attend the meeting to advise the second line manager on the proceedings;
- that if the police officer agrees, any other person specified in the notice may attend the meeting;
- that prior to the meeting the police officer must provide the second line manager with any documentation he or she intends to rely on in the meeting; and
- the police officer's rights i.e. his or her right to seek advice from a representative of his or her staff association (in the case of a member of the police force) and to be accompanied and represented at the meeting by a police friend.

6.3 The notice must also include copies of related documentation relied upon by the line manager in support of the view that the police officer's performance or attendance continues to be unsatisfactory.

6.4 In advance of the meeting, the police officer shall provide the second line manager with any documents on which he or she intends to rely on in support of his or her case.

6.5 Any document or other material that was not submitted in advance of the meeting may be considered at the meeting at the discretion of the second line manager. The purpose of allowing this discretion is to ensure fairness to all parties. However the presumption should be that such documents or other material will not be permitted unless it can be shown that they were not previously available to be submitted in advance. Where such a document or other material is permitted to be considered, a short adjournment may be necessary to enable the second line manager or the police officer, as the case may be, to read or consider the document or other material and consider its implications. The length of the adjournment will depend upon the case. A longer adjournment may be necessary if the material in question is complex.

6.6 The purpose of the meeting is to hear the evidence of the unsatisfactory performance or attendance and to give the police officer the opportunity to put forward his or her views. It will also be an opportunity to hear of any factors that are continuing to affect the police officer's performance or attendance and what the police officer considers can be done to address them.

6.7 The second line manager should explain that there is potentially a further stage to the procedures and that the maximum outcome of stage two is a final improvement notice. The second line manager will also explain that if the procedure is followed to the final stage, dismissal, a reduction in rank (in the case of a member of a police force and in performance cases only), redeployment to alternative duties or an extended improvement notice (in exceptional circumstances) are possible outcomes.

6.8 Wherever possible, the meeting date and time should be agreed between the second line manager and the police officer. However, where agreement cannot be reached the second line manager must specify a time and date. If the police officer or his or her police friend is not available at the date or time specified by the second line manager, the police officer may propose an alternative time. Provided that the alternative time is reasonable and falls within a period of 5 working days beginning with the first working day after that specified by the second line manager, the meeting must be postponed to that time.

6.9 Once a date for the meeting is fixed, the second line manager should send to the police officer a notice in writing of the date, time and place of the second stage meeting.

At the second stage meeting

6.10 At the second stage meeting the second line manager will:

(a) explain to the police officer the reasons why he or she has been required to attend a second stage meeting;

(b) provide the police officer with the opportunity to make representations in response;

(c) provide the police officer's police friend (if he or she has one) with an opportunity to make representations (see Role of Police Friend);

(d) listen to what the police officer (and/or his or her police friend) has to say, ask questions and comment as appropriate.

6.11 The second line manager may adjourn the meeting at any time if he or she considers it is necessary or expedient to do so. An adjournment may be appropriate where information which needs to be checked by the line manager emerges during the course of the meeting or the manager decides that he or she wishes to adjourn the meeting whilst he or she makes a decision.

6.12 Where the line manager finds that the performance or attendance of the police officer has been satisfactory during the period in question, he or she will inform the police officer that no further action will be taken.

6.13 Where, having considered any representations by either the police officer and/ or his or her police friend, the second line manager finds that the performance or attendance of the police officer has been unsatisfactory (either during the period specified in the written improvement notice or during the validity period of the written improvement notice) he or she shall:

(a) inform the police officer in what respect (s) his or her performance or attendance is considered unsatisfactory;

(b) inform the police officer of the improvement that is required in his or her performance or attendance;

(c) inform the police officer that, if a sufficient improvement is not made within the period specified by the second line manager , he or she may be required to attend a third stage meeting.

(d) inform the police officer that he or she will receive a final written improvement notice; and

(e) inform the police officer that if the sufficient improvement in his or her performance or attendance is not maintained during the validity period of such notice, he or she may be required to attend a third stage meeting.

6.14 It is expected that the specified period for improvement would not normally exceed 3 months. However, depending on the nature and circumstances of the matter, it may be appropriate to specify a longer or shorter period for improvement (but which should not exceed 12 months). In determining the specified period of an improvement notice, consideration should also be given to any periods of known extended absence from the police officer's normal role.

Procedure following the second stage meeting

6.15 As soon as reasonably practicable following the meeting, the second line manager will cause to be prepared a written record of the meeting and, where he or she found at the meeting that the performance or attendance of the police officer was unsatisfactory, a final written improvement notice. The written record and any improvement notice shall be sent to the officer as soon as reasonably practicable after they have been prepared. The written record supplied to the police officer should comprise a summary of the proceedings at that meeting.

6.16 The written improvement notice must set out the information conveyed to the police officer in paragraph 6.13, state the period for which it is valid, and be signed and dated by the second line manager. Any improvement notice must be accompanied by a notice informing the police officer of his or her right to appeal and the name of the person to whom the appeal should be sent. The notice must also inform the police officer of his or her right to submit written comments on the written record of the meeting and of the procedure for doing so.

6.17 The police officer may submit written comments on the written record not later than the end of 7 working days after the date that he or she received it (unless an extension has been granted by the second line manager following an application by the police officer). Any written comments provided by the police officer should be retained with the note. However, if the police officer has exercised his or her right to appeal against the finding or outcome of the second stage meeting, the police officer may not submit comments on the written record.

6.18 It is the responsibility of the second line manager to ensure that the written record, written improvement notice and any written comments of the police officer on the written record are retained together and filed in accordance with force policies.

6.19 Normally it will also be appropriate to agree an action plan (see paragraph 4.9) setting out the actions which may assist the police officer to perform his or her duties to an acceptable standard e.g. attending training courses or a recommendation that the police officer seek welfare or medical advice. It is expected that the police officer will co-operate with implementation of the action plan and take responsibility for his or her own development or improvement. Equally, the police officer's managers must ensure that any actions to support the police officer to improve are implemented.

Assessment of performance or attendance

6.20 It is expected that the police officer's performance or attendance will be actively monitored against the improvement notice and, where applicable, the action plan by the line manager throughout the specified period of the final improvement notice. The line manager should discuss with the police officer any concerns that the line manager has during this period as regards his or her performance or attendance and offer advice and guidance where appropriate.

6.21 As soon as reasonably practicable after the specified period of the improvement notice comes to an end, the line manager, in consultation with the second line manager or an HR professional (or both), must formally assess the performance or attendance of the police officer during that period.

6.22 If the line manager considers that the police officer's performance or attendance is satisfactory, the line manager should notify the police officer in writing of this. The line manager must also notify the police officer that whilst the performance or attendance of the police officer is now satisfactory, the final improvement notice is valid for a period of 12 months from the date printed on the notice so that it is possible for stage three of the procedures to be initiated if the performance or attendance of the police officer falls below an acceptable level within the remaining period.

6.23 If the line manager considers that the police officer's performance or attendance is still unsatisfactory, the line manager should notify the police officer in writing of this. The notification should also inform the police officer that he or she is required to attend a third stage meeting to consider these ongoing performance or attendance issues.

6.24 If the police officer has improved his or her performance or attendance to an acceptable standard within the specified improvement period, but then fails to maintain that standard within the 12 month validity period, it is open to the line manager to initiate stage three of the procedures.

6.25 In such circumstances the line manager must notify the police officer in writing of his or her view that the police officer's performance or attendance is unsatisfactory as he or she has failed to maintain a sufficient improvement and that as a consequence the police officer is required to attend a third stage meeting to discuss this failure to maintain a satisfactory standard of performance or attendance.

Second stage appeals

6.26 A police officer has a right of appeal against the finding and the terms of the improvement notice imposed at stage two of the UPPs and against the decision to require him to attend the meeting. However, any finding and outcome of this second stage meeting will continue to apply up to the date that the appeal is determined. Therefore where the police officer contests the finding or outcome, he or she should continue to follow the terms of the improvement notice and any accompanying action plan pending the determination of the appeal.

6.27 Any appeal should be made in writing to the senior manager within 7 working days following the day of the receipt of the improvement notice (unless the period is extended by the senior manager following an application by the police officer). The notice of appeal must clearly set out the grounds and evidence for the appeal.

Appeal grounds

6.28 The grounds for appeal are as follows:

- that the finding of unsatisfactory performance or attendance is unreasonable;
- that any of the terms of the improvement notice are unreasonable;
- that there is evidence that could not reasonably have been considered at the second stage meeting which could have materially affected the finding of unsatisfactory performance or attendance or any of the terms of the improvement notice;
- that there was a breach of the procedures set out in the Police (Performance) Regulations or other unfairness which could have materially affected the finding of unsatisfactory performance or attendance or the terms of the written improvement notice.
- that the police officer should not have been required to attend the second stage meeting as the meeting did not concern unsatisfactory performance or attendance which was similar to or connected with the unsatisfactory performance or attendance referred to in the written improvement notice that followed the first stage meeting.

6.29 On the basis of the above grounds of appeal, the police officer may appeal against the finding of unsatisfactory performance or attendance, the decision to require him to attend the second stage meeting or the terms of the written improvement notice, those being:

- the respect in which the police officer's performance or attendance is considered unsatisfactory;
- the improvement which is required of the police officer;
- the length of the period specified for improvement by the second line manager at the second stage meeting.

6.30 The police officer has the right to be accompanied and represented by a police friend at the second stage appeal meeting.

6.31 Wherever possible, the meeting date and time should be agreed between the senior manager and the police officer. However, where agreement cannot be reached the senior manager must specify a time and date. If the police officer or his or her police friend is not available at the date or time specified by the manager, the police officer may propose an alternative time. Provided that the alternative time is reasonable and falls within a period of 5 working days beginning with the first working day after that specified by the senior manager, the meeting must be postponed to that time.

6.32 Once a date for the meeting is fixed, the senior manager should send to the police officer a notice in writing of the date, time and place of the second stage appeal meeting together with the information required to be provided under Regulation 24 of the Performance Regulations.

At the second stage appeal meeting

6.33 At this meeting the senior manager will:

- provide the police officer with the opportunity to make representations;
- provide his or her police friend (if he or she has one) with an opportunity to make representations (See Role of Police Friend).

6.34 Having considered any representations by either the police officer and/ or his or her police friend, the senior manager may:

- make a finding that the officer should not have been required to attend the second stage meeting, and reverse the finding made at that meeting;
- confirm or reverse the finding of unsatisfactory performance or attendance;
- endorse or vary the terms of the improvement notice.

6.35 The senior manager may deal with the police officer in any manner in which the second line manager could have dealt with him or her at the second stage meeting.

6.36 Within 3 working days of the day following the conclusion of the appeal meeting, the police officer will be given written notice of the senior manager's decision. If the senior manager is in a position to send a written summary of the reasons for that decision, then this may also accompany the written notice of the decision.

6.37 However, where the senior manager sends only the written notice of the decision to the police officer, as soon as reasonably practicable after the conclusion of the meeting, he or she will send a written summary of reasons for that decision.

6.38 Any decision made that changes the finding or outcome of the second stage meeting will take effect by way of substitution for the finding or terms appealed against and as from the date of the second stage meeting.

7. The third stage

Preparation and purpose

7.1 With the exception of gross incompetence cases (see paragraph 7.8), initiation of the third stage must be for matters similar to or connected with the unsatisfactory performance or attendance referred to in the final written improvement notice.

7.2 Where, at the end of the period specified in the final written improvement notice, the line manager finds that the police officer's performance or attendance has not improved to an acceptable standard during that period or that the police officer has not maintained an acceptable level of performance or attendance during the validity period of the notice, then the line manager must notify the police officer in writing that he or she is required to attend a third stage meeting to discuss these issues. As soon as reasonably practicable thereafter, the senior manager must give a notice to the officer informing him:

• that the meeting will be with a panel appointed by the appropriate authority;
• the procedures for determining the date and time of the meeting (see paragraphs 7.31 and 7.32);
• a summary of the reasons why the police officer's performance or attendance is considered unsatisfactory;
• the possible outcomes of a third stage meeting (see paragraph 7.6)
• that an HR professional or a police officer (who should have experience of UPPs and be independent from the line management chain) may attend to advise the panel on the proceedings;
• that counsel or a solicitor may attend the meeting to advise the panel on the proceedings and on any question of law that may arise at the meeting;

where the police officer is a special constable, inform him or her that a member of
• the special constabulary will attend the meeting to advise the panel (see paragraphs 7.27 to 7.30);
• that if the police officer agrees, any other person specified in the notice may attend e.g. a person attending for development reasons; and
• the police officer's rights i.e. his or her right to seek advice from a representative of his or her staff association (in the case of a member of the police force) and to be accompanied and represented at the meeting by a police friend.[8]

7.3 The notice must also include copies of related documentation relied upon by the line manager in support of the view that the police officer's performance or attendance continues to be unsatisfactory. It is important to note that a third stage meeting may not take place unless the officer has been notified of his right to representation by a police friend.

7.4 The notice does not at this stage need to give the names of the panel members as these may not be known at the time of issue. However, as soon as the panel has been appointed by the appropriate authority, the appropriate authority should notify the police officer of the members' names. (For details of panel membership and procedures, see paragraphs 7.16 to 7.22).

7.5 The purpose of the meeting is for the panel to hear the evidence of the unsatisfactory performance or attendance and to give the police officer the opportunity to put forward his or her views. It will also be an opportunity to hear of any factors that are continuing to affect the police officer's performance or attendance and what the police officer considers can be done to address them.

7.6 Where the police officer has reached stage three following stages one and two (i.e. not a gross incompetence meeting), the possible outcomes of this stage three meeting are as follows:

• redeployment;
• reduction in rank (in the case of a member of a police force and for performance cases only);
• dismissal (with a minimum of 28 days' notice); or
• extension of a final improvement notice (in exceptional circumstances)

7.7 Where the panel grants an extension to the final improvement notice, they will specify a new period within which improvement to performance or attendance must be made. The 12 month validity period of the extended final improvement notice will apply in full from the date of extension. The panel may also vary any of the terms in the notice.

---

[8] A third-stage meeting cannot take place unless the police officer concerned has been notified of his or her right to be represented by a police friend.

Gross incompetence third stage meetings

7.8 There may be exceptional circumstances where the appropriate authority[9] considers the performance (not attendance) of the police officer to be so unsatisfactory as to warrant the procedures being initiated at the third stage. This would be as a result of a single incident of "gross incompetence". It is not envisaged that an appropriate authority would initiate the procedures at the third stage in respect of a series of acts over a period of time.

7.9 "Gross incompetence" is defined in the Police (Performance) Regulations 2008 as:

> "…a serious inability or serious failure of a police officer to perform the duties of the rank or role he is currently undertaking to a satisfactory standard or level, to the extent that dismissal would be justified, except that no account shall be taken of the attendance of a police officer when considering whether he has been grossly incompetent."

7.10 Where the appropriate authority determines it is appropriate to initiate the procedures at this stage, then the police officer must be informed in writing that he or she is required to attend a third stage meeting to discuss his or her performance.

7.11 Where the appropriate authority has informed the police officer that he or she is to attend a third stage only meeting, it must, as soon as reasonably practicable, send the police officer a notice in writing which will include the following details:

- that the meeting will be with a panel appointed by the appropriate authority;
- the procedure for determining the date and time of the meeting;
- a summary of the reasons why the police officer's performance is considered to constitute gross incompetence;
- the possible outcomes of a third stage only meeting (see paragraph 7.15);
- that an HR professional and a police officer (who should have experience of UPPs and be independent from the line management chain) may attend to advise the panel on the proceedings;
- that counsel or a solicitor may attend the meeting to advise the panel on the proceedings and on any question of law that may arise at the meeting;

  where the police officer is a special constable, inform him that a ,member of the
- special constabulary will attend the meeting to advise the panel (see paragraphs 7.27 to 7.30);
- if the police officer agrees, any other person specified in the notice may attend e.g. a person attending for development reasons; and
- the police officer's rights: his or her right to seek advice from a representative of his or her staff association (in the case of a member of the police force) and to be accompanied at the meeting by a police friend

In addition, the notice must also set out the effect of regulation 6 of the Performance Regulations.

7.12 The notice must be accompanied by the documentation relied upon by the appropriate authority in support of its view that the police officer's performance constitutes gross incompetence.

7.13 The notice does not have to give the names of the panel members at this stage as these may not be known at the time of issue. However, as soon as reasonably practicable after the panel has been appointed by the appropriate authority, it should notify the police officer of the members' names.

7.14 The purpose of the meeting is for the panel to hear the evidence of the gross incompetence and to give the police officer and his or her representative the opportunity to make representations on the matter.

---

[9] It should be noted that if the decision to initiate the gross incompetence part of the procedures is delegated by the appropriate authority, that decision must be authorized by a senior police officer.

7.15 The appropriate authority will explain that the police officer is required to attend the third stage meeting and that the possible outcomes of the stage three meeting are:

- redeployment to alternative duties;
- the issue of a final written improvement notice;
- reduction in rank (with immediate effect);
- dismissal (with immediate effect) or.
- the issue of a written improvement notice (if the panel considers that there has been unsatisfactory performance and not gross incompetence)

Panel membership and procedure

7.16 The panel will comprise a panel chair and two other members and be appointed by the appropriate authority of the force in which the police officer is a police officer. At least one of the three panel members must be a police officer and one should be an HR professional. Membership will be as follows:

1st panel member (chair)
Senior police officer;[10] or
Senior HR professional (see paragraph 7.18).

2nd panel member
Police officer of at least the rank of
superintendent; or
HR professional who in the
opinion of the appropriate authority is at least
equivalent to that rank.

3rd panel member
Police officer of at least the rank
of superintendent; or
police staff member who in the
opinion of the appropriate authority
is at least equivalent to that rank.

7.17. None of the panel members should be junior in rank to the police officer concerned i.e. they must be of at least the same rank or equivalent (in the opinion of the appropriate authority).

7.18 For the purposes of chairing a third stage meeting, the Police (Performance) Regulations 2008 define a "senior HR professional" as:

"…a human resources professional who, in the opinion of the appropriate authority, has sufficient seniority, skills and experience to be a panel chair".

The panel chair should be senior in rank (or, in the opinion of the appropriate authority, is senior in rank) to the police officer concerned.

7.19 The appropriate authority may appoint police officers or police staff managers from another police force to be members of a panel.

7.20 No panel member should be an interested party i.e. a person whose appointment could reasonably give rise to a concern as to whether he could act impartially under the procedures.

7.21 As soon as the appropriate authority has appointed a third stage panel, it should arrange for copies of all relevant documentation to be sent to those members. In particular, any document:

- that was available to the line manager in relation to any first stage meeting;
- which was available to the second line manager in relation to any second stage meeting;

---

[10] 'Senior police officer' means a police officer holding a rank above that of chief superintendent.

- which was prepared or submitted in advance of the third stage meeting;
- which was prepared or submitted following those meetings i.e. improvement notices, action plans and meeting notes;
- relating to any appeal.

7.22 As soon as the appropriate authority has appointed a third stage panel, it must send the police officer written confirmation of the names of panel members.

Objection to panel members

7.23 The police officer has the right to object to any panel members appointed by the appropriate authority and any such objection must be made in writing to the appropriate authority no later than 3 working days after receipt of the notification of the names of the panel members. The police officer must include the ground of his or her objection to a panel member (s) in that submission.

7.24 The appropriate authority must inform the police officer in writing whether it upholds or rejects an objection to a panel member.

7.25 If the appropriate authority upholds the objection, a new panel member will be appointed as a replacement. As soon as practicable after any such appointment, the police officer will be informed in writing of the name of the new panel member. The appropriate authority must ensure that the requirements for the composition of the panel in paragraph 7.16 continue to be met.

7.26 The police officer may object to the newly appointed panel member in the same way as that described in paragraph 7.23 whereupon the appropriate authority must follow the procedure described above.

Special constables and third stage meetings

7.27 In cases where the police officer is a special constable, as indicated above, the force will appoint a member of the special constabulary to attend the meeting to advise the panel. This is for the purpose of fairness so that any significant differences between the role of a regular and special police constable and which may have a bearing on the police officer's performance or attendance can be taken into account.

7.28 The special constable advising the panel must have sufficient seniority and experience of the special constabulary to be able to advise the panel. The special constable advising the panel can be a police officer serving in a different force.

7.29 The special constable advisor will not form part of the panel and will not have a role in determining whether or not the police officer's performance or attendance is unsatisfactory.

7.30 In arranging a third stage meeting involving special constables, due consideration should be given to the fact that special constables are unpaid volunteers and may therefore have full time employment or other personal commitments.

Meeting dates and timeframes

7.31 Subject to paragraph 7.32, any third stage meeting should take place no later than 30 working days after the date that the notification described in paragraphs 7.2 to 7.4 has been sent to the police officer. Within that timeframe, wherever possible, the meeting date and time should be agreed between the panel chair and the police officer. However, where agreement cannot be reached the panel chair must specify a time and date. If the police officer or his or her police friend is not available at the date or time specified by the panel chair, the police officer may propose an alternative time. Provided that the alternative time is reasonable and falls within a period of 5 working days beginning with the first working day after that specified by the panel chair, the meeting must be postponed to that time.

7.32 If the panel chair considers it to be in the interests of fairness to do so, he or she may extend the 30 working day period within which the meeting should take place and the reasons for any such extension must be notified in writing to both the appropriate authority and the police officer.

7.33 As soon as a date for the meeting is fixed, the panel chair should send to the police officer a notice in writing of the date, time and place of the third stage meeting.

Procedure on receipt of notice of third stage meeting

7.34 Within 14 working days of the date on which a notice (as set out in paragraphs 7.2. and 7.11) has been sent to the police officer (unless this period is extended by the panel chair for exceptional circumstances), the police officer must provide to the appropriate authority:

(a) a written notice of whether or not he or she accepts that his or her performance or attendance has been unsatisfactory or that he or she has been grossly incompetent, as the case may be;

(b) where he or she accepts that his or her performance or attendance has been unsatisfactory or that he or she has been grossly incompetent, any written submission he or she wishes to make in mitigation;

(c) where the police officer does not accept that his or her performance or attendance has been unsatisfactory or that he or she has been grossly incompetent or where he or she disputes part of the matters referred to in the notice that he or she has received, he or she shall provide the appropriate authority with a written notice of:
   • the matters he or she disputes and his or her account of the relevant events; and
   • any arguments on points of law he or she wishes to be considered by the panel.

7.35 The police officer shall provide the appropriate authority and the panel with a copy of any document he or she intends to rely on at the third stage meeting.

Witnesses and evidence

7.36 Before the end of three working days following the officer's compliance with paragraph 7.34, the senior manager and the officer shall each supply a list of proposed witnesses or give notice that they do not have any witnesses. Where witnesses are proposed, this must be accompanied by brief details of their evidence and their address. The officer should try and agree a list of witnesses with the senior manager.

7.37 Where agreement has not been reached as above, the officer shall send to the appropriate authority his or her list of witnesses.

7.38 As soon as reasonably practicable after any list of witnesses has been agreed or, in the case where no agreement could be reached, supplied to the appropriate authority, the appropriate authority must send the list(s) to the panel chair together with, in the latter case, a list of its proposed witnesses. The panel chair will consider the list of proposed witnesses and will determine which, if any, witnesses should attend the third stage meeting.

7.39 The panel chair can determine that persons not named in the list should attend as witnesses.

7.40 No witnesses will give evidence at a third stage meeting unless the panel chair reasonably believes that it is necessary in the interests of fairness for the witness to do so, in which case he or she will:

(a) in the case of a police officer, cause him or her to be ordered to attend the third stage meeting;

(b) in any other case, cause him or her to be given notice that his or her attendance at the third stage meeting is necessary.

Such notices will include the date, time and place of the meeting.

7.41 Where a witness attends to give evidence then any questions to that witness should be made through the panel chair. This would not prevent the panel chair allowing questions to be asked directly if he or she feels that this is appropriate.

7.42 The documents or other material to be relied upon at the meeting are required to be submitted in advance. Any document or other material that was not submitted in advance of the meeting may be considered at the meeting at the discretion of the panel chair. The purpose of allowing this discretion is to ensure fairness to all parties. However, the presumption should be that such documents or other material will not be permitted unless it can be shown that they were not previously available to be submitted in advance or that they relate to mitigation following a finding of unsatisfactory performance or attendance that was contested by the police officer. Where such a document or other material is permitted to be considered, a short adjournment may be necessary to enable those present to read or consider the document or other material and consider its implications. The length of the adjournment will depend upon the case. A longer adjournment may be necessary if the material in question is complex.

At the third stage meeting

7.43 At the third stage meeting the panel chair will conduct the meeting and will:

(a) explain to the police officer the reasons why he or she has been required to attend a third stage meeting;

(b) provide the police officer with the opportunity to make representations in response;

(c) where the case is one of gross incompetence and the police officer has opted for legal representation, provide the police officer's legal representative with the opportunity to make representations;

(d) unless the police officer is entitled to be and has chosen to be legally represented, provide the police officer's police friend (if he or she has one) with an opportunity to make representations (see Role of Police Friend);

(e) listen to what the police officer (and/or his or her police friend) has to say and ask questions as appropriate

7.44 Having considered any representations by either the police officer and/ or his or her police friend or (where applicable) the police officer's legal representative, the panel will come to a finding as to whether or not the performance or attendance of the police officer has been unsatisfactory or whether or not his or her behaviour constitutes gross incompetence, as the case may be.

7.45 If there is a difference of view between the three panel members, the finding or decision will be based on a simple majority vote, but it will not be indicated whether it was taken unanimously or by a majority.

7.46 The panel must prepare (or cause to be prepared) their decision in writing which shall also state the finding. Where the panel have found that the police officer's performance or attendance has been unsatisfactory or that he or she has been grossly incompetent, the decision must also state their reasons and any outcome which they order.

7.47 As soon as reasonably practicable after the conclusion of the meeting, the panel chair shall send a copy of the decision to the police officer and the line manager. However, the police officer must be given written notice of the finding of the panel within 3 working days of the conclusion of the meeting.

7.48 Where the panel have made a finding of unsatisfactory performance or attendance or gross incompetence the copy of the decision sent to the police officer must also be accompanied by a notice informing him or her of the circumstances in which and the timeframe within which he or she may appeal to a police appeals tribunal.

Records

7.49 A verbatim record of the meeting should be taken. The police officer must, on request, be supplied with a copy of the record.

Postponement and adjournment of a third stage meeting

7.50 If the panel chair considers it necessary or expedient, he or she may direct that the third stage meeting should take place at a different time to that originally notified to the police officer.

7.51 The panel chair's alternative time may fall after the period of 30 working days specified in paragraph 7.31.

7.52 In the event that the panel chair postpones a third stage meeting he or she should notify the following relevant parties in writing of his or her reasons and the revised time and place for the meeting:

- the police officer;
- other panel members; and
- the appropriate authority.

7.53 If the police officer informs the panel chair in advance that he or she is unable to attend the third stage meeting on grounds which the panel chair considers reasonable, the panel chair may allow the police officer to participate in the meeting by video link or other means.

7.54 In cases where the police officer is absent (for example through illness or injury) a short delay may be reasonable to allow him or her to attend. If this is not possible or any delay is considered not appropriate in the circumstances then the person(s) conducting the meeting/hearing may allow the police officer to participate by telephone or video link. In these circumstances a police friend will always be permitted to attend the meeting/hearing to represent the police officer in the normal way (and, in the case of a gross incompetence meeting, the police officer's legal representative where appointed).

Assessment of final and extended-final improvement notices issued at the third stage

7.55 Where the police officer has been issued with a final improvement notice or, in exceptional cases, the panel has extended a final improvement notice period, it is expected that the police officer's performance or attendance will be actively monitored by the line manager throughout the specified period of the final/ extended final improvement notice. The line manager should discuss with the police officer any concerns that the line manager has during this period as regards his or her performance or attendance and offer advice and guidance where appropriate.

7.56 As soon as reasonably practicable after the specified period of the final/ extended-final improvement notice comes to an end, the panel will assess the performance or attendance of the police officer during that period. The panel chair must then inform the police officer in writing of the panel's conclusion following assessment i.e. whether there has been sufficient improvement in his or her performance or attendance during the specified period. If the panel considers that there has been insufficient improvement the panel chair shall also notify the officer that he or she is required to attend another third stage meeting.

7.57 If, at the end of the validity period of the final/ extended-final improvement notice, the panel considers that sufficient improvement to the police officer's performance or attendance has not been made or maintained during this period, the panel chair will inform the police officer of the panel's assessment.

7.58 Any such notification to the police officer must also include notification that he or she is required to attend a further third stage meeting.

7.59 Where an officer is required to attend a further third stage meeting, the regulations shall apply as if he were required to attend that meeting for the first time and following a second stage meeting.

7.60 As with the initiation of stages one and two for unsatisfactory performance or attendance, a further third stage meeting must relate to matters similar to or connected with the unsatisfactory performance or attendance or gross incompetence referred to in the final improvement notice extended or issued by the panel.

7.61 The panel should (where possible) be composed of the same persons who conducted the previous third stage meeting. However, there may be cases where re-constitution of the panel is either inappropriate or not possible. For example, original panel members may be on a career break or have left the force. In such circumstances the appropriate authority may substitute members as it sees fit subject to the requirements in the regulations described in paragraph 7.16. As soon as reasonably practicable after the appointment of any new panel member (s), the police officer should be notified in writing of the changes in panel membership. The police officer will have the opportunity to object to any new panel member (s) subject to the restrictions set out in paragraphs 7.23 – 7.26.

7.62 A police officer may only be given an extension to a final improvement notice on one occasion. Therefore where the police officer is required to attend a reconvened third stage meeting and the panel find that the police officer's performance or attendance continues to be unsatisfactory, the only outcomes available to the panel are:

- Re-deployment;
- Reduction in rank (only for a member of a police force and in performance cases)[11]; or
- Dismissal (with notice).

Assessment of improvement notices issued at the third stage

7.63 In cases where a police officer was issued with an improvement notice (as opposed to a final improvement notice) for unsatisfactory performance at a gross incompetence third stage meeting, that written improvement notice will be equivalent to a written improvement notice issued at a first stage meeting. In that case the procedure for assessing the performance of the police officer will be the same as that following the first stage. See paragraphs 5.19 to 5.25.

Third stage appeals

7.64 Following a third stage meeting, a police officer may be able to appeal to a police appeals tribunal. This is dealt with in Annex C.

7.65 However, any finding and outcome of the third stage meeting will continue to apply up to the date that the appeal is determined.

8. Other Matters

Management action and medical and attendance issues

8.1 Where absence is due to genuine cases of illness, either self certified or medically certified, the issue is one of capability and thus falls under the UPPs rather than the procedures relating to misconduct. In such cases management should to take a sympathetic and considerate approach, particularly if the absence is disability related and where reasonable adjustments in the workplace also need to be made which might enable the police officer to return to work.

8.2 On the basis of the occupational health advice, management should consider whether alternative work is available. If there is some doubt about the nature of the police officer's illness or injury, the police officer will be informed that he or she will be examined by a force medical adviser (FMA). If the police officer refuses, he or she will be told in writing that a decision on whether he or she is subject to UPPs will be taken on the basis of the information available. The above will be applied in accordance with forces' own managing attendance procedures.

8.3 In accordance with local force attendance management procedures, the line manager and the police officer should keep in regular contact. If management wish to contact the police officer's doctor, normal force arrangements will be followed.

8.4 The police officer should be made aware at the start of the UPPs that if he or she remains unwell and if necessary adjustments cannot be made dismissal from the force is a possible outcome at stage three.

8.5 For further guidance on sickness and absence matters, see separate guidance on attendance management (Chapter 4).

---

[11] A reduction in rank may also involve redeployment to alternative duties.

Attendance at each stage of the procedures and ill-health

8.6 Attendance at any stage meeting is not subject to the same considerations as reporting for duty and the provisions of Regulation 33 (sick leave) of the Police Regulations 2003 do not apply. An illness or disability may render a police officer unfit for duty without affecting his or her ability to attend a meeting. However, if the police officer is incapacitated, the meeting may be deferred until he or she is sufficiently improved to attend.

8.7 A meeting will not be deferred indefinitely because the police officer is unable to attend, although every effort should be made to make it possible for the police officer to attend if he or she wishes to be present. For example:

• the acute phase of a serious physical illness is usually fairly short-lived, and the meeting may be deferred until the police officer is well enough to attend;
• if the police officer suffers from a physical injury – a broken leg - for instance, it may be possible to hold the meeting at a location convenient to him or her.

8.8 Where such circumstances apply at a stage three meeting, the force may wish to consider the use of video, telephone or other conferencing technology.

8.9 Where, despite such efforts having been made and/or the meeting having been deferred, the police officer either persists in failing to attend the meeting or maintains his or her inability to attend, the person conducting the meeting will need to decide whether to continue to defer the meeting or whether to proceed with it, if necessary in the absence of the police officer. The person conducting the meeting must judge the most appropriate course of action. Nothing in this paragraph should be taken to suggest that, where a police officer's medical condition is found to be such that he or she would normally be retired on medical grounds the UPPs should prevent or delay retirement.

Medical retirement under police pension legislation

8.10 The Police Pensions Regulations 1987 in relation to the Police Pension Scheme and the Police Pensions Regulations 2006 in relation to the New Police Pension Scheme provide that where a police authority is considering whether a police officer is permanently disabled it shall refer the issue to the selected medical practitioner (SMP) for a decision.

8.11 Some cases of unsatisfactory attendance may raise the need to consider whether the police officer is permanently disabled within the meaning of the Police Pension Regulations 1987 or 2006. In such cases, this guidance should be read in conjunction with the PNB Joint Guidance on Improving the Management of Ill-Health.

8.12 Where a police officer is referred to the SMP for consideration of permanent disablement under the Police Pensions Regulations, no action shall be commenced or continued under the Police (Performance) Regulations 2008 with regard to the unsatisfactory attendance of a police officer until the issue of permanent disablement has been considered and the report of the SMP has been received by the Police Authority.

8.13 Where a police officer appeals to a Medical Appeal Board against a decision of the SMP that he or she is not permanently disabled or to a Crown Court against a decision of the Police Authority not to refer the permanent disablement questions to a SMP, no action shall be commenced or continued under the Police (Performance) Regulations 2008 with regard to the unsatisfactory attendance of the police officer until the appeal has been resolved.

8.14 Action can, however, be taken under the UPPs where a case has been referred or is the subject of appeal if the unsatisfactory attendance is unrelated to the condition forming the basis of the referral or appeal. However, forces must be confident that there is no connection as a decision to proceed in such circumstances may be challenged in the courts or tribunals. If the appropriate manager is unsure whether any condition forming the basis of a referral to the SMP or an appeal to either a Medical Appeal Board or Crown Court is related to the unsatisfactory attendance of a police officer, then advice should be sought from the HR professional acting on behalf of the Police Authority before any decision is taken to commence or continue the UPPs. Medical advice from the force medical advisor (FMA) may also be necessary.

For further guidance on medical retirement procedures, see:

http://www.ome.uk.com/downloads/0319%20Ill%20Health%20Retirementfinal.doc

http://www.lge.gov.uk/lge/aio/53547

http://police.homeoffice.gov.uk/human-resources/police-pensions/IHR/

Retirement under A19 of the Police Pensions Regulations 1987 and Regulation 20 of the Police Pensions Regulations 2006 and the 30+ Scheme

8.15 A19 of the Police Pensions Regulations 1987 provides for the compulsory retirement of police officers who have built up 30 years of pensionable service (and are entitled to an immediate full pension) where retention of a police officer would not be in the general interests of force efficiency. Similarly, regulation 20 of the Police Pensions Regulations 2006 provides for the compulsory retirement of those police officers who are members of the new 2006 Police Pension Scheme, and can be retired immediately with a full pension, on the same grounds.

8.16 These regulations should not to be used to remove a police officer in situations of unsatisfactory performance or attendance where there is no issue of wider force efficiency. The UPPs should be used in such cases.

8.17 UPPs can also be used where police officers have resumed service under the 30+ Scheme and where a termination of office under A19 or regulation 20 is not appropriate (as above).

8.18 For detailed guidance on the Police Pension Regulations and 30+ Scheme, see:

http://www.npia.police.uk/en/8395.htm

http://police.homeoffice.gov.uk/human-resources/police-pensions/

Special Priority Payments and Competency Related Threshold Payments

8.19 A finding or admission of unsatisfactory performance or attendance or gross incompetence at a UPP meeting will not automatically result in the removal of a police officer's competency related threshold payment or special priority payment. However, where a police officer has received an improvement notice or final improvement notice, this may trigger a review of the appropriateness of that police officer continuing to receive such payments. Any such review should take into account the qualifying criteria for payments under these schemes.

The use of records under UPPs

8.20 Records of any part of the UPPs should not be taken into account after an improvement notice has ceased to be valid. Equally, where a police officer appeals and that appeal is successful, the record of that procedure should not be taken into consideration in any future proceedings or for any other purpose.

CHAPTER 4 ·

GUIDANCE ON ATTENDANCE MANAGEMENT

Introduction

1. The police service is committed to promoting a good attendance culture and a supportive working environment within police forces. This guidance on attendance management is issued by the Home Office with the full support of the Police Advisory Board for England and Wales.
2. The purpose of this guidance is to highlight the key principles that should guide police forces in developing good attendance management policies and practices.
3. While the guidance is not statutory, it is relevant to the application of the Police (Performance) Regulations 2008. There is a clear expectation that forces will have in place an attendance policy that meets the standards set out in this guidance. Failure to have or to follow such a policy could be taken into account when decisions are being made, or appeals decided under the Unsatisfactory Performance Procedures (UPPs).
4. This guidance has been developed in conjunction with the police staff associations.
5. The Police (Performance) Regulations 2008 define unsatisfactory attendance as 'the inability or failure of a police officer to perform the duties of the role or rank he [she] is currently undertaking to a satisfactory standard or level'. In this context, this would be due to absence during agreed hours of duty.
6. In the case of lateness, there will be a need to establish the reasons for the behaviour. Consideration should be given to whether the matter is properly dealt with under the attendance management policy or as an issue of personal misconduct.

Scope

- This guidance covers an attendance management policy as it relates to police officers, including Special Constables. Arrangements are underway to develop a parallel document in relation to police staff. However, while acknowledging the differing employment status of officers and staff, the principles of effective attendance management set out here are generally applicable to both officers and staff, and forces may chose to develop a single policy to cover both officers and staff.

Key Principles

- All forces should have a clear policy on attendance management that is well-publicised and accessible to all.
- There should be ownership of the policy at the Chief Officer level.
- The policy should be developed in consultation with staff associations, force medical advisors, occupational health practitioners and health and safety advisors.
- To maximise the likelihood of success, forces must adopt a positive, supportive and transparent approach to attendance management that does not unlawfully discriminate. Policies should be reviewed at stipulated regular intervals, the review to include an equality impact assessment.
- Forces must place appropriate emphasis on the prevention of accidents and factors that cause or contribute to ill-health and take all reasonably practicable steps to safeguard the health, safety and welfare of all their officers.
- All officers have a duty to have due regard to health, safety and welfare and to co-operate with their force arrangements in order to safeguard themselves and others.[12]

---

[12] Health and Safety at Work Act 1974, as amended by the Police (Health and Safety) Act 1997, s 7 ('General duties of employees at work') reads: 'It shall be the duty of every employee while at work- (a) to take reasonable care for the health and safety of himself and of other persons who may be affected by his acts or omissions at

- There must be clear and effective communication in relation to attendance management, both generally and in individual cases.
- Any decision to use the Unsatisfactory Performance Procedures (UPPs) to deal with poor attendance should be taken only after all supportive approaches have been offered in line with force policy.
- Where the UPPs are invoked, the primary aim is to improve attendance. However, one available outcome of the UPPs is termination of service.

Policy

1. Each Force must ensure it has in place formal policies and procedures setting out its approach to the management of attendance. These should be endorsed by Chief Officers. The policy should have clear aims and objectives. It is essential that these are communicated to all managers, officers and their representatives and steps taken to ensure that they are familiar with, and fully understand their responsibilities. Officers should have ready access to the policy and procedures.
2. The Chief Officer should appoint a named individual at a senior level who takes the lead on attendance issues.
3. Staff associations have a key role in the development and review of attendance management policies and procedures.
4. The policy should set out clearly the Force's expectations in respect of attendance management. Effective policies have the following features:
   - The policy and procedures should be monitored for effectiveness, and include a stated process and period for review. Publication of regular management reports on attendance management may assist in keeping attendance management in focus.
   - The policy demonstrates senior management's commitment to care for officer health, safety and welfare and to comply with all relevant legislation, using all available data to promote improvement and learning.
   - Support for officers to improve their attendance and assist those who are on sick leave to return to work.
   - Clarity on how information will be captured and recorded, locally and on a force wide basis; this should include the stated recording method. Given many Forces now operate a variety of shift patterns, the recording of absence in hours, as directed by the current Home Office Guidance on Statutory Performance Indicators,[13] is critical in order that accurate comparisons can be made between Forces.
   - Whole organisation ownership, demonstrating effective communication and consultation process with the workforce
   - Transparent and non discriminatory application at all levels in the organisation and for all officers, whilst taking individual circumstances and requirements into account.
   - There will be clarity regarding roles and responsibilities of individual officers, line managers, human resource managers, occupational health practitioners, health and safety advisors and force medical advisors.
   - Forces must clearly set out the relationship of the attendance management policy with other Force policies which may have a link to health-related issues. These could include substance misuse; health promotion; Risk Assessment Based Medical Examination (RABME);[14] Fairness

---

work; and (b) as regards any duty or requirement imposed on his employer or any other person by or under any of the relevant statutory provisions, to co-operate with him so far as is necessary to enable that duty or requirement to be performed or complied with.'

[13] Available online at <http://police.homeoffice.gov.uk>.
[14] Available online at <http://www.npia.police.uk>.

at Work; dispute resolution; disability; maternity; and workplace stress policies and policies on work-life balance.

The Procedure

1. The procedure describes how the objectives of the policy will be achieved in practice, by setting the framework for management action to maintain and where appropriate, to improve attendance levels.

2. An attendance management procedure should seek to ensure the following outcomes:
   - The promotion of a healthy and safe working environment
   - Consistent and transparent application to all officers, regardless of grade or rank, taking into account individual circumstances and requirements.
   - Levels of sickness absence are accurately recorded in line with Home Office guidance on a regular basis, with regular monitoring reports to be used locally and nationally.
   - Communication by forces to all officers on the organisation's objectives around attendance management.
   - Managers at all levels are fully aware of their responsibilities
   - Defined levels of occupational health and other welfare support to be provided.

   An effective procedure should contain the following features:
   - Clear processes for reporting periods of sickness absence, and reasons for absence, both at the start of the period of sickness and at defined periods thereafter.
   - Clear process for either self-certification or the provision of medical certificate(s)
   - Clear process for how lateness should be dealt with
   - Clear processes for reporting and recording injuries incurred on duty
   - Clear process for maintaining contact during periods of absence.
   - Clear process for conducting return to work interviews and the development of rehabilitation and/or action plans to improve attendance
   - Guidance on records to be kept regarding interviews and rehabilitation and/or action plans
   - Guidance on the use of recuperative or restricted duties to encourage early and safe structured return to work
   - Guidance on the recording of absence and action to be taken under special circumstances, eg where absence is maternity or disability related.[15] Where absence is disability related separate records should be kept.
   - Whether, and if so, how, sickness absence will be a factor used in selection for training opportunities/postings/promotion. Where sickness absence is a factor, forces should ensure that this is compliant with other relevant force policies on issues such as disability and equality.

Managing Processes

1. Forces should take a proactive and supportive approach to managing absence, identifying and tackling any barriers to good attendance.

Short term absence

2. Every instance of sickness absence should be considered in line with force procedures. Managers should seek to ascertain any underlying causes of absence, and take appropriate action to prevent absence from escalating further. Using every instance of sickness absence as an opportunity to review the health of the officer concerned is important and such review may prevent the

---

[15] Available online at <http://police.homeoffice.gov.uk>.

sickness becoming more prolonged. Each review will also be an opportunity to consider whether there are any patterns of absence that give rise to any concern.

Long-term absence

1. Long term absence is defined as absence lasting 28 calendar days or more. Once an individual is absent from work for around 28 calendar days, regardless of their medical condition, their return to work can become more problematic, and there is a distancing from the workplace and work colleagues. It is of the utmost importance that clear arrangements are in place to maintain contact from an early stage in any absence.

Maintaining Contact

1. It is important that there are clear, locally published arrangements in place to maintain contact with officers who are absent for extended periods. Such arrangements should set out the purpose for the contact. This is likely to include ensuring medical certificates are regularly supplied and access to internal services such as counselling and rehabilitation are offered.
2. Line managers should maintain or facilitate regular contact with all officers absent on locally defined periods of sickness or long term absence throughout the period of absence and maintain a contact log.
3. Any arrangements should specify the nominated person who is responsible for ensuring contact is maintained.
4. Depending on the reason for absence and whether the officer is at home or in hospital, sensitivity will be required in ensuring that the appropriate level of contact is maintained. Phone calls, letters or regular Force newsletters could all be used. A balance needs to be struck between too much or too little contact as too much could be regarded as intrusive and bordering on harassment, whereas too little could be interpreted as not caring.
5. In rare cases it may be appropriate to have a person who is not in the officer's line management chain as the point of contact. For example, this could arise where the reported cause of the absence is due to management issues. Any Force procedure should ensure there is guidance on this point. Local arrangements should however make clear that the officer has a responsibility to provide the necessary medical certification and information on progress. The officer should also facilitate contact and co-operate with the advice and services provided by occupational health.

Facilitating Return to Work

1. Effective and sensitive management can be effective in facilitating the earliest possible safe return to work, especially in cases of extended sickness absence. Management, in consultation with occupational health, should make the officer's medical practitioners aware that the return to work can be phased, either by reducing hours at the start of the return or adjusting some of the tasks of the role to ensure no undue risk is placed on the officer concerned. Managers should ensure an appropriate 'risk assessment' is undertaken in such cases. Managers can be active in their support and encouragement for an early, safe return to work.
2. It is very likely that in these cases occupational health would have been involved at an earlier stage and their advice to managers is important. There may be some locally funded spend-to-save schemes which could facilitate private health care if undue NHS waiting times are being encountered. The role of occupational health in supporting the management of sickness absence is specifically reflected in the Strategy for a Healthy Police Service.[16]
3. The offer of a discussion with the officer and his or her representative may assist in the return to work. Police officers are key in understanding their condition and how their role may be temporarily adjusted to facilitate a return to work.

---

[16] Available online at <http://www.acpo.police.uk>.

Payment during sickness absence

1. It will be important at the appropriate time to inform the officer of the effect of Regulation 28 of the Police Regulations 2003 and its implications for sick pay. This will be particularly important when the officer concerned is approaching the time when his or her pay may be reduced or removed, to ensure there is clarity regarding this point and where appropriate, application for discretion to extend the period for which a specific rate of pay is payable is made in good time.[17]

Return to work interviews

1. Return to work interviews, conducted effectively, play a fundamental role in ensuring attendance is carefully and fairly managed. Such interviews should be conducted following a return to work after every period of unscheduled absence, even if the absence has been very short.[18]
2. Return to work interviews should apply to all officers regardless of rank, and should be viewed by both the officer and the manager as positive. However there should be reference to the officer's overall sickness record, where this is appropriate, so there can be an open discussion regarding any patterns of absence or other issues affecting his or her ability to attend regularly, or a need for further intervention or support.
3. The return to work interview should:
   - Ensur e that all documentation (such as medical certificates or self-certification) has been completed.
   - Discuss the reasons for absence in a non-confrontational way and whether the officer is able to undertake the full range of duties applicable to his or her role or develop a plan for recuperative duties. Where there is any doubt, the matter should be referred to occupational health for advice.
   - Consider whether, if appropriate, an adjustment could be made to an officer's working environment to enable him or her to return to work.
   - Provide the opportunity for the officer to indicate any areas of concern that may have contributed to his or her period of absence.
   - Where appropriate, update the officer on any matters of significance that have occurred in his or her period of absence; this should cover both his or her own work, and that of the team.
   - Be conducted sensitively and in a manner that enables any particular circumstances to be dealt with.
4. Records of return to work interviews must be securely stored in line with general policies on officer data and in accordance with the Data Protection Act 1998.
5. A return to work interview may raise the question as to whether the principles governing the treatment of disabled officers may need to be considered. Detailed guidance on managing disability can be obtained from the Home Office publication Disability in the Police Service.[19]

Disability

1. The decision as to whether or not an officer is disabled under the Disability Discrimination Act 1995 (as amended) (DDA) is ultimately a matter for an Employment Tribunal to decide. However, whether an officer definitely falls within the scope of the DDA should not be the overriding principle in the process of deciding whether to make reasonable adjustments. If a Force considers that an officer may be covered by the DDA, then it is good practice to treat him or her as such.

---

[17] PNB Circular 2005/1, available online at <http://www.ome.uk.com>.
[18] [Sic]
[19] Available online at <http://www.police.homeoffice.gov.uk>.

Recuperative duties

1. A phased return to work using recuperative duty arrangements can aid an early return to work. Recuperative duties should be used when there is the expectation that an officer will return to full duties upon his or her recovery. They are appropriate as a time-limited measure based on individual circumstances to enable officers to re-integrate into the workforce following a period of sick leave or injury. Any change to tasks should be temporary and a measured increase to return to normal hours and tasks should be actively managed and achieved in the shortest possible time.

Restricted duties

1. Where the condition is likely to be permanent, a return to work on the basis of restricted duties should be considered. Restricted duties are used in order to retain the skills and expertise of police officers and prevent unnecessary and costly early retirement. Police officers who are performing restricted duties are working full hours, as the restriction is predominantly based upon the type of work an officer can perform rather than the hours worked. This work should utilise their police skills and experience.

Ill-health retirement

1. There will be occasions where the medical condition causing the absence will be very serious and potentially with a permanent effect. In such cases the issues of whether the officer is 'permanently disabled' within the definition used in ill-health retirement guidance, will need to be considered.[20]

Unsatisfactory Performance Procedures

1. Where supportive approaches have failed to improve attendance to acceptable levels, and ill-health retirement is inappropriate, it may be necessary to use the Unsatisfactory Performance Procedures (see Chapter 3).

Allocating Responsibilities

1. Chief Officers have responsibilities under the Health and Safety at Work etc Act 1974[21] and related legislation to protect officers whilst at work. If they are vulnerable to risk particularly if they have an illness, injury or disability, Then human resources, health and safety practitioners and occupational health and welfare are the competent advisors.
2. It is the role of HR professionals to support sickness absence policies by providing advice and guidance to the line managers responsible for implementing the policies. This will include the provision of advice which takes into account the requirements of the Disability Discrimination Act 1995 (as amended) and HSE's Stress Management Guidance.[22]
3. Occupational health practitioners should play a major role in evaluating reasons for absence, conducting health assessments, advising HR professionals and line managers in planning returns to work, and promoting good health.
4. All managers have a significant role to play by demonstrating their commitment to managing absence and making it a service priority.
5. The development of good practice in managing attendance is encouraged. The NPIA will be developing a database of good practice, which will be made available to forces.
6. The Strategy for a Healthy Police Service details the specific responsibilities of the various parties who contribute to a healthier police service.

---

[20] Available online at <http://police.homeoffice.gov.uk>.
[21] As amended by the Police (Health and Safety) Act 1997.
[22] Available online at <http://www.hse.gov.uk>.

Role of Occupational Health

1. Occupational health has a role both in giving advice to managers to assist in taking managerial decisions and in supporting officers who seek their advice and assistance. Forces and Police Authorities should ensure that sufficient resources are available to provide a defined level of occupational health service.

2. Occupational health is responsible for providing advice on clinical issues affecting officers in the workplace, where this may be affecting performance or attendance. Where the force is required to conduct a risk assessment, officers can be required to co-operate with occupational health and/or health and safety advisors as part of the risk assessment process.

3. The Force should clearly define for all officers, the role and range of services they can expect from the occupational health service. It is vital that officers have confidence in the service and that managers are clear regarding the professional confidentiality requirements of occupational health practitioners.

4. Advice given to managers should be in a form which enables the manager to make a decision regarding the officer. Managers are responsible for making decisions regarding the officer informed by professional advice, including that provided by occupational health. A manager who has concerns about an officer's health and the effect it may have on his or her ability to attend regularly and perform his or her normal tasks, may refer the officer to occupational health.

5. A manager should set out clearly the questions he or she wants occupational health to advise on, and should provide occupational health with information about the role the officer performs to enable the advice to be relevant. The following issues are examples of medical advice that may be requested. In addition managers should state the reasons for referrals and any management issues:

   - Is the officer fully fit for work in the particular role or are they subject to temporary or permanent limitations?
   - Are there any adjustments required and, if so, what is the nature of any adjustments that can be recommended to enable the officer to carry out his or her role?
   - Are there any issues affecting the workplace that are impacting on the officer's performance?
   - Is the condition one which could recur, and which may in the future affect effective attendance and performance?
   - How does the medical condition directly affect the role undertaken, i.e. what parts of the role can be undertaken and which cannot?
   - Does the impairment affect day-to-day activity?
   - Could the officer return to work on recuperative duties as a step to returning to full duties and if so what functional activities could be performed?
   - Is the condition such that a return on a restricted duty basis is an option and if so what functional activities are capable of being performed regularly?
   - Is there any equipment that could assist in a safe return to work?
   - Is time needed to undertake treatment/rehabilitation?
   - Does the officer's condition fall within the scope of the DDA?
   - How long is the condition likely to last before a return to full duties?
   - Advice as to whether the condition is likely to require consideration of 'permanent disability' as defined in pension arrangements. If so, procedures covering pensions should be followed.[23]
   - Information given to managers by occupational health will not give the medical diagnosis as this is protected by medical confidentiality, but the impact of the condition on the officer's performance, capability and attendance will be identified, together with relevant timescales.

---

[23] See Home Office Circular 21/2003, available online at <http://www.knowledgenetwork.gov.uk>.

Health and Safety

1. The legal responsibility for assurance of proactive preventative measures rests with the Chief Officer and the Police Authority. As part of the requirement to provide a safe and healthy environment for all officers, each Force will have to assess how it will meet those responsibilities. This should include an assessment of a range of proactive preventative measures to reduce the incidence of both physical and psychological ill-health where work may be a factor, for example, access to private health care may be an option available where NHS waiting lists are lengthy.

2. Such measures should be designed to support and promote an environment where safe systems of work are a natural feature. The introduction of a Risk Assessed Based Medical Examination (RABME) process may provide a useful structured approach, identifying posts where there may be higher risks to physical or psychological wellbeing, together with appropriate measures to reduce or mitigate such risks. Analysis of the major causes of absence should guide the delivery of service provision.

Training and Communication

1. All managers who are required to participate in any aspect of attendance management must have clarity about their responsibilities and have confidence in handling attendance management issues. In addition to providing ready access to the policies and procedures, attention should be given to ensuring there is competence in the necessary skills required to conduct all aspects of the process, for example conducting a return to work interview in a non-confrontational way and formulating risk assessment and rehabilitation plans.

2. All new officers should receive information regarding their individual responsibilities in the attendance management process as part of their induction.

3. The organisation should provide accessible regular updates when changes are introduced, and provide opportunity for clarification, while officers should take responsibility for familiarising themselves with information provided.

4. There should be appropriate training and available information in place to ensure that:
   - All parties are familiar with and understand the force's attendance management policy and procedure, and where it can be located.
   - All managers and officers understand the arrangements, including timescales for reporting sickness absence
   - All managers and officers understand their responsibilities in relation to achieving and maintaining good attendance

Monitoring Individual Progress

1. It is the responsibility of all managers, using the Force's attendance management arrangements and taking advice as necessary, to monitor their officers' attendance records.

2. Monitoring and recording absence accurately is essential if absence is to be managed effectively and fairly. Managers should keep a record of every absence of each officer reporting to them. Accurate records are the only way to identify when and where problems are occurring; they also provide a historical record for determining patterns of absence for individual officers and departments.

3. It is the responsibility of all officers to ensure that, in the case of sickness absence they comply with the reporting requirements of the attendance management procedures.

4. Nominated staff should be responsible for recording data at the start and end of periods of absence, in addition to the reasons for absence.

5. Managers should also keep written records of any action (or non action) taken in relation to their officers.

Reviews

1. very instance of sickness absence is an opportunity for managers to take a proactive approach to examining the causes of absence and provide appropriate support.

2. Forces may also set locally defined and published review points, to assist managers in identifying patterns of absence and taking appropriate action.

3. Reviews are intended to act as a gateway to further management support or action, to ensure that officers are accessing all the necessary support to improve their attendance. This could include referral to occupational health, consideration of flexible working arrangements, and/or the involvement of a more senior manager.

4. Such reviews can provide a framework for consistent application of management intervention, but there is a need to ensure that these are not used rigidly without taking into account individual circumstances. Line managers should have the confidence and training to use their discretion in applying the policy.[24] While review points may be of assistance in identifying patterns or unusually high levels of absence, managers should not wait until a review point is reached before any action is taken. Similarly, based on their knowledge of a case, managers may choose not to take action, even where a review point has been reached.

5. The use of reviews should be non-discriminatory, regularly assessed, and subject to a full equality impact assessment.

Audit and Review

1. To be sure that an attendance management procedure is effective in achieving its stated objectives, there is a need to ensure that there is a robust and accurate information collection process, which provides realistic and simple information to enable managers to manage attendance in a timely and fair manner.

2. Monitoring information should be used as a positive tool to identify areas of concern and offer the opportunity for targeted improvement action where necessary. Monitoring information should form a regular input to Chief Officer Review meetings and should also be scrutinised by the appropriate consultative committee. Care should always be taken to ensure that information that is made generally available does not identify individual officers and where significant factors are identified, review whether there are underlying issues that should be addressed.

3. Forces should introduce a structured monitoring regime to:
   - Measure the overall performance of the Force in terms of absolute levels of sickness absence for all groups of officers. This can identify trends and indicate whether in overall terms the attendance management policy/procedures are effective in reducing absence and maintaining levels of attendance.
   - Identify whether the Force is performing against national set targets and whether there is an improvement against the Force's previous levels.
   - Identify areas of low levels of absence which may indicate areas of good practice which could be shared.
   - Identify areas where there is a high level of absence, which may indicate inadequate management attention to the active management of absence, or roles which may be particularly hazardous.
   - Identify where the Force appears to have predominantly short or long term absences and whether there are patterns of absence.
   - Measure the levels of sickness absence of different groups (e.g. gender, ethnicity, age, full or part time) in order to identify whether the Force's procedure impact disproportionately on any group. The information should be factored into regular equality impact assessments of the policy.
   - Allow managers to see how their section is performing alongside other available workforce information.

---

[24] Health and Safety Executive Report RR582, available online at <http://www.hse.gov.uk>.

4. The Home Office has developed a standard method of recording sickness absence, including definitions and criteria. This requires absence to be recorded in hours. These should always be used as it is necessary to supply the Home Office, quarterly, with information so it can prepare service wide monitoring information. Police Authorities will also find the information useful when considering Force performance. Consideration should be given to benchmarking with other forces to assess relative performance. Forces may also find it helpful to consider the cost to the organisation of sickness absence.
5. In the collection of all data, Forces must comply with their statutory requirements under the Data Protection Act 1998.

ANNEX A

FAST TRACK PROCEDURES (SPECIAL CASES)

Introduction

1. The following paragraphs provide guidance on the operation of the fast track misconduct procedures, referred to as "special cases" in the Conduct Regulations. Part 5 of the Conduct Regulations sets out the procedures for dealing with special cases.

2. The special case procedures can only be used if the appropriate authority certifies the case as a special case, having determined that the 'special conditions' are satisfied or if the IPCC has given a direction under paragraph 20H(7) of Schedule 3 to the Police Reform Act 2002.
   The 'special conditions' are that –
   (a) there is sufficient evidence, in the form of written statements or other documents, without the need for further evidence, whether written or oral, to establish on the balance of probabilities, that the conduct of the police officer concerned constitutes gross misconduct; and
   (b) it is in the public interest for the police officer concerned to cease to be a police officer without delay.
   These procedures are therefore designed to deal with cases where the evidence is incontrovertible in the form of statements, documents or other material (e.g. CCTV) and is therefore sufficient without further evidence to prove gross misconduct and it is in the public interest, if the case is found or admitted for the police officer to cease to be a member of the police service forthwith.

3. Even where the criteria for special cases are met there may be circumstances where it would not be appropriate to certify the case as a special case, for instance, where to do so might prematurely alert others (police officers or non-police officers) who are, or may be, the subject of an investigation.

4. In the case of non senior officers the case will be heard by the police officer's Chief Constable (Assistant Commissioner in the Metropolitan Police) or in cases where the Chief Constable is an interested party or is unavailable, another Chief Constable or an Assistant Commissioner. In the case of a senior officer, the case will be heard by a panel as set out in Regulations 47 and 48 of the Conduct Regulations. The police officer will have a right of appeal under regulation 56 of the Conduct Regulations to a Police Appeals Tribunal against any finding of gross misconduct and the disciplinary action imposed.

Complaint cases

5. Where a matter that meets the criteria for using the special case procedures has arisen from a complaint by a member of the public, the complainant or interested person will have the right to attend the special case hearing as an observer subject to any conditions imposed by the person conducting proceedings under regulation 53(3) of the Conduct Regulations.

6. Where a complainant or interested person is to attend a special case hearing he or she will be entitled to be accompanied by one other person and if the complainant or interested person has a special need, by one further person to accommodate that need.

7. A complainant or interested person and any person accompanying the complainant or interested person will be permitted to remain in the hearing up to and including any finding by the person (or persons in the case of a senior officer) conducting the hearing. The complainant or interested person and any person accompanying the complainant or interested person will not be permitted to remain in the hearing whilst character references or mitigation are being given or the decision of the person conducting the hearing (or persons in the case of a senior officer) as to the outcome. However, the appropriate authority will have a duty (in cases investigated locally or supervised by the IPCC) to inform the complainant or interested person of the outcome of the hearing whether the complainant or interested person attends or not.

Evidence

8. There will be no oral witness testimony at the special case hearing other than from the police officer concerned. There will be copies of the notice given to the police officer, the certificate certifying the case as a special case, the notice the police officer has supplied in response, including any documents he or she provides in support of his or her case, a copy of the investigator's report or such parts of that report as relate to the police officer concerned, statements made by the police officer during the investigation, and in a case where the police officer concerned denies the allegation against him or her, copies of all statements and documents that in the opinion of the appropriate authority should be considered at the meeting.

Special case process

Procedure for consideration in advance of the meeting

9. Where the appropriate authority determines that the special conditions (see paragraph 2 above) are satisfied, unless it considers that the circumstances are such to make it inappropriate to do so, he, she or it shall certify the case as a special case and refer it to a special case hearing. The decision as to whether a case is suitable for using the fast track procedure will be taken by the appropriate authority which must determine whether it believes the special conditions are satisfied having regard to the available evidence and any other relevant information. The appropriate authority will be the police authority in the case of a senior officer or the chief officer in the case of a non-senior officer. If the chief officer delegates this decision, that decision must be authorised by a senior officer.
10. If the appropriate authority decides that the special case procedures will not be used then he, she or it will refer it back to the investigator if further investigation is required or to the appropriate authority to proceed under the standard procedures.
11. If the appropriate authority decides that the special case procedures should be used then he, she or it will sign a "Special Case Certificate" and will provide to the police officer concerned notice giving particulars of the conduct that is alleged to constitute gross misconduct and copies of: -
    * the Special Case Certificate
    * any statement the police officer may have made to the investigator during the course of the investigation
    * Subject to the harm test, :-
        * the investigator's report(if any) or such parts of that report as relate to the police officer concerned, together with any documents attached to that report; and
        * any relevant statement or documents gathered during the course of the investigation
    The police officer concerned will also be told the date, time and place of the hearing and of his or her right to legal representation and to advice from a 'police friend'.
12. The date of the meeting will be not less than 10 working days and not more than 15 working days from the date the "Special Case Certificate" and other documents are provided to the police officer concerned.
13. Within 7 working days of the first working day after the day on which the written notice and documents are supplied to the police officer concerned, the police officer shall provide a written notice to the appropriate authority of –
    * whether or not he or she accepts that his or her conduct constituted gross misconduct
    * where he or she accepts that the conduct constituted gross misconduct, any submission he or she wishes to make in mitigation
    * where he or she does not accept that the conduct constituted gross misconduct
        (a) the allegations he or she disputes and his or her version of the relevant events; and
        (b) any arguments on points of law he or she wishes to be considered by the person or persons conducting the meeting.

At the same time the police officer shall provide the person conducting or chairing (in the case of a senior officer) the hearing with copies of any documents he or she intends to rely on at the hearing (see regulation 45).

14. The Chief Constable or Assistant Commissioner (in the MPS) or Commissioner (in the case of the City of London Police) (or the chair of the hearing in the case of a senior officer) should be provided with the papers and it should be seen as good practice to provide them at least 3 working days prior to the hearing.

Outcome of special case hearing

15. Where the person(s) conducting the special case hearing find that the conduct of the police officer concerned constituted gross misconduct, then he, she or they shall impose disciplinary action, which may be: -
    a) Dismissal without notice.
    b) A final written warning (unless a final written warning has been imposed on the police officer concerned within the previous 18 months).
    c) an extension of a final written warning.
    Where the police officer concerned has received a final written warning within the 18 months prior to the assessment of the conduct then in exceptional circumstances only, the final written warning may be extended by a further 18 months. An extension of a final written warning can occur on one occasion only.

16. Where the person(s) conducting the hearing determines that the conduct does not amount to gross misconduct, then he, she or they may dismiss the case.

17. Alternatively, he, she or they may return the case to the appropriate authority to deal with at a misconduct meeting or hearing (where there is a live final written warning) under the standard procedures. This may be because the person(s) conducting the hearing consider that the conduct is misconduct rather than gross misconduct.

18. There is power under regulation 42 for the appropriate authority to remit the case to be dealt with under the standard procedures at any time prior to the start of the special case hearing. This might be because he, she or it considers that a particular witness whose evidence is crucial to the case and is disputed must be called to give oral testimony.

19. Where the police officer admits the allegation or the person(s) conducting the hearing find it proved on the balance of probabilities, then the person(s) conducting the hearing –
    a) shall have regard to the record of police service of the police officer concerned as shown on his or her personal record;
    b) may consider such documentary evidence as would, in his, her or their opinion, assist him, her or them in determining the question; and
    c) shall give the police officer concerned, and his or her police friend or relevant lawyer, an opportunity to make oral or written representations.

20. The police officer concerned shall be informed of the finding and any disciplinary action imposed or a decision to dismiss the case or revert it back to be dealt with under the standard procedures as soon as practicable and in any event shall be provided with written notice of these matters and a summary of the reasons within 5 working days beginning with the first working day after the conclusion of the hearing.

Absence of police officer concerned at the hearing

21. The hearing may proceed in the absence of the police officer concerned, but the person(s) conducting the hearing should ensure that the police officer concerned has been informed of his or her right to be legally represented at the hearing or to be represented by a police friend where the police officer chooses not to be legally represented.

ANNEX B

MISCONDUCT MEETINGS/HEARINGS

Senior Police Officers

1. This section sets out the persons who will hear a misconduct case involving a senior police officer that has been referred to either a misconduct meeting or misconduct hearing.

Misconduct Meeting/Hearings – Chief Constables etc.

2. Where a case is referred to a misconduct meeting and the police officer concerned is—
   (a) a chief constable; or
   (b) in the case of the Metropolitan Police Force—
       (i) the commissioner;
       (ii) the deputy commissioner; or
       (iii) an assistant commissioner; or
   (c) in the case of the City of London police force, the commissioner,
   the misconduct proceedings shall be conducted by the following panel of persons appointed by the appropriate authority: -
   i) the chair of the police authority for the police force concerned, or another member of that police authority nominated by the chair, who shall be the chair; and
   ii) HMCIC or an inspector of constabulary nominated by HMCIC.

3. For a misconduct hearing, those persons are—
   (a) a barrister selected from a list of candidates nominated by the Secretary of State , who shall be the chair;
   (b) the chair of the police authority for the police force concerned or another member of that police authority nominated by that chair;
   (c) HMCIC or an inspector of constabulary nominated by HMCIC;
   (d) a person selected from a list of candidates maintained by a police authority.

Misconduct Meeting/Hearings – Other senior officers.

4. Where the case is referred to a misconduct meeting and the police officer concerned is a senior officer other than one mentioned above, those proceedings shall be conducted by the following panel of persons appointed by the appropriate authority: -
   (i) where the police officer concerned is a member of the Metropolitan Police Force, an assistant commissioner or a senior officer of at least one rank above that of the police officer concerned, nominated by an assistant commissioner, who shall be the chair;
   (ii) where the officer concerned is a member of the City of London police, the commissioner or a senior officer of at least one rank above that of the officer concerned nominated by the commissioner, who shall be chair; or
   (iii) in any other case, the chief officer of the force concerned or a senior officer of at least one rank above that of the police officer concerned, nominated by the chief officer, who shall be the chair; and
   the chair of the police authority for the force concerned or another member of that police authority nominated by the police authority chair.

5. For misconduct hearings, those persons are—
   (a) HMCIC or an inspector of constabulary nominated by HMCIC, who shall be the chair;
   (b) the chief officer of the force concerned or a senior officer of at least one rank above that of the police officer concerned, nominated by the chief officer;
   (c) the chair of the police authority for the force concerned or another member of that police authority nominated by that chair;
   (d) a person selected from a list of candidates maintained by a police authority.

6. The senior officer concerned should be informed of the names of the persons appointed to conduct the misconduct meeting/hearing together with the name of any person appointed to advise such persons at the meeting/hearing as soon as reasonably practicable after they have been appointed.
7. The senior officer may object to any person hearing or advising at a misconduct meeting or hearing in accordance with regulation 21 of the Conduct Regulations. In doing so the senior officer concerned will need to set out clear objections as to why a particular person(s) should not conduct or advise at the meeting.
8. If the senior officer concerned submits a compelling reason why such a person should not be involved in the meeting/hearing then, in the interests of fairness, a replacement should be found. The senior officer will be informed who the replacement is and will have the right to object to such person if he or she submits compelling reasons why the replacement should not be involved in the meeting/hearing in accordance with the procedure set out in regulation 21 of the Conduct Regulations.

Annex C
Appeals to Police Appeals Tribunal

Police Appeals Tribunal Rules 2008

1. Introduction

1.1 This guidance relates to appeals made to a Police Appeals Tribunal for matters that have been dealt with under the Police (Conduct) Regulations 2008 and the Police (Performance) Regulations 2008.

1.2 Appeals made to a Police Appeals Tribunal that were dealt with under the Police (Conduct) Regulations 2004 or the Police (Efficiency) Regulations 1999 will be dealt with under the Police Appeals Tribunal Rules 1999.

1.3 For the purposes of this guidance the following terms will be used: -

- 'Appellant' – The police officer who has submitted an appeal.
- 'Respondent' – In the case of an appeal brought by a police officer up to and including the rank of chief superintendent, the respondent will be the chief officer of that force. For senior officers the respondent is the police authority for that force.
- 'Working Day' – means any day other than a Saturday or Sunday or a day which is a bank holiday or a public holiday in England and Wales

2. Scope

2.1 A police officer has a right of appeal to a Police Appeals Tribunal against any disciplinary finding and/or disciplinary outcome imposed at a misconduct hearing or special case hearing held under the Police (Conduct) Regulations 2008. Senior police officers, in addition, have the right to appeal to a Police Appeals Tribunal against any disciplinary finding and/or outcome imposed at a misconduct meeting. A police officer may not appeal to a tribunal against a finding of misconduct or gross misconduct where that finding was made following acceptance by the officer that his or her conduct amounted to misconduct or gross misconduct (as the case may be).

2.2 A police officer of a rank up to and including chief superintendent has a right of appeal to a Police Appeals Tribunal against the finding and/or the following outcomes imposed following a third stage meeting under the Police (Performance) Regulations 2008: -

i) Dismissal; or
ii) Reduction in rank

2.3 In addition to the outcomes at (i) and (ii), if the case has been dealt with at a stage three meeting, without having progressed through stages 1 and 2, the police officer may appeal against the following outcomes: -

(a) redeployment to alternative duties
(b) the issue of a final written improvement notice
(c) the issue of a written improvement notice

2.4 A police officer may not appeal against a finding of unsatisfactory performance or attendance, or gross incompetence at a third stage performance meeting where that finding was made following acceptance by the officer that his or her performance or attendance has been unsatisfactory or that he or she has been grossly incompetent (as the case may be).

3. Composition and timing of Police Appeals Tribunals

3.1 Where the appeal is made by a police officer who is not a senior officer, the Tribunal appointed by the police authority will consist of; -

a) a legally qualified chair drawn from a list maintained by the Home Office;
b) a member of the police authority nominated by the authority;

c) a serving senior officer (ACPO rank); and

d) a retired member of a police force who was a member of an "appropriate staff association".

3.2 An "appropriate staff association" means if the appellant was of the rank of chief superintendent or superintendent, the Police Superintendents' Association of England and Wales. In any other case, it means the Police Federation of England and Wales.

3.3 The composition of a Police Appeals Tribunal for senior officers is set out in Schedule 6 to the Police Act 1996, as amended by the Criminal Justice and Immigration Act 2008.

3.4 It is expected that a tribunal will take place as soon as reasonably practicable and in any case should take place no later than 3 months of the determination by a tribunal chair that a hearing should be held.

3.5 It will be the responsibility of the police authority to satisfy itself that the members who are to sit on a Police Appeals Tribunal are sufficiently independent of the matter so as not to give rise to any suggestion of unfairness.

4. Grounds of appeal

4.1 A Police Appeals Tribunal is not a re hearing of the original matter; rather its role is to consider an appeal based on specific grounds.

4.2 In the case of matters dealt with under the Police (Conduct) Regulations 2008 the grounds for appeal are: -

a) That the finding or disciplinary action imposed was unreasonable; or

b) that there is evidence that could not reasonably have been considered at the misconduct meeting (in the case of senior police officers), the misconduct hearing or special case hearing (as the case may be); or

c) that there was a breach of the procedures set out in the Police (Conduct) Regulations 2008, the Police (Complaints and Misconduct) Regulations 2004, Schedule 3 to the Police Reform Act 2002 or other unfairness which could have materially affected the finding or decision on disciplinary action.

4.3 In the case of matters dealt with under the Police (Performance) Regulations 2008 the grounds for appeal are: -

a) That the finding of unsatisfactory performance or attendance or gross incompetence, or the outcome imposed, was unreasonable; or

b) that there is evidence that could not reasonably have been considered at the third stage meeting which could have materially affected the finding or decision on the outcome; or

c) that there was a breach of the procedures set out in the Police (Performance) Regulations 2008 or other unfairness which could have materially affected the finding or decision on the outcome; or

d) where the police officer was required to attend a third stage meeting following a first and second stage meeting, that the police officer concerned should not have been required to attend that meeting as his or her unsatisfactory performance or attendance was not similar to or connected with the unsatisfactory performance or attendance referred to in his or her final written improvement notice.

5. Notice of appeal

5.1 Where a police officer wishes to appeal then he or she will need to give notice of his or her appeal in writing to the police authority. The notice of appeal must be given within 10 working days, beginning with the first working day after the police officer is supplied with a written copy of the decision that he or she is appealing against.

5.2 In cases where the police officer fails to submit his or her notice of appeal within the 10 working days period, he or she may, within a reasonable time after the end of that period, submit a notice of appeal which shall be accompanied by the reasons why it was not submitted within that period, and the reasons for the officer's view that it was served within a reasonable time after that period.

5.3 The police authority will appoint a Police Appeals Tribunal chair to deal with the notice of appeal and any applications for extensions to the time limits. (See paragraphs 6 to 8 below). The same chair may, but need not, chair the tribunal that deals with the substantive appeal, if the matter proceeds to that stage.

5.4 Upon receipt of an appeal that has been submitted outside the 10 working day time limit, the police authority shall send a copy of the notice and the reasons to a tribunal chair, who shall determine: -

a) whether or not it was reasonably practicable for the notice to be given within the time limit, and
b) whether the notice was submitted within a reasonable time after the end of the 10 day period for submitting a notice of appeal.

5.5 Where the tribunal chair determines that it was reasonably practicable to have submitted the notice of appeal within the time limit or the chair determines that the notice was not submitted within a reasonable time after the end of the 10 day time limit, the appeal shall be dismissed. Where the tribunal chair determines that it was not reasonably practicable to have submitted the notice within the 10 working day period and that the notice was given within a reasonable time after the end of that period, the appeal shall be allowed to proceed.

5.6 In his or her notice of appeal, the appellant may request a copy of all or part of the transcript of the original hearing.

5.7 The police authority, upon receipt of a notice of appeal, shall, as soon as reasonably practicable, send a copy of the notice to the respondent and (where the appeal is a specified appeal[25]) to the Independent Police Complaints Commission (IPCC).

6. Procedure on notice of appeal

6.1 As soon as reasonably practicable after receipt of a copy of the notice of appeal and in any case within 15 working days (beginning with the first working day following the day of such receipt) the respondent shall provide to the police authority: -

a) a copy of the decision appealed against (namely the written judgement of the original panel/person);
b) any documents that were available to the panel/person conducting the original hearing; and
c) the transcript or part of the transcript of the proceedings at the original hearing requested by the appellant (see 5.6 above)

6.2 A copy of the transcript (if applicable) shall also at the same time be sent to the appellant.

6.3 The appellant, within 20 working days beginning with the first working day following the day on which he or she is supplied with a copy of the transcript or, where no transcript is requested, within 35 working days (beginning with the first working day following the day on which the appellant gave notice of his or her appeal), shall provide to the police authority: -

a) a notice setting out the finding, disciplinary action or outcome appealed against and of his or her grounds for the appeal;
b) any supporting documents

---

[25] A specified appeal is one where the decision appealed against arose from a complaint or conduct matter to which paragraph 17, 18 or 19 of Schedule 3 to the Police Reform Act 2002 (investigations) applied.

c) where the appellant is allowed to call witnesses (for appeals made only on the ground of there being evidence that could not reasonably have been considered at the original hearing and which could have materially affected the finding or outcome): -

    i) a list of any proposed witnesses; and

    ii) a witness statement from each of the proposed witness

d) If he or she consents to the appeal being determined without a hearing (that is, on the basis of the papers alone), notice in writing that he or she so consents.

6.4 In relation to the appellant, a "proposed witness" is a person whom the appellant wishes to call to give evidence at the hearing, whose evidence was not and could not reasonably have been considered at the hearing and whose evidence could have materially affected the decision being appealed against.

6.5 Not later than 20 working days, beginning with the first working day following the day on which the respondent receives the documents from the police authority, the respondent shall send to the police authority: -

a) a statement setting out the respondent's response to the appeal;

b) any supporting documents;

c) where the respondent is permitted to adduce witness evidence: -

    i) a list of any proposed witnesses;

    ii) a witness statement from each of the proposed witnesses; and

d) If he or she consents to the appeal being determined without a hearing (that is, on the basis of the papers alone), notice in writing that he or she so consents

6.6 The respondent should also send to the appellant, at the same time, a copy of the documents in (a),(c) and (d) above, together with a list of any documents submitted under (b).

6.7 The police authority will send a copy of the papers submitted by the respondent and appellant to the tribunal chair appointed to deal with the notice of appeal as soon as practicable following receipt.

6.8 The respondent may only propose a witness to attend where the ground for appeal by the appellant is that there is evidence that could not reasonably have been considered at the original hearing which could have materially affected the finding or decision on disciplinary action or the outcome. In such cases the respondent may propose a witness who may give evidence to deal with the issue raised by the appellant. An example may be where the appellant submits new medical evidence that was not available to the original hearing and the respondent wishes to propose its own witness to give evidence on this issue.

6.9 In the event that the chair decides that there should be a hearing, and the appellant had consented to the matter being determined on the papers, the appellant is under no obligation to attend but is entitled to reconsider his or her position. The appellant may also reconsider his or her consent to the determination of the appeal on the basis of the papers prior to a determination on this issue by the chair. The appellant's withdrawal of consent should be notified to the police authority in writing and if this occurs, a hearing must be held.

6.10 Where the appellant, having seen the documents sent in by the respondent, withdraws his or her consent to the matter being dealt with on the papers, a hearing must be held.

7. Extension of time limits

7.1 The appellant or the respondent can apply to the police authority for an extension to the time limits stated above for providing documents (except the time for giving notice of appeal: see paragraph 5) setting out its reasons for the application and the additional time period it is seeking.

7.2 The police authority will copy any application by the respondent or the appellant to the other party as soon as practicable after receipt and ask whether it consents to the application.

7.3 Where the other party consents to the application for more time then the police authority shall extend the time to the agreed time limit. Where the other party does not consent then the police authority will refer the matter to the tribunal chair who shall determine whether the relevant time period should be extended and if so for how long.

7.4 There is an expectation that the time limits will ordinarily be complied with and only in exceptional circumstances, for example due to the complexity of the case, will a time limit be extended.

8. Review of notice of appeal

8.1 Upon receipt of the documents submitted to him or her by the police authority, the chair appointed to consider the notice of appeal shall determine whether the appeal should be dismissed at this stage. It is expected that the chair will normally make his or her preliminary determination within 10 working days of receiving the documents (see also paragraph 8.4).

8.2 The tribunal chair will dismiss the appeal at this stage if he or she considers that: -

a) the appeal has no real prospect of success; and
b) there is no other compelling reason why the appeal should proceed.

8.3 Where the tribunal chair is minded to dismiss the appeal at this stage, he or she will notify the appellant and the respondent in writing of his or her view together with his or her reasons before making his or her final determination.

8.4 The appellant and the respondent may within 10 working days, beginning with the first working day after the day of being notified of the chair's preliminary view, make written representations to the chair and the chair will consider such representations before coming to his or her final decision.

8.5 The tribunal chair shall inform the appellant, respondent and police authority of his or her final decision. It is expected that the tribunal chair's decision will be made and communicated within 10 working days of receipt of the last of the representations. Where the tribunal chair dismisses the appeal then the notification will include his or her reasons for doing do.

9. Determination of an appeal

9.1 Where the tribunal chair allows the appeal to go forward to a tribunal hearing then the police authority will be responsible for making the administrative arrangements prior to and at the tribunal and for ensuring that the members of the tribunal appointed to deal with the appeal are sent the papers together with a schedule of the documents that each of the members should have.

9.2 The tribunal chair who made the determination as to whether to allow the notice of appeal to proceed to a tribunal need not necessarily be the same tribunal chair who hears the subsequent appeal. However, the chair who makes the decision as to whether the appeal should be dealt with at a hearing or on the papers should be the chair appointed to hear the appeal itself.

9.3 Where an appeal has not been dismissed at the review stage, the tribunal chair shall determine whether the appeal should be dealt with at a hearing. It is expected that this decision will be made by the tribunal chair within 10 working days of receiving the papers. If the appellant has not consented to an appeal being dealt with on the papers then a hearing shall be held. If the appellant has consented, the tribunal chair may determine that the appeal shall be dealt with without a hearing. If the appeal is to be dealt with at a hearing, the chair shall give the appellant and the respondent his or her name and contact address.

10. Power to request disclosure of documents

10.1 At any time after the appellant and respondent have submitted their respective documents, the appellant or respondent may apply to the tribunal chair for disclosure of any document by the other party which is relevant to the appeal.

10.2 The tribunal chair may request the disclosure of any such document and where it is disclosed, a copy shall be given to the tribunal chair and the requesting party.

10.3 Where the appellant or respondent does not comply with a request to disclose any document, then the appellant or respondent (as appropriate) shall give the tribunal chair and the other party their reasons for non-disclosure in writing.

10.4 The tribunal in making its determination of the appeal may take into account any non-disclosure of documents where the tribunal decides that the requested documents may have been relevant to the determination of the appeal.

11. Legal and other representation

11.1 The appellant can be represented at a hearing by a relevant lawyer or a police friend. Where the appellant is represented by a lawyer then the appellant's police friend may also attend. (See the section on 'Police friends' ain the introduction to the Guidance).

11.2 The respondent may be represented at the hearing by a relevant lawyer, a police officer, the chief executive or other officer or employee of the relevant police authority.

12. Procedure at hearing

12.1 Where the case is to be heard at a tribunal hearing, the chair of the tribunal shall cause the appellant and the respondent to be given written notice of the time, date and place of the hearing, at least 20 working days or such shorter period as may with the agreement of both parties be determined, before the hearing begins.

12.2 Subject to the rules set out in the Police Appeals Tribunal Rules 2008, the procedure at the tribunal shall be determined by the tribunal.

12.3 The tribunal chair will determine in advance of the tribunal whether to allow any witness that the appellant or respondent proposes to call to give evidence at the tribunal.

12.4 Witnesses will only be permitted where the ground for appeal is that there is evidence that could not reasonably have been considered at the original hearing which could have materially affected the finding or decision on outcome.

12.5 No witnesses shall give evidence at the hearing unless the chair reasonably believes that it is necessary for the witness to do so.

12.6 Any witness that does attend the tribunal may be subject to questioning and cross questioning.

12.7 It is for the Tribunal to decide on the admissibility of any evidence, or to determine whether or not any question should or should not be put to a witness.

12.8 The police authority shall arrange for a verbatim record of evidence given at the tribunal to be taken and kept by the authority for at least 2 years.

12.9 The Tribunal have discretion to proceed with the hearing in the absence of either party, whether represented or not, if it appears to be just and proper to do so. Where it is decided to proceed in the absence of either party the Tribunal should record its reasons for doing so. The Tribunal may adjourn the appeal as necessary.

12.10 The hearing shall be held in private. The Tribunal may allow a person to attend the hearing as an observer for the purposes of training. On the application of the appellant or the respondent or otherwise, the tribunal chair may require any observer to withdraw from all or any part of the hearing.

13. Attendance of other persons

13.1 Where the matter to be dealt with at the appeal is related directly to a complaint made against the appellant or a conduct matter involving an interested party, then the chair of the tribunal shall cause the complainant or interested party to be given notice of the time, date and place of the tribunal.

13.2 The complainant or interested party may attend the tribunal as an observer. The complainant or interested party may be accompanied by one other person and in addition, if the complainant or interested party has a special need, by one further person to accommodate that need.

13.3 Where the complainant or interested party or any person accompanying them is to give evidence at the tribunal, then he or she or any person accompanying him or her may not attend the hearing before that evidence is given.

13.4 Where the appeal is a 'specified appeal' (see footnote 1), then the tribunal chair shall cause the IPCC to be notified of the time, date and location of the tribunal. In such cases the IPCC may attend as an observer.

14. Determination and Outcome of Appeal

14.1 A tribunal need not be unanimous in its determination of the appeal or of any other decision before it and may reach a decision based on a majority. Where a tribunal finds itself divided equally, the tribunal chair will have the casting vote. The tribunal shall not indicate whether any determination was taken unanimously or by a majority.

14.2 A tribunal, when determining any disciplinary or unsatisfactory performance outcome imposed, may impose any outcome that the original panel/person could have imposed. The tribunal has the power to increase as well as reduce the outcome imposed by the original panel/person.

14.3 The decision of the tribunal will normally be made on the day of the tribunal hearing. Where this is not practicable then the decision will be made as soon as possible.

14.4 The tribunal chair shall, within 3 working days of the tribunal determining the appeal, give written notice to the appellant of the tribunal's decision.

14.5 As soon as reasonably practicable after the determination of the appeal the tribunal chair shall cause to be sent to the appellant, respondent and police authority a written statement of its reasons for its determination of the appeal. It is expected that this will normally be sent within 20 working days of the determination of the appeal.

14.6 A police officer ordered to be reinstated in his or her former force or rank will be deemed to have served in his or her force and/or rank continuously from the date of the original decision to the date of reinstatement. Reinstatement means that the officer is put back in the role that he or she would have been in if not dismissed or reduced in rank. The Tribunal may determine (to such extent as they decide) that the officer is deemed to have served in the force for the purposes of his or her pay from the date of the original decision.

15. Costs

15.1 The fees and expenses of the tribunal members will be borne by the police authority.

15.2 An appellant pays their own costs of the appeal unless the tribunal directs that the whole or part of his or her costs are to be paid by the police authority. Where the Tribunal decides to award costs in favour of the appellant, it is suggested that the Tribunal sets out the reasons for this and identifies any lessons to be learned for the force as a result of the case.

Annex D
Seconded Police Officers

Under Section 97 of the Police Act 1996

1. This guidance sets out the procedures for dealing with matters of unsatisfactory performance or attendance and misconduct allegations in respect of police officers who are seconded under the provisions of Section 97 of the Police Act 1996.

2. The procedures set out in the Police (Conduct) Regulations 2008 and Police (Performance) Regulations 2008 cannot be applied by the organisation to which the police officer is seconded under Section 97 of the Police Act 1996. However the procedures set out in the Regulations can be applied by the parent force in respect of conduct, performance or attendance whilst on secondment.

3. Those responsible for managing police officers on secondment are expected to uphold the principles contained within this guidance, namely to manage any issue of unsatisfactory performance or attendance or minor misconduct in a proportionate, fair and timely manner without returning an officer to his or her parent force. Only if it is necessary to institute the formal procedures should an officer be returned to force, in accordance with the principles and procedures expressed below. [NB where an officer is on secondment under the Police (Overseas Service) Act 1945, with the Police Ombudsman for Northern Ireland or with the Police Service of Northern Ireland, then he can be dealt with by the receiving organisation under their disciplinary arrangements. However, on return to his force, he can still be dealt with under the Police disciplinary arrangements in respect of the same matters.]

4. It is important that police officers on secondment are clear about who has line management responsibility for them. The line managers for such police officers must ensure that the police officer continues to have a PDR and is made aware of these arrangements for dealing with issues of misconduct or unsatisfactory performance or attendance.

Unsatisfactory performance procedures

5. It is recognised that the public is entitled to expect the highest standards of performance of police duties from all seconded police officers. Similarly, managers need a management system which both supports police officers performing their tasks and reinforces the aims of both the service and the organisation to which the police officer is seconded.

6. Unlike the broad policing functions performed by police forces throughout England and Wales, the nature and range of the tasks carried out by police officers who are seconded from their forces are specific and, by their nature may be narrow and/or specialist. It follows that the need to deal fairly with such police officers whose performance is giving rise to concern requires particular attention.

7. Where a pattern of performance by a seconded police officer is giving rise to concern, the line manager should raise his or her concerns with the police officer concerned and seek to identify any underlying causes of the unsatisfactory performance or attendance. The line manager should seek to improve the police officer's performance or attendance to an acceptable standard.

8. Where there is no or insufficient improvement in the performance or attendance of the police officer, the seconded police officer's line manager should prepare a written report which details the nature of the unsatisfactory performance or attendance together with the remedial and other measures taken, and send this report to the head of the organisation to which the police officer is seconded (or his or her nominated representative). The head of the organisation (or nominated representative), in conjunction with the appropriate authority for the police officer concerned, will decide whether it is appropriate that the police officer concerned should be returned to his

or her parent force or whether the unsatisfactory performance or attendance can be addressed with the police officer remaining on secondment.

9. Where a police officer who has been returned to his or her parent force under this procedure continues to demonstrate the same pattern of unsatisfactory performance or attendance then the details of the unsatisfactory performance or attendance whilst on secondment may be used to inform the decision whether it is appropriate to use the UPPs.

Misconduct procedures

10. The public and colleagues with whom police officers work are entitled to expect the highest level of personal and professional standards of police officers. Those serving on secondment are expected to act in accordance with the Standards of Professional Behaviour (see Section 1).

11. Section 2 of this guidance sets out the principles for dealing with allegations of misconduct. This allows for less serious matters to be dealt with in a proportionate and timely manner by means of management action and this principle will apply to police officers who are seconded to other organisations with line managers having the responsibility for dealing with these issues.

12. The organisation to which the police officer has been seconded will need to make an initial assessment of the allegation of misconduct. If that assessment determines that the matter can be dealt with by management action then the seconded officer's manager is expected to deal with the matter in this way. As part of this decision making process, it may be necessary for the line manager to contact the appropriate authority for the seconded officer to assist in determining the nature of the conduct and whether it should be investigated. In this regard, the appropriate authority will need to consider its obligations under the Police Reform Act 2002 and any requirement to refer a matter to the Independent Police Complaints Commission.

13. However, where the line manager considers that an alleged breach of the Standards of Professional Behaviour is more serious and indicates that the police officer concerned may have committed a criminal offence, or behaved in a manner that would justify the bringing of disciplinary proceedings, then the head of the organisation to which the police officer is seconded (or his or her nominated representative) will liaise with the appropriate authority from which the police officer concerned is seconded to assess whether the officer should be returned to the force while a preliminary assessment into the matter is conducted by the parent force. If, as a result of that preliminary assessment, the parent force considers it appropriate to issue a Regulation 15 notice in relation to the matter then the officer must be returned to force.

14. Where it is determined by the appropriate authority for the seconded officer and the organisation to which he or she is seconded, that the conduct, if proved or admitted, would not justify the bringing of disciplinary proceedings then management action may still be taken where appropriate.

15. At the conclusion of any disciplinary proceedings, where the police officer has been returned to the parent force, then the parent force together with the organisation to which the police officer concerned was seconded, will decide if it is appropriate for the police officer to be able to resume his or her secondment.

16. The arrangements set out in this guidance should be agreed to as part of the secondment agreements in force between the police force, the receiving organisation and the officer. This will ensure that the receiving organisation accepts its role as set out above, and that the officer gives his or her consent to the exchange of information between the receiving organisation and the home force.

Annex E

NOTICE OF ALLEGED BREACH OF THE STANDARDS OF PROFESSIONAL BEHAVIOUR

REGULATION 15 POLICE (CONDUCT) REGULATIONS 2008 / REGULATION 14 A POLICE (COMPLAINTS AND MISCONDUCT) REGULATIONS 2004

Name: _____ Warrant number: _____ Rank: _____

Name of complainant (If appropriate):

Case reference number: [_____]

This is to notify you that an allegation has been made that your individual conduct may have breached the Standards of Professional Behaviour and that there will be an investigation into the circumstances.

Whilst you do not have to say anything it may harm your case if you do not mention when interviewed, or when providing any information (under regulations 16(1) or 22(2) or (3) or 45 of the Police (Conduct) Regulations 2008 or regulation 14C of the Police (Complaints and Misconduct) Regulations 2004), something which you later rely on in any misconduct proceedings or special case hearing or any appeal proceedings.

The details of your conduct that it is alleged may have breached the Standards of Professional Behaviour can be found below. (See notes overleaf).

Based on the information available at this time the conduct described above, if proven or admitted, has been assessed as amounting to:

Misconduct [_____]   Gross Misconduct [_____]

This may result in your attendance at a:

Misconduct Meeting [_____]   Misconduct Hearing [_____]

(continue on separate sheet as necessary)

Name of person investigating _____

Contact Details (Address / Tel / E-mail) _____

Signature of person investigating _____ Date:

I acknowledge that I have received a copy of this document and my attention has been drawn to the accompanying notes.

Signature of Officer concerned. _____ Date:

Print Name _____

I authorise a copy of this notice to be forwarded to my Staff Association. Yes ☐ No ☐

Signature of Officer concerned. _____

If the notice is not given to the officer by the person investigating please append the name and signature of the person giving the notice below: -

Name: Signature: Date:

Explanatory Notes

1. This notice has been issued to inform you at the earliest possible stage that an allegation has been made that you may have breached the Standards of Professional Behaviour and that there is to be an investigation into your individual conduct in accordance with the Police (Conduct) Regulations 2008 or the Police (Complaints and Misconduct) Regulations 2004.

2. The fact that you have been given this notice does not necessarily imply that misconduct proceedings will be taken against you but is given to safeguard your interests. It is given in order that you have the opportunity to secure any documentation or other material or make any notes that may assist you in responding to the allegation(s).

3. You have the right to seek advice from your staff association and be advised, represented and accompanied at any interview, meeting or hearing by a 'police friend' who must be a member of the police service or a nominee of your staff association and not otherwise involved in the matter (in accordance with regulation 6 of the Police (Conduct) Regulations 2008 or 14B of the Police (Complaints and Misconduct) Regulations 2004). A special constable may be represented by a police officer or police staff member.

4. Within 10 working days of being served with this notice (starting with the day after this notice is given, unless this period is extended by the investigator) you may provide a written or oral statement relating to any matter under investigation and you or your police friend may provide any relevant documents to the investigator who must consider those documents. Failure to provide a response to this notice may lead to an adverse inference being drawn in any subsequent misconduct proceedings or at any special case hearing or appeal.

5. If, following service of this notice, the assessment of conduct or the determination of the likely form of any misconduct proceedings to be taken is revised then as soon as practicable you will be given a further written notice together with reasons for that change.

6. Prior to being interviewed you will be provided with sufficient information and time to prepare for the interview. The information provided should include full details of the allegations made against you, including the relevant date(s) and place(s) of the alleged misconduct, where known.

7. You are reminded that failure to provide an account or response to any questions at this stage of the investigation may lead to an adverse inference being drawn at a later stage.

8. At the conclusion of the investigation, if direction is given to withdraw the case then upon request you shall, subject to the harm test, be provided with a copy of the investigator's report or such parts of that report as relate to you.

9. Where the case is referred to misconduct proceedings you shall be given written notice of the referral, a copy of any statement made by you to the investigator, a copy, subject to the harm test, of the investigator's report or such parts of that report as relate to you and any other relevant document gathered in the course of the investigation.

10. You should understand that any decision as to whether there is a case to answer that you may have breached the Standards of Professional Behaviour and whether the matter should be referred to misconduct proceedings will be based on an objective assessment of all the evidence provided during the course of the investigation. If the case is referred to misconduct proceedings, the decision at the meeting or hearing will be determined on the standard of proof required in civil cases, which is the balance of probabilities.

11. If the case is referred to a misconduct hearing or special case hearing you have the right to be legally represented by a barrister or solicitor. If you elect not to be so represented you may be represented by a police friend, however if you elect not to be legally represented you may still be dismissed or receive any other disciplinary outcome without being so represented.

12. Outcomes available in misconduct proceedings:

Misconduct Meeting	Misconduct Hearing
• Misconduct not found • No further action • Management advice • Written warning (12 months) • Final written warning (18 months)	• Misconduct not found • No further action • Management advice • Written warning (12 months) • Final written warning (18 months) • Extension of final written warning (exceptional circumstances only) • Dismissal with notice (minimum 28 days) (misconduct plus final written warning) • Dismissal without notice (Gross misconduct)

APPENDIX J

The Police (Amendment) Regulations 2008, SI 2008/2865

STATUTORY INSTRUMENTS

2008 NO. 2865

POLICE, ENGLAND AND WALES

The Police (Amendment) Regulations 2008

Made	*5th November 2008*
Laid before Parliament	*7th November 2008*
Coming into force	*1st December 2008*

The Secretary of State makes the following Regulations in exercise of the powers conferred by section 50 of the Police Act 1996[1].

In accordance with section 63(3) of that Act, the Secretary of State has supplied a draft of these Regulations to the Police Advisory Board for England and Wales and taken into consideration their representations.

Citation, commencement and interpretation

1.—(1) These Regulations may be cited as the Police (Amendment) Regulations 2008.

(2) These Regulations come into force on 1st December 2008.

(3) In these Regulations "the 2003 Regulations" means the Police Regulations 2003[2].

Amendments to the 2003 Regulations

2.—(1) Regulation 15 (contents of personal records) of the 2003 Regulations is amended as follows.

(2) In paragraph (3) after the words "Police (Conduct) Regulations 1999" insert the words ", regulation 35 of the Police (Conduct) Regulations 2004[3]".

(3) After paragraph (4) insert the following paragraphs —

"(4A) Subject to paragraphs (4B), (4C) and (5A), the record of service kept in accordance with paragraph (2)(g) shall also include particulars of all—

(a) disciplinary action, save for management advice—
    (i) taken under regulation 35, 40 or 55 of the Police (Conduct) Regulations 2008[4]; or
    (ii) ordered following an appeal to a police appeals tribunal in accordance with the Police Appeals Tribunals Rules 2008[5];

(b) written improvement notices issued under regulation 15 or varied under regulation 18 of the Police (Performance) Regulations 2008[6];

(c) final written improvement notices issued under regulation 22 or varied under regulation 25 of the Police (Performance) Regulations 2008; and

(d) outcomes, save for redeployment to alternative duties, ordered under regulation 38 of the Police (Performance) Regulations 2008 or following an appeal to a police appeals tribunal in accordance with the Police Appeals Tribunals Rules 2008.

(4B) In relation to a record of service—

(a) a written warning shall be expunged after the expiry of the period of 12 months as referred to in regulation 3(3)(a) of the Police (Conduct) Regulations 2008 (subject to regulation 3(4) of those Regulations);

(b) a final written warning shall be expunged—

   (i) after the period of 18 months as referred to in regulation 3(3)(b) of the Police (Conduct) Regulations 2008 (subject to regulation 3(4) of those Regulations); or

   (ii) in the event of a final written warning being extended under regulation 35(6)(b) or 55(2)(b) of the Police (Conduct) Regulations 2008, on the expiry of that extended warning;

(c) a reduction in rank shall be expunged after 5 years from the date the officer concerned was reduced in rank; and

(d) a written improvement notice or a final written improvement notice issued or extended shall be expunged at the end of the validity period of such notice as defined in the Police (Performance) Regulations 2008 unless in relation to such a notice a period mentioned in regulation 10(2) of those Regulations has been extended beyond 12 months, in which case that notice shall be expunged at the end of such extended period.

(4C) A written warning or final written warning shall not be expunged from the record of service where before the time period expires for the written notice or final written notice to be expunged under paragraph (4A)(a) or (b) a written notice is served on the officer concerned under regulation 15 of the Police (Conduct) Regulations 2008 or under regulation 14A of the Police (Complaints and Misconduct) Regulations 2004[7]. In such cases, the written warning or final written warning shall remain on the record of service until the conclusion of the disciplinary proceedings for which the written notice was served".

(4) After paragraph (5) insert the following paragraph—

"(5A) Where, following an appeal meeting under the Police (Conduct) Regulations 2008, a first stage appeal meeting or second stage appeal meeting under the Police (Performance) Regulations 2008 or an appeal to a police appeals tribunal under the Police Appeals Tribunals Rules 2008, the person or persons hearing the appeal decide to reverse, revoke, vary the terms of or impose a different disciplinary action, outcome or notice, the previous disciplinary action, outcome or notice which was the subject matter of the appeal shall be expunged forthwith".

Home Office   Minister of State

EXPLANATORY NOTE

(This Note is Not Part of the Regulations)

These Regulations amend regulation 15 of the Police Regulations 2003 following changes to the police performance and disciplinary procedures, set out in the Police (Conduct) Regulations 2008, the Police (Performance) Regulations 2008 and the Police Appeals Tribunals Rules 2008.

New paragraphs (4A) to (4C), as inserted by regulation 2(3), set out the length of time that disciplinary action, outcomes or notices imposed under the new police conduct or performance procedures should remain on an officer's personal record. New paragraph (5A), as inserted by regulation 2(4), provides that where there is an appeal against a disciplinary action, outcome or notice, any previous disciplinary action, outcome or notice recorded following the initial misconduct meeting or hearing (in the case of misconduct proceedings) or first, second or third stage meeting (in the case of performance proceedings), shall be expunged where it is reversed, varied or removed or where a different action, outcome or notice is imposed.

Notes:

[1] 1996 c.16. Section 50 was amended by paragraph 95 of Schedule 27 to the Greater London Authority Act 1999 (c.29) and section 125 of the Criminal Justice and Police Act 2001 (c.16). It is also amended by paragraph 3 of Schedule 22 to the Criminal Justice and Immigration Act 2008 (c.4). Section 63 was amended by paragraph 78 of Schedule 4 to the Serious Organised Crime and Police Act 2005 (c.15) and paragraph 6 of Schedule 22 to the Criminal Justice and Immigration Act 2008 (c.4).

[2] S.I. 2003/527, as amended by S.I. 2006/3449, 2005/2834; there are other amendments but none is relevant.

[3] S.I. 2004/645, as amended by S.I. 2006/549.

[4] S.I. 2008/2864.

[5] S.I. 2008/2863.

[6] S.I. 2008/2862.

[7] S.I. 2004/643, as amended by S.I. 2005/3311 and S.I. 2008/2866; there are other amending instruments but none is relevant. Regulation 14A is inserted by S.I. 2008/2866.

INDEX

abuse of process
  conclusion, 12.59–12.64
  delay, 12.55–12.56
  fair hearings, 12.57–12.58
  fair trial (Art 6), 12.59–12.64
  jurisdiction
    exceptional remedy, 12.45–12.46
    executive unlawfulness, 12.27–12.35
    fair hearings and regulatory
      departure, 12.36–12.44
    proof, 12.47–12.48
  overview, 12.01–12.07
  police as regulated profession
    consequences of regulatory
      failure, 12.17–12.23
    judicial review, 12.24–12.26
    primacy of regulation, 12.08–12.16
  regulatory departures
    general principles, 12.49–12.54
accountability
  IPCC, 3.93
  NPIA, 1.128
ACPO *see* **Association of Chief Police Officers**
admissibility, *see* **evidence**
adverse inferences
  misconduct proceedings under 2008
    Regulations, 8.89–8.95
  procedure on receipt of referral notice, 8.37
Advisory, Conciliation and Arbitration Service
  background to 2008 Regulations, 5.07
  basis for regulation, 4.13
anonymity at inquests, 14.127–14.141
APA *see* **Association of Police Authorities**
appeals
  see also **reviews**
  central changes under 2008 regime, 4.14
  chief officers
    conclusion, 11.112–11.113
    overview, 11.01–11.07
    Police Appeals Tribunals, 11.45–11.111
  fast-track procedure
    2004 Conduct regulations, 10.75–10.76
  inherent complexities, 6.03
  local resolution, 6.116–6.118
  Minister's power to make rules, 1.31

  misconduct proceedings under 2008 Regulations
    entitlement, 8.142
    against outcome of hearings, 8.155
    against outcome of meetings, 8.143–8.154
  outcomes of first-stage meetings under 2008
    Regulations
    general entitlement, 5.123–5.135
    meetings, 5.131–5.135
  outcomes of second-stage meetings under 2008
    Regulations, 5.151–5.154
  outcomes of third-stage meetings under 2008
    Regulations, 5.208
  overview of regulatory framework, 4.05, 4.13
  Police Appeals Tribunals Rules 1999, App B
  Police Appeals Tribunals Rules 2008, App H
  proceedings under 2004 Regulations, 9.114
  reports of investigations, 7.189–7.195
  senior officers, 11.44
appointment of investigators
  procedure
    2002 Act, 7.96–7.102
    2008 Regulations, 7.91–7.95
  qualifications
    2002 Act, 7.105–7.109
    2008 Regulations, 7.103–7.104
areas and forces
  inter-force activity, 1.19–1.22
    collaboration agreements, 1.19–1.20
    collaborative arrangements, 1.23–1.25
    international joint investigations, 1.22
    public safety and order, 1.21
  organizational overview, 1.11–1.16
  table of force statistics, App A
assessment of conduct
  background and rationale, 7.74–7.75
  series of graded assessments, 7.83–7.90
  severity assessments, 7.76–7.82
Association of Chief Police Officers
  consultation prior to 2008 Regulations, 5.06
  funding for inquests, 14.113
Association of Police Authorities
  consultation prior to 2008 Regulations, 5.06
  role, 1.102
attendance and participation
  see also **unsatisfactory attendance**

attendance and participation (*cont.*)
1999 PAT Rules, 11.67–11.69
chief officers' reviews, 11.21–11.25, 11.38
misconduct proceedings under 2008 Regulations
appeals, 8.151
complainants and interested
parties, 8.76–8.85
investigators, 8.75
IPCC, 8.68–8.69
nature of 'private' proceedings, 8.66
officer concerned, 8.67
public hearings, 8.70–8.74
authorities *see* Police authorities
Authority, respect and courtesy, 6.46
Autrefois acquit, 9.83–9.84

behaviour *see* misconduct
best value, 1.100–1.101
bias *see* interested parties
burden of proof
abuse of process, 12.47–12.48
inquests, 14.154
misconduct proceedings under 2008
Regulations, 8.105–8.108
procedure under 2008 Regulations, 5.52
business interests, 1.18

capability *see* performance
careless driving, 15.134–15.136
causing death by dangerous driving, 15.134
challenging and reporting improper conduct
Home Office Guidance, 6.58–6.60
Police (Conduct) Regulations 2008, 6.35
character evidence, 8.109–8.110
charges
disclosure, 9.87–9.89
drafting, 9.90–9.93
chief constables, *see also* senior officers
appointment of conducting officers under 2004
Regulations, 9.101–9.105
collaboration agreements, 1.20
rank structure, 1.17
reports to Secretary of State, 1.61
review of fast-track procedure, 10.70–10.74
chief officers
appeals
conclusion, 11.112–11.113
overview, 11.01–11.07
Police Appeals Tribunals, 11.45–11.111
initial handling of complaints, 6.85–6.87
organizational overview, 1.04–1.06
local procedures, 1.09
rank structure, 1.17
removal
combined procedure, 2.16–2.37

conclusion, 2.38
Home Office Protocol, 2.14–2.15
Minister's powers, 2.11–2.13
overview, 2.01–2.06
revised powers of direction under 1996
Act, 1.76–1.77
statutory framework, 2.07–2.10
reviews
2004 Regulations, 11.08–11.43
conclusion, 11.112–11.113
overview, 11.01–11.07
strategic priorities, 1.35
Chief Police Officers' Staff Association, 5.06
civil proceedings, 6.126–6.127
Code of Conduct (2004 Regulations), 9.32–9.44,
10.70
codes of practice
basis for regulation, 4.13
organizational overview, 1.06
revised powers of direction under 1996
Act, 1.66–1.67
cognate expressions, 5.35
collaboration agreements, 1.19–1.20
combined procedure
consultation with HMIC, 2.19–2.20
initial decision, 2.16–2.18
pending resignation or retirement, 2.27–2.37
suspension, 2.20–2.26
competence *see* gross incompetence; performance
complainants
attendance and participation at misconduct
proceedings, 8.76–8.85
information about disciplinary
recommendations, 7.203–7.205
treatment in fast-track cases, 10.24–10.42
complaints
defined, 6.72–6.75
IPCC
conclusions, 3.195–3.196
disciplinary procedure, 3.91–3.194
general functions and duties, 3.51–3.90
legal character, 3.22–3.40
membership and staff, 3.41–3.50
overview, 3.01–3.12
statutory framework, 3.13–3.21
overview of regulatory framework
central changes under 2008
Regulations, 4.14
introduction and history of reform,
4.01–4.09
Taylor Review, 4.10–4.13
process charts, 4.18
revised powers of direction under 1996
Act, 1.68–1.75
summary of specific duties

Police Act 1996, 1.110
Police Reform Act 2002, 1.110–1.118
conditions of service, 1.18
conduct *see* **misconduct**
confidentiality, 6.52–6.53
see also **privacy**
consultation
Association of Police Authorities, 1.102
background to 2008 Regulations, 5.06
police authorities and local community, 1.98
removal of chief officers, 2.19–2.20
Secretary of State
general duties, 1.30
strategic priorities, 1.33
control, *see* **direction and control**
coroners *see* **inquests**
corporate manslaughter
conclusions, 15.126–15.127
inquest verdicts, 14.32
introduction, 15.114–15.117
statutory provisions, 15.118–15.125
costs *see* **funding for legal representation**
IPCC charges for advice, 3.69
CPOSA *see* **Chief Police Officers' Staff Association**
Crime and disorder reduction partnerships
best value, 1.100–1.101
power for Minister to merge areas, 1.27
criminal proceedings
see also **civil proceedings; fast-track procedure**
adjournment of inquests, 14.59–14.67
application of criminal law to police
conclusion, 15.163–15.164
overview, 15.01–15.09
autrefois acquit, 9.83–9.84
driving offences
introduction, 15.128–15.132
police exemptions, 15.138–15.158
statutory provisions, 15.133–15.137
summary of police liability, 15.139–15.162
investigatory regime
effect of outstanding proceedings, 7.50–7.54
harm test for disclosure, 7.16–7.35
notice of criminal proceedings
by DPP, 7.178
overlapping interviews, 7.145–7.154
misconduct in public office
conclusion, 15.73–15.74
essential requirements, 15.15–15.72
overview, 15.10–15.14
proceedings under 2004 Regulations, 9.79
restrictions under 2002 Act, 6.146–6.148
unlawful killing
causation, 15.84–15.87
duty of care, 15.81–15.83
inquest verdicts, 14.168–14.178

introduction, 15.75–15.77
manslaughter, 15.91–15.127
overview of forms of homicide, 15.78–15.80
self-defence, 15.88–15.90
cross-border policing, 1.19
Crown Prosecution Service, 10.09–10.23

dangerous driving
expert driving ability, 15.153–15.154
speed as basis of dangerous driving, 15.155
statutory exemptions, 15.149–15.152
statutory provisions, 15.134
death and serious injury
see also **inquests**
causing death by dangerous driving, 15.134
conduct matters disclosed during DSI
investigation, 6.131
deaths in custody, 14.16–14.20
defined, 6.77–6.79
handling of DSI matters under 2002
Act, 6.140–6.145
initial handling of complaints under 2002 Act
overview, 6.02–6.05
statutory and regulatory
frameworks, 6.61–6.63
statutory provisions, 6.64, 6.61
IPCC powers, 3.06
manslaughter
corporate manslaughter, 15.114–15.127
gross negligence manslaughter, 15.96–15.127
unlawful and dangerous act
manslaughter, 15.91–15.95
reports of investigations, 7.186–7.188
unlawful killing
causation, 15.84–15.87
duty of care, 15.81–15.83
inquest verdicts, 14.168–14.178
introduction, 15.75–15.77
overview of forms of homicide, 15.78–15.80
self-defence, 15.88–15.90
delay
abuse of process, 12.55–12.56
inquests, 14.11
development *see* **learning and development**
directed surveillance, 7.155–7.156
direction and control
organizational overview
local procedures, 1.07–1.10
role of chief officer, 1.04–1.06
Police Reform Act 2002, 6.82
Director of Public Prosecutions, 10.17–10.18
disabled persons
attendance and participation at misconduct
proceedings, 8.79
equality and diversity, 5.88

disciplinary procedure *see* **misconduct**
disclosure
  drafting charges, 9.87–9.89
  fast-track procedure, 10.24–10.42,
    10.87–10.97
  harm test for disclosure, 7.14–7.34
  Home Office Protocol, 2.36
  investigator's report, 8.21–8.22
  IPCC duties, 3.31–3.34
  proceedings under 2004 Regulations, 9.69–9.73
discreditable conduct
  Home Office Guidance, 6.55
  Police (Conduct) Regulations 2008, 6.35
dismissal
  discharge of probationers
    decided authorities, 13.14–13.22
    general provisions, 13.03–13.13
    key points, 13.23
    procedure, 13.24–13.25
  fast-track procedure, 10.109
  gross misconduct, 8.124
  misconduct proceedings under 2008
    Regs, 8.115–8.117
  outcome of proceedings under 2004 Regulations
    non-senior officers, 9.109
    senior officers, 9.116
  outcome of third-stage meeting, 5.195–5.197
  PAT Rules, 11.49
diversity *see* **equality and diversity**
documents
  adverse inferences, 8.91
  first-stage meetings under 2008
    Regulations, 5.102–5.103, 5.100
  misconduct proceedings under 2008 Regulations
    appeals, 8.150
    general principles, 8.61–8.65
    procedure on receipt of referral notice, 8.39
  overview of procedure under 2008
    Regulations, 5.53
  second-stage meetings under 2008
    Regulations, 5.146
  third-stage meetings under 2008
    Regulations, 5.183
driving offences
  introduction, 15.128–15.132
  police exemptions, 15.138–15.158
  statutory provisions, 15.133–15.137
  summary of police liability, 15.139–15.162
DSI *see* **death and serious injury**

employees
  see also **Non-senior officers; Senior officers**
  complaints against IPCC staff, 3.167–3.194
  complaints to IPCC, 3.37

  conditions of service, 1.18
  membership and staff of IPCC, 3.41–3.50
  police as regulated profession, 12.08–12.16
  public offices
    contracted-out staff, 15.26–15.29
    function-led approach, 15.37–15.44
    non-designated staff, 15.30–15.36
    police constables, 15.22–15.25
equality and diversity
  disability discrimination, 5.88
  Home Office Guidance, 6.48
  introduction, 1.103–1.104
European Union
  cross-border policing, 1.19
  international investigations, 1.22
evidence
  fast-track procedure
    2004 Regulations, 10.53
    2008 Regulations, 10.78
  first-stage meetings under 2008
    Regulations, 5.106
  good character evidence, 8.109–8.110
  inquests, 14.147–14.152
  intercept evidence
    admissibility of surveillance
      evidence, 7.155–7.156
    authorization for surveillance
      evidence, 7.162–7.166
    lawful business monitoring, 7.157–7.161
executive unlawfulness, 12.27–12.35

fair hearings
  general principles, 12.57–12.58
  jurisdiction, 12.36–12.44
fair trial (Art 6)
  exclusion of misconduct
    proceedings, 12.59–12.64
  proceedings under 2004 Regulations, 9.08
fast-track procedure
  2004 Conduct regulations
    appeals, 10.75–10.76
    case criteria, 10.48–10.53
    consideration in advance of
      hearing, 10.54–10.63
    Home Office Guidance, 10.64–10.74
    overview, 10.43–10.47
  2008 Regulations
    hearings, 10.98–10.107
    outcomes, 10.108–10.109
    overview, 10.77–10.82
    pre-hearing procedures, 10.83–10.86
    referrals to hearings, 10.87–10.97
  certification by IPCC, 6.149–6.150
  gross incompetence, 5.161–5.166

overview, 10.01–10.08
restrictions under 2002 Act, 6.146
role of IPCC
    keeping complainant informed, 10.24–10.42
    overview, 10.09–10.23
structure of 2008 Regulations, 5.32
final written warnings
fast-track procedure, 10.109
misconduct proceedings under 2008
    Regulations, 8.113
findings
see also **outcomes**
decisions on appeal, 8.152
first-stage meetings under 2008
    Regulations, 5.108–5.109
inquests
    judicial review, 14.179
    leaving all options to jury, 14.162–14.167
    lethal use of firearms, 14.168–14.178
    narrative verdicts, 14.95–14.104
    overview, 14.153–14.155
    reports of findings, 14.105–14.109
    statutory provisions, 14.28
    unlawful killing, 14.168–14.178
    withdrawal from jury, 14.156–14.161
majority findings of misconduct panel, 8.111
Police Appeals Tribunals
    1999 PAT Rules, 11.70–11.71
    2008 PAT Rules, 11.109–11.111
third-stage meetings under 2008
    Regulations, 5.190–5.193
fines
non-senior officers, 9.111–9.112
senior officers, 9.116
firearms, 14.168–14.178
first-stage process under 2008 Regulations
appeals, 5.123–5.135
arrangements at meeting, 5.96–5.103
circumstances when meeting required,
    5.93–5.95
introduction, 5.57–5.58
invoking Regulations by management, 5.92
pre-regulatory action, 5.59–5.62
procedure at meeting, 5.104–5.111
procedure following meeting, 5.112–5.122
structure of 2008 Regulations, 5.23–5.33
unsatisfactory attendance, 5.71–5.91
unsatisfactory performance, 5.63–5.70
fitness for duty, 6.54
force
Code of Conduct (2004 Regulations), 9.40–9.41
Home Office Guidance, 6.50
self-defence, 15.88–15.90
forces *see* **areas and forces**

friends *see* **Police friends**
funding for legal representation
inquests
    police officers, 14.112–14.115
    relatives of deceased, 14.09, 14.116–14.126
NPIA, 1.124

good character evidence, 8.109–8.110
gross incompetence
defined, 5.35
fast-track procedure, 5.161–5.166
findings, 5.190
outcome of third-stage meeting, 5.197
gross misconduct
see also **misconduct**
assessment of conduct
    series of graded assessments, 7.83–7.90
    severity assessments, 7.76–7.82
determination of case to answer, 8.07–8.17
dismissal without notice, 8.124
overview of regulatory framework, 4.06–4.07
procedure on receipt of referral notice,
    8.35–8.39
gross negligence manslaughter
application of basic principles, 15.102–15.110
conclusions, 15.111–15.113
leading authorities, 15.96–15.101
Guidance *see* **Home Office Guidance**

harm test for disclosure
disclosure of investigator's report, 8.21
implied duty of disclosure, 7.14–7.34
Police (Conduct) Regulations 2004, 9.96
hearings
see also **meetings**
central changes under 2008 regime, 4.14
fast-track procedure
    consideration in advance of
        hearing, 10.54–10.63
    pre-hearing procedures, 10.83–10.86
    procedure, 10.98–10.107
    referrals to hearings, 10.87–10.97
misconduct proceedings under 2008
    Regulations
    attendance and participation, 8.66–8.85
    choice of hearing or meeting, 8.14
    outcomes, 8.112–8.141
    procedure, 8.86–8.111
    procedure of receipt of notice, 8.35–8.39
    referral of cases, 8.01–8.34
    witnesses, 8.40–8.65
Police Appeals Tribunals
    1999 PAT Rules, 11.66
    2008 PAT Rules, 11.101–11.108

hearings (*cont.*)
proceedings under 2004 Regulations
disclosure obligations, 9.87–9.89
drafting charges, 9.90–9.93
joint hearings, 9.85–9.86
officers conducting hearing, 9.101–9.105
pre-hearing procedure, 9.97
presenting officers, 9.94–9.96
procedure at hearing, 9.106–9.110
witnesses, 9.98–9.100
Her Majesty's Inspectorate of Constabulary
consultation prior to 2008 Regulations, 5.06
cooperation with IPCC, 3.67
organizational overview, 1.02
removal of chief officers, 2.19–2.20
revised powers under 1996 Act, 1.54,
1.57, 1.52
HMIC *see* Her Majesty's Inspectorate of
Constabulary
Home Office Guidance
see also Secretary of State
background to 2008 Regulations,
5.06–5.19
chief officers' reviews
attendance and participation, 11.23
officer conducting review, 11.10–11.11,
11.14–11.15
outcomes, 11.41
scope of review, 11.27, 11.30
Counting Rules, 1.39
fast-track procedure
2004 Conduct regulations, 10.64–10.74
case criteria, 10.60, 10.51, 10.57
overview, 10.05
pre-hearing procedures, 10.83
procedure for hearing, 10.64
fast-track procedure for gross
incompetence, 5.166
first-stage process under 2008 Regulations
appeals, 5.139
arrangements for meeting, 5.96–5.103
circumstances when meeting
required, 5.93–5.95
invoking Regulations by management, 5.92
pre-regulatory action, 5.59–5.62
procedure following meeting, 5.112–5.122
unsatisfactory attendance, 5.71–5.91
unsatisfactory performance, 5.63–5.70
full text of Guidance, App I
investigatory regime
harm test for disclosure, 7.16
interviews, 7.144
officer response to notice of
investigation, 7.133

overview, 7.05–7.06
police friends, 7.42–7.43, 7.40
pre-interview procedures, 7.140
purpose of investigation, 7.110–7.111
suspension, 7.59–7.60
IPCC duties, 3.58, 3.71–3.90
line management resolutions, 6.12
local procedures, 1.07–1.10
misconduct proceedings under 2008
Regulations
determination of case to answer, 8.12, 8.10
disclosure of investigator's report, 8.21
mitigation, 8.128
notice to officer, 8.28, 8.26
panel membership, 8.33–8.34
questioning of witnesses, 8.98–8.99
witnesses, 8.40
more aggressive approach to
intervention, 1.40–1.44
organizational overview, 1.02, 1.06
Police (Conduct) Regulations 2004
general points and procedural
challenges, 9.45–9.53
joint hearings, 9.85–9.86
overview, 9.01–9.06
relationship with Regulations, 9.12–9.15
structure and purpose, 9.23–9.24
removal of chief officers, 2.14–2.15
revised powers of direction under 1996
Act, 1.68–1.75
standards of professional behaviour, 6.44–6.60
homicide *see* unlawful killing
honesty and integrity
Code of Conduct (2004 Regulations), 9.36
Home Office Guidance, 6.45
Police (Conduct) Regulations 2008, 6.33
HRP *see* human resource professionals
human resource professionals
attendance at first-stage meetings, 5.104
consultation prior to second-stage
process, 5.137
defined, 5.36
investigatory regime, 7.10
misconduct hearings, 8.54
third-stage meeting panels, 5.179–5.181
human rights
equality and diversity, 1.103–1.104
fair trial (Art 6)
exclusion of misconduct
proceedings, 12.59–12.64
proceedings under 2004 Regulations, 9.08
IPCC
disclosure, 3.31–3.34
status as public authority, 3.42–3.43

proceedings under 2004 Regulations, 9.08
removal of chief officers, 2.32
scope of inquest investigation
    anonymity of police officers, 14.138–14.139
    coroner's duty to hold inquest and
        timing, 14.66–14.67
    deaths after HRA 1998, 14.84–14.86
    deaths preceding HRA 1998, 14.77–14.83
    family participation and
        disclosure, 14.89–14.94
    narrative verdicts, 14.95–14.104
    overview, 14.14–14.15, 14.33–14.36
    subsequent developments, 14.87–14.88
surveillance evidence, 7.162–7.166

incompetence *see* **gross incompetence; Performance**
Independent Police Complaints Commission
attendance and participation at
    proceedings, 8.68–8.69
complaints and disciplinary process
    appointment and termination of
        members, 3.97–3.101
    complaints against chairman, 3.109–3.111
    complaints against deputy chair, 3.112–3.113
    complaints against ordinary
        members, 3.114–3.128
    complaints against staff, 3.167–3.194
    'IPCC stages', 3.132–3.166
    non-statutory procedures, 3.102–3.108
    overview, 3.91–3.96
    suspension, 3.129–3.131
conclusion, 3.195–3.196
constitution, 3.44–3.50
consultation prior to 2008 Regulations
fast-track procedure
    keeping complainant informed, 10.24–10.42
    overview, 10.09–10.23
general functions and duties
    'Learning the Lessons Committee', 3.54–3.56
    Police Complaints Authority
        compared, 3.51–3.53
handling of conduct matters under 2002 Act
    discretionary referrals to IPCC, 6.133
    other mandatory referrals to IPCC, 6.132
handling of DSI matters under 2002
    Act, 6.140–6.145
importance to reform process, 4.03
initial handling of complaints under 2002 Act
    dispensation by IPCC, 6.119–6.124
    mandatory referral to IPCC, 6.88–6.99
    overview, 6.01–6.25
investigatory regime
    appointment of investigators, 7.96–7.102
    choice of regime, 7.68–7.72

    enhanced role, 7.04
    purpose of investigation, 7.111
    representation, 7.47
    suspension, 7.61
legal character
    before 2004, 3.26–3.35
    after 2004, 3.36–3.40
    creation and transitional provisions,
        3.22–3.25
miscellaneous aspects of 2002 Act
    fast-track procedure, 6.149–6.150
    power to discontinue
        investigations, 6.151–6.156
    restrictions on proceedings, 6.146–6.148
organizational overview, 1.02
overlap with inquests, 14.20–14.21
overview, 3.01–3.12
as public authority, 3.41–3.43
public hearings, 8.70–8.74
recommendations on appeal, 8.154
reports of investigations
    2002 Act, 7.169–7.172
    2008 Regulations, 7.167–7.168
    action by IPCC in response to
        report, 7.182–7.185
    appeals, 7.189–7.195
    death and serious injury, 7.186–7.188
    notice of criminal proceedings by DPP, 7.178
    notice of determinations to
        IPCC, 7.179–7.181
    recommendations for disciplinary
        proceedings, 7.198–7.205
    response by IPCC, 7.173–7.177
    reviews and reinvestigations, 7.196–7.197
statutory framework, 3.13–3.21
statutory functions and duties, 3.57–3.90
initial handling of complaints
conclusion, 6.157–6.159
dispensation by IPCC, 6.119–6.124
key duties, 6.85–6.87
local resolution, 6.100–6.118
mandatory referral to IPCC, 6.88–6.99
overview, 6.01–6.25
proceedings under 2004 Regulations,
    9.54–9.58
statutory and regulatory frameworks, 6.61–6.70
injury *see* **death and serious injury**
inquests
conclusion, 14.180–14.181
coroner's duty to hold inquest and timing
    adjournments for criminal
        proceedings, 14.59–14.67
    after public inquiry, 14.68–14.70
    challenging decisions, 14.74–14.76

inquests (*cont.*)
  coroner's duty to hold inquest and timing (*cont.*)
    requirements for jury, 14.52–14.58
    scope of resumed inquests, 14.71–14.73
    statutory provisions, 14.43–14.51
  engagement of human rights, 14.14–14.15
  importance of funding, 1.108
  nature and purpose
    Coroners Rules 1984, 14.29–14.32
    introduction, 14.25–14.27
    statutory provisions, 14.28
  other proceedings distinguished, 14.37–14.42
  overview
    deaths in custody, 14.16–14.20
    drawbacks of system, 14.07–14.13
    reform proposals, 14.01–14.06
    relevance of human rights, 14.33–14.36
  procedure
    anonymity, 14.127–14.141
    attendance of witnesses, 14.142–14.143
    interested parties, 14.110–14.126
    self-incrimination, 14.144–14.146
    witness summonses and
        admissibility, 14.147–14.152
  scope of investigation
    deaths after HRA 1998, 14.84–14.86
    deaths preceding HRA 1998, 14.77–14.83
    family participation and
        disclosure, 14.89–14.94
    narrative verdicts, 14.95–14.104
    reports of findings, 14.105–14.109
    subsequent developments, 14.87–14.88
  verdicts
    judicial review, 14.179
    leaving all options to jury, 14.162–14.167
    lethal use of firearms, 14.168–14.178
    overview, 14.153–14.155
    unlawful killing, 14.168–14.178
    withdrawal from jury, 14.156–14.161
inter-force activity
  collaboration agreements, 1.19–1.20
  collaborative arrangements, 1.23–1.25
  international joint investigations, 1.22
  public safety and order, 1.21
intercept evidence
  admissibility of surveillance
      evidence, 7.155–7.156
  authorization for surveillance
      evidence, 7.162–7.166
interested parties
  attendance and participation at
      proceedings, 8.76–8.85
  chief officers' reviews, 11.12–11.20
  defined, 5.37 8

inquests
  defined, 14.110–14.111
  funding for legal
      representation, 14.112–14.126
  third-stage meeting panels, 5.179
interviews
  discretionary procedures, 7.144
  overlapping criminal matters, 7.145–7.154
  pre-interview procedures, 7.137–7.143
  proceedings under 2004 Regulations, 9.79
intrusive surveillance, 7.155–7.156
investigations
  appointment of investigators
    2002 Act, 7.96–7.102
    2008 Regulations, 7.91–7.95
  assessment of conduct
    background and rationale, 7.74–7.75
    series of graded assessments, 7.83–7.90
    severity assessments, 7.76–7.82
  choice of regime
    forms of investigation, 7.67–7.70
    independent investigations, 7.71–7.73
    introduction, 7.63–7.66
  conclusion, 7.206–7.207
  fast-track procedure, 10.56
  inquests
    deaths after HRA 1998, 14.84–14.86
    deaths preceding HRA 1998, 14.77–14.83
    family participation and
        disclosure, 14.89–14.94
    narrative verdicts, 14.95–14.104
    reports of findings, 14.105–14.109
    subsequent developments, 14.87–14.88
  intercept evidence
    admissibility of surveillance
        evidence, 7.155–7.156
    authorization for surveillance
        evidence, 7.162–7.166
    lawful business monitoring, 7.157–7.161
  international investigations, 1.22
  international joint teams, 1.22
  interviews
    discretionary procedures, 7.144
    overlapping criminal matters, 7.145–7.154
    overview, 7.134–7.136
    pre-interview procedures, 7.137–7.143
  IPCC power to discontinue, 6.151–6.156
  overview
    effect of outstanding criminal
        proceedings, 7.50–7.54
    harm test for disclosure, 7.14–7.34
    Home Office Guidance, 7.05–7.06
    parallel regimes, 7.01–7.04
    police friends, 7.35–7.45

preliminaries, 7.07–7.13
representation, 7.35, 7.46–7.49
suspension, 7.55–7.62
proceedings under 2004 Regulations, 9.69–9.81
purpose of investigation, 7.110–7.112
reports of investigations
2002 Act, 7.169–7.172
2008 Regulations, 7.167–7.168
action by IPCC in response to
report, 7.182–7.185
appeals, 7.189–7.195
death and serious injury, 7.186–7.188
notice of criminal proceedings by
DPP, 7.178
notice of determinations to
IPCC, 7.179–7.181
recommendations for disciplinary
proceedings, 7.198–7.205
response by IPCC, 7.173–7.177
reviews and reinvestigations, 7.196–7.197
representation
adverse inferences, 7.128
duty to consider submissions, 7.127
officer response to notice of
investigation, 7.129–7.133
written notices of investigation
content under 2002 Act, 7.122–7.125
content under 2008 Regulations, 7.120–7.121
history and purpose, 7.113–7.119
officer response to notice of
investigation, 7.129–7.133
investigators
appointment
2002 Act, 7.96–7.102, 7.105–7.109
2008 Regulations, 7.91–7.95, 7.103–7.104
attendance and participation at misconduct
proceedings, 8.75
complaints against IPCC, 3.141–3.160
IPCC *see* **Independent Police Complaints
Commission**

joint hearings, 9.85–9.86
judicial review
chief officers' reviews, 11.33–11.37
coroner's duty to hold inquest and
timing, 14.74–14.76
locus of IPCC, 6.18
Police (Conduct) Regulations 2004, 9.50
status of IPCC, 3.42–3.43
timing and availability, 12.24–12.26
jurisdiction
abuse of process
exceptional remedy, 12.45–12.46
executive unlawfulness, 12.27–12.35

fair hearings and regulatory
departure, 12.36–12.44
proof, 12.47–12.48
Police Appeals Tribunals, 8.155
1999 PAT Rules, 11.54–11.60
2008 PAT Rules, 11.75–11.86

lawful business monitoring, 7.157–7.161
lawful orders, 1.18
learning and development, 4.13
'Learning the Lessons Committee', 3.54–3.56
'legacy cases', 3.22–3.25
legal representation
funding
inquests, 14.09, 14.112–14.126
NPIA, 1.124
mitigation after misconduct proceedings, 8.125
overview, 7.35, 7.46–7.49
procedure under 2008 Regulations, 5.49–5.53
lethal use of firearms, 14.168–14.178
line managers
defined, 5.40
second-stage process, 5.136–5.144
triggers for first-stage meeting under 2008
Regulations, 5.93–5.94
listed police forces, 1.122
local resolution
appeals, 6.116–6.118
introduction, 6.02
overview, 6.100–6.115
proceedings under 2004 Regulations
role of police friends, 9.59–9.62
words of advice, 9.63–9.68

majority findings, 8.111
manslaughter
corporate manslaughter
conclusions, 15.126–15.127
inquest verdicts, 14.32
introduction, 15.114–15.117
statutory provisions, 15.118–15.125
gross negligence manslaughter
application of basic principles, 15.102–15.110
conclusions, 15.111–15.113
leading authorities, 15.96–15.101
unlawful and dangerous act
manslaughter, 15.91–15.95
meetings
see also **hearings**
central changes under 2008 regime, 4.14
first-stage process under 2008 Regulations
appeals against first-stage
meetings, 5.131–5.135
arrangements for meeting, 5.96–5.103

meetings (*cont.*)

first-stage process under 2008 Regulations (*cont.*)

circumstances when meeting
required, 5.93–5.95
procedure following meeting, 5.112–5.122

misconduct proceedings under 2008
Regulations
attendance and participation, 8.66–8.85
choice of hearing or meeting, 8.14
outcomes, 8.112–8.141
procedure, 8.86–8.111
procedure of receipt of notice, 8.35–8.39
referral of cases, 8.01–8.34
witnesses, 8.40–8.65

nominees at council meetings, 1.99

second-stage process under 2008 Regulations
appeals, 5.151–5.154
arrangements for meeting, 5.145–5.147
circumstances when meeting
required, 5.136–5.144
procedure at and after meeting, 5.148–5.150

structure of 2008 Regulations, 5.23–5.33

third-stage meetings under 2008 Regulations
arrangements for meeting, 5.160
fast-track procedure for gross
incompetence, 5.161–5.166
procedure at meetings, 5.188–5.189
procedure leading to meeting, 5.167–5.173
witnesses, 5.174–5.176

membership

IPCC, 3.97–3.101
appointment and termination of
members, 3.97–3.101
complaints against chairman, 3.109–3.111
complaints against deputy chair,
3.112–3.113
complaints against ordinary
members, 3.114–3.128
constitution, 3.44–3.50
suspension, 3.129–3.131

NPIA, 1.127

panels
misconduct proceedings under 2008
Regulations, 8.31–8.34, 8.51–8.60
third-stage meeting, 5.178–5.187

police authorities, 1.86–1.93

Metropolitan Police Authority

areas and forces, 1.14–1.15
chief officers' reviews, 11.12
general functions, 1.94
membership, 1.88–1.93
removal of chief officers, 2.04
review of fast-track procedure, 10.70–10.74

Ministry of Defence Police, 1.11

misconduct

see also **gross misconduct**

defined, 6.76

handling of conduct matters under 2002 Act
civil proceedings, 6.126–6.127
discretionary referrals to IPCC, 6.133
matters disclosed during DSI
investigation, 6.131
other mandatory referrals to IPCC, 6.132
recording of other matters, 6.128–6.130

initial handling of complaints under 2002 Act
dispensation by IPCC, 6.119–6.124
key duties, 6.85–6.87
local resolution, 6.100–6.118
mandatory referral to IPCC, 6.88–6.99

investigatory regime
appointment of investigator, 7.91–7.109
assessment of conduct, 7.74–7.90
choice of regime, 7.63–7.73
conclusion, 7.206–7.207
interviews, 7.134–7.166
overview, 7.01–7.13
purpose of investigation, 7.110–7.112
report of investigation, 7.167–7.205
representations, 7.126–7.133
written notices of investigation, 7.113–7.125

IPCC
conclusions, 3.195–3.196
disciplinary procedure, 3.91–3.194
general functions and duties, 3.51–3.56
legal character, 3.22–3.40
membership and staff, 3.41–3.50
overview, 3.01–3.12
statutory framework, 3.13–3.21
statutory functions and duties, 3.57–3.90

overview of regulatory framework
central changes under 2008
Regulations, 4.14
introduction and history of reform, 4.01–4.09
Taylor Review, 4.10–4.13

Police (Conduct) Regulations 2004
code of conduct, 9.32–9.44
conclusion, 9.117–9.118
general points and procedural
challenges, 9.45–9.53
non-senior officers, 9.54–9.114
overview, 9.01–9.21
senior officers, 9.115–9.116
structure and purpose, 9.22–9.31

proceedings under 2008 Regulations
appeals, 8.142–8.155
attendance and participation, 8.66–8.85
outcomes, 8.112–8.141
procedure, 8.86–8.111

procedure of receipt of notice, 8.35–8.39
  referral of cases, 8.01–8.34
  witnesses, 8.40–8.65
process charts, 4.18
relationship to criminal
  proceedings, 15.08–15.09
revised powers of direction under 1996
  Act, 1.68–1.75
summary of specific duties
  Police Act 1996, 1.110
  Police Reform Act 2002, 1.110–1.118
misconduct in public office
conclusion, 15.73–15.74
essential requirements
  abuse of public's trust, 15.66–15.69
  introduction, 15.15–15.19
  public officers acting as such, 15.20–15.44
  wilful neglect or misconduct, 15.45–15.65
  without excuse or justification, 15.70–15.72
overview, 15.10–15.14
mitigation after misconduct
  proceedings, 8.125–8.128
Morris Inquiry, 11.09

narrative verdicts, 14.95–14.104
National Crime Reporting Standards, 1.39
National Policing Improvement Agency
establishment, 1.119
objects and powers, 1.122–1.128
organizational overview, 1.02
statutory framework, 1.120
NCRS *see* **National Crime Reporting Standards**
no case to answer, 8.07–8.17
nominated persons, 5.54–5.56
non-senior officers
see also **probationers**
misconduct in public office, 15.22–15.25
panel membership, 8.51–8.60
proceedings under 2004 Regulations
  disclosure obligations, 9.87–9.89
  drafting charges, 9.90–9.93
  formal investigations, 9.69–9.81
  initial handling, 9.54–9.58
  joint hearings, 9.85–9.86
  local resolution and role of 'friends',
    9.59–9.62
  officers conducting hearing, 9.101–9.105
  pre-hearing procedure, 9.97
  presenting officers, 9.94–9.96
  procedure at hearing, 9.106–9.110
  reviews and appeals, 9.114
  sanctions, 9.111–9.113
  withdrawal of cases, 9.82–9.84
  witnesses, 9.98–9.100

words of advice, 9.63–9.68
rank structure, 1.17
notices
appeals, 8.148
appeals against first-stage meetings
  notice of appeal, 5.128
  notice of meeting, 5.128
dismissal
  gross misconduct, 8.124
  outcome of misconduct
    proceedings, 8.115–8.117
findings of third- stage meeting, 5.193
meetings
  appeals against first-stage meetings, 5.128
  first-stage meetings, 5.96–5.99
  second-stage meetings, 5.145–5.147
  third-stage meetings, 5.168–5.169
misconduct proceedings, 8.45–8.50
proceedings under 2004 Regulations
  duties of disclosure, 9.69–9.73
  formal investigations, 9.74–9.78
  hearings, 9.96
  witnesses, 9.98–9.100
referral of cases under 2008 Regulations
  form of notice, 8.28–8.30
  notice to officer, 8.23–8.24
  procedure on receipt, 8.35–8.39
reports of investigations
  notice of criminal proceedings
    by DPP, 7.178
  notice of determinations to
    IPCC, 7.179–7.181
written notices of investigation
  content under 2002 Act, 7.122–7.125
  content under 2008 Regulations,
    7.120–7.121
  history and purpose, 7.113–7.119
  officer response to notice of
    investigation, 7.129–7.133
NPIA *see* **National Policing Improvement Agency**

orders and instructions, 6.35
outcomes
see also **findings**
chief officers' reviews, 11.39–11.43
complaints against IPCC, 3.161–3.166
fast-track procedure, 10.108–10.109
misconduct proceedings under 2008
  Regulations
  available outcomes, 8.112–8.124
  decisions on appeal, 8.152
  general approaches, 8.129–8.137
  mitigation, 8.125–8.128
  notification, 8.138–8.141

outcomes (*cont.*)
    proceedings under 2004
        Regulations, 9.111–9.113
        non-senior officers, 9.11–9.13
        senior officers, 9.116
    reports of investigations
        2002 Act, 7.169–7.172
        2008 Regulations, 7.167–7.168
        action by IPCC in response to
            report, 7.182–7.185
        appeals, 7.189–7.195
        death and serious injury, 7.186–7.188
        notice of criminal proceedings by DPP, 7.178
        notice of determinations to
            IPCC, 7.179–7.181
        recommendations for disciplinary
            proceedings, 7.198–7.205
        response by IPCC, 7.173–7.177
        reviews and reinvestigations, 7.196–7.197
    review of fast-track procedure, 10.74

participation *see* attendance and participation
PCSD *see* Police and Crime Standards Directorate
performance
    background to 2008 Regulations, 5.12–5.16, 5.20
    Code of Conduct (2004 Regulations), 9.37
    first-stage process under 2008
        Regulations, 5.63–5.70
    more aggressive approach to intervention by
        Home Office, 1.40–1.44
    objectives and performance targets, 1.36–1.39
    overview of regulatory framework
        central changes under 2008 Regulations, 4.14
        introduction and history of reform, 4.01–4.09
        Taylor Review, 4.10–4.13
    Police (Performance) Regulations 2008
        appeals, 5.208
        conclusion, 5.209
        first-stage process, 5.57–5.135
        overview, 5.01–5.33
        preliminaries, 5.34–5.56
        second-stage process, 5.136–5.154
        third-stage process, 5.155–5.207
    process charts, 4.18
    revised powers of direction under 1996
        Act, 1.68–1.75
PNB *see* Police Negotiating Board
Police Act 1996
    organizational overview
        areas and forces, 1.12–1.14
        tripartite structure, 1.03
    revised powers for Secretary of State
        previous powers compared, 1.50–1.54
    summary of specific duties, 1.110

Police Advisory Boards, 1.78–1.81
Police (Amendment) Regulations 2008
    see also Table of Statutory Instruments
    full text of Regulation, App J
Police and Crime Standards
    Directorate, 1.40–1.44
Police and Justice Act 2006
    areas and forces, 1.12
    tripartite structure, 1.03
Police Appeals Tribunals
    1999 PAT Rules
        attendance and participation, 11.67–11.69
        findings, 11.70–11.71
        jurisdiction, 11.54–11.60
        procedure on notice, 11.64–11.65
        respondents, 11.61
        time limits, 11.62–11.63
    2008 PAT Rules
        determinations without hearing, 11.101
        findings, 11.109–11.111
        jurisdiction, 11.75–11.86
        procedure, 11.87–11.98
        procedure at hearing, 11.102–11.108
        statutory changes, 11.72–11.74
    appeals from third-stage meetings, 5.208
    common features, 11.49–11.53
    conclusion, 11.112–11.113
    jurisdiction, 8.155
    statutory basis, 11.45–11.48
    Tribunals Rules 1999, App B
    Tribunals Rules 2008, App H
Police authorities
    APA appointed for consultation, 1.102
    best value, 1.100–1.101
    consultation with local community, 1.98
    equality and diversity, 1.103–1.104
    funding for members, 1.105–1.109
    general functions, 1.94–1.97
    history and membership, 1.86–1.93
    initial handling of complaints, 6.85–6.87
    inter-force activity
        collaboration agreements, 1.19–1.20
        collaborative arrangements, 1.23–1.25
        international joint investigations, 1.22
        public safety and order, 1.21
    nominees at council meetings, 1.99
    powers of direction from Minister,
        1.45–1.49
    removal of chief officers, 2.07–2.10
    revised powers of direction under 1996 Act
        action plans, 1.60
        codes of practice, 1.66–1.67
        consultation, 1.78–1.81
        guidance, 1.68–1.75

making of regulations, 1.62–1.65
miscellaneous powers, 1.45–1.49
previous powers compared, 1.50–1.54
removal of chief officers, 1.76–1.77
reports, 1.61
statutory provisions, 1.54–1.59
strategic priorities, 1.35
summary of specific duties
  Police Act 1996, 1.110
  Police Reform Act 2002, 1.110–1.118
Police (Conduct) Regulations 2004
see also Table of Statutory Instruments
chief officers' reviews
  Home Office Guidance, 11.10–11.11
  introduction, 11.08–11.09
  officer conducting review, 11.12–11.20
Code of Conduct, 9.32–9.44
conclusion, 9.117–9.118
fast-track procedure
  appeals, 10.75–10.76
  case criteria, 10.48–10.53
  consideration in advance of
    hearing, 10.54–10.63
  Home Office Guidance, 10.64–10.74
  overview, 10.43–10.47
full text of Regulation, App C, App D
general points and procedural
    challenges, 9.45–9.53
non-senior officers
  disclosure obligations, 9.87–9.89
  drafting charges, 9.90–9.93
  formal investigations, 9.69–9.81
  initial handling, 9.54–9.58
  joint hearings, 9.85–9.86
  local resolution and role of 'friends', 9.59–9.62
  officers conducting hearing, 9.101–9.105
  pre-hearing procedure, 9.97
  presenting officers, 9.94–9.96
  procedure at hearing, 9.106–9.110
  reviews and appeals, 9.114
  sanctions, 9.111–9.113
  withdrawal of cases, 9.82–9.84
  witnesses, 9.98–9.100
  words of advice, 9.63–9.68
overview
  application, 9.16–9.21
  Home Office Guidance, 9.01–9.06
  purpose of proceedings, 9.07–9.11
  relationship with HMG, 9.12–9.15
senior officers, 9.115–9.116
structure and purpose
  overview, 9.22–9.31
Police (Conduct) Regulations 2008
see also Table of Statutory Instruments

fast-track procedure
  hearings, 10.98–10.107
  outcomes, 10.108–10.109
  overview, 10.77–10.82
  pre-hearing procedures, 10.83–10.86
  referrals to hearings, 10.87–10.97
full text of Regulation, App G
investigatory regime
  appointment of investigator, 7.91–7.109
  assessment of conduct, 7.74–7.90
  choice of regime, 7.63–7.73
  conclusion, 7.206–7.207
  interviews, 7.134–7.166
  overview, 7.01–7.13
  purpose of investigation, 7.110–7.112
  report of investigation, 7.167–7.205
  representations, 7.126–7.133
  written notices of investigation, 7.113–7.125
misconduct proceedings
  appeals, 8.142–8.155
  attendance and participation, 8.66–8.85
  outcomes, 8.112–8.141
  procedure, 8.86–8.111
  procedure of receipt of notice, 8.35–8.39
  referral of cases, 8.01–8.34
  witnesses, 8.40–8.65
overview of regulatory framework
  central changes under 2008 Regulations, 4.14
  introduction and history of reform, 4.01–4.09
  Taylor Review, 4.10–4.13
standards of professional behaviour, 6.26–6.43
police friends
choice of, 5.46
investigatory regime
  overview, 7.35–7.45, 7.46–7.49
  mitigation after misconduct proceedings, 8.125
  pre-interview procedures, 7.142,
    7.138–7.139
  proceedings under 2004 Regulations, 9.59–9.62
  role, 5.47–5.48, 7.36–7.45
Police Negotiating Board, 1.78–1.81
Police (Performance) Regulations 2008
see also Table of Statutory Instruments
conclusion, 5.209–5.210
first-stage process
  appeals, 5.123–5.135
  arrangements for meeting, 5.96–5.103
  circumstances when meeting
    required, 5.93–5.95
  introduction, 5.57–5.58
  invoking Regulations by management, 5.92
  pre-regulatory action, 5.59–5.62
  procedure at meeting, 5.104–5.111
  procedure following meeting, 5.112–5.122

Police (Performance) Regulations 2008 (*cont.*)
  first-stage process (*cont.*)
    unsatisfactory attendance, 5.71–5.91
    unsatisfactory performance, 5.63–5.70
  full text of Regulation, App F
  overview
    background, 5.01–5.22
    structure of Regulations, 5.23–5.33
  overview of regulatory framework
    central changes under 2008 Regulations, 4.14
    introduction and history of reform,
      4.01–4.09
    Taylor Review, 4.10–4.13
  police friends
    procedure, 5.49–5.53
  preliminaries
    definitions, 5.34–5.45
    nominated persons, 5.54–5.56
    procedure, 5.49–5.53
  second-stage process
    appeals, 5.151–5.154
    arrangements for meeting, 5.145–5.147
    circumstances when meeting
      required, 5.136–5.144
    procedure at and after meeting, 5.148–5.150
  third-stage process
    arrangements for meeting, 5.160
    assessment of performance and
      attendance, 5.155–5.159
    assessments after meeting, 5.201–5.207
    fast-track procedure for gross
      incompetence, 5.161–5.166
    findings, 5.190–5.193
    outcomes, 5.194–5.200
    panel members, 5.178–5.187
    procedure at meetings, 5.188–5.189
    procedure leading to meeting, 5.167–5.173
    timing and notice of meeting, 5.177
    witnesses, 5.174–5.176
Police Reform Act 2002
  see also Table of Statutes
  definitions
    complaints, 6.72–6.75
    conduct matters, 6.76
    death and serious injury, 6.77–6.79
    direction and control, 6.82
    former police officers, 6.81
    persons serving with police, 6.80
  handling of conduct matters
    civil proceedings, 6.126–6.127
    discretionary referrals to IPCC, 6.133
    matters disclosed during DSI
      investigation, 6.131
    other mandatory referalls to IPCC, 6.132

    recording of other matters, 6.128–6.130
    handling of DSI matters, 6.140–6.145
  initial handling of complaints
    conclusion, 6.157–6.159
    dispensation by IPCC, 6.119–6.124
    key duties, 6.85–6.87
    local resolution, 6.100–6.118
    mandatory referral to IPCC, 6.88–6.99
  investigatory regime
    appointment of investigator, 7.91–7.109
    assessment of conduct, 7.74–7.90
    choice of regime, 7.63–7.73
    conclusion, 7.206–7.207
    interviews, 7.134–7.166
    overview, 7.01–7.13
    purpose of investigation, 7.110–7.112
    report of investigation, 7.167–7.205
    representations, 7.126–7.133
    written notices of investigation, 7.113–7.125
  miscellaneous aspects of 2002 Act
    fast-track procedure, 6.149–6.150
    power to discontinue
      investigations, 6.151–6.156
    restrictions on proceedings, 6.146–6.148
  organizational overview
    areas and forces, 1.12–1.14
    tripartite structure, 1.03
  overview of regulatory framework
    central changes under 2008 Regulations, 4.14
    introduction and history of reform, 4.01–4.09
    Taylor Review, 4.10–4.13
  preservation of evidence, 6.83
  summary of specific duties, 1.110–1.118
  text of statute, App E
Police staff members, 5.44
Police Standards Unit, 1.40–1.44
**Police Superintendents' Association of England
  and Wales**, 5.06
pre-interview procedures, 7.137–7.143
pre-regulatory action, 5.59–5.62
presenting officers, 9.94–9.96
priorities *see* **Strategies**
privacy (Art 8)
  conditions of service, 1.18
  relevance to inquests, 14.15
  surveillance evidence, 7.162–7.166
private hearings
  fast-track procedure, 10.90
  misconduct proceedings under 2008
    Regulations, 8.66
**privilege against self-
  incrimination**, 14.144–14.146
probationers
  conclusion, 13.26–13.27

discharge under reg 13
  decided authorities, 13.14–13.22
  general provisions, 13.03–13.13
  key points, 13.23
  procedure, 13.24–13.25
  overview, 13.01–13.02
procedure
  see also **fast-track procedure**
  discharge of probationers, 13.24–13.25
  first-stage meetings under 2008 Regulations
    arrangements for meeting, 5.96–5.103
    procedure at meeting, 5.104–5.111
    procedure following meeting, 5.112–5.122
  hearings under 2004 Regulations, 9.106–9.110
  inquests
    anonymity, 14.127–14.141
    attendance of witnesses, 14.142–14.143
    interested parties, 14.110–14.126
    self-incrimination, 14.144–14.146
    witness summonses and
      admissibility, 14.147–14.152
  IPCC complaints and disciplinary process
    appointment and termination of
      members, 3.97–3.101
    complaints against chairman, 3.109–3.111
    complaints against deputy chair, 3.112–3.113
    complaints against ordinary
      members, 3.114–3.128
    complaints against staff, 3.167–3.194
    'IPCC stages', 3.132–3.166
    non-statutory procedures, 3.102–3.108
    overview, 3.91–3.96
    suspension, 3.129–3.131
  Minister's power to make rules, 1.31
  misconduct proceedings under 2008 Regulations
    adverse inferences, 8.89–8.95
    appeals, 8.147
    discretionary powers of chair, 8.86–8.88
    good character evidence, 8.109–8.110
    majority findings, 8.111
    prescribed task of chair, 8.104
    procedure on receipt of referral
      notice, 8.35–8.39
    proof, 8.105–8.108
    questioning of witnesses, 8.96–8.103
    receipt of notice on investigation, 8.35–8.39
    referral of cases, 8.01–8.06
    witnesses, 8.40–8.44
  Police Appeals Tribunals
    1999 PAT Rules, 11.64–11.66
    2008 PAT Rules, 11.87–11.98
  process charts, 4.18
  removal of chief officers, 2.16–2.37
    consultation with HMIC, 2.19–2.20

initial decision, 2.16–2.18
  pending resignation or retirement, 2.27–2.37
  suspension, 2.20–2.26
  second-stage meetings under 2008
    Regulations, 5.148–5.150
  third-stage meetings under 2008 Regulations
    arrangements for meeting, 5.160
    fast-track procedure for gross
      incompetence, 5.161–5.166
    procedure at meetings, 5.188–5.189
    procedure leading to meeting, 5.167–5.173
    witnesses, 5.174–5.176
process charts, 4.18
professional behaviour *see* **misconduct**
proof
  abuse of process, 12.47–12.48
  inquests, 14.154
  misconduct proceedings under 2008
    Regulations, 8.105–8.108
  procedure under 2008 Regulations, 5.52
Protocols, 2.14–2.15
PSAEW *see* **Police Superintendants' Association**
  of England and Wales
PSU *see* **Police Standards Unit**
public hearings
  anonymity at inquests, 14.127–14.141
  fast-track procedure, 10.90
  misconduct proceedings under 2008
    Regulations, 8.70–8.74
public interest
  deaths in custody, 14.18
  fast-track procedure, 10.50
  immunity, 9.95
  proceedings under 2004 Regulations, 9.10
public office
  see also **misconduct in public office**
  contracted-out staff, 15.26–15.29
  function-led approach, 15.37–15.44
  non-designated staff, 15.30–15.36
  police constables, 15.22–15.25
public rights and duties, 1.18
public safety and order, 1.21
public statements, 2.32

ranks
  rank structure, 1.17
  reduction in rank
    outcome of proceedings under 2004
      Regulations, 9.111
    outcome of third- stage meeting,
      5.195–5.198
    PAT Rules, 11.49
recorded crime, 1.39
redeployment, 5.195–5.197

reduction in rank
outcome of third stage meeting, 5.195–5.198
PAT Rules, 11.49
referral of cases
determination of case to answer, 8.07–8.17
notice to officer, 8.23–8.24
procedure, 8.01–8.06
procedure on receipt of notice, 8.35–8.39
regulatory departures
abuse of process, 12.04
general principles, 12.49–12.54
jurisdiction, 12.36–12.44
triggers for first-stage meeting under 2008
Regulations, 5.95
regulatory framework
complaints against IPCC, 3.167–3.194
initial handling of complaints, 6.61–6.70
investigatory regime
appointment of investigator, 7.91–7.109
assessment of conduct, 7.74–7.90
choice of regime, 7.63–7.73
conclusion, 7.206–7.207
interviews, 7.134–7.166
overview, 7.01–7.13
purpose of investigation, 7.110–7.112
report of investigation, 7.167–7.205
representations, 7.126–7.133
written notices of investigation, 7.113–7.125
misconduct proceedings under 2008 Regulations
attendance and participation, 8.66–8.85
outcomes, 8.112–8.141
procedure, 8.86–8.111
procedure of receipt of notice, 8.35–8.39
referral of cases, 8.01–8.34
witnesses, 8.40–8.65
organizational overview, 1.01–1.03, 1.129–1.130
police as regulated profession
consequences of regulatory
failure, 12.17–12.23
judicial review, 12.24–12.26
primacy of regulation, 12.08–12.16
Police (Conduct) Regulations 2004
Code of Conduct, 9.32–9.44
conclusion, 9.117–9.118
general points and procedural
challenges, 9.45–9.53
non-senior officers, 9.54–9.114
overview, 9.01–9.21
senior officers, 9.115–9.116
structure and purpose, 9.22–9.31
Police (Performance) Regulations 2008
appeals, 5.208
conclusion, 5.209
first-stage process, 5.57–5.135

overview, 5.01–5.33
preliminaries, 5.34–5.56
second-stage process, 5.136–5.154
third-stage process, 5.155–5.207
revised powers of direction under 1996
Act, 1.62–1.65
reinvestigations, 7.196–7.197
removal of chief officers
combined procedure, 2.16–2.37
consultation with HMIC, 2.19–2.20
initial decision, 2.16–2.18
pending resignation or retirement, 2.27–2.37
suspension, 2.20–2.26
conclusion, 2.38
Home Office Protocol, 2.14–2.15
overview, 2.01–2.06
revised powers of direction under 1996
Act, 1.76–1.77
statutory framework
Minister's powers, 2.11–2.13
powers and duties of authorities, 2.07–2.10
reports of investigations
2002 Act, 7.169–7.172
2008 Regulations, 7.167–7.168
action by IPCC in response to
report, 7.182–7.185
appeals, 7.189–7.195
death and serious injury, 7.186–7.188
disclosure, 8.21–8.22
inquests, 14.105–14.109
notice of criminal proceedings
by DPP, 7.178
notice of determinations to IPCC, 7.179–7.181
proceedings under 2004 Regulations, 9.80–9.81
recommendations for disciplinary
proceedings, 7.198–7.205
response by IPCC, 7.173–7.177
reviews and reinvestigations, 7.196–7.197
representation
see also **legal representation**
funding for legal representation, 1.105–1.109
investigatory regime
adverse inferences, 7.128
duty to consider submissions, 7.127
officer response to notice of
investigation, 7.129–7.133
overview, 7.35, 7.46–7.49
nominees at council meetings, 1.99
police friends
choice of, 5.46
investigatory regime, 7.35–7.45, 7.46–7.49
mitigation after misconduct
proceedings, 8.125
pre-interview procedures, 7.138–7.139, 7.142

proceedings under 2004
    Regulations, 9.59–9.62
role, 5.47–5.48
representations
first-stage meetings under 2008
    Regulations, 5.106–5.107
mitigation after misconduct
    proceedings, 8.125–8.128
removal of chief officers, 2.33–2.34
reprimands
non-senior officers, 9.111
senior officers, 9.116
resignation
discretionary powers, 2.36
outcome of proceedings under 2004 Regulations
    non-senior officers, 9.111
    senior officers, 9.116
PAT Rules, 11.49
restrictively listed police forces, 1.122
retirement, 2.36
reviews
see also **appeals**
background to 2008 Regulations, 5.20
chief officers
    2004 Regulations, 11.08–11.43
    conclusion, 11.112–11.113
    overview, 11.01–11.07
complaints against IPCC, 3.153–3.160
prescribed task of chair at misconduct
    proceedings, 8.104
proceedings under 2004 Regulations,
    9.111–9.112, 9.114
reports of investigations, 7.196–7.197
right to life (Art 2)
IPCC
    disclosure, 3.31–3.34
    status as public authority, 3.43
scope of inquest investigation
    anonymity of police officers, 14.138–14.139
    coroner's duty to hold inquest and
        timing, 14.66–14.67
    deaths after HRA 1998, 14.84–14.86
    deaths preceding HRA 1998, 14.77–14.83
    family participation and
        disclosure, 14.89–14.94
    narrative verdicts, 14.95–14.104
    overview, 14.14–14.15, 14.22,
        14.33–14.36
    subsequent developments, 14.87–14.88

sanctions *see* **outcomes**
Scarman Inquiry and Report, 3.03–3.04
second line managers, 5.41
second-stage process under 2008 Regulations

circumstances when meeting
    required, 5.136–5.144
structure of 2008 Regulations, 5.23–5.33
Secretary of State
see also **Home Office Guidance**
consultation with APA, 1.102
crime and disorder reduction partnerships, 1.27
general duties, 1.28–1.31
more aggressive approach to
    intervention, 1.40–1.44
objectives and performance targets, 1.36–1.39
organizational overview, 1.02
power to alter areas, 1.15
powers of direction to local
    authorities, 1.45–1.49
removal of chief officers
    approval, 2.35
    Minister's powers, 2.11–2.13
requirements for collaborative arrangements, 1.24
revised powers for Secretary of State
    action plans, 1.60
    codes of practice, 1.66–1.67
    consultation, 1.78–1.81
    guidance, 1.68–1.75
    making of regulations, 1.62–1.65
    miscellaneous powers, 1.82–1.85
    removal of chief officers, 1.76–1.77
    reports, 1.61
    statutory provisions, 1.54–1.59
revised powers under 1996 Act
    action plans, 1.60
    codes of practice, 1.66–1.67
    consultation, 1.78–1.81
    guidance, 1.68–1.75
    making of regulations, 1.62–1.65
    miscellaneous powers, 1.82–1.85
    previous powers compared, 1.50–1.54
    removal of chief officers, 1.76–1.77
    reports, 1.61
    statutory provisions, 1.54–1.59
strategic priorities, 1.32–1.35
usually Home Secretary, 1.26
self-defence, 15.88–15.90
self-incrimination *see* **privilege against**
    self-incrimination
senior officers
see also **chief officers**
appeals, 11.44
nominated persons, 5.54–5.56
proceedings under 2004
    Regulations, 9.115–9.116
rank structure, 1.17
senior managers defined, 5.42
standards of professional behaviour, 6.29

senior officers (*cont.*)
   third-stage meeting panels, 5.179–5.180
serious injury *see* death and serious injury
Serious Organised Crime Agency
   IPCC powers, 3.05
   organizational overview, 1.11
special cases *see* fast-track procedure
speeding police drivers
   application to response drivers, 15.141–15.158
   speed as basis of dangerous driving, 15.155
   statutory exemption, 15.139–15.140
standard of proof
   abuse of process, 12.47–12.48
   inquests, 14.154
   misconduct proceedings under 2008
      Regulations, 8.105–8.108
   procedure under 2008 Regulations, 5.52
standards of professional behaviour
   central changes under 2008 regime, 4.14
   Code of Conduct (2004 Regulations), 9.39
   Home Office Guidance, 6.44–6.60
   overview, 6.01–6.25
   Police (Conduct) Regulations 2008, 6.26–6.43
statutory framework
   initial handling of complaints, 6.61–6.70
   investigatory regime
      appointment of investigator, 7.91–7.109
      assessment of conduct, 7.74–7.90
      choice of regime, 7.63–7.73
      conclusion, 7.206–7.207
      interviews, 7.134–7.166
      overview, 7.01–7.13
      purpose of investigation, 7.110–7.112
      report of investigation, 7.167–7.205
      representations, 7.126–7.133
      written notices of investigation, 7.113–7.125
   IPCC, 3.13–3.21
   organizational overview
      areas and forces, 1.12–1.14
      tripartite structure, 1.03
   removal of chief officers, 2.07–2.10
      Minister's powers, 2.11–2.13
      powers and duties of authorities, 2.07–2.10
   revised powers of direction under 1996 Act
      action plans, 1.60
      codes of practice, 1.66–1.67
      consultation, 1.78–1.81
      guidance, 1.68–1.75
      making of regulations, 1.62–1.65
      miscellaneous powers, 1.45–1.49
      previous powers compared, 1.50–1.54
      removal of chief officers, 1.76–1.77
      reports, 1.61
      statutory text, 1.54–1.59

Statutory guidance *see* Home Office Guidance
Stephen Lawrence Inquiry, 3.04
strategic priorities, 1.32–1.35
surveillance evidence
   admissibility, 7.155–7.156
   authorization, 7.162–7.166
suspension
   chief officers, 2.19–2.20
   investigatory regime
      overview, 7.55–7.62
   IPCC members, 3.129–3.131
   outcome of proceedings under 2004
      Regulations
      non-senior officers, 9.111
      senior officers, 9.116

Taylor Review
   background to 2008 Regulations, 5.05
   chief officers' reviews, 11.09
   overview of regulatory framework, 4.10–4.13
   police as regulated profession, 12.10
third-stage process under 2008 Regulations
   arrangements for meeting, 5.160
   assessment of performance and
      attendance, 5.155–5.159
   assessments after meeting, 5.201–5.207
   fast-track procedure for gross
      incompetence, 5.161–5.166
   findings, 5.190–5.193
   outcomes, 5.194–5.200
   panel members, 5.178–5.187
   procedure at meetings, 5.188–5.189
   procedure leading to meeting, 5.167–5.173
   structure of 2008 Regulations, 5.23–5.33
   timing and notice of meeting, 5.177
   witnesses, 5.174–5.176
time limits
   appeals against first-stage meetings
      meetings, 5.129
      notice of appeal, 5.128
   appeals against misconduct proceedings, 8.145
   compliance with written improvement
      notices, 5.115–5.116
   misconduct proceedings under 2008
      Regulations, 8.45–8.50
   overview of regulatory framework, 4.13
   Police Appeals Tribunals
      1999 PAT Rules, 11.62–11.63
      2008 PAT Rules, 11.87–11.98
   third-stage meetings under 2008
      Regulations, 5.177
transparency
   appointment of investigators, 7.93
   disclosure of investigator's report, 8.21

initial handling of complaints under 2002
    Act, 6.10
overview of regulatory framework, 4.13

unlawful killing
causation, 15.84–15.87
duty of care, 15.81–15.83
inquest verdicts, 14.168–14.178
introduction, 15.75–15.77
manslaughter
    corporate manslaughter, 15.114–15.127
    gross negligence manslaughter, 15.96–15.127
    inquest verdicts, 14.32
    unlawful and dangerous act
        manslaughter, 15.91–15.95
overview of forms of homicide, 15.78–15.80
self-defence, 15.88–15.90
unsatisfactory attendance
defined, 5.43
first-stage process under 2008
    Regulations, 5.71–5.91
unsatisfactory performance
see also **performance**
defined, 5.43
UPP *see* **unsatisfactory performance**
use of force *see* **force**

verdicts *see* **findings**

warnings
fast-track procedure, 10.109
misconduct proceedings under 2008
    Regulations, 8.113
outcome of proceedings under 2004
    Regulations, 9.111
overview, 7.12
proceedings under 2004 Regulations,
    9.63–9.68
WIN *see* **written improvement notices**
withdrawal of cases
misconduct proceedings under 2008
    Regulations, 8.18–8.20

proceedings under 2004 Regulations, 9.82–9.84
witnesses
1999 PAT Rules, 11.67–11.69
central changes under 2008 regime, 4.14
fast-track procedure, 10.53
first-stage meetings under 2008
    Regulations, 5.106
inquests
    presence in court, 14.142–14.143
    witness summonses and
        admissibility, 14.147–14.152
misconduct proceedings under 2008 Regulations
    general practice, 8.40–8.44
    questioning of witnesses, 8.96–8.103
proceedings under 2004 Regulations, 9.98–9.100
right to be accompanied, 8.84
third-stage meetings under 2008 Regulations
    agreed lists, 5.171–5.173
    management, 5.174–5.176
words of advice, 9.63–9.68
written improvement notices
assessment after third stage
    meeting, 5.201–5.207
determination of hearing or meeting, 8.14
extension after third stage meeting, 5.30, 5.196
first-stage process
    appeals, 5.123–5.135
    drafting, 5.110
    procedure following first-stage
        meeting, 5.112–5.122
second-stage process
    appeals, 5.151–5.154
    circumstances when meeting
        required, 5.136–5.144
    procedure at and after meeting, 5.148–5.150
structure of 2008 Regulations, 5.27–5.30
written warnings
misconduct proceedings under 2008
    Regulations, 8.113
no further written warnings, 8.119–8.122
overview, 7.12
proceedings under 2004 Regulations, 9.63–9.68